Österreich
Einwohner: 8,2 Mio
Maßstab 1,5 cm = 50 km

TSCHECHIEN

DEUTSCHLAND

Gmünd
Horn
Krems
Donau
Linz
WIEN
Sankt Pölten
Wien
OBERÖSTERREICH
Melk
Amstetten
Baden
NIEDERÖSTERREICH
Eisenstadt
Gmunden
Wiener Neustadt
Neusiedler See
Salzburg
Bad Ischl
Mariazell
Salzkammergut
Hallstatt
Bruck an der Mur
BURGENLAND
Kufstein
Sankt Johann in Tirol
Liezen
Oberwart
Wörgl
Bischofshofen
STEIERMARK
Bregenz
Kitzbühel
Zell am See
Radstadt
Sankt Georgen
VORARLBERG
Reutte
Bruck
Feldkirch
Arlberg
Innsbruck
Mauterndorf
Güssing
Landeck
SALZBURG
Graz
TIROL
Mur
Osttirol
(zu Tirol)
Wintschgau
Lienz
Spittal an der Drau
Feldkirchen
UNGARN
DIE SCHWEIZ
Drau
Meran
KÄRNTEN
Klagenfurt
SÜDTIROL
Villach
Wörther See
Bozen
ITALIEN
SLOWENIEN
Bodensee

SCHAFFHAUSEN
Schaffhausen
DEUTSCHLAND
Kreuzlingen
BASEL
(STADT)
Rhein
THURGAU
BASEL
Basel
Liestal
Baden
Winterthur
Frauenfeld
Bodensee
St. Margrethen
FRANKREICH
Rhein
ZÜRICH
St. Gallen
AUSSER-RHODEN
Delemont
BASEL
(LAND)
AARGAU
Zürich
Herisau
Appenzell
JURA
Aarau
Zürichsee
INNER-RHODEN
SOLOTHURN
Reuss
Vaduz
Solothurn
LUZERN
Zug
Einsiedeln
SANKT
GALLEN
ÖSTERREICH
Biel
ZUG
LIECHTENSTEIN
JURA
Luzern
SCHWYZ
Glarus
NEUCHÂTEL
Bern
Vierwaldstätter See
Stans
Schwyz
GLARUS
NEUENBURG
BERNER
NIDW.
Braunwald
Neuenburger See
OBERLAND
Sarnen
Altdorf
Chur
UNTERWALDEN
OBW.
Engelberg
BERN
Thun
Brienz
URI
Davos
Fribourg
Thuner See
Brienzer See
Andermatt
Disentis
GRAUBÜNDEN
WAADT
FREIBURG
Interlaken
Jungfrau
Grindelwald
Klosters
Lausanne
Montreux
Jungfraujoch
St. Moritz
Gstaad
Genfer See
Brig
TESSIN
Genf
Sion
Bellinzona
GENF
WALLIS
Rhône
Locarno
Zermatt
Matterhorn
Lugano
Langensee
ITALIEN

NIDW = NIDWALDEN
OBW = OBWALDEN

Die Schweiz
und Liechtenstein
Einwohner
Schweiz: 7,6 Mio
Liechtenstein: 35 000
Maßstab 2,0 cm = 50 km

Kontakte

7e

Kontakte
A Communicative Approach

ERWIN TSCHIRNER
Herder-Institut, Universität Leipzig
University of Arizona

BRIGITTE NIKOLAI
Werner-von-Siemens-Gymnasium, Bad Harzburg

TRACY D. TERRELL
Late, University of California, San Diego

Mc
Graw
Hill

Connect
Learn
Succeed™

Published by McGraw-Hill, an imprint of The McGraw-Hill Companies, Inc., 1221 Avenue of the Americas, New York, NY 10020. Copyright © 2013, 2009, 2004, 2000, 1996, 1992, 1988. All rights reserved. Printed in the United States of America. No part of this publication may be reproduced or distributed in any form or by any means, or stored in a database or retrieval system, without the prior written consent of The McGraw-Hill Companies, Inc., including, but not limited to, in any network or other electronic storage or transmission, or broadcast for distance learning.

This book is printed on acid-free paper.

1 2 3 4 5 6 7 8 9 0 QDB/QDB 10 9 8 7 6 5 4 3 2

ISBN: 978-0-07-338634-8 (Student's edition)
MHID: 0-07-338634-0
ISBN: 978-0-07-741048-3 (Instructor's Edition)
MHID: 0-07-741048-3

Publisher: *Katie Stevens*
Marketing Manager: *Craig Gill*
Managing Developmental Editor: *Susan Blatty*
Developmental Editor: *Paul Listen*
Production Editor: *Holly Irish*
Production Service: *The Left Coast Group, Inc.*
Manuscript Editor: *Marie Deer*
Text Designer: *Lisa Buckley*
Cover Designer: *Preston Thomas*
Photo Research: *Inge King*
Buyer: *Tandra Jorgensen*
Media Project Manager: *Brett Coker*
Digital Product Manager: *Jay Gubernick*
Composition: *10/12 Californian by Aptara®, Inc.*
Printing: *45# New Era Matte Plus Recycled, Quad/Graphics, Dubuque, IA*

Vice President Editorial: *Michael Ryan*

Cover: Eva Dahl: *Abstrakte Formen 1*, 5/2011, Medium: Acryl. © Eva Dahl, Reproduced with permission of the artist.

Credits: The credits section for this book begins on page C-1 and is considered an extension of the copyright page.

Library of Congress Cataloging-in-Publication Data
Tschirner, Erwin P., 1956–
  Kontakte : a communicative approach/Erwin Tschirner, Brigitte Nikolai, Tracy D. Terrell.—7th ed.
    p. cm.
  Text in English and German.
  Includes index.
  ISBN-13: 978-0-07-338634-8 (student's ed. : acid-free paper)
  ISBN-10: 0-07-338634-0 (student's ed. : acid-free paper)
1. German language—Grammar.   2. German language—Textbooks for foreign speakers—English.
I. Nikolai, Brigitte.   II. Terrell, Tracy D.   III. Title.
  PF3112.T425 2012
  438.2'421—dc23

                                                                                        2011046166

The Internet addresses listed in the text were accurate at the time of publication. The inclusion of a website does not indicate an endorsement by the authors or McGraw-Hill, and McGraw-Hill does not guarantee the accuracy of the information presented at these sites.

Contents

To the Instructor   xv

To the Student   xxiii

EINFÜHRUNG A

Themen	Kulturelles	Strukturen

Aufforderungen 4
Namen 6
Kleidung 8
Farben 10
Begrüßen und
   Verabschieden 12
Zahlen 14
Wortschatz 17
	Kunst und Künstler 3
	KLI: Vornamen 6
	KLI: Farben als Symbole 11
	Musikszene: „A-N-N-A"
	   (Freundeskreis) 13
	KLI: So zählt man ... So
	   schreibt man ... 14
	Videoecke: Persönliche
	   Daten 15
		A.1 Giving instructions:
		   polite commands 19
		A.2 What is your name?
		   The verb **heißen** 20
		A.3 The German case
		   system 20
		A.4 Grammatical
		   gender: nouns and
		   pronouns 21
		A.5 Addressing people:
		   Sie versus **du** or **ihr** 22

EINFÜHRUNG B

Themen	Kulturelles	Strukturen

Der Seminarraum 26
Beschreibungen 27
Der Körper 28
Die Familie 29
Wetter und Jahreszeiten 31
Herkunft und Nationalität 34
Wortschatz 38
	Kunst und Künstler 25
	KLI: Was ist wichtig im
	   Leben? 28
	KLI: Wetter und Klima 32
	Musikszene: „36 Grad"
	   (2raumwohnung) 33
	KLI: Die Lage Deutschlands in
	   Europa 35
	Videoecke: Familie 36
		B.1 Definite and indefinite
		   articles 40
		B.2 Who are you? The verb
		   sein 41
		B.3 What do you have?
		   The verb **haben** 42
		B.4 Plural forms of
		   nouns 43
		B.5 Personal pronouns 45
		B.6 Origins: **Woher**
		   kommen Sie? 46
		B.7 Possessive adjectives:
		   mein and **dein/Ihr** 47

KAPITEL 1

Wer ich bin und was ich tue

Themen

Freizeit   50
Schule und Universität   53
Tagesablauf   56
Persönliche Daten   60
Wortschatz   67

KAPITEL 2

Besitz und Vergnügen

Themen

Besitz   80
Geschenke   83
Kleidung und Aussehen   87
Vergnügen   92
Wortschatz   96

KAPITEL 3

Talente, Pläne, Pflichten

Themen

Talente und Pläne   110
Pflichten   114
Ach, wie nett!   119
Körperliche und geistige
   Verfassung   124
Wortschatz   128

Kulturelles	Lektüren	Strukturen
Kunst und Künstler 49	Film: *Hilfe!* (Oliver Dommenget) 58	1.1 The present tense 69
KLI: Freizeit 52	Biografie: Guten Tag, ich	1.2 Expressing likes and dislikes: **gern / nicht gern** 71
KLI: Schule 55	heiße … 64	1.3 Telling time 72
Filmclip: *Hilfe!* (Oliver Dommenget) 60		1.4 Word order in statements 74
Musikszene: „Gewinner" (Clueso) 62		1.5 Separable-prefix verbs 75
Videoecke: Tagesablauf 65		1.6 Word order in questions 76

Kulturelles	Lektüren	Strukturen
Kunst und Künstler 79	Blog Deutsch 101: Frau Schulz hat Geburtstag 85	2.1 The accusative case 98
KLI: Der Euro 81	Film: *Lola rennt* (Tom Tykwer) 89	2.2 The negative article: **kein, keine** 99
Musikszene: „Junge" (Die Ärzte) 88		2.3 What would you like? **Ich möchte …** 100
Filmclip: *Lola rennt* (Tom Tykwer) 91		2.4 Possessive adjectives 101
KLI: Jugend im Netz 93		2.5 The present tense of stem-vowel changing verbs 104
Videoecke: Hobbys 94		2.6 Asking people to do things: the **du**-imperative 106

Kulturelles	Lektüren	Strukturen
Kunst und Künstler 109	Zeitungsartikel: Ringe fürs Leben zu zweit 112	3.1 The modal verbs **können, wollen, mögen** 130
Musikszene: „Müssen nur wollen" (Wir sind Helden) 116	Film: *Soul Kitchen* (Fatih Akin) 121	3.2 The modal verbs **müssen, sollen, dürfen** 131
KLI: Jugendschutz 118		3.3 Accusative case: personal pronouns 133
Filmclip: *Soul Kitchen* (Fatih Akin) 122		3.4 Word order: dependent clauses 135
KLI: Schuljahr und Zeugnisse 123		3.5 Dependent clauses and separable-prefix verbs 137
Videoecke: Fähigkeiten und Pflichten 126		

KAPITEL 4

Ereignisse und Erinnerungen

Themen

Der Alltag   140
Urlaub und Freizeit   142
Geburtstage und Jahrestage   147
Ereignisse   153
Wortschatz   159

KAPITEL 5

Geld und Arbeit

Themen

Geschenke und Gefälligkeiten   172
Berufe   176
Arbeitsplätze   181
In der Küche   184
Wortschatz   190

KAPITEL 6

Wohnen

Themen

Haus und Wohnung   204
Das Stadtviertel   207
Auf Wohnungssuche   213
Hausarbeit   216
Wortschatz   224

Kulturelles	Lektüren	Strukturen
Kunst und Künstler 139 KLI: Universität und Studium 143 Musikszene: „Du hast den Farbfilm vergessen" (Nina Hagen) 146 KLI: Feiertage und Bräuche 148 Filmclip: *Jenseits der Stille* (Caroline Link) 156 **Videoecke:** Feste und Feiern 157	Anekdote: Sternzeichen (Rafik Schami) 151 Film: *Jenseits der Stille* (Caroline Link) 155	4.1 Talking about the past: the perfect tense 161 4.2 Strong and weak past participles 163 4.3 Dates and ordinal numbers 165 4.4 Prepositions of time: **um, am, im** 166 4.5 Past participles with and without **ge-** 167

Kulturelles	Lektüren	Strukturen
Kunst und Künstler 171 KLI: Leipzig 175 Musikszene: „Millionär" (Die Prinzen) 181 KLI: Ausbildung und Beruf 183 Filmclip: *Der Tunnel* (Roland Suso Richter) 188 **Videoecke:** Studium und Arbeit 189	Webartikel: Die coolsten Studentenjobs 179 Film: *Der Tunnel* (Roland Suso Richter) 187	5.1 Dative case: articles and possessive adjectives 193 5.2 Question pronouns: **wer, wen, wem** 195 5.3 Expressing change: the verb **werden** 196 5.4 Location: **in, an, auf** + dative case 197 5.5 Dative case: personal pronouns 199

Kulturelles	Lektüren	Strukturen
Kunst und Künstler 203 KLI: Wohnen 206 KLI: Auf Wohnungssuche 215 Musikszene: „Haus am See" (Peter Fox) 218 Filmclip: *Good bye Lenin!* (Wolfgang Becker) 221 **Videoecke:** Wohnen 222	Sachtext: Städteranking 2010 211 Film: *Good bye Lenin!* (Wolfgang Becker) 220	6.1 Dative verbs 226 6.2 Location vs. destination: two-way prepositions with the dative or accusative case 228 6.3 Word order: time before place 230 6.4 Direction: **in/auf** vs. **zu/nach** 230 6.5 Separable-prefix verbs: the present tense and the perfect tense 232 6.6 The prepositions **mit** and **bei** + dative 234

KAPITEL 7

Unterwegs

Themen

Geografie 238
Transportmittel 242
Das Auto 246
Reiseerlebnisse 250
Wortschatz 255

KAPITEL 8

Essen und Einkaufen

Themen

Essen und Trinken 270
Haushaltsgeräte 275
Einkaufen und Kochen 279
Im Restaurant 284
Wortschatz 289

KAPITEL 9

Kindheit und Jugend

Themen

Kindheit 302
Jugend 305
Geschichten 307
Märchen 313
Wortschatz 323

Kulturelles

Kunst und Künstler 237
Musikszene: „Mädchen, lach doch mal!" (Wise Guys) 243
Filmclip: *Im Juli* (Fatih Akin) 245
KLI: Volkswagen 249
KLI: Die Schweiz 252
Videoecke: Ausflüge und Verkehrsmittel 253

Lektüren

Gedicht: Die Lorelei (Heinrich Heine) 240
Film: *Im Juli* (Fatih Akin) 244

Strukturen

7.1 Relative clauses 257
7.2 Making comparisons: the comparative and superlative forms of adjectives and adverbs 259
7.3 Referring to and asking about things and ideas: **da**-compounds and **wo**-compounds 263
7.4 The perfect tense (review) 265
7.5 The simple past tense of **haben** and **sein** 267

Kulturelles

Kunst und Künstler 269
Musikszene: „Hawaii Toast Song" (Alexander Marcus) 273
KLI: Österreich 274
Filmclip: *Bella Martha* (Sandra Nettelbeck) 283
KLI: Stichwort „Restaurant" 286
Videoecke: Essen 287

Lektüren

Kurzgeschichte: Die Motorradtour (Christina Egger) 277
Film: *Bella Martha* (Sandra Nettelbeck) 282

Strukturen

8.1 Adjectives: an overview 291
8.2 Attributive adjectives in the nominative and accusative cases 292
8.3 Destination vs. location: **stellen/stehen, legen/liegen, setzen/sitzen, hängen/hängen** 293
8.4 Adjectives in the dative case 297
8.5 Talking about the future: the present and future tenses 298

Kulturelles

Kunst und Künstler 301
KLI: Jugend im 21. Jahrhundert 304
KLI: 1989 309
Musikszene: „Wir beide" (Juli) 310
Filmclip: *Nordwand* (Philipp Stölzl) 312
Videoecke: Schule 321

Lektüren

Film: *Nordwand* (Philipp Stölzl) 310
Märchen: Rotkäppchen – (Gebrüder Grimm) 318

Strukturen

9.1 The conjunction **als** with dependent-clause word order 325
9.2 The simple past tense of **werden**, the modal verbs, and **wissen** 325
9.3 Time: **als, wenn, wann** 328
9.4 The simple past tense of strong and weak verbs (receptive) 330
9.5 Sequence of events in past narration: the past perfect tense and the conjunction **nachdem** (receptive) 332

KAPITEL 10

Auf Reisen

Themen

Reisepläne   336
Nach dem Weg fragen   340
Urlaub am Strand   347
Tiere   350
Wortschatz   358

KAPITEL 11

Gesundheit und Krankheit

Themen

Krankheit   372
Körperteile und Körperpflege   375
Arzt, Apotheke, Krankenhaus   381
Unfälle   384
Wortschatz   390

KAPITEL 12

Die moderne Gesellschaft

Themen

Familie, Ehe, Partnerschaft   402
Multikulturelle Gesellschaft   405
Das liebe Geld   412
Kunst und Literatur   415
Wortschatz   420

Kulturelles	**Lektüren**	**Strukturen**
Kunst und Künstler 335	Gedicht: Die Stadt (Theodor Storm) 343	10.1 Prepositions to talk about places: **aus, bei, nach, von, zu** 360
KLI: Reiseziele 338	Reiseführer: Husum 344	10.2 Requests and instructions: the imperative (summary review) 362
Musikszene: „Dieser Weg" (Xavier Naidoo) 346	Film: *Die fetten Jahre sind vorbei* (Hans Weingartner) 354	10.3 Prepositions for giving directions: **an ... vorbei, bis zu, entlang, gegenüber von, über** 364
KLI: Die deutsche Einwanderung in die USA 349		10.4 Being polite: the subjunctive form of modal verbs 365
Filmclip: *Die fetten Jahre sind vorbei* (Hans Weingartner) 355		10.5 Focusing on the action: the passive voice 367
Videoecke: Urlaub 356		

Kulturelles	**Lektüren**	**Strukturen**
Kunst und Künstler 371	Kurzgeschichte: Juttas neue Frisur 379	11.1 Accusative reflexive pronouns 393
KLI: Hausmittel 374	Film: *Das Leben der Anderen* (Florian Henckel von Donnersmarck) 386	11.2 Dative reflexive pronouns 394
Musikszene: „Danke" (Die fantastischen Vier) 376		11.3 Word order of accusative and dative objects 395
KLI: Beim Arzt 382		11.4 Indirect questions: **Wissen Sie, wo ...?** 396
Filmclip: *Das Leben der Anderen* (Florian Henckel von Donnersmarck) 388		11.5 Word order in dependent and independent clauses (summary review) 397
Videoecke: Krankheiten 389		

Kulturelles	**Lektüren**	**Strukturen**
Kunst und Künstler 401	Kurzgeschichte: Deutsche Kastanien (Yüksel Pazarkaya) 408	12.1 The genitive case 423
KLI: Gleichberechtigung 404	Film: *Sophie Scholl – Die letzten Tage* (Marc Rothemund) 417	12.2 Expressing possibility: **würde, hätte,** and **wäre** 426
Musikszene: „Cüs Junge" (Muhabbet [mit Fler]) 407		12.3 Causality and purpose: **weil, damit, um ... zu** 427
KLI: Wie bezahlt man in Europa? 414		12.4 Principles of case (summary review) 428
Filmclip: *Sophie Scholl – Die letzten Tage* (Marc Rothemund) 418		
Videoecke: Familie und Freunde 419		

APPENDIX A   Informationsspiele: 2. Teil   A-1

APPENDIX B   Rollenspiele: 2. Teil   A-13

APPENDIX C   Phonetics Summary Tables   A-16

APPENDIX D   Grammar Summary Tables   A-23

APPENDIX E   Verbs   A-29

APPENDIX F   Answers to Grammar Exercises   A-33

VOKABELN DEUTSCH-ENGLISCH   V-1

VOKABELN ENGLISCH-DEUTSCH   V-33

INDEX   I-1

CREDITS   C-1

To the Instructor

Your students are changing. Technology is changing. The idea of the classroom is changing. Now, the way your students learn German is changing as well.

In preparation for this edition of *Kontakte,* we conducted extensive research, employing a wide array of research tools including surveys, focus groups, and ethnographic studies to identify the key goals and challenges of the introductory German course. Not surprisingly, communication and cultural competence are among the top goals of the majority of instructors, who are facing the challenges of fewer contact hours, budget cuts, and new course formats that make these goals difficult to achieve.

The Seventh Edition of *Kontakte* continues to offer a truly communicative approach that supports functional proficiency while responding to these changing needs in new and exciting ways. As a direct result of our research, we created

Connect German (www.connectgerman.com), a powerful online learning platform that includes the ebook, the online *Arbeitsbuch*, an audio/video chat feature, and a brand-new video filmed in Leipzig, thereby offering a flexible solution for the evolving introductory German landscape.

Enhanced by these powerful new digital tools, the Seventh Edition of *Kontakte*

- engages students in authentic culture and inspires them to communicate with confidence by providing them with the natural contexts they need to develop their language skills,
- provides tools for flexibility and easy administration, and
- achieves consistent results across the different course formats offered: face-to-face, hybrid, and online.

The *Kontakte* Program and the Five Cs

Firmly based on the research on second-language learning, *Kontakte* also supports the National Standards as outlined in the *Standards for Foreign Language Learning in the 21st Century*, third edition (a collaborative project of ACTFL, AATF, AATG, AATI, AATSP, ACL, ACTR, CLASS, and NCJLT-ATJ). As presented in the Standards, the five Cs of Communication, Cultures, Connections, Comparisons, and Communities provide a framework for what students should know and be able to do as a result of their language study. The Seventh Edition of *Kontakte* and **Connect German** provide a solid foundation for the implementation of the five Cs.

Communication and Cultures

Communication

Kontakte emphasizes communication in meaningful contexts in the target language in multiple ways. Throughout the program, students listen to and read comprehensible German and have ample opportunities to use German in autograph, interview, information-gap, role-play, writing, and other personalized activities that are theme-based, not grammar-driven.

The brand-new DVD video segments, **Interviews** and **Perspektiven**, filmed specifically for *Kontakte*, feature interviews with a variety of native speakers that allow students to hear authentic German in context and provide models for talking about topics using authentic, current German. The related activities move from comprehension to interaction and guide students in communicating with one another.

Regardless of course format, in the **Connect German** (**www.connectgerman.com**) *Arbeitsbuch*, students can also take advantage of the audio and video live chat tool to communicate with their classmates online. Each chapter includes one **Rollenspiel** chat activity adapted from the textbook role-plays. After completing pre-listening tasks, students listen to a model role-play. They then connect online with another student and role-play in real time.

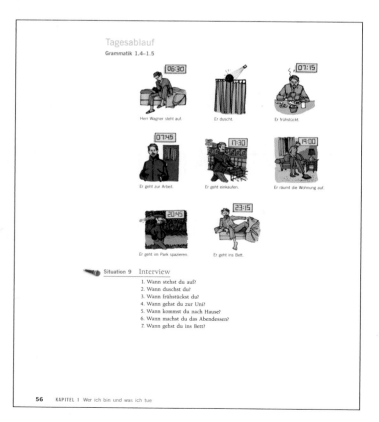

"I have used **Kontakte** for years primarily because of the communicative exercises and the way it is structured."

—*Leslie Taylor,*
Pima Community College

Cultures

Cultural readings called **Kultur ... Landeskunde ... Informationen** develop themes such as geography, history, and society and present various perspectives on the cultures of the German-speaking world. The new **Musikszene** and **Filmclip** features highlight contributions in German-language music and film.

In addition, the new *Kontakte* DVD Program provides a rich source of authentic language and culture that holds students' interest and draws them into interactions and discussion. Students are able to access both the activities and the video in **Connect German.**

Connections

Chapter themes and activities encourage students to link their study of German with their personal lives and with other subjects they are studying.

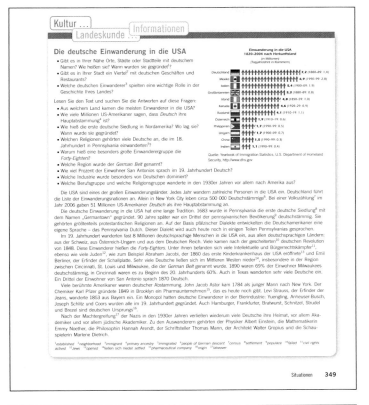

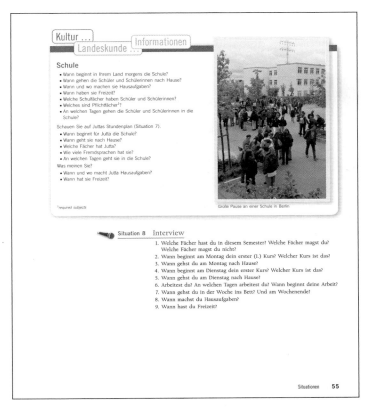

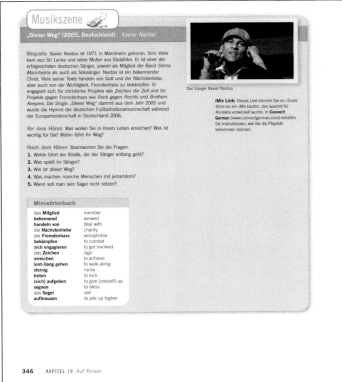

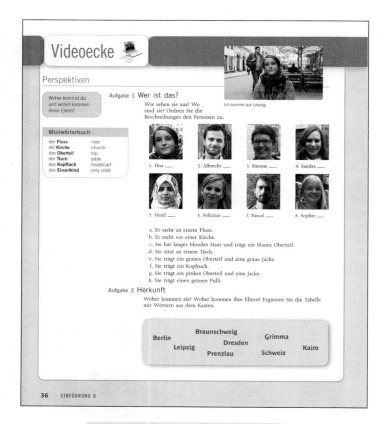

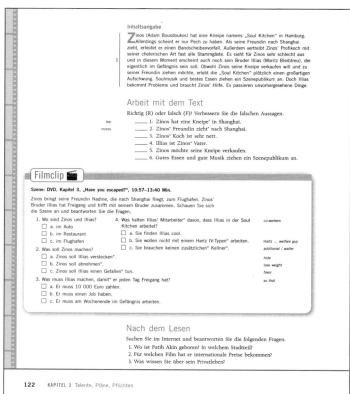

Communities

Students are given direct access to the German-speaking world through a variety of activities. The post-reading **Nach dem Lesen** sections engage students in activities in which they expand the scope of the subject matter or topic to the real-world level. In several **Filmlektüren,** students complete Internet research on topics related to German cinema.

"The **Perspektiven** videos are stellar! Clearly enunciated, slow enough but not artificially so, and beautiful settings; also wonderful introduction and repetition of vocabulary."

—*Stephanie Libbon, Kent State University*

Comparisons

The **Situationen,** the **Kultur ... Landeskunde ... Informationen** boxes, the **Musikszenen,** the **Filmlektüren,** and the **Videoecken** lead students to make comparisons between their world and that of German-speaking people.

The *Kontakte* Program: Administration and Standardization

How does *Kontakte* help instructors overcome the challenges of administering the course and the emerging challenge of providing standard course outcomes across all sections, whether they are face-to-face, hybrid, or online sections?

Administration

The *Kontakte* program now provides online tools to reduce the amount of time and energy that instructors have to invest in administering their course. Here are some of the ways these tools can be used.

- **Assignment Builder.** When creating assignments in the *Arbeitsbuch*, instructors can easily sort them according to a variety of parameters, choosing and using the parameters that are important to their course in particular. Instructors can sort and assign activities based on parameters including skill, grammar structure, vocabulary theme, time on task, and activity type.
- **Connect German Reports.** Instructors are able to pull administrative reports about student performance and coordinators are able to integrate these reports across sections to see the performance of all students in their program.
- **Blackboard.** Instructors and students can access all McGraw-Hill **Connect German** content directly from within the Blackboard course. Not only do you get single sign-on with **Connect German**, you also get deep integration of McGraw-Hill content right in Blackboard. When a student completes an integrated **Connect German** assignment, the grade for that assignment automatically (and instantly) feeds into your Blackboard gradebook.

Standardization

More departments are looking for ways to offer language instruction via hybrid or online sections. Given these trends, *Kontakte* is uniquely designed to provide consistent outcomes no matter which of these formats is used. It achieves this through the following:

- **Activities.** You can be assured that regardless of whether your section is taught online or face to face, all content is directly tied to course learning objectives to ensure consistency across the program.
- **Digital Offerings.** With **Connect German,** students have access in one central location to the ebook, the online *Arbeitsbuch*, the Audio Program, and the video, which provides them with ample opportunities to engage with the rich cultural content of the program anytime and anywhere, regardless of course format.

For Instructors and Students

- **Student Edition.** Full-color textbook with activities, grammar explanations and exercises, and helpful appendices. Available in print and as a digital ebook in **Connect German**.
- *Arbeitsbuch.* This combined workbook and laboratory manual contains both acquisition activities and practice exercises for use outside the classroom. The Answer Key at the end of the *Arbeitsbuch* allows students to correct many of the activities themselves. The *Arbeitsbuch* activities and the related audio recordings are also accessible in **Connect German,** which also features an audio/video chat tool.
- **Text Audio Program.** This audio program contains selected dialogues, listening comprehension passages, cultural readings, poems, a song, and a fairy tale from the textbook. Look for the headphone icon next to relevant activities in the textbook. The program is available on the **Connect German** site (www.connectgerman.com) and as a separate audio CD packaged with the Audio Program.
- **Audio Program.** Available on a set of audio CDs and on the **Connect German** site, this seven-hour program

contains pronunciation practice and listening compre-hension texts, recorded dialogues, and narratives. The Audio Program corresponds to the listening compre-hension activities in the print *Arbeitsbuch* and in the digital *Arbeitsbuch* on **Connect German.** Packaged with the Audio Program is a separate audio CD containing the Text Audio Program that accompanies the textbook.

- **DVD Program.** The *Kontakte* DVD is available to students and instructors. The footage, consisting of **Perspektiven** and **Interviews** video segments, can also be accessed within **Connect German.**

For Instructors

- **Instructor's Edition.** The main text contains margin notes and annotations with suggestions for using and expanding most of the **Situationen** in the text. It also offers the scripts for **Bildgeschichte** narratives, scripts for all materials in the Text Audio Program, additional cultural information, teaching hints for using readings, photos, and realia, and tips on teaching selected grammar points.

Online Instructor Resources

With the exception of the Instructor's Edition, all of the following instructor resources are available within **Connect German:**

- **Instructor's Manual.** The *Instructor's Manual* provides a guided walk through **Einführungen A/B** and **Kapitel 1,** information on Natural Approach theory and practice, and hints and practical guidance for instructors.
- **Testing Program with Audio CD.** This program offers a variety of test components emphasizing pronunciation, listening, speaking, reading, writing, vocabulary, gram-mar, and culture. Available online as a Word document, this program provides you with the flexibility to elec-tronically modify or adapt the tests to suit the particu-lar needs of your class. The listening comprehension passages are available on the accompanying audio CD.
- **Audioscript.** This is a transcript of all the material recorded on the Audio Program.
- **Vocabulary Display PowerPoints.** A set of color images of line art from the textbook for presentation of vocabulary, review, and class activities.

New to This Edition

Throughout the review process, we received valuable input from instructors and students alike. As a result, we have undertaken a number of changes in the Seventh Edition, without altering the basic concept and approach of *Kontakte.*

- **Connect German** (www.connectgerman.com) is McGraw-Hill's powerful online learning platform that includes the ebook, the online *Arbeitsbuch,* an audio/video chat feature, all digital resources, a reporting feature, instructor's resources, and more.
- The *Kontakte* team has produced an all-new DVD featur-ing interviews with young people at the Universität Leipzig. Engaging new **Videoecke** activities correspond to the new video.
- In the new song feature, **Musikszene,** students listen to a German-language song from the *Kontakte* iTunes iMix playlist and complete corresponding activities. The *Kontakte* playlist is available for purchase at the iTunes store.
- In the brand-new activity called **Filmclip,** students view a short clip of a full-length German-language feature film and complete the corresponding activities.
- The **Kultur ... Landeskunde ... Informationen** boxes have been updated to reflect cultural changes since the last edition and to keep abreast of cultural trends in the German-speaking world. A third of the culture features have entirely new and highly relevant cultural topics.
- Eleven of the **Lektüre** reading texts are new to this edition. Responding to user acclaim for the film synopsis readings, half of the readings in the book now deal with contemporary German films. Each numbered chapter has one film-synopsis reading (**Filmlektüre**) as well as one reading in one of a variety of other genres (**Lektüre**).
- Many photographs have been replaced to make the material more appealing to contemporary students.
- Many of the chapter-opening paintings have been replaced with new art selections.
- The chapter-opening art now features an art-viewing activity (**Kunst und Künstler**) which encourages students to develop their skills in reacting verbally to visual imagery in German.
- The latest official spelling-reform guidelines have been implemented, with specific reference to Duden's recommendations in the 25th edition of *Die deutsche Rechtschreibung* (Bibliographisches Institut AG: Mannheim, 2009).
- The Seventh Edition of *Kontakte* has an attractive and inviting new design.

Acknowledgments

We gratefully acknowledge our debt to the many instructors who over the past years have personally shared their experiences with us, especially Peter Ecke and the graduate student instructors at the University of Arizona. In addition, the authors would like to express their gratitude to the following members of the language-teaching profession whose valuable suggestions contributed to the preparation of this revised edition. The appearance of these names does not necessarily constitute an endorsement of *Kontakte* or its methodology.

Auburn University
Iulia Pittman

Brigham Young University
Randall Lund

Brown University
Aminia Brueggemann

Chapman University
Heather Ter-Jung

College of Charleston
Stephen Della Lana

Columbia University
Jutta Schmiers-Heller

Indiana University
Susanne Even

Kent State University
Stephanie E. Libbon
Cynthia Trocchio

Montclair State University
Courtney Glore Crimmins

Northern Arizona University
K. Bernd Conrad
Marilya Veteto Reese

Penn State University
Michael Putnam

Pima Community College
Leslie Taylor

Santa Monica College
Susan V. Wyman

Texas Christian University
Cynthia M. Chapa

University of Arizona
Albrecht Classen
Peter Ecke
Barbara Kosta

University of California, Los Angeles
Christopher M. Stevens

University of Chicago
Catherine C. Baumann

University of Georgia
Brigitte Rossbacher

University of Illinois at Chicago
Susanne Rott

University of Missouri
Monika Fischer

University of Pennsylvania
Christina Frei

University of Rhode Island
Damon Rarick

University of Southern California
Eve Lee

University of Tennessee-Knoxville
Maria Gallmeier

University of Texas at Arlington
Klaus Driessen

University of Washington
Klaus Brandl

University of West Georgia
John Blair
Muriel Cormican

Western Kentucky University
Timothy Straubel

We would like to extend our continuing thanks to all the loyal users, reviewers, consultants, and native readers who contributed to prior editions of *Kontakte* and have helped shape the development of this program over the years; they are too numerous to mention here. We continue to thank Eirik Børve and Thalia Dorwick, who launched the first edition. *Kontakte* also owes enduring thanks to Gregory Trauth, editor extraordinaire of the third and fourth editions and best of friends. We still miss you, Gregory.

The revised Seventh Edition of *Kontakte* is a product of the hardworking efforts of many different language-teaching and publishing professionals. Our gratitude to Arden Smith, who painstakingly compiled the German-English and English-German end vocabularies; to Inge King for researching the many interesting photos; and to Veronica Oliva, who secured reprint permissions for the realia and readings. We owe a debt of gratitude to Marie Deer, our copy editor. Many thanks to Jennifer Rodes at Klic Video Productions and her team for the beautiful new **Interviews** and **Perspektiven** video segments, and to Jupp Möhring, Nicole Mackus, Jenny Fischer, Judith Müller, Juliane Schäfer and Sandra Süring for organizing and helping with the video shoot as well as to Tetyana Chobotar, Michael Dobstadt, Shaimaa Hamdy Mohamed Elsayed, Simone Grossmann, Hend Adel Lotfy Hasan, Tina Hofmann, Maria Jeschke, Albrecht Klemm, Felicitas Krahnert, Tabea Mackel, Inna Meskova, Pascal Müller, Nadezda Mukhina, Michael Seyfarth, Carolyn Teschner, Susan Wagner, Sophia Weber, and Martin Wendig for participating in it. Thanks are also due to Jenny Fischer, Judith Müller, and Gerrit Tschirner for their contributions to the textbook, to Katharina Kley for her contributions to the *Arbeitsbuch*, and to Leonie Schröder and Anneke Peters for their work on the **Test Bank** for this revised edition.

Our heartfelt gratitude also goes to Jason Kooiker, Development Editor of the *Arbeitsbuch*.

The updated look of the interior of *Kontakte* is due to the artistry of Lisa Buckley. We thank Preston Thomas for the imaginative cover. We also thank our project manager, Chris Schabow of The Left Coast Group, whose fine work made our lives so much easier, and the production and design team at McGraw-Hill, whose expertise helped transform manuscript into this book: Holly Irish, Anne Fuzellier, and Tandra Jorgensen. Special thanks as well to Craig Gill, Jorge Arbujas, Kim Sallee, Alexa Recio and the rest of the McGraw-Hill marketing and sales staff, who so actively promote *Kontakte*. Special thanks are due to our Development Editor, Paul Listen, whose amazing attention to detail and fine editorial eye have greatly enhanced this edition. It has been a true pleasure to work with Paul.

Finally, we express our heartfelt gratitude to the McGraw-Hill World Languages editorial staff: Sara Jaeger, our Editorial Coordinator; Susan Blatty, Managing Development Editor; Brett Coker, Media Producer; Katie Stevens, our Publisher, whose support and encouragement are deeply appreciated; and William R. Glass, our Editorial Director, whose guidance and experience helped bring this project to its successful completion.

To the Student

Getting to Know the Characters

The people you will read and talk about in *Kontakte* appear in activities and exercises throughout the book. Some are American students, and others are from Germany, Austria, and Switzerland. First, there is a group of students learning German at the University of California at Berkeley. Although they all have different majors, they are all in Professor Karin Schulz's German class. You will meet eight students in the class: Steve (Stefan), Heidi, Al (Albert), Nora, Monique (Monika), Peter, Kathy (Katrin), and Thomas. Each uses the German version of his or her name. In Göttingen, Germany, you will meet Silvia Mertens and her boyfriend, Jürgen Baumann.

You will also get to know the Schmitz family. Rolf Schmitz, who is studying psychology in the United States, lives with his parents in Göttingen over the university holidays. His grandmother, Helene Schmitz, lives near Düsseldorf, Germany. Rolf has twin sisters, Helga and Sigrid. In Germany, you will also accompany an American student, Claire Martin, on her travels. Her best friends are Melanie Staiger and Josef Bergmann from Regensburg.

In Berlin, you will meet Renate Röder and Mehmet Sengün. In Dresden, you will meet Sofie Pracht, her friend Willi Schuster, and their friend Marta Szerwinski.

In Munich, you will meet the Wagners and the Rufs. Josie and Uli Wagner have three children: Ernst, Andrea, and Paula. Their cousin Jens comes to visit quite often. The Wagners' neighbors are the Rufs: Jochen Ruf, a writer and stay-at-home dad, and Margret, a businesswoman. They have two children: Jutta and Hans.

There are others in the neighborhood as well, such as Herr Günter Thelen and Herr Alexander Siebert, Frau Sybille Gretter, Frau Judith Körner, Michael Pusch, and his girlfriend Maria Schneider. In Austria, you will get to know Richard Augenthaler, who is 18 and has just graduated from high school.

In Zurich, Switzerland, you will meet the Frisch family, Veronika and Bernd and their three children.

We hope you will enjoy meeting these characters and learning more about their personalities, their daily lives, and the German-speaking regions they are from. Enjoy learning German and working with *Kontakte*!

Kontakte

Your goals in **Einführung A** should be to relax, listen to as much German as possible, and get to know your classmates. The focus of this chapter is primarily on listening skills; after you have heard German for several weeks, speaking it will come naturally to you.

GOALS

Einführung A has 4 goals: **(1)** to convince students (sts.) that they will be able to understand the German you speak in class, **(2)** to help lower anxiety levels by letting them get to know their classmates, **(3)** to begin the binding of meaning to key words in the input, and **(4)** to help students learn to use a listening strategy of attending to key words and to context. All activities are designed to make the input comprehensible. You will use three principal techniques to provide comprehensible input that does not require the sts. to produce German words: **(1)** Total Physical Response (TPR), **(2)** descriptions of the sts. themselves, and **(3)** descriptions of pictures from your picture file (PF). Each technique is described in detail in the Instructor's Manual (IM). The IM also contains a "walk-through" with general descriptions and suggestions for *Einführung A–B* and *Kapitel 1*.

Themen

Aufforderungen

Namen

Kleidung

Farben

Begrüßen und Verabschieden

Zahlen

Kulturelles

KLI: Vornamen

KLI: Farben als Symbole

Musikszene: „A-N-N-A" (Freundeskreis)

KLI: So zählt man ... So schreibt man ...

Videoecke: Persönliche Daten

Strukturen

A.1 Giving instructions: polite commands

A.2 What is your name? The verb **heißen**

A.3 The German case system

A.4 Grammatical gender: nouns and pronouns

A.5 Addressing people: **Sie** versus **du** or **ihr**

PRE-TEXT ORAL ACTIVITIES (1) Classroom commands: TPR (See also the IM). Introduce these actions in the first class session: *Stehen Sie auf, Setzen Sie sich, Laufen Sie, Schauen Sie* (hand above eyes to mime), *Singen Sie, Tanzen Sie, Nehmen Sie einen Bleistift usw.* In later class sessions add: *Hören Sie zu* (with hand behind ears), *Öffnen Sie das Buch* (use any book), *Schließen Sie das Buch, Schreiben Sie (Ihren Namen)* (in the air or on the board), *Lesen Sie* (as if reading a book), *Sprechen Sie* (blah! blah!). Finally, introduce the command *Sagen Sie* with short greetings: *Sagen Sie „Guten Tag". Sagen Sie „Auf Wiedersehen".* Have sts. shake hands and pretend to greet and say good-bye to each other. Then, have them say a short dialogue: *Guten Tag. Wie geht's? Gut, danke. Auf Wiedersehen. Auf Wiedersehen.* **(2) Names and descriptions of sts.:** (See the IM for suggestions on st.-centered input in Stage 1.) Write key nouns and adjectives on the board. Introduce the following words for people: *Professor, Professorin, Lehrer, Lehrerin, Student, Studentin, Mann, Frau;* and for physical appearance: *Schnurrbart, Brille, Kleidung (Rock, Jacke, Hose, Hemd, Schuhe, Pullover/ Pulli),* and colors *(weiß, gelb, orange, rosa).* The particular words you introduce will depend on your sts. Other words and expressions you will probably use: *Wer ist ...? Wer hat ...? Wer trägt ...? Wie heißt ...? das, er, sie, ich, Sie, auch, aber, sondern, ja, nein, nicht, kein.* **(3) Numbers:** (See also the IM.)

Introduce numbers by counting things in class for which sts. recognize the words: the number of men, women, total students, women with skirts, men with beards. Then ask sts. to react to statements with numbers. **(4) Additional commands and vocabulary for using the text:** The sts. in Frau Schulz's 8:00 AM German class reappear frequently in all components of *Kontakte.* Review all commands from pre-text activity 1 and add the following commands (many from *Sit. 1*) if you have not already done so: *Schauen Sie nach oben / nach unten, Stehen Sie auf, Springen Sie, Gehen Sie, Laufen Sie, Halten Sie, Setzen Sie sich, Nehmen Sie einen Stift, Legen Sie den Stift weg, Nehmen Sie das Buch, Öffnen Sie das Buch, Lesen Sie, Lachen Sie, Schließen Sie das Buch, Sprechen Sie, Hören Sie zu, Singen Sie, Nehmen Sie ein Blatt Papier, Schreiben Sie, Geben Sie mir die Hausaufgabe usw.* Then, make the commands specific to a group and then to individuals: *Männer mit Brille: stehen Sie auf, setzen Sie sich; Frauen mit braunem Haar: gehen Sie an die Tafel, gehen Sie zurück an Ihren Platz, öffnen Sie das Buch, lesen Sie, schließen Sie das Buch usw.* **(5) Alphabet:** Write the letters of the alphabet on the board, or prepare a large alphabet chart (or cards) and place it in a location visible to all during the activity. After *z,* include the letters *ä, ö, ü,* and *ß.* Pronounce *ä, ö,* and *ü* as they sound (i.e., do not say *a-umlaut,* etc.) and the *ß* as *sz* (es-zett). Practice the letters of the alphabet several times. Then, give short dictations of well-known names, such as cars *(VW, BMW),* cities *(Berlin, Wien),* and words from the chapter. Have sts. spell their names (first and last), first to you and then to a partner who writes them down. Introduce *Wie schreibt man das?* and *Wie, bitte?* During these first few weeks, reserve a few minutes each day to practice spelling. (Check the *Arbeitsbuch* to find out which sounds are practiced in which chapter.)

Wassily Kandinsky: *Herbst in Bayern* (1908), Museé national d'art moderne, Centre Georges Pompidou, Paris

Kunst und Künstler

Wassily Kandinsky (1866–1944) was a Russian-German expressionist painter who lived in Munich and Weimar. Born in Moscow, he later went to Munich to study at the *Kunstakademie München*. Along with Gabriele Münter and Franz Marc, he founded the expressionist group known as *Der blaue Reiter*. From 1922 to 1933 he taught at the Bauhaus in Weimar.

Sehen Sie das im Bild?[1]

	JA	NEIN		JA	NEIN
eine Straße[2]	☒	☐	die Farbe Gelb[4]	☒	☐
eine Kirche[3]	☒	☐	die Farbe Grün[5]	☒	☐
Gras	☒	☐	die Farbe Blau[6]	☒	☐
Autos	☐	☒			

[1]Sehen ... *Do you see that in the picture?* [2]eine ... *a road* [3]*church* [4]die ... *the color yellow* [5]*green* [6]*blue*

Situationen

Aufforderungen

Grammatik A.1

Vocabulary displays can be used to teach new vocabulary, to recycle vocabulary already learned, to enhance input, and to elicit student responses (oral and written). (See also IM Walk-Through). Vocabulary displays are most effectively used with an overhead or data projector (the IM contains masters for all drawings in *Kontakte*). **Presentation:** Introduce the people involved: *Das ist Stefan, Das ist Nora usw.*, and then say what Professor Schulz is telling her students: *Frau Schulz sagt zu Stefan: Schreiben Sie usw.* Pronounce the sentences carefully, and pause briefly after each sentence to make sure sts. get crisp, clear images of them. (See also the IM.)

Receptive recall: During the second phase of the binding process, sts. are asked to recognize the new vocabulary or phrases, but they are not yet asked to produce them. This means that the new vocabulary is contained in the question: *Zu wem sagt Frau Schulz: „Lesen Sie?" Zu Nora oder zu Peter?* Because of the clear context and the forced-choice question format, sts. should have no comprehension difficulties. **Choral response:** If your sts. like to speak at this stage (and many students do), you can go on to teach production as early as the first week of class. (See the IM for discussion of the "Silent Period.")

Productive recall: Ask questions that elicit new vocabulary: *Was sagt Frau Schulz zu Heidi? Stehen Sie auf, oder setzen Sie sich?*

Sit. 1. Your sts. will have to know the alphabet to pronounce the letters *a–h* to match the drawings with the commands. Quickly review numbers 1–10. With books closed, use TPR to review the commands introduced in the pre-text oral activities and featured in *Sit. 1.* Then, tell the sts.: *Öffnen Sie das Buch auf Seite 4, Situation 1, Nummer 1: Geben Sie mir die Hausaufgabe. Welches Bild zeigt: Geben Sie mir die Hausaufgabe-Bild a oder Bild c? Bild a, richtig. Arbeiten Sie jetzt mit einem Partner oder einer Partnerin. Schreiben Sie neben Satz 1 den Buchstaben a. Welchen Buchstaben schreiben Sie neben Satz 2? Sie haben zwei Minuten.* When the time is up, ask the whole class (don't choose individual sts. yet) what the correct matches are (pronounce the sentences, too, not only the numbers): *Also, welches Bild gehört zu Satz 2: Öffnen Sie das Buch? usw.*

schreiben Sie

hören Sie zu

lesen Sie

stehen Sie auf

setzen Sie sich

Stefan   Nora   Peter   Frau Schulz   Albert   Heidi

Situation 1   Aufforderungen

Hausaufgabe

a.

b.

c.

d.

e.

f.

Vocabulary Display (page 6) A. Buchstaben. In this section, we introduce the International Phonetic Alphabet (IPA) to distinguish more clearly between how letters are spelled and how they are pronounced. Do not feel obligated to teach the IPA though. It is sufficient to pronounce the letters as you read them with your students. You may wish to point out the following: **(1)** The colon is used for lengthening, the apostrophe for showing stress. **(2)** [ɛ] and [e] both represent (German) **e**-sounds ([ɛ] is short with the lips more open and [e] is long with the lips more closed). Note that most Germans use a long *and* open sound—i.e., [ɛː]—to pronounce the letter **Ä**. **(3)** [j] is the sound that is usually spelled *y* in English, as in *young*. **(4)** [øː] is pronounced by saying [eː] while at the same time strongly rounding the lips. **(5)** [yː] is pronounced by saying [iː] while strongly rounding the lips. Note that [yː] refers to a vowel sound, not a consonant sound as is the case in English spelling. **(6)** [ɪ] refers to a short (German) **i**-sound with the lips slightly more open than with the long [iː]. **(7)** [ʏ] refers to a short (German) **ü**-sound with the lips slightly more open than with long [yː]. Note that [ˈʏpsilɔn] is stressed on the first syllable.

g.

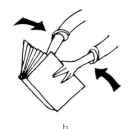

h.

1. Geben Sie mir die Hausaufgabe!
2. Öffnen Sie das Buch!
3. Schließen Sie das Buch!
4. Nehmen Sie einen Stift!

5. Gehen Sie!
6. Springen Sie!
7. Laufen Sie!
8. Schauen Sie an die Tafel!

Situation 2 Wer macht das?

Hören Sie zu und schreiben Sie die Zahlen unter die Bilder.

Sit. 2. Briefly review letters *a–h* and numbers 1-8. Write numbers as words on the board and practice pronunciation. Explain task: *Sie hören acht Aufforderungen. Welche Nummer gehört zu welchem Bild?*

a. ___3___

b. ___6___

c. ___2___

d. ___4___

e. ___5___

f. ___1___

g. ___8___

h. ___7___

Zum Beispiel: Nummer 1. Schreiben Sie „Heidi"! Zu welchem Bild gehört die Nummer 1? Richtig, zum Bild f. Point to drawing f. Ask students to work in pairs: *Arbeiten Sie mit einem Partner!* Read or play sentences twice in a row: *Ich lese Ihnen (spiele Ihnen) jetzt die Sätze vor. Hören Sie zu und schreiben Sie die Nummern zu den Buchstaben. Ich lese Ihnen alle Sätze zweimal vor.* Review activity by asking: *Nummer 2. Sagen Sie „a"! Zu welchem Bild gehört die Nummer 2? Richtig, zum Bild c.* Do the same for all sentences. **Text for listening comprehension.** Nummer 1. Schreiben Sie „Heidi"! Nummer 2. Sagen Sie „a"! Nummer 3. Hören Sie zu! Nummer 4. Stehen Sie auf! Nummer 5. Setzen Sie sich! Nummer 6. Lesen Sie! Nummer 7. Arbeiten Sie mit einem Partner oder einer Partnerin! Nummer 8. Sagen Sie Ihren Namen!

B. Dialog. Presentation: *Das ist Heidi, das ist Stefan. Stefan fragt: „Wie heißt du?" Heidi sagt: „Heidi." Stefan fragt: „Wie schreibt man das?" Heidi sagt: „H-E-I-D-I. Und wie heißt du?"*

Receptive recall: *Wie heißt die Frau? Wie schreibt man das? Wie heißt der Mann? Wissen Sie, wie man das schreibt?* Practice the lines of the dialogue with your sts. a few times. Ask 5 sts. what their names are and how they spell them. Help them with their spelling if they have problems. Then ask sts. to turn to their classmates. Using the lines of the dialogue, they ask each of 5 classmates what his or her name is, how it is spelled, and write it down. *Nehmen Sie ein Blatt Papier! Nehmen Sie einen Stift! Stehen Sie auf! Fragen Sie fünf Personen: „Wie heißt du?" und „Wie schreibt man das?" Schreiben Sie die Namen auf! Bitte beginnen Sie!* As follow-up, ask 5 sts. what their neighbor's name is and how it is spelled.

Namen

Grammatik A.2–A.3

—Wie heißt du?
—Heidi.
—Wie schreibt man das?
—H-E-I-D-I. Und wie heißt du?

Heidi   Stefan

Buchstaben					
Schreiben	*Sprechen*	*Schreiben*	*Sprechen*	*Schreiben*	*Sprechen*
A a	[a:]	J j	[jɔt]	L s	[ɛs]
Ä ä	[ɛ:]	K k	[ka:]	ß	[ɛs'tsɛt]
B b	[be:]	L l	[ɛl]	T t	[te:]
C c	[tse:]	M m	[ɛm]	U u	[u:]
D d	[de:]	N n	[ɛn]	Ü ü	[y:]
E e	[e:]	O o	[o:]	V v	[fau]
F f	[ɛf]	Ö ö	[ø:]	W w	[ve:]
G g	[ge:]	P p	[pe:]	X x	[ɪks]
H h	[ha:]	Q q	[ku:]	Y y	['ʏpsilɔn]
I i	[i:]	R r	[ɛr]	Z z	[tsɛt]

Kultur ... Landeskunde ... Informationen

Vornamen

- Was sind häufige[1] Vornamen in Ihrem Land für Personen über 60 Jahre? für Personen um die 40? für Personen um die 20? für Neugeborene[2]?
- Welche Vornamen gefallen Ihnen[3]?
- Welche deutschen Vornamen gibt es auch in Ihrem Kurs?
- Welche deutschen Familiennamen gibt es in Ihrem Kurs?
- Möchten Sie einen deutschen Vornamen annehmen[4]? Welchen?

[1]*common* [2]*newborns* [3]*gefallen ... do you like* [4]*adopt* [5]*most popular*

Die beliebtesten[5] Vornamen in Deutschland 2009

Mädchen	Jungen
1. Marie	1. Maximilian
2. Sophie/Sofie	2. Alexander
3. Maria	3. Leon
4. Anna	4. Paul
5. Emma	5. Luca/Luka
6. Mia	6. Elias
7. Sophia/Sofia	7. Felix
8. Leonie	8. Lukas/Lucas
9. Lena	9. Jonas
10. Johanna	10. David

Quelle: Gesellschaft für deutsche Sprache, e.V. (Wiesbaden).

Kultur ... Landeskunde ... Informationen (KLI). The *Gesellschaft für deutsche Sprache* publishes this list every year. Prepare activity by reading all questions and names. Ask sts. to work in groups of three to answer the questions. Follow up by asking sts. what their results are. Ask sts. if they want to adopt German names for the remainder of the semester and, if yes, which ones. Also use the list to practice pronunciation.
Comparison: Some of the most popular names in the late 19th and early 20th centuries for girls were: Anneliese, Clara, Elisabeth, Frieda, Gisela, Helga, Irmgard, Luise, Marie, and Ursula. For boys: Ernst, Georg, Hans, Herbert, Joachim, Karl, Kurt, Paul, Werner, and Wolfgang.

Situation 3 Wie heißt ...?

Sit. 3. Begin with *Darf ich vorstellen?* and then describe the characters: *Professorin Karin Schulz steht an der Tafel. Hier ist Thomas. Er hat langes Haar usw.* After introducing the characters, simply ask the questions listed in *Sit. 3.* Sts. answer with the name only or perhaps with *Er/Sie heißt ...* Then switch off the projector and have sts. open their books and do the same activity in pairs. Give them only about 1 minute to do this.

1. Wie heißt die Frau mit dem Buch?
2. Wie heißt der Mann mit dem Stift?
3. Wie heißt die Frau an der Tafel?
4. Wie heißt die Frau an der Tür?
5. Wie heißt der Mann mit der Brille?
6. Wie heißt der Mann mit dem Schnurrbart?
7. Wie heißt die Frau mit dem Ball?
8. Wie heißt der Mann mit dem langen Haar?

 ## Situation 4 Interview: Wie schreibt man deinen Namen?

Sit. 4. Preparation 1: Practice spelling sts.' names. Ask 5-6 sts. to spell their names while you write them on the board. Tell sts. to ask one another what their names are and how they are spelled: *Arbeiten Sie mit einem Partner oder einer Partnerin. Fragen Sie ihn oder sie, wie er heißt oder wie sie heißt. Fragen Sie dann, wie man seinen oder ihren Namen schreibt. Wie fragt man, wie jemand heißt? Richtig: Wie heißt du? Und wie fragt man, wie man das schreibt? Richtig: Wie schreibt man das?* **Preparation 2:** Ask sts. to find people with the characteristics mentioned in *Sit. 4: Wer von uns trägt eine Brille?* etc. **Activity:** Ask sts. to get up and talk to people with the characteristics mentioned in *Sit. 4,* asking them what their names are and how they are spelled. Ask sts. to write down the names. **Follow-up:** Ask sts. what names they wrote down for each characteristic, and ask them to spell these names while you write them on the board.

MODELL: ein Student / eine Studentin mit Brille →
        S1: Wie heißt du?
   S2 (*mit Brille*): Mark.
        S1: Wie schreibt man das?
        S2: M-A-R-K.

NAME

1. ein Student / eine Studentin mit Brille   _____
2. ein Student / eine Studentin in Jeans   _____
3. ein Student / eine Studentin mit langem Haar   _____
4. ein Student / eine Studentin mit einem Buch   _____
5. ein Student / eine Studentin mit Ohrring   _____
6. ein Student / eine Studentin mit kurzem Haar   _____

Kleidung

Grammatik A.4

Vocabulary Display

Vocabulary Display
Presentation: *Was trägt Michael Pusch? Er trägt einen Hut, eine Krawatte und einen Anzug. Der Anzug hat zwei Teile: ein Sakko und eine Hose. Jens Krüger trägt eine Jacke und eine Hose usw.* **Receptive recall:** *Wer trägt eine Krawatte? Wer trägt einen Mantel? usw.* **Productive recall:** *Was trägt Michael? usw.* **Personalization:** *Schreiben Sie auf. Was tragen Sie heute?* **Suggestion:** To help sts. learn the names of the cast of characters in *Kontakte,* have them identify the characters in the drawings. Using a projector, cover up the names on the screen and ask questions such as *Wer trägt einen Hut? Wer trägt einen Rock? usw.*

Situation 5   Kleidung

Sit. 5. Start this activity as a st.-centered writing task with follow-up questions.
Follow-up for Sit. 5: First, all sts. wearing the general article of clothing stand up, and you recycle the colors (presented in pre-text oral activities) by adding: *Mark trägt ein weißes Hemd. Aaron trägt ein blaues Hemd.* After completing *Sit. 5.* the first time, repeat the activity by describing an outfit so specifically that only one student fits the description. *Wer trägt ein gelbes Hemd und eine blaue Hose?* You might wish to introduce new vocabulary, such as *gepunktet, gestreift, kariert,* if sts. in class are wearing clothing with these patterns. You may also wish to teach *niemand,* a word sts. will find useful in similar activities: *Niemand trägt Stiefel.*

Wer im Deutschkurs trägt _____?

1. eine Bluse
2. einen Rock
3. eine Jacke
4. ein Kleid
5. Stiefel
6. ein Hemd
7. eine Hose
8. einen Hut
9. Sportschuhe
10. einen Pullover
11. eine Krawatte
12. einen Anzug

Sit. 6. This activity is the first in a series of information-gap (IG) activities designed to create a genuine exchange of information in a controlled way. (See the IM for more ideas about using IG activities.) Sts. work in pairs. One st. works with the questions and drawing on this page, the other st. turns to the second half of the information-gap activity in Appendix A. They take turns asking each other up to 10 questions to find out what the people in their partner's drawing are wearing. For each *ja*, they get one point. The one with the most points after 10 questions wins. **(1) Preparation:** Practice pronunciation of all questions. Divide sts. into two groups, one working with the activity on this page, the other one working with the activity in Appendix A. An easy way to pair students off is to count 1, 2, 1, 2, etc. All twos turn to the appendix, and all ones work with the chart in the chapter. Remind students not to show their half of the activity to their partners. Explain the task to them. Alternatively, put sts. in groups of three, with two sts. completing the activity and the third st. keeping score. **(2) Activity:** Make sure sts. take turns, speak German, and don't look at one another's books. **(3) Follow-up:** Tell sts. what clothing each person is wearing, so that they hear a native-like pronunciation of the words of the activity again. *Thomas trägt eine Jeans, einen Pullover, ein Stirnband, eine Brille und Schuhe. Nora trägt ein Kleid, einen Hut, eine Jacke und Schuhe. Herr Siebert trägt eine Hose, ein Sakko, eine Krawatte, ein Hemd und Schuhe. Frau Körner trägt eine Bluse, einen Rock, einen Mantel und Stiefel.*

Stellen Sie zehn Fragen. Für jedes „Ja" gibt es einen Punkt.

MODELL: s1: Trägt Thomas einen Anzug?
s2: Nein. Trägt Frau Körner einen Hut?
s1: Nein.

	THOMAS		NORA	
	JA	NEIN	JA	NEIN
einen Anzug	☐	☒	☐	☐
eine Bluse	☐	☐	☐	☐
eine Brille	☐	☐	☐	☐
ein Hemd	☐	☐	☐	☐
eine Hose	☐	☐	☐	☐
einen Hut	☐	☐	☐	☐
eine Jacke	☐	☐	☐	☐
eine Jeans	☐	☐	☐	☐
ein Kleid	☐	☐	☐	☐
eine Krawatte	☐	☐	☐	☐
einen Mantel	☐	☐	☐	☐
einen Pullover	☐	☐	☐	☐
einen Rock	☐	☐	☐	☐
ein Sakko	☐	☐	☐	☐
Schuhe	☐	☐	☐	☐
Socken	☐	☐	☐	☐
Sportschuhe	☐	☐	☐	☐
Stiefel	☐	☐	☐	☐
ein Stirnband	☐	☐	☐	☐
ein T-Shirt	☐	☐	☐	☐

? ?

Thomas   Nora   Herr Siebert   Frau Körner

*This is the first of many information-gap activities in **Kontakte.** Pair up with another student. One of you will work with the pictures on this page. The other will work with different pictures in Appendix A. The goal is to complete the activity speaking only German, while not looking at your partner's pictures.

Farben

Grammatik A.4

Situation 7   Meine Mitstudenten

Schauen Sie Ihre Mitstudenten und Mitstudentinnen an. Was tragen sie?

NAME	KLEIDUNG	FARBE
1. Heidi	Rock	blau
2. _____	_____	_____
3. _____	_____	_____
4. _____	_____	_____
5. _____	_____	_____

 ## Situation 8   Umfrage: Was ist deine Lieblingsfarbe?

MODELL: s1: Ist deine Lieblingsfarbe blau?
      s2: Ja.
      s1: Unterschreib bitte hier.

                                           UNTERSCHRIFT

1. Ist deine Lieblingsfarbe blau?   _____
2. Trägst du gern schwarz?   _____
3. Hast du zu Hause braune Socken?   _____
4. Ist deine Lieblingsfarbe rot?   _____
5. Trägst du gern gelb?   _____
6. Hast du zu Hause ein grünes T-Shirt?   _____
7. Ist deine Lieblingsfarbe lila?   _____
8. Hast du zu Hause ein weißes Hemd?   _____

Farben als Symbole

<u>Rot</u> ist die Liebe[1]
<u>Weiß</u> ist die Unschuld[2]
<u>Schwarz</u> ist die Trauer[3]
<u>Blau</u> ist die Treue[4]
<u>Grün</u> ist die Hoffnung[5]
<u>Gelb</u> ist der Neid[6]

KLI. Write the following color terms on the board: *blau, gelb, grün, rot, schwarz, weiß*. Ask sts. what the color blue symbolizes in English. Tell them that in German it symbolizes *Treue* (loyalty). Have sts. work in groups of three and write the color terms from the board in the spaces provided in the textbook. Tell them to start with the easy colors, e.g., red and black, and guess the rest. Follow up by asking: *Was ist die Liebe? Ja, rot ist die Liebe.*

[1]*love* [2]*innocence* [3]*grief, sorrow* [4]*loyalty* [5]*hope* [6]*envy*

Ich liebe Dich mehr...

...als meinen Teddybär!

Photo questions. *Wo sind diese Personen? Wie sehen sie aus? Was tragen sie? Wie alt sind sie?*

In der Stadt

Begrüßen und Verabschieden

Grammatik A.5

Guten Morgen!   Guten Tag!   Guten Abend!

—Auf Wiedersehen! —Wiedersehen!   —Tschüss! —Bis bald!

 Situation 9   Dialoge

1. Jürgen Baumann spricht mit einer Studentin.

   JÜRGEN: Hallo, bist du __neu__ hier?
   MELANIE: __Ja__. Du auch?
   JÜRGEN: Ja. Sag mal, __wie heißt du__?
   MELANIE: Melanie. Und __du__?
   JÜRGEN: Jürgen.

2. Frau Frisch ruft Herrn Koch an.

   HERR KOCH: Koch.
   FRAU FRISCH: Guten Tag, Herr Koch, __hier ist__ Frisch. Unser Computer ist kaputt.
   HERR KOCH: __Gut__, ich komme morgen vorbei.
   FRAU FRISCH: Gut. Bis dann. __Auf Wiederhören__.

3. Jutta trifft ihren Freund Jens.

   JUTTA: Servus, Jens.
   JENS: Ach, __servus__, Jutta.
   JUTTA: Wo willst __du__ denn hin?
   JENS: __Ich__ muss zum Fußballtraining.
   JUTTA: Na, dann __viel Spaß__!
   JENS: __Danke__. Mach's gut, Jutta.

Musikszene

„A-N-N-A" (1997, Deutschland) *Freundeskreis*

Biografie *Freundeskreis* ist aus Stuttgart. Der Gründer und Lead-Sänger heißt Max Herre. „A-N-N-A" war die 1. Hitsingle der Gruppe aus dem Jahr 1997. Andere große Hits waren „Tabula rasa" und „Mit dir".

Freundeskreis

Vor dem Hören Was ist das Besondere an dem Namen *Anna*?

☐ **1.** Er beginnt mit *A*.

☐ **2.** Er hat vier Buchstaben.

☒ **3.** Er ist von hinten und von vorne gleich.

Nach dem Hören

A. Hören Sie den Refrain! Richtig (R) oder falsch (F)?

R **1.** Max denkt an Anna, wenn es regnet.

R **2.** Anna war nass bis auf die Haut.

R **3.** Max liebt Anna.

B. Wie heißt dein Freund oder deine Freundin?

iMix Link: This song is available for purchase at the iTunes store in a special iMix created for *Kontakte*. For more information about accessing the playlist, go to **Connect German** (www.connectgerman.com).

Miniwörterbuch

das Besondere an	special about	**denkt an**	thinks about
von hinten	backwards	**regnet**	rains
von vorne	forwards	**nass**	wet
gleich	the same	**bis auf die Haut**	*here:* to the bone

Situation 10* Rollenspiel: Begrüßen

s1: Begrüßen Sie einen Mitstudenten oder eine Mitstudentin. Schütteln Sie dem Mitstudenten oder der Mitstudentin die Hand. Sagen Sie Ihren Namen. Fragen Sie, wie alt er oder sie ist. Verabschieden Sie sich.

Photo questions. *Welche Farben sehen Sie auf diesem Bild? Wo sind diese Personen? Was sagen sie? Wie sehen sie aus? Was tragen sie?*

Begrüßen

*This is the first of many role-playing activities in **Kontakte.** Pair up with another student. One of you takes the role of S1. The corresponding role for the other person (S2) appears in Appendix B.

Zahlen

Vocabulary Display
Introduction: *Wie viele Brillen sehen Sie? (Zwei.) Richtig, zwei. Zählen Sie bitte mit mir mit: eins, zwei. Wie viele CDs sehen Sie? (Neun.) Richtig, neun. Zählen Sie bitte mit mir mit: eins, zwei, drei … neun, usw.* **Practice:** While pronouncing them, write the numbers from 1 to 10 on the board or display them using a projector. Point to these numbers in quick, random succession, asking sts. to call out the numbers you are pointing to. Do the same for numbers 11 to 20, 21 to 30, and 10 to 100 in steps of ten. Present and review these numbers over the course of several class periods while giving short number dictations. **Game:** Sts. count to 100 (or however far they get in, say, 2 to 3 minutes) using the following procedure: **(1)** clap your hands; **(2)** tap your hands on your knees; **(3)** say the next higher number. Numbers with a 7 in them and multiples of 7 may not be called out loud. Sts. snap their fingers instead when they get to the "forbidden" numbers, e.g., 7, 14, 17, 21, 27, 28, 35, 37, etc. When a st. calls out one of these forbidden numbers by mistake, everybody has to start over from the beginning. Set up the game in German. **Point out:** *dreißig* is spelled with an *ß*.

0	null	10	zehn	20	zwanzig	30	dreißig
1	eins	11	elf	21	einundzwanzig	40	vierzig
2	zwei	12	zwölf	22	zweiundzwanzig	50	fünfzig
3	drei	13	dreizehn	23	dreiundzwanzig	60	sechzig
4	vier	14	vierzehn	24	vierundzwanzig	70	siebzig
5	fünf	15	fünfzehn	25	fünfundzwanzig	80	achtzig
6	sechs	16	sechzehn	26	sechsundzwanzig	90	neunzig
7	sieben	17	siebzehn	27	siebenundzwanzig	100	hundert
8	acht	18	achtzehn	28	achtundzwanzig		
9	neun	19	neunzehn	29	neunundzwanzig		

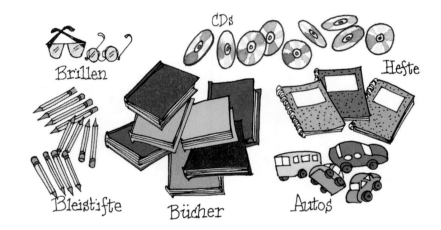

CDs · Brillen · Hefte · Bleistifte · Bücher · Autos

Situation 11 Wie viele?

Sit. 11. Have sts. count the number of persons in the class who fit the descriptions given in the activity. Ask questions such as: *Wie viele Studenten und Studentinnen tragen eine Brille? Studenten und Studentinnen mit Brille: Stehen Sie bitte auf! (Fünf - John trägt eine Brille, Ann trägt eine Brille, …) Wie viele Frauen tragen eine Brille? (Drei.)* Sts. can say the number or hold up 2 fingers and 1 thumb. *Ja, drei Studentinnen tragen eine Brille. Und wie viele Männer?*

Wie viele Studenten/Studentinnen im Kurs tragen …?

eine Hose	_____	eine Bluse	_____
eine Brille	_____	einen Rock	_____
eine Armbanduhr	_____	Sportschuhe	_____

Kultur … Landeskunde … Informationen

So zählt man …

eins, zwei, drei…

So schreibt man …

1 — eine Eins

7 — eine Sieben

KLI. Use TPR to show sts. how to count in German. Use your hands as follows: **(1)** thumb up, **(2)** thumb + index finger, **(3)** thumb + index finger + middle finger, **(4)** thumb + index finger + middle finger + ring finger, **(5)** full hand, **(6)** full hand + thumb of other hand, and so on. Demonstrate how the number 1 and the number 7 are written in German. Use TPR: *Das ist eine Eins. Zeigen Sie die Eins.* Then use with *Sit. 12.*

Situation 12 Informationsspiel: Zahlenrätsel

Sit. 12. *Das eine Bild zeigt ein Auto, das andere einen Teddybären.*

Verbinden Sie die Punkte. Sagen Sie Ihrem Partner oder Ihrer Partnerin, wie er oder sie die Punkte verbinden soll. Dann sagt Ihr Partner oder Ihre Partnerin Ihnen, wie Sie die Punkte verbinden sollen. Was zeigen Ihre Bilder?

s1: Start ist Nummer 1. Geh zu 18, zu 7, zu 29, zu 13, zu 60, zu 32, zu 12, zu 5, zu 14, zu 20, zu 11, zu 9, zu 3, zu 80, zu 23, zu 19, zu 4, zu 27, zu 8, zu 15, zu 35, zu 26, zu 2, und zum Schluss zu 17. Was zeigt dein Bild?

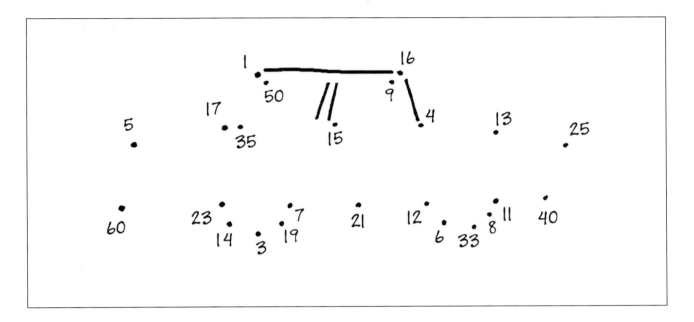

Videoecke

Perspektiven

Aufgabe 1 Wie viele?

Miniwörterbuch	
die **Paare**	pairs
umarmen	embrace
sich	*here:* each other
küssen	kiss
zueinander	to each other

„Hey, wie geht's?"

Wie viele Paare machen das?

__5__ 1. Wie viele Paare schütteln sich die Hand?

__4__ 2. Wie viele Paare umarmen sich?

__2__ 3. Wie viele Paare küssen sich?

__2, 6__ 4. Wie viele Paare sitzen, wie viele stehen?

__alle__ 5. Wie viele Paare sagen: „Wie geht's?"?

__1__ 6. Wie viele Paare sagen **Sie** zueinander?

Videoecke. Perspektiven: Ask sts. *Wie geht's?* Then ask: *Was machen Leute, wenn sie sich grüßen?* Elicit actions such as shaking hands, embracing, and kissing, and write the German equivalents on the board. Next explain *Aufgabe 1.* Read out all questions and make sure sts. understand them. Play video twice and elicit answers.

Aufgabe 2 Was sagen sie?

Miniwörterbuch

der **Zopf**	braid
die **Strickjacke**	cardigan sweater
der **Schal**	scarf
beide	both

Aufgabe 2: Go over descriptions of people and what they say, reading everything out loud. Play video twice and ask sts. to match descriptions and expressions in pairs or small groups. Elicit answers.

Was sagen die folgenden Personen?

____a____ 1. junger Mann mit lila Hemd

____e____ 2. junge Frau mit Zopf und blondem Haar

____c____ 3. junge Frau mit langem schwarzem Haar und schwarzer Strickjacke

____h____ 4. Frau mit kurzem dunkel-braunem Haar und brauner Jacke

____b____ 5. junge Frau mit langem blondem Haar und lila Sweatshirt

____d____ 6. junger Mann mit grün-kariertem Hemd

____f____ 7. junge Frau mit langem dunkel-braunem Haar, lila T-Shirt und schwarzer Hose

____g____ 8. junge Frau mit hellbrauner Jacke und Schal

a. „Hallo Susi."

b. „Gut, und dir?"

c. „Na, wie geht's dir?"

d. „Hey, wie geht's dir?"

e. „Hey, wie geht's?"

f. „Mir geht's gut und dir?"

g. „Ach, ganz gut und dir?"

h. „Guten Tag!"

Interviews

- Wie heißt du?
- Wie schreibt man das?
- Welche Kleidung trägst du gern?
- Welche Farben trägst du gern?
- Wie alt bist du?
- Hast du eine Glückszahl?

Nicole

Michael

Interviews: Introduce Nicole and Michael and ask sts. to find out what they say about themselves. Play video segment first to listen to how they spell their names. Stop after each one has spelled his or her name and ask sts. to write it down as it is spelled. Then play segment a couple of times for sts. to complete *Aufgabe 3* in pairs or small groups. Elicit answers. For *Aufgabe 4*, ask sts. to think about their own answers to the questions posed in *Aufgabe 3* and to write down their answers. Finally, ask them to interview each other.

Aufgabe 3 Persönliche Daten

Wer sagt das, Nicole oder Michael oder beide?

	Nicole	Michael	Beide
1. Ich trage gern Jeans und Pullover.	☐	☐	☒
2. Ich trage gern türkis, blau und grün.	☒	☐	☐
3. Ich trage gern rot und braun.	☐	☒	☐
4. Ich bin 45 Jahre alt.	☐	☒	☐
5. Ich bin 28 Jahre alt.	☒	☐	☐
6. Meine Glückszahl ist sieben.	☐	☒	☐
7. Meine Glückszahl ist dreizehn.	☒	☐	☐

Aufgabe 4 Interview

Interviewen Sie eine Partnerin oder einen Partner. Stellen Sie dieselben Fragen.

Wortschatz (next page). The *Wortschatz* follows each *Videoecke* section; it contains new words that have been introduced in the displays and activities in that chapter. These are the words sts. should recognize in a communicative context. Many of these words will be used actively by sts. in later chapters. Most words are grouped thematically to help sts. bind meaning to words. Note that all nouns are grouped by gender (feminine, masculine, neuter), with a separate listing for nouns used only in the plural. *Ähnliche Wörter* lists consist of true cognates and, in later chapters, of compound words with components that sts. will be able to recognize (e.g., *Spielplatz* from *spielen* and *Platz*). Advise sts. that if they have difficulty guessing the meaning of words in these lists, they can find the meanings in the German-English vocabulary at the end of the book.

Wortschatz

öffnete

Aufforderungen	Instructions
arbeiten Sie mit einem Partner*	work with a partner
geben Sie mir	give me
gehen Sie	go, walk
hören Sie zu	listen
✓ laufen Sie	go, run
lesen Sie	read
nehmen Sie	take
öffnen Sie	open
sagen Sie	say
schauen Sie	look
schließen Sie	close, shut
schreiben Sie	write; spell
setzen Sie sich	sit down
springen Sie	jump
stehen Sie auf	get up, stand up

Kleidung	Clothes
er/sie hat ...	he/she has . . .
hast du ...?	do you have . . . ?
er/sie trägt ...	he/she is wearing . . .
trägst du ...?	do you wear . . . ? / are you wearing . . . ?
die eine Armbanduhr	a watch
die eine Brille	glasses
die eine Hose	pants
die eine Krawatte	a tie
der einen Anzug	a suit
der einen Mantel	a coat; an overcoat
die einen Ohrring	an earring
der einen Rock	a skirt
das ein Hemd	a shirt
das ein Kleid	a dress
das ein Sakko	a sports jacket
die ein Stirnband	a headband
die Stiefel	boots

Ähnliche Wörter†

er/sie trägt ... eine Bluse, eine Jacke; einen Hut; Schuhe, Sportschuhe

Farben	Colors
gelb	yellow
lila	purple
rosa	pink
schwarz	black

Ähnliche Wörter

blau, braun, grau, grün, orange [oraŋʒə], rot, weiß

Zahlen		Numbers	
0	null	20	zwanzig
1	eins	21	einundzwanzig
2	zwei	22	zweiundzwanzig
3	drei	23	dreiundzwanzig
✓ 4	vier	24	vierundzwanzig
5	fünf	25	fünfundzwanzig
6	sechs	26	sechsundzwanzig
7	sieben	27	siebenundzwanzig
8	acht	28	achtundzwanzig
9	neun	29	neunundzwanzig
10	zehn	30	dreißig
11	elf	40	vierzig
12	zwölf	50	fünfzig
13	dreizehn	60	sechzig
14	vierzehn	70	siebzig
15	fünfzehn	80	achtzig
16	sechzehn	90	neunzig
17	siebzehn	100	hundert
18	achtzehn		
19	neunzehn		

Begrüßen und Verabschieden	Greeting and Leave-Taking
auf Wiedersehen	good-bye
bis bald	so long; see you soon
grüezi	hi (Switzerland)
grüß Gott	good afternoon; hello (formal; southern Germany, Austria)
guten Abend	good evening
guten Morgen	good morning
guten Tag	good afternoon; hello (formal)
hallo	hi (informal)
die Hand schütteln	to shake hands
mach's gut	take care (informal)
servus	hello; good-bye (informal; southern Germany, Austria)
tschüss	bye (informal)
viel Spaß	have fun

*The diacritic marks in the **Wortschatz** list are meant to help you learn which vowels are stressed. A dot below a single vowel indicates a short stressed vowel. An underline below a single vowel, double vowel, or diphthong (combination of two different vowels) indicates a long stressed vowel. Note that these markings are not used in written German but are provided here as an aid to pronunciation.

†**Ähnliche Wörter** (similar words; cognates) lists contain words that are closely related to English words in sound, form, and meaning and compound words that are composed of previously introduced vocabulary.

Personen — People

die **Frau**	woman; Mrs.; Ms.
die **Lehrerin**	female teacher, instructor
der **Herr**	gentleman; Mr.
der **Lehrer**	male teacher, instructor
die **Mitstudenten**	fellow (male) students
die **Mitstudentinnen**	fellow (female) students

Ähnliche Wörter

die **Freundin**, die **Professorin**, die **Studentin**; der **Freund**, der **Mann**, der **Professor**, der **Student**

Sonstige Substantive — Other Nouns

die **Tafel**	blackboard/whiteboard
die **Tür**	door
der **Stift**	pen
der **Bleistift**	pencil
Lieblings-	favorite
die **Lieblingsfarbe**	favorite color
der **Lieblingsname**	favorite name

Ähnliche Wörter

die **CD**; der **Ball**, der **Fußball**, der **Kurs**, der **Deutschkurs**, der **Name**, der **Familienname**, der **Vorname**, der **Teddybär**; das **Auto**, das **Buch**

Fragen — Questions

heißen	to be called, be named
wie **heißen** Sie?	what's your name? (*formal*)
wie **heißt** du?	what's your name? (*informal*)
ich **heiße** ...	my name is . . .
was **zeigen** Ihre **Bilder**?	what do your pictures show?
welche **Farbe** hat ...?	what color is . . . ?
wer ...?	who . . . ?
wie **schreibt** man das?	how do you spell that?
wie **viele** ...?	how many . . . ?
wo willst du denn hin?	where are you going?

Wörter im Deutschkurs — Words in German Class

die **Antwort**	answer
die **Einführung**	introduction

die **Frage**	question
die **Grammatik**	grammar
die **Hausaufgabe**	homework
die **Sprechsituation**	conversational situation
die **Übung**	exercise
der **Punkt**	point
der **Wortschatz**	vocabulary
das **Kapitel**	chapter
stellen Sie **Fragen**	ask questions
unterschreib bitte hier	sign here, please
verbinden	to connect

Sonstige Wörter und Ausdrücke — Other Words and Expressions

aber	but
auch	also, too; as well
bitte	please
gibt es ...?	is there . . . ? / are there . . . ?
hübsch	pretty
kaputt	broken
mein(e)	my
mit	with
mit dem kurzen **Haar**	with the short hair
mit dem langen **Haar**	with the long hair
mit dem **Ohrring**	with the earring
mit dem **Schnurrbart**	with the mustache
nein	no
nicht	not
oder	or
schmutzig	dirty
sein	to be
sondern	but (rather/on the contrary)
trägst du gern ...?	do you like to wear . . . ?
viel	a lot, much
viele	many
von	of; from
zählen	to count
zu Hause	at home

Ähnliche Wörter

alt, **danke**, **dann**, **hier**, **in**, **neu**, **oft**, **so**, **und**

Strukturen und Übungen

A.1 Giving instructions: polite commands

command form = verb + **Sie**

Strukturen. The grammar explanations in *Einführung A* are meant to be used as "advance organizers" to help sts. understand your input. In general, sts. are not expected to be able to produce forms and structures that are explained in this chapter. All grammar points in *Einführung A* are presented again in later chapters. Marginal grammar notes provide sts. with rules of thumb and pointers to help them understand and learn the grammar concepts.

The instructions your instructor gives you in class consist of a verb, which ends in **-en,** and the pronoun **Sie** (*you*).* Like the English *you*, the German **Sie** can be used with one person (*you*) or with more than one (*you* [*all*]). In English instructions the pronoun *you* is normally understood but not said. In German, **Sie** is a necessary part of the sentence.

Stehen Sie bitte **auf.**	*Please stand up.*
Nehmen Sie bitte das Buch.	*Please take the book.*

With certain instructions, you will also hear the word **sich** (*yourself*).†

Setzen Sie sich, bitte.	*Sit down, please.*

A.1. *Aufforderungen.* The goal of A.1 is recognition of commands. Forms like separable prefixes and reflexive pronouns will be explained later.

Note. Answers to the *Übungen* are in Appendix F.

Übung 1

Im Seminarraum

Was sagt Frau Schulz zu den Studenten?

Nehmen Sie einen Stift!
Sagen Sie „Guten Tag"!
Schauen Sie an die Tafel!
Schließen Sie das Buch!
Schreiben Sie „Tschüss"!
Öffnen Sie das Buch!
Hören Sie zu!
Geben Sie mir die Hausaufgabe!

1. Peter

2. Heidi

3. Monika

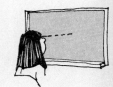

4. Nora

5. Albert

6. Stefan

7. Thomas

8. Katrin

*The pronoun **Sie** (*you*) is capitalized to distinguish it from another pronoun, **sie** (*she; it; they*).
†**Sich** is a reflexive pronoun; its use will be explained in **Kapitel 11.**

A.2 What is your name? The verb *heißen*

heißen = *to be called*
Wie heißen Sie? (*formal*)
Wie heißt du? (*informal*)

A.2. Point out the meaning of *Wie* in the question *Wie heißen Sie?* This is the sts.' first encounter with verb conjugation in German, so only the most useful forms are included here. The complete conjugations of *sein* and *haben* and the first full conjugation of a regular verb (*kommen*) appear in *Einführung B*.

Use a form of the verb **heißen** (*to be called*) to tell your name and to ask for the names of others.

Wie heißen Sie? / Wie heißt du?*	*What is your name?*
Ich heiße ...	*My name is . . .*

heißen (singular forms)	
ich heiße	*my name is*
du heißt Sie heißen	*your name is*
er heißt sie heißt	*his name is* *her name is*

Übung 2   Minidialoge

Üb.2. *Minidialoge* appear frequently in the exercises. One way to use them is to assign them as homework and, in the next class, give the roles to sts. to perform. Familiarize sts. with the *er/sie*-form by using it in class. When taking attendance, ask: *Wie heißt Ihre Nachbarin? Heißt sie Anna?* etc. This procedure also helps sts. learn one another's names.

Ergänzen Sie[1] das Verb **heißen**: heiße, heißt, heißen.

1. ERNST: Hallo, wie _____ª du?
   JUTTA: Ich _____ᵇ Jutta. Und du?
   ERNST: Ich _____ᶜ Ernst.

2. HERR THELEN: Guten Tag, wie _____ª Sie bitte?
   HERR SIEBERT: Ich _____ᵇ Siebert, Alexander Siebert.

3. CLAIRE: Hallo, ich _____ª Claire und wie heißt ihr?
   MELANIE: Ich _____ᵇ Melanie und er _____ᶜ Josef.

A.3 The German case system

Case shows how nouns function in a sentence.

A.3. *Das deutsche Kasussystem.* Point out to sts. here that they will not need to know the reason for the endings on articles and adjectives to understand your speech. The context and your gestures will help them interpret what you say. Occasionally, a st. will insist on knowing the reason for every form. Avoid long grammar explanations in class. The forms will be explained when sts. are asked to produce them.

German speakers use a *case system* (nominative for the subject, accusative for the direct object, and so on) to indicate the function of a particular noun in a sentence. The article[†] or adjective that precedes the noun shows its case. You will learn the correct endings in future lessons. For now, be aware that you will hear and read articles and adjectives with a variety of endings. These various forms will not prevent you from understanding German. Here are all the possibilities.

der, das, die, dem, den, des	*the*
ein, eine, einen, einem, einer, eines	*a, an*
blau, blaue, blauer, blaues, blauen, blauem	*blue*

*The difference between **Sie** (*formal*) and **du** (*informal*) will be explained in Section A.5.
[†]Articles are words such as *the, a,* and *an,* which precede nouns.
[1]**Ergänzen ...** *Supply*

In addition, definite articles may contract with some prepositions, just as *do* and *not* contract to *don't* in English. Here are some common contractions you will hear and read.

in + das	= ins		*into the*
in + dem	= im		*in the*
zu + der	= zur	}	*to the*
zu + dem	= zum		
an + das	= ans		*to/on the*
an + dem	= am		*to/at the*

A.4 Grammatical gender: nouns and pronouns

A.4. *Genus: Nomen und Pronomen.* The two main points in this section are the notion of grammatical gender in German and the replacement of nouns by pronouns according to grammatical gender. Emphasize the usefulness of color-coded lists for learning gender. Use classroom objects and your PF (picture file) to help sts. bind articles to nouns and acquire correct pronoun substitution. The most frequent error in pronoun replacement is the use of es for all inanimate nouns. Articles and personal pronouns are discussed again in *Einführung B.*

masculine = **der**

neuter = **das**

feminine = **die**

plurals (all genders) = **die**

In German, all nouns are classified grammatically as masculine, neuter, or feminine. When referring to people, grammatical gender usually matches biological sex.

MASCULINE	FEMININE
der Mann	**die** Frau
der Student	**die** Studentin

When referring to things or concepts, however, grammatical gender obviously has nothing to do with biological sex.

MASCULINE	NEUTER	FEMININE
der Rock	**das** Hemd	**die** Hose
der Hut	**das** Buch	**die** Jacke

The definite article indicates the grammatical gender of a noun. German has three nominative singular definite articles: **der** (*masculine*), **das** (*neuter*), and **die** (*feminine*). The plural article is **die** for all genders. All mean *the*.

	Singular	Plural
Masculine	der	die
Neuter	das	die
Feminine	die	die

der → **er** = *he, it*

das → **es** = *it*

die → **sie** = *she, it*

die (*pl.*) → **sie** = *they*

Note. You may need to point out the distinction in usage: *Haben* is used in a question about colors, *sein* in a statement.

Suggestion. You may wish to provide further tips to your sts.—e.g., nouns ending in *-er* are mostly masculine.

The personal pronouns **er, es, sie** (*he, it, she*) reflect the gender of the nouns they replace. For example, **er** (*he, it*) refers to **der Rock** because the grammatical gender is masculine; **es** (*it*) refers to **das Hemd** (*neuter*); **sie** (*she, it*) refers to **die Jacke** (*feminine*). The personal pronoun **sie** (*they*) refers to all plural nouns.

—Welche Farbe hat **der Rock?**	*What color is the skirt?*
—Er ist gelb.	*It is yellow.*
—Welche Farbe hat **das Hemd?**	*What color is the shirt?*
—Es ist weiß.	*It is white.*
—Welche Farbe hat **die Jacke?**	*What color is the jacket?*
—Sie ist braun.	*It is brown.*
—Welche Farbe haben **die Bleistifte?**	*What color are the pencils?*
—Sie sind gelb.	*They are yellow.*

Sometimes gender can be determined from the ending of the noun; for example, nouns that end in **-e**, such as **die Jacke** or **die Bluse**, are usually feminine. The ending **-in** indicates a female person: **die Studentin, die Professorin.**

In most cases, however, gender cannot be predicted from the form of the word. It is best, therefore, to learn the corresponding definite article along with each new noun.*

Übung 3   Kleidung

Üb. 3–4. Use as examples articles of clothing sts. can see in the classroom. Alternating between exercise items and examples from the classroom makes the learning process more interesting.

Frau Schulz spricht über die Kleidung. Ergänzen Sie **er, es, sie** oder **sie** (Plural).

Frau Schulz:

1. Hier ist die Jacke. _____ ist neu.
2. Und hier ist das Kleid. _____ ist modern.
3. Hier ist der Rock. _____ ist kurz.
4. Und hier ist die Bluse. _____ ist hübsch.
5. Hier ist das Hemd. _____ ist grün.
6. Und hier sind die Schuhe. _____ sind schmutzig.
7. Hier ist der Hut. _____ ist rot.
8. Und hier ist die Hose. _____ ist weiß.
9. Hier sind die Stiefel. _____ sind schwarz.
10. Und hier ist der Anzug. _____ ist alt.

Übung 4   Welche Farbe?

Welche Farbe haben diese Kleidungsstücke? Ergänzen Sie **er, es, sie** oder **sie** (Plural) und die richtige Farbe.

1. A: Welche Farbe hat Marias Rock?
   B: _____ ist _____.

2. A: Welche Farbe hat Michaels Hose?
   B: _____ ist _____.

3. A: Welche Farbe hat Michaels Hemd?
   B: _____ ist _____.

4. A: Welche Farbe hat Michaels Hut?
   B: _____ ist _____ und _____.

5. A: Welche Farbe haben Marias Schuhe?
   B: _____ sind _____.

6. A: Welche Farbe haben Michaels Schuhe?
   B: _____ sind _____.

7. A: Welche Farbe hat Marias Bluse?
   B: _____ ist _____.

*Some students find the following suggestion helpful. When you hear or read new nouns you consider useful, write them down in a vocabulary notebook, using different colors for the three genders; for example, use blue for masculine, black for neuter, and red for feminine. Some students also write nouns in three separate columns according to gender.

A.5 Addressing people: *Sie* versus *du* or *ihr*

A.5. *Jemanden ansprechen.* Sts. who have not encountered the formal/informal distinction in other languages may need further explanation in class.

German speakers use two modes of addressing others: the formal **Sie** (*singular* and *plural*) and the informal **du** (*singular*) or **ihr** (*plural*). You usually use **Sie** with someone you don't know or when you want to show respect or social distance. Children are addressed as **du.** Students generally call one another **du.**

Use **du** and **ihr** with friends, family, and children. Use **Sie** with almost everyone else.

	Singular	Plural
Informal	du	ihr
Formal	Sie	Sie

Frau Ruf, **Sie** sind 38, nicht wahr?
Jens und Jutta, **ihr** seid 16, nicht wahr?
Hans, **du** bist 13, nicht wahr?

Ms. Ruf, you are 38, aren't you?
Jens and Jutta, you are 16, aren't you?
Hans, you are 13, aren't you?

Übung 5 *Sie, du* oder *ihr*?

Üb. 5. Sts. should have no difficulty understanding the meaning of the plural nouns. Plural forms of nouns will be presented in *Einführung B*. **Item 5.** The usage depends on the relationship between the women. Explain that *Sie* would be used at first but could later change to *du* if the women became friends. This lends itself to discussion in class.

Was sagen diese Personen: **Sie, du** oder **ihr**?

1. Student → Student *du*
2. Professor → Student *Sie (uni or college)*
3. Freund → Freund *du*
4. Studentin → zwei Studenten *ihr*
5. Frau (40 Jahre alt) → Frau (50 Jahre alt) *Sie*
6. Student → Sekretärin *Sie*
7. Doktor → Patient *Sie (du if child)*
8. Frau → zwei Kinder *ihr*

GOALS

The purpose of *Einführung B* is to give sts. opportunities to make the transition from Comprehension to Early Speech. Continue to emphasize the development of the ability to comprehend German, but, at the same time, encourage sts. to begin to respond using single words and short phrases. In many activities throughout the text sts. will work in pairs or in small groups rather than having a strictly teacher-centered lesson. The semantic focus continues to be on identification and descriptions of common items and people in the sts.' environment.

In **Einführung B,** you will continue to develop your listening skills and will begin to speak more German. You will learn to talk about your classroom, the weather, and people: their character traits, family relationships, and national origins.

Themen

Der Seminarraum

Beschreibungen

Der Körper

Die Familie

Wetter und Jahreszeiten

Herkunft und Nationalität

Kulturelles

KLI: Was ist wichtig im Leben?

KLI: Wetter und Klima

Musikszene: „36 Grad" (2raumwohnung)

KLI: Die Lage Deutschlands in Europa

Videoecke: Familie

Strukturen

B.1 Definite and indefinite articles

B.2 Who are you? The verb **sein**

B.3 What do you have? The verb **haben**

B.4 Plural forms of nouns

B.5 Personal pronouns

B.6 Origins: **Woher kommen Sie?**

B.7 Possessive adjectives: **mein** and **dein/Ihr**

PRE-TEXT ORAL ACTIVITIES

(1) Classroom commands. Use TPR to review classroom commands from *Einführung A*. Sample sequence: *Stehen Sie auf, öffnen Sie das Buch, schließen Sie das Buch, setzen Sie sich.* Repeat and recombine commands during the sequence. Narrow the size of the group participating in individual commands by giving selective descriptions: *Männer, die Jeans tragen, stehen Sie bitte auf, heben Sie die rechte Hand, setzen Sie sich.* **(2) Transition to Stage II:** Use the topics from *Einführung A* to make the transition from Stage I to Stage II. (See the IM for suggestions of the types of questions appropriate for Stage II activities.) Talk about numbers, clothes, and colors. Hold up fingers and ask either/or questions such as *Sind es fünf oder sechs?* Expand answers: *Ja, richtig, das sind fünf.* Create sequences using several types of questions: *Wer trägt ein weißes Hemd? (Robert.) Ja, das stimmt. Heute trägt Robert ein weißes Hemd.* (Use subject-verb inversion naturally to get the sts. used to both word orders.) *Trägt Tom eine gelbe Hose? (Ja.) Ja? Ist die Hose gelb? Nicht orange? Wirklich? Und welche Farbe hat Janes Bluse? Ist sie grün oder braun?*

Doris Ziegler: *Familienbild* (c. 1978), Privatbesitz

Chapter opening artwork: This painting is a good example of Doris Ziegler's realistic but rather harsh style. The dominant colors, mainly blue and grey, underline the distance and lack of emotion and warmth in this painting. The couple seems to be represented as individuals, detached and lonely, with the father looking directly at the viewer almost portrait-like and the mother concentrating on the baby in her lap.

Suggestion: Use Ziegler's painting as a starting point for input and to introduce the chapter themes. Ask the following questions and answer them yourself, or expand them to yes/no or forced-choice questions.

Kunst und Künstler

Doris Ziegler (b. 1949) is a well-known contemporary German painter associated with the *Leipziger Schule*. Born in Weimar, she studied painting and graphic design in Leipzig from 1969 to 1974 at the *Hochschule für Grafik und Buchkunst* (HGB, Academy of Visual Arts), one of the oldest art schools in Germany. She has taught at the HGB since 1993.

Was sehen Sie auf dem Gemälde[1]?

1. Welche Farben sind dominant: rot, blau, grün, grau, schwarz, braun, weiß, rosa oder orange?
2. Welche Personen und Lebewesen sehen Sie: einen Mann, eine Frau, ein Kind, einen Hund, eine Katze?
3. Was ist im Vordergrund[2], was im Hintergrund[3]: der Mann, die Frau, ein Sofa, ein Tisch, eine Lampe, ein Radio, Bilder, Fenster, Häuser?
4. Welche Gefühle[4] evoziert das Gemälde: Familie, Hierarchie, Treue, Ruhe, Hoffnung, Liebe, Unschuld, Glück?

[1]*painting* [2]*foreground* [3]*background* [4]*feelings*

Situationen

Vocabulary Display Presentation: Start with the screen that shows the classroom, so you are sure to include all vocabulary items introduced in this section. *Das ist ein Tisch. Das ist ein Buch. Das Buch liegt auf dem Tisch. Das ist die Wand; das ist die Uhr. Die Uhr hängt an der Wand. usw.* Afterward, review the items by pointing to the real articles in your classroom and saying each word. **Receptive recall:** Point to the items in your classroom and ask: *Ist das ein Stuhl oder ein Tisch? Ist das ein Heft oder ein Buch? usw.* Or: (hold book) *Das ist ein Stuhl, nicht wahr? (Nein.) Richtig. Das ist kein Stuhl. Das ist ein Buch.* Or: *die Lampe. Gibt es in unserem Seminarraum eine Lampe? Ja oder nein?* **Productive recall:** Cover the item's label on the screen and ask *Was ist das?* Or simply point to the item in the classroom and ask: *Was ist das?* **Personalization:** *Nehmen Sie ein Blatt Papier und einen Stift. Schreiben Sie sieben Dinge auf, die Sie zu Hause in Ihrem Zimmer haben.* **Expansion:** Review/Introduce common adjectives to describe items in the classroom: *schön, hässlich, groß, hoch, kurz, alt, neu; sauber, schmutzig* (some of these will be used in later situations). Ask either/or questions: *Ist der Tisch alt oder neu? Sind die Wände grün oder weiß?*

Sit. 1. First, prepare the sts. for this activity, and then ask them to work in pairs. This activity gives sts. the opportunity to recognize plural forms (introduced formally in B.4) and use indefinite articles. **Preparation:** Sts.' books are closed. Ask all questions and have sts. count. When the answer is 1, make sure they use *ein* and *eine* correctly and change the nouns to singular. Introduce the word *viele* for items that are difficult to count because there are so many of them or because you can't see them very well. Establish the pattern by asking your sts. to repeat the first question a few times. Then, point to or hold up the next item so that sts. can ask the second question. Do that for all items. **Activity:** Ask sts. to do the activity in pairs. Set a time limit (2 minutes). One st. asks all questions in a row and writes down the answers. The st. who answers has his or her book closed. Then, ask sts. to switch roles. Encourage sts. to go beyond the items in the book. **Wrap-up:** Ask the same questions in a different order.

Sit. 2. Introduce new vocabulary and review old vocabulary by pointing and saying (or asking) *Das ist … (Was ist das?).* Review nouns by doing a TPR activity: *Zeigen Sie auf den Boden (das Fenster usw.)!* Then ask sts. to do *Sit. 2* in pairs: first, one st. asks all questions, then the other asks. This activity gives sts. the chance to produce the definite articles with nouns and to hear that adjectives in predicate position are not inflected. For #6, encourage sts. to think of additional adjectives such as *klein, groß, grün,* and so forth, as well as other classroom objects.

Der Seminarraum

Grammatik B.1

Situation 1 Der Seminarraum

Wie viele _____ sind im Seminarraum?

1. Studenten
2. Tische
3. Fenster
4. Lampen

5. Uhren
6. Türen
7. Bücher
8. Tafeln

9. Professoren/ Professorinnen
10. Hefte
11. Laptops

Situation 2 Gegenstände[1] im Seminarraum

MODELL: S1: Was ist weiß?
S2: Die Tafel (ist weiß).

1. weiß
2. schmutzig
3. sauber
4. neu
5. alt
6. _____

a. der Boden
b. das Fenster
c. die Tafel
d. die Uhr
e. der Beamer
f. _____

[1]objects

Beschreibungen

Grammatik B.2–B.3

Vocabulary Display
Presentation: *Das ist Michael Pusch. Er ist groß* (show with your hands that this means "tall," not "heavy," or contrast immediately with *klein*), *und er hat einen Schnurrbart. Herr Siebert steht neben Michael. Herr Siebert ist alt und er hat einen Schnurrbart und einen Bart usw.* **Receptive recall:** (covering up vocabulary above the characters but allowing their names to show) *Wer ist groß? Wer ist klein? Wer ist alt? usw.* When possible, ask about contrasting opposites (*groß/klein, alt/jung, usw.*). **Choral response. Productive recall:** *Wie ist Michael? Ist er groß oder klein? Und wie ist Jens? Ist er auch groß? Hat Michael einen Bart oder einen Schnurrbart? Was hat Herr Siebert? usw.* **Personalization:** *Wer im Deutschkurs hat blondes/ kurzes Haar? Wer ist klein/groß? usw.*

groß
schlank

alt
Bart

jung
klein

langes, braunes Haar

kurzes, blondes Haar

kurzes, graues Haar

Michael Pusch — Herr Siebert — Jens Krüger — Maria Schneider — Jutta Ruf — Frau Körner

Situation 3   Im Deutschkurs

Sit. 3. Ask sts. to write a classmate's name for each description. If they don't know a name, they should go to that person and ask his or her name. It is usually easier to do this activity standing up so sts. are more inclined to move around. As a follow-up, ask the whole class: *Wer ist blond? Ja, Janet ist blond und Robert auch usw.*

Alternate Activity (AA). Have sts. write a description of someone in the classroom, using lists of words or phrases, and ask others to guess the identity.

1. Wer ist _____?
   a. blond
   b. groß
   c. klein
   d. schlank
   e. jung
   f. alt

2. Wer hat _____?
   a. braunes Haar
   b. graues Haar
   c. kurzes Haar
   d. langes Haar
   e. einen Bart
   f. blaue Augen
   g. braune Augen

Situation 4   Interaktion: Wie bist du?

Sit. 4. Throughout *Kontakte*, new vocabulary is introduced both in the illustrations that begin each section and in the activities that follow them. Always make sure that students understand all the new words before asking them to work on their own or in groups. In *Sit. 4*, sts. first check the characteristics that apply to themselves. Next, each st. asks one male and one female st. what they are like: *Bist du fröhlich, traurig, konservativ, usw.?* The students questioned answer either *ja* or *nein*, according to what they have already checked. Those asking the questions should write down the name of the interviewee and check the boxes for which the answer is *ja*.

Photo questions. *Wie sieht der Mann / die Frau aus? Wie alt ist er/sie? Wie ist er/sie? (konservativ, schüchtern, sportlich)? Ist er/sie verheiratet? Hat er/sie eine große Familie? Warum ist er/sie froh/ traurig?*

MODELL: s1: Bist du glücklich?
          s2: Ja, ich bin glücklich.
          oder Nein, ich bin nicht glücklich.

	ICH	MEIN PARTNER	MEINE PARTNERIN
glücklich	☐	☐	☐
traurig	☐	☐	☐
konservativ	☐	☐	☐
schüchtern	☐	☐	☐
religiös	☐	☐	☐
ruhig	☐	☐	☐
freundlich	☐	☐	☐
verrückt	☐	☐	☐
sportlich	☐	☐	☐

Mir geht's gut.

Ach, wie traurig!

Was ist wichtig im Leben?

Was ist für Sie wichtig? Was ist am wichtigsten, was ist weniger wichtig? Bringen Sie die Aussagen in die Reihenfolge ihrer Wichtigkeit für Sie!

_____ Ich möchte gute Freunde haben[1].
_____ Ich möchte einen hohen Lebensstandard[2] haben.
_____ Ich möchte sozial Benachteiligten[3] helfen.
_____ Ich glaube an Gott.
_____ Ich möchte das Leben in vollen Zügen genießen[4].
_____ Ich möchte meine Bedürfnisse[5] durchsetzen[6].
_____ Ich möchte ein gutes Familienleben haben.

Schauen Sie sich die Grafik an. Welche Werte[7] haben junge Deutsche?

1. Was steht auf Platz 1?
2. Was ist wichtiger[8] für die jungen Deutschen: ein gutes Familienleben oder ein hoher Lebensstandard?
3. Was ist wichtiger für sie: eigene Bedürfnisse durchzusetzen oder sozial Benachteiligten zu helfen?
4. Wie viel Prozent der jungen Deutschen glauben an Gott?
5. Wie viel Prozent der jungen Deutschen wollen das Leben in vollen Zügen genießen?

Freunde beim Grillen im Park

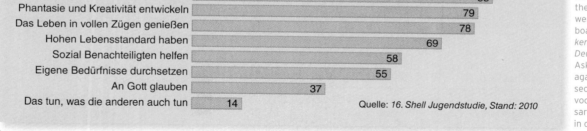

Wertorientierungen: Pragmatisch, aber nicht angepasst
Jugendliche im Alter von 12 bis 25 Jahren (Angaben in %)

Gute Freunde haben	97
Gutes Familienleben führen	92
Eigenverantwortlich leben und handeln	90
Fleißig und ehrgeizig sein	83
Phantasie und Kreativität entwickeln	79
Das Leben in vollen Zügen genießen	78
Hohen Lebensstandard haben	69
Sozial Benachteiligten helfen	58
Eigene Bedürfnisse durchsetzen	55
An Gott glauben	37
Das tun, was die anderen auch tun	14

Quelle: *16. Shell Jugendstudie, Stand: 2010*

[1]möchte haben *would like to have*   [2]*standard of living*   [3]*disadvantaged people*   [4]das Leben ... *live life to its fullest*   [5]*needs*   [6]*make known*   [7]*values*   [8]*more important*

Kultur ... Landeskunde ... Informationen. Establish the context by asking sts. *Was ist im Leben wichtig: viel Geld? ein guter Job? eine gute Familie? gute Freunde?* Then ask them to work in pairs to complete the first task. Help with vocabulary where necessary. Ask 5–6 pairs what their top three priorities were and write them on the board. Then ask: *Was denken Sie? Was ist für junge Deutsche wichtig? Dasselbe?* Ask sts. to work in pairs again to complete the second activity. Help with vocabulary where necessary. Follow up by discussing in class.

Der Körper

Grammatik B.4

Vocabulary Display
Use TPR to introduce parts of the body. Begin with the hand: *Das ist die Hand. Das ist der Arm.* Add other parts one by one, repeating each new word several times: *Haar, Augen, Rücken usw.* Alternate with the touch command: *Berühren Sie den Arm. Berühren Sie Ihren rechten Arm mit Ihrer linken Hand. Berühren Sie das Bein.*

AA. „*Simon sagt*": ask sts. to touch parts of their body, but this time precede (almost) every request with „*Simon sagt*": *Simon sagt, berühren Sie die Augen. Simon sagt, berühren Sie die Nase usw.* If you give a command without first saying „*Simon sagt*," any sts. who indicate the body part mentioned must sit down. Even adults enjoy this.

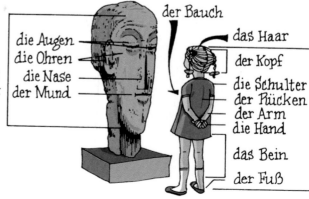

der Bauch
die Augen
die Ohren
die Nase
der Mund
das Gesicht
das Haar
der Kopf
die Schulter
der Rücken
der Arm
die Hand
das Bein
der Fuß
der Körper

Situation 5   Welches Monster ist das?

Sit. 5. Preparation: First, describe all the creatures to sts. Then, describe one creature at a time in random order, and ask sts. to name the creature you are describing. **Activity:** Explain the task to sts. Working in pairs, one person chooses one creature without naming it and describes it to his/her partner. If the partner correctly names the creature, he or she receives a point and the right to describe a creature. If the partner does not correctly name the creature, the st. describing gets a point and gets to describe another creature. Allow sts. 3–4 min. to do the activity in pairs and then ask them to describe creatures for you to guess.

MODELL: S1: Mein Monster hat fünf Beine und vier Arme.
S2: Das ist Momo.

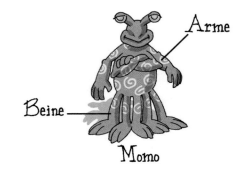

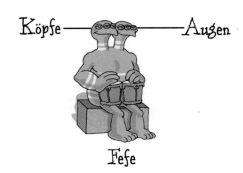

Die Familie

Grammatik B.5

Vocabulary Display
Presentation and receptive recall: Introduce the people and their relationship to one another: *Das ist Dora Schmitz. Ihr Mann heißt Johannes Schmitz. Dora und Johannes haben drei Kinder: zwei Töchter und einen Sohn. Wie heißt der Sohn? (Rolf.) Rolf, richtig. Und wie heißen die Töchter? (Helga und Sigrid.) Helga und Sigrid, richtig. Wie heißt der Mann von Ursula Köhnen? Wie viele Kinder haben Ursula and Viktor? Wie viele Töchter? Wie viele Söhne? Wie heißt die Tochter? Und die Söhne?* Introduce in a similar way (about 4–6 at a time): *Vater, Mutter, Onkel, Tante, Neffe, Nichte; Opa, Oma, Enkelkinder; Geschwister, Bruder, Schwester, Vetter, Kusine.* When working with the display at another time, you can introduce *Schwiegereltern, -vater, -mutter, -sohn, -tochter, Schwager, Schwägerin.*
Choral response: Point to Helga and say: *Das ist Helgas Familie. Sigrid ist die Schwester. Wiederholen Sie bitte: die Schwester usw.* Students repeat only the family relationship. **Productive recall:** Similar to choral response. Pick a focal person (e.g., Dora Schmitz) and say: *Wer ist Johannes Schmitz? Johannes ist Doras _____. usw.* **Personalization:** *Schreiben Sie auf: den Namen von Ihrem Vater, von Ihrer Mutter, von einem Bruder (wenn Sie einen haben) usw.*

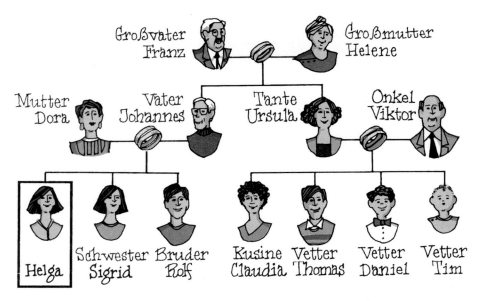

Dora und Johannes Schmitz sind verheiratet. Sie haben drei Kinder: einen Sohn und zwei Töchter.

Situation 6 Interview: Die Familie

Sit. 6. (See the IM Walk-Through.)

1. Wie heißt dein Vater/Stiefvater? Wie alt ist er? Wo wohnt er?
2. Wie heißt deine Mutter/Stiefmutter? Wie alt ist sie? Wo wohnt sie?
3. Hast du Geschwister? Wie viele? Wie heißen sie? Wie alt sind sie? Wo wohnen sie?

 Situation 7* Informationsspiel: Familie

Sit. 7. This is the first information-gap activity in table form. As with previous information-gap activities, it is designed to create a genuine exchange of information in a controlled way. Sts. work in pairs. One st. works with the chart on this page, the other with the corresponding chart in Appendix A. Each has only half the information in the chart and must ask a partner questions to fill in the missing pieces. Model question-and-answer pairs are given.

MODELL: s2: Wie heißt Richards Vater?
s1: Er heißt Werner.
s2: Wie schreibt man das?
s1: W-E-R-N-E-R. Wie alt ist er?
s2: Er ist _____ Jahre alt. Wo wohnt er?
s1: Er wohnt in Innsbruck. Wie heißt Richards Mutter?
s2: Sie heißt _____.
s1: Wie schreibt man das?
s2: _____.

		Richard	Sofie	Mehmet
Vater	Name	Werner	Erwin	Kenan
	Alter	39	50	59
	Wohnort	Innsbruck	Dresden	Izmir
Mutter	Name	Maria	Elfriede	Sule
	Alter	38	47	54
	Wohnort	Innsbruck	Dresden	Izmir
Bruder	Name	Alexander	Erwin	Yakup
	Alter	15	27	34
	Wohnort	Innsbruck	Leipzig	Istanbul
Schwester	Name	Elisabeth	—	Fatima
	Alter	16	—	31
	Wohnort	Innsbruck	—	Izmir

To start the activity, pair sts. off by counting 1, 2, 1, 2, etc. All twos turn to the appendix, and all ones work with the chart in the chapter. Remind sts. not to show their half of the activity to their partners. Students alternate, asking questions for each person listed, moving vertically down the columns.
s2: *Wie heißt Richards Vater?*
s1: *Er heißt Werner.*
s2: *Wie schreibt man das?*
s1: *W-E-R-N-E-R. Wie alt ist er?*
s2: *Er ist 39 Jahre alt. Wo wohnt er?*
s1: *Er wohnt in Innsbruck. Wie heißt Richards Mutter?*
s2: *Sie heißt Maria.*
s1: *Wie schreibt man das?*
s2: *M-A-R-I-A. usw.*

Teach sts. phrases such as *Wie bitte? Noch einmal, bitte! Wie schreibt man das? Wie heißt das? Ich verstehe nicht. Danke.* to enable them to keep the complete interaction in German.

*This is an information-gap activity in table form. Pair up with another student. One of you will work with the following chart, the other with the corresponding chart in Appendix A. Different information is missing from each chart.

Wetter und Jahreszeiten

Vocabulary Display
Presentation: Use the projector or your PF to introduce weather expressions. Then use a calendar to teach names of months and seasons.
Receptive recall: Ask: *Welches Bild zeigt: Es ist heiß? usw.* Months and seasons: Ask: *Welche Jahreszeit haben wir im Januar? im Juli? In welchen Monaten ist es kalt? Wann ist es warm? usw.* **Choral response. Productive recall:** Cover the labels on the transparency and ask sts. what the weather is, which are winter months, in what season it is hot, windy, etc. Or bring in other pictures and ask: *Wie ist das Wetter?*

WIE IST DAS WETTER?

1. Es ist sonnig und warm.

2. Es ist sehr heiß.

3. Es ist kalt.

4. Es regnet.

5. Es ist kühl.

6. Es schneit.

7. Es ist windig.

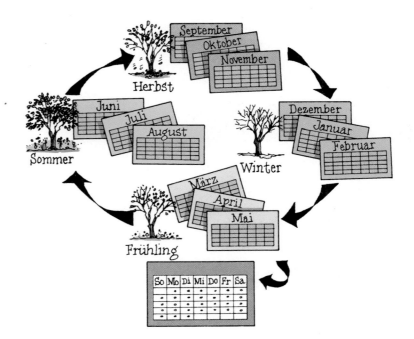

 Situation 8 Dialog: Das Wetter in Regensburg

Josef trifft Claire an der Uni.

Sit. 8. Use this dialogue as an exercise in listening comprehension, following the steps outlined in *Sit. 9* of *Einführung A:* **(1)** Set the scene; **(2)** Play the dialogue several times while sts. fill in the blanks; **(3)** Ask sts. to check their answers in pairs or groups; **(4)** Write answers on the board.

JOSEF: Schön heute, nicht?
CLAIRE: Ja, sehr <u>warm</u> und <u>sonnig</u> – wirklich schön!
JOSEF: Leider <u>regnet</u> es so oft hier in Bayern – auch im <u>Sommer</u>.
CLAIRE: Ist es auch oft <u>kühl</u> und <u>windig</u> hier?
JOSEF: Ja, im <u>Frühling</u>. Und manchmal <u>schneit</u> es noch im April.

Wetter und Klima

Winterwetter in München

Wie ist das Wetter in Ihrer Stadt? Kreuzen Sie an.

	IM WINTER	IM SOMMER
sonnig	☐	☐
warm	☐	☐
(sehr) heiß	☐	☐
(sehr) feucht	☐	☐
mild	☐	☐
(sehr) kalt	☐	☐
viele Niederschläge[1] (Schnee/Regen)	☐	☐
windig	☐	☐
große Temperaturunterschiede[2]	☐	☐
geringe[3] Temperaturunterschiede	☐	☐

Deutschland hat ein gemäßigtes[4] Klima mit Niederschlägen in allen Jahreszeiten. Im Nordwesten ist das Klima mehr ozeanisch mit warmen, aber selten heißen Sommern und relativ milden Wintern. Im Osten ist es eher[5] kontinental. Im Winter liegen die Temperaturen im Durchschnitt[6] zwischen 1,5 Grad Celsius (°C) im Tiefland[7] und minus 6°C im Gebirge[8], im Juli liegen sie zwischen 18 und 20°C.

Ausnahmen[9]: Am Rhein ist das Klima sehr mild, hier wächst[10] sogar Wein. Oberbayern hat einen warmen alpinen Südwind, den Föhn. Im Harz sind die Sommer oft kühl und im Winter gibt es viel Schnee.

Wie sind die Temperaturen in Deutschland? Benutzen Sie die Tabelle.

	Sommer	Winter Tiefland	Winter Gebirge
in °C			
in °F			

Welche Gebiete[11] bilden Ausnahmen?

> *wo* _____
>
> *Klima*   sehr _____   warmer _____   Sommer: _____
>   Winter: _____

[1]precipitation   [2]temperature variations   [3]minor   [4]moderate   [5]more   [6]im ... on average   [7]lowlands   [8]mountains
[9]exceptions   [10]grows   [11]areas

Temperaturen in Fahrenheit und Celsius

Fahrenheit → Celsius

32 subtrahieren und mit 5/9 multiplizieren

°F		°C
0		-17,8
32		0
50	~	10
70		21,1
90		32,2
98,6		37
212		100

Celsius → Fahrenheit

Mit 9/5 multiplizieren und 32 addieren

°C		°F
-10		14
0		32
10	~	50
20		68
30		86
37		98,6
100		212

Sit. 9. (See also the IM.) As in *Sit. 7*, one st. uses the chart on this page, the other st. uses the chart in Appendix A. Use the following steps: **(1)** Introduce the topic: *Wissen Sie, wie viel Grad Celsius 65 Grad Fahrenheit sind? Nein? Das werden Sie jetzt erfahren.* **(2)** Preteach vocabulary: Review numbers from 0 to 100 and introduce how to express negative numbers, e.g., *minus fünf.* **(3)** Set up activity: Practice the sample exchange. Remind sts. to use phrases such as *Wie bitte?* and not to look at each other's charts. Divide sts. into two groups and set a time limit of 2-3 minutes. **(4)** Follow-up: Ask students to convert additional Fahrenheit temperatures such as today's high and low temperatures. To convert Fahrenheit into Celsius, subtract 32 and multiply by 5/9.

Musikszene. The goal of this feature is to provide sts. with a view of contemporary German popular music, to motivate them to listen to songs in German, and to pay attention to the lyrics. The song can be downloaded from iTunes. **Suggestion:** Tell sts. that they will hear a contemporary German pop song. Tell them that the song is by a group called *2raumwohnung* (pronounced: *Zweiraumwohnung*) and tell them what it means: *ein Apartment mit zwei Zimmern oder Räumen.* Ask them to read the musician bio and find the answers to the following questions: *Aus wie viel Personen besteht die Gruppe? Wie heißen die Personen? Wann war ihre Single „36 Grad" der Sommerhit in Deutschland?* Then ask sts. to read the *Vor dem Hören* question. Ask them: *Ist 36 Grad kalt oder heiß?* Then ask them to convert 36 degrees Celsius into Fahrenheit. (Answer: 96.8°.) Next, ask sts. to read the true/false statements in part A of *Nach dem Hören.* Play the beginning of the song up to and including the chorus. Ask sts. to determine if the statements are true or false. You may need to replay the chorus several times. Discuss in class. Finally, tell sts. that the singer will say that she takes off her shoes and puts on her bikini in verse two and ask them to listen to what happens then. (Answer: They go outside and dance in the rain.) Play several times and discuss in class.

 Situation 9 Informationsspiel: Temperaturen

MODELL: s1: Wie viel Grad Celsius sind 90 Grad Fahrenheit?
s2: _____ Grad Celsius.

°F	90	65	32	0	−5	−39
°C	32	18	0	−18	−21	−39

Sommer im Voralpenland

Musikszene

„36 Grad" (2007, Deutschland) *2raumwohnung*

2raumwohnung im Konzert

Biografie *2raumwohnung* (Zweiraumwohnung) ist ein Duo aus Berlin. Das Duo besteht aus Inga Humpe und Tommi Eckart. „36 Grad" war der Sommerhit des Jahres 2007 in Deutschland.

Vor dem Hören Wie viel Grad Fahrenheit sind 36 Grad Celsius?

Nach dem Hören

A. Hören Sie den Refrain! Richtig oder falsch?

R **1.** Es ist heiß und wird noch heißer.

R **2.** Es gibt keinen Ventilator.

R **3.** Die Sängerin meint, das Leben ist leicht.

B. Die Sängerin zieht die Schuhe aus und den Bikini an. Was macht sie dann?

iMix Link: This song is available for purchase at the iTunes store in a special iMix created for *Kontakte*. For more information about accessing the playlist, go to **Connect German** (www.connectgerman.com).

Miniwörterbuch

der **Refrain**	chorus	(zieht ...) an	(puts) on
keinen	no, not a	regnen	to rain
das **Leben**	life	tanzen	to dance
leicht	easy	singen	to sing
zieht ... aus	takes off		

Note: *2raumwohnung (Zweiraumwohnung)* is a duo founded in Berlin in 2000. It consists of Inga Humpe and Tommi Eckart. "36 Grad" was Germany's summer hit in 2007 and was the group's most successful single.

Herkunft und Nationalität

Grammatik B.6–B.7

Vocabulary Display Presentation: Introduce countries by using the map on the projector and saying: *Hugh Grant kommt aus Großbritannien. Er spricht Englisch.* [Juliette Binoche: Frankreich (*Schauspielerin*), Federico Fellini: Italien (*Regisseur*), Vladimir Putin: Russland (*Politiker*), Luciano Pavarotti: Italien (*Sänger*), *usw.*] Use names students will know and concentrate on those countries of most interest to sts. **Receptive recall:** Ask either/or questions (*Kommt Nicolas Sarkozy aus Spanien oder Frankreich?*) or make false claims (*Juan Carlos kommt aus Schweden, nicht wahr?*) **Productive recall:** *Woher kommt _____?* or *Wo spricht man Französisch? Deutsch? Spanisch? usw.* Alternatively, quiz sts. about capital cities: *Wie heißt die Hauptstadt von _____?* Or use directions (*Welches Land liegt westlich von Spanien?*) and other geographical features (*Welche Länder liegen in Skandinavien?*). **Personalization:** Ask who has been to which country, who comes from where, or who has friends anywhere in Europe. Develop an association activity by using this information (see the IM) or by asking *Wer möchte mal nach Ungarn reisen? usw.*

 ## Situation 10   Dialog: Woher kommst du?

Sit. 10. This dialogue lends itself to serving as a model for sts.' own interactions and to their moving from comprehension to production via a series of steps. The following steps are intended for use with the textbooks closed. **(1)** Set the scene: *Sie hören ein kurzes Gespräch zwischen Claire und Melanie. Claire und Melanie sind auf einer Party.* **(2)** Ask focus questions: *Ist Claire Deutsche? Woher kommt sie? Ist Melanie Deutsche? Woher kommt sie?* **(3)** Play the dialogue. **(4)** Ask sts. to tell you the answers to the focus questions. **(5)** Ask sts. to count the words in each sentence. **(6)** Divide sts. into two groups, assign 1 role to each group, and ask each group to repeat their lines. **(7)** Ask groups to repeat their lines from memory. **(8)** Ask 2-3 pairs of volunteers (1 from each group) to present the dialogue in front of the class. Instead of assuming their previous roles, however, they should change the lines of the dialogue to talk about themselves. **(9)** Sts. get up and work in pairs. While moving from one person to the next, they act out their personalized versions several times.

Claire trifft Melanie auf einer Party.

CLAIRE: Wie heißt du?
MELANIE: Melanie. _Und du_?
CLAIRE: Claire.
MELANIE: Bist du _Amerikanerin_?
CLAIRE: Ja.
MELANIE: Und _woher_ kommst du?
CLAIRE: _Aus_ New York. Und du?
MELANIE: Aus Regensburg. Ich _bin_ von hier.

Situation 11　Herkunft

Sit. 11. Practice model questions and answers with your sts. Also practice the character names. Then ask sts. to write 7 questions, based on information in the display: 2 questions with *woher*, 2 questions with *wer*, and 3 *ja/nein* questions. Sts. then get together in pairs to ask and answer their questions. As always, they should take notes about their partner's responses, and you should conclude with a brief whole-class follow-up.

MODELL:　s1: Woher kommt Silvia Mertens?
　　　　s2: Sie kommt aus _____.
　　　　s1: Wer kommt aus Dresden?
　　　　s2: _____.
　　　　s1: Kommt Bernd Frisch aus Innsbruck?
　　　　s2: Nein, er kommt aus _____.

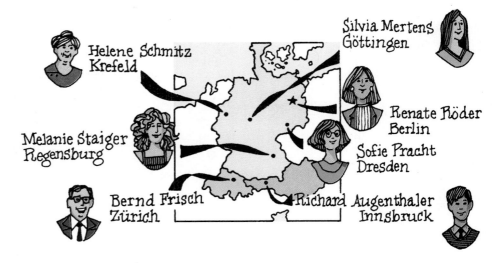

 ## Situation 12　Rollenspiel: Herkunft

Sit. 12. First set the scene: *Sie sind Studenten in Deutschland, und ich bin ein neuer Student / eine neue Studentin. Sie sind neugierig und stellen mir Fragen. Ich spreche über meine Familie und meine Freunde.* Brainstorm with students what questions one might ask. Write them on the board. Model pronunciation, have them repeat, and then answer the questions as they apply to you. Then have students work in pairs. S1 will work from here; S2 will turn to the appendix. Ask sts. to write down the answers.

s1: Sie sind ein neuer Student / eine neue Studentin an einer Universität in Deutschland. Sie lernen einen anderen Studenten / eine andere Studentin kennen. Fragen Sie, wie er/sie heißt und woher er/sie kommt. Fragen Sie auch, ob er/sie Freunde/Freundinnen in anderen Ländern hat und welche Sprachen sie sprechen.

Follow-up: Ask three to six students questions about themselves or about what they learned from their partners. **Note:** If your students are using McGraw-Hill's **Connect** online *Arbeitsbuch*, they can do this *Rollenspiel* using the real-time, interactive **Video-Chat** feature.

Kultur ... Landeskunde ... Informationen

Die Lage Deutschlands in Europa

Deutschland liegt mitten in Europa. Es grenzt an[1] Dänemark, _Polen_, Tschechien, Österreich, die _Schweiz_, Frankreich, Luxemburg, _Belgien_ und die Niederlande. Die Grenzen[2] Deutschlands sind _3 757_ Kilometer lang. Die längste Grenze ist die mit Österreich. Sie ist _815_ Kilometer lang. Die Grenze zu Dänemark ist nur _67_ Kilometer lang, die Grenze zu Polen _442_, zu Tschechien 811, zur Schweiz _316_, zu Frankreich 448, zu Luxemburg _135_, zu Belgien 156 und zu den Niederlanden _567_ Kilometer. Im Norden grenzt Deutschland an zwei Meere, die Nordsee und die _Ostsee_.

- Deutschland gehört[3] zur Europäischen Union. Welche Länder gehören noch zur Europäischen Union? Schauen Sie auf die Karte auf Seite 34.

[1]grenzt ... *has borders with*　[2]*borders*　[3]*belongs*

KLI. This text practices comprehension of numbers over 100 in addition to providing geographical information about Germany. Source: *Statistisches Bundesamt* **(1)** Establish the context by asking, e.g.: *Wo liegt Deutschland? Wo genau in Europa? Wie heißen seine Nachbarländer? Wie viele Nachbarn hat Deutschland insgesamt? Dazu hören wir jetzt einen Text.* **(2)** Read the text at least twice while sts. fill in the blanks. **(3)** Review sts.' answers. **(4)** Follow-up: Ask sts. to group the neighboring countries according to whether they lie to the West, the South, the East, or the North of Germany. Additional questions: *Wie heißt das Meer zwischen Großbritannien und Deutschland? zwischen Schweden und Polen? Welche Länder gehören zur Europäischen Union?* Refer sts. to the map of Europe on the previous page.

Videoecke

Perspektiven

Ich komme aus Leipzig.

> Woher kommst du und woher kommen deine Eltern?

Miniwörterbuch

der **Fluss**	river
die **Kirche**	church
das **Oberteil**	top
der **Tisch**	table
das **Kopftuch**	headscarf
das **Einzelkind**	only child

Videoecke. Perspektiven: Ask several sts. *Woher kommen Sie? Woher kommen Ihre Eltern?* Explain *Aufgabe 1.* Read all the statements out loud and make sure sts. understand them. Play the video segment twice and elicit answers. (The volume can be muted for *Aufgabe 1* if desired.) Then turn to *Aufgabe 2.* Go over the information already present and explain what sts. have to listen for. Play the segment twice and ask sts. to work in pairs or small groups. Elicit answers. **Interviews:** Next introduce Pascal and Nadezda and ask sts. what they already know about them based on the previous activities: *Was wissen Sie schon über Pascal und Nadezda?* Play the video segment a couple of times for sts. to complete *Aufgabe 3* in pairs or small groups. Elicit answers. Suggestions for additional questions: *An welchem Fluss liegt Moskau? An der Moskwa. Was sind Pascals Eltern? Sie sind Rentner* (retired). *Was antwortet Nadezda auf die Frage, wie das Wetter morgen wird? Sie weiß es nicht. Was sagt Pascal? Wunderschön.* For *Aufgabe 4*, ask sts. to think about their own answers to the questions posed in *Aufgabe 3* and to write them down. Finally, ask them to interview each other.

Aufgabe 1 Wer ist das?

Wie sehen sie aus? Wo sind sie? Ordnen Sie die Beschreibungen den Personen zu.

1. Tina _d_   2. Albrecht _b_   3. Simone _g_   4. Sandra _h_

5. Hend _f_   6. Felicitas _e_   7. Pascal _a_   8. Sophie _c_

a. Er steht an einem Fluss.
b. Er steht vor einer Kirche.
c. Sie hat langes blondes Haar und trägt ein blaues Oberteil.
d. Sie sitzt an einem Tisch.
e. Sie trägt ein graues Oberteil und eine graue Jacke.
f. Sie trägt ein Kopftuch.
g. Sie trägt ein pinkes Oberteil und eine Jacke.
h. Sie trägt einen grünen Pulli.

Aufgabe 2 Herkunft

Woher kommen sie? Woher kommen ihre Eltern? Ergänzen Sie die Tabelle mit Wörtern aus dem Kasten.

> Braunschweig
> Berlin   Grimma
>   Dresden
>   Leipzig
>   Prenzlau   Schweiz   Kairo

Name	Woher?	Woher kommen die Eltern?
Tina	Leipzig	Leipzig
Albrecht	Dresden	Dresden
Simone	Braunschweig	Salzgitter
Sandra	Prenzlau	Prenzlau
Hend	Kairo	Kairo
Felicitas	Grimma	Grimma
Pascal	Schweiz	aus der Schweiz und aus Holland
Sophie	Berlin	aus Würzburg und aus Braunschweig

Interviews

- Woher kommst du?
- Wo liegt das?
- Woher kommt deine Familie?
- Erzähl mir ein bisschen von deiner Familie!
- Welche Sprachen sprichst du?
- Wie wird morgen das Wetter?

Pascal

Nadezda

Aufgabe 3 Familie

Wer sagt das, Pascal oder Nadezda?

	Pascal	Nadezda
1. Ich komme aus Moskau.	☐	☒
2. Ich komme aus Zürich.	☒	☐
3. Meine Familie kommt aus Holland und aus der Schweiz.	☒	☐
4. Meine Familie kommt aus Russland und aus Europa.	☐	☒
5. Ich bin Einzelkind.	☐	☒
6. Meine Geschwister arbeiten.	☒	☐
7. Ich spreche Holländisch, Französisch, Englisch und Italienisch.	☒	☐
8. Ich spreche Deutsch, Englisch und Russisch.	☐	☒

Aufgabe 4 Interview

Interviewen Sie eine Partnerin oder einen Partner. Stellen Sie dieselben Fragen.

Wortschatz

Der Seminarraum	The Classroom
die Decke, -n*	ceiling
✓ die Tafel, -n (R)†	blackboard/whiteboard
die Uhr, -en	clock
die Wand, ⸚e	wall
der Beamer, - [bi:mɐ]	data projector
der Boden, ⸚	floor
der Laptop, -s [lɛptɔp]	laptop (computer)
der Stift, -e (R)	pen
der Bleistift, -e (R)	pencil
der Tisch, -e	table
das Fenster, -	window
das Heft, -e	notebook

Ähnliche Wörter

die Lampe, -n; die Professorin, -nen (R); die Studentin, -nen (R); die Uni, -s; die Universität, -en; der Professor, Professoren (R); der Student, -en (R); der Stuhl, ⸚e; das Buch, ⸚er (R); das Papier

Beschreibungen	Descriptions
er/sie hat ...	he/she has . . .
einen Bart	a beard
blaue Augen	blue eyes
blondes Haar	blond hair
✓ kurzes Haar	short hair
er/sie ist ...	he/she is . . .
glücklich	happy
groß	tall; big
klein	short; small
ruhig	quiet, calm
sauber	clean
schlank	slender, slim
schön	pretty, beautiful
schüchtern	shy
traurig	sad
verrückt	crazy

Ähnliche Wörter

blond, freundlich, jung, konservativ, lang, religiös, sportlich

Der Körper	The Body
der Bauch, ⸚e	belly, stomach
der Kopf, ⸚e	head
✓ der Mund, ⸚er	mouth
der Rücken, -	back

das Auge, -n	eye
das Bein, -e	leg
das Gesicht, -er	face
das Ohr, -en	ear

Ähnliche Wörter

die Hand, ⸚e; die Schulter, -n; der Arm, -e; der Fuß, ⸚e; das Haar, -e

Die Familie	The Family
die Frau, -en (R)	woman; wife
die Nichte, -n	niece
die Schwester, -n	sister
die Tante, -n	aunt
✓ der Mann, ⸚er (R)	man; husband
der Vetter, -n	male cousin
das Kind, -er	child
die Eltern	parents
die Großeltern	grandparents
die Geschwister	siblings

Ähnliche Wörter

die Kusine, -n; die Mutter, ⸚; die Großmutter, ⸚; die Tochter, ⸚; der Bruder, ⸚; der Neffe, -n; der Onkel, -; der Sohn, ⸚e; der Vater, ⸚; der Großvater, ⸚

Wetter und Jahreszeiten	Weather and Seasons
der Frühling	spring
im Frühling	in the spring
der Herbst	fall, autumn
der Monat, -e	month
das Jahr, -e	year
es ...	it . . .
ist 18 Grad Celsius	is 18 degrees Celsius
ist feucht	is humid
ist schön	is nice
regnet	is raining; rains
schneit	is snowing; snows

Ähnliche Wörter

der Januar, im Januar, der Februar, der März, der April, der Mai, der Juni, der Juli, der August, der September, der Oktober, der November, der Dezember; der Sommer, der Winter; Fahrenheit, heiß, kalt, kühl, sonnig, warm, windig

---

*Beginning with this chapter, the plural endings of nouns are indicated in the vocabulary lists. See grammar section B.4 for more explanation.

†(R) indicates words that were listed in a previous chapter and are presented again for review.

Geografie	Geography
Deutschland	Germany
Frankreich	France
Griechenland	Greece
Österreich	Austria
Russland	Russia
Tschechien	Czech Republic
Ungarn	Hungary
die Hauptstadt, ⸚e	capital city
die Ostsee	Baltic Sea
die Schweiz	Switzerland
das Mittelmeer	Mediterranean Sea

Ähnliche Wörter

Afrika, Amerika, Asien, Australien, Belgien, Bulgarien, China, Dänemark, England, Europa, Finnland, Großbritannien, Holland, Irland, Italien, Kanada, Liechtenstein, Neuseeland, Nordamerika, Norwegen, Polen, Portugal, Rumänien, Schweden, Slowenien, Spanien, Südamerika; die Nordsee, die Slowakei, die Türkei; die Niederlande (*pl.*), die USA (*pl.*)

Herkunft	Origin
der/die Deutsche, -n	German (person)
Ich bin Deutsche/r.	I am German.
der Franzose, -n / die Französin, -nen	French (person)
der Österreicher, - / die Österreicherin, -nen	Austrian (person)
der Schweizer, - / die Schweizerin, -nen	Swiss (person)

Ähnliche Wörter

die Amerikanerin, -nen; die Australierin, -nen; die Engländerin, -nen; die Kanadierin, -nen; die Mexikanerin, -nen; der Amerikaner, -; der Australier, -; der Engländer, -; der Kanadier, -; der Mexikaner, -

Sprachen	Languages
Deutsch	German
Französisch	French

Ähnliche Wörter

Arabisch, Chinesisch, Englisch, Italienisch, Portugiesisch, Russisch, Schwedisch, Spanisch, Türkisch

Sonstige Wörter und Ausdrücke	Other Words and Expressions
das ist ...	this/that is . . .
das sind ...	these/those are . . .
dein(e)	your (*informal*)
genau	exactly
heute	today
Ihr(e)	your (*formal*)
kennen	to know
kommen (aus)	to come (*from*)
leider	unfortunately
manchmal	sometimes
noch	even, still
sehr	very
sprechen	to speak
wann	when
was	what
welch-	which
wer	who
wie	how
wirklich	really
wo	where
woher	from where
wohnen (in)	to live (in)

Strukturen und Übungen

B.1. *Bestimmter und unbestimmter Artikel.* This section reviews the definite article and introduces the indefinite article. Mention that this form is the nominative, the first of the German cases that students will learn.

B.1 Definite and indefinite articles

Wissen Sie noch?

masculine = **der**
neuter = **das**
feminine = **die**
plural (all genders) = **die**

Review grammar section A.4.

Recall that the definite article **der, das, die** (*the*) varies by gender, number, and case.* Similarly, the indefinite article **ein, eine** (*a, an*) has various forms.

Das ist **ein** Buch. Welche Farbe hat **das** Buch? *This is a book. What color is the book?*

Das ist **eine** Tür. Welche Farbe hat **die** Tür? *This is a door. What color is the door?*

Here are the definite and indefinite articles for all three genders in the singular and plural, nominative case. There is only one plural definite article for all three genders: **die.** The indefinite article (*a, an*) has no plural.

der → ein
das → ein
die → eine
die (*pl.*) → ø

	Singular	Plural
Masculine	**der** Stift **ein** Stift	**die** Stifte Stifte
Neuter	**das** Buch **ein** Buch	**die** Bücher Bücher
Feminine	**die** Tür **eine** Tür	**die** Türen Türen

Übung 1 Im Seminarraum

Frau Schulz spricht über die Gegenstände und die Farben im Seminarraum. Ergänzen Sie den unbestimmten[1] Artikel, den bestimmten[2] Artikel und die Farbe.

Note. Answers to the *Übungen* are in Appendix F.

MODELL: FRAU SCHULZ: Das ist eine Lampe.
  Welche Farbe hat die Lampe?
STUDENT(IN): Sie ist gelb.

1. Und das ist _____ᵃ Stift.
   Welche Farbe hat _____ᵇ Stift?
   Er ist _____ᶜ.

2. Und das ist _____ᵃ Stuhl.
   Welche Farbe hat _____ᵇ Stuhl?
   Er ist _____ᶜ.

3. Und das ist _____ᵃ Tafel.
   Welche Farbe hat _____ᵇ Tafel?
   Sie ist _____ᶜ.

*See Sections A.3 and A.4.
[1]indefinite [2]definite

4. Und das ist _____ª Uhr.
   Welche Farbe hat _____ᵇ Uhr?
   Sie ist _____ᶜ.

5. Und das ist _____ª Buch.
   Welche Farbe hat _____ᵇ Buch?
   Es ist _____ᶜ.

6. Und das ist _____ª Brille.
   Welche Farbe hat _____ᵇ Brille?
   Sie ist _____ᶜ.

Übung 2   Was ist das?

Herr Frisch spricht mit seiner kleinen Tochter.

MODELL: Ist das eine Decke? →
        Nein, das ist ein Bleistift.

1. Ist das eine Tür?

2. Ist das eine Uhr?

3. Ist das eine Lampe?

4. Ist das ein Tisch?

5. Ist das ein Stuhl?

6. Ist das eine Studentin?

7. Ist das ein Heft?

8. Ist das eine Tafel?

B.2 Who are you? The verb *sein*

sein = *to be*

Use a form of the verb **sein** (*to be*) to identify or describe people and things.

—**Sind Jutta und er** blond?   *Are Jutta and he blond?*
—Ja, **sie sind** blond.   *Yes, they are blond.*

Peter ist groß.   *Peter is tall.*
Das Fenster ist klein.   *The window is small.*

Achtung!

NOT = **NICHT**

—Ist Jens groß?
—Nein, er ist **nicht** groß, er ist klein.

sein					
Singular			*Plural*		
ich	bin	*I am*	wir	sind	*we are*
du	bist	*you are*	ihr	seid	*you are*
Sie	sind		Sie	sind	
er		*he*	sie	sind	*they are*
sie	ist	*she* is			
es		*it*			

Ergänzen Sie das Verb **sein**: bin, bist, ist, sind, seid.

1. MICHAEL: Ich bin Michael. Wer _____ᵃ du?
   JENS: Ich _____ᵇ Jens. Jutta und ich, wir _____ᶜ gute Freunde.

2. FRAU SCHULZ: Das ist Herr Thelen. Er _____ᵃ alt.
   STEFAN: Herr Thelen ist alt?
   FRAU SCHULZ: Ja, Stefan. Herr Thelen ist alt, aber Maria und Michael
   _____ᵇ jung.

3. HERR THELEN: Jutta und Hans, wie alt _____ᵃ ihr?
   JUTTA: Ich _____ᵇ 16 und Hans _____ᶜ 13.

4. MICHAEL: Wer bist du?
   HANS: Ich _____ᵃ Hans.
   MICHAEL: Wie alt bist du?
   HANS: Ich _____ᵇ 13.

B.3 What do you have? The verb *haben*

haben = *to have*

B.3. This is the full conjugation of another useful irregular verb. (The forms of the regular verb *kommen* appear in *B.6*.) Verb conjugation is introduced gradually in the early chapters, because we want sts. to learn to understand and produce forms of these verbs through meaningful practice, without focusing too much on conjugation patterns or endings. You might want to have sts. play the roles in the *Minidialoge (Üb. 4)*.

The verb **haben** (*to have*) is often used to show possession or to describe physical characteristics.

Ich habe eine Brille.   *I have glasses.*
Hast du das Buch?   *Do you have the book?*
Nora hat braune Augen.   *Nora has brown eyes.*

haben					
Singular			*Plural*		
ich	habe	*I have*	wir	haben	*we have*
du	hast	*you have*	ihr	habt	*you have*
Sie	haben		Sie	haben	
er		*he*			
sie	hat	*she* } *has*	sie	haben	*they have*
es		*it*			

Ergänzen Sie das Verb **haben**: habe, hast, hat, habt, haben.

1. FRAU SCHULZ: Nora, _____ᵃ Sie viele Freunde und Freundinnen?
   NORA: Ja, ich _____ᵇ viele Freunde und Freundinnen.

2. MONIKA: Stefan, _____ du einen Stift?
   STEFAN: Nein.

3. PETER: Hallo, Heidi und Katrin! _____ᵃ ihr das Deutschbuch?
   HEIDI: Katrin _____ᵇ es, aber ich nicht.
   PETER: Dann _____ᶜ wir zwei. Ich _____ᵈ es auch.

B.4 Plural forms of nouns

B.4. *Plural der Substantive.* The many plural forms are something new for most sts. There are few rules to reliably predict the endings. Acquisition will take place gradually as sts. have the opportunity to hear and use the nouns with their plural endings. The chart summarizes some common associations between gender and plural forms in German. Sts. should also use the *Wortschatz* lists to help them discover patterns in plural formation. Because the nouns in the *Wortschatz* have been grouped according to gender, the correspondences between gender and plural forms are more apparent.

Just as in English, there are different ways to form plurals in German.

Albert hat ein Heft. Peter hat zwei Hefte.	*Albert has one notebook. Peter has two notebooks.*
Heidi hat eine Kusine. Katrin hat zwei Kusinen.	*Heidi has one cousin. Katrin has two cousins.*

These guidelines will help you to recognize and form the plural of German nouns.

1. Most feminine nouns add **-n** or **-en**. They add **-n** when the singular ends in **-e**; otherwise, they add **-en**. Nouns that end in **-in** add **-nen**.

eine Lampe, zwei Lampe**n**	eine Frau, zwei Frau**en**
eine Tür, zwei Tür**en**	eine Studentin, zwei Studentin**nen**

2. Masculine and neuter nouns usually add **-e** or **-er**. Those plurals that end in **-er** have an umlaut when the stem vowel is **a, o, u,** or **au.** Many masculine plural nouns ending in **-e** have an umlaut as well. Neuter plural nouns ending in **-e** do not have an umlaut.

MASCULINE (der)	NEUTER (das)
ein Rock, zwei Röck**e**	ein Heft, zwei Heft**e**
ein Mann, zwei Männ**er**	ein Buch, zwei Büch**er**

3. Masculine and neuter nouns that end in **-er** either add an umlaut or change nothing at all in the plural. Many nouns with a stem vowel of **a, o, u,** or **au** add an umlaut.

MASCULINE (der)	NEUTER (das)
ein Bruder, zwei Brüder	ein Fenster, zwei Fenster
ein Computer, zwei Computer	

4. Nouns that end in a vowel other than unstressed **-e** and many nouns of English or French origin add **-s.**

ein Laptop, zwei Laptop**s**	ein Auto, zwei Auto**s**

The following chart summarizes the guidelines provided above.

Singular	Plural	Examples
ein _____er	no ending: some words add an umlaut where possible	ein Lehrer, zwei Lehrer ein Vater, zwei V**ä**ter
ein _____	add **-e**; masculine words often add an umlaut, neuter words do not	ein Rock, zwei R**ö**ck**e** ein Haar, zwei Haar**e**
ein _____	add **-er**; add an umlaut where possible	ein Mann, zwei M**ä**nn**er** ein Buch, zwei B**ü**ch**er**
eine _____	add **-n, -en,** or **-nen,** depending on final letter of the word	eine Lampe, zwei Lampe**n** eine Tür, zwei Tür**en** eine Freundin, zwei Freundin**nen**
ein(e) _____ *(foreign words)*	add **-s**	ein Hobby, zwei Hobby**s** eine Kamera, zwei Kamera**s**

Beginning with this chapter, the plural endings of nouns are indicated in the vocabulary lists as follows.

LISTING	PLURAL FORM
das **Fenster**, -	die **Fenster**
der **Bruder**, ⸚	die **Brüder**
der **Tisch**, -e	die **Tische**
der **Stuhl**, ⸚e	die **Stühle**
das **Kleid**, -er	die **Kleider**
der **Mann**, ⸚er	die **Männer**
die **Tante**, -n	die **Tanten**
die **Uhr**, -en	die **Uhren**
die **Studentin**, -nen	die **Studentinnen**
das **Auto**, -s	die **Autos**

Übung 5   Der Körper

Üb. 5-6 can be illustrated and supplemented with objects in the classroom. Assign for homework or use for oral work.

Wie viele der folgenden Körperteile hat der Mensch[1]?

MODELL: Der Mensch hat zwei Arme.

Arm
Auge
Bein
Finger
Fuß
Haar
Hand
Nase
Ohr
Schulter

Übung 6   Das Zimmer

Üb. 6. Model and encourage positive responses. Discourage sts. from using *nicht* in their answer. *Kein* is introduced in *Kapitel 2*.

Wie viele der folgenden Dinge sind in Ihrem[2] Zimmer? (ein[e], zwei, ..., viele, nicht viele)

das Buch
der Computer
das Fenster
die Lampe
der Stuhl
der Tisch
die Tür
die Uhr
die Wand

In meinem Zimmer ist/sind _____ Buch/Bücher, ...

[1] *person* [2] *your*

B.5 Personal pronouns

B.5. *Personalpronomen.* This section reviews what sts. have previously learned about personal pronouns. Note that the plural pronouns *ihr* and *sie* are often the last to be acquired.

Personal pronouns refer to the speaker (first person), to the person addressed (second person), or to the person(s) or object(s) talked about (third person).

		Singular		Plural
First person	ich	*I*	wir	*we*
Second-person informal	du	*you*	ihr	*you*
Second-person formal	Sie	*you*	Sie	*you*
Third person	er	*he, it*		
	es	*it*	sie	*they*
	sie	*she, it*		

Wissen Sie noch?

der → er = *he, it*
das → es = *it*
die → sie = *she, it*
die (*pl.*) **→ sie** = *they*

Review grammar section A.4.

As you know, third-person singular pronouns reflect the grammatical gender of the nouns they replace.

—Welche Farbe hat **der Hut?**	*What color is the hat?*
—**Er** ist braun.	*It is brown.*
—Welche Farbe hat **das Kleid?**	*What color is the dress?*
—**Es** ist grün.	*It is green.*
—Welche Farbe hat **die Bluse?**	*What color is the blouse?*
—**Sie** ist gelb.	*It is yellow.*

The third-person plural pronoun is **sie** for all three genders.

—Welche Farbe haben **die Schuhe?**	*What color are the shoes?*
—**Sie** sind schwarz.	*They are black.*

Übung 7   Welche Farbe?

Üb. 7. Remind sts. that while *haben* is used in the question, their response will use *sein: Welche Farbe hat der Hut? Er ist schwarz.*

Frau Schulz spricht über die Farbe der Kleidung. Antworten Sie!

1. Welche Farbe hat der Hut?
2. Welche Farbe hat das Hemd?
3. Welche Farbe hat die Hose?
4. Welche Farbe hat die Bluse?
5. Welche Farbe haben die Socken?
6. Welche Farbe hat das Kleid?
7. Welche Farbe hat der Rock?
8. Welche Farbe haben die Stiefel?
9. Welche Farbe hat die Jacke?
10. Welche Farbe hat der Mantel?

B.6 Origins: *Woher kommen Sie?*

kommen aus = *to come from* (a place)

B.6. The full regular conjugation of the present tense is presented here for the first time with *kommen*. Present-tense forms of other regular verbs will appear in *Kapitel 1*.

To ask about someone's origins, use the question word **woher** (*from where*) followed by the verb **kommen** (*to come*). In the answer, use the preposition **aus** (*from, out of*).

—Woher kommst du / kommen Sie? *Where do you come from?*
—Ich komme aus Berlin. *I'm from Berlin.*

kommen			
ich	komme	wir	kommen
du	kommst	ihr	kommt
Sie	kommen	Sie	kommen
er sie es	kommt	sie	kommen

The infinitive of German verbs, that is, the basic form of the verb, ends in **-n** or **-en.** Most verbs follow a conjugation pattern similar to that of **kommen.**

Kommen Sie heute Abend? *Are you coming this evening?*
Warten Sie! **Ich komme** mit! *Wait! I'll come along.*

Übung 8 Minidialoge

Üb. 8. Assign for homework and have the dialogues performed in class.

Ergänzen Sie **kommen, woher** und **aus** und die Personalpronomen.

1. MEHMET: Woher _____ᵃ du, Renate?
   RENATE: Ich _____ᵇ aus Berlin.

2. FRAU SCHULZ: Woher _____ᵃ Lydia?
   KATRIN: Lydia kommt _____ᵇ Zürich.
   FRAU SCHULZ: _____ᶜ kommen Josef und Melanie?
   STEFAN: Sie _____ᵈ aus Regensburg.
   FRAU SCHULZ: Und woher komme _____ᵉ?
   ALBERT: Sie, Frau Schulz, Sie kommen _____ᶠ Kalifornien.

3. FRAU SCHULZ: Kommt Sofie aus Regensburg?
   HEIDI: Nein, _____ᵃ kommt aus Dresden.
   FRAU SCHULZ: Kommen Josef und Melanie aus Innsbruck?
   STEFAN: Nein, sie _____ᵇ aus Regensburg.

4. ANDREAS: Silvia und Jürgen, kommt _____ᵃ aus Göttingen?
   SILVIA: Ja, _____ᵇ kommen aus Göttingen.

B.7 Possessive adjectives: *mein* and *dein/Ihr*

der → mein, dein, Ihr
das → mein, dein, Ihr
die → meine, deine, Ihre
die (*pl.*) → meine, deine, Ihre

B.7. *Possessivadjektiv.* We have divided the introduction of possessive adjectives into 2 parts to make the acquisition of these forms easier. The 3 most frequently used forms are described here; they will serve as a reference point for learning the others, which will be introduced in *Kapitel 2*. Point out to sts. that German masculine and neuter forms, on the one hand, and feminine and plural forms, on the other hand, are often the same, as they are here.

The possessive adjectives **mein** (*my*), **dein** (*informal your*), and **Ihr** (*formal your*) have the same endings as the indefinite article **ein.** In the plural, the ending is **-e.** Here are the nominative forms of these possessive adjectives.

	Onkel (*m.*)	Auto (*n.*)	Tante (*f.*)	Eltern (*pl.*)
ich	mein	mein	meine	meine
du	dein	dein	deine	deine
Sie	Ihr	Ihr	Ihre	Ihre

Achtung!

Note that the forms of **Ihr** are capitalized, just as **Sie** is, when they mean *your.*

—Woher kommen **deine** Eltern, Albert?
—**Meine** Eltern kommen aus Mexiko.

Wie heißt **Ihr** Vater, Frau Schulz?
Und **Ihre** Mutter?

Where are your parents from, Albert?
My parents are from Mexico.

What is your father's name, Ms. Schulz?
And your mother's name?

Üb. 9. Assign as homework, and have sts. perform the dialogues in class.

Achtung!

Just as in English, an **s** added onto someone's name in German indicates possession. In German, however, there is no apostrophe before the **s.**

Das ist Helga. Das ist Helgas Vater.
This is Helga. That is Helga's father.

Übung 9   Minidialoge

Ergänzen Sie die Possessivpronomen.

1. FRAU SCHULZ: Wo sind _____ Hausaufgaben?
   PETER: Sie liegen leider zu Hause.
2. ONKEL: Ist das _____ᵃ Hund?
   NICHTE: Nein, das ist nicht _____ᵇ Hund. Ich habe keinen[1] Hund.
3. LYDIA: He, Rosemarie! Das ist _____ᵃ Kleid.
   ROSEMARIE: Nein, das ist _____ᵇ Kleid. _____ᶜ Kleid ist schmutzig.
4. KATRIN: Woher kommen _____ᵃ Eltern, Frau Schulz?
   FRAU SCHULZ: _____ᵇ Mutter kommt aus Schwabing und _____ᶜ Vater kommt aus Germering.

Übung 10   Woher kommen sie?

Üb. 10. Suitable for oral work in class or for a written homework assignment.

Beantworten Sie die Fragen.

1. Woher kommen Sie?
2. Woher kommt Ihre Mutter?
3. Woher kommt Ihr Vater?
4. Woher kommen Ihre Großeltern?
5. Woher kommt Ihr Professor / Ihre Professorin?
6. Wie heißt ein Student aus Ihrem Deutschkurs und woher kommt er?
7. Wie heißt eine Studentin aus Ihrem Deutschkurs und woher kommt sie?

[1]*no*

Wer ich bin und was ich tue

GOALS

This chapter extends sts.' listening and speaking skills to exchange personal information. Sts. will continue to respond with single words, but short phrases will become increasingly common in their speech, and they will use more complete sentences in guided activities. They will learn to recognize and understand the various forms of the present tense, including verbs with separable prefixes.

In **Kapitel 1** you will learn to talk about how you spend your time: your studies, your recreational pursuits, and what you like and don't like to do.

PRE-TEXT ACTIVITIES

Provide input by using yourself as a model: *Am Wochenende spiele ich oft Tennis. Ich spiele auch Karten mit meinem Freund Peter. Ich spiele gern Karten, aber Peter nicht. Er spielt gern Gitarre.* Mime the meaning of words sts. don't recognize. Make sure sts. understand the meaning of *gern: Ich tanze gern. Tanzen Sie gern, Melanie? (Nein.) Melanie tanzt nicht gern. (Ja.) Monika tanzt gern. usw.*

Review the present-tense forms that were introduced in the preliminary chapters with *sein, haben, heißen,* and *kommen.* In *Kapitel 1* the sts. need to understand and use many more present-tense forms. Note that regular present-tense forms are introduced in grammar Section 1.1, and verbs with separable prefixes and associated nouns in 1.5. It is unlikely, however, that you will be able to maintain this neat separation of categories within an activity when the focus is on meaning. Most sts. have no trouble with present-tense endings in German and quickly become accustomed to the variation of verb forms owing to person-number agreement. However, for those sts. with no prior foreign language experience, the concept of verb endings may take some time to grasp. In any case, sts. will not be able to use verb forms easily until they have had multiple opportunities to hear them used in communicative contexts.

Themen

Freizeit

Schule und Universität

Tagesablauf

Persönliche Daten

Kulturelles

KLI: Freizeit

KLI: Schule

Filmclip: *Hilfe!* (Oliver Dommenget)

Musikszene: „Gewinner" (Clueso)

Videoecke: Tagesablauf

Lektüren

Film: *Hilfe!* (Oliver Dommenget)

Biografie: Guten Tag, ich heiße …

Strukturen

1.1 The present tense

1.2 Expressing likes and dislikes: **gern / nicht gern**

1.3 Telling time

1.4 Word order in statements

1.5 Separable-prefix verbs

1.6 Word order in questions

Kunst und Künstler

Carl Spitzweg (1808–1885) war ein deutscher Maler und Dichter aus der Umgebung[1] von München. Seine Bilder sind oft ironisch. „Der Bücherwurm" ist ein gutes Beispiel[2] für Spitzwegs humorvolle Perspektive.

Schauen Sie sich das Gemälde[3] an und beantworten Sie folgende Fragen.

1. Wie sieht der Mann aus: jung, alt, dünn, dick, klein, groß, interessant, langweilig, spitze Nase, braunes Haar, in Jeans, im Anzug?
2. Wo ist er: in einer alten Bibliothek, in einer neuen Bibliothek, auf einer Leiter, auf einem Sofa?
3. Wo hat er Bücher: in den Händen, unter dem Arm, unter den Füßen, auf dem Kopf, zwischen den Knien?
4. Welche Farben dominieren?
5. Welche Gefühle evoziert das Gemälde?

[1] *vicinity*   [2] *example*   [3] *painting*

Carl Spitzweg: *Der Bücherwurm* (1850), Museum Georg Schäfer, Schweinfurt/ Deutschland

Situationen

Vocabulary Display
First state the infinitive of each activity, then read the sentences and have sts. repeat: *wandern – Peter und Stefan wandern gern usw.* After pronouncing each activity, do an association activity. (See the IM for suggestions on using association activities in Stage III.) *Peter und Stefan wandern gern. Wer von Ihnen wandert gern? Heben Sie bitte die Hand.* Associate one st. with each activity. *Lisa wandert gern usw.* After going through all the activities, see if sts. can remember the names matched with each hobby: *Wer wandert gern? (Lisa.)* Then ask students to produce the sentences by asking: *Was macht Lisa gern? (Sie wandert gern.) usw.*

Grammatik 1.1–1.2

Peter und Stefan wandern gern.

Ernst spielt gern Fußball.

Jutta und Gabi spielen gern Karten.

Melanie tanzt gern.

Michael spielt gern Gitarre.

Veronika reitet gern.

Thomas segelt gern.

Herr und Frau Ruf gehen gern spazieren.

Hobbys

Sagen Sie ja oder nein.

1. In den Ferien ...
   a. reise ich gern.
   b. koche ich gern.
   c. spiele ich gern Volleyball.
   d. arbeite ich gern.

2. Im Winter ...
   a. gehe ich gern ins Museum.
   b. spiele ich gern Karten.
   c. gehe ich gern Snowboard fahren.
   d. schwimme ich gern.

3. Meine Eltern ...
   a. chatten gern.
   b. spielen gern Golf.
   c. gehen gern ins Kino.
   d. singen gern.

4. Mein Bruder / Meine Schwester ...
   a. wandert gern in den Bergen.
   b. zeltet gern.
   c. boxt gern.
   d. spielt gern Gitarre.

5. Mein Deutschlehrer / Meine Deutschlehrerin ...
   a. simst gern.
   b. reitet gern.
   c. geht gern ins Konzert.
   d. spielt gern Fußball.

 Situation 2 Informationsspiel: Freizeit

MODELL: s1: Wie alt ist Rolf?
s2: __20__.
s1: Woher kommt Richard?
s2: Aus __Innsbruck__.
s1: Was macht Richard gern?
s2: Er __geht gern in die Berge__.
s1: Wie alt bist du?
s2: _____.
s1: Woher kommst du?
s2: _____.
s1: Was machst du gern?
s2: _____.

	Alter	Wohnort	Hobby
Richard	18	Innsbruck	geht gern in die Berge
Rolf	20	Berkeley	spielt gern Tennis
Jürgen	21	Göttingen	geht gern tanzen
Sofie	22	Dresden	kocht gern
Jutta	16	München	hört gern Musik
Melanie	25	Regensburg	chattet gern
mein Partner / meine Partnerin			

Interview: Was machst du gern?

MODELL: s1: Ich spiele gern Karten. Du auch?
s2: Ja, ich spiele auch gern Karten.
Nein, ich spiele nicht gern Karten.

1. Ich spiele gern Schach.
2. Ich wandere gern.
3. Ich gehe gern spazieren.
4. Ich schreibe gern E-Mails.
5. Ich singe gern.
6. Ich simse gern.
7. Ich höre gern Musik.
8. Ich koche gern.
9. Ich tanze gern.
10. Ich lerne gern Deutsch.
11. Ich fliege gern.

Kultur ...
Landeskunde ...
Informationen

Freizeit

- Was machen Menschen in Ihrem Land in ihrer Freizeit?
- Was machen Sie in Ihrer Freizeit? am Wochenende? abends? in den Ferien?
- Was machen Ihre Eltern in ihrer Freizeit? am Wochenende? abends? in den Ferien?
- Wie viele Stunden Freizeit haben Sie am Tag?
- Sehen Sie sich die Grafik an. Was machen Deutsche öfter[1] als Sie? Was machen sie weniger[2] oft als Sie?
- Wie viele Stunden Freizeit haben Deutsche am Tag? Raten[3] Sie!

Die häufigsten Freizeitbeschäftigungen der Deutschen

(täglich)

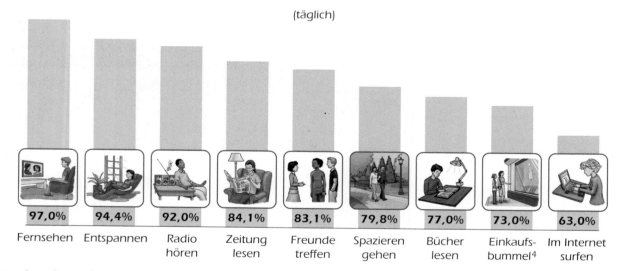

| 97,0% | 94,4% | 92,0% | 84,1% | 83,1% | 79,8% | 77,0% | 73,0% | 63,0% |
| Fernsehen | Entspannen | Radio hören | Zeitung lesen | Freunde treffen | Spazieren gehen | Bücher lesen | Einkaufs- bummel[4] | Im Internet surfen |

[1]*more often* [2]*less* [3]*Guess* [4]*window shopping*

 **Situation 4** Umfrage

Sit. 4. This is an autograph activity. (See the IM for suggestions on the use of autograph activities.) Sts. move around the classroom and try to find someone who can answer *ja* to a question in the activity. 1 asks 2 a question, and if 2 answers *ja*, he/she signs the line next to that activity. Once 2 answers *ja*, 1 moves on and asks a different person the next question. If 2 answers *nein*, 1 can then ask another question. Sts. try to get as many different signatures as possible within a certain time limit, perhaps 5 minutes. The person who gets the most signatures wins.
Follow-up. Ask sts. about their responses. *Wer spielt gern Gitarre? Wer schwimmt gern?* Then address the person identified and ask for confirmation. *Schwimmen Sie gern, Katy?*

MODELL: S1: Schwimmst du gern im Meer?
          S2: Ja.
          S1: Unterschreib bitte hier.

UNTERSCHRIFT

1. Schwimmst du gern im Schwimmbad?   _____
2. Trinkst du gern Kaffee?   _____
3. Spielst du gern Gitarre?   _____
4. Hörst du gern Musik?   _____
5. Gehst du gern zelten?   _____
6. Arbeitest du gern?   _____
7. Gehst du gern joggen?   _____
8. Tanzt du gern?   _____
9. Spielst du gern Golf?   _____
10. Machst du gern Fotos?   _____

Schule und Universität

Grammatik 1.3

Vocabulary Display
Pronounce the subjects with the appropriate definite article and have sts. repeat. Sts. will have little difficulty understanding the subjects, but pronunciation may be a problem. Have sts. repeat in chorus. Then associate each subject with a st. *Wer studiert Kunst?* If no one studies a particular subject, make up a person's name and write it on the board (without a subject) and say *Michael studiert Kunst.* Go through all the subjects. Then go through the names asking: *Was studiert Michael?* (*Er studiert Kunst.*) You may wish to point out that all the subjects in this display are feminine, except for *der Sport* and *der Maschinenbau.*

Situation 5 Dialog: Was studierst du?

Sit. 5. (See the IM.) Set the scene and introduce the characters. Work either with sts.' books open or closed. With books closed, ask the following focus questions: **1.** *Woher kommt Rolf?* **2.** *Was macht er in den USA?* **3.** *Was studiert Stefan?* At the end, have sts. work in pairs to produce a similar dialogue.

Stefan trifft Rolf in der Cafeteria der Universität Berkeley.

STEFAN: Hallo, bist du __neu__ hier?
ROLF: Ja, ich __komme__ aus Deutschland.
STEFAN: Und was machst __du__ hier?
ROLF: Ich __studiere__ Psychologie. Und du?
STEFAN: __Chemie__.

Situation 6 Wie spät ist es?

Sit. 6. Present ways to tell time using the projector or a toy clock before doing the activity in class. Introduce vocabulary contextually with questions such as *Wie viele Sekunden gibt es in einer Minute? wie viele Minuten in einer Stunde? wie viele Stunden in einem Tag? usw.* Enliven your presentation and recycle verbs with commentary: *Es ist acht Uhr. Um acht Uhr gehe ich zur Uni. usw.*

AA. Point out the time difference between Germany and your time zone and ask sts. to calculate the current time in Germany.

MODELL: S1: Wie spät ist es?
S2: Es ist _____.

1. 2. 3. 4. 5.

6. 7. 8. 9. 10.

Cultural note (Sit. 7.) Although this chart still represents a typical *Gymnasium* schedule for 5th to 10th grade, including breaks and regular school hours, several reforms induced by the poor results of the PISA study have brought about changes in the traditional structure of German schools. In many German states, sts. at the *Gymnasium* now graduate after 12 years instead of 13. Afternoon classes are also becoming more common. What has stayed the same is that two foreign languages are mandatory, besides German and math (*Lang-* or *Hauptfächer*, usually 4 periods per week). *Kurz-* or *Nebenfächer* such as history, biology, and physics are taught twice a week. Every student in a given grade takes the same courses.

Situation 7 Informationsspiel: Juttas Stundenplan

MODELL: S2: Was hat Jutta am Montag um acht Uhr fünfzig?
S1: Sie hat Deutsch.

Sit. 7. (See the IM.) Introduce days of the week and, if necessary, review the pronunciation of the academic subjects, before doing the activity. Model the question before having sts. work in pairs. The corresponding chart is in Appendix A.

Uhr	Montag	Dienstag	Mittwoch	Donnerstag	Freitag
8.00–8.45	Latein	Mathematik	Deutsch	Biologie	Französisch
8.50–9.35	Deutsch	Englisch	Englisch	Latein	Physik
9.35–9.50	←		Pause		→
9.50–10.35	Biologie	Sozialkunde	Mathematik	Geschichte	Religion
10.40–11.25	Geschichte	Französisch	Physik	Mathematik	Deutsch
11.25–11.35	←		Pause		→
11.35–12.20	Sport	Musik	Erdkunde	Sport	Latein
12.25–13.10	Erdkunde	Deutsch	Kunst	Sozialkunde	frei

Schule

- Wann beginnt in Ihrem Land morgens die Schule?
- Wann gehen die Schüler und Schülerinnen nach Hause?
- Wann und wo machen sie Hausaufgaben?
- Wann haben sie Freizeit?
- Welche Schulfächer haben Schüler und Schülerinnen?
- Welches sind Pflichtfächer[1]?
- An welchen Tagen gehen die Schüler und Schülerinnen in die Schule?

Schauen Sie auf Juttas Stundenplan (Situation 7).

- Wann beginnt für Jutta die Schule?
- Wann geht sie nach Hause?
- Welche Fächer hat Jutta?
- Wie viele Fremdsprachen hat sie?
- An welchen Tagen geht sie in die Schule?

Was meinen Sie?

- Wann und wo macht Jutta Hausaufgaben?
- Wann hat sie Freizeit?

Cultural note. Point out that while the word "student" is used for both school and university students in English, in German a distinction is made between *Schüler/in* (*Grundschule* [elementary school] through *Gymnasium*) and *Student/in* (university only).

Photo questions. *Wer sind diese Leute? Was machen sie? Wie alt sind sie? Was fragen sie? Welche Jahreszeit ist es?*

[1]*required subjects*

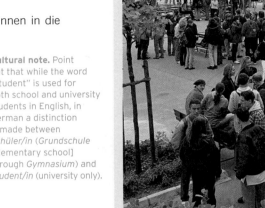

Große Pause an einer Schule in Berlin

 Situation 8 Interview

1. Welche Fächer hast du in diesem Semester? Welche Fächer magst du? Welche Fächer magst du nicht?
2. Wann beginnt am Montag dein erster (1.) Kurs? Welcher Kurs ist das?
3. Wann gehst du am Montag nach Hause?
4. Wann beginnt am Dienstag dein erster Kurs? Welcher Kurs ist das?
5. Wann gehst du am Dienstag nach Hause?
6. Arbeitest du? An welchen Tagen arbeitest du? Wann beginnt deine Arbeit?
7. Wann gehst du in der Woche ins Bett? Und am Wochenende?
8. Wann machst du Hausaufgaben?
9. Wann hast du Freizeit?

Tagesablauf

Grammatik 1.4–1.5

Herr Wagner steht auf.

Er duscht.

Er frühstückt.

Er geht zur Arbeit.

Er geht einkaufen.

Er räumt die Wohnung auf.

Er geht im Park spazieren.

Er geht ins Bett.

 Situation 9 Interview

1. Wann stehst du auf?
2. Wann duschst du?
3. Wann frühstückst du?
4. Wann gehst du zur Uni?
5. Wann kommst du nach Hause?
6. Wann machst du das Abendessen?
7. Wann gehst du ins Bett?

Situation 10 Am Wochenende

Sit. 10. Preteach any unfamiliar vocabulary. Ask sts. to record answers for themselves using S, W, or V. After they have finished for themselves, have them compare their results with a partner: *Ich spiele sicher Computerspiele. Spielst du am Wochenende Computerspiele?* and record the partner's answers.

Was machen Sie am Wochenende sicher, wahrscheinlich, vielleicht?

S = sicher
W = wahrscheinlich
V = vielleicht

	ICH	PARTNER/PARTNERIN
1. Ich spiele Computerspiele.	———	———
2. Ich stehe spät auf.	———	———
3. Ich kaufe ein.	———	———
4. Ich surfe im Internet.	———	———
5. Ich schreibe E-Mails.	———	———
6. Ich höre Musik.	———	———
7. Ich arbeite fürs Studium.	———	———
8. Ich rufe Freunde oder meine Familie an.	———	———
9. Ich räume mein Zimmer oder meine Wohnung auf.	———	———
10. Ich gehe mit Freunden aus.	———	———
11. Ich gehe ins Kino.	———	———
12. Ich jobbe.	———	———

Situation 11 Bildgeschichte: Ein Tag in Sofies Leben

Sit. 11. This is the first "narration series," a set of sketches that form a connected narrative. These series are included to give sts. a chance to hear and use verb forms and tenses and to practice narration in past, present, and future. Use the same approach as with the vocabulary displays, followed by an oral or written practice of narration. In this situation sts. practice separable-prefix verbs in a meaningful context. Note: Narration series are also on tape in the laboratory program. **Presentation** (using projector): *Das ist Sofie. Was macht Sofie an einem normalen Tag? Bild 1. Sofie steht früh auf. 2. Sie duscht. 3. Sie frühstückt. 4. Sie packt ihre Bücher ein. 5. Sie geht zur Uni. 6. Sie füllt ein Formular aus. 7. Sie geht zur Post. 8. Sie holt ein Paket ab. 9. Sie geht nach Hause. 10. Sie ruft ihre Freundin an. 11. Sie gehen zusammen aus.* **Receptive recall** (random order): *Welches Bild zeigt „Sofie geht zur Uni?"* (*Bild 5.*) usw. **Choral response. Productive recall** (normal sequence): *Was macht Sofie in Bild 1? usw.* **Personalization:** *Schreiben Sie auf, was auch Sie an einem ganz normalen Tag machen.* **Focus on narration:** Ask sts. to write down the sentences from memory (with the help of the drawings). Put sts. in groups of 3 to proofread one another's writing. Follow up by writing the story on the board according to your students' dictation.

Situation 12 Informationsspiel: Diese Woche

Sit. 12. (See the IM.) The corresponding chart is in Appendix A.

MODELL: S2: Was macht Silvia am Dienstag?
S1: Sie arbeitet am Abend in einer Bar.
S2: Was machst du am Montag?
S1: Ich _____.

	Silvia Mertens	**Mehmet Sengün**	**mein(e) Partner(in)**
Montag	Sie steht um 6 Uhr auf.	Er geht um 7 Uhr zur Arbeit.	
Dienstag	Sie arbeitet am Abend in einer Bar.	Er lernt eine neue Kollegin kennen.	
Mittwoch	Sie schreibt eine Prüfung.	Er surft im Internet.	
Donnerstag	Sie ruft ihre Eltern an.	Er geht einkaufen.	
Freitag	Sie geht tanzen.	Er hört um 15 Uhr mit der Arbeit auf.	
Samstag	Sie geht mit Freunden ins Kino.	Er räumt seine Wohnung auf.	
Sonntag	Sie besucht ihre Eltern.	Er repariert sein Motorrad.	

Filmlektüre
Hilfe!

 Vor dem Lesen

A. Beantworten Sie die folgenden Fragen.

1. Was sehen Sie auf dem Bild? Machen Sie eine Liste, z. B. Papier, ...

cap

2. Mickey trägt ein gelbes T-Shirt und Emma trägt eine Mütze°, eine weiße Jacke und Jeans. Identifizieren Sie Emma und Mickey. Schreiben Sie die Namen unter das Foto.

Filmangaben

Titel: *Hilfe!*
Genre: Komödie
Erscheinungsjahr: 2002
Land: Deutschland
Dauer: 91 Min
Regisseur: Oliver Dommenget
Hauptrollen: Sarah Hannemann, Nick Seidensticker, Nina Petri, Dominique Horwitz, Philipp Blank, Pinkas Braun

a. _____ b. _____

B. Lesen Sie die Wörter im Miniwörterbuch. Suchen Sie sie im Text und unterstreichen Sie sie.

Miniwörterbuch

das **Leben**	life
mögen	to like
ärgern	to tease, pick on
einmal	for once
wäre	would be
entdecken	to discover
der **Zauberspruch**	spell
der **Wunsch**	wish
in Erfüllung gehen	to come true
man	one, you
rückgängig machen	to reverse
die **Lösung**	solution
der **Mut**	courage
die **Freundschaft**	friendship
einander	one another

Inhaltsangabe

Emma (Sarah Hannemann) wohnt in Hamburg. Sie ist 11 Jahre alt, Schülerin und geht in die Brecht-Schule. Sie ist sehr talentiert und in ihrer Freizeit schwimmt sie gern. Ihr Leben ist nicht leicht. Mickey (Nick Seidensticker) und seine Freunde mögen sie nicht. In der Schule ärgern sie sie oft. Emma denkt:

5 „Einmal eine andere Person sein. Das wäre toll." Emmas Freund Freddy „Vierauge" (Philipp Blank) entdeckt in einem alten Buch einen Zauberspruch, mit dem ihr Wunsch in Erfüllung geht.

Am nächsten Morgen wacht Emma auf. Emma ist nicht mehr Emma. Sie ist jetzt Mickey, und Mickey ist nicht mehr Mickey. Er ist jetzt Emma. Das ist natürlich ein
10 großes Problem. Wie kann man den Zauber rückgängig machen? Emma, Mickey und Vierauge suchen zusammen eine Lösung, aber sie haben nur 54 Stunden Zeit. Am Ende finden sie Mut, Freundschaft und einander.

Arbeit mit dem Text

Richtig (R) oder falsch (F)? Verbessern Sie die falschen Aussagen.

__R__ 1. Emmas Hobby ist Schwimmen.

__R__ 2. Emma hat viel Talent.

__R__ 3. Mickey mag Emma nicht.

__F__ 4. Emma und Mickey sind gute Freunde.

__R__ 5. Freddy findet einen Zauberspruch.

__F__ 6. Emma ist jetzt Mickey und Mickey ist jetzt Freddy.

__F__ 7. Sie haben drei Tage Zeit eine Lösung zu finden.

__R__ 8. Am Ende sind Mickey und Emma Freunde.

Filmclip

Szene: DVD Kapitel 3, „In der Schule", 17:35–19:15 Min.

Emma und Freddy („Vierauge") gehen zusammen in die Schule.

Ergänzen Sie!

1. Vierauge und Emma ___d___ in die Schule.
2. Die Schüler ___b___ heute einen Mathetest.
3. Mickey ___c___ Probleme mit dem Test.
4. Der Schüler mit dem Gameboy ___f___ eine braune Mütze.
5. Emma ___e___ einen Zettel°.
6. Die Lehrerin ___a___, dass Mickey spickt°.

a. glaubt°   *believes*
b. haben
c. hat
d. kommen
e. schreibt   *note*
f. trägt   *is cheating*

Nach dem Lesen

Kennen Sie andere Filme mit Zauberern? Wie heißen diese Filme? Mögen Sie diese Filme?

Persönliche Daten

Vocabulary Display
The goal of this section is to introduce question forms. Ask sts. to scan the ID application form. Reassure them that they need not understand every word. They should try to figure out the meanings of the technical words from context. Ask questions such as: *Wie heißt die Frau? Wo wohnt sie? Welche Farbe haben ihre Augen? Wie groß ist sie? Wie alt ist sie? Wann ist sie geboren? Wo ist sie geboren?* Write questions on the board, and have sts. repeat them. Now personalize by asking similar questions: *Wo wohnen Sie? und Ihre Familie? Wo sind Sie geboren? usw.* Use an association activity to review sts.' answers: *Wo wohnt Claudia? Wie alt ist sie? usw.* If sts. seem ready to produce a few questions themselves, have them ask you your name, age, etc.

Grammatik 1.6

Antrag auf Ausstellung eines Personalausweises

Familienname: Ruf

geborene(r): Schuler

Vornamen: Margret

Geburtstag: 13. April 1973

Geburtsort: Augsburg

Staatsangehörigkeit: deutsch

Augenfarbe: blau, grau, (grün), braun   Größe 172 cm

München   Sonnenstr.   11
             Straße   Hausnummer

München, den 30.5.2012

Margret Ruf
Unterschrift des Antragstellers

Situation 13 Dialog: Auf dem Rathaus

Sit. 13. (See the IM.) This dialogue provides a model for the interview that follows it. We suggest moving from comprehension to production via a series of steps. The following steps are intended for use with the textbooks closed. (1) Set the scene: *Melanie braucht einen neuen Personalausweis* (show picture of a *Personalausweis*). *Sie wohnt in Regensburg. Also geht sie auf das Rathaus in Regensburg* (show picture of a *Rathaus*). *Sie spricht mit einem Beamten.* (2) Ask focus questions: *Wie heißt Melanie mit Nachnamen? Was ist ihre Adresse? Was ist ihre Telefonnummer? Was ist sie von Beruf? Ist sie verheiratet?* (3) Play the dialogue. (4) Review sts.' answers. (5) Ask sts. to count the words in each sentence. (6) Divide sts. into two groups, assign one role to each group, and ask each group to repeat their lines. (7) Ask groups to repeat their lines from memory. To help sts. remember, write the first word or words of each question on the board. (8) Ask 2-3 pairs of volunteers (1 from each group) to present the dialogue in front of the class. Instead of assuming their previous roles, however, they should change the lines of the dialogue to talk about themselves. (9) Sts. get up and work in pairs. While moving from one person to the next, they act out their personalized versions several times.

Melanie Staiger ist auf dem Rathaus in Regensburg. Sie braucht einen neuen Personalausweis.

BEAMTER: Grüß Gott!
MELANIE: Grüß Gott. Ich brauche einen neuen <u>Personalausweis</u>.
BEAMTER: <u>Wie</u> ist Ihr Name, bitte?
MELANIE: Staiger, Melanie Staiger.
BEAMTER: Und <u>wo</u> wohnen Sie?
MELANIE: In Regensburg.
BEAMTER: <u>Was</u> ist die genaue Adresse?
MELANIE: Gesandtenstraße 8.
BEAMTER: Haben Sie auch <u>Telefon</u>?
MELANIE: Ja, die Nummer ist 24352.
BEAMTER: Was sind Sie <u>von Beruf</u>?
MELANIE: Ich bin Studentin.
BEAMTER: Sind Sie verheiratet?
MELANIE: <u>Nein</u>. Ich bin ledig.

Cultural note. In German-speaking countries, you are required to register with the local town administration when you take residence somewhere (*einen Wohnsitz anmelden*). You must also inform them whenever you move (*ummelden/abmelden*) so that the government always has your current address. The *Einwohnermeldeamt*, or an administrative subdivision, also issues passports and ID cards.

Sit. 14. (See cultural note under *Sit. 13*.) Have sts. work in pairs. 2's book should be closed, and 1 should write down the information as 2 answers. Sts. might also need to ask: *Wie schreibt man Ihren Namen? Wie, bitte? usw.*

Situation 14 Interview: Auf dem Rathaus

1. Wie heißen Sie?
2. Wie alt sind Sie?
3. Wo sind Sie geboren?
4. Wo wohnen Sie?
5. Was ist Ihre genaue Adresse?
6. Was ist Ihre E-Mail-Adresse?
7. Was studieren Sie?
8. Sind Sie verheiratet?
9. Welche Augenfarbe haben Sie?
10. Welche Haarfarbe?

Das Regensburger Rathaus

Musikszene

Clueso

Biografie Clueso kommt aus Erfurt. Sein richtiger Name ist Thomas Hübner. Er wurde 1980 geboren. Sein Künstlername kommt von Inspektor Clouseau aus dem Film *The Pink Panther.*

Vor dem Hören Wie fühlt man sich am Ende einer Beziehung?

Nach dem Hören

A. Was sagt der Sänger zu seiner Freundin? Richtig (R) oder falsch (F)?

_R_ 1. An allem, was man sagt, ist auch was dran.

_F_ 2. Ich glaub' an mich.

_R_ 3. Wir sind dabei, uns zu verlier'n.

_F_ 4. Ich gebe auf.

B. Es fehlen die Verben. Ergänzen Sie sie!

1. Ich __glaube__ nichts. Ich __glaub__ an dich. __Glaubst__ du an mich? Ich __glaub__, ich auch.

2. Ich __frage__ mich. Ich __frage__ dich. Doch __frag__ ich nicht, __fragst__ du dich auch?

3. Ich __bin__ dabei, du __bist__ dabei, wir __sind__ dabei, uns zu verlier'n.

iMix Link: This song is available for purchase at the iTunes store in a special iMix created for *Kontakte.* For more information about accessing the playlist, go to **Connect German** (www.connectgerman.com).

Musikszene. **Suggestion:** Ask sts. to look at the photo and read the musician's biography. Ask a few questions about the artist. Then ask sts. to think about the *Vor dem Hören* question and write down some of the questions one might have when a relationship is coming to an end. Next read through the true/false statements in *Nach dem Hören* activity A. Ask sts. to listen to the first and second stanza of the song and determine if the statements are true or false. Then ask sts. to listen to the first stanza and the chorus (*Ich bin dabei, du bist dabei,* …) and determine which verb forms fit in the gaps in activity B. (You could also include the verb *suchen,* from the second stanza, in this activity.) Next ask sts. to listen to the end of the song and to copy the last six lines: *Ich bin dabei. Du bist dabei. Wir sind dabei. Ich bin dabei. Bist du dabei? Sind wir dabei?* Ask them what they think these lines might mean. Finally, ask them why the song is titled *Gewinner.* (Clueso said in an interview that he gave it this title because the end of a relationship can also be seen as the beginning of something new.) **Note:** Clueso is a singer/songwriter from Erfurt. His real name is Thomas Hübner and he was born in 1980. His stage name derives from inspector Clouseau from the *Pink Panther.* In 2005 he went on a tour through Italy for the Goethe-Institut. His hit single *Gewinner,* about the end of a relationship, was recorded in 2009.

Miniwörterbuch

fühlt sich	feels	**dabei sein**	to be close to or on the verge of
die **Beziehung**	relationship		
ist auch was dran	there's something to it	**verlieren**	to lose
		aufgeben	to give up
glauben	to believe		

Lyrics from "Gewinner": words and music by Thomas Huebner, Ralf Mayer and Baris Aladag. Copyright © 2009 EDITIONS 10 VOR 10 in the United States and Canada Controlled and Administered by UNIVERSAL MUSIC PUBLISHING LTD. All Rights Reserved. Used by Permission. Reprinted by permission of Hal Leonard Corporation.

Situation 15 Rollenspiel: Auf dem Auslandsamt

s1: Sie sind Student/Studentin und möchten ein Jahr lang in Österreich studieren. Gehen Sie aufs Auslandsamt und sagen Sie, dass Sie ein Stipendium möchten. Beantworten Sie die Fragen des Beamten / der Beamtin. Sagen Sie am Ende des Gesprächs „Auf Wiedersehen".

Sit. 15. *Rollenspiel.* This is one of many role-plays in *Kontakte.* (See the IM.) The role for student 1 (S1) appears here, the role for student 2 (S2) appears in Appendix B. **(1)** Set the scene as described in the role for s1. **(2)** Provide sts. with a model by working with the enactment of the role-play found in the workbook/lab manual. **(3)** Write the structure of the role-play on the board: *begrüßen; fragen und antworten; bedanken und verabschieden.* **(4)** Elicit possible greetings, questions, and how to say good-bye from sts. and write on board. Ask for appropriate responses to the greeting and leave-taking and for possible answers to the questions, and write them on the board as well. **(5)** Divide the class into 2 groups and assign 1 part of the role-play to each group. Ask sts. to practice the role-play in pairs. **(6)** Ask 2-3 pairs of sts. to perform their role-play in class. Provide feedback as to appropriateness and accuracy of language used, after sts. have returned to their seats. The intention here is not to correct all or even most mistakes but rather to focus on a few phrases and sentences that are the most useful for all or most sts. in the context of this role-play. **(7)** Ask sts. to find new partners and to practice the role-play in pairs again. **(8)** Optional homework assignment: Ask sts. to write up their version of the role-play. **Note:** If your students are using McGraw-Hill's **Connect** online *Arbeitsbuch,* they can do this *Rollenspiel* using the real-time, interactive **Video-Chat** feature.

Situation 16 Gesucht¹!

Sit. 16. Preview *Nützliche Wörter* and the information missing in the poster. Ask sts. to guess what the missing information might be. Write guesses on the board. Ask sts. to work in pairs. Read or play the complete text at least twice. Ask sts. to correct their guesses on the board. Read or play one last time asking sts. to knock on the table when they hear the following words: *Spitzname, Narbe, Vollbart, Sonnenbrille, Halstuch.* **Text for listening comprehension:** *Gesucht wird der Bankräuber Paul Steckel, bekannt unter dem Spitznamen Narben-Paule. Er ist 35 Jahre alt, sieht aber älter aus. Seine Haare sind mittelblond, zuletzt hatte er einen Vollbart. Seine Augen sind graublau. Er trägt oft eine Sonnenbrille. Besonderes Kennzeichen ist eine circa drei Zentimeter lange Narbe unter dem rechten Auge. Steckel ist einen Meter fünfundachtzig groß, schlank und spricht mit Berliner Akzent. Meistens trägt er eine schwarze Jeansjacke und Cowboystiefel, dazu ein Halstuch. Vorsicht, er ist bewaffnet!*

Schreiben Sie die fehlenden Angaben² in den Steckbrief.

NÜTZLICHE WÖRTER

der Bankräuber	*bank robber*
der Spitzname	*nickname*
die Narbe	*scar*
besonderes Kennzeichen	*distinguishing feature*
das Halstuch	*bandanna*
bewaffnet	*armed*

GESUCHT

Paul Steckel

Spitzname: _____-Paule

Alter: _____ Jahre, sieht älter aus

Haarfarbe: mittel_____, Voll_____

_____: graublau

Besonderes Kennzeichen: _____

unter dem rechten _____

Größe: _____ cm, schlank

Akzent: _____

Kleidung: meistens _____ Jeansjacke

und _____, dazu ein _____

¹*Wanted* ²*information*

Lektüre 📖

Vor dem Lesen

Welche Informationen geben Sie, wenn Sie sich vorstellen?[1] Kreuzen Sie an.

- [ ] Name
- [ ] Alter
- [ ] Beruf/Studienfach
- [ ] Familie
- [ ] Freunde
- [ ] Geburtsdatum

- [ ] Gewicht[2]
- [ ] Hobbys
- [ ] Herkunft
- [ ] Noten[3]
- [ ] Interessen
- [ ] Adresse

Miniwörterbuch

das **Fahrrad**	bicycle	**seit**	since; *here:* for
die **Gärtnerei**	nursery (gardening)	die **Sozialkunde**	social studies
der **Geschäftsmann**	businessman	die **Speditionsfirma**	trucking company
der **Lastwagen**	truck	**unterrichten**	to teach
der **Ort**	town	**unterwegs**	on the road

Guten Tag, ich heiße ...

Guten Tag, ich heiße Veronika Frisch. Ich bin verheiratet und habe drei Töchter. Sie heißen Natalie, Rosemarie und Lydia. Ich lebe mit meinem Mann Bernd und unseren Töchtern in der Schweiz. Wir wohnen in Zürich. Ich komme aus Zürich und mein Mann kommt aus Luzern. Ich bin dreiunddreißig Jahre alt und Bernd ist
5 fünfzig. Bernd ist Geschäftsmann hier in Zürich und ich bin Lehrerin. Ich unterrichte Französisch und Sozialkunde. Meine Freizeit verbringe ich am liebsten mit meiner Familie. Außerdem reise ich gern.

Guten Tag, ich heiße Sofie Pracht, bin 22 und komme aus Dresden. Ich studiere Biologie an der Technischen Universität Dresden. Ein paar Stunden in der
10 Woche arbeite ich in einer großen Gärtnerei. In meiner Freizeit gehe ich oft ins Kino oder ich besuche Freunde. Ich spiele Gitarre und tanze sehr gern. Mein Freund heißt Willi Schuster. Er studiert auch hier in Dresden an der Technischen Universität. Er kommt aus Radebeul. Das ist ein kleiner Ort ganz in der Nähe von Dresden. Am Wochenende fahren wir manchmal mit dem Fahrrad nach Radebeul und besuchen
15 seine Familie.

Guten Tag, ich heiße Mehmet Sengün. Ich bin 29 und in Izmir, in der Türkei, geboren. Ich lebe jetzt seit 19 Jahren hier in Berlin. Ich wohne in Kreuzberg, einem Stadtteil von Berlin, in einer kleinen Wohnung. In Kreuzberg leben sehr viele Türken–die Berliner nennen es Klein-Istanbul–und viele meiner türkischen Freunde
20 wohnen ganz in der Nähe. Im Moment arbeite ich für eine Speditionsfirma hier in der Stadt. Ich fahre einen Lastwagen und bin viel unterwegs. Ich weiß nicht, aber richtig zu Hause fühle ich mich in Berlin auch nicht und für die Deutschen bin ich immer der Türke.

[1]sich ... *introduce yourself* [2]*weight* [3]*grades*

Arbeit mit dem Text

Was erfahren Sie über Veronika Frisch, Sofie Pracht und Mehmet Sengün? Vervollständigen Sie die Tabelle.

Name	Veronika Frisch	Sofie Pracht	Mehmet Sengün
Alter			
Geburtsort			
Familie/Freunde			
Wohnort			
Beruf			
Studienfach			
Freizeit			
Sonstiges[1]			

Nach dem Lesen

Stellen Sie sich vor.[2] Schreiben Sie einen kurzen Text. Kleben[3] Sie ein Foto auf das Papier oder zeichnen[4] Sie ein Selbstporträt. Hängen Sie Ihre Texte im Seminarraum an die Wand.

[1]*other information*   [2]Stellen … *Introduce yourself.*   [3]*Glue*   [4]*draw*

Videoecke

Perspektiven

Aufgabe 1 Uhren

Wie spät ist es?

Worauf schauen sie?   Wie spät ist es?

1. Wie viele Leute schauen auf ihre Armbanduhr? vier
2. Wie viele Leute schauen auf ihr Handy? zwei
3. Wie viele Leute schauen auf die Turmuhr? eine

Aufgabe 2 Wer sagt das?

Wie spät ist es? Acht Personen werden gefragt. Ordnen Sie die Aussagen den Personen zu.

Videoecke. Perspektiven: Ask sts. *Wie spät ist es?* Then ask: *Was studieren Sie? Wann beginnt Ihr erstes Seminar? Wann stehen Sie auf? Was machen Sie dann? Wie kommen Sie zur Universität? Was machen Sie in Ihrer Freizeit?* Next, ask sts. to open their books to page 61, to look at the photo of the *Rathausturm* and to tell you what time it is. Explain *Aufgabe 1* by saying: *Sie fragen mich, wie spät es ist. Worauf schaue ich? Ich schaue auf meine Armbanduhr, or, auf mein Handy. Sehen Sie sich das Video an. Worauf schauen die Leute? Wie viele schauen auf ihre Armbanduhr, wie viele auf ihr Handy und wie viele auf die Turmuhr?* Play video once and elicit answers. Then turn to *Aufgabe 2.* Go over responses a through h, reading everything out loud. Play the video twice and ask sts. to match pictures and expressions in pairs or small groups. Elicit answers. If there are errors, simply play the video again and ask sts. to make sure everything is correct. **Interviews:** Introduce Sandra and Susan. Play the video segment a couple of times and ask sts. to work in pairs and small groups to determine who does what. Elicit answers.

1. ___h___   2. ___a___   3. ___b___   4. ___g___

5. ___f___   6. ___c___   7. ___d___   8. ___e___

a. Es ist 10 Uhr 10.   e. Ich weiß es nicht. Ich habe keine Uhr.
b. Es ist 12 Uhr 25.   f. Es ist drei vor sechs.
c. Es ist 13 Uhr 28.   g. Es ist dreiviertel fünf.
d. Es ist 14 Uhr 38.   h. Es ist neun Uhr.

Interviews

- Was studierst du?
- Welche Seminare hast du in diesem Semester?
- Wann beginnen deine Seminare?
- Wann stehst du da auf?
- Was machst du dann?
- Was machst du in deiner Freizeit?

Miniwörterbuch

die **Fremdsprache**	*foreign language*
belegen	*to take*

Sandra

Susan

Aufgabe 3 Tagesablauf

Wer macht das? Sandra, Susan oder beide? Kreuzen Sie an.

	Sandra	Susan	Beide
1. Sie studiert Deutsch als Fremdsprache.	☐	☐	☒
2. Sie belegt Seminare zur Phonetik, Phonologie und Grammatik.	☒	☐	☐
3. Ihre Seminare beginnen um 9 Uhr.	☐	☒	☐
4. Sie steht um halb acht auf.	☐	☒	☐
5. Sie steht um 7 Uhr auf.	☒	☐	☐
6. Sie fährt mit dem Fahrrad zur Universität.	☐	☒	☐
7. Sie geht zuerst duschen.	☒	☐	☐
8. Sie geht gern laufen und sie liest gern.	☒	☐	☐
9. Sie geht schwimmen und singt im Chor.	☐	☒	☐

Wortschatz

Freizeit	Leisure Time
chatten [tschɛt-]	to chat
lesen (R)	to read
er/sie liest	he/she reads
Zeitung lesen	to read the newspaper
liegen	to lie
in der Sonne liegen	to lie in the sun
reisen	to travel
schreiben (R)	to write
eine SMS schreiben	to write a text message
segeln	to sail
simsen	to text
spielen	to play
wandern	to hike
zelten	to camp

Ähnliche Wörter

die E-Mail, -s; die Gitarre, -n; die Karte, -n; die Musik; die Sonnenbrille, -n; der Ball, ⸚e (R); der Fußball, ⸚e (R); der Kaffee; der Volleyball, ⸚e; das Foto, -s; das Golf; das Hobby, -s; das Schach; das Snowboard, -s; das Tennis; boxen; hören; kochen; reiten; schwimmen gehen; singen; im Internet surfen; tanzen

Orte	Places
die Arbeit	work
zur Arbeit gehen	to go to work
der Berg, -e	mountain
in die Berge gehen	to go to the mountains
in den Bergen wandern	to hike in the mountains
das Kino, -s	movie theater, cinema
ins Kino gehen	to go to the movies
das Meer, -e	sea
im Meer schwimmen	to swim in the sea
das Rathaus, ⸚er	town hall
auf dem Rathaus	at the town hall
das Schwimmbad, ⸚er	swimming pool
ins Schwimmbad fahren	to go to the swimming pool

Ähnliche Wörter

die Party, -s; auf eine Party gehen; die Uni, -s (R); zur Uni gehen; auf der Uni sein; der Park, -s; im Park spazieren gehen; das Bett, -en; ins Bett gehen; das Haus, ⸚er; zu Hause sein; nach Hause gehen; das Konzert, -e; ins Konzert gehen; das Museum, Museen; ins Museum gehen

Schule und Universität	School and University
die Geschichte	history
die Kunstgeschichte	art history
die Informatik	computer science
die Kunst	art
die Lehrerin, -nen (R)	female teacher, instructor
die Prüfung, -en	test
die Schule, -n	school
die Schülerin, -nen	female pupil
die Sozialkunde	social studies
die Wirtschaft	economics
der Lehrer, - (R)	male teacher, instructor
der Maschinenbau	mechanical engineering
der Schüler, -	male pupil
der Stundenplan, ⸚e	schedule
das Auslandsamt, ⸚er	center for study abroad
das Fach, ⸚er	academic subject
das Stipendium, Stipendien	scholarship
das Studium, Studien	university studies
die Ferien (*pl.*)	vacation

Ähnliche Wörter

die Biologie, die Chemie, die Geografie, die Linguistik, die Literatur; die Mathematik; die Musik; die Pause, -n; die Physik; die Religion; die Soziologie; der Kurs, -e (R); der Sport; das Latein; das Semester, -; lernen; studieren

Persönliche Daten	Biographical Information
die Farbe, -n	color
die Größe, -n	height
die Narbe, -n	scar
die Staatsangehörigkeit, -en	nationality, citizenship
die Unterschrift, -en	signature
der Beruf, -e	profession
was sind Sie von Beruf?	what's your profession?
der Geburtstag, -e	birthday
der Personalausweis, -e	(personal) ID card
der Reisepass, ⸚e	passport
der Spitzname, -n	nickname
der Wohnort, -e	residence
das Alter	age
ledig	unmarried
verheiratet	married

Ähnliche Wörter

die Adresse, -n; die Augenfarbe; die Haarfarbe; die Nummer, -n; die Hausnummer, -n; die Telefonnummer, -n; die Person, -en; der Name, -n (R); der Familienname, -n (R); der Vorname, -n (R); das Telefon, -e; geboren; wann sind Sie geboren?

Tagesablauf — Daily Routine

die Stunde, -n	hour
die Woche, -n	week
in der Woche	during the week
der Abend, -e	evening
der Tag, -e	day
den ganzen Tag	all day long
der Montag	Monday
der Dienstag	Tuesday
der Mittwoch	Wednesday
der Donnerstag	Thursday
der Freitag	Friday
der Samstag	Saturday
der Sonntag	Sunday
das Wochenende, -n	weekend
am Wochenende	over the weekend
früh	early
spät(er)	late(r)
Um wie viel Uhr ...?	At what time . . . ?
Wann?	When?
um halb drei	at two thirty
um sechs (Uhr)	at six o'clock
um sieben Uhr zwanzig	at seven twenty
um Viertel vor vier	at a quarter to four
um zwanzig nach fünf	at twenty after/past five
Welcher Tag ist heute?	What day is today?
Wie spät ist es?	What time is it?
Wie viel Uhr ist es?	What time is it?

Ähnliche Wörter

die Sekunde, -n; der Moment, -e; im Moment

Sonstige Substantive — Other Nouns

die Tasche, -n	bag; purse; pocket
die Wohnung, -en	apartment
der Brief, -e	letter
das Abendessen, -	supper, evening meal
das Halstuch, ̈-er	bandanna
das Motorrad, ̈-er	motorcycle
Motorrad fahren	to ride a motorcycle
das Zimmer, -	room

Verben mit trennbaren Präfixen — Verbs with Separable Prefixes

ab·holen	to pick (somebody) up (from a place)
an·kommen	to arrive
an·rufen	to call up
auf·hören (mit)	to stop (doing something)
auf·räumen	to clean (up)
auf·stehen	to get up
aus·füllen	to fill out
aus·gehen	to go out
ein·kaufen (gehen)	to (go) shop(ping), shop for
ein·packen	to pack up
fern·sehen	to watch TV
er/sie sieht fern	he/she is watching TV
kennen·lernen	to get acquainted with

Sonstige Verben — Other Verbs

arbeiten	to work
besuchen	to visit
brauchen	to need; to use
duschen	to (take a) shower
fliegen	to fly
frühstücken	to eat breakfast
kaufen	to buy
mögen	to like
ich mag	I like
du magst	you like
spazieren gehen	to go for a walk
suchen	to look for
tun	to do
unterschreiben	to sign

Ähnliche Wörter

beginnen, reparieren, trinken

Sonstige Wörter und Ausdrücke — Other Words and Expressions

gern	gladly, with pleasure
wir singen gern	we like to sing
ihr(e)	her
nervös	nervous
sein(e)	his
sicher	sure
wahrscheinlich	probably

Strukturen und Übungen

1.1 The present tense

1.1. *Präsens: regelmäßige Verben.* This section introduces more regular verbs in the present tense. Verbs that change their stem vowel appear in *Kapitel 2.* We do not expect sts. to use all endings correctly in speech at this stage. The *ich-, du-,* and *Sie-*forms are likely to be acquired first. Include the other forms in your input, too, so sts. can become familiar with them.

Wissen Sie noch?

ich	-e
du	-st
er/sie/es	-t
wir	-en
ihr	-t
Sie, sie	-en

Review grammar B.6

Note. You might wish to point out to sts. that Appendix E summarizes verb conjugations. Appendix D contains summaries of other important grammar points.

One German present-tense form expresses three different ideas in English.

Ich spiele Gitarre.
$$\begin{cases} \textit{I play the guitar.} \\ \textit{I'm playing the guitar.} \\ \textit{I'm going to play the guitar.} \end{cases}$$

Most German verbs form the present tense just like **kommen (Einführung B).**

spielen			
ich	spiele	wir	spielen
du	spielst	ihr	spielt
Sie	spielen	Sie	spielen
er sie es	spielt	sie	spielen

Gabi und Jutta **spielen** gern Karten.	*Gabi and Jutta like to play cards.*

Verbs whose stems end in an **s**-sound, such as **-s, -ss, -ß, -z (-ts),** or **-x (-ks),** do not add an additional **-s-** in the **du**-form: **du tanzt, du heißt, du reist.**

—Wie **heißt du?**	*What's your name?*
—Ich **heiße** Natalie.	*My name's Natalie.*

Verbs whose stems end in **-d** or **-t** (and a few other verbs such as **regnen** [*to rain*] and **öffnen** [*to open*]) insert an **-e-** between the stem and the **-st** or **-t** endings. This happens in the **du-, ihr-,** and **er/sie/es**-forms.

Reitest du jeden Tag?	*Do you go horseback riding every day?*

reiten			
ich	reite	wir	reiten
du	reitest	ihr	reitet
Sie	reiten	Sie	reiten
er sie es	reitet	sie	reiten

Übung 1   Was machen sie?

Note. Answers to the *Übungen* are in Appendix F.

Üb. 1. This is the first example of an exercise in which there are restrictions of both a grammatical and a semantic kind as to what combinations are possible. First, sts. need to select a verb that agrees in person and number with the subject at hand. Then, they need to select an object that makes sense to use with the verb selected during the first step. This two-step approach is based on the following two goals: **(1)** to sensitize sts. to paying attention to word endings; and **(2)** to focus sts. on meaning even during grammar exercises by making it difficult to come up with correct sentences without understanding what they mean. Work with the first two or three sentences as sample sentences in class.

Kombinieren Sie die Wörter. Achten Sie auf die Verbendungen.

MODELL: Ich besuche Freunde.

1. ich	lernen	Freunde
2. ihr	besuche	ins Kino
3. Jutta und Jens	studiert	Spaghetti
4. du	hört	ein Buch
5. Melanie	reisen	gut Tennis
6. ich	kochen	nach Deutschland
7. wir	lese	in Regensburg
8. Richard	spielst	Spanisch
9. Jürgen und Silvia	geht	gern Musik

Übung 2   Minidialoge

Üb. 2–3. Assign the next two exercises for homework. In class have pairs of sts. read the dialogues aloud. Sts. must choose the subject pronoun in *Üb. 2* and the verb ending in *Üb. 3*.

Ergänzen Sie das Pronomen.

1. CLAIRE: Arbeitet Melanie?
   JOSEF: Nein, _____ arbeitet nicht.

2. MICHAEL: Schwimmen _____ gern im Meer?
   FRAU KÖRNER: Ja, sehr gern. Und Sie?

3. MEHMET: Was machst _____ª im Sommer?
   RENATE: _____ᵇ fliege nach Spanien.

4. CLAIRE: Woher kommt _____ª?
   HELGA UND SIGRID: _____ᵇ kommen aus Krefeld.

5. JÜRGEN: _____ª studiere in Göttingen. Und _____ᵇ?
   KLAUS UND CHRISTINA: _____ᶜ studieren in Berlin.

Übung 3   Minidialoge

Ergänzen Sie die Verbendungen.

1. CLAIRE: Du tanz_____ª gern, nicht?
   MELANIE: Ja, ich tanz_____ᵇ sehr gern, aber mein Freund tanz_____ᶜ nicht gern.

2. FRAU SCHULZ: Richard geh_____ª im Sommer in den Bergen wandern.
   STEFAN: Und was mach_____ᵇ seine Eltern?
   FRAU SCHULZ: Seine Mutter reis_____ᶜ nach Frankreich und sein Vater arbeit_____ᵈ.

3. JÜRGEN: Wir koch_____ª heute Abend. Was mach_____ᵇ ihr?
   KLAUS: Wir besuch_____ᶜ Freunde.

4. DANIEL: Schreib_____ª du mir eine E-Mail?
   TIM: Ja, ich schreibe dir eine E-Mail. Chatt_____ᵇ du auch?
   DANIEL: Ja, das mach_____ᶜ ich auch.

1.2 Expressing likes and dislikes: *gern / nicht gern*

verb + **gern** = *to like to do something*

verb + **nicht gern** = *to dislike doing something*

To say that you like doing something, use the word **gern** after the verb. To say that you don't like to do something, use **nicht gern.**

Ernst spielt **gern** Fußball.   Ernst likes to play soccer.
Josef spielt **nicht gern** Fußball.   Josef doesn't like to play soccer.

I	II	III	IV
Sofie	spielt	gern	Schach.
Willi	spielt	auch gern	Schach.
Ich	spiele	nicht gern	Schach.
Monika	spielt	auch nicht gern	Schach.

The position of **auch/nicht/gern** (in that order) is between the verb and its complement.*

1.2. *Gern* and *nicht gern* do not correspond directly to any English forms, but sts. usually have no difficulty using them in simple sentences.

Übung 4   Was machen die Studenten gern?

Üb. 4–5. Assign for homework, which may be written. Follow up in class with questions to sts. about their own likes and dislikes.

Bilden Sie Sätze.

MODELL: Heidi und Nora schwimmen gern.

Heidi / Nora

Monika / Albert
1.

Heidi
2.

Stefan
3.

Nora
4.

Peter
5.

Katrin
6.

Monika
7.

Albert
8.

*The complement provides additional information and thus "completes" the meaning of the verb:
ich spiele → **ich spiele Tennis; ich höre** → **ich höre Musik.**

Sagen Sie, was die folgenden Personen gern machen.

MODELL: Frau Ruf liegt gern in der Sonne. Jutta liegt auch gern in der Sonne, aber Herr Ruf liegt nicht gern in der Sonne.

1. Frau Ruf   Jutta   Herr Ruf

2. Jens   Ernst   Jutta

3. Jens   Jutta   Andrea

4. Michael   Maria   die Rufs   die Wagners

1.3 Telling time

Ask the time in German in one of two ways.

Wie spät ist es?   *What time is it?*
Wie viel Uhr ist es?

Es ist eins.
Es ist ein Uhr.

Es ist drei.
Es ist drei Uhr.

Es ist Viertel vor elf.
Es ist zehn Uhr fünfundvierzig.

Es ist Viertel nach elf.
Es ist elf Uhr fünfzehn.

vor = *to*
nach = *after*

Es ist zehn (Minuten) vor acht.
Es ist sieben Uhr fünfzig.

Es ist zehn (Minuten) nach acht.
Es ist acht Uhr zehn.

The expressions **Viertel, nach, vor,** and **halb** are used in everyday speech. In German, the half hour is expressed as "half before" the following hour, not as "half after" the preceding hour, as in English.

halb = *half, thirty*

halb zehn = *half past nine, nine thirty*

Es ist halb zehn.   *It is nine thirty (halfway to ten).*

The 24-hour clock (0.00 to 24.00) is used when giving exact or official times, as in time announcements, schedules, programs, and the like. With the 24-hour clock only the pattern [(*number*) **Uhr** (*number of minutes*)] is used.

AA. Use the excerpt from a *Zugbegleiter* as an opportunity to ask further questions about times. *Wann kommt der Zug in Potsdam an? Wann fährt er ab?*

Ankunft	km	Abfahrt	Anschlüsse
14.22 Potsdam Stadt		**14.24**	
↓		14.43	Wildpark 14.49 Werder (Havel) 14.56 (204)
	24	*E* 15.01	Wustermark 15.39 Nauen 15.57 (204.4)
			S-Bahnanschlüsse (Taktverkehr) bestehen in Richtung: Wannsee – Westkreuz – Charlottenburg – Zool Garten (Ⓢ 3)

Der Zug geht um vierzehn Uhr vierundzwanzig.   *The train leaves at two twenty-four p.m.*

Übung 6   Die Uhrzeit

Üb. 6. For oral work in pairs.

Wie spät ist es?

MODELL: Es ist acht Uhr.

1.   2.   3.   4.

5.   6.   7.   8.

1.4 Word order in statements

1.4. *Wortstellung in Aussagen.* The placement of the verb in second position when the subject is not the first element appears to be a simple rule, but it is acquired relatively late. Early mastery of this rule in speech is not expected.

In English, the verb usually follows the subject of a sentence.

SUBJECT	VERB	COMPLEMENT
Peter	takes	a walk.

Even when another word or phrase begins the sentence, the word order does not change.

	SUBJECT	VERB	COMPLEMENT
Every day,	Peter	takes	a walk.

In statements, verb second.

In German statements, the verb is always in second position. If the sentence begins with an element other than the subject, the subject follows the verb.

I	II	III	IV
SUBJECT	VERB		COMPLEMENT
Wir	spielen	heute	Tennis.
	VERB	SUBJECT	COMPLEMENT
Heute	spielen	wir	Tennis.

Übung 7   Rolf

Üb. 7. Assign as homework or do in class. If assigned as homework, explain to sts. what the task is beforehand. The verb-second rule is practiced for reading purposes only. Identifying the subject is an important technique when reading. However, we do not practice this rule for speaking purposes at this stage, since it is very unlikely that sts. will profit from it this early in their acquisition of German.

Unterstreichen[1] Sie das Subjekt des Satzes. Steht das konjugierte Verb vor[2] oder nach[3] dem Subjekt?

1. <u>Rolf</u> kommt aus Krefeld.   *nach*
2. Im Moment studiert er in Berkeley. _____
3. Seine Großmutter wohnt noch in Krefeld. _____
4. Samstags geht Rolf oft ins Kino. _____
5. Am Wochenende wandert er oft in den Bergen. _____
6. In der Woche treibt er gern Sport. _____
7. Im Sommer geht er surfen. _____
8. Er geht auch ins Schwimmbad der Uni. _____

Übung 8   Sie und Ihr Freund

Üb. 8. Before assigning this exercise for written homework, explain the task and do a few sample sentences with your sts. Follow up in class by having sts. read their answers aloud. Combine with oral questions.

Bilden Sie Sätze. Beginnen Sie die Sätze mit dem ersten Wort oder den ersten Wörtern in jeder Zeile. Beachten[4] Sie die Satzstellung[5].

MODELL: Heute (ich / sein _____) → Heute bin ich fröhlich.

1. Ich (studieren _____)
2. Im Moment (ich / wohnen in _____)
3. Heute (ich / kochen _____)
4. Manchmal (ich / trinken _____)
5. Ich (spielen gern _____)
6. Mein Freund (heißen _____)
7. Jetzt (er / wohnen in _____)
8. Manchmal (wir / spielen _____)

[1]Underline [2]before [3]after [4]Pay attention to [5]word order

1.5 Separable-prefix verbs

1.5. *Verben mit trennbaren Präfixen.* In this chapter, sts. will mostly need to use the structure with the prefix at the end of the sentence. Infinitive forms will be used in *Kapitel 2.* Point out that this is the first encounter with *Satzklammer,* a characteristic feature of German sentence structure. The next example of *Satzklammer* occurs with the modal *möchte* in *Kapitel 2.*

Many German verbs have prefixes that change the verb's meaning. They combine with the infinitive to form a single word.

stehen	*to stand*
gehen	*to go*
kommen	*to come*
aufstehen	*to stand up*
ausgehen	*to go out*
ankommen	*to arrive*

In statements, verb second, prefix last.

When you use a present-tense form of these verbs, put the conjugated form in second position and put the prefix at the end of the sentence. The two parts of the verb form a frame or bracket, called a **Satzklammer,** that encloses the rest of the sentence.

Claire <u>kommt</u> <u>an</u>.

Claire <u>kommt</u> am Donnerstag <u>an</u>.

Claire <u>kommt</u> am Donnerstag in Frankfurt <u>an</u>.

Here are some common verbs with separable prefixes.

abholen	*to pick up, fetch*
ankommen	*to arrive*
anrufen	*to call up*
aufhören	*to stop, be over*
aufräumen	*to clean up, tidy up*
aufstehen	*to get up*
ausfüllen	*to fill out*
ausgehen	*to go out*
einkaufen	*to shop, shop for*
einpacken	*to pack up*
kennenlernen	*to get acquainted with*

Übung 9   Eine Reise in die Türkei

Mehmet fliegt morgen in die Türkei. Was macht er heute? Ergänzen Sie die folgenden Wörter: **ab, an, auf, auf, auf, aus, aus, ein, ein.**

1. Er steht um 7 Uhr _____.
2. Er räumt die Wohnung _____.
3. Er packt seine Sachen[1] _____.
4. Er ruft Renate _____.
5. Er füllt ein Formular _____.
6. Er holt seinen Reisepass _____.
7. Er kauft Essen[2] _____.
8. Abends geht er _____.
9. Er geht ins Kino. Der Film hört um 22 Uhr _____.

Mehmet

[1]*things* [2]*food*

Was machen die Leute?

Verwenden Sie die folgenden Verben.

abholen
ankommen
anrufen
aufräumen
aufstehen
ausfüllen
ausgehen
einkaufen
einpacken
kennenlernen

MODELL: Frau Schulz kauft ein paar Lebensmittel ein.

1.

2.

Heidi / Thomas

3.

Albert

4.

Peter / Monika

5.

Peter / Monika

6.

Frau Schulz

7.

Stefan

8.

Katrin   Rolf

9.

1.6 Word order in questions

1.6. *Wortstellung in Fragesätzen.* Word order in German questions is generally not a problem for English-speaking learners. Students will already have heard many yes/no questions as well as questions beginning with a question word.

In **w**-questions, verb second.

When you begin a question with a question word (for example, **wie, wo, wer, was, wann, woher**), the verb follows in second position. The subject of the sentence is in third position. Any further elements appear in fourth position.

I	II	III	IV	
Wann	beginnt	das Spiel?		*When does the game start?*
Was	machst	du	heute Abend?	*What are you doing this evening?*
Wo	wohnst	du?		*Where do you live?*
Welches Fach	studierst	du?		*What subject are you studying?*

Here are the question words you have encountered so far.

wann	*when*
was	*what*
welcher*	*which*
wer	*who*
wie	*how*
wie viel(e)	*how much (many)*
wo	*where*
woher	*from where*

Questions that can be answered by *yes* or *no* begin with the verb.

Tanzt du gern?	*Do you like to dance?*
Arbeitest du hier?	*Do you work here?*
Gehst du ins Kino?	*Are you going to the movies?*

Übung 11 Ein Interview mit Marta Szerwinski

Üb. 11. Students need to change the form and order of the words. Assign as written homework. Follow up in class with oral pair work.

Schreiben Sie die Fragen.

MODELL: du + heißen + wie + ? → Wie heißt du?

Marta

1. du + sein + geboren + wann + ?
2. du + kommen + woher + ?
3. du + wohnen + wo + ?
4. du + haben + Augenfarbe + welch- + ?
5. du + sein + groß + wie + ?
6. du + studieren + ?
7. du + studieren + Fächer + welch- + ?
8. du + arbeiten + Stunden + wie viele + ?
9. du + machen + gern + was + ?

Übung 12 Noch ein Interview

Üb. 12. Assign for homework. In class, ask sts. to interview someone who plays Sofie, or else play the role of Sofie yourself.

AA. After doing the exercise with the given responses, sts. could be encouraged to make slight variations in both questions and answers.

Stellen Sie die Fragen.

Sofie

1. —Ich heiße Sofie.
2. —Nein, ich komme nicht aus München.
3. —Ich komme aus Dresden.
4. —Ich studiere Biologie.
5. —Er heißt Willi.
6. —Er wohnt in Dresden.
7. —Nein, ich spiele nicht Tennis.
8. —Ja, ich tanze sehr gern.
9. —Ja, ich trinke gern Cola.
10. —Ja, Willi trinkt gern Bier.

*The endings of **welcher** vary according to gender, number, and case of the following noun. They are the same endings as those of the definite article. Therefore, **welcher** is called a **der**-word.

(M)	(N)	(F)	(Pl)
welch**er** Name	welch**es** Alter	welch**e** Adresse	welch**e** Studienfächer

Besitz und Vergnügen

In **Kapitel 2** you will learn to talk more about things: your own possessions and things you give others. You will also learn how to describe what you have and don't have and to give your opinion on matters of taste or style.

GOALS The focus of *Kapitel 2* is the sts.' immediate environment outside the class: things they have, things they would like to have, and what they like to do. The suggested additional activities provide further chances for talking about daily activities, as a review of the topics from *Kapitel 1*.

PRE-TEXT ACTIVITIES Bring in pictures of items found in the sts.' environment. First identify and talk briefly about the items, then pass each picture to a different st. Ask: *Wer hat den/das/die _____?* Then ask another st.: *Was möchten Sie haben? Den _____, das _____ oder die _____?* (If sts. ask, point out that *der* changes to *den* in these sentences.)

Themen

Besitz
Geschenke
Kleidung und Aussehen
Vergnügen

Kulturelles

KLI: Der Euro
Musikszene: „Junge" (Die Ärzte)
Filmclip: *Lola rennt* (Tom Tykwer)
KLI: Jugend im Netz
Videoecke: Hobbys

Lektüren

Blog Deutsch 101: Frau Schulz hat Geburtstag
Film: *Lola rennt* (Tom Tykwer)

Strukturen

2.1 The accusative case
2.2 The negative article: **kein, keine**
2.3 What would you like? **Ich möchte ...**
2.4 Possessive adjectives
2.5 The present tense of stem-vowel changing verbs
2.6 Asking people to do things: the **du**-imperative

Suggestion: Use Hofheinz-Döring's painting as a starting point to review colors, the symbolic use of colors and characteristics of people in general. You might ask: *Welche Farben kennen Sie? Welche Farbe hat die Liebe? Welche Farbe hat der Neid? etc. Das Bild heißt Der Geizhals, wie ist ein Geizhals (z.B. egoistisch, ehrgeizig, glücklich, freundlich, konservativ?)*

Kunst und Künstler

Margret Hofheinz-Döring (1910–1994) ist eine deutsche Malerin und Grafikerin der sogenannten Verschollenen[1] Generation, die sich während der Nazizeit und des 2. Weltkriegs nicht weiterentwickeln[2] konnte. Hofheinz-Dörings Themen sind vor allem Menschen und Bilder zur Weltliteratur. Immer wieder stellt sie typisch menschliche Situationen oder Märchenhaftes dar[3]. Dazu gehört auch ihr Bild „Der Geizhals[4]".

Schauen Sie sich das Bild an und beant-worten Sie die folgenden Fragen.

1. Welche Farben dominieren?
2. Welche Linien dominieren: runde, eckige[5], spitze[6]?
3. Wie sieht der Geizhals aus? Wo ist er? Was macht er? Worauf schaut er? Was ist im Hintergrund?
4. Welche Gefühle evoziert das Bild?

[1]*lost* [2]*continue to develop* [3]stellt dar *portrays* [4]*miser* [5]*angular* [6]*pointed*

Margret Hofheinz-Döring: *Geizhals* (1926), Galerie Brigitte Mauch, Göppingen

Chapter opening artwork: *Der Geizhals* is an early painting by Margret Hofheinz-Döring in which she combines a typical human trait with elements of the fairy tale. The figure in the center of the painting seems to be hoarding something valuable in a cave in the forest at night. The contrast between the vivid colors in the background and the spidery representation of the figure in black underlines the negative perception of miserly behavior in society. The secretive and compulsive behavior of the miser is presented in a slightly grotesque way typical for Hofheinz-Döring's work. Her style is often described as sensitive, poetic, and idiosyncratic with a tendency to the grotesque.

Situationen

Besitz

Grammatik 2.1–2.2

Vocabulary Display
Introduce vocabulary as usual: presentation, receptive recall (*Wo steht der Schrank? Links, rechts oder in der Mitte?*), choral response, productive recall, personalization: *Schreiben Sie auf, was alles in Ihrem Zimmer ist!* (See the IM for suggestions on introducing vocabulary.)

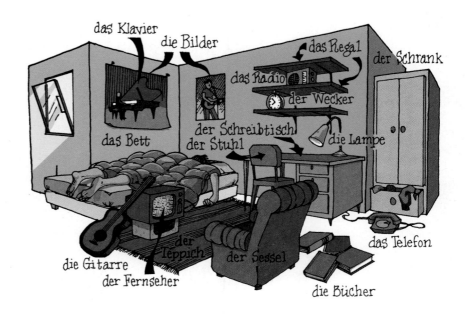

Situation 1 Hast du einen Schlafsack?

Sit. 1. In this activity, sts. use the accusative forms *einen/ein/eine* and *keinen/kein/keine*. The masculine is stressed in this interaction, since it is the only gender that changes in the accusative. Demonstrate the model question and answer. Use the data projector to point to the item mentioned. Then repeat the model with 1-2 other items from the list. Make sure sts. understand the meaning of all new words before they work in pairs. Cover the labels on the screen, and ask *Was ist das?* The response to this question will be in the nominative, and it may be necessary to point this out. Have sts. alternate asking and answering. You may want to point out that *kein* will have the same ending as *ein* in their responses. Afterward, to make sure that sts. understand the relationship between the definite and indefinite articles, you could ask: *Welche Sachen/Dinge im Bild sind maskulin/feminin/neutral? Wie wissen Sie das?*

MODELL: S1: Hast du einen Schlafsack?
S2: Ja, ich habe einen Schlafsack.
Nein, ich habe keinen Schlafsack.

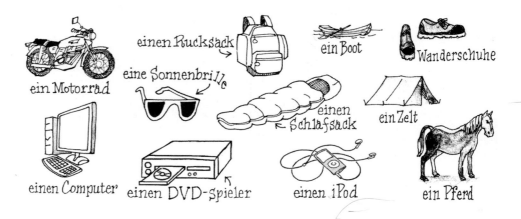

500 Euro

Der Euro

Fragen Sie Ihren Partner oder Ihre Partnerin.

1. Wie heißt die Währung[1] in dem Land, in dem du geboren bist?
2. Welche Münzen[2] gibt es, z. B. 1-Cent-Münzen, 2-Cent-Münzen?
3. Welche Geldscheine[3] gibt es, z. B. 1-Dollar-Scheine, 2-Dollar-Scheine?
4. Welche Farbe haben die Geldscheine?
5. Welche Bilder und Symbole gibt es auf den Geldscheinen und Münzen?

50 Euro

Lesen Sie die Fragen und suchen Sie die Informationen im Text.

1. Was ist der Euro?
2. In welchen Ländern der Europäischen Union zahlt[4] man mit dem Euro?
3. In welchen Ländern der Europäischen Union benutzt[5] man den Euro nicht?
4. Welche Euroscheine gibt es? Wie sehen sie aus?
5. Welche Euromünzen gibt es? Wie sehen sie aus?

10 Euro

Den Euro gibt es seit[6] dem 1. Januar 2002. Der Euro ist die gemeinsame Währung[7] der Europäischen Union (EU). Zwölf Länder haben den Euro seit 2002: Belgien, Deutschland, Finnland, Frankreich, Griechenland, Irland, Italien, Luxemburg, die Niederlande, Österreich, Portugal und Spanien. Auch Estland, Malta, die Slowakei, Slowenien und Zypern gehören zur Eurozone.

5 Euro

Doch nicht alle Länder der EU haben den Euro. Dazu gehören[8] die folgenden 10 Länder: Bulgarien, Dänemark, Großbritannien, Lettland, Litauen, Polen, Rumänien, Schweden, Tschechien und Ungarn. Manche Länder akzeptieren den Euro, obwohl[9] sie nicht in der Europäischen Union sind. Dazu gehört zum Beispiel die Schweiz.

Es gibt Euroscheine und Euromünzen. Die Euroscheine sind 5€, 10€, 20€, 50€, 100€, 200€ und 500€ wert[10]. Die Scheine sind in allen Ländern gleich[11]. Alle Scheine haben auf der Rückseite ein Bild von einer Brücke[12].

10 cent

2 Euro

Die Euromünzen sind 1 Cent (ct), 2ct, 5ct, 10ct, 20ct und 50ct wert. 100 Cent sind 1 Euro. Es gibt auch 1€ und 2€ Münzen. Die Vorderseite[13] zeigt die Länder der Eurozone. Auf der Rückseite hat jedes Land ein anderes Bild.

10 cent (D)

2 Euro (D)

KLI. Have sts. research the back of all Austrian coins and ask them how they would design the back of the German Euro coins. Raise the question of how a nation can be visually represented on coins or bills.

10 cent (A)

2 Euro (A)

[1]currency [2]coins [3]der Schein *bill* [4]pays [5]uses [6]since [7]gemeinsame ... *common currency* [8]Dazu ... *Among these are*
[9]although [10]worth [11]the same [12]bridge [13]front side

Situation 2   Dialog: Stefan zieht in sein neues Zimmer

Sit. 2. (See the IM.) Establish the context: *Stefan studiert jetzt und er will nicht bei seinen Eltern wohnen. Er möchte im Studentenheim wohnen, aber er hat keine Möbel. Stefan trifft Katrin im Möbelgeschäft.* (Show a picture or explain.) Questions to focus attention: **(1)** *Was macht Stefan morgen?* **(2)** *Was braucht Stefan?* **(3)** *Was hat er schon?* **(4)** *Wie viel Geld hat er?* Questions for second reading: **(1)** *Was glaubt Katrin?* **(2)** *Was schlägt sie vor?*

Katrin trifft Stefan im Möbelgeschäft.

KATRIN: Hallo, Stefan. Was machst du denn hier?

STEFAN: Ach, ich brauche noch ein paar Sachen. Morgen ziehe ich in ___mein neues Zimmer___ .

KATRIN: Was brauchst du denn?

STEFAN: Ach, alles Mögliche.

KATRIN: Was hast du denn schon?

STEFAN: Ich habe einen ___Schlafsack___ , eine ___Gitarre___ und ... und ... und einen ___Wecker___ .

KATRIN: Das ist aber nicht viel. ___Wie viel Geld___ hast du denn?

STEFAN: So 30 Dollar.

KATRIN: Ich glaube, du bist im falschen Geschäft. Der Flohmarkt ist viel besser ___für dich___ .

STEFAN: Ja, vielleicht hast du recht.

Situation 3   Informationsspiel: Was machen sie morgen?

Sit. 3. (See the IM.) The corresponding chart is in Appendix A. In this version, sts. must ask their partners the same questions that they ask about the characters in the book. To do this activity, sts. must clearly understand how to conjugate regular and separable-prefix verbs in 2nd- and 3rd-person singular. Model the first 4 questions using *Jürgen* as your subject and the last 4 questions using *du* as the subject, to make sure that sts. hear the correct pronunciation and to alert them to the separable-prefix verbs, which are not modeled in the example. Have the sts. repeat after you. It is more efficient for S1 to complete the entire chart and then allow S2 to ask questions. For additional speaking practice, ask sts. to switch partners and ask: *Was macht Ihr Partner / Ihre Partnerin morgen?* Sts. can list everything their partner plans to do the next day: *Morgen schreibt Ann einen Brief, sie lernt den Wortschatz auswendig und sie besucht einen Freund.* Your follow-up can be similar: *Ann, wer war Ihr Partner / Ihre Partnerin? Was macht er/sie morgen?* Ann must then answer as above; alternatively simply ask 3-4 sts.: *Tony, was machst du morgen?* or *Braden, sag uns bitte drei Sachen, die du morgen machst.*

MODELL: S2: Schreibt Jürgen morgen eine E-Mail?
S1: Nein.
S2: Schreibst du morgen eine E-Mail?
S1: Ja. (Nein.)

	Jürgen	Silvia	mein(e) Partner(in)
1. schreibt/schreibst ... eine E-Mail	−	+	
2. kauft/kaufst ... ein Buch	+	+	
3. schaut/schaust ... einen Film an	−	+	
4. ruft/rufst ... eine Freundin an	−	+	
5. macht/machst ... Hausaufgaben	+	+	
6. isst/isst ... einen Hamburger	−	+	
7. besucht/besuchst ... einen Freund	+	+	
8. räumt/räumst ... das Zimmer auf	−	−	

Situation 4   Interview: Besitz

Sit. 4. (See the IM for suggestions on using interviews.) First, set the scene by asking a few of the interview questions. Then model pronunciation of the interview questions. As sts. repeat, answer the questions as they apply to you and encourage sts. to write down any of your answers that might help them to formulate their responses. You will need to review types of jewelry and perhaps write the vocabulary on the board. Some sts. may have unusual pets as well, so be prepared to supply other animal vocabulary to individual sts. Remind your sts. to write down their partner's answers, since afterward they will find new partners and discuss what they learned about the first interviewee.

1. Was hast du in deinem Zimmer? Was möchtest du haben?
2. Hast du wertvolle Sachen? DVD-Spieler, Auto, Laptop, Fernseher, I-Pad, Handy? Was möchtest du haben?
3. Hast du einen Hund oder eine Katze? Möchtest du einen Hund oder eine Katze haben?

Geschenke

Grammatik 2.3

der Hund   der Koffer   das Handy   die Kinokarte   der Film

die Tasche   die Kamera   das Videospiel   der Pullover   das Geld

Situation 5   Was möchten sie?

MODELL: S1: Was möchte Herr Siebert?
S2: Er möchte _____.

ein Auto   ein Surfbrett   ein Fahrrad   eine Katze   ein Haus

Herr Siebert   Jutta   Ernst   Josie   Herr Ruf

Situation 6   Dialog: Ein Geschenk für Josef

Melanie trifft Claire in der Mensa.

MELANIE: Josef hat nächsten Donnerstag Geburtstag.
CLAIRE: Wirklich? Dann brauche ich ja noch ein Geschenk für ihn. Mensch, das ist schwierig. Hat er denn Hobbys?
MELANIE: Er spielt Gitarre und hört gern Musik.
CLAIRE: Hast du schon ein Geschenk?
MELANIE: Ich möchte ein Songbuch kaufen. Aber es ist ziemlich teuer. Kaufen wir es zusammen?
CLAIRE: Ja, klar. Welche Art Musik hat er denn gern?
MELANIE: Ich glaube, Soft-Rock und Oldies. Elton John, Céline Dion und so.

Situation 7 Zum Schreiben: Eine Einladung

Schreiben Sie eine Einladung zu einer Party. Benutzen Sie das Modell unten und Ihre Phantasie!

CALIGULA* PARTY

Wann: Mittwoch den 11. Juni - ab 20 Uhr.
Wo: Ludwig-Thomaheim - Neubau 5. Stock.
Wie: Im Kostüm der Epoche, mit
      eigenem Kissen, um darauf
      zu ruhen.

B. D. E. A. (Bring Deinen Eigenen Alkohol)
* Der wahnsinnige römische Kaiser

Situation 8 Rollenspiel: Am Telefon

S1: Sie rufen einen Freund / eine Freundin an. Sie machen am Samstag eine Party. Laden Sie Ihren Freund / Ihre Freundin ein.

Sit. 8. *Rollenspiel:* The role for S1 appears here, the role for S2 appears in Appendix B. **(1)** Set the scene as described in the role for S1. **(2)** Provide sts. with a model by working with the enactment of the role-play found in the workbook/lab manual. **(3)** Write the structure of the role-play on the board: *Begrüßen; Erkundigen (nach Interesse und/oder Verfügbarkeit); Einladen; Zeit und Ort vereinbaren; Verabschieden.* **(4)** Elicit sample greetings, questions, etc. and write on the board. Ask for appropriate responses and also write on the board. **(5)** Divide the class into 2 groups and assign one part of the role-play to each group. Ask sts. to practice the role-play in pairs. **(6)** Ask 2-3 pairs of sts. to perform their role-play in class. Provide feedback as to appropriateness and accuracy of language used after sts. have returned to their seats. **(7)** Ask sts. to find new partners and to practice the role-play in pairs again. **(8)** Optional homework assignment: Ask sts. to write up their version of the role-play. **Sit. 8.** *Cultural note.* Tell your sts. about German telephone etiquette. When answering the phone, people usually say only their last name. At the end of their conversation, they say „*Auf Wiederhören.*" **Note:** If your students are using McGraw-Hill's **Connect** online *Arbeitsbuch,* they can do this *Rollenspiel* using the real-time, interactive **Video-Chat** feature.

Lektüre 📖

Vor dem Lesen

A. Frau Schulz hat bald Geburtstag. Die Studenten wollen ihr ein Geschenk machen. Im Internet diskutieren sie über ihre Ideen. Welche Geschenke kann man einer Professorin machen, wenn sie Geburtstag hat? Kreuzen Sie an.

☐ Blumen
☐ einen Rucksack
☐ ein Foto der Klasse
☐ ein Snowboard
☐ eine Kinokarte
☐ Schmuck
☐ eine Reise nach Europa
☐ ein Fahrrad
☐ einen deutschen Film auf DVD
cake ☐ einen Kuchen°
☐ einen Laptop
☐ ein Buch
☐ ein Klavier
☐ sie zu einer Party einladen

B. Suchen Sie die Wörter von A, oben, im Text. Unterstreichen Sie die Wörter, die Sie finden.

Blog Deutsch 101: Frau Schulz hat Geburtstag

Pinnwand	Etwas schreiben	Alle ansehen
Zeige 19 von 19 Einträgen		

Heidi schrieb
am Donnerstag um 14:36 Uhr

Frau Schulz hat morgen Geburtstag. Wir sollten ihr eine Freude machen. Hat jemand eine Idee?

Monika schrieb
am Donnerstag um 14:48 Uhr

Wir können einen Kuchen backen. Sie mag sehr gern Schokolade.

Thomas schrieb
am Donnerstag um 15:01 Uhr

Ich wusste gar nicht, dass Frau Schulz Geburtstag hat. Wir sollten sie überraschen!

Heidi schrieb
am Donnerstag um 15:05 Uhr

Aber womit? Sollen wir ihr etwas kaufen? Ein Buch? Oder eine Kinokarte?

Nora schrieb
am Donnerstag um 17:10 Uhr

Nein, ein Buch ist langweilig! Wir können selbst etwas machen. Ein Foto von uns allen – dann vergisst sie uns nicht.

Peter schrieb
am Donnerstag um 17:18 Uhr

Ich habe ein Bild von unserer letzten Kursfahrt. Wir sitzen alle am Tisch im Restaurant und Stefan ist ganz nass, weil die Kellnerin die Limonade verschüttet hat :)

Nora schrieb
am Donnerstag um 17:20 Uhr

Haha, daran erinnere ich mich noch sehr gut.

Katrin schrieb
am Donnerstag um 17:27 Uhr

Ich finde beide Ideen gut – den Kuchen und das Bild. Ich habe noch einen schönen Bilderrahmen.

Stefan schrieb
am Donnerstag um 17:32 Uhr

Das mit der Limonade war nicht lustig! :P Alles hat geklebt! ... Wir können alle gemeinsam etwas unternehmen. Wie alt wird Frau Schulz?

Katrin schrieb
am Donnerstag um 17:41 Uhr

Über das Alter einer Frau spricht man nicht! Wir können abends bowlen gehen. Oder wie Heidi sagte: Wir schenken ihr eine Kinokarte und gehen gemeinsam mit ihr.

Nora schrieb
am Donnerstag um 17:47 Uhr

Au ja, Bowlen wäre super! Im Kino kann man nicht reden.

Thomas schrieb
am Donnerstag um 17:49 Uhr

Wir geben ihr morgen früh nur das Bild und schreiben dazu: „Treffen Sie uns heute Abend um 20 Uhr bei der Bowlingbahn!"

Heidi schrieb
am Donnerstag um 17:55 Uhr

Ja, das ist eine tolle Idee. Peter bringt das Bild mit. Katrin, bringst du bitte den Bilderrahmen mit? Monika, es wäre toll, wenn du einen Schokoladenkuchen bäckst und abends mitbringst.

Katrin schrieb
am Donnerstag um 17:58 Uhr

Mache ich!

Monika schrieb
am Donnerstag um 17:59 Uhr

Ja, das ist kein Problem. Der wird lecker! Hat jemand etwas von Albert gehört? Weiß er Bescheid?

Albert schrieb
am Donnerstag um 22:45 Uhr

Tut mir leid, dass ich das jetzt erst lese. Ich bin morgen auch dabei!

Arbeit mit dem Text

Beantworten Sie die Fragen.

1. Wann hat Frau Schulz Geburtstag?
2. Wer wusste nicht°, dass Frau Schulz Geburtstag hat?
3. Welche Art° von Kuchen mag Frau Schulz gern?
4. Was für eine Idee hat Nora? / Was möchte Nora schenken?
5. Wo waren die Studenten mit Frau Schulz auf der letzten Kursfahrt?
6. Wer hat noch einen Bilderrahmen°?
7. Welche Idee hat Stefan?
8. Wie alt wird Frau Schulz?
9. Was möchten die Studierenden am Abend machen?
10. Wer bäckt den Kuchen?
11. Kommt Albert auch mit?

wusste ... did not know
kind

picture frame

Nach dem Lesen

Fragen Sie einen Partner oder eine Partnerin. Schreiben Sie die Antworten auf.

1. Wie bleibst du mit deinen Freunden in Kontakt?
2. Wann hast du Geburtstag?
3. Was möchtest du zum Geburtstag?
4. Was machst du gern, wenn du mit Freunden weggehst? Wohin geht ihr?

Vocabulary Display. Presentation. *Was trägt Michael? Er trägt ein Unterhemd, eine Unterhose, Sandalen und Socken.* Go over all four people. **Receptive recall.** Cover up labels for clothing: *Wer trägt Ohrringe? Wer trägt ein Nachthemd?* Go over all items. **Choral response.** Practice pronunciation of new words with questions containing possessive adjectives: *Sprechen wir über Michael. Wiederholen Sie bitte! Wie findest du sein Unterhemd? Wie findest du seine Unterhose?* etc. **Productive recall 1.** Cover up labels: *Was trägt Michael?* etc. **Productive recall 2.** *Schreiben Sie auf, was diese vier Personen tragen. Schreiben Sie „Michael trägt" und ergänzen Sie die Kleidungsstücke. Achten Sie auf die richtige Form von „ein".* **Follow-up.** Write value judgments on the board such as: *Super. Sexy. Toll. Langweilig. Zum Gähnen. Hässlich. Todschick.* Write display items in four gender/plural columns with the headings: *seinen/ihren, sein/ihr, seine/ihre, seine/ihre.* Ask sts. to work in pairs asking each other *Wie findest du Michaels Unterhemd? Und seine Unterhose?* Alternatively, ask sts. to work in groups of 3 with 2 people asking each other questions and the third person keeping tabs on who likes what and on whether they use the correct form of the possessive adjective each time.

der Haarschnitt
der Ohrring
die Halskette
die Sporthose

Silvia

HELGA: Wie findest du ihren Haarschnitt?
SIGRID: Sieht gut aus!

die Sonnenbrille
der Bademantel
die Handschuhe
der Gürtel

Rolf

SIGRID: Wie findest du seinen Bademantel?
HELGA: Nicht schlecht!

das Piercing
der Schal
das Armband
das Nachthemd

Melanie

CLAIRE: Wie findest du ihr Nachthemd?
JOSEF: Klasse!

das Unterhemd
die Unterhose
die Socken
die Sandalen

Michael

JUTTA: Na, wie findest du seine Socken?
JENS: Hässlich!

Situation 9   Umfrage: Hast du einen neuen Haarschnitt?

Sit. 9. Review vocabulary and explain new items: *manchmal, Schmuck.* Practice pronunciation. Ask sts. to collect signatures. Recycle information, e.g., by adding an association activity: *Wer hat einen neuen Haarschnitt?* etc. followed by *Was wissen wir von [Name]?* (See the IM for working with association activities.)

MODELL: S1: Hast du einen neuen Haarschnitt?
S2: Ja.
S1: Unterschreib bitte hier.

UNTERSCHRIFT

1. Hast du einen neuen Haarschnitt?   _____
2. Trägst du heute eine Kette?   _____
3. Hast du ein Piercing?   _____
4. Schläfst du im Schlafanzug?   _____
5. Trägst du manchmal eine Brille?   _____
6. Findest du mein Hemd / meine Bluse toll?   _____
7. Trägst du gern Schmuck?   _____

Situation 10 Interaktion: Wie findest du meine Sportschuhe?

1. Kreuzen Sie an, was Sie heute tragen.
2. Fragen Sie, wie Ihr Partner / Ihre Partnerin das findet.

Preparation 2: Introduce more descriptive adjectives in reference to your own clothing: *Wie finden Sie meine Schuhe? Wie finden Sie meinen Pullover? toll, schön, ganz nett, hässlich, furchtbar?* Then demonstrate the model with a student. **Part 2:** Sts. work in pairs to complete the chart.

MODELL: S1: Wie findest du meine Schuhe?
S2: Deine Schuhe? Nicht schlecht.

echt stark   klasse

hübsch   super

voll süß   grell

Finde ich ganz toll!

schick

Sieht/Sehen gut aus

Steht/Stehen dir gut!

krass

	Was Sie heute tragen	Wie Ihr(e) Partner(in) das findet
meine Hose		
meine Schuhe		
meinen Schal		
meinen Gürtel		
mein Armband		
meine Halskette		
meinen Ohrring / meine Ohrringe		

Musikszene

„Junge" (2007, Deutschland) *Die Ärzte*

Die Ärzte

Miniwörterbuch

erfolgreich	successful	**sollen**	are supposed to
das **Schlagzeug**	drums	die **Nachbarn**	neighbors
was gefällt	what do your	die **Löcher**	holes
Ihren Eltern	parents like	**stören**	to bother
an Ihnen	about you	**an dem Jungen**	about the boy

Biografie *Die Ärzte* sind eine der erfolgreichsten deutschen Punkrock-Bands. Es gibt sie seit 1982. Sie kommen aus Hamburg und aus Berlin. Farin Urlaub spielt Gitarre, Rod spielt Bass und Bela B. spielt Schlagzeug. Sie singen alle drei. Ihr Hit „Junge" stammt aus dem Jahre 2007.

iMix Link: This song is available for purchase at the iTunes store in a special iMix created for *Kontakte*. For more information about accessing the playlist, go to **Connect German** (www.connectgerman.com).

Vor dem Hören Was gefällt Ihren Eltern an Ihnen? Was gefällt Ihren Eltern nicht?

Nach dem Hören

1. Was fragt die Mutter den Jungen?
   - ☒ **a.** Junge, warum hast du nichts gelernt?
   - ☐ **b.** Warum gehst du nicht in die Stadt?
   - ☒ **c.** Was sollen die Nachbarn sagen?
   - ☐ **d.** Was sollen die Mitbewohner sagen?

2. Wie sieht der Junge aus?
   - ☒ **a.** Er hat Löcher in der Hose.
   - ☐ **b.** Er trägt kaputte Schuhe.
   - ☐ **c.** Seine Haare sind schwarz.
   - ☒ **d.** Er hat Löcher in der Nase.

3. Was stört die Eltern an dem Jungen?
   - ☒ **a.** Er hört laute Musik.
   - ☐ **b.** Er ist den ganzen Tag zu Hause.
   - ☐ **c.** Er hat lange Haare.
   - ☒ **d.** Seine Freunde nehmen Drogen.

Vor dem Hören: Ask sts. to think about the question in pairs or small groups; elicit several answers. **Nach dem Hören:** Explain the task to sts.—they are to check all that apply—and then play the song. You may wish to play it more than once. You may find it helpful to download the lyrics from the Internet and work with them to help sts. complete the task. **Follow-up:** Play the song again, pausing after every line of text that is referred to in the activity. When sts. correctly identify that *Er hat lange Haare* is incorrect, ask them what his hair is like. Similarly, with *Er ist den ganzen Tag zu Hause*, ask them what his parents complain about: *Nie kommst du nach Hause.*

Situation 11 Frau Gretters neuer Mantel

Sit. 11. Have sts. reorder the lines of the dialogue, working in groups of 3. Then put the sts. into groups of 7 and hand out all the lines of the dialogue (each line written on a separate piece of paper and one line to each person) to each group, and ask sts. to line themselves up within their groups according to the correct sequence of their dialogue lines. Then ask each st. to read his or her line.

Bringen Sie die Sätze in die richtige Reihenfolge.

___5___ Von Kaufland. Er ist wirklich sehr schön.

___4___ Finde ich ganz toll. Woher haben Sie ihn?

___1___ Guten Tag, Frau Körner.

___6___ Ach, mein Mantel ist auch schon so alt. Ich brauche dringend etwas für den Winter.

___2___ Guten Tag, Frau Gretter. Wie geht's denn so?

___7___ Gehen Sie doch auch mal zu Kaufland. Da gibt es gute Preise.

___3___ Danke, ganz gut. Wie finden Sie denn meinen neuen Mantel?

Filmlektüre
Lola rennt

 Vor dem Lesen

A. Schauen Sie auf das Foto und die Filmangaben und beantworten Sie die folgenden Fragen.

1. Was macht Lola?
2. Welche Haarfarbe hat Lola? Was kann das bedeuten?
3. Wer sind der Schauspieler und die Schauspielerin in den Hauptrollen?

Filmangaben

Titel: *Lola rennt*
Genre: Spielfilm
Erscheinungsjahr: 1998
Land: Deutschland
Dauer: 81 min
Regisseur: Tom Tykwer
Hauptrollen: Franka Potente, Moritz Bleibtreu

Lola hat es sehr eilig.

B. Lesen Sie die Wörter im Miniwörterbuch. Suchen Sie sie im Text und unterstreichen Sie sie.

Miniwörterbuch

der **Geldbote**	money courier
die **U-Bahn**	subway
beschaffen	to find, raise
umbringen	to kill
überfallen	to rob
verfolgen	to chase
erschießen	to kill
von vorne	from the beginning
ausrauben	to rob
überqueren	to cross
der **Krankenwagen**	ambulance
überfahren	to run over
sterben, stirbt	to die, dies

Inhaltsangabe

Manni (Moritz Bleibtreu) arbeitet als Geldbote für die Mafia. Er lässt 100 000 DM in der U-Bahn liegen. Er hat 20 Minuten Zeit, um 100 000 DM zu beschaffen. Wenn nicht, bringt ihn sein Boss, Ronnie, um. Lola (Franka Potente) ist die Freundin von Manni und versucht, ihm zu helfen. Sie rennt los.

5   Zuerst rennt Lola zur Bank ihres Vaters und bittet ihn um Geld. Als er ihr nicht helfen kann, überfallen Lola und Manni einen Supermarkt. Sie laufen weg. Die Polizei verfolgt sie und erschießt Lola.

Der Film beginnt von vorne. Lola rennt wieder zur Bank ihres Vaters. Diesmal raubt sie die Bank aus und bringt Manni die 100 000 DM. Manni sieht Lola auf der 10 anderen Seite der Straße. Er überquert die Straße. Ein Krankenwagen überfährt ihn und er stirbt.

Der Film beginnt ein drittes Mal. Lola rennt zur Bank, aber ihr Vater ist nicht da. Sie rennt zu einem Casino und gewinnt beim Roulette 100 000 DM. Sie rennt zurück zu Manni. Manni hat aber die 100 000 DM wieder gefunden und sie seinem 15 Boss gegeben. Jetzt sind sie reich.

Arbeit mit dem Text

Beantworten Sie die folgenden Fragen.

1. Für wen arbeitet Manni?
2. Wo vergisst Manni das Geld?
3. Wie viel Zeit bleibt Lola und Manni, um 100 000 DM zu finden?
4. Wen bittet Lola zuerst um[1] Geld?
5. Was passiert[2], nachdem Lola und Manni den Supermarkt überfallen?
6. Was passiert, nachdem Lola eine Bank ausraubt?
7. Wie bekommen Lola und Manni zum Schluss[3] das Geld?

[1]bittet um *asks for* [2]*happens* [3]zum ... *in the end*

Filmclip

Szene: DVD Kapitel 5 „Ronnie", 8:45–11:00 Min.

Manni erzählt Lola am Telefon, dass er das Geld für Ronnie in der U-Bahn vergessen hat. Er ist verzweifelt°. Wenn er nicht in 20 Minuten 100 000 DM beschafft, bringt Ronnie ihn um.

desperate

Schauen Sie sich die Szene an und beantworten Sie die Fragen. Es sind mehrere Antworten möglich.

1. Wo ist Manni?
   - ☐ a. in der U-Bahn
   - ☐ b. in einer Telefonzelle
   - ☐ c. in der Innenstadt°

2. Was hat Manni bei sich?
   - ☐ a. eine Pistole
   - ☐ b. eine Tasche mit Geld
   - ☐ c. ein Handy

3. Was hat Manni vor°?
   - ☐ a. Er geht zurück zur U-Bahn.
   - ☐ b. Er überfällt einen Supermarkt.
   - ☐ c. Er weiß es nicht.

4. Was verspricht° Lola?
   - ☐ a. Sie holt Hilfe°.
   - ☐ b. Sie ist in 20 Minuten da.
   - ☐ c. Sie kann das Geld beschaffen.

5. Wie lange wartet Manni auf Lola?
   - ☐ a. bis sie kommt
   - ☐ b. bis sie das Geld hat
   - ☐ c. bis um 12 Uhr

promises

help

in … downtown

hat vor is planning

Filmclip. Suggestion: Paraphrase the introduction to the *Filmclip* and make sure students understand the context in which the scene takes place. If necessary, review the setting from the *Inhaltsangabe* activity. This scene contains a lot of rapid, colloquial speech, much of which will be above students at this level. The goal is not to understand everything, but to listen and watch for specific information. In preparation for viewing, go over the multiple-choice questions with students, clarifying any unfamiliar vocabulary. You may wish to play the sequence several times.

Nach dem Lesen. Franka Potente has written several books and is also a successful songwriter.

Nach dem Lesen

Suchen Sie nach Informationen über die Schauspielerin Franka Potente im Internet.

1. Wann und wo ist Franka Potente geboren?
2. Wie heißt ihr erster Film?
3. In welchen anderen Filmen spielt sie mit?
4. Franka Potente ist nicht nur Schauspielerin. Womit ist sie noch erfolgreich?

Sit. 12. Explain the activity and ask sts. to write down five items they want to sell. Then, write four columns on the board, labeled *meinen/deinen, mein/dein, meine/deine,* and *meine/deine.* Ask sts. to tell you what they want to sell, and in which column to write the item. Practice model exchange with several items on the board. Model and make sure sts. understand the relevant vocabulary: *verkaufen, kaufen, brauchen, kosten, nehmen, zeig mal, teuer, billig.* Ask sts. to find five different buyers by engaging in the model exchange and by writing down the names of the buyers. Encourage sts. to expand on the model, e.g., *Nein, ich brauche keine Ohrringe, aber ich finde dein T-Shirt toll. Verkaufst du es?* **Follow-up:** Ask who sold what to whom: *Was haben Sie verkauft? Wer hat es gekauft? Für wie viel hat er (sie) es gekauft?* Don't expect students to produce the present perfect forms yet. **Alternative.** Change the activity into a *Flohmarkt* role-play either by bringing a few small items to class yourself or by asking students to bring some.

Situation 12 Flohmarkt

Schreiben Sie fünf Sachen auf, die Sie verkaufen. Schreiben Sie auf, wer sie kauft und wie viel sie kosten.

MODELL: s1: Ich verkaufe meine Ohrringe. Brauchst du Ohrringe?
s2: Nein danke, ich brauche keine Ohrringe.
oder Zeig mal. Ja, ich finde deine Ohrringe toll. Was kosten sie?
s1: 2 Euro.
s2: Gut, ich nehme sie.

ZU VERKAUFEN	KÄUFER/KÄUFERIN	PREIS
1. _____	_____	_____
2. _____	_____	_____
3. _____	_____	_____
4. _____	_____	_____
5. _____	_____	_____

Vergnügen

Grammatik 2.5–2.6

Herr Wagner schläft gern.

Jens fährt gern Motorrad.

Sofie trägt gern Hosen.

Melanie lädt gern Freunde ein.

Mehmet läuft gern im Wald.

Ernst isst gern Eis.

Hans liest gern Bücher.

Natalie sieht gern fern.

Situation 13 Interview: Was machst du lieber?

MODELL: S1: Schwimmst du lieber im Meer oder lieber im Schwimmbad?
S2: Lieber im Meer.

1. Isst du lieber zu Hause oder lieber im Restaurant?
2. Spielst du lieber Volleyball oder lieber Basketball?
3. Fährst du lieber Fahrrad oder lieber Motorrad?
4. Schreibst du lieber E-Mails oder lieber Briefe?
5. Liest du lieber online oder lieber auf Papier?
6. Lädst du lieber Freunde oder lieber Verwandte ein?
7. Läufst du lieber im Wald oder lieber in der Stadt?
8. Schläfst du lieber im Hotel oder lieber im Zelt?

Situation 14 Umfrage: Fährst du jedes Wochenende nach Hause?

MODELL: S1: Fährst du jedes Wochenende nach Hause?
S2: Ja.
S1: Unterschreib bitte hier.

UNTERSCHRIFT

1. Fährst du jedes Wochenende nach Hause? _____
2. Schläfst du manchmal in der Vorlesung? _____
3. Vergisst du oft wichtige Geburtstage? _____
4. Siehst du mehr als vier Stunden pro Tag fern? _____
5. Trägst du oft eine Krawatte? _____
6. Liest du jeden Tag eine Zeitung? _____
7. Sprichst du mehr als zwei Sprachen? _____

Situation 15 Informationsspiel: Was machen sie gern?

Sit. 15. (See the IM.) The corresponding chart is in Appendix A.

MODELL: s2: Was fährt Richard gern?
s1: Motorrad.
s2: Was fährst du gern?
s1: _____

	Richard	Josef und Melanie	mein(e) Partner(in)
fahren	Motorrad	Zug	
tragen	Pullis	Jeans	
essen	Wiener Schnitzel	Pizza	
sehen	Fußball	Gruselfilme	
vergessen	seine Hausaufgaben	ihr Alter	
waschen	sein Auto	ihr Auto	
treffen	seine Freundin	ihre Lehrer	
einladen	seinen Bruder	ihre Eltern	
sprechen	Italienisch	Englisch	

Kultur ... Landeskunde ... Informationen

KLI. Answers: **1.** 138 Minuten; **2.** Kommunikation; **3.** E-Mails; **4.** Musik hören (am Computer und im Internet)

Jugend im Netz

Was ist im Internet für Sie am wichtigsten[1]?

Lesen Sie in der Grafik zuerst, was deutsche Teenager im Internet machen. Beantworten Sie dann die Fragen.

1. Wie viel Zeit verbringen[2] deutsche Jugendliche von montags bis freitags pro Tag im Netz?
2. Womit verbringen deutsche Jugendliche im Netz die meiste Zeit: Kommunikation, Unterhaltung, Spiele oder Informationssuche?
3. Womit verbringen mehr Jugendliche ihre Zeit: mit E-Mails oder mit Chatten?
4. Womit verbringen mehr Jugendliche ihre Zeit: mit Musik hören oder mit Videos gucken?

[1]am ... *most important* [2]*spend* [3]*im ... on average*
[4]*use* [5]*entertainment* [6]*Browsing* [7]*researching*

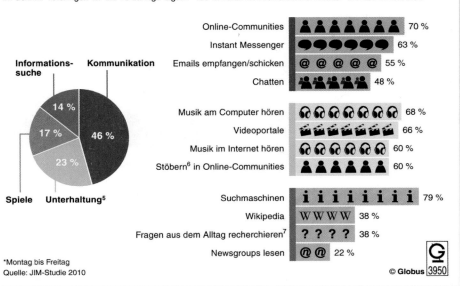

Jugend im Netz: Chatten, Mailen, Musik hören

Im Schnitt[3] verbringen 12- bis 19-Jährige täglich* 138 Minuten im Internet. Dafür nutzen[4] sie ihre Online-Zeit:

Online-Communities 70 %
Instant Messenger 63 %
Emails empfangen/schicken 55 %
Chatten 48 %

Musik am Computer hören 68 %
Videoportale 66 %
Musik im Internet hören 60 %
Stöbern[6] in Online-Communities 60 %

Suchmaschinen 79 %
Wikipedia 38 %
Fragen aus dem Alltag recherchieren[7] 38 %
Newsgroups lesen 22 %

Informationssuche 14 %
Kommunikation 46 %
Unterhaltung[5] 23 %
Spiele 17 %

*Montag bis Freitag
Quelle: JIM-Studie 2010

© Globus 3950

Situation 16 Bildgeschichte: Ein Tag in Silvias Leben

Sit. 16. (See the IM for suggestions on using narration series.) *Sit. 16* contains stem-changing verbs and separable-prefix verbs and uses subject-verb inversion. Sentences: 1. *Silvia schläft bis acht Uhr.* 2. *Vor dem Frühstück läuft sie fünf Kilometer.* 3. *Heute trägt sie Jeans und eine Jacke.* 4. *Sie fährt mit dem Bus zur Uni.* 5. *Um zwölf Uhr isst sie in der Mensa.* 6. *Sie trifft Jürgen.* 7. *Jürgen lädt sie zum Abendessen ein.* 8. *Nach dem Essen geht sie nach Hause und sieht fern.* 9. *Dann liest sie noch eine halbe Stunde im Bett.* 10. *Um 12.30 schläft sie ein.*
Receptive recall: *Welches Bild zeigt: Silvia fährt mit dem Bus zur Uni?* (Bild 4.) *Nach dem Essen geht Silvia nach Hause und sieht fern?* (Bild 8.) *Um 12.30 schläft Silvia ein?* (Bild 10.) *Vor dem Frühstück läuft Silvia fünf Kilometer?* (Bild 2.) *Heute trägt sie Jeans und eine Jacke?* (Bild 3.) *Mittags isst sie in der Mensa?* (Bild 5.) *Sie liest noch eine halbe Stunde im Bett?* (Bild 9.) *Sie trifft Jürgen?* (Bild 6.) *Silvia schläft bis 8 Uhr?* (Bild 1.) *Jürgen lädt Silvia zum Abendessen ein?* (Bild 7.) **Choral response.**
Productive recall: *Was zeigt Bild 1? usw.*
Personalization: Then ask sts. to work in small groups as they describe their day to one another.

AA. Have sts. describe Jürgen's day.

Videoecke

Perspektiven

> Welches elektronische Gerät[1] ist für dich am wichtigsten[2]? Warum?

Aufgabe 1 Hintergrund[3]

Schauen Sie sich den Clip an.
Was sehen Sie hinter[4] diesen Personen?

Am wichtigsten ist mir mein Laptop.

1. Judith ___g___   2. Sandra ___h___   3. Tina ___c___   4. Susan ___d___

5. Pascal ___a___   6. Martin ___e___   7. Felicitas ___b___   8. Albrecht ___f___

[1]*device*   [2]*am … most important*   [3]*background*   [4]*behind*

a. Ein Boot fährt vorbei.

b. Wir sehen ein schönes historisches Gebäude[1] auf einem großen Platz.

c. Zwei junge Leute schieben ihre Fahrräder vorbei[2].

d. Wir sehen schöne Blumen[3].

e. Ein Taxi fährt vorbei.

f. Ein paar Leute stehen unter einer Laterne.

g. Wir sehen ein Café.

h. Wir sehen eine Statue mit der Inschrift[4] „Johann Sebastian Bach".

Aufgabe 2 Gründe[5]

Warum sind diese elektronischen Geräte so wichtig? Ordnen Sie die Geräte und Gründe den Personen zu.

PERSON	GERÄT	GRUND
1. Judith	ihr Handy	Er kann ohne ihn keine Musik machen.
2. Sandra	ihr Laptop	Er schreibt seine Dissertation und schaut Filme an.
3. Tina	ihr MP3-Player	Er trägt es den ganzen Tag herum.
4. Susan	ihr Radio	Sie braucht ihn für Unisachen und das Internet.
5. Pascal	ihr Telefon	Sie hört gern Musik.
6. Martin	sein Gitarrenverstärker[6]	Sie hört gern Musik.
7. Felicitas	sein Handy	Sie möchte immer erreichbar[7] sein.
8. Albrecht	sein Laptop	Sie ruft gern ihre Freunde und ihre Schwestern an.

Interviews

Maria

Simone

- Was für Hobbys hast du?
- Welche elektronischen Geräte hast du?
- Bist du bei Facebook oder einem anderen sozialen Netzwerk?
- Was machst du damit?
- Was hältst du davon?
- Was machst du sonst? Twitterst du? Chattest du?
- Trägst du gern Schmuck?
- Hast du ein besonderes Schmuckstück?

Aufgabe 3 Hobbys

Wer ist das, Maria, Simone oder beide?

	Maria	Simone	Beide
1. Sie geht gern schwimmen und macht Hula-Hoop.	☒	☐	☐
2. Sie macht ganz viel Sport.	☐	☒	☐
3. Sie hat ein Notebook, einen I-Pod und ein Handy.	☐	☒	☐
4. Sie hat einen Laptop und eine Stereoanlage.	☒	☐	☐
5. Sie ist bei Facebook.	☐	☐	☒
6. Sie chattet über Skype.	☒	☐	☐
7. Sie schreibt nur E-Mails.	☐	☒	☐
8. Sie trägt keinen Schmuck.	☒	☐	☐
9. Sie trägt gern Ketten und Ringe.	☐	☒	☐

Aufgabe 4 Interview

Interviewen Sie eine Partnerin oder einen Partner. Stellen Sie dieselben Fragen.

[1]building [2]ihre Fahrräder vorbeischieben *walk their bicycles past* [3]*flowers* [4]*inscription* [5]*reasons*
[6]*guitar amplifier* [7]*reachable*

Wortschatz

Besitz	Possessions
der Fernseher, -	TV set
der Rucksack, ̈e	backpack
der Schlafsack, ̈e	sleeping bag
der Schmuck	jewelry
der Schreibtisch, -e	desk
der Wecker, -	alarm clock
das Bild, -er	picture
das Boot, -e	boat
das Fahrrad, ̈er	bicycle
das Handy, -s [hɛndi]	cellular phone
das Klavier, -e	piano
das Pferd, -e	horse
das Surfbrett, -er	surfboard

Ähnliche Wörter

die Kamera, -s; die Kinokarte, -n; der CD-Spieler, -; der Computer, -; der DVD-Spieler, -; der I-Pod, -s [aipɔt]; der MP3-Spieler, -; der Wanderschuh, -e; das Buch, ̈er (R); das Songbuch, ̈er; das Wörterbuch, ̈er; das Radio, -s; das Telefon, -e (R); das Videospiel, -e

Haus und Wohnung	Home and Apartment
der Schrank, ̈e	wardrobe
der Sessel, -	armchair
der Stuhl, ̈e (R)	chair
der Teppich, -e	carpet
das Regal, -e	bookshelf, bookcase
das Zimmer, - (R)	room

Ähnliche Wörter

die Katze, -n; der Hund, -e; das Haus, ̈er (R)

Kleidung und Schmuck	Clothes and Jewelry
die Halskette, -n	necklace
die Sonnenbrille, -n (R)	sunglasses
die Sporthose, -n	tights, sports pants
die Unterhose, -n	underpants
der Bademantel, ̈	bathrobe
der Gürtel, -	belt
der Handschuh, -e	glove
der Schmuck	jewelry
das Armband, ̈er	bracelet
das Nachthemd, -en	nightshirt
das Unterhemd, -en	undershirt

Ähnliche Wörter

die Jeans (pl.); die Socke, -n; der Pullover, -; der Pulli, -s; der Ring, -e; der Ohrring, -e (R); der Schal, -s; das Piercing; das T-Shirt, -s

Sonstige Substantive	Other Nouns
die Art, -en	kind, type
die Einladung, -en	invitation
die Mensa, Mensen	student cafeteria
die Mitbewohnerin, -nen	female roommate, housemate
die Reihenfolge, -n	order, sequence
die Sache, -n	thing
die Stadt, ̈e	city
die Stunde, -n (R)	hour
die Tasse, -n	cup
die Telefonzelle, -n	telephone booth
die Zeitung, -en	newspaper
der Gruselfilm, -e	horror film
der Haarschnitt, -e	haircut
der Mensch, -en	person
Mensch!	Man! Oh boy! (coll.)
der Mitbewohner, -	male roommate, housemate
der Wald, ̈er	forest, woods
im Wald laufen	to run in the woods
das Frühstück, -e	breakfast
das Geld	money
das Geschäft, -e	store
das Geschenk, -e	present
das Studentenheim, -e	dorm
das Vergnügen	pleasure
das Zelt, -e	tent
die Verwandten (pl.)	relatives

Ähnliche Wörter

die E-Mail [i:me:l], -s; die Karte, -n (R); die Geburtstags- karte, -n; die Postkarte, -n; die Telefonkarte, -n; die Party, -s (R); die Pizza, Pizzen; der Basketball, ̈e; der Bus, -se; der Film, -e; der Flohmarkt, ̈e; der Geburtstag, -e (R); der Kilometer, -; das Bier, -e; das Ding, -e; das Eis; das Hotel, -s; das Restaurant, -s

Verben	Verbs
an·schauen	to look at
aus·sehen, sieht ... aus	to look
es sieht gut aus	it looks good
ein·laden, lädt ... ein	to invite
essen, isst	to eat
fahren, fährt	to drive, ride
glauben	to believe
klingeln	to ring
laufen, läuft (R)	to run
möchte	would like
recht haben	to be right
schicken	to send
schlafen, schläft	to sleep

Sport treiben	to do sports
stehen	to stand
Das steht / Die	That looks / Those look
stehen dir gut!	good on you!
treffen, trifft	to meet
treffen wir uns ...	let's meet ...
verkaufen	to sell
wissen, weiß	to know
ziehen	to move

Ähnliche Wörter

bringen; finden; kosten; sehen, sieht; vergessen, vergisst; waschen, wäscht

Adjektive und Adverbien / Adjectives and Adverbs

billig	cheap, inexpensive
dick	large, fat
dringend	urgent(ly)
echt	real(ly)
einfach	simple, simply
falsch	wrong
ganz	whole; *here:* quite
grell	gaudy, shrill; *here:* cool, neat
hässlich	ugly
hübsch (R)	pretty
langweilig	boring
richtig	right, correct
schlecht	bad
schwierig	difficult
süß	sweet
voll süß	totally sweet
teuer	expensive
toll	neat, great
wertvoll	valuable, expensive
wichtig	important
ziemlich	rather
ziemlich groß	pretty big
zu	too

Ähnliche Wörter

besser; schick

Possessivpronomen / Possessive Adjectives

dein, deine, deinen	your (*informal sg.*)
euer, eure, euren	your (*informal pl.*)
ihr, ihre, ihren	her, its; their

Ihr, Ihre, Ihren	your (*formal*)
mein, meine, meinen	my
sein, seine, seinen	his, its
unser, unsere, unseren	our

Präpositionen / Prepositions

an	at; on; to
am Samstag	on Saturday
am Telefon	on the phone
ans Meer	to the sea
bei	with; at
bei Monika	at Monika's
bis	until
bis acht Uhr	until eight o'clock
für	for
zu	to; for (*an occasion*)
zum Geburtstag	for someone's birthday
zur Uni	to the university

Sonstige Wörter und Ausdrücke / Other Words and Expressions

alles	everything
alles Mögliche	everything possible
da	there
dich	you (*accusative case*)
diese, diesen, dieser, dieses	this; these
ein paar	a few
etwas	something
heute Abend	this evening
ihn	him; it (*accusative case*)
kein, keine, keinen	no; none
Klar!	Of course!
lieber	rather
ich gehe lieber ...	I'd rather go . . .
mittags	at noon
morgen	tomorrow
natürlich	naturally
nie	never
niemand	no one, nobody
pro	per
schon	already
vielleicht	perhaps
wenn	if; when
zusammen	together

Strukturen und Übungen

2.1 The accusative case

nominative = subject

accusative = direct object

2.1. *Akkusativ.* The focus here is on the use of the accusative for direct objects. (The other major use of the accusative—with accusative prepositions—will be introduced later, in 6.2. Accusative pronouns are covered in 3.3.) The rule of thumb for sts. is to change the masculine singular ending to *-en;* all other forms stay the same. Encourage sts. to associate this ending with the masculine singular accusative, because it is the characteristic ending of this case.

The nominative case designates the subject of a sentence; the accusative case commonly denotes the object of the action implied by the verb, such as what is being possessed, looked at, or acted on by the subject of the sentence.

Jutta hat einen Wecker.	*Jutta has an alarm clock.*
Jens kauft eine Lampe.	*Jens buys a lamp.*

Here are the nominative and accusative forms of the definite and indefinite articles.

	Tisch (*m.*)	Bett (*n.*)	Lampe (*f.*)	Bücher (*pl.*)
Nominative	der	das	die	die
Accusative	den			
Nominative	ein	ein	eine	—
Accusative	einen			

Note that only the masculine has a different form in the accusative case.

Der Teppich ist schön. Kaufst du **den** Teppich?	*The rug is beautiful. Are you going to buy the rug?*

Übung 1 Im Kaufhaus

Üb. 1. You can introduce the chart on the next page and allow sts. to hear accusative forms by creating sentences that they will judge true or false. Then assign the exercise for homework and have sts. check their answers against the answer key (Appendix F).

Was kaufen diese Leute? Was kaufen Sie?

MODELL: Jens kauft den Wecker, **das** Regal und **den** DVD-Spieler.

	Jens	Ernst	Melanie	Jutta	ich
der Pullover	−	−	−	+	
der Wecker	+	−	−	−	
die Tasche	−	+	+	−	
das Regal	+	−	+	−	
die Lampe	−	−	−	+	
die Stühle	−	+	−	−	
der DVD-Spieler	+	−	−	+	
der Schreibtisch	−	+	+	−	

Übung 2   Besitz

Üb. 2. Remind sts. to use indefinite (rather than definite) articles in the singular and no article in the plural. Have sts. tell a partner or the class what they have.

Was haben Sie?

MODELL: Ich habe einen/eine/ein/ _____, …

das Bett
das Bild / die Bilder
die Bücher
der CD-Spieler
der Fernseher
die Gitarre
das Handy
das Klavier
die Lampe / die Lampen
der Laptop
der MP3-Spieler

das Radio
das Regal / die Regale
der Schrank
der Schreibtisch
der Sessel
der Stuhl / die Stühle
das Telefon
der Teppich
der Wecker
_____

2.2 The negative article: *kein, keine*

2.2. *Negativer Artikel: kein, keine.* Point out that, in general, *kein* is used to negate a noun that has either an indefinite article or no article and that, otherwise, negation is expressed using *nicht*.

Kein and **keine** (*not a, not any, no*) are the negative forms of **ein** and **eine**.

Im Klassenzimmer sind **keine** Fenster.	*There aren't any / are no windows in the classroom.*
Stefan hat **keinen** Schreibtisch.	*Stefan doesn't have a desk.*

The negative article has the same endings as the indefinite article **ein**. It also has a plural form: **keine.**

ein → kein
einen → keinen
eine → keine
[plural] → keine

	Teppich (*m.*)	Regal (*n.*)	Uhr (*f.*)	Stühle (*pl.*)
Nominative/Accusative	ein/einen	ein	eine	−
Nominative/Accusative	kein/keinen	kein	keine	keine

—Hat Katrin **einen** Schrank?	*Does Katrin have a wardrobe?*
—Nein, sie hat **keinen** Schrank.	*No, she doesn't have a wardrobe.*
—Hat Katrin **Bilder** an der Wand?	*Does Katrin have pictures on the wall?*
—Nein, sie hat **keine** Bilder an der Wand.	*No, she has no pictures on the wall.*

Übung 3 Vergleiche[1]

Üb. 3. Assign for homework and follow up in class by asking questions about the chart.

Wer hat was? Was haben Sie?

MODELL: Albert hat keinen Teppich. Er hat einen Fernseher und eine Gitarre, aber er hat kein Fahrrad. Er hat einen Computer und Bilder, aber er hat kein Handy.

	Albert	Heidi	Monika	ich
der Teppich	−	+	−	
der Fernseher	+	−	−	
die Gitarre	+	+	−	
das Fahrrad	−	−	+	
der Computer	+	+	+	
die Bilder	+	−	+	
das Handy	−	+	+	

2.3 What would you like? *Ich möchte …*

2.3. The formal introduction of modal verbs begins here with *möchte*. Other modal verbs are presented as a group in 3.1 and 3.2. In this chapter, *möchte* appears mostly without a dependent infinitive. This is the first verb conjugation in which 1st- and 3rd-person singular forms are the same. It is not necessary, at this stage, to point out that *möchte* is a subjunctive form of *mögen*.

Use **möchte** (*would like*) to express that you would like to have something. The thing you want is in the accusative case.

Ich möchte **eine Tasse Kaffee,** bitte.   *I'd like a cup of coffee, please.*
Hans möchte **einen iPad** zum   *Hans would like an iPad for his*
Geburtstag.   *birthday.*

Möchte is particularly common in polite exchanges, for example in shops or restaurants.

KELLNER: Was möchten Sie?   WAITER: *What would you like?*
GAST: Ich möchte ein Bier.   CUSTOMER: *I'd like a beer.*

[1]*Comparisons*

Following are the forms of **möchte.** Note that the **er/sie/es**-form does not follow the regular pattern; it does not end in **-t.**

möchte			
ich	möchte	wir	möchten
du	möchtest	ihr	möchtet
Sie	möchten	Sie	möchten
er sie es	möchte	sie	möchten

Wissen Sie noch?

The **Satzklammer** forms a frame or a bracket consisting of the main verb and either a separable prefix or an infinitive.

Review grammar 1.5.

To say that someone would like to do something, use **möchte** with the infinitive of the verb that expresses the action. This infinitive appears at the end of the sentence. Think of the **Satzklammer** used with separable-prefix verbs, and pattern your **möchte** sentences after it. Other verbs similar to **möchte** are explained in **Kapitel 3.**

Peter **möchte** einen Mantel **kaufen.**   Sofie **möchte** ein Eis **essen.**

Übung 4   Der Wunschzettel

Üb. 4. Use as a written homework assignment or for oral work in class. Sts. should convert the definite article to an indefinite article for the answer.

Was, glauben Sie, möchten diese Personen?

MODELL: Meine beste Freundin möchte einen Ring.

das Auto	der Hund	der Pullover
die Digitalkamera	die Katze	das Radio
der DVD-Spieler	der Koffer	der Ring
das E-Book	der Laptop	die Sonnenbrille
der Fernseher	das Motorrad	die Sportschuhe
die Hose	die Ohrringe	der Teppich

1. Ich _____
2. Mein bester Freund / Meine beste Freundin _____
3. Meine Eltern _____
4. Mein Mitbewohner / Meine Mitbewohnerin und ich _____
5. Mein Nachbar / Meine Nachbarin in der Klasse _____
6. Mein Professor / Meine Professorin _____
7. Mein Bruder / Meine Schwester _____

2.4. *Possessivadjektive:* This section completes the introduction of possessive adjectives. The combination of new words and their endings is difficult. We expect recognition of all forms, but mastery of case and gender/number agreement will come slowly. Use all possessive adjectives in varied, comprehensible input. The meanings of the plural forms are usually the last to be acquired. Confusion between *sein* and *ihr* may also persist. Provide as much input and repetition of these forms as possible. To aid understanding of these forms, emphasize that the endings of the possessive adjectives are the same as those of *ein* and *kein*.

2.4 Possessive adjectives

Use the possessive adjectives **mein, dein,** and so forth to express ownership.

—Ist das **dein** MP3-Spieler?   *Is this your MP3 player?*
—Nein, das ist nicht **mein** MP3-Spieler.   *No, that's not my MP3 player.*
—Ist das Sofies Gitarre?   *Is this Sofie's guitar?*
—Ja, das ist **ihre** Gitarre.   *Yes, that's her guitar.*

Here are the nominative neuter forms of the possessive adjectives.

Singular	Plural
mein Auto (*my car*)	**unser** Auto (*our car*)
dein Auto (*your car*) **Ihr** Auto (*your car*)	**euer** Auto (*your car*) **Ihr** Auto (*your car*)
sein Auto (*his/its car*) **ihr** Auto (*her/its car*)	**ihr** Auto (*their car*)

Just as the personal pronoun **sie** can mean either *she* or *they*, the possessive adjective **ihr** can mean either *her* or *their*. When it is capitalized as **Ihr**, it means *your* and corresponds to the formal **Sie** (*you*).

Note the three forms for English *your*: **dein** (*informal singular*), **euer** (*informal plural*), and **Ihr** (*formal singular or plural*).

Albert und Peter, wo sind **eure** Bücher?	*Albert and Peter, where are your books?*
Öffnen Sie **Ihre** Bücher auf Seite 133.	*Open your books to page 133.*

Possessive adjectives have the same endings as the indefinite article **ein**. They agree in case (*nominative* or *accusative*), gender (*masculine, neuter,* or *feminine*), and number (*singular* or *plural*) with the noun that they precede.

Possessive adjectives have the same endings as **ein** and **eine**.

ein → mein

eine → meine

einen → meinen

[plural] → meine

Mein Pulli ist warm. Möchtest du **meinen** Pulli tragen?	*My sweater is warm. Would you like to wear my sweater?*
Josef verkauft **seinen** Computer.	*Josef is selling his computer.*

Like **ein**, the forms of possessive adjectives are the same in the nominative and accusative cases—except for the masculine singular, which has an **-en** ending in the accusative.

	Ring (*m.*)	Armband (*n.*)	Halskette (*f.*)	Ohrringe (*pl.*)
my	mein/meinen	mein	meine	meine
your	dein/deinen	dein	deine	deine
your	Ihr/Ihren	Ihr	Ihre	Ihre
his, its	sein/seinen	sein	seine	seine
her, its	ihr/ihren	ihr	ihre	ihre
our	unser/unseren	unser	unsere	unsere
your	euer/euren	euer	eure	eure
your	Ihr/Ihren	Ihr	Ihre	Ihre
their	ihr/ihren	ihr	ihre	ihre

**Possessive Adjectives
Nominative and Accusative Cases**

Hans und Helga

Beschreiben Sie Hans und Helga.

Seine Haare sind braun.	Ihre Haare sind blond.
_____ Augen sind grün.	_____ Augen sind blau.
_____ Halskette ist lang.	_____ Halskette ist …
_____ Schuhe sind schmutzig.	…
_____ Gitarre ist alt.	…
_____ Zimmer ist groß.	…
_____ Fenster ist klein.	…

Übung 6   Minidialoge

Ergänzen Sie **dein, euer** oder **Ihr.** Verwenden Sie die richtige Endung.

1. FRAU GRETTER: Wie finden Sie meinen Pullover?
   HERR WAGNER: Ich finde _____ Pullover sehr schön.
2. BERND: Weißt du, wo meine Brille ist, Veronika?
   VERONIKA: _____ Brille ist auf dem Tisch.
3. OMA SCHMITZ: Helga! Sigrid! Räumt _____ Schuhe auf!
   HELGA UND SIGRID: Ja, gleich, Oma.
4. HERR RUF: Jutta! _____ Freundin war da. Sie braucht ihr Buch zurück.
   JUTTA: Ja, gut. Ich nehme es morgen mit in die Schule.
5. HERR SIEBERT: Beißt _____ Hund?
   FRAU KÖRNER: Was glauben Sie denn! Natürlich beißt mein Hund nicht.
6. NORA: Morgen möchte ich zu meinen Eltern fahren.
   PETER: Wo wohnen _____ Eltern?
   NORA: In Santa Cruz.
7. JÜRGEN: Silvia und ich, wir verkaufen unseren Computer.
   ANDREAS: _____ Computer! Der ist so alt, den kauft doch niemand!

Wissen Sie noch?

Use **du (dein)** and **ihr (euer)** to address people whom you know well and whom you address by their first name. Use **Sie (Ihr)** for all other people.

Review grammar A.5.

Üb. 7. This is another example of an exercise type first introduced in *Kapitel 1, Üb. 1*, in which sts. need to pay attention to both grammar and meaning when selecting elements to construct sentences. Explain the task and do a few sample sentences with your sts. before assigning it as homework. First, sts. need to select a form of *verkaufen* that agrees in person and number with the subject at hand. Next, they need to choose an object in column 4 that is likely owned by the person in the subject position. Finally, they need to choose a form of the possessive adjective that agrees with the subject and that agrees with the gender and number of the object selected from column 4. These objects are followed by their definite article in the nominative to remind sts. of their gender. You may wish to remind your sts. that no ending on the possessive adjective is associated with the neuter gender in the accusative case, etc.

Sie und die Studenten und Studentinnen in Frau Schulz' Deutschkurs brauchen Geld und organisieren einen Flohmarkt. Schreiben Sie Sätze. Wer verkauft was?

MODELL: Monika verkauft ihre CDs.

Monika	verkaufe	ihr	Computer (der)
Thomas	verkaufen	ihre	Ohrring (der)
ich	verkaufen	ihre	Wörterbuch (das)
Katrin	verkaufen	ihren	DVD-Spieler (der)
Peter und Heidi	verkauft	ihren	CDs (pl.)
wir	verkauft	mein	Bücher (pl.)
Stefan	verkauft	seine	Gitarre (die)
Nora und Albert	verkauft	seinen	Bilder (pl.)
Frau Schulz	verkauft	unsere	Telefon (das)

2.5 The present tense of stem-vowel changing verbs

2.5. *Präsens: Verben mit Vokalwechsel.* The presentation of stem-vowel changing verbs completes the introduction of the present tense of verbs that are not modals. (For modals see 3.1 and 3.2.) Point out that there are four patterns. Not all verbs with these vowels in the infinitive make these vowel changes (e.g., *machen* and *kaufen* do not); the changes are restricted to strong verbs, a term that will become meaningful to sts. only when the perfect tense has been introduced in *Kapitel 4.*

There are four types of stem vowel changes:
a → ä, au → äu, e → i, e → ie.

In some verbs, the stem vowel changes in the **du-** and the **er/sie/es-**forms.

—**Schläfst** du gern?	*Do you like to sleep?*
—Ja, ich **schlafe** sehr gern.	*Yes, I like to sleep very much.*
Ich **lese** viel, aber Ernst **liest** mehr.	*I read a lot, but Ernst reads more.*

These are the types of vowel changes you will encounter.

a → ä	fahren:	du fährst	er/sie/es fährt	*to drive*
	schlafen:	du schläfst	er/sie/es schläft	*to sleep*
	tragen:	du trägst	er/sie/es trägt	*to wear*
	waschen:	du wäschst	er/sie/es wäscht	*to wash*
	einladen*:	du lädst ... ein	er/sie/es lädt ... ein	*to invite*
au → äu†	laufen:	du läufst	er/sie/es läuft	*to run*
e → i	essen:	du isst‡	er/sie/es isst	*to eat*
	geben:	du gibst	er/sie/es gibt	*to give*
	sprechen:	du sprichst	er/sie/es spricht	*to speak*
	treffen:	du triffst	er/sie/es trifft	*to meet*
	vergessen:	du vergisst‡	er/sie/es vergisst	*to forget*
e → ie§	lesen:	du liest‡	er/sie/es liest	*to read*
	sehen:	du siehst	er/sie/es sieht	*to see*
	fernsehen:	du siehst ... fern	er/sie/es sieht ... fern	*to watch TV*

Jürgen **läuft** jeden Tag 10 Kilometer.	*Jürgen runs 10 kilometers every day.*
Ernst **isst** gern Pizza.	*Ernst likes to eat pizza.*
Michael **sieht** gern **fern.**	*Michael likes to watch TV.*

*Recall that verb stems ending in **-d** or **-t** insert an **-e-** before another consonant: **ich arbeite, du arbeitest.** Verb forms that contain a vowel change do not insert an **-e-: du lädst ein.** Verb forms without this vowel change, however, do insert an **-e-: ihr ladet ein.**

†Recall that **äu** is pronounced as in English *boy.*

‡Recall that verb stems that end in **-s, -ß, -z,** or **-x** do not add **-st** in the **du-**form, but only **-t.**

§Recall that **ie** is pronounced as in English *niece.*

Übung 8   Minidialoge

Achtung!

—Läufst du **gern** *Do you like to jog*
in der Stadt? *in the city?*
—Nein, ich *No, I prefer*
laufe **lieber** im *jogging in the*
Wald. *forest.*

Ergänzen Sie das Pronomen.

1. OMA SCHMITZ: Seht _____ᵃ gern fern?
   HELGA UND SIGRID: Ja, _____ᵇ sehen sehr gern fern.
2. FRAU GRETTER: Lesen _____ᵃ die Zeitung?
   MARIA: Im Moment nicht. _____ᵇ lese gerade ein Buch.
3. HERR SIEBERT: Isst Ihre Tochter gern Eis?
   HERR RUF: Nein, _____ᵃ isst lieber Joghurt. Aber da kommt mein Sohn, _____ᵇ isst sehr gern Eis.
4. SILVIA: Wohin¹ fährst _____ᵃ im Sommer?
   ANDREAS: _____ᵇ fahre nach Spanien. Und wohin fahrt _____ᶜ?
   SILVIA: _____ᵈ fahren nach England.

Übung 9   Jens und Jutta

Ergänzen Sie das Verb. Verwenden Sie die folgenden Wörter.

essen (3×)
fahren (2×)
lesen
machen (2×)
schlafen
sehen

MICHAEL: Was _____ᵃ Jutta und Jens gern?
ANDREA: Jutta _____ᵇ sehr gern Motorrad. Jens _____ᶜ lieber fern.
MICHAEL: Was essen sie gern? _____ᵈ Jens gern Chinesisch?
ERNST: Jens _____ᵉ gern Italienisch, aber nicht Chinesisch. Und Jutta _____ᶠ gern Fast Food.
MICHAEL: Und ihr, was _____ᵍ ihr gern?
ANDREA: Ich _____ʰ gern Bücher und Ernst _____ⁱ gern. Und im Winter _____ʲ wir gern Snowboard.

Üb. 8–10. This sequence of exercises focuses first receptively on the meaning of verb endings (*Üb. 8*), before moving on to producing verb forms (*Üb. 9*), and finally, to contrasting the forms of the stem-vowel changing verbs. You may wish to alert your sts. to the fact that *machen* in *Üb. 9* is not a stem-changing verb. Use *Üb. 10* as an activity in class after having assigned it for homework: using the statement-question format of the assignment, sts. interview each other about their preferences.

Übung 10   Was machen Sie gern?

Sagen Sie, was Sie gern machen, und bilden Sie Fragen.

MODELL: ich/du: Fast Food essen →
Ich esse (nicht) gern Fast Food: Isst du auch (nicht) gern Fast Food?

1. wir/ihr: Deutsch sprechen
2. ich/du: Freunde einladen
3. ich/du: im Wald laufen
4. ich/du: Pullis tragen
5. wir/ihr: fernsehen
6. ich/du: Fahrrad fahren
7. wir/ihr: die Hausaufgabe vergessen
8. ich/du: schlafen
9. wir/ihr: online lesen

¹*Where*

2.6 Asking people to do things: the *du*-imperative

2.6. The formal *Sie*-imperative was introduced in *Einführung A. Kapitel 10* will complete the presentation of the imperative by adding the *ihr-* and *wir-*forms to a summary of all forms.

Drop the **-(s)t** from the **du**-form to get the **du**-imperative.

Use the **du**-imperative when addressing people you normally address with **du**, such as friends, relatives, other students, and the like. It is formed by dropping the **-(s)t** ending from the present-tense **du**-form of the verb. The pronoun **du** is not used.

(du) arbeitest →	Arbeite!	*Work!*
(du) isst →	Iss!	*Eat!*
(du) kommst →	Komm!	*Come!*
(du) öffnest →	Öffne!	*Open!*
(du) siehst →	Sieh!	*See!*
(du) tanzt →	Tanz!	*Dance!*

Verbs whose stem vowel changes from **a(u)** to **ä(u)** drop the umlaut in the **du**-imperative.

(du) fährst →	Fahr!	*Drive!*
(du) läufst →	Lauf!	*Run!*

Wissen Sie noch?

To form commands for people you address with **Sie,** invert the subject and verb: **Sie kommen mit. → Kommen Sie mit!**

Review grammar A.1.

Imperative sentences always begin with the verb.

Trag mir bitte die Tasche.	*Please carry the bag for me.*
Öffne bitte das Fenster.	*Open the window, please.*
Reite nicht so schnell!	*Don't ride so fast!*
Sieh nicht so viel fern!	*Don't watch so much TV!*

Übung 11   Probleme, Probleme

Üb. 11. This exercise is divided into two sections to make the task more manageable. Sentences 1-5 go with a-e, 6-10 with f-j.

Peter spricht mit Heidi über seine Probleme. Heidi sagt ihm, was er machen soll.

MODELL: PETER: Ich vergesse alles. (1)
        HEIDI: Schreib es dir auf! (e)

1. Ich vergesse alles.
2. Ich sehe den ganzen Tag fern.
3. Ich arbeite zu viel.
4. Ich bin zu dick.
5. Ich trinke zu viel Kaffee.

6. Ich esse zu viel Eis.
7. Mein Pullover ist alt.
8. Ich koche nicht gern Italienisch.
9. Das Wochenende ist langweilig.
10. Ich fahre nicht gern Auto.

a. Treib Sport!
b. Trink Cola!
c. Lies ein Buch!
d. Mach eine Pause!
e. Schreib es dir auf!

f. Fahr Fahrrad!
g. Iss lieber Joghurt!
h. Lade deine Freunde ein!
i. Kauf dir einen neuen Pullover!
j. Koch Chinesisch!

Übung 12   Ach, diese Geschwister!

Üb. 12. Watch sts.' sentences closely for the position of *nicht* before the complements in the negative commands.

Ihr kleiner Bruder macht alles falsch. Sagen Sie ihm, was er machen soll.

MODELL: Ihr kleiner Bruder isst zu viel. → Iss nicht so viel!

1. Ihr kleiner Bruder schläft den ganzen Tag.
2. Er liegt den ganzen Tag in der Sonne.
3. Er vergisst seine Hausaufgaben.
4. Er liest seine Bücher nicht.
5. Er sieht den ganzen Tag fern.
6. Er trinkt zu viel Cola.
7. Er sitzt den ganzen Tag am Computer.
8. Er trägt seine Brille nicht.
9. Er spielt immer Computerspiele.
10. Er treibt keinen Sport.

Übung 13   Vorschläge[1]

Üb. 13. Alert sts. to the separable-prefix verbs in sentences 4, 7, and 10.

Machen Sie Ihrem Freund / Ihrer Freundin Vorschläge.

MODELL: deinen Eltern einen Brief / schreiben →
Schreib deinen Eltern einen Brief.

1. heute ein T-Shirt / tragen
2. keine laute Musik / spielen
3. den Wortschatz / lernen
4. deine Freunde / anrufen
5. nicht allein im Park / laufen
6. nicht zu lange in der Sonne / liegen
7. dein Zimmer / aufräumen
8. heute Abend in einem Restaurant / essen
9. nicht zu spät ins Bett / gehen
10. früh / aufstehen

[1]*Suggestions*

Talente, Pläne, Pflichten

In **Kapitel 3**, you will learn how to describe your talents and those of others. You will learn how to express your intentions and how to talk about obligation and necessity. You will also learn additional ways to describe how you or other people feel.

GOALS

The focus of *Kapitel 3* is on abilities, future plans, obligations, states, and conditions.

To introduce the presentation of *können*, ask sts. to think of one thing they know how to do well. Introduce the modal verb: *Peter kann gut kochen.* Follow up with yes/no questions based on what you already know about sts.' talents: *Kathy, kannst du gut kochen?* For *wollen*, ask what sts. want to do on the weekend.

Themen

Talente und Pläne
Pflichten
Ach, wie nett!
Körperliche und geistige Verfassung

Kulturelles

Musikszene: „Müssen nur wollen" (Wir sind Helden)
KLI: Jugendschutz
Filmclip: *Soul Kitchen* (Fatih Akin)
KLI: Schuljahr und Zeugnisse
Videoecke: Fähigkeiten und Pflichten

Lektüren

Zeitungsartikel: Ringe fürs Leben zu zweit
Film: *Soul Kitchen* (Fatih Akin)

Strukturen

3.1 The modal verbs **können, wollen, mögen**
3.2 The modal verbs **müssen, sollen, dürfen**
3.3 Accusative case: personal pronouns
3.4 Word order: dependent clauses
3.5 Dependent clauses and separable-prefix verbs

Chapter opening artwork: Ambrosius Holbein was a brother of the more famous Hans Holbein the Younger. This painting was used as a kind of advertising tool to attract potential students. At a time when schooling was a privilege, it would have been comparable to the signs craftsmen used to show the kind of service they provided. Humanist and Renaissance artists were discovering the bourgeois world as a motif for their works. The text above the picture reads roughly: *Ist jemand hier, der gern Deutsch schreiben und lesen lernen wollte aus dem aller einfachsten Grund, den sich jemand erdenken kann, und wer auch keinen Buchstaben kennt, der wird es bald können. Er kann es lernen, seine eigenen Schulden aufzuschreiben und zu lesen. Und ist einer so ungeschickt, dass er es nicht lernen kann, den habe ich vergebens gelehrt und nehme gar keinen Lohn von ihm. Wer immer es ist, Bürger oder Handwerksgesellen, Frauen und Jungfrauen, wer es nötig hat, der komme her und er wird treulich um einen günstigen Lohn gelehrt. Aber die jungen Knaben und Mädchen nach den Fronfasten, wie Gewohnheit ist. 1516.*

Suggestion: Use the painting as a starting point to review classroom vocabulary and to introduce some new words. *Was sehen Sie auf dem Bild? Wie viele Personen sind auf dem Bild? Wer ist der Mann auf der linken Seite? Wer ist die Frau auf der rechten Seite? Was machen die Kinder? Was ist das Zimmer? Was hat der Mann in der Hand? Was macht er damit? Ist das eine moderne Schule?*

Wer Jemandt hie der gern welt lernen Dütsch schriben vnd läsen
vß dem aller kürtzisten grundt den Jeman erdencken kan Do durch
ein jeder der vor nit ein büchstaben kan der mag kürtzlich vnd bald
begriffen ein grundt do durch er mag von jm selbs lernen sin schuld
uff schribe vnd läsen vnd wer es nit gelernen kan so vngeschickt
were Den will ich vm̄ nut vnd vergeben glert haben vnd gantz nüt
von jm zü lon nemen er sig wer er well burger oder hantwercks ge
sellen frouwen vnd junchfrouwen wer sin bedarff der kum har jn der
wirt drüwlich glert vm̄ ein zimlichen lon · Aber die junge knabe
und meitlin noch den fronvasten wie gewonheit ist · 1 5 1 6 ·

Kunst und Künstler

Ambrosius Holbein (ca. 1494 – ca. 1519) war ein deutsch-schweizerischer Maler und Grafiker der Renaissance. Er wurde in Augsburg geboren und starb in Basel. Seine bekanntesten Werke sind das Bildnis eines Jungen mit blondem Haar und das Bildnis eines Jungen mit braunem Haar. Das Bild hier entstand als Aushängeschild[1] eines echten Schulmeisters.

Schauen Sie sich das Bild an und beantworten Sie die folgenden Fragen.

1. Wo sind die Personen? Welche Möbel sehen Sie? Was sehen Sie noch?
2. Wie viele Personen sehen Sie? Was machen sie? Wo stehen sie? Wie sind sie gekleidet[2]? Was haben sie in der Hand?
3. Welche Farben dominieren? welche Linien?
4. Welche Gefühle evoziert das Bild?

[1] signboard [2] dressed

Situationen

Talente und Pläne

Grammatik 3.1

Peter kann ausgezeichnet kochen.

Rosemarie und Natalie können gut zeichnen.

Claire kann gut Deutsch.

Melanie und Josef wollen heute Abend zu Hause bleiben und lesen.

Silvia will für Jürgen einen Pullover stricken.

Sofie und Willi wollen tanzen gehen.

Situation 1   Kochen

Sit. 1. (See notes to *Kapitel 2, Sit. 11.*) Be sure to set the scene before asking sts. to put the sentences in order. *Zwei Studenten sitzen in der Mensa / im Cafe / usw. und sprechen miteinander. S1 lädt S2 zum Abendessen / zum Kochen ein. Was kochen sie?* You might ask sts. to do this activity as a race and award an extra point, or a prize, to the pair or group that first places the sentences in the correct order. Have sts. finish by playing the roles, varying content as they wish. You may need to give sts. some guidance in replacing words–*Spaghetti, Chinesisch usw.*

Bringen Sie die Sätze in die richtige Reihenfolge.

_5_ Spaghetti esse ich besonders gern.

_6_ Dann komm doch mal vorbei.

_4_ Nicht so gut. Aber ich kann sehr gut Spaghetti machen.

_3_ Kannst du Chinesisch kochen?

_1_ Kochst du gern?

_2_ Ja, ich koche sehr gern.

_7_ Ja, gern! Vielleicht Samstag?

_8_ Gut! Bis Samstag.

Situation 2 Informationsspiel: Kann Katrin kochen?

Sit. 2. The corresponding chart is in Appendix A. Establish the context and model pronunciation in the example given, and then pronounce the adverbs (*ausgezeichnet, fantastisch usw.*) and the activities in the chart, having the sts. repeat after you immediately: *Kann Katrin zeichnen? Wie heißt diese Frage, wenn Sie einen Partner fragen? (Kannst du zeichnen?) Richtig.*

For extra practice of the *du-* and *ich*-forms, sts. could switch partners and repeat the activity with someone new, omitting the questions about Katrin and Peter and simply questioning their partner. To wrap up the activity, ask 3–4 sts. to describe either what they can do or what their partners can do.

MODELL: S2: Kann Katrin kochen?
S1: Ja, ganz gut.
S2: Kannst du kochen?
S1: Ja, aber nicht so gut.

[+]
ausgezeichnet
fantastisch
sehr gut
gut

[0] ganz gut

[−]
nicht so gut
nur ein bisschen
gar nicht
kein bisschen

	Katrin	Peter	mein(e) Partner(in)
kochen	ganz gut	fantastisch	
zeichnen	sehr gut	kein bisschen	
tippen	nur ein bisschen	ganz gut	
Witze erzählen	ganz gut	ganz gut	
tanzen	fantastisch	sehr gut	
stricken	gar nicht	kein bisschen	
Skateboard fahren	ganz gut	nicht so gut	
Geige spielen	ausgezeichnet	nur ein bisschen	
schwimmen	gut	nur ein bisschen	
ein Auto reparieren	nicht so gut	nicht so gut	

Situation 3 Interview: Kannst du das?

Sit. 3. Ask sts. first to record answers for themselves using B, N, or K. After they have finished for themselves, have them compare their results with a partner: *Ich kann besonders gut Walzer tanzen. Kannst du das?*—and record the partner's answers.

Alternate Activity. Ask sts. to draw a grid with columns headed *besonders gut, nicht so gut, kein bisschen* and to fill in their personal preferences and weaknesses using the given expressions as a starting point, but expanding or altering with more personal information, e.g. *Tennis spielen, Hip-Hop tanzen* etc. Then interview a partner and record the results.

Was können Sie besonders gut, nicht so gut, kein bisschen?

B = besonders gut
N = nicht so gut
K = kein bisschen

MODELL: S1: Ich kann besonders gut tauchen. Kannst du das?
S2: Ich kann nicht so gut tauchen.

	Ich	Partner/Partnerin
1. *tauchen*		
2. *Gitarre spielen*		
3. *ein Fahrrad reparieren*		
4. *Schlittschuh laufen*		
5. *Französisch*		
6. *Karaoke singen*		
7. *Haare schneiden*		
8. *Walzer tanzen*		
9. *Tischtennis spielen*		
10. *Fotos machen*		

Situation 4   Ferienpläne

Sit. 4. Remind sts. who Melanie and Josef are and where they live, and tell them what the context of the situation is. Play the audio (or read the text) several times while sts. jot down what Melanie and Josef plan to do during their vacation. Ask them to work in groups of three and to compare notes after each listening. In addition, you may wish to put the table on the board and to fill in any information as it is provided by the sts. Do not volunteer any information; rather, play the audio again and provide them with one word or two or the first two or three letters of a word. When the table is complete, ask sts. what Melanie and Josef can do together. Finally, ask sts. which of Melanie's and Josef's activities they like and what plans they have for their own next vacation. Focus on activities rather than on going places. **Text for listening comprehension:** *MELANIE: Ich freue mich schon auf die Ferien, denn da kann ich viel machen, wozu ich sonst keine Zeit habe. Ich will zum Beispiel nach München fahren und eine Ausstellung für Fotografie besuchen. Außerdem will ich tauchen lernen. Im Schwimmbad der Universität kann man einen Tauchkurs für Anfänger machen. Ich möchte viel Querflöte spielen, denn das macht mir großen Spaß. Im Sommerurlaub muss man natürlich auch verreisen, irgendwohin, wo man schwimmen und in der Sonne liegen kann. Ich weiß noch nicht genau, wohin ich fahren möchte, aber vielleicht hat Josef ja eine Idee. JOSEF: Ich will in den Ferien mindestens drei Wochen verreisen. Am liebsten möchte ich nach Italien fahren, irgendwohin ans Meer, wo man schwimmen und in der Sonne liegen kann. Ich möchte jeden Tag lange schlafen und abends in Straßencafés sitzen. Vorher muss ich allerdings noch die Garage aufräumen und mein Motorrad reparieren. Das wird sicher auch ein paar Tage dauern.*

Melanie und Josef wollen beide einen Teil[1] ihrer Ferien zu Hause in Regensburg verbringen, aber auch eine Reise machen. Was wollen sie wo machen? Können sie etwas zusammen machen? Hören Sie zu und ergänzen Sie die Tabelle.

NÜTZLICHE WÖRTER

die Ausstellung	*exhibition*
die Garage	*garage*
die Querflöte	*transverse flute*
sitzen	*to sit*

	Melanie	Josef	beide zusammen
in München	Ausstellung für Fotografie		
zu Hause in Regensburg	tauchen lernen	Garage aufräumen	
	Querflöte spielen	Motorrad reparieren	
auf der Reise	schwimmen	schwimmen	
	in der Sonne liegen	in der Sonne liegen	
		lange schlafen	
		in Cafés sitzen	

[1]*part*

Lektüre 📖

Lesehilfe

Before starting to read, it is always useful to look at the complete text, the title, and any subtitles, accompanying pictures, tables, photos, or drawings, in order to get a general idea of what the text will be about. Look at this text, its title, subtitles and its accompanying pictures. Then write down what the main topic of the text probably is and what subtopics it suggests.

Vor dem Lesen

German and English are closely related languages and share many words. Sometimes the words look almost identical, with minor spelling variations such as German **k** or **z** for English *c*. Sometimes you have to use a little guesswork to see the English word in the German one, as in the word **Ägypter** (*Egyptian*). In the following text, underline the words whose meanings you think you can guess by knowing English.

Ringe fürs Leben zu zweit

Symbole ewiger[1] Liebe

D er Ehering symbolisiert ewige Liebe: er hat keinen Anfang und kein Ende. So wie der Ring kein Ende hat, soll auch die Liebe nie aufhören. Er signalisiert aller Welt: Dieser Mann / Diese Frau ist verheiratet. Jeder Ring kann zum Ehering werden. In Deutschland ist der Ehering oft ein einfacher goldener Ring. Zum Ehering
5 wird ein Ring durch die eingravierte Schrift. Auch auf sehr schmale Ringe kann man die Vornamen der Eheleute und das Hochzeitsdatum eingravieren.

[1]*of eternal*

Wenn[1] der Ring einmal am Finger ist, darf er nie[2] mehr herunter kommen. Wenn der Ring kalt wird, wird auch die Liebe kalt. Wenn der Ring zerbricht oder wenn er verloren geht, dann ist das schlecht für die Liebe.

Das Herz als Sitz der Liebe

Die alten Griechen und Ägypter trugen den Ehering am linken Ringfinger. Sie glaubten[3], dass eine Ader[4] von diesem Finger direkt zum Herzen führt. Sie glaubten, dass das Herz der Sitz der Liebe ist. Ein bekannter Kinderreim lautet:

Er (oder sie) liebt mich von Herzen,
mit Schmerzen[5],
oder gar nicht.

Wenn man wissen möchte, ob der Freund oder die Freundin einen[6] liebt, dann pflückt man eine Blume und reißt ihr nacheinander alle Blütenblätter ab[7]. Bei jedem Blütenblatt sagt man eine Zeile des Reims. Das, was man beim letzten Blütenblatt sagt, gilt[8].

In Italien trägt man den Ring noch heute an der linken Hand. In Deutschland trägt man nur den Verlobungsring[9] an der linken Hand. Den Ehering trägt man an der rechten Hand.

Arbeit mit dem Text

A. Guess the meaning of the following words by looking at the context of the sentences in which they appear. Some hints are provided.

1. **Ehering** (Zeile 1) HINT: **Ehering** is a compound of **Ehe** and **Ring**. Look at the drawing. What kind of rings are these? What might **Ehe** mean?

2. **Anfang** (Zeile 1) HINT: the opposite of the noun **Ende**

3. **aufhören** (Zeile 2) HINT: a verb similar in meaning to the noun **Ende**

4. **Eheleute** (Zeile 6) HINT: You already guessed **Ehe**. **Leute** means people; what might the combination of these two words mean?

5. **herunter** (Zeile 7) HINT: Because the second clause contains the phrase *must never*, **herunter** is probably the opposite of **am Finger.**

6. **zerbricht** (Zeile 8) HINT: What bad things can happen to a ring? The root of this word is **brich.** German **ch** is often English *k*. What English word is spelled *br__k* and is something bad?

7. **verloren** (Zeile 8) HINT: Ignore the prefix **ver-** and the **-n** for a moment. German **r** is sometimes related to English *s*. What verb is this?

8. **Herzen/Herz** (Zeile 11) HINT: What might be called the seat of love (line 12) and be connected to other parts of the body by a vein?

[1]*When, If* [2]*darf … it must never* [3]*believed* [4]*vein, artery* [5]*pain* [6]*here: you* [7]*reißt … plucks all its petals off one at a time* [8]*is valid* [9]*engagement ring*

9. **Kinderreim** (Zeile 12) HINT: You know what **Kinder** means. If you pronounce **Reim**, it sounds like *rhyme*, which is its meaning. What might the combination of these two words mean?

B. Beantworten Sie die folgenden Fragen.

1. Warum symbolisiert ein Ring ewige Liebe?
2. Was signalisiert ein Ehering der Welt[1]?
3. Welche Ringe trägt man in Deutschland oft als Eheringe?
4. Was ist oft in Eheringen eingraviert?
5. Was passiert, wenn der Ring vom Finger herunter kommt? Was glauben viele Leute?
6. Was macht man in Deutschland, wenn man wissen möchte, ob der Freund oder die Freundin einen liebt?
7. Was trägt man in Deutschland an der linken Hand und was an der rechten Hand?

Nach dem Lesen

A. Gibt es in Ihrer Klasse unterschiedliche Traditionen und Kulturen? Sammeln Sie in Ihrer Klasse Antworten auf die folgenden Fragen.

1. Trägt man in Ihrer Kultur Eheringe? Wenn ja, an welchem Finger welcher Hand trägt man sie? Wenn nicht, wie signalisiert man, dass Menschen verheiratet sind? Oder signalisiert man es gar nicht?
2. Was macht man in Ihrer Kultur, wenn man herausfinden möchte, ob jemand einen liebt?

B. Was halten Sie von Symbolen, die zeigen, dass zwei Menschen miteinander durchs Leben gehen wollen? Finden Sie sie wichtig? Warum (nicht)?

C. Sind Sie verheiratet? Wenn nicht, haben Sie Heiratspläne für die Zukunft?

[1]der ... *to the world*

Pflichten

Vocabulary Display
(See the IM).

Grammatik 3.2

Jens hat schlechte Noten. Er muss mehr lernen.

Er darf nicht mit seinen Freunden Skateboard fahren.

Jutta muss in der Schule besser aufpassen.

Sie darf in der Stunde nicht mit ihrer Freundin reden.

Jutta muss nach der Schule ihre Hausaufgaben machen.

Situation 5 Schlechtes Zeugnis!

Sit. 5. Tell sts. about the German grading system (see the KLI on *Schuljahr und Zeugnisse*).
Preparation: First talk about Jens's report card: In *welchen Fächern hat Jens eine Eins? eine Zwei? usw. Ist Jens ein guter oder ein schlechter Schüler? Was muss er tun, um ein guter Schüler zu sein?* Sts. work in groups of 3-4, treating this situation as a problem-solving activity. You should establish the pattern for the conversation by asking the first 3-4 questions and demonstrating the use of *muss* and *darf: Darf Jens Freitagabend in die Disko gehen? Nein, er darf Freitagabend nicht in die Disko gehen. Jens hat ein schlechtes Zeugnis. Muss er Latein lernen? Ja, er muss Latein lernen. Er hat eine Fünf in Latein.* Encourage sts. to make up as many additional responses as possible for the last two items. Afterward, write the responses on the board, correcting the grammar if necessary.

Follow-up: *In welcher Klasse ist Jens? In welche Klasse kommt er? Welches Fach haben amerikanische Schüler nicht?* Have sts. look at the drawing of Jens in the vocabulary display. Ask: *In welchen Fächern muss Jens mehr lernen?*

Jens hat drei Fünfen auf dem Zeugnis.

- Was muss er machen? Was darf er nicht machen? Kreuzen Sie an.
- Schreiben Sie dann noch eine Sache dazu, die er machen muss, und eine, die er nicht machen darf.
- Entscheiden Sie schließlich, was am wichtigsten ist (1), was weniger wichtig (2–9) und was am unwichtigsten (10).

MUSS	DARF NICHT		WIE WICHTIG? (1–10)
☐	☐	in die Disko gehen	_____
☐	☐	Latein lernen	_____
☐	☐	den ganzen Tag in der Sonne liegen	_____
☐	☐	seine Hausaufgaben machen	_____
☐	☐	jeden Tag ins Schwimmbad gehen	_____
☐	☐	eine Woche nach Italien fahren	_____
☐	☐	Nachhilfe nehmen	_____
☐	☐	mit seinen Lehrern sprechen	_____
☒	☐	_____	_____
☐	☒	_____	_____

 Situation 6 Umfrage: Musst du neben dem Studium arbeiten?

Sit. 6. (See the IM for suggestions on working with autograph activities). Explain new vocabulary, e.g., *neben dem Studium, Tiere, bis Mittag* and practice pronunciation. Set up the task and give sts. about 5 min. to walk around and ask questions. Turn the follow-up into an association activity (see the IM) to practice the 3rd-person singular forms of the modal verbs.

AA. Practice the modal *dürfen* by asking sts. what they are not permitted to do in class, at home, in the student cafeteria, in the dorms, etc.

MODELL: S1: Musst du neben dem Studium arbeiten?
S2: Ja.
S1: Unterschreib bitte hier.

UNTERSCHRIFT

1. Musst du neben dem Studium arbeiten?   _____
2. Kannst du gut Auto fahren?   _____
3. Musst du mal wieder deine Eltern besuchen?   _____
4. Darfst du in deiner Wohnung Tiere haben?   _____
5. Musst du heute noch Hausaufgaben machen?   _____
6. Kannst du jeden Tag bis Mittag schlafen?   _____
7. Musst du oft einkaufen gehen?   _____
8. Darfst du schon Bier trinken?   _____

Musikszene

„Müssen nur wollen" (2003, Deutschland) *Wir sind Helden*

Wir sind Helden

Biografie *Wir sind Helden* kommen aus Berlin. Die Lead-Sängerin heißt Judith Holofernes. Sie schreibt auch die meisten Texte und Songs der Gruppe. Die Songs sind oft sehr kritisch. Der Hit „Müssen nur wollen" stammt aus dem Jahr 2003.

Vor dem Hören Was musst du tun, was willst du tun? Willst du, was du musst?

iMix Link: This song is available for purchase at the iTunes store in a special iMix created for *Kontakte*. For more information about accessing the playlist, go to **Connect German** (www.connectgerman.com).

Nach dem Hören

A. Was sagt die Sängerin? Richtig (R) oder falsch (F)?

___ **1.** In einer Hand trägt sie die Welt, mit der anderen Hand bietet sie Getränke an.

___ **2.** Sie kann gar nichts.

___ **3.** Alle sollen etwas wollen.

___ **4.** Dressierte Affen können alles schaffen.

___ **5.** Sie kann glücklich sein und Konzerne leiten.

B. Was meinen Sie?

1. Kann man glücklich sein und Konzerne leiten?

2. Muss man alles tun, was man tun kann?

Musikszene. Wir sind Helden are a band from Berlin whose songs are reminiscent of the *Neue Deutsche Welle* of the 1980s and 1990s. They inspired bands like *Silbermond* and *Juli*. These bands and others are sometimes referred to as the *Neue Neue Deutsche Welle*. The lead singer and songwriter is Judith Holofernes, who criticizes many aspects of modern consumer-oriented societies. The hit "Müssen nur wollen", in which she makes fun of people who work too hard, is from their 2003 debut album *Die Reklamation*. **Suggestion:** Ask sts. to look at the photo and to read the musician biography. Ask a few questions to verify understanding. Then ask sts. to think about the *Vor dem Hören* task in pairs or groups of three and to write down some of the things they have to do but don't want to do. (You may wish to explain to sts. that modal verbs in German don't always have a dependent infinitive to go with them, especially when the meaning of the expected infinitive is clear, as with verbs like *machen* or *tun* as in this case.) Discuss the results in class. Next go over the statements in Activity A of *Nach dem Hören* and make sure sts. understand them. Ask them to find the words explained in the *Miniwörterbuch* in Activity A and to underline them. Play the song and ask sts. to determine if the statements are true or false. Finally, ask sts.' opinion of the questions in Activity B.

Miniwörterbuch

tragen	to carry	die **Affen**	monkeys
anbieten	to offer	**schaffen**	to achieve
die **Getränke**	drinks	der **Konzern**	corporation
gar nichts	nothing at all	**leiten**	to lead, be head of
dressiert	trained (animals)		

 Situation 7   Dialog

Sit. 7. (See the IM for suggestions on presenting dialogues.) **(1)** Set the scene by reminding sts. who Rolf and Katrin are, where they are, and what they are discussing. **(2)** Preteach vocabulary: *stören; Viel Glück!* **(3)** Ask sts. to open their books; play the dialogue for them at least twice while they fill in the blanks. **(4)** Write sts.' answers on the board, or ask them to write their answers on the board, while making any necessary corrections. **(5)** Play the dialogue one last time for the benefit of sts. who did not get the right answers. **(6)** Follow-up: *Wer hat morgen (diese Woche noch) eine Prüfung? In welchem Fach? Müssen Sie noch viel lernen? usw.*

Rolf trifft Katrin in der Cafeteria.

ROLF: Hallo, Katrin, ist hier noch ___frei___?

KATRIN: Ja, klar.

ROLF: Ich hoffe, ich störe ___dich___ nicht beim Lernen.

KATRIN: Nein, ich muss auch mal ___Pause___ machen.

ROLF: Was machst du denn?

KATRIN: Wir haben morgen eine ___Prüfung___ und ich ___muss___ noch das Arbeitsbuch machen.

ROLF: ___Müsst___ ihr viel für euren Kurs arbeiten?

KATRIN: Ja, ganz schön viel. Heute Abend ___kann___ ich bestimmt nicht fernsehen, ___weil___ ich so viel lernen muss.

ROLF: Ich glaube, ich störe dich nicht länger. ___Viel Glück___ für die Prüfung.

KATRIN: Danke, tschüss.

Stefans Zimmer

Stefans Mutter kommt zu Besuch.

Das ist Stefans Zimmer.

So soll es sein.

Was muss Stefan machen?

den Tisch abräumen	**die Kerzen anzünden**	**seine Kleidung aufräumen**
das Bett machen	**den Schrank zumachen**	**den Boden sauber machen**
den Papierkorb ausleeren		**die Pflanze gießen**
	die Bücher gerade stellen	
das Bild an die Wand hängen		**das Fenster zumachen**
den Fernseher ausmachen	**die Katze aus dem Zimmer werfen**	

Jugendschutz

Nicht in jedem Alter darf man alles. In Deutschland regelt das Jugendschutz-gesetz[1], in welchem Alter Kinder und Jugendliche etwas dürfen oder können.

Mit 17 darf man Auto fahren.

Mit 13 ...

- darf man in den Ferien arbeiten.
  aber: Die Eltern müssen es erlauben[2] und die Arbeit muss leicht sein.

Mit 14 ...

- darf man im Restaurant Bier oder Wein trinken.
  aber: Die Eltern müssen dabei sein[3].

Mit 15 ...

- kann man mit der Arbeit anfangen.
  aber: Man darf nur 8 Stunden am Tag und 5 Tage in der Woche arbeiten.

Mit 16 ...

- darf man im Restaurant Bier oder Wein trinken (ohne Eltern).
- darf man von zu Hause wegziehen[4].
  aber: Die Eltern müssen es erlauben.
- darf man heiraten[5].
  aber: Die Eltern müssen es erlauben.
  und: Der Partner muss über 18 Jahre alt sein.
- darf man bis 24.00 Uhr in die Disko gehen.

Mit 17 ...

- darf man den Führerschein[6] für ein Auto machen.

Mit 18 ...

- darf man den Führerschein für ein Motorrad machen.
- darf man ohne Erlaubnis heiraten.
- darf man wählen[7].
- darf man im Kino alle Filme sehen.
- darf man im Restaurant Alkohol trinken.
- darf man so lange in die Disko gehen, wie man will.
- darf man rauchen.

In Deutschland ist man mit 18 Jahren erwachsen[8].

Wie ist es in Ihrem Land? Machen Sie eine Tabelle.

KLI. In addition to providing cultural information, the KLI practices the modal verbs *dürfen, können, müssen.* Start by asking, e.g.: *Dürfen Kinder Auto fahren? Alkohol trinken? in den Ferien arbeiten? Wie alt muss man sein, damit man Auto fahren darf?* etc. Write the following items on the board: *in den Ferien arbeiten, im Restaurant Bier oder Wein trinken, von zu Hause wegziehen, heiraten, Auto fahren, wählen.* Explain or paraphrase new vocabulary. Then ask: *Was glauben Sie: Wie alt muss man in Deutschland sein, damit man diese Dinge machen kann?* Let sts. guess and write guessed age limits next to the items on the board. Then, sts. open their textbooks and verify how close they came by guessing. Let them work in pairs for a few minutes, then collect their responses. Ask them to work on the activity *Wie ist es in Ihrem Land?* in small groups. Rather than writing in this book, they may wish to create a table on a piece of paper with the relevant ages for their country/countries. Encourage them to go beyond the items mentioned in the box. If they don't know the correct age, let them guess. During the follow-up insist on complete sentences, e.g., *Mit sechzehn darf man Auto fahren.*

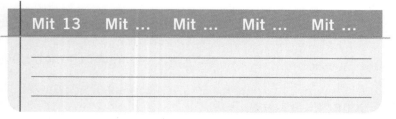

Mit 13	Mit ...	Mit ...	Mit ...	Mit ...

heiraten	wählen	Alkohol trinken
in die Disko gehen	alle Filme sehen	Auto fahren
arbeiten	erwachsen sein	rauchen

[1]*law for the protection of minors*   [2]*permit*   [3]*dabei ... be present*   [4]*move away*   [5]*marry*
[6]*driver's license*   [7]*vote*   [8]*grown-up*

Ach, wie nett!

Grammatik 3.3

Vocabulary Display
(1) Presentation: Tell (or ask sts. to tell) who and where the people are as you read what they are saying. *Maria und Michael zu Hause vor dem Fernseher; Frau Gretter und Frau Körner vor einem Schaufenster; Oma Schmitz und Helga auf dem Nachhauseweg; Jutta und Jens in einem Schauspiel, das im Mittelalter spielt; Silvias Freundin, die Silvia und Jürgen auf eine Party ein-lädt; zwei Tramperinnen, die mit Melanie und Josef nach Regensburg fahren wollen.* **(2) Recall:** Ask sts. to repeat the lines of the first dialogue after you. Cover up the lines and ask sts. to write them down from memory. Uncover and ask sts. to check their answers. Do the same for the other drawings. **(3) Focus on form:** Ask sts. to work in small groups and to find all accusative pronouns, to write them on a piece of paper, and to write the nominative form next to each accusative one.

MARIA: Der Fernseher läuft ja den ganzen Tag.
MICHAEL: Soll ich ihn ausmachen?

FRAU KÖRNER: Ich finde den Mantel einfach toll!
FRAU GRETTER: Kaufen Sie ihn doch!

OMA SCHMITZ: Die Tasche ist so schwer.
HELGA: Komm, Oma, ich trage sie.

PRINZESSIN: Hier ist mein Taschentuch. Du darfst mich nie vergessen.
PRINZ: Nein, Geliebte, ich vergesse dich nie!

SILVIAS FREUNDIN: Samstag geben wir eine Party. Ich möchte euch gern einladen.

ZWEI TRAMPERINNEN: Hallo, wir wollen nach Regensburg. Nehmt ihr uns mit?

Situation 9   Minidialoge

Sit. 9. Preparation: This is a problem-solving activity, so simply establish the context and describe the task. Point out to sts. that the gender of the pronoun will help them match the lines. **Activity:** Have sts. work in groups of three. **Follow-up:** Establish correct matches. Then ask sts. to create 2 more lines for each dialogue.

Was passt?

1. Es ist kalt und das Fenster ist offen!
2. Der Wein ist gut.
3. Du hast nächste Woche Geburtstag?
4. Der Koffer ist so schwer.
5. Die Suppe ist wirklich gut!
6. Wie findest du Paul Simon?
7. Das Haus ist schmutzig.

a. Komm, ich trage ihn.
b. Machen Sie es bitte zu.
c. Darf ich ihn probieren?
d. Ich mag sie aber nicht.
e. Ja, ich gebe eine Party und ich lade euch ein.
f. Ich mache es morgen sauber.
g. Ich mag ihn ganz gern.

Situation 10 Dialog

Sit. 10. (See the IM.) This dialogue provides a model for the role-play (*Sit. 11*). Use these steps while textbooks are closed: **(1)** Set the scene: *Heidi ist Studentin in Frau Schulz' Kurs. Sie hat Hunger und sucht einen Platz in der Mensa. Die Mensa ist ziemlich voll, aber ein Platz ist noch frei.* **(2)** Ask focus questions. First listening: *Wie heißt der Student? Woher kennen sich Heidi und der Student? Woher kommt der Student? Woher kommt Heidi?* Second listening: *Was ist Heidis Hauptfach? Was studiert Stefan? Wo möchte Stefan arbeiten?* **(3)** Play the dialogue. **(4)** Review sts.' answers. **(5)** Ask sts. to count the words in each sentence. **(6)** Divide sts. into 2 groups, assign one role to each group, and ask each group to repeat their lines. **(7)** Ask groups to repeat their lines from memory. **(8)** Ask 2 or 3 pairs of volunteers to present the dialogue in front of the class. Ask sts. to use their own names and their own personal information instead of that of the dialogue characters. **(9)** Sts. get up and work in pairs. While moving from one person to the next, they act out their own version of the dialogue several times.

Heidi sucht einen Platz in der Cafeteria.

HEIDI: Entschuldigung, <u>ist hier noch frei</u>?

STEFAN: Ja, sicher.

HEIDI: Danke.

STEFAN: <u>Kennen wir uns nicht</u>?

HEIDI: Ja, ich glaube schon. Bist du nicht auch in dem Deutschkurs um neun?

STEFAN: Na, klar. Jetzt <u>weiß</u> ich's wieder. Du <u>heißt</u> Stefanie, nicht wahr?

HEIDI: Nein, ich heiße Heidi.

STEFAN: Ach ja, richtig … Heidi. Ich heiße Stefan.

HEIDI: <u>Woher</u> kommst du eigentlich, Stefan?

STEFAN: <u>Aus</u> Iowa City, und du?

HEIDI: Ich bin aus Berkeley.

STEFAN: Und was studierst du?

HEIDI: <u>Ich weiß noch nicht</u>. Vielleicht Sport, vielleicht Geschichte oder vielleicht Deutsch.

STEFAN: Ich studiere auch Deutsch, Deutsch und <u>Wirtsch</u>. Ich möchte in Deutschland bei einer amerikanischen Firma arbeiten.

HEIDI: Toll! Da verdienst du sicherlich viel Geld.

STEFAN: <u>Hoffentlich</u>.

 Situation 11 Rollenspiel: In der Mensa

Sit. 11. Rollenspiel. (See the IM.) The role for S1 appears here, the role for S2 appears in Appendix B. **(1)** Set the scene as described in the role for S1 **(2)** Provide sts. with a model by working with the enactment of the role-play found in the workbook/lab manual. **(3)** Write the structure of the role-play on the board: *Begrüßen/Erkundigen (ob noch ein Platz frei ist); Fragen stellen; Verabschieden.* **(4)** Elicit sample greetings, questions, etc. and write on the board. Ask for appropriate responses and also write on the board. **(5)** Divide the class into two groups and assign one part of the role-play to each group. Ask sts. to practice the role-play in pairs. **(6)** Ask 2 or 3 pairs of sts. to perform their role-play in class. Provide feedback as to appropriateness and accuracy of language used after sts. have returned to their seats. **(7)** Ask sts. to find new partners and to practice the role-play in pairs again. **(8)** Optional homework assignment: Ask sts. to write up their version of the role-play. **Note:** If your students are using McGraw-Hill's **Connect** online *Arbeitsbuch*, they can do this *Rollenspiel* using the real-time, interactive **Video-Chat** feature.

Photo questions. *Essen Sie zu Hause oder an der Uni? Warum essen so viele Studenten in der Mensa? Möchten Sie in dieser Mensa essen? Sehen Sie nur Studenten im Bild? Sehen die Studenten aus wie amerikanische Studenten? Was trinken sie?*

Cultural note. Sharing tables is expected when restaurants are filling up. People do not usually engage in small talk, however. *Guten Tag, Guten Appetit,* and *Auf Wiedersehen* are the only exchanges necessary.

S1: Sie sind Student/Studentin an der Uni in Regensburg. Sie gehen in die Mensa und setzen sich zu jemand an den Tisch. Fragen Sie, wie er/sie heißt, woher er/sie kommt und was er/sie studiert.

In der Mensa

Situation 12 Ratespiel

Sit. 12. This activity is intended to give sts. more practice with 3rd-person pronouns referring to things. Review items of clothing and accessories with the clothing screen from *Kap. 2*. Explain any unfamiliar vocabulary in the numbered sentences. Model sentences and practice pronunciation. Tell sts. that the pronouns in the sentences provide them with clues as to what choices they have. Ask them which pronouns correspond to which articles. Ask them to complete the activity in pairs or small groups.
Follow-up: Ask sts. to come up with additional *Ratespiel* items to test one another's knowledge of clothing and of pronouns.

Was ist das?

1. __f__ Man trägt sie im Sommer an den Füßen.
2. __e__ Man trägt ihn nach dem Duschen.
3. __g__ Man trägt es im Bett.
4. __a__ Man trägt ihn im Winter um den Hals.
5. __b__ Man trägt sie im Ohr.
6. __d__ Man trägt sie unter der Kleidung.
7. __c__ Man trägt sie im Winter an den Händen.

a. der Schal
b. die Ohrringe
c. die Handschuhe
d. die Unterhose
e. der Bademantel
f. die Sandalen
g. das Nachthemd

Filmlektüre
Soul Kitchen

 Vor dem Lesen

Filmlektüre: (1) Ask the questions in *Vor dem Lesen* and some additional ones about the *Filmangaben* such as: *Wann ist der Film erschienen? In welchem Land? Was für ein Film ist er? Wie lange dauert er? Wer hat die Hauptrollen?* **(2)** Next, ask sts. to read the words in the *Miniwörterbuch*, to find them in the *Inhaltsangabe* and to underline them. Tell them that it will help them get a first impression of what the text will be about. **(3)** Then, go over the *Arbeit mit dem Text* making sure sts. understand all the words. Write unfamiliar words on the board with translations or convey the meanings

A. Beantworten Sie die folgenden Fragen.

1. Was sehen Sie im Bild?
2. Was ist die *Soul Kitchen*? Was glauben Sie?
3. Wer ist der Regisseur?

Filmangaben

Titel: *Soul Kitchen*
Genre: Komödie
Land: Deutschland
Erscheinungsjahr: 2009
Dauer: 99 Min.
Regisseur: Fatih Akin
Hauptrollen: Adam Bousdoukos, Moritz Bleibtreu, Birol Ünel

Zinos und sein Bruder Illias im Restaurant

in another manner. **(4)** Ask sts. to work in pairs and to determine whether the statements are true or false according to the text and ask them to correct false statements. **(5)** Next, work with the *Filmclip*. Paraphrase the introduction to the *Filmclip* and go over the multiple-choice questions making sure sts. understand the questions and the choices. Tell sts. that you will play the clip twice and that they should check the correct answers. **(6)** Elicit answers and write sts. choices on the board including incorrect ones. Tell them that you will play the clip one more time and ask them to determine which of their choices are correct. **(7)** Tell them what the correct choices are. **(8)** Play the clip one last time asking sts. to knock when they hear the correct choice pausing the clip briefly. **(9)** Assign the *Nach dem Lesen* for homework.

B. Lesen Sie die Wörter im Miniwörterbuch. Suchen Sie sie im Text und unterstreichen Sie sie.

Miniwörterbuch

das **Pech**	bad luck	das **Gefängnis**	jail
erleidet einen	suffers from a	der **Aufschwung**	boom
Bandscheibenvorfall	slipped disc	**anziehen**	to attract
vertreiben	to drive away	das **Szenepublikum**	the in crowd
cholerische Art	short-tempered nature	**unvorhergesehen**	unforeseen

Inhaltsangabe

Zinos (Adam Bousdoukos) hat eine Kneipe namens „Soul Kitchen" in Hamburg. Allerdings scheint er nur Pech zu haben. Als seine Freundin nach Shanghai zieht, erleidet er einen Bandscheibenvorfall. Außerdem vertreibt Zinos' Profikoch mit seiner cholerischen Art fast alle Stammgäste. Es sieht für Zinos sehr schlecht aus

5 und in diesem Moment erscheint auch noch sein Bruder Illias (Moritz Bleibtreu), der eigentlich im Gefängnis sein soll. Obwohl Zinos seine Kneipe verkaufen will und zu seiner Freundin ziehen möchte, erlebt die „Soul Kitchen" plötzlich einen großartigen Aufschwung. Soulmusik und bestes Essen ziehen ein Szenepublikum an. Doch Illias bekommt Probleme und braucht Zinos' Hilfe. Es passieren unvorhergesehene Dinge.

Arbeit mit dem Text

Richtig (R) oder falsch (F)? Verbessern Sie die falschen Aussagen.

bar

moves

_____ 1. Zinos hat eine Kneipe° in Shanghai.

_____ 2. Zinos' Freundin zieht° nach Shanghai.

_____ 3. Zinos' Koch ist sehr nett.

_____ 4. Illias ist Zinos' Vater.

_____ 5. Zinos möchte seine Kneipe verkaufen.

_____ 6. Gutes Essen und gute Musik ziehen ein Szenepublikum an.

Filmclip 🎬

Szene: DVD, Kapitel 3, „Have you escaped?", 10:57–13:40 Min.

Zinos bringt seine Freundin Nadine, die nach Shanghai fliegt, zum Flughafen. Zinos' Bruder Illias hat Freigang und trifft mit seinem Bruder zusammen. Schauen Sie sich die Szene an und beantworten Sie die Fragen.

1. Wo sind Zinos und Illias?
   - ☐ a. im Auto
   - ☐ b. im Restaurant
   - ☐ c. im Flughafen

2. Was soll Zinos machen?
   - ☐ a. Zinos soll Illias verstecken°.
   - ☐ b. Zinos soll abnehmen°.
   - ☐ c. Zinos soll Illias einen Gefallen° tun.

3. Was muss Illias machen, damit° er jeden Tag Freigang hat?
   - ☐ a. Er muss 10 000 Euro zahlen.
   - ☐ b. Er muss einen Job haben.
   - ☐ c. Er muss am Wochenende im Gefängnis arbeiten.

4. Was halten Illias' Mitarbeiter° davon, dass Illias in der Soul Kitchen arbeitet?
   - ☐ a. Sie finden Illias cool.
   - ☐ b. Sie wollen nicht mit einem Hartz IV-Typen° arbeiten.
   - ☐ c. Sie brauchen keinen zusätzlichen° Kellner°.

co-workers

Hartz ... *welfare guy*

additional / waiter

hide

lose weight

favor

so that

Nach dem Lesen

Suchen Sie im Internet und beantworten Sie die folgenden Fragen.

1. Wo ist Fatih Akin geboren? In welchem Stadtteil?

2. Für welchen Film hat er internationale Preise bekommen?

3. Was wissen Sie über sein Privatleben?

Schuljahr und Zeugnisse

Wie ist das in Ihrem Land?

1. Wann beginnt das Schuljahr? Wann endet es?
2. Welche Fächer hat man in der 9. Klasse?
3. Welche Fremdsprachen lernt man in der 9. Klasse?
4. Wie oft gibt es Zeugnisse[1]? Wann?
5. Muss jemand die Zeugnisse unterschreiben? Wer?
6. Was passiert, wenn ein Schüler in vielen Fächern sehr schlechte Noten[2] hat?

Sie hören einen Text über die deutschen Schulen. Hören Sie gut zu und beantworten Sie dann die Fragen.

- Das Schuljahr beginnt im _August_ oder _September_.
- Das Schuljahr ist im _Juni_, _Juli_ oder _August_ zu Ende.
- Wann gibt es Zeugnisse? In der _Mitte_ und am _Ende_ des Schuljahres.
- Schreiben Sie neben die Wörter die richtige Note (Zahl) und was es in Ihrem Land ist.

	IN DEUTSCHLAND	IN IHREM LAND
„sehr gut"	1	
„gut"	2	
„befriedigend"[3]	3	
„ausreichend"[4]	4	
„mangelhaft"[5]	5	
„ungenügend"[6]	6	

- Wann bleibt man sitzen[7]?

Miniwörterbuch

entscheiden	to decide
die **Klasse, -n**	grade, level
das **Resultat, -e**	result
die **Versetzung**	promotion into the next grade

[1]report cards [2]grades [3]satisfactory [4]sufficient [5]poor [6]insufficient [7]bleibt sitzen flunks, is held back a grade

---

ZEUGNIS

Schuljahr 20 _11/12_   1. Halbjahr   Klasse _9 b_

Jens Krüger
Vor- und Zuname des Schülers/der Schülerin
geboren am _22. 8. 97_ in _München_

Pflichtunterricht

Deutsch	4	Mathematik (Fachleistungskurs___)	4
Rechtschreiben	4	Physik/Chemie	5
Englisch (Fachleistungskurs___) _Latein_	5	Biologie	3
	5	Musik	2
Welt- und Umweltkunde	3	Kunst	2
Religion	4	Werken	2
Werte und Normen	4	Textiles Gestalten	/
		Sport	1

Wahlpflichtunterricht und wahlfreier Unterricht

Italienisch   4

Bemerkungen

Jens ist bei seinen Mitschülern beliebt.

Goslar, den _1. Feb. 2011_
Datum der Ausstellung

Cramer   _U. Möller_
Klassenlehrer(in)   Schulleiter(in)

gesehen: _Arnd Krüger_
Unterschrift eines Erziehungsberechtigten

Cultural note. Austria uses the same grading system as Germany, whereas in Switzerland the opposite system is used: 6 is the best, 1 the worst.

KLI. (See the IM on how to present KLI notes.) Read the text or play the recording. *Das Schuljahr dauert von August oder September bis Juni, Juli oder August des nächsten Jahres. In jedem Fach schreiben die Schüler Klassenarbeiten und Tests. Die Resultate dieser Arbeiten und Tests ergeben die Noten im Zeugnis. Zweimal im Jahr – in der Mitte und am Ende – gibt es Zeugnisse. Das Zeugnis am Ende des Jahres entscheidet über die Versetzung, d.h. ob der Schüler oder die Schülerin in die nächste Klasse kommt oder nicht. Die Noten im Zeugnis gehen von 1 bis 6. Dabei ist 1 „sehr gut", 2 „gut", 3 „befriedigend", 4 „ausreichend", 5 „mangelhaft" und 6 „ungenügend". Bei zwei Fünfen oder einer Sechs müssen die Schüler eine Klasse noch einmal machen.*

Körperliche und geistige Verfassung

Grammatik 3.4–3.5

Vocabulary Display
Use pictures to teach adjectives that describe particular physical and mental states. Ask *Wie geht es der Frau / dem Mann / dem Hund usw.?* so sts. learn to recognize the question. Put the sketches on the projector, cover the captions, and ask similar questions. (See the IM on using vocabulary displays.) You might want to ask sts. to identify the characters in each sketch.

 Er ist glücklich.

 Sie sind traurig.

 Er ist wütend.

 Sie ist krank.

 Sie sind in Eile.

 Sie ist müde.

 Sie haben Hunger.

 Er hat Langeweile.

 Er hat Durst.

Er hat Angst.

 Situation 13 Informationsspiel: Was machen sie, wenn ...?

Sit. 13. Have sts. work in pairs. The corresponding chart is in Appendix A. Remember to set a time limit for the activity. Sts. do not need to complete the entire chart. Make sure, however, that they ask each other all the questions that pertain to themselves (*Was machst du, wenn du traurig bist? müde bist? usw.*).

MODELL: s2: Was macht Renate, wenn sie traurig ist?
s1: Sie ruft ihre Freundin an.
s2: Was machst du, wenn du traurig bist?
s1: Ich gehe ins Bett.

	Renate	Ernst	mein(e) Partner(in)
1. *traurig ist/bist*	ruft ihre Freundin an	weint	
2. *müde ist/bist*	trinkt Kaffee	schläft	
3. *in Eile ist/bist*	nimmt ein Taxi	ist nie in Eile	
4. *wütend ist/bist*	wirft mit Tellern	schreit ganz laut	
5. *krank ist/bist*	geht zum Arzt	isst Hühnersuppe	
6. *glücklich ist/bist*	lädt Freunde ein	lacht ganz laut	
7. *Hunger hat/hast*	isst einen Apfel	schreit laut „Hunger!"	
8. *Langeweile hat/hast*	liest ein Buch	ärgert seine Schwester	
9. *Durst hat/hast*	trinkt Mineralwasser	trinkt Limo	
10. *Angst hat/hast*	schließt die Tür ab	läuft zu Mama	

Situation 14 Interview: Wie fühlst du dich, wenn ...?

Sit. 14. Model pronunciation in the example given, and review the pronunciation of *ausgezeichnet*. Make sure sts. understand that adjectives are ordered from positive to negative (+ 0 −). Pronounce *mies* and explain that it is *Umgangssprache*, and pronounce the phrases in 1-11 (add *Wie fühlst du dich?* before each one), having the sts. repeat after you. Then have sts. work in pairs. Afterward, you might choose to give them some additional (and preferably entertaining) situations to help them become familiar with word order when the *wenn*-clause is in the second half of the sentence: *Stellen Sie sich vor, Sie sind Präsident oder Präsidentin der USA. Wie fühlen Sie sich, wenn Sie mit einem Journalisten sprechen müssen? Sie sind in der Footballmannschaft von* [your university]. *Wie fühlen Sie sich, wenn Sie ein Spiel gegen* [your rival university] *gewinnen? verlieren? usw.*

MODELL: s1: Wie fühlst du dich, wenn du um fünf Uhr morgens aufstehst?
s2: Ausgezeichnet!

[+]	[0]	[−]
ausgezeichnet		nicht besonders gut
fantastisch		ziemlich schlecht
sehr gut	ganz gut	mies
gut		total mies

1. wenn du um fünf Uhr morgens aufstehst
2. wenn du die ganze Nacht nicht schlafen kannst
3. wenn deine Freunde dich auf eine Party einladen
4. wenn du eine Arbeit oder einen Test zurückbekommst
5. wenn du ein Referat halten musst
6. wenn das Semester zu Ende ist
7. wenn du einkaufen gehen willst, aber kein Geld hast
8. wenn alle deine T-Shirts schmutzig sind
9. wenn du eine gute Note bekommst
10. wenn du Heimweh hast
11. wenn du eifersüchtig bist

Situation 15 Warum fährt Frau Ruf mit dem Bus?

Sit. 15. The goal of this *Sit.* is for sts. to become accustomed to placing the verb at the end of clauses that begin with the subordinating conjunction *weil*. First introduce any new vocabulary, e.g., *Lust haben.* Have sts. (in groups of 3) match the sentences in column A with those in column B. This exercise is divided into two sections to make the task more manageable. Sentences 1-5 go with a-e, 6-10 with f-j.

Kombinieren Sie!

MODELL: s1: Warum fährt Frau Ruf mit dem Bus?
s2: Weil ihr Auto kaputt ist.

1. Warum fährt Frau Ruf mit dem Bus?
2. Warum hat Hans Angst?
3. Warum geht Jutta nicht ins Kino?
4. Warum geht Jens nicht in die Schule?
5. Warum kauft Andrea Hans eine CD?

a. weil er Geburtstag hat
b. weil ihr Auto kaputt ist
c. weil sein Referat noch nicht fertig ist
d. weil sie für eine Klassenarbeit lernen muss
e. weil er keine Lust hat

6. Warum fährt Herr Wagner nach Leipzig?
7. Warum ist Ernst wütend?
8. Warum fährt Frau Gretter in die Berge?
9. Warum geht Herr Siebert um zehn Uhr ins Bett?
10. Warum ruft Maria ihre Freundin an?

f. weil er seinen Bruder besuchen will
g. weil sie wandern geht
h. weil er in Mathe so viele Hausaufgaben hat
i. weil sie sie ins Kino einladen will
j. weil er jeden Tag um sechs Uhr aufsteht

Situation 16 Zum Schreiben: Auch in Ihnen steckt ein Dichter!

Sit. 16. Brainstorm possible topics with sts. Some ideas might include *Hund, Oma, Wochenende, Uni, Deutsch,* and so forth. Have students work in pairs and put their poems on the projector to present to the class. Students could also write on the board.

Schreiben Sie ein Gedicht!

MODELL:

Wasser	ein Nomen = Thema
kühl, nass	zwei Adjektive
schwimmen, segeln, tauchen	drei Verben
Sonne auf meiner Haut	vier Wörter, die ein Gefühl ausdrücken[1]
Sommer	ein Nomen = Zusammenfassung[2]

[1]express [2]summary

Videoecke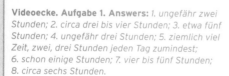

Perspektiven

Wie viel Zeit verbringst du pro Tag am Computer? Womit verbringst du die meiste Zeit?

Aufgabe 1 Zeit am Computer

Wie viel Zeit verbringen sie am Computer? Schreiben Sie die Antworten auf.

Ich arbeite oder ich chatte.

Videoecke. Aufgabe 1. Answers: *1. ungefähr zwei Stunden; 2. circa drei bis vier Stunden; 3. etwa fünf Stunden; 4. ungefähr drei Stunden; 5. ziemlich viel Zeit, zwei, drei Stunden jeden Tag zumindest; 6. schon einige Stunden; 7. vier bis fünf Stunden; 8. circa sechs Stunden.*

1. Susan ____

2. Felicitas ____

3. Michael ____

4. Shaimaa ____

5. Nadezda ____

6. Pascal ____

7. Judith ____

8. Martin ____

Aufgabe 2 Tätigkeiten am Computer

Was machen sie am Computer? Ordnen Sie die Tätigkeiten den Personen unter Aufgabe 1 zu.

__f__ 1. Susan   a. Die meiste Zeit verbringt sie auf Facebook.

__a__ 2. Felicitas   b. Er liest E-Mails und Nachrichten.

__b__ 3. Michael   c. Er macht Layout und Grafik.

__e__ 4 Shaimaa   d. Er sucht potentielle Kunden[1] für seine Firma.

__h__ 5. Nadezda   e. Sie arbeitet die meiste Zeit.

__c__ 6. Pascal   f. Sie arbeitet oder sie chattet.

__g__ 7. Judith   g. Sie checkt ihre E-Mails und ist oft bei Facebook.

__d__ 8. Martin   h. Sie verwendet die meiste Zeit für ihr Studium.

Interviews

- Hast du handwerkliche oder künstlerische Fähigkeiten?
- Was kannst du besonders gut?
- Was gefällt dir daran?
- Was kannst du nicht besonders gut?
- Gibt es etwas, was du nicht gern machst?
- Wie fühlst du dich, wenn du eine Prüfung hast?
- Wie bereitest du dich darauf vor?

Carolyn

Michael

Aufgabe 3 Fähigkeiten und Pflichten

Carolyn oder Michael?

	Carolyn	Michael
1. Wer tanzt und gestaltet[2] gerne T-Shirts?	☒	☐
2. Wer hat keine handwerklichen Fähigkeiten?	☐	☒
3. Wer mag es total, sich zu den Rhythmen der Musik zu bewegen?	☒	☐
4. Wer spielt Gitarre, Akkordeon und Klavier?	☐	☒
5. Wer kann nicht gut kochen?	☐	☒
6. Wer putzt nicht gern?	☒	☐
7. Wer macht nicht gern Sport?	☐	☒
8. Wessen[3] Hände schwitzen[4], wenn er oder sie eine Prüfung hat?	☒	☐
9. Wer geht regelmäßig zu Seminaren und Vorlesungen, damit er oder sie gut vorbereitet ist?	☐	☒

Aufgabe 4 Interview

Interviewen Sie eine Partnerin oder einen Partner. Stellen Sie dieselben Fragen.

[1]customers [2]designs [3]whose [4]sweat

Wortschatz

Talente und Pläne — Talents and Plans

der Besuch, -e	visit
zu Besuch kommen	to visit
der Schlittschuh, -e	ice skate
Schlittschuh laufen, läuft	to go ice-skating
der Witz, -e	joke
Witze erzählen	to tell jokes
schneiden	to cut
Haare schneiden	to cut hair
stricken	to knit
tauchen	to dive
tippen	to type
zeichnen	to draw

Ähnliche Wörter

der Ski, -er; Ski fahren, fährt; der Walzer, -;
das Skateboard, -s; Skateboard fahren, fährt

Pflichten — Obligations

ab·räumen	to clear
den Tisch ab·räumen	to clear the table
gerade stellen	to straighten
gießen	to water
die Blumen gießen	to water the flowers
sauber machen	to clean

Körperliche und geistige Verfassung — Physical and Mental State

die Angst, ⁻e	fear
Angst haben	to be afraid
die Eile	hurry
in Eile sein	to be in a hurry
die Langeweile	boredom
Langeweile haben	to be bored
die Lust	desire
Lust haben	to feel like (doing something)
das Glück	luck; happiness
viel Glück!	lots of luck! good luck!
das Heimweh	homesickness
Heimweh haben	to be homesick
ärgern	to annoy; to tease
schreien	to scream, yell
stören	to disturb
weinen	to cry
eifersüchtig	jealous
krank	sick

nett	nice
müde	tired
wütend	angry

Ähnliche Wörter

der Durst; Durst haben; der Hunger; Hunger haben; das
Gefühl, -e; fühlen; wie fühlst du dich?; ich fühle mich ...

Schule — School

die Nachhilfe	tutoring
die Sprechstunde, -n	office hour
der Satz, ⁻e	sentence
das Arbeitsbuch, ⁻er	workbook
das Beispiel, -e	example
zum Beispiel (z. B.)	for example
das Referat, -e	report
das Studium, Studien (R)	course of studies

Sonstige Substantive — Other Nouns

die Ärztin, -nen	female physician
die Blume, -n	flower
die Geige, -n	violin
die Geliebte, -n	beloved female friend, love
die Kerze, -n	candle
die Oma, -s	grandma
die Pflicht, -en	duty; requirement
der Arzt, ⁻e	male physician
der Papierkorb, ⁻e	wastebasket
das Gedicht, -e	poem
das Krankenhaus, ⁻er	hospital
das Mittagessen	midday meal, lunch
das Taschentuch, ⁻er	handkerchief
das Tier, -e	animal

Ähnliche Wörter

die CD, -s (R); die Disko, -s; die Firma, Firmen; die
Nacht, ⁻e; die Pflanze, -n; der DVD-Spieler, - (R); der
Mittag, -e; der Plan, ⁻e; der Platz, ⁻e; das Alphabet; das
Licht, -er; das Talent, -e; das Taxi, -s; das Tischtennis

Modalverben — Modal Verbs

dürfen, darf	to be permitted (to), may
können, kann	to be able (to), can; may
mögen, mag (R)	to like, care for
möchte	would like (to)
müssen, muss	to have to, must
sollen, soll	to be supposed to
wollen, will	to want; to intend, plan (to)

Sonstige Verben — Other Verbs

an·machen	to turn on, switch on
an·sehen, sieht ... an	to look at; to watch
an·ziehen	to put on (clothes)
an·zünden	to light
auf·machen	to open
auf·passen	to pay attention
aus·leeren	to empty
aus·machen	to turn off
aus·ziehen	to take off (clothes)
bekommen	to get, receive
bleiben	to remain, stay
erleben	to experience
erzählen	to tell
heiraten	to marry
lieben	to love
mit·nehmen, nimmt ... mit	to take along
probieren	to try, taste
rauchen	to smoke
stellen	to put, place (upright)
verbringen	to spend (*time*)
verreisen	to go on a trip
vorbei·kommen	to come by, visit
werfen, wirft	to throw
zu·machen	to close

Ähnliche Wörter

baden, hängen, hoffen, kämmen, kombinieren, lachen, leben, mit·bringen; das Bild an die Wand hängen

Adjektive und Adverbien — Adjectives and Adverbs

ausgezeichnet	excellent
beliebt	popular
besonders	particularly
bestimmt	definitely, certainly
eigentlich	actually
fertig	ready; finished
genug	enough

nass	wet
schwer	heavy; hard, difficult
wahr	true

Sonstige Wörter und Ausdrücke — Other Words and Expressions

außerdem	besides
blau machen	to take the day off
dreimal	three times
einander	one another, each other
hintereinander	in a row
miteinander	with each other
ein bisschen	a little bit
Entschuldigung!	excuse me
die ganze Nacht	all night long
ganz schön viel	quite a bit
gar nicht	not a bit
immer	always
jede	each, every
jede Woche	every week
jemand	someone, somebody
jetzt	now
kein bisschen	not at all
mit mir	with me
na	well
nach	after; to
neben	beside, in addition to
nur	only
sicherlich	certainly
sofort	immediately
von der Arbeit	from work
warum	why
weil	because
wieder	again
schon wieder	once again
wohin	where to
zu Fuß	on foot
zum Arzt	to the doctor
zum Mittagessen	for lunch

Strukturen und Übungen

3.1 The modal verbs *können, wollen, mögen*

Wissen Sie noch?

The **Satzklammer** forms a frame or a bracket consisting of a verb and either a separable prefix or an infinitive. This same structure is used with the modal verbs.

Review grammar 1.5 and 2.3.

3.1. *Modalverben: möchte* in Section 2.3 was a preview of modal auxiliary verbs. In this chapter, the forms and meanings of the 6 German modal verbs are introduced. If sts. can hear modal verbs repeatedly, the *Satzklammer* (which they have already encountered in Section 1.5 with separable-prefix verbs) will not cause much difficulty.

Point out the differences from the regular verb conjugation. Typical mistakes are using the vowel of the infinitive in the singular and adding endings to the *ich*- and *er/sie/es*-forms. Stress that the singular has a different vowel from the infinitive (except in *sollen*), whereas the vowel of the plural is always the same as the infinitive.

können = *can*
wollen = *to want to*
mögen = *to like (to)*

Modal verbs, such as **können** (*can, to be able to, know how to*), **wollen** (*to want to*), and **mögen** (*to like to*) are auxiliary verbs that modify the meaning of the main verb. The main verb appears as an infinitive at the end of the clause.

The modal **können** usually indicates an ability or talent but may also be used to ask permission. The modal **wollen** expresses a desire or an intention to do something. The modal **mögen** expresses a liking; just like its English equivalent, *to like*, it is commonly used with an accusative object.

Kannst du kochen?	*Can you cook?*
Kann ich mitkommen?	*Can I come along?*
Sofie und Willi wollen tanzen gehen.	*Sofie and Willi want to go dancing.*
Ich mag aber nicht tanzen.	*I don't like to dance though.*
Magst du Spaghetti?	*Do you like spaghetti?*

Modals do not have endings in the **ich-** and **er/sie/es**-forms. Note also that these modal verbs have one stem vowel in all plural forms and in the polite **Sie**-form, and a different stem vowel in the **ich-, du-,** and **er/sie/es**-forms.

	können	**wollen**	**mögen**
ich	kann	will	mag
du	kannst	willst	magst
Sie	können	wollen	mögen
er/sie/es	kann	will	mag
wir	können	wollen	mögen
ihr	könnt	wollt	mögt
Sie	können	wollen	mögen
sie	können	wollen	mögen

Übung 1   Talente

Üb. 1. This exercise is restricted to the forms of *können*. Assign for homework and have sts. read individual sentences in class.

A. **Wer kann das?**

MODELL: Ich kann Deutsch.
    oder Wir können Deutsch.

1. Deutsch
2. Golf spielen
3. Ski fahren
4. Klavier spielen
5. gut kochen
6. gut Karaoke singen
7. Witze erzählen
8. Snowboard fahren

mein Freund / meine Freundin
meine Eltern
ich/wir
mein Bruder / meine Schwester
der Professor / die Professorin

B. **Kannst du das?**

MODELL: Gedichte schreiben → Kannst du Gedichte schreiben?
                oder   Könnt ihr Gedichte schreiben?

1. Gedichte schreiben   du
2. Auto fahren   ihr
3. tippen
4. stricken
5. zeichnen

Übung 2   Pläne und Fähigkeiten

Üb. 2. Remind sts. that German *will* is not the equivalent of English "will." Give sts. many chances to hear this form of *wollen* used in a meaningful context

Was können oder wollen diese Personen (nicht) machen?

MODELL: am Samstag / ich / wollen →
       Am Samstag **will** ich **Schlittschuh laufen.**

> **Achtung!**
>
> German **will** is not the equivalent of English *will* but means rather "want(s)" or "intend(s) to."

E-Mails lesen
Golf spielen
Haare schneiden
ins Kino gehen
nach Europa fliegen
schlafen
simsen
Ski fahren
Witze erzählen
zeichnen
_____ ?

1. heute Abend / ich / wollen
2. morgen / ich / nicht können
3. mein Freund (meine Freundin) / gut können
4. am Samstag / mein Freund (meine Freundin) / wollen
5. mein Freund (meine Freundin) und ich / wollen
6. im Winter / meine Eltern (meine Freunde) / wollen
7. meine Eltern (meine Freunde) / gut können

3.2 The modal verbs *müssen, sollen, dürfen*

3.2. The meaning of *sollen* as introduced here is "to be supposed to," primarily as a request by a person other than the speaker. Since the subjunctive is used more appropriately in German (*sollte* = "should") for making suggestions, this meaning is not introduced here.

Sts. may grasp the difference between *nicht dürfen* and *nicht müssen* and their relationship to *müssen* and *dürfen* better if it is explained in class.

The modal **müssen** stresses the necessity to do something. The modal **sollen** is less emphatic than **müssen** and may imply an obligation or a strong suggestion made by another person. The modal **dürfen,** used primarily to indicate permission, can also be used in polite requests.

Jens muss mehr lernen.	*Jens has to study more.*
Vati sagt, du sollst sofort nach Hause kommen.	*Dad says you're supposed to come home immediately.*
Frau Schulz sagt, du sollst morgen zu ihr kommen.	*Ms. Schulz says you should come to see her tomorrow.*
Darf ich die Kerzen anzünden?	*May I light the candles?*

	müssen	sollen	dürfen
ich	muss	soll	darf
du	musst	sollst	darfst
Sie	müssen	sollen	dürfen
er/sie/es	muss	soll	darf
wir	müssen	sollen	dürfen
ihr	müsst	sollt	dürft
Sie	müssen	sollen	dürfen
sie	müssen	sollen	dürfen

müssen = *must*
sollen = *to be supposed to*
dürfen = *may*

When negated, the English expressions *to have to* and *must* undergo a change in meaning. The expression *not have to* implies that there is no need to do something, while *must not* implies a strong warning. These two distinct meanings are expressed in German by **nicht müssen** and **nicht dürfen,** respectively.

nicht müssen = *not to have to, not to need to*
nicht dürfen = *mustn't*

Du musst das nicht tun.   *You don't have to do that.*
                           or: *You don't need to do that.*
Du darfst das nicht tun.   *You mustn't do that.*

Übung 3   Jutta hat eine Fünf in Englisch.

Üb. 3. Assign this exercise for *müssen* and *nicht dürfen* as homework and check it in class.

Was muss sie machen? Was darf sie nicht machen?

1. mit Jens zusammen lernen
2. den ganzen Abend chatten
3. in der Klasse aufpassen und mitschreiben
4. jeden Tag tanzen gehen
5. jeden Tag ihren Wortschatz lernen
6. amerikanische Filme im Original sehen
7. ihren Englischlehrer zum Abendessen einladen
8. für eine Woche nach London fahren
9. die englische Grammatik fleißig[1] lernen

Übung 4   Minidialoge

Üb. 4. Assign for homework and have sts. perform the dialogues in class.

Ergänzen Sie **können, wollen, müssen, sollen, dürfen.**

1. ALBERT: Hallo, Nora. Peter und ich gehen ins Kino. _____[a] du nicht mitkommen?
   NORA: Ich _____[b] schon, aber leider _____[c] ich nicht mitkommen. Ich _____[d] arbeiten.

2. JENS: Vati, _____[a] ich mit Hans fischen gehen?
   HERR WAGNER: Nein! Du hast eine Fünf in Physik, eine Fünf in Latein und eine Fünf in Englisch. Du _____[b] zu Hause bleiben und deine Hausaufgaben machen.
   JENS: Aber, Vati! Meine Hausaufgaben _____[c] ich doch heute Abend machen.
   HERR WAGNER: Nein, aber du _____[d] zu Hans gehen und dann _____[e] ihr eure Hausaufgaben zusammen machen.

[1]*diligently*

Achtung!

Remember the two characteristics of modal verbs:

1. no ending in the **ich-** and **er/sie/es-**forms;
2. one stem vowel in the **ich-, du-,** and **er/sie/es-**forms and a different one in the plural, the formal **Sie,** and the infinitive. (Note, however, that **sollen** has the same stem vowel in all forms.)

3. HEIDI: Hallo, Stefan. Frau Schulz sagt, du _____ª morgen in ihre Sprechstunde kommen.
STEFAN: Morgen _____ᵇ ich nicht, ich habe keine Zeit.
HEIDI: Das _____ᶜ du Frau Schulz schon selbst sagen. Bis bald.

3.3 Accusative case: personal pronouns

3.3. *Personalpronomen: Akkusativ.* This section continues the presentation of accusative forms that was begun in *Kapitel 2*.

Mich causes no problems because of the equivalent English form, but there will be confusion with *mir* when it is introduced in Section 5.5. The plural forms take longer to acquire, although giving sts. the chance to hear the forms used meaningfully will help.

As in English, certain German pronouns change depending on whether they are the subject or the object of a verb.

Ich möchte mitkommen. Nimmst du **mich** mit?
I would like to come along. Will you take me with you?

Er kommt aus Wien. Kennst du **ihn**?
He is from Vienna. Do you know him?

A. First- and second-person pronouns: nominative and accusative forms

Wissen Sie noch?

The accusative case is used to indicate direct objects of verbs.

Review grammar 2.1.

Nominative	Accusative	
ich	mich	*me*
du	dich	*you*
Sie	Sie	*you*
wir	uns	*us*
ihr	euch	*you*
Sie	Sie	*you*

Wer bist **du**? Ich kenne **dich** nicht.
Who are you? I don't know you.

Wer seid **ihr**? Ich kenne **euch** nicht.
Who are you (people)? I don't know you.

B. Third-person pronouns: nominative and accusative forms

	Nominative	Accusative	
Masculine	er	ihn	*him, it*
Feminine	sie		*her, it*
Neuter	es		*it*
Plural	sie		*them*

der → er
den → ihn
das → es
die → sie

Recall that third-person pronouns reflect the grammatical gender of the noun they stand for: **der Film → er; die Gitarre → sie; das Foto → es.** This relationship also holds true for the accusative case: **den Film → ihn; die Gitarre → sie; das Foto → es.** Note that only the masculine singular pronoun has a different form in the accusative case.

Wo ist der Spiegel? Ich sehe **ihn** nicht.
Where is the mirror? I don't see it.

Das ist meine Schwester Jasmin. Du kennst **sie** noch nicht.
This is my sister Jasmin. You don't know her yet.

—Wann kaufst du die Bücher?
—When will you buy the books?

—Ich kaufe **sie** morgen.
—I'll buy them tomorrow.

Strukturen und Übungen **133**

Minidialoge

Üb. 5. 1st- and 2nd-person forms are used in this exercise. Assign for homework and ask sts. to perform the roles in class.

Ergänzen Sie **mich, dich, uns, euch, Sie.**

1. KATRIN: Holst du mich heute Abend ab, wenn wir ins Kino gehen?
   THOMAS: Natürlich hole ich _____ ab!

2. STEFAN: Hallooo! Hier bin ich, Albert! Siehst du _____^a denn nicht?
   ALBERT: Ach, *da* bist du. Ja, jetzt sehe ich _____^b.

3. SARAH: Guten Tag, Frau Schulz. Sie kennen _____ noch nicht. Wir sind neu in Ihrer Klasse. Das ist Rick, und ich bin Sarah.
   FRAU SCHULZ: Guten Tag, Rick. Guten Tag, Sarah.

4. MONIKA: Hallo, Albert. Hallo, Thomas. Katrin und ich besuchen _____ heute.
   ALBERT UND THOMAS: Toll! Bringt Kuchen mit!

5. STEFAN: Heidi, ich mag _____^a!
   HEIDI: Das ist schön, Stefan. Ich mag _____^b auch.

6. FRAU SCHULZ: Spreche ich laut genug? Verstehen Sie _____^a?
   KLASSE: Ja, wir verstehen _____^b sehr gut, Frau Schulz.

7. STEFAN UND ALBERT: Auf Wiedersehen, Frau Schulz! Schöne Ferien! Und vergessen Sie uns nicht!
   FRAU SCHULZ: Natürlich nicht! Wie kann ich _____ denn je vergessen?

Der Deutschkurs

Üb. 6. Point out to sts. in item 8 that they should think of a specific teacher and use the appropriate pronoun: *ihn* for a male teacher or *sie* for a female one.

MODELL: Machst du gern **das** Arbeitsbuch für *Kontakte*?
ja, ich mache **es** gern. *Oder:* nein, ich mache **es** nicht gern.

Tipp: das → es   den → ihn   die → sie

1. Machst du gern **das** Arbeitsbuch für *Kontakte*?
2. Kannst du **das deutsche Alphabet** aufsagen?
3. Kennst du **den beliebtesten deutschen Vornamen für Jungen**?
4. Liest du gern **die Grammatik**?
5. Lernst du gern **den Wortschatz**?
6. Kennst du **die Studenten und Studentinnen** in der Klasse?
7. Vergisst du oft **die Hausaufgaben**?
8. Magst du **deinen** Lehrer oder **deine** Lehrerin?

Was machen diese Personen?

Üb. 7. For practice of 3rd-person pronouns. Stress that *ihn, sie,* and *es* are all equivalent to "it." Assign for homework or use in class with partners.

Beantworten Sie die Fragen negativ.

MODELL: Kauft Michael das Buch? →
Nein, er kauft es nicht, er liest es.

Verwenden Sie diese Verben.

anrufen, ruft an
anziehen, zieht an
anzünden, zündet an
ausmachen, macht aus
essen, isst
kaufen
schreiben
trinken
verkaufen
waschen, wäscht

1. Liest Maria den Brief?

2. Isst Michael die Suppe?

3. Macht Maria den Fernseher an?

4. Kauft Michael das Auto?

5. Zieht Michael die Hose aus?

6. Trägt Maria den Rock?

7. Bestellt[1] Michael das Schnitzel?

8. Besucht Michael seinen Freund?

9. Kämmt Maria ihr Haar?

10. Bläst Michael die Kerzen aus[2]?

3.4 Word order: dependent clauses

3.4 *Wortstellung: Nebensätze.* Word order in dependent clauses in German is formally introduced here with the subordinating conjunctions *wenn* and *weil*. Though sts. can place the verb correctly in exercises, few will achieve this in spontaneous speech in the first year. Many will not even try to use dependent clauses. Verb-last position in dependent clauses is one of the last word-order rules acquired. Sts. will have fewer problems if they are given many chances to hear this word order in your speech before they are required to use it.

Sts. may be familiar with other terms. Point out that the terms "main clause" and "independent clause" can be used interchangeably, as can "dependent clause" and "subordinate clause."

Use a conjunction such as **wenn** (*when, if*) or **weil** (*because*) to add a modifying clause to a sentence.

Mehmet hört Musik, **wenn** er traurig ist.	*Mehmet listens to music whenever he is sad.*
Renate geht nach Hause, **weil** sie müde ist.	*Renate is going home because she is tired.*

In the preceding examples, the first clause is the main clause. The clause introduced by a conjunction is called a *dependent clause*. In German, the verb in a dependent clause occurs at the end of the clause.

[1]bestellen *to order* (*in a restaurant*) [2]Bläst ... aus? *Is* [*he*] *blowing out . . . ?*

When **wenn** or **weil** begins a clause, the conjugated verb appears at the end of the clause.

MAIN CLAUSE	DEPENDENT CLAUSE
Ich bleibe im Bett,	wenn ich krank **bin.**
I stay in bed	*when I am sick.*

In sentences beginning with a dependent clause, the entire clause acts as the first element in the sentence. The verb of the main clause comes directly after the dependent clause, separated by a comma. As in all German statements, the verb is in second position. The subject of the main clause follows the verb.

I	II	III
DEPENDENT CLAUSE	VERB	SUBJECT
Wenn ich krank bin,	bleibe	ich	im Bett.
When I'm sick, I stay in bed.		
Weil sie müde ist,	geht	Renate	nach Hause.
Because she's tired, Renate is going home.		

Übung 8   Warum denn?

Beantworten Sie die Fragen.

MODELL: Warum gehst du nicht in die Schule? → Weil ich krank bin.

1. Warum gehst du nicht in die Schule?   a. Durst haben
2. Warum liegt dein Bruder im Bett?   b. krank sein
3. Warum esst ihr denn schon wieder?   c. traurig sein
4. Warum kommt Nora nicht mit ins Kino?   d. Langeweile haben
5. Warum sieht Jutta schon wieder fern?   e. Angst haben
6. Warum sitzt du allein in deinem Zimmer?   f. glücklich sein
7. Warum trinken sie Bier?   g. lernen müssen
8. Warum machst du denn das Licht an?   h. müde sein
9. Warum singt Jens den ganzen Tag?   i. Hunger haben
10. Warum bleibst du zu Hause?   j. keine Zeit haben

Übung 9   Ist das immer so?

Sagen Sie, wie das für andere Personen ist und wie das für Sie ist.

MODELL: s1: Was macht Albert, wenn er müde ist?
s2: Wenn Albert müde ist, geht er nach Hause.
s1: Und du?
s2: Wenn ich müde bin, trinke ich einen Kaffee.

1. Albert ist müde.   a. Sie trifft Michael.
2. Maria ist glücklich.   b. Er geht nach Hause.
3. Herr Ruf hat Durst.   c. Sie fährt mit dem Taxi.
4. Frau Wagner ist in Eile.   d. Sie kauft einen Hamburger.
5. Heidi hat Hunger.   e. Er trinkt eine Cola.
6. Frau Schulz hat Ferien.   f. Er geht zum Arzt.
7. Hans hat Angst.   g. Er ruft: „Mama, Mama".
8. Stefan ist krank.   h. Sie fliegt nach Deutschland.

3.5 Dependent clauses and separable-prefix verbs

3.5. As was pointed out in section 3.4, most sts. cannot be expected to handle word order in dependent clauses correctly in spontaneous speech. Many will not even try to use dependent clauses. We introduce dependent word order here primarily for reading purposes so that sts. learn to look for the main verb of a clause in the right places.

As you know, the prefix of a separable-prefix verb occurs at the end of an independent clause.

Rolf **steht** immer früh **auf.**	*Rolf always gets up early.*

In a dependent clause, the prefix is attached to the verb form, which is placed at the end of the clause.

Rolf ist immer müde, wenn er früh **aufsteht.**	*Rolf is always tired when he gets up early.*
Helga, bitte **mach** das Fenster nicht **auf!** Es wird kalt, wenn du es **aufmachst.**	*Helga, please don't open the window. It gets cold when you open it.*

When there are two verbs in a dependent clause, such as a modal verb and an infinitive, the modal verb comes last, following the infinitive.

INDEPENDENT CLAUSE	Rolf **muss** früh **aufstehen.**	*Rolf has to get up early.*
DEPENDENT CLAUSE	Er ist müde, wenn er früh **aufstehen muss.**	*He is tired when he has to get up early.*
INDEPENDENT CLAUSE	Helga hat kein Geld. Sie **kann** nichts **machen.**	*Helga doesn't have any money. She can't do anything.*
DEPENDENT CLAUSE	Sie hat Langeweile, weil sie nichts **machen kann.**	*She's bored because she can't do anything.*

Übung 10   Warum ist das so?

Üb. 10. Tell sts. that the choice of subject pronoun in column 2 helps them identify suitable responses for the questions in column 1 more quickly. Follow up next day in class by pairing sts. up to do the exercise orally.

MODELL: Jürgen ist wütend, weil er immer so früh aufstehen muss.

1. Jürgen ist wütend.	a. Sie muss noch einkaufen.
2. Silvia ist froh.	b. Er muss immer so früh aufstehen.
3. Claire ist in Eile.	c. Seine Freundin nimmt ihn zur Uni mit.
4. Josef ist traurig.	d. Er sieht immer fern.
5. Thomas geht nicht zu Fuß.	e. Sie kann nicht schwimmen.
6. Willi hat selten Langeweile.	f. Er will seine Eltern besuchen.
7. Marta hat Angst vor Wasser.	g. Melanie ruft ihn nicht an.
8. Mehmet fährt in die Türkei.	h. Sie muss heute nicht arbeiten.

Ereignisse und Erinnerungen

GOALS

The purpose of *Kapitel 4* is to give sts. chances to interact in situations dealing with past events. We formally introduce the perfect tense for this purpose. The simple past forms will be formally introduced in *Kapitel 7* and *9*.

In **Kapitel 4,** you will begin to talk about things that happened in the past: your own experiences and those of others. You will also talk about different kinds of memories.

PRE-TEXT ACTIVITIES
1. Use association techniques to introduce the forms of the perfect tense. In these activities, remember to follow the natural sequence of having sts. listen before they speak. **2.** Before each class period, spend about 5 minutes telling the sts. what you did the previous day. Clarify any new vocabulary. For additional listening practice, ask the sts. what they did the day before, but state the questions so they can answer with *ja* or *nein* or by raising their hands: *Wer hat gestern Hausaufgaben gemacht? Heben Sie bitte die Hand! Wer ist gestern in die Bibliothek gegangen? Wer hat gestern die Wäsche gewaschen? Wer hat gestern ferngesehen? usw.*

Themen

Der Alltag
Urlaub und Freizeit
Geburtstage und Jahrestage
Ereignisse

Kulturelles

KLI: Universität und Studium
Musikszene: „Du hast den Farbfilm vergessen" (Nina Hagen)
KLI: Feiertage und Bräuche
Filmclip: *Jenseits der Stille* (Caroline Link)
Videoecke: Feste und Feiern

Lektüren

Anekdote: Sternzeichen (Rafik Schami)
Film: *Jenseits der Stille* (Caroline Link)

Strukturen

4.1 Talking about the past: the perfect tense
4.2 Strong and weak past participles
4.3 Dates and ordinal numbers
4.4 Prepositions of time: **um, am, im**
4.5 Past participles with and without **ge–**

Kiymet Benita Bock:
Kindheitserinnerungen (1996)

Chapter opening artwork: The naive or childlike appearance of this painting might be due to the fact that the artist is not professionally trained and is expressing her feelings and memories in a very original way. The artist calls this picture *"Meine Pferde."*

Suggestion: Let students look at the picture. Use an *Assoziogramm* on the board to record their ideas. The following questions may help them get started. *Was sehen Sie auf dem Bild? Welches Tier ist das vielleicht? Wer hat das Bild gemalt? Wie alt ist der/die Maler/in? Wo hat er/sie das Bild gemalt? Welche Farben hat er/sie benutzt?*

Kunst und Künstler

Kiymet Benita Bock (geb. 1958) ist eine türkisch-deutsche Künstlerin aus der Gruppe der „Schlumper". Diese Gruppe wurde 1984 gegründet. Sie nannte sich Schlumper, weil ihr Atelier[1] im Stadthaus Schlump in Hamburg war. Die Schlumper sind geistig behinderte[2] Künstler, die in den letzten Jahren weltweite Anerkennung[3] gefunden haben. Das Bild von Kiymet Benita Bock entstand 1996 und ist ein Beispiel für Naive Kunst.

Schauen Sie sich das Bild an und beantworten Sie die folgenden Fragen.

1. Welche Personen und Tiere sehen Sie auf dem Bild? Wie sehen sie aus?
2. Welche Farben gibt es auf dem Bild? Welchen Eindruck[4] gibt das dem Bild?
3. Welche Assoziationen weckt das Bild?
4. Warum, glauben Sie, heißt das Bild *Kindheitserinnerungen*?

[1]*studio*   [2]*geistig ... mentally handicapped*   [3]*recognition*   [4]*impression*

Situationen

Der Alltag

Grammatik 4.1

Vocabulary Display
In this section the focus is on the past participles of verbs without separable prefixes. Present the vocabulary in the usual manner: (1) presentation, (2) receptive recall, (3) choral response, (4) productive recall. If your sts. enjoy performing for one another, you can turn off the projector and ask for volunteers to act out scenes from the transparency while the other sts. guess the expression. When talking about another st., they must use the 2nd-person form: *Du bist in die Uni gegangen* or *Du hast geduscht* rather than *ich bin* or *ich habe*. Also have them use the expression in the form of a question: *Hast du geduscht? gefrühstückt? usw.* Books should be closed. Next, have sts. work in pairs for 1–2 minutes, describing their activities of the previous day. You can also use the PF to present and review activities in the perfect tense. To help sts. remember which verbs take *haben* and which ones take *sein*, the verbs appearing in this display and in the one introducing the following section are color-coded: red with *sein* to help them associate the verbs with change and blue with *haben* for no such association.

Ich habe geduscht.

Ich habe gefrühstückt.

die Universität

Ich bin in die Uni gegangen.

Ich bin in einem Kurs gewesen.

Ich habe mit meinen Freunden Kaffee getrunken.

nach Hause

Ich bin nach Hause gekommen.

Ich habe zu Mittag gegessen.

Ich bin nachmittags zu Hause geblieben.

Ich habe abends gelernt.

Situation 1   Umfrage: Letzte Woche

Sit. 1. Preteach/review vocabulary *vor Mitternacht, stundenlang* and practice pronunciation. Turn the follow-up into an association activity (see the IM) to practice the present perfect verb forms in the 3rd-person singular.

MODELL: s1: Hast du Pizza zum Frühstück gegessen?
s2: Ja.
s1: Unterschreib bitte hier.

UNTERSCHRIFT

1. Hast du Pizza zum Frühstück gegessen?   _____
2. Hast du kalten Kaffee getrunken?   _____
3. Bist du mit dem Fahrrad zur Uni gefahren?   _____
4. Bist du abends zu Hause geblieben?   _____
5. Hast du im Bett Cola getrunken?   _____
6. Hast du stundenlang telefoniert?   _____
7. Hast du in der Bibliothek gearbeitet?   _____
8. Hast du viele Hausaufgaben gemacht?   _____

9. Bist du vor Mitternacht ins Bett
gegangen?   _____

10. Hast du deine Freunde zum Essen
eingeladen?   _____

11. Hast du viele E-Mails geschrieben?   _____

 Situation 2   Dialog: Das Fest

Sit. 2. (See the IM.) Work with sts.' books either opened or closed. With sts.' books closed, ask the following focus questions. Questions for first listening: *Wie geht es Silvia? Wo war sie gestern Abend? Was hat sie da gemacht?* Questions for second listening: *Warum, glaubt Jürgen, ist Silvia müde? Wann ist sie nach Hause gekommen?*

Silvia und Jürgen sitzen in der Mensa und essen zu Mittag.

SILVIA: Ich bin furchtbar <u>müde</u>.

JÜRGEN: Bist du wieder so spät ins Bett <u>gegangen</u>?

SILVIA: Ja. Ich bin heute früh erst um vier Uhr nach Hause <u>gekommen</u>.

JÜRGEN: Wo <u>warst</u> du denn so lange?

SILVIA: Auf einem Fest.

JÜRGEN: <u>Bis um vier Uhr früh</u>?

SILVIA: Ja, ich habe ein paar alte Freunde <u>getroffen</u> und wir haben uns sehr gut unterhalten.

JÜRGEN: Kein Wunder, <u>dass du müde bist</u>!

Situation 3   Das letzte Mal

Sit. 3. First, review the time expressions and days of the week. Point out that *vor* can be used with other time expressions: *vor zwei Wochen, Monaten, Jahren.* Then, model pronunciation for sentences 1–12, and respond to the questions creatively as sts. repeat them. Model possible responses using *nie* for sts. who may never have done a certain activity: **1.** *Ich habe noch nie mein Auto gewaschen. Ich habe kein Auto.* **3.** *Ich bin noch nie ins Theater gegangen. Ich gehe lieber ins Kino.* **6.** *Ich bin noch nie in die Disko gegangen. Ich tanze nicht. usw.*

MODELL: Wann hast du mit deiner Mutter gesprochen? →
Ich habe gestern mit meiner Mutter gesprochen.

heute	gestern Abend	noch nie
gestern	vorgestern	vor zwei Tagen
letzten Montag	letztes Jahr	letzte Woche

1. Wann hast du dein Auto gewaschen?
2. Wann hast du geduscht?
3. Wann bist du ins Theater gegangen?
4. Wann hast du deine beste Freundin / deinen besten Freund getroffen?
5. Wann hast du einen Film gesehen?
6. Wann bist du in die Disko gegangen?
7. Wann hast du gelernt?
8. Wann bist du einkaufen gegangen?
9. Wann hast du eine Zeitung gelesen?
10. Wann hast du das Geschirr gespült?
11. Wann bist du spät ins Bett gegangen?
12. Wann bist du den ganzen Abend zu Hause geblieben?

Zum Schreiben: Ein Tagebuch

Schreiben Sie auch ein Tagebuch. Vielleicht haben Sie das früher schon einmal auf Englisch gemacht. Machen Sie sich zuerst ein paar Notizen. Was ist letzte Woche passiert? Was haben Sie gemacht? Was wollen Sie nicht vergessen?

MODELL: Letzte Woche habe/bin ich ...

> 28. Juli 2011
>
> Habe einen total coolen Jungen kennengelernt! Er heißt Billy, eigentlich Paul, aber er sieht aus wie Billy Idol. Er ist total süß!! Habe gleich einen Brief an Geli geschrieben und ihr von Billy erzählt. Warte jetzt auf Gelis Antwort... Außerdem haben wir Zeugnisse bekommen. Das war nicht so gut...

Juttas Tagebuch

Urlaub und Freizeit

Grammatik 4.2

Jutta ist ins Schwimmbad gefahren.

Sie hat in der Sonne gelegen.

Sie ist geschwommen.

Sie hat Musik gehört.

Jens und Robert haben Postkarten geschrieben.

Sie sind in den Bergen gewandert.

Sie haben Tennis gespielt.

Sie haben viel gelesen.

Universität und Studium

- Wann haben Sie mit dem Studium am College oder an der Universität angefangen?
- Welche Voraussetzungen[1] (High-School-Abschluss, Prüfungen usw.) braucht man für ein Studium?
- An welchen Universitäten haben Sie sich beworben[2]?
- Studieren Sie an einer privaten oder einer staatlichen Hochschule[3]?
- Müssen Sie Studiengebühren[4] bezahlen?
- Wie lange dauert Ihr Studium voraussichtlich?
- Welchen Abschluss[5] haben Sie am Ende Ihres Studiums?
- Was für Kurse müssen Sie belegen?

Eine Demonstration gegen Studiengebühren in Hamburg

Die meisten Universitäten in Deutschland sind öffentliche Universitäten. Es gibt nur wenige private Hochschulen. Bis 2005 mussten Studenten für ihr erstes Studium keine Studiengebühren zahlen. Das ist jetzt anders. Die Bundesländer dürfen Studierende nun zur Kasse bitten und viele, z. B. Bayern, tun das seit einigen Jahren auch. Die Gebühren liegen in den meisten Bundesländern bei circa 500 Euro pro Semester. In anderen Bundesländern, z. B. in Sachsen, müssen Studierende für ihr Erststudium weiterhin keine Studiengebühren bezahlen.

Viele Studenten arbeiten während des Semesters und in den Semesterferien. Nur knapp 20% bekommen ein Stipendium oder eine finanzielle Hilfe vom Staat, das sogenannte BAföG (Bundesausbildungsförderungsgesetz[6]). Der BAföG-Höchstsatz[7] beträgt zur Zeit 670 Euro im Monat.

Um an einer Universität zu studieren, braucht man normalerweise das Abitur[8]. Die traditionellen Abschlüsse an deutschen Universitäten waren das Diplom, das Staatsexamen und der Magister. Nun gibt es in Deutschland und in Europa die neuen Bachelor- und Masterstudiengänge. Diese Studiengänge wurden eingeführt, um international vergleichbare[9] Studienabschlüsse zu haben. Ein Bachelorstudium dauert meist drei Jahre, ein Masterstudium zwei weitere Jahre.

Etwa 12% der Studierenden in Deutschland kommen aus dem Ausland[10], die meisten aus China (10,3%), aus der Türkei (9,3%), aus Polen (5%) und aus Russland (5%). Zum Vergleich: Der Anteil ausländischer Studenten in den USA beträgt 3,5%. Allerdings studieren relativ wenige Deutsche im Ausland, nämlich nur ca. 5%, die meisten in den Niederlanden, in Österreich und in Großbritannien. US-amerikanische Studenten gehen allerdings noch seltener für ein Semester oder länger ins Ausland, nämlich nur 1%.

[1]prerequisites [2]sich ... applied [3]college, university [4]fees, tuition [5]degree; diploma [6]federal law for the promotion of higher education [7]maximum amount [8]roughly: high school diploma [9]comparable [10]aus ... from abroad

KLI. (1) Set up the prereading questions as an interview. Practice changing the questions from *Sie* to *du*. Then ask sts. to interview each other while jotting down their partner's answers. Finally, put a summary on the board. Use three columns: an abbreviated question column, a column for your sts.' country to be filled in now, and a column for Germany to be filled in later. (2) Ask sts. to work in groups, to read the KLI note, and to find and jot down the differences between Germany and their country following the format on the board. Set a time limit of approximately 5 minutes. When the time is up, complete the chart on the board by filling in the column for Germany according to your sts.' answers. (3) Follow up by summarizing the major differences between the two systems.

Situation 5 Bildgeschichte: Familie Wagner im Urlaub am Strand

Sit. 5. (See the IM for suggestions on using a narration series.) Sentences: **1.** *Familie Wagner ist ganz früh mit dem Auto losgefahren.* **2.** *Sie sind pünktlich an ihrem Ferienhaus angekommen.* **3.** *Paula und Ernst haben am Strand eine große Sandburg gebaut.* **4.** *Ernst und Andrea haben Volleyball gespielt.* **5.** *Josie hat in der Sonne gelegen und ein Buch gelesen.* **6.** *Uli hat in einem Liegestuhl geschlafen.* **7.** *Andrea hat neue Spielkameraden gefunden und mit ihnen Frisbee gespielt.* **8.** *Am letzten Tag hat es geregnet. Deshalb sind alle den ganzen Tag im Ferienhaus geblieben.*

Receptive recall: Ask sts. to tell you which pictures you are describing: *Andrea hat neue Spielkameraden gefunden und mit ihnen Frisbee gespielt. (Bild 7); Familie Wagner ist ganz früh mit dem Auto losgefahren. (Bild 1); Josie hat in der Sonne gelegen und ein Buch gelesen. (Bild 5) usw.*
Choral repetition. Productive recall: Now ask the sts. to tell you what occurs in each picture: *Was haben die Wagners in Bild 1 gemacht? In Bild 2? usw.* Personalization: *Von den Dingen, die Familie Wagner gemacht hat, schreiben Sie 3 Dinge auf, die Sie in Ihrem letzten Urlaub gemacht haben. Haben Sie etwas getan, gesehen, unternommen usw., was Familie Wagner nicht gemacht hat?*

AA. Use the narration series to review vocabulary about months, seasons, and weather, and have sts. describe the members of the family.

Situation 6 Dialog: Jens' und Juttas Wochenende

Sit. 6. (See the IM.) **(1)** Set the scene by reminding sts. who Jens and Jutta are and by telling them where they are and what they are discussing. **(2)** Preteach the new vocabulary: *das hört sich wirklich toll an* (as a stock phrase), *auf jeden Fall.* **(3)** Ask sts. to open their books; play the dialogue for them at least twice while they fill in the blanks. **(4)** Write sts.' answers on the board, or ask them to write their answers on the board, while making any necessary corrections. **(5)** Ask sts. to work in groups to determine the infinitives of the participles, and to put these verbs in groups according to their past participle formation and their choice of auxiliary. **(6)** Review sts.' answers.

Es ist Montag. Jutta und Jens treffen sich auf dem Schulhof ihrer Schule und reden über ihr Wochenende.

> JENS: Hallo, Jutta!
> JUTTA: Grüß dich, Jens! Was hast du am Wochenende <u>gemacht</u>?
> JENS: Ach, nichts Besonderes. Ich habe <u>ferngesehen</u> und Musik <u>gehört</u>. Es war langweilig. Und du?
> JUTTA: Ich bin mit meinen Eltern in die Berge <u>gefahren</u>. Wir sind viel <u>gewandert</u> und haben sogar ein Picknick gemacht. Das war ganz super.
> JENS: Das hört sich wirklich toll an!
> JUTTA: Ja, auf jeden Fall. Komm doch das nächste Mal mit.
> JENS: Au ja, gern.

Am Wochenende haben wir gefeiert.

Schauen Sie auf die Bilder und finden Sie die passende Antwort auf jede Frage.

Sit. 7. Tell sts. that there are two strategies for completing the task: **1.** their knowledge of the characters' identities and **2.** the grammatical number of the subject pronoun and verb in the responses. Sts. will recognize most of the characters based on their appearance in activities in *Kontakte* thus far. Sts. can look at the pictures and find the proper responses based on what they see the characters doing. When students are not sure of a character's identity, they can look at the form of the pronoun and the verb. Point out that sentences 1-2 go with *sie* plus singular verb, sentences 3-4 with *sie* plus plural verb, and sentences 5-8 with *er* plus singular verb. The activities in this exercise are consistent with what sts. have discovered and will discover about these characters. For example, in Sit. 4 sts. read Jutta's diary entry in which she writes *Habe einen total coolen Jungen kennengelernt*. Mention other related facts as well, to make the contexts come alive. *Die Frischs wohnen in der Schweiz. Michael ist mit Maria verlobt.*

1. ____f____ Was hat Frau Ruf am Freitag gemacht?
2. ____e____ Was hat Jutta am Samstag gemacht?
3. ____a____ Was haben Jutta und Hans am Sonntag gemacht?
4. ____c____ Was haben die Frischs am Sonntag gemacht?
5. ____b____ Was hat Michael am Samstag gemacht?
6. ____d____ Was hat Jens am Sonntag gemacht?
7. ____g____ Was hat Herr Ruf am Freitag gemacht?
8. ____h____ Was hat Richard am Samstag gemacht?

a. Sie haben den Hund gebadet.
b. Er hat mit Maria zu Abend gegessen.
c. Sie sind in den Bergen gewandert.
d. Er hat stundenlang ferngesehen.
e. Sie hat Billy kennengelernt.
f. Sie ist nach Augsburg gefahren.
g. Er hat für seine Familie die Wäsche gewaschen.
h. Er ist zum Strand gefahren.

Musikszene

Musikszene. Note: The version included in the *Kontakte* iTunes iMix is actually sung by Gesine Franke and the Traminer from Dresden who recorded the film clip „Du hast den Farbfilm vergessen" on the island of Hiddensee in 2007. It is available on YouTube and provides a nice visual rendering of the lyrics.

„Du hast den Farbfilm vergessen" (1974, Ostdeutschland)   *Nina Hagen*

Nina Hagen

Biografie Nina Hagen wurde 1955 in der damaligen DDR geboren. Sie ist die Stieftochter von Wolf Biermann, einem bekannten Liedermacher. Beide verließen 1976 die DDR. Nina Hagen gilt als die deutsche „Godmother" des Punk. Neben ihrer Karriere als Sängerin und Songwriterin ist sie auch als Schauspielerin berühmt geworden. Ihr Hit „Du hast den Farbfilm vergessen" wird von vielen gesungen. Die Version hier stammt von Gesine Franke und den Traminern.

Vor dem Hören Machen Sie gern Fotos? Haben Sie schon mal Schwarz-Weiß-Fotos gemacht?

Nach dem Hören
Beantworten Sie die Fragen.

1. Wo ist die Sängerin?
2. Wie heißt ihr Freund?
3. Welche Farben nennt sie?
4. Welche Fotos hat der Freund von ihr gemacht?
5. Warum ist es schlimm, dass der Freund den Farbfilm vergessen hat?
6. Was passiert, wenn der Freund den Farbfilm noch einmal vergisst?

Answers: 1. am Strand (von Hiddensee); 2. Micha or Michael; 3. blau, weiß, grün; 4. im Bikini, am FKK, im Mini; 5. weil niemand glaubt, wie schön es dort war; 6. sie verlässt ihn. **Notes:** Hiddensee is an island just west of Rügen. It used to be a favorite vacation destination in GDR times and continues to attract a great number of tourists. *FKK* is short for *Freikörperkultur*. Here it refers to a nudist beach. *Mini* is short for *Minirock*.

iMix Link: This song is available for purchase at the iTunes store in a special iMix created for *Kontakte*. For more information about accessing the playlist, go to **Connect German** (www.connectgerman.com).

Miniwörterbuch

damalig	former	**gelten als**	to be known as
verlassen, verließ, verlassen	to leave	der **Strand**, die **Strände**	beach

Suggestion: Ask sts. to look at the photo and read the short *Biografie*. Ask a few questions to verify understanding. Ask the *Vor dem Hören* questions and elicit a few answers. Then go over the *Nach dem Hören* questions, making sure that sts. understand them, and play the song several times. After each playing ask sts. what they have understood so far. Write it on the board. Play the first two stanzas for questions 1 and 2, the chorus for question 3, and the second set of stanzas for questions 4, 5, and 6.

 Situation 8   Umfrage: Hast du das gemacht?

Musikszene. Note: Nina Hagen is a German singer, songwriter, and actress. She was born in 1955 in East Berlin. When her stepfather, Wolf Biermann, was forced to leave the GDR in 1976, she openly declared her solidarity with him. Because of her own and her stepfather's popularity, she and her mother were allowed to emigrate the same year. Nina Hagen started her singing career in the 1970s with the band *Automobil*. The song "Du hast den Farbfilm vergessen" (1974) made her a young star. It is the most famous song of her early career and has achieved cult status. Nina Hagen has released many albums—first with her *Nina Hagen Band*, founded in 1977, later as a solo artist—and is known today as the German godmother of punk. In addition to her singing and acting careers, she continues to attract media attention with her theories about UFOs, spirituality, and religion as well as her work in animal welfare.

Was hast du am Wochenende gemacht?

UNTERSCHRIFT

1. Hast du bis mittags geschlafen? _____
2. Bist du tanzen gegangen? _____
3. Hast du mit jemandem gefrühstückt? _____
4. Hast du Sport getrieben? _____
5. Hast du Hausaufgaben gemacht? _____
6. Hast du eine E-Mail geschrieben? _____
7. Bist du ins Kino gegangen? _____
8. Hast du ein Buch gelesen? _____
9. Hast du Wäsche gewaschen? _____
10. Hast du gesimst? _____

Geburtstage und Jahrestage

Grammatik 4.3–4.4

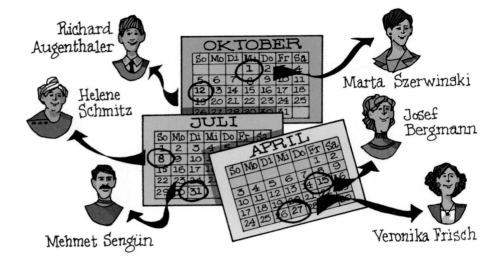

Marta hat am ersten Oktober Geburtstag.
Richard hat am zwölften Oktober Geburtstag.
Frau Schmitz hat am achten Juli Hochzeitstag.
Mehmet ist am einunddreißigsten Juli geboren.
Josef ist am fünfzehnten April geboren.
Veronika hat am siebenundzwanzigsten April Geburtstag.

 Situation 9   Dialog: Welcher Tag ist heute?

Bringen Sie die Sätze in die richtige Reihenfolge.

Marta und Sofie sitzen im Café. Sofie fragt:

   _3_   Nein, welches Datum?

   _2_   Montag.

   _6_   Wirklich? Ich dachte, er hat im August Geburtstag.

   _8_   Hast du denn schon ein Geschenk?

   _1_   Welcher Tag ist heute?

   _4_   Ach so, der dreißigste.

   _5_   Der dreißigste? Mann, dann ist ja heute Willis Geburtstag!

   _9_   Das ist es ja! Ich hab' noch nicht einmal ein Geschenk.

   _7_   Nein, Christian hat im August Geburtstag, aber Willi im Mai.

  _10_   Na, dann viel Spaß beim Geschenke kaufen!

Feiertage und Bräuche[1]

- Welches sind die Familienfeste in Ihrem Land?
- Was macht man an diesen Festen?
- Wer feiert[2] zusammen?
- Kennen Sie deutsche Feiertage und Bräuche?
  Wenn ja, welche?

Photo questions. *Wie ist das Wetter? Was sehen Sie? Was machen die Leute? Wie sehen sie aus?*

Der Adventskalender: Ein deutscher Exportartikel in christlicher Tradition ist über 100 Jahre alt. Amerika ist das Importland Nummer 1.

- Weihnachten in Deutschland: An welchen Tagen feiert man?
- Welche deutschen Weihnachtstraditionen kennen Sie?
- Wie feiern die Deutschen am liebsten Weihnachten? Analysieren Sie die Umfrage.

Auf dem Christkindlmarkt in München im Jahre 1897

TAG FÜR TAG: Adventskalender lassen die Erwartungen steigen

Cultural note. This is a reproduction of a colored woodcut made in 1897 after a drawing by P. Bauer. **KLI.** (See the IM.) Bring in an *Adventskalender* and have sts. take turns opening windows/doors and describing what they see behind them. Sts. may not be familiar with these calendars and not know that the window for each day in December is opened until Christmas Eve arrives.

[1]*customs*   [2]*celebrates*

FOCUS-FRAGE

„Wo verbringen Sie Weihnachten?"

EIN FAMILIENFEST ZU HAUSE

von 1300 Befragten* antworteten

zu Hause	**73 %**
bei den Eltern/Kindern	**21 %**
bei Freunden	**3 %**
im Urlaub	**3 %**

83 Prozent der Deutschen verbringen Weihnachten im Kreis der Familie, 7 Prozent zusammen mit dem Partner, 6 Prozent mit Freunden, 4 Prozent feiern alleine.

* Repräsentative Umfrage des Sample-Instituts für FOCUS im Dezember

Cultural note. Apart from *Neujahr* (January 1), *Maifeiertag / Tag der Arbeit* (May 1), and the national holidays (Germany, October 3; Austria, October 26; Switzerland, August 1), most holidays are of religious origin. The most important ones are the following: *Karfreitag* (the Friday before Easter), *Ostern* (the first Sunday and Monday after the first full moon in spring, i.e., on or after March 21), *Christi Himmelfahrt* (the 6th Thursday after Easter), *Pfingsten* (the 7th Sunday and Monday after Easter), *Weihnachten* (December 25 and 26). Germany is 31% Catholic, 30% Protestant, 5% Muslim, and 2.5% Jewish. Austria is 66% Catholic, 4% Protestant, and 5% Muslim; Switzerland is 41% Catholic, 40% Protestant, and 5% Muslim.

Situation 10 Informationsspiel: Geburtstage

Sit. 10. The corresponding chart is in Appendix A.

MODELL: S2: Wann ist Willi geboren?
S1: Am dreißigsten Mai 1987.

Person	Geburtstag
Willi	30. Mai 1987
Sofie	9. November 1991
Claire	1. Dezember 1986
Melanie	3. April 1988
Nora	4. Juli 1994
Thomas	17. Januar 1994
Heidi	23. Juni 1991
mein(e) Partner(in)	
sein/ihr Vater	
seine/ihre Mutter	

Situation 11 Erfindungen und Entdeckungen

Sit. 11. Review numbers by having sts. first read the years. Ask sts. to work in pairs, alternating asking and answering questions. The sts. asking the questions cover the captions and write the name and date spoken by their partner. Nationality: Cyril Demian (Austria), Friedrich Staedtler (Germany), Emil Berliner (Germany), Joseph Cayetti (USA), Melitta Bentz (Germany), Laszlo Biro (Hungary), Peter Mitterhofer (Germany), Marie Curie (originally from Poland, lived and worked in France), Friedrich Herschel (originally German but lived in England), Alexander Fleming (England), Leif Eriksson (Norway).

MODELL: S1: Wer hat den Bleistift erfunden?
S2: _____.
S1: Wann hat er ihn erfunden?
S2: _____.

Cyril Demian
1829

Friedrich Staedtler
1662

Emil Berliner
1887

Joseph Cayetti
1857

Melitta Bentz
1908

Laszlo Biro
1938

Peter Mitterhofer
1864

das Toilettenpapier   **der Kugelschreiber**

der Bleistift   **der Kaffeefilter**   **die Schallplatte**

die Schreibmaschine   **das Akkordeon**

MODELL: S1: Wer hat das Radium entdeckt?

S2: _____.

S1: Wann hat sie es entdeckt?

S2: _____.

Suggestion: Have students look up additional information about these inventors and discoverers online.

Marie Curie
1898

Friedrich Herschel
1781

Alexander Fleming
1928

Leif Eriksson
1000

das Penizillin   **Amerika**   **das Radium**   **der Uranus**

 ### Situation 12 Interview

Sit. 12. Preteach any new vocabulary. Do the first half of the activity in one sitting and the second half in another. Or, select three lines of questions that are most pertinent to your class.

1. Wann bist du geboren (Tag, Monat, Jahr)? Wann ist dein Freund / deine Freundin geboren (Tag, Monat, Jahr)? Wann ist dein Vater / deine Mutter geboren (Tag, Monat, Jahr)?

2. Wann bist du in die Schule gekommen (Monat, Jahr)? Wann hast du angefangen zu studieren (Monat, Jahr)?

3. Was war der wichtigste Tag in deinem Leben? Was ist da passiert? In welchem Monat war das? In welchem Jahr?

4. In welchem Monat warst du zum ersten Mal verliebt? hast du zum ersten Mal Geld verdient? hast du einen Unfall gehabt?

5. An welchen Tagen in der Woche arbeitest du? hast du frei? gehst du ins Kino? besuchst du deine Eltern? gehst du in Vorlesungen? gehst du ins Computerlabor? gehst du in die Bibliothek?

6. Um wie viel Uhr stehst du auf? ist dein erster Kurs? gehst du nach Hause? gehst du ins Bett?

Lektüre

Vor dem Lesen

Lesen. Suggestions: Introduce the word *Sternzeichen*. Write several signs of the zodiac in German on the board: *Steinbock, Wassermann, Fische, Widder, Stier, Zwilling, Krebs, Löwe, Jungfrau, Waage, Skorpion, Schütze.* Ask sts. to complete *Vor dem Lesen* individually, then ask them to interview each other. Ask a few sts. what they found out about their partner. Next, ask sts. to read the *Miniwörterbuch,* to locate the words in *Vor dem Lesen* and in the text proper and to underline them.

A. Beantworten Sie die folgenden Fragen.

1. Wann haben Sie Geburtstag? Wissen Sie, um wie viel Uhr Sie geboren sind? Wie war das Wetter? Welche berühmten Persönlichkeiten sind am gleichen Tag wie Sie geboren?

2. Welches Sternzeichen sind Sie? Welche Eigenschaften hat Ihr Sternzeichen? Spielen Sternzeichen eine Rolle in Ihrem Leben?

B. Lesen Sie die Wörter im Miniwörterbuch. Suchen Sie sie in den Aktivitäten und im Text und unterstreichen Sie sie.

Miniwörterbuch

die **Eigenschaft**	characteristic	die **Geburt**	birth
Krebs	Cancer	**berühmt**	famous
sei	*here:* was	die **Persönlichkeit**	personality
ablehnen	to refuse	das **Sternzeichen**	sign of the zodiac
die **Schüchternheit**	shyness	der **Ausweis**	identification card
meiden	to avoid	die **Aprikose, -n**	apricot
die **Neigung**	inclination	der **Kampf**, die **Kämpfe**	battle, fight
trotz	despite	der **Berg, -e**	mountain
der **Schriftsteller**	writer	**hämisch**	gloatingly
der **Bahnhof**	train station	die **Begegnung**	encounter

Note: You may wish to explain that trains are generally very punctual in Germany. The phrase *am Bahnhof geboren* thus refers to Europeans being very conscious of time.

Sternzeichen

von Rafik Schami

„Typisch Krebs", sagt H., ein Bekannter aus Heidelberg. Er glaubt noch genau zu wissen, daß ich Ende Juni geboren sei. Wir haben zusammen studiert. Heute ist er erfolgreicher Astrologe. Nach fünfzehn Jahren sehen wir uns zum ersten Mal wieder. Er will mir sofort ein exaktes Horoskop erstellen. Als ich es ablehne,
5   führt er das auf die für Krebse angeblich typische Schüchternheit zurück.

„Nicht von ungefähr geht der Krebs seitlich. Er meidet jeden Konflikt, aber wenn es darauf ankommt, ist er sehr wehrhaft", denke ich laut. H. lacht. Typisch für den Krebs sei seine Neigung zur Kunst, entgegnet er.

Entscheidend für die gesamte Ausrichtung meines Lebens ist also seiner Meinung
10 nach mein Geburtstag gewesen. Und er spricht ständig von Achsen und Sternenkonstellationen. Er habe schon damals in Heidelberg sicher gewußt, daß ich trotz des Chemiestudiums in meinem tiefsten Innern ein Künstler sei. „Und was ist dann aus dir geworden, hm? Vielleicht ein Chemiker? Nein, ein Schriftsteller."

Araber feiern vieles, aber Geburtstage nie. Denn wenn man seinen Geburtstag
15 genau kennt, wird man nur älter. Mir kommen die Europäer manchmal so vor, als wären sie alle am Bahnhof geboren. Sie wissen nicht bloß das Datum, sondern sogar die genaue Uhrzeit ihrer Geburt. H., mein Bekannter, weiß auch die Temperatur und das Himmelsbild jenes Tages, sogar die berühmten Persönlichkeiten, die unter demselben Sternzeichen wie er auf die Welt kamen, hat er parat.

20 Als er geht, rufe ich meine Mutter in Damaskus an und frage sie, wann ich geboren wurde, denn ich mißtraue meinem Ausweis. „Anfang bis Mitte April", antwortet sie. „Die Aprikosen standen in voller Blüte. Wir mußten uns aber wegen der Kämpfe in der Hauptstadt in den Bergen verstecken. Deshalb konnten wir dich erst danach in der Hauptstadt registrieren lassen, das war dann Ende Juni."
25 Und ich freue mich hämisch auf die nächste Begegnung mit H., dem Astrologen.

Arbeit mit dem Text

A. Personen. Es gibt drei Personen im Text: H., Rafik Schami und Rafiks Mutter. Was erfahren wir über sie? Kreuzen Sie alles an, was richtig ist.

    1. H.
        ☒ a. Er hat mit Rafik Schami studiert.
        ☒ b. Er ist Astrologe.
        ☒ c. Er ist aus Heidelberg
        ☐ d. Er hat Chemie studiert.

2. Rafik Schami
☐ a. Er ist Krebs.
☐ b. Er hat Astrologie studiert.
☒ c. Er ist Schriftsteller.
☒ d. Er hat H. 15 Jahre nicht gesehen.

3. Rafiks Mutter
☒ a. Sie wohnt in Damaskus.
☐ b. Sie feiert gern ihren Geburtstag.
☒ c. Als Rafik geboren wurde, war sie in den Bergen.
☐ d. Sie liebt Aprikosen.

B. **Handlung.** Die folgenden Sätze fassen die Handlung zusammen. Bringen Sie sie in die richtige Reihenfolge.

___3___ Rafik lehnt ab.

___6___ Die Mutter erzählt Rafik, dass er im April geboren ist.

___2___ H. will für Rafik ein Horoskop erstellen.

___1___ H. trifft Rafik nach 15 Jahren wieder.

___5___ Als H. geht, ruft Rafik seine Mutter an.

___4___ H. meint, dass Rafik schon immer ein Künstler war.

C. **Inhalt.** Beantworten Sie die Fragen.

1. Welche Eigenschaften hat ein Krebs?
2. Warum feiern Araber ihren Geburtstag nicht?
3. Warum, glaubt Rafik, sind Europäer am Bahnhof geboren? (TIPP: Was sagt man über die Pünktlichkeit der deutschen Züge?)
4. Was weiß H. alles über seine eigene Geburt?
5. Warum steht in Rafiks Ausweis, dass er Ende Juni geboren ist?
6. Warum freut sich Rafik hämisch auf die nächste Begegnung mit seinem Bekannten?

Nach dem Lesen

Suggestions: Ask sts. to do the *Arbeit mit dem Text* activities in small groups. Collect and correct sts.' results after each activity. Ask sts. if they have had similar experiences, either with zodiac signs or with crosscultural encounters. Finally, go over the *Nach dem Lesen*, verifying that sts. understand Rafik Schami's short biography and what information they are supposed to find online. **Answers:** *Nach dem Lesen:* 1. 1946; 2. in Marnheim (Pfalz); 3. *Eine Hand voller Sterne* (1987), *Erzähler der Nacht* (1989), *Die dunkle Seite der Liebe* (2004), *Das Geheimnis des Kalligraphen* (2008), and others; 4. Nelly-Sachs-Preis (2007), Foreword Reviews' Book of the Year Awards (2009), Silver, for the English translation of *Die dunkle Seite der Liebe,* and others; 5. in 25 Sprachen; 6. Rafik Schami sagt, dass er den Olivenbaum, Oliven und Olivenkerne liebt. Er hat als Kind mit Olivenkernen Fußball gespielt. Er sagt, dass Olivenkerne, genau wie seine Geschichten, satt machen, aber nicht jedem schmecken.

Rafik Schami kommt aus Syrien. Er ist 1971 nach Deutschland ausgewandert, hat dort Chemie studiert und 1979 seinen Doktortitel bekommen. Seit 1982 ist er freier Schriftsteller und seit 2002 ist er Mitglied der Bayerischen Akademie der Künste. Die Geschichte *Sternzeichen* stammt aus dem Buch *Gesammelte Olivenkerne* von 1997. In diesem Buch schreibt Rafik Schami über seine Begegnungen mit Deutschen und Arabern. Suchen Sie im Internet Antworten auf die folgenden Fragen.

1. Wann ist Rafik Schami geboren?
2. Wo wohnt er?
3. Welche weiteren Bücher hat er geschrieben?
4. Welche Preise hat er bekommen?
5. In wie viele Sprachen wurden seine Bücher übersetzt?
6. Warum hat er sein Buch von 1997 *Gesammelte Olivenkerne* genannt?

Ereignisse

Grammatik 4.5

Vocabulary Display
This section introduces the participles for separable-
prefix verbs and reviews question forms. The first
picture series shows Frau Schulz's day. Assume the
role of Frau Schulz and have your sts. ask you
the questions, to which you make up suitable
responses in accordance with the pictures.

For the second picture series, ask the sts. to form
pairs; one st. should assume the role of Albert. Tell
sts. the setting is last Saturday. After completing
the sequence, the questioner should make up one
more question (Frame 7) to which "Albert" should
respond.

1. Wann sind Sie aufgewacht?
2. Wann sind Sie aufgestanden?
3. Wann sind Sie von zu Hause weggegangen?
4. Wann hat Ihr Kurs angefangen?
5. Wann hat Ihr Kurs aufgehört?
6. Wann sind Sie nach Hause gekommen?
7. Wann haben Sie unsere Prüfungen korrigiert?

1. Wann hast du eingekauft?
2. Wann hast du das Geschirr gespült?
3. Wann hast du mit deiner Freundin telefoniert?
4. Wann hast du ferngesehen?
5. Wann hast du dein Fahrrad repariert?
6. Wann bist du abends ausgegangen?

Situation 13 Michaels freier Tag

Sit. 13. Preteach new vocabulary: *tut mir leid* (as a set phrase), *denken an, zuerst, Keller, versuchen, dauern*. **Suggestion:** Photocopy the lines and cut them into strips. Then have sts. work in small groups to sequence them.

Michael telefoniert mit Maria. Sie reden über Michaels freien Tag. Bringen Sie die Sätze in die richtige Reihenfolge.

_10_ Tut mir leid, Maria, an dich habe ich leider nicht gedacht. Aber wenn du willst, können wir heute Abend etwas machen.

_2_ Hallo Maria. Hier ist Michael. Wie geht's?

_4_ Also, zuerst habe ich meinen kleinen Bruder besucht und sein Motorrad repariert.

_13_ Tschüss.

_8_ Dann habe ich meinen Keller aufgeräumt. Und am Abend bin ich ausgegangen, in die Kneipe, mit zwei Arbeitskollegen.

_6_ Nein, natürlich nicht. Mittags habe ich meinen neuen Nachbarn kennengelernt und wir haben zusammen Kaffee getrunken.

_7_ Und dann?

_1_ Schneider, guten Tag.

_9_ Und an mich hast du den ganzen Tag nicht gedacht, oder doch?

_11_ Also gut. Kannst du mich um acht Uhr abholen?

_3_ Ganz gut, danke. Du, sag mal, ich habe versucht, dich gestern anzurufen. Was hast du denn den ganzen Tag gemacht?

_12_ Ja gern. Bis dann um acht. Tschüss.

_5_ So, und das hat den ganzen Tag gedauert?

Situation 14 Interview: Gestern

Sit. 14. Have sts. do this activity in pairs. This is the first occurrence of the simple past *war*. It should not hinder comprehension. Follow-up questions: *Wer hat Italienisch gegessen? Was hat Barbara getrunken? Wann ist Tom ins Bett gegangen?*

1. Wann bist du aufgestanden?
2. Was hast du gefrühstückt?
3. Wie bist du zur Uni gekommen?
4. Was war dein erster Kurs?
5. Was hast du zu Mittag gegessen?
6. Was hast du getrunken?
7. Wen hast du getroffen?
8. Was hast du nachmittags gemacht?
9. Wie war das Wetter?
10. Wo bist du um sechs Uhr abends gewesen?
11. Was hast du abends gemacht?
12. Wann bist du ins Bett gegangen?
13. Ist gestern etwas Interessantes passiert? Was?

Situation 15 Informationsspiel: Zum ersten Mal

MODELL: S2: Wann hat Frau Gretter ihren ersten Kuss bekommen?
S1: Als sie dreizehn war.

	Herr Thelen	Frau Gretter	mein(e) Partner(in)
seinen/ihren/deinen ersten Kuss bekommen	als er 12 war	als sie 13 war	
zum ersten Mal ausgegangen	als er 14 war	als sie 15 war	
seinen/ihren/deinen Führerschein gemacht	mit 18	mit 25	
sein/ihr/dein erstes Bier getrunken	mit 16	mit 18	
seine/ihre/deine erste Zigarette geraucht	mit 21	noch nie	
zum ersten Mal nachts nicht nach Hause gekommen	noch nie	mit 21	

Sit. 15. The corresponding chart is in Appendix A. If your students do not respond well to the personal questions, you can ask them to adopt another persona (TV personality, pop star, politician, etc.) to answer the questions for the right column. Model pronunciation and have sts. repeat key words: *zum ersten Mal, Kuss, Führerschein, Zigarette, noch nie*. Write sample answers on the board, e.g., *Als ich 15 war.* or *Mit 15*. Also write the phrase *Ich habe/bin noch nie _____.* for students who have never done some of these things.

Filmlektüre
Jenseits der Stille

 Vor dem Lesen

A. Beantworten Sie die folgenden Fragen.

1. Was assoziieren Sie mit Stille?
2. Schauen Sie sich das Filmposter an: Wie sehen die beiden jungen Leute auf dem Poster aus?
3. Welche Charaktereigenschaften haben sie vielleicht? Finden Sie Adjektive.
4. Was machen sie mit ihren Händen?

Filmangaben

Titel: *Jenseits der Stille*
Genre: Drama
Erscheinungsjahr: 1996
Land: Deutschland
Dauer: 107 min
Regisseur: Caroline Link
Hauptrollen: Sylvie Testud, Tatjana Trieb, Howie Seago, Emmanuelle Laborit, Sibylle Canonica

Zeichensprache

B. Lesen Sie die Wörter im Miniwörterbuch. Suchen Sie sie im Text und unterstreichen Sie sie.

Inhaltsangabe

Die achtjährige Lara (Tatjana Trieb) lebt mit ihren Eltern in Bayern. Sie ist die Einzige in der Familie, die sprechen und hören kann. Ihre Eltern sind beide gehörlos. Lara muss ihnen bei der Verständigung im Alltag oft helfen. Weil sie die Zeichensprache und die Sprache der Außenwelt beherrscht, übersetzt sie für ihre Eltern: bei jedem Telefonat, auf der Bank, in der Schule. Zu ihrem Vater hat Lara ein besonders gutes Verhältnis.

Eines Tages bekommt Lara eine Klarinette von ihrer Tante Clarissa (Sibylle Canonica). Lara lernt auf dem Instrument zu spielen und ist richtig gut. Sie hat Talent. Doch nicht nur das: Sie entdeckt eine große Welt außerhalb der häuslichen Stille, nämlich die Musik. Mit 18 (Sylvie Testud) will sie nach Berlin auf das Konservatorium und dort Musik studieren. Ihren Eltern sagt sie zunächst nichts davon. Als sie es dann doch erfahren, gibt es Ärger. Vor allem ihr Vater (Howie Seago) ist wütend und eifersüchtig. Er weiß, dass Lara dabei ist, sich von ihnen zu lösen und Welten zu entdecken, die ihnen verschlossen bleiben.

Lara geht trotzdem nach Berlin und bereitet sich auf die Aufnahmeprüfung vor. Auch als ihre Mutter (Emmanuelle Laborit) plötzlich bei einem Verkehrsunfall ums Leben kommt, bessert sich das angespannte Verhältnis zwischen Vater und Tochter nicht. Aber in dem Moment, in dem Lara vor die Prüfungskommission des Konservatoriums tritt, sieht sie ihren Vater im Konzertsaal. Er will sie spielen sehen.

Miniwörterbuch

angespannt	tense
der **Ärger**	trouble
die **Aufnahme-**	entrance exam
prüfung	
beherrschen	to master
gehörlos	deaf
die **Prüfungs-**	examining
kommission	board
sich lösen	to free oneself
übersetzen	to translate
ums Leben kommen	to die
das **Verhältnis**	relationship
die **Verständigung**	communication
vorbereiten	to prepare
die **Zeichensprache**	sign language
zunächst	at first

Arbeit mit dem Text

Suggestion: Go over *Arbeit mit dem Text* making sure sts. understand all the words. Write unfamiliar words on the board with translations or convey the meaning in another manner. Ask sts. to work in pairs and decide whether the statements are true or false.

Welche Aussagen sind falsch? Verbessern Sie die falschen Aussagen.

1. Lara kann hören und sprechen, ihre Eltern aber nicht.
2. Lara hilft ihren Eltern im Alltag, weil sie gehörlos sind.
3. Lara hat ein besonders gutes Verhältnis zu ihrer Mutter.
4. Lara bekommt von ihrer Kusine Clarissa eine Klarinette.
5. Laras Eltern möchten, dass Lara nach Berlin auf das Konservatorium geht.
6. Das Verhältnis zwischen Lara und ihrem Vater wird nach dem Tod der Mutter auch nicht besser.
7. Laras Vater akzeptiert am Ende des Films Laras Wunsch, Musik zu studieren.

Filmclip

DVD, Kapitel 3, „Merry Christmas", 14:20–17:36 Min.

Laras Tante, Clarissa, ist eine begeisterte Musikerin. Es ist die Weihnachtszeit. Jedes Weihnachten spielt sie auf ihrer Klarinette, begleitet von ihrem Vater auf dem Klavier, allen Gästen etwas vor.

Schauen Sie sich die Szene an. Die folgenden Aussagen beschreiben die Szene in der falschen Reihenfolge. Bringen Sie die Sätze in die richtige Reihenfolge.

<u>3</u> Lara, ihre Mutter, ihre Tante und ihre Großmutter sind in der Küche und sprechen über das neue Baby.

<u>1</u> Lara hört ihrer Tante Clarissa und ihrem Großvater zu, wie sie Klavier und Klarinette spielen.

<u>2</u> Laras Vater erinnert sich°, als er ein Junge war und seine Schwester spielen sah.

<u>7</u> Tante Clarissa möchte, dass Lara bei ihr bleibt, und bittet sie, ihre Mutter zu fragen, ob sie darf.

<u>4</u> Tante Clarissa schenkt Lara ihre erste Klarinette zu Weihnachten.

<u>6</u> Tante Clarissa sagt, sie ist ein Talent.

<u>5</u> Lara spielt mit der Klarinette und schafft° es, einen Ton zu spielen.

<u>8</u> Laras Mutter sagt widerwillig° ja.

Filmclip. In diesem Filmausschnitt beginnt Lara, sich von der Welt ihrer Eltern zu entfernen. Sie entdeckt die Musik und ihr Talent. Ihr Vater erinnert sich daran, wie sich seine Schwester von ihm entfremdet hat, als sie die Musik entdeckte und er ihr nicht folgen konnte. Er hat Angst, dass sich dasselbe mit Lara wiederholt.

erinnert ... *remembers*

manages

reluctantly

Nach dem Lesen

Nach dem Lesen. Have sts. develop the open-ended story into a creative writing activity. Hints: Is Lara accepted into the conservatory? How does the relationship with her father develop? How does she feel about the development of events?

Kreatives Schreiben. Wie geht die Geschichte weiter? Lara schreibt einen Brief an ihre beste Freundin oder ihren besten Freund und erzählt, wie es nach dem Vorspielen weitergegangen ist. Liebe ... (Lieber ...), wie geht es dir? Letzte Woche habe ich hier in Berlin am Konservatorium vorgespielt ...

Situation 16 Rollenspiel: Das Studentenleben

Sit. 16. (See the IM.) Role for S2 appears in Appendix B. **Note:** If your students are using McGraw-Hill's **Connect** online *Arbeitsbuch,* they can do this *Rollenspiel* using the real-time, interactive **Video-Chat** feature.

s1: Sie sind Reporter/Reporterin einer Unizeitung in Österreich und machen ein Interview zum Thema: Studentenleben in Ihrem Land. Fragen Sie, was Ihr Partner / Ihre Partnerin gestern alles gemacht hat: am Vormittag, am Mittag, am Nachmittag und am Abend.

Videoecke

Perspektiven

> Was hast du gestern Abend gemacht?

Aufgabe 1 Gestern Abend

Wer hat das gestern Abend gemacht? Ordnen Sie die Aussagen den Personen zu.

Gestern Abend habe ich ein Buch gelesen.

Miniwörterbuch

die **Probe**	rehearsal	**zuwinken, zugewunken**	to wave
verbringen, verbracht	to spend	**ausprobieren**	to try out
aufpassen	to watch, look after	**sich beschäftigen**	to be busy
unternehmen, unternommen	to do, undertake	**(mit etwas)**	(with sth.)

1. Sandra _b_   2. Hend _a_   3. Martin _h_   4. Simone _c_

5. Sophie _d_   6. Jenny _g_   7. Pascal _e_   8. Tina _f_

a. Ich habe ein ägyptisches Essen gekocht.
b. Ich habe ein Buch gelesen.
c. Ich habe etwas in einer Kneipe getrunken.
d. Ich habe mit einer Freundin etwas Schönes gekocht.
e. Ich habe mir beim Chinesen etwas zu essen geholt.
f. Ich habe mit meiner Freundin Wein getrunken.
g. Ich habe zu Hause eine DVD geguckt.
h. Ich hatte Probe mit meiner Band.

Interviews

Tanja

Felicitas

- Wie hast du das letzte Wochenende verbracht?
- Was war das Interessanteste, was dir in den letzten Tagen passiert ist?
- Wann hast du Geburtstag?
- Wie hast du deinen letzten Geburtstag gefeiert?
- Welchen Feiertag findest du am besten? Warum?
- Was war der schönste Tag in deinem Leben?

Aufgabe 2 Tanja und Felicitas

Auf wen treffen die folgenden Aussagen zu, Tanja oder Felicitas?

	Tanja	Felicitas
1. Letztes Wochenende bin ich zu meinem Freund nach Jena gefahren.	☒	☐
2. Ich habe auf die Kinder von meiner Schwester aufgepasst.	☐	☒
3. Ich habe am 2. März Geburtstag.	☐	☒
4. Ich habe ein Fußballspiel der Champions League gesehen.	☒	☐
5. An meinem letzten Geburtstag habe ich Sushi gegessen.	☒	☐
6. An meinem letzten Geburtstag habe ich abends etwas mit Freunden unternommen.	☐	☒
7. Ich finde den Tag der Deutschen Einheit am besten.	☐	☒
8. Ich finde Weihnachten am schönsten.	☒	☐
9. Ich habe ein Stipendium gewonnen, um in Deutschland zu studieren.	☒	☐
10. Justin Timberlake hat mir zugewunken.	☐	☒

Aufgabe 3 Tanjas Wochenende

Was ist passiert? Bringen Sie die Sätze in die richtige Reihenfolge.

_1_ Ich bin am Samstag zu meinem Freund nach Jena gefahren.

_3_ Ich habe mir einen neuen Laptop gekauft.

_5_ Wir haben Programme installiert und alles ausprobiert.

_4_ Am Abend haben wir uns die ganze Zeit mit dem neuen Laptop beschäftigt.

_2_ Wir sind einkaufen gegangen.

Aufgabe 4 Dies und das

Beantworten Sie die folgenden Fragen.

1. Wer hat in Tanjas Heimatstadt das Champions League Spiel gewonnen?
2. Wann hat Tanja Geburtstag?
3. Warum findet Tanja Weihnachten so schön?
4. Was ist am schönsten Tag in Tanjas Leben passiert?
5. Wo war Felicitas mit den Kindern ihrer Schwester?
6. Warum findet Felicitas den Tag der deutschen Einheit so gut?
7. Was ist passiert, als Felicitas beim Justin Timberlake-Konzert war?

Wortschatz

Unterwegs	On the Road
die **Fahrkarte**, -n	ticket
der **Bahnhof**, ⸚e	train station
der **Führerschein**, -e	driver's license
der **Schlafwagen**, -	sleeping car
der **Unfall**, ⸚e	accident
der **Urlaub**, -e	vacation

Zeit und Reihenfolge	Time and Sequence
der **Abend**, -e (R)	evening
am **Abend**	in the evening
der **Alltag**	daily routine
der **Nachmittag**, -e	afternoon
der **Vormittag**, -e	late morning
das **Datum**, **Daten**	date
welches **Datum** ist heute?	what is today's date?
das **Mal**, -e	time
das letzte **Mal**	the last time
zum ersten **Mal**	for the first time
abends	evenings, in the evening
gestern	yesterday
gestern Abend	last night
letzt-	last
letzte **Woche**	last week
letzten **Montag**	last Monday
letzten **Sommer**	last summer
letztes **Wochenende**	last weekend
nachmittags	afternoons, in the afternoon
nachts	nights, at night
vorgestern	the day before yesterday
an (R)	on; in
am **Abend**	in the evening
am ersten **Oktober**	on the first of October
an welchem **Tag**?	on what day?
bis (R)	until
bis um **vier Uhr**	until four o'clock
einmal	once
warst du schon einmal ...?	were you ever . . . ?
erst	not until
erst um **vier Uhr**	not until four o'clock
früh (R)	in the morning
bis um vier Uhr **früh**	until four in the morning
schon (R)	already

seit	since; for
seit zwei **Jahren**	for two years
über	over
übers **Wochenende**	over the weekend
vor	ago
vor zwei **Tagen**	two days ago

Schule und Universität	School and University
die **Aufgabe**, -n	assignment
die **Bibliothek**, -en	library
die **Vorlesung**, -en	lecture
der **Kugelschreiber**, -	ballpoint pen
das **Abitur**	high school graduation exam
belegen	to take (a course)
halten, **hält**, **gehalten***	to hold
ein **Referat** halten	to give a paper / oral report

Feste und Feiertage	Holidays
der **Feiertag**, -e	holiday
der **Nationalfeiertag**, -e	national holiday
das **Familienfest**, -e	family celebration
(das) **Weihnachten**	Christmas

Ähnliche Wörter

die **Tradition**, -en; der **Muttertag**; der **Valentinstag**; das **Picknick**, -s

Ordinalzahlen	Ordinal Numbers
erst-	**acht-**
der erste **Oktober**	**neunt-**
zweit-	**zehnt-**
dritt-	**elft-**
viert-	**zwölft-**
fünft-	**dreizehnt-**
sechst-	**zwanzigst-**
siebt-	**hundertst-**

Sonstige Substantive	Other Nouns
die **Erinnerung**, -en	memory, remembrance
die **Kneipe**, -n	bar, tavern
die **Nachbarin**, -nen	female neighbor
die **Rechnung**, -en	bill; check (in restaurant)
die **Sandburg**, -en	sandcastle

*Strong and irregular verbs are listed in the **Wortschatz** with the third-person singular, if there is a stem-vowel change, and with the past participle. All verbs that use **sein** as the auxiliary in the present perfect tense are listed with **ist**.

die Umfrage, -n	survey
die Unizeitung, -en	university newspaper
der Keller, -	basement, cellar
der Kuss, ⸚e	kiss
der Liegestuhl, ⸚e	deck chair
der Nachbar, -n	male neighbor
der Strand, ⸚e	beach
das Ferienhaus, ⸚er	vacation house
das Geschirr	dishes
Geschirr spülen	to wash the dishes
das Jahrzehnt, -e	decade
das Sprachlabor, -s	language laboratory
das Tagebuch, ⸚er	diary

Ähnliche Wörter

die Information, -en; die Reporterin, -nen; die Rolle, -n; die Wäsche; die Zigarette, -n; der Kaffeefilter, -; der Reporter, -; der Tee; der Uranus; das Akkordeon, -s; das Café, -s; das Interview, -s; das Penizillin; das Prozent, -e; das Studentenleben; das Theater, -; das Thema, Themen; das Toilettenpapier; das Wunder, -; kein Wunder

Sonstige Verben	Other Verbs
ab·fahren, fährt ... ab, ist abgefahren	to depart
an·fangen, fängt ... an, angefangen	to begin
antworten*	to answer
auf·wachen, ist aufgewacht	to wake up
bezahlen	to pay (for)
dauern	to last
denken (an + *akk.*), gedacht	to think (of)
entdecken	to discover
entscheiden, entschieden	to decide
erfinden, erfunden	to invent
ergänzen	to complete, fill in the blanks
feiern	to celebrate
los·fahren, fährt ... los, ist losgefahren	to drive off
passieren, ist passiert	to happen
spülen	to wash; to rinse

verdienen	to earn
verstehen, verstanden	to understand
versuchen	to try, attempt
war, warst, waren	was, were

Ähnliche Wörter

diskutieren; essen, isst, gegessen (R); zu Abend essen; fotografieren; gewinnen, gewonnen; korrigieren; sitzen, gesessen; telefonieren; weg.gehen, ist weggegangen

Adjektive und Adverbien	Adjectives and Adverbs
furchtbar	terrible
knapp	just, barely
links	left
mit dem linken Fuß auf·stehen, ist aufgestanden	to get up on the wrong side of bed
pünktlich	punctual; on time
verliebt	in love

Ähnliche Wörter

total

Sonstige Wörter und Ausdrücke	Other Words and Expressions
also	well, so, thus
auf jeden Fall	by all means
das hört sich toll an	that sounds great
deshalb	therefore; that's why
diese, dieser, dieses (R)	this, that, these, those
doch!	yes (on the contrary)!
etwas (R)	something
etwas Interessantes/ Neues	something interesting/new
in (R)	in; at
im Garten	in the garden
im Café	at the cafe
ja	indeed
das ist es ja!	that's just it!
tut mir leid	I'm sorry
wen	whom (*accusative*)
zuerst	first

*Regular weak verbs are listed only with their infinitive.

Strukturen und Übungen

4.1 Talking about the past: the perfect tense

4.1. *Perfekt: haben und sein.* In this section, we formally present for the first time the perfect tense. (The simple past tense of *haben* and *sein* are introduced in **Kapitel 7,** the simple past of other verbs in **Kapitel 9.**) The emphasis is on the use of the auxiliaries *haben* and *sein*. The formation of the participles will be explained in Section 4.2, and verbs with separable and inseparable prefixes are covered in Section 4.5. The perfect tense is another important instance of the sentence bracket. The word order itself causes sts. fewer →

In conversation, German speakers generally use the perfect tense to describe past events. The simple past tense, which you will study in **Kapitel 9,** is used more often in writing.

Ich **habe** gestern Abend ein Glas Wein **getrunken.**	*I drank a glass of wine last night.*
Nora **hat** gestern Basketball **gespielt.**	*Nora played basketball yesterday.*

German forms the perfect tense with an auxiliary (**haben** or **sein**) and a past participle (**gewaschen**). Participles usually begin with the prefix **ge-**.

	AUXILIARY		PARTICIPLE
Ich	**habe**	mein Auto	**gewaschen.**

The auxiliary is in first position in yes/no questions and in second position in statements and **w**-word questions. The past participle is at the end of the clause.

Hat Heidi gestern einen Film **gesehen?**	*Did Heidi see a movie last night?*
Ich **habe** gestern zu viel Kaffee **getrunken.**	*I drank too much coffee yesterday.*
Wann **bist** du ins Bett **gegangen?**	*When did you go to bed?*

Wissen Sie noch?

You've already seen how a **Satzklammer** forms a frame or a bracket consisting of a verb and either a separable prefix or an infinitive (grammar 1.5, 2.3, and 3.1). Note here how the **Satzklammer** is composed of **haben/sein** and the past participle.

Verbs with **sein** = no direct object; change of location or condition.

Although most verbs form the present perfect tense with **haben**, many use **sein**. To use **sein**, a verb must fulfill two conditions.

1. It cannot take a direct object.
2. It must indicate change of location or condition.

sein	**haben**
Ich **bin aufgestanden.**	Ich **habe gefrühstückt.**
I got out of bed.	*I ate breakfast.*
Stefan **ist** ins Kino **gegangen.**	Er **hat** einen Film **gesehen.**
Stefan went to the movies.	*He saw a film.*

difficulties than the choice of auxiliary and the formation of the past participle. Use perfect forms in your speech as often as possible before asking sts. to use them.

Here is a list of common verbs that take **sein** as an auxiliary. For a more complete list, see Appendix E.

ankommen	*to arrive*	ich bin angekommen
aufstehen	*to get up*	ich bin aufgestanden
fahren	*to go, drive*	ich bin gefahren
gehen	*to go, walk*	ich bin gegangen
kommen	*to come*	ich bin gekommen
schwimmen	*to swim*	ich bin geschwommen
wandern	*to hike*	ich bin gewandert

In addition to these verbs, **sein** itself and the verb **bleiben** (*to stay*) take **sein** as an auxiliary.

Bist du schon in China **gewesen?**	*Have you ever been to China?*
Gestern **bin** ich zu Hause **geblieben.**	*Yesterday I stayed home.*

Rosemaries erster Schultag

Üb. 1–2. These exercises ask the sts. to provide only the auxiliary verb. Point out the rule that, if the verb has a direct object, the auxiliary is always *haben*. Assign for homework and check in class. Ask sts. to write out the answers to the questions following both texts in complete sentences. As a follow-up in class, ask sts. to group the verbs according to their choice of auxiliary while writing them in two columns (*sein* and *haben*) on the board.

Ergänzen Sie **haben** oder **sein**. Beantworten Sie dann die Fragen.

Rosemarie _____ᵃ bis sieben Uhr geschlafen. Dann _____ᵇ sie aufgestanden und _____ᶜ mit ihren Eltern und ihren Schwestern gefrühstückt. Sie _____ᵈ ihre Tasche genommen und _____ᵉ mit ihrer Mutter zur Schule gegangen. Ihre Mutter und sie _____ᶠ ins Klassenzimmer gegangen und ihre Mutter _____ᵍ noch ein bisschen dageblieben. Die Lehrerin, Frau Dehne, _____ʰ alle begrüßt. Dann _____ⁱ Frau Dehne „Herzlich willkommen" an die Tafel geschrieben.

1. Wann ist Rosemarie aufgestanden?
2. Wohin sind Rosemarie und ihre Mutter gegangen?
3. Wer ist Frau Dehne?
4. Was hat Frau Dehne an die Tafel geschrieben?

Übung 2 Eine Reise nach Istanbul

Ergänzen Sie **haben** oder **sein**. Beantworten Sie dann die Fragen.

JOSEF UND MELANIE:

Wir _____ᵃ ein Taxi genommen. Mit dem Taxi _____ᵇ wir zum Bahnhof gefahren. Dort _____ᶜ wir uns Fahrkarten gekauft. Dann _____ᵈ wir in den Orientexpress eingestiegen. Um 5.30 _____ᵉ wir abgefahren. Wir _____ᶠ im Speisewagen[1] gefrühstückt. Den ganzen Tag _____ᵍ wir Karten gespielt. Nachts _____ʰ wir in den Schlafwagen gegangen. Wir _____ⁱ schlecht geschlafen. Aber wir _____ʲ gut in Istanbul angekommen.

1. Wohin sind Josef und Melanie mit dem Taxi gefahren?
2. Wann sind sie mit dem Zug abgefahren?
3. Wo haben sie gefrühstückt?
4. Was haben sie nachts gemacht?

Übung 3 Ein ganz normaler Tag

Üb. 3. Before assigning as homework, go through the list of verbs with your sts., determining which verbs use *sein* and which ones use *haben*.

Ergänzen Sie das Partizip.

> **aufgestanden** **gefrühstückt** **gehört**
>
> **gearbeitet** **gegangen** **getroffen**
>
> **geduscht** **gegessen** **getrunken**

Heute bin ich um 7.00 Uhr _____ᵃ. Ich habe _____ᵇ, _____ᶜ und bin an die Uni _____ᵈ. Ich habe einen Vortrag _____ᵉ. Um 10 Uhr habe ich ein paar Mitstudenten _____ᶠ und Kaffee _____ᵍ. Dann habe ich bis 12.30 Uhr in der Bibliothek _____ʰ und habe in der Mensa zu Mittag _____ⁱ.

[1]dining car

4.2 Strong and weak past participles

weak verbs = **ge-** + verb stem + **-(e)t**

German verbs that form the past participle with **-(e)t** are called *weak verbs*.

| arbeiten | gearbeitet | *work* | *worked* |
| spielen | gespielt | *play* | *played* |

To form the regular past participle, take the present tense **er/sie/es**-form and precede it with **ge-**.

er	spielt	→	er	hat	gespielt
sie	arbeitet	→	sie	hat	gearbeitet
es	regnet	→	es	hat	geregnet

4.2. *Regelmäßige und unregelmäßige Partizipien.* Point out that the forms of weak verbs are not listed in vocabulary lists because they are predictable. Sts. may be interested to know that German strong and weak participles and English participles ending in *-en* (*eaten, written*) and *-ed* (*asked, waited*) are related.

strong verbs = **ge-** + verb stem + **-en;** the verb stem may have vowel or consonant changes.

Verbs that form the past participle with **-en** are called *strong verbs.* Many verbs have the same stem vowel in the infinitive and the past participle.

| kommen | → | gekommen |

Some verbs have a change in the stem vowel.

| schwimmen | → | geschwommen |

Some also have a change in consonants.

| gehen | → | ge**g**angen |

Here is a reference list of common irregular past participles.

PARTICIPLES WITH **haben**

essen, gegessen	*to eat*
halten, gehalten	*to hold*
lesen, gelesen	*to read*
liegen, gelegen	*to lie, be situated*
nehmen, genommen	*to take*
schlafen, geschlafen	*to sleep*
schreiben, geschrieben	*to write*
sehen, gesehen	*to see*
sprechen, gesprochen	*to speak*
tragen, getragen	*to wear, carry*
treffen, getroffen	*to meet*
trinken, getrunken	*to drink*
waschen, gewaschen	*to wash*

PARTICIPLES WITH **sein**

ankommen, angekommen	*to arrive*
aufstehen, aufgestanden	*to get up*
bleiben, geblieben	*to stay, remain*
fahren, gefahren	*to go (using a vehicle), drive*
gehen, gegangen	*to go (walk)*
kommen, gekommen	*to come*
schwimmen, geschwommen	*to swim*
sein, gewesen	*to be*

Übung 4   Das ungezogene¹ Kind

Üb. 4. Assign for homework. Have pairs of sts. play the roles in class.

Stellen Sie die Fragen!

MODELL: SIE: Hast du schon geduscht?
DAS KIND: Heute will ich nicht duschen.

1. Heute will ich nicht frühstücken.
2. Heute will ich nicht schwimmen.
3. Heute will ich keine Geschichte lesen.
4. Heute will ich nicht Klavier spielen.
5. Heute will ich nicht schlafen.
6. Heute will ich nicht essen.
7. Heute will ich nicht Geschirr spülen.
8. Heute will ich den Brief nicht schreiben.
9. Heute will ich nicht ins Bett gehen.

Übung 5   Katrins Tagesablauf

Üb. 5. Assign as written homework. You might wish to add a creative section by asking students to describe an imaginary 11th picture.

Wie war Katrins Tag gestern? Schreiben Sie zu jedem Bild einen Satz. Verwenden Sie diese Ausdrücke.

MODELL: Katrin hat bis 9 Uhr im Bett gelegen.

arbeiten
abends zu Hause bleiben
ein Referat halten
nach Hause kommen
bis neun im Bett liegen
regnen
mit Frau Schulz sprechen
einen Rock tragen
Freunde treffen
ihre Wäsche waschen

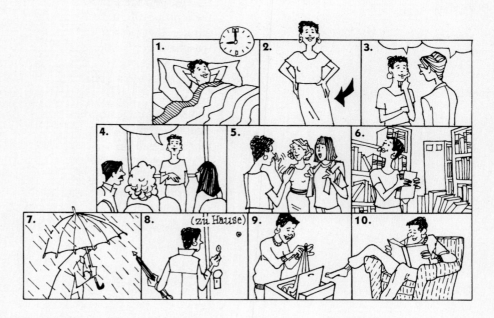

¹naughty

4.3 Dates and ordinal numbers

To form ordinal numbers, add **-te** to the cardinal numbers 1 through 19 and **-ste** to the numbers 20 and above. Exceptions to this pattern are **erste** (*first*), **dritte** (*third*), **siebte** (*seventh*), and **achte** (*eighth*).

4.3. *Datum und Ordnungszahlen.* We expect sts. to recognize the ordinal numbers and to state important dates in the 2 ways described, but we do not yet expect mastery of all the ordinal numbers.

Ordinals 1–19 add **-te** to the cardinal number (but note: **erste, dritte, siebte, achte**).

eins	**erste**	*first*
zwei	zweite	*second*
drei	**dritte**	*third*
vier	vierte	*fourth*
fünf	fünfte	*fifth*
sechs	sechste	*sixth*
sieben	**siebte**	*seventh*
acht	**achte**	*eighth*
neun	neunte	*ninth*
. . .		

Ordinals 20 and higher add **-ste** to the cardinal number.

neunzehn	neunzehnte	*nineteenth*
zwanzig	zwanzigste	*twentieth*
einundzwanzig	einundzwanzigste	*twenty-first*
zweiundzwanzig	zweiundzwanzigste	*twenty-second*
. . .		
dreißig	dreißigste	*thirtieth*
vierzig	vierzigste	*fortieth*
. . .		
hundert	hundertste	*hundredth*
. . .		

Ordinal numbers usually end in **-e** or **-en.** Use the construction **der + -e** to answer the question **Welches Datum ...?**

Welches Datum ist heute?	*What is today's date?*
Heute ist **der** achte Mai.	*Today is May 8th.*

All dates are masculine:
der zweit*e* Mai
am zweit*en* Mai

Use **am + -en** to answer the question **Wann ...?**

Wann sind Sie geboren?	*When were you born?*
Am achtzehnten Juni 1983.	*On the eighteenth of June, 1983.*

Ordinal numbers in German can be written as words or figures.

am zweiten Februar	*on the second of February*
am 2. Februar	*on the 2nd of February*

Übung 6   Wichtige Daten

Üb. 6. For oral pair-work in class.

Beantworten Sie die Fragen.

1. Welches Datum ist heute?
2. Welches Datum ist morgen?
3. Wann feiert man Weihnachten?
4. Wann feiert man den Nationalfeiertag in Ihrem Land?
5. Wann feiert man das neue Jahr?
6. Wann feiert man Valentinstag?
7. Wann ist dieses Jahr Muttertag?
8. Wann ist nächstes Jahr Ostern?
9. Wann beginnt der Frühling?
10. Wann beginnt der Sommer?

4.4 Prepositions of time: *um, am, im*

Use the question word **wann** to ask for a specific time. The preposition in the answer will vary depending on whether it refers to clock time, days or parts of days, months, or seasons.

um CLOCK TIME

—Wann beginnt der Film?   When does the film start?
—**Um** neun Uhr.   At nine o'clock.

um

am DAYS AND PARTS OF DAYS*

—Wann ist das Konzert?   When is the concert?
—**Am** Montag.   On Monday.

—Wann arbeitest du?   When do you work?
—**Am** Abend.   In the evening.

am

im SEASONS AND MONTHS

—Wann ist das Wetter schön?   When is the weather nice?
—**Im** Sommer und besonders   In the summer and especially
  im August.   in August.

im

No preposition is used when stating the year in which something takes place.

—Wann bist du geboren?   When were you born?
—Ich bin 1995 geboren.   I was born in 1995.

*Note the exceptions: **in der Nacht** (*at night*) and **um Mitternacht** (*at midnight*).

Übung 7   Melanies Geburtstag

Üb. 7. Assign for homework and check in class.

Ergänzen Sie **um, am, im** oder —.

Melanie hat _____ª Frühling Geburtstag, _____ᵇ April. Sie ist _____ᶜ 1988 geboren, _____ᵈ 3. April 1988. _____ᵉ Dienstag kommen Claire und Josef _____ᶠ halb vier zum Kaffee. Melanies Mutter kommt _____ᵍ 16 Uhr. _____ʰ Abend gehen Melanie, Claire und Josef ins Kino. Josef hat auch _____ⁱ April Geburtstag, aber erst _____ʲ 15. April.

Übung 8   Interview

Üb. 8. Set up as an in-class interview.

Beantworten Sie die Fragen.

1. Was machst du im Winter? im Sommer?
2. Wie ist das Wetter im Frühling? im Herbst?
3. Was machst du am Morgen? am Abend?
4. Was machst du am Freitag? am Samstag?
5. Was machst du heute um sechs Uhr abends? um zehn Uhr abends?
6. Was machst du am Sonntag um Mitternacht?

4.5 Past participles with and without *ge-*

Separable-prefix verbs form their past participles with **-ge-** before the verb stem.

WEAK VERBS

prefix + **-ge-** + stem + **-(e)t**

STRONG VERBS

prefix + **-ge-** + stem + **-en**

The verb stem may have vowel or consonant changes.

A. Participles with ge-

German past participles usually begin with **ge-**. The past participles of separable-prefix verbs begin with the prefix; the **ge-** goes between the prefix and the verb.

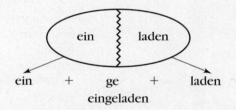

ein   +   ge   +   laden

eingeladen

4.5. *Partizipien mit ge-.* This section deals with the participles of verbs with separable prefixes. Stress that the separable prefix and the participle constitute a single word. Point out that if sts. know the participle of the base verb, they can simply add the prefix to it.

Frau Schulz **hat** Heidi und Nora zum Essen **eingeladen.**

Frau Schulz invited Heidi and Nora for dinner.

Here are the infinitives and past participles of some common separable-prefix verbs.

SEPARABLE PREFIXES

an

auf

aus

ein

mit

weg

wieder

zusammen

and others

PAST PARTICIPLES WITH **haben**

anfangen	angefangen	*to start*
anrufen	angerufen	*to call up*
aufräumen	aufgeräumt	*to tidy up*
auspacken	ausgepackt	*to unpack*
fernsehen	ferngesehen	*to watch TV*

PAST PARTICIPLES WITH **sein**

ankommen	angekommen	*to arrive*
aufstehen	aufgestanden	*to get up*
ausgehen	ausgegangen	*to go out*
weggehen	weggegangen	*to go away, leave*

B. Participles without ge-

There are two types of verbs that do not add **ge-** to form the past participle: verbs that end in **-ieren** and verbs with inseparable prefixes.

Verbs ending in **-ieren** are weak: verb stem + **-t.**

1. Verbs ending in **-ieren** form the past participle with **-t: studieren** → **studiert.**

   Paula **hat** Deutsch **studiert.**   *Paula studied German.*

   Here is a list of common verbs that end in **-ieren.**

4.5. *Partizipien ohne ge-.* For verbs ending in *-ieren*, emphasize that participles end in *-t* and do not add *ge-*.

diskutieren	diskutiert	*to discuss*
fotografieren	fotografiert	*to take pictures*
korrigieren	korrigiert	*to correct*
probieren	probiert	*to try, taste*
reparieren	repariert	*to repair, fix*
studieren	studiert	*to study*
telefonieren	telefoniert	*to telephone*

Almost all verbs ending in **-ieren** form the perfect tense with **haben.** The verb **passieren** (*to happen*) requires **sein** as an auxiliary: **Was ist passiert?** (*What happened?*)

Verbs with inseparable prefixes may be weak or strong:

WEAK VERBS
verb stem + **-(e)t**
STRONG VERBS
verb stem + **-en**

The verb stem may have vowel or consonant changes.

INSEPARABLE PREFIXES
be-
ent-
er-
ge-
ver-
zer-

Separable prefixes can stand alone as whole words; inseparable prefixes are always unstressed syllables.

2. The past participles of inseparable-prefix verbs do not include **ge-:** **verstehen** → **verstanden.**

   Stefan **hat** nicht **verstanden.**   *Stefan didn't understand.*

Whereas separable prefixes are words that can stand alone (**auf, aus, wieder,** and so forth), inseparable prefixes are simply syllables: **be-, ent-, er-, ge-, ver-,** and **zer-.** The past participles of most inseparable-prefix verbs require **haben** as an auxiliary. Here is a list of common inseparable-prefix verbs and their past participles.

bekommen	bekommen	*to get*
besuchen	besucht	*to visit*
bezahlen	bezahlt	*to pay*
entdecken	entdeckt	*to discover*
erfinden	erfunden	*to invent*
erzählen	erzählt	*to tell*
verdienen	verdient	*to earn*
vergessen	vergessen	*to forget*
verlieren	verloren	*to lose*
verstehen	verstanden	*to understand*

Übung 9   Ein schlechter Tag

Üb. 9. Assign as homework and check in class.

AA Ask sts. to form groups and describe a bad day in their own lives. They could report back orally or with written texts that you then put on the projector to show to the class.

Herr Thelen ist gestern mit dem linken Fuß aufgestanden. Zuerst hat er seinen Wecker nicht gehört und hat verschlafen. Dann ist er in die Küche gegangen und hat Kaffee gekocht. Nach dem Frühstück ist er mit seinem Auto in die Stadt zum Einkaufen gefahren. Er hat geparkt und ist erst nach zwei Stunden zurückgekommen. Herr Thelen hat einen Strafzettel[1] bekommen und 20 Euro bezahlt für falsches Parken. Er ist nach Hause gefahren, hat die Wäsche gewaschen und hat aufgeräumt. Beim Aufräumen ist eine teure Vase auf den Boden gefallen und zerbrochen[2]. Als die Wäsche fertig war, war ein Pullover eingelaufen[3]. Herr Thelen ist dann schnell ins Bett gegangen. Fünf Minuten vor Mitternacht ist das Haus abgebrannt[4].

[1]*ticket* [2]*broken* [3]*shrunk* [4]*burned down*

A. Richtig (R) oder falsch (F)?

1. _____ Herr Thelen hat gestern verschlafen.
2. _____ Vor dem Frühstück ist er in die Stadt gefahren.
3. _____ Herr Thelen hat falsch geparkt.
4. _____ Er hat seine Wohnung aufgeräumt.
5. _____ Herr Thelen braucht ein neues Haus.

B. Suchen Sie die Partizipien heraus, bilden Sie die Infinitive und schreiben Sie sie auf.

PARTIZIPIEN MIT ge-   INFINITIVE

_____   _____

_____   _____

⋮   ⋮

PARTIZIPIEN OHNE ge-   INFINITIVE

_____   _____

_____   _____

⋮   ⋮

Übung 10   In der Türkei

Üb. 10. For homework. Tell students that auxiliary verbs have separate blanks but not their own letters.

Mehmet ist in der Türkei. Was hat er gestern gemacht? Verwenden Sie die Verben am Rand[1].

Mehmet ist in der Türkei bei seinen Eltern. Gestern _____ er um 17 Uhr _____[a]. Er _____ seine Eltern und Geschwister _____[b] und einen Tee mit ihnen _____[c]. Dann _____ er in sein Zimmer _____[d] und _____ _____[e].

gehen   schlafen
trinken
ankommen   begrüßen

Nach einer Stunde _____ er zum Abendessen in die Küche _____[f]. Seine Eltern _____ ihn viel über sein Leben in Deutschland _____[g] und Mehmet _____ über seine Arbeit und seine Freunde _____[h]. Sie _____ noch einen Tee _____[i] und _____ um 23 Uhr ins Bett _____[j].

gehen   sprechen
trinken
fragen   gehen

Übung 11   Interview

Üb. 11. Assign the questions for homework. Do the first 2 or 3 examples orally in class. As follow-up the next day in class, ask sts. to interview each other. Have them take notes, then ask them to tell the class something particularly amusing or interesting about their partners. If you tell them ahead of time that they will be relating information to the class, they are more likely to be creative in their interviews.

Fragen Sie Ihren Partner / Ihre Partnerin. Schreiben Sie die Antworten auf.

MODELL: mit deinen Eltern telefonieren (wie lange?) →

    s1: Hast du gestern mit deinen Eltern telefoniert?
    s2: Ja.
    s1: Wie lange?
    s2: Eine halbe Stunde.

1. früh aufstehen (wann?)
2. jemanden fotografieren (wen?)
3. jemanden besuchen (wen?)
4. ausgehen (wohin?)
5. etwas bezahlen (was?)
6. etwas reparieren (was?)
7. etwas Neues probieren (was?)
8. fernsehen (wie lange?)
9. etwas nicht verstehen (was?)
10. dein Zimmer aufräumen (wann?)

[1]margin

5

Geld und Arbeit

In **Kapitel 5,** you will talk about shopping, jobs and the workplace, and daily life at home. You will expand your ability to express your likes and dislikes and learn to describe your career plans.

GOALS

In *Kapitel 5,* sts. talk about professions and work environments in addition to work performed in kitchens. (Other household chores are introduced in *Kapitel 6.*)

The grammar in this chapter focuses on the dative case, expressing change with *werden* and asking "who(m)." We do not expect sts. to master the dative forms in this lesson, simply to recognize them and use them in certain fixed expressions.

Themen

Geschenke und Gefälligkeiten
Berufe
Arbeitsplätze
In der Küche

Kulturelles

KLI: Leipzig
Musikszene: „Millionär" (Die Prinzen)
KLI: Ausbildung und Beruf
Filmclip: *Der Tunnel* (Roland Suso Richter)
Videoecke: Studium und Arbeit

Lektüren

Webartikel: Die coolsten Studentenjobs
Film: *Der Tunnel* (Roland Suso Richter)

Strukturen

5.1 Dative case: articles and possessive adjectives
5.2 Question pronouns: **wer, wen, wem**
5.3 Expressing change: the verb **werden**
5.4 Location: **in, an, auf** + dative case
5.5 Dative case: personal pronouns

Adolph von Menzel: *Eisenwalzwerk* (1872–75), Alte Nationalgalerie, Berlin

Kunst und Künstler

Adolph von Menzel (1815–1905) war der bedeutendste[1] Maler des Realismus. Vor allem war er ein Maler des damaligen modernen Lebens. Für sein Bild *Eisenwalzwerk* reiste[2] Menzel nach Königshütte in Schlesien, damals eine der modernsten Industrieregionen Deutschlands. Das Bild zeigt die Herstellung[3] von Eisenbahnschienen[4].

Schauen Sie sich das Bild an und beantworten Sie die folgenden Fragen.

1. Was ist im Zentrum des Bildes? Was machen die Arbeiter mit den Zangen[5]? Wie wird es dargestellt?
2. Was machen die Arbeiter vorne rechts? Wer ist die Person, die sie ansieht?
3. Was machen die Arbeiter vorne links?
4. Wer ist die Person mit dem Hut links im Hintergrund? Was macht er?
5. Welche Farben werden verwendet? Welchen Eindruck[6] gibt das dem Bild?
6. Welche Assoziationen weckt das Bild?

[1]*most significant* [2]*traveled* [3]*production* [4]*rails for railroad tracks* [5]*tongs* [6]*impression*

Situationen

Geschenke und Gefälligkeiten

Grammatik 5.1–5.2

1. Peter kauft seinem Freund Albert eine Konzertkarte.

2. Ernst gibt seinem Vater die Tageszeitung.

3. Michael schenkt seiner Freundin Maria einen Ausflug an die Ostsee.

4. Hans leiht seiner Schwester einen MP3-Spieler.

5. Oma Schmitz kocht ihrem Enkel Rolf das Abendessen.

6. Heidi verkauft ihrem Mitstudenten Stefan ein Wörterbuch.

7. Melanie erzählt ihrer Freundin Claire ein Geheimnis.

8. Claire schreibt ihrer Mutter einen Brief.

Situation 1   Ist das normal?

Sit. 1. Have sts. match each sentence with the picture it describes, then have them tell you how the two sentences differ in meaning. Although the spelling differences between the dative and accusative possessive articles are obvious to you, some sts. may not notice them unless you point them out.

AA. Bring pictures from the PF that show someone doing something for someone else: repairing a bicycle, selling flowers, etc. Describe the pictures: *A repariert B das Fahrrad. Und hier verkauft X Y Blumen.* Now ask: *Was verkauft X? (Blumen.) Wem verkauft X die Blumen? (Y.) Richtig, und wem repariert A das Fahrrad? (B.) Genau, A repariert B das Fahrrad.* Stress the question words *was* and *wer/wem* to make it clear that the former refers to things; the latter, to people. This will help students when they do *Sit. 2.* You can also write a list of verbs on the board and have sts. make up sentences of their own. Encourage them to make up humorous and therefore memorable examples. Verbs: *geben, (ein)gießen, kaufen, kochen, renovieren, reparieren usw.*

Welches Bild gehört zu welchem Satz?

1. a.   b.

_____ Jens gießt seiner Tante die Blumen.
_____ Jens gießt seine Tante.

2. a.   b.

_____ Jutta repariert ihren Bruder.
_____ Jutta repariert ihrem Bruder das Radio.

3. a.   b.

_____ Silvia kauft das Kind.
_____ Silvia kauft dem Kind die Schokolade.

4. a.   b.

_____ Herr Ruf kocht der Familie das Essen.
_____ Herr Ruf kocht die Familie.

Sagen Sie *ja*, *nein* oder *vielleicht*.

Sit. 2. Demonstrate the activity by reading through the first example with a st. Read the question, emphasizing *wem,* then continue with the responses: *dem Professor?* (*Ja.*) *ihren Eltern?* (*Vielleicht.*) *usw.* As you pronounce the items in a–d, emphasize the dative form of the articles and the possessives. Quickly model pronunciation for the remaining questions and responses, having sts. repeat. Now have them work in pairs. It is acceptable to use *niemand* (as opposed to *niemandem*) as the negative answer to a dative question.

1. Wem geben die Studenten ihre Hausaufgaben?
   a. dem Professor
   b. ihren Eltern
   c. dem Hausmeister
   d. dem Taxifahrer

2. Wem schreibt Rolf einen Brief?
   a. seiner Katze
   b. dem Präsidenten
   c. seinem Friseur
   d. seinen Eltern

3. Wem kauft Andrea das Hundefutter?
   a. ihrer Mutter
   b. ihrem Freund Lukas
   c. ihrem Hund
   d. ihren Geschwistern

4. Wem repariert Herr Ruf das Fahrrad?
   a. seinem Hund
   b. seiner Mutter
   c. seinen Nachbarn
   d. seinem Sohn

Interaktion: Was schenkst du deiner Mutter?

Sit. 3. Preteach vocabulary: *Roman, Mütze, Fahrradhelm, Badehose, Bikini, Regenschirm, Reiseführer, Kaffeemaschine, Parfüm.* Ask sts. to repeat after you as you read the words. Encourage sts. to use items above and beyond those in the display in their answers if they choose. Tell sts. the current exchange rate. (You may wish to ask sts. to check the financial pages of newspapers for current exchange rates.) Then model some responses, mentioning some humorous gifts to encourage creativity. You could have your examples written out on a projector with the dative and accusative endings underlined in different colors. Remind sts. of word order with indirect and direct objects. Expand on your responses to reinforce the use of *weil,* to recycle old vocabulary, and to give the sts. as much input as possible: *Ich kaufe mein**er** Mutter ein**e** Reise nach Deutschland, weil sie deutsch**es** Bier trinken möchte / weil sie ein Dirndl kaufen möchte. Ich kaufe mein**em** Vater ein**en** Mercedes, weil er jetzt ein**en** Golf fährt. Ich kaufe mein**em** Bruder ein**en** Fahrradhelm, weil er gern Rad fährt. Ich habe kein**e** Schwester.* Some sts. may need to say "stepfather," "-mother," etc.: *Stiefvater, -mutter usw.* Also, some may need to know *Mein/e _____ lebt nicht mehr.* Remind sts. that "I don't have a" is *Ich habe kein/keine ...* Afterward, have each st. tell the class the most unusual thing he or she bought.

Sie haben in der Lotterie 2 000 Euro gewonnen. Für 500 Euro wollen Sie Ihrer Familie und Ihren Freunden Geschenke kaufen. Was schenken Sie ihnen?

MODELL: S1: Was schenkst du deiner Mutter?
S2: Einen/Ein/Eine _____.
S1: Was schenkst du deinem Vater?
S2: Einen/Ein/Eine _____.

der Bikini
der Regenschirm
die Badehose
der Reiseführer (Baedeker *Mallorca*)
der Roman (Thomas Mann *Der Zauberberg*)
die Mütze
das Parfüm
die Kaffeemaschine
der Fahrradhelm

	ich	mein(e) Partner(in)
deiner Mutter		
deinem Vater		
deiner Schwester		
deinem Bruder		
deinem Großvater		
deiner Großmutter		
deinem Freund / deiner Freundin		
deinem Professor / deiner Professorin		
deinem Mitbewohner / deiner Mitbewohnerin		

600 JAHRE UNIVERSITÄT LEIPZIG
DEUTSCHLAND
55

2009: die Leipziger Universität ist 600 Jahre alt.

Leipzig

Beantworten Sie die folgenden Fragen.

- Wo liegt Leipzig? Lokalisieren Sie die Stadt auf einer Landkarte.
- Was wissen Sie über Leipzig?
- Was wissen Sie über Johann Sebastian Bach und Richard Wagner?
- Was ist 1989 in Deutschland passiert?

Lesen Sie den Text und suchen Sie die Antworten auf die folgenden Fragen:

- Wann hatte Leipzig die meisten Einwohner[1]? Wie viele hat es jetzt?
- Wann wurde die Universität Leipzig gegründet? Wie viele Studierende hat sie?
- Welchen Beruf hatten die folgenden Personen: Heisenberg, Ostwald, Mommsen, Wundt, Wagner und Leibniz?
- Welche berühmte Messe[2] findet jedes Jahr in Leipzig im März statt, und welches Festival im Juni?
- Wie lange war Johann Sebastian Bach Thomaskantor in Leipzig?
- Warum nennt man Leipzig die Heldenstadt[3]?
- In welcher Straße gibt es besonders viele Cafés, Kneipen[4] und Clubs?

Leipzig ist eine der größten und bedeutendsten Städte Deutschlands. Leipzig ist die Stadt der zweitältesten Universität Deutschlands, die Stadt des Buches, die Stadt der Musik und die Stadt der friedlichen[5] Revolution von 1989.

Leipzig erhielt 1165 das Stadtrecht[6], damals mit nur 500 Einwohnern. Vor Beginn des 1. Weltkriegs[7] war sie mit 590 000 Einwohnern die viertgrößte Stadt Deutschlands. 1930 hatte sie mehr als 700 000 Einwohner. Heute hat sie ca. 518 000 Einwohner, ist aber immer noch ein wichtiger Verkehrsknotenpunkt[8] und eines der wichtigsten Wirtschaftszentren Ostdeutschlands.

Die Universität Leipzig wurde 1409 gegründet und ist nach Heidelberg die zweitälteste Universität Deutschlands. Im 19. Jahrhundert war sie eine der drei wichtigsten Universitäten Deutschlands. An ihr unterrichteten die Dichter[9] Gottsched und Lessing, der Physiker Werner Heisenberg (Nobelpreis 1932), der Chemiker Wilhelm Ostwald (Nobelpreis 1909), der Historiker Theodor Mommsen (Nobelpreis in Literatur 1902), Wilhelm Wundt, der Begründer der experimentellen Psychologie und der Philosoph Ernst Bloch. An ihr studierten Goethe (Jura), Nietzsche (Altphilologie) und de Saussure (Indogermanistik), die

Buchmesse in Leipzig

Komponisten Robert Schumann und Richard Wagner sowie Gottfried Wilhelm Leibniz (Philosophie), dessen Statue eines der Wahrzeichen[10] der Universität ist. Jetzt studieren an ihr ca. 29 000 Studenten.

Eine besonders große Rolle spielt in der Geschichte Leipzigs die Musik. Johann Sebastian Bach war Thomaskantor in Leipzig und leitete den Thomanerchor von 1723 bis 1750. Jedes Jahr im Juni erinnert das Bach Leipzig Festival an[11] diesen berühmten Musiker.

1989 begannen in Leipzig die Montagsdemonstrationen, die zum Fall der Berliner Mauer und zur Wiedervereinigung Deutschlands 1990 führten. Seitdem wird Leipzig auch die Heldenstadt genannt.

Da es in Leipzig viele Studentinnen und Studenten gibt, gibt es viele Möglichkeiten auszugehen oder zu feiern. Wöchentlich finden Partys in den Studentenclubs „Moritzbastei", „TV-Club" und „StuK" statt. Die Karl-Liebknecht-Straße, liebevoll „Karli" genannt, bietet jede Menge Cafés, Kneipen und Clubs zum gemütlichen Cocktailtrinken oder zum Tanzen bis in die frühen Morgenstunden.

Leipzig hat eine lange Tradition als Messestadt. Neben vielen anderen Messen findet jedes Jahr im März die Leipziger Buchmesse statt. Sie war bis 1945 die größte Buchmesse Deutschlands, heute ist sie nach Frankfurt am Main die zweitgrößte.

[1]inhabitants [2]trade fair [3]city of heroes [4]bars [5]peaceful [6]town privileges [7]world war
[8]transportation hub [9]poets [10]landmarks [11]erinnert an commemorates

KLI. Suggestion: Ask sts. to locate Leipzig on the map of Germany in the front of the book.

Situation 4 Bildgeschichte: Josef kauft Weihnachtsgeschenke.

Sit. 4. Sentences for narration series: **1.** *Josef macht sich eine Liste und geht einkaufen.* **2.** *Er kauft seinem Vater einen Roman.* **3.** *Er kauft seiner Mutter Parfüm.* **4.** *Er kauft seinem Bruder ein Videospiel.* **5.** *Er kauft seiner Schwester eine Halskette.* **6.** *Er kauft seinem Großvater eine Sonnenbrille.* **7.** *Er kauft seiner Großmutter einen Regenschirm.* **8.** *Er kauft seiner Freundin Melanie einen MP3-Spieler.* **9.** *Es ist sechs Uhr abends und Josef hat alles, was er braucht.* **Receptive recall:** *Welches Bild zeigt …?* **Choral response. Productive recall:** *Was macht Josef im Bild …?* **Personalization:** *Was kaufen Sie Ihren Verwandten und Freunden zu Weihnachten oder zum Geburtstag?*

Es ist fast Weihnachten und Josef hat noch keine Geschenke.

Vocabulary Display
(See the IM.) Show sts. how to derive female professions from the male professions, using the *-in* suffix or *-frau*. Note that professions with *-mann* form their plural with *-leute* (e.g., *Geschäftsmann → Geschäftsleute*). After introducing several professions, use the verb *werden* in natural interactions. *Was studieren Sie? Was wollen Sie werden? Was möchten Sie werden? Jennifer studiert Jura. Sie wird Anwältin usw.*

Berufe

Grammatik 5.3

1. Der Arzt hilft kranken Menschen.

2. Der Verkäufer arbeitet in einem Laden.

3. Die Anwältin verteidigt den Angeklagten.

4. Der Pilot fliegt ein Flugzeug.

5. Der Richter arbeitet im Gericht.

6. Die Bauarbeiterin baut ein Parkhaus.

7. Die Architektin zeichnet ein Haus.

8. Die Krankenpflegerin arbeitet im Krankenhaus.

Situation 5 Definitionen

Sit. 5. Point out that standard German generally has no article with professions, nationalities, and religions: *Er ist Pilot. Sie ist Ärztin.* Ask sts. to work in groups of 3. During the wrap-up, ask sts. if they can name other duties of these people—e.g., *Was muss ein/e Lehrer/in noch machen?*

AA. Show pictures of various people doing different jobs. Ask the question *Was macht er/sie?* Try to introduce verbs that describe what people do on the job, similar to what sts. have just learned in *Sit. 5*, and put them on the projector.

AA. Give sts. a list of professions and have them give simple definitions to encourage the use of verbs associated with each profession.
S1: *Was macht ein Sekretär?*
S2: *Er schreibt Briefe. Er tippt am Computer usw.*

Finden Sie den richtigen Beruf.

Anwältin	Verkäufer	Schriftsteller
Architekt(in)	Krankenpflegerin	Pilot
Ärztin		Lehrer

1. Dieser Mann unterrichtet an einer Schule. Er ist _____.
2. Diese Frau untersucht Patienten im Krankenhaus. Sie ist _____.
3. Dieser Mann fliegt ein Flugzeug. Er ist _____.
4. Dieser Mann verkauft Computer in einem Laden. Er ist _____.
5. Diese Person zeichnet Pläne für Häuser. Sie ist _____.
6. Diese Frau arbeitet auf dem Gericht. Sie ist _____.
7. Diese Frau pflegt kranke Menschen. Sie ist _____.
8. Dieser Mann schreibt Romane. Er ist _____.

Situation 6 Bildgeschichte: Was Michael Pusch schon alles gemacht hat

Sit. 6. Sentences for narration series:
1. *Als Michael 10 war, hat er seinen Nachbarn den Rasen gemäht.* **2.** *Als er 12 war, hat er Zeitungen ausgetragen.* **3.** *Als er 14 war, hat er dem Jungen von nebenan Nachhilfe in Mathematik gegeben.* **4.** *Als er mit der Schule fertig war, hat er Krankenpfleger gelernt.* **5.** *Als er bei der Bundeswehr war, hat er als Koch gearbeitet.* **6.** *Nach der Bundeswehr hat er als Taxifahrer gearbeitet.* **7.** *Als er 25 war, hat er Maria kennengelernt.* **8.** *Damals hat er in einem Schwimmbad als Bademeister gearbeitet.* **9.** *Später hat er Versicherungen verkauft.* Ask sts. if they remember what Michael now does professionally (*Werbeagent*).

AA. Ask sts. what jobs they think Maria may have had, and, to personalize the activity, ask if they have held any of these jobs.

Sit. 7. Review the professions so that the vocabulary is fresh in sts.' minds. Have them work in pairs or groups of 3-4. After giving them 3-4 minutes to make their lists, have them close their books, keeping lists available. Then ask questions 1-8, but in a different order and without giving the number, so sts. must listen rather than simply read off their answers in the order they wrote them down. After hearing one group answer, ask the others if they agree or have other suggestions not yet mentioned: *Stimmt das? Haben Sie noch Vorschläge?*

Situation 7 Berufe

Machen Sie Listen. Suchen Sie zu jeder Frage drei Berufe.

In welchen Berufen ...

1. verdient man sehr viel Geld?
2. verdient man nur wenig Geld?
3. gibt es mehr Männer als Frauen?
4. gibt es mehr Frauen als Männer?
5. muss man gut in Mathematik sein?
6. muss man gut in Sprachen sein?
7. muss man viel reisen?
8. muss man viel Kraft[1] haben?

Situation 8 Interview

Sit. 8. This interview also recycles the perfect tense (4, 5) and ways of expressing time. Be sure that sts. understand the difference between *lernen* and *studieren*. Model pronunciation and have sts. repeat. Then call on individuals to address questions to you so you can model responses as well. Now have sts. work in pairs. The st. asking the questions should take notes. Afterward, have 3-4 sts. report on their partners' responses.

1. Arbeitest du? Wo? Als was? Was machst du? An welchen Tagen arbeitest du? Wann fängst du an? Wann hörst du auf?
2. Was studierst du? Wie lange dauert das Studium?
3. Was möchtest du werden? Verdient man da viel Geld? Ist das ein Beruf mit viel Prestige?
4. Was ist dein Vater von Beruf? Was hat er gelernt (studiert)?
5. Was ist deine Mutter von Beruf? Was hat sie gelernt (studiert)?

[1]*strength* **Cultural note.** *Grundsätzlich ist in Deutschland eine Erwerbstätigkeit von Kindern unter 16 Jahren verboten. Ausnahmen sind auf leichte Arbeiten (wie die Austragung von Werbebroschüren) beschränkt, wobei maximal 2 Std. pro Schultag gearbeitet werden darf und die Nachtarbeit (20-6 Uhr) verboten ist. Etwa 40% der Kinder im Alter von 13 bis 15 Jahren arbeiten in Deutschland, wovon sich circa die Hälfte nicht an die gesetzlichen Bestimmungen hält.*

Lektüre

Lektüre. Ask sts. to quickly go over the *Vor dem Lesen* activity, jotting down their answers. Then pair them up and ask them to interview each other, using those questions. Discuss in class. Ask sts. to look at the photo and the title and try to imagine what the text might be about. Next, ask them to go over the *Miniwörterbuch*, to find the words in the text and to underline them. Then, ask them to do the *Arbeit mit dem Text* in small groups. Discuss afterwards. Make sure sts. understand BAföG (*Bundesausbildungsförderungsgesetz*). Assign the *Nach dem Lesen* as group homework or do as an in-class activity. **Additional activity:** Have sts. script a *Schlussmachgespräch* in the two ways suggested: *nachsichtig* vs. *unbarmherzig*.

Vor dem Lesen

A. Beantworten Sie die folgenden Fragen.

1. Arbeiten Sie neben dem Studium? Was machen Sie?
2. Wie viele Stunden pro Woche arbeiten Sie? Warum?
3. Was machen Sie mit Ihrem Geld?
4. Arbeiten Sie auch in den Semesterferien? Was machen Sie?
5. Macht Ihnen Ihr Job Spaß? Was macht Ihnen Spaß?

B. Lesen Sie die Wörter im Miniwörterbuch. Suchen Sie sie im Text und unterstreichen Sie sie.

Miniwörterbuch

unterstützen	to support	**zusammenstoßen**	to smash into
ausreichen	to be enough, to last	der **Unfall**	accident
kellnern	to wait tables	**beschäftigen**	to employ
die **Nachhilfe**	tutoring	der **Straßenbahnführer**	streetcar driver
der **Heißluftballon**	hot air balloon	die **Trennungsagentur**	separation agency
jagen	to chase	**Schluss machen**	to end (*here:* end a relationship)
hingeweht werden	to be blown to	der **Kunde**	customer
der **Flughafen**	airport	**nachsichtig**	considerately
der **Vogel**, die **Vögel**	bird	**unbarmherzig**	ruthlessly
vertreiben	to chase away	**zurückzahlen**	to pay back

Dieser Student jobbt als Straßenbahnfahrer.

Lesehilfe

Scanning a text is one way to find details without reading word for word. How many familiar words can you identify by scanning the text?

Die coolsten Studentenjobs

Mehr als die Hälfte der Studenten in Deutschland arbeiten. Sie sind jung und brauchen das Geld. Welche Jobs sind besonders populär? Welche sind besonders interessant?

Mehr als die Hälfte der Studenten in Deutschland arbeiten neben dem Studium und in den Semesterferien. Der Staat unterstützt junge Leute mit Stipendien und BAföG und die Familie hilft auch oft. Aber das Geld reicht nicht aus.

Besonders beliebt bei den Studenten sind kellnern, Nachhilfe geben, babysitten oder
5 im Supermarkt kassieren. Doch wer die Augen offen hält, findet auch interessantere Jobs. Man kann zum Beispiel Heißluftballons jagen: Die „Verfolger" beobachten, wo ein Ballon hingeweht wird, um die Passagiere am Landeplatz abzuholen und zurück zum Startpunkt zu fahren.

Flughäfen beschäftigen sogenannte Vogelvertreiber, denn Vögel sind auf Flughäfen
10 nicht gern gesehen. Wenn sie mit Flugzeugen zusammenstoßen oder in die Triebwerke der Maschinen fliegen, kann es zu schweren Unfällen kommen. Die Vogelvertreiber beobachten die Start- und Landebahnen und vertreiben die Störenfriede. Die Kölner Verkehrsbetriebe beschäftigen auch Studenten als Fahrer. Sie bilden die jungen Leute in einem siebenwöchigen Intensivkurs zum Straßenbahnführer aus.

15 Mutige Studenten melden sich bei Trennungsagenturen. Diese beschäftigen „Schlussmacher", die einem Partner die Botschaft vom Beziehungsende telefonisch oder im direkten Gespräch übermitteln. Der Kunde kann vorher sagen, ob er möchte, dass der Schlussmacher den Partner nachsichtig oder unbarmherzig behandeln soll.

Für Studenten, die BAföG erhalten, ist es wichtig darauf zu achten, nicht mehr
20 als rund 400 Euro im Monat zu verdienen. Wenn sie mehr verdienen, müssen sie das Geld an den Staat zurückzahlen. Es gibt viele „Minijobs", die das berücksichtigen und gerne Studenten beschäftigen.

Bearbeitung des Textes „Die verrücktesten Nebenjobs", http://home.1und1.de/themen/beruf, 19. April 2011

Arbeit mit dem Text

A. Beliebte Jobs und interessante Jobs. Welche der folgenden Jobs sind beliebt, welche sind interessant? Schreiben Sie B neben die Jobs, die beliebt sind, und *I* neben die Jobs, die interessant sind.

_____ als Babysitter/in arbeiten

_____ als Kassierer/in im Supermarkt arbeiten

_____ als Kellner/in arbeiten

_____ als Straßenbahnführer/in arbeiten

_____ bei einer Trennungsagentur arbeiten

_____ Heißluftballons jagen

_____ Nachhilfe geben

_____ Vögel vom Flughafen vertreiben

B. Beantworten Sie die Fragen.

1. Woher können Studierende in Deutschland Geld bekommen?
2. Was machen Heißluftballonjäger?
3. Wo arbeiten Vogelvertreiber? Warum ist ihre Arbeit wichtig?
4. In welcher Stadt kann man als Student als Straßenbahnführer arbeiten? Wie lange dauert der Vorbereitungskurs[1]?
5. Was machen Schlussmacher? Welche Optionen gibt es für die Kunden?
6. Wie viel darf man im Monat verdienen, wenn man BAföG bekommt?

Nach dem Lesen

1. Machen Sie eine Umfrage im Kurs. Stellen Sie die folgenden Fragen:

   - Welche Jobs hattest du?
   - Wie alt warst du, als du deinen ersten Job hattest?
   - Wie viel hast du gearbeitet?
   - Wie viel hast du verdient?
   - Was hast du dir von deinem Geld gekauft?

   Benutzen Sie die folgende Tabelle.

Name	Alter	Job	Stundenlohn	Geld für ...

2. Sammeln Sie die Antworten und machen Sie ein Plakat mit dem Titel: *Die Jobs unserer Kursteilnehmer.* Hängen Sie das Plakat aus.

[1]*preparatory course*

Musikszene

„Millionär" (1991, Deutschland) *Die Prinzen*

Biografie Die Prinzen sind eine Musikgruppe aus Leipzig. Sie sind für ihre A-cappella-Musik und ihre witzigen Texte bekannt. Ihre Mitglieder lernten sich an der Thomanerschule in Leipzig kennen. Sebastian Krumbiegel studierte an der Hochschule für Musik und Theater Felix Mendelssohn Bartholdy Schlagzeug und Gesang. Tobias Künzel und Wolfgang Lenk waren Mitglieder des Thomanerchors. Die zwei weiteren Sänger heißen Jens Sembdner und Henri Schmidt.

Vor dem Hören Wie bekommt man eine Million Euro?

Nach dem Hören Welche Antworten sind richtig?

1. Als Millionär wäre das ...
   - ☐ **a.** Portemonnaie sehr schwer.
   - ☒ **b.** Konto nie leer.

2. Der Sänger ist
   - ☐ **a.** Professor
   - ☒ **b.** faul

3. Der Sänger möchte ...
   - ☐ **a.** eine Bank knacken.
   - ☒ **b.** Popstar werden.

4. Eine Bank auszurauben ...
   - ☐ **a.** ist nicht gefährlich.
   - ☒ **b.** bringt einen in den Knast.

5. Viele reiche Witwen wollen ...
   - ☒ **a.** seinen Körper.
   - ☐ **b.** sein Geld.

Die Prinzen, eine Musikgruppe aus Leipzig

iMix Link: This song is available for purchase at the iTunes store in a special iMix created for *Kontakte*. For more information about accessing the playlist, go to **Connect German** (www.connectgerman.com).

Miniwörterbuch

witzig	funny	**weder ... noch**	neither . . . nor
das **Mitglied, -er**	member	**faul**	lazy
das **Schlagzeug**	drums	**knacken**	to break into (*slang*)
wäre	would be	**ausrauben**	to rob
wäre gern	would like to be	**gefährlich**	dangerous
das **Portemonnaie**	wallet	der **Knast**	slammer (*slang for* jail)
das **Konto**	(bank) account	die **Witwe**	widow

Musikszene. Die Prinzen are a German pop band founded in the former GDR in 1987. The group members Sebastian Krumbiegel, Tobias Künzel, Wolfgang Lenk, Jens Sembdner, and Henri Schmidt met in Leipzig where they studied music. In high school, Sebastian, Tobias, and Wolfgang were members of the famous *Thomanerchor* of the *Thomasschule* in Leipzig. Die Prinzen became famous for their a cappella singing and their humorous lyrics.

Arbeitsplätze

Grammatik 5.4

Vocabulary Display

In this section, we introduce the concept of expressing a fixed location using the dative case while also introducing vocabulary for workplaces.
(1) Presentation: *Was macht man an der Tankstelle? Wenn das Auto kein Benzin mehr hat, wenn es Benzin braucht, fährt man zur Tankstelle und tankt Benzin. usw.* **(2) Choral repetition. (3)** Based on the information you gave in step 1, ask short questions to elicit the locations in the display: *Wo tankt man? Wo schwimmt man? usw.*

auf der Bank · auf der Post · in der Gaststätte · an der Kinokasse · im Hotel · im Schwimmbad · an der Tankstelle · auf der Polizei

Situation 9 Der Arbeitsplatz

Sit. 9. Before having sts. do this activity on their own, you can introduce the location phrases and reinforce the professions in the following way: Bring in pictures of the 10 locations mentioned; show them to the sts. as you model the pronunciation. As sts. repeat each phrase, tape the pictures at various locations around the room. To test sts.' recall, do two quick exercises.

First, say to sts. (books closed): *Ich bin Anwältin. Wo arbeite ich?* (*Auf dem Gericht.*) Walk to the picture of the courtroom, and, as you stand in front of it, continue: *Ja, ich bin Anwältin und eine Anwältin arbeitet auf dem Gericht.* Continue this, always standing in front of the appropriate picture. Or, mention TV characters representative of the various professions. Present the professions in a different order from that in the book.

Second, go to the various locations and say, for example, *Ich arbeite auf der Bank. Was bin ich von Beruf?* (*Sie sind Bankangestellte.*) *Ich arbeite in der Schule. Was bin ich von Beruf?* (*Sie sind Lehrerin.*) Now have sts. work in pairs to do the exercise. Partners can switch roles after S1 has asked 5 questions.

MODELL: S1: Wo arbeitet eine Anwältin?
S2: Auf dem Gericht.

> **im Krankenhaus** **in der Kirche** **auf der Post**
> **auf der Polizei** **auf der Universität** **auf dem Gericht**
> **im Schwimmbad** **in der Schule** **im Kaufhaus**
> **auf der Bank**

1. eine Anwältin
2. ein Arzt
3. eine Bademeisterin
4. ein Bankangestellter
5. ein Lehrer

6. eine Polizistin
7. ein Postbeamter
8. ein Priester
9. eine Professorin
10. eine Verkäuferin

Situation 10 Minidialoge

Sit. 10. Model pronunciation of the locations. Give sts. a few minutes to do the activity. If you have pictures of each location in your PF, place them around the classroom. To model pronunciation, act out each minidialogue while standing in front of the appropriate picture. Have sts. repeat several times, with their books closed. After sts. have a good grasp of each minidialogue, have them choose partners. Send each pair to one of the pictures, where they should act out the appropriate exchange. Encourage them to be inventive; they need not simply repeat what they have heard. After performing for the class, one of the pair concludes, *Wo findet dieser Dialog statt?* to which the class must respond appropriately.

AA. Sts. could also create their own dialogues to present to the class. Classmates should then guess where they take place.

AA. Here is a guessing game about professions, similar to 20 Questions. It enables sts. to combine much of what they have learned in other situations. Say: *An welchen Beruf denke ich?* and have sts. ask you questions to determine the profession you have in mind. You could write sample questions down ahead of time to help sts. get from the more general, i.e., *Arbeitest du zu Hause? Arbeitest du im Büro? Arbeitest du im Krankenhaus? Arbeitest du im Freien? Verdienst du viel Geld? Musst du jeden Tag einen Anzug / ein Kostüm tragen? Musst du ein Diplom haben? usw.*, to the more specific job tasks learned in earlier activities: *Pflegst du kranke Menschen? Zeichnest du Pläne für Häuser? Untersuchst du Patienten? usw.*

Wo finden diese Dialoge statt?

> **auf der Post** **an der Tankstelle** **auf dem Bahnhof**
> **im Hotel** **in der Bäckerei** **in der Gaststätte**
> **an der Kinokasse** **im Schwimmbad** **auf der Bank**

1. —Guten Tag, ich möchte ein Konto eröffnen.
   —Füllen Sie bitte dieses Formular aus und gehen Sie zum Schalter 3.
2. —Ich hätte gern eine Fahrkarte nach Bonn.
   —Hin und zurück oder einfach?
3. —Zwei Briefmarken für Postkarten in die USA, bitte.
   —Das sind zweimal 75 Cent, ein Euro fünfzig zusammen.
4. —Guten Tag, einmal volltanken und kontrollieren Sie bitte das Öl.
   —Wird gemacht.
5. —Grüß Gott, geben Sie mir bitte ein Bauernbrot.
   —Bitte sehr! Sonst noch etwas?
6. —Guten Abend, ich hätte gern ein Doppelzimmer für eine Nacht.
   —Mit oder ohne Dusche?
7. —Könnten Sie mir sagen, wo die Umkleidekabinen sind?
   —Ja, die sind gleich hier um die Ecke.
8. —Zwei Eintrittskarten für *Goethe!*, bitte.
   —Tut mir leid, der Film ist leider schon ausverkauft.
9. —Hallo! Zahlen bitte!
   —Gerne. Zusammen oder getrennt?

Ausbildung und Beruf

Wie ist es in Ihrem Land?

- Welchen Schulabschluss[1] braucht man für eine Berufsausbildung?
- Wie bekommt man eine Berufsausbildung?
- Wo lernt man die praktische Seite des Berufs? Wie lange dauert das?
- Wo lernt man die theoretische Seite? Wie lange dauert das?
- Macht man am Ende eine Prüfung? Was ist man dann?

Max hat keine Lust auf Schule und später Studium. Wenn er die zehnte Klasse erfolgreich[2] abschließt[3], hat er den Realschulabschluss. Er möchte am liebsten eine praktische Ausbildung machen, z. B. als Tischler oder Koch. Ein Facharbeiter[4] verdient mehr als ein ungelernter Arbeiter. Die Grafik zeigt, wie die Ausbildung für Max weitergeht.

Wie ist es in Deutschland?

- Wie lange dauert eine Ausbildung oder Lehre?
- Wo bekommt man die theoretische Ausbildung?
- Wo lernt man die praktische Seite des Berufs?
- Was bekommt man am Ende der Gesellenprüfung?
- Was ist man am Schluss[5]?

Photo questions. (*Praktische Ausbildung*) *Was lernt man in dieser Schule? Was lernen die Leute auf diesem Bild? Was tragen die jungen Männer auf dem Kopf? Warum? Wie alt sind sie? Wo werden Bäcker in Ihrer Stadt oder Ihrem Staat ausgebildet? (Theoretische Ausbildung) Wie alt sind die Berufsschüler? Was sehen Sie auf den Tischen? Was lernt man in diesem Raum? Sehen Sie mehr Männer oder Frauen? Wer spricht auf diesem Bild? Schauen die Schüler den Lehrer an? Warum (nicht)?*

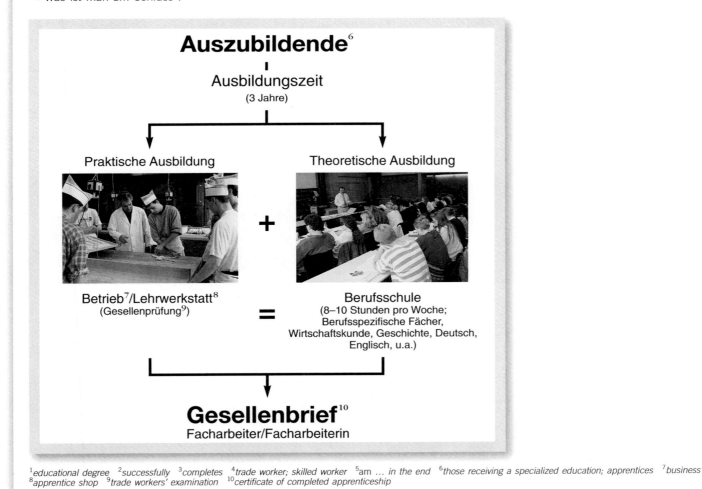

Auszubildende[6]

Ausbildungszeit
(3 Jahre)

Praktische Ausbildung   +   Theoretische Ausbildung

Betrieb[7]/Lehrwerkstatt[8]   =   Berufsschule
(Gesellenprüfung[9])   (8–10 Stunden pro Woche;
Berufsspezifische Fächer,
Wirtschaftskunde, Geschichte, Deutsch,
Englisch, u.a.)

Gesellenbrief[10]
Facharbeiter/Facharbeiterin

[1]*educational degree* [2]*successfully* [3]*completes* [4]*trade worker; skilled worker* [5]*am ... in the end* [6]*those receiving a specialized education; apprentices* [7]*business* [8]*apprentice shop* [9]*trade workers' examination* [10]*certificate of completed apprenticeship*

Situation 11 Zum Schreiben: Vor der Berufsberatung

Sit. 11. This activity prepares sts. for the role-play in *Sit. 12*. Assign as homework. Ask sts. to write complete sentences and to provide as much detail as possible. **Note:** A *Berufsberater* helps high school and college students to find a profession or a field of study that fits their skills, interests, and personality. Every school and university offers consultations with a *Berufsberater*.

Morgen haben Sie einen Termin beim Berufsberater. Bereiten Sie sich auf das Gespräch vor. Machen Sie sich Notizen zu den Stichwörtern von der Liste.

- Schulbildung
- familiärer[1] Hintergrund (Beruf der Eltern usw.)
- Interessen, Hobbys
- Lieblingsfächer, besondere Fähigkeiten
- Qualifikationen (Fremdsprachen, Computerkenntnisse usw.)
- Erwartungen[2] an den zukünftigen[3] Beruf (Geld, Arbeitszeiten, Urlaub usw.)

Situation 12 Rollenspiel: Bei der Berufsberatung

Sit. 12. (See the IM on how to present *Rollenspiele*.) Role for S2 appears in Appendix B. In preparation for this activity, have sts. do *Sit. 11*. You may wish to go over proper question formation with your sts. before doing the role-play.

Note: If your students are using McGraw-Hill's **Connect** online *Arbeitsbuch*, they can do this *Rollenspiel* using the real-time, interactive **Video-Chat** feature.

s1: Sie arbeiten bei der Berufsberatung. Ein Student / Eine Studentin kommt in Ihre Sprechstunde. Stellen Sie ihm/ihr Fragen zu diesen Themen: Schulbildung, Interessen und Hobbys, besondere Kenntnisse, Lieblingsfächer.

In der Küche

Grammatik 5.4–5.5

Vocabulary Display
This section exposes sts. to more dative prepositional phrases and introduces dative personal pronouns. **(1)** Ask sts. to repeat after you as you read the words of the display. **(2)** Ask sts. to write down which of these items they have in their possession. **(3)** Prepare the following interview by asking sts. to practice the sentence „*Hast du ein/e/n _____?*" with all the words in the display. **(4)** Ask sts. to interview each other about what items they have, jotting down what their partner owns.

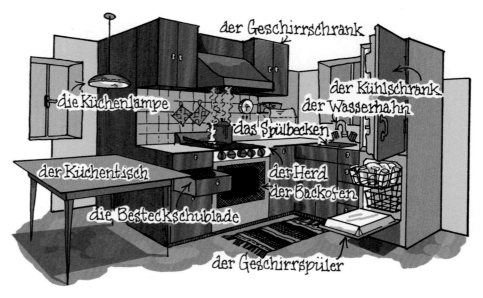

[1]*family* [2]*expectations* [3]*future*

Situation 13 Wo ist ...?

Sit. 13. This activity is based on the vocabulary display for this section. Have sts. work in pairs.

MODELL: s1: Wo ist der Küchentisch?
s2: Unter der Küchenlampe.

> am Fenster   unter dem Herd
>
> unter dem Geschirrschrank
>
> im Geschirrschrank   auf dem Herd   im Geschirrspüler
>
> im Kühlschrank   unter dem Kühlschrank
>
> in der Besteckschublade

1. Wo ist der Geschirrspüler?
2. Wo ist die Küchenuhr?
3. Wo ist der Backofen?
4. Wo ist das Spülbecken?
5. Wo sind die Papiertücher?
6. Wo ist die Pfanne?
7. Wo ist das Geschirr?
8. Wo ist der Topf?
9. Wo sind die Gläser?
10. Wo ist das Besteck?

Situation 14 Interaktion: Küchenarbeit

Sit. 14. Sts. who live in a dorm should be asked what they do (or did) when at home.

Cultural note. In Germany many bottles carry a deposit value, and so people are motivated to return them. For bottles without a deposit, there are recycling bins, one for each color of glass.

Wie oft spülst du das Geschirr?

mehrmals am Tag
jeden Tag
fast jeden Tag
zwei- bis dreimal in der Woche
einmal in der Woche
einmal im Monat
selten
nie

Wie oft ...?	ich	mein(e) Partner(in)
gehst du einkaufen		
kochst du		
deckst du den Tisch		
spülst du das Geschirr		
stellst du das Geschirr weg		
machst du den Herd sauber		
machst du den Tisch sauber		
machst du den Kühlschrank sauber		
fegst du den Boden		
bringst du die leeren Flaschen weg		

Situation 15 Umfrage: Kochst du mir ein Abendessen?

MODELL: s1: Kochst du mir morgen ein Abendessen?
s2: Ja.
s1: Unterschreib bitte hier.

UNTERSCHRIFT

1. Kochst du mir morgen ein Abendessen? _____
2. Backst du mir einen Kuchen zum Geburtstag? _____
3. Kaufst du mir ein Eis? _____
4. Schenkst du mir deinen Kugelschreiber? _____
5. Hilfst du mir heute bei der Hausaufgabe? _____
6. Kannst du mir die Grammatik erklären? _____
7. Schreibst du mir in den Ferien eine Postkarte? _____
8. Kannst du mir mein Zimmer aufräumen? _____
9. Kannst du mir fünf Dollar leihen? _____

Situation 16 Dialog: Chaos in der Küche

In der Küche herrscht Chaos und Herr Ruf ist sauer.

HERR RUF: Jutta, komm mal her!

JUTTA: Ja, Papa. Warum schreist du denn so?

HERR RUF: Weil es hier aussieht wie im Schweinestall! Warum ist Marmelade in der Besteckschublade?

JUTTA: Ich habe mir ein Brot gemacht und das ist dann in die Schublade gefallen.

HERR RUF: Und warum ist die Kaffeemaschine auf dem Fußboden?

JUTTA: Hans brauchte Platz auf dem Küchentisch für seine Legos.

HERR RUF: Das Kochbuch liegt im Backofen! Unglaublich!

JUTTA: Weil es da warm ist. Es war leider nass.

HERR RUF: Und warum ist der Kuchen im Spülbecken?

JUTTA: Keine Ahnung!

HERR RUF: Ihr glaubt wohl, dass Aufräumen meine Lieblingsbeschäftigung ist!

JUTTA: Ach, Papa, das ist doch nicht so schlimm. Ich hole Hans und dann helfen wir dir.

Filmlektüre
Der Tunnel

Filmlektüre. Suggestions: (1) Ask the questions in *Vor dem Lesen* and some additional ones such as: *Wann ist der Film erschienen? In welchem Land? Was für ein Film ist es? Wie lange dauert er? Wer hat die Hauptrollen? Wie heißt der Regisseur?* **(2)** Next, ask students to read the words in the *Miniwörterbuch*, to find them in the *Inhaltsangabe* and to underline them. **(3)** Then, go over the *Arbeit mit dem Text* making sure sts. understand all the words. Write unfamiliar words on the board with translations or convey the meaning in another manner. **(4)** Ask sts. to work in pairs and match the sentence parts giving an example *Welcher Buchstabe gehört zu Nummer 1? (e.)* **Answers:** 1. e.; 2. c.; 3. a.; 4. d.; 5. b.

Vor dem Lesen

A. Sehen Sie sich das Filmposter an.
1. Wie viele Leute sehen Sie?
2. Wie sehen sie aus?
3. Wie ist die Stimmung?
4. Sehen Sie Werkzeuge oder Materialien?
5. Warum bauen Menschen eigentlich Tunnel?

Filmangaben

Titel: *Der Tunnel*
Genre: Drama
Erscheinungsjahr: 2001
Land: Deutschland
Dauer: 150 min
Regisseur: Roland Suso Richter
Hauptrollen: Alexandra Maria Lara, Claudia Michelsen, Heino Ferch, Nicolette Krebitz, Sebastian Koch, Felix Eitner

Szene aus dem Film *Der Tunnel*

B. Lesen Sie die Wörter im Miniwörterbuch. Suchen Sie sie im Text und unterstreichen Sie sie.

Miniwörterbuch

abgrenzen	to fence off	hinter jemandem her sein	to be after someone
sich anschließen (schließt sich an)	to join (joins)	kriegen	to get, to catch
beschließen	to decide	der **Oberst**	colonel
durchkreuzen	to thwart	die **Stasi** (Staatssicherheit)	East German secret service
fliehen	to flee	der **Verlobte**	fiancé
gefährlich	dangerous	versperrt sein	to be blocked
der **Geheimdienst**	secret service	vertrauen	to trust
graben	to dig	zusammenbrechen	to collapse
das **Grundwasser**	groundwater		

Inhaltsangabe

13. August 1961: Die DDR-Regierung baut eine Mauer durch Berlin und grenzt den Osten der Stadt vom Westen ab. Schwimmstar Harry Melchior (Heino Ferch) hat genug von der DDR und will weg. Noch im Herbst, kurz nach dem Bau der Berliner Mauer, flieht er mit seinem Freund Matthis Hiller (Sebastian Koch) in den
5 Westteil Berlins. Die beiden beschließen, Harrys Schwester Lotte (Alexandra Maria

Suggestions (continued): (5) Next, work with the *Filmclip*. Paraphrase the introduction to the *Filmclip* and go over the questions making sure sts. understand them. Tell sts. that you will play the clip twice and that they should take notes on the questions. **(6)** Elicit answers and write them on the board including incorrect ones. Tell them that you will play the clip one more time and ask them to determine which of their answers are correct. **(7)** Provide sts. with the correct answers or have sts. work in groups or pairs to determine the correct answers. **(8)** Assign *Nach dem Lesen* for homework.

Lara) und Matthis' Frau Carola (Claudia Michelsen) in den Westen zu holen. Zusammen mit Fred von Klausnitz und dem Ex-GI Vittorio „Vic" Castanza wollen sie einen Tunnel von West nach Ost graben, weil alle anderen Fluchtwege versperrt sind. Im Keller einer alten Fabrik an der Bernauer Straße finden sie den idealen Ort für den Tunnel. Die junge, attraktive Friederike „Fritzi" (Nicolette Krebitz) schließt sich der Gruppe an. Sie will für ihren Verlobten Heiner die Flucht in den Westen möglich machen.

Die Gruppe um Harry rekrutiert mehr Helfer, um die schwierige Aufgabe zu schaffen. Die Frage dabei ist immer: Wem kann man vertrauen? Einfach ist das Tunnelprojekt nicht. Einmal bricht der Tunnel beinah zusammen und ein anderes Mal läuft Grundwasser ein. Auch müssen die Fluchthelfer ihre Aktion finanzieren: Sie verkaufen die Rechte ihrer Geschichte an die NBC und werden dafür bei ihrer Arbeit gefilmt. Und dann gibt es noch die Stasi, den Geheimdienst der DDR. Vor allem Stasi-Oberst Krüger ist hinter Harry und Matthis her. Er will ihren Plan durchkreuzen. Am Ende wird es gefährlich für Harry und seine Freunde, aber Krüger kriegt sie nicht!

Arbeit mit dem Text

Was gehört zusammen?

1. Harry hat genug von der DDR, …
2. Alle Fluchtwege sind versperrt, …
3. Harry und seine Freunde können den Tunnel nicht allein bauen, …
4. Harry und seine Leute haben nicht genug Geld, …
5. Kein DDR-Bürger darf das Land verlassen, …

a. deshalb helfen mehr Menschen beim Graben.
b. deshalb verfolgt Stasi-Oberst Krüger Fluchthelfer wie Harry und seine Freunde.
c. deshalb ist der Tunnel eine der letzten Möglichkeiten, die DDR zu verlassen.
d. deshalb verkaufen sie ihre Geschichte an das amerikanische Fernsehen.
e. deshalb will er weg.

 Filmclip

DVD, Kapitel 1, Vorspann, 0:00:00–0:03:00 Min.

Harry Melchior, die Hauptfigur des Films, stellt sich und andere vor.

Schauen Sie sich die Szene an und beantworten Sie die Fragen.

1. Wann hat Harry sein Land verlassen?
2. Was genau ist „sein Land"?
3. Bei welchem Wettkampf° tritt Harry an°? Wie schneidet er ab°?
4. Wer ist Lotte?
5. Wer ist Matthis?
6. Matthis erzählt, dass man große Mengen Steine von seiner Baustelle° wegschafft°. Warum macht man das?

competition / tritt … an *does . . . compete* / schneidet … ab *does . . . perform*

construction site

carries away

Nach dem Lesen

Kreatives Schreiben. Oberst Krüger verfolgt Harry im Tunnel. Es kommt zu einem Gespräch zwischen den beiden. Was sagen sie? Schreiben Sie einen Dialog zwischen Harry und Oberst Krüger.

Videoecke

Perspektiven

> Wie finanzierst du dir dein Studium?

Aufgabe 1 Das Studium

Ich bekomme BAföG.

Wer bekommt BAföG? Wer hat einen Nebenjob? Schreiben Sie auf, wie sich die Studentinnen und Studenten ihr Studium finanzieren. ACHTUNG: Manche bekommen Geld aus unterschiedlichen Quellen.

Miniwörterbuch

einen Kredit aufnehmen	to take out a loan
der Nebenjob	side job
sparen	to save
die Kulturwissenschaften	cultural sciences
eigentlich	actually
die Forschung	research
die Entwicklungshilfe	developmental aid
das Fließband	assembly line
basteln	to do crafts

1. Judith _b, e_

2. Susan _e_

3. Shaimaa _f_

4. Martin _a_

5. Tina _d, a_

6. Inna _f_

7. Nadezda _d, c_

8. Sophie _b_

a. arbeiten
b. BAföG
c. einen Kredit aufnehmen
d. Eltern
e. Nebenjobs
f. Stipendium

Interviews

- Was studierst du?
- Was gefällt dir an deinem Studium?
- Was willst du damit mal machen?
- Arbeitest du neben deinem Studium?
- Was machst du da genau?
- Wie viel Geld verdienst du damit?
- Gibt es etwas, worauf du sparst?

Tabea

Tina

Aufgabe 2 Wer sagt was?

Wer sagt das, Tabea oder Tina?

	Tabea	Tina
1. Ich studiere Biochemie und Mathematik.	☒	☐
2. Ich studiere Kulturwissenschaften.	☐	☒
3. Eigentlich wollte[1] ich Medizin studieren.	☒	☐
4. Ich möchte gern in die Forschung gehen.	☒	☐
5. Ich möchte vielleicht in die Entwicklungshilfe gehen.	☐	☒
6. Ich arbeite in den Semesterferien am Fließband.	☒	☐
7. Ich passe auf ein dreijähriges Kind auf.	☐	☒
8. Ich verdiene 8 Euro 50 pro Stunde.	☒	☐
9. Ich möchte einmal nach Japan reisen.	☒	☐
10. Ich ziehe um und brauche eine neue Küche.	☐	☒

Aufgabe 3 Dies und das

Beantworten Sie die folgenden Fragen.

1. Warum kann Tabea nicht Medizin studieren?
2. Was möchte Tabea machen, wenn sie in die Forschung geht?
3. Was gefällt Tina an ihrem Studium?
4. Was macht Tina mit dem dreijährigen Kind?
5. Wie viel verdient Tina?

Aufgabe 4 Interview

Interviewen Sie eine Partnerin oder einen Partner. Stellen Sie die Interviewfragen.

[1]wanted to

Wortschatz

Berufe	Professions
der Anwalt, ⸚e / die Anwältin, -nen	lawyer
der Arzt (R), ⸚e / die Ärztin, -nen	physician, doctor
der Bademeister, - / die Bademeisterin, -nen	swimming-pool attendant
der/die Bankangestellte, -n	bank employee
der Bauarbeiter, - / die Bauarbeiterin, -nen	construction worker
der Berufsberater, - / die Berufsberaterin, -nen	career counselor
der Dirigent, -en (*wk. masc.*) / die Dirigentin, -nen	(orchestra) conductor

der Friseur, -e / die Friseurin, -nen	hairdresser
der Hausmeister, - / die Hausmeisterin, -nen	custodian
der Krankenpfleger, - / die Krankenpflegerin, -nen	nurse
der Richter, - / die Richterin, -nen	judge
der Schriftsteller, - / die Schriftstellerin, -nen	writer
der Verkäufer, - / die Verkäuferin, -nen	salesperson

Ähnliche Wörter

der Arbeiter, - / die Arbeiterin, -nen; der Architekt, -en (*wk. masc.*) / die Architektin, -nen; der Bibliothekar, -e /

die Bibliothekarin, -nen; der Koch, -̈e / die Köchin, -nen; der Pilot, -en (wk. masc.) / die Pilotin, -nen; der Polizist, -en (wk. masc.) / die Polizistin, -nen; der Präsident, -en (wk. masc.) / die Präsidentin, -nen; der Priester, - / die Priesterin, -nen; der Sekretär, -e / die Sekretärin, -nen; der Taxifahrer, - / die Taxifahrerin, -nen

Orte	Places
die Ecke, -n	corner
um die Ecke	around the corner
die Fabrik, -en	factory
in der Fabrik	in the factory
die Gaststätte, -n	restaurant
in der Gaststätte	at the restaurant
die Kasse, -n	ticket booth
an der Kasse	at the ticket booth
die Kirche, -n	church
in der Kirche	at church
die Polizei	police station
auf der Polizei	at the police station
die Post	post office
auf der Post	at the post office
die Tankstelle, -n	gas station
an der Tankstelle	at the gas station
der Bahnhof, -̈e (R)	train station
auf dem Bahnhof	at the train station
der Schalter, -	ticket booth
am Schalter	at the ticket booth
das Büro, -s	office
im Büro	at the office
das Gericht, -e	courthouse
auf dem Gericht	at the courthouse
das Kaufhaus, -̈er	department store
im Kaufhaus	at the department store
das Krankenhaus, -̈er (R)	hospital
im Krankenhaus	in the hospital
das Schwimmbad, -̈er (R)	swimming pool
im Schwimmbad	at the swimming pool

Ähnliche Wörter

die Bäckerei, -en; in der Bäckerei; die Bank, -en; auf der Bank; die Schule, -n (R); in der Schule; die Universität, -en (R); auf der Universität; der Supermarkt, -̈e; im Supermarkt; das Hotel, -s (R); im Hotel

In der Küche	In the Kitchen
die Fensterbank, -̈e	windowsill
die Flasche, -n	bottle
die Küche, -n	kitchen
die Küchenwaage, -n	kitchen scale
die Salatschüssel, -n	salad (mixing) bowl
die Schublade, -n	drawer
die Tasse, -n (R)	cup

der Backofen, -̈	oven
der Geschirrspüler, -	dishwasher
der Herd, -e	stove
der Kühlschrank, -̈e	refrigerator
der Topf, -̈e	pot, pan
der Topflappen, -	potholder
der Wasserhahn, -̈e	faucet
das Besteck	silverware, cutlery
das Geschirr (R)	dishes
das Papiertuch, -̈er	paper towel
das Spülbecken, -	sink

Ähnliche Wörter

die Kaffeemaschine, -n; die Küchenarbeit, -en; die Küchenlampe, -n; die Küchenuhr, -en; die Pfanne, -n; der Küchentisch, -e; das Glas, -̈er

Einkäufe und Geschenke	Purchases and Presents
die Badehose, -n	swim(ming) trunks
die Briefmarke, -n	stamp
die Halskette, -n (R)	necklace
die Mütze, -n	cap
der Regenschirm, -e	umbrella
der Reiseführer, -	travel guidebook
der Roman, -e	novel
das Weihnachtsgeschenk, -e	Christmas present

Ähnliche Wörter

die Konzertkarte, -n; die Tageszeitung, -en; der Bikini, -s; der Fahrradhelm, -e; der MP3-Spieler, - (R); das Parfüm, -e

Schule und Beruf	School and Career
die Ausbildung	specialized training
praktische Ausbildung	practical (career) training
die Bundeswehr	German army
bei der Bundeswehr	in the German army
die Schulbildung	education, schooling

Sonstige Substantive	Other Nouns
die Dusche, -n	shower
die Eintrittskarte, -n	admissions ticket
die Enkelin, -nen	granddaughter
die Fremdsprache, -n	foreign language
die Lehre, -n	apprenticeship
die Lieblingsbeschäftigung, -en	favorite activity
die Möglichkeit, -en	possibility
die Umkleidekabine, -n	dressing room

die Versicherung, -en	insurance
die Werkstatt, ⁻en	repair shop, garage
der Enkel, -	grandson
der Kuchen, -	cake
der Rasen	lawn
der Rat, Ratschläge	advice
der Schweinestall, ⁻e	pigpen
der Termin, -e	appointment
der Urlaub, -e (R)	vacation
der Vorschlag, ⁻e	suggestion
das Bauernbrot, -e	(loaf of) farmer's bread
das Doppelzimmer, -	double room
das Geheimnis, -se	secret
das Hundefutter	dog food
das Interesse, -n	interest
Interesse haben an	to be interested in
(+ dat.)	
das Konto, Konten	bank account
ein Konto eröffnen	to open a bank account
das Lieblingsfach, ⁻er	favorite subject
das Öl	oil
das Öl kontrollieren	to check the oil
die Kenntnisse (pl.)	skills; knowledge about a field

Ähnliche Wörter

die Klasse, -n; die Liste, -n; die Lotterie, -n; in der Lotterie gewinnen; die Patientin, -nen; der Patient, -en (wk. masc.); das Chaos; das Prestige [prestiːʒ]

Verben	Verbs
aus·tragen, trägt ...	to deliver
aus, ausgetragen	
Zeitungen austragen	to deliver newspapers
decken	to cover; set
den Tisch decken	to set the table
ein·kaufen gehen, ist	to go shopping
einkaufen	
gegangen (R)	
erklären	to explain
erzählen (R)	to tell (a story, joke)
fegen	to sweep
feiern (R)	to celebrate
heiraten (R)	to marry
interessieren	to interest
sich interessieren für	to be interested in
leid·tun, leidgetan (+ dat.)	to be sorry
tut mir leid (R)	I'm sorry
leihen, geliehen	to lend
mähen	to mow
pflegen	to attend to; to nurse

sagen (R)	to say, tell
schenken	to give (as a present)
statt·finden, stattgefunden	to take place
stellen (R)	to place, put
eine Frage stellen	to ask a question
unterrichten	to teach, instruct
untersuchen	to investigate; to examine
verkaufen (R)	to sell
voll·tanken	to fill up (with gas)
weg·stellen	to put away
werden, wird, ist	to become
geworden	
zahlen	to pay
zeichnen (R)	to draw

Ähnliche Wörter

backen, gebacken; heilen; weg·bringen, weggebracht

Adjektive und Adverbien	Adjectives and Adverbs
ausverkauft	sold out
dunkel	dark
getrennt	separately; separate checks
leer	empty
sauer	angry
unglaublich	incredible

Ähnliche Wörter

normal, praktisch

Sonstige Wörter und Ausdrücke	Other Words and Expressions
als	as; when
als was?	as what?
als ich acht Jahre alt war	when I was eight years old
etwas (R)	something, anything
sonst noch etwas?	anything else?
fast	almost
gern (R)	gladly
ich hätte gern	I would like
hin und zurück	round-trip
jede, jeder, jedes (R)	each
mehrmals	several times
nebenan	next door
von nebenan	from next door
sonst	otherwise
unter	under, underneath
unter dem Fenster	under the window
wem	whom (dative)
zweimal	twice

Strukturen und Übungen

5.1 Dative case: articles and possessive adjectives

The dative case indicates the person to or for whom something is done.

Wissen Sie noch?

The nominative case designates the subject of a sentence. The accusative case designates the object of the action of the verb.

Review grammar 2.1.

5.1. *Dativ: Artikel und Possessiva.* This is the first formal presentation of the dative case. The forms of articles and possessive adjectives are introduced here; the dative forms of personal pronouns will be described in Section 5.5. Point out that here the dative is used to indicate the indirect object. Other important uses of the dative are presented later: two-way prepositions with the dative in Sections 5.4, 6.2, and 6.4; dative verbs in Section 6.1; *mit* and *bei* + dative in Section 6.6; and other prepositions with the dative in Section 10.1. The concept of case and the use of case forms are among the most difficult areas of German grammar for sts. Accuracy in speech is not expected at this stage. Not all sts. will achieve a good understanding of case in the first year. Even when monitoring in written work, some will have difficulty with the selection of correct forms. Give sts. as much input with case forms as possible to aid acquisition. Emphasize these markers for the dative. Another useful rule is that dative plural forms of all determiners and nouns (and, later, attributive adjectives) end in *-n* (except nouns with a plural in *-s*).

A noun or pronoun in the dative case is used to designate the person to or for whom something is done.

Ernst schenkt **seiner Mutter** ein Buch.	*Ernst gives his mother a book.*
Sofie gibt **ihrem Freund** einen Kuss.	*Sofie gives her boyfriend a kiss.*

Note that the dative case frequently appears in sentences with three nouns: a person who does something, a person who receives something, and the object that is passed from the doer to the receiver. The doer, the subject of the sentence, is in the nominative case; the recipient, or beneficiary, of the action is in the dative case; and the object is in the accusative case.

Doer		Recipient	Object
Nominative Case	*Verb*	*Dative Case*	*Accusative Case*
Maria	kauft	ihrem Freund	ein Hemd.

Maria is buying her boyfriend a shirt.

In German, the signal for the dative case is the ending **-m** in the masculine and neuter, **-r** in the feminine, and **-n** in the plural. Here are the dative forms of the definite, indefinite, and negative articles, and of the possessive adjectives.

	Masculine and Neuter	Feminine	Plural
Definite Article	dem	der	den
Indefinite	einem	einer	—
Negative Article	keinem	keiner	keinen
Possessive Adjective	meinem	meiner	meinen
	deinem	deiner	deinen
	seinem	seiner	seinen
	ihrem	ihrer	ihren
	unserem	unserer	unseren
	eurem	eurer	euren

Jutta schreibt **einem Freund** einen Brief.	*Jutta is writing a letter to a friend.*
Jens erzählt **seinen Eltern** einen Witz.	*Jens is telling his parents a joke.*

All plural nouns end in **-n** in the dative unless they form their plural with **-s**.

All plural nouns add an **-n** in the dative unless they already end in **-n** or in **-s**.

> Claire erzählt **ihren Freunden** von ihrer Reise nach Deutschland.
>
> *Claire is telling her friends about her trip to Germany.*

Here is a short list of verbs that often take an accusative object and a dative recipient.

erklären	*to explain something to someone*
erzählen	*to tell someone (a story)*
geben	*to give someone something*
leihen	*to lend someone something*
sagen	*to tell someone something*
schenken	*to give someone something as a gift*

> Certain masculine nouns, in particular a number of nouns denoting professions, add **-(e)n** in the dative and accusative singular as well as in the plural. They are often called weak masculine nouns.

	Singular	Plural
Nominative	der Student	die Studenten
Accusative	den Studenten	die Studenten
Dative	dem Studenten	den Studenten

Übung 1   Was machen Sie für diese Leute?

Üb. 1-2. Assign these exercises for homework and have sts. read their answers in class.

Schreiben Sie mit jedem Verb einen Satz.

MODELL: Ich schenke meiner Mutter eine Kamera.

backen	Bruder/Schwester	ein Abendessen
erklären	Freund/Freundin	meine Bilder
erzählen	Großvater/Großmutter	einen Brief
geben	Mitbewohner/Mitbewohnerin	ein Buch
kaufen	Onkel/Tante	eine CD
kochen	Partner/Partnerin	mein Deutschbuch
leihen	Professor/Professorin	50 Dollar
schenken	Vater/Mutter	eine E-mail
schreiben	Vetter/Kusine	ein Geheimnis
verkaufen		eine Geschichte
		Kaffee
		eine Konzertkarte
		eine Krawatte
		einen Kuchen
		einen Kuss
		einen MP3-Spieler
		einen Witz

Übung 2   Was machen diese Leute?

Bilden Sie Sätze.

MODELL: Heidi schreibt ihren Eltern eine Karte.

Bikini (m.) = der Bikini
Grammatik (f.) = die Grammatik
Zelt (n.) = das Zelt

Heidi	erklären	*ihren* Eltern	Armband (n.)
Peter	erzählen	Freund	Bikini (m.)
Thomas	geben	Freundin	Geheimnis (n.)
Katrin	kaufen	Mann	Grammatik (f.)
Stefan	kochen	Mutter	*eine* Karte (f.)
Albert	leihen	Professor	Regenschirm (m.)
Monika	schenken	Schwester	Rucksack (m.)
Frau Schulz	schreiben	Tante	Suppe (f.)
Nora	verkaufen	Vetter	Zelt (n.)

5.2 Question pronouns: *wer, wen, wem*

5.2. *Interrogativpronomen*. Point out that the endings are the same as those of the masculine definite article. These German forms correspond to the formal English *who, whom,* and *to/for whom.*

wer (Who is it?) = nominative
wen (Whom do you know?) = accusative
wem (Whom did you give it to?) = dative

Use the pronouns **wer, wen,** and **wem** to ask questions about people: **wer** indicates the subject, the person who performs the action; **wen** indicates the accusative object; **wem** indicates the dative object.

Wer arbeitet heute Abend um acht?	*Who's working tonight at eight?*
Wen triffst du heute Abend?	*Whom are you meeting tonight?*
Wem leihst du das Zelt?	*To whom are you lending the tent?*

Übung 3   Minidialoge

Ergänzen Sie **wer, wen** oder **wem.**

1. JÜRGEN: _____ hat meinen Regenschirm?
   SILVIA: Ich habe ihn.

2. MELANIE: _____ hast du in der Stadt gesehen?
   JOSEF: Claire.

3. SOFIE: _____ willst du die DVD schenken?
   WILLI: Marta. Sie wünscht sie sich schon lange.

4. FRAU AUGENTHALER: Na, erzähl doch mal. _____ hast du letztes Wochenende kennengelernt?
   RICHARD: Also, sie heißt Uschi und ...

5. MEHMET: _____ wollt ihr denn euren neuen Computer verkaufen?
   RENATE: Schülern und Studenten.

6. NATALIE: Weißt du, _____ heute Abend zu uns kommt?
   LYDIA: Nein, du?
   NATALIE: Tante Christa, natürlich.

5.3 Expressing change: the verb *werden*

Use a form of **werden** to talk about changing conditions.

Ich werde alt.	*I am getting old.*
Es wird dunkel.	*It is getting dark.*

werden			
ich	werde	*wir*	werden
du	wirst	*ihr*	werdet
Sie	werden	*Sie*	werden
er *sie* *es*	wird	*sie*	werden

In German, **werden** is also used to talk about what somebody wants to be.

Was willst du werden?	*What do you want to be (become)?*
Natalie will Ärztin werden.	*Natalie wants to be (become) a physician.*

Übung 4   Was passiert?

Bilden Sie Fragen und suchen Sie dann eine logische Antwort darauf.

MODELL: Was passiert im Winter? —Es wird kalt.

1. am Abend
2. wenn man Bücher schreibt
3. wenn man krank wird
4. im Frühling
5. im Herbst
6. wenn Kinder älter werden
7. wenn man in der Lotterie gewinnt
8. wenn man Medizin studiert
9. am Morgen
10. im Sommer

a. Man wird Arzt.
b. Man wird bekannt[1].
c. Die Blätter werden bunt[2].
d. Es wird dunkel.
e. Sie werden größer.
f. Es wird wärmer.
g. Es wird hell[3].
h. Man bekommt Fieber.
i. Die Tage werden länger.
j. Man wird reich.

Übung 5   Was werden sie vielleicht?

Suchen Sie einen möglichen Beruf für jede Person.

MODELL: Jens hilft gern kranken Menschen. →
        Vielleicht wird er Arzt.

[1]*well-known* [2]*colorful* [3]*bright; light*

1. Lydia kocht gern.
2. Sigrid interessiert sich für Medikamente.
3. Ernst fliegt gern.
4. Jürgen hat Interesse an Pädagogik.
5. Jutta zeichnet gern Pläne für Häuser.
6. Helga geht gern in die Bibliothek.
7. Hans möchte gern kranke Menschen heilen.
8. Andrea hört gern klassische Musik.

Apotheker/Apothekerin
Architekt/Architektin
Bibliothekar/Bibliothekarin
Dirigent/Dirigentin
Koch/Köchin
Krankenpfleger/Krankenpflegerin
Lehrer/Lehrerin
Pilot/Pilotin

5.4 Location: *in, an, auf* + dative case

When indicating where something is located, **in, an,** and **auf** take the dative case.

5.4. *Akkusativ-/Dativpräpositionen.* This is the first presentation of two-way prepositions. We limit it to the 3 most common prepositions and their use with the dative only, so that students acquire this complex set of forms through meaningful practice without having to focus simultaneously on all the prepositions and both cases. Two-way prepositions with the dative are dealt with as a group in Section 6.2. For their use with the accusative, see Sections 6.2, 6.4, and 10.3.

To express the location of someone or something, use the following prepositions with the dative case.

$$
\left.\begin{array}{l}
\textbf{in } (in, at) \\
\textbf{auf } (on, at) \\
\textbf{an } (on, at)
\end{array}\right\} + \left\{\begin{array}{l}
\textbf{dem/einem} \underline{\quad} (m., n.) \\
\textbf{der/einer} \underline{\quad} (f.) \\
\textbf{den} \underline{\quad} (pl.)
\end{array}\right.
$$

Katrin wohnt **in der Stadt.**
Stefan und Albert sind **auf der Bank.**

Katrin lives in the city.
Stefan and Albert are at the bank.

A. Forms and Contractions

Remember the signals for dative case.

	Masculine and Neuter	Feminine	Plural
Dative	dem	der	den
	einem	einer	—

in + dem = im
an + dem = am

Note that the prepositions **in + dem** and **an + dem** are contracted to **im** and **am.**

Masculine and Neuter	Feminine	Plural
im Kino	**in der** Stadt	**in den** Wäldern
in einem Kino	**in einer** Stadt	**in** Wäldern
am See	**an der** Tankstelle	**an den** Wänden
an einem See	**an einer** Tankstelle	**an** Wänden
auf dem Berg	**auf der** Bank	**auf den** Bäumen
auf einem Berg	**auf einer** Bank	**auf** Bäumen

B. Uses

1. Use **in** when referring to enclosed spaces.

im Supermarkt	*in the supermarket (enclosed)*
in der Stadt	*in (within) the city*

2. **An,** in the sense of English *at,* denotes some kind of border or limiting area.

am Fenster	*at the window*
an der Tankstelle	*at the gas pump*
am See	*at the lake*

3. Use **auf,** in the sense of English *on,* when referring to surfaces.

auf dem Tisch	*on the table*
auf dem Herd	*on the stove*

4. **Auf** is also used to express location in public buildings such as the bank, the post office, or the police station.

auf der Bank	*at the bank*
auf der Post	*at the post office*
auf der Polizei	*at the police station*

Übung 6   ## Was macht man dort?

Üb. 6. Assign for homework or use for pair work in class.

Stellen Sie einem Partner / einer Partnerin Fragen. Er/Sie soll eine Antwort darauf geben.

MODELL: S1: Was macht man am Strand?
         S2: Man spielt Volleyball.

Benzin[1] tanken	**Geld wechseln[3]**	**tanzen**
beten[2]	**ein Buch lesen**	**schwimmen**
einen Film sehen	**Volleyball spielen**	**?**
	Briefmarken kaufen	**spazieren gehen**

1. im Kino
2. auf der Post
3. an der Tankstelle
4. in der Disko
5. in der Kirche
6. auf der Bank
7. im Meer
8. in der Bibliothek
9. im Park

[1]*gasoline*   [2]*to pray*   [3]*to exchange*

Übung 7   Wo?

Üb. 7. Have sts. also describe the location of objects and persons in the classroom and in pictures from your PF.

Wo sind die Leute? Wo sind das Poster, der Topf und der Wein?

MODELL: Stefan ist am Strand.

1.   2.   3.

4.   5.   6.

7.   8.   9.   10.

5.5 Dative case: personal pronouns

Wissen Sie noch?

The dative case designates the person to whom or for whom something is done.

Review grammar 5.1.

5.5. *Dativ: Personalpronomen.* This section continues the introduction of dative forms begun earlier in the chapter.

Mir and *mich*, *dir* and *dich* may be confused, because there is only one corresponding English form for both: *me* and *you*.

Personal pronouns in the dative case designate the person to or for whom something is done. (See also **Strukturen 5.1.**)

Kaufst du **mir** ein Buch?   *Are you buying me a book?*
Nein, ich schenke **dir** eine CD.   *No, I'm giving you a CD.*

A. First- and Second-Person Pronouns

Here are the nominative and dative forms of the first- and second-person pronouns.

Singular		Plural	
Nominative	*Dative*	*Nominative*	*Dative*
ich	mir	wir	uns
du	dir	ihr	euch
Sie	Ihnen	Sie	Ihnen

Note that German speakers use three different pronouns to express the recipient or beneficiary in the second person (English *you*): **dir, euch,** and **Ihnen.**

RICHARD: Leihst du mir dein Auto, Mutti? (*Will you lend me your car, Mom?*)
FRAU AUGENTHALER: Ja, ich leihe **dir** mein Auto. (*Yes, I'll lend you my car.*)

HERR THELEN: Viel Spaß in Wien! (*Have fun in Vienna!*)
HERR WAGNER: Danke! Wir schreiben **Ihnen** eine Postkarte. (*Thank you! We'll write you a postcard.*)

HANS: Ernst und Andrea! Kommt in mein Zimmer! Ich zeige **euch** meine Briefmarken. (*Ernst and Andrea! Come to my room! I'll show you my stamp collection.*)

B. Third-Person Pronouns

The third-person pronouns have the same signals as the dative articles: **-m** in the masculine and neuter, **-r** in the feminine, and **-n** in the plural.

	Masculine and Neuter	Feminine	Plural
Article	dem	der	den
Pronoun	**ihm**	**ihr**	**ihnen**

Was kaufst du deinem Vater?	*What are you going to buy your dad?*
Ich kaufe **ihm** ein Buch.	*I'll buy him a book.*
Was schenkst du deiner Schwester?	*What are you going to give your sister?*
Ich schenke **ihr** eine Bluse.	*I'll give her a blouse.*
Was kochen Sie Ihren Kindern?	*What are you going to cook for your kids?*
Ich koche **ihnen** Spaghetti.	*I'm making them spaghetti.*

Note that the dative-case pronoun precedes the accusative-case noun.

Ich schreibe dir einen Brief.   *I'll write you a letter.*

Übung 8   Minidialoge

Ergänzen Sie **mir, dir, uns, euch** oder **Ihnen.**

1. HANS: Mutti, kaufst du _____ Schokolade?
   FRAU RUF: Ja, aber du weißt, dass du vor dem Essen nichts Süßes essen sollst.

2. MARIA: Was hat denn Frau Körner gesagt?
   MICHAEL: Das erzähle ich _____ nicht.

3. ERNST: Mutti, kochst du Andrea und mir einen Pudding?
   FRAU WAGNER: Natürlich koche ich _____ einen Pudding.

4. HERR SIEBERT: Sie schulden[1] mir noch zehn Euro, Herr Pusch.
   HERR PUSCH: Was!? Wofür denn?
   HERR SIEBERT: Ich habe _____ doch für 100 Euro mein altes Motorrad verkauft, und Sie hatten nur 90 Euro dabei.
   HERR PUSCH: Ach, ja, richtig.

5. FRAU KÖRNER: Mein Mann und ich gehen heute Abend aus. Können Sie _____ vielleicht ein gutes Restaurant empfehlen, Herr Pusch?
   MICHAEL: Ja, gern ...

[1]*owe*

Note the potential for confusion here, too. German *ihn* and *ihm* correspond to English *him*, German *sie* and *ihr* to English *her*.

dem → ih**m**
der → ih**r**
den → ih**nen**

Üb. 8. This exercise uses 1st- and 2nd-person pronouns.

Übung 9   Wer? Wem? Was?

Üb. 9. For practice of 3rd-person pronouns. The exercise can be used for homework or for pair work in class. If sts. need additional practice, this activity could be expanded with personalizations. *Was haben Sie Ihrem Bruder gekauft?*

Beantworten Sie die Fragen mit Hilfe der Tabelle.

MODELL: Was hat Renate ihrem Freund geschenkt?
          Sie hat ihm ein T-Shirt geschenkt.

	Renate	Mehmet
schenken	ein T-Shirt	einen Regenschirm
leihen	ihr Auto	500 Euro
erzählen	ein Geheimnis	eine Geschichte
verkaufen	ihre Sonnenbrille	seinen Fernseher
zeigen	ihr Büro	seine Wohnung
kaufen	eine neue Brille	einen Kinderwagen

1. Was hat Mehmet seiner Mutter geschenkt?
2. Was hat Renate ihrem Vater geliehen?
3. Was hat Mehmet seinem Bruder geliehen?
4. Was hat Renate ihrer Friseurin erzählt?
5. Was hat Mehmet seinen Nichten erzählt?
6. Was hat Renate ihrer Freundin verkauft?
7. Was hat Mehmet seinen Eltern verkauft?
8. Was hat Renate ihrem Schwager gezeigt?
9. Was hat Mehmet seinem Freund gezeigt?
10. Was hat Renate ihrer Großmutter gekauft?
11. Was hat Mehmet seiner Schwägerin gekauft?

Wohnen

In **Kapitel 6,** you will learn vocabulary and expressions for describing where you live, for finding a place to live, and for talking about housework.

GOALS

In *Kapitel 6* sts. talk about living arrangements, how to look for an apartment, and about household chores. They also learn to specify location and direction, using both two-way prepositions and prepositions + fixed case (dative or accusative). In addition, they will learn more about separable-prefix verbs and about placement of adverbs and adverbial phrases of time and place. They are also introduced to the dative verbs.

Themen

Haus und Wohnung
Das Stadtviertel
Auf Wohnungssuche
Hausarbeit

Kulturelles

KLI: Wohnen
KLI: Auf Wohnungssuche
Musikszene: „Haus am See" (Peter Fox)
Filmclip: *Good bye Lenin!* (Wolfgang Becker)
Videoecke: Wohnen

Lektüren

Sachtext: Städteranking 2010
Film: *Good bye Lenin!* (Wolfgang Becker)

Strukturen

6.1 Dative verbs
6.2 Location vs. destination: two-way prepositions with the dative or accusative case
6.3 Word order: time before place
6.4 Direction: **in/auf** vs. **zu/nach**
6.5 Separable-prefix verbs: the present tense and the perfect tense
6.6 The prepositions **mit** and **bei** + dative

Friedensreich Hundertwasser: *(630A) Mit der Liebe warten tut weh, wenn die Liebe woanders ist* (1971), Galerie Koller, Zürich

Chapter opening artwork: The artist adopted the name "Hundertwasser" in 1949. ("Sto" means "hundred" in several Slavic languages.) One of his favorite projects was *kreative Architektur*, in which nature and architecture harmoniously connect. He was buried on his land in New Zealand in the *Garten der glücklichen Toten* underneath a tulip tree. The "630A" in the title of the work actually appears on the piece itself, center left just outside the frame.

Suggestion: Use this colorful and extravagant presentation of architecture for an association activity. Students need to use their imagination to come up with possible answers to most of the following questions. *Was sehen Sie auf dem Bild? Welche Farben hat der Maler benutzt? Wo stehen diese Häuser? Wer könnte da wohnen? Wie sind die Menschen, die da wohnen? Wie wirken diese Häuser auf Sie? Was könnte der Titel „Mit der Liebe warten tut weh, wenn die Liebe woanders ist" bedeuten?*

Kunst und Künstler

Friedensreich Hundertwasser (1928–2000), mit bürgerlichem Namen[1] Friedrich Stowasser, ist einer der bedeutendsten österreichischen Künstler des 20. Jahrhunderts. Er war Maler und Architekt, entwarf[2] aber auch Briefmarken und Bucheinbände[3]. Er war Sohn einer Jüdin. Aufgrund seiner Erfahrungen im Dritten Reich war er politisch aktiv, vor allem gegen Diktaturen. Weiterhin engagierte er sich sehr für den Umweltschutz. Mit seinen Gebäuden schuf er Beispiele für eine natur- und menschengerechte Architektur. Seine Bilder sind von kräftigen Farben, organischen Formen und einer Ablehnung[4] von geraden[5] Linien gekennzeichnet.

Schauen Sie sich das Bild an und beantworten Sie die folgenden Fragen.

1. Welche Farben dominieren im Bild? Welche Farbe dominiert besonders? Was symbolisiert diese Farbe? Denken Sie an den Titel.
2. Was ist das Besondere an den Häusern? Laden sie ein oder schließen sie aus? Woran erkennt man das?
3. Was sehen Sie links unten im rechten Haus? Wer könnte das sein?
4. Weckt das Bild eher fröhliche oder traurige Assoziationen? Warum?

[1]mit … *born* [2]*designed* [3]*book covers* [4]*rejection* [5]*straight*

Situationen

Haus und Wohnung

Grammatik 6.1–6.2

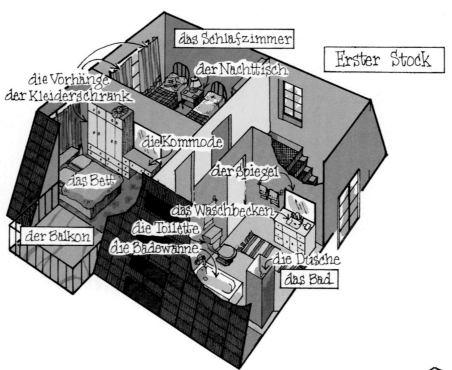

das Schlafzimmer

Erster Stock

der Nachttisch

die Vorhänge
der Kleiderschrank

die Kommode

der Spiegel

das Bett

das Waschbecken

der Balkon

die Toilette
die Badewanne

die Dusche

das Bad

Vocabulary Display

Use the projector to teach the words for rooms in a house and common articles of furniture. For receptive recall ask: *Haben Sie ein/e/n _____ in Ihrer Wohnung?* Tell sts. to imagine they are moving into an apartment and need to buy furniture (money is no problem). Then begin the activity by saying: *Ich ziehe um und ich kaufe ein Bett.* You could show pictures of the items from your PF at the same time. Then call on a st.: *Chad, was kaufen Sie?* Chad must now list what you bought and add something he is buying. *Ich kaufe ein Bett und einen Stuhl.* Chad now asks someone else: *Matt, was kaufst du?* to which Matt responds, *Ich kaufe ein Bett und einen Stuhl und einen Spiegel* and so on. (Provide hints from your PF.)

Introduce the term *Einweihungsfeier* to the sts. and tell them that house/apartment-warming parties are popular among young Germans. Traditional gifts are a loaf of bread and salt. The bread symbolizes having plenty to eat, and salt represents prosperity.

Cultural note. Toilets are often in a separate room from bathrooms.

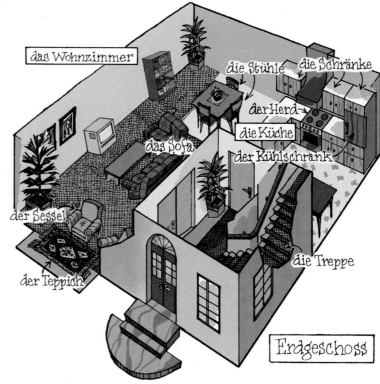

das Wohnzimmer

die Stühle

die Schränke

der Herd

die Küche

das Sofa

der Kühlschrank

der Sessel

die Treppe

der Teppich

Erdgeschoss

Situation 1   Wo ist das?

Sit. 1. This introduces new words, recycles the display vocabulary, and familiarizes sts. with using *in* as a dative preposition: *im_____, in der_____*. Have sts. work in pairs, alternating who asks and who answers. Words for additional practice: *Das Bücherregal, der Fernseher, die Mikrowelle, die Stereoanlage, die Toilette, das Waschbecken.*

AA. Show sts. how to make new words (compounds) to expand their vocabulary. Say: *Ein Tisch zum Essen ist ein Esstisch.* (Stress the compound.) *Ein Tisch zum Arbeiten ist ein Arbeitstisch. Ein Tisch zum Schreiben ist ein _____* (Schreibtisch). Then go to *Schrank: Ein Schrank für Kleider ist ein Kleiderschrank. Ein Schrank in der Küche ist ein _____* (Küchenschrank) *usw.* Then *Lampe, Stuhl usw.* Compound three words: *Eine Lampe für den Schreibtisch ist eine Schreibtischlampe usw.* Point out that the last part of the compound always determines the gender.

MODELL: s1: Wo ist die Badewanne?
         s2: Im Bad.

die Badewanne
das Bett
die Dusche
der Geschirrspüler
der Herd
das Klavier
die Kopfkissen
der Kühlschrank
der Nachttisch
der Schrank
das Sofa
der Spiegel
der Teppich

Cultural note. There are very few walk-in or built-in closets in German houses and apartments. Tenants have to provide their own freestanding closets.

> **im Bad**   **im Esszimmer**
> **im Schlafzimmer**
> **in der Küche**   **im Wohnzimmer**

Situation 2   Das Zimmer

Sit. 2. Begin by reviewing the names and genders of the items in the picture. Write these on the board, perhaps grouped according to gender, to make sure that sts. ask about all 8 items. Then focus sts.' attention on form: **(1)** write the prepositions in a row on the board, **(2)** list the nouns used in the prepositional phrases, grouping them by gender (*der Tisch, der Schrank; die Wand; das Fenster*), and **(3)** be explicit about what happens to the article, depending on gender, with each preposition, e.g., **der** Tisch: am Tisch, auf dem Tisch, neben dem Tisch usw. Look at the whole picture on the projector with the class. Describe the pictures in random order and ask sts. which picture you are describing, e.g.: „*Das Sofa steht an der Wand. Der Schrank steht neben dem Sofa. Der Tisch steht vor dem Schrank. Die Uhr hängt über dem Schrank. Die Katze ist auf → dem Tisch. Die Zeitung liegt auf dem Sofa.*" (picture 4). Make sure sts. recognize all the things that are different in the pictures and have access to the phrases required to ask the right questions.

Wählen Sie ein Bild, aber sagen Sie die Nummer nicht. Ihr Partner oder Ihre Partnerin stellt Fragen und sagt, welches Bild Sie gewählt haben.

MODELL: s1: Ist die Katze auf dem Sofa?
         s2: Ja.
         s1: Ist es neun Uhr?
         s2: Ja.
         s1: Dann ist es Bild 1.
         s2: Richtig. Jetzt bist du dran.

> **am Fenster**   **?**
> **auf dem Tisch**
> **vor dem Sofa**
> **auf dem Sofa**
> **über dem Schrank**
> **neben dem Sofa**
> **an der Wand**
> **unter dem Tisch**

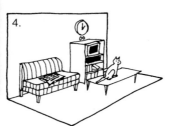

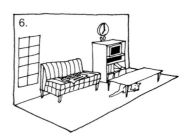

Ask sts. to work in pairs. S2 selects one of the six pictures, but does not tell his or her partner which one it is. S1 then asks yes/no questions to determine which picture S2 has selected. You may want to write model questions on the board, e.g. *Hängt die Uhr über dem Regal? Ist es neun Uhr? Gibt es ein Fenster?* To give the activity more structure, you may want to limit the number of questions to five or so.

Wohnen

In Ihrem Land:

- Haben moderne Häuser in Ihrem Land einen Keller[1], eine Terrasse, einen Balkon?
- Haben sie einen Garten vor oder hinter dem Haus?
- Aus welchem Material sind die Häuser normalerweise? (aus Stein, aus Holz[2], aus Beton[3])
- Gibt es einen Zaun[4] um das ganze Grundstück[5] herum oder nur um den Garten hinter dem Haus?
- Wie viele Garagen sind üblich[6]? Wie groß sind die Garagen? (Platz für ein Auto, zwei Autos, drei Autos)
- Aus welchem Material ist das Dach? (aus Asphaltschindeln[7], aus Holzschindeln[8], aus Ziegeln[9])

Einfamilienhaus in einer Neubausiedlung

Wohnblöcke im Ostteil Berlins

Zweifamilienhaus aus Backstein

In Deutschland:

- Schauen Sie sich die Fotos an. Welche Unterschiede[10] gibt es zu Häusern in Ihrem Land?

Hören Sie sich den Text an und beantworten Sie die folgenden Fragen.

- Wie viele Menschen leben in Deutschland?
- Wie groß ist Deutschland?
- In Deutschland leben ungefähr[11] 200 Menschen auf einem Quadratkilometer[12], das sind 563 auf einer Quadratmeile. In den USA z. B. sind es im Durchschnitt[13] 80. Wie viele sind es in Ihrem Bundesland?

KLI. Play recording or read passage to sts: *Ein modernes Einfamilienhaus in Deutschland hat einen Keller, eine Terrasse und oft auch einen Balkon. Es ist sehr massiv und aus Stein gebaut und von einem Zaun, einer Mauer oder Hecke umgeben. Das Dach ist meistens aus Ziegeln und hat einen Schornstein. Natürlich gibt es regionale Unterschiede. Ein typisches Haus in Süddeutschland sieht anders aus als ein Haus an der Nordseeküste. Weil Deutschland so dicht bevölkert ist–über 82 Millionen Menschen leben auf 357 000 Quadratkilometern–sind Häuser teuer. Nur 30% der Deutschen wohnen im eigenen Heim. Die anderen 70% wohnen zur Miete.* Ask sts. to discuss the questions relative to their countries. Collect sts.' answers and write on the board. Then, ask sts. to respond to the questions on Germany, again in small groups. Write sts.' answers on the board. Summarize the major differences between your country and Germany in simple German.

[1]basement [2]wood [3]concrete [4]fence [5]property [6]customary [7]asphalt shingles [8]wooden shingles [9]clay tiles [10]differences [11]approximately [12]square kilometer [13]im ... on average

Photo questions. *Wo spielen die Kinder, die hier wohnen? Wann hat man diese Häuser gebaut? Können Sie viele Blumen und Bäume sehen? Können Sie viele Autos sehen? Wo kann man hier parken? Möchten Sie lieber in einem Einfamilienhaus, einem Zweifamilienhaus oder in einem Wohnblock wohnen?*

Situation 3 Interview

Sit. 3. Model pronunciation and have sts. repeat. Have individual sts. ask you the questions and answer appropriately. Then have sts. work in pairs. Sts. asking the questions should also take notes. After each st. has asked all the questions, tell sts. to find a new partner. One st. could ask *Mit wem hast du gesprochen?* and then ask the interview questions regarding that person. This will give sts. practice using the possessive adjectives *sein/ihr* and their endings (*Kapitel 2*).

1. Wo wohnst du? (in einer Wohnung, in einem Studentenheim, in einem Haus, auf dem Land, in der Stadt, _____)
2. Wohnst du allein? (in einer WG [Wohngemeinschaft], bei deinen Eltern, bei einer Familie, mit einem Mitbewohner, mit einer Mitbewohnerin, _____)
3. Wie lange brauchst du zur Uni? (zehn Minuten zu Fuß, fünf Minuten mit dem Fahrrad, eine halbe Stunde mit dem Auto oder mit dem Bus, _____)
4. Was kostet dein Zimmer / deine Wohnung pro Monat?
5. Was für Möbel hast du in deinem Zimmer / in deiner Wohnung?

Situation 4 Interaktion: In der Wohnung

Beantworten Sie die Fragen für sich selbst und schreiben Sie Ihre Antworten auf. Stellen Sie dann die gleichen Fragen an Ihren Partner oder Ihre Partnerin.

	ich	mein(e) Partner(in)
Wie gefällt dir deine Wohnung oder dein Zimmer?		
Welches Möbelstück fehlt dir?		
Welches Möbelstück gehört dir nicht?		
Wie gefällt dir das Aufräumen und Putzen?		
Wer hilft dir beim Aufräumen und Putzen?		

Das Stadtviertel

Grammatik 6.3–6.4

Vocabulary Display
(See the IM.) Introduce nonguessable vocabulary by pointing to buildings and providing a simple definition using familiar words: *Im Rathaus arbeitet der Bürgermeister. In einer Metzgerei kann man Fleisch und Wurst kaufen. Ins Gefängnis kommt man, wenn man gestohlen oder getötet hat.* (You may need to act this out too.) Point out the difference between an *Apotheke* and a *Drogerie.* (*Metzgerei = Fleischerei* in northern Germany.)

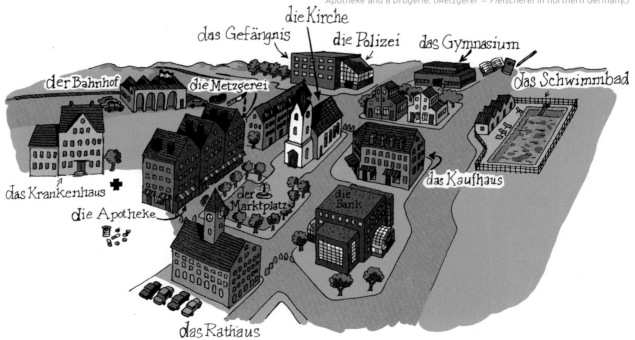

die Kirche

das Gefängnis

die Polizei

das Gymnasium

der Bahnhof

die Metzgerei

das Schwimmbad

das Krankenhaus

das Kaufhaus

der Marktplatz

die Bank

die Apotheke

das Rathaus

Situation 5 Wie weit weg?

MODELL: S1: Wie weit weg sollte die Apotheke von deiner Wohnung sein?
S2: _____

1. die Apotheke	5. das Kino	9. der Supermarkt
2. die Universität	6. das Krankenhaus	10. die Kirche
3. die Polizei	7. das Gefängnis	
4. der Flughafen	8. der Kindergarten	

gleich um die Ecke   am anderen Ende der Stadt

gleich gegenüber   so weit weg wie möglich

fünf Minuten zu Fuß   zehn Minuten mit dem Fahrrad

zwei Straßen weiter

eine halbe Stunde mit dem Auto   mir egal

Situation 6 Umfrage

Sit. 6. This poll provides examples of the "time before place" rule. Model pronunciation before sts. work in pairs.

MODELL: S1: Wohnst du in der Nähe der Universität?
S2: Ja.
S1: Unterschreib bitte hier.

UNTERSCHRIFT

1. Wohnst du in der Nähe der Universität? _____
2. Übernachtest du manchmal in Hotels? _____
3. Gibt es in deiner Heimatstadt ein Schwimmbad? _____
4. Warst du letzte Woche auf der Post? _____
5. Warst du gestern im Supermarkt? _____
6. Gibt es in deiner Heimatstadt ein Rathaus? _____
7. Warst du letzten Freitag in der Disko? _____
8. Bist du oft in der Bibliothek? _____
9. Warst du letzten Sonntag in der Kirche? _____

Sit. 7. This activity works with word order in subordinate clauses. Model pronunciation. Then, have sts. work in pairs. Afterward, ask sts. individually, *Wohin gehst du, wenn du ...,* and then turn it around and ask as well, *Wann fährst du zur Tankstelle? usw.,* to which sts. must answer, *Wenn ich Benzin brauche.* This gives them additional practice with word order and conjugating verbs at the end of the clause. Sts. who complete the exercise quickly can redo it in this manner until the rest of the class has finished.

Situation 7 Wohin gehst du, wenn ...?

MODELL: S1: Wohin gehst du, wenn du ein Buch lesen willst?
S2: Wenn ich ein Buch lesen will? In die Bibliothek.

1. du schwimmen gehen willst?	zum Bahnhof
2. du Briefmarken kaufen willst?	in die Bäckerei
3. du Geld brauchst?	zum Flughafen
4. du Benzin brauchst?	zum Arzt
5. du Brot brauchst?	auf die Bank
6. du krank bist?	zur Tankstelle
7. du verreisen willst?	auf die Post
8. du eine Zugfahrkarte kaufen willst?	ins Schwimmbad
9. _____?	_____

Wohin fahren Sie, wenn Sie Benzin brauchen?

Situation 8 Informationsspiel: Gestern und heute

Sit. 8. This is an information-gap activity that involves both scenes at once. Ask sts. to work in pairs. S1 works from the two scenes on this page, and S2 works from the corresponding pair of scenes in Appendix A. Eight locations are identified in the scenes, but each st. has complete information (*früher* and *heute*) for only four of them. For the remaining four locations, the st. knows either the previous or the current identity, but not both. Remind sts. to negotiate meaning in German by using such phrases as *Wie bitte? Wie schreibt man das? Was ist das?* usw.

Arbeiten Sie zu zweit und stellen Sie Fragen wie im Modell.

MODELL: S2: Heute ist hier ein Schuhgeschäft. Was war früher hier?
S1: Früher war hier eine Disko.

FRÜHER

HEUTE

Situationen **209**

Lektüre 📖

Lesehilfe

This reading, „**Städteranking 2010,**" is a **Sachtext** (informational, nonfiction text). German **Sachtexte** are usually filled with passive constructions such as **wird gefragt** (*is asked*) or **wurden untersucht** (*were studied*). When you see a form of **werden** plus a past participle, it is usually a passive construction. You will learn how to create and use passive constructions in **Kapitel 10**.

Vor dem Lesen

A. Beantworten Sie die folgenden Fragen.

1. Welche Städte sind die beliebtesten Städte in Ihrem Land? Warum sind sie beliebt?

2. Was ist Ihre Lieblingsstadt? Warum?

3. Welche Merkmale[1] einer Stadt sind für Sie wichtig? Welche sind weniger wichtig? Sortieren Sie die folgenden Merkmale von *am wichtigsten* zu *am wenigsten wichtig:* gute Schulen, viele Arbeitsplätze, große Universität, Alter und Geschichte, Größe der Stadt, Kulturangebot, Nähe zum Meer oder zu den Bergen, geringe Kriminalität, Größe des Flughafens, viele junge Leute.

4. Welche großen Städte kennen Sie in Deutschland, in Österreich oder in der Schweiz? Warum kennen Sie diese Stadt oder diese Städte? Was wissen Sie über sie?

B. Suchen Sie die Städtenamen im Text und unterstreichen Sie sie. Suchen Sie dann die Städte auf einer Landkarte.

C. Suchen Sie nun die Wörter des Miniwörterbuchs im Text und in den darauffolgenden Aktivitäten und unterstreichen Sie sie.

Miniwörterbuch

aktuell	current
blass	pale
der **Lichtblick**	ray of hope
erscheinen	to appear, be published
der **Zustand**	conditions, circumstances
der **Wohlstand**	quality of life
die **Wirtschaft**	economy
der **Arbeitsmarkt**	job market
das **Bevölkerungswachstum**	population growth
die **Anzahl**	number, amount
das **Ergebnis**	result
unterschiedlich	different
die **Behörde**	government agency
umgehen mit (etwas)	to handle (sth.)
sicher	secure
das **Einkommen**	income
die **Sicherheit**	safety
schaffen, schaffte	to manage (to do sth.), managed
punkten	to score
der **Vertreter**	representative
die **Arbeitslosenquote**	unemployment rate
der **Durchschnitt**	average
die **Leistung**	performance
bewerten	to rate

Städteranking

● Niveauranking
● Dynamikranking

Stralsund (1)
Greifswald (3)
SCHLESWIG-HOLSTEIN
MECKLENBURG-VORPOMMERN
HAMBURG
BREMEN
NIEDERSACHSEN
BRANDENBURG
Wolfsburg (5)
BERLIN
Frankfurt/Oder (5)
NORDRHEIN-WESTFALEN
SACHSEN-ANHALT
SACHSEN
THÜRINGEN
HESSEN
RHEINLAND-PFALZ
Bamberg (4)
Bayreuth (2)
SAARLAND
Erlangen (2)
BAYERN
BADEN-WÜRTTEMBERG
Ingolstadt (3)
Ulm (4)
München (1)

[1]*features*

Lektüre. Note: This reading selection is a summary of the German city rankings for 2010 as published by the Initiative Neue Soziale Marktwirtschaft GmbH in Berlin. The map and the graph make the reading accessible to a high degree in spite of the level of vocabulary and grammatical structures in the text. Furthermore, cognates facilitate comprehension. The task in *Vor dem Lesen* Part A involves drawing upon sts. world knowledge about cities in general as well as prompting them to begin thinking about what features of a city are desirable. *Vor dem Lesen* Part B aims to familiarize sts. with some of the lesser-known cities mentioned in the text. *Vor dem Lesen* Part C allows sts. to preview unfamiliar vocabulary. *Arbeit mit dem Text* Part A is a series of straight-forward comprehension questions. *Arbeit mit dem Text* Part B exposes sts. to journalistic compound nouns. *Nach dem Lesen* asks sts. to do Internet research and synthesize findings and preferences for a presentation.

Städteranking 2010

Wohnkomfort nur im Süden? Auch das aktuelle Städteranking lässt die Städte im Westen, Osten und Norden Deutschlands blass aussehen. Lichtblick für die neuen Bundesländer: das Dynamikranking. Stralsund auf Platz 1, Greifswald auf Platz 3, Frankfurt an der Oder auf Platz 5.

Die „Initiative Neue Soziale Marktwirtschaft" und die Zeitschrift *Wirtschaftswoche* haben für das Jahr 2010 ein Städteranking für Deutschland erarbeitet. Seit 2004 erscheint jährlich eine neue Studie. Das Niveauranking zeigt den aktuellen Zustand. Das Dynamikranking zeigt, wie sich die Städte in der Zeit von 2004 bis 2009 entwickelt haben. Aus dem Niveau- und dem Dynamikranking ergibt sich ein Gesamtranking. Es wird gefragt: In welcher deutschen Stadt ist der Wohlstand am größten? Und: Wo findet man die höchste wirtschaftliche Dynamik? Wichtige Faktoren sind der Arbeitsmarkt, der Wohlstand, die Kriminalitätsrate, das Bevölkerungswachstum, die Anzahl Hochqualifizierter, die Anzahl junger Leute und die Anzahl der Gästeübernachtungen. Einhundert deutsche Städte wurden untersucht.

Beim Niveauranking belegte München den ersten Platz. München ist die Landeshauptstadt von Bayern. Die Ergebnisse beruhen auf unterschiedlichen Fragen. Es wurde z. B. gefragt: Wie gehen die Behörden der jeweiligen Stadt mit den Finanzen um? Wie sicher fühlen sich die Bürger der Stadt? Wie hoch ist das Jahreseinkommen der Bürger? Bei all diesen Fragen lag München jeweils sehr weit vorn. 97,5 Prozent der Menschen sagten, dass die öffentliche Sicherheit in München sehr hoch ist. Das Jahreseinkommen liegt in München bei 23 145 Euro. In den anderen deutschen Städten beträgt es nur 18 418 Euro.

Viele andere süddeutsche Städte lagen beim Niveauranking auf den ersten 10 Plätzen. Die bayrischen Städte Erlangen, Ingolstadt, Landshut, Aschaffenburg und Kempten sowie die baden-württembergischen Städte Ulm, Baden-Baden und Stuttgart schafften es unter die Top-Ten. Nur eine norddeutsche Stadt kam auf einen der ersten 10 Plätze: Wolfsburg in Niedersachsen. Andere große deutsche Städte schafften es nicht unter die ersten 10. So kam Frankfurt am Main auf Platz 18, Köln auf 43 und Berlin sogar nur auf Platz 90.

Beim Dynamikranking konnten allerdings einige Städte aus den neuen Bundesländern punkten. Stralsund schaffte es auf den ersten Platz. Stralsund liegt in Mecklenburg-Vorpommern an der Ostseeküste. Für die Top-Ten des Dynamikrankings ist Stralsund ein typischer Vertreter. Die Arbeitslosenquote sank in den letzten 5 Jahren um 7,8% und die Wirtschaftsleistung stieg um 26,5%. Der deutschlandweite Durchschnitt war 11,6%.

Unter den Top-Ten des Dynamikrankings lagen weitere Städte aus den neuen Bundesländern und einige aus Ost- und Nordbayern. Greifswald und Neubrandenburg, wie Stralsund in Mecklenburg-Vorpommern gelegen, schafften es in die Top-Ten. Weitere Städte aus den neuen Bundesländern sind Frankfurt an der Oder (Brandenburg) und

Gesamtranking, sortiert nach Platzierung

Platz	Stadt	Punkte
1	Erlangen	128,3
2	Ingolstadt	125,6
3	Ulm	122,9
4	München	121,1
5	Aschaffenburg	118,9
6	Wolfsburg	117,7
7	Bamberg	117,2
8	Rosenheim	117,2
9	Kempten (Allgäu)	117,2
10	Baden-Baden	116,6

In Erlangen lebt man besser.

35 Weimar (Thüringen). Aber auch Bayern war gut vertreten, mit Bayreuth, Bamberg, Hof und Ingolstadt. Bremerhaven schaffte es als einzige nicht süddeutsche und nicht ostdeutsche Stadt unter die ersten zehn Plätze des Dynamikrankings.

40 Aus beiden Rankings wurde abschließend ein Gesamtranking ermittelt. Dabei liegen ebenfalls wieder viele bayrische Städte auf den ersten Plätzen. Die Top-Ten sieht man in der Grafik. Auf Platz 1 im Gesamtranking kam Erlangen. Dort lag die Arbeitslosenquote bei nur 4,4%; dazu hatten 26,4% der Einwohner einen Hochschulabschluss. Viele große deutsche Städte folgen erst auf den hinteren Plätzen: 19. Düsseldorf, 23. Stuttgart, 27. Hamburg, 29. Frankfurt am Main, 40. Bonn, 53. Köln, 81. Berlin, 87. Essen, 90. Leipzig, 100. Gelsenkirchen.

Arbeit mit dem Text

A. Fragen zum Text. Beantworten Sie die folgenden Fragen.

1. Wie viele deutsche Städte werden im Städteranking untersucht? Wie lange gibt es das Städteranking schon?
2. Welche Faktoren sind besonders wichtig?
3. Welche Stadt liegt beim Niveauranking auf Platz 1? Warum?
4. In welchem Bundesland liegen die meisten der Top-Ten-Städte des Niveaurankings? Aus welchen anderen Bundesländern gab es weitere Top-Ten-Städte?
5. Welche Stadt liegt beim Dynamikranking auf Platz 1? Warum?
6. In welchen Bundesländern liegen die anderen Top-Ten-Städte des Dynamikrankings?
7. Was ist besonders an Bremerhaven?
8. Welche großen Städte werden im Gesamtranking besonders schlecht bewertet?

B. Zeitungssprache. In journalistischen Texten gibt es viele Komposita. Komposita setzen sich aus zwei oder mehr einfachen Wörtern zusammen. Bilden Sie aus den folgenden Wörtern Komposita und suchen Sie sie im Text. Was bedeuten sie?

die Arbeit	der Blick
arbeitslos	das Einkommen
die Bevölkerung	die Hauptstadt
der Gast	der Komfort
das Jahr	die Leistung
die Kriminalität	der Markt
das Land	die Quote
das Licht	die Rate
die Wirtschaft	die Übernachtung
wohnen	das Wachstum

Nach dem Lesen

Suchen Sie im Internet das aktuelle Städteranking für Deutschland, Österreich oder die Schweiz. Welche der Top-Ten-Städte eines dieser Länder finden Sie am interessantesten? Tragen Sie Informationen zu dieser Stadt zusammen und präsentieren Sie sie im Seminar.

Auf Wohnungssuche

das Reihenhaus

das Einfamilienhaus

die Villa

die Altbauwohnung

das Bauernhaus

die Skihütte

das Hochhaus

das Studentenheim

der Wohnwagen

Situation 9   Wo möchtest du gern wohnen?

Sit. 9. Model pronunciation. Sts. work with a partner, first asking each other to rank the buildings in order of desirability and then working on attributes and locations for their top three choices. In your follow-up, ask sts. to give full information and possibly reasons for choices.

Fragen Sie fünf Personen und schreiben Sie die Antworten auf.

MODELL: S1: Wo möchtest du gern wohnen?
         S2: In einem Bauernhaus mit alten Möbeln.
         S1: Und wo soll es stehen?
         S2: Auf dem Land.

in einem Bauernhaus	mit Weinkeller	in der Innenstadt
in einem Wohnwagen	mit schönem Ausblick	am Stadtrand
in einem Hochhaus	mit Terrasse	im Ausland
in einem Einfamilienhaus	mit Balkon	auf dem Land
in einem Reihenhaus	mit alten Möbeln	in den Bergen
in einer Skihütte	mit vielen Fenstern	an einem See
in einer Villa	mit einem Garten	in der Nähe der Stadt
im Studentenheim	mit Garage	in der Nähe der Uni

Situation 10   Umfrage

MODELL: S1: Möchtest du gern in der Innenstadt leben?
         S2: Ja.
         S1: Unterschreib bitte hier.

UNTERSCHRIFT

1. Möchtest du gern in der Innenstadt leben? _____
2. Möchtest du gern am Stadtrand leben? _____
3. Kannst du dir ein Leben auf dem Land vorstellen? _____
4. Möchtest du gern im Ausland wohnen? _____
5. Möchtest du in einer Villa wohnen? _____
6. Möchtest du in einem Wohnwagen leben? _____
7. Kannst du dir ein Leben auf einem Hausboot vorstellen? _____
8. Möchtest du gern im Studentenheim wohnen? _____
9. Möchtest du gern eine Woche unter Wasser wohnen? _____
10. Möchtest du gern im Wald leben? _____

Auf Wohnungssuche

Wie haben Sie Ihr Zimmer / Ihre Wohnung gefunden? Kreuzen
Sie an.

durch eine Anzeige[1] in der Zeitung ☐
mit Hilfe der Uni ☐
durch Freunde oder Bekannte ☐
durch eine Anzeige am schwarzen Brett ☐
durch die Gelben Seiten ☐
über das Internet ☐

① **ER IST WIEDER DA ...**
ALIEN XIV
—DER NACHMIETER[3]—
... Ein halbes Jahr war er in Schweden. Aber plötzlich[4] ist er wieder in Hamburg.
Manche nennen[5] ihn EL SYMPATICO. Doch die meisten Karsten. Er will nur eines:
DEINE WOHNUNG! (1-2 Zi bis 250 Euro inkl.)
Wenn Du ihn anrufst, ruft er zurück ...
Niemand hat es bis jetzt gewagt[6]. . .

04451 -83591	04451 -83591	04451 -83591	04451 -83591	04451 -83591	04451 -83591	04451 -83591	04451 -83591	04451 -83591

Schauen Sie sich die Anzeigen an.

- Welche der Anzeigen suchen nach einer Wohnung?
- Welche bieten eine Wohnung oder ein Zimmer an[2]?
- Unter welchen Umständen gibt es die Wohnung in
  St. Pauli billiger?
- Wann kann man in die Wohnung in Ottensen einziehen?

Schreiben Sie selbst eine Suchanzeige für eine Wohnung
oder ein Zimmer in einer WG für ein Schwarzes Brett.
Wohnungen sind sehr knapp. Machen Sie Ihre Anzeige
so attraktiv wie möglich!

② Vermiete[7] im September
2-Zimmer-Whg in St. Pauli (Hinterhof).
Miete 350 Euro + Heizung, Strom, Telefon.
wenn Katzenliebhaber/in[8] auch den Kater
mitversorgt,[9] gibt es die Wohnung billiger.

2te Person für 3-Zimmer
Wohnung in Ottensen (HH50)
ab Juli gesucht.
Miete: EUR 250 + Kaution[10]
Tel. (040) 39 22 93 ③

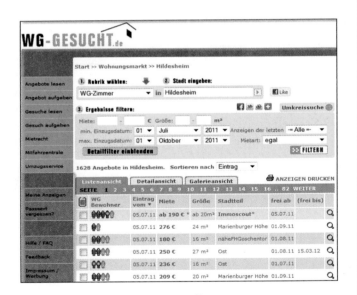

[1]ad [2]anbieten: to offer [3]person who takes over a lease [4]suddenly [5]call [6]dared [7]renting out [8]cat lover [9]helps take care of [10]security deposit

KLI. (See the IM.) The three print ads were found at the University of Hamburg. St. Pauli and Ottensen are parts or suburbs of Hamburg. *HH* (Hansestadt Hamburg) is the
license plate code for the city. In Hamburg, with its severe housing shortage, the *Kaution* (security deposit) is usually very high—twice or even three times the monthly rent.
The large ad is by far the most creative in style. The author is playing with several images or phrases from movies. Ask sts.: *An welche Filme denken Sie?* for the writing task,
ask sts. to be creative and to compose a housing ad that is likely to get noticed on a crowded bulletin board in Hamburg. The webpage reflects the growing trend to use
online services to look for housing. As a follow-up, bring a bulletin board to class and have sts. post their ads, or create an online ad. Ask sts. to select the most creative ad,
or ask each st. to pick an ad they like and role-play a "looking for a room" encounter based on the ad with the person who composed it.

Situation 11 Dialog: Auf Wohnungssuche

Sit. 11. (See the IM.) This dialogue provides a model for the role-play following it. You may wish to follow the steps for presenting the dialogue without the use of the textbook. Remind sts. they can listen to this dialogue in the laboratory. Questions for first listening: **1.** *Wie meldet man sich am Telefon?* **2.** *Was will Silvia wissen?* **3.** *Was ist die genaue Adresse?* Questions for second listening: **1.** *In welchem Stockwerk ist das Zimmer?* **2.** *Was kostet das Zimmer?* **3.** *Welche Möbel stehen darin?* **4.** *Wo kann Silvia baden?*

Cultural note. In Germany, the first floor (*1. Stock*) is equivalent to the second floor in the U.S. The first floor in the U.S. is the ground floor (*Erdgeschoss*) in Germany. (See also the following cultural note.)

Cultural note. Although renting a furnished room from a landlord/lady is not as widespread as it used to be among students, this is still a realistic dialogue. Arrangements to rent are made well in advance, often 2 or 3 months. Notice before moving out (*Kündigungsfrist*) is required.

Silvia ist auf Wohnungssuche.

FRAU SCHUSTER: Schuster)

SILVIA: Guten Tag. Hier Silvia Mertens. Ich rufe wegen des Zimmers an. Ist es noch frei?

FRAU SCHUSTER: Ja, das ist noch zu haben.

SILVIA: Prima, in welchem Stadtteil ist es denn?

FRAU SCHUSTER: Frankfurt-Süd, Waldschulstraße 22.

SILVIA: Und in welchem Stock liegt das Zimmer?

FRAU SCHUSTER: Im fünften, gleich unter dem Dach.

SILVIA: Gibt es einen Aufzug?

FRAU SCHUSTER: Nein, leider nicht.

SILVIA: Schade. Was kostet denn das Zimmer?

FRAU SCHUSTER: Dreihundert Euro möbliert.

SILVIA: Möbliert? Was steht denn drin?

FRAU SCHUSTER: Also, ein Bett natürlich, ein Tisch mit zwei Stühlen und ein Kleiderschrank.

SILVIA: Ist auch ein Bad dabei?

FRAU SCHUSTER: Nein, aber baden können Sie bei mir. Und Sie haben natürlich Ihre eigene Toilette.

SILVIA: Wann könnte ich mir denn das Zimmer mal anschauen?

FRAU SCHUSTER: Wenn Sie wollen, können Sie gleich vorbeikommen.

SILVIA: Gut, dann komme ich gleich mal vorbei. Auf Wiederhören.

FRAU SCHUSTER: Auf Wiederhören.

Situation 12 Rollenspiel: Zimmer zu vermieten

Sit. 12. The role for S2 appears in Appendix B. **Note:** If your students are using McGraw-Hill's *Connect* online *Arbeitsbuch*, they can do this *Rollenspiel* using the real-time, interactive **Video-Chat** feature.

S1: Sie sind Student/Studentin und suchen ein schönes, großes Zimmer. Das Zimmer soll hell und ruhig sein. Sie haben nicht viel Geld und können nur bis zu 300 Euro Miete zahlen, inklusive Nebenkosten. Sie rauchen nicht und hören keine laute Musik. Fragen Sie den Vermieter / die Vermieterin, wie groß das Zimmer ist, was es kostet, ob es im Winter warm ist, ob Sie kochen dürfen und ob Ihre Freunde Sie besuchen dürfen. Sagen Sie dann, ob Sie das Zimmer mieten möchten.

Hausarbeit

Grammatik 6.5–6.6

Vocabulary Display
This section reviews present-tense verb forms, especially separable-prefix verbs, while teaching vocabulary for housework.

Andrea putzt ihre Schuhe.

Paula wischt den Tisch ab.

Ernst mäht den Rasen.

der Besen

Jens fegt den Boden.

Josie saugt Staub.

Uli bügelt sein Hemd.

Jochen macht die
Toilette sauber.

Jutta wäscht die
Wäsche.

Margret wischt den
Boden.

Hans macht sein Bett.

Situation 13 Was macht man mit einem Besen?

MODELL: S1: Was macht man mit einem Besen?
S2: Mit einem Besen fegt man den Boden.

Staub saugen   den Rasen mähen

Hemden oder Blusen bügeln

die Wäsche waschen   den Boden fegen

den Rasen sprengen

die Schuhe putzen   das Geschirr spülen

die Blumen gießen

den Tisch abwischen

1. mit einem Staubsauger
2. mit einem Geschirrspüler
3. mit einer Waschmaschine
4. mit einem Besen
5. mit einem Rasenmäher
6. mit einer Gießkanne
7. mit einem Bügeleisen
8. mit einem Putzlappen
9. mit einem Gartenschlauch

Situation 14 Angenehm oder unangenehm?

Sit. 14. This activity recycles phrases from *Sit. 13* and introduces some new ones using familiar vocabulary. **Preparation:** Introduce new vocabulary: *Müll, (un)angenehm.* Pick two household chores, one which you like and one which you dislike. Ask sts. whether they like these chores. *Ich mache gar nicht gern das Bett. Das ist mir unangenehm. Machen Sie gern das Bett? Ist das angenehm? Ich putze sehr gern die Fenster. Putzen Sie gern die Fenster?* Explain the activity to sts. Ask sts. to work alone to rank the tasks. **Follow-up:** Ask how many chose each task as number 1, number 2, etc. Use this information to present on the board the class's most popular and least popular tasks. **Alternative:** Ask sts. to work in groups of 3 and come to a consensus within each group as to how to rank the tasks.

Welche Hausarbeit machen Sie gern, weniger gern oder gar nicht gern? Ordnen Sie die folgenden Tätigkeiten von sehr angenehm (1) zu sehr unangenehm (10).

_____ Hosen bügeln

_____ Regale abwischen

_____ eine Einkaufsliste schreiben

_____ die Toilette putzen

_____ den Müll wegbringen

_____ die Sessel absaugen

_____ die Vorhänge waschen

_____ Töpfe und Pfannen spülen

_____ das Bett machen

_____ Fenster putzen

Musikszene

„Haus am See" (2008, Deutschland) *Peter Fox*

Biografie Peter Fox ist ein Reggae- und Hip-Hop-Musiker aus Berlin. Sein bürgerlicher Name ist Pierre Baigorry. Seine Mutter kommt aus dem französischen Baskenland. Wegen seiner roten Haare wurde er als Kind Foxi genannt. Deshalb nennt er sich jetzt Fox. Peter Fox studierte Musik, Sonderschulpädagogik und Englisch, beendete sein Studium aber nicht. Peter Fox ist einer der Sänger der Reggae-Gruppe Seeed. Von 2007 bis 2009 hatte er eine Solokarriere. Sein Album *Stadtaffe* (2008), aus der die Single „Haus am See" ausgekoppelt wurde, war in Deutschland und Österreich auf Platz 1 der Charts und in der Schweiz auf Platz 4.

Vor dem Hören Wie stellen Sie sich Ihr Traumhaus vor? Wo liegt es? Wer wohnt da? Wie sieht es aus?

Peter Fox vor einem Konzert in Lörrach

iMix Link: This song is available for purchase at the iTunes store in a special iMix created for *Kontakte*. For more information about accessing the playlist, go to **Connect German** (www.connectgerman.com).

Nach dem Hören

1. Warum sagt der Sänger in der ersten Strophe, dass er weg muss?

☒ **a.** Er kennt jedes Haus und jeden Laden und sogar jede Taube.

☐ **b.** Er wartet auf eine schicke Frau mit einem schnellen Wagen.

☐ **c.** Ein Frauenchor singt am Straßenrand für ihn.

2. Was gefällt dem Sänger an seinem Haus am See? (Mehrere Antworten sind möglich)

☒ **a.** Er hat 20 Kinder und eine schöne Frau.

☒ **b.** Auf dem Weg dorthin liegen Orangenbaumblätter.

☒ **c.** Alle Menschen kommen ihn dort besuchen.

3. Wie kommt der Sänger zurück?

☐ **a.** Er kommt zurück mit einer Frau.

☐ **b.** Er kommt zurück mit Schnee und Sand.

☒ **c.** Er kommt zurück mit beiden Taschen voll Gold.

4. Was passiert, als er wieder zu Hause ist?

☒ **a.** Er fängt vor Freude an zu weinen.

☐ **b.** Alle Leute laden ihn ein.

☒ **c.** Er feiert eine Woche lang jede Nacht.

Musikszene. Suggestion: Ask sts. to read the *Biografie* and ask questions about it to verify understanding. Then ask sts. to do the *Vor dem Hören* section in pairs, interviewing each other and taking notes. Ask several groups to report on their results. Next ask sts. to find the words presented in the *Miniwörterbuch* in the *Nach dem Hören* section and to underline them. Make sure sts. understand the questions and answers. Play the entire song through uninterrupted. Then play the first stanza several times for question 1, the chorus for question 2, and the second stanza for questions 3 and 4.

Miniwörterbuch

die **Strophe**	stanza	der **Orangenbaum, die -bäume**	orange tree
die **Taube, -n**	pigeon		
der **Chor, die Chöre**	choir	das **Blatt, die Blätter**	leaf, blossom
der **Straßenrand**	side of the street	**vor Freude**	for joy

Situation 15 Bildgeschichte: Frühjahrsputz

Sit. 15. Sentences for the narration series: **1.** *Gestern war bei Wagners der große Frühjahrsputz. Alle haben geholfen.* **2.** *Herr Wagner hat zuerst die Terrasse gefegt.* **3.** *Dann hat er den Keller aufgeräumt.* **4.** *Frau Wagner hat zuerst die Fenster geputzt.* **5.** *Dann hat sie im ganzen Haus Staub gesaugt.* **6.** *Jens hat zuerst die Flaschen weggebracht.* **7.** *Und Ernst hat zuerst sein Zimmer aufgeräumt.* **8.** *Dann hat Jens das Geschirr gespült.* **9.** *Und Ernst hat abgetrocknet.* **10.** *Und Andrea? Andrea war bei ihrer Freundin und hat ferngesehen.* Point out that spring cleaning is still an important tradition in much of the German-speaking world.

Sit. 16. (See the IM.) The corresponding chart is in Appendix A. **(1)** Establish the topic by asking such questions as: *Wer von Ihnen mäht gern den Rasen? hat heute sein Bett gemacht? usw.* **(2)** Preteach vocabulary: *Staub wischen, nichts von alledem,* and practice model sentences both for Nora and Thomas (3rd person) and for a partner (2nd person). Ask sts. which time expressions in the chart signal present tense (the first 4), perfect tense (the following 2), and a sentence with the modal verb *muss* (the last 2). **(3)** Remind sts. to use phrases such as *Wie bitte?* and *Wie schreibt man das?* when comprehension problems arise and not to revert to English or look into each other's charts. Pair sts. up. Allow at least 5 minutes for completing the activity. **(4)** Follow up by asking questions about the *mein Partner / meine Partnerin* column and turn it into an association activity (see the IM) if time allows.

❓ Situation 16 Informationsspiel: Haus- und Gartenarbeit

MODELL: s2: Was macht Thomas am liebsten?
s1: Er mäht am liebsten den Rasen.
s2: Was hat Nora letztes Wochenende gemacht?
s1: Sie hat ihre Bluse gebügelt.
s2: Was muss Thomas diese Woche noch machen?
s1: Er muss seine Wäsche waschen.

s1: Was machst du am liebsten?
s2: Ich _____ am liebsten _____.

	Thomas	Nora	mein(e) Partner(in)
am liebsten	den Rasen mähen	einkaufen gehen	
am wenigsten gern	das Bad putzen	die Fenster putzen	
jeden Tag	nichts von alledem	den Tisch abwischen	
einmal in der Woche	sein Bett machen	die Wäsche waschen	
letztes Wochenende	das Geschirr spülen	ihre Bluse bügeln	
gestern	die Blumen gießen	ihr Zimmer aufräumen	
diese Woche	seine Wäsche waschen	den Boden wischen	
bald mal wieder	die Flaschen wegbringen	Staub wischen	

Filmlektüre
Good bye Lenin!

📖 Vor dem Lesen

Filmlektüre. Suggestions: (1) Ask the questions in *Vor dem Lesen* and some additional ones such as: *Wann ist der Film erschienen? In welchem Land? Was für ein Film ist es? Wie lange dauert er? Wer hat die Hauptrollen? Wie heißt der Regisseur?* **(2)** Next, ask students to read the words in the *Miniwörterbuch,* to find them in the *Inhaltsangabe* and to underline them.

A. Sehen Sie sich das Foto aus dem Film an.

1. Welche Art[1] Fernsehsendung ist das?
2. Der Mann im Hintergrund war 1971 bis 1989 Staatschef[2] der DDR. Wie hieß er?
3. Was wissen Sie über die ehemalige[3] DDR und die Wiedervereinigung[4]? Sammeln Sie Informationen.

„Guten Abend, meine Damen und Herren"

Filmangaben

Titel: *Good bye Lenin!*
Genre: Komödie
Erscheinungsjahr: 2003
Land: Deutschland
Dauer: 150 min
Regisseur: Wolfgang Becker
Hauptrollen: Daniel Brühl, Katrin Saß, Maria Simon

Photo. Note: The photo in the background shows Erich Honecker, who was head of state in the GDR from 1971 until 1989. Egon Krenz succeeded him for a very short time, from October 18 to December 13, 1989.

B. Lesen Sie die Wörter im Miniwörterbuch. Suchen Sie sie im Text und unterstreichen Sie sie. Lesen Sie dann den Text.

Miniwörterbuch

die **Aufregung**	excitement	der **Kosmonaut**	East German word for astronaut
der **Bürger** / die **Bürgerin**	citizen	**schaden**	to harm
DDR (Deutsche Demokratische Republik	GDR (German Democratic Republic)	der **Sperrmüll**	bulk refuse (heap)
entschlossen	determined	der **Tod**	death
flüchten	to flee	**überzeugt**	staunch
gefälscht	fake	die **Veränderung**	change
geht es nach Alex	if you believe Alex	**verheimlichen**	to conceal
die **Gesundheit**	health	**vorspielen**	to feign
der **Herzinfarkt**	heart attack	**wohlbekannt**	well-known
		der **Zusammenbruch**	collapse

Inhaltsangabe

Christiane Kerner (Katrin Saß) – eine engagierte DDR-Bürgerin und überzeugte Sozialistin – hat am 7. Oktober 1989 einen Herzinfarkt und fällt ins Koma. Während sie im Krankenhaus liegt und bewusstlos ist, fällt zwei Tage später die Berliner Mauer und die DDR wird ein Teil der Bundesrepublik Deutschland. Acht
5 Monate später wacht sie auf und die DDR existiert nicht mehr.

[1]*type* [2]*head of state* [3]*former* [4]*reunification*

Suggestions (continued): (3) Go over the *Arbeit mit dem Text* making sure sts. understand all the words. Write unfamiliar words on the board with translations or convey the meaning in another manner. (4) Ask sts. to work in pairs and answer the questions. (5) Next, work with the *Filmclip*. Paraphrase the introduction to the *Filmclip* and go over the questions making sure sts. understand them. Tell sts. that you will play the clip twice and that they should take notes on the questions. (6) Elicit answers and write them on the board including incorrect ones. Tell them that you will play the clip one more time and ask them to determine which of their answers are correct. (7) Provide sts. with the correct answers or have sts. work in groups or pairs to determine the correct answers. (8) Assign *Nach dem Lesen* for homework.

Jede Art von Aufregung schadet Christiane Kerners Gesundheit, deshalb beschließt ihr Sohn Alex (Daniel Brühl) die politischen Veränderungen vor seiner Mutter zu verheimlichen. Gemeinsam mit seiner Schwester Ariane (Maria Simon) will Alex seiner Mutter den ganz normalen DDR-Alltag vorspielen. Leichter gesagt als getan:
10 Die alten DDR-Möbel der Familie sind out und stehen im Keller oder liegen auf dem Sperrmüll; im Supermarkt gibt es jetzt westdeutsche Lebensmittel und keine aus DDR-Produktion; die wohlbekannten DDR-Fernsehsendungen laufen auch nicht mehr; West-Autos und Fast-Food-Restaurants überrollen den Osten; und am Haus gegenüber hängt ein großes Coca-Cola Werbeplakat. Dies alles ist für Alex und Ariane ein großes Prob-
15 lem. Aber Alex ist entschlossen und kreativ. Selbst Freunde und Nachbarn spielen mit.

Am Ende, kurz vor ihrem Tod, erfährt Mutter Christiane aber doch vom Zusammenbruch der DDR. Sie sagt Alex nichts davon. Alex' DDR, die er mit gefälschten DDR-Nachrichtensendungen belebt, ist ganz anders als die alte DDR: Geht es nach Alex, ist die DDR das Wunschland aller Menschen; Westdeutsche flüchten in den
20 Osten; und Staatschef ist natürlich Alex' Idol, der DDR-Kosmonaut Sigmund Jähn.

Arbeit mit dem Text

Beantworten Sie die folgenden Fragen.

1. Warum sagt Alex seiner Mutter nicht, dass die DDR nicht mehr existiert?
2. In welchen alltäglichen Bereichen[1] ändert sich das Leben der Kerners nach dem Fall der Mauer?
3. Wie wünscht[2] sich Alex die DDR?

[1]*domains, spheres*   [2]*wishes*

Filmclip

Szene: DVD, Kapitel 17, Geburtstagsfeier, 00:59:50–1:02:02 Min.

Christiane, die Mutter von Alex und Ariane, hat Geburtstag. Nachdem sie aus dem Koma erwacht ist, wird sie zu Hause von ihren Kindern gepflegt. Deshalb lädt Alex die Geburtstagsgäste nach Hause ein. Die Gäste dürfen aber nicht sagen, dass es die DDR nicht mehr gibt, weil sich Christiane nicht aufregen[1] soll. Nachdem die Pioniere gesungen und die Genossen[2] Ansprachen gehalten haben, beginnt Alex zu sprechen.

Schauen Sie sich die Szene an und beantworten Sie die Fragen.

1. Was sagt Alex über seine Mutter?
2. Welches Plakat wird während der Geburtstagfeier am Gebäude[3] gegenüber angebracht? Wofür steht dieses Plakat? Warum ist Christiane so entsetzt[4]?
3. Was macht Lara, als sie mit Alex im Nebenzimmer ist?
4. Worüber beschwert sich[5] Lara? Was war ihr Vater in Wirklichkeit?

[1]*sich aufregen   to get excited*   [2]*comrades*   [3]*building*   [4]*upset*   [5]*beschwert … complains*

Filmclip. Answers: 1. Er sagt, dass sie die beste Mutter auf der Welt ist. 2. Ein Coca-Cola-Plakat. Es steht für den Westen und den Kapitalismus, die größten Gegner der DDR. 3. Sie zieht die alten DDR-Klamotten aus. 4. Sie findet es nicht richtig, dass Alex so lügt. Ihr Vater war ein einfacher Koch und kein Lehrer für Taubstumme.

Nach dem Lesen

A. Recherchieren Sie im Internet über den Schauspieler Daniel Brühl, der im Film Alex Kerner spielt. Woher kommt er? Welche Filme hat er noch gemacht? Welche Preise hat er mit *Good bye Lenin!* gewonnen? Welche Projekte hat er gerade?

response

B. Die Resonanz° auf *Good bye Lenin!* war sehr groß in Ost- und Westdeutschland. Warum ist der Film in Deutschland so beliebt? Finden Sie Antworten (auch im Internet) und präsentieren Sie Ihre Gedanken und Lösungen auf einem Poster in der Klasse.

Videoecke

Perspektiven

Wie hast du deine
Wohnung gefunden?

Aufgabe 1 Wohnungssuche

Wie haben die Leute ihre Wohnung
gefunden?

Ich habe meine Wohnung über ein
Internetportal gefunden.

Miniwörterbuch

das **Studentenwerk**	student services
die **Annonce**	ad
einteilen	to arrange, divide up
unsaniert	unrenovated
der **Altbau**	old building

1. Albrecht __d__

2. Nadezda __b__

3. Simone __e__

4. Jenny __b__

5. Michael __f__

6. Sophie __c__

7. Pascal __b__

8. Sandra __a__

a. über eine Annonce in der Zeitung
b. durch/über einen Freund
c. über das Internet
d. über ein Internetportal
e. durch eine ehemalige Kollegin
f. durch das Studentenwerk

Interviews

- Wo wohnst du?
- Kannst du mir deine Wohnung beschreiben?
- Was bezahlst du für deine Wohnung?
- Wohnst du gern mit Leuten zusammen?
- Wie teilt ihr euch die gemeinsame Arbeit ein?
- Gibt es da oder gab es da schon mal Probleme?

Sophie

Maria

Aufgabe 2 Sophie oder Maria?

Sehen Sie sich das Video an und kreuzen Sie an.

	Sophie	Maria
1. Wer wohnt im Süden von Leipzig in einer kleinen Wohnung?	☒	☐
2. Wer wohnt in der Nähe vom Bahnhof?	☐	☒
3. Wer wohnt in einem unsanierten Altbau?	☐	☒
4. Wer bezahlt 150 Euro plus Nebenkosten?	☒	☐
5. Wer möchte nicht mit mehr Leuten zusammen wohnen?	☒	☐
6. Wer hat einen Wochenplan?	☒	☐

Aufgabe 3 Sophies Wohnung

Aufgabe 3. Answers: 1. F; zwei Zimmer 2. F; im 6. Stock 3. R 4. F; sehr klein

Richtig (R) oder falsch (F)? Verbessern Sie die falschen Antworten.

_____ 1. Ihre Wohnung hat drei Zimmer, eine Küche und ein Bad.

_____ 2. Ihre Wohnung ist im 2. Stock.

_____ 3. Die Zimmer sind sehr groß und haben jeweils zwei Fenster.

_____ 4. Das Bad ist groß.

Aufgabe 4 Arbeiten im Haushalt

Welche Hausarbeiten nennt Sophie, welche nennt Maria, welche nennt keine von beiden?

	Sophie	Maria	keine von beiden
1. das Bad putzen	☐	☒	☐
2. das Geschirr spülen	☐	☐	☒
3. den Müll runterbringen	☐	☒	☐
4. die Betten machen	☐	☐	☒
5. die Küche aufräumen	☐	☐	☒
6. die Küche putzen	☐	☒	☐
7. kochen	☒	☐	☐
8. sauber machen	☒	☐	☐
9. Staub saugen	☐	☐	☒
10. die Waschmaschine füllen	☒	☐	☐

Aufgabe 5 Interview

Interviewen Sie eine Partnerin oder einen Partner. Stellen Sie dieselben Fragen.

Wortschatz

In der Stadt	In the City
die Apotheke, -n	pharmacy
die Drogerie, -n	drugstore
die Metzgerei, -en	butcher shop
die Reinigung, -en	dry cleaner's
die Stadt, ⸚e (R)	town, city
die Heimatstadt, ⸚e	hometown
die Innenstadt, ⸚e	downtown
die Straße, -n	street, road
der Flughafen, ⸚	airport
der Stadtrand, ⸚er	city limits
der Stadtteil, -e	district, neighborhood
das Eisenwarengeschäft, -e	hardware store
das Gefängnis, -se	prison, jail
das Gymnasium, Gymnasien	high school, college preparatory school
das Rathaus, ⸚er (R)	town hall
das Schreibwarengeschäft, -e	stationery store
das Stadtviertel, -	district, neighborhood

Ähnliche Wörter

die Boutique, -n; der Kindergarten, ⸚; der Marktplatz, ⸚e; der Supermarkt, ⸚e (R); das Reisebüro, -s; das Schuhgeschäft, -e

Haus und Wohnung	House and Apartment
die Badewanne, -n	bathtub
die Treppe, -n	stairway
die Zentralheizung	central heating
der Aufzug, ⸚e	elevator
der Ausblick, -e	view
der Quadratmeter (qm), -	square meter (m²)
der Stock, Stockwerke	floor, story
im ersten Stock*	on the second floor
das Dach, ⸚er	roof
das Waschbecken, -	(wash)basin

Ähnliche Wörter

die Garage, -n [gara:ʒə]; die Terrasse, -n; die Toilette, -n; der Balkon, -e; der Keller, - (R); der Weinkeller, -; das Bad, ⸚er; das Esszimmer, -; das Schlafzimmer, -; das Wohnzimmer, -

Haus und Garten	House and Garden
die Bürste, -n	brush
die Gießkanne, -n	watering can
die Kommode, -n	dresser

der Besen, -	broom
der Frühjahrsputz	spring cleaning
der Gartenschlauch, ⸚e	garden hose
der Müll	trash, garbage
der Putzlappen, -	cloth, rag (for cleaning)
der Rasenmäher, -	lawn mower
der Schrank, ⸚e (R)	closet; cupboard
der Kleiderschrank, ⸚e	clothes closet, wardrobe
der Sessel, - (R)	armchair
der Spiegel, -	mirror
der Staubsauger, -	vacuum cleaner
der Vorhang, ⸚e	drapery, curtain
das Bügeleisen, -	iron
das Kopfkissen, -	pillow
die Möbel (pl.)	furniture

Ähnliche Wörter

die Pflanze, -n (R); die Stereoanlage, -n; die Waschmaschine, -n; der Nachttisch, -e; das Bett, -en (R); das Möbelstück, -e; das Poster, -; das Sofa, -s

Wohnmöglichkeiten	Living Arrangements
die Skihütte, -n	ski lodge
die Villa, Villen	mansion
die WG, -s (Wohngemeinschaft, -en)	shared housing
das Haus, ⸚er (R)	house
das Bauernhaus, ⸚er	farmhouse
das Einfamilienhaus, ⸚er	single-family home
das Hochhaus, ⸚er	high-rise building
das Reihenhaus, ⸚er	row house, town house

Ähnliche Wörter

das Hausboot, -e; das Iglu, -s; das Studentenheim, -e (R)

Auf Wohnungssuche	Looking for a Room or Apartment
die Anzeige, -n	ad
die Miete, -n	rent
die Mieterin, -nen	female renter
die Suchanzeige, -n	housing-wanted ad
die Vermieterin, -nen	landlady
der Mieter, -	male renter
der Vermieter, -	landlord
die Nebenkosten (pl.)	extra costs (e.g., utilities)

*The first floor is called **das Erdgeschoss.** All levels above the first floor are referred to as **Stock** or **Stockwerke.** Thus, **der erste Stock** refers to the second floor, and so on.

Sonstige Substantive — Other Nouns

die **Nähe**	vicinity
in der **Nähe**	in the vicinity
die **Seite**, -n	side; page
die **Tätigkeit**, -en	activity
die **Zugfahrkarte**, -n	train ticket
das **Ausland**	foreign countries
im **Ausland**	abroad
das **Benzin**	gasoline
das **Land**, ⁼er	country (*rural*)
auf dem **Land**	in the country

Verben — Verbs

ab·trocknen	to dry (dishes)
begegnen (+ *dat.*)	to meet
bügeln	to iron
fehlen (+ *dat.*)	to be missing
geben, gibt, gegeben	to give
es **gibt** ...	there is/are . . .
gibt es ...? (R)	is/are there . . . ?
gefallen, gefällt, gefallen (+ *dat.*)	to be to one's liking, to please
es **gefällt** mir	I like it
gehören (+ *dat.*)	to belong to
gratulieren (+ *dat.*)	to congratulate
helfen, hilft, geholfen (+ *dat.*)	to help
mieten	to rent
passen (+ *dat.*)	to fit
putzen	to clean
schaden (+ *dat.*)	to be harmful to
schmecken (+ *dat.*)	to taste good to
Staub saugen	to vacuum
stehen, gestanden (R)	to stand
stehen, gestanden (+ *dat.*)	to suit
tippen (R)	to type
übernachten	to stay overnight
vermieten	to rent out
vor·stellen	to introduce, present
sich etwas **vorstellen**	to imagine something
wiederholen	to repeat

wischen	to mop
ab·wischen	to wipe clean
zu·hören (+ *dat.*)	to listen to

Ähnliche Wörter

kosten (R); **zurück·kommen, ist zurückgekommen**

Adjektive und Adverbien — Adjectives and Adverbs

angenehm	pleasant
eigen	own
hell	light
möbliert	furnished
warm	heated, heat included
weit	far
Wie **weit** weg?	How far away?
wunderschön	exceedingly beautiful

Ähnliche Wörter

attraktiv, dumm, leicht, modern

Sonstige Wörter und Ausdrücke — Other Words and Expressions

auf **Wiederhören**	*good bye*
bei (R)	at; with
bei deinen Eltern	with/at your parents'
bei einer Bank	at a bank
Ist ein/eine ... dabei?	Does it come with a . . . ?
drin/darin	in it
egal	equal, same
Das ist mir **egal.**	It doesn't matter to me.
gegenüber	opposite; across
gleich **gegenüber**	right across the way
gleich	right away; right, directly
gleich um die Ecke	right around the corner
inklusive	included (utilities)
möglichst (+ *adverb*)	as . . . as possible
ob	if, whether
prima!	great!
schade!	too bad!
unter (R)	below, beneath; among
wegen	on account of; about

Strukturen und Übungen

6.1 Dative verbs

Dative verbs are verbs that require a dative object.

The dative object usually indicates the person to whom or for whom something is done. The dative case can be seen as the partner case. The "something" that is done (or given) is in the accusative case (it is the direct object).

Ich schenke **dir ein Bügeleisen.**	*I'll give you an iron. (I'll give an iron to you.)*
Ich kaufe **meinem Bruder ein Buch.**	*I'll buy my brother a book. (I'll buy a book for my brother.)*

Wissen Sie noch?

The dative case is used primarily to indicate to whom or for whom something is done (or given).

Review grammar 5.1.

6.1 *Dativverben.* This section introduces another major use of the dative case. Verbs with dative and accusative objects were introduced in Section 5.1. Of all the dative verbs, *gefallen* is probably used most. Provide sts. with a lot of input containing the verb. Point out that the English equivalent is *to please* and that the thing *liked* is the subject of the verb. Sts. frequently equate *gefallen* with *to like*, and errors in its use may persist for a long time.

Certain verbs, called "dative verbs," require only a subject and a dative object; there is no accusative object. These verbs fall into two groups.

In Group 1, both the subject and the dative object are persons.

antworten	*to answer*
begegnen	*to meet*
gratulieren	*to congratulate*
helfen	*to help*
zuhören	*to listen to*

Er antwortete mir nicht.	*He didn't answer me.*
Wir begegneten dem alten Vermieter.	*We met the old landlord.*
Ich gratuliere dir zum Geburtstag.	*Happy Birthday! (I congratulate you on your birthday.)*
Soll ich dir helfen?	*Do you want me to help you?*
Ich höre dir genau zu.	*I'm listening to you carefully.*

In Group 2, the subject is usually a thing; the dative object is the person who experiences or owns the thing.

gehören	*to belong to*
passen	*to fit*
schaden	*to be harmful to*
schmecken	*to taste good to*
stehen	*to suit*

Diese Poster gehören mir.	*These posters belong to me.*
Diese Hose passt mir nicht.	*These pants don't fit me.*
Rauchen schadet der Gesundheit.	*Smoking is bad for (damages) your health.*
Schmeckt Ihnen der Fisch?	*Does the fish taste good to you?*
Blau steht dir gut.	*Blue suits you well.*

Note that the following Group 2 verbs express ideas that are rendered very differently in English.

fehlen	*to be missing*
gefallen	*to be to one's liking, to please*

Mir fehlt ein Buch.	*I'm missing a book.*
Gefällt Ihnen dieser Schrank?	*Do you like this cupboard? (Does this cupboard please you?)*

Übung 1   Minidialoge

Üb. 1. Assign as homework. Have sts. perform the dialogues in class.

Ergänzen Sie das Verb. Nützliche Wörter:

> antworten   gefallen   passen   schaden
>
> begegnen   gehören   schmecken
>
> fehlen   gratulieren   stehen   zuhören
>
> helfen

1. MONIKA: Schau, ich habe mir einen neuen MP3-Spieler gekauft.
   KATRIN: Der ist aber toll! Der _____ mir!

2. MARTA: Hallo, Willi. Ich habe gehört, du hast endlich eine Wohnung gefunden. Ich _____ dir ganz herzlich.
   WILLI: Danke. Das ist aber lieb von dir.

3. FRAU RUF: Jochen, kannst du mir bitte _____? Ich kann die Vorhänge nicht allein tragen.
   HERR RUF: Ja, ich komme.

4. FRAU GRETTER: _____ Ihnen der Salat?
   HERR SIEBERT: Ja, sehr gut, die Soße ist ausgezeichnet.

5. FRAU KÖRNER: Dieser Rock _____ mir nicht. Ich brauche doch Größe 42.
   VERKÄUFER: Ich seh mal nach, ob wir Größe 42 haben.

6. JÜRGEN: Wem _____ denn dieser neue Staubsauger?
   SILVIA: Mir. Ich habe ihn gestern gekauft.

7. FRAU SCHULZ: Was suchst du, Albert? _____ dir etwas?
   ALBERT: Ja, ich kann mein Heft nicht finden.

8. FRAU KÖRNER: Wissen Sie, wer mir am Marktplatz _____ ist, Herr Siebert?
   HERR SIEBERT: Nein, wer denn?
   FRAU KÖRNER: Die Mutter von Maria. Und wissen Sie, was die mir erzählt hat?
   HERR SIEBERT: Nein, was denn?
   FRAU KÖRNER: Also, ...

9. ARZT: Also, Herr Ruf, Sie müssen jetzt wirklich mit dem Rauchen aufhören. Nikotin _____ Ihrer Gesundheit!
   HERR RUF: Aber, Herr Doktor, dann habe ich ja gar keine Freude mehr im Leben.

10. STEFAN: Entschuldigung, Frau Schulz, ich habe Ihnen nicht _____. Können Sie das noch mal wiederholen?
    FRAU SCHULZ: Na, gut.

Übung 2   Interview

Üb. 2. Assign as homework or do in class. Ask sts. to answer in complete sentences.

1. Wem haben Sie neulich[1] gratuliert?
2. Wem sind Sie neulich begegnet?
3. Welches Essen schmeckt Ihnen am besten?
4. Wie steht Ihnen Ihr Lieblingshemd?
5. Wie gefällt Ihnen Ihre Wohnung oder Ihr Zimmer?
6. Welches Möbelstück fehlt Ihnen in der Wohnung oder im Zimmer?

[1]recently

6.2 Location vs. destination: two-way prepositions with the dative or accusative case

Wo asks about location. Questions about location are answered with a preposition + dative.

The prepositions **in** (*in*), **an** (*on, at*), **auf** (*on top of*), **vor** (*before*), **hinter** (*behind*), **über** (*above*), **unter** (*underneath*), **neben** (*next to*), and **zwischen** (*between*) are used with both the dative and accusative cases. When they refer to a fixed location, the dative case is required. In these instances, the prepositional phrase answers the question **wo** (*where [at]*).

Wissen Sie noch?

The prepositions **in, an,** and **auf** use the dative case when they indicate location.

Review grammar 5.4.

6.2. *Akkusativ-/Dativpräpositionen.* This section completes the introduction of the use of two-way prepositions with the dative which was begun in Section 5.4 with *in, an,* and *auf.*

To keep meaning (and a little humor) in this presentation and practice of preposition usage, you might want to ask sts. why things are where they are in the various illustrations—why the tennis shoes are in the bookcase, the cat under the sofa, etc.

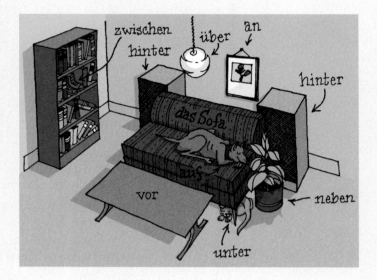

Im Wohnzimmer steht ein Sofa.
Hinter dem Sofa stehen zwei große Boxen.
An der Wand hängt ein Bild.
Auf dem Sofa liegt ein Hund.
Unter dem Sofa liegt eine Katze.
Vor dem Sofa steht ein Tisch.
Über dem Sofa hängt eine Lampe.
Neben dem Sofa steht eine große Pflanze.
Zwischen den Büchern stehen Tennisschuhe.

Wohin asks about placement or destination. Questions about placement or destination are answered with a preposition + accusative.

When these prepositions describe movement toward a place or a destination, they are used with the accusative case. In these instances, the prepositional phrase answers the question **wohin** (*where [to]*).

Peter hat das Sofa **ins Wohnzimmer** gestellt.
Die Boxen hat er **hinter das Sofa** gestellt.
Das Bild hat er **an die Wand** gehängt.
Der Hund hat sich gleich **auf das Sofa** gelegt.
Die Katze hat sich **unter das Sofa** gelegt.
Peter hat den Tisch **vor das Sofa** gestellt.
Die Lampe hat er **über das Sofa** gehängt.
Die große Pflanze hat er **neben das Sofa** gestellt.
Und seine Tennisschuhe hat er **zwischen die Bücher** gestellt.

	Wo?	Wohin?
	Location *Dative*	Placement/Destination *Accusative*
Masculine	Es ist auf **dem** Stuhl. *It is on the table.*	Leg es auf **den** Stuhl. *Put it on the table.*
Neuter	Es ist auf **dem** Bett. *It is on the bed.*	Leg es auf **das** Bett. *Put it on the bed.*
Feminine	Es ist auf **der** Kommode. *It is on the bureau.*	Leg es auf **die** Kommode. *Put it on the bureau.*
Plural	Es steht vor **den** Boxen. *It is in front of the speakers.*	Stell es vor **die** Boxen. *Put it in front of the speakers.*

Übung 3   Alberts Zimmer

Üb. 3. For homework or class work. Use your PF and objects and people in the classroom for additional practice.

Schauen Sie sich Alberts Zimmer an.

1. Wo ist Albert?
2. Wo ist der Spiegel?
3. Wo ist der Kühlschrank?
4. Wo ist das Deutschbuch?
5. Wo ist die Lampe?
6. Wo ist der Computer?
7. Wo sind die Schuhe?
8. Wo ist die Hose?
9. Wo ist das Poster von Berlin?
10. Wo ist die Katze?

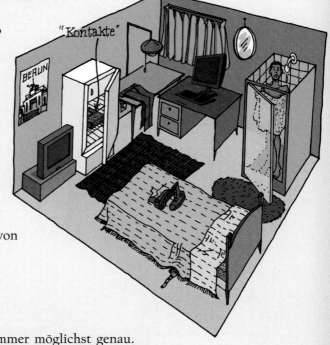

Achtung!

in + dem = im
an + dem = am

in + das = ins
an + das = ans

Übung 4   Mein Zimmer

Üb. 4. Assign as written homework and check in class. Have one st. read his or her description out loud in class while the other sts. draw a picture of the room described. Then ask sts. to compare their drawings in groups of 3 and to ask questions in cases of disagreement.

Beschreiben Sie Ihr Zimmer möglichst genau. Schreiben Sie mindestens acht Sätze mit verschiedenen Präpositionen.

MODELL: Das Bett ist unter dem Fenster. Rechts neben dem Bett steht ein Nachttisch ...

6.3 Word order: time before place

Time before place

In a German sentence, a time expression usually precedes a place expression. Note that this sequence is often reversed in English sentences.

Ich gehe heute Abend in die Bibliothek.

I'm going to the library tonight.

Übung 5   Wo sind Sie wann?

Üb. 5. Assign for homework. Remind sts. to begin the sentences with *ich* and to create their own answers besides using those listed.

Bilden Sie Sätze aus den Satzteilen.

MODELL: heute Abend → Ich bin heute Abend im Kino.

WANN	WO
1. heute Abend	in der Klasse
2. am Nachmittag	bei meinen Eltern
3. um 16 Uhr	im Bett
4. in der Nacht	auf einer Party
5. am frühen Morgen	im Urlaub
6. am Montag	am Frühstückstisch
7. am ersten August	in der Mensa
8. an Weihnachten	in der Bibliothek
9. im Winter	?
10. am Wochenende	

6.4. *Präpositionen: Antwort auf wohin?* This section presents sets of prepositions grouped according to their meaning rather than their form. Answers to the question *Wohin?* include both two-way and dative prepositions. This is a complex topic, and the correct choice of preposition and use of case are acquired only very gradually.

6.4 Direction: *in/auf* vs. *zu/nach*

Direction:

in/auf + accusative; **zu/nach** + dative

To refer to the place where you are going, use either **in** or **auf** + accusative, **zu** + dative, or **nach** + place name.

Albert geht **in die** Kirche.	*Albert goes to church.*
Katrin geht **auf die** Bank.	*Katrin goes to the bank.*
Heidi fährt **zum** Flughafen.	*Heidi drives to the airport.*
Rolf fliegt **nach** Deutschland.	*Rolf is flying to Germany.*

A. **in** + Accusative

in for most buildings and enclosed spaces

In general, use **in** when you plan to enter a building or an enclosed space.

Heute Nachmittag gehe ich **in die Bibliothek.**	*This afternoon I'll go to (into) the library.*
Abends gehe ich **ins Kino.**	*In the evening I go to (into) the movies.*
Morgen fahre ich **in die Stadt.**	*Tomorrow I'll drive to (into) the city.*

in for countries with a definite article

Also use **in** with the names of countries that have a definite article, such as **die Schweiz, die Türkei,** and **die USA.**

Herr Frisch fliegt oft **in die** USA.	*Mr. Frisch often flies to the USA.*
Claire fährt **in die** Schweiz.	*Claire is going to Switzerland.*
Mehmet fährt alle zwei Jahre **in die** Türkei.	*Mehmet goes to Turkey every two years.*

Zu and *nach* are the first dative prepositions presented. In this usage, *nach* is not followed by an article that indicates case. *Mit* and *bei* are introduced in Section 6.6; other dative prepositions are presented in Section 10.1.

auf for public buildings

B. auf + Accusative

Use **auf** instead of **in** when the destination is a public building such as the post office, the bank, or the police station.

Ich brauche Briefmarken. Ich gehe **auf die** Post.	*I need stamps. I'm going to the post office.*
Ich brauche Geld. Ich gehe **auf die** Bank.	*I need money. I'm going to the bank.*

C. zu + Dative

zu for specifically named buildings, places in general, open spaces, and people's places

Use **zu** to refer to destinations that are specific names of buildings, places or open spaces such as a playing field, or people.

Ernst geht **zu** McDonald's.	*Ernst is going to McDonald's.*
Hans geht **zum** Sportplatz.	*Hans goes to the playing field.*
Andrea geht **zum** Arzt.	*Andrea goes to the doctor.*

zu Hause = *at home*

Note that **zu Hause** (*at home*) does not indicate destination but rather location.

D. nach + place name

Use **nach** with names of countries and cities that have no article. Note that this applies to the vast majority of countries and cities.

Renate fliegt **nach Paris.**	*Renate is flying to Paris.*
Melanie fährt **nach Österreich.**	*Melanie is driving to Austria.*

nach Hause = (*going/coming*) *home*

Also use **nach** in the idiomatic construction **nach Hause** (*going/coming home*).

Übung 6   Situationen

Heute ist Montag. Wohin gehen oder fahren die folgenden Personen?

MODELL: Katrin sucht ein Buch. → Sie geht in die Bibliothek.

Achtung!

in + das	= ins
auf + das	= aufs
zu + dem	= zum
zu + der	= zur

zum Arzt   zum Fußballplatz   zur Tankstelle
zum Flughafen   ins Hotel   ins Theater
auf die Post   in die Schule
zu ihrem Freund   in den Supermarkt   in den Wald

1. Albert ist krank.
2. Hans möchte Fußball spielen.
3. Frau Schulz ist auf Reisen in einer fremden[1] Stadt. Sie braucht einen Platz zum Schlafen.
4. Herr Ruf braucht Benzin.
5. Herr Thelen braucht Lebensmittel.
6. Herr Wagner muss Briefmarken kaufen.
7. Jürgen und Silvia gehen Pilze[2] suchen.
8. Maria möchte mit ihrem Freund sprechen.
9. Mehmet möchte in die Türkei fliegen.
10. Renate möchte ein Musical sehen.
11. Jutta muss ein Referat halten.

[1]here: *unfamiliar*   [2]*mushrooms*

6.5 Separable-prefix verbs: the present tense and the perfect tense

Wissen Sie noch?

Separable-prefix verbs consist of a prefix plus an infinitive. In the present tense, the verb and the prefix form the **Satzklammer.**

Review grammar 1.5 and 3.5.

The infinitive of a separable-prefix verb consists of a prefix such as **auf, mit,** or **zu** followed by the base verb.

aufstehen	*to get up*
mitkommen	*to come along*
zuschauen	*to watch*

Most prefixes are derived from prepositions and adverbs.

abwaschen	*to do the dishes*
fernsehen	*to watch TV*

A. The Present Tense

Separable prefixes are placed at the end of the independent clause.

1. Independent clauses: In an independent clause in the present tense, the conjugated form of the base verb is in second position and the prefix is in last position.

Ich **stehe** jeden Morgen um sieben Uhr **auf.**	*I get up at seven every morning.*

Separable prefixes are "reconnected" to the base verb in dependent clauses.

2. Dependent clauses: In a dependent clause, the prefix and the base verb form a single verb. It appears at the end of the clause and is conjugated.

Rolf sagt, dass er jeden Morgen um sechs Uhr **aufsteht.**	*Rolf says that he gets up at six every morning.*
Hast du nicht gesagt, dass du heute **abwäschst?**	*Didn't you say that you would do the dishes today?*

Separable prefixes stay attached to the infinitive.

3. Modal verb constructions: In an independent clause with a modal verb (**wollen, müssen,** etc.), the infinitive of the separable-prefix verb is in last position. In a dependent clause with a modal verb, the separable-prefix verb is in the second-to-last position, and the modal verb is in the last position.

Jutta möchte ihren Freund **anrufen.**	*Jutta wants to call her boyfriend.*
Ernst hat schlechte Laune, wenn er nicht **fernsehen** darf.	*Ernst is in a bad mood when he's not allowed to watch TV.*

Wissen Sie noch?

The perfect tense is formed with **haben/sein** plus the past participle.

Review grammar 4.5.

B. The Perfect Tense

The past participle of a separable-prefix verb is a single word, consisting of the past participle of the base verb + the prefix.

Separable prefixes precede the **-ge-** marker in past participles.

6.5. Zweiteilige Verben: Präsens und Perfekt. This section consolidates the descriptions of separable-prefix verbs given in Sections 1.5, 3.5, and 4.5. It summarizes the use of the present and perfect tenses of these verbs in main and dependent clauses and with modals. For changes resulting from the spelling reform, see the IM.

Infinitive	Past Participle
auf**stehen**	auf**gestanden**
um**ziehen**	um**gezogen**
weg**bringen**	weg**gebracht**

Note that the prefix does not influence the formation of the past participle of the base verb; it is simply attached to it.

Herr Wagner **hat** gestern die Garage **aufgeräumt.**	*Mr. Wagner cleaned up his garage yesterday.*
Ich **habe** vor einer Stunde **angerufen.**	*I called an hour ago.*

Übung 7 Minidialoge

Üb. 7. Point out that some blanks are to be filled with either a prefix or a verb form, but others represent the prefix and verb form in a single word.

Ergänzen Sie die Sätze.

> aufstehen
>
> ankommen   mitkommen
>
> ausmachen
>
> anrufen   einladen   mitnehmen
>
> aufräumen   fernsehen   umziehen

1. HERR WAGNER: Ernst, aufwachen! Hast du nicht gestern gesagt, dass du heute um 7 Uhr _____?
   ERNST: Ich bin aber noch so müde!

2. FRAU WAGNER: Andrea, jetzt aber Schluss[1]! Ich _____[a] den Fernseher jetzt _____[b]. Du wirst noch dumm, wenn du den ganzen Tag nur_____[c].
   ANDREA: Aber, Mami, nur noch das Ende. Der Film ist doch gleich vorbei!

3. SILVIA: Entschuldigen Sie bitte! Wann _____[a] der Zug aus Hamburg _____[b]?
   BAHNANGESTELLTER: Um 14 Uhr 56.

4. ANDREAS: Hallo, Jürgen. Ich habe gehört, dass ihr bald eine neue Wohnung habt. Wann _____[a] ihr denn _____[b]?
   JÜRGEN: Nächstes Wochenende.

5. MARTA: Hallo, Sofie. Ich habe morgen Geburtstag und ich möchte dich gern zu einer kleinen Feier _____.
   SOFIE: Das ist aber nett von dir. Ich komme gern.

6. CLAIRE: Hallo, Melanie. Wo ist Josef?
   MELANIE: Er ist zu Hause. Er _____[a] heute sein Zimmer _____[b] und das dauert bei ihm immer etwas länger.

7. JÜRGEN: Hallo, Silvia. Ich fahre heute mit dem Auto zur Uni. Willst du _____[a]?
   SILVIA: Ja, gern. Schön, dass du mich _____[b].

8. KATRIN: Hier ist meine Telefonnummer. Warum _____[a] du mich nicht mal _____[b]!
   HEIDI: Gut, das mach' ich mal.

Übung 8 Am Sonntag

Üb 8. Assign for homework and check in class.

Gestern war Sonntag. Was haben die folgenden Personen gestern gemacht?

Nützliche Wörter: abtrocknen, anrufen, anziehen, aufwachen, ausgehen, ausziehen, fernsehen, zurückkommen

[1]jetzt ... *finish up now*

Andrea

Kino →
Katrin und Peter

Heidi
Frau Schulz

Herr Ruf

Jürgen
Schlaf-zimmer
BAD
KÜCHE

Abendkleid
Jutta

aus Bulgarien
Maria

Herr Thelen

6.6 *Dativpräpositionen: mit und bei.* The introduction of dative prepositions continues here with *mit* and *bei*. Point out the difference between *mit* the preposition and *mit* the separable prefix, which occurred in *Üb. 7.* Sts. sometimes confuse prepositions and prefixes that have the same form (*an, auf, usw*).

6.6 The prepositions *mit* and *bei* + dative

The prepositions **mit** (*with, by*) and **bei** (*near, with*) are followed by the dative case.

Masculine	Neuter	Feminine	Plural
mit dem Staubsauger	mit dem Bügeleisen	mit der Bürste	mit den Eltern
beim Onkel	beim Fenster	bei der Tür	bei den Eltern

Mit corresponds to the preposition *with* in English and is used in similar ways.

Herr Wagner fegt die Terrasse **mit** seinem neuen Besen.

Mr. Wagner sweeps the patio with his new broom.

Ich gehe **mit** meinen Freunden ins Kino.

I'm going to the movies with my friends.

Ich möchte ein Haus **mit** einem offenen Kamin.

I want a house with a fireplace.

Use **mit** with means of transportation.

The preposition **mit** also indicates the means of transportation; in this instance it corresponds to the English preposition *by*. Note the use of the definite article in German.

Rolf fährt **mit** dem Bus zur Uni.

Rolf goes to the university by bus.

Renate fährt **mit** dem Auto zur Arbeit.

Renate drives to work (goes to work by car).

The preposition **bei** may refer to a place in the vicinity of another place; in this instance it corresponds to the English preposition *near*.

Bad Harzburg liegt **bei** Goslar.

Bad Harzburg is near Goslar.

The preposition **bei** also indicates placement with a person, a company, or an institution; in these instances it corresponds to the English preposition *with*, *at*, or *for*.

Ich wohne **bei** meinen Eltern.

I'm living (staying) with my parents / at my parents'.

Hans arbeitet **bei** McDonald's.

Hans works at (for) McDonald's.

	German	English
Instrument	mit dem Hammer	*with the hammer*
Togetherness	mit Freunden	*with friends*
Means of transportation	mit dem Flugzeug	*by airplane*
Vicinity	bei München	*near Munich*
Somebody's place	bei den Eltern	*(staying) with parents*
Place of employment	bei McDonald's	*at McDonald's*

Übung 9 Im Haus und im Garten

Üb 9. Assign as homework and check in class.

Womit machen Sie die folgenden Aktivitäten?

MODELL: S1: Womit mähst du den Rasen?
S2: Mit dem Rasenmäher.

1. Kaffee kochen
2. Staub saugen
3. den Boden fegen
4. bügeln
5. einen Brief tippen
6. die Blumen im Garten gießen
7. den Boden wischen
8. die Blumen in der Wohnung gießen

> **der Besen**   **das Bügeleisen**   **der Computer**
>
> **der Gartenschlauch**   **die Gießkanne**
>
> **die Kaffeemaschine**   **der Putzlappen**   **der Staubsauger**

Übung 10 Minidialoge

Ergänzen Sie die Sätze mit der Präposition **mit** oder **bei.**

1. FRAU KÖRNER: Fahren Sie _____[a] dem Bus oder _____[b] dem Fahrrad zur Arbeit?
   MICHAEL PUSCH: _____[c] dem Bus. Ich arbeite jetzt _____[d] Siemens. Das ist am anderen Ende von München.

2. PETER: Wohnst du in Krefeld _____[a] deinen Eltern?
   ROLF: Ja, sie haben ein wunderschönes Haus _____[b] einem riesigen Garten.
   PETER: Liegt Krefeld eigentlich _____[c] Dortmund?
   ROLF: Nein, nach Dortmund fährt man über eine Stunde _____[d] dem Auto.

3. JÜRGEN: Oh je, jetzt habe ich deinen Gummibaum[1] umgeworfen[2]! Soll ich die Erde[3] _____[a] dem Staubsauger aufsaugen?
   SILVIA: Mach es lieber _____[b] dem Besen. Er steht _____[c] der Kellertür.

[1]*rubber plant* [2]*knocked over* [3]*dirt*

Unterwegs

Kapitel 7 is about geography and transportation. You will learn more about the geography of the German-speaking world and about the kinds of transportation used by people who live there.

GOALS

The focus of this chapter is travel, with emphasis on sts.' own experiences. Relative pronouns are introduced, although we don't yet expect sts. to use them productively in speaking. The comparative and superlative are introduced as well.

Themen

Geografie
Transportmittel
Das Auto
Reiseerlebnisse

Kulturelles

Musikszene: „Mädchen, lach doch mal!" (Wise Guys)
Filmclip: *Im Juli* (Fatih Akin)
KLI: Volkswagen
KLI: Die Schweiz
Videoecke: Ausflüge und Verkehrsmittel

Lektüren

Gedicht: Die Lorelei (Heinrich Heine)
Film: *Im Juli* (Fatih Akin)

Strukturen

7.1 Relative clauses
7.2 Making comparisons: the comparative and superlative forms of adjectives and adverbs
7.3 Referring to and asking about things and ideas: **da**-compounds and **wo**-compounds
7.4 The perfect tense (review)
7.5 The simple past tense of **haben** and **sein**

Elfriede Lohse-Wächtler: *Loschwitzer Brücke (Blaues Wunder)* (1931), Privatbesitz

Kunst und Künstler

Elfriede Lohse-Wächtler (1899–1940) war eine Dresdner Malerin der Avantgarde. Sie studierte in Dresden an der Kunstgewerbe-schule[1] und der Kunstakademie. Als sie an Schizophrenie erkrankte, wurde sie von den Nazis entmündigt[2], in ein Krankenhaus eingewiesen[3] und schließlich 1940 umgebracht[4]. Neben Stadt- und Landschaftsporträts malte sie viele Kopf- und Körperstudien von psychisch Kranken. Ihre Kunst wurde von den Nazis als *Entartete Kunst*[5] bezeichnet und viele ihrer Bilder wurden vernichtet[6]. Die Loschwitzer Brücke wurde 1883 gebaut. Sie wird das *Blaue Wunder* genannt und ist eines der Wahrzeichen von Dresden.

Schauen Sie sich das Bild an und beantworten Sie die folgenden Fragen.

1. Was sehen Sie auf dem Bild? Beschreiben Sie es.
2. Welche Farben und Linien dominieren im Bild? Welche Perspektive wird eingenommen[7]?
3. Was ist das Besondere an den Gebäuden? Wie wird die Brücke dargestellt[8]? Und der Fluss?
4. Welche Assoziationen weckt das Bild?

[1] *School of Arts and Crafts* [2] *declared mentally incompetent* [3] *committed* [4] *killed* [5] *degenerate art* [6] *destroyed* [7] *assumed* [8] *represented*

Situationen

Geografie

Vocabulary Display
Model pronunciation of geographical
terms and have sts. repeat. Then ask
questions related to the topic: *Gibt
es in (your state) Berge oder Hügel?
Wo gibt es Berge? Welche Staaten liegen am Meer?
an den großen Seen? Wie heißt die größte Insel der
Welt? (Grönland) Wo gibt es die schönsten Strände
der Welt? usw.*

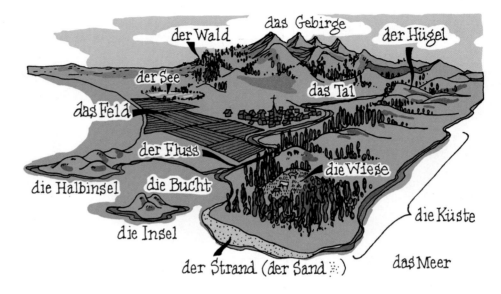

Situation 1   Erdkunde: Wer weiß – gewinnt

Sit. 1. (See the IM for the use of content-based
activities.) This activity uses relative pronouns.
Stress that this is a guessing game, like "Trivial
Pursuit," not a research task. Sts. can figure out
the answers based on clues given. Have sts. work
in small groups. Afterward, restate definitions as
questions and have sts. answer: *Welcher Fluss fließt
durch Wien? In welchem Wald haben die Germanen
die Römer besiegt? usw.* **Answers:** 1. h, 2. d, 3. i,
4. b, 5. e, 6. a, 7. c, 8. f, 9. j, 10. g.

Cultural note. See the IM for detailed information
on the places and events mentioned here. Bring
in a large map to give sts. an idea where these
places are.

1. Fluss, der durch Wien fließt
2. Wald, in dem die Germanen[1] die Römer[2] besiegt haben
3. Insel in der Ostsee, auf der weiße Kreidefelsen[3] sind
4. Berg, auf dem sich die Hexen treffen
5. See, der zwischen Deutschland, Österreich und der Schweiz liegt
6. Meer, das Europa von Afrika trennt
7. Gebirge in Österreich, in dem man sehr gut Ski fahren kann
8. berühmte Wüste, die in Ostasien liegt
9. Inseln, die vor der Küste von Ostfriesland liegen
10. Fluss, an dem die Lorelei ihr Haar kämmt

a. das Mittelmeer
b. der Brocken im Harz (1 142 Meter hoch)
c. die Kitzbühler Alpen
d. der Teutoburger Wald
e. der Bodensee
f. die Wüste Gobi
g. der Rhein
h. die Donau
i. Rügen
j. die Ostfriesischen Inseln

[1]*Teutons* [2]*Romans* [3]*chalk cliffs*

Situation 2   Ratespiel: Stadt, Land, Fluss

Sit. 2. This activity demonstrates the superlative form of adjectives. Sts. work in small groups with whole-class follow-up. Again, encourage them to approach the activity playfully. **Answers:** 1. c, 2. d, 3. f, 4. b, 5. h, 6. e, 7. i, 8. g, 9. a.

Suggestion. Invert columns and play "Jeopardy." Read the answers first, and have sts. respond with the corresponding question.

Cultural note. See the IM for detailed information on the geographic features mentioned here and for ideas for additional activities.

1. Wie heißt der tiefste See der Schweiz?
2. Wie heißt der höchste Berg Österreichs?
3. Wie heißt der längste Fluss Deutschlands?
4. Wie heißt das salzigste Meer der Welt?
5. Wie heißt der größte Gletscher der Alpen?
6. Was ist die heißeste Wüste der Welt?
7. Wie heißt die älteste Universitätsstadt Deutschlands?
8. Wie heißt das kleinste Land, in dem man Deutsch spricht?
9. Wie heißt die berühmteste Höhle in Österreich?

a. die Dachstein-Mammuthöhle
b. das Tote Meer
c. der Genfer See
d. der Großglockner
e. die Wüste Sahara
f. der Rhein
g. Liechtenstein
h. der Große Aletschgletscher
i. Heidelberg

 ## Situation 3   Informationsspiel: Deutschlandreise

Sit. 3. The corresponding chart is in Appendix A. S1 asks the location of cities labeled with a blank on the map; S2 consults the corresponding map in Appendix A, where missing cities are labeled. S2 tells S1 where to write in the name of each city, using the compass points. Then sts. switch roles: S2 asks about cities labeled with a blank on the map in the appendix; S1 gives location, using the map in the chapter.

Wo liegen die folgenden Städte? Schreiben Sie die Namen der Städte auf die Landkarte.

Aachen, Bayreuth, Dresden, Erfurt, Flensburg, Freiburg, Hannover, Heidelberg, Magdeburg, Wiesbaden

MODELL: s2: Wo liegt Braunschweig?
s1: Braunschweig liegt im Norden.
s2: Wo genau?
s1: Südlich von Hamburg.

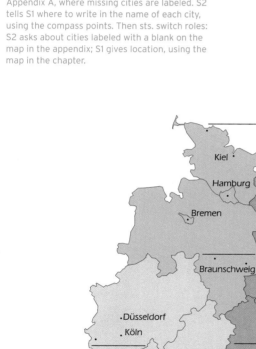

AA. As a follow-up, put the map on the projector and provide one or two *Bundesländer*. Introduce the *Länder* to sts. by saying, e.g., *Halle liegt in Sachsen-Anhalt. Sachsen-Anhalt liegt nördlich von Thüringen, etc.* Then ask sts. a few questions such as *Was liegt östlich von Sachsen-Anhalt? Welches Bundesland liegt im Norden? Welches im Süden? usw.*

Situationen   **239**

Lektüre

Lektüre. (1) Set the scene by asking sts. to look at the picture and describe what is taking place. Ask if they know what river is depicted: *Wie heißt der Fluss, an dem die Lorelei ihr Haar kämmt?* (2) Ask sts. to work on *Vor dem Lesen* in small groups. Discuss afterwards. (3) Tell sts. that the language of the poem is archaic in some respects, and give them examples. Let sts. read the complete text. Play the audio recording in class. If you and your sts. enjoy singing, sing along after they've heard it once. Later in the semester/quarter, sts. could be challenged to sing the song without accompaniment. (4) Make sure sts. understand that they are to complete Part A of *Arbeit mit dem Text* without looking at the text again. Then compare their answers with the text. (5) Assign Part B of *Arbeit mit dem Text* for written homework. (6) Ask sts. to discuss *Nach dem Lesen* in small groups.

Vor dem Lesen

Schreiben Sie mögliche[1] Antworten auf die folgenden Fragen.

1. Ist das eine lustige oder eine traurige Geschichte? Woher wissen Sie das?
2. Was macht die Frau auf dem Bild? Warum macht sie das?
3. Neben ihr liegt eine Leier[2]. Warum liegt sie da?
4. Was macht der Mann im Boot? Was sollte er machen?
5. Was passiert mit dem Mann im Boot? Spekulieren Sie!

Die Lorelei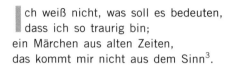

von Heinrich Heine

Die Loreley.

Die schönste Jungfrau sitzet
Dort oben wunderbar,
Ihr goldnes Geschmeide blitzet,
Sie kämmt ihr goldenes Haar.

Sie kämmt es mit goldenem Kamme
Und singt ein Lied dabei
Das hat eine wundersame,
Gewaltige Melodei.

Ich weiß nicht, was soll es bedeuten,
dass ich so traurig bin;
ein Märchen aus alten Zeiten,
das kommt mir nicht aus dem Sinn[3].

5   Die Luft ist kühl und es dunkelt[4],
und ruhig fließt der Rhein;
der Gipfel[5] des Berges funkelt[6]
im Abendsonnenschein.

Die schönste Jungfrau[7] sitzet
10   dort oben wunderbar;
ihr goldnes Geschmeide[8] blitzet,
sie kämmt ihr goldenes Haar.

Sie kämmt es mit goldenem Kamme[9]
und singt ein Lied dabei;
15   das hat eine wundersame,
gewaltige[10] Melodei.

Den Schiffer im kleinen Schiffe
ergreift[11] es mit wildem Weh[12];
er schaut nicht die Felsenriffe[13],
20   er schaut nur hinauf in die Höh'.

Ich glaube, die Wellen[14] verschlingen[15]
am Ende Schiffer und Kahn[16];
und das hat mit ihrem Singen
die Lore-Ley getan.

[1]possible   [2]lyre   [3]das ... I can't forget it   [4]is growing dark   [5]peak   [6]is sparkling   [7]virgin; young woman
[8]jewelry   [9]comb   [10]powerful   [11]seizes   [12]pain, longing   [13]cliffs   [14]waves   [15]devour, swallow up   [16]boat

Arbeit mit dem Text

A. Ergänzen Sie die folgenden Sätze mit Wörtern aus dem Kasten, ohne den Text noch einmal zu lesen. Schauen Sie dann auf das Gedicht und korrigieren Sie Ihre Antworten.

> funkelt   kühl
>
> kommt   fließt
>
> blitzet   kämmt
>
> verschlingen
>
> singt

1. Ein Lied _____ mir nicht aus dem Sinn.
2. Die Luft ist _____.
3. Der Fluss _____ ruhig.
4. Der Gipfel _____ im Abendsonnenschein.
5. Das goldene Geschmeide _____.
6. Sie _____ ihr goldenes Haar.
7. Sie _____ ein Lied.
8. Die Wellen _____ das Boot.

B. Zeit, Ort, Personen und Handlung. Beantworten Sie die folgenden Fragen und Aufgaben. Schreiben Sie dazu, in welcher Zeile[1] Sie jede Antwort gefunden haben.

1. Wann spielt die Geschichte (vor wie vielen Jahren)? Zu welcher Jahreszeit oder Tageszeit spielt die Geschichte? Wie viel Zeit vergeht[2]?
2. Wo spielt die Geschichte (an welchem Fluss)? Beschreiben Sie den Ort!
3. Welche Personen treten auf[3]? Was wissen wir über sie? Was machen sie?
4. Handlung: Bringen Sie die Sätze in die richtige Reihenfolge.

   _4_ Unten auf dem Rhein hört ein Schiffer ihr Singen.

   _1_ Eine schöne Frau sitzt oben auf einem Berg am Rhein.

   _5_ Er schaut fasziniert nach oben zu der Frau.

   _2_ Ihr Schmuck funkelt in der Abendsonne.

   _7_ Sein Schiff sinkt und er ertrinkt[4].

   _3_ Sie kämmt sich und singt ein Lied dabei.

   _6_ Weil er nicht aufpasst, fährt er auf einen Felsen.

Nach dem Lesen

Welche Geschichten kennen Sie, in denen Frauen mit ihrer Schönheit oder mit ihrem Gesang Männer ins Unglück locken[5]? Erzählen Sie!

[1]*line* [2]*passes* [3]*treten … appear* [4]*drowns* [5]*ins … lure into misfortune*

 Situation 4   Interview: Landschaften

1. Warst du schon mal im Gebirge? Wo? Was hast du da gemacht? Wie heißt der höchste Berg, den du gesehen (oder bestiegen) hast?
2. Warst du schon mal am Meer? Wo und wann war das? Hast du gebadet? Was hast du sonst noch gemacht?
3. Wohnst du in der Nähe von einem großen Fluss? Wie heißt er? Wie heißt der größte Fluss, an dem du schon warst? Was hast du da gemacht?
4. Wie heißt die interessanteste Stadt, in der du schon warst?
5. Warst du schon mal in der Wüste oder im Dschungel? Wie war das?

Transportmittel

Grammatik 7.1, 7.4

Vocabulary Display
Pronounce the vocabulary and have sts. repeat. Then cover up vocabulary and ask: *Was ist größer: ein Bus oder ein Auto? Was ist schneller: ein Fahrrad oder ein Motorrad? Gibt es in der Nähe von hier eine U-Bahn? Welches Transportmittel benutzen Sie, wenn Sie nach Europa wollen? nach New York City? nach Hause? usw.*

das Auto

das Taxi

das Fahrrad

der Lastwagen

der Bus

die U-Bahn

das Motorrad

der Zug

die Straßenbahn

das Flugzeug

die Autobahn

Situation 5   Definitionen: Transportmittel

Sit. 5. Definitions and instructor's questions following the activity demonstrate use of relative pronouns. Have sts. work in small groups, and then ask: *Wie nennt man ein Transportmittel, das fliegt? Wie nennt man das Auto, das in Deutschland die Farbe beige hat und ein Schild auf dem Dach hat? usw.*

1. das Flugzeug
2. die Rakete
3. das Kamel
4. das Fahrrad
5. der Kinderwagen
6. der Zeppelin
7. der Zug
8. das Taxi

a. Transportmittel, das Waggons und eine Lokomotive hat
b. Transportmittel, das fliegt
c. Tier, das viele Beduinen als Transportmittel benutzen
d. Transportmittel, mit dem man zum Mond fliegen kann
e. Auto, das in Deutschland ein gelbes Schild auf dem Dach hat
f. Transportmittel in der Luft, das wie eine Zigarre aussieht
g. Transportmittel mit zwei Rädern, das ohne Benzin fährt
h. Wagen, in dem man Babys transportiert

Musikszene

„Mädchen, lach doch mal!" (1999, Deutschland) *Wise Guys*

Biografie Die *Wise Guys* kommen aus Köln. Sie singen vor allem a cappella. Viele von ihnen sind an das selbe Gymnasium in Köln gegangen, wo ihre Lehrer sie die Besserwisser genannt haben. Daher stammt auch ihr Name. Ihre Alben *Frei* (2008) und *Klassenfahrt* (2010) haben Platz 2 der deutschen Charts erreicht. Sie treten regelmäßig auf dem Deutschen Evangelischen Kirchentag auf ebenso wie auf anderen großen öffentlichen Veranstaltungen. Der Hit „Mädchen, lach doch mal" stammt aus dem Album *Skandal* von 1999.

Die Wise Guys aus Köln

Vor dem Hören Wer könnte das Mädchen sein? Warum lacht sie nicht?

Nach dem Hören Kreuzen Sie die richtigen Antworten an. Nur jeweils eine Antwort pro Frage ist falsch.

1. Wo trifft der junge Mann das Mädchen?
    - ☒ **a.** in der Straßenbahn
    - ☒ **b.** in seiner Stammkneipe
    - ☐ **c.** im Dom
    - ☒ **d.** im Traum
2. Wie beschreibt er das Mädchen?
    - ☒ **a.** Sie hat ein geheimnisvolles Gesicht.
    - ☒ **b.** Sie hat eine Topfigur.
    - ☐ **c.** Sie hat einen festen Freund.
    - ☒ **d.** Sie hat strahlend weiße Zähne.
3. Was würde er tun, wenn das Mädchen lachen würde?
    - ☒ **a.** Er würde sich vom Dom stürzen.
    - ☐ **b.** Er würde über den Rhein schwimmen.
    - ☒ **c.** Er würde mit dem Rad nach Rom fahren.
    - ☒ **d.** Er würde ihren Namen auf sein Grab schreiben.

iMix Link: This song is available for purchase at the iTunes store in a special iMix created for *Kontakte*. For more information about accessing the playlist, go to **Connect German** (www.connectgerman.com).

Musikszene. Suggestion: Ask sts. to read the *Biografie* and ask a few questions to verify understanding. Discuss *Vor dem Hören* in class and elicit suggestions. Explain *Nach dem Hören*. Go over the activity, pointing out which words are covered in the *Miniwörterbuch*. Make sure sts. understand the remaining words. Explain that the group comes from Cologne and tell them that Cologne is on the river Rhine and that it boasts the tallest cathedral in Germany (*Kölner Dom*). Show photos. Then ask sts. to do *Nach dem Hören* in pairs or small groups while playing the song several times. **Follow-up:** You may wish to ask sts. to write out the chorus. You will need to play it several times for this, as the pace is rather quick. Point out that *doch* and *mal* are flavoring particles that soften or intensify commands. For sts. to accomplish this task, it might be useful to provide some of the unfamiliar vocabulary: *lächeln, in Frieden, sterben, erben, funktionieren.*

Miniwörterbuch

der **Besserwisser**	wise guy, know-it-all	**geheimnisvoll**	mysterious
auftreten	to perform	**der feste Freund**	steady boyfriend
der **Kirchentag**	church congress	die **Zähne**	teeth
die **Stammkneipe**	favorite bar	**würde**	would
der **Dom**	cathedral	**sich stürzen**	to jump (to one's death)
der **Traum**	dream	das **Grab**	grave

Situation 6 Interview

Sit. 6. You will notice that the interview activities are becoming increasingly more like discussions, involving follow-up questions that require sts. to explain their responses. Be sure to model possible answers–e.g., *Ich fahre selten mit dem Bus, weil die Verbindungen so schlecht sind und weil ich nicht gern warte. Ich fahre gern mit dem Zug, weil ich dabei lesen oder stricken kann.* Sts. should take notes on their partner's responses so that they can report them in the follow-up.

1. Welche Transportmittel hast du schon benutzt?
2. Fährst du oft mit der U-Bahn oder mit dem Bus? Warum (nicht)?
3. Fährst du gern mit dem Zug (oder möchtest du gern mal mit dem Zug fahren)? Welche Vorteile/Nachteile hat das Reisen mit dem Zug?
4. Fliegst du gern? Warum (nicht)? Welche Vorteile/Nachteile hat das Reisen mit dem Flugzeug?
5. Fährst du lieber mit dem Auto oder mit öffentlichen Verkehrsmitteln? Warum? Womit fährst du am liebsten?
6. Denkst du an die Umwelt, wenn du Transportmittel benutzt?

Situation 7　Dialog: Eine Bahnfahrt online buchen

Cultural note. Train travel is fast in Germany and a convenient alternative to flying or driving. The ICE (Inter-City-Express) train connects all major German cities. It travels at speeds of up to 330 km per hour.

Sit. 7. (See the IM.) You may wish to follow the steps for presenting the dialogue without the use of the textbook. Questions for first listening: *1. Wohin möchten Renate und Mehmet fahren? 2. Wann müssen sie da sein?* Questions for second listening: *1. Wann fährt der ICE ab? 2. Wann kommt er in München an? 3. Fahren Mehmet und Renate erster oder zweiter Klasse?*

RENATE: Okay, Mehmet, dann lass uns mal unsere Bahnfahrt nach München <u>buchen</u>. Bist du schon online?

MEHMET: Ja. Was ist noch mal dein <u>Passwort</u> bei bahn.de?

RENATE: 16. Oktober.

MEHMET: Also, wann wollen wir denn fahren? <u>So</u> früh <u>wie</u> möglich?

RENATE: Nein, wir müssen um 17 Uhr da sein. Aber bitte ohne Umsteigen.

MEHMET: Okay, Abfahrt um 10.39 Uhr, <u>Ankunft</u> um 16.39, mit ICE, ohne Umsteigen.

RENATE: Was kostet das?

MEHMET: Mit Sparpreis <u>in der zweiten Klasse</u>, Hin- und Rückfahrt, 140 Euro pro Person.

RENATE: Müssen wir Sitzplätze reservieren?

MEHMET: Um diese Zeit <u>vielleicht</u> nicht. Soll ich zwei Plätze für uns buchen?

RENATE: Ja.

Situation 8　Rollenspiel: Am Fahrkartenschalter

Sit. 8. The role for S2 appears in Appendix B. **Note:** If your students are using McGraw-Hill's *Connect* online *Arbeitsbuch*, they can do this *Rollenspiel* using the real-time, interactive **Video-Chat** feature.

S1: Sie stehen am Fahrkartenschalter im Bahnhof von Bremen und wollen eine Fahrkarte nach München kaufen. Sie wollen billig fahren, müssen aber vor 16.30 Uhr am Bahnhof in München ankommen. Fragen Sie, wann und wo der Zug abfährt und über welche Städte der Zug fährt.

Filmlektüre
Im Juli

Vor dem Lesen

Filmlektüre. Suggestion: Have sts. look at the photograph and talk about it. Ask them questions such as: *Was assoziieren Sie mit den Personen auf dem Foto? Wie sehen sie aus? Was machen sie? Sind sie Freunde, Verwandte oder Fremde? Warum heißt der Film „Im Juli"? Was für ein Film kann das sein (Krimi, Liebesfilm, etc.)?* Collect sts.' answers on the board and by doing so create a possible story line with sts.' help.

A. Beantworten Sie die folgenden Fragen.

1. Was sehen Sie auf dem Foto?
2. Warum heißt der Film wohl *Im Juli?*
3. Wer ist der Regisseur?
4. Wann startete der Film im Kino?

Filmangaben

Titel: *Im Juli*
Genre: Roadmovie
Erscheinungsjahr: 2000
Land: Deutschland
Dauer: 99 min
Regisseur: Fatih Akin
Hauptrollen: Moritz Bleibtreu, Christiane Paul, Idil Üner

Szene aus dem Film *Im Juli*. Daniel küsst seine neue Freundin.

B. Lesen Sie die Wörter im Miniwörterbuch. Suchen Sie sie in der Inhaltsangabe und unterstreichen Sie sie.

Miniwörterbuch

langweilig	boring	fahren	to drive
flippig	weird, funky	der **Liebeskummer**	love problems
der **Schmuck**	jewelry	schüchtern	shy
das **Pech**	bad luck		

Inhaltsangabe

Der junge Lehrer Daniel (Moritz Bleibtreu) lebt in Hamburg und ist ein sehr langweiliger Typ. Nur die flippige Schmuckverkäuferin Juli (Christiane Paul) interessiert sich für ihn. In den Sommerferien trifft Daniel auf einer Party die Türkin Melek (Idil Üner). Sie ist auf dem Weg nach Istanbul. Daniel verliebt sich sofort in seine

5 „Traumfrau". Das ist aber Pech für Juli, die auch auf die Party kommt! Als Melek am nächsten Morgen in die Türkei fliegt, fährt Daniel seiner großen Liebe mit dem Auto nach – 2 700 Kilometer bis nach Istanbul. Auf der Autobahn trifft er Juli wieder. Sie will aus Liebeskummer einfach wegtrampen. Daniel nimmt sie in seinem Auto mit. Für Juli und Daniel beginnt eine wilde Odyssee und eine Reise in ein

10 neues Leben. Am Ende ist Daniel ein anderer Typ: nicht mehr der schüchterne und langweilige Lehrer, sondern ein cooler Lover und auch Juli ist keine traurige junge Frau mit Liebeskummer mehr.

Filmclip

Szene: DVD, Kapitel 2, „School's out", 7:28–11:00 Min.

Daniel ist Referendar in einer Schule in Hamburg. Er geht jeden Tag an Julis Stand auf dem Markt vorbei … bis sie ihn eines Tages anspricht.

Schauen Sie sich die Szene an. Die folgenden Aussagen beschreiben die Szene in der falschen Reihenfolge. Bringen Sie die Sätze in die richtige Reihenfolge.

___5___ Daniel fällt seine Tüte zu Boden. Juli sagt zu Daniel, „He du, komm doch mal her."

___1___ Daniel ist Lehrer in einer Schule. Es ist die letzte Stunde vor den Ferien.

___2___ Die Schüler passen nicht auf und wollen Daniels Fragen nicht beantworten.

___9___ Juli verkauft Daniel den Ring für 35 Euro, weil sie ihn gern hat.

___10___ Juli lädt Daniel auf eine Party ein.

___8___ Juli sagt, Daniel wird ein Mädchen kennenlernen, das eine Sonne trägt.

___7___ Juli sagt: „Die Sonne macht Licht", und „Ein anderes Wort für Licht ist Glück".

___4___ Juli (mit Dreadlocks) und ihre Freundin (mit blonden Haaren) unterhalten sich über Daniel. Juli sagt, sie ist schüchtern.

___6___ Juli zeigt Daniel einen Ring. Darauf sieht man eine Sonne.

___3___ Die Schülerin Kira sagt: „Wir machen Schluss." Alle Schüler stehen auf und gehen.

Note. Fatih Akin, born in 1973, is the son of Turkish immigrants who came to Germany in the 1960s. Akin made his debut as a movie director in 1998 with his short film *Kurz und schmerzlos*, and has become very successful since then. His fourth movie, *Gegen die Wand* (2004), in particular, earned a lot of praise and received many awards. *Im Juli* is his second film, which is a road movie, romantic and funny. Daniel, the main character, falls in love with Melek, a Turkish woman, whom he even follows to Turkey. Convinced that Melek is the love of his life, Daniel does not notice that Juli, who has loved him for a long time, is the one. Juli's and Daniel's journey through Eastern Europe turns out to be an exciting undertaking, as almost everything goes wrong: they fall into the Danube river, are involved in a car chase, and even end up in prison.

Arbeit mit dem Text

Richtig (R) oder falsch (F)? Verbessern Sie die falschen Aussagen.

_____ 1. Daniel kommt aus Hamburg.

_____ 2. Auf einer Reise lernt Daniel die Türkin Melek kennen.

_____ 3. Juli liebt den langweiligen Daniel.

_____ 4. Daniel fährt mit dem Motorrad nach Istanbul.

_____ 5. Juli fliegt mit Melek in die Türkei.

_____ 6. Am Ende der Reise ist Daniel nicht mehr langweilig.

Nach dem Lesen

A. Suchen Sie weitere Informationen über den Regisseur Fatih Akin im Internet.

1. Woher kommt Fatih Akin?

2. Woher kommen seine Eltern?

3. Wie alt ist er?

4. Wie heißt sein erster Film?

5. Welche Preise haben seine Filme bekommen?

B. Sehen Sie den Trailer zum Film im Internet an und machen Sie ein Poster zum Film.

Das Auto

Grammatik 7.3

Vocabulary Display. Model pronunciation and have sts. repeat. Then ask: _Ist der Kofferraum vorn oder hinten? Was braucht man, wenn es regnet? Muss man in (your state) mit Sicherheitsgurt fahren? Woher kommt das Auto, dessen Nummernschild Sie sehen? (Neuss) Worauf tritt man, wenn man halten will? usw._ Have sts. guess where the following license plates are from: M (München); H (Hannover); B (Berlin); R (Regensburg); BN (Bonn); L (Leipzig); DD (Dresden); C (Chemnitz).

AA. You might want to ask your sts. to speculate further on the drawing: _Was legt der Mann in den Kofferraum? Warum ist der Mann, der eine Reifenpanne hat, so wütend? usw._

1. Damit kann man hupen.
2. Daran sieht man, woher das Auto kommt.
3. Darin kann man seine Koffer verstauen.
4. Damit wischt man die Scheiben.

Situation 9 Definitionen: Die Teile des Autos

Sit. 9. This activity demonstrates the use of *da*-compounds. Have sts. work in small groups to figure out the answers. As a wrap-up, ask: *Worauf setzt man sich? Was braucht man, wenn man bei Regen fährt? usw.*

1. die Bremsen
2. die Scheibenwischer
3. das Autoradio
4. das Lenkrad
5. die Hupe
6. das Nummernschild
7. die Sitze
8. das Benzin
9. der Tank

a. Man setzt sich darauf.
b. Man braucht sie, wenn man bei Regen fährt.
c. Damit lenkt man das Auto.
d. Damit warnt man andere Fahrer oder Fußgänger.
e. Daran sieht man, woher das Auto kommt.
f. Damit hört man Musik und Nachrichten.
g. Damit fährt das Auto.
h. Darin ist das Benzin.
i. Damit hält man den Wagen an.

Situation 10 Rollenspiel: Ein Auto kaufen

Sit. 10. The role for S2 and the corresponding chart appear in Appendix B.

Cultural note. All cars in Germany must be inspected every two years by the *TÜV (Technischer Überwachungsverein)*, the agency that checks brakes, steering, lights, tires, and even rust damage for safety hazards. Once a car has passed the TÜV test, the owner gets a sticker for the license plate that indicates when the next inspection is due.

Cultural note. Because of high gasoline prices in Europe, fuel efficiency is a major concern for many Europeans when selecting a car. It is figured differently from U.S. standards: how many liters per 100 km rather than miles per gallon.

s1: Sie wollen einen älteren Gebrauchtwagen kaufen und lesen deshalb die Anzeigen in der Zeitung. Die Anzeigen für einen Opel Corsa und einen Ford Fiesta sind interessant. Rufen Sie an und stellen Sie Fragen.

Sie haben auch eine Anzeige in die Zeitung gesetzt, weil Sie Ihren VW Golf und Ihren VW Beetle verkaufen wollen. Antworten Sie auf die Fragen der Leute über Ihre Autos.

MODELL: Guten Tag, ich rufe wegen des Opel Corsa an.
Wie alt ist der Wagen?
Welche Farbe hat er?
Wie ist der Kilometerstand?
Wie lange hat er noch TÜV?
Wie viel Benzin braucht er?
Was kostet der Wagen?

Modell	VW Golf	VW Touareg Hybrid	Opel Corsa	Ford Fiesta
Baujahr	2010	2012	2006	2007
Farbe	rot	grau	schwarz	blaugrün
Kilometerstand	65 000 km	5 000 km	84 500 km	52 000 km
TÜV	noch 1 Jahr	2 Jahre	6 Monate	fast 2 Jahre
Benzinverbrauch pro 100 km	5,5 Liter	8,2 Liter	6 Liter	6,5 Liter
Preis	12 500 Euro	69 000 Euro	5 000 Euro	4 000 Euro

Situation 11 Interview: Das Auto

Sit. 11. In this interview, sts. use the superlative as an attributive adjective, as a predicate adjective, and as an adverb.

Cultural note. You must be 18 to get a driver's license in Germany. (At age 17 you can get a restricted one that requires an accompanying adult.) New drivers take a class at a driving school (*Fahrschule*) and also drive a certain number of hours with a professional instructor. A driver's license doesn't serve as an ID. It is valid for a lifetime. Regarding question 8: Germany is the only country in Europe with no general speed limit on the freeways.

1. Hast du einen Führerschein? Wann hast du ihn gemacht?
2. Was für ein Auto möchtest du am liebsten haben? Warum?
3. Welche Autos findest du am schönsten?
4. Welche Autos findest du am praktischsten (unpraktischsten)? Warum?
5. Wer von deinen Freunden hat das älteste Auto? Wie alt ist es ungefähr? Und wer hat das hässlichste (schnellste, interessanteste)?
6. Mit was für einem Auto möchtest du am liebsten in Urlaub fahren?
7. Was glaubst du: Was ist das teuerste Auto der Welt?
8. Was glaubst du: In welchem Land fährt man am schnellsten?
9. Was glaubst du: Was ist das kleinste Auto der Welt?

Kennen Sie diese Verkehrsschilder? Was bedeuten sie?

1. Dieses Verkehrsschild bedeutet „Halt".
2. Hier darf man nicht halten.
3. Wer von rechts kommt, hat Vorfahrt.
4. Hier darf man nur in eine Richtung fahren.
5. Hier darf man nur mit dem Rad fahren.
6. Hier darf man auf dem Fußgängerweg parken.
7. Hier dürfen keine Autos fahren.
8. Achtung Radfahrer!
9. Dieser Weg ist nur für Fußgänger.
10. Hier dürfen keine Motorräder fahren.

Situation 13 Zum Schreiben: Eine Anzeige

Sit. 13. Discuss the model ad provided. Ask sts. if they think this is a good ad and likely to get noticed on a crowded bulletin board. Ask what is missing (an address or telephone number) and ask for other improvements. Assign the writing task for homework. Sts. should write their own ads and write their name on the back of the ad. As a follow-up, bring a bulletin board to class and have sts. post their ads. Ask sts. to select the most creative ad, or ask each st. to pick an ad they like and role-play a purchase encounter based on the ad with the person who composed it.

Sie wollen ein Fahrzeug (Auto, Boot, Motorrad, Fahrrad usw.) verkaufen. Schreiben Sie eine Anzeige. Machen Sie sie interessant!

Kultur ... Landeskunde ... Informationen

Volkswagen

- Haben Sie ein Auto? Wenn ja, was für eins? Wie lange haben Sie es schon? Was gefällt Ihnen daran?
- Welche deutschen Automarken[1] kennen Sie? Was halten Sie von deutschen Autos?

Lesen Sie den Text und suchen Sie die Antworten auf die folgenden Fragen:

- Wie viel Prozent der Autos in Europa sind Volkswagen?
- Wo liegt der Firmensitz[2] des Volkswagenkonzerns?
- Wer hat den ersten Prototyp des Volkswagen Käfers gebaut?
- Wo hat Ferdinand Porsche Produktionsmethoden von Autos studiert?
- Welches Auto ist das meistverkaufte der Welt?
- In welchen Ländern hat VW große Standorte[3]?
- Wie lange gibt es den VW-Bus schon?

Ein VW-Bus von 1969 ist ein Oldtimer.

Jedes fünfte Auto in Europa ist ein Volkswagen. Schon seit vielen Jahren ist der VW Golf in Deutschland das meistverkaufte Auto. Auf Platz 2 steht meistens der VW Polo. Volkswagen ist der größte Automobilhersteller[4] Europas und der drittgrößte der Welt. Zum Volkswagenkonzern gehören nicht nur die Marken VW und Audi, sondern auch so schicke Autos wie Bugatti und Lamborghini, die Edelmarke Bentley, sowie seit 2011 auch Porsche. Der Firmensitz befindet sich in Deutschland, im niedersächsischen Wolfsburg.

Den ersten Prototyp des Volkswagen Käfer baute der Österreicher Ferdinand Porsche 1934. Der Volkswagen sollte[5] ein Auto für die breite Masse werden. Um ihn möglichst billig bauen zu können, ging Porsche nach Detroit und studierte die Produktionsmethoden von Ford. Das erste Volkswagenwerk wurde[6] 1938 in Niedersachsen in der Nähe von Braunschweig gebaut. Der Ausbruch des 2. Weltkriegs[7] verhinderte die Massenproduktion des VW Käfer. Erst nach dem Krieg kam es dazu. Aus dem Volkswagenwerk entstand die Stadt Wolfsburg, die heute 100 000 Einwohner hat, und der Siegeszug[8] des Käfers war nicht aufzuhalten. Bis 2002 war der Käfer mit 21,5 Millionen Exemplaren das meistverkaufte Auto der Welt. Dann wurde er vom VW Golf überholt[9], der jetzt diesen Titel besitzt.

Der VW-Konzern hat viele Standorte in der ganzen Welt. Die größten Standorte außerhalb Europas befinden sich in Mexiko (Puebla), Brasilien (Saõ Paulo) und China (Shanghai). Weitere große Standorte befinden sich in Südafrika (Uitenhage), Kenia (Nairobi) und in den USA (Chattanooga).

Beliebte Modelle sind neben dem Golf und dem Polo der Passat, die Vans Touran und Sharan sowie der Geländewagen[10] Touareg. Von 1997 bis 2010 gab es auch den New Beetle, den neuen Käfer im Retrolook, den es auch als Cabrio gab. Unschlagbar[11] unter Studenten und auf der ganzen Welt bekannt ist allerdings der VW-Bus, den es seit 1950 gibt und der immer noch hergestellt wird.

[1]*automobile makes* [2]*company headquarters* [3]*production sites* [4]*auto maker* [5]*was supposed to* [6]*was* [7]*world war* [8]*triumph* [9]*overtaken* [10]*SUV* [11]*Unbeatable*

Reiseerlebnisse

Grammatik 7.4–7.5

Vocabulary Display
This section introduces travel vocabulary and reviews the perfect tense.

AA. Show pictures of one of your trips to a German-speaking country, or, if you are a native of a German-speaking country, show slides of your hometown. Describe each slide and have sts. take notes. Then, show the slides again, but this time have the sts. describe what is happening in each scene. Also, invite sts. in the class to bring in slides from a trip and talk about them.

Im letzten Urlaub waren Herr und Frau Frisch in Italien.

1. Am Morgen sind Herr und Frau Frisch am Strand spazieren gegangen.

2. Dann sind sie im Meer geschwommen.

3. Zu Mittag haben sie Spaghetti gegessen.

4. Später sind sie in die Stadt gefahren.

5. Zuerst hat Frau Frisch dort Souvenirs gekauft.

6. Dann haben sie eine Stadtrundfahrt gemacht.

7. Am Abend haben sie Wein getrunken.

Situation 14 Umfrage: Warst du schon mal im Ausland?

MODELL: S1: Warst du schon mal im Ausland?
S2: Ja!
S1: Unterschreib bitte hier.

UNTERSCHRIFT

1. Warst du schon mal im Ausland? _____
2. Bist du schon mal am Strand spazieren gegangen? _____
3. Hattest du schon mal einen Autounfall? _____
4. Warst du schon mal auf einem Oktoberfest? _____
5. Bist du schon mal Zug gefahren? _____
6. Hast du schon mal eine Stadtrundfahrt gemacht? _____
7. Hattest du schon mal eine Reifenpanne? _____
8. Warst du schon mal auf einer Insel? _____
9. Hast du schon mal deinen Pass verloren? _____
10. Bist du schon mal im Meer geschwommen?

Situation 15 Bildgeschichte: Stefans Reise nach Österreich

Sit. 15. Sentences for narration series: **1.** *Stefan ist zuerst nach Frankfurt geflogen.* **2.** *Er hat sich auf dem Bahnhof eine Fahrkarte gekauft.* **3.** *Dann ist er mit dem Zug nach Österreich gefahren.* **4.** *Erst hat er eine Wanderung in den Alpen gemacht.* **5.** *Dann hat er Salzburg besichtigt.* **6.** *In einem Café hat er Christine, eine nette Österreicherin, kennengelernt.* **7.** *Sie sind in ein Konzert gegangen und haben in einer Disko getanzt.* **8.** *Schließlich sind sie auf dem Wolfgangsee Boot gefahren.* **9.** *Jetzt schreibt Stefan immer Briefe nach Salzburg.*

Suggestion. Have sts. form groups and create a 10th picture with commentary on transparencies to present to the class.

Sit. 16. Begin by relating to sts. a story about one of your own travel experiences. Before beginning the narration, ask sts. to listen for how you introduce people, how you talk about time and place, and what you do to make the story come alive. After telling your story, write four words on the board as column headers: *Personen, Ort, Zeit, Handlung.* Elicit responses from sts. as you recreate the structure of the story you just told in key words and phrases. *Wer war in meiner Geschichte dabei? Wo war es? Wann war es? Was ist zuerst passiert?* Write the key words and phrases in the four categories. Then, ask sts. to think about one of their own travel experiences and jot down notes following the same structure. Allow sts. to invent stories if they are so inclined. Move around the classroom and help sts. with vocabulary. Allow sts. to practice their stories twice, each time with a different partner. Then, ask two or three sts. to tell their stories to the class. Finally, ask sts. to write up their stories and turn them in as homework.

Situation 16 Ein Reiseerlebnis erzählen

Hatten Sie schon mal ein interessantes Reiseerlebnis? Erzählen Sie darüber! Machen Sie sich zuerst Notizen und denken Sie an die folgenden Fragen.

1. Personen: Wer war dabei? Was muss man über diese Personen wissen, um Ihre Geschichte besser zu verstehen?
2. Ort: Wo hatten Sie das Erlebnis? Was war interessant an diesem Ort? Versuchen Sie den Ort zu visualisieren und beschreiben Sie ihn.
3. Zeit: Wann hatten Sie das Erlebnis? Vor wie vielen Jahren? Welche Tageszeit war es? War es ein besonderer Tag?
4. Handlung: Was ist zuerst passiert? Was haben Sie gefühlt und gedacht? Was ist dann passiert? Was war der Höhepunkt des Erlebnisses? Was war das Besondere?

Die Schweiz

- Woran denken Sie, wenn Sie *Schweiz* hören?
- Kennen Sie eine Schweizerin oder einen Schweizer? Waren Sie schon mal in der Schweiz? Was sind Ihre Eindrücke?
- Finden Sie die Schweiz auf einer Landkarte. Lokalisieren Sie die Städte Bern, Genf und Zürich.

Ein typisches Schweizer Dorf

Lesen Sie den Text und suchen Sie die Antworten auf die folgenden Fragen:

- Was für ein Land ist die Schweiz?
- Welche Sprachen spricht man dort? Wie sind sie verteilt[1]?
- Wie heißen die größten Städte?
- Wann wurde die Schweiz gegründet[2]? Wie hießen die ersten Kantone?
- Wie ist die Schweiz politisch? Welchen Organisationen gehört sie (nicht) an?
- Wofür ist die Schweiz bekannt?
- Wofür ist Genf bekannt?
- Was sagen Fußballfans, wenn sie wollen, dass die Schweiz gewinnt?

KLI. Suggestion: Have sts. complete small research projects on Swiss personalities/historical figures, Swiss languages, or other topics covered in the reading.

Einer für alle, alle für einen. So lautet das Motto der Schweiz, eines kleinen Alpenlandes, das eines der reichsten Länder der Welt ist. Nach Fläche[3] ist die Schweiz auf Platz 133, nach der Bevölkerungszahl auf Platz 94 der Länder der Welt. 64 Prozent der Schweizer sprechen Deutsch, 20% Französisch, knapp 7% Italienisch und nur 0,5% Rätoromanisch. Diese Sprachen sind die offiziellen Sprachen der Schweiz. Französisch spricht man im Westen; Italienisch im Südosten, im Tessin; Rätoromanisch im Osten; und Deutsch im Norden, in der Mitte und im Süden. Die größten Städte sind die deutschsprachigen Städte Zürich und Basel und das französischsprachige Genf. Allerdings[4] darf man nicht glauben, dass das Deutsch der Schweizer so einfach zu verstehen ist. Die Deutschschweizer sprechen alemannische Dialekte, die sich sehr von der deutschen Standardsprache unterscheiden. Die Schriftsprache dagegen[5] weist nur wenige Unterschiede auf.

Die Schweiz besteht aus 26 Kantonen[6]. Der Legende nach entstand die Schweiz im Jahre 1291 auf dem Rütliberg, als sich die drei Kantone Uri, Schwyz und Unterwalden zu einem Bund zusammenschlossen[7]. Seit 1815 ist die Schweiz politisch neutral. Sie ist nicht Teil der EU und auch nicht in der NATO. Seit 2002 ist sie aber Mitglied in der UNO.

Wofür ist die Schweiz am Bekanntesten? Für ihre Schokolade? Für ihren Käse? Für ihre Uhren? Für ihre Berge? Für ihr Eisenbahnnetz[8]? Wer kennt nicht Johanna Spyri, die Schöpferin[9] von Heidi; den Psychologen Jean Piaget; die Reformatoren Calvin und Zwingli? Die ETH (Eidgenössische Technische Hochschule) in Zürich ist eine der besten Universitäten der Welt. Die UNO-Stadt Genf ist nicht nur der Ort, wo das Rote Kreuz gegründet wurde, sondern eine sehr schöne Stadt, Sitz von 25 großen internationalen Organisationen, unter anderen die Welthandelsorganisation (WTO) und die Weltgesundheitsorganisation (WHO). Das Matterhorn ist

Die Schweiz hat das dichteste[10] Eisenbahnnetz der Welt.

einer der schönsten und höchsten Berge der Schweiz (4 478 m). In der Schweiz entspringen der Rhein und die Rhône, die längsten Flüsse Deutschlands und Frankreichs. Nicht nur im Fußball sagen deshalb viele Leute: „Hopp Schwiiz!" (Los, Schweiz!)

[1]*distributed* [2]*founded* [3]*area* [4]*However* [5]*on the other hand* [6]*cantons (roughly equivalent to a province or state)* [7]*joined* [8]*railway network* [9]*creator* [10]*densest*

Videoecke

Perspektiven

Aufgabe 1 Wer sagt das?

Ordnen Sie die Aussagen den Personen zu.

Ich achte darauf, wo die Produkte herkommen.

> Lebst du umwelt-
> bewusst? Was
> machst du?

Miniwörterbuch

den Müll trennen	to sort trash (for recycling)
die **Führerscheinprüfung**	driver's license test

1. Pascal _a_

2. Felicitas _d_

3. Nadezda _g_

4. Simone _c_

5. Michael _h_

6. Hend _f_

7. Sophie _e_

8. Albrecht _b_

a. Ich achte darauf, wo die Produkte herkommen.
b. Ich fahre viel Fahrrad und kaufe im Bioladen ein.
c. Ich habe kein Auto und ich trenne den Müll.
d. Ich mache das Wasser beim Zähneputzen aus.
e. Ich nutze wenig Wasser.
f. Ich recycle.
g. Ich trenne den Müll.
h. Nein, ich verbrauche sehr viel Wasser.

Interviews

- Woher kommst du?
- Wo liegt das?
- Was ist dort besonders interessant?
- Wie bist du in Leipzig unterwegs?
- Hast du einen Führerschein?
- War es schwer, ihn zu bekommen?

Albrecht

Simone

Aufgabe 2 Albrecht und Simone

Sehen Sie sich das Video an und ergänzen Sie die Tabelle.

	Albrecht	**Simone**
Woher kommen sie?	aus Leipzig bzw. Dresden	aus Braunschweig
Wo liegt die Stadt?	im Osten, südlich von Berlin	im Norden, nahe Hannover
Was ist dort interessant?	viele Kneipen, viel Grün	alte Burg, Fluss (die Oker)
Wie unterwegs?	immer mit dem Fahrrad	zu Fuß
Führerschein?	ja, fährt aber fast nie Auto	ja
Schwer, ihn zu bekommen?	ja	ja

Aufgabe 3 Fragen

Aufgabe 3. Answers: 1. schon sehr lange 2. ungefähr 150 km 3. im Süden von Leipzig 4. bei jedem Wetter 5. es hat lange gedauert und es war teuer 6. die Stadt anschauen 7. nächste Woche 8. kein Auto 9. vor der Führerscheinprüfung

Beantworten Sie die folgenden Fragen.

1. Wie lange wohnt Albrecht schon in Leipzig?
2. Wie viele Kilometer sind es von Leipzig nach Berlin?
3. Wo gibt es viele Seen?
4. Wann fährt Albrecht mit dem Fahrrad?
5. Warum war es für Albrecht schwer, den Führerschein zu bekommen?
6. Was kann man vom Fluss Oker aus machen?
7. Wann bekommt Simone ihr Fahrrad?
8. Was hat Simone nicht?
9. Wovor hatte Simone große Angst?

Aufgabe 4 Interview

Interviewen Sie eine Partnerin oder einen Partner. Stellen Sie dieselben Interviewfragen.

Wortschatz

Geografie	Geography
die Bucht, -en	bay
die Insel, -n	island
die Halbinsel, -n	peninsula
die Richtung, -en	direction
die Wiese, -n	meadow, pasture
die Wüste, -n	desert
der Fluss, ⸚e	river
der Gipfel, -	mountaintop
der Gletscher, -	glacier
der Hügel, -	hill
der See, -n	lake
der Strand, ⸚e (R)	shore, beach
der Wald, ⸚er (R)	forest, woods
das Feld, -er	field
das Gebirge, -	(range of) mountains
das Meer, -e (R)	sea
das Tal, ⸚er	valley

Ähnliche Wörter

die Küste, -n; die Landkarte, -n; der Dschungel, -; die Alpen (*pl.*); nördlich (von); nordöstlich (von); nordwestlich (von); östlich (von); südlich (von); südöstlich (von); südwestlich (von); westlich (von)

Auto	Car
die Bremse, -n	brake
die Hupe, -n	horn
die Reifenpanne, -n	flat tire
der Gang, ⸚e	gear
der Gebrauchtwagen, -	used car
der Kilometerstand	mileage
der Kofferraum, ⸚e	trunk
der Reifen, -	tire
der Scheibenwischer, -	windshield wiper
der Sicherheitsgurt, -e	seat belt
der Sitz, -e	seat
der Tank, -s	(fuel) tank
das Autoradio, -s	car radio
das Lenkrad, ⸚er	steering wheel
das Nummernschild, -er	license plate
das Rad, ⸚er	wheel

Verkehr und Transportmittel	Traffic and Means of Transportation
die Abfahrt, -en	departure
die Ankunft, ⸚e	arrival
die Bahn, -en	railroad
die Autobahn, -en	freeway
die Straßenbahn, -en	streetcar
die U-Bahn, -en (Untergrundbahn)	subway
die Bahnfahrt, -en	train trip
die Einbahnstraße, -n	one-way street
die Hin- und Rückfahrt	round-trip
die Radfahrerin, -nen	(female) bicyclist
die Rakete, -n	rocket
die Vorfahrt, -en	right-of-way
der Fahrkartenschalter, -	ticket window
der Fußgänger, -	pedestrian
der Fußgängerweg, -e	sidewalk
der Radfahrer, -	(male) bicyclist
der Wagen, -	car
der Kinderwagen, -	baby carriage
der Lastwagen, -	truck
der Waggon [vagon], -s	train car
der Zug, ⸚e	train
das Fahrrad, ⸚er (R)	bicycle
das Fahrzeug, -e	vehicle
das Flugzeug, -e	airplane
das Motorrad, ⸚er (R)	motorcycle
das Schild, -er	sign
das Verkehrsschild, -er	traffic sign
die öffentlichen Verkehrsmittel (*pl.*)	public transportation

Ähnliche Wörter

die Fahrerin, -nen; die Lokomotive, -n; der Bus, -se (R); der Fahrer, -; der Zeppelin, -e; das Passwort, ⸚er; das Taxi, -s (R); buchen; parken; transportieren

Reiseerlebnisse	Travel Experiences
die Reise, -n	trip, journey
auf Reisen sein	to be on a trip
die Stadtrundfahrt, -en	tour of the city
die Wanderung, -en	hike
die Welt, -en	world
der Höhepunkt, -e	highlight
das Erlebnis, -se	experience
besichtigen	to visit, sightsee
besteigen, bestiegen	to climb

Ähnliche Wörter

der Pass, ⸚e; der Wein, -e; das Souvenir, -s; die Spaghetti (*pl.*); reservieren

Sonstige Substantive — Other Nouns

die Achtung	attention
die Angestellte, -n	female clerk
die Fläche, -n	surface
die Hexe, -n	witch
die Luft	air
die Scheibe, -n	windowpane
der Angestellte, -n	male clerk
der Regen	rain
bei Regen	in rainy weather
der Teil, -e	part
der Nachteil, -e	disadvantage
der Vorteil, -e	advantage
das Lied, -er	song
das Tier, -e (R)	animal
die Leute (*pl.*)	people
die Nachrichten (*pl.*)	news

Ähnliche Wörter

die Zigarre, -n; der Euro, -; der Liter, -; der Preis, -e; der Sand; das Baby [be:bi], -s; das Oktoberfest, -e

Sonstige Verben — Other Verbs

an·halten, hält ... an, angehalten	to stop
benutzen	to use
besiegen	to conquer
ein·schlafen, schläft ... ein, ist eingeschlafen	to fall asleep
erlauben	to permit
fließen, ist geflossen	to flow
halten, hält, gehalten	to stop
hupen	to honk
nach·denken (über + *akk.*), nachgedacht	to think (about), consider
Rad fahren, fährt ... Rad, ist Rad gefahren	to ride a bicycle
rennen, ist gerannt	to run
rufen, gerufen	to call, shout

schwimmen, ist geschwommen	to swim; to float
setzen	to put, place, set
trennen	to separate
übernehmen, übernimmt, übernommen	to take on
um·steigen, ist umgestiegen	to change (trains)
vergleichen, verglichen	to compare
verlieren, verloren	to lose
versprechen, verspricht, versprochen	to promise
verstauen	to stow
warten	to wait
wischen (R)	to wipe

Ähnliche Wörter

beantworten, warnen, wecken

Sonstige Wörter und Ausdrücke — Other Words and Expressions

berühmt	famous
bitte schön?	yes please?; may I help you?
dort	there
durch	through
hoch	high
lieb	dear
am liebsten	like (*to do*) best
nah	close, nearby
rechts	to the right
schließlich	finally
schnell	quick, fast
ungefähr	approximately
zuerst (R)	first
zwischen	between

Ähnliche Wörter

exotisch, intelligent, interessant, mehr, salzig, tief, tolerant

Strukturen und Übungen

7.1 Relative clauses

7.1. *Relativsätze und Relativpronomen.* We want to help sts. to understand the relative clauses they hear and see and to monitor the ones they write. First-year sts. rarely attempt to use relative clauses when speaking. Point out that relative clauses are another kind of dependent clause. (Unlike the adverbial *wenn-* and *weil-* clauses introduced in Section 3.4, they are adjectival clauses.)

The selection of the correct relative pronoun is often a difficult matter for sts. at this level. They can easily find the gender and number from the antecedent, but the determination of case from the relative clause can present a problem.

Relative clauses add information about a person, place, thing, or idea already mentioned in the sentence. The relative pronoun begins the relative clause, which usually follows the noun it describes. The relative pronoun corresponds to the English words *who, whom, that,* and *which.* The conjugated verb is in the end position.

RELATIVE CLAUSE

Der Atlantik ist das Meer, **das** Europa und Afrika von Amerika trennt.

VERB IN END POSITION

The Atlantic is the ocean that separates Europe and Africa from America.

While relative pronouns may sometimes be omitted in English, they cannot be omitted from German sentences.

Do not omit the relative pronoun in the German sentence.

> Das ist der Mantel, **den** ich letzte Woche gekauft habe.
> *That is the coat (that) I bought last week.*

Likewise, the comma is not always necessary in an English sentence, but it must precede a relative clause in German. If the relative clause comes in the middle of a German sentence, it is followed by a comma as well.

Relative clauses are preceded by a comma.

> Der See, **der** zwischen Deutschland und der Schweiz liegt, heißt Bodensee.
> *The lake that lies between Germany and Switzerland is called Lake Constance.*

Wissen Sie noch?

A relative clause is a type of dependent clause. As in other dependent clauses, the conjugated verb appears at the end of the clause.

Review grammar 3.4.

A. Relative Pronouns in the Nominative Case

In the nominative (subject) case, the forms of the relative pronoun are the same as the forms of the definite article **der, das, die.**

> **Der** Fluss, **der** durch Wien fließt, heißt Donau.
> Gobi heißt **die** Wüste, **die** in Innerasien liegt.

The relative pronoun has the same gender and number as the noun it refers to.

The relative pronoun and the noun it refers to have the same number and gender.

Masculine	der Mann, **der** ...	*the man who . . .*
Neuter	das Auto, **das** ...	*the car that . . .*
Feminine	die Frau, **die** ...	*the woman who . . .*
Plural	die Leute, **die** ...	*the people who . . .*

B. Relative Pronouns in the Accusative and Dative Cases

When the relative pronoun functions as an accusative object or as a dative object within the relative clause, then the relative pronoun is in the accusative or dative case, respectively.

The case of a relative pronoun depends on its function within the relative clause.

ACCUSATIVE

Nur wenige Menschen haben **den Mount Everest** bestiegen.

Only a few people have climbed Mount Everest.

Der Mount Everest ist ein Berg, **den** nur wenige Menschen bestiegen haben.

Mount Everest is a mountain that only a few people have climbed.

DATIVE

| Ich habe **meinem Vater** nichts davon erzählt. | *I haven't told my father anything about it.* |
| Mein Vater ist der einzige Mensch, **dem** ich nichts davon erzählt habe. | *My father is the only person whom I haven't told anything about it.* |

As in the nominative case, the accusative and dative relative pronouns have the same forms as the definite article, except for the dative plural, **denen.**

	Masculine	Neuter	Feminine	Plural
Accusative	den	das	die	die
Dative	dem	dem	der	denen

C. Relative Pronouns Following a Preposition

The case of the relative pronoun depends on the preposition that precedes it.

When a relative pronoun follows a preposition, the case is determined by that preposition. The gender and number of the pronoun are determined by the noun.

Ich spreche am liebsten **mit meinem** Bruder.	*Most of all I like to talk with my brother.*
Mein Bruder ist der Mensch, **mit dem** ich am liebsten spreche.	*My brother is the person (whom) I like to talk with most.*
Auf der Insel Rügen sind weiße Kreidefelsen.	*There are white chalk cliffs on the island of Rügen.*
Rügen ist eine Insel in der Ostsee, **auf der** weiße Kreidefelsen sind.	*Rügen is an island in the Baltic Sea on which there are white chalk cliffs.*

Point out that the German sequence of preposition and pronoun corresponds to formal English usage: *Who was the woman with whom I saw you yesterday?*

Preposition + relative pronoun = inseparable unit

The preposition and the pronoun stay together as a unit in German.

| Wer war die Frau, **mit der** ich dich gestern gesehen habe? | *Who was the woman (whom) I saw you with yesterday?* |

Übung 1 **Das mag ich, das mag ich nicht!**

Üb. 1. The relative pronouns (all nominative) are already provided, and sts. get practice in forming relative clauses with the verb last. Assign for homework and have sts. state their preferences in class.

Bilden Sie Sätze!

MODELL: Ich mag Leute, die spät ins Bett gehen.

1. Ich mag Leute, die …
2. Ich mag keine Leute, die …
3. Ich mag eine Stadt, die …
4. Ich mag keine Stadt, die …
5. Ich mag einen Mann, der …
6. Ich mag keinen Mann, der …
7. Ich mag eine Frau, die …
8. Ich mag keine Frau, die …
9. Ich mag einen Urlaub, der …
10. Ich mag ein Auto, das …

nett sein   interessant aussehen   laut lachen

exotisch sein   Spaß machen   langweilig sein

gern verreisen   schnell fahren

viel sprechen   gern im Sand spielen   betrunken sein   ?

Übung 2   Risiko[1]

Üb. 2. Sts. convert the sentences in the righthand column into a question and match it with the correct answer from the left. You can help them by pointing out that the relative pronoun in the question will have the same case as the noun it stands for in the original sentence. Assign for homework and have sts. read out the question for the class to answer.

Hier sind die Antworten. Stellen Sie die Fragen!

MODELL: Diesen Kontinent hat Kolumbus entdeckt. →
Wie heißt der Kontinent, den Kolumbus entdeckt hat? (Amerika)

1. Europa
2. Mississippi
3. San Francisco
4. die Alpen
5. Washington
6. das Tal des Todes
7. Ellis
8. der Pazifik
9. die Sahara
10. der Große Salzsee

a. Auf diesem See in Utah kann man segeln.
b. Diese Insel sieht man von New York.
c. Diese Stadt liegt an einer Bucht.
d. Diese Wüste kennt man aus vielen Filmen.
e. Diesem Staat in den USA hat ein Präsident seinen Namen gegeben.
f. In diesem Tal ist es sehr heiß.
g. In diesen Bergen kann man sehr gut Ski fahren.
h. Dieser Kontinent ist eigentlich eine Halbinsel von Asien.
i. Über dieses Meer fliegt man nach Hawaii.
j. Von diesem Fluss erzählt Mark Twain.

7.2 Making comparisons: the comparative and superlative forms of adjectives and adverbs

7.2. *Komparativ und Superlativ.* This section deals with predicate adjectives and adverbs together, since their forms are the same. You might want to point out the distinction between adjectives and adverbs.

so … wie = *as … as*

A. Comparisons of Equality: so … wie

To say that two or more persons or things are alike or equal in some way, use the phrase **so … wie** (*as . . . as*) with an adjective or adverb.

Deutschland ist ungefähr **so groß wie** Montana.	*Germany is about as big as Montana.*
Der Mount Whitney ist fast **so hoch wie** das Matterhorn.	*Mount Whitney is almost as high as the Matterhorn.*

Inequality can also be expressed with this formula and the addition of **nicht.**

Die Zugspitze ist **nicht so hoch wie** der Mount Everest.	*The Zugspitze is not as high as Mount Everest.*
Österreich ist **nicht ganz so groß wie** Maine.	*Austria is not quite as big as Maine.*

B. Comparisons of Superiority and Inferiority

All comparatives in German are formed with **-er.**

To compare two unequal persons or things, add **-er** to the adjective or adverb. Note that the comparative form of German adjectives and adverbs always ends in **-er**, whereas English sometimes uses the adjective with the word *more*.

als = *than*

Sts. generally have few problems with the comparative forms of adverbs and predicate adjectives presented here. Point out that the noun that occurs after *als* is in the nominative case.

Ein Fahrrad ist **billiger als** ein Motorrad.	*A bicycle is cheaper than a motorcycle.*
Lydia ist **intelligenter als** ihre Schwester.	*Lydia is more intelligent than her sister.*
Jens läuft **schneller als** Ernst.	*Jens runs faster than Ernst.*

[1]*Jeopardy*

Some adjectives that end in **-el** and **-er** drop the **-e-** in the comparative form.

teuer → teu~e~rer
dunkel → dunk~e~ler

Eine Wohnung in Regensburg ist teuer, aber eine Wohnung in München ist noch **teurer.**	*An apartment in Regensburg is expensive, but an apartment in Munich is even more expensive.*
Gestern war es dunkel, aber heute ist es **dunkler.**	*Yesterday it was dark, but today it is darker.*

C. The Superlative

To express the superlative in German, use the contraction **am** with a predicate adjective or adverb plus the ending **-sten.**

Ein Porsche ist schnell, ein Flugzeug ist schneller, und eine Rakete ist am schnellsten.	*A Porsche is fast, an airplane is faster, and a rocket is the fastest.*

Superlatives: am + -sten

Unlike the English superlative, which has two forms, all German adjectives and adverbs form the superlative in this way.

Hans ist **am jüngsten.**	*Hans is the youngest.*
Jens ist **am tolerantesten.**	*Jens is the most tolerant.*

When the adjective or adverb ends in **-d** or **-t**, or an s-sound such as **-s, -ß, -sch, -x,** or **-z,** an **-e-** is inserted between the stem and the ending.

frisch → am frisch**esten**
gesund → am gesünd**esten**
heiß → am heiß**esten**
intelligent → am intelligent**esten**

Um die Mittagszeit ist es oft am heißesten.	*The hottest (weather) is often around noontime.*

Groß is an exception to the rule: **am größten.**

D. Irregular Comparative and Superlative Forms

Irregular comparatives and superlatives have an umlaut whenever possible.

The following adjectives have an umlaut in the comparative and the superlative.

alt	älter	am ältesten
gesund	gesünder	am gesündesten
groß	größer	am größten
jung	jünger	am jüngsten
kalt	kälter	am kältesten
krank	kränker	am kränksten
kurz	kürzer	am kürzesten
lang	länger	am längsten
warm	wärmer	am wärmsten

Im März ist es oft **wärmer** als im Januar. Im August ist es **am wärmsten.**	*In March it's often warmer than in January. It's warmest in August.*

As in English, some superlative forms are very different from their base forms:

gern	lieber	am liebsten
gut	besser	am besten
hoch	höher	am höchsten
nah	näher	am nächsten
viel	mehr	am meisten

Ich spreche Deutsch, Englisch und Spanisch. Englisch spreche ich **am besten** und Deutsch spreche ich **am liebsten.**	*I speak German, English, and Spanish. I speak English the best, and I like to speak German the most.*

E. Superlative Forms Preceding Nouns

When the superlative form of an adjective is used with a definite article (**der, das, die**) directly *before* a noun, it has an **-(e)ste** ending in all forms of the nominative singular and an **-(e)sten** ending in the plural. You will get used to the -e/-en distribution as you have more experience listening to and reading German. (A more detailed description of adjectives that precede nouns will follow in **Kapitel 8.**)

Superlatives before nouns in the nominative:
der/das/die + **-(e)ste**
die (*pl.*) + **-(e)sten**

	Fluss (*m.*)	Tal (*n.*)	Wüste (*f.*)	Berge (*pl.*)
Nominative	der längst**e**	das tiefst**e**	die größt**e**	die höchst**en**

Only nominative case endings are introduced now. These are the forms most often used, and the two endings, -e for the singular and -en for the plural, can be handled relatively easily. This is the first formal introduction of attributive adjective endings. The main presentation of these endings is found in Sections 8.1, 8.2, and 8.4.

—Wie heißt der längste Fluss Europas? —Wolga.	*What is the name of the longest river in Europe?* *The Volga.*
—In welchem Land wohnen die meisten Menschen? —In China.	*What country has the most people?* *China.*

Übung 3 ## Vergleiche

Üb. 3. Assign for homework and check in class. Remind sts. to think about the meaning of the comparison before forming the sentence.

Vergleichen Sie.

MODELL: Wien / Göttingen / klein → Göttingen ist kleiner als Wien.

1. Berlin / Zürich / groß
2. San Francisco / München / alt
3. Hamburg / Athen / warm
4. das Matterhorn / der Mount Everest / hoch
5. der Mississippi / der Rhein / lang
6. die Schweiz / Liechtenstein / klein
7. Leipzig / Kairo / kalt
8. ein Fernseher / eine Waschmaschine / billig
9. Schnaps / Bier / stark
10. ein Haus in der Stadt / ein Haus auf dem Land / schön
11. zehn Euro / zehn Cent / viel
12. eine Wohnung in einem Studentenheim / ein Appartement / teuer
13. ein Fahrrad / ein Motorrad / schnell
14. ein Sofa / ein Stuhl / schwer
15. Milch / Bier / gut

Übung 4 Biografische Daten

Vergleichen Sie. [(+) = Superlativ]

MODELL: alt / Thomas / Stefan → Thomas ist **älter** als Stefan.
alt (+) → Heidi ist **am ältesten.**

	Thomas	Heidi	Stefan	Monika
Alter	19	22	18	21
Größe	1,89 m	1,75 m	1,82 m	1,69 m
Gewicht	75 kg	65 kg	75 kg	57 kg
Haarlänge	20 cm	15 cm	5 cm	25 cm
Note in Deutsch	B	A	C	B

1. schwer / Monika / Heidi
2. schwer (+)
3. gut in Deutsch / Thomas / Stefan
4. gut in Deutsch (+)
5. klein / Heidi / Stefan
6. klein (+)
7. jung / Thomas / Stefan
8. jung (+)
9. lang / Heidis Haare / Thomas' Haare
10. lang (+)
11. kurz / Monikas Haare / Heidis Haare
12. kurz (+)
13. schlecht in Deutsch / Heidi / Monika
14. schlecht in Deutsch (+)

Übung 5 Geografie und Geschichte

MODELL: Das Tal des Todes (−86 m) liegt tiefer als das Kaspische Meer (−28 m). →
Das Tote Meer (−396 m) liegt am tiefsten.

1. In Rom (25,6°C) ist es im Sommer heißer als in München (17,2°C).
2. In Wien (−1,4°C) ist es im Winter kälter als in Paris (3,5°C).
3. Liechtenstein (157 km^2)* ist kleiner als Luxemburg (2 586 km^2).
4. Deutschland (911) ist älter als die Schweiz (1291).
5. Kanada (1840) ist jünger als die USA (1776).
6. Der Mississippi (6 021 km) ist länger als die Donau (2 850 km).
7. Philadelphia (40° nördliche Breite) liegt nördlicher als Kairo (30° nördliche Breite).
8. Der Mont Blanc (4 807 m) ist höher als der Mount Whitney (4 418 m).
9. Österreich (83 849 km^2) ist größer als die Schweiz (41 288 km^2).

a. Athen (27,6°C)
b. das Tote Meer (−396 m)
c. Deutschland (357 050 km^2)
d. Frankfurt (50° nördliche Breite)
e. Frankreich (498)
f. Monaco (1,49 km^2)
g. Moskau (−9,9°C)
h. der Mount Everest (8 848 m)
i. der Nil (6 671 km)
j. Südafrika (1884)

*km^2 = Quadratkilometer

7.3 Referring to and asking about things and ideas: *da*-compounds and *wo*-compounds

7.3. *Pronominaladverbien.* Sts. may be interested to know that these German words with *da*- correspond to English words with *there-*, such as *therefore* and *thereafter.*

In both German and English, personal pronouns are used directly after prepositions when these pronouns refer to people or animals.

Ich werde bald **mit ihr** sprechen.	*I'll talk to her soon.*
—Bist du mit Josef gefahren?	*Did you go with Josef?*
—Ja, ich bin **mit ihm** gefahren.	*Yes, I went with him.*

da- or **dar-** + preposition

When the object of the preposition is a thing or concept, it is common in English to use the pronoun *it* or *them* with a preposition: *with it, for them,* and so on. In German, it is preferable to use compounds that begin with **da-** (or **dar-** if the preposition begins with a vowel).

dadurch	*through it/them*	daraus	*out of it/them*
dafür	*for it/them*	darin	*in it/them*
dagegen	*against it/them*	darüber	*over it/them*
dahinter	*behind it/them*	darunter	*underneath it/them*
damit	*with it/them*	davon	*from it/them*
daneben	*next to it/them*	davor	*in front of it/them*
daran	*on it/them*	dazu	*to it/them*
darauf	*on top of it/them*	dazwischen	*between it/them*

Note that the following prepositions cannot be preceded by **da(r)-: ohne, außer, seit.**

—Was macht man mit einer Hupe?	*What do you do with a horn?*
—Man warnt andere Leute **damit.**	*You warn other people with it.*
—Hast du etwas gegen das Rauchen?	*Do you have something against smoking?*
—Nein, ich habe nichts **dagegen.**	*No, I don't have anything against it.*

Some **da**-compounds are idiomatic.

Hast du Geld **dabei?**	*Do you have any money on you?*
Darum hast du auch kein Glück.	*That's why you don't have any luck.*

Use a preposition + **wem** or **wen** to ask about people.

Questions about people begin with **wer** (*who*) or **wen/wem** (*whom*). If a preposition is involved, it precedes the question word.

—Mit **wem** gehst du ins Theater?	*Who will you go to the theater with? (With whom . . .?)*
—Mit Melanie.	*With Melanie.*
—In **wen** hast du dich diesmal verliebt?	*Who did you fall in love with this time? (With whom . . .?)*

Use **wo-** + a preposition to ask about things or ideas.

Questions about things and concepts begin with **was** (*what*). If a preposition is involved, German speakers use compound words that begin with **wo-** (or **wor-** if the preposition begins with a vowel).

—**Womit** fährst du nach Berlin?	*How are you getting to Berlin?*
—Mit dem Bus.	*By bus.*
—**Worüber** sprichst du?	*What are you talking about?*
—Ich spreche über den neuen Film von Doris Dörrie.	*I'm talking about Doris Dörrie's new film.*

People	Things and Concepts
mit wem	womit
von wem	wovon
zu wem	wozu
an wen	woran
für wen	wofür
über wen	worüber
auf wen	worauf
um wen	worum

—**Von wem** ist die Oper „Parsifal"?   *Who is the opera Parzival by?*
—Von Richard Wagner.   *By Richard Wagner.*
—**Wovon** handelt diese Oper?   *What is the opera about?*
—Von der Suche nach dem Gral.   *About the search for the Holy Grail.*

Übung 6   Juttas Zimmer

Da-compounds:

dahinter

daneben

daran

darauf

darin

darüber

darunter

davor

dazwischen

Ergänzen Sie!

Links[1] ist eine Kommode. Eine Lampe steht *darauf* [a]. Rechts _____[b] steht der Schreibtisch. _____[c] steht Juttas Tasche. An der Wand steht ein Schrank. _____[d] hängen Juttas Sachen. Links an der Wand steht Juttas Bett. _____[e] liegt die Katze auf dem Teppich. An der Wand _____[f] hängt ein Bild. Auf dem Bild ist eine Wiese mit einem Baum. _____[g] hängen Äpfel. Mitten im Zimmer steht ein Sessel. _____[h] sieht man Juttas Schuhe und _____[i] hat sich Hans versteckt[2].

[1] *To the left*   [2] hat ... *Hans has hidden himself*

Übung 7   Ein Interview mit Richard

Üb. 7. Assign as homework and have sts. play the roles in class.

Das folgende Interview ist nicht vollständig. Es fehlen die Fragen. Rekonstruieren Sie die Fragen aus den Antworten.

1. Ich gehe am liebsten **mit meiner Kusine** ins Theater.
2. Am meisten freue ich mich **auf die Ferien.**
3. Ich muss immer **auf meinen Freund** warten. Er kommt immer zu spät.
4. In letzter Zeit habe ich mich **über meinen Physiklehrer** geärgert.
5. Wenn ich „USA" höre, denke ich **an Hochhäuser und Gettos, an den Grand Canyon und die Rocky Mountains und natürlich an Iowa.**
6. Zur Schule fahre ich meistens **mit dem Fahrrad, manchmal auch mit dem Bus.**
7. Ich schreibe nicht gern **über Sachen,** die mich nicht interessieren, wie zum Beispiel die Vorteile und Nachteile des Kapitalismus.
8. Meinen letzten Brief habe ich **an einen alten Freund von mir** geschrieben. Der ist vor kurzem nach Graz gezogen, um dort Jura zu studieren.
9. Ich halte nicht viel **von meinen Lehrern.** Die tun nur immer so, als wüssten sie alles; in Wirklichkeit wissen die gar nichts.

7.4 The perfect tense (review)

Wissen Sie noch?

The perfect tense consists of a form of the present tense of **haben** or **sein** + the past participle.

Review grammar 4.1.

As you remember from **Kapitel 4,** it is preferable to use the perfect tense in oral communication when talking about past events.

Ich **habe** im Garten Äpfel **gepflückt.**	*I picked apples in the garden.*

To form the perfect tense, use **haben** or **sein** as an auxiliary with the past participle of the verb.

A. **haben** or **sein**

Use **haben** with most verbs.
Use **sein** if the verb:
• cannot take an accusative object
• indicates change of location or condition.
See Appendix E (II) for a list of common verbs and their auxiliaries.

Haben is by far the more commonly used auxiliary. **Sein** is normally used only when both of the following conditions are met: (1) The verb cannot take an accusative object. (2) The verb implies a change of location or condition.

7.4. *Perfekt.* The perfect tense, introduced in *Kapitel 4,* is reviewed here to give students more practice in the oral narration of past events. Weak verbs with a stem change in the past participle (*denken, usw.*) are included here for the first time. Point out: *werden* implies a change of condition and is, therefore, used with the auxiliary *sein* in the perfect tense.

Bertolt Brecht **ist** 1956 in Berlin **gestorben.**	*Bertolt Brecht died in Berlin in 1956.*
Ernst **ist** mit seinem Hund **spazieren gegangen.**	*Ernst went for a walk with his dog.*

In spite of the fact that there is no change of location or condition, the following verbs also take **sein** as an auxiliary: **sein, bleiben,** and **passieren.**

Letztes Jahr **bin** ich in St. Moritz **gewesen.**	*Last year I was in St. Moritz.*
Was **ist passiert?**	*What happened?*

Past participles of strong verbs end in **-en;** past participles of weak verbs end in **-t** or **-et.**

B. Forming the Past Participle

There are basically two ways to form the past participle. Strong verbs add the prefix **ge-** and the ending **-en** to the stem. Weak verbs add the prefix **ge-** and the ending **-t** or **-et.**

Suggestion. Have sts. identify which verbs in these lists are weak and which are strong.

rufen	hat **gerufen**	*to shout, call*
reisen	ist **gereist**	*to travel*
arbeiten	hat **gearbeitet**	*to work*

In the past-participle form, most, but not all, strong verbs have a changed stem vowel or stem.

gehen	ist ge**g**angen	*to walk*
werfen	hat gew**o**rfen	*to throw*
but: laufen	ist gelaufen	*to run*

Very few weak verbs have a change in the stem vowel. Here are some common weak verbs that do change.

bringen	hat gebr**acht**	*to bring*
denken	hat ged**acht**	*to think*
dürfen	hat ged**urft**	*to be allowed to*
können	hat gek**onnt**	*to be able to*
müssen	hat gem**usst**	*to have to*
rennen	ist ger**annt**	*to run*
wissen	hat gew**usst**	*to know (as a fact)*

no **ge**- with
- verbs ending in **-ieren**
- inseparable-prefix verbs

Point out. *Verlieren* is not considered to be a verb ending in *-ieren*. Instead it is a strong inseparable-prefix verb with the stem *verlier-*, which changes to *verlor-* in the perfect tense.

common inseparable prefixes

be-
ent-
er-
ge-
ver-

C. Past Participles with and without **ge**-

Another group of verbs forms the past participle without **ge**-. You will recognize them because, unlike most verbs, they are not pronounced with an emphasis on the first syllable. These verbs fall into two major groups: those that end in **-ieren** and those that have inseparable prefixes.

passieren	ist passiert	*to happen*
studieren	hat studiert	*to study, go to college*
verlieren	hat verloren	*to lose*

The most common inseparable prefixes are **be-**, **ent-**, **er-**, **ge-**, and **ver-**.

besuchen	hat besucht	*to visit*
entdecken	hat entdeckt	*to discover*
erzählen	hat erzählt	*to tell*
gewinnen	hat gewonnen	*to win*
versprechen	hat versprochen	*to promise*

The past participle of separable-prefix verbs is formed by adding the prefix to the past participle of the base verb.

| anfangen | hat angefangen | *to begin* |
| aufstehen | ist aufgestanden | *to get up* |

Übung 8   Renate

Üb. 8. Remind sts. that a verb with a direct object always has *haben* as its auxiliary verb. Assign the exercise for homework and check it in class.

Ergänzen Sie **haben** oder **sein**.

1. In meiner Schulzeit _____ ich nie gern aufgestanden.
2. Meine Mutter _____^{a} mich immer geweckt, denn ich _____^{b} nie von allein aufgewacht.
3. Ich _____^{a} ganz schnell etwas gegessen und _____^{b} zur Schule gerannt.
4. Meistens hatte es schon zur Stunde geklingelt, wenn ich angekommen _____.
5. In der Schule war es oft langweilig; in Biologie _____ ich sogar einmal eingeschlafen.
6. Einmal in der Woche hatten wir nachmittags Sport. Am liebsten _____^{a} ich Basketball gespielt und _____^{b} geschwommen.
7. Auf dem Weg nach Hause _____^{a} ich einmal einen Autounfall gesehen. Zum Glück _____^{b} nichts passiert.
8. Aber viele Leute _____^{a} herumgestanden, bis die Polizei gekommen _____^{b}.
9. Sie _____^{a} geblieben, bis eine Autowerkstatt die kaputten Autos abgeholt _____^{b}.

Ernst war fleißig. Er hat schon alles gemacht. Und spielt jetzt Fußball. Übernehmen Sie seine Rolle.

MODELL: Steh bitte endlich auf! → Ich bin schon aufgestanden.

1. Mach bitte Frühstück!
2. Trink bitte deine Milch!
3. Mach bitte den Tisch sauber!
4. Lauf mal schnell zum Bäcker!
5. Bring bitte Brötchen mit!
6. Nimm bitte Geld mit!
7. Füttere bitte den Hund!
8. Mach bitte die Tür zu!

7.5 The simple past tense of *haben* and *sein*

7.5 Präteritum. This is the first formal presentation of the simple past tense. We begin with two of the verbs that generally use this tense for conversation: *haben* and *sein*. Sts. will have heard these forms in your speech. They became acquainted with verbs with identical *ich-* and *er/sie/es*-forms when they learned modal verbs in *Kapitel 3.* The use of the simple past tense of all other verbs is presented in *Kapitel 9*, where the focus is on fairy tales and narrative.

When talking about events that have already happened, people commonly use the verbs **haben** and **sein** in the simple past tense instead of the perfect tense. The conjugations appear below; notice that the **ich-** and the **er/sie/es-**forms are the same.

Warst du schon mal im Ausland?
Letzte Woche **hatte** ich einen Autounfall.

Have you ever been abroad?
Last week I had a car accident.

sein				haben			
ich	war	wir	waren	ich	hatte	wir	hatten
du	warst	ihr	wart	du	hattest	ihr	hattet
Sie	waren	Sie	waren	Sie	hatten	Sie	hatten
er sie es	war	sie	waren	er sie es	hatte	sie	hatten

Übung 10   Minidialoge

Ergänzen Sie eine Form von **war** oder **hatte**.

1. FRAU GRETTER: Ihr Auto sieht ja so kaputt aus. _____ᵃ Sie einen Unfall?
   HERR THELEN: Ja, leider _____ᵇ ich wieder mal einen Unfall. Das ist schon der dritte in dieser Woche.

2. FRAU KÖRNER: Sie sind aber braun geworden. _____ Sie im Urlaub?
   MICHAEL PUSCH: Ja, ich war drei Wochen in der Türkei.

3. HANS: Warum _____ᵃ ihr gestern nicht in der Schule?
   JENS UND JUTTA: Wir _____ᵇ keine Zeit.

4. CLAIRE: _____ᵃ du schon mal in Linz, Melanie?
   MELANIE: Ja, ich _____ᵇ schon ein paar Mal da.

5. MARIA SCHNEIDER: Wo warst du letzte Woche, Jens?
   JENS: Ich _____ Ferien und war bei meinen Großeltern auf dem Land.

6. JUTTA: Michael, sag mal, _____ du schon mal eine Reifenpanne?
   MICHAEL PUSCH: Nein, Gott sei Dank noch nie.

7. CLAIRE: Ich habe dich gestern im Kino gesehen. _____ᵃ du allein?
   JOSEF: Ja, Melanie _____ᵇ gestern zu Hause. Sie _____ᶜ keine Lust, ins Kino zu gehen.

Essen und Einkaufen

In **Kapitel 8,** you will learn to talk about shopping for food and cooking and about the kinds of foods you like. You will also talk about household appliances and about dining out.

GOALS

The food section of this chapter focuses on foods and meals of the German-speaking countries. Sts. learn about shopping for food and ordering meals in a restaurant. The chapter presents an overview of attributive and predicate adjectives.

Themen

Essen und Trinken
Haushaltsgeräte
Einkaufen und Kochen
Im Restaurant

Kulturelles

Musikszene: „Hawaii Toast Song" (Alexander Marcus)
KLI: Österreich
Filmclip: *Bella Martha* (Sandra Nettelbeck)
KLI: Stichwort „Restaurant"
Videoecke: Essen

Lektüren

Kurzgeschichte: Die Motorradtour (Christine Egger)
Film: *Bella Martha* (Sandra Nettelbeck)

Strukturen

8.1 Adjectives: an overview
8.2 Attributive adjectives in the nominative and accusative cases
8.3 Destination vs. location: **stellen/stehen, legen/liegen, setzen/sitzen, hängen/hängen**
8.4 Adjectives in the dative case
8.5 Talking about the future: the present and future tenses

Georg Flegel: *Stillleben mit Obst und Krebsen* (ca. 1630), Nationalgalerie, Warschau

Kunst und Künstler

Georg Flegel (1566–1638) war der erste und vielleicht wichtigste Stilllebenmaler in Deutschland. Er wurde in Olmütz in Mähren (heute Tschechische Republik) geboren, arbeitete dann im österreichischen Linz in der Werkstatt des niederländischen Malers Lucas von Valckenborch und zog mit ihm um 1592 nach Frankfurt am Main, wo Flegel bis zu seinem Tode als Maler arbeitete. Seine Bilder sind ein perfektes Abbild der Gegenstände[1], aber im Sinne[2] des Barock haben sie ein fast magisches Eigenleben[3]. Typisch für Flegels Werke ist, dass oft ein kleines Tier in Kontrast zu den leblosen Objekten des Stillebens tritt.

Schauen Sie sich das Bild an und beantworten Sie die folgenden Fragen.

1. Was sehen Sie auf dem Bild? Identifizieren Sie die Gegenstände und Früchte.
2. Welche Farben und Linien dominieren im Bild? Wie sind die Gegenstände verteilt?
3. Welches Tier tritt in Kontrast zu den Gegenständen? Was macht es?
4. Welche Assoziationen und Gefühle weckt das Bild in Ihnen?

[1]*objects* [2]*sense* [3]*life of their own*

Essen und Trinken

Grammatik 8.1–8.2

der Honig · der Zucker · der Kakao · der Käse · der Orangensaft · der Schinken

das Brot · die Kaffeesahne · der Kaffee · der Tee · das Ei · die Marmelade · die Brötchen

das Frühstück

Vocabulary Display
Work with 1 set of food items at a time. **(1)** Read and have sts. repeat the words of the picture. Then ask, e.g.: *Schreiben Sie bitte auf: Was haben Sie heute zum Frühstück gegessen und getrunken? Was essen oder trinken Sie manchmal zum Frühstück? Was essen oder trinken Sie nie zum Frühstück?* **(2)** Read the text underneath the photo. Then write *Brötchen, Ei, Marmelade,* and *Kaffee* on the board and ask sts. what the gender of each of these nouns is. Tell them that the sentences you just read give them clues to gender.

RENATE: Meistens esse ich ein frisches Brötchen, ein gekochtes Ei und selbst gemachte Marmelade zum Frühstück. Außerdem brauche ich einen starken Kaffee. Am Wochenende esse ich auch Schinken und Käse und trinke einen frisch gepressten Orangensaft. Als ich ein Kind war, habe ich meistens Milch mit Honig getrunken, später auch Tee.

HERR THELEN: Zu Mittag esse ich am liebsten einen gemischten Salat, gebratenes Fleisch oder gegrillten Fisch mit gekochten Kartoffeln. Auch Hähnchen mag ich ganz gern und Karotten mit viel Salz und Pfeffer. Meistens trinke ich eine Apfelschorle. Das ist ein Gemisch aus Apfelsaft und Mineralwasser. Am Sonntag trinke ich vielleicht auch mal ein Glas Wein, am liebsten Rotwein.

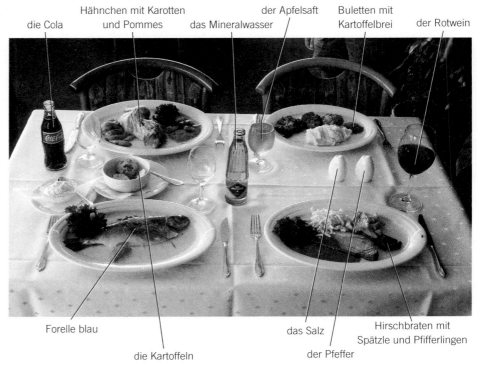

die Cola — Hähnchen mit Karotten und Pommes — das Mineralwasser — der Apfelsaft — Buletten mit Kartoffelbrei — der Rotwein

Forelle blau — die Kartoffeln — das Salz — der Pfeffer — Hirschbraten mit Spätzle und Pfifferlingen

das Mittagessen

FRAU FRISCH: Am Abend esse ich gern rustikal: Brot, Butter, Schinken, Käse. Rohen Schinken esse ich gern mit Meerrettich. Manchmal mache ich mir auch ein paar warme Würstchen. Die esse ich dann mit Senf. Emmentaler esse ich gern mit sauren Essiggurken. Dazu trinke ich entweder ein Glas Milch oder Saft mit Mineralwasser.

das Mineralwasser — das Brot — der Camembert — der Meerrettich — der Emmentaler — das Bier — die Essiggurken

die Milch — die Butter — der Aufschnitt — der Schinken — die Würstchen — der Senf

das Abendessen

Situation 1 Umfrage: Isst du gern fettige Hamburger?

Sit. 1. Preteach vocabulary: *gebratene Eier mit Speck, würzen, belegtes Brot,* and practice pronunciation.

MODELL: s1: Isst du gern fettige Hamburger?
s2: Ja!
s1: Unterschreib bitte hier!

UNTERSCHRIFT

1. Isst du gern fettige Hamburger? _____
2. Isst du oft Chinesisch? _____
3. Isst du oft frisches Obst? _____
4. Frühstückst du selten? _____
5. Isst du zum Frühstück gern gebratene
   Eier mit Speck? _____
6. Isst du meistens in der Mensa? _____
7. Isst du manchmal Pizza? _____
8. Würzt du dein Essen mit viel Pfeffer? _____
9. Isst du selten zu Hause? _____
10. Hast du für heute ein belegtes Brot dabei? _____

 Situation 2 Informationsspiel: Mahlzeiten und Getränke

MODELL: s1: Was isst Stefan zum Frühstück?
s2: _____

	Frau Gretter	**Stefan**	**Andrea**
zum Frühstück essen	frische Brötchen	frisches Müsli	Brot mit selbst gemachter Marmelade
zum Frühstück trinken	schwarzen Kaffee	kalten Orangensaft	heißen Kakao
zu Mittag essen	kalorienarmes Gemüse und Hähnchen	belegte Brote und Kartoffelchips	heiße Würstchen
zu Abend essen	nichts, sie will abnehmen	italienische Spaghetti	Brot mit Honig
nach dem Sport trinken	nichts, sie treibt keinen Sport	kalten Tee mit Zitrone	Apfelsaft
auf einem Fest trinken	deutschen Sekt	mexikanisches Bier	eiskalte Limonade
essen, wenn er/sie groß ausgeht	etwas für Kalorienbewusste	frischen Fisch mit französischer Soße	den schönsten Kinderteller

Sit. 2. Focus: adjective endings. The corresponding chart is in Appendix A. Before doing this activity, comment on the different names and functions of the 3 meals in Germany. **(1)** Preteach vocabulary and write on the board: *Müsli, Gemüse, Hähnchen, belegte Brote, Kartoffelchips, Zitrone, Apfelsaft, Sekt, Soße, Kinderteller, selbst gemacht, kalorienarm, kalorienbewusst, abnehmen.* **(2)** Remind sts. to use *„Wie bitte?", „Wie schreibt man das?", „Weißt du, was das heißt?"* usw. instead of using English or looking at each other's charts. Allow at least 5 minutes for completion of the charts. **(3)** Focus on form: Tell sts. that most adjectives are in the accusative case (except the 1 adjective that is preceded by the preposition *mit*), and ask them to come up with the rules for adjective endings for the 3 genders and the plural in the accusative.

„Hawaii Toast Song" (2009, Deutschland) *Alexander Marcus*

Alexander Marcus

Biografie Alexander Marcus ist ein Berliner Musiker und Entertainer. Er singt einfache dümmliche Schlagertexte zu einer Mischung aus Volksmusik und Techno. Marcus nennt seinen Stil *Electrolore,* eine Mischung aus Elektro und Folklore[1]. Der „Hawaii Toast Song" ist von seinem zweiten Album *Mega.*

Vor dem Hören Kennen Sie Hawaii Toast? Welche Zutaten, glauben Sie, braucht man dafür? (Denken Sie an Hawaii Pizza.)

Nach dem Hören Beantworten Sie die folgenden Fragen.
1. Welche Zutaten braucht man für einen Hawaii Toast?
2. Wie macht man ihn?
3. Was bewirkt er?
4. Haben Sie schon mal einen Hawaii Toast gemacht oder gegessen?

iMix Link: This song is available for purchase at the iTunes store in a special iMix created for *Kontakte.* For more information about accessing the playlist, go to **Connect German** (www.connectgerman.com).

Miniwörterbuch

dümmlich	silly	**die mittlere Schiene**	the middle oven rack
der **Schlager**	German pop song of the 1950s and 60s	die **Not**	time of need
der **Scheiblettenkäse**	individually wrapped cheese slices	**Trost spenden**	to provide solace
vorheizen	to preheat	**bewirken**	to have an effect

[1]*folk music*

Musikszene. Nach dem Hören. Answers: 1. Ananas aus der Dose, Scheiblettenkäse und Schinken 2. den Ofen vorheizen, auf die mittlere Schiene legen 3. er schmeckt allen gut, er schmeckt klein und groß, er spendet in der Not Trost.

Situation 3   Ratespiel: Regionale Spezialitäten

Sit. 3. (1) Present the new vocabulary: *deftig, Berliner Weiße* (relatively sour wheat beer, often drunk with raspberry juice), *Fleischchüechli (Frikadellen), Knödel (Kartoffelklöße), Semmeln (Brötchen), Rote Grütze (Mus aus roten Früchten).* **(2)** Introduce the concept of regional cuisine. Let sts. who have been to a German-speaking country talk about their eating experiences. **(3)** Then, ask sts. to work in groups and encourage them to guess when they don't know. **(4) Focus on form.** Ask sts. what gender or number the nouns have. Tell them that they can tell gender by looking at the adjective ending. Ask them to figure out what adjective ending goes with which gender or number. Answers may vary somewhat. Expected answers are: 1. *in Berlin* 2. *in der Schweiz* 3. *in den USA* 4. *in Bayern* 5. *in Norddeutschland* 6. *überall* 7. *in Bayern* or *in Österreich* 8. *in den USA* 9. *in Norddeutschland* 10. *in Sachsen.*

Was glauben Sie? Wo isst oder trinkt man diese regionalen Spezialitäten? Es gibt viele richtige Antworten.

1. Wo trinkt man Berliner Weiße?
2. Wo isst man selbst gemachte Fleischchüechli?
3. Wo isst man gebratene Eier und Speck?
4. Wo isst man deftige Knödel?
5. Wo isst man frischen Fisch aus der Nordsee?
6. Wo trinkt man frisch gepressten Orangensaft?
7. Wo isst man frische Semmeln?
8. Wo trinkt man eiskalten Eistee?
9. Wo isst man Rote Grütze?
10. Wo trinkt man sächsisches Schwarzbier?

in Österreich	**in Berlin**	**überall**	**in Sachsen**
in Bayern	**in den USA**		**in der Schweiz**
	in Norddeutschland		

Österreich

- Was wissen Sie über Österreich? Wofür ist es bekannt?
- Wo liegt es? Was ist die Hauptstadt? Schauen Sie auf die Landkarte in **Kontakte.**
- Welche berühmten Österreicherinnen und Österreicher kennen Sie?
- Kennen Sie eine Österreicherin oder einen Österreicher persönlich? Was erzählt er oder sie über sein Land?
- Waren Sie schon mal in Österreich? Erzählen Sie!

Lesen Sie den Text und suchen Sie die Antworten auf diese Fragen:
- Woher kommt der Ausdruck[1] „Felix Austria"?
- Wann wurde der Name Österreich zum ersten Mal erwähnt[2]?
- Was geschah 1804?
- Welche heutigen Länder umfasste die k. u. k. Monarchie?
- Wie lange wurde Österreich nach dem Zweiten Weltkrieg von den Alliierten verwaltet[3]?
- Wo wohnen die meisten Österreicher?
- Aus welchen Bundesländern besteht Österreich?
- Wofür ist das Reiseland Österreich vor allem bekannt?
- Welche deutschen Komponisten wirkten in Wien?
- Für welche kulinarischen Köstlichkeiten[4] ist Österreich bekannt?

Kaffee, Kuchen und ein Glas Wasser

Felix Austria! „Andere mögen[5] Kriege führen, du, glückliches Österreich, heirate!" Ein Motto, das ursprünglich auf die Heiratspolitik der Habsburger verwies[6], drückt das Lebensgefühl[7] eines Landes aus, das zum Großteil (ca. 60 Prozent) in den Alpen liegt und zum anderen Teil an der Donau.

Österreich wurde 976 als Ostarrîchi zum ersten Male urkundlich erwähnt. 1156 wurde es ein eigenes Herzogtum[8]. Die Habsburger, die über viele Jahrhunderte hinweg die deutschen Könige und Kaiser waren, erhoben[9] es 1278 zum Erzherzogtum. In der frühen Neuzeit (15.–17. Jahrhundert) musste sich Österreich vor allem gegen die Türken wehren[10], die zweimal Wien belagerten[11]. 1804 wurde das Kaiserreich Österreich gegründet und 1867 die kaiserlich-königliche (k. u. k.) Monarchie Österreich-Ungarn, die neben Österreich und Ungarn auch die heutigen Länder Tschechien, die Slowakei, Slowenien, Kroatien, Bosnien sowie Teile Italiens, Rumäniens, Polens und der Ukraine umfasste. Nach dem Ersten Weltkrieg wurde der Vielvölkerstaat Österreich-Ungarn zerschlagen[12] und Österreich wurde in seinen jetzigen Grenzen gegründet. Nach dem Zweiten Weltkrieg wurde Österreich zehn Jahre lang von den Alliierten verwaltet und erst 1955 entstand die jetzige Zweite Republik. Über die Zeit nach dem Zweiten Weltkrieg erzählt der britische Spielfilm *Der dritte Mann* mit Orson Welles in der Hauptrolle und mit dem immer noch bekannten Harry-Lime-Thema, das von dem Österreicher Anton Karas komponiert und auf der Zither gespielt wurde.

Österreich ist ein relativ kleines Land, etwas größer als die Schweiz, und steht auf Platz 113 der Länder der Welt von seiner Fläche[13] her und auf Platz 92 von der Bevölkerungszahl. Von den 8,4 Millionen Einwohnern wohnen 2,4 Millionen in der Metropolregion Wien. Die Bundesländer Vorarlberg, Tirol, Salzburg, Kärnten und die Steiermark liegen in den Alpen und die Bundesländer Oberösterreich, Niederösterreich und Wien an der Donau. Das Burgenland liegt im Südosten an der Grenze zu Ungarn. Seit 1995 ist Österreich Mitglied der EU; seine Währung ist der Euro.

Die zentrale Lage in Europa, seine wunderschönen Berg- und Flußlandschaften und seine historischen Städte machen Österreich zu einem Reiseland *par excellence.* In Europa liegt Österreich auf Platz 2 der Länder, die durch den Tourismus besonders viel Geld verdienen. Die meisten Touristen kommen aus Deutschland. Im Winter kommen viele Leute zum Skifahren oder Snowboarden. Im Sommer gibt es viele Touristen, die wandern oder klettern. Im 18. und 19. Jahrhundert war Wien das Zentrum klassischer Musik. Die Wiener Klassik um Joseph Haydn und Wolfgang Amadeus Mozart zog den in Bonn geborenen Ludwig van Beethoven an, die Romantik um Franz Schubert und Anton Bruckner den in Hamburg geborenen Johannes Brahms. Sowohl Beethoven wie Brahms lebten bis zu ihrem Lebensende in Wien.

Kulinarisch ist Österreich für vieles bekannt. Das Wiener Schnitzel, die Sachertorte, der Apfelstrudel, der Kaiserschmarren und die Palatschinke sind nur einige wenige Beispiele für österreichische Köstlichkeiten. Eine der schönsten Erfindungen[14] sind jedoch die Wiener Kaffeehäuser, in denen man stundenlang vor einer Kaffeeköstlichkeit sitzen und Zeitung lesen oder sich unterhalten kann.

[1]*expression* [2]*mentioned* [3]*governed* [4]*delicacies* [5]*may* [6]*referred* [7]*attitude to life* [8]*duchy* [9]*elevated* [10]*defend* [11]*laid siege to* [12]*broken apart* [13]*area* [14]*inventions*

 **Situation 4** Interview: Die Mahlzeiten

Sit. 4. Sts. might want to add these questions. *Was ist dein Lieblingsessen/Lieblingsgetränk?*

AA. If some of your sts. have relatives from German-speaking countries, you might ask them to talk about special dishes or mealtime customs in their families. Similarly, many sts. may have German ancestors who have passed mealtime traditions down from generation to generation.

1. Was isst du normalerweise zum Frühstück? Was zu Mittag?
2. Isst du viel zu Abend? Was?
3. Isst du immer eine Nachspeise? Was isst du am liebsten als Nachspeise?
4. Trinkst du viel Kaffee? Energydrinks? Warum (nicht)?
5. Isst du zwischen den Mahlzeiten? Warum (nicht)?
6. Was isst du, wenn du mitten in der Nacht großen Hunger hast?
7. Was trinkst du, wenn du auf Feste gehst?
8. Was hast du heute Morgen gegessen und getrunken?
9. Was isst du heute zu Mittag?
10. Was isst du heute zu Abend?

Haushaltsgeräte

Vocabulary Display

This section provides examples of the verbs *stellen, stehen, legen, liegen, setzen, sitzen,* and *hängen.* Introduce vocabulary and the concept of 2-way prepositions and then reinforce them with TPR activities. For example, bring in plastic knives and forks, paper plates, glasses, and napkins, and tell each pair of sts. to pick up a set. Then demonstrate setting a table yourself with a commentary: *Ich stelle einen Teller auf den Tisch, dann lege ich eine Gabel links neben den Teller und ein Messer rechts. Ich stelle ein Glas rechts vor den Teller usw.* Then step back and describe the table setting: *Ein Teller steht auf dem Tisch. Neben dem Teller liegt eine Gabel, und vor dem Teller steht ein Glas.* In pairs, sts. should now follow your example except that one sets the table and narrates and the other describes the locations afterward. They then reverse roles.

Cultural note. WGs are common in Germany. Young people—often sts.—prefer to share apartments not only for economic reasons but as an alternative way of living.

Grammatik 8.3

Stefan stellt die Schüsseln und Teller in den Geschirrspüler.
Nora stellt die Teekanne in den Schrank.
Marion legt die Servietten in die Schublade.
Rainer hängt das Handtuch an den Haken.
Die schmutzigen Töpfe und Pfannen stehen auf dem Herd.
Messer, Gabeln und Löffel liegen auf dem Tisch.

Situation 5   Was kosten diese Gegenstände?

Sit. 5. Sts. work together in small groups. Preteach vocabulary with pictures from your PF. For each item, ask how much it might cost. When students give you prices in dollars, simply use the same price and say euros. Explain the two tasks and ask sts. to work in groups of 3. Follow up by asking them to explain why they cannot do without certain items.

Listen Sie die Gegenstände in jeder Gruppe dem Preis nach. Beginnen Sie mit dem teuersten Gegenstand. Wählen Sie dann aus jeder Gruppe die vier Gegen-stände aus, auf die Sie am wenigsten verzichten[1] könnten.

GRUPPE A

1. eine Kaffeemaschine
2. ein elektrischer Dosenöffner
3. eine Küchenmaschine
4. ein Korkenzieher
5. eine Kaffeemühle
6. ein Bügeleisen
7. eine Küchenwaage
8. ein Toaster

GRUPPE B

1. eine Mikrowelle
2. ein Kühlschrank
3. ein Geschirrspüler
4. eine Waschmaschine
5. ein Wäschetrockner
6. ein Grill
7. ein Staubsauger
8. eine Gefriertruhe

Situation 6   Was brauchen Sie dazu?

Sit. 6. Sts. read through the list of tasks and decide what items they need for each. If time permits, put sts. in small groups to think of other situations in which they would need these items. Afterward, they can read their lists to the class and have the class decide what would be useful in that situation. Encourage sts. to be imaginative, as well: *Ich habe ein Geburtstagsgeschenk bekommen und möchte die Schnur durchschneiden. Ich möchte für meine Freundin ein Wiener Schnitzel machen und muss das Fleisch zuschneiden usw.* In doing this, sts. reinforce not only the particular vocabulary items but many other phrases and grammatical structures as well.

1. Sie bekommen ein Paket, das mit einer Schnur zugebunden ist. Sie wollen die Schnur durchschneiden.
2. Sie wollen sich ein belegtes Brot machen und eine Scheibe Wurst abschneiden.
3. Sie wollen sich eine Dose Suppe heiß machen und müssen die Dose aufmachen.
4. Sie haben Gäste und wollen ein paar Flaschen Bier aufmachen.
5. Sie wollen eine Kerze anzünden.
6. Sie wollen Tee kochen und müssen Wasser heiß machen.
7. Sie haben eine Reifenpanne und müssen einen rostigen Nagel aus einem Autoreifen ziehen.
8. Sie wollen ein Bild aufhängen und müssen einen Nagel in die Wand schlagen.
9. Beim Gewitter ist der Strom ausgefallen. In Ihrem Zimmer ist es total dunkel.

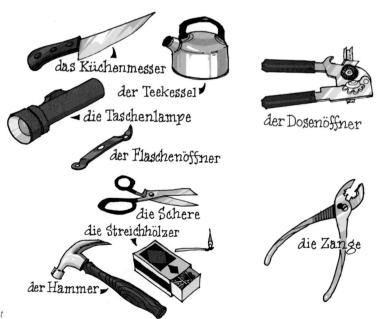

[1]*do without*

Situation 7 Diskussion: Haushaltsgeräte

Sit. 7. Sts. work in groups of 3–4. Ask them to choose one person to be spokesperson for each question. After sts. have discussed the questions for a few minutes, each spokesperson then tells how the group answered.

1. Welche elektrischen Haushaltsgeräte haben Sie, Ihre Eltern oder Freunde? Welches Gerät finden Sie am wichtigsten?
2. Stellen Sie sich vor, Sie dürfen nur ein Gerät im Hause haben. Welches wählen Sie und warum?
3. Welche Werkzeuge sollte es in jedem Haushalt geben?
4. Sie wollen übers Wochenende zum Zelten. Machen Sie eine Liste, welche Geräte Sie zum Essen und Kochen brauchen.
5. Sie planen ein elegantes Picknick. Was packen Sie alles ein?

Lektüre

Lesehilfe

In the following story, detective Julia Falk uses her well-honed skills to investigate a crime. As you read it, you become a detective, too. At right, under **Vor dem Lesen,** are some hints from her "Handbook for a Rookie Detective." They will help you to catch the important details as you read the story. As you might expect, taking notes is part of the investigation. When you take notes during the **Vor dem Lesen** activity, be sure to include: 1) important words to look up in the dictionary, three per paragraph at most; 2) words that seem key to the plot; and 3) interesting facts.

Vor dem Lesen

So lesen Sie wie ein Detektiv …

1. Setzen Sie sich an einen ruhigen Ort, wo Sie sich konzentrieren können.
2. Legen Sie sich Papier und Schreibzeug bereit.
3. Lesen Sie den ganzen Text durch, um zu wissen, worum es geht.
4. Lesen Sie den Text jetzt absatzweise[1] etwas genauer und machen Sie sich dabei Notizen.
5. Vergleichen Sie Ihre Notizen mit Ihrem Partner oder mit Ihrer Partnerin.

Die Motorradtour

Hallo, Kollegin, wie war's in den Ferien?" Oberinspektor Eichhorn begrüßt Julia Falk mit einem freundschaftlichen Handschlag. „Hoffentlich ist es Ihnen nicht genauso ergangen wie der Familie Andres am Blumenweg 1. Als die von ihrer Reise zurückkehrte, fand sie ein gründlich ausgeraubtes Haus vor." Oberinspektor Eichhorn greift nach einem Bündel Akten[2]. „Na ja, wenn Sie den Fall[3] gleich weiterverfolgen könnten …? Die meisten Anwohner am Blumenweg haben wir bereits vernommen[4]. Zu befragen wären da noch ein Rentnerpaar, Familie Wächter im Haus Nummer 7, und deren junger Untermieter Heinz Hurtig."

Julia Falk drückt zum dritten Mal den Knopf[5] über dem Schildchen „Heinz Hurtig". Eigenartig, dass er nicht aufmacht. Dabei hat sie doch gerade eben noch einen jungen Mann am Fenster oben stehen sehen. Julia schüttelt verwundert den Kopf. Sie dreht sich um und lässt ihren Blick[6] über den verlassenen[7] Hof und das funkelnagelneue Motorrad unter dem Garagenvordach schweifen.

Ein paar Minuten später klingelt Julia noch ein Mal. Ein Geräusch ist von drinnen zu hören. Na endlich, das hat aber lange gedauert! Heinz Hurtig guckt durch den Türspalt. „Guten Tag, Herr Hurtig." Julia Falk zückt ihren Ausweis. „Darf ich einen Moment reinkommen? Ich ermittle[8] wegen des Einbruchs bei Familie Andres."

Erst im Flur bemerkt Julia, dass Hurtigs rechter Arm dick einbandagiert in einer Armschlinge liegt. „Hatten Sie einen Unfall[9]?" Heinz Hurtig nickt. „Ich habe letzte Woche mit meinem Motorrad eine Kurve zu schnell genommen. Aber ich hatte noch Glück, ich habe mir bloß den Arm gebrochen."

Heinz Hurtig führt die Inspektorin in die Küche. Auf dem Küchentisch steht ein Teller mit Speck[10] und Rührei[11], daneben eine Tasse mit dampfend heißem Kaffee. „Darf ich Ihnen auch eine Tasse Kaffee anbieten? – Nein? Keinen Kaffee? Nun, was den Einbruch betrifft[12], ich bin ja erst vorgestern von meiner Motorradtour heimgekommen, habe nichts gesehen und gehört. Und, sorry, falls ich ein Alibi brauche – mit meinem verletzten Arm hätte ich wirklich kein Haus ausrauben können, nicht wahr?"

[1]one paragraph at a time [2]files [3]case [4]questioned [5]here: doorbell [6]glance [7]deserted [8]am investigating
[9]accident [10]bacon [11]scrambled eggs [12]was … betrifft as far as … is concerned

30 „Leben Sie allein hier?", fragt die Inspektorin. „Nein, mit Schnurrli, meinem Kater." Heinz Hurtig grinst und weist mit dem Kinn zum Fenstersims, wo sich eine prächtige rote Katze wohlig in der Sonne ausstreckt. „Tut mir leid, Herr Hurtig", meint Julia Falk sachlich. „Sie begleiten mich jetzt aufs Präsidium[1]. Mit Ihrem Alibi stimmt nämlich etwas ganz und gar nicht[2]."

Aus: *Aufgepasst, Julia Falk!* von Christine Egger

Arbeit mit dem Text

A. Locate each of the following words in the text, read the hint below, and write down what you think its English equivalent might be. Then check yourself by looking up the words in the glossary at the end of the book.

1. **Handschlag** (Zeile 2) HINT: You already know the word **Hand. Schlagen** means *to beat*, *strike*, or *hit*. How do people sometimes greet with their hands?

2. **ausgeraubt** (Zeile 4) HINT: This is the past participle of the verb **ausrauben.** What English word is similar to **raub** and is related to crime and houses?

3. **weiterverfolgen** (Zeile 5) HINT: **Weiter** is the comparative form of **weit.** The prefix **ver** adds a sense of continuation. The verb **folgen** means *to follow.*

4. **verwundert** (Zeile 11) HINT: The verb **verwundern** means *to surprise;* **verwundert** is the past participle.

5. **funkelnagelneu** (Zeile 12) HINT: The verb **funkeln** means *to sparkle* and **Nagel** means *nail.*

6. **Einbruch** (Zeile 17) HINT: The prefix **ein** often means *in.* The word **Bruch** is a noun related to the verb **brechen,** which means *to break.*

7. **Armschlinge** (Zeile 19) HINT: You already know the word for the body part **Arm.** What English word is like **Schlinge** and has to do with an arm injury?

8. **heimgekommen** (Zeile 25) HINT: You know what **Heimweh** means. What English word is like **heim** and combines with *come* to indicate a destination?

9. **ausstrecken** (Zeile 31) HINT: German -ck- is occasionally equivalent to English -tch-. What might a cat do on a sunny **Fenstersims?**

B. Was ist passiert? Bringen Sie die folgenden Sätze in die richtige Reihenfolge.

___3___ Als Frau Falk bei Heinz Hurtig klingelt, macht er zuerst nicht auf.

___5___ Endlich macht Hurtig auf und lässt sie in seine Wohnung.

___7___ Er erzählt der Kommissarin von seinem Motorradunfall in der vergangenen Woche.

___6___ Julia bemerkt, dass Hurtig seinen rechten Arm einbandagiert hat.

___4___ Julia Falk schaut sich inzwischen aufmerksam im Hof um.

___10___ Julia Falk zweifelt stark an Heinz Hurtigs Alibi.

___1___ Kommissarin Falk ist gerade aus dem Urlaub zurückgekommen.

___9___ Sein Alibi ist sein verletzter Arm.

___2___ Sie soll wegen des Einbruchs bei Familie Andres ermitteln.

___8___ Weil er erst vor zwei Tagen von der Motorradtour zurückgekommen ist, hat er nichts gesehen und gehört.

Nach dem Lesen

1. Beschreiben Sie die Szene in Heinz Hurtigs Küche so genau wie möglich. Notieren Sie alle Einzelheiten.

2. Warum zweifelt Julia Falk am Alibi von Heinz Hurtig? Sammeln Sie alles, was nicht zusammenpasst.

[1]*police station* [2]*stimmt … something isn't right at all*

Einkaufen und Kochen

Grammatik 8.4

das Fleisch und der Fisch

das Gemüse

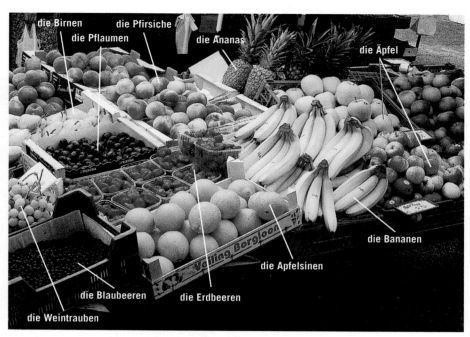

die Birnen die Pfirsiche

die Pflaumen die Ananas

die Äpfel

die Bananen

die Apfelsinen

die Blaubeeren die Erdbeeren

die Weintrauben

das Obst

Situation 8 Bildgeschichte: Michaels bestes Gericht

Michael kocht heute wieder sein bestes Gericht: Omelett *à la haute cuisine* ...

Sit. 8. Sentences for narration series: **1.** *Michael wäscht die Tomaten und Pilze mit kaltem Wasser.* **2.** *Dann schneidet er die Tomaten und Pilze in Scheiben.* **3.** *Dann schneidet er den Schinken in kleine Stücke.* **4.** *Dann schlägt Michael drei Eier in eine Schüssel.* **5.** *Er würzt die Eier mit Salz, Pfeffer und Paprika.* **6.** *Jetzt erhitzt er Öl in einer Pfanne.* **7.** *Michael gibt den Schinken in die Pfanne und bräunt ihn.* **8.** *Dann kommen die Tomaten und Pilze hinzu.* **9.** *Zum Schluss gießt er die Eier darüber.* **10.** *Wenn das Omelett fast fertig ist, bestreut er es noch mit Käse.*

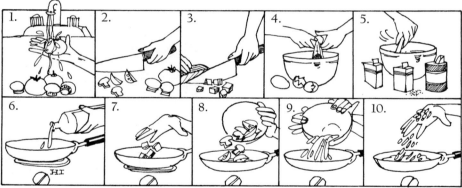

Deutsche Bioeier: Bioprodukte werden immer beliebter.

Situation 9   Einkaufsliste

Sit. 9 Depending on whether or not your sts. like to cook, you might mention a few of the spices (*die Gewürze*): Basil = *Basilikum;* bay leaves = *Lorbeerblätter;* cinnamon = *Zimt;* cloves = *Gewürznelken;* ginger = *Ingwer;* nutmeg = *Muskatnuss;* oregano = *Oregano;* parsley = *Petersilie;* herbs = *Kräuter.*

Sie wollen heute Abend kochen. Was wollen Sie kochen? Was brauchen Sie? (Sie finden Ideen im Wortkasten.) Machen Sie für jedes Gericht eine Einkaufsliste. Denken Sie auch an Salat, Gemüse und Gewürze, an Vorspeise und Nachspeise und an Getränke.

1. ein italienisches Gericht
2. ein amerikanisches Gericht
3. ein türkisches Gericht
4. ein deutsches Gericht
5. ein französisches Gericht

Fisch	**Nudeln**	**Salz**	**Bohnen**
Paprika	**Erbsen**	**Oliven**	
Zwiebeln	**Knoblauch**	**Gurken**	**Pilze**
Schnitzel	**Kopfsalat**	**Pfeffer**	
Tomaten	**Schafskäse**	**Tomatensoße**	**Kartoffeln**
Karotten	**Hackfleisch**	**Essig und Öl**	

Situation 10   Zum Schreiben: Ein Rezept

Sit. 10. AA. Depending on the interests of the class, you might compile everyone's favorite recipes. Each st. could choose a favorite recipe and translate the directions into German. Don't convert ingredient quantities to the metric system; just use *Tasse, Esslöffel,* and *Teelöffel.* Give sts. examples of recipes to use as models for writing cooking directions.

Ein Austauschstudent aus Deutschland möchte ein Rezept für ein typisches Gericht aus Ihrem Land. Geben Sie ihm/ihr Ihr persönliches Lieblingsrezept. Schreiben Sie zuerst auf, was man alles braucht und wie viel. Dann beschreiben Sie, wie man es zubereitet. Machen Sie auch kleine Zeichnungen dazu. (Keine Mikrowellenmahlzeit, bitte!)

ZUTATEN   ZUBEREITUNG

_____   _____

_____   _____

_____   _____

Situation 11   Interview: Einkaufen und Kochen

Sit. 11. Model pronunciation. Sts. repeat. Sts. interview each other, then switch partners and report on the first partner's answers. Then, address questions to the whole class, and expand on some of them. If sts. are married or have partners, or roommates, who does the cooking and the shopping? Always one or the other person, or do they share the responsibilities?

1. Kannst du kochen? Was zum Beispiel?
2. Kochst du oft? Wer kocht in deiner Familie?
3. Was kochst du am liebsten? Welche Zutaten braucht man dazu?
4. Kaufst du jeden Tag ein? Wenn nicht, wie oft in der Woche? An welchen Tagen? Wo kaufst du meistens ein?

Filmlektüre
Bella Martha

 Vor dem Lesen

A. Sehen Sie sich das Foto an und beantworten Sie die folgenden Fragen.

1. Wo sind die Personen?
2. Was sind sie von Beruf? Was machen sie? Wie ist ihre Arbeit?
3. Wer, glauben Sie, ist das kleine Mädchen?

Filmangaben

Titel: *Bella Martha*
Genre: Komödie/Drama
Erscheinungsjahr: 2001
Land: Deutschland
Dauer: 109 min
Regisseurin: Sandra Nettelbeck
Hauptrollen: Martina Gedeck,
Maxime Foerste,
Sergio Castellitto

Szene aus dem Film *Bella Martha*

B. Lesen Sie die Wörter im Miniwörterbuch. Suchen Sie sie in der Inhaltsangabe und unterstreichen Sie sie.

Miniwörterbuch

alleinstehende	single	**zurechtkommen**	to get along
die **Leidenschaft**	passion	**einstellen**	to hire
im Sinn haben	to have in mind	**ernst nehmen**	to take seriously
ertragen	to tolerate	**argwöhnisch**	suspicious
verunglücken	to have an accident	**sich verstehen mit**	to get along with
		kündigen	to quit, to resign
aufnehmen	to take in	**schaffen**	to manage
die **Umstellung**	adjustment	das **Verhältnis**	relationship
dickköpfige	headstrong	**letztendlich**	in the end

Inhaltsangabe

Martha Klein (Martina Gedeck) ist eine alleinstehende Frau, die nur eine Leidenschaft hat: Kochen. Als Chefköchin eines vornehmen Restaurants hat sie nichts anderes im Sinn und für niemanden Zeit. Sie ist Perfektionistin und kann es nicht ertragen, nicht die beste zu sein. Als eines Tages ihre Schwester bei einem Autounfall tödlich verunglückt, nimmt Martha ihre achtjährige Nichte Lina (Maxime Foerste) bei sich auf. Über den Vater von Lina weiß sie nur, dass er Italiener ist und Giuseppe heißt. Um Lina zu helfen, verspricht Martha herauszufinden, wo ihr Vater lebt. Martha versucht für Lina da zu sein, doch die Umstellung ist für beide sehr schwer. Die dickköpfige Lina vermisst ihre Mutter sehr, mag die Schule nicht und isst nur wenig.

Indem Martha versucht mit dieser neuen Situation zurechtzukommen, stellt das Restaurant den charmanten Mario (Sergio Castellitto) als Koch ein. Mario, ein bisschen exzentrisch und ganz anders als Martha, hat ein besonderes Rezept für

Suggestions: Go over the *Arbeit mit dem Text* making sure sts. understand all the words. Write unfamiliar words on the board with translations or convey the meanings in another manner. Ask sts. to read the text silently and answer the questions, then in pairs compare their answers. Follow up on students' answers and provide feedback if necessary.

Assign the questions in *Nach dem Lesen as a mingling activity. Have sts ask at least 4-5 other students.* Follow up and find out what sts found out from each other.

15 sein Leben: Er nimmt das Leben nicht so ernst. Mario bewundert die Kochkünste von Martha, doch Martha ist sehr argwöhnisch und mag Mario zuerst nicht. Mario aber versteht sich gut mit Lina, und schafft es, dass sie wieder anfängt zu essen. Dadurch wird das Verhältnis zwischen Mario und Martha langsam besser und sie verlieben sich.

20 Letztendlich findet Martha Linas Vater, der ein LKW Fahrer aus Italien ist, und Lina zieht mit ihrem Vater nach Italien. Auch Martha wartet nicht mehr lange. Sie kündigt im Restaurant, fährt nach Italien, eröffnet dort ein Restaurant und heiratet Mario.

Arbeit mit dem Text

Beantworten Sie die folgenden Fragen.

1. Beschreiben Sie Martha. Wie ist sie? Was macht sie von Beruf? Was macht sie gern?
2. Wie stirbt ihre Schwester?
3. Wer ist der Vater von ihrer Nichte? Woher kommt er? Was ist er von Beruf?
4. Wie ist die Beziehung zwischen Martha und Mario am Anfang?
5. Wie endet der Film?

Filmclip

Szene: DVD, Szene 2, „Tragedy", 13:55–18:15 Min.

Martha ist im Restaurant und sehr beschäftigt. Das Restaurant ist voll und es ist hektisch. Plötzlich klingelt das Telefon.

Schauen Sie sich die Szene an und beantworten Sie die folgenden Fragen.

1. Wer, glaubt Martha, ist am Telefon?
   a. Mario   b. ihre Schwester   c. die Polizei
2. Wer ist wahrscheinlich am Telefon?
   a. Mario   b. ihre Schwester   c. die Polizei
3. Wie reagiert Martha auf die Nachricht?
   a. froh   b. gleichgültig   c. geschockt
4. Martha bricht zusammen und weint. Wo ist sie wahrscheinlich?
   a. zu Hause   b. im Restaurant   c. im Krankenhaus
5. Als Martha nach Hause kommt, hört sie eine Nachricht von ihrer Schwester auf dem Anrufbeantworter an. Ihre Schwester sagt, …
   a. dass sie gleich   b. dass sie erst   c. dass sie noch 100
      da ist.   späte r kommt.   km fahren muss.

Am nächsten Tag spricht Martha mit einem Arzt im Krankenhaus. Richtig oder falsch? Verbessern Sie die falschen Aussagen.

_____ 6. Der Arzt sagt: „Lina weiß, dass ihre Mutter tot ist."
_____ 7. Der Arzt will wissen, wo Linas Vater ist.

Filmclip. Suggestion: Play the first 90 seconds of this scene, then pause the video and have students answers questions 1, 2, and 3. Then ask students to read questions 4 through 7 and play the remainder of this scene. **Answers:** 1. b 2. c 3. c 4. c 5. b 6. F, Der Arzt sagt, dass man es ihr noch nicht gesagt hat. 7. R

Nach dem Lesen

Was ist Ihre Leidenschaft im Leben? Was machen Sie gern?

Im Restaurant

Grammatik 8.5

a. —Ist hier noch frei?
  —Ja, bitte schön.

b. —Was darf ich Ihnen bringen?
  —Kann ich bitte die Speisekarte haben?
  —Ja, gern, einen Moment, bitte.

c. —Ein Wasser, bitte.
  —Ein Mineralwasser. Kommt sofort!

d. —Wir würden gern zahlen.
  —Gern. Das waren zwei Wiener Schnitzel, ein Glas Wein und eine Limo …

e. —38,80 Franken, bitte schön.
  —Das stimmt so.
  —Vielen Dank.
  —Können Sie mir dafür eine Quittung geben?
  —Selbstverständlich.

f. —Darf ich Sie noch zu einem Kaffee einladen?
  —Das ist nett, aber leider muss ich mich jetzt beeilen.

Situation 12 Was sagen Sie?

Sit. 12. Have sts. work in groups of 3.

Cultural note. Quite often, especially when a restaurant is full or someone is sitting alone, newly arriving customers will ask to share a table where there are empty seats.

Wählen Sie für jede Situation eine passende Aussage.

> **Nein, danke.**
>
> **Ja, bitte sehr.**
>
> **Zahlen, bitte.**
>
> **Leider habe ich kein Geld.**
>
> **Herr Kellner, bitte, sehen Sie sich das mal an.**
>
> **Das kann nicht stimmen. Ich habe doch einen Sauerbraten bestellt.**
>
> **Morgen fliege ich in die USA.**
>
> **Das stimmt so.**
>
> **Ich liebe Schweinebraten.**
>
> **Die Speisekarte, bitte.**

1. Sie sitzen an einem Tisch im Restaurant. Sie haben Hunger, aber noch keine Speisekarte. Sie sehen die Kellnerin und sagen: _____
2. Sie haben mit Ihren Freunden im Restaurant gegessen. Sie haben es eilig und möchten zahlen. Sie rufen den Kellner und sagen: _____
3. Ihr Essen und Trinken hat 19 Euro 20 gekostet. Sie haben der Kellnerin einen Zwanzigeuroschein gegeben. 80 Cent sind Trinkgeld. Sie sagen: _____
4. Sie essen mit Ihren Eltern in einem feinen Restaurant. Da stellen Sie fest, dass eine Fliege in der Suppe schwimmt. Sie rufen den Kellner und sagen: _____
5. Sie haben einen Sauerbraten mit Knödeln bestellt. Die Kellnerin bringt Ihnen einen Schweinebraten. Sie sagen: _____

Situation 13 Dialog: Melanie und Josef gehen aus.

Sit. 13. (See the IM.) This dialogue provides a model for the role-play following it. You may wish to follow the steps for presenting the dialogue without the use of the textbook. You may then want to have sts. complete the dialogue as homework. (Some main text dialogues are on the workbook/lab manual recordings. All are on the text recording.) Questions for listening comprehension: **1.** *Was möchten Melanie und Josef haben?* **2.** *Was möchte Melanie trinken? Und Josef?* **3.** *Was isst Melanie? Und Josef?*

Cultural note. In German-speaking countries, people usually drink sparkling mineral water instead of tap water (*Leitungswasser*). Tap water is not served in restaurants, and there are no drinking fountains in public places.

Melanie und Josef haben sich einen Tisch ausgesucht und sich hingesetzt. Der Kellner kommt an ihren Tisch.

KELLNER: Bitte schön?
MELANIE: Können wir die <u>Speisekarte</u> haben?
KELLNER: Natürlich. Möchten Sie etwas trinken?
MELANIE: Für mich ein <u>Mineralwasser</u> bitte.
JOSEF: Und <u>für mich</u> ein Bier.
KELLNER: Gern.
[*etwas später*]
KELLNER: <u>Wissen Sie schon</u>, was Sie essen möchten?
MELANIE: Ich möchte das Rumpsteak mit Pilzen und Kroketten.
JOSEF: Und ich hätte gern die Forelle „blau" mit Kräuterbutter, grünem Salat und Salzkartoffeln. Dazu <u>noch ein Bier</u> bitte.
KELLNER: Gern. Darf ich <u>Ihnen</u> auch noch etwas zu trinken bringen?
MELANIE: Nein, danke, im Moment nicht.

Situation 14 Rollenspiel: Im Restaurant

Sit. 14. The role for S2 appears in Appendix B. Bring a menu to class, find one on the web, or have sts. refer to the vocabulary displays for ideas on what they might order.

S1: Sie sind im Restaurant und möchten etwas zu essen und zu trinken bestellen. Wenn Sie mit dem Essen fertig sind, bezahlen Sie und geben Sie der Bedienung ein Trinkgeld.

Note: If your students are using McGraw-Hill's *Connect* online *Arbeitsbuch,* they can do this *Rollenspiel* using the real-time, interactive **Video-Chat** feature.

Stichwort „Restaurant"

- Gehen Sie oft ins Restaurant?
- Haben Sie ein Lieblingsrestaurant?
- Was machen Sie, wenn alle Tische besetzt sind?
- Wie lange bleiben Sie normalerweise im Restaurant sitzen, nachdem Sie gegessen haben?

Wie ist es in deutschen Restaurants? Hören Sie zu.

Vergleichen Sie! Deutschland (D) oder Nordamerika (N)?

___D___ Platz selbst aussuchen

___N___ auf einen freien Tisch warten

___N___ nach dem Essen bald gehen

___D___ nach dem Essen noch eine Weile sitzen bleiben

___D___ weniger Trinkgeld geben

___N___ 15%–20% Trinkgeld geben

KLI. Have students review the vocabulary in the *Miniwörterbuch* before playing the recording or reading the passage to sts. Read or play recording: *Wenn man in Deutschland ins Restaurant geht, sucht man sich selbst einen Platz. Wenn es voll ist und man keinen Tisch reserviert hat, geht man wieder. Kaum jemand kommt auf die Idee, auf einen freien Tisch zu warten. Das kann auch lange dauern, denn viele Leute bleiben nach dem Essen noch bei einem Bier, Wein oder einem alkoholfreien Getränk sitzen, um sich zu unterhalten. Beim Essengehen geht es auch um die Geselligkeit. Als Trinkgeld für die Bedienung rundet man die Rechnung auf oder gibt je nach Betrag ca. 5% bis 10% dazu. In Deutschland bekommen Kellner und Kellnerinnen in Restaurants und Lokalen einen festen Lohn, meist zwischen 10% und 15% des Umsatzes. Trinkgeld ist daher kein Muss, sondern eine Anerkennung für nette und aufmerksame Bewirtung.*

In einem Restaurant in Berlin

Miniwörterbuch

die **Anerkennung**	acknowledgment
aufmerksam	attentive
die **Bewirtung**	service
die **Geselligkeit**	sociability, social life
je nach Betrag	depending on the amount
der **Umsatz**	sales

Situation 15 Bildgeschichte: Abendessen mit Hindernissen

Sit. 15. Sentences for narration series: **1.** *Gestern sind Maria und Michael ins Restaurant Zum Löwen gegangen.* **2.** *Sie haben beim Kellner ihre Getränke und ihr Essen bestellt.* **3.** *Zuerst hat ihnen der Wein nicht geschmeckt.* **4.** *Dann hat Maria die falsche Suppe bekommen.* **5.** *Danach hat Michael eine Fliege in seiner Suppe gefunden.* **6.** *Zum Schluss hat der Kellner ihnen zu viel berechnet.* **7.** *Schließlich haben sich Maria und Michael beim Geschäftsführer beschwert.* **8.** *Sie haben bezahlt.* **9.** *Danach sind sie in ein Eiscafé gegangen und haben ein großes Eis als Nachspeise gegessen.*

Situation 16 Interview

Sit. 16. Model pronunciation and have sts. repeat, then have them work in pairs. Ask everyone to switch partners, but for a change of pace, they should simply do the interview again, rather than having the second partner ask about the first partner's answers. Bring in any *Speisekarten* you might have saved from trips.

1. Gehst du oft essen? Wie oft in der Woche isst du nicht zu Hause? Wirst du heute Abend zu Hause essen?

2. Isst du oft im Studentenheim? Wirst du morgen im Studentenheim essen? Schmeckt dir das Essen da?

3. Gehst du oft in Fast-Food-Restaurants? Wirst du vielleicht noch diese Woche in so einem Restaurant essen?

4. Warst du schon mal in einem deutschen Restaurant? Wenn ja, was hast du gegessen? Wenn nein, was wirst du bestellen, wenn du mal in einem deutschen Restaurant bist?

5. In welchem Restaurant schmeckt es dir am besten? Gibt es ein Restaurant, in dem du oft isst? Wie heißt es? Was isst du da? Wirst du diese Woche noch einmal hingehen?

6. Was ist das feinste Restaurant in unserer Stadt? Wie viel muss man da für ein gutes Essen bezahlen?

Videoecke

Perspektiven

> Was ist für dich *gesundes Essen*?

Aufgabe 1 Fleisch oder Gemüse?

Lebensmittel vom Biomarkt

Was ist für diese Leute *gesundes Essen*?

1. Sandra _d, j_   2. Simone _h_   3. Hend _b_   4. Martin _i_

5. Tina _a_   6. Nadezda _c, f_   7. Felicitas _f, e_   8. Pascal _g_

a. das Essen genießen
b. Joghurt und Vollkornbrot
c. keine Pommes
d. Lebensmittel vom Biomarkt
e. nicht zu viel Fleisch
f. Obst und Gemüse

g. ökologisches Essen
h. viel Obst und möglichst wenig Schokolade
i. wenig Fett und wenig Zucker
j. viel selber anbauen

Interviews

Tanja   Susan

- Was isst du zum Frühstück?
- Was isst du zum Mittag?
- Wie oft gehst du essen?
- Wo isst du am liebsten?
- Was isst du da?
- Was isst du nicht gerne?
- Was kannst du besonders gut kochen?
- Wie macht man das?

Aufgabe 2 Tanja oder Susan?

Sehen Sie sich das Video an und kreuzen Sie an.

	Tanja	Susan
1. Wer isst zum Frühstück etwas Süßes vom Bäcker?	☒	☐
2. Wer isst zum Frühstück einen Joghurt?	☐	☒
3. Wer isst zum Mittag normalerweise einen Salat oder eine Suppe?	☒	☐
4. Wer geht jeden Tag in der Mensa essen?	☒	☐
5. Wer isst am liebsten in der Mensa?	☐	☒
6. Wer isst am liebsten in Auerbachs Keller?	☒	☐
7. Wer isst gern Kassler mit Sauerkraut und Klößen?	☒	☐
8. Wer mag kein Rindfleisch?	☒	☐
9. Wer mag keinen Rosenkohl und keinen Spinat[1]?	☐	☒

Aufgabe 3 Nudeln mit Shrimps

Susan macht Nudeln mit Shrimps. Bringen Sie die Sätze in die richtige Reihenfolge.

___4___ Am Ende kommt noch Sahne dazu.

___2___ Dann gebe ich die Shrimps hinein.

___3___ Dann würze ich es mit Chili, Salz und Pfeffer.

___5___ Ganz zum Schluss kommt oben drauf noch Parmesan-Käse.

___1___ Zuerst brate ich die Zwiebeln an.

Aufgabe 4 Interview

Interviewen Sie eine Partnerin oder einen Partner. Stellen Sie dieselben Fragen.

[1]spinach

Wortschatz

Frühstück	Breakfast
die Wurst, ⸚e	sausage
der Käse	cheese
der Schinken	ham
der Speck	bacon
das Brötchen, -	roll
das Ei, -er	egg
gebratene Eier	fried eggs
gekochte Eier	boiled eggs
das Würstchen, -	frank(furter); hot dog

Ähnliche Wörter

die Marmelade, -n; der Honig; das Omelett, -s

Mittagessen und Abendessen	Lunch and Dinner
die Forelle, -n	trout
die Krabbe, -n	shrimp
die Mahlzeit, -en	meal
die Nachspeise, -n	dessert
die Vorspeise, -n	appetizer
der Braten, -	roast
der Knödel, -	dumpling
der Pilz, -e	mushroom
das Brot, -e	bread
das belegte Brot, die belegten Brote	open-face sandwich
das Fleisch	meat
das Hackfleisch	ground beef (or pork)
das Rindfleisch	beef
das Schweinefleisch	pork
die Pommes (frites) [frit] or [frits] (pl.)	French fries

Ähnliche Wörter

die Krokette, -n; die Muschel, -n; die Nudel, -n; der Fisch, -e; der Reis; das Rumpsteak, -s; das Schnitzel, -

Obst und Nüsse	Fruit and Nuts
die Apfelsine, -n	orange
die Birne, -n	pear
die Erdbeere, -n	strawberry
die Weintraube, -n	grape
die Zitrone, -n	lemon
der Pfirsich, -e	peach

Ähnliche Wörter

die Banane, -n; die Nuss, ⸚e; die Pflaume, -n

Gemüse	Vegetables
die Bohne, -n	bean
die Erbse, -n	pea
die Gurke, -n	cucumber
saure Gurken	pickles
die Kartoffel, -n	potato
die Salzkartoffeln	boiled potatoes
die Zwiebel, -n	onion
der Kohl	cabbage
der Blumenkohl	cauliflower
der Rosenkohl	Brussels sprouts

Ähnliche Wörter

die Karotte, -n; die Olive, -n; die Tomate, -n; der Salat, -e (R); der Kopfsalat

Getränke	Beverages
der Saft, ⸚e	juice
der Apfelsaft	apple juice
der Orangensaft	orange juice

Ähnliche Wörter

die Milch; der Kakao [kakau]; das Mineralwasser

Zutaten	Ingredients
der Essig	vinegar
der Knoblauch	garlic
der Senf	mustard
das Gewürz, -e	spice; seasoning
die Kräuter (pl.)	herbs

Ähnliche Wörter

die Butter; die Kräuterbutter; die Soße, -n; der Pfeffer; der Zucker; das Öl (R); das Salz

Küche und Zubereitung	Cooking and Preparation
bestreuen	to sprinkle
braten, brät, gebraten	to fry
bräunen	to brown, fry
erhitzen	to heat
geben, gibt, gegeben (in + akk.)	to put (into)
gießen, gegossen	to pour
schlagen, schlägt, geschlagen	to beat
würzen	to season

Im Restaurant — At the Restaurant

die **Bedienung**	service; waiter, waitress
die **Fliege, -n**	fly
die **Geschäfts-**	manager (female)
führerin, -nen	
die **Kellnerin, -nen**	waitress
die **Quittung, -en**	receipt, check
die **Speisekarte, -n**	menu
die **Suppe, -n**	soup
der **Geschäftsführer, -**	manager (male)
der **Kellner, -**	waiter
der **Schein, -e**	bill, note (*of currency*)
der **Zwanzigeuro-**	twenty-euro note
schein, -e	
der **Teller, -**	plate
das **Gericht, -e**	dish
das **Stück, -e**	slice; piece

Ähnliche Wörter

der **Schweizer Franken, -**; das **Eiscafé, -s**; das **Trinkgeld, -er**

Im Haushalt — In the Household

die **Dose, -n**	can
die **Gabel, -n**	fork
die **Gefriertruhe, -n**	freezer
die **Küchenmaschine, -n**	mixer
die **Schere, -n**	scissors
die **Schnur, ⸚e**	string
die **Schüssel, -n**	bowl
die **Serviette, -n**	napkin
die **Zange, -n**	pliers, tongs
der **Dosenöffner, -**	can opener
der **Haken, -**	hook
der **Löffel, -**	spoon
der **Mülleimer, -**	garbage can
der **Nagel, ⸚**	nail
der **Strom**	electricity, power
der **Wäschetrockner, -**	clothes dryer
das **Gerät, -e**	appliance
das **Handtuch, ⸚er**	hand towel
das **Messer, -**	knife
das **Paket, -e**	package
das **Streichholz, ⸚er**	match
das **Werkzeug, -e**	tool

Ähnliche Wörter

die **Kaffeemühle, -n**; die **Teekanne, -n**; der **Flaschenöffner, -**; der **Grill, -s**; der **Hammer, ⸚**; der **Korkenzieher, -**; der **Teekessel, -**; der **Toaster, -** [tosta]

Sonstige Verben — Other Verbs

ạb·nehmen, nimmt ... ạb, abgenommen	to lose weight
ạb·schneiden, abgeschnitten	to cut off
auf·hängen	to hang up
aus·fallen, fällt ... aus, ist ausgefallen	to go out (*power*)
sich **beeilen**	to hurry
berechnen (+ *dat.*)	to charge
sich **beschweren (bei)**	to complain (to)
bestellen	to order (*food*)
durch·schneiden	to cut through
fest·stellen	to establish
stimmen	to be right
das **stimmt so**	that's right; keep the change
ziehen, gezogen	to pull
zu·bereiten, zubereitet	to prepare (*food*)

Adjektive und Adverbien — Adjectives and Adverbs

fettig	fat; greasy
frei	free, empty, available
ist hier noch frei?	is this seat available?
gebraten	roasted; broiled; fried
gesund	healthy
kalorienarm	low in calories
kalorienbewusst	calorie-conscious
zart	tender
zugebunden	tied shut

Ähnliche Wörter

eiskalt, elegant, elektrisch, fein, frisch, gegrillt, gekocht, gemischt, gesalzen, holländisch, japanisch, mexikanisch, rostig, russisch, sauer

Sonstige Wörter und Ausdrücke — Other Words and Expressions

am wenigsten	the least
danach	afterward
dazu	in addition
eilig	rushed
es **eilig haben**	to be in a hurry
meistens	usually, mostly
normalerweise	normally
der **Schluss, ⸚e**	end
zum Schluss	in the end, finally
selbst gemacht	homemade
selten	rare(ly), seldom

Strukturen und Übungen

8.1 Adjectives: an overview

Attributive adjectives precede nouns and have endings. Predicate adjectives follow the verb **sein** and have no endings.

8.1. *Adjektive.* Adjective endings are, of course, complex, and we do not expect first-year sts. to use most of them correctly in speaking. They can, however, use the description given here for focusing on endings when they read and for monitoring their own written work.

A. Attributive and Predicate Adjectives

Adjectives that precede nouns are called *attributive adjectives* and have endings similar to the forms of the definite article: **kalter, kaltes, kalte, kalten, kaltem.** Adjectives that follow the verb **sein** and a few other verbs are called *predicate adjectives* and do not have any endings.

VERKÄUFER: **Heiße** Würstchen! Ich verkaufe **heiße** Würstchen!	VENDOR: *Hot dogs! I'm selling hot dogs!*
KUNDE: Verzeihung, sind die Würstchen auch wirklich **heiß?**	CUSTOMER: *Excuse me, are the hot dogs really hot?*
VERKÄUFER: Natürlich, was denken Sie denn?!	VENDOR: *Of course, what do you think?!*

B. Attributive Adjectives with and without Preceding Article

If *no* article or article-like word (**mein, dein, dieser,** or the like) precedes the adjective, then the adjective itself has the ending of the definite article **(der, das, die).** This means that the adjective provides the information about the gender, number, and case of the noun that follows.

Ich esse gern gegrill**ten** Fisch. *I like to eat grilled fish.*	**den** Fisch = masculine accusative
Stefan isst gern frisch**es** Müsli. *Stefan likes to eat fresh cereal.*	**das** Müsli = neuter accusative

If an article or article-like word precedes the adjective but does not have an ending, the adjective—again—has the ending of the definite article. **Ein**-words (the indefinite article **ein,** the negative article **kein,** and the possessive adjectives **mein, dein,** etc.) do *not* have an ending in the masculine nominative and in the neuter nominative and accusative. In these instances, as expected, the adjective gives the information about the gender, number, and case of the noun that follows.

Ein groß**er** Topf steht auf dem Herd. *There is a large pot on the stove.*	**der** Topf = masculine nominative
Ich esse ein frisch**es** Brötchen. *I am eating a fresh roll.*	**das** Brötchen = neuter accusative

If an article or article-like word with an ending precedes the adjective, the adjective ends in either **-e** or **-en.** (See Sections 8.2 and 8.4.)

Ich nehme das holländisch**e** Bier.	*I'll take the Dutch beer.*
Ich nehme die deutsch**en** Äpfel.	*I'll take the German apples.*

8.2 Attributive adjectives in the nominative and accusative cases

Rules of thumb:

1. In many instances, the adjective ending is the same as the ending of the definite article.
2. *But:* after **der** (nominative masculine) and **das,** the adjective ending is **-e.***
3. *But:* after **die** (plural), the adjective ending is **-en.**

As described in Section 8.1, adjective endings vary according to the gender, number, and case of the noun they describe and according to whether this information is already indicated by an article or article-like word. In essence, however, there are only a very limited number of possibilities. Study the following chart carefully and try to come up with some easy rules of thumb that will help you remember the adjective endings.

	Masculine	Neuter	Feminine	Plural
Nominative	der kalt**e** Tee	das kalt**e** Bier	die kalt**e** Milch	die kalt**en** Getränke
	ein kalt**er** Tee	ein kalt**es** Bier	eine kalt**e** Milch	
	kalt**er** Tee	kalt**es** Bier	kalt**e** Milch	kalt**e** Getränke
Accusative	den kalt**en** Tee	das kalt**e** Bier	die kalt**e** Milch	die kalt**en** Getränke
	einen kalt**en** Tee	ein kalt**es** Bier	eine kalt**e** Milch	
	kalt**en** Tee	kalt**es** Bier	kalt**e** Milch	kalt**e** Getränke

Üb. 1. All answers contain nominative inflections, which sts. may generate directly from the definite article. Stress the connection so that sts. will not think that the adjective endings are something different from endings on articles. Tell sts. to note that the gender of each noun is provided in parentheses.

Übung 1   Spezialitäten!

Jedes Land hat eine Spezialität: ein Gericht oder ein Getränk, das aus diesem Land einfach am besten schmeckt. An welche Länder denken Sie bei den folgenden Gerichten oder Getränken?

MODELL: Salami → Italienische Salami!

amerikanisch
dänisch
deutsch
englisch
französisch
griechisch
holländisch
italienisch
japanisch
kolumbianisch
neuseeländisch
norwegisch
polnisch
russisch
ungarisch

1. Steak (*n.*)
2. Kaviar (*m.*)
3. Oliven (*pl.*)
4. Sushi (*n.*)
5. Champagner (*m.*)
6. Wurst (*f.*)
7. Käse (*m.*)
8. Spaghetti (*pl.*)
9. Paprika (*m.*)
10. Marmelade (*f.*)
11. Kaffee (*m.*)
12. Kiwis (*pl.*)

Übung 2   Der Gourmet

Üb. 2. This exercise focuses on unpreceded accusative forms. Assign for homework and review in class.

Michael isst und trinkt nicht alles, sondern nur, was er für fein hält. Übernehmen Sie Michaels Rolle.

MODELL: Kognak (*m.*) / französisch →
Ich trinke nur französischen Kognak!

1. Brot (*n.*) / deutsch
2. Kaviar (*m.*) / russisch
3. Salami (*f.*) / italienisch
4. Kaffee (*m.*) / kolumbianisch
5. Kiwis (*pl.*) / neuseeländisch
6. Wein (*m.*) / französisch
7. Bier (*n.*) / belgisch
8. Muscheln (*pl.*) / spanisch
9. Marmelade (*f.*) / englisch
10. Thunfisch (*m.*) / japanisch

*Remember this rule as "**der** (nominative masculine)" because, as you will learn in Section 8.4, when **der** refers to the dative feminine, the adjective ending will be **-en.**

Übung 3   Im Geschäft

Michael hat kein Geld, aber er möchte alles kaufen. Maria muss ihn immer bremsen.

MODELL: der schicke Anzug / teuer →

MICHAEL: Ich möchte den schicken Anzug da.

MARIA: Nein, der schicke Anzug ist viel zu teuer.

1. der graue Wintermantel / schwer
2. die gelbe Hose / bunt
3. das schicke Hemd / teuer
4. die roten Socken / warm
5. der schwarze Schlafanzug / dünn
6. die grünen Schuhe / groß
7. der modische Hut / klein
8. die schwarzen Winterstiefel / leicht
9. die elegante Sonnenbrille / bunt
10. die roten Tennisschuhe / grell

Übung 4   Minidialoge

Ergänzen Sie die Adjektivendungen.

1. HERR RUF: Na, wie ist denn Ihr neu_____ᵃ Auto?

    FRAU WAGNER: Ach, der alt_____ᵇ Mercedes war mir lieber.

    HERR RUF: Dann hätte ich mir aber keinen neu_____ᶜ Wagen gekauft!

2. KELLNER: Wie schmeckt Ihnen denn der italienisch_____ᵃ Wein?

    MICHAEL: Sehr gut. Ich bestelle gleich noch eine weiter_____ᵇ Flasche.

3. MICHAEL: Heute repariere ich mein kaputt_____ᵃ Fahrrad.

    MARIA: Prima! Dann kannst du meinen blöd_____ᵇ Computer auch reparieren. Er ist schon wieder kaputt.

    MICHAEL: Na gut, aber dann habe ich wieder kein frei_____ᶜ Wochenende.

8.3 Destination vs. location: *stellen/stehen, legen/liegen, setzen/sitzen, hängen/hängen*

Destination implies the accusative case; location implies the dative case.

DESTINATION	LOCATION
Verbs of action and direction used with two-way prepositions followed by the accusative	Verbs of condition and location used with two-way prepositions followed by the dative

Maria stellt eine Flasche Wein **auf den** Tisch.

Die Flasche Wein steht **auf dem** Tisch.

stellen/stehen = vertical position

Stellen and **stehen** designate vertical placement or position. They are used with people and animals, as well as with objects that have a base and can "stand" without falling over.

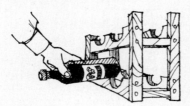 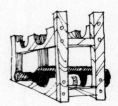

Michael legt eine Flasche Wein **ins** Weinregal.   Die Flasche Wein liegt **im** Weinregal.

legen/liegen = horizontal position

Legen and **liegen** designate horizontal placement or position. They are used with people and animals, as well as with objects that do not have a base and cannot "stand" without falling over.

DESTINATION   LOCATION

Frau Wagner setzt Paula **in den** Hochstuhl.   Paula sitzt **im** Hochstuhl.

sitzen/setzen = sitting position (people and certain animals)

Setzen designates the act of being seated; **sitzen** the state of sitting. These verbs are used only with people and with animals that are capable of sitting.

Helga hängt das Handtuch **an den** Haken.

Das Handtuch hängt **am** Haken.

hängen/hängen = hanging position

Hängen (gehängt) designates the act of being hung; **hängen (gehangen)** the state of hanging.

The verbs **stellen, legen, setzen,** and **hängen** are weak verbs that require an accusative object. The two-way preposition is used with the accusative case.

stellen	hat gestellt
legen	hat gelegt
setzen	hat gesetzt
hängen	hat gehängt

The verbs **stehen, liegen, sitzen,** and **hängen** are strong verbs that cannot take an accusative object. The two-way preposition is used with the dative case.

stehen	hat gestanden
liegen	hat gelegen
sitzen	hat gesessen
hängen	hat gehangen

Übung 5   Minidialoge

Üb. 5. Use as homework and have sts. play the roles in class. Questions about the location and movement of people and objects in the classroom can provide further practice, but we do not expect sts. to acquire these forms quickly.

Ergänzen Sie den Artikel, die Präposition plus Artikel oder das Pronomen.

Genus der Wörter:

> **die Bank**   **das Bett**   **die Gläser (*pl.*)**   **der Herd**
>
> **das Regal**   **der Schrank**   **der Schreibtisch**   **das Sofa**
>
> **die Tasche**   **der Tisch**

1. SILVIA: Wohin stellst du die Blumen?
   JÜRGEN: Auf _____ Tisch.
2. JOSEF: Warum setzt du dich nicht an _____ᵃ Tisch?
   MELANIE: Ich sitze lieber hier auf _____ᵇ Sofa.
3. MARIA: Meine Bücher liegen auf _____ᵃ Tisch. Bitte stell sie auf _____ᵇ Regal.
   MICHAEL: Okay.
4. ALBERT: Ich kann Melanie nicht finden.
   STEFAN: Sie sitzt auf _____ Bank im Garten.
5. MONIKA: Hast du die Weinflaschen in _____ᵃ Schrank gestellt?
   HEIDI: Ja, sie stehen neben _____ᵇ Gläsern.

6. SOFIE: (*am Telefon*) Was machst du heute?
   MARTA: Nichts! Ich lege mich (in) _____ ^a Bett.
   SOFIE: Liegst du schon (in) _____ ^b Bett?
   MARTA: Nein, jetzt sitze ich noch (an) _____ ^c Schreibtisch.

7. KATRIN: Darf ich mich neben _____ ^a (du) setzen?
   STEFAN: Ja, bitte setz _____ ^b (du).

8. FRAU RUF: Hast du die Suppe auf _____ ^a Herd gestellt?
   HERR RUF: Sie steht schon seit einer Stunde auf _____ ^b Herd.

9. HERR RUF: Wo ist der Stadtplan?
   FRAU RUF: Er liegt unter _____ Tasche.

Übung 6   Vor dem Abendessen

Üb. 6. Assign for homework and check in class.

Beschreiben Sie die Bilder. Nützliche Wörter:

legen/liegen	der Küchenschrank
setzen/sitzen	der Schrank
stehen/stellen	die Schublade
	die Serviette
	das Sofa
	der Teller
	der Tisch

MODELL: Die Schuhe → Die Schuhe liegen auf dem Boden.

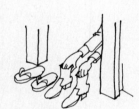

Peter → Peter stellt die Schuhe vor die Tür.

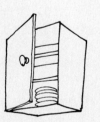

1. Die Teller _____.

2. Albert _____.

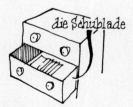

3. Die Servietten _____.

4. Monika _____.

5. Messer und Gabeln _____.

6. Stefan _____.

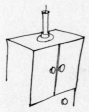

7. Die Kerze _____.   8. Heidi _____.   9. Thomas _____.

8.4 Adjectives in the dative case

8.4. *Adjektive im Dativ.* Unpreceded adjectives in the dative case are common only after prepositions and in the plural. In the singular, they are not very frequent, even with prepositions, and are exceedingly rare with datives referring to people. In the plural, the strong ending–that is, the unpreceded one–is also *-en.* Associating *-en* with dative will help sts. choose the correct pattern in the vast majority of cases and so will help them to learn the German case system a little more easily. The complete chart of adjective endings can be found in Appendix D.

In the dative case, nouns are usually preceded by an article (**dem, der, den; einem, einer**) or an article-like word (**diesem, dieser, diesen; meinem, meiner, meinen**). When adjectives occur before such nouns they end in **-en.*

Jutta geht mit ihrem neuen Freund spazieren.	*Jutta is going for a walk with her new friend.*
Jens gießt seiner kranken Tante die Blumen.	*Jens is watering the flowers for his sick aunt.*
Ich spreche nicht mehr mit diesen unhöflichen Menschen.	*I'm not talking with these impolite people any more.*

	Masculine	Neuter	Feminine	Plural
Dative	dies**em** lieb**en** Vater mein**em** lieb**en** Vater	dies**em** lieb**en** Kind mein**em** lieb**en** Kind	dies**er** lieb**en** Mutter mein**er** lieb**en** Mutter	dies**en** lieb**en** Eltern mein**en** lieb**en** Eltern

Übung 7   Was machen diese Leute?

Achtung!

All nouns have an **-n** in the dative plural unless their plural ends in **-s.**

Nominative: die Freunde

Dative: den Freunde**n**   *but:* den Hobbys

Üb. 7. The focus is on dative forms. Assign for homework and check in class. When doing so, vary how you ask the questions: use both forms such as *Was macht Jens?* and *Wem zeigt Ernst die Ratte?* so that sts. connect the interrogative *wem* with dative forms.

Schreiben Sie Sätze.

MODELL: Jens / seine alte Tante / einen Brief schreiben →
        Jens schreibt seiner alten Tante einen Brief.

1. Jutta / ihr neuer Freund / ihre Lieblings-CD leihen
2. Jens / der kleine Bruder von Jutta / eine Ratte verkaufen
3. Hans / nur seine besten Freunde / die Ratte zeigen
4. Jutta / ihre beste Freundin / ein Buch schenken
5. Jens / sein wütender Lehrer / eine Krawatte kaufen
6. Ernst / seine große Schwester / einen Witz erzählen
7. Jutta / die netten Leute von nebenan / Kaffee kochen
8. Ernst / das süße Baby von nebenan / einen Kuss geben

*Unpreceded adjectives in the dative case follow the same pattern as in the nominative and accusative case, that is, they have the ending of the definite article. For example, **mit frischem Honig** (*with fresh honey*), **mit kalter Milch** (*with cold milk*).

8.5 Talking about the future: the present and future tenses

future tense = **werden** + infinitive

You already know that **werden** is the equivalent of English *to become*.

Ich möchte Ärztin werden.	*I'd like to become a physician.*

You can also use a form of **werden** plus infinitive to talk about future events.

Wo wirst du morgen sein?	*Where will you be tomorrow?*
Morgen werde ich wahrscheinlich zu Hause sein.	*Tomorrow I will probably be at home.*

8.5. *Präsens und Futur.* The future tense is the second use that German makes of *werden.* (It was introduced as a main verb in Section 5.3 and will be introduced as the passive auxiliary in Section 10.5.) Sts. find the future construction relatively easy.

Point out to sts. that they have already often used the present tense in German to talk about the future.

When an adverb of time is present or when it is otherwise clear that future actions or events are indicated, German speakers normally use the present tense rather than the future tense to talk about what will happen in the future.

Nächstes Jahr **fahren** wir nach Schweden.	*Next year we're going to Sweden.*
Was **machst** du, wenn du in Schweden bist?	*What are you going to do when you're in Sweden?*

Use **wohl** with the future tense to express present or future probability.

The future tense with **werden** can express present or future probability. In such cases, the sentence often includes an adverb such as **wohl** (*probably*).

Mein Freund wird jetzt **wohl** zu Hause sein.	*My friend should be home now.*
Morgen Abend werden wir **wohl** zu Hause bleiben.	*Tomorrow evening we'll probably stay home.*

Don't forget to put **werden** at the end of the dependent clause.

Ich weiß nicht, ob ich einmal heiraten **werde.**	*I don't know if I'm ever going to get married.*

Übung 8   Vorsätze

Sie wollen ein neues Leben beginnen? Schreiben Sie sechs Dinge auf, die Sie ab morgen machen werden oder nicht mehr machen werden.

MODELL: Ich werde nicht mehr so oft in Fast-Food-Restaurants gehen.
Ich werde mehr Obst und Gemüse essen.

> weniger/mehr fernsehen   weniger/mehr Kurse belegen
>
> früher/später ins Bett gehen   weniger/mehr arbeiten
>
> weniger/mehr lernen   weniger oft/öfter ins Kino gehen
>
> weniger/mehr SMS schicken
>
> weniger oft/öfter selbst kochen
>
> weniger gesund/gesünder essen

Übung 9   Morgen ist Samstag

Üb. 9. Assign for homework. Check and compare sts.' answers in class.

Was machen Frau Schulz und ihre Studenten morgen?

MODELL: Katrin geht morgen ins Kino.

Katrin

1. Frau Schulz

2. Heidi

3. Peter

4. Monika

5. Stefan

6. Nora

7. Albert

8. Thomas

Übung 10   Vorhersagen

Machen Sie sechs Vorhersagen, die in diesem oder im nächsten Jahr eintreffen werden.

MODELL: Dieses Jahr werden die Broncos den Superbowl gewinnen.
Nächstes Jahr werden wir einen republikanischen Gouverneur wählen.

die Wimbledon-Spiele gewinnen

einen tollen Job bekommen

in eine andere Wohnung ziehen

mit dem Studium fertig werden

die Studiengebühren fallen/steigen

weniger Steuern bezahlen

der Papst nach Mexiko fliegen   **gute Noten bekommen**

Kindheit und Jugend

Kapitel 9 deals with memories and past events. You will have the opportunity to talk about your childhood and you will learn more about the tales that are an important part of childhood in the German-speaking world.

GOALS

In this chapter, sts. talk about childhood memories and learn to tell all kinds of stories using the perfect tense. They are introduced to the simple past and the past perfect by reading a variety of texts and retelling some of Grimm's fairy tales. We expect sts. to use the simple past of *haben, sein, werden, wissen,* and the modal verbs actively. All other simple past forms and the past perfect are presented here primarily for receptive mastery, i.e., for reading and listening comprehension.

Themen

Kindheit

Jugend

Geschichten

Märchen

Kulturelles

KLI: Jugend im 21. Jahrhundert

KLI: 1989

Musikszene: „Wir beide" (Juli)

Filmclip: *Nordwand* (Philipp Stölzl)

Videoecke: Schule

Lektüren

Film: *Nordwand* (Philipp Stölzl)

Märchen: *Rotkäppchen – Ein Märchen der Gebrüder Grimm*

Strukturen

9.1   The conjunction **als** with dependent-clause word order

9.2   The simple past tense of **werden,** the modal verbs, and **wissen**

9.3   Time: **als, wenn, wann**

9.4   The simple past tense of strong and weak verbs (receptive)

9.5   Sequence of events in past narration: the past perfect tense and the conjunction **nachdem** (receptive)

Ingrid M. Schmeck: *Plön Prinzeninsel* (1981), Privatbesitz

Kunst und Künstler

Ingrid Schmeck wurde 1944 in Posen im heutigen Polen geboren und studierte in Kiel an der Muthesius Werkkunstschule und an der Fachhochschule für Gestaltung in Hamburg. Sie ist bekannt für ihre „schiefen"[1] Häuser- und Stadtbilder, in denen sie mit Proportionen und Perspektiven spielt.

Schauen Sie sich das Bild an und beantworten Sie die folgenden Fragen.

1. In welchem Teil Deutschlands könnte so ein Haus stehen?
2. Beschreiben Sie die Gegenstände, die Sie um das Haus herum sehen.
3. Schauen Sie sich das Haus genauer an. Fällt Ihnen etwas auf, wenn Sie die vordere und die hintere Haushälfte vergleichen? Was für eine Bedeutung könnte das haben?
4. Wie wirkt das Bild auf[2] Sie? Wie könnte man die Atmosphäre beschreiben?

[1] *lopsided* [2] wirkt auf *affects*

Situationen

Vocabulary Display
Before projecting the vocabulary display, explain to sts. that you are going to talk about things you did when you were a child. Mix predictable statements with slightly shocking statements. You could then ask sts. to recall your statements. Do not expect perfect recall. Next project the vocabulary and ask about the characters. Do not let sts. see the captions at first, but encourage them to guess. Then uncover the text; model and have sts. repeat.

Kindheit

Grammatik 9.1

Jens hat seinem Onkel den Rasen gemäht.

Uli hat im Garten Äpfel gepflückt.

Richard hat mit seiner Mutter Kuchen gebacken.

Bernd hat Staub gesaugt und sauber gemacht.

Willi hat seiner Oma die Blumen gegossen.

Jochen hat seinem kleinen Bruder Geschichten vorgelesen.

Situation 1 Melanies erstes Haustier

Sit. 1. In this activity, sts. continue to use the perfect tense they learned earlier. Introduce unfamiliar vocabulary: *Korb, füttern, Schleife, Knochen.* Model pronunciation and have sts. repeat the sentences. Then have them work in small groups to decide which activities would match which times. Several sequences are possible. You could also ask sts. to give reasons for their choices.

Als Melanie sechs Jahre alt war, hat sie einen Hund zum Geburtstag bekommen. Sie hat ihn Bruno genannt. Was hat sie wohl am nächsten Tag mit ihm gemacht? Ordnen Sie die Aktivitäten den Zeiten zu.

MODELL: Um sechs Uhr ist sie gemeinsam mit Bruno aufgestanden.

6.00 Uhr	**10.15 Uhr**	**16.00 Uhr**
6.30 Uhr	**12.00 Uhr**	
7.00 Uhr	**14.30 Uhr**	**19.30 Uhr**
10.00 Uhr	**15.00 Uhr**	

1. Sie ist zusammen mit Bruno eingeschlafen.
2. Sie hat mit ihm gespielt.
3. Sie hat Brunos Korb[1] sauber gemacht.
4. Sie ist mit Bruno spazieren gegangen.
5. Sie ist gemeinsam mit Bruno aufgestanden.
6. Sie hat Bruno gefüttert.
7. Sie hat ihn ihren Freunden gezeigt.
8. Sie hat ihm eine Schleife[2] ins Haar gebunden.
9. Sie hat Bruno in der Badewanne gewaschen.
10. Sie hat ihm einen großen Knochen[3] gekauft.

 Situation 2   Umfrage

Sit. 2. First, ask the sts. the questions that they will ask each other afterward: *Wer von Ihnen hat als Kind Karten gespielt? Heben Sie bitte die Hand! Wer von Ihnen hat als Kind viel ferngesehen? usw.* Then have them ask you the questions: *Haben Sie ...*, and encourage them to ask you anything else they can think of. Finally, have them do the autograph activity.

MODELL: S1: Hast du als Kind Karten gespielt?
          S2: Ja.
          S1: Unterschreib bitte hier.

UNTERSCHRIFT

1. Karten gespielt _____
2. viel ferngesehen _____
3. dich mit den Geschwistern gestritten _____
4. manchmal die Nachbarn geärgert _____
5. einen Hund oder eine Katze gehabt _____
6. in einer Baseballmannschaft gespielt _____
7. Ballettunterricht genommen _____
8. Fensterscheiben kaputt gemacht _____

Situation 3   Interaktion: Als ich 12 Jahre alt war ...

Sit. 3. Sts. first answer these questions for themselves and then ask their partners the same questions. Before they work in pairs, ask them to tell you how they will ask the questions, as there is no model supplied: *Sie sprechen jetzt mit Ihrem Partner / mit Ihrer Partnerin. Wie stellen Sie ihm/ ihr die Fragen, z.B. Nummer 1? (Wie oft hast du dein Zimmer aufgeräumt?) und 2?* Tell sts. to watch for verbs that have the auxiliary *sein*.

Wie oft haben Sie das gemacht, als Sie 12 Jahre alt waren: **oft, manchmal, selten** oder **nie?**

1. mein Zimmer aufgeräumt
2. Kuchen gebacken
3. Liebesromane gelesen
4. Videos angeschaut
5. heimlich jemanden geliebt
6. spät aufgestanden
7. Freunde eingeladen
8. allein verreist
9. zu einem Fußballspiel gegangen

[1]*basket* [2]*bow* [3]*bone*

Jugend im 21. Jahrhundert

Welche verbotenen Dinge tun Sie manchmal? Wie sieht der ideale Freitagabend aus? Diese und viele andere Fragen haben 2 034 deutsche Jugendliche zwischen 14 und 29 Jahren für eine repräsentative Umfrage beantwortet. Die Antworten zeigen das Selbstporträt einer eigensinnigen[1], illusionslosen[2] Generation.

Beantworten Sie die folgenden Fragen zuerst für sich selbst. Vergleichen Sie dann Ihre Antworten mit den Antworten der anderen Studenten in Ihrem Deutschkurs und dann mit denen der deutschen Jugendlichen.

Photo questions. Encourage students to speculate if answers are not apparent. *Wie finden Sie diesen jungen Mann / diese junge Frau? Was macht er/sie beruflich? Was für eine Familie hat er/sie? Was für Musik hört er/sie gern? Was sind seine/ihre Hobbys? Wie war er/sie als Kind?*

Timo Schacht, 22, Elektrotechniker.
Motto: Immer positiv denken.

Sandra Paul, 26, Modezeichnerin.
Motto: Sich immer wieder neu entdecken.

1. Wie haben Ihre Eltern Sie erzogen?

liebevoll	40%
liberal	26%
streng	19%
antiautoritär	6%
nachlässig[3]	5%
mit Prügel[4] und Hausarrest	4%
gar nicht	2%

2. Wo sind Sie aufgewachsen?

bei beiden Elternteilen[5]	85%
bei einem Elternteil	14%
bei Verwandten	1%

3. Wo wohnen Sie zur Zeit?

bei den Eltern	50%
mit meinem Lebenspartner	24%
allein	18%
in einer WG	6%
im Wohnheim	1%

4. Wie viele Stunden sehen Sie jeden Tag fern?

gar nicht	3%
unter 1 Stunde	21%
1 bis 2 Stunden	42%
2 bis 4 Stunden	28%
4 bis 6 Stunden	5%
mehr als 6 Stunden	1%

5. Wie viele Videos sehen Sie pro Woche?

keines	46%
ein bis zwei	42%
drei bis fünf	10%
mehr als zehn	1%

6. Wie häufig sehen Sie die Nachrichten im Fernsehen?

fast jeden Tag	39%
oft	32%
selten	23%
nie	4%

7. Wie oft lesen Sie eine Tageszeitung?

fast jeden Tag	42%
oft	25%
selten	26%
nie	7%

8. Wie viele Bücher haben Sie in den letzten drei Monaten gelesen?

keines	41%
ein bis zwei	33%
drei oder mehr	25%

[1]*stubborn* [2]*without illusions* [3]*negligently* [4]*beatings* [5]*parents*

KLI. Ask questions from the introductory paragraph in class or let sts. poll one another. After sts. have checked answers to the 8 questions, have them compare their answers with those of the German young people. Provide one or two model responses. **AA:** Use the information for an interactive activity. Have sts. first check off their own answers for each question. Then in small groups have them guess their classmates' answers. **Note:** Some categories do not total exactly 100%, because the percentages are rounded to the nearest whole number.

 **Situation 4** Interview

Sit. 4. Sts. should work with a partner and interview each other alternately: S1: *Wo hast du gewohnt, als du acht Jahre alt warst?* S2: *In Pittsburgh. Und du? Wo hast du gewohnt?* S1: *In San Francisco. Hattest du Geschwister?* S2: *Ja. Zwei Brüder. Und du? Hattest du auch Geschwister? usw.* Sts. should take notes. Then have sts. change partners and describe the childhood of their first partner to their second partner. Finally, have sts. interview you.

Vocabulary Display
This display introduces simple past-tense forms of *haben, sein,* and the modals. Sts. will already be familiar with some of these forms, especially *sein.* Present by covering the captions and narrating the events. Then follow the regular method. (See the IM.) As a follow-up let students speculate on what happened to Sybille after picture 8 and ask them to draw or describe a picture 9.

Als du acht Jahre alt warst ...

1. Wo hast du gewohnt? Hattest du Geschwister? Freunde? Wo hat dein Vater gearbeitet? deine Mutter? Was hast du am liebsten gegessen?

2. In welche Grundschule bist du gegangen? Wann hat die Schule angefangen? Wann hat sie aufgehört? Welchen Lehrer / Welche Lehrerin hattest du am liebsten? Welche Fächer hattest du am liebsten? Was hast du in den Pausen gespielt? Was hast du nach der Schule gemacht?

3. Hast du viel ferngesehen? Was hast du am liebsten gesehen? Hast du gern gelesen? Was? Hast du Sport getrieben? Was? Was hast du gar nicht gern gemacht?

Jugend

Grammatik 9.2–9.3

1. Sybille Gretter war sehr begabt. In der Schule wusste sie immer alles.

2. Sie brauchte für die Prüfungen nicht viel zu lernen.

3. Sie konnte auch sehr gut tanzen und wollte Ballerina werden.

4. Dreimal in der Woche musste sie zum Ballettunterricht.

5. Als sie in der letzten Klasse war, hatte sie einen Freund.

6. Ihr Vater durfte nichts davon wissen, denn er war sehr streng.

7. Eines Tages hat sie ihren Freund ihren Eltern vorgestellt.

8. Aber ihr Vater mochte ihn nicht und sie mussten sich trennen.

Situation 5 Dialog: Jugendsünden

Sit. 5. (See the IM.) **(1)** Set the scene. **(2)** Preteach vocabulary: *sich erinnern an, damals, zufällig, der Ärger, der Direktor, stehlen.* **(3)** You may wish to have sts. keep their books closed while answering the following questions. Write them on the board. Questions for first listening: **1.** *Was macht Alexander heute?* **2.** *Was haben Michael, Alexander und ihre Mitschüler in Frau Müllers Klasse gemacht?* **3.** *Mit welcher Person haben die Schüler dann Ärger bekommen?* Questions for second listening: **1.** *Wie heißen die zwei anderen Lehrer, über die Michael und Alexander sprechen?* **2.** *Welche Fächer haben sie unterrichtet?* **3.** *Warum möchte Alexander nicht wieder Gymnasiast sein?* **(4)** Compare sts.' answers. Ask sts. to open their books. Play the dialogue for them once more while they fill in the blanks. **(5)** Write sts.' answers on the board or ask them to write their answers on the board themselves, while making any necessary corrections. **(6)** Ask sts. to work in groups to determine the infinitives of the participles. **(7)** Review sts.' answers.

Michael Pusch geht zum zehnten Klassentreffen seiner Abiturklasse. Er trifft seinen alten Freund Alexander. Die beiden sprechen über ihre gemeinsame Schulzeit.

MICHAEL: Schön, dich mal wieder zu sehen, Alex. Was hast du eigentlich nach dem Abi _gemacht_?

ALEXANDER: Ich habe eine Tanzschule _eröffnet_.

MICHAEL: Nicht schlecht. Gern und gut _getanzt_ hast du ja früher schon.

ALEXANDER: Stimmt. Erinnerst du dich an das Drama mit Frau Müller damals?

MICHAEL: Ach, als wir in ihrem Deutschunterricht laut Musik _gehört_ und getanzt haben?

ALEXANDER: Genau. Sie war noch nicht in der Klasse, uns war langweilig und Hans hatte zufällig ein bisschen Musik dabei.

MICHAEL: Und als Frau Müller hereinkam, haben alle wild getanzt und _gesungen_. Das war ein Spaß.

ALEXANDER: Danach hat es nur leider viel Ärger mit dem Direktor _gegeben_.

MICHAEL: Richtig. Dabei hatten wir diese Sache noch nicht einmal _geplant_.

ALEXANDER: Und als wir Herrn Riedel die Geschichtsklausuren[1] _gestohlen_ oder das Auto der Französischlehrerin Frau Häuser mit Toilettenpapier _eingepackt_ haben …

MICHAEL: Es war eigentlich eine schöne Zeit auf dem Gymnasium.

ALEXANDER: Na ja. Denk doch nur an die vielen Klassenarbeiten.

 Situation 6 Interview

Sit. 6. Sts. use the simple past-tense forms of the modals intensively in this situation, as well as *wenn, wann,* and *als.* Have sts. work in pairs and take notes on their partner's answers. At the end, have them report back to the class.

1. Musstest du früh aufstehen, als du zur Schule gegangen bist? Wann?
2. Wann musstest du von zu Hause weggehen?
3. Musstest du zur Schule, wenn du krank warst?
4. Durftest du abends lange fernsehen oder im Internet surfen, wenn du morgens früh aufstehen musstest?
5. Konntest du zu Fuß zur Schule gehen?
6. Wolltest du manchmal lieber zu Hause bleiben? Warum?
7. Was wolltest du werden, als du ein Kind warst?
8. Durftest du abends ausgehen? Wann musstest du zu Hause sein?

Situation 7 Geständnisse

Sit. 7. This activity reinforces the difference between *als* and *wenn.* Sts. work in small groups and write what they did in each situation. Encourage playfulness and provide a few models about yourself. Afterward, ask the class as a whole: *Was haben Sie gemacht, als Sie einmal mit einem Jungen / mit einem Mädchen im Kino waren?* and call on individuals.

Sagen Sie, was in diesen Situationen passiert ist oder was Sie gemacht haben.

MODELL: Als ich zum ersten Mal allein verreist bin, habe ich meinen Teddy mitgenommen.

1. Als ich einmal mit einem Jungen / einem Mädchen im Kino war
2. Als ich zum ersten Mal Kaffee getrunken hatte
3. Wenn ich zu spät nach Hause gekommen bin
4. Als ich mein erstes F bekommen hatte
5. Wenn ich keine Hausaufgaben gemacht habe
6. Wenn ich total verliebt war
7. Als ich zum ersten Mal verliebt war
8. Als ich einmal meinen Hausschlüssel verloren hatte
9. Wenn ich eine schlechte Note bekommen habe

[1] *history exams*

Situation 8   Rollenspiel: Das Klassentreffen

Sit. 8. The role for S2: appears in Appendix B.

Note: If your students are using McGraw-Hill's *Connect* online *Arbeitsbuch*, they can do this *Rollenspiel* using the real-time, interactive **Video-Chat** feature.

S1: Sie sind auf dem fünften Klassentreffen Ihrer alten High-School-Klasse. Sie unterhalten sich mit einem alten Schulfreund / einer alten Schulfreundin. Fragen Sie: was er/sie nach Abschluss der High School gemacht hat, was er/sie jetzt macht und was seine/ihre Pläne für die nächsten Jahre sind. Sprechen Sie auch über die gemeinsame Schulzeit.

Geschichten

Grammatik 9.4

Vocabulary Display

Sentences for narration series: **1.** *Eines Abends war Willi allein zu Hause.* **2.** *Seine Eltern waren ins Theater gegangen.* **3.** *Willi lag im Bett und konnte nicht einschlafen.* **4.** *Plötzlich hörte er durch das Fenster ein Geräusch.* **5.** *Er schaute aus dem Fenster und sah einen Schatten.* **6.** *„Ein Einbrecher!", dachte Willi.* **7.** *Er hatte große Angst und rief die Großeltern an.* **8.** *Dann versteckte Willi sich mit einem Tennisschläger im Keller.* **9.** *Der Großvater fuhr sofort mit dem Fahrrad los.* **10.** *Unterwegs fing es an zu regnen und der Großvater wurde ganz nass.* **11.** *Großvater ging mit einer Taschenlampe in den Garten.* **12.** *Aber er fand keinen Einbrecher, nur Büsche und eine kleine Katze.*

After narrating the story and having sts. repeat, pass out a sheet of paper with the same drawings out of sequence. Reread the passage, and have sts. number the pictures correctly. To add a focus on form, ask sts. to work in small groups and to write down from memory all simple past forms they remember, to determine their infinitive forms, and to categorize them as weak or strong verbs.

Als Willi mal allein zu Hause war …

 Situation 9   Informationsspiel: Was ist passiert?

Sit. 9. The corresponding chart is in Appendix A. This activity practices the past-tense forms that German speakers typically use in relating personal stories or events, i.e. the perfect tense for all verbs except *haben* and *sein* and the modal verbs, which are in the simple past. You may want to point out

MODELL: Was ist Sofie passiert? / Was ist dir passiert?
Wann ist es passiert?
Wo ist es passiert?
Warum ist es passiert?

	Sofie	Mehmet	Ernst	mein Partner / meine Partnerin
Was?	hat ihre Schlüssel verloren	hat sein Flugzeug verpasst	hat seine Hose zerrissen	
Wann?	als sie im Kino war	als er in die Türkei fliegen wollte	als er über den Zaun geklettert ist	
Wo?	in Leipzig	in Frankfurt	bei seiner Tante	
Warum?	weil ihre Jackentasche ein Loch hatte	weil der Flug aus Berlin Verspätung hatte	weil der Zaun zu hoch war	

that the simple past tense for other verb forms is commonly used in speaking only when retelling fairy tales or other tales referring to distant times or fictitious people. Preteach the new vocabulary (*Loch, Schlüssel, verpassen, Verspätung, Zaun, zerreißen*), e.g., by telling Sofie's, Mehmet's, and Ernst's misfortunes as if they had happened to you, acting out any new vocabulary items and writing them on the board. Ask sts. to think of something that happened to them before having them begin this activity with a partner.

Situation 10 Und dann?

Sit. 10. This activity demonstrates use of the simple past in narration of past events. Have sts. work in small groups to match the events (1-9) with the outcomes (a-i). **Possible answers:** 1. e, 2. f, 3. g, 4. d, 5. b, 6. a, 7. c, 8. i, 9. h.

Suchen Sie für jede Situation eine logische Folge.

MODELL: Jutta konnte ihren Hausschlüssel nicht finden und kletterte durch das Fenster.

1. Ernst machte die Fensterscheibe kaputt
2. Jens reparierte sein Fahrrad
3. Richard sparte ein ganzes Jahr
4. Claire kam in Innsbruck an
5. Michael bekam ein neues Fahrrad
6. Rolf lernte sechs Jahre Englisch
7. Josef arbeitete drei Monate im Krankenhaus
8. Silvia wohnte zwei Semester allein
9. Melanie bekam ihren ersten Kuss

a. machte dann Urlaub in Spanien.
b. fuhr gleich gegen einen Baum.
c. kaufte sich ein Motorrad.
d. kaufte sich einen neuen Pulli.
e. lief weg.
f. machte eine Radtour.
g. flog dann nach Amerika.
h. sagte leise: „Ach du lieber Gott!"
i. zog dann in eine WG.
j. ?

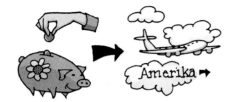

Situation 11 Bildgeschichte: Beim Zirkus

Sit. 11. This narration series also demonstrates the simple past-tense forms of all types of verbs: weak, strong, *haben, sein,* and the modals. Sentences for narration series: **1.** *Als Michael Pusch fünfzehn Jahre alt war, kam eines Tages ein Zirkus in die Stadt.* **2.** *Am Abend ging Michael mit seinen Freunden in den Zirkus.* **3.** *Dort gab es Clowns und Artisten und die junge Seiltänzerin war sehr schön.* **4.** *Am nächsten Morgen musste Michael immer an die Seiltänzerin denken.* **5.** *Nach der Schule lief er sofort zurück zum Zirkus.* **6.** *Er wollte beim Zirkus bleiben, dort arbeiten und die schöne Seiltänzerin heiraten.* **7.** *Michael wurde Tierpfleger. Er fütterte die Pferde und die Elefanten.* **8.** *Aber nach ein paar Tagen kamen Michaels Eltern und er musste wieder nach Hause.* **9.** *Er ging wieder zur Schule und machte langweilige Hausaufgaben.* **10.** *Manchmal aber träumte er vom Zirkus und der schönen Seiltänzerin.*

To add a focus on form, ask sts. to work in small groups and to write down from memory all simple past forms they remember, to determine their infinitive forms, and to categorize them as weak or strong verbs. **AA.** You could also have sts. draw an 11th picture to show on the projector and present it to the class with a commentary.

Kultur … Landeskunde … Informationen

1989

KLI. First question: Weitere Ereignisse im Jahr 1989 sind Massaker auf dem Tian'anmen-Platz in Peking; die UdSSR zieht ihre Truppen aus Afghanistan ab; George H. W. Bush wird Präsident der USA.

- Was geschah 1989?
- Wo liegt Leipzig? Wie viele Einwohner hat Leipzig? Was wissen Sie über Leipzig?
- Fragen Sie ältere Kommilitonen, Ihre Eltern oder Ihren Dozenten / Ihre Dozentin, ob er oder sie sich erinnert, wo er oder sie war, als die Mauer fiel. Was haben sie damals gedacht?

Deutschland vor 1990
Rostock
Ost-Berlin
West-Berlin
Potsdam
Magdeburg
DDR
Leipzig
Dresden
BRD

Die Mauer ist gefallen.

Lesen Sie den Text und suchen Sie die Antworten auf die folgenden Fragen:

- Wie nennt man in Deutschland das Jahr 1989?
- Wie lange war Deutschland geteilt[1]?
- Wie hieß der östliche Teil Deutschlands? Wann wurde er gegründet[2]?
- Was war mit West-Berlin?
- Wie ging es der DDR in den 1980er Jahren wirtschaftlich[3]?
- Was empörte[4] die DDR-Bürger besonders?
- Welches sozialistische Land öffnete seine Grenzen als erstes?
- Wo fanden die Montagsdemonstrationen statt?
- War es gefahrlos[5], an den Montagsdemonstrationen teilzunehmen?
- Wie viele Menschen demonstrierten am 9. Oktober?
- Wann fiel die Berliner Mauer?
- An welches Ereignis erinnert der deutsche Nationalfeiertag?
- Was findet jedes Jahr am 9. Oktober in Leipzig statt?
- Nun eine Frage an Sie persönlich: Welche historischen Ereignisse des 20. Jahrhunderts waren für Sie und Ihre Familie wichtig? Welche Ereignisse waren für die Welt wichtig?

1989 ist als das Wendejahr[6] bekannt, das Jahr der friedlichen Revolution. Nach dem verlorenen 2. Weltkrieg[7] war Deutschland zuerst vier Jahre lang besetzt[8] und dann 40 Jahre lang geteilt. 1949 schlossen sich die Besatzungszonen der Westalliierten zur Bundesrepublik Deutschland (BRD) zusammen und aus der sowjetischen Besatzungszone wurde die Deutsche Demokratische Republik, die DDR. Der Kalte Krieg zwischen den USA und der Sowjetunion teilte nicht nur Deutschland, sondern Europa und die ganze Welt. Westdeutschland war eine Demokratie und Teil des kapitalistischen Westens und die DDR war eine Diktatur und Teil des sozialistischen Ostens. West-Berlin war eine westdeutsche Insel in der DDR.

1989 wurde immer deutlicher, dass das diktatorische und sozialistische System der DDR zum Scheitern verurteilt[9] war. Wirtschaftlich stand das Land vor dem Staatsbankrott, die Altstädte verfielen[10] und die Umwelt verkam[11]. Gesellschaftlich[12] empörten sich immer mehr Menschen über den Überwachungsstaat[13], der seine Bürger in Unmündigkeit[14] hielt und ihnen Vieles verbot, insbesondere den Kontakt zum Westen. Viele Leute kamen ins Gefängnis und wurden dort auch gefoltert[15]. Mindestens 200 DDR-Bürger, die versuchten, über die Grenze[16] zu fliehen[17], waren erschossen[18] worden.

1989 flohen immer mehr Bürger der DDR über Ungarn, das als erstes seine Grenzen öffnete, in den Westen. Am 4. September fand die erste Montagsdemonstration in Leipzig statt. Sie begann im Anschluss an die Friedensgebete[19] in der Nikolaikirche, die seit Mitte der 1980er Jahre immer montags um 17 Uhr stattfanden. Diesen Montagsdemonstrationen schlossen sich von Woche zu Woche immer mehr Menschen an[20], obwohl die Sicherheitskräfte der DDR brutal gegen die Demonstranten vorgingen[21]. Auch in anderen Städten der DDR kam es zu Demonstrationen. Am 9. Oktober demonstrierten 70 000 Menschen in Leipzig unter der Parole: Wir sind das Volk. Eine Woche später waren es bereits 120 000 und an den folgenden Montagen waren es jeweils 300 000. Ende Oktober trat die gesamte DDR-Regierung[22] zurück und am 9. November wurde die Berliner Mauer geöffnet. Die Bürger der DDR waren frei.

Am 18. März 1990 gab es die ersten freien Wahlen[23] in der DDR und am 3. Oktober 1990 trat die DDR der Bundesrepublik Deutschland bei[24]. Deutschland war wiedervereinigt[25]. Der 3. Oktober wurde zum Nationalfeiertag Deutschlands. In Leipzig wird jedes Jahr am 9. Oktober ein großes Lichtfest gefeiert, in Erinnerung an die *friedliche Revolution*, bei dem ebenso wie 1989 viele Menschen mit Kerzen[26] durch die Innenstadt Leipzigs ziehen.

Suggestion: Have sts. write a short narrative in the past tense about an important historical event from their youth.

[1]*divided* [2]*established* [3]*economically* [4]*outraged* [5]*without danger* [6]*turning-point year* [7]*world war* [8]*occupied* [9]zum … *doomed to collapse* [10]*fell into disrepair* [11]*deteriorated* [12]*Societally* [13]*surveillance state* [14]*powerlessness* [15]*tortured* [16]*border* [17]*flee* [18]*shot dead* [19]*prayers of peace* [20]schlossen sich an *joined* [21]*acted* [22]*government* [23]*elections* [24]trat bei *joined* [25]*reunited* [26]*candles*

Musikszene

„Wir beide" (2006, Deutschland) *Juli*

Eva Briegel

Biografie Juli ist in Deutschland eine der meist gespielten Bands im Radio. Sie nennen ihren Musikstil Alternativ-Pop und wollen vor allem interessante Texte schreiben. Die Band gibt es seit 2002. Die Leadsängerin Eva Briegel und die Gitarristen Simon Triebel und Jonas Pfetzing schreiben alle Lieder der Band und sie schreiben sie alle auf Deutsch. Ihre erste Single *Perfekte Welle* wurde eine Art Hymne der neuen deutschsprachigen Popmusik seit dem Jahr 2004. Die Single „Wir beide" stammt aus dem Jahr 2006. Sie ist eine Hymne an die Freundschaft und war 10 Wochen in den deutschen Charts.

iMix Link: Dieses Lied können Sie im *iTunes Store* als ein *iMix* kaufen, das speziell für *Kontakte* entwickelt wurde. In **Connect German** (www.connectgerman.com) erhalten Sie Instruktionen, wie Sie die Playliste bekommen können.

Vor dem Hören Haben Sie einen besten Freund / eine beste Freundin? Was macht ihn oder sie so besonders? Was erwarten Sie, dass Ihr bester Freund oder Ihre beste Freundin für Sie tut? Was würden Sie für Ihren besten Freund oder Ihre beste Freundin tun?

Nach dem Hören Was ist richtig? Korrigieren Sie die fett gedruckten Wörter.

1. Du bist mir jederzeit ~~untreu~~. *loyal*
2. Keine **findet** mich so gut wie du.
3. Immer werden wir **uns ändern**.
4. Wir beide sind jung und frei und **reich**.
5. Wir stehen **Tag für Tag** auf der guten Seite.
6. Wir **weinen** über schlechte Zeiten.
7. Deine **Probleme** sind auch meine.
8. Du schlägst dich mit meinen **Freunden**.
9. Ich vertraue **mir** mehr als **dir**.
10. Du vergisst niemals, was das **Schöne** ist.

Miniwörterbuch

die **Welle**	wave
eine **Art**	a kind of
untreu	unfaithful
(sich) ändern	to change (oneself)
der **Schmerz, -en**	pain
der **Feind, -e**	enemy
vertrauen	to trust

Musikszene. Suggestion: Introduce the song as in previous chapters. See the IM for general suggestions. **Answers:** 1. loyal; 2. kennt; 3. so bleiben; 4. schön; 5. Jahr für Jahr; 6. lachen; 7. Schmerzen; 8. Feinden; 9. dir/mir; 10. Wichtige.

Filmlektüre
Nordwand

 Vor dem Lesen

Filmlektüre. Suggestion: (1) Ask the questions in *Vor dem Lesen* and some additional ones about the *Filmangaben* such as: *Wann ist der Film erschienen? In welchem Land? Was für ein Film ist es? Wie lange dauert er? Wer hat die Hauptrollen?* **(2)** Next, ask sts. to read the words in the *Miniwörterbuch*, to find them in the *Inhaltsangabe* and to underline them. Tell them that it will help them get a first impression of what the text will be about.
(Continued on pg 312.)

A. Beantworten Sie die folgenden Fragen.

1. Wer sind die Personen auf dem Poster? Wie alt sind sie? Was haben sie vor?
2. Schauen Sie sich den Hintergrund° an. Wie finden Sie das, was sie vorhaben? — *background*
3. Suchen Sie im Internet. Auf welchem Berg finden Sie die berühmte „Nordwand"? Wie heißt das Gebirge? In welchem Land ist dieser Berg?

Filmangaben

Titel: Nordwand
Genre: Drama
Erscheinungsjahr: 2008
Land: Deutschland, Österreich, Schweiz
Regisseur: Phillip Stölzl
Hauptrollen: Benno Fürmann,
Florian Lukas, Johanna Wokalek,
Georg Friedrich, Simon Schwarz,
Ulrich Tukur

Miniwörterbuch

die **Begebenheit**	event
spannend	suspenseful
das **Abenteuer**	adventure
die **Nordwand**	north wall; *here:* north face
erklettern	to climb
schaffen	to achieve
besteigen	to climb
jdn. aufrufen	to call on
etwas zu machen	someone to do something
der **Bergsteiger**	mountaineer
erfahren	experienced
überzeugt	convinced
bezwingen	to defeat
vorhaben	to intend
die **Vorbereitung**	preparation
überraschend	by surprise
der **Stein**	stone
ihren Lauf nehmen	to take its course
umschlagen	to change
der **Nullpunkt**	zero point on a scale measuring degrees Celsius
toben	to rampage
die **Lawine**	avalanche
der **Drang**	quest
der **Ruhm**	fame
der **Erfolg**	success

B. Lesen Sie die Wörter im Miniwörterbuch. Suchen Sie sie im Text und unterstreichen Sie sie.

Inhaltsangabe

Der Film basiert auf einer wahren Begebenheit und berichtet von dem spannenden und dramatischen Abenteuer einer Expedition, die 1936 stattgefunden hat. Das Ziel war es, die Eiger-Nordwand, die nicht nur extrem gefährlich sondern auch unter dem Namen „die Mordwand" bekannt war, zu erklettern. Schon viele hatten es probiert, doch bisher hatte es noch niemand geschafft, diese Wand zu besteigen. Als im Jahre 1936, kurz vor den Olympischen Spielen, die Nazis dazu aufrufen, wird es der Traum von vielen Bergsteigern aus ganz Europa. Auch die erfahrenen Kletterer Toni Kurz (Benno Fürmann) aus Berchtesgaden und Andreas Hinterstoißer (Florian Lukas) denken an nichts anderes und sind davon überzeugt, dass sie den Berg bezwingen können. Zwei ehrgeizige Österreicher, Willy (Simon Schwarz) und Edi (Georg Friedrich), haben es ebenso vor, und glauben, die ersten zu sein.

Während der Vorbereitungen am Fuß der Nordwand treffen Toni und Andi überraschend auf Luise (Johanna Wokalek), die sie schon aus ihrer frühen Kindheit kennen. Luise arbeitet jetzt als Fotoreporterin für eine Berliner Zeitung und soll über die Erstbesteigung berichten. Luise merkt bald, dass sie in Andi verliebt ist. Bald beginnt der Aufstieg und das Rennen beginnt. Zunächst läuft alles hervorragend, und beide Teams kommen schnell voran. Doch bereits am Anfang hat Willy einen Unfall. Ein Stein verletzt ihn am Kopf. Die Katastrophe nimmt ihren Lauf, als das Wetter umschlägt. Die Temperaturen fallen tief unter den Nullpunkt. Ein Schneesturm tobt. Lawinen drohen. Der Drang nach Ruhm und Erfolg führt zu einem Kampf auf Leben und Tod.

(Continued from pg 310.) **(3)** Go over the *Arbeit mit dem Text* making sure sts. understand all the words. Write unfamiliar words on the board with translations or convey the meanings in another manner. Ask sts. to read the text silently and answer the questions, then in pairs compare their answers. Follow up on sts.' answers and provide feedback if necessary. **(4)** Next work with the *Filmclip*. Before playing the scene, ask sts. to read through all the questions and go over the vocabulary. Play the scene until right before Andi and Toni reach the peak and take a break. Have sts. answer questions 1–3. Play the remainder of the scene and have students answer questions 4 and 5, and revisit 1. Answers are: 1. b, c, d; 2 b; 3. b; 4. a, b, c; 5. a. R; b. F. **(5)** Assign questions 1 and 2 in *Nach dem Lesen* for sts. to discuss in pairs. Assign question 3 as homework.

Arbeit mit dem Text

Richtig oder falsch? Verbessern Sie die falschen Aussagen.

___F___ 1. Der Film ist eine erfundene Geschichte.

___F___ 2. Bergsteigen war Teil der Olympischen Spiele.

___F___ 3. Luise lernt Toni und Andi während der Vorbereitungen am Fuß der Nordwand kennen.

___F___ 4. Toni hat sich sehr früh verletzt.

___R___ 5. Die Österreicher glauben, dass sie schneller sind als Toni und Andi.

___R___ 6. Viele Bergsteiger haben schon versucht, die Nordwand zu besteigen.

___F___ 7. Luise ist in Toni verliebt.

Filmclip 🎬

Szene: DVD, Kapitel 1, „Ersteigung eines Berges", 7:47–13:18 Min.

Toni und Andi verlassen die Kaserne° und Toni bereitet sich auf die Besteigung eines Berges vor. Die Szene zeigt, wie sie (Toni im blauen Hemd und Andi im rotkarierten Hemd) zusammen den Gipfel° der Zugspitze erklettern.

barracks

summit

Sehen Sie sich die Szene an und beantworten Sie die folgenden Fragen.

1. Welche Begrüßungen kommen vor? Kreuzen Sie alle richtigen Antworten an.
   - ☐ a. Grüß Gott!
   - ☐ b. Heil Hitler!
   - ☐ c. Servus!
   - ☐ d. Berg Heil!

2. Toni und Andi haben Probleme und können nicht weiter klettern. Toni will …
   - ☐ a. umkehren.
   - ☐ b. woanders hochklettern (unten überqueren).
   - ☐ c. direkt hochklettern.

3. Was passiert beim Hochklettern?
   - ☐ a. Andi rutscht aus°.
   - ☐ b. Ein Haken bricht los°.
   - ☐ c. Das Seil reißt.

4. Was machen die beiden, nachdem sie auf dem Gipfel angekommen sind? Kreuzen Sie alle richtigen Antworten an.
   - ☐ a. Toni markiert die Route in seinem Tagebuch.
   - ☐ b. Andi ruht sich aus.
   - ☐ c. Sie essen etwas.

5. Richtig oder falsch? Verbessern Sie die falschen Aussagen.
   - ___R___ a. Andi versucht, Toni zu überreden°, die Eiger-Nordwand zu besteigen.
   - ___F___ b. Toni sagt, dass er Schiss° hat.

convince

Angst

rutscht … *slips*

bricht … *breaks loose*

Nach dem Lesen

Beantworten Sie die folgenden Fragen.

1. Haben Sie schon einmal einen Berg bestiegen? Wie war dieses Erlebnis?

2. Hatten Sie schon einmal ein Erlebnis, das sehr aufregend oder gefährlich war? Was haben Sie gemacht?

3. Suchen Sie im Internet. Wie viele Menschen haben versucht, die Eiger-Nordwand zu besteigen? Wie viele sind dabei tödlich verunglückt?

Märchen

Vocabulary Display
These vocabulary words will help sts. work with the fairy tales in the following activities. Make sure sts. understand the importance of the fairy tale tradition in the German-speaking world. Although there is a lot of new vocabulary in this section, much of it is guessable because sts. are already familiar with the stories.

der König die Königin

die böse Hexe

der Frosch →
(der verwunschene Prinz)

der Schatz

die gute Fee

das Schloss

der Jäger

Die böse Stiefmutter vergiftet
Schneewittchen.

Der Prinz erlöst die
Prinzessin.

Der Prinz tötet den Drachen.

Situation 12 Schneewittchen

Bringen Sie die Sätze in die richtige Reihenfolge.

___2___ Die Königin starb bald darauf, und der König heiratete wieder.

___12___ Der Prinz und Schneewittchen heirateten, aber die böse Stiefmutter musste sterben.

___4___ Ein Jäger brachte Schneewittchen in den dunklen Wald.

___10___ Eines Tages kam ein Königssohn. Als er Schneewittchen sah, verliebte er sich in sie und wollte sie mit nach Hause nehmen.

___3___ Die böse Stiefmutter hasste Schneewittchen, weil sie so schön war.

___6___ Schneewittchen blieb bei den Zwergen und führte ihnen den Haushalt.

___1___ Es war einmal eine Königin, die bekam eine Tochter, die so weiß war wie Schnee, so rot wie Blut und so schwarzhaarig wie Ebenholz[1].

___7___ Die Stiefmutter hörte bald von ihrem Spiegel, dass Schneewittchen noch am Leben war.

___5___ Schneewittchen lief durch den Wald und kam zu den sieben Zwergen.

___9___ Die Zwerge weinten und legten sie in einen gläsernen Sarg.

___11___ Als seine Diener den Sarg wegtrugen, stolperte ein Diener. Das giftige Apfelstück rutschte aus Schneewittchens Hals und sie wachte auf.

___8___ Die Stiefmutter verkaufte Schneewittchen einen giftigen Apfel, Schneewittchen biss hinein und fiel tot um.

[1]ebony

Situation 13 Bildgeschichte: Dornröschen

Sit. 13. Use only for listening comprehension, i.e., read the fairy tale to your sts. and then do the receptive recall phase by reading the sentences out of order and asking: *Welches Bild zeigt: ...?* As follow-up, distribute 12 slips of paper, with one sentence from the tale written on each, to twelve sts. or groups of sts. Then, sts. line themselves up according to their sequence of sentences.

Sentences for narration series: **(1)** *Es waren einmal ein König und eine Königin, die wollten so gern ein Kind.* **(2)** *Als die Königin endlich eine Tochter bekam, war die Freude groß.* **(3)** *Sie veranstalteten ein Fest und luden zwölf Feen ein, vergaßen aber die dreizehnte.* **(4)** *Die dreizehnte Fee kam und verwünschte Dornröschen. Sie sollte sich an einer Spindel stechen und sterben.* **(5)** *Die zwölfte Fee änderte den bösen Wunsch. Dornröschen sollte nur hundert Jahre schlafen.* **(6)** *Als Dornröschen fünfzehn Jahre alt war, ging der böse Wunsch in Erfüllung. Sie stach sich an einer Spindel und fiel in einen tiefen Schlaf.* **(7)** *Mit ihr schlief das ganze Schloss ein, alle Menschen und alle Tiere.* **(8)** *Rund um das Schloss wuchs eine große Dornenhecke.* **(9)** *Als 100 Jahre vorbei waren, kam ein junger Prinz zur Hecke und die Dornen verwandelten sich in Blumen.* **(10)** *Er ging ins Schloss, fand Dornröschen und als er sie küsste, wachte sie auf.* **(11)** *Alle anderen Menschen und alle Tiere wachten auch auf.* **(12)** *Der Prinz und Dornröschen heirateten. Und wenn sie nicht gestorben sind, dann leben sie noch heute.*

Situation 14 Was ist passiert?

Sit. 14. This activity provides examples of the past perfect tense with *nachdem.* **Answers:** 1. d, 2. g, 3. e, 4. h, 5. f, 6. a, 7. c, 8. b.

1. Nachdem Schneewittchen den giftigen Apfel gegessen hatte,
2. Nachdem Hänsel und Gretel durch den dunklen Wald gelaufen waren,
3. Nachdem die Prinzessin den Frosch geküsst hatte,
4. Nachdem die Müllerstochter keinen Schmuck mehr hatte,
5. Nachdem Aschenputtel alle Linsen[1] eingesammelt[2] hatte,
6. Nachdem der Wolf die Großmutter gefressen hatte,
7. Nachdem der Prinz Dornröschen geküsst hatte,
8. Nachdem Rumpelstilzchen seinen Namen gehört hatte,

a. legte er sich in ihr Bett.
b. wurde er sehr wütend.
c. wachte sie auf.
d. fiel sie tot um.
e. verwandelte er sich in einen Prinzen.
f. ging sie auf den Ball.
g. kamen sie zum Haus der Hexe.
h. versprach sie Rumpelstilzchen ihr erstes Kind.

[1]*lentils* [2]*gathered*

Situationen **315**

Sit. 15. Have sts. work in groups to match the quotations with the correct fairy tale. **Answers:**
1. Hänsel und Gretel, 2. Schneewittchen,
3. Rotkäppchen, 4. Dornröschen, 5. Der Froschkönig,
6. Aschenputtel, 7. Rumpelstilzchen.

Aus welchem Märchen ist das?

Dornröschen

Rumpelstilzchen

Aschenputtel

Der Froschkönig

Rotkäppchen

Hänsel und Gretel

Schneewittchen

1. „Knusper, knusper, knäuschen, wer knuspert an meinem Häuschen?" „Der Wind, der Wind, das himmlische Kind."

2. „Spieglein, Spieglein an der Wand, wer ist die Schönste im ganzen Land?" „Frau Königin, Ihr seid die Schönste hier, aber die junge Königin ist tausendmal schöner als Ihr."

3. „Ei, Großmutter, was hast du für große Ohren!" „Damit ich dich besser hören kann." „Ei, Großmutter, was hast du für große Augen!" „Damit ich dich besser sehen kann." „Ei, Großmutter, was hast du für ein großes Maul!" „Damit ich dich besser fressen kann."

4. „Die Königstochter soll an ihrem fünfzehnten Geburtstag in einen tiefen Schlaf fallen, der hundert Jahre dauert."

5. „Wenn ich am Tisch neben dir sitzen und von deinem Teller essen und aus deinem Becher trinken und in deinem Bett schlafen darf, dann will ich deinen goldenen Ball aus dem Brunnen heraufholen."

6. „Rucke di guh, rucke di guh, Blut ist im Schuh: Der Schuh ist zu klein, die rechte Braut sitzt noch daheim."

7. „Heute back ich, morgen brau ich, übermorgen hol' ich der Königin ihr Kind: ach, wie gut, dass niemand weiß, dass ich _____ heiß!"

Situation 16 Zum Schreiben: Es war einmal ...

Sit. 16. Do first in class as an oral group activity. Sts. can practice building simple story lines and working with known vocabulary and structures. Start them off with *Es war einmal ...* Tell sts. something about the structure of fairy tales: Time and place are of no importance. There are good characters, bad characters, and a problem–often caused by evil forces–that has to be solved by the hero or heroine. Encourage sts. to be creative.

AA. You could also ask sts. to illustrate their stories and then present them to the class. This could be a group project.

Lektüre: Ask sts. to look at the painting and ask them what fairy tale it depicts. Ask them to tell you who the main characters are (point them to the thumbnail pictures in the four corners of the painting for help). Then ask sts. to complete *Vor dem Lesen A*. Explain the task and ask them to work in pairs or small groups. Elicit answers giving appropriate feedback. Then ask sts. to complete *Vor dem Lesen B*. Ask them to study the *Miniwörterbuch*, to find the vocabulary items in the text of the fairy tale and to underline them. Ask them to do the same for the words that are glossed in *Vor dem Lesen A*. Next, ask sts. to work in pairs or small groups again and to complete *Arbeit mit dem Text A*. Ask them first to make sure they understand the sentences before they look for them in the text. Help them with unknown words that are not glossed or in the *Miniwörterbuch*. As follow-up, read the fairy tale to your sts., asking them to stop you whenever you read one of the sentences for which they were asked to determine who said it; when they stop you, have them tell you who the speaker was. Assign *Arbeit mit dem Text B* and *C* as homework. Follow up on these activities in the next class period. Then ask sts. to prepare the *Nach dem Lesen* activity in groups of five. Allow at least 15 minutes for the group work. Then ask one or two groups to act out the scene in front of the class.

Schreiben Sie ein Märchen. Wählen Sie aus den vier Kategorien etwas aus oder erfinden Sie etwas.

DIE GUTEN

eine schöne Prinzessin
ein armer Student
eine tapfere Königin
ein treuer Diener
?

DIE BÖSEN

eine böse Hexe
eine grausame Professorin
ein hungriger Drache
ein böser Stiefvater
?

DIE AUSGANGSLAGE

frisst Menschen und Tiere
hat lange Zeit geschlafen
bekommt immer nur Fs
vergiftet das Wasser
?

DIE AUFGABE

drei Rätsel lösen
mit einem Riesen kämpfen
etwas Verlorenes wiederfinden
eine List erfinden
?

Lektüre

Vor dem Lesen

A. Märchenfiguren. Märchen, auch wenn man sie nicht kennt, sind vorhersagbar[1]. Im Märchen vom Rotkäppchen kommen vier wichtige Figuren vor: ein kleines Mädchen namens Rotkäppchen, ihre Großmutter, der Wolf und der Jäger. Welche Eigenschaften und Tätigkeiten sind typisch für sie? Schreiben Sie neben jede Eigenschaft oder Tätigkeit, ob sie typisch für Rotkäppchen, die Großmutter, den Wolf oder den Jäger ist.

1. Er hat große Ohren und ein großes Maul.
2. Er ist listig[2].
3. Er schießt mit seinem Gewehr.
4. Er schnarcht sehr laut.
5. Er schneidet ihm den Bauch auf.
6. Er sieht nach, ob jemand was fehlt[3].
7. Er verschlingt[4] die Großmutter.
8. Er zieht ihm den Pelz ab[5].
9. Er zieht ihre Kleider an.
10. Jeder hat sie lieb.
11. Sie guckt sich gern um[6].
12. Sie hört gern die Vöglein singen.
13. Sie ist klein und süß.
14. Sie ist krank und schwach.
15. Sie pflückt gern Blumen.
16. Sie trinkt gern Wein und isst gern Kuchen.
17. Sie wohnt draußen im Wald.

B. Suchen Sie die Wörter im Miniwörterbuch im Text und unterstreichen Sie sie.

[1]*predictable* [2]*cunning* [3]ob ... *whether someone needs something* [4]*devours* [5]zieht den Pelz ab *skins*
[6]guckt sich um *explores*

das **Maul**	mouth (*of animals*)
das **Gewehr**	rifle
schnarchen	to snore
der **Bauch**	belly
pflücken	to pick
zerbrechen	to break
der **Korb**	basket
zart	tender
packen	*here:* to grab
erschrocken	startled, scared
das **Dorf**	village
verraten	to tell (*a secret*)
atmen	to breathe

Lesehilfe

The fairy tale "Rotkäppchen" is one of many fairy tales that are well-known across cultures. Just as in English, a fairy tale in German typically contains certain formulaic expressions or phrases. English fairy tales often begin with the phrase *Once upon a time*. Look at the beginning of this fairy tale to see how German fairy tales typically begin.

Fairy tales in German are typically written and told in the simple past tense. As you read this one, you will encounter many such verb forms. Avoid the temptation to look them up upon the first reading; you will deal with them during the **Arbeit mit dem Text** activities at the end of the reading.

Rotkäppchen – Ein Märchen der Gebrüder Grimm

Es war einmal ein kleines, süßes Mädchen, das hatte jeder lieb, der sie nur ansah, am allerliebsten aber ihre Großmutter, die wusste gar nicht, was sie dem Kind alles geben sollte. Einmal schenkte sie dem Mädchen ein Käppchen aus rotem Samt, und weil es Rotkäppchen so gut stand und sie nichts anders mehr tragen wollte, hieß sie nur das Rotkäppchen. Eines Tages sprach ihre Mutter zu ihr: "Komm, Rotkäppchen, da hast du ein Stück Kuchen und eine Flasche Wein, bring das der Großmutter hinaus; sie ist krank und schwach. Dadurch wird sie zu Kräften kommen. Gehe los, bevor es heiß wird, und wenn du aus dem Dorf gehst, so geh anständig und komm nicht vom Weg ab, sonst fällst du und zerbrichst das Glas, und die Großmutter hat nichts. Und wenn du in ihr Haus kommst, vergiss nicht, guten Morgen zu sagen."

"Ich werde schon alles richtig machen", sagte Rotkäppchen zur Mutter und gab ihr die Hand darauf. Die Großmutter aber wohnte draußen im Wald, eine halbe Stunde vom Dorf. Als Rotkäppchen in den Wald kam, begegnete ihr der Wolf. Rotkäppchen aber wusste nicht, was das für ein böses Tier war, und fürchtete sich nicht vor ihm. "Guten Tag, Rotkäppchen", sprach er. "Guten Tag, Wolf." "Wo gehst du so früh hin, Rotkäppchen?" "Zur Großmutter." "Was trägst du in deinem Korb?" "Kuchen und Wein: gestern haben wir gebacken, davon soll sich die kranke und schwache Großmutter etwas stärken." "Rotkäppchen, wo wohnt deine Großmutter?" "Noch eine gute Viertelstunde weiter im Wald hinein, unter den drei großen Eichbäumen, da steht ihr Haus. Da unten sind die Nusshecken, das wirst du ja kennen", sagte Rotkäppchen. Der Wolf dachte bei sich: "Das junge zarte Ding, das ist ein fetter Bissen, der wird noch besser schmecken als die Alte: ich muss es listig anfangen, damit ich beide bekomme." Da ging er ein Weilchen neben Rotkäppchen her, dann sprach er: "Rotkäppchen, sieh einmal die schönen Blumen, die hier überall stehen, warum guckst du dich nicht um? Ich glaube, du hörst gar nicht, wie die Vöglein so lieblich singen? Du läufst als wärst du auf dem Weg zur Schule. Dabei ist es so lustig im Wald!"

Rotkäppchen schlug die Augen auf, und als sie sah, wie die Sonnenstrahlen durch die Bäume hin und her tanzten und alles voll schöner Blumen war, dachte sie: "Wenn ich der Großmutter einen frischen Strauß mitbringe, der wird ihr auch Freude machen. Es ist noch so früh am Tag, dass ich doch nicht zu spät komme." Rotkäppchen lief vom Weg in den Wald hinein und suchte Blumen. Und wenn sie eine Blume gepflückt hatte, meinte sie, weiter im Wald steht eine schönere, lief dorthin, und geriet immer tiefer in den Wald hinein. Der Wolf aber ging geradeswegs zum Haus der Großmutter und klopfte an die Tür. "Wer ist da?" "Rotkäppchen, ich bringe Kuchen und Wein. Mach auf!" "Die Tür ist offen, komm herein", rief die Großmutter, "ich bin zu schwach und kann nicht aufstehen." Der Wolf drückte auf die Klinke, die Tür sprang auf. Er ging, ohne ein Wort zu sagen, direkt zum Bett der Großmutter und verschluckte sie. Dann zog er ihre Kleider an, setzte ihre Haube auf, legte sich in ihr Bett und zog die Vorhänge zu.

Rotkäppchen aber suchte immer noch Blumen, und als sie so viele gesammelt hatte, dass sie keine mehr tragen konnte, fiel ihr die Großmutter wieder ein, und sie machte sich auf den Weg zu ihr. Sie wunderte sich, dass die Tür von Großmutters Haus offen stand. Als sie in das Haus trat, so kam es ihr seltsam darin vor. Rotkäppchen dachte: "Ach, du meine Güte! Warum graut es mich heute so, obwohl ich sonst so gerne bei der Großmutter bin?" Rotkäppchen rief "Guten Morgen", bekam aber keine Antwort. Darauf ging sie zum Bett und zog die Vorhänge zurück. Da lag die Großmutter und hatte die Haube tief ins Gesicht gezogen und sah so wunderlich aus. "Ei, Großmutter, was hast du für große Ohren!" "Dass ich dich besser hören kann." "Ei, Großmutter, was hast du für große Augen!" "Dass ich dich besser sehen kann." "Ei, Großmutter, was hast du für große Hände!" "Dass ich dich besser packen kann." "Aber, Großmutter, was hast du für ein entsetzlich großes Maul!" "Dass ich dich besser fressen kann." Kaum hatte der Wolf das gesagt, sprang er aus dem Bett und verschlang das arme Rotkäppchen.

Als der Wolf seine Gelüste gestillt hatte, legte er sich wieder ins Bett, schlief ein
und fing an, sehr laut zu schnarchen. Da ging der Jäger an dem Haus vorbei und
dachte: „Wie die alte Frau schnarcht, ich muss mal sehen, ob ihr etwas fehlt." Da trat
er in das Haus, und als er zum Bett kam, sah er, dass der Wolf darin lag. „Finde ich
dich hier, du alter Sünder", sagte er, „ich habe dich lange gesucht." Nun wollte er sein
Gewehr anlegen, da fiel ihm ein, dass der Wolf die Großmutter vielleicht gefressen
hatte und er könnte sie noch retten. Der Jäger schoss nicht, sondern nahm eine Schere
und begann, dem schlafenden Wolf den Bauch aufzuschneiden. Als er ein paar Schnitte
gemacht hatte, sah er das rote Käppchen leuchten, und noch ein paar Schnitte, da
sprang das Mädchen heraus und rief: „Ach, wie war ich erschrocken! Es war so dunkel
in dem Bauch des Wolfes!" Und dann kam die alte Großmutter auch noch lebendig
heraus und konnte kaum atmen. Rotkäppchen aber holte schnell große Steine. Damit
füllten sie den Leib des Wolfes, und als er aufwachte, wollte er davon springen. Aber
die Steine waren so schwer, dass er zurück in das Bett fiel und nie wieder aufwachte.

Da waren alle drei vergnügt: Der Jäger zog dem Wolf den Pelz ab und ging damit
nach Hause. Die Großmutter aß den Kuchen und trank den Wein, den Rotkäppchen
ihr gebracht hatte, und erholte sich wieder. Rotkäppchen aber dachte: „Ich werde nie
wieder allein vom Weg in den Wald laufen, wenn die Mutter es mir verboten hat."

—frei nach den Gebrüdern Grimm

Arbeit mit dem Text

A. Wer sagt das? Lesen Sie den Text und finden Sie heraus, wer die folgenden Sätze denkt oder sagt.

1. Geh anständig¹ und komm nicht vom Weg ab², sonst fällst du und zerbrichst das Glas.
2. Ich werde schon alles richtig machen.
3. Was trägst du in deinem Korb?
4. Ihr Haus steht unter den drei großen Eichbäumen³.
5. Das junge, zarte Ding, das wird noch besser schmecken als die Alte.
6. Ich muss es listig anfangen, damit ich beide bekomme.
7. Du läufst als wärst du⁴ auf dem Weg zur Schule.
8. Es ist noch so früh am Tag, dass ich doch nicht zu spät komme.
9. Die Tür ist offen, komm herein.
10. Ach, du meine Güte⁵! Warum graut es mich⁶ heute so?
11. Was hast du für große Augen!
12. Dass ich dich besser packen kann.
13. Wie die alte Frau schnarcht, ich muss mal sehen, ob ihr etwas fehlt.
14. Finde ich dich hier, du alter Sünder⁷, ich habe dich lange gesucht.
15. Ach, wie war ich erschrocken!
16. Ich werde nie wieder allein vom Weg in den Wald laufen.

B. Richtig oder falsch? Verbessern Sie die falschen Aussagen.

_____ 1. Die Mutter schenkte ihrer Tochter ein Käppchen aus rotem Samt⁸.

_____ 2. Rotkäppchen versprach ihrer Mutter, dass sie alles richtig machen wird.

_____ 3. Die Großmutter wohnte draußen im Wald, eine Stunde vom Dorf.

_____ 4. Rotkäppchen hatte Angst vor dem Wolf.

_____ 5. Rotkäppchen verriet dem Wolf, wo ihre Großmutter wohnt.

_____ 6. Der Wolf fraß Rotkäppchen und ging dann zum Haus ihrer Großmutter.

¹properly ²abkommen *diverge* ³*oak trees* ⁴als wärst du *as though you were* ⁵*goodness* ⁶graut ... *am I afraid*
⁷du ... *you old rascal* ⁸*velvet*

_____ 7. Rotkäppchen lief immer tiefer in den Wald hinein, weil sie immer mehr Blumen pflücken wollte.

_____ 8. Der Wolf machte das Licht aus und legte sich ins Bett der Großmutter.

_____ 9. Als Rotkäppchen zum Haus der Großmutter kam, war die Tür verschlossen.

_____ 10. Als der Jäger zum Haus der Großmutter kam, war alles ruhig.

_____ 11. Der Jäger schoss den Wolf in den Bauch.

_____ 12. Als die Großmutter aus dem Bauch des Wolfes heraus kam, konnte sie kaum noch atmen.

_____ 13. Rotkäppchen füllte den Leib[1] des Wolfes mit großen Steinen.

_____ 14. Der Wolf lief davon und wurde[2] nie wieder gesehen.

_____ 15. Rotkäppchen wollte nie wieder etwas tun, was ihr ihre Mutter verboten hatte.

C. Suchen Sie die folgenden Wörter im Text. Ergänzen Sie die Tabelle mit Zeilennummer, Infinitiv und englischer Übersetzung.

Präteritum	Zeilennummer	Infinitiv	Englisch
ansah			
wusste			
stand			
sprach			
gab			
kam			
dachte			
ging			
schlug … auf			
lief			
geriet … hinein			
rief			
sprang … auf			
zog … an			
zog … zu			
fiel … ein			
trat			
kam … vor			
bekam			
zog … zurück			
lag			
sah … aus			
schlief … ein			
fing … an			

[1]body [2]was

Präteritum	Zeilennummer	Infinitiv	Englisch
schoss			
begann			
sprang ... heraus			
fiel			
zog ... ab			
aß			
trank			

Nach dem Lesen

Vor Gericht[1] (Alternativende). Der Wolf hat überlebt[2] und bringt Rotkäppchen vor Gericht. Sie soll ins Gefängnis[3], weil sie seinen Bauch mit Steinen gefüllt hat und ihn umbringen[4] wollte. Spielen Sie die Szene im Gericht mit verteilten Rollen. Sie brauchen einen Richter[5], der die Fragen stellt. Rotkäppchen erzählt ihre Geschichte, der Wolf erzählt seine Geschichte. Die Großmutter und der Jäger sind die Zeugen[6] und erzählen, was sie gesehen und erlebt haben. Am Ende spricht der Richter sein Urteil[7].

[1]Vor ... *In court* [2]*survived* [3]*prison* [4]*kill* [5]*judge* [6]*witnesses* [7]spricht sein Urteil *reaches his verdict*

Videoecke

Perspektiven

Was ist gut, was ist schlecht an der Schule in Deutschland?

Aufgabe 1 Gut oder schlecht?

Was finden die Leute gut, was finden sie schlecht? Schreiben Sie *gut* oder *schlecht* neben die Aussagen.

Gut finde ich, dass man nicht dafür bezahlen muss.

1. Die Materialien sind kostenlos.   gut
2. Es gibt unterschiedliche Systeme in den Bundesländern.   schlecht
3. Man lernt Inhalte, die für das spätere Leben nicht so nützlich sind.   schlecht
4. Jeder kann die Schule besuchen, die er will.   gut
5. Es werden immer weniger Lehrer eingestellt.   schlecht
6. Die Klassen sind groß.   schlecht
7. Die Lehrer sind gut ausgebildet.   gut
8. Es gibt keine Schuluniformen.   schlecht
9. Die Schulen sind öffentlich.   gut
10. Es gibt ein dreigliedriges Schulsystem.   schlecht

Interviews

Carolyn

Martin

- Wann hast du Abitur gemacht?
- Hattest du gute Noten?
- In welchen Fächern warst du besonders gut?
- Was hat dir daran gefallen?
- Welchen Lehrer oder welche Lehrerin fandest du besonders gut? Warum?
- Erzähl etwas, was dieser Lehrer gemacht hat.

Aufgabe 2 Die Lehrergeschichte

Auf wen treffen die folgenden Aussagen zu, auf den Lehrer von Carolyn oder auf den Lehrer von Martin? Schreiben Sie C für Carolyn oder M für Martin neben die Aussagen.

1. Er war sehr engagiert. C
2. Er hat auf Schulfesten immer aufgepasst. C
3. Er war mit seinen Schülern auf Klassenfahrt in Amsterdam. M
4. Einmal hat ihm die Musik sehr gut gefallen. C
5. Er hat im Hotel ein Bier ausgegeben. M
6. Er ist mit ihm/ihr ins Gespräch gekommen. M
7. Er hat auf der Tanzfläche eine ganze Nacht lang getanzt. C
8. Auch Lehrer sind nur Menschen. M

Aufgabe 3 Abitur

Wann haben sie Abitur gemacht? Sehen Sie sich das Video an und schreiben Sie Carolyns und Martins Antworten auf.

	Carolyn	**Martin**
Wann hat sie/er Abitur gemacht?	2005	2004
Hatte sie/er gute Noten?	ja	nein
In welchen Fächern war sie/er besonders gut?	Englisch, Geografie, Kunst, Musik	Englisch, Geschichte
Was hat ihr/ihm daran gefallen?	Sprache und Kultur eines anderen Landes; Entstehung von Gebirgen und vom Wetter	historische Ereignisse beeinflussen die heutige Zeit; mit anderen Leuten in einer zweiten Sprache zu kommunizieren
Welche/n Lehrer/in fand sie/er besonders gut?	Deutschlehrer	Englischlehrer
Warum?	lustig, sarkastisch, Unterricht belebt	konnte die Sprache sehr gut; war darauf bedacht, dass die Schüler die Sprache gut lernen

Aufgabe 4 Interview

Interviewen Sie eine Partnerin oder einen Partner. Stellen Sie dieselben Fragen.

Wortschatz

Kindheit und Jugend — Childhood and Youth

die Grundschule, -n	elementary school
die Klasse, -n	grade (level)
die Note, -n	grade
der Abschluss	graduation
der Ballettunterricht	ballet class
das Klassentreffen, -	class reunion
das Mädchen, -	girl

Ähnliche Wörter

der Clown, -s; der Spielplatz, ⸚e; der Teddy, -s; der Zirkus, -se

Märchen — Fairy Tales

die Braut, ⸚e	bride
die Fee, -n	fairy
die Hexe, -n (R)	witch
die Königin, -nen	queen
die List, -en	deception, trick
der Brunnen, -	well; fountain
der Diener, -	servant
der Drache, -n (wk. masc.)	dragon
der Jäger, -	hunter
der König, -e	king
der Riese, -n (wk. masc.)	giant
der Sarg, ⸚e	coffin
der Schatz, ⸚e	treasure
der Zwerg, -e	dwarf
das Märchen, -	fairy tale
das Rätsel, -	puzzle, riddle
ein Rätsel lösen	to solve a puzzle/riddle
das Schloss, ⸚er	castle
erlösen	to rescue, free
kämpfen	to fight
klettern, ist geklettert	to climb
küssen	to kiss
sterben, stirbt, starb, ist gestorben	to die
töten	to kill
träumen	to dream
um·fallen, fällt ... um, fiel ... um, ist umgefallen	to fall over
vergiften	to poison
sich verwandeln in (+ akk.)	to change into
verwünschen	to curse, cast a spell on
böse	evil, mean
giftig	poisonous
gläsern	glass
grausam	cruel

heimlich	secret
tapfer	brave
tot	dead
treu	loyal, true
verwunschen	cursed; enchanted

Ähnliche Wörter

die Prinzessin, -nen; die Stiefmutter, ⸚; der Prinz, -en (wk. masc.); der Stiefvater, ⸚; das Blut; das Feuer, -

Natur und Tiere — Nature and Animals

der Baum, ⸚e	tree
der Frosch, ⸚e	frog
der Schnee	snow
das Maul, ⸚er	mouth (of an animal)
das Pferd, -e (R)	horse
beißen, biss, gebissen	to bite
fressen, frisst, fraß, gefressen	to eat (said of an animal)
füttern	to feed
pflücken	to pick

Ähnliche Wörter

der Busch, ⸚e; der Dorn, -en; der Elefant, -en (wk. masc.); der Wind, -e; der Wolf, ⸚e; das Schwein, -e

Sonstige Substantive — Other Nouns

die Direktorin, -nen	female (school) principal, director
die Einbrecherin, -nen	female burglar
die Feier, -n	celebration, party
die Fensterscheibe, -n	windowpane
die Freude, -n	joy, pleasure
die Mannschaft, -en	team
die Baseballmannschaft, -en	baseball team
die Radtour, -en	bicycle tour
die Taschenlampe, -n	flashlight
die Verspätung, -en	delay
der Ärger	trouble
der Becher, -	cup, mug
der Direktor, -en	male (school) principal, director
der Einbrecher, -	male burglar
der Flug, ⸚e	flight
der Gruß, ⸚e	greeting
der Hals, ⸚e	neck; throat
der Liebesroman, -e	romance novel
der Schatten, -	shadow, shade
der Schlüssel, -	key
der Hausschlüssel, -	house key

der Zaun, ⸚e	fence
das Geräusch, -e	sound, noise
das Leben, -	life
am Leben sein	to be alive
das Loch, ⸚er	hole

Ähnliche Wörter

die Ballerina, -s; der Haushalt, -e; der Schlaf;
das Video, -s; das Werk, -e

Sonstige Verben	Other Verbs
ändern	to change
sich erinnern (an + *akk.*)	to remember
eröffnen	to open
hassen	to hate
holen	to fetch, (go) get
los·fahren, fährt ... los, fuhr ... los, ist losgefahren (R)	to drive/ride off
rutschen, ist gerutscht	to slide, slip
schimpfen	to cuss; to scold
stehlen, stiehlt, stahl, gestohlen	to steal
stolpern, ist gestolpert	to trip
streiten, gestritten	to argue, quarrel
übersetzen	to translate
sich unterhalten, unterhält, unterhielt, unterhalten	to converse
sich verlieben (in + *akk.*)	to fall in love (with)
verpassen	to miss
sich verstecken	to hide
vor·lesen, liest ... vor, las ... vor, vorgelesen	to read aloud
wachsen, wächst, wuchs, ist gewachsen	to grow
zerreißen, zerriss, zerrissen	to tear

Ähnliche Wörter

fallen, fällt, fiel, ist gefallen; planen; weg·tragen, trägt ... weg, trug ... weg, weggetragen

Adjektive und Adverbien	Adjectives and Adverbs
arm	poor
bald	soon
bald darauf	soon thereafter
begabt	gifted
daheim	at home
damals	back then
endlich	finally
hinein	in(ward)
leise	quiet(ly)
mitten	in the middle
neulich	recently
plötzlich	suddenly
streng	strict
übermorgen	the day after tomorrow
unterwegs	on the road
verboten	forbidden, prohibited
vorbei	past, over
zufällig	accidental(ly)
zurück	back

Ähnliche Wörter

hungrig, liberal, schwarzhaarig

Sonstige Wörter und Ausdrücke	Other Words and Expressions
denn	for, because
gegen (+ *akk.*)	against
nachdem	after (*conj.*)
neben	next to
nichts	nothing

Strukturen und Übungen

9.1 The conjunction *als* with dependent-clause word order

9.1. *Als* was introduced as a lexical item in *Kapitel 5* (*Sit. 6*). It is presented here formally as a subordinating conjunction. Section 9.3 completes the introduction of *als* by contrasting it with *wenn* and *wann*.

> **Wissen Sie noch?**
>
> An **als**-clause is a type of dependent clause. As in other dependent clauses, the conjugated verb appears at the end of the clause.
>
> Review grammar 3.4 and 7.1.

The conjunction **als** (*when*) is commonly used to express that two events or circumstances happened at the same time. The **als**-clause establishes a point of reference in the past for an action or event described in the main clause.

Als ich zwölf Jahre alt war, bin ich zum ersten Mal allein verreist.
When I was twelve years old, I traveled alone for the first time.

When an **als**-clause introduces a sentence, it occupies the first position. Consequently, the conjugated verb in the main clause occupies the second position and the subject of the main clause is in the third position.

$$\underline{\text{Als ich 12 Jahre alt } \textbf{war,}} \quad \overset{1}{\underset{}{}} \quad \overset{2}{\textbf{bin}} \; \overset{3}{\textbf{ich}} \text{ zum ersten Mal allein verreist.}$$

Note that the conjugated verb in the **als**-clause appears at the end of that clause.

Übung 1   Meilensteine

Üb. 1. Assign for homework and discuss in class. It should be interesting to compare sts.' answers in class. Ask 4 or 5 sts. to read their 1st line, then their 2nd, and so forth.

Schreiben Sie 10–15 Sätze über Ihr Leben. Beginnen Sie jeden Satz mit **als.**

MODELL: Als ich eins war, habe ich laufen gelernt.
Als ich zwei war, habe ich sprechen gelernt.
Als ich fünf war, bin ich in die Schule gekommen.
Als ich …

9.2 The simple past tense of *werden,* the modal verbs, and *wissen*

Use the simple past tense of **haben, sein, werden, wissen,** and the modal verbs in both writing and conversation.

9.2. *Präteritum.* The simple past of *haben* and *sein* was introduced in 7.5. Here, we introduce additional verbs that generally use the simple past tense for conversation. Sts. will be familiar with some of these forms, having heard them in your speech. They became acquainted with verbs with identical *ich*- and *er/sie/es*-forms when they learned modal verbs in *Kapitel 3.* The use of the simple past tense of strong and weak verbs in written texts is presented in Section 9.4.

The simple past tense is preferred over the perfect tense with some frequently used verbs, even in conversational German. These verbs include **haben, sein, werden,** the modal verbs, and the verb **wissen.**

Frau Gretter **war** sehr begabt.
In der Schule **wusste** sie immer alles.
Sie **hatte** viele Freundinnen und Freunde.

Mrs. Gretter was very talented.
In school she always knew everything.
She had many friends.

The conjugations of **werden,** the modal verbs, and **wissen** appear on the following pages. For **haben** and **sein,** refer back to **Strukturen 7.5.** Notice that the **ich**- and **er/sie/es**-forms are the same.

A. The Verb **werden**

Michael **wurde** Tierpfleger.
Im August **wurde** er sehr krank.

Michael became an animal caretaker.
In August he became very sick.

werden			
ich	wurde	*wir*	wurden
du	wurdest	*ihr*	wurdet
Sie	wurden	*Sie*	wurden
er *sie* *es*	wurde	*sie*	wurden

B. Modal Verbs

To form the simple past tense of modal verbs, use the stem, drop any umlauts, and add -**te**- plus the appropriate ending.

können → könn → konn → konnte → du konntest

Gestern **wollten** wir ins Kino gehen.
Mehmet **musste** jeden Tag um sechs aufstehen.
Helga und Sigrid **durften** mit sechs Jahren noch nicht fernsehen.

Yesterday, we wanted to go to the movies.
Mehmet had to get up at six every morning.
When they were six, Helga and Sigrid weren't yet allowed to watch TV.

Here are the simple past-tense forms of the modal verbs.

	können	**müssen**	**dürfen**	**sollen**	**wollen**	**mögen**
ich	konnte	musste	durfte	sollte	wollte	mochte
du	konntest	musstest	durftest	solltest	wolltest	mochtest
Sie	konnten	mussten	durften	sollten	wollten	mochten
er *sie* *es*	konnte	musste	durfte	sollte	wollte	mochte
wir	konnten	mussten	durften	sollten	wollten	mochten
ihr	konntet	musstet	durftet	solltet	wolltet	mochtet
Sie	konnten	mussten	durften	sollten	wollten	mochten
sie	konnten	mussten	durften	sollten	wollten	mochten

Note the consonant change in the past tense of **mögen: mochte.**

C. The Verb **wissen**

The forms of the verb **wissen** are similar to those of the modal verbs.

Ich **wusste** nicht, dass du keine
Erdbeeren magst.

*I didn't know that you don't
like strawberries.*

Here are the simple past-tense forms.

wissen			
ich	wusste	*wir*	wussten
du	wusstest	*ihr*	wusstet
Sie	wussten	*Sie*	wussten
er *sie* *es*	wusste	*sie*	wussten

Übung 2   Fragen und Antworten

Üb. 2. Assign this exercise and *Üb. 3* for homework and check in class by having sts. take the roles. *Üb. 2* requires only 1st-person-singular forms.

Hier sind die Fragen. Was sind die Antworten?

MODELL: Lydia, warum bist du nicht mit ins Kino gegangen? (nicht können)
→ Ich konnte nicht.

1. Ernst, warum bist du nicht mit zum Schwimmen gekommen? (nicht dürfen)
2. Maria, warum bist du nicht gekommen? (nicht wollen)
3. Jens, gestern war Juttas Geburtstag! (das / nicht wissen)
4. Jutta, warum hast du eine neue Frisur? (eine/wollen)
5. Jochen, warum hast du das Essen nicht gekocht? (das / nicht sollen)

Übung 3   Minidialoge

Setzen Sie Modalverben oder **wissen** ein.

1. SILVIA: Was hast du gemacht, wenn du nicht zur Schule gehen _____ᵃ,
Jürgen?
JÜRGEN: Ich habe gesagt: „Ich bin krank."
SILVIA: Haben deine Eltern das geglaubt?
JÜRGEN: Nein, meine Mutter _____ᵇ immer, was los war.
2. ERNST: Hans, warum bist du gestern nicht auf den Spielplatz gekommen?
HANS: Ich _____ᵃ nicht. Ich habe eine Fünf in Mathe geschrieben und
_____ᵇ zu Hause bleiben.
ERNST: Schade. Wir _____ᶜ Fußball spielen, aber dann _____ᵈ wir nicht
genug Spieler finden.
3. HERR RUF: Guten Tag, Frau Gretter. Tut mir leid, dass ich neulich nicht zu
Ihrer kleinen Feier kommen _____ᵃ. Aber ich _____ᵇ meine alte Tante
in Würzburg besuchen.
FRAU GRETTER: Ja, wirklich schade. Ich _____ᶜ gar nicht, dass Sie eine Tante
in Würzburg haben.
HERR RUF: Sie zieht diese Woche nach Düsseldorf zu ihrer Tochter, und
ich _____ᵈ sie noch einmal besuchen.

9.3 Time: *als, wenn, wann*

9.3. *Temporale Konjunktionen.* The choice of the correct conjunction is not easy for sts. at this stage. Except for direct questions with *wann*, they rarely attempt to use clauses of this type in speech. Some have difficulties even when they have time to monitor their work in writing. Point out that *als* and *wenn* introduce dependent clauses and that the rules of word order they learned for *wenn-* and *weil*-clauses (Section 3.4) apply here, too.

Als refers to a circumstance (time period) in the past or to a single event (point in time) in the past or present, but never in the future.

TIME PERIOD

Als ich 15 Jahre alt war, sind meine Eltern nach Texas gezogen.
When I was 15 years old, my parents moved to Texas.

POINT IN TIME

Als wir in Texas angekommen sind, war es sehr heiß.
When we arrived in Texas, it was very hot.

Als Veronika ins Zimmer kommt, klingelt das Telefon.
When (As) Veronika comes into the room, the phone rings.

Wenn has three distinct meanings: a conditional meaning and two temporal meanings. In conditional sentences, **wenn** means *if*. In the temporal sense, **wenn** may be used to describe events that happen or happened one or more times (*when*[*ever*]) or to describe events that will happen in the future (*when*).

CONDITION

Wenn man auf diesen Knopf drückt, öffnet sich die Tür.
If you press this button, the door will open.

REPEATED EVENTS

Wenn Herr Wagner nach Hause kam, freuten sich die Kinder.
When(ever) Mr. Wagner came home, the children were happy.

Wenn Herr Wagner nach Hause kommt, freuen sich die Kinder.
When(ever) Mr. Wagner comes home, the children are happy.

FUTURE EVENT

Wenn ich in Frankfurt ankomme, rufe ich dich an.
When I arrive in Frankfurt, I'll call you.

In the simple past, **wenn** refers to a habit or an action or event that happened repeatedly or customarily; **als** refers to a specific action or event that happened once, over a particular time period or at a particular point in time in the past.

Wenn ich nicht zur Schule gehen wollte, habe ich gesagt, dass ich krank bin.	*When(ever) I didn't want to go to school, I said that I was sick.*
Als ich mein erstes F bekommen habe, habe ich geweint.	*When I got my first F, I cried.*

Wann is an adverb of time meaning *at what time*. It is used in both direct and indirect questions.

Wann hast du deinen ersten Kuss bekommen?	*When did you get your first kiss?*
Ich weiß nicht, **wann** der Zug kommt.	*I don't know when the train is coming.*

Note that when **wann** is used in an indirect question, the conjugated verb comes at the end of the clause.

When	
Single event in past or present (*at one time*) Circumstance in the past	**als**
Condition (*if*) Repeated event in past, present, or future (*whenever*) Single event in the future (*when*)	**wenn**
Adverb of time (*at what time?*)	**wann**

Übung 4

Minidialoge

Üb. 4. Sts. do not find it easy to recognize indirect questions. If *wann* is associated only with questions, there can be difficulties because indirect questions are often statements. A useful rule of thumb is that if *when* means "at what time," German uses *wann*. You can point out, too, that indirect questions are often introduced by a verb such as *wissen* or *fragen*.

Wann, wenn oder **als?**

1. ERNST: _____ᵃ darf ich fernsehen?
   FRAU WAGNER: _____ᵇ du deine Hausaufgaben gemacht hast.
2. ROLF: Oma, _____ᵃ hast du Opa kennengelernt?
   OMA: _____ᵇ ich siebzehn war.
3. STEFAN: Was habt ihr gemacht, _____ ihr in München wart?
   NORA: Wir haben sehr viele Filme gesehen.
4. MARTHA: _____ᵃ hast du Sofie getroffen?
   WILLI: Gestern, _____ᵇ ich an der Uni war.
5. ALBERT: _____ᵃ fliegst du nach Europa?
   PETER: _____ᵇ ich genug Geld habe.
6. MONIKA: Du spielst sehr gut Tennis. _____ᵃ hast du das gelernt?
   HEIDI: _____ᵇ ich noch klein war.

Übung 5

Ein Brief

Üb. 5. Assign for homework and check in class. If sts. have noticed the similarity between Jutta's letter and the tale of *Rotkäppchen,* you could ask who the wolf is and how this modern version might have developed.

Wann, wenn oder **als?**

Liebe Tina,

gestern Nachmittag musste ich meiner Oma mal wieder Kuchen und Wein bringen. Immer _____ᵃ ich mich mit meinen Freunden verabrede[1], will mein Vater irgendetwas[2] von mir. Ich war ganz schön wütend. _____ᵇ ich den Korb[3] zusammengepackt habe, habe ich leise geschimpft. _____ᶜ ich meine Oma besuche, muss ich immer ein bisschen dableiben und mich mit ihr unterhalten. Das ist langweilig und anstrengend[4], denn die Oma hört nicht mehr so gut. Außerdem wohnt sie am anderen Ende der Stadt. Auch _____ᵈ ich mit dem Bus fahre, dauert es mindestens zwei Stunden.

_____ᵉ ich aus dem Haus gekommen bin, habe ich an der Ecke Billy auf seinem Moped gesehen. _____ᶠ ich ihn das letzte Mal gesehen habe, haben wir uns prima unterhalten.

„_____ᵍ kommst du mal wieder ins Jugendzentrum?" hat Billy gerufen. „Vielleicht heute gegen Abend", habe ich geantwortet. _____ʰ ich mich auf den Weg gemacht habe, hat es auch noch angefangen zu regnen. Und natürlich … wie immer … _____ⁱ es regnet, habe ich keinen Regenschirm dabei. So viel für heute.

Tausend Grüße

deine Jutta

[1]*make a date* [2]*something* [3]*basket* [4]*strenuous*

9.4 The simple past tense of strong and weak verbs (receptive)

In written texts, the simple past tense is frequently used instead of the perfect to refer to past events.

Jutta **fuhr** allein in Urlaub.	*Jutta went on vacation alone.*
Ihr Vater **brachte** sie zum Bahnhof.	*Her father took her to the train station.*

In the simple past tense, just as in the present tense, separable-prefix verbs are separated in independent clauses but joined in dependent clauses.

Rolf **stand** um acht Uhr **auf.** Es war selten, dass er so früh **aufstand.**	*Rolf got up at eight. It was rare that he got up so early.*

A. Weak Verbs

weak verbs = **-(e)te-**

You can recognize the simple past of weak verbs by the **-(e)te-** that is inserted between the stem and the ending.

PRESENT	SIMPLE PAST		PRESENT	SIMPLE PAST
du sagst :	du sagtest		sie arbeitet :	sie arbeitete

Wir **badeten, bauten** Sandburgen und **spielten** Volleyball.	*We went swimming, built sand castles, and played volleyball.*

Like modal verbs, simple past-tense forms do not have an ending in the **ich-** or the **er/sie/es-**forms: **ich sagte, er sagte.** Here are the simple past-tense forms of the verb **machen.**

machen			
ich machte		*wir* machten	
du machtest		*ihr* machtet	
Sie machten		*Sie* machten	
er/*sie*/*es* machte		*sie* machten	

irregular weak verbs = stem-vowel change + **-te-**

For a few weak verbs, the stem of the simple past is the same as the one used to form the past participle.

PRESENT	SIMPLE PAST	PERFECT	
bringen	brachte	hat gebracht	*to bring*
denken	dachte	hat gedacht	*to think*
kennen	kannte	hat gekannt	*to know, be acquainted with*
wissen	wusste	hat gewusst	*to know (as a fact)*

B. Strong Verbs

All strong verbs have a different stem in the simple past: **schwimmen/ schwamm, singen/sang, essen/aß.** Since English also has a number of verbs with irregular stems in the past (*swim/swam, sing/sang, eat/ate*), you will usually have no trouble recognizing simple past stems. You will recognize the **ich-** and **er/sie/es-**forms of strong verbs easily, because they do not have an ending.

Through practice reading texts in the simple past, you will gradually become familiar with the various patterns of stem change that exist. Here are some common past-tense forms you are likely to encounter in your reading.* A more complete list of stem-changing verbs can be found in Appendix E.

bleiben	blieb	*to stay*
essen	aß	*to eat*
fahren	fuhr	*to drive*
fliegen	flog	*to fly*
geben	gab	*to give*
gehen	ging	*to go*
lesen	las	*to read*
nehmen	nahm	*to take*
rufen	rief	*to call*
schlafen	schlief	*to sleep*
schreiben	schrieb	*to write*
sehen	sah	*to see*
sprechen	sprach	*to speak*
stehen	stand	*to stand*
tragen	trug	*to carry*
waschen	wusch	*to wash*

Der Bus fuhr um sieben Uhr ab.	*The bus left at seven o'clock.*
Sechs Kinder schliefen in einem Zimmer.	*Six children were sleeping in one room.*
Jutta aß frische Krabben.	*Jutta ate fresh shrimp.*

Übung 6   Die Radtour

> aßen   gingen
>   kamen
> schwammen   standen
>   schliefen
> fuhren   hielten
>   sprangen

Setzen Sie die Verben ein:

Willi und Sofie wollten eine Radtour machen, aber ihre Räder waren kaputt. Sie mussten sie reparieren, bevor sie losfahren konnten. Am Morgen der Tour _____ᵃ sie um sechs Uhr auf, _____ᵇ in die Garage, wo die Räder waren und machten sich an die Arbeit. Gegen acht waren sie fertig, sie frühstückten noch und dann _____ᶜ sie ab. Gegen elf _____ᵈ sie an einen kleinen See. Sie _____ᵉ an und setzten sich ins Gras. Willis Mutter hatte ihnen Essen eingepackt. Sie waren hungrig und _____ᶠ alles auf. Sie _____ᵍ im See und legten sich dann in den Schatten und _____ʰ. Am späten Nachmittag _____ⁱ sie noch mal ins Was-ser und radelten dann zurück nach Hause. Die Rückfahrt dauerte eine Stunde länger als die Hinfahrt.

---

*It is fairly easy to make an educated guess about the form of the infinitive when encountering new simple past-tense forms. The following vowel correspondences are the most common.

SIMPLE PAST	INFINITIVE	EXAMPLES
a	e/i	gab - geben, fand - finden
i/ie	a/ei	ritt - reiten, hielt - halten, schrieb - schreiben

Übung 7 Hänsel und Gretel

Ergänzen Sie die Verben.

brachten, fanden, gab, kamen, liefen, rannte, sahen, saß, schliefen, schloss, tötete, trug, wohnte

1. Vor einem großen Wald _____ eine arme Familie mit den beiden Kindern Hänsel und Gretel.

2. Als sie eines Tages nichts mehr zu essen hatten, _____ die Eltern die Kinder in den Wald.

3. Die Kinder _____ ein und als sie aufwachten, waren sie allein.

4. Dann _____ sie durch den Wald, bis sie an ein kleines Haus _____.

5. Durch das Fenster _____ sie eine alte Frau, die vor einem Kamin[1] _____ und strickte.

6. Als die Alte die Kinder bemerkte[2], holte sie sie herein und _____ ihnen etwas zu essen. Die Kinder _____ die Frau sehr freundlich.

7. Aber leider war sie eine böse Hexe. Sie packte[3] Hänsel, _____ ihn in einen Käfig und _____ die Tür. Er sollte dick werden, damit sie ihn essen konnte.

8. Gretel weinte und versuchte, Hänsel zu helfen. Sie _____ die Hexe und _____ mit Hänsel weg.

9.5 Sequence of events in past narration: the past perfect tense and the conjunction *nachdem* (receptive)

9.5. *Plusquamperfekt.* We focus here especially on the use of the past perfect with *nachdem* to make the relationship with the simple past tense clear. The sequence of tenses in past time is not an easy concept. This is a tense that sts. will need only to recognize. Remind them that the *nachdem*-clause counts as the first element in the sentence, so that the simple past-tense form will stand immediately after the comma.

A. Uses of the Past Perfect Tense

The past perfect tense is used to describe past actions and events that were completed before other past actions and events.

Nachdem Luca zwei Stunden **ferngesehen hatte,** ging er ins Bett.

Nachdem Jutta mit ihrer Freundin **telefoniert hatte,** machte sie ihre Hausaufgaben.

After Luca had watched TV for two hours, he went to bed.

After Jutta had talked with her friend on the phone, she did her homework.

[1]hearth [2]noticed [3]grabbed

332   KAPITEL 9 Kindheit und Jugend

The past perfect tense is often used in the clause with **nachdem**. The simple past tense is then used in the concluding (main) clause.

The past perfect tense often occurs in a dependent clause with the conjunction **nachdem** (*after*); the verb of the main clause is in the simple past or the perfect tense.

> Nachdem Jens seine erste Zigarette **geraucht hatte, wurde** ihm schlecht.
>
> *After Jens had smoked his first cigarette, he got sick.*

A dependent clause introduced by **nachdem** usually precedes the main clause. This results in the pattern "verb, verb."

DEPENDENT CLAUSE   MAIN CLAUSE

1   2

Nachdem ich die Schule **beendet hatte,** **machte** ich eine Lehre.

After I had finished school, I learned a trade.

The conjugated verb of the dependent clause is at the end of the dependent clause; the conjugated verb of the main clause is at the beginning of the main clause. Because the entire dependent clause holds the first position in the sentence, the verb-second rule applies here.

B. Formation of the Past Perfect Tense

past perfect tense = **hatte/war** + past participle

The past perfect tense of a verb consists of the simple past tense of the auxiliary **haben** or **sein** and the past participle of the verb.

> Ich **hatte** schon **bezahlt** und wir konnten gehen.
>
> *I had already paid, and we could go.*
>
> Als wir ankamen, **waren** sie schon **weggegangen.**
>
> *When we arrived, they had already left.*

Übung 8   Was ist zuerst passiert?

Üb. 8. Assign for homework and compare responses or have sts. do the exercise in class in pairs. Since items 6 and 9 refer to narration series earlier in the chapter, you might use the exercise to review the stories.

Bilden Sie logische Sätze mit Satzteilen aus beiden Spalten.

MODELL: Nachdem Jutta den Schlüssel verloren hatte, kletterte sie durch das Fenster.

1. Nachdem Jutta den Schlüssel verloren hatte,
2. Nachdem Ernst die Fensterscheibe eingeworfen hatte,
3. Nachdem Claire angekommen war,
4. Nachdem Hans seine Hausaufgaben gemacht hatte,
5. Nachdem Jens sein Fahrrad repariert hatte,
6. Nachdem Michael die Seiltänzerin[1] gesehen hatte,
7. Nachdem Richard ein ganzes Jahr gespart hatte,
8. Nachdem Silvia zwei Semester allein gewohnt hatte,
9. Nachdem Willi ein Geräusch gehört hatte,

a. flog er nach Australien.
b. ging er ins Bett.
c. kletterte sie durch das Fenster.
d. lief er weg.
e. machte er eine Radtour.
f. rief er den Großvater an.
g. rief sie Melanie an.
h. war er ganz verliebt.
i. zog sie in eine WG.

[1]*tightrope walker*

Auf Reisen

Kapitel 10 focuses on travel. You will also learn to get around in the German-speaking world by following directions and reading maps.

GOALS

This chapter focuses on travel. Targeted skills: making travel plans and reservations, using maps, giving and asking for directions, going to hotels, youth hostels, etc. Sts. learn additional polite forms, and they are introduced to the passive voice.

Themen

Reisepläne
Nach dem Weg fragen
Urlaub am Strand
Tiere

Kulturelles

KLI: Reiseziele
Musikszene: „Dieser Weg" (Xavier Naidoo)
KLI: Die deutsche Einwanderung in die USA
Filmclip: *Die fetten Jahre sind vorbei* (Hans Weingartner)
Videoecke: Urlaub

Lektüren

Gedicht: Die Stadt (Theodor Storm)
Reiseführer: Husum
Film: *Die fetten Jahre sind vorbei* (Hans Weingartner)

Strukturen

10.1 Prepositions to talk about places: **aus, bei, nach, von, zu**
10.2 Requests and instructions: the imperative (summary review)
10.3 Prepositions for giving directions: **an ... vorbei, bis zu, entlang, gegenüber von, über**
10.4 Being polite: the subjunctive form of modal verbs
10.5 Focusing on the action: the passive voice

Franz Marc: *Turm der blauen Pferde* (1913), verschollen

Kunst und Künstler

Franz Marc (1880–1916) ist ein führender Vertreter des deutschen Expressionismus. Er studierte an der Münchner Kunstakademie und war Mitbegründer des Kunstalmanachs *Der Blaue Reiter*, für den er auch Artikel über Kunsttheorie schrieb. Im August 1914 meldete er sich freiwillig zum Kriegsdienst. Er fiel 1916 bei seinem letzten Einsatz nahe Verdun in Frankreich. Die Nazis bezeichneten sein Werk als Entartete Kunst. Manche seiner Bilder wurden anschließend ins Ausland verkauft oder zerstört. Viele seiner Bilder sind von geometrischen und abstrakten Formen gekennzeichnet[1] und stellen oft Tiermotive, zum Beispiel Pferde, dar. Die Farben Blau, Gelb und Rot hatten für ihn eine symbolische Bedeutung. Blau steht für das Männliche, Herbe[2] und Geistige[3], Gelb für das Weibliche, Sanfte, Heitere[4] und Sinnliche[5], und Rot für das Brutale und Schwere.

Schauen Sie sich das Bild an und beantworten Sie die folgenden Fragen.

1. Welche Farben überwiegen[6] in dem Bild?
2. Beschreiben Sie die Atmosphäre des Bildes und gehen Sie dabei auf Marcs Farbensymbolik ein[7].
3. Was könnte die Körperhaltung[8] des Pferdes ausdrücken[9]?
4. Stellen Sie sich vor, Sie wären der Künstler oder die Künstlerin. Welche Farbe hätten Sie dem Pferd gegeben, Blau oder Gelb? Warum?

[1]gekennzeichnet von *characterized by* [2]*harsh*
[3]*intellectual* [4]*cheerful* [5]*sensual* [6]*dominate*
[7]eingehen auf *consider* [8]*posture* [9]*express*

Chapter opening artwork: Franz Marc was born in Munich in 1880. He studied art at the *Münchner Kunstakademie* and traveled several times to Paris, the art center at the turn of the century. With Wassily Kandinsky he founded the artists' group *Der Blaue Reiter*. Marc is an important representative of Expressionism in Germany. His works often feature animals in bright colors. He liked animals and understood them as creatures that live in harmony with nature. His favorite motif is the horse. The painting *Turm der blauen Pferde* is considered one of the masterpieces of German Expressionism. The painting has been missing since World War II. The blue in this painting symbolizes spiritual integrity and harmony.

Suggestion: Use this colorful and unusual representation of horses–including the title–for an association activity. The painting also lends itself to introducing or reviewing animals. *Welche Tiere sehen Sie auf dem Bild? Welche Farbe haben sie? Welche Farben sind auf dem Gemälde noch wichtig? Was für Farben sind das? Sehen die Tiere realistisch aus? Warum (nicht)? Wie sind die Formen auf dem Gemälde? Warum heißt das Bild „Turm der blauen Pferde"? Was ist am linken Rand? Was ist im Hintergrund am Himmel?*

Situationen

Reisepläne

Vocabulary Display

Bring in a passport, ticket stubs, and foreign currency and talk about a trip you made recently, as a way of introducing new vocabulary items. Encourage sts. to talk about their travels.

Grammatik 10.1

WILLI: Wo warst du in deinem letzten Urlaub?
MARTA: Ich war in Schweden.

WILLI: Was hast du dort gemacht?
MARTA: Ich bin Kanu gefahren und viel gewandert.

WILLI: Bist du geflogen?
MARTA: Nein, ich bin mit dem Auto gefahren und war die ganzen zwei Wochen dort auch mit dem Auto unterwegs.

WILLI: Wo hast du gewohnt?
MARTA: Ich habe auf Campingplätzen gezeltet.

THOMAS: Ich will nächsten Sommer nach Australien fliegen.
PETER: Wie lange möchtest du dort bleiben?

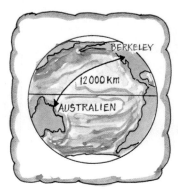

THOMAS: Vielleicht drei Wochen.
PETER: Warum willst du nach Australien? Das ist doch so weit weg und der Flug ist sehr teuer.

das Känguru

THOMAS: Ich möchte die vielen
interessanten Tiere sehen,
zum Beispiel Kängurus. Und
dann will ich meine Freundin
in Sydney besuchen.
PETER: Da musst du dir
bestimmt ein Auto mieten.

THOMAS: Nein, ich trampe.
Und wohnen werde ich bei
meiner Freundin und in
Jugendherbergen. Dann wird
alles ein bisschen billiger.
PETER: Gute Idee. Viel Spaß in
Australien.

Situation 1 Urlaub

Sit. 1. This could be done as a partner activity
where one person has his/her book closed. As a
follow-up the sentences can be used as a starting
point to write a short connected paragraph about
Marta's holiday in Sweden and Thomas's holiday
plans.

Wer ist das, Marta (M) oder Thomas (T)?

_____ ist Kanu gefahren und viel gewandert.

_____ möchte Kängurus sehen.

_____ war in Schweden.

_____ hat auf Campingplätzen gezeltet.

_____ will in Jugendherbergen wohnen.

_____ war mit dem Auto unterwegs.

_____ möchte drei Wochen bleiben.

_____ will seine Freundin in Sydney besuchen.

 ## Situation 2 Informationsspiel: Reisen

Sit. 2. The corresponding chart is in Appendix A.
Have sts. work with a partner. The model demonstrates asking for all the missing information referring to one character before moving on to the next
person, but sts. might prefer to take turns asking
all the woher questions, wohin questions, etc.

MODELL: s1: Woher kommt Sofie?
s2: Aus _____.
s1: Wohin fährt sie in den Ferien?
s2: Nach/In _____.
s1: Wo wohnt sie?
s2: Bei _____. Was macht sie da?
s1: Sie kauft Bücher und besucht
Verwandte. Wann kommt sie
zurück?
s2: In _____.

	Richard	Sofie	Mehmet	Peter	Jürgen	mein(e) Partner(in)
Woher?	aus Innsbruck	aus Dresden	aus Izmir	aus Berkeley	aus Bad Harzburg	
Wohin?	nach Frankreich	nach Düsseldorf	nach Italien	nach Hawaii	in die Alpen	
Wo?	bei einer Gastfamilie	bei ihrer Tante	bei alten Freunden	bei seiner Schwester	bei einem Freund	
Was?	Französisch lernen	Bücher kaufen; Verwandte besuchen	am Strand liegen; schwimmen	einen Vulkan besteigen	Ski fahren natürlich	
Wann?	in drei Monaten	in einer Woche	in zwei Wochen	nächstes Wochenende	in zwei Wochen	

Kultur ... Landeskunde ... Informationen

Reiseziele

Wenn einer eine Reise tut,
So kann er was erzählen;
Drum[1] nähm[2] ich meinen Stock und Hut
Und tät das Reisen wählen[3].

—Matthias Claudius (1740–1815)

- Welche Länder oder Städte sind für Sie beliebte Reiseziele? Warum?
- Was mögen Touristen an Ihrem Land besonders? Wohin fahren sie am liebsten?
- Welche Andenken (Souvenirs) bringen sie mit nach Hause? Spekulieren Sie!
- Welche Urlaubsländer sind bei Ihren Landsleuten beliebt?

[1]*Therefore* [2]*would take* [3]tät wählen *would choose*

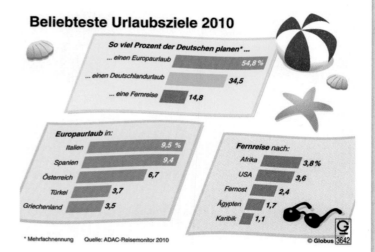

Beliebteste Urlaubsziele 2010

So viel Prozent der Deutschen planen* ...

... einen Europaurlaub	54,8 %
... einen Deutschlandurlaub	34,5
... eine Fernreise	14,8

Europaurlaub in:

Italien	9,5 %
Spanien	9,4
Österreich	6,7
Türkei	3,7
Griechenland	3,5

Fernreise nach:

Afrika	3,8 %
USA	3,6
Fernost	2,4
Ägypten	1,7
Karibik	1,1

* Mehrfachnennung   Quelle: ADAC-Reisemonitor 2010

© Globus 3642

Schauen Sie sich die Grafik an.
- Wo machen Deutsche am liebsten Urlaub?
- Was macht Spanien, Italien und Österreich attraktiv für deutsche Urlauber?
  - ☐ Man spricht dort Deutsch.
  - ☐ Der Urlaub ist relativ preisgünstig.
  - ☐ Man kann mit dem Auto hinfahren.
  - ☐ Es ist warm und die Sonne scheint.
  - ☐ Das Essen schmeckt sehr gut.
  - ☐ ?

KLI. Poem. You might want to use the poem as an introductory activity. In small groups have sts. answer the following questions: *Was will Claudius sagen? Warum kann man etwas erzählen, wenn man reist? Warum wollen Menschen außerdem noch reisen?* Sts. could also write a four-line poem about their own travels or favorite destinations and present it in class. It is interesting to note that over 30% of Germans stay in their own country for vacations (the favorite destinations are Schleswig-Holstein in the far north and Bavaria in the south). The top three foreign countries are favorite destinations for different reasons: Spain, primarily because of its climate; Austria, because it is a German-speaking country and just across the border; and Italy, the longtime favorite of Germans in search of the sun, because of its climate and its vicinity. For many Germans, price is certainly a factor when selecting vacation destinations (which may explain why so many stay in Germany), while food plays a minor role. As to "deutschfreundlich," German tourists are probably considered a necessary evil, as most tourists are, particularly when they number in the millions.

Photo questions. *Wie sind die Leute auf den Berg gekommen? Wo liegt die Zugspitze? Ist sie möglicherweise ein beliebtes Ausflugziel der Deutschen? Warum? Was können Urlauber in den Alpen machen?*

Die Zugspitze

Situation 3 Dialog: Am Fahrkartenschalter

Sit. 3. This dialogue contains a number of useful speech patterns. Preteach new vocabulary before working with the dialogue. You may wish to follow the steps for presenting the dialogue without the use of the textbook. Alternatively, use as a cloze dictation. When presenting without the book, ask the following focus questions. **(1)** Questions for first listening: 1. *Wohin möchte Silvia fahren?* 2. *Wann möchte sie dort sein?* 3. *Womit möchte sie bezahlen?* 4. *Wie viel kostet die Fahrkarte?* **(2)** Questions for second listening: 1. *Fährt sie einfach oder hin und zurück?* 2. *Fährt sie erster oder zweiter Klasse?* 3. *Wann genau fährt sie ab, wann genau kommt sie an?* 4. *Aus welchem Gleis fährt der Zug ab?*

Cultural note. Train travel is fast in Germany and a convenient alternative to flying or driving. The ICE train (Inter-City-Express) connects all major German cities on an hourly basis. It travels at speeds of up to 330 km per hour and covers, e.g., the 530 km (330 miles) between Göttingen and Munich in about 4 hours. Frequent travelers can travel more cheaply with a BahnCard issued by the Deutsche Bahn. In 2011, a BahnCard for second-class travel cost between 50 and 200 euros and entitled the bearer to travel on all trains for one year while paying either 75% or even as little as 50% of the full ticket price.

Suggestion. Have sts. write plans for a vacation in a place of their choice. *Was möchten Sie an diesem Ort / in diesem Land machen? Wann? Warum? usw.* Sts. could also present their plans in class and compare them.

Silvia steht am Fahrkartenschalter und möchte mit dem Zug von Göttingen nach München fahren.

BAHNANGESTELLTER: Bitte schön?

SILVIA: Eine <u>Fahrkarte</u> nach München, bitte.

BAHNANGESTELLTER: Einfach oder hin und zurück?

SILVIA: Hin und zurück bitte, mit BahnCard <u>zweiter</u> Klasse.

BAHNANGESTELLTER: Wann wollen Sie fahren?

SILVIA: Ich würde gern <u>so gegen Mittag</u> in München sein.

BAHNANGESTELLTER: Wenn Sie um 8.06 Uhr fahren, sind Sie um 12.11 Uhr in München.

SILVIA: Das ist gut. Wissen Sie, wo der Zug <u>abfährt</u>?

BAHNANGESTELLTER: Aus Gleis 10.

SILVIA: Ach ja, ich würde gern mit VISA bezahlen. <u>Geht das</u>?

BAHNANGESTELLTER: Selbstverständlich. Das macht dann 115 Euro 20.

SILVIA: Bitte sehr.

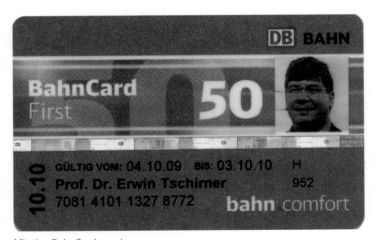

Göttingen → München Hbf
530 km

Ab	Zug		Umsteigen	An	Ab	Zug		An	Verkehrstage
5.56	ICE	997	Fulda	6.49	7.00	ICE	987	10.11	01
5.56	ICE	997	Fulda	6.52	7.02	ICE	987	10.11	02
7.03	ICE	581						10.58	täglich
8.06	ICE	783						12.11	täglich
9.03	ICE	583						12.58	täglich
9.47	IC	1081	Augsburg Hbf	14.04	14.10	SE	21139	14.54	täglich
10.03	ICE	91	Nürnberg Hbf	12.26	12.30	IC	523	14.17	täglich
10.30	IC	1087	Nürnberg Hbf	13.23	13.34	IC	813	15.17	03

Mit der BahnCard spart man.

 Situation 4 Interview

Sit. 4. Model pronunciation, have sts. repeat, and answer, based on your own experiences. Then have sts. work in pairs. Leave enough time for as many sts. as possible to tell about their trips, or arrange to do this during another class period.

1. Wo machst du gern Urlaub?
2. Fliegst du gern? Was gefällt dir daran? Stört dich etwas beim Fliegen? Was?
3. Wie suchst du dir deine Urlaubsziele aus? Wie besorgst du dir dein Ticket?
4. Wie packst du für eine Flugreise? Was nimmst du alles mit?
5. Erzähl von einer deiner letzten Reisen. Wo warst du? Wie bist du dahin gekommen? Warst du allein? Hast du jemanden kennengelernt? Was hast du am liebsten gemacht? Was war das Interessanteste, was dir passiert ist?

Nach dem Weg fragen

Grammatik 10.2–10.3

Biegen Sie an der Ampel nach links ab.

Gehen Sie über den Zebrastreifen.

Gehen Sie geradeaus, bis Sie eine Kirche sehen.

Gehen Sie an der Kirche vorbei, immer geradeaus.

Gehen Sie die Goetheallee entlang bis zur Bushaltestelle.

Gehen Sie über die Brücke. Auf der linken Seite ist dann das Rathaus.

Die U-Bahnhaltestelle ist gegenüber vom Markthotel.

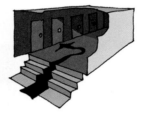

Gehen Sie die Treppe hinauf und dann ist es die zweite Tür links.

Situation 5   Mit dem Stadtplan unterwegs in Regensburg

Suchen Sie sich ein Ziel in Regensburg aus dem Stadtplan auf der nächsten Seite aus. Beschreiben Sie Ihrem Partner / Ihrer Partnerin den Weg, ohne das Ziel zu verraten[1]. Wenn er/sie dort richtig ankommt, bekommen Sie einen Punkt und es wird gewechselt. Achtung: Ausgangspunkt[2] und Ziel dürfen nicht im selben Quadrat liegen!

MODELL: Also, wir sind jetzt an der Steinernen Brücke, auf dem Stadtplan oben in der Mitte. Siehst du die Steinerne Brücke? Gut. Von der Steinernen Brücke aus geh bitte nach links in die Goldene-Bären-Straße hinein und an der nächsten Straße gleich wieder rechts. Du kommst dann zum Krauterermarkt und zum Dom. Geh geradeaus über den Krauterermarkt hinüber und durch die Residenzstraße zum Neupfarrplatz. Dort gehst du bitte wieder links, die Schwarze-Bären-Straße ganz durch und über die Maximilianstraße hinüber. Noch ein paar Schritte weiter und du bist am _____.

[1]*give away*   [2]*starting point*

links/rechts die (Goliath)straße entlang
links/rechts in die (Kram)gasse hinein
geradeaus über den (Krauterer)markt / über die (Kepler)straße hinüber
weiter bis zum/zur _____
an der (Steinernen Brücke) vorbei

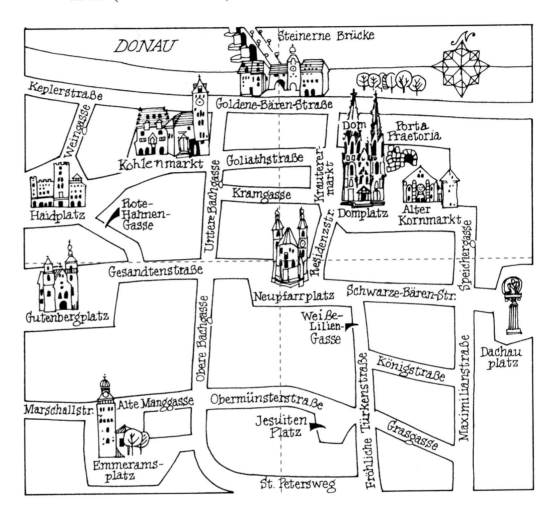

 Situation 6 Dialoge

Sit. 6. Work with one dialogue at a time. **(1)** Set the scene by briefly reminding sts. who the characters are, where they are, where they want to go, and why. **(2)** Play (or read) each dialogue at least twice while sts. fill in the blanks. **(3)** Have sts. compare their answers with a partner. Ask sts. for their answers and write them on the board. **(4)** Ask sts. to work in small groups and to sketch a map according to the directions. **(5)** As grammatical follow-up, ask sts. to find all prepositional phrases and to group the prepositions according to case.

l. Jürgen ist bei Silvias Mutter zum Geburtstag eingeladen.

JÜRGEN: Wie komme ich denn zu eurem Haus?

SILVIA: Das ist ganz einfach. Wenn du <u>aus dem</u> Bahnhofsgebäude herauskommst, siehst du rechts <u>auf der</u> anderen Seite der Straße einen Supermarkt. Geh <u>über die</u> Straße, links <u>am</u> Supermarkt vorbei, und wenn du einfach geradeaus weitergehst, kommst du <u>auf die</u> Bismarckstraße. Die musst du nur ganz hinaufgehen, bis du <u>zu einem</u> Kreisverkehr kommst. Direkt <u>auf der</u> anderen Seite ist unser Haus.

2. Claire und Melanie sind in Göttingen und suchen die Universitätsbibliothek.

MELANIE: Entschuldige, kannst du uns sagen, wo die Universitätsbibliothek ist?

STUDENT: Ach, da seid ihr aber ganz schön falsch. Also, geht erst die Straße mal wieder zurück <u>bis zu der</u> großen Kreuzung. <u>Über die</u> Kreuzung <u>hinüber</u> und <u>in die</u> Fußgängerzone <u>hinein</u>. Immer geradeaus <u>durch die</u> Fußgängerzone <u>bis zur</u> Prinzenstraße. Da rechts. <u>Auf der</u> rechten Seite seht ihr dann die Post. Direkt <u>gegenüber von der</u> Post ist die Bibliothek. Könnt ihr gar nicht verfehlen.

MELANIE
UND CLAIRE: Danke.

3. Frau Frisch findet ein Zimmer im Rathaus nicht.

FRAU FRISCH: Entschuldigen Sie, ich suche Zimmer 204.

SEKRETÄRIN: Das ist <u>im</u> dritten Stock. Gehen Sie den Korridor entlang <u>bis zum</u> Treppenhaus. Dann eine Treppe <u>hinauf</u> und oben links. Zimmer 204 ist die zweite Tür <u>auf der</u> rechten Seite.

FRAU FRISCH: Vielen Dank. Da hätte ich ja lange suchen können …

Situation 7   Wie komme ich …?

Sit. 7. Have sts. use the classroom building as the starting point for their directions. First go over proper question formation with sts. After they have worked with their partners, ask for a volunteer to describe a route to a well-known destination and see if the others can guess where they will arrive.

Beschreiben Sie Ihrem Partner / Ihrer Partnerin,

1. wie man zu Ihrem Studentenheim oder zu Ihrer Wohnung kommt.
2. wo die nächste Post ist und wie man dahinkommt.
3. wo die beste Kneipe/Disko in der Stadt ist und wie man dahinkommt.
4. wie man zum Schwimmbad kommt.
5. wie man zur Bibliothek kommt.
6. wo der nächste billige Kopierladen ist und wie man dahinkommt.
7. wie man zum Büro von Ihrem Lehrer / Ihrer Lehrerin kommt.
8. wo der nächste Waschsalon ist und wie man dahinkommt.

Lektüre 📖

Lesehilfe

A short text like a poem usually requires intensive reading. Every single word is carefully chosen to convey the meaning and feelings one desires to express. One of the most famous poems of Theodor Storm, a well-known German poet and novelist, describes his hometown, Husum.

Vor dem Lesen 1. The prereading task asks sts. to free-associate feelings, colors, sounds, smells, activities, and memories with the two seasons spring and fall. Give them a minute to write down associations before writing them on the board. Read or play the poem. Then ask sts. to do *Arbeit mit dem Text 1* in small groups.

Vor dem Lesen 1

Was assoziieren Sie mit den Jahreszeiten Frühling und Herbst? Schreiben Sie Gefühle, Farben, Geräusche, Gerüche, Tätigkeiten und Erinnerungen auf.

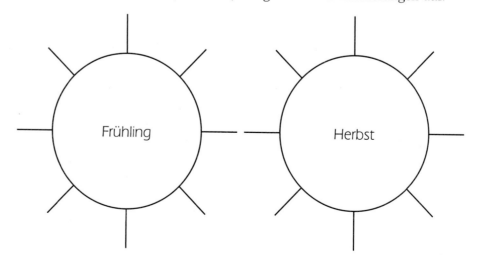

Die Stadt

Theodor Storm

Am grauen Strand, am grauen Meer
Und seitab liegt die Stadt;
Der Nebel drückt die Dächer schwer,
Und durch die Stille braust das Meer
5 Eintönig um die Stadt.

Es rauscht kein Wald, es schlägt im Mai
Kein Vogel ohn' Unterlaß;
Die Wandergans mit hartem Schrei
Nur fliegt in Herbstesnacht vorbei,
10 Am Strande weht das Gras.

Doch hängt mein ganzes Herz an dir,
Du graue Stadt am Meer;
Der Jugend Zauber für und für
Ruht lächelnd doch auf dir, auf dir,
15 Du graue Stadt am Meer.

Miniwörterbuch

brausen	to rage
eintönig	monotonously
für und für	forever
ohne Unterlass	incessantly
rauschen	to rustle
seitab	off to the side
wehen	to blow
der Zauber	charm

Arbeit mit dem Text 1

A. Suchen Sie Beispiele aus dem Gedicht für die folgenden Kategorien: Landschaft, Wetter/Jahreszeit, Fauna und Flora, Geräusche. Schreiben Sie sie in die Tabelle.

Landschaft	Wetter/Jahreszeit	Fauna und Flora	Geräusche

B. Kontraste

1. Die ersten beiden Zeilen der zweiten Strophe und die drei weiteren bilden einen Kontrast. Welches Bild oder welche Farbe hat man bei Wald, Mai, Vögel vor Augen und woran denkt man bei Wandergans, Herbstesnacht, Strand und Gras? Welche Wörter (Negation und Adverb) sind typisch für einen Kontrast?

2. Die dritte Strophe steht im Kontrast zu den ersten beiden. Warum? Welches Wort ist hier sehr wichtig?

C. Wie ist die Stimmung in dem Gedicht? Fröhlich, melancholisch, dramatisch? Wie erreicht der Dichter das? Denken Sie an Rhythmus, Klang[1] und Lautmalerei[2].

Nach dem Lesen 1

Sind Sie Dichter oder Dichterin? Schreiben Sie ein Gedicht über Ihre Heimatstadt, über die Natur, über die Liebe oder über sich selbst. Das Gedicht muss sich nicht reimen. Es kann auch ein modernes Gedicht sein.

Aktivität B. 1. *Frühling, grün, helle Farben* might come to mind in connection with woods, the month of May, and birds; migrating geese, autumn nights, the beach and grass might evoke *dunkle Erdfarben, Wind, Kälte, Dunkelheit;* typical words for contrast *kein, nur.* **2.** The negative associations the poet evokes in the first two stanzas are contrasted with his nevertheless positive feelings for his hometown in the third; the important word is *doch.*

Nach dem Lesen 1. You may want to have sts. write their poems on poster board and hang them in the classroom. You could also have some sts. recite their poems in front of the class.

[1]*sound* [2]*onomatopoeia*

Vor dem Lesen 2

Vor dem Lesen 2. Husum, a small North Sea town close to the border with Denmark in the north of Germany, is most famous for being the birthplace of Theodor Storm, who described it in one of his most famous poems as the *graue Stadt am grauen Meer*. The text presented in this reading section is a tour guide description of Husum, which stresses its association with the poet. Begin by asking your sts. what the main attractions of your college town are, the kinds of things a travel guide might list. Then do the two prereading activities.

Give a time limit of 1-2 minutes for Activity B to encourage sts. to skim the text. After discussing the activity, read the text out loud while your sts. read along silently. Then go to the *Arbeit mit dem Text 2*. First ask sts. to complete Activity A in small groups. Then read the instructions for B out loud and explain any difficult vocabulary. Ask sts. to solve the task by working in groups of 2 or 3.

A. Was für Informationen erwartet man in einem Reiseführer? Kreuzen Sie an.

☐ Museen   ☐ Unterkunft
☐ Restaurants und Kneipen   ☐ Stadtplan
☐ Wetter und Klima   ☐ Kultur und Feste
☐ Attraktionen   ☐ Zugfahrplan
☐ Rezepte   ☐ Nachtleben
☐ berühmte Personen   ☐ Wörterbuch

B. Überfliegen Sie den Text „Husum" und bestimmen Sie, in welcher Reihenfolge die folgenden Informationen gegeben werden.

_____ Anziehungspunkte in Husum

_____ Informationen zu Theodor Storm, der in Husum geboren wurde

_____ Kirchen und Museen

_____ Vorschläge für einen Stadtrundgang

Miniwörterbuch

der **Amtsrichter**	district judge
der **Anziehungspunkt**	attraction
sich **befinden**	to be located
der **Bestandteil**	part
das **Freilichtmuseum**	open-air museum
gewidmet	dedicated
das **Herzogtum**	duchy
der **Rundgang**	(walking) tour
die **Sache**	*here*: cause
schaffen, schuf	to create
schildern	to portray
vertreten, vertrat	to plead for

Lesehilfe

This selection is taken from a travel guide published by the German automobile association ADAC. Husum, a small town of 25,000, is best known for being the birthplace of Theodor Storm.

Husum

Husum ist die Stadt Theodor Storms. Als „Graue Stadt am Meer" hat er sie liebevoll in seinem ihr gewidmeten Gedicht angeredet. Storm wurde 1817 in Husum geboren und schuf hier einen Teil seiner Gedichte und Novellen. Husum gehörte damals zu den Herzogtümern Schleswig und Holstein und war Bestandteil des deutsch-dänischen Gesamtstaates. Von 1852 bis 1864 konnte der Dichter, der
5 im bürgerlichen Leben als Anwalt, später als Amtsrichter tätig war, nicht in seiner Vaterstadt leben, weil er gegenüber der dänischen Herrschaft die deutsche Sache vertrat. Er starb 1888 in Hademarschen, doch liegt er in Husum begraben.

Sie können in Husum Häuser anschauen, in denen Storm gelebt, und andere, die er
10 in seinen Novellen geschildert hat. Weitere Anziehungspunkte sind der Hafen mit den Krabbenkuttern, das Schloss mit seinen Wiesen, auf denen im Frühling Millionen von Krokussen blühen, sowie die alten Kaufmannshäuser am Markt und in der Großstraße.

Ein Rundgang beginnt am Markt an der Großstraße, führt durch die Hohle Gasse und die Wasserreihe zum Hafen, durch das Westerende und die Nordhusumer Straße
15 zum „Ostenfelder Haus", einem Freilichtmuseum mit einem Niedersachsenhaus des 16./17. Jahrhunderts. Über den alten Friedhof und den Totengang geht man über die Neustadt zum Schloss (Sitz des Kreisarchivs) mit dem als „Cornils'sches Haus" bekannten Torhaus (1612) und durch den Schlossgang zum Markt zurück. Storms Grab auf dem Klosterkirchhof erreichen Sie vom Markt aus durch die Norderstraße.

20 | Das Haus in der Wasserreihe 31, in dem der Dichter zwischen 1866 und 1880 wohnte, dient heute als Storm-Museum (täglich geöffnet von April bis Oktober). Im Nissenhaus befindet sich das Nordfriesische Museum zu den Themen Erd- und Vorgeschichte, Landschaftskunde und Kulturgeschichte (täglich geöffnet). Die Marktkirche Husums gilt als der bedeutendste klassizistische Kirchenbau Schleswig-Holsteins.

(aus: ADAC-Reiseführer Norddeutschland)

Arbeit mit dem Text 2

A. Ein Rundgang durch Husum. Zeichnen Sie den Weg, der im Reiseführer beschrieben wird, in den Stadtplan ein.

B. Storms Leben. Welche dieser Jahreszahlen und Ereignisse stehen im Text, welche nicht? Schreiben Sie die Zeilennummern dazu.

		ZEILE
1817	wird Theodor Storm in Husum geboren	———
1843–1852	ist er Rechtsanwalt in Husum	———
1846	erste Heirat mit Konstanze Esmarch	———
1852–1856	ist er Assessor in Potsdam	———
1852–1864	lebt er aus politischen Gründen nicht in Husum	———
1856–1864	ist er Richter in Heiligenstadt	———
1864–1867	ist er Landvogt[1] in Husum	———
1866	zweite Heirat mit Dorothea Jensen	———
1866–1880	wohnt er in der Wasserreihe 31	———
1867	wird er Amtsrichter	———
1888	stirbt er in Hademarschen	———

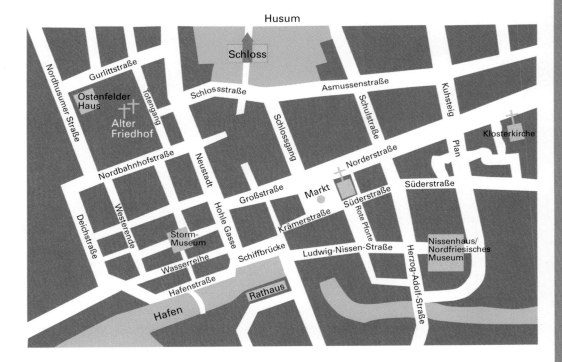

Nach dem Lesen 2

Suchen Sie im Internet mehr Informationen über Husum und über Theodor Storm und stellen Sie sie in der Klasse vor.

[1]*governor*

„Dieser Weg" (2005, Deutschland) *Xavier Naidoo*

Der Sänger Xavier Naidoo

Biografie Xavier Naidoo ist 1971 in Mannheim geboren. Sein Vater kam aus Sri Lanka und seine Mutter aus Südafrika. Er ist einer der erfolgreichsten deutschen Sänger, sowohl als Mitglied der Band *Söhne Mannheims* als auch als Solosänger. Naidoo ist ein bekennender Christ. Viele seiner Texte handeln von Gott und der Nächstenliebe, aber auch von der Wichtigkeit, Fremdenhass zu bekämpfen. Er engagiert sich für christliche Projekte wie *Zeichen der Zeit* und für Projekte gegen Fremdenhass wie *Rock gegen Rechts* und *Brothers Keepers*. Die Single „Dieser Weg" stammt aus dem Jahr 2005 und wurde die Hymne der deutschen Fußballnationalmannschaft während der Europameisterschaft in Deutschland 2006.

Vor dem Hören Was wollen Sie in Ihrem Leben erreichen? Was ist wichtig für Sie? Wohin führt Ihr Weg?

Nach dem Hören Beantworten Sie die Fragen.

1. Wohin führt die Straße, die der Sänger entlang geht?
2. Was spielt im Sänger?
3. Wie ist *dieser* Weg?
4. Was machen manche Menschen mit jemandem?
5. Wann soll man sein Segel nicht setzen?

iMix Link: Dieses Lied können Sie im *iTunes Store* als ein *iMix* kaufen, das speziell für *Kontakte* entwickelt wurde. In **Connect German** (www.connectgerman.com) erhalten Sie Instruktionen, wie Sie die Playliste bekommen können.

Miniwörterbuch

das **Mitglied**	member
bekennend	avowed
handeln von	deal with
die **Nächstenliebe**	charity
der **Fremdenhass**	xenophobia
bekämpfen	to combat
sich engagieren	to get involved
das **Zeichen**	sign
erreichen	to achieve
(ent-)lang gehen	to walk along
steinig	rocky
treten	to kick
(sich) aufgeben	to give (oneself) up
segnen	to bless
das **Segel**	sail
aufbrausen	to pile up higher

Urlaub am Strand

Grammatik 10.4

Situation 8 Umfrage: Urlaub am Strand

MODELL: S1: Hast du schon mal eine Sandburg gebaut?
S2: Ja.
S1: Unterschreib bitte hier.

UNTERSCHRIFT

1. Hast du schon einmal eine Sandburg gebaut? _____
2. Hast du eine Luftmatratze? _____
3. Bist du schon mal im Meer geschwommen? _____
4. Kannst du Wellen reiten? _____
5. Sammelst du gern Muscheln? _____
6. Warst du schon einmal windsurfen? _____
7. Liegst du gern im Liegestuhl? _____
8. Bist du schon mal Schlauchboot gefahren? _____
9. Bekommst du leicht einen Sonnenbrand? _____
10. Benutzt du oft Sonnenmilch? _____

Situation 9 Informationsspiel: Wo wollen wir übernachten?

Sit. 9. The corresponding chart appears in Appendix A. Go over the questions with sts. before doing the activity to assure that they are using grammatically correct formulations with *im* and *in der*. Tell sts. that in most hotels and especially in *Pensionen*, breakfast is included in the price. Also mention that not all rooms in *Pensionen* have a private bath or shower. Preteach the following words: *Aufenthaltsraum, Herbergseltern, inbegriffen*.

MODELL: Wie viel kostet _____?

Haben die Zimmer im (in der) _____ eine eigene Dusche und Toilette?

Gibt es im (in der) _____ Einzelzimmer?

Gibt es im (in der, auf dem) _____ einen Fernseher?

Ist das Frühstück im (in der, auf dem) _____ inbegriffen?

Ist die Lage von dem (von der) _____ zentral/ruhig?

Gibt es im (in der, auf dem) _____ Telefon?

	das Hotel Strandpromenade	das Gästehaus Ostseeblick	die Jugendherberge	der Campingplatz
Preis pro Person	78,- Euro	42,- Euro	12,50 Euro	11,- Euro
Dusche/Toilette	ja	nicht in allen Zimmern	nein	nein
Einzelzimmer	ja	ja	nein	natürlich nicht
Fernseher	in jedem Zimmer	im Fernsehzimmer	im Aufenthaltsraum	natürlich nicht
Frühstück	inbegriffen	inbegriffen	kostet extra	nein
zentrale Lage	ja	ja	im Wald	direkt am Strand
ruhige Lage	an der Strandpromenade	ja	ja	ja
Telefon	in jedem Zimmer	im Telefonzimmer	bei den Herbergseltern	Telefonzelle

 Situation 10 Dialog: Auf Zimmersuche

Sit. 10. (See the IM). This dialogue provides a model for the role-play following it. Follow the steps for presenting the dialogue without the use of the textbook and assign the dialogue for homework. (The dialogue is on the st. tape for the workbook/lab manual.) Questions for listening comprehension: 1. *Was für ein Zimmer möchten die Rufs?* 2. *Wie lange wollen sie bleiben?* 3. *Was kostet das Zimmer?* 4. *Wann und wo können sie frühstücken?*

Herr und Frau Ruf suchen ein Zimmer.

HERR RUF: Guten Tag, haben Sie noch ein Doppelzimmer mit Dusche frei?

WIRTIN: Wie lange möchten Sie denn <u>bleiben</u>?

HERR RUF: <u>Drei Nächte</u>.

WIRTIN: Ja, da habe ich ein Zimmer <u>mit Dusche</u> und Toilette.

FRAU RUF: Ist das Zimmer auch ruhig?

WIRTIN: Natürlich. Unsere Zimmer sind alle ruhig.

FRAU RUF: <u>Was kostet</u> das Zimmer denn?

WIRTIN: 54 Euro <u>pro Nacht</u>.

HERR RUF: Ist Frühstück dabei?

WIRTIN: Selbstverständlich ist Frühstück dabei.

FRAU RUF: Gut, wir nehmen das Zimmer.

HERR RUF: Und wann können wir <u>frühstücken</u>?

WIRTIN: <u>Von acht bis zehn</u> im Frühstückszimmer.

 Situation 11 Rollenspiel: Im Hotel

Sit. 11. The role for S2 appears in Appendix B.

Note: If your students are using McGraw-Hill's **Connect** online *Arbeitsbuch*, they can do this *Rollenspiel* using the real-time, interactive **Video-Chat** feature.

S1: Sie sind im Hotel und möchten ein Zimmer mit Dusche und Toilette. Außerdem möchten Sie ein ruhiges Zimmer. Fragen Sie auch nach Preisen, Frühstück, Telefon und wann Sie morgens abreisen müssen.

Die deutsche Einwanderung in die USA

- Gibt es in Ihrer Nähe Orte, Städte oder Stadtteile mit deutschem Namen? Wie heißen sie? Wann wurden sie gegründet[1]?
- Gibt es in Ihrer Stadt ein Viertel[2] mit deutschen Geschäften und Restaurants?
- Welche deutschen Einwanderer[3] spielten eine wichtige Rolle in der Geschichte Ihres Landes?

Lesen Sie den Text und suchen Sie die Antworten auf diese Fragen:

- Aus welchem Land kamen die meisten Einwanderer in die USA?
- Wie viele Millionen US-Amerikaner sagen, dass *Deutsch* ihre Hauptabstammung[4] ist?
- Wie hieß die erste deutsche Siedlung in Nordamerika? Wo lag sie? Wann wurde sie gegründet?
- Welchen Religionen gehörten viele Deutsche an, die im 18. Jahrhundert in Pennsylvania einwanderten[5]?
- Warum hieß eine besonders große Einwanderergruppe die *Forty-Eighters*?
- Welche Region wurde der *German Belt* genannt?
- Wie viel Prozent der Einwohner San Antonios sprach im 19. Jahrhundert Deutsch?
- Welche Industrie wurde besonders von Deutschen dominiert?
- Welche Berufsgruppe und welche Religionsgruppe wanderte in den 1930er Jahren vor allem nach Amerika aus?

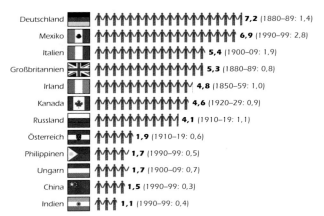

**Einwanderung in die USA
1820–2004 nach Herkunftsland**
(in Millionen)
(Topjahrzehnt in Klammern)

Deutschland		**7,2** (1880–89: 1,4)
Mexiko		**6,9** (1990–99: 2,8)
Italien		**5,4** (1900–09: 1,9)
Großbritannien		**5,3** (1880–89: 0,8)
Irland		**4,8** (1850–59: 1,0)
Kanada		**4,6** (1920–29: 0,9)
Russland		**4,1** (1910–19: 1,1)
Österreich		**1,9** (1910–19: 0,6)
Philippinen		**1,7** (1990–99: 0,5)
Ungarn		**1,7** (1900–09: 0,7)
China		**1,5** (1990–99: 0,3)
Indien		**1,1** (1990–99: 0,4)

Quelle: Yearbook of Immigration Statistics, U.S. Department of Homeland Security, http://www.dhs.gov

Die USA sind eines der großen Einwanderungsländer. Jedes Jahr wandern zahlreiche Personen in die USA ein. Deutschland führt die Liste der Einwanderungsnationen an. Allein in New York City leben circa 500 000 Deutschstämmige[6]. Bei einer Volkszählung[7] im Jahr 2006 gaben 51 Millionen US-Amerikaner *Deutsch* als ihre Hauptabstammung an.

Die deutsche Einwanderung in die USA hat eine lange Tradition. 1683 wurde in Pennsylvania die erste deutsche Siedlung[8] mit dem Namen „Germantown" gegründet. 90 Jahre später war ein Drittel der pennsylvanischen Bevölkerung[9] deutschstämmig. Sie gehörten größtenteils protestantischen Religionen an. Auf der Basis pfälzischer Dialekte entwickelten die Deutschamerikaner eine eigene Sprache – das Pennsylvania Dutch. Dieser Dialekt wird auch heute noch in einigen Teilen Pennsylvanias gesprochen.

Im 19. Jahrhundert wanderten fast 8 Millionen deutschsprachige Menschen in die USA ein, aus allen deutschsprachigen Ländern: aus der Schweiz, aus Österreich-Ungarn und aus dem Deutschen Reich. Viele kamen nach der gescheiterten[10] deutschen Revolution von 1848. Diese Einwanderer hießen die *Forty-Eighters*. Unter ihnen befanden sich viele Intellektuelle und Bürgerrechtskämpfer[11], ebenso wie viele Juden[12], wie zum Beispiel Abraham Jacobi, der 1860 das erste Kinderkrankenhaus der USA eröffnete[13] und Emil Berliner, der Erfinder der Schallplatte. Sehr viele Deutsche ließen sich im Mittleren Westen nieder[14], insbesondere in der Region zwischen Cincinnati, St. Louis und Milwaukee, die der *German Belt* genannt wurde. 1890 waren 69% der Einwohner Milwaukees deutschstämmig, in Cincinnati waren es zu Beginn des 20. Jahrhunderts 60%. Auch in Texas wanderten sehr viele Deutsche ein. Ein Drittel der Einwohner von San Antonio sprach 1870 Deutsch.

Viele berühmte Amerikaner waren deutscher Abstammung. John Jacob Astor kam 1784 als junger Mann nach New York. Der Chemiker Karl Pfizer gründete 1849 in Brooklyn ein Pharmaunternehmen[15], das es heute noch gibt. Levi Strauss, der Erfinder der Jeans, wanderte 1853 aus Bayern ein. Ein Monopol hatten deutsche Einwanderer in der Bierindustrie: Yuengling, Anheuser-Busch, Joseph Schlitz und Coors wurden alle im 19. Jahrhundert gegründet. Auch Hamburger, Frankfurter, Bratwurst, Schnitzel, Strudel und Brezel sind deutschen Ursprungs[16].

Nach der Machtergreifung[17] der Nazis in den 1930er Jahren verließen wiederum viele Deutsche ihre Heimat, vor allem Akademiker und vor allem jüdische Akademiker. Zu den Auswanderern gehörten der Physiker Albert Einstein, die Mathematikerin Emmy Noether, die Philosophin Hannah Arendt, der Schriftsteller Thomas Mann, der Architekt Walter Gropius und die Schauspielerin Marlene Dietrich.

[1]*established* [2]*neighborhood* [3]*immigrant* [4]*primary ancestry* [5]*immigrated* [6]*people of German descent* [7]*census* [8]*settlement* [9]*populace* [10]*failed* [11]*civil rights activist* [12]*Jews* [13]*opened* [14]*ließen sich nieder settled* [15]*pharmaceutical company* [16]*origin* [17]*takeover*

Tiere

Grammatik 10.5

Juttas Ratte wird gegen Tollwut geimpft.

Ernsts Meerschweinchen wird oft gebadet.

Schildkröten werden oft als Haustiere gehalten.

In der Wüste muss man aufpassen, dass man nicht von einer Schlange gebissen wird.

Gestern wurde Silvia von einer Biene gestochen.

Als Josef und Melanie gestern beim Baden waren, wurden sie von tausend Mücken gestochen.

Situation 12 Ratespiel

die Klapperschlange

die Schildkröte

die Schnecke

der Kolibri

der Gepard

die Fledermaus

1. Das größte Landsäugetier: Es hat einen Rüssel und zwei Stoßzähne aus Elfenbein; wegen des Elfenbeins wird es oft illegal gejagt.
2. Die schnellste Katze der Welt: Sie läuft mindestens 80 Kilometer in der Stunde.
3. Das schwerste Tier: Es lebt im Wasser, aber es ist kein Fisch.
4. Das langsamste Tier: Es trägt oft ein Haus auf seinem Rücken und hat keine Beine.
5. Es sieht aus wie ein Hund, ist aber nicht so zahm.
6. Dieses Tier lebt länger als der Elefant.
7. Das ist die giftigste Schlange in Nordamerika.
8. Dieser Wasservogel hat eine Spannweite von mehr als drei Metern.
9. Dieses Tier hat die höchste Herzfrequenz, mit zirka 1 000 Schlägen pro Minute.
10. Dieses Tier hört besser als ein Delfin.

a. der Kolibri
b. der Elefant
c. die Riesenschildkröte
d. die Schnecke
e. die Fledermaus
f. der Blauwal
g. der Gepard
h. die Klapperschlange
i. der Albatros
j. der Wolf

der Blauwal

Situation 13 Informationsspiel: Tiere

Sit. 12. Sts. read and complete the activity individually. Then ask for their answers. Find out how many other animals sts. know/remember. Focus by asking: *Welche Tiere findet man nur im Dschungel? Welche Tiere findet man in Australien? Welche Tiere findet man in der Wüste? Welche Tiere findet man in Nordamerika? in Südamerika? in Europa? in Asien?* As a warm-up exercise some time, have sts. quickly draw pictures of various animals on the board. The first person to guess the animal correctly, wins and draws the next picture. **Answers:** 1. b, 2. g, 3. f, 4. d, 5. j, 6. c, 7. h, 8. i, 9. a, 10. e.

Sit. 13. The corresponding chart is in Appendix A. In the follow-up, focus on the choices made by the sts. and ask them to explain their responses.

MODELL: Welche Tiere findet _____ am tollsten?
    Vor welchem Tier hat _____ am meisten Angst?
    Welches Tier hätte _____ gern als Haustier?
    Welches wilde Tier würde _____ gern in freier Natur sehen?
    Wenn _____ an Afrika denkt, an welche Tiere denkt er/sie?
    Wenn _____ an die Wüste denkt, an welches Tier denkt er/sie dann zuerst?
    Welche Vögel findet _____ am schönsten?
    Welchen Fisch findet _____ am gefährlichsten?
    Welchem Tier möchte _____ nicht in Wald begegnen?

	Ernst	Maria	mein(e) Partner(in)
Lieblingstier	ein Krokodil	eine Katze	
Angst	vor dem Hund von nebenan	vor Mäusen	
Haustier	eine Schlange	einen Papagei	
wildes Tier	einen Elefanten	eine Giraffe	
Afrika	an Löwen	an Zebras	
Wüste	an einen Skorpion	an ein Kamel	
Vögel	Adler	Eulen	
Fisch	den weißen Hai	den Piranha	
Wald	einem Wolf	einem Wildschwein	

Situation 14 Interview: Tiere

1. Was ist dein Lieblingstier? Warum?
2. Hast du oder hattest du ein Haustier? Was für eins? Wie heißt oder wie hieß es? Beschreib es. Erzähl eine Geschichte von ihm!
3. Vor welchen Tieren fürchtest du dich?
4. Welches Tier findest du am interessantesten?
5. Welches Tier findest du am hässlichsten?
6. Welches Tier wärst du am liebsten? Warum?
7. Findest du es wichtig, dass Kinder mit Tieren aufwachsen? Wenn ja, mit welchen? Warum?

Situation 15 Bildgeschichte: Lydias Hamster

Sit. 15. Sentences for narration series: **1.** *Lydia Frisch bekam zum Geburtstag einen Hamster.* **2.** *Sie spielte jeden Tag mit ihrem Hamster.* **3.** *Eines Abends vergaß sie, die Käfigtür richtig zuzumachen.* **4.** *Als sie am nächsten Morgen aufstand, war der Hamster verschwunden.* **5.** *Lydia suchte den Hamster im ganzen Haus.* **6.** *Sie war sehr traurig, weil sie ihn nicht fand.* **7.** *Eine Woche später entdeckte sie ein komisches Loch in ihrer Jacke.* **8.** *Außerdem war die Pflanze in ihrer Fensterbank angefressen.* **9.** *Lydia suchte noch einmal überall. Mit ihrem Vater schaute sie sogar hinter den Kleiderschrank.* **10.** *Da fand sie schließlich den Hamster. Er hatte sich ein gemütliches Nest gebaut.*

Photo Questions. *Was macht dieses Paar? Wie nennt man diese Hunderasse? Wie oft gehen sie zusammen spazieren? Was sieht man sonst auf diesem Bild? Welche Jahreszeit ist es?*

Zwei ältere Menschen gehen mit Hunden Gassi.

Situation 16 Tiere in Sprichwörtern

In vielen Sprachen gibt es Sprichwörter, in denen Tiere vorkommen. Welche Sprichwörter fallen Ihnen auf Englisch ein? Ordnen Sie jeder Zeichnung das passende Sprichwort zu.

1. Wenn dem Esel zu wohl ist, geht er aufs Eis.
2. Einem geschenkten Gaul (= Pferd) sieht man nicht ins Maul.
3. Kaum ist die Katze aus dem Haus, tanzen die Mäuse auf dem Tisch.
4. Den letzten beißen die Hunde.
5. In der Not[1] frisst der Teufel Fliegen.
6. Ein blindes Huhn findet auch mal ein Korn.

—

—

—

—

—

Was bedeuten die Sprichwörter? Kombinieren Sie die Definitionen mit den Sprichwörtern.

a. Wenn man etwas geschenkt bekommt, sollte man nicht zu kritisch damit sein.
b. Wenn man etwas nötig braucht, muss man nehmen, was da ist.
c. Wenn der Chef nicht da ist, machen die Angestellten, was sie wollen.
d. Jemandem, der sonst wenig Erfolg hat, kann auch etwas gelingen.
e. Wenn man sich nicht beeilt, ergeht es einem schlecht.
f. Leute, die zu viel Erfolg oder Glück haben, werden übermütig[2].

[1]*emergency* [2]*cocky*

Filmlektüre
Die fetten Jahre sind vorbei

 Vor dem Lesen

A. Schauen Sie sich das Foto an.

1. Welche Personen sehen Sie auf dem Foto?
2. Beschreiben Sie die junge Frau.
3. Welchen der beiden jungen Männer finden Sie am sympathischsten? Warum?

Filmangaben

Titel: *Die fetten Jahre sind vorbei*
Genre: Drama
Land: Österreich
Erscheinungsjahr: 2004
Dauer: 127 Min.
Regisseur: Hans Weingartner
Hauptrollen: Daniel Brühl, Julia Jentsch, Stipe Erceg, Burghart Klaußner

... denn sie wissen nicht, was sie tun

B. Lesen Sie die Wörter im Miniwörterbuch. Suchen Sie sie im Text und unterstreichen Sie sie.

Miniwörterbuch

verteilt	distributed	schulden	to owe
einbrechen	to break in	das **Vermögen**	fortune
verrücken	to move, to disarrange	beschädigen	to damage
verstecken	to hide	entführen	to kidnap
die **Nachricht**	message	die **Berghütte**	mountain cabin
unterzeichnen	to sign	aufbegehren	to revolt
die **Erziehungsberechtigten**	legal guardians	verraten	to betray
im **Überschwang der** **Gefühle**	in exuberance	auf etwas verzichten	to go without something
		aufbrechen	to take off

Inhaltsangabe

Besitz und Geld sind auf der Welt ungerecht verteilt. Jan (Daniel Brühl) und Peter (Stipe Erceg), zwei junge Berliner, wollen diese Situation ändern und haben eine eigene Methode dafür gefunden: Sie brechen nachts in Villen reicher Leute ein. Sie stehlen nichts, sondern verrücken Möbel, hängen Bilder um und
5   verstecken wertvolle Gegenstände im Kühlschrank oder werfen sie in den Swimmingpool. Die Nachrichten, die sie für die Hausbesitzer hinterlassen, lauten: „Die fetten Jahre sind vorbei" oder „Sie haben zu viel Geld", unterzeichnet mit „Die Erziehungsberechtigten". Ihr Ziel: Die Reichen sollen über ihren Luxus nachdenken.
    Alles läuft immer nach Plan. Jan und Peter haben ihren Spaß und die Villenbe-
10 wohner sind geschockt beim Anblick ihrer Häuser. Doch als sich dann Jan und Jule

Miniwörterbuch

das **Entwicklungsland**	developing country
festnehmen	to apprehend
umkippen	to topple
verhindern	to prevent
durchgreifen	to crack down
anpöbeln	to accost
sich einmischen	to intervene
der **Obdachlose**	homeless person
behandeln	to treat
die **Räumungsklage**	eviction notice
zwar ... aber	to be sure . . . but
verzweifelt	desperate
herstellen	to make

(Julia Jentsch), Peters Freundin, ineinander verlieben, brechen die beiden im Überschwang der Gefühle und ohne Peter in die Villa des Geschäftsmannes Justus Hardenberg (Burghart Klaußner) ein. Dem schuldet Jule ein halbes Vermögen, weil sie bei einem Unfall sein teures Auto beschädigt hat. Ein harmloser Einbruch wie die anderen wird es nicht, denn sie werden vom Hausbesitzer überrascht. Jan und Jule schlagen Hardenberg nieder, entführen ihn und bringen ihn mit Peters Hilfe in die Berghütte von Jules Onkel am Tiroler Achensee. In der Berghütte stellt sich heraus, dass Hardenberg in seinen jungen Jahren genauso gegen das etablierte Bürgertum aufbegehrte wie Jan, Peter und Jule jetzt. Seine Ideale von früher hat Hardenberg jedoch verraten.

Am Ende bringen die drei Entführer Hardenberg in seine Villa zurück. Er verzichtet auf das Geld, das ihm Jule wegen des Autounfalls schuldet. Als die Polizei wenig später die Wohnung der drei jungen Leute stürmt, sind sie schon verschwunden. Am Schluss brechen sie mit Hardenbergs Motorjacht zu neuen Taten auf.

Arbeit mit dem Text

Welche Aussagen sind falsch? Verbessern Sie die falschen Aussagen.

1. Peter und Jan brechen in Villen ein, weil sie Geld brauchen.
2. Jule ist Peters Freundin, verliebt sich aber in Jan.
3. Peter und Jan brechen in die Villa von Justus Hardenberg ein.
4. Hardenberg schuldet Jule sehr viel Geld.
5. Jan, Peter und Jule entführen Hardenberg, weil er sie beim Einbruch in seine Villa überrascht hat.
6. Die drei Entführer lassen Hardenberg in Tirol frei.
7. Jan, Peter und Jule melden sich° bei der Polizei.

Filmclip 🎬

Szene: DVD, Kapitel 1, „Start", 4:30–8:25 Min.

Jule nimmt an einer Demonstration gegen Sweatshops teil. Jan sitzt im Park und fährt dann mit der Straßenbahn nach Hause. Schauen Sie sich den Filmclip an. Bringen Sie die Sätze in die richtige Reihenfolge.

- **1** Jule nimmt an einer Demo gegen Sweatshops teil und erklärt zwei Mädchen, wie viel die kleinen Kinder in Entwicklungsländern arbeiten müssen.
- **6** Als die Polizisten und die zwei festgenommenen jungen Leute im Polizeiwagen sitzen, versuchen die Demonstranten ihn umzukippen.
- **5** Die Demonstranten wollen das verhindern, die Polizei greift aber brutal durch.
- **4** Die Polizei nimmt die zwei jungen Männer fest und bringt sie in den Polizeiwagen.
- **13** Ein Kontrolleur geht hinter Jan her und will ihn anpöbeln, Jan aber lässt sich das nicht gefallen.
- **7** Jan (Brühl) sitzt im Park und sieht einer jungen Familie zu.
- **12** Jan mischt sich ein und gibt dem alten Mann seine Karte.
- **11** Jan sitzt in der Straßenbahn und sieht, wie drei Kontrolleure einen Obdachlosen schlecht behandeln.
- **8** Jule geht nach Hause und bekommt eine Räumungsklage.
- **9** Jule hat zwar die Miete bezahlt, aber sechs Monate zu spät.
- **10** Jule liest die Räumungsklage und ist völlig verzweifelt.
- **3** Zwei Angestellte des Sportladens werfen die zwei jungen Männer hinaus.
- **2** Zwei junge Männer gehen in einen Sportladen und erklären, wie die Turnschuhe hergestellt werden.

Nach dem Lesen

Beantworten Sie die folgenden Fragen.

success

rüttelt wach *shakes awake*

seriously

1. Glauben Sie, dass Jan, Peter und Jule mit ihren Aktionen Erfolg° haben? Rüttelt man mit so etwas die Gesellschaft wach°? Kann oder muss man die drei ernst° nehmen? Warum? Warum nicht?

2. Justus Hardenberg gehörte zu den sogenannten „68ern". 1968 war ein aufregendes Jahr in der alten BRD. Forschen Sie im Internet nach, was in diesem Jahr in Westdeutschland passierte und welche Rolle die Studenten gespielt haben.

Videoecke

Perspektiven

> Was machst du gern im Urlaub?

Aufgabe 1 Wer sagt das?

Ordnen Sie die Aussagen den Personen zu.

Ich wandere gerne und mache viel Sport.

1. Sandra __c__   2. Shaimaa __h__   3. Tina __d__   4. Jenny __a__

5. Nadezda __f__   6. Pascal __e__   7. Simone __g__   8. Michael __b__

a. Ich entspanne am liebsten am Strand.
b. Ich erhole mich gern.
c. Ich fahre am liebsten ans Meer.
d. Ich gucke mir Gebäude an und treffe Menschen, die dort leben.
e. Ich mache gerne gar nichts.
f. Ich schwimme sehr gerne.
g. Ich wandere gerne.
h. Reisen und schlafen.

Interviews

Tina

Tabea

- Wohin fährst du gern in Urlaub?
- Was war dein bisher schönster Urlaub?
- Was war daran so besonders?
- Gab es mal einen Urlaub, in dem etwas schief ging?
- Hast du oder hattest du ein Haustier?
- Gibt es über dein Haustier eine lustige Geschichte?

Aufgabe 2 Tina oder Tabea?

Sehen Sie sich das Video an und schreiben Sie Tina oder Tabea neben die Aussagen.

1. Mein schönster Urlaub war meine Reise nach Spanien. Tina
2. Mein schönster Urlaub war am Meer. Tabea
3. Wir haben den tollen Sternenhimmel gesehen. Tabea
4. Ich habe dort drei Monate gearbeitet. Tina
5. Mir wurde einmal die Tasche geklaut. Tina
6. Wir haben Flusskrebse gebraten. Tabea
7. Wir haben die Hälfte des Essens vergessen. Tabea
8. Ich hatte ein Zwergkaninchen. Tabea
9. Ich hatte einen Hasen namens Milan. Tina
10. Ich dachte immer, es wär ein Junge. Tina

Aufgabe 3 Tinas Tasche

Tina wird die Tasche geklaut. Hören Sie sich die Geschichte an und erzählen Sie sie dann mithilfe der folgenden Notizen.

> **Tasche neben sich stellen**   **im Bus sitzen**
>
> **einen Moment unachtsam**   **Tasche weg**
>
> **gut aufpassen**   **problematisch**
>
> **Personalausweis und Portemonnaie drin**

Aufgabe 4 Tinas Hase

Videoecke. Aufgabe 4. Answers: *Sts. to make use of the following in their narration*: Hase namens Milan; in einem Wohnhaus wohnen; Hase lebt auf dem Hof; Familie kümmert sich nicht um ihn; ausziehen; Hasen mitnehmen; dachte immer, es wär ein Junge; zwei Jahre später kastrieren lassen; es war ein Mädchen.

Tina hatte einen Hasen. Hören Sie sich die Geschichte an, machen Sie sich Notizen und erzählen Sie dann die Geschichte mithilfe Ihrer Notizen.

Aufgabe 5 Interview

Interviewen Sie eine Partnerin oder einen Partner. Stellen Sie dieselben Fragen.

Wortschatz

Reisen und Tourismus — Travel and Tourism

die Bahnangestellte, -n	female train agent
die Fahrt, -en	trip
die Haltestelle, -n	stop
die Jugendherberge, -n	youth hostel
die Klasse, -n (R)	class
erster Klasse fahren	to travel first class
die Lage, -n	place; position
die Luftmatratze, -n	air mattress
die Möwe, -n	seagull
die Reisende, -n	female traveler
die Schiene, -n	train track
die Sonnenmilch	suntan lotion
die Unterkunft, ⸚e	lodging
die Welle, -n	wave
der Aufenthaltsraum, ⸚e	lounge, recreation room
der Ausweis, -e	identification card
der Bahnangestellte, -n	male train agent
der Hafen, ⸚	harbor, port
der Reisende, -n (ein Reisender)	male traveler
der Sonnenbrand, ⸚e	sunburn
der Sonnenschirm, -e	sunshade, beach parasol
der Strandkorb, ⸚e	beach chair
der Wirt, -e	host, innkeeper; barkeeper
der Zug, ⸚e (R)	train
das Andenken, -	souvenir
das Einzelzimmer, -	single room
das Gästehaus, ⸚er	bed-and-breakfast (inn)
das Gleis, -e	(set of) train tracks
das Kanu, -s	canoe
Kanu fahren	to go canoeing
das Schlauchboot, -e	inflatable dinghy
das Ziel, -e	destination

Ähnliche Wörter

die Idee, -n; die Rezeption, -en; der Campingplatz, ⸚e; das Camping; das Doppelzimmer, - (R); das Fernsehzimmer, -; das Frühstückszimmer; packen

Den Weg beschreiben — Giving Directions

ab·biegen, bog ... ab, ist abgebogen	to turn
entlang·gehen	to go along
verfehlen	to miss, not notice
vorbei·gehen (an + dat.)	to go by
weiter·gehen	to keep on walking

entlang	along
gegenüber von (R)	across from
geradeaus	straight ahead
her(·kommen)	(to come) this way
heraus(·kommen)	(to come) out this way
herein(·kommen)	(to get/go) in this way
hin(·gehen)	(to go) that way
hinauf(·gehen)	(to go) up that way
hinüber(·gehen)	(to go) over that way
links (R)	left
oben	above
rechts (R)	right

In der Stadt — In the City

die Brücke, -n	bridge
die Bushaltestelle, -n	bus stop
die Gasse, -n	narrow street; alley
die Kreuzung, -en	intersection
der Dom, -e	cathedral
der Kopierladen, ⸚	copy shop
der Kreisverkehr, -e	traffic roundabout
der Waschsalon, -s	laundromat
der Zebrastreifen, -	crosswalk
das Gebäude, -	building

Ähnliche Wörter

die Fußgängerzone, -n; der Markt, ⸚e; der Stadtplan, ⸚e

Tiere — Animals

die Biene, -n	bee
die Fledermaus, ⸚e	bat
die Mücke, -n	mosquito
die Schildkröte, -n	turtle
die Schlange, -n	snake
die Klapperschlange, -n	rattlesnake
die Schnecke, -n	snail
der Adler, -	eagle
der Gepard, -e	cheetah
der Hai, -e	shark
der Kolibri, -s	hummingbird
der Löwe, -n (wk. masc.)	lion
der Papagei, -en	parrot
der Rüssel, -	trunk (of an elephant)
der Stoßzahn, ⸚e	tusk
der Vogel, ⸚	bird
der Wasservogel, ⸚	waterfowl

das Meerschweinchen, -	guinea pig
das Tier, -e (R)	animal
das Haustier, -e	pet
das Landsäugetier, -e	land mammal

Ähnliche Wörter

die Giraffe, -n; die Maus, ⁻e; die Ratte, -n; der Albatros, -se; der Blauwal, -e; der Delfin, -e; der Hamster, -; der Piranha, -s; der Skorpion, -e; das Känguru, -s; das Krokodil, -e; das Wildschwein, -e; das Zebra, -s

Sonstige Substantive	Other Nouns
die Bürgerin, -nen	female citizen
die Fensterbank, ⁻e (R)	windowsill
die Tollwut	rabies
der Bürger, -	male citizen
der Käfig, -e	cage
das Elfenbein	ivory
das Treppenhaus, ⁻er	stairwell

Ähnliche Wörter

der Staat, -en; das Nest, -er; in freier Natur

Sonstige Verben	Other Verbs
ab·reisen, ist abgereist	to depart
ein·schalten	to turn on
ein·steigen (R), stieg ... ein, ist eingestiegen	to board
entschuldigen	to excuse
entschuldigen Sie!	excuse me!
sich erkundigen nach	to ask about, get information about
sich fürchten vor (+ *dat.*)	to be afraid of
grüßen	to greet, say hello to
impfen gegen	to vaccinate against
sammeln	to collect
sonnenbaden gehen	to go sunbathing
stechen, sticht, stach, gestochen	to sting; to bite (*of insects*)
trampen, ist getrampt	to hitchhike

Ähnliche Wörter

antworten (+ *dat.*) (R); windsurfen gehen

Adjektive und Adverbien	Adjectives and Adverbs
einfach	one-way (trip)
gefährlich	dangerous
gemütlich	cozy
komisch	funny, strange
nützlich	useful
überall	everywhere
ungeduldig	impatient
zahm	tame

Ähnliche Wörter

extra, voll, zentral

Sonstige Wörter und Ausdrücke	Other Words and Expressions
an ... vorbei	by
aus	of; from; out of
außerdem (R)	besides
bei (R)	at; with; near
bis zu	as far as; up to
danach (R)	afterward
hin und zurück (R)	there and back; round-trip
inbegriffen	included
nach (R)	to (*a place*)
nach Hause (R)	(to) home
selbstverständlich	of course
vielen Dank	many thanks
von (R)	of; from
zu (R)	to (*a place*)
zu Hause (R)	at home

Strukturen und Übungen

10.1 Prepositions to talk about places:
aus, bei, nach, von, zu

10.1 *Präpositionen des Orts.* We have introduced the dative prepositions in different chapters according to their meanings, rather than as a single group of prepositions taking the dative. The idea of a dative preposition was introduced with *zu* in Section 6.4 and *mit* and *bei* in Section 6.6. In the present section, we describe the use of 5 dative prepositions that refer to place. *Aus* as a way of expressing origin appeared first in Section B.6. The use of *nach* and *zu* for indicating direction was introduced in Section 6.4. (See that section for other details.) In Section 10.3, *bis zu* and *gegenüber von*, which also take the dative, are introduced as a means of giving directions.

Point out that the preposition *in* with the accusative, not *nach*, is used with the names of countries that have a definite article.

Use the prepositions **aus** and **von** to indicate origin; **bei** to indicate a fixed location; and **nach** and **zu** to indicate destination. These five prepositions are always used with nouns and pronouns in the dative case.

Woher (kommt sie?)	Wo (ist sie?)	Wohin (geht/fährt sie?)
aus Spanien		nach Spanien
aus dem Zimmer		nach Hause
von rechts		nach links
von Erika	bei Erika	zu Erika
vom Strand		zum Strand

A. The Prepositions **aus** and **von**

1. Use **aus** to indicate that someone or something comes from an enclosed or defined space, such as a country, a town, or a building.

Diese Fische kommen **aus der Donau.**	*These fish come from the Danube river.*
Jens kam **aus seinem Zimmer.**	*Jens came out of his room.*

aus: enclosed spaces
  countries
  towns
  buildings

Most country and city names are neuter; no article is used with these names.

> Josef kommt **aus Deutschland.**

Wissen Sie noch?

The prepositions **aus** (*from*), **bei** (*near, with*), **mit** (*with*), **nach** (*to*), **von** (*from*), **zu** (*to*) are prepositions that take the dative case.

Review grammar B.6, 6.4, and 6.6.

However, the article is included when the country name is masculine, feminine, or plural.

> Richards Freund Ali kommt **aus dem Iran.**
> Mehmets Familie kommt **aus der Türkei.**
> Ich komme **aus den USA.**

2. Use **von** to indicate that someone or something comes not from an enclosed space but from an open space, from a particular direction, or from a person.

von: open spaces
  directions
  persons

Melanie kommt gerade **vom Markt** zurück.	*Melanie's just returning from the market.*
Das rote Auto kam **von rechts.**	*The red car came from the right.*
Michael hat es mir gesagt. Ich weiß es **von ihm.**	*Michael told me. I know it through (from) him.*

B. The Preposition **bei**

Achtung!

von + dem = vom
bei + dem = beim
zu + dem = zum
zu + der = zur

Use **bei** before the name of a place where someone works or a place where someone lives or is staying.

Albert arbeitet **bei McDonald's.**	*Albert works at McDonald's.*
Rolf wohnt **bei einer Gastfamilie.**	*Rolf is staying with a host family.*
Treffen wir uns **bei Katrin.**	*Let's meet at Katrin's.*

bei: place of work
  residence

nach: cities
    countries without articles
    direction
    nach Hause (idiom)

C. The Prepositions nach and zu

Use **nach** with neuter names of cities and countries (no article), to indicate direction, and in the idiom **nach Hause** ([*going*] *home*).

Wir fahren morgen **nach Salzburg.**	*We'll go to Salzburg tomorrow.*
Biegen Sie an der Ampel **nach links ab.**	*Turn left at the light.*
Gehen Sie **nach Westen.**	*Go west.*
Ich muss jetzt **nach Hause.**	*I have to go home now.*

zu: places
    persons
    zu Hause (idiom)

Use **zu** to indicate movement toward a place or a person, and in the idiom **zu Hause** (*at home*).

Wir fahren heute **zum Strand.**	*We'll go to the beach today.*
Wir gehen morgen **zu Tante Julia.**	*We'll go to Aunt Julia's tomorrow.*
Rolf ist nicht **zu Hause.**	*Rolf is not at home.*

Übung 1   Die Familie Ruf

Kombinieren Sie Fragen und Antworten.

Üb. 1. Assign for homework and check in class. Alert sts. to the fact that they can reduce the number of choices by focusing on the question word, e.g., *woher* matches up with *aus* and *von*, and sometimes on the gender of the subject, e.g., *Herr Ruf* goes with *aus seinem Zimmer.*

1. Hier kommt Herr Ruf. Er hat seine Hausschuhe an. Woher kommt er gerade?
2. Hans hat noch seine Schultasche auf dem Rücken. Woher kommt er?
3. Frau Ruf kommt mit zwei Taschen voll Obst und Gemüse herein. Woher kommt sie?
4. Jutta kommt herein. Sie hat eine neue Frisur[1]. Woher kommt sie?
5. Gestern Abend war Jutta nicht zu Hause. Wo war sie?
6. Ihre Mutter war auch nicht zu Hause. Wo war sie?
7. Morgen geht Herr Ruf aus. Wohin geht er?
8. Hans fährt am Wochenende weg. Wohin fährt er?
9. Frau Ruf ist am Wochenende geschäftlich unterwegs. Wohin fährt sie?
10. Jutta möchte mit ihrem Freund einen Skiurlaub machen. Wohin wollen sie?

a. Aus der Schule.
b. Aus seinem Zimmer.
c. Bei ihrem Freund.
d. Bei Frau Körner.
e. Nach Innsbruck.
f. Nach Berlin.
g. Vom Friseur.
h. Vom Markt.
i. Zu Herrn Thelen, Karten spielen.
j. Zu seiner Tante.

Übung 2   Melanies Reise nach Dänemark

Üb. 2. Assign for homework. Ask sts. to act out the dialogue between Claire and Melanie in class.

Beantworten Sie die Fragen. Verwenden Sie die Präpositionen **aus, bei, nach, von** oder **zu**.

MODELL: CLAIRE: Wohin bist du gefahren? (Dänemark) →
      MELANIE: Nach Dänemark.

1. Wohin genau? (Kopenhagen)
2. Wohin bist du am ersten Tag gegangen? (der Strand)
3. Und deine Freundin Fatima? Wohin ist sie gegangen? (ihre Tante Sule)

[1]*hairstyle*

4. Woher kommt die Tante deiner Freundin? (die Türkei)

5. Kommt deine Freundin auch aus der Türkei? (nein / der Iran)

6. Am Strand hast du Peter getroffen, nicht? Woher ist der plötzlich gekommen? (das Wasser)

7. Sein Freund war auch dabei, nicht? Woher ist der gekommen? (der Markt)

8. Weißt du, wo die beiden übernachten wollten? (ja/uns)

9. Und wo haben sie übernachtet? (Fatimas Tante)

10. Wohin seid ihr am nächsten Morgen gefahren? (Hause)

10.2 Requests and instructions: the imperative (summary review)

10.2. *Aufforderungen und Anweisungen: Der Imperativ.* This section reviews the *Sie*-imperative (introduced in Section A.1) and the *du*-imperative (introduced in Section 2.6) and describes for the first time the *ihr*-imperative and the imperative with *wir*. The rules for the formation of all forms except the *du*-imperative are straightforward and cause few difficulties.

Wissen Sie noch?

The imperative is used to form commands, sentences in which you tell others how to act.

Review grammar 2.6.

As you have already learned, the imperative (command form) in German is used to make requests, to give instructions and directions, and to issue orders. To soften requests or to make them more polite, words such as **doch, mal,** and **bitte** are often included in imperative sentences.

Mach mal das Fenster **zu!**	*Close the window!*
Bringen Sie mir **bitte** noch einen Kaffee.	*Bring me another cup of coffee, please.*

The imperative has four forms: the familiar singular (**du**), the familiar plural (**ihr**), the polite (**Sie**), and the first-person plural (**wir**).

A. Sie and wir

In both the **Sie**- and the **wir**-forms, the verb begins the sentence and the pronoun follows.

Kontrollieren Sie bitte das Öl.	*Please check the oil.*
Gehen wir doch heute ins Kino!	*Let's go to the movies today.*

B. ihr

The familiar plural imperative consists of the present-tense **ihr**-form of the verb but does not include the pronoun **ihr**.

Lydia und Rosemarie, **kommt her** und **hört** mir **zu!**	*Lydia and Rosemarie, come here and listen to me.*
Sagt immer die Wahrheit!	*Always tell the truth.*

C. du

The familiar singular imperative consists of the present-tense **du**-form of the verb without the -(s)t ending and without the pronoun **du**.

du kommst	**Komm!**
du tanzt	**Tanz!**
du isst	**Iss!**

In written German, you will sometimes see a final **-e (komme, gehe),** but this **-e** is usually omitted in the spoken language for all verbs except those for which the present-tense **du**-form ends in **-est.**

du arbeitest	**Arbeite!**
du öffnest	**Öffne!**

Verbs that have a stem-vowel change from **-a-** to **-ä-** or **-au-** to **-äu-** do not have an umlaut in the **du**-imperative.

du fährst	**Fahr!**
du läufst	**Lauf!**

D. sein

The verb **sein** has irregular imperative forms.

du	→ **Sei** leise!	⎫		*(Paul!)*
ihr	→ **Seid** leise!	⎬ *Be quiet!*	*(You two!)*
Sie	→ **Seien Sie** leise!	⎭		*(Mrs. Smith!)*
wir	→ **Seien wir** leise!	*Let's be quiet!*

Sei so gut und gib mir die   *Be so kind and pass me the*
    Butter, Andrea.   *butter, Andrea.*
Seid keine Egoisten!   *Don't be such egotists!*

Übung 3   ## Hans und sein Vater

Hans und sein Vater sind zu Hause. Hans fragt seinen Vater, was er tun darf oder tun muss. Spielen Sie die Rolle seines Vaters. Sie brauchen auch einen guten Grund!

MODELL: Darf ich den Fernseher einschalten? →
        Ja, schalte ihn ein. Es kommt ein guter Film.
  oder Nein, schalte ihn nicht ein. Ich möchte Musik hören.

1. Muss ich jetzt Klavier üben?
2. Darf ich Jens anrufen?
3. Darf ich die Schokolade essen?
4. Darf ich das Fenster aufmachen?
5. Muss ich dir einen Kuss geben?
6. Kann ich mit dir reden?
7. Muss ich das Geschirr spülen?
8. Darf ich in den Garten gehen?
9. Darf ich morgen mit dem Fahrrad in die Schule fahren?

Übung 4   ## Aufforderungen!

Üb. 4. Remind sts. of the convention that *du*-forms are to be used with a single first name, *ihr*-forms with more than one first name, and *Sie*-forms with names preceded by *Herr* and/or *Frau*.

Sie sind die erste Person in jeder Zeile. Was sagen Sie?

MODELL: Frau Wagner: Jens und Ernst / Zimmer aufräumen →
        Jens und Ernst, räumt euer Zimmer auf!

1. Herr Wagner: Jens und Ernst / nicht so laut sein
2. Michael: Maria / bitte an der nächsten Ampel halten
3. Frau Wagner: Uli / an der nächsten Straße nach links abbiegen
4. Herr Ruf: Jutta / mehr Obst essen
5. Herr Siebert: Herr Pusch / nicht so schnell fahren
6. Jutta: Jens / an der Ecke auf mich warten
7. Frau Frisch: Natalie und Rosemarie / nicht ungeduldig sein
8. Herr Thelen: Andrea und Paula / Vater von mir grüßen
9. Frau Ruf: Hans / mal schnell zu Papa laufen
10. Oma Schmitz: Helga und Sigrid / jeden Tag die Zeitung lesen

Verwenden Sie die Verben im Kasten.

> helfen   machen
>
>   vergessen
>
> warten   sprechen

1. FRAU RUF: Ich sitze jetzt schon wieder seit sechs Stunden vor dem Computer.
   HERR RUF: Du arbeitest zu viel. _____ mal eine Pause.

2. HERR SIEBERT: _____ bitte lauter, ich verstehe Sie nicht.
   MARIA: Ja, wie laut soll ich denn sprechen? Wollen Sie, dass ich schreie?

3. MICHAEL: Na, was ist? Kommen Sie nun oder kommen Sie nicht?
   FRAU KÖRNER: Ich bin ja gleich fertig. Bitte _____ doch noch einen Moment.

4. HANS: Kann ich mit euch zum Schwimmen gehen?
   JENS: Ja, komm und _____ deine Badehose nicht.

5. OMA SCHMITZ: _____ mir bitte, ich kann die Koffer nicht allein tragen.
   HELGA UND SIGRID: Aber natürlich, Großmutter, wir helfen dir doch gern.

ACCUSATIVE:
   entlang (follows the noun)
   über (precedes the noun)

10.3 Prepositions for giving directions: *an ... vorbei, bis zu, entlang, gegenüber von, über*

A. **entlang** (*along*) and **über** (*over*) + Accusative

Use the prepositions **entlang** and **über** with nouns in the accusative case. Note that **entlang** follows the noun.

Fahren Sie **den Fluß entlang.**	*Drive along the river.*
Gehen Sie **über den Zebrastreifen.**	*Walk across the crosswalk.*

The preposition **über** may also be used as the equivalent of English *via.*

Der Zug fährt **über** Frankfurt und Hannover nach Hamburg.	*The train goes to Hamburg via Frankfurt and Hanover.*

DATIVE:
   an ... vorbei (encloses the noun)
   bis zu (precedes the noun)
   gegenüber von (precedes the noun)

B. **an ... vorbei** (*past*), **bis zu** (*up to, as far as*), **gegenüber von** (*across from*) + Dative

Use **an ... vorbei, bis zu,** and **gegenüber von** with the noun in the dative case. Note that **an ... vorbei** encloses the noun.

Gehen Sie **am Supermarkt vorbei.**	*Go past the supermarket.*
Fahren Sie **bis zur Fußgängerzone** und biegen Sie links ab.	*Drive to the pedestrian zone and turn left.*
Die U-Bahnhaltestelle ist **gegenüber vom Markthotel.**	*The subway station is across from the Markthotel.*

Übung 6   Wie komme ich dahin?

Ein Ortsfremder[1] fragt Sie nach dem Weg. Antworten Sie! Nützliche Wörter:

entlang	an ... vorbei	gegenüber von
über	bis zu	

1. Wie muss ich fahren?

2. Wie muss ich gehen?

3. Wie muss ich gehen?

4. Wie muss ich fahren?

[1]stranger

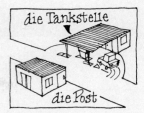

5. Wo ist die Tankstelle?

6. Wie komme ich zum Zug?

7. Immer geradeaus?

8. Vor dem Rathaus links?

9. Das Hotel „Zum Patrizier"?

10. Wie komme ich nach Nürnberg?

10.4. *Höflichkeitsformen: Konjunktiv der Modalverben.* The form we call subjunctive here is often referred to in other textbooks as the present subjunctive. In *Kontakte* we provide subjunctive forms only for certain frequently used verbs. The forms are presented according to their different uses. (We do not introduce the use of subjunctive forms in indirect speech.) Polite requests with the subjunctive of modal verbs are described in this section. Hypothetical statements with *würde, wäre,* and *hätte* will be introduced in Section 12.2. We do not introduce the subjunctive forms of any other verbs or the forms

The subjunctive is formed from the simple past-tense stem. Add an umlaut if there is an umlaut in the infinitive.

often called past subjunctive (*ich hätte gearbeitet, ich wäre gegangen*).

10.4 Being polite: the subjunctive form of modal verbs

Use the subjunctive form of modal verbs to be more polite.

Könnten Sie mir bitte dafür eine Quittung geben?
Ich **müsste** mal telefonieren. **Dürfte** ich Ihr Telefon benutzen?

Could you please give me a receipt for that?
I have to make a phone call. Could I use your phone?

To form the subjunctive of a modal verb, add an umlaut to the simple past form if there is also one in the infinitive. If the modal verb has no umlaut in the infinitive (**sollen** and **wollen**), the subjunctive form is the same as the simple past form.

Infinitive	Past	Subjunctive
dürfen	ich durfte	ich d**ü**rfte
können	ich konnte	ich k**ö**nnte
mögen	ich mochte	ich m**ö**chte
müssen	ich musste	ich m**ü**sste
sollen	ich sollte	ich sollte
wollen	ich wollte	ich wollte

On the following page are the subjunctive forms of **können** and **wollen.**

könnten			
ich	könnte	wir	könnten
du	könntest	ihr	könntet
Sie	könnten	Sie	könnten
er sie es	könnte	sie	könnten

wollen			
ich	wollte	wir	wollten
du	wolltest	ihr	wolltet
Sie	wollten	Sie	wollten
er sie es	wollte	sie	wollten

In modern German, **möchte,** the subjunctive form of **mögen,** has become almost a synonym of **wollen.**

—Wohin wollen Sie fliegen?   *Where do you want to go (fly)?*
—Wir möchten nach Kanada fliegen.   *We want / would like to fly to Canada.*

Another polite form, **hätte gern,** is now used more and more, especially in conversational exchanges involving goods and services.

Ich hätte gern eine Cola, bitte.   *I'd like a Coke, please.*
Wir hätten gern die Speisekarte, bitte.   *We'd like the menu, please.*

Übung 7   Überredungskünste

Üb. 7. The exercise can be done by pairs of sts. in class. The answers use the *du*- and *wir*-forms of the subjunctive of *können*.

Versuchen Sie, jemanden zu überreden[1], etwas anderes zu machen als das, was er/sie machen will.

MODELL: s1: Ich fahre jetzt. (bleiben)
          s2: Ach, könntest du nicht bleiben?

1. Ich koche Kaffee. (Tee, Suppe, ?)
2. Ich lese jetzt. (später, morgen, ?)
3. Ich sehe jetzt fern. (etwas Klavier spielen, mit mir sprechen, ?)
4. Ich rufe meine Mutter an. (deinen Vater, deine Tante, ?)
5. Ich gehe nach Hause. (noch eine Stunde bleiben, bis morgen bleiben, ?)

MODELL: s1: Wir fahren nach Spanien. (Italien)
          s2: Könnten wir nicht mal nach Italien fahren?

6. Wir übernachten im Zelt. (Hotel, Campingbus, ?)
7. Wir kochen selbst. (essen gehen, fasten, ?)
8. Wir gehen jeden Tag wandern. (schwimmen, ins Kino, ?)
9. Wir schreiben viele Briefe. (nur eine E-Mail, nur Postkarten, ?)
10. Wir sehen uns alle Museen an. (in der Sonne liegen, viel schlafen, ?)

[1]*convince*

Übung 8   Eine Autofahrt

Üb. 8. Assign for homework and check in class. The subjunctive forms of all modal verbs except *mögen* are practiced here.

Sie wollen mit einem Freund ausgehen und fahren in seinem Auto mit. Stellen Sie Fragen. Versuchen Sie, besonders freundlich und höflich zu sein.

MODELL: wir / jetzt nicht fahren können →
Könnten wir jetzt nicht fahren?

1. du / nicht noch tanken müssen
2. wir / nicht Jens abholen sollen
3. zwei Freunde von mir / auch mitfahren können
4. wir / nicht zuerst in die Stadt fahren sollen
5. du / nicht zur Bank wollen
6. du / etwas langsamer fahren können
7. ich / das Autoradio anmachen dürfen
8. ich / das Fenster aufmachen dürfen

10.5 Focusing on the action: the passive voice

10.5. *Passiv.* Here we treat only the present- and simple past-tense forms of the passive, which are relatively easy for sts. to understand. We believe that the introduction of the other, more complex tenses can well be left until the second year. *Werden* as a main verb was introduced in Section 5.3. *Werden* as the future auxiliary verb was presented in Section 8.5. Stress that active and passive sentences are not necessarily interchangeable and that the use of the passive is appropriate when the doer of the action is not known or does not need to be specified.

A. Uses of the Passive Voice

The passive voice is used in German to focus on the action of the sentence itself rather than on the person or thing performing the action.

ACTIVE VOICE

Der Arzt impft die Kinder.   *The physician inoculates the children.*

PASSIVE VOICE

Die Kinder **werden geimpft.**   *The children are (being) inoculated.*

Note that the accusative (direct) object of the active sentence, **die Kinder,** becomes the nominative subject of the passive sentence.

In passive sentences, the agent of the action is often unknown or unspecified. In the following sentences, there is no mention of who performs each action.

Schildkröten werden oft als Haustiere gehalten.   *Turtles are often kept as pets.*

1088 wurde die erste Universität gegründet.   *The first university was founded in 1088.*

Wissen Sie noch?

In addition to the passive auxiliary, **werden** can be used as a main verb meaning "to become" or as a future auxiliary with an infinitive to form the future tense.

Review grammar 5.3 and 8.5.

passive = **werden** + past participle

B. Forming the Passive Voice

The passive voice is formed with the auxiliary **werden** and the past participle of the verb. The present-tense and simple past-tense forms are the tenses you will encounter most frequently in the passive voice.

Passive Voice: fragen Present Tense			
ich	werde gefragt	*wir*	werden gefragt
du	wirst gefragt	*ihr*	werdet gefragt
Sie	werden gefragt	*Sie*	werden gefragt
er *sie* *es*	wird gefragt	*sie*	werden gefragt

Past Tense			
ich	wurde gefragt	*wir*	wurden gefragt
du	wurdest gefragt	*ihr*	wurdet gefragt
Sie	wurden gefragt	*Sie*	wurden gefragt
er *sie* *es* }	wurde gefragt	*sie*	wurden gefragt

Passive agents are indicated by **von** + noun.

C. Expressing the Agent in the Passive Voice

In most passive sentences in German, the agent (the person or thing performing the action) is not mentioned. When the agent is expressed, the construction **von** + dative is used.

ACTIVE VOICE

Die Kinder füttern die Tiere.   *The children are feeding the animals.*

PASSIVE VOICE

AGENT: **von** + DATIVE

Die Tiere werden **von den**   *The animals are being fed by*   **Kindern** gefüttert.   *the children.*

Übung 9   Geschichte

Üb. 9. The answers use the simple past tense of the passive. Remind sts. that a plural subject requires a plural verb form. **Answers:** 1. j, 2. f, 3. g, 4. i, 5. d, 6. c, 7. h, 8. e, 9. b, 10. a.

Hier sind die Antworten. Was sind die Fragen?

MODELL: 1492 → Wann wurde Amerika entdeckt?

1. vor 50 000 Jahren
2. um 2500 v. Chr.[1]
3. 44 v. Chr.
4. 800 n. Chr.[2]
5. 1088
6. 1789
7. 1885
8. 1945
9. 1963
10. 1990

a. Deutschland vereinigen
b. John F. Kennedy erschießen
c. die amerikanische Verfassung unterschreiben
d. die erste Universität (Bologna) gründen
e. die Atombomben auf Hiroshima und Nagasaki werfen
f. die ersten Pyramiden bauen
g. Cäsar ermorden
h. in Kanada die transkontinentale Eisenbahn vollenden
i. Karl den Großen zum Kaiser krönen
j. Australien von den Aborigines besiedeln

[1]vor Christus   [2]nach Christus

Übung 10 Der Mensch und das Tier

Üb. 10. Although some of the items listed can combine logically with more than one verb phrase in the box, each has a best answer based on the pictures. The answers use the present-tense forms. Remind sts. that some of the subjects are singular, while others are plural.

MODELL: die Giraffe / langsam aus ihrem Lebensraum verdrängt →
Die Giraffe wird langsam aus ihrem Lebensraum verdrängt.

1. Mäuse
2. Meerschweinchen
3. Bienen
4. Mücken
5. die Fledermaus

6. Schnecken
7. der Gepard
8. die meisten Papageien
9. Delfine
10. viele Haie

jedes Jahr gefischt   in der Wildnis gefangen   wegen ihrer Intelligenz bewundert[1]

durch Parfum und Kosmetikprodukte angelockt[2]   in vielen Labortests benutzt

oft mit Butter- und Knoblauchsoße gegessen   oft als Haustiere gehalten

wegen ihrer Honigproduktion geschätzt[3]   langsam aus ihrem Lebensraum verdrängt[4]

immer noch für seinen Pelz getötet   in vielen Kulturen mit Vampiren assoziiert

[1]admired [2]attracted [3]valued [4]displaced

Gesundheit und Krankheit

Kapitel 11 focuses on health and fitness. You will talk about how to stay fit and about illness and accidents.

GOALS

Kapitel 11 gives sts. a chance to talk about their illnesses, accidents, emergencies, and health in general. Reflexive verbs occur naturally in these contexts.

Themen

Krankheit
Körperteile und Körperpflege
Arzt, Apotheke, Krankenhaus
Unfälle

Kulturelles

KLI: Hausmittel
Musikszene: „Danke" (Die Fantastischen Vier)
KLI: Beim Arzt
Filmclip: *Das Leben der Anderen* (Florian Henckel von Donnersmarck)
Videoecke: Krankheiten

Lektüren

Kurzgeschichte: Juttas neue Frisur
Film: *Das Leben der Anderen* (Florian Henckel von Donnersmarck)

Strukturen

11.1 Accusative reflexive pronouns
11.2 Dative reflexive pronouns
11.3 Word order of accusative and dative objects
11.4 Indirect questions: **Wissen Sie, wo ...?**
11.5 Word order in dependent and independent clauses (summary review)

Hannah Höch: *Grotesk* (1963),
ifa, Stuttgart

Chapter opening artwork: The collage *Grotesk* is a
good example of Hannah Höch's unique Dada style.
The confident pose the two women—or rather their
legs—strike looks both modern and timeless. They
demonstrate Höch's ability to balance multiple
elements in a natural composition. The piece is an
example of a female artist expressing her belief in
the power of women.

Kunst und Künstler

Hannah Höch (1889–1978) ist eine deutsche
Vertreterin[1] des Dadaismus. Sie studierte an
der Kunstgewerbeschule in Berlin, lernte 1917
den Dadaismus kennen und nahm 1920 an
der 1. Internationalen Dada-Messe teil. Ihre
Werke wurden unter anderem in den USA und
in der Sowjetunion ausgestellt. In der Zeit des
Dritten Reiches wurden sie von den Nazis der
Entarteten Kunst zugeordnet und durften
nicht mehr ausgestellt werden. Höch war
eine der Vorreiterinnen[2] der Fotomontage. Ihre
Werke spiegeln ihre kritische Einstellung
gegenüber der Weimarer Gesellschaft sowie
den traditionellen Geschlechterrollen und
Schönheitsidealen wider. In ihren Werken sind
androgyne Figuren und gleichgeschlechtliche[3]
Partnerschaften ein wiederkehrendes[4] Motiv.

Schauen Sie sich das Bild an und beantworten Sie die folgenden Fragen.

1. Was sehen Sie in dem Bild?
2. Welche Farbe überwiegt? Was
   assoziieren Sie mit dieser Farbe?
3. Schauen Sie sich die Augen der
   linken Figur an. Was fällt Ihnen auf?
   Was wollte die Künstlerin vielleicht
   damit sagen?
4. Beschreiben Sie die Kopfbedeckung[5]
   der Frau rechts. Was ist daran
   seltsam[6]?

[1] *representative* [2] *pioneers* [3] *same-sex*
[4] *recurring* [5] *head covering* [6] *odd*

Situationen

Krankheit

Grammatik 11.1

Stefan hat sich erkältet.

Er fühlt sich nicht wohl.

Er hat Husten.

Er hat Schnupfen.

Er hat Kopfschmerzen.

Er hat Halsschmerzen.

Und er hat Fieber.

Er darf sich nicht aufregen.

Er muss sich ins Bett legen.

Er muss sich ausruhen.

Situation 1 Hausmittel[1]

Was machst du immer, manchmal, nie?

1. Wenn ich Fieber habe,
   a. lege ich mich ins Bett.
   b. nehme ich zwei Aspirin.
   c. gehe ich zum Arzt.
   d. rege ich mich auf.

2. Wenn ich Husten habe,
   a. nehme ich Hustensaft.
   b. trinke ich heißen Tee mit Zitrone.
   c. rauche ich eine Zigarette.
   d. lutsche ich Hustenbonbons.

3. Wenn ich mich erkältet habe,
   a. gehe ich schwimmen.
   b. ruhe ich mich aus.
   c. gehe ich in die Sauna.
   d. ärgere ich mich furchtbar.

[1]Home remedies

4. Wenn ich Kopfschmerzen habe,
  a. gehe ich zum Friseur. c. bleibe ich im Bett.
  b. nehme ich zwei Aspirin. d. nehme ich ein heißes Bad.

5. Wenn ich Zahnschmerzen habe,
  a. trinke ich heißen Kaffee. c. nehme ich Tabletten.
  b. gehe ich zum Zahnarzt. d. setze ich mich aufs Sofa.

6. Wenn ich mich verletzt habe,
  a. desinfiziere ich die Wunde. c. hole ich ein Pflaster.
  b. falle ich in Ohnmacht. d. ziehe ich mich aus.

7. Wenn ich Muskelkater habe,
  a. lasse ich mich massieren. c. mache ich Muskeltraining.
  b. gehe ich zum Arzt. d. lege ich mich aufs Sofa.

8. Wenn ich mich in den Finger geschnitten habe,
  a. ärgere ich mich furchtbar. c. nehme ich Hustensaft.
  b. hole ich ein Pflaster. d. desinfiziere ich die Wunde.

9. Wenn ich einen Kater habe,
  a. gehe ich ins Krankenhaus. c. schlafe ich den ganzen Tag.
  b. nehme ich zwei Aspirin. d. gehe ich joggen.

10. Wenn ich Magenschmerzen habe,
  a. lege ich mich aufs Sofa. c. ziehe ich mich aus.
  b. trinke ich Kamillentee. d. esse ich viel Schokolade.

Situation 2   Was tut dir weh?

Sit. 2. Have sts. work in groups of 3, then ask the class for responses. Point out that an alternative structure to the answer given in the model is *Die Ohren tun mir weh.*

MODELL: Du warst in einem Rockkonzert. →
Ich habe Ohrenschmerzen.

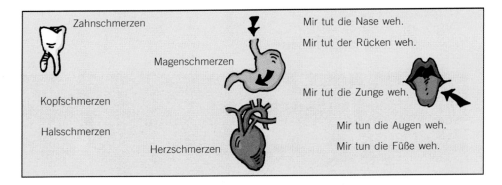

1. Du hast den ganzen Tag in der Bibliothek gesessen und Bücher gelesen.
2. Du hast zwei große Teller Chili gegessen.
3. Jemand hat dich auf die Nase geschlagen.
4. Du bist 20 Kilometer gewandert.
5. Du hast gestern Abend zu viel Kaffee getrunken.
6. Du warst bei einem Basketballspiel und hast viel geschrien.
7. Du hast zu viele Bonbons gegessen.
8. Du hast furchtbaren Liebeskummer.
9. Du hast zwei Stunden Schnee geschaufelt.
10. Der Kaffee, den du getrunken hast, war zu heiß.

Hausmittel

- Welche von diesen Hausmitteln kennen Sie? Wogegen helfen sie?
  - ☐ Eisbeutel
  - ☐ grüner Tee
  - ☐ heißer Tee mit Zitrone
  - ☐ Hühnersuppe
  - ☐ Kamillentee
  - ☐ Knoblauch
  - ☐ Salzwasser
  - ☐ warme Umschläge[1]
- Benutzen Sie Hausmittel, wenn Sie sich nicht wohl fühlen? Wenn ja, welche?

Lesen Sie die drei Zeitungstexte. Kennen Sie diese Hausmittel? Glauben Sie, dass sie wirken? Warum?

> Bei Husten warmes Zuckerwasser mit Eidotter[2] vermischen. Das mildert den Hustenreiz[3]. Oder Hustenbier trinken: Einen halben Liter Bier erhitzen, mit fünf Löffeln flüssigem Honig verrühren[4] und abends trinken.

> Wenn die Augen müde sind, Hände reiben[5] bis sie warm sind, sie auf die geschlossenen Augen legen und an die Farbe Schwarz denken.

> Bei Fieber Zitronenscheiben auf die Schläfen[6] legen. Oder eine Kette aus Rettichscheiben[7] über Nacht um den Hals binden.

KLI. Natural remedies play an important role in Germany. Health insurance groups publish pamphlets about them, health food stores and pharmacies advertise homeopathic remedies, and a great variety of teas and herbs is available. People are sometimes reluctant to take pills, especially antibiotics.

Hausmittel stehen oftmals der Pflanzenheilkunde[8] nahe[9]. Die Arnikapflanze ist nur ein Beispiel. Lesen Sie den Text und beantworten Sie die Fragen.

- Wo wächst die Arnika?
- Wofür wird Arnika verwendet?
- In welcher Form kann man heute Arnika bekommen?

Arnika ist eine beliebte Heilpflanze.

Die Arnika wächst in den Alpen. Seit jeher wird die Alpenpflanze von den Menschen in den Bergen bei Prellungen[10], Stauchungen[11] und schmerzenden Beinen verwendet. Man hat herausgefunden, dass die Arnika die Beine besonders gut durchblutet, Schmerzen lindert, Schwellungen[12] abbaut und entzündungshemmend[13] wirkt. Deshalb eignet sich Arnika bei Sportverletzungen sehr gut. Heute kann man Arnika-Salben, -Gels und -Beinsprays kaufen.

[1]compresses [2]egg yolk [3]irritation of the throat [4]stir [5]rub [6]temples [7]radish slices [8]herbal medicine
[9]nahestehen to be closely connected to [10]bruises [11]sprains [12]swelling [13]as an anti-inflammatory

Situation 3 Umfrage

Sit. 3. In this autograph activity, sts. use reflexive verbs requiring the accusative case. Model pronunciation, have sts. repeat, and then have them collect signatures. Follow up with general questions: *Wer ist gegen Hunde allergisch? usw.*

MODELL: S1: Legst du dich ins Bett, wenn du dich erkältet hast?
S2: Ja.
S1: Unterschreib bitte hier.

UNTERSCHRIFT

1. Ruhst du dich aus, wenn du Kopfschmerzen hast? _____
2. Ärgerst du dich, wenn du in den Ferien krank wirst? _____
3. Legst du dich ins Bett, wenn du eine Grippe hast? _____
4. Bist du gegen Katzen allergisch? _____
5. Hast du einen niedrigen Blutdruck? _____
6. Freust du dich, wenn dein Lehrer / deine Lehrerin krank ist? _____
7. Regst du dich auf, wenn du dich verletzt hast? _____
8. Erkältest du dich oft? _____
9. Nimmst du Tabletten, wenn du dich nicht wohl fühlst? _____

Körperteile und Körperpflege

Grammatik 11.2–11.3

Vocabulary Display
This section introduces dative reflexive pronouns with body parts and contrasts them with accusative reflexive pronouns. The rule of thumb sts. should acquire is to use the dative when there is another object in the utterance and otherwise to use the accusative.

Ich wasche mich.

Ich wasche mir die Haare.

Ich trockne mich ab.

Ich trockne mir die Hände ab.

Ich kämme mir die Haare.

Ich schminke mich.

Ich rasiere mich.

Ich putze mir die Zähne.

Ich ziehe mich an.

Musikszene

„Danke" (2010, Deutschland)   *Die Fantastischen Vier*

Die Fantastischen Vier

Biografie Die Fantastischen Vier (kurz: Fanta 4) machten den deutschsprachigen Hip-Hop populär. Sie nannten ihn den deutschen Sprechgesang. Fanta 4 besteht aus Michael Bernd Schmidt alias Smudo, Thomas Dürr, Michael Beck und Andreas Rieke und kommt aus Stuttgart. Ihren ersten Auftritt hatte die Gruppe schon 1989. 2000 nahmen sie ein MTV-Unplugged-Album auf, nach Herbert Grönemeyer damals erst die zweiten deutschen Künstler, die so geehrt wurden. 2009 erhielten sie als erste Musikgruppe den Paul-Lincke-Ring der Stadt Goslar für ihre Verdienste im deutschen Sprechgesang. Die Single „Danke" entstammt ihrem Album *Für dich immer noch Fanta Sie* aus dem Jahre 2010.

Vor dem Hören Waren Sie schon mal in Todesgefahr? Was ist passiert?

Nach dem Hören

A. Beantworten Sie die Fragen zum Anfang und zum Refrain.

1. Was wäre schön gewesen?

2. Wo liegt der Sänger?

3. Was wollen die Leute mit ihm noch machen?

4. Wann nur könnte der Sänger noch einmal *danke* sagen?

B. Der erste Tod. Bringen Sie die Sätze in die richtige Reihenfolge.

___ Er fragt sich, warum es auch hinter ihm eine Schranke gibt.

___ Er fragt sich, wo es eine Tankstelle gibt.

___ Er steht mit seinem Auto vor einer Schranke.

___ Er verheddert sich in seinem Gurt.

C. Woran stirbt der Sänger in den vier Strophen? Verbinden Sie Ort und Todesart.

1. auf dem Bahngleis   **a.** Er bekommt einen elektrischen Schock.

2. im Restaurant   **b.** Der Wagen hängt sich aus und er ist nicht angeschnallt.

3. auf der Achterbahn   **c.** Er verschluckt sich an einem Fisch.

4. im Bad   **d.** Er wird von einem Zug überfahren.

iMix Link: Dieses Lied können Sie im *iTunes Store* als ein *iMix* kaufen, das speziell für *Kontakte* entwickelt wurde. In **Connect German** (www.connectgerman.com) erhalten Sie Instruktionen, wie Sie die Playliste bekommen können.

Musikszene. Answers: A. 1. ein längeres Leben 2. im Krankenwagen 3. ihn zwangsbeatmen 4. falls sie ihn nicht begraben B. 3, 2, 1, 4 C. 1. d 2. c 3. b 4. a

Miniwörterbuch

der **Sprechgesang**	rap	die **Schranke**	gate (at a railway crossing)
ehren	to honor	**sich verheddern**	to get tangled up
der **Verdienst**	merit	der **Gurt**	(seat) belt
die **Todesgefahr**	danger of death	das **Bahngleis**	railway track
wäre gewesen	would have been	die **Achterbahn**	roller coaster
zwangsbeatmen	to resuscitate (forcefully)	**sich aushängen**	to get unhinged, uncoupled
begraben	to bury	**anschnallen**	to buckle up
der **Tod**	death	**sich verschlucken**	to choke (on sth.)

Körperteile

Sit. 4. Use TPR to introduce new verbs before beginning the activity. Then have sts. work in pairs.

MODELL: s1: Was macht man mit den Augen?
s2: Mit den Augen sieht man.

greifen   sprechen
atmen
kauen   hören
riechen   küssen
denken
fühlen   gehen

1. mit den Ohren
2. mit den Händen
3. mit dem Gehirn
4. mit der Nase
5. mit der Lunge
6. mit den Zähnen
7. mit den Lippen
8. mit den Beinen
9. mit dem Mund
10. mit dem Herzen

Situation 5 **Körperpflege**

Sit. 5. Sts. use reflexive verbs requiring dative pronouns. Have sts. read the situations and decide what they do in each case. Then address questions to the class as a whole, calling on individuals to answer: *Was machen Sie, wenn Ihre Haut trocken ist? (Ich creme sie ein.) Diane cremt ihre Haut ein. usw.*

AA. You could also have sts. act out the verbs for others to guess.

1. Wenn meine Haut trocken ist,
   a. creme ich sie ein.
   b. gehe ich schwimmen.
   c. gehe ich zum Arzt.

2. Wenn meine Fingernägel lang sind,
   a. bade ich mich.
   b. schneide ich sie mir.
   c. kaue ich sie ab.

3. Wenn meine Haare fettig sind,
   a. putze ich mir die Zähne.
   b. schneide ich sie mir.
   c. wasche ich sie mir.

4. Wenn ich ins Theater gehe,
   a. schminke ich mich.
   b. rasiere ich mich.
   c. schneide ich mir die Haare.

5. Wenn ich ins Bett gehe,
   a. ziehe ich mir warme Schuhe an.
   b. putze ich mir die Zähne.
   c. schneide ich mir die Fingernägel.

6. Wenn ich mich geduscht habe,
   a. ziehe ich mich aus.
   b. trockne ich mich ab.
   c. föhne ich mir die Haare.

7. Wenn ich mich erholen will,
   a. gehe ich in die Sauna.
   b. rasiere ich mir die Beine.
   c. nehme ich Tabletten.

8. Wenn es draußen kalt ist,
   a. dusche ich mich heiß.
   b. ziehe ich mir eine warme Hose an.
   c. ziehe ich mich aus.

9. Wenn ich eine Verabredung habe,
   a. schminke ich mich.
   b. wasche ich mir die Haare.
   c. esse ich viel Knoblauch.

Situation 6   Bildgeschichte: Maria hat eine Verabredung.

Sit. 6. This narration series reviews the perfect tense and provides practice of the use of reflexive pronouns. Sentences for narration series: **1.** *Maria ist von der Arbeit nach Hause gekommen.* **2.** *Sie hat sich ausgezogen.* **3.** *Sie hat sich geduscht.* **4.** *Sie hat sich abgetrocknet.* **5.** *Dann hat sie sich die Zähne geputzt.* **6.** *Sie hat sich die Fingernägel geschnitten.* **7.** *Sie hat sich die Haare geföhnt.* **8.** *Sie hat sich die Beine eingecremt.* **9.** *Dann hat sie sich geschminkt.* **10.** *Schließlich hat sie sich ein schönes Kleid angezogen.*

AA. After narrating Maria's activities, you could discuss with sts. who her date is and what he does in preparation for their meeting–e.g., *Cremt er sich die Beine ein? Schminkt er sich?*

Situation 7   Interview: Körperpflege

Sit 7. Additional vocabulary for makeup: *sich die Wimpern tuschen* = to apply mascara; *der Lippenstift* = lipstick; *Lippenstift auflegen* = to apply lipstick; *der Lidschatten* = eyeshadow; *Lidschatten auflegen* = to apply eyeshadow.

1. (für Frauen) Schminkst du dich jeden Tag? Was machst du?
2. (für Männer) Rasierst du dich jeden Tag? Hattest du schon mal einen Bart? Was für einen (Schnurrbart, Vollbart, Spitzbart, Backenbart)? Wie war das? Wenn du einen Bart hast: Seit wann hast du einen Bart?
3. Wäschst du dir jeden Tag die Haare? Föhnst du sie dir auch? Was für Haar hast du (trockenes, fettiges, normales Haar)?
4. Putzt du dir jeden Tag die Zähne? Gehst du oft zum Zahnarzt?
5. Wie oft gehst du zum Friseur? Hattest du mal eine Dauerwelle? Wie hast du ausgesehen?
6. Hast du trockene Haut? Cremst du dich oft ein?
7. Treibst du regelmäßig Sport? Was machst du? Wie oft? Gehst du manchmal in die Sauna oder ins Solarium?

Lektüre

Vor dem Lesen

Suggestion. You could also have your sts. tell you something about Billy Idol–his appearance, his music, etc.

A. Was wissen Sie über Jutta Ruf?
B. Lesen Sie den Cartoon auf der nächsten Seite. Welche „Haarmoden" (Frisuren) sind noch „kontrovers"? Zeichnen Sie eine „kontroverse" Haarmode oder bringen Sie Fotos mit in den Kurs.

Miniwörterbuch

allerdings	of course	**sprühen**	to spray
begeistert	thrilled	die **Stirn**	forehead
sich nicht hineintrauen	to be afraid to go inside	die **Strumpfhosen**	(*pl.*) tights
kahl	bald	**tätowiert**	tattooed
kaum	hardly	der **Totenkopf**	skull
die **Kette**	chain	das **Vorbild**	role model
der **Nacken**	neck	**vor Lachen**	from laughing (so hard)
die **Narbe**	scar	**zerrissen**	torn
die **Rasierklinge**	razor blade		

Lesehilfe

In this reading, Jutta Ruf takes on a new persona. Recall what you already know about Jutta and her boyfriend "Billy." Go back and read Jutta's diary entry in **Situation 4** of **Kapitel 4.** What kind of persona do you think Jutta will take on?

Juttas neue Frisur

Jutta Ruf hat einen neuen Freund, Billy. Eigentlich heißt er nicht Billy, sondern Paul, aber sein Vorbild ist Billy Idol und so nennt er sich nach ihm. Er hat sich auch die Haare ganz kurz geschnitten und hellblond gebleicht und trägt immer alte, kaputte Jeans, zerrissene T-Shirts und eine Lederjacke mit Ketten. Auf dem Oberarm

5 hat er einen Totenkopf tätowiert und auf seiner linken Hand steht „no future". Auf beiden Wangen hat er je drei parallele Narben. Die hat er sich auf einer Fete nach einem Billy-Idol-Konzert mit einer Rasierklinge geschnitten ... Jutta findet ihn toll! Sie trägt jetzt immer zerrissene schwarze Strumpfhosen, Turnschuhe, die sie silbern gesprüht hat, ein T-Shirt, auf dem „I love Billy" steht, und eine alte Jeansjacke.

10 Es ist Mittwochabend nach acht Uhr. Jutta steht vor der Tür und traut sich nicht hinein. Sie hat Angst, dass ihre Eltern ihre neue Frisur nicht so toll finden wie ihre Freunde, besonders Billy.

Am Morgen ist sie nicht zur Schule gegangen, sondern hat sich mit Billy in einer Kneipe getroffen. Da haben sie noch eine Stunde über die neue Frisur gesprochen

15 und dann sind sie zum Friseur gegangen. Jutta hatte darauf gespart, denn so eine Frisur ist nicht billig. Nach drei Stunden war alles fertig und Billy war begeistert. Allerdings hat es dann auch 50,- Euro gekostet, wegen der neuen Farbe und so.

Jutta hat jetzt einen ziemlich ungewöhnlichen Haarschnitt. In der Mitte steht ein zehn Zentimeter breiter Haarstreifen, der von der Stirn bis in den Nacken läuft. Die

20 Haare sind fünfzehn Zentimeter lang, stehen fest und gerade nach oben und sind violett und grün. Der Rest des Kopfes ist kahl. Billy wollte dann noch mit ihr zu einem Tätowierer gehen und ihr „Billy" auf die rechte Seite des Kopfes tätowieren lassen, aber sie hatten kein Geld mehr. Alle Freunde fanden es toll ... aber jetzt steht sie allein vor der Tür. Sie will warten, bis ihre Eltern ins Bett gegangen sind.

25 Plötzlich hört sie jemanden.

„Mensch, das bist ja du, Jutta!" Es ist ihr Bruder Hans, der aus dem Fenster schaut. „Wie siehst du denn aus?" Hans kann vor Lachen kaum sprechen. „Das sieht ja unmöglich aus!"

„Ach, du hast doch keine Ahnung!"

30 „Mutti und Papi finden es sicher toll. Komm schnell herein!"

„Nein, ich will noch warten, bis sie ins Bett gegangen sind."

„Da kannst du lange warten, es ist doch erst acht Uhr! Komm, das will ich sehen, wie die reagieren!"

Arbeit mit dem Text

A. Wie sehen sie aus?

	Haarschnitt	Haarfarbe	Kleidung
Billy			
Jutta			

B. Mittwochmorgen oder Mittwochabend? Schreiben Sie ein M oder ein A vor jeden Satz und bringen Sie die Sätze dann in die richtige Reihenfolge.

_____ Jutta steht vor der Tür und hat Angst.

_____ Hans will sehen, wie die Eltern reagieren.

_____ Jutta ist nicht in die Schule gegangen.

_____ Jutta hat Billy in einer Kneipe getroffen.

_____ Hans schaut aus dem Fenster.

_____ Jutta ist zum Friseur gegangen.

_____ Billy wollte mit Jutta zu einem Tätowierer gehen.

C. Fragen

1. Warum sind Jutta und Billy nicht mehr zum Tätowieren gegangen?
2. Wie findet Hans Juttas Frisur?
3. Was, glauben Sie, werden Juttas Eltern sagen?
4. Warum kleidet sich Jutta so wie im Text beschrieben? Warum bekommt sie eine solche außergewöhnliche Frisur und will sich sogar tätowieren lassen? Denken Sie an Juttas Alter.

Nach dem Lesen

Hatten Sie schon mal Schwierigkeiten mit Ihren Eltern, weil Sie einen anderen Geschmack hatten als sie? Im Aussehen? In der Wahl Ihrer Freunde? In der Wahl Ihrer Tätigkeiten? Erzählen Sie! Machen Sie sich zuerst Gedanken und schreiben Sie sich Stichwörter auf. Arbeiten Sie dann in Kleingruppen und erzählen Sie Ihre Geschichte. Die anderen Gruppenmitglieder helfen mit Fragen und kommentieren.

Arzt, Apotheke, Krankenhaus

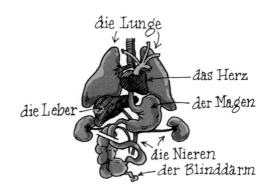

Jürgen hat sich das Bein gebrochen. Jetzt muss er einen Gips tragen.

Silvia bekommt eine Spritze.

Josef bekommt einen Verband.

Der Zahnarzt zieht Melanie einen Zahn.

Die Ärztin gibt Claire ein Rezept.

Situation 8 Medizinische Berufe

Wohin gehen Sie?

ins Krankenhaus	**in die Drogerie**
in die Apotheke **zum Zahnarzt**	**zum Hausarzt**
zum Tierarzt **zum Psychiater**	**zum Augenarzt**

1. Sie haben sich erkältet und brauchen Hustensaft.
2. Sie haben schon seit zwei Wochen eine schlimme Halsentzündung und wollen Antibiotika.
3. Ihr Freund / Ihre Freundin hat sich in den Finger geschnitten. Der Finger blutet stark.
4. Ihr Freund / Ihre Freundin hat Sie verlassen und Sie sind sehr deprimiert.
5. Ihr Goldfisch frisst schon seit mehreren Tagen nicht mehr.
6. Sie haben furchtbare Zahnschmerzen.
7. Sie können im Unterricht nicht lesen, was an der Tafel steht.
8. Ihr Arzt hat Ihnen ein Rezept ausgeschrieben und Sie wollen sich das Medikament abholen.

Interaktion: Ich bin krank

Sit. 9. Sts. use the *du*-form of the imperative.

Ein Mitstudent / Eine Mitstudentin ist krank. Was raten Sie ihm/ihr?

MODELL: s1: Ich habe Fieber.
s2: Leg dich ins Bett.

1. Ich habe Fieber.
2. Ich habe Kopfschmerzen.
3. Ich fühle mich nicht wohl.
4. Ich habe starken Husten.
5. Ich habe mich in den Finger geschnitten.
6. Ich habe mich erkältet.
7. Ich habe Zahnschmerzen.
8. Ich bin allergisch gegen Katzen.
9. Mir tun die Augen weh.
10. Ich habe Magenschmerzen.

a. Geh zum Arzt.
b. Nimm Hustensaft.
c. Leg dich ins Bett.
d. Geh nach Hause.
e. Kauf dir Kopfschmerztabletten.
f. Ruh dich aus.
g. Nimm ein warmes Bad.
h. Zieh dich warm an.
i. Verkauf deine Katze.
j. Geh zum Zahnarzt.
k. Kauf dir eine Brille.
l. _____ ?

Kultur ...
Landeskunde ... Informationen

Beim Arzt

Lesen Sie das Gedicht von Ernst Jandl. Welche Situation beschreibt es?

fünfter sein

tür auf
einer raus
einer rein
vierter sein

tür auf
einer raus
einer rein
dritter sein

tür auf
einer raus
einer rein
zweiter sein

tür auf
einer raus
einer rein
nächster sein

tür auf
einer raus
selber rein
tagherrdoktor

—Ernst Jandl

Bevor man im Wartezimmer einer Arztpraxis Platz nehmen kann, muss man in Deutschland an der Anmeldung[1] seine Chipkarte abgeben. Jeder bekommt von seiner Krankenversicherung diese Karte. Auf ihr sind alle Informationen gespeichert[2]. Sie wird beim Arzt abgegeben und der Arzt rechnet nach der Behandlung[3] mit der Krankenversicherung ab[4]. In Deutschland ist eigentlich jeder krankenversichert.

KLI cultural note. There are two kinds of health insurance, public and private, depending on income. For people on welfare or unemployed, the insurance is paid for by the *Sozialamt* or *Arbeitsamt*. Although the system is not perfect, no one is without insurance for lack of money. *Soziale Sicherheit* is also assured by *Arbeitslosenversicherung*, *Rentenversicherung*, and *Unfallversicherung*, payment for which is mandatory and shared by employers and employees. The present insurance system

(*Sozialversicherung*) has existed since Bismarck's era (1883–1889). AOK (*Allgemeine Ortskrankenkasse*) is the most common health insurance.

Rollenspiel: Beim Arzt. Bauen Sie alle Stationen ein: Anmeldung, Wartezimmer und das Gespräch mit dem Arzt.

[1]reception [2]stored [3]treatment [4]rechnet ab *settles*

Sit. 10. The corresponding chart is in Appendix A. Model pronunciation and have sts. repeat. Ask sts. to choose partners, and set a time limit for the activity. Suggest that they fill in all the information for Claire and Herr Thelen, then take turns asking about each other. Afterward, ask the class as a group: *Wer von Ihnen hat sich schon mal etwas gebrochen? Jim hat sich schon mal etwas gebrochen. Was haben Sie sich gebrochen? usw.* After asking several questions, review to see how well sts. remember: *Was hat Jim sich schon mal gebrochen? Warum ist Laura schon im Krankenhaus gewesen? usw.*

 Situation 10 Informationsspiel: Krankheitsgeschichte

MODELL: Hat Claire sich (Hast du dir) schon mal etwas gebrochen? Was?
Ist Claire (Bist du) schon mal im Krankenhaus gewesen? Warum?
Hat Herr Thelen (Hast du) schon mal eine Spritze bekommen? Gegen was?
Erkältet sich Herr Thelen (Erkältest du dich) oft?
Ist Claire (Bist du) gegen etwas allergisch? Gegen was?
Hat man Claire (Hat man dir) schon mal einen Zahn gezogen?
Hatte Herr Thelen (Hattest du) schon mal hohes Fieber? Wie hoch?

	Claire	Herr Thelen	mein(e) Partner(in)
sich etwas brechen	den Arm	das Bein	
im Krankenhaus sein	Nierenentzündung	Lungenentzündung	
eine Spritze bekommen	Diphtherie	Tetanus	
sich oft erkälten	ja	nein	
gegen etwas allergisch sein	Sonne	Katzen	
einen Zahn gezogen haben	nein	ja	
hohes Fieber haben	104° F	41,2° C	

 Situation 11 Dialoge

Sit. 11. (1) Set the scene. (2) Preteach vocabulary. *Termin; das passt gut; dagegen* (here: for it); *wirken.* (3) Ask sts. to open their books and play the dialogue for them at least twice while they fill in the blanks. (4) Write sts.' answers on the board, or ask them to write their answers on the board, while making any necessary corrections. (5) Ask sts. to practice the dialogues in pairs and ask a few pairs to act out the dialogues in front of the class.

1. Herr Thelen möchte einen Termin beim Arzt.

HERR THELEN: Guten Tag, ich hätte gern <u>einen Termin</u> für nächste Woche.
SPRECHSTUNDENHILFE: Gern, vormittags oder nachmittags?
HERR THELEN: Das ist mir eigentlich <u>egal</u>.
SPRECHSTUNDENHILFE: Mittwochmorgen um neun?
HERR THELEN: Ja, <u>das passt gut</u>. Vielen Dank.

2. Frau Körner geht in die Apotheke.

FRAU KÖRNER: Ich habe schon seit Tagen <u>Magenschmerzen</u>. Können Sie mir etwas <u>dagegen</u> geben?
APOTHEKERIN: Wir haben gerade etwas ganz Neues bekommen, Magenex.
FRAU KÖRNER: Hauptsache, <u>es hilft schnell</u>.
APOTHEKERIN: Es soll sehr gut <u>wirken</u>. Hier ist es.

3. Frau Frisch ist bei ihrem Hausarzt.

HAUSARZT: Guten Tag, Frau Frisch, wie geht es Ihnen?
FRAU FRISCH: Ich fühle mich gar nicht wohl. <u>Halsschmerzen, Fieber</u> ... alles tut mir weh.
HAUSARZT: Das klingt nach <u>Grippe</u>. Sagen Sie mal bitte „Ah".

Sit. 12. The role for S2 appears in Appendix B. Assign roles and have sts. prepare schedules as homework without consulting with their partners; the doctor's secretary prepares an appointment schedule and the patient a class schedule. In class they try to come up with a time that suits both. **Note:** If your students are using McGraw-Hill's **Connect** online *Arbeitsbuch,* they can do this *Rollenspiel* using the real-time, interactive **Video-Chat** feature.

Situation 12 Rollenspiel: Anruf beim Arzt

S1: Sie fühlen sich nicht wohl. Wahrscheinlich haben Sie Grippe. Rufen Sie beim Arzt an und lassen Sie sich einen Termin geben. Es ist dringend, aber Sie haben einen vollen Stundenplan.

Situation 13 Interview

Sit. 13. Note the extensive use of the reflexive. This situation recycles many of the expressions used in *Sit. 10*.

1. Warst du schon mal schwer krank? Wann? Was hat dir gefehlt?
2. Warst du schon mal im Krankenhaus? Wann? Warum? Wie lange? Hat man dich untersucht? Hat man dir Blut abgenommen? Hast du eine Spritze bekommen?
3. Hast du dir schon mal etwas gebrochen? Was? Hattest du einen Gips? Wie lange?
4. Hat man dich schon mal geröntgt? Wann? Warum?
5. Erkältest du dich oft? Was machst du, wenn du eine Erkältung hast?
6. Bist du gegen etwas allergisch? Gegen was?
7. Bist du schon mal in Ohnmacht gefallen? Warum?

Unfälle

Vocabulary Display
This section focuses on accidents and injuries and what to do in such instances. It reviews the *als/wenn* contrast and gives additional practice in past narration.

Grammatik 11.4–11.5

Zwei Autos sind zusammengestoßen. Eine Frau ist schwer verletzt.

Situation 14 Ein Autounfall

Sit. 14. Have sts. work in pairs to arrange the sentences in their logical order. Point out that, in this type of interview, the format will be a question followed by an answer. After the sts. have determined the correct sequence of events, have them prepare the situation as a role-play. Then have 3-4 pairs perform for the class.

Eine Polizistin spricht mit einem Zeugen über einen Unfall. Bringen Sie die Sätze in eine logische Reihenfolge.

___3___ Können Sie mir sagen, wie spät es ungefähr war?

___2___ Also, heute Morgen war ich auf dem Weg zur Uni.

___1___ Bitte erzählen Sie genau, was passiert ist.

___6___ Ein Auto ist aus einer Einfahrt gekommen.

___10___ Ich glaube nicht, er hat jedenfalls nicht gebremst, bevor er auf die Straße gefahren ist.

___9___ Wissen Sie, ob der Fahrer auf den Verkehr geachtet hat?

___8___ Ja, ein anderes Auto kam von rechts und dann sind sie zusammengestoßen.

___4___ So zwischen halb und Viertel vor neun.

___5___ Was haben Sie da gesehen?

___7___ Und dann?

___11___ Vielen Dank für Ihre Hilfe.

Situation 15 Unfälle

Sit. 15. Have sts. work in small groups to match the descriptions with the pictures. First team to finish, wins. For more listening practice, have sts. cover the text so they can only see the pictures (or use a projector to show the pictures) while you read through the descriptions at random, one at a time. After reading each sentence, ask sts. to identify the picture you described.

Sit. 15. AA. After sts. have matched the sentences to the pictures, you might ask them what happened next—e.g., *Hat Ernst sehr laut geschrien? Hat Maria oder ihr Freund dem Kind geholfen? Hat Herr Frisch schnell genug gebremst? Hat Jürgen weiter gelesen?*

Welcher Satz passt zu welchem Bild?

a.

b.

c.

d.

e.

f.

g.

h.

1. Michael und Maria waren beim Segeln, als das Boot umkippte.
2. Sofie schnitt gerade Tomaten, als plötzlich vor ihrem Haus ein Mann von einem Auto überfahren wurde.
3. Jutta und Hans waren auf dem Weg ins Konzert, als Jutta ausrutschte und hinfiel.
4. Jürgen saß gerade in der Bibliothek, als auf der Straße zwei Autos zusammenstießen.
5. Herr Frisch fuhr gerade zur Arbeit, als ihm ein Hund vors Auto lief.
6. Als Ernst mit seinen Freunden Fußball spielte, brach er sich das Bein.
7. Maria und ihr Freund liefen Schlittschuh, als ein Kind ins Eis einbrach.
8. Rolf wollte gerade nach Hawaii fliegen, als ein Flugzeug abstürzte.

Situation 16 Notfälle

Sit. 16. Have sts. work in pairs. Then, question the class as a whole and have individuals respond. Ask if anyone might do something not mentioned in the text.

Was machst du, wenn ...

1. du einen Unfall siehst?
2. der Verletzte einen Schock hat?
3. der Fahrer von dem anderen Auto flüchtet?
4. du im Fahrstuhl stecken bleibst?
5. du ausrutschst und hinfällst?
6. du dir den Arm gebrochen hast?
7. du ins Wasser fällst?
8. es im Nachbarhaus brennt?
9. du dir die Zunge verbrannt hast?

a. den Krankenwagen rufen
b. die Feuerwehr rufen
c. die Autonummer aufschreiben
d. die Polizei rufen
e. eine Decke holen und den Verletzten zudecken
f. fluchen
g. liegen bleiben und warten, dass jemand kommt
h. schwimmen
i. um Hilfe rufen
j. ____?

Situation 17 Bildgeschichte: Paulas Unfall

Sit. 17. Sentences for narration series. **1.** *Herr und Frau Wagner sind ausgegangen.* **2.** *Paula ist auf einen Stuhl geklettert und hat die Schranktür aufgemacht.* **3.** *Sie hat eine Tüte mit Bonbons aus dem Schrank geholt.* **4.** *Als sie herunterklettern wollte, ist sie ausgerutscht und auf den Boden gefallen.* **5.** *Ihr Arm hat sehr wehgetan, und sie hat angefangen zu weinen.* **6.** *Sie hat um Hilfe gerufen.* **7.** *Andrea ist gleich zur Nachbarin gelaufen.* **8.** *Die Nachbarin ist mit Andrea und Paula ins Krankenhaus gefahren.* **9.** *Eine Ärztin hat Paula untersucht.* **10.** *Dann hat Paula einen Gips bekommen, weil sie sich den Arm gebrochen hat.*

Sit. 17. AA. You might ask sts. to provide a moral to this narrative–e.g., *Eltern sollten hungrige Kinder nicht allein zu Hause lassen. Man sollte Bonbons nicht in einem hohen Schrank verstecken. Man sollte versteckte Bonbons nicht klauen. usw.*

AA. *Beschreiben Sie einen Unfall, den Sie einmal hatten, entweder einen Unfall im Haus oder einen Autounfall. Denken Sie an einen Unfall, bei dem etwas Seltsames passiert ist. Was ist passiert? Wie haben Sie reagiert? Was haben Sie gemacht? Was ist dann passiert?*

Filmlektüre
Das Leben der Anderen

 Vor dem Lesen

A. Beantworten Sie die folgenden Fragen.

1. Was macht der Mann auf dem Bild? Warum macht er das?
2. Beschreiben Sie das Gesicht des Mannes. Was hört er?
3. Was wissen Sie über die DDR und die Rolle der Stasi[1]?

[1]Ministerium für <u>Staatssicherheit</u>

Filmangaben

Titel: *Das Leben der Anderen*
Genre: Drama
Erscheinungsjahr: 2006
Land: Deutschland
Dauer: 137 min
Regisseur: Florian Henckel von Donnersmarck
Hauptrollen: Ulrich Mühe, Sebastian Koch, Thomas Thieme, Martina Gedeck

Der Lauscher auf dem Dachboden

B. Lesen Sie die Wörter im Miniwörterbuch. Suchen Sie sie im Text und unterstreichen Sie sie.

Miniwörterbuch

pflichtbewusst	conscientious	**belastendes Material**	incriminating evidence
regimetreu	loyal to the regime	das **Versteck**	hiding place
bespitzeln	to spy on	**verschwinden lassen**	to make disappear
der **Spürsinn**	perceptiveness	das **Opfer**	victim
die **Bewachung**	guarding	**verraten**	to reveal
jemanden aus dem Weg schaffen	to get rid of someone	**widmen**	to dedicate
verwanzt	bugged		
das **Abhörgerät**	bugging device		

Filmlektüre. Suggestion: (1) Ask the questions in *Vor dem Lesen* and some additional ones about the *Filmangaben* such as: *Wann ist der Film erschienen? In welchem Land? Was für ein Film ist es? Wie lange dauert er? Wer hat die Hauptrollen?* **(2)** Next, ask sts. to read the words in the *Miniwörterbuch,* to find them in the *Inhaltsangabe* and to underline them. Tell them that it will help them get a first impression of what the text will be about. **(3)** Go over the *Arbeit mit dem Text* making sure sts. understand all the words. Write unfamiliar words on the board with translations or convey the meanings in another manner. Ask sts. to read the text silently and answer the questions, then in pairs compare their answers. Follow up on sts.' answers and provide feedback if necessary. **(4)** Next work with the *Filmclip*. Before playing the scene, spend some time with the scene-setting context, making sure students understand who each character is and the context in which the interaction in the film clip takes place. Ask sts. to read through all the questions and go over the vocabulary. Have sts. answer questions in pairs or small groups. **(5)** Assign *Nach dem Lesen* as homework.

Inhaltsangabe

Ost-Berlin 1984. Der pflichtbewusste Stasi-Mitarbeiter Gerd Wiesler (Ulrich Mühe) soll den bekannten und angeblich regimetreuen Dramaturgen Georg Dreyman (Sebastian Koch) bespitzeln. Wiesler hat einen guten Spürsinn und glaubt, dass Dreyman nicht so treu ist, wie er tut. Kulturminister Hempf (Thomas Thieme) unter-
5 stützt die Bewachung des Theaterschriftstellers, weil er ihn aus dem Weg schaffen will, um freie Bahn bei dessen Freundin, der Schauspielerin Christa-Maria Sieland (Martina Gedeck) zu haben.

Dreymans Wohnung wird verwanzt, und auf dem Dachboden des Hauses installiert Wiesler Abhörgeräte. Wiesler, der allein in einer Neubauwohnung lebt und kein aufre-
10 gendes Privatleben hat, erlebt durch die Bewachung Dreymans eine für ihn völlig neue Welt: nämlich die der Kunst, der Literatur, des freien Geistes und der Liebe. Das Leben des Dramaturgen und der Schauspielerin beeindruckt den Stasi-Mann so sehr, dass er aufhört, belastendes Material über Dreyman zu sammeln. Wieslers Berichte über den Theaterschriftsteller sind trivial. Er unternimmt auch nichts, als Dreyman nach dem Selbstmord eines befreundeten Regisseurs anonym einen Essay über die
15 hohe Selbstmordrate in der DDR veröffentlicht. Wiesler schützt Dreyman sogar, indem er die Schreibmaschine, auf der Dreyman den Essay für den *Spiegel* geschrieben hat, aus ihrem Versteck nimmt und verschwinden lässt.

Ein Opfer gibt es dennoch: Die psychisch labile Schauspielerin Christa-Maria Sie-
20 land verrät der Stasi, dass Dreyman den Essay geschrieben hat und wo die Schreib-maschine versteckt ist. Dann flüchtet sie, läuft vor ein Auto und stirbt. Als Dreyman nach der Wende Einsicht in seine Stasi-Akten bekommt, erfährt er, dass ein Stasi-Mitarbeiter ihn geschützt hat. Seine Erinnerungen schreibt Dreyman in einem Roman nieder. Sein Buch widmet er seinem Stasi-Spitzel Wiesler unter dessen Stasi-
25 Deckcode-Namen HGW XX/7–in Dankbarkeit.

Miniwörterbuch

zufällig	by chance
zwingen, gezwungen	to coerce
sonst	otherwise
das **Berufsverbot**	occupational ban
aufmuntern	to cheer up
schmücken	to decorate
die **Beziehung**	relationship
Schlips binden	to tie a tie
zusperren, zugesperrt	to lock

Arbeit mit dem Text

Welche Aussagen sind falsch? Verbessern Sie die falschen Aussagen.

1. „Das Leben der Anderen" spielt vor dem Fall der Berliner Mauer.
2. Der Dramaturg Dreyman scheint ein Fan des DDR-Regimes zu sein.
3. Gerd Wiesler arbeitet für die Polizei und den Kulturminister.
4. Wiesler hat den Auftrag, den Dramaturgen Dreyman und dessen Freundin zu überwachen.
5. Dreyman unterschreibt den Essay im *Spiegel* mit seinem Namen.
6. Wiesler meldet seinem Chef, dass sich Dreyman nicht regimetreu verhält.
7. Christa-Maria Sieland schützt Dreyman und muss deshalb sterben.
8. Nach der Wiedervereinigung schreibt Dreyman ein Buch über seine Erinnerungen.

Filmclip 🎬

Szene: DVD Kapitel 4, 25.06–29.08 Min.

Die Männer der Stasi verwanzen die Wohnung von Georg und Christa-Maria. Die Nachbarin Frau Meineke sieht dies zufällig und wird von den Stasi-Leuten gezwungen, niemandem etwas davon zu sagen. Sonst würde man ihrer Tochter den Medizinstudienplatz wegnehmen. Georg ist in der Zwischenzeit bei seinem Freund, Albert Jerska. Jerska war Regisseur. Vor sieben Jahren hat man ihm ein Berufsverbot erteilt, weil er das Regime kritisiert hatte. Georg versucht, seinen Freund aufzumuntern und möchte ihn zu seiner Geburtstagsfeier einladen. Das vergisst er aber. Als Georg nach Hause kommt, schmückt Christa-Maria gerade die Wohnung für die Feier.

Schauen Sie sich die Szene an und beantworten Sie die Fragen.

1. Welche Beziehung haben Georg und Christa-Maria?
2. Was soll in ihrer Wohnung stattfinden? Was macht Christa-Maria dafür?
3. Was erzählt Georg Christa-Maria über seinen Besuch bei Albert Jerska?
4. Was hält Christa-Maria von Albert?
5. Wie alt wird Georg?
6. Was schenkt ihm Christa-Maria zum Geburtstag?
7. Was sagt Georg, dass er tun kann? Stimmt das?
8. Warum braucht Georg die Hilfe der Nachbarin Frau Meineke?
9. Wie reagiert die Nachbarin auf Georg? Warum?
10. Warum verlässt Georg die Wohnung?
11. Was macht Christa-Maria, als Georg gegangen ist? Warum macht sie das vielleicht?
12. Was denken Sie? Wie geht die Beziehung zwischen Georg und Christa-Maria weiter?

Nach dem Lesen

Georg Dreymans Tagebuch: Schreiben Sie zu einer der folgenden Situationen einen Eintrag aus Dreymans Perspektive.

a. nach der Veröffentlichung des Essays im *Spiegel*
b. nach dem Unfall von Christa-Maria Sieland
c. nach Einsicht in die eigenen Stasi-Akten nach der Wende

Videoecke

Perspektiven

Aufgabe 1 Tattoos und Piercings

Sie gehören zum Zeitgeschmack.

Wer mag Tattoos? Wer mag Piercings? Wer mag weder Tattoos noch Piercings? Ordnen Sie die Personen in drei Kategorien.

1. Michael

2. Judith

3. Nadezda

4. Pascal

5. Sophie

6. Felicitas

7. Tina

8. Martin

Tattoos	Piercings	Weder/noch
Judith	Judith	Michael
Pascal		Nadezda
Tina		Sophie
		Felicitas
		Martin: denkt, dass sie wieder aus der Mode kommen

Aufgabe 2 Wer sagt das?

Schreiben Sie die Namen neben die Aussagen.

1. Ich finde Tattoos und Piercings absolut hässlich. Michael
2. Ich habe ein Tattoo. Judith
3. Ich habe zu große Angst vor den Schmerzen. Tina
4. Man soll möglichst natürlich aussehen. Sophie
5. Piercings sind nicht so mein Ding. Pascal
6. Tattoos und Piercings kommen irgendwann wieder aus der Mode. Martin

Interviews

- Wann warst du das letzte Mal krank?
- Was hattest du?
- Was machst du, wenn du dich erkältet hast?
- Hattest du schon mal einen Unfall? Erzähl mal.
- Was für eine Krankenversicherung hast du?
- Wie viel kostet sie?
- Bist du mit ihr zufrieden?

Albrecht

Michael

Aufgabe 3 Albrecht oder Michael?

Sehen Sie sich das Video an und ergänzen Sie die Tabelle.

	Albrecht	Michael
Wann war er das letzte Mal krank?	im letzten Winter	vor zwei Wochen
Was hatte er?	Grippe; hohes Fieber, Husten, Schnupfen, Halsschmerzen	Magen-Darm-Grippe; ihm war die ganze Zeit übel
Was macht er, wenn er sich erkältet hat?	Hausmittel: Tee trinken, ausruhen, viel schlafen; Medikamente nehmen	im Bett liegen, Tee trinken
Was für eine Krankenversicherung hat er?	gesetzliche Krankenversicherung	über die Mutter familienversichert
Wie viel kostet sie?	15% vom Bruttogehalt, 150 Euro pro Monat	kostet nichts
Ist er damit zufrieden?	ja	ja

Interviews. Additional activities: (1) Provide students a list of phrases relating to Albrecht's accident: *war klein, ein Wettrennen mit dem Fahrrad gefahren, gestürzt, Bein und Arm haben geblutet, hat immer noch Narbe.* Ask sts. listen to his story and to put them in order and finish by re-telling Albrecht's story. (2) Ask sts. to listen to Michael's story about his accident and re-tell it. You may wish to provide students with phrases as necessary: *mit Mutter im Auto; Auto vor ihnen blieb plötzlich stehen; konnten nicht mehr bremsen; in das andere Auto hineingefahren; das andere Auto völlig kaputt; eigenes Auto war ganz*

Wortschatz

Krankheit und Gesundheit	Illness and Health
die Entzündung, -en	infection
die Lungenentzündung	pneumonia
die Nierenentzündung	kidney infection
die Erkältung, -en	(head) cold
die Gesundheit	health
die Grippe	influenza, flu
die Krankheit, -en	illness, sickness
die Ohnmacht	unconsciousness
in Ohnmacht fallen	to faint
der Blutdruck	blood pressure
niedrigen/hohen Blutdruck haben	to have low/high blood pressure
der Husten	cough
der Hustensaft, ⸚e	cough syrup

der Kater, -	hangover
der Liebeskummer	lovesickness
der Muskelkater, -	sore muscles
der Schmerz, -en	pain
die Halsschmerzen	sore throat
die Herzschmerzen	heartache
die Kopfschmerzen	headache
die Magenschmerzen	stomachache
die Ohrenschmerzen	earache
die Zahnschmerzen	toothache
der Schnupfen, -	cold (*with a runny nose*), sniffles
das Bonbon, -s	drop, lozenge
das Hustenbonbon, -s	cough drop
sich ärgern (R)	to get angry
sich auf·regen	to get excited, get upset

sich erkälten	to catch a cold
fehlen (+ *dat.*) (R)	to be wrong with, be the matter with (*a person*)
weh·tun, tat ... weh, wehgetan	to hurt

Ähnliche Wörter

das Fieber; (sich) fühlen; sich wohl fühlen

Der Körper — The Body

die Haut, ⸚e	skin
die Niere, -n	kidney
die Zunge, -n	tongue
der Blinddarm, ⸚e	appendix
der Magen, ⸚	stomach
der Zahn, ⸚e	tooth
das Gehirn, -e	brain
atmen	to breathe
greifen, griff, gegriffen	to grab, grasp
kauen	to chew
lutschen	to suck
riechen, roch, gerochen	to smell

Ähnliche Wörter

die Leber, -n; die Lippe, -n; die Lunge, -n; die Nase, -n; der Finger, -; der Fingernagel, ⸚; das Haar, -e (R); das Herz, -en

Apotheke und Krankenhaus — Pharmacy and Hospital

die Apothekerin, -nen	female pharmacist
die Ärztin, -nen (R)	female doctor, physician
die Augenärztin, -nen	eye doctor
die Hausärztin, -nen	family doctor
die Zahnärztin, -nen	dentist
die Arztpraxis, Arztpraxen	doctor's office
die Psychiaterin, -nen	female psychiatrist
die Spritze, -n	shot, injection
die Tierärztin, -nen	female veterinarian
der Apotheker, -	male pharmacist
der Arzt, ⸚e (R)	male doctor, physician
der Augenarzt, ⸚e	eye doctor
der Hausarzt, ⸚e	family doctor
der Zahnarzt, ⸚e	dentist
der Gips	cast (*plaster*)
der Psychiater, -	male psychiatrist
der Tierarzt, ⸚e	male veterinarian
der Verband, ⸚e	bandage
das Medikament, -e	medicine
ein Medikament gegen	medicine for
das Pflaster, -	adhesive bandage
das Rezept, -e	prescription

ab·nehmen, nimmt ... ab, nahm ... ab, abgenommen	to remove; to lose weight
Blut abnehmen	to take blood
röntgen	to X-ray
wirken	to work, take effect

Ähnliche Wörter

die Diphtherie; die Tablette, -n; die Kopfschmerztablette, -n; die Wunde, -n; der Schock; der Tetanus; das Aspirin; das Blut (R); die Antibiotika (*pl.*); bluten; desinfizieren

Unfälle — Accidents

die Feuerwehr	fire department
die Verletzte, -n	female injured person
die Zeugin, -nen	female witness
der Verletzte, -n (ein Verletzter)	male injured person
der Zeuge, -n (*wk. masc.*)	male witness
ab·stürzen, ist abgestürzt	to crash
aus·rutschen, ist ausgerutscht	to slip
bremsen	to brake
brennen, brannte, gebrannt	to burn
hin·fallen, fällt ... hin, fiel ... hin, ist hingefallen	to fall down
schlagen, schlägt, schlug, geschlagen (R)	to hit
stecken bleiben, blieb ... stecken, ist stecken geblieben	to get stuck
überfahren, überfährt, überfuhr, überfahren	to run over
um·kippen	to knock over
verbrennen, verbrannte, verbrannt	to burn
sich (die Zunge) verbrennen	to burn (one's tongue)
sich verletzen	to injure oneself
zu·decken	to cover
zusammen·stoßen, stößt ... zusammen, stieß ... zusammen, ist zusammengestoßen	to crash

Ähnliche Wörter

der Krankenwagen, -; brechen, bricht, brach, gebrochen; sich (den Arm) brechen

Körperpflege — Personal Hygiene

die Dauerwelle, -n	perm
die Seife, -n	soap
das Solarium, Solarien	tanning salon

sich ab·trocknen (R)	to dry oneself off
sich an·ziehen, zog ... an, angezogen (R)	to get dressed
sich aus·ruhen (R)	to rest
sich aus·ziehen, zog ... aus, ausgezogen (R)	to get undressed
(sich) duschen (R)	to shower (take a shower)
sich ein·cremen	to put lotion on
sich erholen	to recuperate
sich (die Haare) föhnen	to blow-dry (one's hair)
sich (die Zähne) putzen	to brush (one's teeth)
sich rasieren	to shave
sich schminken	to put makeup on
(sich) schneiden, schnitt, geschnitten (R)	to cut (oneself)

Ähnliche Wörter

die Sauna, -s; (sich) baden (R); sich (die Haare) kämmen (R); (sich) waschen, wäscht, wusch, gewaschen (R)

Sonstige Substantive	Other Noun
die Decke, -n	blanket
die Einfahrt, -en	driveway
die Tüte, -n	(paper or plastic) bag
die Verabredung, -en	appointment; date
der Rat, Ratschläge	advice
der Termin, -e (R)	appointment
der Terminkalender, -	appointment calendar
der Unterricht	class, instruction
der Verkehr	traffic
das Fahrzeug, -e	vehicle

Ähnliche Wörter

die Autonummer, -n; der Chili; der Goldfisch, -e; das Rockkonzert, -e

Sonstige Verben	Other Verbs
achten auf (+ akk.)	to watch out for; to pay attention to
auf·schreiben, schrieb ... auf, aufgeschrieben	to write down
beschreiben, beschrieb, beschrieben	to describe
fluchen	to curse, swear
flüchten, ist geflüchtet	to flee
sich freuen über (+ akk.)	to be happy about
herunter·klettern, ist heruntergeklettert	to climb down
sich hin·legen	to lie down
klingen (wie), klang, geklungen	to sound (like)
lassen, lässt, ließ, gelassen	to let
sich einen Termin geben lassen	to get an appointment

passen (R)	to fit
das passt gut	that fits well
raten, rät, riet, geraten (+ dat.)	to advise
rufen, rief, gerufen (R)	to call
schaufeln	to shovel
verlassen, verlässt, verließ, verlassen	to leave; to abandon

Ähnliche Wörter

sich setzen (R)

Adjektive und Adverbien	Adjectives and Adverbs
deprimiert	depressed
fettig (R)	greasy
regelmäßig	regularly
schlimm	bad
stark	heavy, severe
trocken	dry
verletzt	injured
schwer verletzt	critically injured

Ähnliche Wörter

allergisch, medizinisch

Sonstige Wörter und Ausdrücke	Other Words and Expressions
aber (R)	but
als (R)	when (conj.)
bevor	before (conj.)
bis (R)	until (prep., conj.)
dagegen	here: for it
Haben Sie etwas dagegen?	Do you have something for it (illness)?
damit	so that
dass	that (conj.)
denn (R)	for, because
draußen	outside
gemeinsam	together; common
herunter	down (toward the speaker)
Hilfe!	Help!
jedenfalls	in any case
mal	(word used to soften commands)
Komm mal vorbei!	Come on over!
nachdem (R)	after (conj.)
ob (R)	whether
obwohl	although
oder (R)	or
seit (R)	since, for (prep.)
seit mehreren Tagen	for several days
sondern (R)	on the contrary
und (R)	and
während	during
weil (R)	because
wenn (R)	if; whenever

Strukturen und Übungen

11.1 Accusative reflexive pronouns

11.1. *Reflexivpronomen und reflexive Verben.* We introduce accusative reflexive pronouns first to reduce confusion between accusative and dative forms. The dative forms are covered in Section 11.2. Include plural forms in your input so sts. can begin to acquire these forms, too.

Sts. will probably realize that they have already seen or heard some of these verbs, now being introduced as reflexive verbs, in their nonreflexive forms, without a reflexive pronoun. Point out that some verbs are used only reflexively, and others can be either reflexive or nonreflexive.

Reflexive pronouns are generally used to express the fact that someone is doing something to or for himself or herself.

Ich lege das Baby ins Bett.	*I'm putting the baby to bed.*
Ich lege mich ins Bett.	*I'm putting myself to bed (lying down).*

Some verbs are always used with a reflexive pronoun in German, whereas their English counterparts may not be.

Ich habe mich erkältet.	*I caught a cold.*
Warum regst du dich auf?	*Why are you getting excited?*

Here are some common reflexive verbs.

sich ärgern	*to get angry*
sich aufregen	*to get excited, get upset*
sich ausruhen	*to rest*
sich erkälten	*to catch a cold*
sich freuen	*to be happy*
sich (wohl) fühlen	*to feel (well)*
sich hinlegen	*to lie down*
sich verletzen	*to get hurt*

In most instances the forms of the reflexive pronoun are the same as those of the personal object pronouns. The only reflexive form that is distinct is **sich,** which corresponds to **er, sie** (*she*), **es, sie** (*they*), and **Sie*** (*you*).

Accusative Reflexive Pronouns	
ich → mich	*wir* → uns
du → dich	*ihr* → euch
Sie → sich	*Sie* → sich
er *sie* } → sich *es*	*sie* → sich

Ich fühle mich nicht wohl.	*I don't feel well.*
Michael hat sich verletzt.	*Michael hurt himself.*

Verbs with reflexive pronouns use the auxiliary **haben** in the perfect and past perfect tenses.

Heidi hat sich in den Finger geschnitten.	*Heidi cut her finger.*

*Even when it refers to **Sie,** the polite form of *you,* **sich** is not capitalized.

Übung 1   Minidialoge

Üb. 1. Point out that the reflexive verbs in this exercise may be used in the present or perfect tense, or they may be used with a modal verb.

Ergänzen Sie das Verb und das Reflexivpronomen.

sich ärgern (geärgert)
sich aufregen (aufgeregt)
sich ausruhen (ausgeruht)
sich erkälten (erkältet)
sich freuen (gefreut)
sich fühlen (gefühlt)
sich legen (gelegt)
sich schneiden (geschnitten)
sich verletzen (verletzt)

1. SILVIA: Ich _____ _____ᵃ gar nicht wohl.
   JÜRGEN: Warum denn?
   SILVIA: Ich glaube, ich habe _____ _____ᵇ.
   JÜRGEN: Du Ärmste! Du musst _____ gleich ins Bett _____ᶜ.

2. MICHAEL: Du, weißt du, dass Herr Thelen einen Herzinfarkt¹ hatte?
   MARIA: Kein Wunder, er hat _____ auch immer so furchtbar _____ᵃ.
   MICHAEL: Na, jetzt muss er _____ erst mal ein paar Wochen _____ᵇ.

3. FRAU RUF: Du blutest ja! Hast du _____ _____ᵃ?
   HERR RUF: Ja, ich habe _____ in den Finger _____ᵇ.

4. HEIDI: Warum _____ du _____ᵃ, Stefan?
   STEFAN: Ich habe in meiner Prüfung ein D bekommen.
   HEIDI: Du solltest _____ _____ᵇ, dass du kein F bekommen hast.

11.2 Dative reflexive pronouns

11.2. *Reflexivpronomen und reflexive Verben.* A useful rule of thumb is that if there is no other object, the reflexive pronoun will be accusative. If the sentence already has an accusative object, the reflexive pronoun will be dative. Sts. sometimes falsely assume that adverbial phrases of time like *jeden Tag* and phrases beginning with a preposition are objects.

When a clause contains another object in addition to the reflexive pronoun, then the reflexive pronoun is in the dative case; the other object, usually a thing or a part of the body, is in the accusative case.

DAT.   ACC.

Ich ziehe mir den Mantel aus.   *I'm taking off my coat.*

Note that the accusative object (the piece of clothing or part of the body) is preceded by the definite article.

Wäschst du dir jeden Tag **die** Haare?   *Do you wash your hair every day?*
Natalie hat sich **den** Arm gebrochen.   *Natalie broke her arm.*

Only the reflexive pronouns that correspond to **ich** and **du** have different dative and accusative forms.

Reflexive Pronouns

	SINGULAR		PLURAL		
	Accusative	*Dative*	*Accusative*		*Dative*
ich	**mich**	**mir**	**uns**		wir
du	**dich**	**dir**	**euch**		ihr
Sie					Sie
er/sie/es	**sich**				sie

¹*heart attack*

Übung 2   Meine Morgentoilette

Üb. 2. This exercise is limited to *ich*-forms and requires both accusative and dative reflexive pronouns. Sts. may begin adding a reflexive pronoun to a nonreflexive verb like *aufstehen* now that they have learned reflexive pronouns; watch out for this.

In welcher Reihenfolge machen Sie das?

MODELL: Erst stehe ich auf. Dann dusche ich mich. Dann ...

sich abtrocknen	sich die Haare föhnen
sich anziehen	sich die Haare kämmen
aufstehen	sich die Haare waschen
sich duschen	sich rasieren
sich die Fingernägel putzen	sich schminken
frühstücken	sich die Zähne putzen
sich das Gesicht waschen	zur Uni gehen

Übung 3   Körperpflege

Üb. 3. 1st- and 3rd-person forms only. Use for homework and/or oral work in class.

Wer macht das? Sie, Ihre Freundin, Ihr Vater ...?

1. sich jeden Morgen rasieren
2. sich zu sehr schminken
3. sich nicht oft genug die Haare waschen
4. sich nach jeder Mahlzeit die Zähne putzen
5. sich immer verrückt anziehen
6. sich jeden Tag duschen
7. sich nie kämmen
8. sich nie die Haare föhnen
9. sich nicht gern baden
10. sich immer elegant anziehen

ich
meine Freundin
mein Freund
mein Vater
meine Mutter
meine Schwester
meine Oma
mein Onkel
_____?

11.3 Word order of accusative and dative objects

11.3. *Wortstellung: Akkusativ- und Dativobjekt.* This rule states that the dative object usually precedes the accusative object, unless the accusative object is a pronoun. At this stage, sts. do not often attempt to use 2 object pronouns when speaking.

When the accusative object and the dative object are both *nouns*, then the dative object precedes the accusative object.

            DAT.   ACC.

Ich schenke **meiner Mutter einen Ring.**   *I'm giving my mother a ring.*

When either the accusative object or the dative object is a *pronoun* and the other object is a *noun*, then the pronoun precedes the noun regardless of case.

            DAT.   ACC.

Ich schenke **ihr einen Ring.**   *I'm giving her a ring.*

            ACC.   DAT.

Ich schenke **ihn meiner Mutter.**   *I'm giving it to my mother.*

The dative object precedes the accusative object, unless the accusative object is a pronoun.

When the accusative object and the dative object are both *pronouns*, then the accusative object precedes the dative object.

Ich schenke **ihn ihr.**   *I'm giving it to her.*

Note that English speakers use a similar word order. Remember that German speakers do *not* use a preposition to emphasize the dative object as English speakers often do (*to my mother, to her*).

Üb. 4. This exercise can be used for oral practice in class. Remind sts. that the choice of 3rd-person pronoun depends on the grammatical gender of the noun.

AA. To help sts. with vocabulary, you might bring in a collection of travel-size toilet articles (shampoo, soap, lotion, aftershave, etc.), so that the activity can be acted out.

Übung 4   Im Hotel

Sie sind mit Ihrem Partner / Ihrer Partnerin in einem Hotel. Sie sind gerade aufgestanden und packen Ihre gemeinsame Toilettentasche aus.

MODELL: S1: Brauchst du den Lippenstift?
S2: Ja, kannst du ihn mir geben?
oder Nein, ich brauche ihn nicht.

1. Brauchst du das Shampoo?
2. Brauchst du den Spiegel?
3. Brauchst du den Rasierapparat?
4. Brauchst du die Seife?
5. Brauchst du das Handtuch?
6. Brauchst du den Föhn?
7. Brauchst du die Creme?
8. Brauchst du das Rasierwasser?
9. Brauchst du den Kamm?

Übung 5   Gute Ratschläge!

Geben Sie Ihrem Partner / Ihrer Partnerin Rat.

MODELL: S1: Meine Hände sind schmutzig.
S2: Warum wäschst du sie dir nicht?

eincremen   waschen

putzen

schneiden   föhnen

1. Mein Bart ist zu lang.
2. Meine Füße sind schmutzig.
3. Meine Fingernägel sind zu lang.
4. Meine Haut ist ganz trocken.
5. Meine Haare sind nass.
6. Mein Hals ist schmutzig.
7. Meine Nase läuft.
8. Meine Haare sind zu lang.
9. Mein Gesicht ist ganz trocken.
10. Meine Haare sind fettig.

11.4 Indirect questions: *Wissen Sie, wo ...?*

Indirect questions:
- dependent clause begins with a question word or **ob**
- conjugated verb in the dependent clause appears at the end of the clause

11.4. *Indirekte Fragen.* This section continues the discussion of subordinating conjunctions and dependent word order begun in Section 3.4 (*wenn, weil*) and carried on in Sections 7.1 (relative pronouns), 9.1 and 9.3 (*als, wenn, wann*), and 9.5 (*nachdem*). This discussion will be completed in 11.5 (summary review) and picked up again in 12.3 (*weil, damit*).

Indirect questions are dependent clauses that are commonly preceded by an introductory clause such as **Wissen Sie, ...** or **Ich weiß nicht, ...** Recall that the conjugated verb is in last position in a dependent clause.

Wissen Sie, **wo** das Kind gefunden **wurde**?	*Do you know where the child was found?*
Können Sie mir sagen, **wann** die Polizei **ankommt**?	*Can you tell me when the police will arrive?*

The question word of the direct question functions as a subordinating conjunction in an indirect question.

DIRECT QUESTION: **Wie** komme ich zur Apotheke?
INDIRECT QUESTION: Ich weiß nicht, **wie** ich zur Apotheke **komme**.

Use the conjunction **ob** (*whether*, *if*) when the corresponding direct question does not begin with a question word but with a verb.

DIRECT QUESTION: **Kommt** Michael heute Abend?
INDIRECT QUESTION: Ich weiß nicht, **ob** Michael heute Abend **kommt.**

Übung 6   Bitte etwas freundlicher!

Üb. 6. Assign for homework. You may want to remind sts. that there is no question word in 2, 5, or 6, and so they will need to use *ob*.

Verwandeln Sie die folgenden direkten Fragen in etwas höflichere indirekte Fragen. Beginnen Sie mit **Wissen Sie, ...** oder **Können Sie mir sagen, ...**

MODELL: Wo war Herr Langen um sieben Uhr fünfzehn? →
Wissen Sie, wo Herr Langen um sieben Uhr fünfzehn war?
oder Können Sie mir sagen, wo Herr Langen um sieben Uhr fünfzehn war?

1. Was ist hier passiert?
2. Hat das Kind das Auto gesehen?
3. Wer war daran Schuld?
4. Warum hat Herr Langen das Kind nicht gesehen?
5. Hat Herr Langen gebremst?
6. Wann hat er gebremst?
7. Wie oft fährt Herr Langen diese Straße zur Arbeit?
8. Wie lange lag Lothar auf der Straße?
9. Wann hat die Polizei Lothars Mutter angerufen?

11.5 Word order in dependent and independent clauses (summary review)

11.5. *Wortstellung in Hauptsätzen und Nebensätzen.* This section provides a review of the coordination and subordination of clauses and lists the most common conjunctions used for each.

Stress that the coordinating conjunction does not count as the first element of the second clause. The subject is often the first element, but an adverbial phrase may also stand in first position.

Dependent clauses were introduced first in Section 3.4 (*wenn* and *weil*). Section 7.1 presented relative clauses, Sections 9.1 and 9.3 the conjunctions *als* and *wenn*, Section 9.5 *nachdem*, and Section 11.4 indirect questions. Section 12.3 will contrast the conjunctions *weil*, *damit*, and *um ... zu*.

To connect thoughts more effectively, two or more clauses may be combined in one sentence. There are essentially two kinds of combinations:

1. Coordination: both clauses are equally important and do not depend on each other structurally.
2. Subordination: one clause depends on the other one; it does not make sense when it stands alone.

COORDINATION

Heute ist ein kalter Tag und es schneit.	*Today is a cold day, and it is snowing.*

SUBORDINATION

Gestern war es wärmer, weil die Sonne schien.	*Yesterday was warmer because the sun was shining.*

A. Coordination

These are the five most common coordinating conjunctions.

und	*and*
oder	*or*
aber	*but*
sondern	*but, on the contrary*
denn	*because*

In clauses joined with these conjunctions, the conjugated verb is in second position in both statements.

CLAUSE 1	CONJ.	CLAUSE 2
I II		I II
Ich muss noch viel lernen,	denn	ich habe morgen eine Prüfung.

(*I still have to study a lot, since I have a test tomorrow.*)

B. Subordination

Clauses joined by subordinating conjunctions follow one of two word order patterns.

1. When the sentence begins with the main clause, that clause has regular word order (verb second in statements) and the dependent clause introduced by the conjunction has dependent word order (verb last).

CLAUSE 1	CONJ.	CLAUSE 2
I II		I LAST
Ich muss noch viel lernen,	weil	ich morgen eine Prüfung habe.

(*I still have to study a lot because I have a test tomorrow.*)

2. When a sentence begins with a dependent clause, the entire dependent clause is considered the first part of the main clause and occupies first position. The verb-second rule applies, then, moving the subject of the main clause after the verb.

CLAUSE 1	CLAUSE 2
I	II SUBJECT
Weil ich morgen eine Prüfung habe,	muss ich noch viel lernen.

(*Because I have a test tomorrow, I still have to study a lot.*)

Here are the most commonly used subordinating conjunctions.

als	*when*
bevor	*before*
bis	*until*
damit	*so that*
dass	*that*
nachdem	*after*
ob	*whether, if*
obwohl	*although*
während	*while*
weil	*because, since*
wenn	*if, when*

Übung 7   Opa Schmitz ist im Garten

Ergänzen Sie **dass, ob, weil, damit** oder **wenn.**

1. OMA SCHMITZ: Weißt du, _____a Opa schon den Rasen gemäht hat?
   HELGA: Ich weiß nur, _____b er schon seit zwei Stunden im Garten ist.
   OMA SCHMITZ: _____c Opa schon so lange im Garten ist, liegt er bestimmt in der Sonne.

2. HELGA: Du, Opi, was machst du denn im Gras?

OPA SCHMITZ: Ich habe mich nur kurz hingelegt, _____[a] mich die Nachbarn nicht sehen.

HELGA: Aber warum sollen die dich denn nicht sehen?

OPA SCHMITZ: _____[b] sich mich heute noch nicht rasiert habe.

Übung 8　Minidialoge

Ergänzen Sie **obwohl, als, nachdem, bevor** oder **während.**

1. HERR THELEN: Was hat denn deine Tochter gesagt, _____[a] du mit deiner neuen Frisur nach Hause gekommen bist?

HERR SIEBERT: Zuerst gar nichts. Erst _____[b] sie ein paar Mal um mich herumgegangen war, hat sie angefangen zu lachen und gesagt: „Aber, Papi, erst fast eine Glatze und jetzt so viele Haare. Das sieht aber komisch aus!"

2. FRAU ROWOHLT: Guten Tag, Herr Frisch! Kommen Sie doch bitte erst zu mir, _____ Sie mit Ihrer Arbeit beginnen.

HERR FRISCH: Aber natürlich, Frau Direktorin.

3. JOSEF: Ja, seid ihr denn immer noch nicht fertig? Was habt ihr eigentlich die ganze Zeit gemacht?

MELANIE: _____ du dich stundenlang geduscht hast, haben wir die ganze Wohnung aufgeräumt.

4. MARIA: Aber, Herr Wachtmeister, könnten Sie nicht mal ein Auge zudrücken? Die Ampel war doch schon fast wieder grün.

POLIZIST: Nein, leider nicht, _____ ich es gern tun würde, meine gnädige[1] Frau. Aber Sie wissen ja, Pflicht ist Pflicht.

---

[1]*dear*

12

Die moderne Gesellschaft

In **Kapitel 12,** you will discuss social relationships and some of the issues that arise in modern multicultural societies. In addition, you will learn to talk about money matters and about German art and literature.

GOALS

In this chapter, sts. learn to express their opinions about contemporary social issues, the economy, and German art and literature. Expressing causality and purpose and using case are reviewed, while the genitive case and the subjunctive to express possibility are presented formally for the first time.

Themen

Familie, Ehe, Partnerschaft
Multikulturelle Gesellschaft
Das liebe Geld
Kunst und Literatur

Kulturelles

KLI: Gleichberechtigung
Musikszene: „Cüs Junge" (Muhabbet [mit Fler])
KLI: Wie bezahlt man in Europa?
Filmclip: *Sophie Scholl – Die letzten Tage* (Marc Rothemund)
Videoecke: Medien und Finanzen

Lektüren

Kurzgeschichte: Deutsche Kastanien (Yüksel Pazarkaya)
Film: *Sophie Scholl – Die letzten Tage* (Marc Rothemund)

Strukturen

12.1 The genitive case
12.2 Expressing possibility: **würde, hätte,** and **wäre**
12.3 Causality and purpose: **weil, damit, um ... zu**
12.4 Principles of case (summary review)

Suzan Emine Kaube: *Derwische*
(1990), Privatbesitz

Kunst und Künstler

Suzan Emine Kaube ist eine deutsch-türkische Autorin, Malerin und Pädagogin. Sie wurde 1942 in Istanbul geboren und lernte einen Deutschen kennen, mit dem sie 1964 nach Deutschland zog. Als Lehrerin engagierte sie sich stark für Kinder mit Migrationshintergrund, die wegen ihrer fehlenden Deutschkenntnisse Probleme in der Schule hatten. Vielen dieser Kinder ermöglichte sie den Besuch eines Gymnasiums oder einer anderen Oberschule oder ein Studium. Außerdem arbeitete sie als Dozentin an einem Institut für die pädagogische Weiterbildung von Lehrkräften[1]. Auch dabei konzentrierte sie sich vor allem auf den Umgang[2] mit Kindern mit Migrationshintergrund. Kaubes Bilder sind von abstrakten Formen und meist kräftigen[3] Farben gekennzeichnet, außerdem verwendet sie oft Collagetechnik.

Schauen Sie sich das Bild an und beantworten Sie die folgenden Fragen.

1. Was für Assoziationen weckt der Titel des Bildes in Ihnen? Passt das zu dem Eindruck[4], den das Bild auf Sie macht?
2. Welche Farben dominieren in dem Bild?
3. Beschreiben Sie die Derwische und ihre Gesichter. Wie wirken die Derwische auf Sie?
4. Betrachten Sie den Hintergrund des Bildes. Warum hat die Künstlerin in den Hintergrund ein Paar Augen gemalt?

[1] *teachers* [2] *dealings* [3] *bold* [4] *impression*

Chapter opening artwork: Suzan Emine Kaube aquired her techniques in various summer schools in Germany and through private lessons by artist friends. She creates expressive and abstract works of art with charcoal, watercolors, oil and acrylic as well as the collage technique. Her main themes include environmental pollution, terror, escape, and fear, the entire array of modern-day concerns. The painting *Derwische* in acrylic, with the intimidating eyes in the background, is a good example, especially with the dark and rather gloomy colors that dominate the scene.

Suggestion: You may wish to use the painting to introduce sts. to the chapter theme *Multikulturelle Gesellschaft* since the artist is a Turkish woman married to a German. She lives both in Germany and Turkey. The piece can also serve as an introduction to the topic of *Kunst und Literatur* in general.

Situationen

Familie, Ehe, Partnerschaft
Grammatik 12.1–12.2

Vocabulary Display
This display provides examples of the genitive case. Sts. will probably not yet learn to use the genitive correctly in speaking, but they should learn to recognize its meaning when they read or hear it.

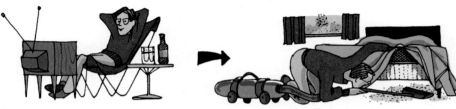

Die gute alte Zeit: der Herr im Haus

Eine Rolle des modernen Mannes

Kinder und Haushalt: eine mögliche Rolle der modernen Frau

Das Leben vieler Frauen: Erfolg im Beruf

Verliebt, verlobt, verheiratet

Er kümmert sich um die Kinder und sie kümmert sich um das Geld.

Situation 1   Wer im Kurs ...?

Sit. 1. This is a variation on the regular autograph activity. Practice forming the questions before asking sts. to do the activity. Follow up by turning sts.' findings into an optional association activity.

1. ist verheiratet
2. ist verlobt
3. hat einen Sohn oder eine Tochter
4. war noch nie verliebt
5. möchte einen Arzt / eine Ärztin heiraten
6. möchte keine Hausfrau / kein Hausmann sein
7. will mehr als drei Kinder haben
8. wird leicht eifersüchtig
9. findet gemeinsame Hobbys wichtig
10. ist gerade glücklich verliebt

Sit. 2. The corresponding chart is in Appendix A.

MODELL: Wie soll Rolfs ideale Partnerin aussehen?
Was für einen Charakter soll sie haben?
Welchen Beruf soll Heidis idealer Partner haben?
Welche Interessen sollte er haben?
Wie alt sollte er sein?
Welche Konfession sollte er haben?
Welcher Nationalität sollte Rolfs Partnerin angehören?
Welche politische Einstellung sollte sie haben?

	Rolf	Heidi	mein(e) Partner(in)
Aussehen	schlank und sportlich	klein und dick	
Charakter	lustig und neugierig	fleißig und geduldig	
Beruf	egal	Rechtsanwalt	
Interessen	Kunst und Kultur	Sport und Reisen	
Alter	so alt wie er	ein paar Jahre jünger als sie	
Konfession	egal	kein Fanatiker	
Nationalität	deutsch	egal	
politische Einstellung	eher konservativ	liberal	

Situation 3   Interview

Sit. 3. Sts. discuss these questions in small groups, then with the entire class. You could ask sts. to write their answers so that you can take them home and construct a summary chart. For yes/no questions, note the percentage of people answering yes/no, and then break these percentages down by gender. For descriptive questions, list the most frequent responses, perhaps computing percentages here as well. Tally the results and distribute to sts. the next day for a follow-up discussion.

1. Willst du heiraten? (Bist du verheiratet?)
2. Wie sollte dein Partner / deine Partnerin sein? Welche Eigenschaften findest du an deinem Partner / deiner Partnerin wichtig?
3. Sind Aussehen und Beruf wichtig für dich? Was ist sonst noch wichtig?
4. Willst du Kinder haben? Wie viele? (Hast du Kinder? Wie viele?)
5. Würdest du zu Hause bleiben, wenn du Kinder hättest?
6. Was hältst du von einem Ehevertrag vor der Ehe?
7. Was würdest du tun, wenn du dich mit deinem Partner / mit deiner Partnerin nicht mehr verstehst?
8. Was wäre für dich ein Grund zur Scheidung?
9. Sollte sich vor allem die Mutter um die Kinder kümmern? Warum (nicht)?
10. Welche Eigenschaften hat ein guter Vater?

Junge Familie beim Frühstück

Kultur ... Landeskunde ... Informationen

Gleichberechtigung

Haben sich Ihr Vater (V), Ihre Mutter (M) oder beide zusammen (b) um die folgenden Aufgaben im Alltag[1] gekümmert?

_____ Auto warten[2]
_____ einkaufen
_____ Geschirr spülen
_____ Kinder betreuen[3]
_____ kochen
_____ putzen
_____ Rasen mähen
_____ Rechnungen bezahlen
_____ Reparaturen im Haus
_____ waschen

Cartoons für Frauen und für emanzipierte Männer

Berufstätige Frauen arbeiten doppelt – am Arbeitsplatz und zu Hause, denn Hausarbeit ist immer noch meistens Frauensache[4]. Zwar[5] wollen 27% der Männer ihren Frauen grundsätzlich[6] helfen, aber Sache der Frauen ist es: zu waschen (90%), zu kochen (88%), zu putzen (80%), einzukaufen (75%) und zu spülen (71%).

Am Anfang des Zusammenlebens sind viele Männer noch bereit, ihrer Partnerin im Haushalt zu helfen. Doch nach der Geburt des ersten Kindes ziehen sich viele fast vollständig[7] von der Hausarbeit zurück[8]. Ebenso gibt es immer noch traditionelle Männeraufgaben: Reparaturen (80%) und das Auto (66%).

Die alte Rollenverteilung setzt sich im Berufsleben fort. Fast die Hälfte aller Frauen und Männer arbeiten in geschlechtertypischen[9] Berufen, in denen die Männer beziehungsweise die Frauen jeweils mit bis zu 80% aller Beschäftigten dominieren. Auch die Forderung: *gleicher Lohn*[10] *für gleiche Arbeit* ist immer noch eine Utopie. Frauen verdienen durchschnittlich ein Drittel weniger als ihre männlichen Kollegen und sind zu einem großen Teil in unteren Lohngruppen[11] oder in Wirtschaftsbereichen[12] mit geringeren Verdienstmöglichkeiten[13] beschäftigt. In der Wirtschaft oder Verwaltung sind Frauen in Führungspositionen[14] eher selten. Außerdem sind sie von Arbeitslosigkeit stärker betroffen[15] als Männer.

- Vergleichen Sie die Angaben im Text mit Ihren eigenen Erfahrungen. Hat Ihre Familie eine ähnliche Arbeitsteilung? Wo gibt es Unterschiede?
- Machen Sie eine Umfrage im Kurs und vergleichen Sie die Prozentzahlen.
- Arbeiten beide Eltern oder nur ein Elternteil? Wer verdient mehr, Ihr Vater oder Ihre Mutter?
- Gibt es bei Ihnen geschlechtertypische Berufe? Welche? Welche Gründe sprechen dafür, dass mehr Frauen oder Männer in diesen Berufen arbeiten?
- In welchen Berufen kann man mehr verdienen und besser Karriere machen: in den typischen Männerberufen oder in den Frauenberufen?

[1]im ... *day-to-day* [2]*doing maintenance on* [3]*taking care of* [4]*a woman's job* [5]*To be sure* [6]*in principle* [7]*completely* [8]ziehen sich zurück *withdraw* [9]*gender-typical* [10]*wages, salary* [11]*wage brackets* [12]*economic sectors* [13]*earning potential* [14]*leadership positions* [15]stärker ... *more strongly affected*

KLI. Discuss the cartoon first. Question: *Mit welchem Märchen assoziieren Sie den Text dieses Cartoons?* Ask sts. to complete the prereading task in small groups and discuss. Then ask sts. to work with the text in small groups, writing down the information they consider important or interesting. After sts. have answered the questions following the text, tally the results and discuss. Throughout this section, you probably want to be sensitive about issues regarding nontraditional families. **Suggestion.** Have sts. write a personal ad in which they describe themselves and give an idea of the partner they are looking for. Sts. should also say what they expect their partner's role to be in terms of family and household. To make this activity more interactive, have sts. exchange their personal ads and then guess who wrote which ad.

Multikulturelle Gesellschaft

Grammatik 12.3

CLAIRE: Ist Deutschland eigentlich ein multikulturelles Land?
JOSEF: Ja, natürlich. Ungefähr 7 Millionen Ausländer leben hier.

RENATE: Unsere ausländischen Mitbürger bereichern Deutschland mit ihrer Kultur und ihren Traditionen.

MEHMET: Deutschland braucht in bestimmten Branchen ausländische Arbeitskräfte, zum Beispiel im EDV-Bereich.

JÜRGEN: Wie in jedem anderen Land müssen Ausländer auch in Deutschland ihre Aufenthalts- und Arbeitserlaubnis beantragen. Dazu müssen sie viele Formulare ausfüllen.

Situation 4   Definitionen

1. das Formular
2. die Aufenthaltserlaubnis
3. die Arbeitserlaubnis
4. der EDV-Bereich
5. das multikulturelle Land
6. etwas beantragen

a. Die braucht man, damit man in Deutschland wohnen darf.
b. Das muss man ausfüllen, um zum Beispiel eine Arbeitserlaubnis zu bekommen.
c. Die braucht man, damit man arbeiten kann.
d. Land, in dem Menschen aus verschiedenen Kulturen zusammen leben
e. Formulare ausfüllen und in einem Büro abgeben
f. Alles, was mit Computern zu tun hat

Situation 5   Interview

1. Weißt du, wann deine Vorfahren eingewandert sind? Woher kamen sie? Welche Sprache haben sie gesprochen? Warum haben sie ihre Heimat verlassen?
2. Spricht man in deiner Familie mehr als eine Sprache? Welche? Welche Vorteile oder Nachteile hat das für dich?
3. Kennst du Einwanderer? Woher kommen sie? Sprechen sie Englisch? Warum sind sie eingewandert?
4. Weißt du, welche Formalitäten man erfüllen muss, um legal hier wohnen und arbeiten zu dürfen?
5. Welche Probleme können Einwanderer haben? Wie kann man diese Probleme lösen? (4–5 Probleme und Lösungsvorschläge bitte)

Situation 6 Diskussion: Leben in einer fremden Kultur

Was ist an der Situation von Ausländern ein Problem? Was ist für die Integration von Ausländern wichtig? Arbeiten Sie in kleinen Gruppen. Schreiben Sie in jede Spalte fünf Dinge, die Sie für wichtig halten. Ordnen Sie die Dinge: das Wichtigste zuerst. Einige Ideen finden Sie im Wortkasten.

Probleme von Ausländern	für die Integration wichtig

Geld verdienen   eine Wohnung finden

eine gute Schulbildung bekommen

Feste gemeinsam feiern   Heimweh haben

Freunde finden   gemeinsam Sport treiben

ein Kulturzentrum gründen   die Sprache lernen

sich über die Kultur des anderen informieren

_____?

einen Arbeitsplatz finden   seine Religion ausüben

Situation 7 Diskussion: Extremismus

Sit. 7. Set the scene by briefly talking about and perhaps showing photos of radicalism, e.g., the federal building in Oklahoma City after the terrorist attack of 1995 or members of the Ku Klux Klan in "uniform." Then ask sts. to complete the activity in small groups and discuss afterward.

Cultural note: *Ende 2009 gab es in Deutschland 195 rechtsextremistische Organisationen. Die Zahl ihrer Mitglieder und anderer nicht organisierter Rechtsextremisten betrug 26 600. 34% von ihnen galten als gewaltbereit. 959 Gewaltdelikte wurden 2009 verzeichnet. Eigentlich ist die Zahl der Straftaten viel höher. Sie lag für 2009 bei cira 20 000. Dazu gehören Propagandadelikte wie das Tragen verfassungsfeindlicher Symbole und das Rufen verbotener Parolen. An der Spitze bei den Straftaten liegen die neuen Bundesländer. Die meisten Rechtsextremen sind junge Männer zwischen 15 und 24 Jahren mit niedrigem Bildungsniveau. Manchmal sind die Gewalttaten politisch motiviert, oft beruhen sie jedoch auf einem diffusen Gefühl einer generellen Bedrohung oder Benachteiligung der Deutschen durch Ausländer. Die Gewalttaten werden oft durch übermäßigen Alkoholkonsum, Musik und rechtsextremistische Hetze ausgelöst. Die Regierung versucht, dem Rechtsradikalismus u.a. durch ein Verbot rechtsradikaler politischer Gruppierungen und Verbot von gewaltverherrlichenden und rassistischen Schriften, Musiktexten und Symbolen Herr zu werden.*

1. Gibt es Extremisten in Ihrem Land? Wo? Was für Ziele haben sie? Was machen sie?
2. Was ist, Ihrer Meinung nach, ein typischer Extremist?

☐ Frau
☐ jung
☐ schlecht ausgebildet
☐ arm
☐ sympathisches Äußeres
☐ arbeitslos
☐ Einzelgänger

☐ Mann
☐ alt
☐ gut ausgebildet
☐ reich
☐ unsympathisches Äußeres
☐ mit gutem Arbeitsplatz
☐ nur in der Gruppe stark

3. Wodurch fallen Extreme auf?
4. Was kann man gegen Extremismus tun?

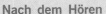
„Cüs Junge" (2007, Deutschland)   *Muhabbet (mit Fler)*

Muhabbet und der deutsche Außenminister
nehmen den Song „Deutschland" auf.

Biografie Muhabbet (Murat Ersen) ist 1984 in Köln geboren. Er singt auf
Deutsch und auf Türkisch. Seine Musik verbindet arabeske Elemente orientalischer
Popmusik mit R'n'B. Muhabbet nennt diesen Stil R'n'Besk, so auch der Titel
seines zweiten Albums. 2007 spielte er auf dem Sommerfest des damaligen
Bundespräsidenten, Horst Köhler, und er nahm das Lied „Deutschland" mit dem
damaligen Außenminister Deutschlands, Frank-Walter Steinmeier, auf. Mit diesem
Lied wollte er für ein modernes und tolerantes Deutschland werben. Der Song „Cüs
Junge" entstand 2006 aus einer Zusammenarbeit mit dem deutschen Rapper Fler.

Vor dem Hören Sind Sie bi-kulturell oder kennen Sie jemanden, der zwei
Kulturen in sich vereint? Welche Vorteile haben bi-kulturelle Menschen? Welchen
Herausforderungen müssen sie sich stellen?

iMix Link: Das Lied „Cüs Junge" können Sie
im *iTunes Store* als ein *iMix* kaufen, das speziell
für *Kontakte* entwickelt wurde. In **Connect
German** (www.connectgerman.com) erhalten
Sie Instruktionen, wie Sie die Playliste
bekommen können.

Nach dem Hören

1. Beantworten Sie die Fragen zum Anfang und zum Refrain.

   a. Für wen ist dieser Song?

   b. Wie ist der Klub?

   c. Wer sitzt an der Bar?

   d. Was sagt der Sänger, als er sie sieht?

2. Was sagt der Sänger NICHT über die junge Frau im Klub?

   a. Sie hat Klasse.

   b. Sie ist seine Traumfrau.

   c. Sie ist der pure Wahnsinn.

   d. Sie ist heute Abend der Star.

   e. Sie ist in ihn verliebt.

   f. Sie füllt den Raum mit Licht.

   g. Sie macht alle schwach.

   h. Sie ist das Beste aus zwei Welten.

   i. Sie ist eine Mischung aus Gold und Platin.

Musikszene. Note: Das Wort *cüs*, gesprochen *tschüsch*, kommt
aus dem Türkischen und wird von türkischen Jugendlichen in
Deutschland als ein Ausruf des Erstaunens und der Begrüßung
verwendet, ähnlich wie *hey* im Englischen. In der Türkei selbst hat
es eine negative Bedeutung, denn damit werden Esel vertrieben.
In diesem Lied hat es aber die erste Bedeutung. **Answers:** 1.a. für
die deutsch-türkischen Girls und für die deutsch-türkischen Gangs
im Klub b. voll c. das Mädchen d. wow 2. e

Miniwörterbuch			
verbinden	to combine	**werben**	to promote
der **Außenminister**	foreign minister, secretary of state	die **Herausforderung**	challenge
		der **Wahnsinn**	madness
aufnehmen	to record		

Lektüre 📖

Vor dem Lesen

In den 1960er Jahren fehlten in Westdeutschland Arbeiter. Deshalb wurden
Ausländer angeworben[1], um in Deutschland zu arbeiten. Sie wurden auch
„Gastarbeiter" genannt. Die ausländischen Arbeiter waren wichtig: Der
millionste „Gastarbeiter", der in Westdeutschland ankam, erhielt ein
Motorrad als Geschenk. Bis zum Stopp der Anwerbung im Jahre 1973 sind
insgesamt 2,3 Millionen „Gastarbeiter" nach Westdeutschland gekommen.
Ungefähr 50% der ausländischen Arbeitskräfte leben seit über 10 Jahren in
Deutschland und fast 30% von ihnen schon mehr als 30 Jahre. In einigen
Großstädten liegt der Anteil der ausländischen Bevölkerung bei 20%. Die

[1]*recruited*

sozialdemokratische Regierung änderte 1999 das Staatsbürgerschaftsrecht[1]. Kinder von Ausländern mit rechtlich zulässiger Aufenthaltsgenehmigung[2] bekommen die deutsche Staatsbürgerschaft, wenn sie in Deutschland geboren wurden. Bis zu ihrem 23. Lebensjahr haben diese Kinder die doppelte Staatsbürgerschaft. Dann müssen sie sich für eine Staatsbürgerschaft entscheiden.

1. Welche Gründe haben Menschen, ihr Heimatland zu verlassen?
2. Was für Probleme haben Fremde in Ihrem Land?
3. Was wissen Sie über ausländische Arbeitnehmer oder „Gastarbeiter" in der Bundesrepublik? Welche Probleme könnten sie haben?
4. Der Schriftsteller hat die folgende Kurzgeschichte in zwei Sprachen geschrieben, auf Deutsch und auf Türkisch. Warum?

Deutsche Kastanien

von Yüksel Pazarkaya

TEIL I

Lesehilfe

This story consists of two parts: first, an incident taking place in the school yard, followed by the recollection of an earlier incident in a park; second, a discussion between a boy and his parents that ensues from the earlier incidents. Note also that this piece was written before the German spelling reform of 1998; therefore, you will find some words spelled differently from the way you have learned them.

Miniwörterbuch

anfassen	to touch
jemandem Angst einjagen	to scare someone
sich aufrichten	to get (i.e., stand) back up
sich bücken	to bend over
erstarren	to stand paralyzed
das Fangen	tag (*children's game*)
fassen	to grab
fortrennen, rannte … fort	to run away
sich halten für	to consider oneself
herausfordernd	challenging
hinzufügen	to add
das Innere	inside
die Kastanie, -n	chestnut
die Mengenlehre	set theory
die Murmel, -n	marble
sich nähern	to approach
die Rechenart, -en	arithmetical operation
schießen, schoss	to shoot
schweigen	to become silent
sich sträuben	to bristle
verdutzt	taken aback
verstummt	speechless
weshalb	why
wieso	why
zerbrechen, zerbrach	to break into pieces
sich etwas zuschulden kommen lassen	to do something wrong
zuwenden, zugewandt	to turn toward
zwar	to be sure

„Du bist kein Deutscher!" sagte Stefan zu Ender in der Pause auf dem Schulhof. Weshalb nur wollte er heute mit Ender nicht Fangen spielen? Um eben einen Grund dafür zu nennen, sagte er einfach: „Du bist doch kein Deutscher." Ender war verdutzt und betroffen. Stefan war sein liebster Klassenkamerad, sein bester Spielfreund.
5 „Wieso?" konnte er nur fragen.

[1]citizenship law [2]rechtlich … *legally valid residence permit*

Stefan verstand ihn nicht. Was heißt da „wieso"? Oder hält sich Ender wohl für einen Deutschen? „Du bist eben kein Deutscher", sagte er. „Du bist kein Deutscher wie ich." Enders schöne dunkle Augen wurden traurig. Sein Inneres sträubte sich, als hätte er sich etwas zuschulden kommen lassen. In seinem Herzen zerbrach
10 etwas. Er schwieg. Er ließ den Kopf hängen. Er ging weg. An diesem Tag sprach er mit Stefan kein Wort mehr. Dem Unterricht konnte er nicht folgen. Dem Lehrer konnte er nicht zuhören. Sein Kopf wurde immer schwerer.

Auch im letzten Herbst war es ihm einmal so ergangen. In dem Wohnviertel gibt es einen hübschen kleinen Park, voll Blumen und Bäume. Im Herbst ist er am
15 schönsten. Dann ziehen die Kastanien alle Kinder in der Umgebung an. Die Kinder werfen die Kastanien mit Steinen herunter. Wer viel sammelt, verkauft sie an den Zoo als Futter für die Elefanten und Kamele. Andere bringen sie in die Schule mit. Man kann sie nämlich im Mathematikunterricht brauchen. Und die kleinen, die noch nicht zur Schule gehen, spielen mit den Kastanien wie mit Murmeln.
20 Der Lehrer sagte: „Jedes Kind bringt zehn Stück mit." Sie sind 34 Kinder in der Klasse. Wenn jedes Kind zehn Kastanien mitbringt, macht es genau 340 Stück. Und damit lassen sich ganz gut Mengenlehre und die vier Rechenarten üben.

Am Nachmittag ging Ender in den Park. Zwei Kinder warfen mit Steinen nach den Kastanien. Sie waren zwar keine Freunde von ihm, aber er kannte sie. Er sah
25 sie öfters in diesem Wohnviertel.

Ender näherte sich ihnen. Er bückte sich nach einer Kastanie, die auf dem Boden lag. Eines von den beiden Kindern sagte zu ihm: „Finger weg!" – „Ich will auch Kastanien sammeln", sagte Ender. Das zweite Kind rief: „Du darfst sie nicht sammeln, das sind deutsche Kastanien." Ender verstand nichts. Das erste Kind fügte hinzu:
30 „Du bist kein Deutscher." Dann sagte das andere: „Du bist Ausländer." Sie stellten sich herausfordernd vor Ender hin. Er verharrte gebückt und mit ausgestreckter Hand. Wenn er sich noch ein bißchen bückte, könnte er die Kastanie fassen. Doch er konnte sie nicht erreichen. Den Kopf nach oben, den Kindern zugewandt, erstarrte er eine Weile in gebückter Haltung. Dann richtete er sich auf. Natürlich ohne Kastanie.
35 Verstummt. Er wollte zwar sagen: „Der Park gehört allen, jeder kann Kastanien sammeln", doch er brachte kein Wort heraus. Dafür waren die anderen um so lauter: „Du bist Ausländer. Das sind deutsche Kastanien. Wenn du sie anfaßt, kannst du was erleben", wollten sie ihm Angst einjagen.

Ender war völlig durcheinander. „Soll ich mit denen kämpfen?" schoß es ihm durch
40 den Kopf. Dann sah er mal den einen, mal den anderen an. „Gegen zwei zu kämpfen ist unklug", dachte er. Er rannte fort, ohne die beiden noch einmal anzusehen.

TEIL II

Miniwörterbuch

ablenken	to change the subject	hoppla	oops, oh boy
annehmen, nahm ... an	to accept	im Grunde	in principle
		einen Jux machen	to be joking
		der Kummer	trouble
sich ärgern	to get angry	nützen	to do some good
jemanden auf den Arm nehmen	to tease someone	quälen	to torment
		der Ranzen	school bag
darauf eingehen, ging darauf ein	to get into something	schleudern	to hurl
		das Staunen	amazement
entschlossen	determined	die Türschwelle	threshold
ersticken	to suffocate	das Überlegen	consideration
hartnäckig	obstinate	der Unterschied	difference, distinction
herumschwirren	to buzz around	zuschnüren	to constrict

Als er an jenem Tag nach Hause kam, stellte Ender seiner Mutter einige Fragen. Aber seine Mutter ging nicht darauf ein. Sie lenkte ab.

Nun war Ender entschlossen, nach dem, was heute zwischen Stefan und ihm passiert war, die Frage endlich zu lösen, die den ganzen Tag wieder in seinem Kopf herumschwirrte. Sobald er den Fuß über die Türschwelle setzte, schleuderte er der Mutter seine Frage ins Gesicht: „Mutti, was bin ich?"

Das war eine unerwartete Frage für seine Mutter. Ebenso unerwartet war ihre Antwort: „Du bist Ender."

„Ich weiß, ich heiße Ender. Das habe ich nicht gefragt. Aber was bin ich?" blieb Ender hartnäckig.

„Komm erstmal herein. Nimm deinen Ranzen ab, zieh die Schuhe aus", sagte seine Mutter.

„Gut", sagte Ender. „Aber sag du mir auch, was ich bin."

Daraufhin dachte Enders Mutter, daß er mit ihr einen Jux machte oder ihr vielleicht ein Rätsel aufgab. „Du bist ein Schüler", sagte sie.

Ender ärgerte sich. „Du nimmst mich auf den Arm", sagte er. „Ich frage dich, was ich bin. Bin ich nun Deutscher oder Türke, was ich bin?"

Hoppla! Solche Fragen gefielen Enders Mutter gar nicht. Denn die Antwort darauf fiel ihr schwer. Was sollte sie da sagen? Im Grunde war das keine schwere Frage. Sie kannte auch die genaue Antwort auf diese Frage. Aber würde Ender sie auch verstehen können? Würde er sie akzeptieren, akzeptieren können? Wenn er sie auch annahm, würde ihm das überhaupt nützen?

Seine Mutter und sein Vater sind Türken. In der Türkei sind sie geboren, aufgewachsen und in die Schule gegangen. Nach Deutschland sind sie nur gekommen, um zu arbeiten und Geld verdienen zu können. Sie können auch gar nicht gut Deutsch. Wenn sie Deutsch sprechen, muß Ender lachen. Denn sie sprechen oft falsch. Sie können nicht alles richtig sagen.

Bei Ender ist es aber ganz anders. Er ist in Deutschland geboren. Hier ist er in den Kindergarten gegangen. Jetzt geht er in die erste Klasse, in eine deutsche Schule. Deutsche Kinder sind seine Freunde. In seiner Klasse sind auch einige ausländische Kinder. Ender macht aber zwischen ihnen keinen Unterschied, er kann keinen machen, dieser Deutscher, dieser nicht oder so, denn außer einem sprechen sie alle sehr gut Deutsch. Da gibt es nur einen, Alfonso. Alfonso tut Ender etwas leid. Alfonso kann nicht so gut Deutsch sprechen wie die anderen Kinder. Ender denkt, daß Alfonso noch gar nicht sprechen gelernt hat. Die kleinen Kinder können doch auch nicht sprechen: so wie ein großes Baby kommt ihm Alfonso vor.

Ender spricht auch Türkisch, aber nicht so gut wie Deutsch. Wenn er Türkisch spricht, mischt er oft deutsche Wörter hinein. Wie eine Muttersprache hat er Deutsch gelernt. Nicht anders als die deutschen Kinder. Manchmal hat er das Gefühl, daß zwischen ihnen doch ein Unterschied ist, weil deutsche Kinder nicht Türkisch können. Doch wenn in der Klasse der Unterricht oder auf dem Schulhof das Spielen beginnt, vergeht dieses Gefühl wieder ganz schnell. Gerade wenn er mit Stefan spielt, ist es unmöglich, daß ihm ein solches Gefühl kommt.

Deshalb war sein Staunen so groß über die Worte Stefans. Und wenn Stefan nie wieder mit ihm spielte? Dann wird er sehr allein sein. Er wird sich langweilen.

Am Abend kam Enders Vater von der Arbeit nach Hause. Noch bevor die Tür sich richtig öffnete, fragte Ender: „Vati, bin ich Türke oder Deutscher?"

Sein Vater war sprachlos.

„Warum fragst du?" sagte er nach kurzem Überlegen.

„Ich möchte es wissen", sagte Ender entschlossen.

„Was würdest du lieber sein, ein Türke oder ein Deutscher?" fragte sein Vater.

„Was ist besser?" gab Ender die Frage wieder zurück.

„Beides ist gut, mein Sohn", sagte sein Vater.

„Warum hat dann Stefan heute nicht mit mir gespielt?"

So kam Ender mit seinem Kummer heraus, der ihn den ganzen Tag gequält hatte.

„Warum hat er nicht mit dir gespielt?" fragte sein Vater.

Point out: *dieser Deutscher, dieser nicht oder so is elliptical for dieser [ist] Deutscher, dieser [ist] nicht oder so.*

"„Du bist kein Deutscher!' hat er gesagt. Was bin ich, Vati?"

"Du bist Türke, mein Sohn, aber du bist in Deutschland geboren", sagte darauf
100 sein Vater hilflos.

"Aber die Namen der deutschen Kinder sind anders als mein Name."

Sein Vater begann zu stottern.

"Dein Name ist ein türkischer Name", sagte er. „Ist Ender kein schöner Name?"

Ender mochte seinen Namen. „Doch! Aber er ist nicht so wie die Namen anderer
105 Kinder", sagte er.

"Macht nichts, Hauptsache, es ist ein schöner Name!" sagte sein Vater.

"Aber Stefan spielt nicht mehr mit mir."

Enders Vater schnürte es den Hals zu. Ihm war, als ob er ersticken müßte. „Sei
nicht traurig", sagte er nach längerem Schweigen zu Ender. „Ich werde morgen mit
110 Stefan sprechen. Er wird wieder mit dir spielen. Er hat sicher Spaß gemacht."

Ender schwieg.

Arbeit mit dem Text

A. Deutsche oder Ausländer? Ordnen Sie die Personen in der Geschichte
   den zwei Kategorien zu.

B. Wer sagt das im Text?

Ender	Enders Lehrer
Enders Vater	Stefan
Enders Mutter	Kinder im Park

1. „Du bist kein Deutscher wie ich." _____
2. „Jedes Kind bringt zehn Stück mit." _____
3. „Ich will auch Kastanien sammeln." _____
4. „Das sind deutsche Kastanien." _____
5. „Du bist Ausländer." _____
6. „Du bist Ender." _____
7. „Du bist ein Schüler." _____
8. „Bin ich nun Deutscher oder Türke, was bin ich?" _____
9. „Was würdest du lieber sein, ein Türke oder ein Deutscher?" _____
10. „Dein Name ist ein türkischer Name." _____

C. Kombinieren Sie die Satzteile.

1. Stefan sagte, dass er nicht mit Ender spielen wollte,
2. Ender ging weg,
3. Alle Kinder sammeln im Herbst Kastanien,
4. Die Kinder im Park waren keine Freunde von Ender,
5. Ender sammelte keine Kastanien,
6. Als Ender nach Hause kam,
7. Die Fragen gefielen der Mutter nicht,
8. Wenn Ender Türkisch spricht,
9. Deutsche Kinder sind anders,
10. Der Vater will mit Stefan sprechen,

aber er kannte sie.
damit er wieder mit Ender spielt.
denn man kann sie gut gebrauchen.
denn sie wusste keine Antwort.
mischt er oft deutsche Wörter hinein.
nachdem er mit den Kindern gesprochen hatte.
stellte er seiner Mutter Fragen.
weil er kein Deutscher war.
weil er traurig war.
weil sie kein Türkisch können.

Nach dem Lesen

Wie geht es weiter? Spricht Enders Vater mit Stefan? Spricht er mit Stefans Vater? Bleiben Ender und Stefan Freunde? Welche Identität entwickelt Ender? Schreiben Sie eine Fortsetzung der Geschichte. Suchen Sie sich eine der folgenden Möglichkeiten aus oder erfinden Sie etwas Eigenes.

- der nächste Tag: Enders Vater spricht mit Stefans Vater
- Enders neuer Freund
- fünf Jahre später: Ender spricht über seine Identität
- Enders Kinder: Ender erzählt seinen Kindern eine Geschichte

Das liebe Geld

Grammatik 12.4

—Ich möchte gern ein Konto eröffnen.
—Ein Spar- oder ein Girokonto?

Für diesen Geldautomaten braucht man eine Euroscheckkarte.

Wenn man Geld auf einem Sparkonto hat, bekommt man Zinsen.

Wenn man Schulden hat, muss man Zinsen zahlen.

Wenn man Geld überweisen möchte, kann man das auch per Internet tun.

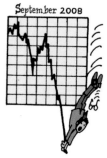

Der Börsenkrach vom September 2008 war einer der schlimmsten in der Geschichte.

Situation 8   Wer weiß–gewinnt: Geld

Sit. 8. Read definitions and answers out loud and have sts. repeat before asking them to work in groups of 3 or 4. During the follow-up phase ask for or provide expansion on the terms and concepts relating German examples to comparable ones in the sts.' own country, e.g. *Wie steht der Wechselkurs heute? In welcher Stadt ist die Börse in Deutschland?* **Answers:** 1. e, 2. f, 3. h, 4. d, 5. c, 6. a, 7. g, 8. j, 9. b, 10. i.

1. der Ort, an dem mit Aktien gehandelt wird
2. die Karte, mit der man bargeldlos bezahlen kann
3. die zahlt man, wenn man seine Kreditkarte nicht abzahlen kann
4. der Kurs, zu dem man ausländische Währung kaufen oder verkaufen kann
5. Automat, aus dem man Bargeld holen kann
6. die Münzen und Geldscheine einer Währung
7. das offizielle Zahlungsmittel eines Landes
8. das macht man, wenn man Rechnungen bargeldlos bezahlt
9. das Konto für den täglichen Gebrauch
10. das macht man, wenn man bei einer Bank neu ist

a. das Bargeld
b. das Girokonto
c. der Geldautomat
d. der Wechselkurs
e. die Börse
f. die Kreditkarte
g. die Währung
h. die Zinsen
i. ein Konto eröffnen
j. Geld überweisen

Situation 9   Dialog: Auf der Bank

PETER: Guten Tag, ich möchte ein Konto eröffnen.
BANKANGESTELLTE: Ein Spar- oder ein Girokonto?
PETER: Ein Girokonto.
BANKANGESTELLTE: Würden Sie dann bitte dieses Formular ausfüllen?
PETER: Bekomme ich bei dem Konto auch eine EC-Karte?
BANKANGESTELLTE: Die müssen Sie extra beantragen, aber das ist kein Problem, wenn regelmäßig auf das Konto eingezahlt wird.
PETER: Ich bekomme ein Stipendium. Das soll auf dieses Konto überwiesen werden.
BANKANGESTELLTE: Gut. Die EC-Karte und Ihre Geheimzahl bekommen Sie mit der Post.
PETER: Bekomme ich auf mein Guthaben auch Zinsen?
BANKANGESTELLTE: Nein, Zinsen gibt es nur auf Sparkonten.
PETER: Habe ich bei dem Girokonto einen Überziehungskredit?
BANKANGESTELLTE: Ja, die Höhe richtet sich nach Ihrem Einkommen.
PETER: Kann ich meine Überweisungen auch übers Internet ausführen?
BANKANGESTELLTE: Natürlich. Meine Kollegin, Frau Schröder, hilft Ihnen da weiter.
PETER: Vielen Dank. Auf Wiedersehen.
BANKANGESTELLTE: Auf Wiedersehen.

Situation 10   Interview

Sit. 10. If sts. are uncomfortable sharing personal financial information, allow them to pretend to be someone else, such as a movie star or entertainer, and give answers based on that alter ego.

1. Hast du ein Konto bei der Bank? Welche Konten hast du?
2. Hast du eine Kreditkarte? Wie viel kannst du damit ausgeben? Wie viel Zinsen musst du bezahlen?
3. Wie viel sparst du im Monat? Worauf sparst du? Wenn du jetzt nicht sparen kannst: Worauf würdest du sparen, wenn du Geld hättest?
4. Womit zahlst du öfter: mit Schecks, mit Kreditkarte oder mit Bargeld?
5. Wie viel Geld hast du im Monat? Wie viel Geld gibst du aus? Wofür gibst du das meiste Geld aus?
6. Hast du schon einmal einen Kredit aufgenommen? Wie hast du das gemacht?

Wie bezahlt man in Europa?

Wie ist es bei Ihnen?

- Wie bezahlen Sie meistens, wenn Sie im Supermarkt einkaufen?
- Wie bezahlen Sie, wenn Sie Ihre Miete bezahlen?
- Wie bezahlen Sie Ihre Telefonrechnung?
- Wie bezahlen Sie, wenn Sie ein Kleidungsstück oder etwas Größeres wie ein Fahrrad, ein Auto oder einen Computer kaufen?
- Wie werden Sie bei Ihrem Job bezahlt, z. B. in Bargeld, mit Scheck oder Überweisung?
- In welcher Form bekommen Sie Geld von Ihren Eltern oder finanzielle Unterstützung für Ihr Studium?

In manchen Restaurants werden keine Kreditkarten akzeptiert.

Wie ist es in Europa? Lesen Sie den Text und beantworten Sie die Fragen.

1. Wie heißt die Karte, die in Deutschland am häufigsten zum Einkaufen benutzt wird?
2. Was muss man für diese Karte bei der Bank haben?
3. Wie heißt die „elektronische Geldbörse", die man in Österreich benutzt?
4. Wie wird in Österreich immer noch am häufigsten bezahlt?
5. Wie bezahlt man normalerweise in Deutschland Miete und Rechnungen?
6. Was ist ein Dauerauftrag?
7. Wie viel Prozent der Deutschen nehmen am Onlinebanking teil?

Man zahlt daher meistens bar.

Auch in vielen Ländern Europas bezahlt man inzwischen nicht mehr so häufig mit Bargeld wie noch vor einigen Jahren. Für bargeldlose[1] Transaktionen wird in Deutschland die EC-Karte am häufigsten benutzt. Man kann mit ihr im Supermarkt, beim Tanken und in den meisten Einzelhandelsgeschäften[2] bezahlen und Geld aus dem Geldautomaten bekommen. Für eine EC-Karte braucht man ein Konto bei einer Bank, das – anders als bei Kreditkarten – bei jeder Transaktion sofort belastet[3] wird. Manchmal muss man allerdings beim Einkauf außerdem noch seinen Personalausweis zeigen.

In Österreich ist die Quickcard eine beliebte Alternative zum Bargeld. Sie funktioniert wie eine elektronische Geldbörse[4]. Man muss sie „aufladen[5]" und kann dann z. B. an Parkautomaten, in Geschäften und an Tankstellen auch kleine Beträge[6] bezahlen. Die dominierende Zahlungsform in Österreich ist aber immer noch die Bargeldtransaktion. Die beliebteste Kreditkarte in Deutschland ist die Eurocard, die zu der Organisation von Mastercard (USA) gehört. Danach kommt die Visakarte.

Rechnungen für Telefon, Nebenkosten oder Miete bezahlt man bargeldlos mit Überweisungen vom Girokonto oder Bankeinzug[7] (der Betrag wird automatisch von der Bank des Empfängers[8] eingezogen). Damit man die monatlichen Zahlungen nicht vergisst, kann man sie per Dauerauftrag[9] überweisen lassen. Das heißt, man gibt seiner Bank einmal den Auftrag[10] und zu einem bestimmten Termin wird der Betrag automatisch überwiesen. Immer beliebter wird auch das Onlinebanking, das inzwischen von ungefähr 40% der Deutschen genutzt wird, vor allem für Überweisungen und Daueraufträge oder zum Überprüfen des Kontostandes.

[1]cash-free [2]retail shops [3]debited [4]wallet [5]charge, recharge [6]amounts [7]automatic withdrawal, i.e. electronic funds transfer [8]payee
[9]standing order, i.e. recurring bill-pay [10]order

 Situation 11 Rollenspiel: Auf der Bank

Sit. 11. The role for S2 appears in Appendix B.

s1: Sie haben ein Stipendium für ein Jahr an der Universität Leipzig. Sie wollen bei der Deutschen Bank ein Konto eröffnen. Fragen Sie auch nach den Zinsen, nach Onlinezugang und EC-Karte und ob Sie Ihr Konto überziehen dürfen.

Kunst und Literatur

Vocabulary Display
Follow the regular pattern of presentation, receptive recall, choral response, and productive recall.

die Mundharmonika
die Trompete
das Schlagzeug
die Orgel
die Blockflöte
die Querflöte

die Töpferscheibe
der Brennofen
die Figur aus Ton

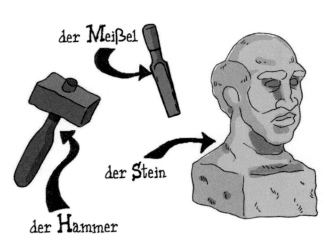

die Ölfarben
die Staffelei
der Pinsel
der Meißel
der Hammer
der Stein

Situation 12 Wer weiß–gewinnt: Kunst und Literatur

Sit. 12. Read questions and answers out loud and have sts. repeat before asking them to work in groups of 3 or 4. Sts. will know only some of these, but they can mark the ones they know and find others by process of elimination. During the follow-up phase ask for or give additional information on the people mentioned according to the interests of your particular class. **Answers:** 1. a, 2. c, 3. e, 4. g, 5. f, 6. d, 7. h, 8. b.

1. Welches Instrument gehört normalerweise nicht in ein Symphonieorchester?
2. Was braucht ein Bildhauer für seine Kunst?
3. Was war Theodor Storm von Beruf?
4. Von wem sind die Brandenburgischen Konzerte?
5. Was war Marlene Dietrich von Beruf?
6. Was brauchte Paul Klee für seine Kunst?
7. Wer schrieb die Tragödie *Faust*?
8. Welches Instrument spielt die Musikerin Anne-Sophie Mutter?

a. Blockflöte
b. Geige
c. Stein, Hammer und Meißel
d. Staffelei, Pinsel und Farben
e. Schriftsteller/in
f. Schauspieler/in
g. Johann Sebastian Bach
h. Johann Wolfgang von Goethe

1. Hörst du gern Musik? Was für Musik? Hast du einen Lieblingskomponisten oder eine Lieblingskomponistin?
2. Spielst du ein Instrument oder singst du?
3. Liest du gern? Was liest du gern: Romane, Gedichte, Dramen, Comics? Welche Schriftsteller magst du besonders gern? Hast du etwas von deutschen Schriftstellern gelesen?
4. Hast du schon mal etwas geschrieben? Was?
5. Welche Maler, Bildhauer oder Grafiker magst du am liebsten?
6. Malst oder zeichnest du? Welche Motive magst du am liebsten? (Berge? das Meer? eine Blumenvase?) Arbeitest du mit anderen Materialien wie Holz, Ton oder Stein?
7. Gehst du gern ins Theater? Welche Stücke gefallen dir besonders gut?
8. Hast du schon mal Theater gespielt? Welche Rollen hast du gespielt? Wie war das?

Situation 14 Faust: Die einfache Version

Eins der bekanntesten Werke der deutschen Literatur ist die Tragödie *Faust* von Goethe. Was in *Faust* geschieht, finden Sie in den folgenden Sätzen. Bringen Sie die Sätze in die richtige Reihenfolge.

TEIL 1

_2_ Als Faust an einem Osternachmittag spazieren geht, sieht er einen schwarzen Pudel, der ihm nach Hause folgt.

_5_ Nach ihrer Unterhaltung gehen Mephisto und Faust in eine Hexenküche. Dort zeigt ihm Mephisto einen magischen Spiegel.

_1_ Faust ist ein berühmter Wissenschaftler, der sehr unzufrieden ist, weil er nicht alles weiß.

_4_ Faust spricht lange mit Mephisto und verspricht ihm seine Seele für einen Augenblick vollkommenen Glücks.

_3_ In Fausts Studierzimmer verwandelt sich der Pudel in Mephisto.

_6_ Im Spiegel sieht Faust eine wunderschöne Frau.

_7_ Kurz danach lernt Faust Gretchen kennen und verliebt sich in sie.

TEIL 2

_7_ Aber Gretchen will nicht vom Teufel gerettet werden und bittet Gott um Vergebung.

_8_ Als Gretchen stirbt, hört man eine Stimme von oben, die sagt: „Sie ist gerettet."

_3_ Als Gretchen vom Tod ihres Bruders hört, wird sie wahnsinnig, und als ihr Kind geboren wird, tötet sie es.

_6_ Auf dem Brocken hat Faust eine Vision von Gretchen, und er und Mephisto eilen ins Gefängnis, um sie zu retten.

_2_ Faust und Valentin kämpfen. Faust tötet Valentin und verlässt die Stadt.

_4_ Gretchen wird ins Gefängnis geworfen und zum Tode verurteilt.

_1_ Gretchen wird schwanger. Valentin, ihr Bruder, will Faust deshalb töten.

_5_ Während Gretchen im Gefängnis sitzt, steigen Faust und Mephisto in der Walpurgisnacht auf den Brocken und feiern mit den Hexen.

Sit. 14. Before sts. mark the statements, summarize the play with books closed, loosely following the description in the activity, e.g.: *Faust ist eine der berühmtesten Geschichten der deutschen Literatur. Faust selbst ist ein Wissenschaftler, der mit seinem Leben sehr unzufrieden ist, weil er nicht alles weiß. Er hat viele Fächer studiert, aber es gibt vieles, was er nicht weiß und das macht ihn sehr unzufrieden.*

Situation 15 Rollenspiel: An der Kinokasse

Rollenspiel. Note: If your students are using McGraw-Hill's **Connect** online *Arbeitsbuch*, they can do this *Rollenspiel* using the real-time, interactive **Video-Chat** feature.

s1: Sie wollen mit vier Freunden in die „Rocky Horror Picture Show". Das Kino ist schon ziemlich ausverkauft. Sie wollen aber unbedingt mit ihren Freunden zusammensitzen und Reis werfen. Fragen Sie, wann, zu welchem Preis und wo noch fünf Plätze übrig sind.

Filmlektüre
Sophie Scholl – Die letzten Tage

 Vor dem Lesen

A. Filmplakat. Sehen Sie sich das Foto an. Welche Assoziationen weckt das Foto? An welche Zeit denken Sie? Welcher Ort könnte das sein? Was könnte die Frau gemacht haben? Wer könnten die Männer sein?

Filmangaben

Titel: *Sophie Scholl – Die letzten Tage*
Genre: Drama
Erscheinungsjahr: 2005
Land: Deutschland
Dauer: 116 Min.
Regisseur: Marc Rothemund
Hauptrollen: Julia Jentsch, Fabian Hinrichs, Alexander Held

Sophie Scholl wird verhaftet.

B. Lesen Sie die Wörter im Miniwörterbuch. Suchen Sie sie im Text und in den Aufgaben und unterstreichen Sie sie.

Miniwörterbuch

das **Mitglied**	member	der **Hochverrat**	high treason
der **Widerstand**	resistance	**anklagen**	to accuse
das **Flugblatt**	pamphlet	**gnadenlos**	merciless
verteilen	to distribute	der **Gerichtssaal**	court room
erwischen	to catch	**verurteilen**	to sentence
die **Gestapo**	*Geheime Staatspolizei* (secret police)	die **Abschlusserklärung**	final declaration
verhören	to interrogate	**hinrichten**	to kill by execution
überzeugen	to convince	**verraten**	to betray
gestehen	to admit	der **Umschlag**	envelope
der **Prozess**	(court) trial	**sich durchsetzen**	to prevail
		der **Hörsaaldiener**	lecture hall attendant

Inhaltsangabe

Sophie Scholl (Julia Jentsch) und ihr Bruder Hans (Fabian Hinrichs) sind Mitglieder der *Weißen Rose*, einer Widerstandsgruppe im Dritten Reich. Als sie ein Flugblatt an der Universität München verteilen wollen, werden sie erwischt und kommen ins Gefängnis. Dort werden sie vom Gestapobeamten Mohr (Alexander Held) verhört. Zuerst gelingt es Sophie, Mohr von ihrer Unschuld zu überzeugen. Als aber Hans gesteht, dass er die Flugblätter geschrieben hat, gesteht auch Sophie und versucht alle Schuld auf sich zu nehmen. Die Geschwister behaupten, sie hätten ganz alleine gehandelt, um die anderen Mitglieder der *Weißen Rose* zu schützen. Es kommt zum Prozess. Sophie, Hans und ein weiteres Mitglied werden wegen Hochverrat angeklagt. Der Nazirichter Freisler ist gnadenlos, aber Sophie hat keine Angst und es kommt zu großen Rededuellen zwischen den beiden im Gerichtssaal. Am Ende werden alle drei zum Tode verurteilt. Sophie sagt in ihrer Abschlusserklärung: „Wo wir heute stehen, werdet ihr bald stehen." Noch am selben Tag werden die drei hingerichtet.

Arbeit mit dem Text

Welche Aussagen sind falsch? Verbessern Sie die falschen Aussagen.

_____ 1. Die *Weiße Rose* war eine Widerstandsgruppe im Dritten Reich.

_____ 2. Sophie und Hans Scholl werden erwischt, als sie ein Flugblatt drucken.

_____ 3. Die Geschwister Scholl werden vom Gestapobeamten Freisler verhört.

_____ 4. Sophie verrät die Namen der anderen Mitglieder der *Weißen Rose*.

_____ 5. Während des Prozesses fängt Sophie Scholl an zu weinen.

_____ 6. Die Geschwister werden zum Tode verurteilt und einen Monat später hingerichtet.

Filmclip 🎬

Szene: DVD, Kapitel 3, 4 „Peaceful Resistance, Arrested" 9:45–16:50 Min.

Die Mitglieder der *Weißen Rose* haben ein neues Flugblatt gedruckt, aber sie haben nicht mehr genügend Umschläge, um es zu versenden. Deshalb kommen sie auf die Idee, die Flugblätter an der Uni zu verteilen. Das ist sehr gefährlich, aber Hans setzt sich durch. Am nächsten Tag gehen Sophie und Hans an die Uni.

Schauen Sie sich die Szene an und beantworten Sie die Fragen.

1. Wo sind Sophie und Hans?
2. Was machen sie?
3. Warum gehen sie noch einmal ganz nach oben?
4. Was macht Sophie, als es klingelt?
5. Was passiert, als Sophie und Hans mit den anderen Studenten die Treppe hinuntergehen?
6. Was gibt Sophie zu?
7. Was findet der Hörsaaldiener bei Hans im Büro des Universitätsdirektors?
8. Wer betritt dann das Zimmer?
9. Wie erklärt Hans dem Gestapobeamten, dass er das Flugblatt hat?

Nach dem Lesen

Dieser Film basiert auf einer wahren Begebenheit. Recherchieren Sie im Internet und suchen Sie Antworten auf die folgenden Fragen.

1. Wer waren die Mitglieder der *Weißen Rose*?
2. Von wann bis wann gab es sie?
3. Was empörte die Mitglieder der *Weißen Rose* besonders?
4. Welche Ziele verfolgten sie?
5. Woher kam der Name?
6. Was erinnert in München an die *Weiße Rose*?

Videoecke

Perspektiven

| Wie informierst du dich? Wie hältst du dich auf dem Laufenden? |

Aufgabe 1 Internet, Radio, Zeitungen oder Fernsehen?

Ich informiere mich über das Internet.

Wie informieren sich die Personen? Ordnen Sie die Medien den Personen zu.

1. Shaimaa _2_   2. Martin _2_   3. Michael _2_   4. Felicitas _1, 2_

5. Sandra _3, 4_   6. Pascal _2, 3, 4_   7. Tina _1, 4_   8. Sophie _2, 3, 4_

| 1. Fernsehen | 3. Radio |
| 2. Internet | 4. Zeitung |

Interviews

- Was hältst du von der Ehe?
- Wie erledigst du deine Geldgeschäfte?
- Wie viel Geld steht dir pro Monat zur Verfügung?
- Wofür gibst du es aus?
- Hast du schon mal einen Kredit aufgenommen?
- Wie hast du das gemacht?

Jenny

Nadezda

Aufgabe 2 Jenny, Nadezda oder beide?

Sehen Sie sich das Video an und beantworten Sie die Fragen.

	Jenny	Nadezda	Beide
1. Wer findet Hochzeiten schön, möchte aber trotzdem nicht heiraten?	☒	☐	☐
2. Wer erledigt Geldgeschäfte per Onlinebanking?	☒	☐	☐
3. Wer hat eine Kreditkarte?	☐	☐	☒
4. Wer bekommt BaföG?	☒	☐	☐
5. Wer gibt das meiste Geld für die Miete aus?	☐	☐	☒
6. Wer hat schon mal einen Kredit aufgenommen?	☐	☐	☒

Aufgabe 3 Jenny

Wie viel Geld hat Jenny, und wofür gibt sie es aus? Ergänzen Sie die Sätze.

1. Jenny bekommt im Monat __643__ Euro BAföG.
2. Sie bezahlt __250__ Euro Miete.
3. __40__ Euro gibt sie monatlich für Telefon und Internet aus.
4. Dazu braucht sie noch Geld für __Lebensmittel__, __Bücher__ und Hobbys.

Aufgabe 4 Interview

Interviewen Sie eine Partnerin oder einen Partner. Stellen Sie dieselben Fragen.

Wortschatz

Partner und Familie	Partners and Family
die E̲he, -n	marriage
die Konfessio̲n, -en	religious denomination, church
die Sche̲idung, -en	divorce
der Vertra̲g, ⸚e	contract
der E̲hevertrag, ⸚e	prenuptial agreement
das Beru̲fsleben	career, professional life
sich kü̲mmern um	to take care of

sich verhe̲iraten mit	to get married to
verhe̲iratet sein	to be married
sich verlie̲ben in	to fall in love with
(+ *akk.*) (R)	
verlie̲bt sein	to be in love
sich verlo̲ben mit	to get engaged to
verlo̲bt sein	to be engaged

Ähnliche Wörter

die Ha̲usfrau, -en; die Pa̲rtnerin, -nen; die Pa̲rtnerschaft, -en; der Ha̲usmann, ⸚er; der Pa̲rtner, -

Multikulturelle Gesellschaft / Multicultural Society

die Arbeitserlaubnis, -se	work permit
die Arbeitskraft, -̈e	labor; employee
die Aufenthaltserlaubnis, -se	residence permit
die Ausländerin, -nen	female foreigner
die Branche, -n	sector
die EDV = elektronische Datenverarbeitung	electronic data processing
die Formalität, -en	formality
die Türkin, -nen	Turkish woman
der Ausländer, -	male foreigner
der Bereich, -e	sector, area
der Einwanderer, -	immigrant
der Einzelgänger, -	loner
der Türke, -n (wk. masc.)	Turkish man
der Vorfahre, -n (wk. masc.)	ancestor
auf·fallen, fällt ... auf, fiel ... auf, ist aufgefallen	to be noticeable
aus·üben	to practice
aus·wandern, ist ausgewandert	to emigrate
beantragen	to apply for
bereichern	to enrich
ein·wandern, ist eingewandert	to immigrate

Ähnliche Wörter

die Heimat; die Integration; die Kultur, -en; die Million, -en; die Tradition, -en (R); der Extremist, -en (wk. masc.); das Heimatland, -̈er

Das liebe Geld / Beloved Money

die Aktie, -n	share, stock
die Börse, -n	stock exchange
die Euroscheckkarte, -n	Eurocheque Card
die Geheimzahl, -en	secret PIN (personal identification number)
die Höhe, -n	height; amount (of money)
die Kundin, -nen	female customer
die Überweisung, -en	transfer (of money)
die Währung, -en	currency
der Börsenkrach, -̈e	stock market crash
der Gebrauch, -̈e	use
der Geldautomat, -en (wk. masc.)	automatic teller machine (ATM)
der Kunde, -n (wk. masc.)	male customer
der Überziehungskredit, -e	overdraft protection
der Zugang	access
das Bargeld	cash
das Einkommen	income
das Formular, -e	form
das Girokonto, Girokonten	checking account
das Guthaben	bank balance
das Sparkonto, Sparkonten	savings account
das Zahlungsmittel	means of payment
die Zinsen (pl.)	interest
ab·zahlen	to pay off
auf·nehmen, nimmt ... auf, nahm ... auf, aufgenommen	to take out (a loan)
aus·geben, gibt ... aus, gab ... aus, ausgegeben	to spend
aus·führen	to carry out, execute

Ähnliche Wörter

der Geldschein, -e

Kunst und Literatur / Art and Literature

die Bildhauerin, -nen	female sculptor
die Blockflöte, -n	recorder (type of flute)
die Kasse, -n (R)	cashier window
die Ölfarbe, -n	oil color (paint)
die Orgel, -n	organ
die Querflöte, -n	(transverse) flute
die Seele, -n	soul
die Staffelei, -en	easel
die Stimme, -n	voice
die Töpferscheibe, -n	potter's wheel
die Wissenschaftlerin, -nen	female scientist
der Bildhauer, -	male sculptor
der Brennofen, -̈	kiln
der Meißel, -	chisel
der Pinsel, -	paintbrush
der Stein, -e	stone
der Teufel, -	devil
der Tod, -e	death
der Ton	clay
der Wissenschaftler, -	male scientist
das Holz, -̈er	wood
das Motiv, -e	motif, theme
das Schlagzeug, -e	percussion, drums
malen	to paint
vollkommen	flawless, perfect
wahnsinnig	crazy, insane

Ähnliche Wörter

die Figur, -en; die Mundharmonika, -s; die Tragödie, -n; die Trompete, -n; der Gott, -̈er; das Instrument, -e; das Material, -ien; magisch

Sonstige Substantive — Other Nouns

die **Einstellung**, -en	attitude
die **Gewalt**	violence
die **Schuld**, -en	debt; guilt

Ähnliche Wörter
der **Charakter**; der **Fanatiker**, -; der **Preis**, -e (R); der **Text**, -e

Sonstige Verben — Other Verbs

an·gehören (+ *dat.*)	to belong to (*an organization*)
auf·wachsen, wächst ... **auf**, wuchs ... **auf**, ist **aufgewachsen**	to grow up
bitten (um + *akk.*), **bat**, gebeten	to ask (for)
erreichen	to reach
erwarten	to expect
halten von, **hält**, **hielt**, gehalten	to think of
sich **informieren über** (+ *akk.*)	to inform oneself about

Adjektive und Adverbien — Adjectives and Adverbs

arbeitslos	unemployed
ausgebildet	educated
ausländisch	foreign
bargeldlos	cash-free
eng	tight; narrow; small
fleißig	industrious
geduldig	patient
gleich	equal, same
lustig	fun, funny
neugierig	curious
täglich	daily
trotzdem	nonetheless
verschieden	different, various

Ähnliche Wörter
afro-deutsch, **ideal**, **illegal**, **politisch**

Sonstige Wörter und Ausdrücke — Other Words and Expressions

anstatt (+ *gen.*)	instead of
eher	rather
statt (+ *gen.*)	instead of
trotz (+ *gen.*)	in spite of
um ... zu	in order to
wohl	probably

Strukturen und Übungen

12.1 The genitive case

Spoken German: Possession may be indicated by **von**.

Written German: Use the genitive case to indicate possession.

As you have learned, the preposition **von** followed by the dative case is commonly used in spoken German to express possession.

Das ist das Haus **von meinen Eltern.**	*This is my parents' house.*

In writing, and sometimes in speech, this relationship between two noun phrases may also be expressed with the genitive case. The genitive case in German is equivalent to both the *of*-phrase and the possessive with 's in English.

Wissen Sie noch?

You can show possession using possessive adjectives, such as **mein** (*my*), **dein** (*your*), and **sein** (*his/its*), or by placing an **-s** after someone's name, for example **Julias Buch.**

Review grammar B.5 and 2.4.

Kennst du den Freund **meiner Schwester?**	*Do you know my sister's friend?*
Die Farbe **des Mantels** gefällt mir nicht.	*I don't like the color of the coat.*

The genitive is also required by certain prepositions. The most common ones are these:

(an)statt	*instead of*
trotz	*in spite of*
während	*during*
wegen	*because of*

Anstatt eines Fernsehers hätte ich mir ein neues Fahrrad gekauft.	*Instead of a TV, I would have bought myself a new bike.*
Trotz des vielen Regens ist noch nicht genügend Wasser in den Tanks.	*In spite of all the rain, there's still not enough water in the tanks.*
Während der letzten Tage bin ich nicht viel aus dem Haus gekommen.	*During the last few days I haven't gotten out of the house much.*
Wegen dieser dummen Situation kann ich jetzt nicht zur Hochzeit kommen.	*Because of this stupid situation, I can't come to the wedding now.*

12.1. *Genitiv.* We emphasize that the genitive case is used mostly in writing and that the construction *von* + dative usually indicates possession in speech. At this point, we do not expect sts. to be able to produce genitive endings with consistent accuracy when speaking.

Stress that, with the exception of names, word order in German with both the genitive and with *von* + dative corresponds to the word order of the English pattern with *of*.

When the attributive adjective is preceded by a determiner, sts. can use the following strategy: Look to see if the noun is dative, genitive, or plural. If it is, the adjective ending is always *-en*.

English tends to use the possessive 's with nouns denoting people (for example, *the girl's mother*). In German, **-s** (without the apostrophe) is added only to *proper names* of people and places.

Noras Vater	*Nora's father*
Englands Rettung	*England's salvation*

A. Nouns in the Genitive

Feminine nouns and plural nouns do not add any endings in the genitive case. In the singular genitive, masculine and neuter nouns of more than one syllable add -s and those of one syllable add -es: **die Farbe des Vogels, die Größe des Hauses.**

Masculine	Neuter	Feminine	Plural
des Vater**s**	des Kind**es**	der Mutter	der Eltern

B. Articles and Article-like Words in the Genitive

In the genitive case, all determiners (**der**-words and **ein**-words) end in **-es** in the masculine and neuter singular, and in **-er** in the feminine singular and all plural forms.

Masculine	Neuter	Feminine	Plural
d**es** Mannes	d**es** Kindes	d**er** Frau	d**er** Eltern
ein**es** Mannes	ein**es** Kindes	ein**er** Frau	
mein**es** Mannes	mein**es** Kindes	mein**er** Frau	mein**er** Eltern
dies**es** Mannes	dies**es** Kindes	dies**er** Frau	dies**er** Eltern

C. Adjectives in the Genitive

In the genitive, all adjectives end in **-en** when preceded by a determiner.*

Masculine and Neuter	Feminine and Plural
des arm**en** Mannes	der arm**en** Frau
des arm**en** Kindes	der arm**en** Leute

Eine mögliche Rolle des modernen Mannes ist es, zu Hause zu bleiben und auf die Kinder aufzupassen.	*A possible role for a modern man is to stay home and take care of the children.*

Übung 1   Minidialoge

Üb. 1-3. The three exercises on the genitive can be given as homework and checked in class.

Ergänzen Sie die Wörter in Klammern.

1. KATRIN: Ist das dein Auto?
   ALBERT: Nein, das ist das Auto _____ Bruders. (mein)

2. BEAMTER: Was ist das Alter _____ Kinder? (Ihr)
   FRAU FRISCH: Natalie ist fünf, Rosemarie ist sechs und Lydia ist neun Jahre alt.

3. FRAU SCHULZ: Ist es wichtig, dass der Partner einen guten Beruf hat?
   THOMAS: Also, ich muss sagen, der Beruf _____ zukünftigen Partnerin ist mir ziemlich egal. (mein)

4. MONIKA: Möchtest du mit mir in die Berge fahren? Meine Eltern haben da ein Wochenendhaus.
   ROLF: Wo ist denn das Wochenendhaus _____ Eltern? (dein)
   MONIKA: In der Nähe von Lake Tahoe.

5. HEIDI: Kennst du den Film „M–Mörder unter uns"?
   ROLF: Ja.
   HEIDI: Wie heißt doch noch mal der Regisseur _____ Films? (dies-)

6. ROLF: Brauchst du denn kein neues Nummernschild?
   PETER: Ach, ich nehme einfach das Nummernschild meines _____ Autos. (alt)

*Unpreceded masculine and neuter adjectives also end in **-en;** unpreceded feminine and plural adjectives end in **-er.** Unpreceded adjectives, however, rarely occur in the genitive.

7. FRAU GRETTER: Wer ist denn das?
   FRAU KÖRNER: Das ist die zweite Frau meines _____ Mannes. (erst-)

8. FRAU AUGENTHALER: 24352 – was ist denn das für eine Telefonnummer?
   RICHARD: Das ist die Telefonnummer meiner _____ Freundin. (neu)

Übung 2   Worüber sprechen sie?

Bilden Sie Sätze.

MODELL: Albert sagt, dass sein Auto rot ist. →
Albert spricht über die Farbe seines Autos.

> **das Alter**   **der Beruf**   **das Bild**
>
> **die Kleidung**   **die Länge**   **die Qualität**
>
> **die Situation**   **die Sprache**

1. Monika sagt, dass ihre Schwester als Lehrerin arbeitet.
2. Thomas sagt, dass sein Vater einen Picasso besitzt.
3. Frau Schulz sagt, dass ihre Nichten fünf und acht Jahre alt sind.
4. Stefan sagt, dass sein Studium insgesamt fünf Jahre dauert.
5. Albert sagt, dass seine Großeltern nur Spanisch sprechen.
6. Nora sagt, dass ihr Freund gern Jeans und lange Pullover trägt.
7. Thomas sagt, dass das Leitungswasser in Berkeley sehr gut ist.
8. Katrin sagt, dass Frauen für die gleiche Arbeit immer noch weniger verdienen als Männer.

Übung 3   Minidialoge

Ergänzen Sie **statt, trotz, während** oder **wegen**.

1. KATRIN: Bist du _____ des Regens spazieren gegangen?
   THOMAS: Ja, so ein bisschen Regen macht doch nichts.

2. MONIKA: Warst du gestern im Kino?
   HEIDI: Nein, _____ der Prüfung bin ich zu Hause geblieben.

3. ALBERT: Was machst du _____ der Ferien?
   PETER: Ich fliege nach Bali.

4. JÜRGEN: Ich muss _____ meiner Erkältung zur Uni.
   SILVIA: Du Ärmster, leg dich lieber ins Bett!

5. PETER: Fährst du nächste Woche weg?
   KATRIN: Ich kann doch _____ des Semesters nicht verreisen!

6. JOCHEN: Warum bist du mit dem Bus gefahren?
   JUTTA: _____ des schlechten Wetters.

7. MARIA: Hast du dir ein neues Auto gekauft?
   MICHAEL: Nein, _____ des Autos habe ich mir einen Computer gekauft.

8. KATRIN: In deinem Zimmer ist es _____ der Heizung kalt!
   STEFAN: Tut mir leid, sie funktioniert nicht richtig.

12.2 Expressing possibility: *würde*, *hätte*, and *wäre*

12.2. *Möglichkeit: würde + Infinitiv.* The forms of *würde* are straightforward – this use is relatively easy for sts.

würde = would

Use the construction **würde** + infinitive to talk about possibilities: things you would do, if you were in that particular situation.

Stell dir vor, du würdest nach Deutschland fliegen	*Imagine you were flying to Germany.*
Wo würdest du übernachten?	*Where would you stay for the night?*

Here are the forms of **würde,** which are the subjunctive forms of the verb **werden.**

Wissen Sie noch?

Würde functions like a modal verb. In sentences with modal verbs, the infinitive appears at the end of the sentence.

Review grammar 3.1 and 3.2.

werden			
ich	würde	*wir*	würden
du	würdest	*ihr*	würdet
Sie	würden	*Sie*	würden
er *sie* *es*	würde	*sie*	würden

Instead of using **würde sein** and **würde haben,** German speakers prefer to say **wäre** (*would be*) and **hätte** (*would have*).

Ich glaube, dass ich eine gute Mutter **wäre.**	*I believe I would be a good mother.*
Ich **hätte** sicher viel Zeit für meine Kinder.	*I'm sure I would have plenty of time for my kids.*

Here are the forms of **wäre** and **hätte,** which are the subjunctive forms of **sein** and **haben.**

sein				haben			
ich	wäre	*wir*	wären	*ich*	hätte	*wir*	hätten
du	wärst	*ihr*	wärt	*du*	hättest	*ihr*	hättet
Sie	wären	*Sie*	wären	*Sie*	hätten	*Sie*	hättet
er *sie* *es*	wäre	*sie*	wären	*er* *sie* *es*	hätte	*sie*	hätten

Übung 4   Kein Problem

Was würden Sie in diesen Situationen machen? Beantworten Sie die Fragen! Was würden Sie machen, …

1. wenn Sie sich in Ihren Lehrer / Ihre Lehrerin verlieben würden?
2. wenn Sie sich um Ihre Eltern kümmern müssten?
3. wenn Ihr Partner / Ihre Partnerin eine andere Konfession hätte als Sie?
4. wenn Sie / Ihre Partnerin schwanger werden würden/würde?
5. wenn Sie sich mit Ihrem Partner / Ihrer Partnerin nicht mehr verstehen würden?

Übung 5 **Was wäre, wenn ...**

Schreiben Sie für jede Perspektive drei Sätze darüber, wie Ihr Leben aussehen würde. Verwenden Sie **hätte, wäre** und **würde** in Ihrer Antwort. Sie müssen nicht nur über sich selbst, sondern können auch über andere (z. B. Kinder, Eltern, Partner und Freunde) schreiben.

MODELL: Wenn ich Kinder hätte, würde ich nicht so oft ins Kino gehen. Ich hätte wahrscheinlich viel mehr Arbeit. Abends wäre ich bestimmt müder.

Was wäre, wenn ...

12.3. *Kausalsätze und Finalsätze.* We contrast here the use of *um ... zu* and *damit* for expressing a purpose. Point out that the word *damit* can be both a conjunction and a *da*-compound. This section also reviews *weil*-clauses, which were introduced in Section 3.4.

1. Sie (keine) Kinder hätten?
2. Sie (nicht) verheiratet wären?
3. Sie (kein) Geld hätten?
4. Sie in einem anderen Land leben würden?
5. Sie ein berühmter Schauspieler / eine berühmte Schauspielerin wären?

12.3 Causality and purpose: *weil, damit, um ... zu*

weil = reason for action

damit = goal of action

um ... zu = goal of action

Use **weil** + dependent clause to express the reason for a particular action. Use **damit** or **um ... zu** to express the goal of an action.

Viele Deutsche wanderten nach Australien aus, **weil ihnen Deutschland zu eng war.**	*Many Germans emigrated to Australia because Germany was too crowded for them.*
Sie wanderten nach Australien aus, **um dort eine bessere Arbeit zu finden.**	*They emigrated to Australia in order to find better jobs there.*

Wissen Sie noch?

You can show reasons for action with the conjunctions **weil** and **denn**.

Review grammar 3.4 and 11.5.

Weil and **damit** introduce a dependent clause. Recall that the conjugated verb is in last position in a dependent clause.

Albert steht auf, damit Frau Schulz sich setzen **kann.**	*Albert gets up so that Frau Schulz can sit down.*

Um ... zu clauses have no expressed subjects.

Damit and **um ... zu** both express the aim or goal of an action. But whereas **damit** introduces a dependent clause complete with subject and conjugated verb, **um ... zu** introduces a dependent infinitive without a subject and without a conjugated verb. Use **damit** when the subject of the main clause is different from the subject of the dependent clause.

Heidi macht das Fenster zu, **damit** Stefan nicht friert.
Heidi closes the window so that Stefan won't be cold.

Use **um ... zu** when the understood subject of the dependent infinitive is the same as the subject of the main clause.

Heidi macht das Fenster zu, **damit** sie nicht friert.

→ Heidi macht das Fenster zu, **um** nicht **zu** frieren.

Heidi closes the window so that she won't be cold.

→ *Heidi closes the window so as not to be cold.*

Erfolgsgeschichten

Üb. 6. Point out that when the *um ... zu* clause is first, as it is here, it counts as the first sentence element, and the verb of the main clause follows the comma. Assign for homework and check in class.

Was muss man tun, um Erfolg an der Universität zu haben?

MODELL: Um gute Noten zu bekommen, muss man fleißig lernen.

1. morgens munter[1] sein
2. die Professoren kennenlernen
3. die Mitstudenten kennenlernen
4. am Wochenende nicht allein sein
5. die Kurse bekommen, die man will
6. in vier Jahren fertig werden
7. nicht verhungern
8. eine gute Note in Deutsch bekommen

a. früh ins Bett gehen
b. in die Sprechstunde gehen
c. jeden Tag zum Unterricht kommen
d. Leute einladen
e. regelmäßig essen
f. sich so früh wie möglich einschreiben
g. viel Gruppenarbeit machen
h. viel lernen and wenig Feste feiern

Übung 7   Gute Gründe?

Verbinden Sie Sätze aus der ersten Gruppe mit Sätzen aus der zweiten Gruppe mit Hilfe der Konjunktionen **weil, damit, um ... zu.** Wenn Ihnen ein Grund nicht gefällt, suchen Sie einen besseren Grund.

MODELL: Ich möchte immer hier leben. Dieses Land ist das beste Land der Welt. →
Ich möchte immer hier leben, weil dieses Land das beste Land der Welt ist.

GRUPPE 1

Ich möchte immer hier leben.
Ich möchte für ein paar Jahre in Deutschland leben.
Ausländer haben oft Probleme.
Wenn ich Kinder habe, möchte ich hier leben.
Viele Ausländer kommen hierher.
Englisch sollte die einzige offizielle Sprache (der USA, Kanadas, Australiens, usw.) sein.

GRUPPE 2

Ausländer verstehen die Sprache und Kultur des Gastlandes nicht.
Ich möchte richtig gut Deutsch lernen.
Dieses Land ist das beste Land der Welt.
Hier kann man gut Geld verdienen.
Meine Kinder sollen als (Amerikaner, Kanadier, Australier, usw.) aufwachsen.
Aus der multikulturellen Bevölkerung soll eine homogene Gemeinschaft werden.

12.4 Principles of case (summary review)

Three main factors determine the choice of a particular case for a given noun: function, prepositions, and verbs.

A. Function

Function refers to the role a particular noun plays within a sentence: the subject, the direct object, the indirect object, or the possessive. The subject

[1]*wide awake*

of a sentence (who or what is doing something) is in the nominative case; the direct object (the thing or person to which or to whom the action is done) is in the accusative case; and the indirect object (usually the person who benefits from the action) is in the dative case.

NOM		DAT	ACC	
Maria	schreibt	ihrer Freundin	einen Scheck.	*Maria is writing her friend a check.*

Possessives express relationships of various kinds, such as belonging to or being part of someone or something. Possessives are in the genitive case.

Der Kurs **des Euro** ist leider wieder gestiegen.	*The exchange rate of the euro has unfortunately risen again.*

B. Prepositions

Nouns or pronouns that follow prepositions are always in a case other than the nominative. You have encountered four groups of prepositions so far: those that take the accusative, those that take the dative, two-way prepositions that take either the accusative or the dative according to the meaning of the clause, and those that take the genitive.

Accusative	Dative	Accusative or Dative	Genitive
durch	aus	an	(an)statt
für	außer	auf	trotz
gegen	bei	hinter	während
ohne	mit	in	wegen
um	nach	neben	
	seit	über	
	von	unter	
	zu	vor	
		zwischen	

Bargeld können Sie **aus dem Geldautomaten** bekommen.	*You can get cash from the ATM.*
Wegen des Feiertags bleiben die Banken geschlossen.	*Because of the holiday, the banks remain closed.*

Two-way prepositions require accusative objects when movement toward a *destination* is involved. They require dative objects when no such destination is expressed, when the focus is on the setting of the action or state (*location*).

Ich habe kein Geld **auf meinem Sparkonto.**	*I don't have any money in my savings account.*
Ich muss Geld **auf mein Sparkonto** überweisen.	*I have to transfer money to my savings account.*

C. Verbs

Certain verbs, just like prepositions, require a noun or pronoun to be in a particular case. The verbs **sein, werden, bleiben,** and **heißen** establish identity relationships between the subject and the predicate, and therefore require a predicate noun in the *nominative* case.

Thomas ist **ein fleißiger Student.**	*Thomas is a conscientious student.*

The following verbs are among those that require *dative* objects.

antworten	*to answer*
begegnen	*to meet*
fehlen	*to be missing*
gefallen	*to be to one's liking*
gehören	*to belong to*
gratulieren	*to congratulate*
helfen	*to help*
passen	*to fit*
schaden	*to be harmful (to)*
schmecken	*to taste good (to)*
stehen	*to suit, look good on* (e.g., clothing)
zuhören	*to listen to*

Die Aktien gehören **meiner Mutter.**	*The stocks belong to my mother.*
Eine schwache Wirtschaft schadet **den Aktienmärkten.**	*A weak economy hurts the stock markets.*

Most other verbs require the accusative, if they require an object at all.

Ich habe für mein Konto **keinen Überziehungskredit.**	*I don't have any overdraft protection for my account.*

Übung 8   Der Umzug

Bestimmen Sie den Kasus (**Nom, Akk, Dat** oder **Gen**) der unterstrichenen Nominalphrasen und geben Sie an, ob dieser Kasus wegen der Funktion (**F**), wegen der Präposition (**P**) oder wegen des Verbs (**V**) benutzt wurde.

		KASUS	GRUND
1.	<u>Meine Freundin</u> braucht einen neuen Schrank.	*Nom*	*F*
2.	Sie möchte <u>Schriftstellerin</u> werden.	____	____
3.	Die Möbel <u>meiner Freundin</u> sind ultramodern.	____	____
4.	Morgen kaufe ich <u>ihr</u> eine schöne Lampe.	____	____
5.	Diesen Teppich mag <u>sie</u> sicher nicht.	____	____
6.	Meine Tapeten gefallen <u>ihr</u> sicher auch nicht.	____	____
7.	Setzen wir uns doch an <u>diesen Tisch</u>.	____	____
8.	Ich habe nichts gegen <u>Vorhänge</u>.	____	____
9.	<u>Das Bett</u> tragen wir am besten zusammen.	____	____
10.	Der Wecker steht auf <u>dem Regal</u>.	____	____
11.	Diese Decke gehört <u>mir</u>.	____	____
12.	Der Umzug findet wegen <u>schlechten Wetters</u> nicht statt.	____	____

Übung 9   Jutta hat sich wieder verliebt!

Ergänzen Sie die richtigen Endungen. Unten finden Sie das Genus wichtiger Substantive.

die **Adresse**	das **Fest**	der **Park**
die **Augen** (*pl.*)	die **Hausaufgaben** (*pl.*)	die **Schule**
der **Brief**	die **Hose**	die **Stadt**
die **Disko**	die **Jacke**	die **Tür**
die **Eltern** (*pl.*)	der **Mann**	der **Weg**
der **Fernseher**	der **Name**	

Jutta hat sich total verliebt. Sie sah vor einem Monat auf ein____¹ Klassenfest ein____² jungen Mann, und jetzt denkt sie nur noch an ihn.

Er trug an jenem Abend ein____³ Jeansjacke, unter sein____⁴ Jacke ein altes Unterhemd und ein____⁵ uralte Hose. Er stand die ganze Zeit neben d____⁶ Tür. Seine Kleidung und sein____⁷ blauen Augen gefielen ihr sehr. Er schaute oft zu ihr hin, aber sie sprach ihn nicht an, sie war zu schüchtern.

Jetzt träumt sie von ihm. Sie möchte mit ihm durch d____⁸ Park gehen und in d____⁹ Stadt. Vielleicht könnten sie auch mal für ein paar Tage ohne d____¹⁰ Eltern wegfahren. Sie möchte ihm gern ein____¹¹ Brief schreiben, aber sie weiß sein____¹² Adresse nicht. Sie kennt nur sein____¹³ Vornamen, Florian. Dies____¹⁴ Namen wird sie nie mehr vergessen!

Morgens in d____¹⁵ Schule denkt sie an ihn, mittags auf d____¹⁶ Weg nach Hause, nachmittags bei d____¹⁷ Hausaufgaben, abends vor d____¹⁸ Fernseher oder in d____¹⁹ Disko.

Ach, wenn sie ihn doch nur noch einmal treffen könnte! Diesmal würde sie sicher zu ihm gehen und ihn ansprechen.

Appendix A Informationsspiele: 2. Teil

Einführung A

Situation 6   10 Fragen

Stellen Sie zehn Fragen. Für jedes „Ja" gibt es einen Punkt.

MODELL: S2: Trägt Frau Körner einen Hut?
        S1: Nein. Trägt Nora einen Mantel?
        S1: Nein.

	HERR SIEBERT		FRAU KÖRNER			HERR SIEBERT		FRAU KÖRNER	
	JA	NEIN	JA	NEIN		JA	NEIN	JA	NEIN
einen Anzug	☐	☐	☐	☐	einen Mantel	☐	☐	☐	☐
eine Bluse	☐	☐	☐	☐	einen Pullover	☐	☐	☐	☐
eine Brille	☐	☐	☐	☐	einen Rock	☐	☐	☐	☐
ein Hemd	☐	☐	☐	☐	ein Sakko	☐	☐	☐	☐
eine Hose	☐	☐	☐	☐	Schuhe	☐	☐	☐	☐
einen Hut	☐	☐	☐	☒	Socken	☐	☐	☐	☐
eine Jacke	☐	☐	☐	☐	Sportschuhe	☐	☐	☐	☐
eine Jeans	☐	☐	☐	☐	Stiefel	☐	☐	☐	☐
ein Kleid	☐	☐	☐	☐	ein Stirnband	☐	☐	☐	☐
eine Krawatte	☐	☐	☐	☐	ein T-Shirt	☐	☐	☐	☐

Thomas   Nora   ?   ?   Herr Siebert   Frau Körner

Situation 12 Zahlenrätsel

Verbinden Sie die Punkte. Sagen Sie Ihrem Partner oder Ihrer Partnerin, wie er oder sie die Punkte verbinden soll. Dann sagt Ihr Partner oder Ihre Partnerin Ihnen, wie Sie die Punkte verbinden sollen. Was zeigen Ihre Bilder?

s2: Start ist Nummer 1. Geh zu 17, zu 5, zu 60, zu 23, zu 14, zu 3, zu 19, zu 7, zu 21, zu 12, zu 6, zu 33, zu 8, zu 11, zu 40, zu 25, zu 13, zu 4, zu 15, zu 35, zu 50, zu 9, und zum Schluss zu 16. Was zeigt dein Bild?

Einführung B

Situation 7 Familie

MODELL: s2: Wie heißt Richards Vater?
    s1: Er heißt _____.
    s2: Wie schreibt man das?
    s1: _____. Wie alt ist er?
    s2: Er ist 39 Jahre alt. Wo wohnt er?
    s1: Er wohnt in _____. Wie heißt Richards Mutter?
    s2: Sie heißt Maria.
    s1: Wie schreibt man das?
    s2: M-A-R-I-A.

		Richard	Sofie	Mehmet
Vater	Name			Kenan
	Alter	39		
	Wohnort		Dresden	
Mutter	Name	Maria		
	Alter	38	47	54
	Wohnort			Izmir
Bruder	Name		Erwin	
	Alter			
	Wohnort	Innsbruck	Leipzig	Istanbul
Schwester	Name	Elisabeth	—	Fatima
	Alter	16	—	31
	Wohnort		—	

Situation 9   Temperaturen

MODELL: S2: Wie viel Grad Fahrenheit sind 18 Grad Celsius?
       S1: _____ Grad Fahrenheit.

°F	90		32		−5	
°C	32	18	0	−18	−21	−39

Kapitel 1

Situation 2   Freizeit

MODELL: S2: Wie alt ist Richard?
       S1: _____.
       S2: Woher kommt Rolf?
       S1: Aus _____.
       S2: Was macht Jürgen gern?
       S1: Er _____.
       S2: Wie alt bist du?
       S1: _____.
       S2: Woher kommst du?
       S1: _____.
       S2: Was machst du gern?
       S1: _____.

	Alter	Wohnort	Hobby
Richard		Innsbruck	geht gern in die Berge
Rolf	20		spielt gern Tennis
Jürgen		Göttingen	
Sofie			kocht gern
Jutta	16	München	
Melanie		Regensburg	
mein Partner / meine Partnerin			

Situation 7   Juttas Stundenplan

MODELL: S1: Was hat Jutta am Montag um acht Uhr?
       S2: Sie hat Latein.

Uhr	Montag	Dienstag	Mittwoch	Donnerstag	Freitag
8.00–8.45	Latein			Biologie	
8.50–9.35		Englisch	Englisch		Physik
9.35–9.50	←		Pause		→
9.50–10.35			Mathematik		Religion
10.40–11.25	Geschichte	Französisch		Mathematik	
11.25–11.35	←		Pause		→
11.35–12.20		Musik		Sport	
12.25–13.10	Erdkunde		Kunst		frei

Situation 12 Diese Woche

MODELL: S1: Was macht Silvia am Montag?
S2: Sie steht um 6 Uhr auf.
S1: Was machst du am Montag?
S2: Ich _____.

	Silvia Mertens	Mehmet Sengün	mein(e) Partner(in)
Montag	Sie steht um 6 Uhr auf.		
Dienstag		Er lernt eine neue Kollegin kennen.	
Mittwoch	Sie schreibt eine Prüfung.		
Donnerstag	Sie ruft ihre Eltern an.		
Freitag		Er hört um 15 Uhr mit der Arbeit auf.	
Samstag		Er räumt seine Wohnung auf.	
Sonntag		Er repariert sein Motorrad.	

Kapitel 2

Situation 3 Was machen sie morgen?

MODELL: S1: Schreibt Silvia morgen eine E-Mail?
S2: Ja.
S1: Schreibst du morgen eine E-Mail?
S2: Ja. (Nein.)

	Jürgen	Silvia	mein(e) Partner(in)
1. schreibt/schreibst ... eine E-Mail		+	
2. kauft/kaufst ... ein Buch		+	
3. schaut/schaust ... einen Film an	–	–	
4. ruft/rufst ... eine Freundin an			
5. macht/machst ... Hausaufgaben		+	
6. isst/isst ... einen Hamburger	–	–	
7. besucht/besuchst ... einen Freund			
8. räumt/räumst ... das Zimmer auf		–	

Situation 15   Was machen sie gern?

MODELL: S1: Was trägt Richard gern?
         S2: Pullis.
         S1: Was trägst du gern?
         S2: _____

	Richard	Josef und Melanie	mein(e) Partner(in)
fahren		Zug	
tragen	Pullis		
essen		Pizza	
sehen		Gruselfilme	
vergessen	seine Hausaufgaben		
waschen		ihr Auto	
treffen		ihre Lehrer	
einladen		ihre Eltern	
sprechen	Italienisch		

Kapitel 3

Situation 2   Kann Katrin kochen?

MODELL: S1: Kann Peter kochen?
         S2: Ja, fantastisch.
         S1: Kannst du kochen?
         S2: Ja, aber nicht so gut.

[+]	[0]	[−]
ausgezeichnet	ganz gut	nicht so gut
fantastisch		nur ein bisschen
sehr gut		gar nicht
gut		kein bisschen

	Katrin	Peter	mein(e) Partner(in)
kochen		fantastisch	
zeichnen	sehr gut		
tippen		ganz gut	
Witze erzählen		ganz gut	
tanzen	fantastisch		
stricken	gar nicht		
Skateboard fahren		nicht so gut	
Geige spielen		nur ein bisschen	
schwimmen		nur ein bisschen	
ein Auto reparieren	nicht so gut		

Situation 13   Was machen sie, wenn ...?

MODELL: s1: Was macht Renate, wenn sie müde ist?
s2: Sie trinkt Kaffee.
s1: Was machst du, wenn du müde bist?
s2: Ich gehe ins Bett.

	Renate	Ernst	mein(e) Partner(in)
1. *traurig ist/bist*		weint	
2. *müde ist/bist*	trinkt Kaffee		
3. *in Eile ist/bist*	nimmt ein Taxi		
4. *wütend ist/bist*		schreit ganz laut	
5. *krank ist/bist*	geht zum Arzt		
6. *glücklich ist/bist*		lacht ganz laut	
7. *Hunger hat/hast*			
8. *Langeweile hat/hast*	liest ein Buch	ärgert seine Schwester	
9. *Durst hat/hast*		trinkt Limo	
10. *Angst hat/hast*	schließt die Tür ab		

Kapitel 4

Situation 10   Geburtstage

MODELL: s1: Wann ist Sofie geboren?
s2: Am neunten November 1991.

Person	Geburtstag
Willi	
Sofie	9. November 1991
Claire	
Melanie	3. April 1988
Nora	

Person	Geburtstag
Thomas	17. Januar 1994
Heidi	
mein(e) Partner(in)	
sein/ihr Vater	
seine/ihre Mutter	

Situation 15   Zum ersten Mal

MODELL: s1: Wann hat Herr Thelen seinen ersten Kuss bekommen?
s2: Als er zwölf war.

	Herr Thelen	Frau Gretter	mein(e) Partner(in)
seinen/ihren/deinen ersten Kuss bekommen	als er 12 war		
zum ersten Mal ausgegangen		als sie 15 war	
seinen/ihren/deinen Führerschein gemacht	mit 18		
sein/ihr/dein erstes Bier getrunken		mit 18	
seine/ihre/deine erste Zigarette geraucht	mit 21		
zum ersten Mal nachts nicht nach Hause gekommen	noch nie		

Kapitel 6

Situation 8   Gestern und heute

Arbeiten Sie zu zweit und stellen Sie Fragen wie im Modell.

MODELL: S1: Früher war hier eine Reinigung. Was ist heute hier?
          S2: Heute ist hier ein Schreibwarengeschäft.

FRÜHER

die Reinigung
der Friseur
das Café
das Lebensmittelgeschäft
das Reisebüro
die Drogerie

HEUTE

das Schreibwarengeschäft
das Schuhgeschäft
die Boutique
der Supermarkt
die Bäckerei
der Buchladen

Situation 16   Haus- und Gartenarbeit

MODELL: s1: Was macht Nora am liebsten?
          s2: Sie geht am liebsten einkaufen.
          s1: Was hat Thomas letztes Wochenende gemacht?
          s2: Er hat das Geschirr gespült.
          s1: Was muss Nora diese Woche noch machen?
          s2: Sie muss den Boden wischen.

          s2: Was machst du am liebsten?
          s1: Ich _____ am liebsten _____.

	Thomas	Nora	mein(e) Partner(in)
am liebsten		einkaufen gehen	
am wenigsten gern	das Bad putzen		
jeden Tag	nichts von alledem		
einmal in der Woche		die Wäsche waschen	
letztes Wochenende	das Geschirr spülen		
gestern	die Blumen gießen		
diese Woche		den Boden wischen	
bald mal wieder		Staub wischen	

Kapitel 7

Situation 3   Deutschlandreise

Wo liegen die folgenden Städte? Schreiben Sie die Namen der Städte auf die Landkarte.

Augsburg, Braunschweig, Bremen, Düsseldorf, Frankfurt/Oder, Halle, Kiel, Nürnberg, Rostock, Stuttgart

MODELL: s1: Wo liegt Hannover?
          s2: Hannover liegt im Norden.
          s1: Wo genau?
          s2: Südlich von Hamburg.

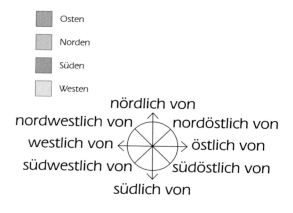

Kapitel 8

Situation 2   Mahlzeiten und Getränke

MODELL: S2: Was isst Frau Gretter zum Frühstück?
       S1: _____.

	Frau Gretter	Stefan	Andrea
zum Frühstück essen		frisches Müsli	Brot mit selbst gemachter Marmelade
zum Frühstück trinken		kalten Orangensaft	
zu Mittag essen	kalorienarmes Gemüse und Hähnchen		heiße Würstchen
zu Abend essen		italienische Spaghetti	
nach dem Sport trinken	nichts, sie treibt keinen Sport	kalten Tee mit Zitrone	
auf einem Fest trinken	deutschen Sekt		eiskalte Limonade
essen, wenn er/sie groß ausgeht		frischen Fisch mit französischer Soße	

Kapitel 9

Situation 9   Was ist passiert?

MODELL: Was ist Mehmet passiert? / Was ist dir passiert?
        Wann ist es passiert?
        Wo ist es passiert?
        Warum ist es passiert?

	Sofie	Mehmet	Ernst	mein(e) Partner / meine Partnerin
Was?	hat ihre Schlüssel verloren		hat seine Hose zerrissen	
Wann?		als er in die Türkei fliegen wollte		
Wo?	in Leipzig		bei seiner Tante	
Warum?		weil der Flug aus Berlin Verspätung hatte		

Kapitel 10

Situation 2   Reisen

MODELL: s2: Woher kommt Richard?
        s1: Aus _____.
        s2: Wohin fährt er in den Ferien?
        s1: Nach/In _____.
        s2: Wo wohnt er?
        s1: Bei _____. Was macht er da?
        s2: Er lernt Französisch. Wann kommt er zurück?
        s1: In _____.

	Richard	Sofie	Mehmet	Peter	Jürgen	mein(e) Partner(in)
Woher?		aus Dresden		aus Berkeley		
Wohin?		nach Düsseldorf		nach Hawaii		
Wo?		bei ihrer Tante	bei alten Freunden		bei einem Freund	
Was?	Französisch lernen		am Strand liegen; schwimmen		Ski fahren natürlich	
Wann?		in einer Woche	in zwei Wochen	nächstes Wochenende		

Situation 9   Wo wollen wir übernachten?

MODELL: Wie viel kostet _____?
        Haben die Zimmer im (in der) _____ eine eigene Dusche und Toilette?
        Gibt es im (in der) _____ Einzelzimmer?
        Gibt es im (in der, auf dem) _____ einen Fernseher?
        Ist das Frühstück im (in der, auf dem) _____ inbegriffen?
        Ist die Lage von dem (von der) _____ zentral/ruhig?
        Gibt es im (in der, auf dem) _____ Telefon?

	das Hotel Strandpromenade	das Gästehaus Ostseeblick	die Jugendherberge	der Campingplatz
Preis pro Person		42 Euro		
Dusche/Toilette			nein	nein
Einzelzimmer				natürlich nicht
Fernseher	in jedem Zimmer	im Fernsehzimmer		natürlich nicht
Frühstück	inbegriffen		kostet extra	nein
zentrale Lage				
ruhige Lage				ja
Telefon	in jedem Zimmer	im Telefonzimmer	bei den Herbergseltern	Telefonzelle

Tiere

MODELL: Welche Tiere findet _____ am tollsten?
Vor welchem Tier hat _____ am meisten Angst?
Welches Tier hätte _____ gern als Haustier?
Welches wilde Tier würde _____ gern in freier Natur sehen?
Wenn _____ an Afrika denkt, an welche Tiere denkt er/sie?
Wenn _____ an die Wüste denkt, an welches Tier denkt er/sie dann zuerst?
Welche Vögel findet _____ am schönsten?
Welchen Fisch findet _____ am gefährlichsten?
Welchem Tier möchte _____ nicht im Wald begegnen?

	Ernst	Maria	mein(e) Partner(in)
Lieblingstier	ein Krokodil		
Angst		vor Mäusen	
Haustier		einen Papagei	
wildes Tier	einen Elefanten		
Afrika		an Zebras	
Wüste	an einen Skorpion		
Vögel	Adler		
Fisch		den Piranha	
Wald		einem Wildschwein	

Kapitel 11

Situation 10   Krankheitsgeschichte

MODELL: Hat Herr Thelen sich (Hast du dir) schon mal etwas gebrochen? Was?
Ist Herr Thelen (Bist du) schon mal im Krankenhaus gewesen? Warum?
Hat Claire (Hast du) schon mal eine Spritze bekommen? Gegen was?
Erkältet sich Claire (Erkältest du dich) oft?
Ist Herr Thelen (Bist du) gegen etwas allergisch? Gegen was?
Hat man Herrn Thelen (Hat man dir) schon mal einen Zahn gezogen?
Hatte Claire (Hattest du) schon mal hohes Fieber? Wie hoch?

	Claire	Herr Thelen	mein(e) Partner(in)
sich etwas brechen	den Arm		
im Krankenhaus sein	Nierenentzündung		
eine Spritze bekommen		Tetanus	
sich oft erkälten		nein	
gegen etwas allergisch sein	Sonne		
einen Zahn gezogen haben	nein		
hohes Fieber haben		41,2° C	

Kapitel 12

Situation 2 Der ideale Partner / Die ideale Partnerin

MODELL: Wie soll Heidis idealer Partner aussehen?
Was für einen Charakter soll er haben?
Welchen Beruf soll Rolfs ideale Partnerin haben?
Welche Interessen sollte sie haben?
Wie alt sollte sie sein?
Welche Konfession sollte sie haben?
Welcher Nationalität sollte Heidis Partner angehören?
Welche politische Einstellung sollte er haben?

	Rolf	Heidi	mein(e) Partner(in)
Aussehen	schlank und sportlich		
Charakter	lustig und neugierig		
Beruf		Rechtsanwalt	
Interessen		Sport und Reisen	
Alter		ein paar Jahre jünger als sie	
Konfession		kein Fanatiker	
Nationalität	deutsch		
politische Einstellung	eher konservativ		

Einführung A

Situation 10   Begrüßen

s2: Begrüßen Sie einen Mitstudenten oder eine Mitstudentin. Schütteln Sie dem Mitstudenten oder der Mitstudentin die Hand. Sagen Sie Ihren Namen. Fragen Sie, wie alt er oder sie ist. Verabschieden Sie sich.

Einführung B

Situation 12   Herkunft

s2: Sie sind Student/Studentin an einer Universität in Deutschland. Sie lernen einen neuen Studenten/eine neue Studentin kennen. Fragen Sie, wie er/sie heißt, woher er/sie kommt, woher seine/ihre Familie kommt und welche Sprachen er/sie spricht.

Kapitel 1

Situation 15   Auf dem Auslandsamt

s2: Sie arbeiten auf dem Auslandsamt der Universität. Ein Student / Eine Studentin kommt zu Ihnen und möchte ein Stipendium für Österreich.

- Fragen Sie nach den persönlichen Daten und schreiben Sie sie auf: Name, Adresse, Telefon, Geburtstag, Studienfach.
- Sagen Sie „Auf Wiedersehen".

Kapitel 2

Situation 8   Am Telefon

s2: Das Telefon klingelt. Ein Freund / Eine Freundin ruft an. Er/Sie lädt Sie ein. Fragen Sie: **wo, wann, um wie viel Uhr, wer kommt mit.** Sagen Sie „ja" oder „nein", und sagen Sie „tschüss".

Kapitel 3

Situation 11   In der Mensa

s2: Sie sind Student/Studentin an der Uni in Regensburg und sind in der Mensa. Jemand möchte sich an Ihren Tisch setzen. Fragen Sie, wie er/sie heißt, woher er/sie kommt und was er/sie studiert.

Kapitel 4

Situation 16   Das Studentenleben

s2: Sie sind Student/Studentin an einer Uni in Ihrem Land. Ein Reporter / Eine Reporterin aus Österreich fragt Sie viel und Sie antworten gern. Sie wollen aber auch wissen, was der Reporter / die Reporterin gestern alles gemacht hat: am Vormittag, am Mittag, am Nachmittag und am Abend.

Kapitel 5

Situation 12   Bei der Berufsberatung

s2: Sie sind Student/Studentin und gehen zur Berufsberatung, weil Sie nicht wissen, was Sie nach dem Studium machen sollen. Beantworten Sie die Fragen des Berufsberaters / der Berufsberaterin.

Kapitel 6

s2: Sie möchten ein Zimmer in Ihrem Haus vermieten. Das Zimmer ist 25 Quadratmeter groß und hat Zentralheizung. Es kostet warm 310 Euro im Monat. Es hat große Fenster und ist sehr ruhig. Das Zimmer hat keine Küche und auch kein Bad, aber der Mieter / die Mieterin darf Ihre Küche und Ihr Bad benutzen. Der Mieter / Die Mieterin darf Freunde einladen, aber sie dürfen nicht zu lange bleiben. Sie haben kleine Kinder, die früh ins Bett müssen. Fragen Sie, was der Student / die Studentin studiert, ob er/sie raucht, ob er/sie oft laute Musik hört, ob er/sie Haustiere hat und ob er/sie Möbel hat.

Kapitel 7

Situation 8   Am Fahrkartenschalter

s2: Sie arbeiten am Fahrkartenschalter im Bahnhof von Bremen. Ein Fahrgast möchte eine Fahrkarte nach München kaufen. Hier ist der Fahrplan. Alle Züge fahren über Hannover und Würzburg.

	Abfahrt	Ankunft	2. Kl.	1. Kl.
IC	4.25	15.40	109 Euro	169 Euro
ICE	7.15	14.05	116 Euro	182 Euro
IC	7.30	20.45	109 Euro	169 Euro

Situation 10   Ein Auto kaufen

s2: Sie wollen einen neueren Gebrauchtwagen kaufen und lesen deshalb die Anzeigen in der Zeitung. Die Anzeigen für einen VW Golf und einen VW Beetle sind interessant. Rufen Sie an und stellen Sie Fragen.
Sie haben auch eine Anzeige in die Zeitung gesetzt, weil Sie Ihren Opel Corsa und Ihren Ford Fiesta verkaufen wollen. Antworten Sie auf die Fragen der Leute.

MODELL: Guten Tag, ich rufe wegen des VW Golf an.
Wie alt ist der Wagen?   Wie lange hat er noch TÜV?
Welche Farbe hat er?   Wie viel Benzin braucht er?
Wie ist der Kilometerstand?   Was kostet der Wagen?

Modell	VW Golf	VW Touareg Hybrid	Opel Corsa	Ford Fiesta
Baujahr			2006	2007
Farbe			schwarz	blaugrün
Kilometerstand			84 500 km	52 000 km
TÜV			6 Monate	fast 2 Jahre
Benzinverbrauch pro 100 km			6 Liter	6,5 Liter
Preis			5 000 Euro	4 000 Euro

Kapitel 8

Situation 14   Im Restaurant

s2: Sie arbeiten als Kellner/Kellnerin in einem Restaurant. Ein Gast setzt sich an einen freien Tisch. Bedienen Sie ihn.

Kapitel 9

Situation 8   Das Klassentreffen

s2: Sie sind auf dem fünften Klassentreffen Ihrer alten High-School-Klasse. Sie unterhalten sich mit einem alten Schulfreund / einer alten Schulfreundin. Fragen Sie: was er/sie nach Abschluss der High School gemacht hat, was er/sie jetzt macht und was seine/ihre Pläne für die nächsten Jahre sind. Sprechen Sie auch über die gemeinsame Schulzeit.

Kapitel 10

Situation 11   Im Hotel

s2: Sie arbeiten an der Rezeption von einem Hotel. Alle Zimmer haben Dusche und Toilette. Manche haben auch Telefon. Frühstück ist inklusive. Das Hotel ist im Moment ziemlich voll. Ein Reisender / Eine Reisende kommt herein und erkundigt sich nach Zimmern. Denken Sie zuerst darüber nach: Was für Zimmer sind noch frei? Was kosten die Zimmer? Bis wann müssen die Gäste abreisen?

Kapitel 11

Situation 12   Anruf beim Arzt

s2: Sie arbeiten in einer Arztpraxis. Ein Patient / Eine Patientin ruft an und möchte einen Termin. Fragen Sie, was er/sie hat und wie dringend es ist. Der Terminkalender für diesen Tag ist schon sehr voll.

Kapitel 12

Situation 11   Auf der Bank

s2: Sie sind Bankangestellte(r) bei der Deutschen Bank und ein Kunde / eine Kundin möchte ein Konto eröffnen. Fragen Sie, ob der Kunde / die Kundin ein Girokonto oder ein Sparkonto eröffnen möchte. Zinsen gibt es nur auf Sparkonten. Eine EC-Karte bekommt man nur, wenn man ein festes Einkommen hat. Onlinezugang ist kostenlos. Man darf das Konto nicht überziehen.

Situation 15   An der Kinokasse

s2: Sie arbeiten an der Kinokasse und sind gestresst, weil Sie den ganzen Tag Karten verkauft haben. Sie haben vielleicht noch zehn Karten für die „Rocky Horror Picture Show" heute Abend, alles Einzelplätze. Auch die nächsten Tage sind schon völlig ausverkauft. Jetzt freuen Sie sich auf Ihren Feierabend, weil Sie dann mit Ihren Freunden selbst in die „Rocky Horror Picture Show" gehen wollen. Sie haben sich fünf ganz tolle Plätze besorgt, in der ersten Reihe. Da kommt noch ein Kunde.

I. Phoneme-Grapheme Relationships (Overview)

Note: The **Arbeitsbuch** presents the phoneme-grapheme relationship in reverse: The graphemes (letters of the alphabet) are the starting point for variations in pronunciation.

Vowels

Sound Group	Phonemes/Sounds	Graphemes	Examples
a-sounds	[aː]	a	Tafel
		ah	Zahl
		aa	Haar
	[a]	a	Hallo
i-sounds	[iː]	i	Ida
		ie	Liebe
		ih	ihr
		ieh	sich anziehen
	[ɪ]	i	Stift
e-sounds	[eː]	e	Peter
		eh	sehen
		ee	Tee
	[ɛ]	e	Herr
		ä	Ärger
	[ɛː]	ä	Cäsar
		äh	zählen
o-sounds	[oː]	o	Hose
		oh	Ohr
		oo	Boot
	[ɔ]	o	Kopf
u-sounds	[uː]	u	Fuß
		uh	Uhr
	[ʊ]	u	Mund
ö-sounds	[øː]	ö	hören
		öh	fröhlich
	[œ]	ö	öffnen
ü-sounds	[yː]	ü	Übung
		üh	früh
		y	Typ
	[ʏ]	ü	tschüss
		y	Ypsilon

(*cont.*)

Sound Group	Phonemes/Sounds	Graphemes	Examples
reduced vowels	[ə]	e	beginnen
	[ɐ]	er	Vater
	[ɐ̯]	r	Ohr
diphthongs	[ae̯]	ei	Kleid
		ai	Mai
		ey/ay	Meyer, Bayern
	[aʊ̯]	au	Auge
	[ɔø̯]	eu	neun
		äu	Häuser

Rules

1. **Long vowels** may be represented in writing by doubled vowels and by <ie>—for example, T*ee*, B*oo*t, L*ie*be.
2. **Long vowels** may also be represented by a vowel followed by <h>, which is not pronounced but only indicates vowel length—for example, Z*ah*l, s*eh*en, fr*üh*.
3. **Single vowels** are often long when they appear in an open or potentially open syllable. Such syllables end in vowels—that is, they have no following end-consonant—for example, Ü-bung, Ho-se, hörst (from hö-ren), gut (from gu-te), Fuß (from Fü-ße). This rule applies above all to verbs, nouns, and adjectives.
4. **Diphthongs** consist of two closely associated short vowels within a syllable. Diphthongs are always long vowels—for example, A*u*ge, Kl*ei*d, n*eu*n.
5. **Short vowels** generally precede double consonants—for example: ö*ff*en, Bri*ll*e, do*pp*elt.
6. **Short vowels** may precede, though not always, a cluster of multiple consonants—for example, W*urst*, Gesi*cht*, Her*bst*.

Consonants

plosives	[p]	p	**P**aula
		pp	do**pp**elt
		-b	gel**b**
	[b]	b	**B**rille
		bb	Kra**bb**e
	[t]	t	**T**ür
		tt	bi**tt**e
		-d	Hem**d**
		th	**Th**eorie
		dt	Sta**dt**
	[d]	d	re**d**en
		dd	Te**dd**y
	[k]	k	**K**leid
		ck	Ro**ck**
		-g	Ta**g**
	[g]	g	Au**g**e

(cont.)

fricatives	[f]	**f**	**F**rau
		ff	ö**ff**nen
		v	**V**ater
	[v]	**w**	**W**ort
		v	**V**iktor
		(q)u	be**qu**em
	[s]	**s**	Hau**s**
		ss	Profe**ss**or
		ß	hei**ß**en
	[z]	**s**	Ho**s**e
	[ʃ]	**sch**	**Sch**ule
		s(t)	**S**tiefel
		s(p)	**S**prache
	[ʒ]	**j**	**J**ournalist
		g	Eta**g**e
(**ich**-sound)	[ç]	**ch**	Gesi**ch**t
		-ig	zwanz**ig**
(**ach**-sound)	[j]	**j**	**j**a
	[x]	**ch**	Bau**ch**
r-sounds	[r]	**r**	**r**ot
		rr	He**rr**
		rh	**Rh**ythmus
	[ʁ]	**r**	Tü**r**
	[ɐ]	**er**	Vat**er**
nasals	[m]	**m**	**M**antel
		mm	ko**mm**en
	[n]	**n**	**N**ame
		nn	Ma**nn**
	[ŋ]	**ng**	spri**ng**en
		n(k)	da**n**ke
liquids	[l]	**l**	**L**ehrer
		ll	Bri**ll**e
aspirants	[h]	**h**	**H**ose
glottal stops	[ʔ]		be·antworten
affricates	[pf]	**pf**	Ko**pf**
	[ts]	**z**	**z**ählen
		tz	se**tz**en
		ts	rech**ts**
		-t(ion)	Lek**t**ion
		zz	Pi**zz**a
	[ks]	**x**	Te**x**t
		ks	lin**ks**
		gs	du sa**gs**t
		chs	se**chs**

Rules

1. Double consonants are pronounced the same as single consonants; they merely indicate that the preceding vowel is short.
2. The letter pair <ch> is pronounced as:
   - a so-called "**ach**-sound" [x] after <u, o, a, au>, for example, *suchen*, To*chter*, *Sprache*, *auch*;
   - a so-called "**ich**-sound" [ç] after all other vowels as well as after <l, n, r> and in *-chen*—for example, *nicht*, *Bücher*, *Töchter*, *Nächte*, *leicht*, *euch*, *Milch*, *durch*, *manchmal*, *Mädchen*;
   - [k] in the cluster <chs> as well as at the beginning of certain foreign words and German names—for example, *sechs*, *Charakter*, *Chemnitz*.
3. [ʃ] is represented:
   - by the letters <sch>: *schön*, *Tasche*; but not in *Häuschen* (*Häus-chen*);
   - by <s(t)>: *Straße*; <s(p)>: *Sprache*.
4. <r> can be clearly heard pronounced as a fricative, uvular, or trilled consonant [r]:
   - at the beginning of a word or syllable: *rot*, *hö-ren*;
   - after consonants and before vowels: *grün*;
   - after short vowels (when clearly enunciated): *Wort*, *Herr*.
5. <r> is pronounced as a vowel [ɐ]:
   - after long vowels: *Uhr*;
   - in the unstressed combinations *er-*, *ver-*, *zer-*, and *-er*: *erzählen*, *Verkäufer*, *zerstören*, *Lehrer*, *aber*.

II. German Vowels and Their Features (Overview)

There are 16 or 17 vowels (+ the vocalic pronunciation of <r>). They can be differentiated by:

- **quantity** (in their length)—they are either short or long;
- **quality** (in their tenseness)—they are either lax or tense.
  Quantity and quality are combined in German. The short vowels are lax; that is, in contrast to long vowels, they are formed with less muscular tension, less use of the lips, and less raising of the tongue. The **a**-vowels are only long and short. In addition, there is a long, open [ɛ:] as well as the reduced [ə] and [ɐ] (schwa).

The following minimal pairs illustrate these differences:

[a:] – [a]	Herr Mahler – Herr Maller
[e:] – [ɛ]	Herr Mehler – Herr Meller
[i:] – [ɪ]	Herr Mieler – Herr Miller
[o:] – [ɔ]	Herr Mohler – Herr Moller
[u:] – [ʊ]	Herr Muhler – Herr Muller
[ø:] – [œ]	Herr Möhler – Herr Möller
[y:] – [ʏ]	Herr Mühler – Herr Müller

Quality and quantity do not play a role with the reduced vowels [ə] as in *eine* and [ɐ] as in *einer*.

- the raising of the tongue—either the front, middle, or back of the tongue is raised. The following minimal pairs illustrate the differences in front vowels:

[e:] – [ɛ]	Herr Mehler – Herr Meller
[i:] – [ɪ]	Herr Mieler – Herr Miller
[ø] – [œ]	Herr Möhler – Herr Möller
[y:] – [ʏ]	Herr Mühler – Herr Müller

The following minimal pairs illustrate the differences in mid vowels:

[a:] – [a]	Herr Mahler – Herr Maller
[ə] – [ɐ]	eine – einer

The following minimal pairs illustrate the differences in back vowels:

[o:] – [ɔ]	Herr Mohler – Herr Moller
[u:] – [ʊ]	Herr Muhler – Herr Muller

- the rounding of the lips—there are rounded and unrounded vowels. The following minimal pairs illustrate the differences between rounded and unrounded vowels:

[ø:] – [e:]	Herr Möhler – Herr Mehler
[œ] – [ɛ]	Herr Möller – Herr Meller
[y:] – [i:]	Herr Mühler – Herr Mieler
[ʏ] – [ɪ]	Herr Müller – Herr Miller

The German vowels can be systematized according to features:

	front		mid	back
long + tense	i: e: ɛ :	y: ø:	a:	u: o:
short + lax	ɪ ɛ	ʏ œ	a	ʊ ɔ
unstressed			ə ɐ	
		rounded		rounded

III. German Consonants and Their Features (Overview)

German consonants are differentiated according to:

- point of articulation: they are formed from the lips (in the front) to the velum (in the back) at different points in the mouth (see overview table on the next page);
- type of articulation:
There are plosives/stops, in which the passage of air is interrupted:

[p] as in Lippen, [b] as in lieben, [t] as in retten, [d] as in reden, [k] as in wecken, [g] as in wegen

There are fricatives, in which the passage of air creates friction:

[f] as in vier, [v] as in wir, [s] as in Haus, [z] as in Häuser, [ʃ] as in Tasche, [ʒ] as in Garage, [ç] as in Mädchen, [j] as in ja, [x] as in Tochter, [r] as in Torte

There are nasals, in which air passes through the nose:

[m] as in *Mai*, [n] as in *nie*, [ŋ] as in *lange*

There are isolated consonants—the liquid [l] as in *hell*, the aspirant [h] as in *hier*.

- tension—there are tense consonants that are always voiceless:

  [p] as in *Lippen*, [t] as in *retten*, [k] as in *wecken*, [f] as in *vier*, [s] as in *Haus*, [ʃ] as in *Tasche*, [ç] as in *Mädchen*, [x] as in *Tochter*

  There are lax consonants that are voiced after vowels and voiced consonants:

  [b] as in *lieben*, [d] as in *reden*, [g] as in *wegen*, [v] as in *bewegen*, [z] as in *Häuser*, [ʒ] as in *Garage*, [j] as in *Kajak*

After a pause in speech (for example at the beginning of a sentence after a pause) and after voiceless consonants, these consonants are also pronounced voiceless:

[b̥] as in *mitbringen*, [d̥] as in *bis drei*, [g̥] as in *ins Haus gehen*, [v̥] as in *auch wir*, [z̥] as in *ab sieben*, [ʒ̊] as in *das Journal*, [j̊] as in *ach ja*

At the end of words and syllables, the following consonants are pronounced voiceless and tense—that is, as fortis consonants. This phenomenon is known as final devoicing:

[b → p] as in *lieb*, [d → t] as in *und*, [g → k] as in *weg*, [v → f] as in *explosiv*, [z → s] as in *Haus*

The German consonants can be systematized according to their features as follows:

front					back
PLOSIVE					
fortis	p		t		k
lenis	b		d		g
FRICATIVE					
fortis	f	s	ʃ	ç	x
lenis	v	z	ʒ	j	r
NASAL	m	n			ŋ
ISOLATED		l			h

IV. Rules for Melody and Accentuation

Melody

1. Melody falls at the end of a sentence (terminal) in:
   - statements—*Ich heiße Anna.* ↘
   - questions with question words—*Woher kommst du?* ↘
   - double questions—*Kommst du aus Bonn oder aus Berlin?* ↘
   - imperatives—*Setz dich!* ↘

2. Melody rises at the end of a sentence (interrogative) in:
   - yes-no questions—*Kommst du aus Bonn?* ↗
   - follow-up questions—*Woher kommst du?* ↘ *Aus Bonn?* ↗
   - questions posed in a friendly or curious tone of voice—*Wie heißt du?* ↗ *Was möchtest du trinken?* ↗
   - imperatives and statements made in a friendly tone of voice—*Bleib noch hier!* ↗ *Die Blumen sind für dich.* ↗
3. Melody remains neutral (doesn't change) directly before pauses in incomplete sentences (progredient)—*Peter kommt aus Bonn,* → *Anna kommt aus Berlin* → *und Ute kommt aus Wien.* ↘

Sentence Stress

1. The most important word is stressed:
   *Ich möchte ein Glas **Wein.*** (kein Bier)
   *Ich möchte ein **Glas** Wein.* (keine Flasche)
   *Ich möchte **ein** Glas Wein.* (nicht zwei)
2. Longer sentences are divided by pauses into accent (rhythmic) groups, in which there is always a main accent:
   *Ich möchte ein Glas **Wein,** / ein Stück **Brot,** / etwas **Käse** / und viel **Wasser.***

Word Stress

1. The stem is stressed:
   - in simple German words: *Mode, **hö**ren;*
   - in words with the prefixes **be-, ge-, er-, ver-, zer-:** be**hal**ten;
   - in verbs with inseparable prefixes and in nouns ending in *-ung* that are derived from them—for example, *wieder**hol**en* → *Wieder**hol**ung.*
2. The beginning of a word (prefix) is stressed:
   - in verbs with separable prefixes and in nouns derived from them—**aus**sprechen → *die **Aus**sprache;*
   - in compounds with *un-* and *ur- —**Ur**laub, **un**genau.*
3. The principally defining word is stressed:
   - in compound nouns and adjectives—**Schlaf***zimmer,* **dunkel***grün.*
4. The final syllable is stressed:
   - in German words with the suffix *-ei—Poli**zei**;*
   - in abbreviations in which each letter is pronounced separately—*AB**C**;*
   - in words that end in *-ion—Explo**sion**.*

Appendix D Grammar Summary Tables

I. Personal Pronouns

Nominative	Accusative	Accusative Reflexive	Dative	Dative Reflexive
ich	mich	mich	mir	mir
du	dich	dich	dir	dir
Sie	Sie	sich	Ihnen	sich
er	ihn	sich	ihm	sich
sie	sie	sich	ihr	sich
es	es	sich	ihm	sich
wir	uns	uns	uns	uns
ihr	euch	euch	euch	euch
Sie	Sie	sich	Ihnen	sich
sie	sie	sich	ihnen	sich

II. Definite Articles / Pronouns Declined Like Definite Articles

dieser/dieses/diese	*this*
mancher/manches/manche	*some, many a*
welcher/welches/welche	*which*
jeder/jedes/jede (*singular*)	*each, every*
alle (*plural*)	*all*

	Singular			Plural
	MASCULINE	NEUTER	FEMININE	
Nominative	der	das	die	die
	dieser	dieses	diese	diese
Accusative	den	das	die	die
	diesen	dieses	diese	diese
Dative	dem	dem	der	den
	diesem	diesem	dieser	diesen
Genitive	des	des	der	der
	dieses	dieses	dieser	dieser

III. Indefinite Articles / Negative Articles / Possessive Adjectives

mein/meine	*my*
dein/deine	*your (familiar singular)*
Ihr/Ihre	*your (polite singular)*
sein/seine	*his, its*
ihr/ihre	*her, its*
unser/unsere	*our*
euer/eure	*your (familiar plural)*
Ihr/Ihre	*your (polite plural)*
ihr/ihre	*their*

	Singular			Plural
	MASCULINE	NEUTER	FEMININE	
Nominative	ein	ein	eine	
	kein	kein	keine	keine
	mein	mein	meine	meine
Accusative	einen	ein	eine	
	keinen	kein	keine	keine
	meinen	mein	meine	meine
Dative	einem	einem	einer	
	keinem	keinem	keiner	keinen
	meinem	meinem	meiner	meinen
Genitive	eines	eines	einer	
	keines	keines	keiner	keiner
	meines	meines	meiner	meiner

IV. Relative Pronouns

	Singular			Plural
	MASCULINE	NEUTER	FEMININE	
Nominative	der	das	die	die
Accusative	den	das	die	die
Dative	dem	dem	der	denen
Genitive	dessen	dessen	deren	deren

V. Question Pronouns

	People	Things and Concepts
Nominative	wer	was
Accusative	wen	was
Dative	wem	
Genitive	wessen	

VI. Attributive Adjectives

		Masculine	Neuter	Feminine	Plural
Nominative	*strong*	guter	gutes	gute	gute
	weak	gute	gute	gute	guten
Accusative	*strong*	guten	gutes	gute	gute
	weak	guten	gute	gute	guten
Dative	*strong*	gutem	gutem	guter	guten
	weak	guten	guten	guten	guten
Genitive	*strong*	guten	guten	guter	guter
	weak	guten	guten	guten	guten

Nouns declined like adjectives: Angestellte, Deutsche, Geliebte, Reisende, Verletzte, Verwandte

VII. Comparative and Superlative

A. *Regular Patterns*

schnell	schneller	am schnellsten
intelligent	intelligenter	am intelligentesten
heiß	heißer	am heißesten
teuer	teurer	am teuersten
dunkel	dunkler	am dunkelsten

B. *Umlaut Patterns*

alt	älter	am ältesten
groß	größer	am größten
jung	jünger	am jüngsten

Similarly: arm, dumm, hart, kalt, krank, kurz, lang, oft, scharf, schwach, stark, warm

C. *Irregular Patterns*

gern	lieber	am liebsten
gut	besser	am besten
hoch	höher	am höchsten
nah	näher	am nächsten
viel	mehr	am meisten

VIII. Weak Masculine Nouns

These nouns add -**(e)n** in the accusative, dative, and genitive.

A. *International nouns ending in* -**t** *denoting male persons:* Dirigent, Komponist, Patient, Polizist, Präsident, Soldat, Student, Tourist
B. *Nouns ending in* -**e** *denoting male persons or animals:* Drache, Junge, Kunde, Löwe, Neffe, Riese, Vorfahre, Zeuge
C. *The following nouns:* Elefant, Herr, Mensch, Nachbar, Name[1]

	Singular	Plural
Nominative	der Student	die Studenten
	der Junge	die Jungen
Accusative	den Studenten	die Studenten
	den Jungen	die Jungen
Dative	dem Studenten	den Studenten
	dem Jungen	den Jungen
Genitive	des Studenten	der Studenten
	des Jungen	der Jungen

IX. Prepositions

Accusative	Dative	Accusative/Dative	Genitive
durch	aus	an	(an)statt
für	außer	auf	trotz
gegen	bei	hinter	während
ohne	mit	in	wegen
um	nach	neben	
	seit	über	
	von	unter	
	zu	vor	
		zwischen	

[1] *genitive:* des Namens

X. Dative Verbs

antworten	*to answer*
begegnen	*to meet*
danken	*to thank*
erlauben	*to allow*
fehlen	*to be missing*
folgen	*to follow*
gefallen	*to please, be pleasing to*
gehören	*to belong to*
glauben	*to believe*
gratulieren	*to congratulate*
helfen	*to help*
leidtun	*to be sorry; to feel sorry for*
passen	*to fit*
passieren	*to happen*
raten	*to advise*
schaden	*to be harmful*
schmecken	*to taste (good)*
stehen	*to suit*
wehtun	*to hurt*
zuhören	*to listen to*

XI. Reflexive Verbs

sich anziehen	*to get dressed*
sich ärgern	*to get angry*
sich aufregen	*to get excited*
sich ausruhen	*to rest*
sich ausziehen	*to get undressed*
sich beeilen	*to hurry*
sich erholen	*to relax, recover*
sich erkälten	*to catch a cold*
sich erkundigen	*to ask*
sich (die Haare) föhnen	*to blow-dry (one's hair)*
sich fragen (ob)	*to wonder (if)*
sich freuen	*to be happy*
sich (wohl) fühlen	*to feel (well)*
sich fürchten	*to be afraid*
sich gewöhnen an	*to get used to*
sich hinlegen	*to lie down*
sich infizieren	*to get infected*
sich informieren	*to get information*
sich interessieren für	*to be interested in*
sich kümmern um	*to take care of*
sich rasieren	*to shave*
sich schminken	*to put on makeup*
sich setzen	*to sit down*
sich umsehen	*to look around*
sich unterhalten	*to have a conversation*
sich verletzen	*to get hurt*
sich verloben	*to get engaged*
sich vorstellen	*to imagine*

XII. Verbs + Prepositions

ACCUSATIVE

bitten um	*to ask for*
denken an	*to think about*
glauben an	*to believe in*
nachdenken über	*to think about; to ponder*
schreiben an	*to write to*
schreiben/sprechen über	*to write/talk about*
sorgen für	*to care for*
verzichten auf	*to renounce, do without*
warten auf	*to wait for*

SICH + ACCUSATIVE

sich ärgern über	*to be angry at/about*
sich erinnern an	*to remember*
sich freuen über	*to be happy about*
sich gewöhnen an	*to get used to*
sich interessieren für	*to be interested in*
sich kümmern um	*to take care of*
sich verlieben in	*to fall in love with*

DATIVE

fahren/reisen mit	*to go/travel by*
halten von	*to think of; to value*
handeln von	*to deal with*
träumen von	*to dream of*

SICH + DATIVE

sich erkundigen nach	*to ask about*
sich fürchten vor	*to be afraid of*

XIII. Inseparable Prefixes of Verbs

A. *Common*

be-	bedeuten, bekommen, bestellen, besuchen, bezahlen
er-	erfinden, erkälten, erklären, erlauben, erreichen
ver-	verbrennen, verdienen, vergessen, verlassen, verletzen

B. *Less Common*

ent-	entdecken, entscheiden, entschuldigen
ge-	gefallen, gehören, gewinnen, gewöhnen
zer-	zerreißen, zerstören

Appendix E Verbs

I. Conjugation Patterns

A. *Simple tenses and principal parts*

		Present	Simple Past	Subjunctive	Aux. + Past Participle
Strong	ich	komme	kam	käme	bin gekommen
	du	kommst	kamst	kämst	bist gekommen
	er/sie/es	kommt	kam	käme	ist gekommen
	wir	kommen	kamen	kämen	sind gekommen
	ihr	kommt	kamt	kämt	seid gekommen
	sie, Sie	kommen	kamen	kämen	sind gekommen
Weak	ich	glaube	glaubte	glaubte	habe geglaubt
	du	glaubst	glaubtest	glaubtest	hast geglaubt
	er/sie/es	glaubt	glaubte	glaubte	hat geglaubt
	wir	glauben	glaubten	glaubten	haben geglaubt
	ihr	glaubt	glaubtet	glaubtet	habt geglaubt
	sie, Sie	glauben	glaubten	glaubten	haben geglaubt
Irregular Weak	ich	weiß	wusste	wüsste	habe gewusst
	du	weißt	wusstest	wüsstest	hast gewusst
	er/sie/es	weiß	wusste	wüsste	hat gewusst
	wir	wissen	wussten	wüssten	haben gewusst
	ihr	wisst	wusstet	wüsstet	habt gewusst
	sie, Sie	wissen	wussten	wüssten	haben gewusst
Modal	ich	kann	konnte	könnte	habe gekonnt
	du	kannst	konntest	könntest	hast gekonnt
	er/sie/es	kann	konnte	könnte	hat gekonnt
	wir	können	konnten	könnten	haben gekonnt
	ihr	könnt	konntet	könntet	habt gekonnt
	sie, Sie	können	konnten	könnten	haben gekonnt
haben	ich	habe	hatte	hätte	habe gehabt
	du	hast	hattest	hättest	hast gehabt
	er/sie/es	hat	hatte	hätte	hat gehabt
	wir	haben	hatten	hätten	haben gehabt
	ihr	habt	hattet	hättet	habt gehabt
	sie, Sie	haben	hatten	hätten	haben gehabt
sein	ich	bin	war	wäre	bin gewesen
	du	bist	warst	wärst	bist gewesen
	er/sie/es	ist	war	wäre	ist gewesen
	wir	sind	waren	wären	sind gewesen
	ihr	seid	wart	wärt	seid gewesen
	sie, Sie	sind	waren	wären	sind gewesen
werden	ich	werde	wurde	würde	bin geworden
	du	wirst	wurdest	würdest	bist geworden
	er/sie/es	wird	wurde	würde	ist geworden
	wir	werden	wurden	würden	sind geworden
	ihr	werdet	wurdet	würdet	seid geworden
	sie, Sie	werden	wurden	würden	sind geworden

B. *Compound tenses*

1. *Active voice*

	Perfect	Past Perfect	Future	Subjunctive
Strong	ich habe genommen	hatte genommen	werde nehmen	würde nehmen
	ich bin gefahren	war gefahren	werde fahren	würde fahren
Weak	ich habe gekauft	hatte gekauft	werde kaufen	würde kaufen
	ich bin gesegelt	war gesegelt	werde segeln	würde segeln
Irregular Weak	ich habe gewusst	hatte gewusst	werde wissen	würde wissen
Modal	ich habe gekonnt	hatte gekonnt	werde können	würde können
haben	ich habe gehabt	hatte gehabt	werde haben	würde haben
sein	ich bin gewesen	war gewesen	werde sein	würde sein
werden	ich bin geworden	war geworden	werde werden	würde werden

2. *Passive voice*

	Present	Simple Past	Perfect
Strong	es wird genommen	wurde genommen	ist genommen worden
Weak	es wird gekauft	wurde gekauft	ist gekauft worden

II. Strong and Irregular Weak Verbs

backen (backt)	backte	hat gebacken	*to bake*
beginnen (beginnt)	begann	hat begonnen	*to begin*
beißen (beißt)	biss	hat gebissen	*to bite*
bekommen (bekommt)	bekam	hat bekommen	*to get, receive*
beschreiben (beschreibt)	beschrieb	hat beschrieben	*to describe*
besitzen (besitzt)	besaß	hat besessen	*to own, possess*
besteigen (besteigt)	bestieg	hat bestiegen	*to climb*
bitten (bittet)	bat	hat gebeten	*to ask*
bleiben (bleibt)	blieb	ist geblieben	*to stay*
braten (brät)	briet	hat gebraten	*to roast, fry*
brechen (bricht)	brach	hat gebrochen	*to break*
brennen (brennt)	brannte	hat gebrannt	*to burn*
bringen (bringt)	brachte	hat gebracht	*to bring*
denken (denkt)	dachte	hat gedacht	*to think*
dürfen (darf)	durfte	hat gedurft	*to be allowed to*
empfehlen (empfiehlt)	empfahl	hat empfohlen	*to recommend*
entscheiden (entscheidet)	entschied	hat entschieden	*to decide*
erfinden (erfindet)	erfand	hat erfunden	*to invent*
essen (isst)	aß	hat gegessen	*to eat*
fahren (fährt)	fuhr	ist gefahren	*to go, drive*
fallen (fällt)	fiel	ist gefallen	*to fall*
fangen (fängt)	fing	hat gefangen	*to catch*

finden (findet)	fand	hat gefunden	*to find*
fliegen (fliegt)	flog	ist geflogen	*to fly*
fliehen (flieht)	floh	ist geflohen	*to flee*
fließen (fließt)	floss	ist geflossen	*to flow*
fressen (frisst)	fraß	hat gefressen	*to eat*
geben (gibt)	gab	hat gegeben	*to give*
gefallen (gefällt)	gefiel	hat gefallen	*to please, be pleasing to*
gehen (geht)	ging	ist gegangen	*to go, walk*
gewinnen (gewinnt)	gewann	hat gewonnen	*to win*
gießen (gießt)	goss	hat gegossen	*to water*
haben (hat)	hatte	hat gehabt	*to have*
halten (hält)	hielt	hat gehalten	*to hold*
hängen (hängt)	hing	hat gehangen	*to hang, be suspended*
heben (hebt)	hob	hat gehoben	*to lift*
heißen (heißt)	hieß	hat geheißen	*to be called*
helfen (hilft)	half	hat geholfen	*to help*
kennen (kennt)	kannte	hat gekannt	*to know*
klingen (klingt)	klang	hat geklungen	*to sound*
kommen (kommt)	kam	ist gekommen	*to come*
können (kann)	konnte	hat gekonnt	*to be able to*
laden (lädt)	lud	hat geladen	*to load*
lassen (lässt)	ließ	hat gelassen	*to let, leave*
laufen (läuft)	lief	ist gelaufen	*to run*
leihen (leiht)	lieh	hat geliehen	*to lend, borrow*
lesen (liest)	las	hat gelesen	*to read*
liegen (liegt)	lag	hat gelegen	*to lie*
mögen (mag)	mochte	hat gemocht	*to like*
müssen (muss)	musste	hat gemusst	*to have to*
nehmen (nimmt)	nahm	hat genommen	*to take*
nennen (nennt)	nannte	hat genannt	*to name*
raten (rät)	riet	hat geraten	*to advise*
reiten (reitet)	ritt	ist geritten	*to ride*
riechen (riecht)	roch	hat gerochen	*to smell*
rufen (ruft)	rief	hat gerufen	*to call*
scheiden (scheidet)	schied	hat geschieden	*to separate*
schießen (schießt)	schoss	hat geschossen	*to shoot*
schlafen (schläft)	schlief	hat geschlafen	*to sleep*
schlagen (schlägt)	schlug	hat geschlagen	*to strike, beat*
schließen (schließt)	schloss	hat geschlossen	*to shut, close*
schneiden (schneidet)	schnitt	hat geschnitten	*to cut*
schreiben (schreibt)	schrieb	hat geschrieben	*to write*
schwimmen (schwimmt)	schwamm	ist geschwommen	*to swim*
sehen (sieht)	sah	hat gesehen	*to see*
sein (ist)	war	ist gewesen	*to be*
senden (sendet)	sandte	hat gesandt	*to send*
singen (singt)	sang	hat gesungen	*to sing*
sinken (sinkt)	sank	ist gesunken	*to sink*
sitzen (sitzt)	saß	hat gesessen	*to sit*
sprechen (spricht)	sprach	hat gesprochen	*to speak*
springen (springt)	sprang	ist gesprungen	*to spring, jump*
stehen (steht)	stand	hat gestanden	*to stand*
steigen (steigt)	stieg	ist gestiegen	*to climb*

sterben (stirbt)	starb	ist gestorben	*to die*
stoßen (stößt)	stieß	hat gestoßen	*to shove, push*
streiten (streitet)	stritt	hat gestritten	*to quarrel, fight*
tragen (trägt)	trug	hat getragen	*to wear, carry*
treffen (trifft)	traf	hat getroffen	*to meet, hit*
treiben (treibt)	trieb	hat getrieben	*to do (sports)*
trinken (trinkt)	trank	hat getrunken	*to drink*
tun (tut)	tat	hat getan	*to do*
verbrennen (verbrennt)	verbrannte	hat verbrannt	*to burn; to incinerate*
verbringen (verbringt)	verbrachte	hat verbracht	*to spend (time)*
vergessen (vergisst)	vergaß	hat vergessen	*to forget*
verlassen (verlässt)	verließ	hat verlassen	*to leave (a place)*
verlieren (verliert)	verlor	hat verloren	*to lose*
verschwinden (verschwindet)	verschwand	ist verschwunden	*to disappear*
versprechen (verspricht)	versprach	hat versprochen	*to promise*
wachsen (wächst)	wuchs	ist gewachsen	*to grow*
waschen (wäscht)	wusch	hat gewaschen	*to wash*
werden (wird)	wurde	ist geworden	*to become*
wissen (weiß)	wusste	hat gewusst	*to know*

Appendix F Answers to Grammar Exercises

Einführung A

Übung 1: 1. Hören Sie zu! 2. Geben Sie mir die Hausaufgabe! 3. Öffnen Sie das Buch! 4. Schauen Sie an die Tafel! 5. Nehmen Sie einen Stift! 6. Sagen Sie „Guten Tag"! 7. Schließen Sie das Buch! 8. Schreiben Sie „Tschüss"! **Übung 2:** 1.a. heißt b. heiße c. heiße 2.a. heißen b. heiße 3.a. heiße b. heiße c. heißt **Übung 3:** 1. Sie 2. Es 3. Er 4. Sie 5. Es 6. Sie 7. Er 8. Sie 9. Sie 10. Er **Übung 4:** 1. Er ist orange. 2. Sie ist grün. 3. Es ist gelb. 4. Er ist schwarz und rot. 5. Sie sind rosa. 6. Sie sind braun. 7. Sie ist weiß. **Übung 5:** 1. du 2. Sie 3. du 4. ihr 5. Sie 6. Sie 7. Sie 8. ihr

Einführung B

Übung 1: 1.a. ein b. der c. rot 2.a. ein b. der c. grün 3.a. eine b. die c. grau 4.a. eine b. die c. braun 5.a. ein b. das c. orange 6.a. eine b. die c. schwarz **Übung 2:** 1. Nein, das ist eine Lampe. 2. Nein, das ist eine Tafel. 3. Nein, das ist ein Fenster. 4. Nein, das ist ein Heft. 5. Nein, das ist eine Uhr. 6. Nein, das ist ein Tisch. 7. Nein, das ist eine Tür. **Übung 3:** 1.a. bist b. bin c. sind 2.a. ist b. sind 3.a. seid b. bin c. ist. 4.a. bin b. bin **Übung 4:** 1.a. haben b. habe 2. hast 3.a. Habt b. hat c. haben d. habe **Übung 5:** Der Mensch hat zwei Arme, zwei Augen, zwei Beine, zehn Finger, zwei Füße, viele Haare, zwei Hände, eine Nase, zwei Ohren, zwei Schultern. **Übung 6:** (*Numbers will vary.*) In meinem Zimmer sind viele Bücher, vier Computer, ein Fenster, zwei Lampen, zwei Stühle, ein Tisch, eine Tür, eine Uhr, vier Wände. **Übung 7:** 1. Er ist schwarz. 2. Es ist weiß. 3. Sie ist blau. 4. Sie ist gelb. 5. Sie sind weiß. 6. Es ist rot. 7. Er ist lila. 8. Sie sind braun. 9. Sie ist grün. 10. Er ist rosa. **Übung 8:** 1.a. kommst b. komme 2.a. kommt b. aus c. Woher d. kommen e. ich f. aus 3.a. sie b. kommen c. aus **Übung 9:** 1. Ihre 2.a. dein b. mein a. mein c. Dein 4.a. Ihre b. Meine c. mein **Übung 10:** (*Answers will vary.*) 1. Ich komme aus _____. 2. Meine Mutter kommt aus _____. 3. Mein Vater kommt aus _____. 4. Meine Großeltern kommen aus _____. / Mein Großvater kommt aus _____ und meine Großmutter kommt aus _____. 5. Mein Professor / Meine Professorin kommt aus _____. 6. Ein Student aus meinem Deutschkurs heißt _____ und er kommt aus _____. 7. Eine Studentin aus meinem Deutschkurs heißt _____ und sie kommt aus _____.

Kapitel 1

Übung 1: (*Answers may vary.*) 1. Ich besuche Freunde. 2. Ihr geht ins Kino. 3. Jutta und Jens lernen Spanisch. 4. Du spielst gut Tennis. 5. Melanie studiert in Regensburg. 6. Ich lese ein Buch. 7. Wir reisen nach Deutschland. 8. Richard hört gern Musik. 9. Jürgen und Silvia kochen Spaghetti. **Übung 2:** 1. sie 2. Sie 3.a. du b. Ich 4.a. ihr b. Wir 5.a. Ich b. Wir **Übung 3:** 1.a. (tanz)t b. (tanz)e c. (tanz)t 2.a. (geh)t b. (mach)en c. (reis)t d. (arbeit)et 3.a. (koch)en b. (mach)t c. (besuch)en 4.a. (Schreib)st b. (Chatt)est c. (mach)e **Übung 4:** (*Answers may vary slightly.*) 1. Monika und Albert spielen gern Schach. 2. Heidi arbeitet gern. 3. Stefan besucht gern Freunde. 4. Nora geht gern ins Kino. 5. Peter hört gern Musik. 6. Katrin macht gern Fotos. 7. Monika zeltet gern. 8. Albert trinkt gern Tee. **Übung 5:** 1. Frau Ruf liegt gern in der Sonne. Jutta liegt auch gern in der Sonne, aber Herr Ruf liegt nicht gern in der Sonne. 2. Jens reitet gern. Ernst reitet auch gern, aber Jutta reitet nicht gern. 3. Jens kocht gern. Jutta kocht auch gern, aber Andrea kocht nicht gern. 4. Michael und Maria spielen gern Karten. Die Rufs spielen auch gern Karten, aber die Wagners spielen nicht gern Karten. **Übung 6:** 1. Es ist halb acht. 2. Es ist elf Uhr. 3. Es ist Viertel vor fünf. 4. Es ist halb eins. 5. Es ist zehn vor sieben. 6. Es ist Viertel nach zwei. 7. Es ist fünfundzwanzig nach fünf. 8. Es ist halb elf. **Übung 7:** 1. (Rolf) nach 2. (er) vor 3. (Seine Großmutter) nach 4. (Rolf) vor 5. (er) vor 6. (er) vor 7. (er) vor 8. (Er) nach **Übung 8:** (*Answers will vary.*) 1. Ich studiere _____. 2. Im Moment wohne ich in _____. 3. Heute koche ich _____. 4. Manchmal trinke ich _____. 5. Ich spiele gern _____. 6. Mein Freund heißt _____. 7. Jetzt wohnt er in _____. 8. Manchmal spielen wir _____. **Übung 9:** 1. auf 2. auf 3. ein 4. an 5. aus 6. ab 7. ein 8. aus 9. auf **Übung 10:** (*Answers may vary.*) 1. Rolf kommt in San Francisco an. 2. Thomas räumt das Zimmer auf. 3. Heidi ruft Thomas an. 4. Albert füllt das Formular aus. 5. Peter holt Monika ab. 6. Peter und Monika gehen aus. 7. Frau Schulz packt die Bücher ein. 8. Stefan steht um halb elf auf. 9. Katrin lernt Rolf kennen. **Übung 11:** 1. Wann bist du geboren? 2. Woher kommst du? 3. Wo wohnst du? 4. Welche Augenfarbe hast du? 5. Wie groß bist du? 6. Studierst du? 7. Welche Fächer studierst du? 8. Wie viele Stunden arbeitest du? 9. Was machst du gern? **Übung 12:** (*Answers may vary.*) 1. Wie heißt du? 2. Kommst du aus München? 3. Woher kommst du? 4. Was studierst du? 5. Wie heißt dein Freund? 6. Wo wohnt er? 7. Spielst du Tennis? 8. Tanzt du gern? 9. Trinkst du gern Cola? 10. Trinkt Willi gern Bier?

Kapitel 2

Übung 1: Ernst kauft die Tasche, die Stühle und den Schreibtisch. Melanie kauft die Tasche, das Regal und den Schreibtisch. Jutta kauft den Pullover, die Lampe und den DVD-Spieler. Ich kaufe ... (*Answers will vary.*) **Übung 2:** (*Answers will vary.*) Ich habe ein Bett, Bilder, Bücher, einen Fernseher, ein Handy, eine Lampe, einen Laptop, einen Sessel und ein Telefon. **Übung 3:** (*Sentences may vary.*) Heidi hat einen Teppich, aber keinen Fernseher. Sie hat eine Gitarre, aber kein Fahrrad. Sie hat einen Computer, aber keine Bilder. Sie hat ein Handy. Monika hat keinen Teppich, keinen Fernseher und keine Gitarre. Aber sie hat ein Fahrrad, einen Computer, Bilder und ein Handy. Ich habe _____. **Übung 4:** (*Answers will vary.*) 1. Ich möchte ein Auto und eine Sonnenbrille. 2. Mein bester Freund möchte eine Katze. 3. Meine Eltern möchten einen Laptop. 4. Meine Mitbewohnerin und ich möchten einen Fernseher. 5. Mein Nachbar in der Klasse möchte ein Motorrad. 6. Meine Professorin möchte einen Koffer. 7. Mein Bruder möchte einen Hund. **Übung 5:** Seine Haare; Seine Augen; Seine Halskette; Seine Schuhe; Seine Gitarre; Sein Zimmer; Sein Fenster; Ihre Haare; Ihre Augen; Ihre Halskette ist kurz. Ihre Schuhe sind sauber. Ihre Gitarre ist neu. Ihr Zimmer ist klein. Ihr Fenster ist groß. **Übung 6:** 1. Ihren 2. Deine 3. eure 4. Deine 5. Ihre 6. deine 7. Euren **Übung 7:** (*Answers may vary.*) **Übung 8:** 1.a. ihr b. wir 2.a. Sie b. Ich 3.a. sie b. er 4.a. du b. Ich c. ihr d. Wir **Übung 9:** a. machen b. fährt c. sieht d. Isst e. isst f. isst g. macht h. lese i. schläft j. fahren **Übung 10:** (*Answers will vary.*) 1. Wir sprechen (nicht) gern Deutsch. Sprecht ihr auch (nicht) gern Deutsch? 2. Ich lade (nicht) gern Freunde ein. Lädst du auch (nicht) gern Freunde ein? 3. Ich laufe (nicht) gern im Wald. Läufst du auch (nicht) gern im Wald? 4. Ich trage (nicht) gern Pullis. Trägst du auch (nicht) gern Pullis? 5. Wir sehen (nicht) gern fern. Seht ihr auch (nicht) gern fern? 6. Ich fahre (nicht) gern Fahrrad. Fährst du auch (nicht) gern Fahrrad? 7. Wir vergessen (nicht) gern die Hausaufgabe. Vergesst ihr auch (nicht) gern die Hausaufgabe? 8. Ich schlafe (nicht) gern. Schläfst du auch (nicht) gern? 9. Wir lesen (nicht) gern online. Lest ihr auch (nicht) gern online? **Übung 11:** 1. e. Schreib es dir auf! 2. c. Lies ein Buch! 3. d. Mach eine Pause! 4. a. Treib Sport! 5. b. Trink Cola! 6. g. Iss lieber Joghurt! 7. i. Kauf dir einen neuen Pullover! 8. j. Koch Chinesisch! 9. h. Lade deine Freunde ein! 10. f. Fahr Fahrrad! **Übung 12:** 1. Schlaf nicht den ganzen Tag! 2. Lieg nicht den ganzen Tag in der Sonne! 3. Vergiss deine Hausaufgaben nicht! 4. Lies deine Bücher! 5. Sieh nicht den ganzen Tag fern! 6. Trink nicht zu viel Cola! 7. Sitz nicht den ganzen Tag am Computer! 8. Trag deine Brille! 9. Spiel nicht immer Computerspiele! 10. Treib Sport! **Übung 13:** 1. Trag heute ein T-Shirt! 2. Spiel keine laute Musik! 3. Lern den Wortschatz! 4. Ruf deine Freunde an! 5. Lauf nicht allein im Park! 6. Lieg nicht zu lange in der Sonne! 7. Räum dein Zimmer auf! 8. Iss heute Abend in einem Restaurant! 9. Geh nicht zu spät ins Bett! 10. Steh früh auf!

Kapitel 3

Übung 1: (*Predicates and sequence will vary.*) A.1. Mein Freund / Meine Freundin kann _____. 2. Meine Eltern können _____. 3. Ich kann / Wir können _____. 4. Mein Bruder / Meine Schwester kann _____. 5. Der Professor / Die Professorin kann _____. B.1. Kannst du / Könnt ihr Gedichte schreiben? 2. Kannst du / Könnt ihr Auto fahren? 3. Kannst du / Könnt ihr tippen? 4. Kannst du / Könnt ihr stricken? 5. Kannst du / Könnt ihr zeichnen? **Übung 2:** (*Answers will vary.*) 1. Heute Abend will ich _____. 2. Morgen kann ich nicht _____. 3. Mein Freund / Meine Freundin kann gut _____. 4. Am Samstag will mein Freund / meine Freundin _____. 5. Mein Freund / Meine Freundin und ich wollen _____. 6. Im Winter wollen meine Eltern / meine Freunde _____. 7. Meine Eltern / Meine Freunde können gut _____. **Übung 3:** 1. Sie darf nicht mit Jens zusammen lernen. 2. Sie darf nicht den ganzen Abend chatten. 3. Sie muss in der Klasse aufpassen und mitschreiben. 4. Sie darf nicht jeden Tag tanzen gehen. 5. Sie muss jeden Tag ihren Wortschatz lernen. 6. Sie muss amerikanische Filme im Original sehen. 7. Sie muss ihren Englischlehrer zum Abendessen einladen. 8. Sie muss für eine Woche nach London fahren. 9. Sie muss die englische Grammatik fleißig lernen. **Übung 4:** 1.a. Willst b. will c. kann d. muss 2.a. darf b. musst c. kann d. darfst e. könnt 3.a. sollst b. kann c. musst **Übung 5:** 1. dich 2.a. mich b. dich 3. uns 4. euch 5.a. dich b. dich 6.a. mich b. Sie 7. Sie **Übung 6:** 1. Ja, ich mache es gern. / Nein, ich mache es nicht gern. 2. Ja, ich kann es aufsagen. / Nein, ich kann es nicht aufsagen. 3. Ja, ich kenne ihn. / Nein, ich kenne ihn nicht. 4. Ja, ich lese sie gern. / Nein, ich lese sie nicht gern. 5. Ja, ich lerne ihn gern. / Nein, ich lerne ihn nicht gern. 6. Ja, ich kenne sie. / Nein, ich kenne sie nicht. 7. Ja, ich vergesse sie oft. / Nein, ich vergesse sie nicht oft. 8. Ja, ich mag ihn/sie. / Nein, ich mag ihn/sie nicht. **Übung 7:** 1. Nein, sie liest ihn nicht, sie schreibt ihn. 2. Nein, er isst sie nicht, er trinkt sie. 3. Nein, sie macht ihn nicht an, sie macht ihn aus. 4. Nein, er kauft es nicht, er verkauft es. 5. Nein, er zieht sie nicht aus, er zieht sie an. 6. Nein, sie trägt ihn nicht, sie kauft ihn. 7. Nein, er bestellt es nicht, er isst es. 8. Nein, er besucht ihn nicht, er ruft ihn an. 9. Nein, sie kämmt es nicht, sie wäscht es. 10. Nein, er bläst sie nicht aus, er zündet sie an. **Übung 8:** 1. Weil ich krank bin. 2. Weil er müde ist. 3. Weil wir Hunger haben. 4. Weil sie keine Zeit hat. 5. Weil sie Langeweile hat. 6. Weil sie traurig bin. 7. Weil sie Durst haben. 8. Weil ich Angst habe. 9. Weil er glücklich ist. 10. Weil ich lernen muss. **Übung 9:** (*Answers will vary.*) 1. s1: Was macht Albert, wenn er müde ist? s2: Wenn Albert müde ist, geht er nach Hause. s1: Und du? s2: Wenn ich müde bin, _____. 2. s1: Was macht Maria, wenn sie glücklich ist? s2: Wenn Maria glücklich ist, trifft sie Michael. s1: Und du? s2: Wenn ich glücklich bin, _____. 3. s1: Was macht Herr Ruf, wenn er Durst hat? s2: Wenn Herr Ruf Durst hat, trinkt er eine Cola. s1: Und du? s2: Wenn ich Durst habe, _____. 4. s1: Was macht Frau Wagner, wenn sie in Eile ist? s2: Wenn Frau Wagner in Eile ist, fährt sie mit dem Taxi. s1: Und du? s2: Wenn ich in Eile bin, _____. 5. s1: Was macht Heidi, wenn sie Hunger hat? s2: Wenn Heidi Hunger hat, kauft sie einen Hamburger. s1: Und du? s2: Wenn ich Hunger habe, _____. 6. s1: Was macht Frau Schulz, wenn sie Ferien hat? s2: Wenn Frau Schulz Ferien hat, fliegt sie nach Deutschland. s1: Und du? s2: Wenn ich Ferien habe, _____. 7. s1: Was macht Hans, wenn er Angst hat? s2: Wenn Hans Angst hat, ruft er „Mama, Mama". s1: Und du? s2: Wenn ich Angst habe, _____. 8. s1: Was macht Stefan, wenn er krank ist? s2: Wenn Stefan krank ist, geht er zum Arzt. s1: Und du? s2: Wenn ich krank bin, _____. **Übung 10:** 1. Jürgen ist wütend, weil er immer so früh aufstehen muss. 2. Silvia ist froh, weil sie heute nicht arbeiten muss. 3. Claire ist in Eile, weil sie noch einkaufen muss. 4. Josef ist traurig, weil Melanie ihn nicht anruft. 5. Thomas geht nicht zu Fuß, weil seine Freundin ihn zur Uni mitnimmt. 6. Willi hat selten Langeweile, weil er immer fernsieht. 7. Marta hat Angst vor Wasser, weil sie nicht schwimmen kann. 8. Mehmet fährt in die Türkei, weil er seine Eltern besuchen will.

Kapitel 4

Übung 1: a. hat b. ist c. hat d. hat e. ist f. sind g. ist h. hat i. hat **Fragen:** 1. Rosemarie ist um 7 Uhr aufgestanden. 2. Sie sind zur Schule gegangen. 3. Frau Dehne ist die Lehrerin. 4. Sie hat „Herzlich Willkommen" an die Tafel geschrieben. **Übung 2:** a. haben b. sind c. haben d. sind e. sind f. haben g. haben h. sind i. haben j. sind **Fragen:** 1. Josef und Melanie sind mit dem Taxi zum Bahnhof gefahren. 2. Sie sind um 5.30 mit dem Zug abgefahren. 3. Sie haben im Speisewagen gefrühstückt. 4. Nachts sind sie in den Schlafwagen gegangen und haben schlecht geschlafen. **Übung 3:** a. aufgestanden b. geduscht c. gefrühstückt d. gegangen e. gehört f. getroffen g. getrunken h. gearbeitet i. gegessen **Übung 4:** 1. Hast du schon gefrühstückt? 2. Bist du schon geschwommen? 3. Hast du schon eine Geschichte gelesen? 4. Hast du schon Klavier gespielt? 5. Hast du schon geschlafen? 6. Hast du schon gegessen? 7. Hast du schon Geschirr gespült? 8. Hast du den Brief schon geschrieben? 9. Bist du schon ins Bett gegangen? **Übung 5:** 1. Katrin hat bis 9 Uhr im Bett gelegen. 2. Sie hat einen Rock getragen. 3. Sie hat mit Frau Schulz gesprochen. 4. Sie hat ein Referat gehalten. 5. Sie hat Freunde getroffen. 6. Sie hat gearbeitet. 7. Es hat geregnet. 8. Sie ist nach Hause gekommen. 9. Sie hat ihre Wäsche gewaschen. 10. Sie ist abends zu Hause geblieben. **Übung 6:** 1. (*Answers will vary.*) 2. (*Answers will vary.*) 3. Am fünfundzwanzigsten Dezember. 4. (*Answers will vary according to country.*) 5. Am ersten Januar. 6. Am vierzehnten Februar. 7. (*Answers will vary.*) 8. (*Answers will vary.*) 9. (*Answers will vary according to country.*) 10. (*Answers will vary according to country.*) **Übung 7:** a. im b. im c. — d. am e. Am f. um g. um h. Am i. im j. am **Übung 8:** (*Answers will vary.*) **Übung 9:** A: 1. R 2. F 3. R 4. R 5. R

B: Partizipien mit ge-:

aufgestanden	aufstehen
gehört	hören
gegangen	gehen
gekocht	kochen
gefahren	fahren
geparkt	parken
zurückgekommen	zurückkommen
gewaschen	waschen
aufgeräumt	aufräumen
gefallen	fallen
eingelaufen	einlaufen
abgebrannt	abbrennen

Partizipien ohne ge-:

verschlafen	verschlafen
bekommen	bekommen
bezahlt	bezahlen
zerbrochen	zerbrechen

Übung 10: a. ist ... angekommen b. hat ... begrüßt c. getrunken d. ist ... gegangen e. hat ... geschlafen f. ist ... gegangen g. haben ... gefragt h. hat ... gesprochen i. haben ... getrunken j. sind ... gegangen **Übung 11:** (*Answers will vary.*) 1. —Bist du gestern früh aufgestanden? —Ja. —Wann? —Um 6 Uhr. 2. —Hast du gestern jemanden fotografiert? —Ja. —Wen? —Jane. 3. —Hast du gestern jemanden besucht? —Ja. —Wen? —Alan. 4. —Bist du gestern ausgegangen? —Ja. —Wohin? —Ins Kino. 5. —Hast du gestern etwas bezahlt? —Ja. —Was? —Die Rechnung. 6. —Hast du gestern etwas repariert? —Ja. —Was? —Mein Auto. 7. —Hast du gestern etwas Neues probiert? —Ja. —Was? —Segeln. 8. —Hast du gestern ferngesehen? —Ja. —Wie lange? —Eine Stunde. 9. —Hast du gestern etwas nicht verstanden? —Ja. —Was? —Sophies Referat. 10. —Hast du gestern dein Zimmer aufgeräumt? —Ja. —Wann? —Um 4 Uhr.

Kapitel 5

Übung 1: (*Answers will vary.*) Ich backe meiner Tante einen Kuchen. Ich erkläre meinem Partner einen Witz. Ich erzähle meiner Kusine ein Geheimnis. Ich gebe meinem Freund einen Kuss. Ich kaufe meinem Vater eine Krawatte. Ich koche meiner Mitbewohnerin Kaffee. Ich leihe meinem Bruder fünfzig Dollar. Ich schenke meiner Großmutter ein Buch. Ich schreibe meiner Mutter einen Brief. Ich verkaufe meinem Mitbewohner mein Deutschbuch. **Übung 2:** (*Answers will vary.*) Heidi erklärt ihrer Freundin die Grammatik. Peter erzählt seinem Vetter ein Geheimnis. Thomas gibt seiner Mutter ein Armband. Katrin kauft ihrem Mann einen Rucksack. Stefan kocht seinem Freund eine Suppe. Albert leiht seinen Eltern einen

Regenschirm. Monika schenkt ihrer Schwester einen Bikini. Frau Schulz schreibt ihrer Tante eine Karte. Nora verkauft ihrem Professor ein Zelt. **Übung 3:** 1. Wer 2. Wen 3. Wem 4. Wen 5. Wem 6. wer **Übung 4:** 1. Was passiert am Abend? d. Es wird dunkel. 2. Was passiert, wenn man Bücher schreibt? b. Man wird bekannt. 3. Was passiert, wenn man krank wird? h. Man bekommt Fieber. 4. Was passiert im Frühling? i. Die Tage werden länger. 5. Was passiert im Herbst? c. Die Blätter werden bunt. 6. Was passiert, wenn Kinder älter werden? e. Sie werden größer. 7. Was passiert, wenn man in der Lotterie gewinnt? j. Man wird reich. 8. Was passiert, wenn man Medizin studiert? a. Man wird Arzt. 9. Was passiert am Morgen? g. Es wird hell. 10. Was passiert im Sommer? f. Es wird wärmer. **Übung 5:** 1. Vielleicht wird sie Köchin. 2. Vielleicht wird sie Apothekerin. 3. Vielleicht wird er Pilot. 4. Vielleicht wird er Lehrer. 5. Vielleicht wird sie Architektin. 6. Vielleicht wird sie Bibliothekarin. 7. Vielleicht wird er Krankenpfleger. 8. Vielleicht wird sie Dirigentin. **Übung 6:** 1. Was macht man im Kino? Man sieht einen Film. 2. Was macht man auf der Post? Man kauft Briefmarken. 3. Was macht man an der Tankstelle? Man tankt Benzin. 4. Was macht man in der Disko? Man tanzt. 5. Was macht man in der Kirche? Man betet. 6. Was macht man auf der Bank? Man wechselt Geld. 7. Was macht man im Meer? Man schwimmt. 8. Was macht man in der Bibliothek? Man liest ein Buch. 9. Was macht man im Park? Man geht spazieren. **Übung 7:** 1. Monika ist in der Kirche. 2. Albert ist im Meer. 3. Heidi ist auf der Polizei. 4. Nora ist in einem Hotel. 5. Katrin ist im Schwimmbad. 6. Thomas ist auf der Post. 7. Frau Schulz ist in der Küche. 8. Das Poster ist an der Wand. 9. Der Topf ist auf dem Herd. 10. Der Wein ist im Kühlschrank. **Übung 8:** 1. mir 2. dir 3. euch 4. Ihnen 5. uns **Übung 9:** 1. Er hat ihr einen Regenschirm geschenkt. 2. Sie hat ihm ihr Auto geliehen. 3. Er hat ihm 500 Euro geliehen. 4. Sie hat ihr ein Geheimnis erzählt. 5. Er hat ihnen eine Geschichte erzählt. 6. Sie hat ihr ihre Sonnenbrille verkauft. 7. Er hat ihnen seinen Fernseher verkauft. 8. Sie hat ihm ihr Büro gezeigt. 9. Er hat ihm seine Wohnung gezeigt. 10. Sie hat ihr eine neue Brille gekauft. 11. Er hat ihr einen Kinderwagen gekauft.

Kapitel 6

Übung 1: 1. gefällt 2. gratuliere 3. helfen 4. Schmeckt 5. passt 6. gehört 7. Fehlt 8. begegnet 9. schadet 10. zugehört **Übung 2:** (*Answers will vary.*) **Übung 3:** (*Answers may vary.*) 1. Albert ist unter der Dusche. 2. Der Spiegel hängt an der Wand. 3. Der Kühlschrank steht neben dem Fernseher. 4. Das Deutschbuch liegt im Kühlschrank. 5. Die Lampe hängt über dem Tisch. 6. Der Computer steht auf dem Schreibtisch. 7. Die Schuhe liegen auf dem Bett. 8. Die Hose liegt auf dem Tisch. 9. Das Poster von Berlin hängt über dem Fernseher. 10. Die Katze liegt unter dem Bett. **Übung 4:** (*Answers will vary.*) **Übung 5:** (*Answers may vary*). 1. Ich bin heute Abend in der Bibliothek. 2. Ich bin am Nachmittag in der Mensa. 3. Ich bin um 16 Uhr bei Freunden. 4. Ich bin in der Nacht im Bett. 5. Ich bin am frühen Morgen am Frühstückstisch. 6. Ich bin am Montag in der Klasse. 7. Ich bin am 1. August im Urlaub. 8. Ich bin an Weihnachten auf einer Party. 9. Ich bin im Winter bei meinen Eltern. 10. Ich bin am Wochenende auf einer Party. **Übung 6:** 1. Er geht zum Arzt. 2. Er geht zum Fußballplatz. 3. Sie geht ins Hotel. 4. Er fährt zur Tankstelle. 5. Er geht in den Supermarkt. 6. Er geht auf die Post. 7. Sie gehen in den Wald. 8. Sie geht zu ihrem Freund. 9. Er fährt zum Flughafen. 10. Sie geht ins Theater. 11. Sie geht in die Schule. **Übung 7:** 1. aufstehst 2.a. mache b. aus c. fernsiehst 3.a. kommt b. an 4.a. zieht b. um 5. einladen 6.a. räumt b. auf 7.a. mitkommen b. mitnimmst 8.a. rufst b. an **Übung 8:** Andrea hat ferngesehen. Katrin und Peter sind ausgegangen. Heidi hat Frau Schulz angerufen. Herr Ruf hat das Geschirr abgetrocknet. Jürgen ist ausgezogen. Jutta hat ihr Abendkleid angezogen. Maria ist aus Bulgarien zurückgekommen. Herr Thelen ist aufgewacht. **Übung 9:** 1. Womit kochst du Kaffee? Mit der Kaffeemaschine. 2. Womit saugst du Staub? Mit dem Staubsauger. 3. Womit fegst du den Boden? Mit dem Besen. 4. Womit bügelst du? Mit dem Bügeleisen. 5. Womit tippst du einen Brief? Mit dem Computer. 6. Womit gießt du die Blumen im Garten? Mit dem Gartenschlauch. 7. Womit wischst du den Boden? Mit dem Putzlappen. 8. Womit gießt du die Blumen in der Wohnung? Mit der Gießkanne. **Übung 10:** 1.a. mit b. mit c. Mit d. bei 2.a. bei b. mit c. bei d. mit 3.a. mit b. mit c. bei.

Kapitel 7

Übung 1: (*Answers will vary.*) 1. Ich mag Leute, die laut lachen. 2. Ich mag keine Leute, die viel sprechen. 3. Ich mag eine Stadt, die Spaß macht. 4. Ich mag keine Stadt, die langweilig ist. 5. Ich mag einen Mann, der gern verreist. 6. Ich mag keinen Mann, der interessant aussieht. 7. Ich mag eine Frau, die nett ist. 8. Ich mag keine Frau, die betrunken ist. 9. Ich mag einen Urlaub, der exotisch ist. 10. Ich mag ein Auto, das schnell fährt. **Übung 2:** 1. Europa → Wie heißt der Kontinent, der eigentlich eine Halbinsel von Asien ist? 2. Mississippi → Wie heißt der Fluss, von dem Mark Twain erzählt? 3. San Francisco → Wie heißt die Stadt, die an einer Bucht liegt? 4. die Alpen → Wie heißen die Berge, in denen man sehr gut Ski fahren kann? 5. Washington → Wie heißt der Staat in den USA, dem ein Präsident seinen Namen gegeben hat? 6. das Tal des Todes → Wie heißt das Tal, in dem es sehr heiß ist? 7. Ellis → Wie heißt die Insel, die man von New York sieht? 8. der Pazifik → Wie heißt das Meer, über das man nach Hawaii fliegt? 9. die Sahara → Wie heißt die Wüste, die man aus vielen Filmen kennt? 10. der Große Salzsee → Wie heißt der See in Utah, auf dem man segeln kann? **Übung 3:** 1. Berlin ist größer als Zürich. 2. München ist älter als San Francisco. 3. Athen ist wärmer als Hamburg. 4. Der Mount Everest ist höher als das Matterhorn. 5. Der Mississippi ist länger als der Rhein. 6. Liechtenstein ist kleiner als die Schweiz. 7. Leipzig ist kälter als Kairo. 8. Ein Fernseher ist billiger als eine Waschmaschine. 9. Schnaps ist stärker als Bier. 10. Ein Haus auf dem Land ist schöner als ein Haus in der Stadt. (*oder* Ein Haus in der Stadt ist schöner als ein Haus auf dem Land.) 11. Zehn Euro sind mehr als zehn Cent. 12. Ein Appartement ist teurer als eine Wohnung in einem Studentenheim. 13. Ein Motorrad ist schneller als ein Fahrrad. 14. Ein Sofa ist schwerer als ein Stuhl. 15. Bier ist besser als Milch. (*oder* Milch ist besser als Bier.) **Übung 4:** 1. Heidi ist schwerer als Monika. 2. Thomas und Stefan sind am schwersten. 3. Thomas ist besser in Deutsch als Stefan. 4. Heidi ist in Deutsch am besten. 5. Heidi ist kleiner als Stefan. 6. Monika ist am kleinsten. 7. Stefan ist jünger als Thomas. 8. Stefan ist am jüngsten. 9. Thomas' Haare sind länger als Heidis. 10. Monikas Haare sind am längsten. 11. Heidis Haare sind kürzer als Monikas. 12. Stefans Haare sind am kürzesten. 13. Monika ist schlechter in Deutsch als Heidi. 14. Stefan ist in Deutsch am schlechtesten. **Übung 5:** 1. In Athen ist es am heißesten. 2. In Moskau ist es am kältesten. 3. Monaco ist am kleinsten. 4. Frankreich ist am ältesten. 5. Südafrika ist am jüngsten. 6. Der Nil ist am längsten. 7. Frankfurt liegt am nördlichsten. 8. Der Mount Everest ist am höchsten. 9. Deutschland ist am größten. **Übung 6:** a. darauf b. daneben c. Dazwischen d. Darin e. Davor/daneben f. darüber g. Daran h. Darunter i. dahinter **Übung 7:** 1. Mit wem gehen Sie am liebsten ins Theater? 2. Worauf freuen Sie sich meistens? 3. Auf wen müssen Sie immer warten? 4. Über wen haben Sie sich in letzter Zeit geärgert? 5. Woran denken Sie, wenn Sie „USA" hören? 6. Womit fahren Sie zur Schule? 7. Worüber schreiben Sie nicht gern? 8. An wen haben Sie Ihren letzten Brief geschrieben? 9. Von wem halten Sie nicht viel? **Übung 8:** 1. bin 2.a. hat b. bin 3.a. habe b. bin 4. bin 5. bin 6.a. habe b. bin 7.a. habe b. ist 8.a. haben b. ist 9.a. ist/sind b. hat **Übung 9:** 1. Ich habe schon Frühstück gemacht. 2. Ich habe meine Milch schon getrunken. 3. Ich habe den Tisch schon sauber gemacht. 4. Ich bin schon zum Bäcker gelaufen. 5. Ich habe schon Brötchen mitgebracht. 6. Ich habe schon Geld mitgenommen. 7. Ich habe den Hund schon gefüttert. 8. Ich habe die Tür schon zugemacht. **Übung 10:** 1.a. Hatten b. hatte 2. Waren 3.a. wart b. hatten 4.a. Warst b. war 5. hatte 6. hattest 7.a. Warst b. war c. hatte.

Kapitel 8

Übung 1: (*Answers will vary.*) 1. Amerikanisches Steak! 2. Russischer Kaviar! 3. Griechische Oliven! 4. Japanisches Sushi! 5. Französischer Champagner! 6. Deutsche Wurst! 7. Dänischer Käse! 8. Italienische Spaghetti! 9. Ungarischer Paprika! 10. Englische Marmelade! 11. Kolumbianischer Kaffee! 12. Neuseeländische Kiwis! **Übung 2:** 1. Ich esse nur deutsches Brot. 2. Ich esse nur russischen Kaviar. 3. Ich esse nur italienische Salami. 4. Ich trinke nur kolumbianischen Kaffee. 5. Ich esse nur neuseeländische Kiwis. 6. Ich trinke nur französischen Wein. 7. Ich trinke nur belgisches Bier. 8. Ich esse nur spanische Muscheln. 9. Ich esse nur englische Marmelade. 10. Ich esse nur japanischen Thunfisch. **Übung 3:** 1. Michael:

Ich möchte den grauen Wintermantel da. Maria: Nein, der graue Wintermantel ist viel zu schwer. 2. Michael: Ich möchte die gelbe Hose da. Maria: Nein, die gelbe Hose ist viel zu bunt. 3. Michael: Ich möchte das schicke Hemd da. Maria: Nein, das schicke Hemd ist viel zu teuer. 4. Michael: Ich möchte die roten Socken da. Maria: Nein, die roten Socken sind viel zu warm. 5. Michael: Ich möchte den schwarzen Schlafanzug da. Maria: Nein, der schwarze Schlafanzug ist viel zu dünn. 6. Michael: Ich möchte die grünen Schuhe da. Maria: Nein, die grünen Schuhe sind viel zu groß. 7. Michael: Ich möchte den modischen Hut da. Maria: Nein, der modische Hut ist viel zu klein. 8. Michael: Ich möchte die schwarzen Winterstiefel da. Maria: Nein, die schwarzen Winterstiefel sind viel zu leicht. 9. Michael: Ich möchte die elegante Sonnenbrille da. Maria: Nein, die elegante Sonnenbrille ist viel zu bunt. 10. Michael: Ich möchte die roten Tennisschuhe da. Maria: Nein, die roten Tennisschuhe sind viel zu grell. **Übung 4:** 1.a. Ihr neues Auto b. der alte Mercedes c. keinen neuen Wagen 2.a. der italienische Wein b. eine weitere Flasche 3.a. mein kaputtes Fahrrad b. meinen blöden Computer c. kein freies Wochenende **Übung 5:** 1. den 2.a. den b. dem 3.a. dem b. das 4. der 5.a. den b, den 6.a. ins b. im c. am 7.a. dich b. dich 8.a. den b. dem 9. der **Übung 6:** 1. Die Teller stehen im Küchenschrank. 2. Albert stellt die Teller auf den Tisch. 3. Die Servietten liegen in der Schublade. 4. Monika legt die Servietten auf den Tisch. 5. Messer und Gabeln liegen in der Schublade. 6. Stefan legt Messer und Gabeln auf den Tisch. 7. Die Kerze steht auf dem Schrank. 8. Heidi stellt die Kerze auf den Tisch. 9. Thomas sitzt auf dem Sofa. **Übung 7:** 1. Jutta leiht ihrem neuen Freund ihre Lieblings-CD. 2. Jens verkauft dem kleinen Bruder von Jutta eine Ratte. 3. Hans zeigt die Ratte nur seinen besten Freunden. 4. Jutta schenkt ihrer besten Freundin ein Buch. 5. Jens kauft seinem wütenden Lehrer eine Krawatte. 6. Ernst erzählt seiner großen Schwester einen Witz. 7. Jutta kocht den netten Leuten von nebenan Kaffee. 8. Ernst gibt dem süßen Baby von nebenan einen Kuss. **Übung 8:** (*Answers and sequence will vary.*) 1. Ich werde weniger fernsehen. 2. Ich werde mehr lernen. 3. Ich werde weniger oft ins Kino gehen. 4. Ich werde früher ins Bett gehen. 5. Ich werde mehr arbeiten. 6. Ich werde öfter selbst kochen. **Übung 9:** (*Answers may vary.*) 1. Frau Schulz repariert morgen das Auto. 2. Heidi fährt morgen aufs Land. 3. Peter spielt morgen Fußball. 4. Monika schreibt morgen einen Brief. 5. Stefan geht morgen einkaufen. 6. Nora heiratet morgen. 7. Albert geht morgen in den Supermarkt. 8. Thomas räumt morgen sein Zimmer auf. **Übung 10:** (*Answers will vary.*)

Kapitel 9

Übung 1: (*Answers will vary.*) **Übung 2:** (*Answers will vary*). 1. Ich durfte nicht. 2. Ich wollte nicht. 3. Das wusste ich nicht. 4. Ich wollte eine. 5. Ich sollte das nicht. **Übung 3:** 1.a. wolltest b. wusste 2.a. durfte b. musste c. wollten d. konnten 3.a. konnte b. musste c. wusste d. wollte **Übung 4:** 1.a. Wann b. Wenn 2.a. wann b. Als 3. als 4.a. Wann b. als 5.a. Wann b. Wenn 6.a. Wann b. Als **Übung 5:** a. wenn b. Als c. Wenn d. wenn e. Als f. Als g. Wann h. Als i. wenn **Übung 6:** a. standen b. gingen c. fuhren d. kamen e. hielten f. aßen g. schwammen h. schliefen i. sprangen **Übung 7:** 1. wohnte 2. brachten 3. schliefen 4. liefen 5. kamen 6. sahen, saß 6. gab, fanden 7. trug, schloss 8. tötete, rannte **Übung 8:** 1. Nachdem Jutta den Schlüssel verloren hatte, kletterte sie durch das Fenster. 2. Nachdem Ernst die Fensterscheibe eingeworfen hatte, lief er weg. 3. Nachdem Claire angekommen war, rief sie Melanie an. 4. Nachdem Hans seine Hausaufgaben gemacht hatte, ging er ins Bett. 5. Nachdem Jens sein Fahrrad repariert hatte, machte er eine Radtour. 6. Nachdem Michael die Seiltänzerin gesehen hatte, war er ganz verliebt. 7. Nachdem Richard ein ganzes Jahr gespart hatte, flog er nach Australien. 8. Nachdem Silvia zwei Semester allein gewohnt hatte, zog sie in eine WG. 9. Nachdem Willi ein Geräusch gehört hatte, rief er den Großvater an.

Kapitel 10

Übung 1: 1. b. 2. a. 3. h. 4. g. 5. c. 6. d. 7. i. 8. j. 9. f. 10. e. **Übung 2:** 1. Nach Kopenhagen. 2. Zum Strand. 3. Zu ihrer Tante Sule. 4. Aus der Türkei. 5. Nein, aus dem Iran. 6. Aus dem Wasser. 7. Vom Markt. 8. Ja, bei uns. 9. Bei Fatimas Tante. 10. Nach Hause. **Übung 3:** (*Answers will vary.*) 1. Ja, üb jetzt Klavier. Du hast morgen Klavierstunde. (*oder* Nein, üb jetzt

nicht Klavier. Wir gehen gleich aus.) 2. Ja, ruf ihn an. Er wollte mit dir sprechen. (*oder* Nein, ruf ihn nicht an. Du musst deine Hausaufgaben machen.) 3. Ja, iss sie mal. Du hast heute noch keine Süßigkeiten gegessen. (*oder* Nein, iss sie nicht. Wir essen gleich zu Abend.) 4. Ja, mach es auf. Die Luft ist hier schlecht. (*oder* Nein, mach es nicht auf. Es ist draußen zu kalt.) 5. Ja, gib mir einen Kuss. Ich fahre weg. (*oder* Nein, gib mir keinen Kuss. Du hast gerade Schokolade auf den Lippen.) 6. Ja, rede doch mal mit mir. Du hast wohl etwas zu erklären. (*oder* Nein, rede im Moment nicht mit mir. Ich bin beschäftigt.) 7. Ja, spül bitte das Geschirr. Ich bin nicht dazu gekommen. (*oder* Nein, spül das Geschirr nicht. Ich mache es nachher.) 8. Ja, geh mal in den Garten. Du brauchst die frische Luft. (*oder* Nein, geh nicht in den Garten. Es regnet.) 9. Ja, fahr mal morgen mit dem Fahrrad in die Schule. Ich kann dich mit dem Auto nicht hinbringen. (*oder* Nein, fahr morgen nicht mit dem Fahrrad in die Schule. Ich bringe dich mit dem Auto hin.) **Übung 4:** 1. Jens und Ernst, seid nicht so laut! 2. Maria, halte bitte an der nächsten Ampel! 3. Uli, bieg an der nächsten Straße nach links ab! 4. Jutta, iss mehr Obst! 5. Herr Pusch, fahren Sie nicht so schnell! 6. Jens, warte an der Ecke auf mich! 7. Natalie und Rosemarie, seid nicht ungeduldig! 8. Andrea und Paula, grüßt euren Vater von mir! 9. Hans, lauf mal schnell zu Papa! 10. Helga und Sigrid, lest jeden Tag die Zeitung! **Übung 5:** 1. Mach 2. Sprechen Sie 3. warten Sie 4. vergiss 5. Helft **Übung 6:** (*Answers may vary.*) 1. Fahren Sie den Fluss entlang. 2. Gehen Sie über die Brücke. 3. Gehen Sie an der Kirche vorbei. 4. Fahren Sie bis zum Bahnhof und dann links. 5. Die Tankstelle ist gegenüber von der Post. 6. Gehen Sie über die Schienen. 7. Ja, bis zur Bismarckstraße und dann rechts. 8. Nein, gehen Sie am Rathaus vorbei und dann links. 9. Das Hotel „Zum Patrizier" ist gegenüber vom Rathaus. 10. Fahren Sie 10 km die Straße entlang. **Übung 7:** (*Answers will vary.*) **Übung 8:** 1. Müsstest du nicht noch tanken? 2. Sollten wir nicht Jens abholen? 3. Könnten zwei Freunde von mir auch mitfahren? 4. Sollten wir nicht zuerst in die Stadt fahren? 5. Wolltest du nicht zur Bank? 6. Könntest du etwas langsamer fahren? 7. Dürfte ich das Autoradio anmachen? 8. Dürfte ich das Fenster aufmachen? **Übung 9:** 1. vor 50 000 Jahren → Wann wurde Australien von den Aborigines besiedelt? 2. um 2500 v. Chr. → Wann wurden die ersten Pyramiden gebaut? 3. 44 v. Chr. → Wann wurde Cäsar ermordet? 4. 800 n. Chr. → Wann wurde Karl der Große zum Kaiser gekrönt? 5. 1088 → Wann wurde die erste Universität (Bologna) gegründet? 6. 1789 → Wann wurde die amerikanische Verfassung unterschrieben? 7. 1885 → Wann wurde in Kanada die transkontinentale Eisenbahn vollendet? 8. 1945 → Wann wurden die Atombomben auf Hiroshima und Nagasaki geworfen? 9. 1963 → Wann wurde John F. Kennedy erschossen? 10. 1990 → Wann wurde Deutschland vereinigt? **Übung 10:** 1. Mäuse werden in vielen Labortests benutzt. 2. Meerschweinchen werden oft als Haustiere gehalten. 3. Bienen werden wegen ihrer Honigproduktion geschätzt. 4. Mücken werden durch Parfum und Kosmetikprodukte angelockt. 5. Die Fledermaus wird in vielen Kulturen mit Vampiren assoziiert. 6. Schnecken werden oft mit Butter- und Knoblauchsoße gegessen. 7. Der Gepard wird immer noch für seinen Pelz getötet. 8. Die meisten Papageien werden in der Wildnis gefangen. 9. Delfine werden wegen ihrer Intelligenz bewundert. 10. Viele Haie werden jedes Jahr gefischt.

Kapitel 11

Übung 1: 1.a. fühle mich b. mich erkältet c. dich ... legen 2.a. sich ... aufgeregt b. sich ... ausruhen 3.a. dich verletzt b. mich ... geschnitten 4.a. ärgerst ... dich b. dich freuen **Übung 2:** (*Answers will vary.*) Erst stehe ich auf. Dann dusche ich mich. Dann wasche ich mir das Gesicht. Dann wasche ich mir die Haare. Dann trockne ich mich ab. Dann putze ich mir die Fingernägel. Dann rasiere ich mich. Dann kämme ich mir die Haare. Dann ziehe ich mich an. Dann frühstücke ich. Dann putze ich mir die Zähne und gehe zur Uni. **Übung 3:** (*Answers will vary.*) 1. Ich rasiere mich jeden Morgen. 2. Meine Oma schminkt sich zu sehr. 3. Mein Freund wäscht sich nicht oft genug die Haare. 4. Mein Vater putzt sich nach jeder Mahlzeit die Zähne. 5. Mein Onkel zieht sich immer verrückt an. 6. Meine Schwester duscht sich jeden Tag. 7. Meine Freundin kämmt sich nie. 8. Mein Bruder föhnt sich nie die Haare. 9. Meine Kusine badet sich nicht gern. 10. Meine Mutter zieht sich immer elegant an. **Übung 4:** 1. Ja, kannst du es mir geben? / Nein, ich brauche es nicht. 2. Ja, kannst du ihn mir geben? / Nein, ich brauche ihn nicht. 3. Ja, kannst du ihn mir geben? / Nein, ich brauche ihn nicht. 4. Ja, kannst du sie mir geben? / Nein, ich brauche sie nicht. 5. Ja, kannst du es mir geben? /Nein, ich brauche es nicht. 6. Ja, kannst du ihn mir geben? / Nein, ich brauche ihn nicht. 7. Ja, kannst du sie mir geben? / Nein, ich brauche sie nicht. 8. Ja, kannst du es mir geben? / Nein, ich brauche es nicht. 9. Ja, kannst du ihn mir geben? / Nein, ich brauche ihn nicht. **Übung 5:** 1. Warum schneidest du ihn dir nicht? 2. Warum wäschst du sie dir nicht? 3. Warum schneidest du sie dir nicht? 4. Warum cremst du sie dir nicht ein? 5. Warum föhnst du sie dir nicht? 6. Warum wäschst du ihn dir nicht? 7. Warum putzt du sie dir nicht? 8. Warum lässt du sie dir nicht schneiden? 9. Warum cremst du es dir nicht ein? 10. Warum wäschst du sie dir nicht? **Übung 6:** (*Some answers will vary.*) 1. Wissen Sie, was hier passiert ist? (*oder* Können Sie mir sagen, was hier passiert ist?) 2. Wissen Sie, ob das Kind das Auto gesehen hat? (*oder* Können Sie mir sagen, ob das Kind das Auto gesehen hat?) 3. Wissen Sie, wer daran Schuld war? (*oder* Können Sie mir sagen, wer daran Schuld war?) 4. Wissen Sie, warum Herr Langen das Kind nicht gesehen hat? (*oder* Können Sie mir sagen, warum Herr Langen das Kind nicht gesehen hat?) 5. Wissen Sie, ob Herr Langen gebremst hat? (*oder* Können Sie mir sagen, ob Herr Langen gebremst hat?) 6. Wissen Sie, wann er gebremst hat? (*oder* Können Sie mir sagen, wann er gebremst hat?) 7. Wissen Sie, wie oft Herr Langen diese Straße zur Arbeit fährt? (*oder* Können Sie mir sagen, wie oft Herr Langen diese Straße zur Arbeit fährt?) 8. Wissen Sie, wie lange Lothar auf der Straße lag? (*oder* Können Sie mir sagen, wie lange Lothar auf der Straße lag?) 9. Wissen Sie, wann die Polizei Lothars Mutter angerufen hat? (*oder* Können Sie mir sagen, wann die Polizei Lothars Mutter angerufen hat?) **Übung 7:** 1.a. ob b. dass c. Wenn 2.a. damit b. Weil **Übung 8:** 1.a. als b. nachdem 2. bevor 3. Während 4. obwohl

Kapitel 12

Übung 1: 1. meines 2. Ihrer 3. meiner 4. deiner 5. dieses 6. alten 7. ersten 8. neuen **Übung 2:** 1. Monika spricht über den Beruf ihrer Schwester. 2. Thomas spricht über das Bild seines Vaters. 3. Frau Schulz spricht über das Alter ihrer Nichten. 4. Stefan spricht über die Länge seines Studiums. 5. Albert spricht über die Sprache seiner Großeltern. 6. Nora spricht über die Kleidung ihres Freundes. 7. Thomas spricht über die Qualität des Leitungswassers in Berkeley. 8. Katrin spricht über die Situation der Frauen. **Übung 3:** 1. trotz 2. wegen 3. während 4. trotz 5. während 6. Wegen 7. statt 8. trotz **Übung 4:** (*Answers will vary.*) **Übung 5:** (*Answers will vary.*) **Übung 6:** 1. Um morgens munter zu sein, muss man früh ins Bett gehen. 2. Um die Professoren kennenzulernen, muss man in die Sprechstunde gehen. 3. Um die Mitstudenten kennenzulernen, muss man viel Gruppenarbeit machen. 4. Um am Wochenende nicht allein zu sein, muss man Leute einladen. 5. Um die Kurse zu bekommen, die man will, muss man sich so früh wie möglich einschreiben. 6. Um in vier Jahren fertig zu werden, muss man viel lernen und wenig Feste feiern. 7. Um nicht zu verhungern, muss man regelmäßig essen. 8. Um eine gute Note in Deutsch zu bekommen, muss man jeden Tag zum Unterricht kommen. **Übung 7:** (*Answers may vary.*) 1. Ich möchte immer hier leben, weil dieses Land das beste Land der Welt ist. 2. Ich möchte für ein paar Jahre in Deutschland leben, um richtig gut Deutsch zu lernen. 3. Ausländer haben oft Probleme, weil sie die Sprache und Kultur des Gastlandes nicht verstehen. 4. Wenn ich Kinder habe, möchte ich hier leben, damit meine Kinder als (Amerikaner, Kanadier, Australier usw.) aufwachsen. 5. Viele Ausländer kommen hierher, weil man hier gut Geld verdienen kann. 6. Englisch sollte die einzige offizielle Sprache (der USA, Kanadas, Australiens usw.) sein, damit aus der multikulturellen Bevölkerung eine homogene Gemeinschaft wird. **Übung 8:** 1. Nom, F 2. Nom, V 3. Gen, F 4. Dat, F 5. Nom, F 6. Dat, V 7. Akk, P 8. Akk, P 9. Akk, F 10. Dat, P 11. Dat, V 12. Gen, P **Übung 9:** 1. em 2. en 3. e 4. er 5. e 6. er 7. e 8. en 9. ie 10. ie 11. en 12. e 13. en 14. en 15. er 16. em 17. en 18. em 19. er

Vokabeln

Deutsch-Englisch

Note to Students: The definitions in this vocabulary are based on the words as used in this text. For additional meanings, please refer to a dictionary.

Proper nouns are given only if the name is feminine or masculine or if the spelling is different from that in English. Compound words that do not appear in the chapter vocabulary lists have generally been omitted if they are easily analyzable and their constituent parts appear elsewhere in the vocabulary.

The letters or numbers in parentheses following the entries refer to the chapters in which the words occur in the chapter vocabulary lists.

ABBREVIATIONS

acc.	accusative	*gen.*	genitive	*p.p.*	past participle
adj.	adjective	*inf.*	infinitive	*prep.*	preposition
adv.	adverb	*infor.*	informal	*pron.*	pronoun
coll.	colloquial	*interj.*	interjection	*rel. pron.*	relative pronoun
coord. conj.	coordinating conjunction	*masc.*	masculine	*sg.*	singular
dat.	dative	*n.*	noun	*s.o.*	someone
def. art.	definite article	*neut.*	neuter	*s.th.*	something
dem. pron.	demonstrative pronoun	*nom.*	nominative	*subord. conj.*	subordinating conjunction
fem.	feminine	*o.s.*	oneself	*v.*	verb
for.	formal	*pl.*	plural	*wk.*	weak masculine noun

ab (+ *dat.*) from; as of, effective

ab·bauen, abgebaut to reduce

ab·biegen (biegt ... ab), bog ... ab, ist abgebogen to turn (10)

das **Abbild, -er** likeness

ab·brennen (brennt ... ab), brannte ... ab, ist abgebrannt to burn down

der **Abend, -e** evening (1, 4); **am Abend** in the evening (4); **gestern Abend** last night (4); **guten Abend** good evening (A); **heute Abend** this evening (2); **morgen Abend** tomorrow evening; **zu Abend essen** to dine, have dinner (4)

das **Abendessen, -** dinner, supper, evening meal (1); **zum Abendessen** for dinner

abends evenings, in the evening (4)

aber (*coord. conj.*) but (A, 11)

ab·fahren (fährt ... ab), fuhr ... ab, ist abgefahren to leave, depart (4)

die **Abfahrt, -en** departure (7)

ab·geben (gibt ... ab), gab ... ab, abgegeben to hand over (to); to deliver (to)

ab·holen, abgeholt to pick (*s.o./s.th.*) up (from a place) (1)

das **Abhörgerät, -e** listening device, bug

das **Abi** (*coll.*) = das **Abitur** high school graduation exam (4)

ab·kauen, abgekaut to chew off

ab·kommen (kommt ... ab), kam ... ab, ist abgekommen: vom Weg abkommen to leave the path, go off course

ab·lehnen, abgelehnt to reject

die **Ablehnung, -en** rejection

ab·lenken, abgelenkt to divert; to change / get off the subject

ab·nehmen (nimmt ... ab), nahm ... ab, abgenommen to remove (11); to lose weight (8, 11); **Blut abnehmen** to take blood (11)

ab·räumen, abgeräumt to clear (3); to remove; **den Tisch abräumen** to clear the table (3)

ab·rechnen, abgerechnet to tally up; to settle an account

ab·reisen, ist abgereist to depart (10)

ab·saugen, abgesaugt to vacuum

ab·schließen (schließt ... ab), schloss ... ab, abgeschlossen to lock (up)

abschließend in conclusion

der **Abschluss, ⸚e** completion; graduation (9)

die **Abschlusserklärung, -en** closing statement

ab·schneiden (schneidet ... ab), schnitt ... ab, abgeschnitten to cut off (8)

absolut absolute(ly)

die **Abstammung, -en** descent

abstrakt abstract(ly)

ab·stürzen, ist abgestürzt to crash (11)

ab·trocknen, abgetrocknet to dry (*dishes*) (6); **sich abtrocknen** to dry oneself off (11)

ab·waschen (wäscht ... ab), wusch ... ab, abgewaschen to wash (dishes)

ab·wischen, abgewischt to wipe clean (6)

ab·zahlen, abgezahlt to pay off (12)

ab·ziehen (zieht ... ab), zog ... ab, abgezogen to pull off; to withdraw (*troops*)

ach oh; **ach so** I see

die **Achse, -n** axis

acht eight (A)

acht- eighth (4)

achten (auf + *acc.*)**, geachtet** to watch out (for); to pay attention (to) (11)

die **Achterbahn, -en** roller coaster

achtundzwanzig twenty-eight (A)

die **Achtung** attention (7)

achtzehn eighteen (A)

achtzig eighty (A)

das **Adjektiv, -e** adjective

der **Adler, -** eagle (10)

die **Adresse, -n** address (1)

der **Adventskalender, -** Advent calendar

das **Adverb, -ien** adverb

der **Affe, -n** (*wk.*) monkey; ape

(das) **Afrika** Africa (B)

afro-deutsch Afro-German (*adj.*) (12)

aggressiv aggressive(ly)

ägyptisch Egyptian (*adj.*)

ähnlich similar(ly)

die Ahnung, -en idea; suspicion

die Akademie, -n academy

der Akademiker, - / **die Akademikerin, -nen** academic (*person*)

das Akkordeon, -s accordion (4)

die Akte, -n (document) file

die Aktie, -n share, stock (12)

die Aktion, -en action

aktiv active(ly)

die Aktivität, -en activity

aktuell current(ly); present-day

akzeptieren, akzeptiert to accept

der Albatros, -se albatross (10)

das Album, Alben album

der Alkohol alcohol

all all; **alle** (*pl.*) everybody; **alle zwei Jahre** every two years; **nichts von alledem** none of this; **vor allem** above all

die Allee, -n avenue

allein(e) alone; by oneself

alleinstehend single

allerdings however; of course

allergisch (gegen + acc.) allergic (to) (11)

allerliebst- most favorite

alles everything (2); **alles Mögliche** everything possible (2)

die Alliierten (*pl.*) the Allies

der Alltag, -e daily routine (4)

alltäglich everyday, daily

die Alpen (*pl.*) the Alps (7)

das Alphabet, -e alphabet (3)

als (*after comparative*) than; (*subord. conj.*) as; when (5, 11); **als ich acht Jahre alt war** when I was eight years old (5); **als ob** as if; as though; **als was?** as what? (5); **anders als** different from

also well; so; thus (4)

alt old (A)

der Altbau, -ten *building built before the end of World War II*

das Alter, - age (1)

alternativ alternative(ly)

die Alternative, -n alternative

der Altgeselle, -n (*wk.*) senior journeyman

die Altstadt, -̈e old part of town

am = an dem at/on the

(das) Amerika America, the USA (B)

der Amerikaner, - / **die Amerikanerin, -nen** American (*person*) (B)

amerikanisch American (*adj.*)

die Ampel, -n traffic light

der Amtsrichter, - / **die Amtsrichterin, -nen** local or district court judge

an (+ acc./dat.) at; on; to; in (2, 4); **am Abend** in the evening (4); **am Leben sein** to be alive (9); **am liebsten** (*like to do s.th.*) best (7); **am Samstag** on Saturday (2); **am Schalter** at the ticket booth (5); **am Telefon** on the phone (2);

am wenigsten the least (8); **am Wochenende** over the weekend (1); **an der Tankstelle** at the gas station (5); **an (+ dat.) ... vorbei** by (10); **an welchem Tag?** on what day? (4); **ans Meer** to the sea (2); **das Bild an die Wand hängen** to hang the picture on the wall (3)

analysieren, analysiert to analyze

die Ananas, - *or* **-se** pineapple

an·bauen, angebaut to grow, cultivate

an·bieten (bietet ... an), bot ... an, angeboten to offer

der Anblick, -e sight

an·braten (brät ... an), briet ... an, angebraten to brown, fry

an·bringen (bringt ... an), brachte ... an, angebracht to put up; to display

das Andenken, - souvenir (10)

ander- other; different; **anders** different(ly); **etwas anderes** something else; **unter anderem** among other things

(sich) ändern, geändert to change (9)

androgyn androgynous(ly)

die Anerkennung, -en acknowledgment, appreciation

der Anfang, -̈e beginning

an·fangen (fängt ... an), fing ... an, angefangen to begin (4)

an·fassen, angefasst to touch

an·führen, angeführt to lead

die Angabe, -n information

an·geben (gibt ... an), gab ... an, angegeben to state

angeblich alleged(ly)

das Angebot, -e offer; offering

an·gehören (+ dat.), angehört to belong to (*an organization*) (12)

angenehm pleasant(ly) (6)

angespannt tense

der/die Angestellte, -n (ein Angestellter) employee; clerk (7)

die Angst, -̈e fear (3); **Angst einjagen (+ dat.)** to scare; **Angst haben (vor + dat.)** to be afraid (of) (3)

sich (dat.) an·gucken, angeguckt (*coll.*) to look at

an·halten (hält ... an), hielt ... an, angehalten to stop (7)

sich (acc.) an·hören, angehört to sound; **das hört sich toll an** that sounds great (4)

sich (dat.) an·hören, angehört to listen to

an·klagen, angeklagt to accuse

an·kommen (kommt ... an), kam ... an, ist angekommen to arrive (1)

an·kreuzen, angekreuzt to mark with an X

die Ankunft, -̈e arrival (7)

an·legen, angelegt to put on; to aim

an·locken, angelockt to attract

an·machen, angemacht to turn on, switch on (3)

die Anmeldung, -en registration

an·nehmen (nimmt ... an), nahm ... an, angenommen to accept; to take; to adopt

die Annonce, -n advertisement

anonym anonymous(ly)

an·pöbeln, angepöbelt (*coll.*) to abuse

an·reden, angeredet to speak to; to address

der Anruf, -e phone call

an·rufen (ruft ... an), rief ... an, angerufen to call up (*on the telephone*) (1)

ans = an das to/on the

(sich) (dat.) an·schauen, angeschaut to look at (2); to watch

sich an·schließen (+ dat.) (schließt ... an), schloss ... an, angeschlossen to join; to follow

anschließend subsequent(ly)

der Anschluss, -̈e connection

an·schnallen, angeschnallt to strap in

(sich) (dat.) an·sehen (sieht ... an), sah ... an, angesehen to look at; to watch (3)

an·sprechen (spricht ... an), sprach ... an, angesprochen to speak to (*s.o.*)

anständig respectable, respectably

anstatt (+ gen.) instead of (12)

anstrengend strenuous; tiring

der Anteil, -e share

antiautoritär anti-authoritarian

das Antibiotikum, Antibiotika antibiotic (11)

die Antwort, -en answer (A)

antworten (+ dat.), geantwortet to answer (*s.o.*) (4, 10); **auf eine Frage antworten** to answer a question

der Anwalt, -̈e / **die Anwältin, -nen** lawyer (5)

an·werben (wirbt ... an), warb ... an, angeworben to recruit

die Anwerbung, -en recruitment

die Anzahl number

die Anzeige, -n ad (6)

an·ziehen (zieht ... an), zog ... an, angezogen to put on (*clothes*) (3); to attract; **sich anziehen** to get dressed (11)

der Anziehungspunkt, -e attraction

der Anzug, -̈e suit (A)

an·zünden, angezündet to light (3); to set on fire

der Apfel, -̈ apple

der Apfelsaft apple juice (8)

die Apfelschorle, -n mixture of apple juice and mineral water

die Apfelsine, -n orange (8)

die Apotheke, -n pharmacy (6)

der Apotheker, - / **die Apothekerin, -nen** pharmacist (11)

das Appartement, -s apartment

die Aprikose, -n apricot

der April April (B)

der Araber, - / **die Araberin, -nen** Arab

die Arabeske, -n arabesque

(das) Arabisch Arabic (*language*) (B)

die Arbeit, -en work (1); **sich an die Arbeit machen** to get down to work; **von der Arbeit** from work (3); **zur Arbeit gehen** to go to work (1)

arbeiten, gearbeitet to work (1); **Arbeiten Sie mit einem Partner.** Work with a partner. (A)

der Arbeiter, - / **die Arbeiterin, -nen** worker (5)

der **Arbeitnehmer**, - / die **Arbeitnehmerin**, -nen employee

das **Arbeitsbuch**, ⸚er workbook (3)

die **Arbeitserlaubnis**, -se work permit (12)

die **Arbeitskraft**, ⸚e labor; employee (12)

arbeitslos unemployed (12)

die **Arbeitslosigkeit** unemployment

die **Arbeitsteilung** division of labor

der **Architekt**, -en (*wk.*) / die **Architektin**, -nen architect (5)

die **Architektur**, -en architecture

der **Ärger** trouble (9); annoyance

ärgern, **geärgert** to annoy; to tease (3); **sich ärgern (über** + *acc.***)** to get angry (about) (11)

argwöhnisch suspicious

arm poor (9)

der **Arm**, -e arm (B); **jemanden auf den Arm nehmen** to tease someone; to pull someone's leg; **sich den Arm brechen** to break one's arm (11)

das **Armband**, ⸚er bracelet (2)

die **Armbanduhr**, -en (wrist)watch (A)

die **Arnika** arnica

die **Art**, -en kind, type (2)

der **Artikel**, - article

der **Arzt**, ⸚e / die **Ärztin**, -nen doctor; physician (3, 5, 11); **zum Arzt** to the doctor (3)

die **Arztpraxis**, **Arztpraxen** doctor's office (11)

(das) **Aschenputtel** Cinderella

(das) **Asien** Asia (B)

die **Asphaltschindel**, -n asphalt shingle

das **Aspirin** aspirin (11)

der **Assessor**, -en / die **Assessorin**, -nen assistant judge

die **Assoziation**, -en association

assoziieren (mit + *dat.***)**, **assoziiert** to associate (with)

der **Astrologe**, -n (*wk.*) / die **Astrologin**, -nen astrologer

die **Astrologie** astrology

das **Atelier**, -s studio

(das) **Athen** Athens

atmen, **geatmet** to breathe (11)

die **Atmosphäre**, -n atmosphere

die **Atombombe**, -n atomic bomb

die **Attraktion**, -en attraction

attraktiv attractive(ly) (6)

au oh

auch also; too; as well (A); **auch wenn** (*subord. conj.*) even if

auf (+ *dat./acc.*) on; upon; on top of; onto; to; at; **auf dem Bahnhof** at the train station (5); **auf dem Land** in the country (*rural*) (6); **auf der Uni(versität)** at the university (1, 5); **auf Deutsch** in German; **auf eine Party gehen** to go to a party (1); **auf jeden Fall** by all means (4); **auf Reisen sein** to be on a trip (7); **auf Wiederhören** good-bye (*on the telephone*) (6); **auf Wiedersehen** good-bye (A)

auf·begehren, **aufbegehrt** to rebel

auf·brausen, **ist aufgebraust** to surge up

auf·brechen (bricht ... auf), **brach ... auf**, **ist aufgebrochen** to set out; to start off

der **Aufenthalt**, -e stay

die **Aufenthaltserlaubnis**, -se residence permit (12)

die **Aufenthaltsgenehmigung**, -en residence permit

der **Aufenthaltsraum**, ⸚e lounge, recreation room (10)

auf·fallen (fällt ... auf), **fiel ... auf**, **ist aufgefallen** to be noticeable (12)

die **Aufforderung**, -en request; instruction

die **Aufgabe**, -n assignment (4); task; homework; job

auf·geben (gibt ... auf), **gab ... auf**, **aufgegeben** to give up; to hand in; to assign

aufgrund (+ *gen.*) on the basis of

auf·hängen, **aufgehängt** to hang up (8)

auf·hören (mit + *dat.***)**, **aufgehört** to stop (*doing s.th.*) (1); to be over

auf·laden (lädt ... auf), **lud ... auf**, **aufgeladen** to load; to charge

auf·leben, **ist aufgelebt** to revive

auf·machen, **aufgemacht** to open (3)

aufmerksam attentive(ly)

auf·muntern, **aufgemuntert** to cheer up

die **Aufnahmeprüfung**, -en entrance examination

auf·nehmen (nimmt ... auf), **nahm ... auf**, **aufgenommen** to pick up; to record; to take in; to take out (*a loan*) (12); **einen Kredit aufnehmen** to take out a loan

auf·passen (auf + *acc.***)**, **aufgepasst** to pay attention (to) (3); to watch out (for)

auf·räumen, **aufgeräumt** to clean (up) (1); to tidy up

sich **auf·regen**, **aufgeregt** to get excited; to get upset (11)

aufregend exciting

die **Aufregung** excitement; agitation

sich **auf·richten**, **aufgerichtet** to stand up; to get back up

auf·rufen (zu + *inf.***) (ruft ... auf)**, **rief ... auf**, **aufgerufen** to call on (*to do s.th*)

aufs = **auf das** on/onto/to the

auf·sagen, **aufgesagt** to recite

auf·saugen, **aufgesaugt** to vacuum

auf·schlagen (schlägt ... auf), **schlug ... auf**, **aufgeschlagen** to open

auf·schneiden (schneidet ... auf), **schnitt ... auf**, **aufgeschnitten** to chop; to cut open

der **Aufschnitt** cold cuts

auf·schreiben (schreibt ... auf), **schrieb ... auf**, **aufgeschrieben** to write down (11)

der **Aufschwung** upswing

auf·setzen, **aufgesetzt** to put on

auf·springen (springt ... auf), **sprang ... auf**, **ist aufgesprungen** to spring open

auf·stehen (steht ... auf), **stand ... auf**, **ist aufgestanden** to get up (1); to rise; to stand up; **mit dem linken Fuß aufstehen** to get up on the wrong side of bed (4); **stehen Sie auf** get up, stand up (A)

der **Auftrag**, ⸚e instruction; task; order

der **Auftritt**, -e appearance

auf·wachen, **ist aufgewacht** to wake up (4)

auf·wachsen (wächst ... auf), **wuchs ... auf**, **ist aufgewachsen** to grow up (12)

auf·wischen, **aufgewischt** to mop (up)

der **Aufzug**, ⸚e elevator (6)

das **Auge**, -n eye (B)

der **Augenarzt**, ⸚e / die **Augenärztin**, -nen eye doctor (11)

der **Augenblick**, -e moment

die **Augenfarbe**, -n color of eyes (1)

der **August** August (B)

aus (+ *dat.*) from; of; out of (10); **aus Stein** made (out) of stone

aus·blasen (bläst ... aus), **blies ... aus**, **ausgeblasen** to blow out

der **Ausblick**, -e view (6)

der **Ausdruck**, ⸚e expression

aus·drücken, **ausgedrückt** to express

aus·fallen (fällt ... aus), **fiel ... aus**, **ist ausgefallen** to fall out; to fail; to go out (*power*) (8)

das **Ausflugsziel**, -e destination of an excursion

aus·führen, **ausgeführt** to carry out, execute (12)

aus·füllen, **ausgefüllt** to fill out (1)

die **Ausgangslage**, -n starting position; initial situation

der **Ausgangspunkt**, -e starting point

aus·geben (gibt ... aus), **gab ... aus**, **ausgegeben** to spend (*money*) (12)

ausgebildet educated (12)

aus·gehen (geht ... aus), **ging ... aus**, **ist ausgegangen** to go out (1)

ausgezeichnet excellent(ly) (3)

sich **aus·hängen**, **ausgehängt** to become unfastened; to get uncoupled

das **Aushängeschild**, -er advertising sign

aus·koppeln, **ausgekoppelt** to uncouple

das **Ausland** foreign countries (6); **im Ausland** abroad (6)

der **Ausländer**, - / die **Ausländerin**, -nen foreigner (12)

ausländisch foreign (12)

das **Auslandsamt**, ⸚er center for study abroad (1)

aus·leeren, **ausgeleert** to empty (3)

aus·machen, **ausgemacht** to turn off (3)

aus·packen, **ausgepackt** to unpack

aus·probieren, **ausprobiert** to try out

aus·rauben, **ausgeraubt** to rob (completely)

ausreichend sufficient(ly)

die **Ausrichtung**, -en orientation; organization

der **Ausruf**, -e cry

sich **aus·ruhen**, **ausgeruht** to rest (11)

aus·rutschen, **ist ausgerutscht** to slip (11)

die **Aussage**, -n statement

aus·schließen (schließt ... aus), **schloss ... aus**, **ausgeschlossen** to exclude

der **Ausschnitt**, -e excerpt

aus·schreiben (schreibt ... aus), **schrieb ... aus**, **ausgeschrieben** to write out

das **Aussehen** appearance

aus·sehen (sieht ... aus), sah ... aus, ausgesehen to look (2); to appear; Es sieht gut aus. It looks good. (2)

der Außenminister, - / die Außenministerin, -nen foreign minister

die Außenwelt outside world

außer (+ dat.) except, besides

außerdem besides (3, 10)

das Äußere (ein Äußeres) outward appearance

außergewöhnlich unusual(ly)

außerhalb (+ gen.) outside of

aus·stellen, ausgestellt to exhibit

die Ausstellung, -en exhibition

aus·strecken, ausgestreckt to stretch out

aus·suchen, ausgesucht to choose; to pick out

der Austauschstudent, -en (wk.) / die Austauschstudentin, -nen exchange student

aus·tragen (trägt ... aus), trug ... aus, ausgetragen to deliver (5); Zeitungen austragen to deliver newspapers (5)

(das) Australien Australia (B)

der Australier, - / die Australierin, -nen Australian (person) (B)

aus·üben, ausgeübt to practice (12)

ausverkauft sold out (5)

aus·wandern, ist ausgewandert to emigrate (12)

der Ausweis, -e identification card (10)

aus·ziehen (zieht ... aus), zog ... aus, ausgezogen to take off (clothes) (3); sich ausziehen to get undressed (11)

das Auto, -s car (A); Auto fahren to drive (a car)

die Autobahn, -en freeway (7)

der Automat, -en (wk.) vending machine

automatisch automatic(ally)

die Autonummer, -n license plate number (11)

der Autor, -en / die Autorin, -nen author

das Autoradio, -s car radio (7)

das Baby, -s baby (7)

der Bachelor, -s bachelor's degree

backen (bäckt), backte, gebacken to bake (5)

der Backenbart, ⸚e sideburns

der Bäcker, - / die Bäckerin, -nen baker

die Bäckerei, -en bakery (5); in der Bäckerei at the bakery (5)

der Backofen, ⸚ oven (5)

das Bad, ⸚er bathroom; bath (6)

die Badehose, -n swim(ming) trunks (5)

der Bademantel, ⸚ bathrobe (2)

der Bademeister, - / die Bademeisterin, -nen swimming-pool attendant (5)

baden, gebadet to bathe (3, 11); to swim; sich baden to bathe (o.s.) (11)

baden-württembergisch of Baden-Württemberg (German state)

die Badewanne, -n bathtub (6)

das BAföG = das Bundesausbildungsförderungsgesetz financial aid for students from the German government

die Bahn, -en path, way; railroad (7)

der/die Bahnangestellte, -n (ein Bahnangestellter) train agent (10); railway employee

die Bahncard, -s discount card for rail travel in Germany

die Bahnfahrt, -en train trip (7)

der Bahnhof, ⸚e train station (4, 5); auf dem Bahnhof at the train station (5)

bald soon (9); bald darauf soon thereafter (9); bis bald so long; see you soon (A)

der Balkon, -e balcony (6)

der Ball, ⸚e ball (A, 1)

die Ballerina, -s ballerina (9)

der Ballettunterricht ballet class (9)

die Banane, -n banana (8)

die Band, -s band, music group

der Bandscheibenvorfall, ⸚e slipped disc

die Bank, ⸚e bench

die Bank, -en bank (5); auf der Bank at the bank (5); bei einer Bank at a bank (6)

der/die Bankangestellte, -n (ein Bankangestellter) bank employee (5)

der Bankeinzug, ⸚e automatic withdrawal; electronic transfer of funds

bar (in) cash

die Bar, -s bar

der Bär, -en (wk.) bear

das Bargeld cash (12)

bargeldlos cash-free (12)

das/der Barock (n.) baroque

der Bart, ⸚e beard (B)

der Baseball, ⸚e baseball

die Baseballmannschaft, -en baseball team (9)

(das) Basel Basel

basieren (auf + dat.), basiert to be based (on)

die Basis, Basen basis

das Baskenland Basque country

der Basketball, ⸚e basketball (2)

der Bass, ⸚e bass (guitar)

der Bauarbeiter, - / die Bauarbeiterin, -nen construction worker (5)

der Bauch, ⸚e belly, stomach (B)

bauen, gebaut to build

das Bauernbrot, -e (loaf of) farmer's bread (5)

das Bauernhaus, ⸚er farmhouse (6)

das Baujahr, -e year of construction

der Baum, ⸚e tree (9)

bayerisch Bavarian (adj.)

(das) Bayern Bavaria

bayrisch Bavarian (adj.)

der Beamer, - data projector (B)

der Beamte, -n (ein Beamter) / die Beamtin, -nen civil servant; official

beantragen, beantragt to apply for (12)

beantworten, beantwortet to answer (7)

der Becher, - cup; mug (9); glass

bedeuten, bedeutet to mean

bedeutend important, significant(ly)

die Bedeutung , -en meaning

bedienen, bedient to serve

die Bedienung service; waiter, waitress (8)

sich beeilen, beeilt to hurry (8)

beeindrucken, beeindruckt to impress

beenden, beendet to end

sich befinden (befindet), befand, befunden to be located; to be situated

befragen, befragt to interview; to interrogate

befreien, befreit to set free

die Befreiung liberation

befreundet (adj.) friends with

befriedigend satisfactory, satisfactorily

begabt gifted (9)

die Begebenheit, -en event, occurrence

begegnen (+ dat.), ist begegnet to meet (6); to encounter

die Begegnung, -en meeting, encounter

begeistert (p.p. of begeistern) thrilled; enthusiastic

der Beginn beginning

beginnen (beginnt), begann, begonnen to begin, start (1)

begleiten, begleitet to accompany

begraben (begräbt), begrub, begraben to bury

begrüßen, begrüßt to greet

die Begrüßung, -en greeting

behandeln, behandelt to handle, treat, deal with

die Behandlung, -en treatment

behaupten, behauptet to maintain, assert

beherrschen, beherrscht to have a command of

behindert (p.p. of behindern) handicapped

die Behörde, -n public authority

bei (+ dat.) with; at; near (2, 6, 10); during; upon; among; bei deinen Eltern with your parents, at your parents' (6); bei einer Bank at a bank (6); bei Monika at Monika's (2); bei Regen in rainy weather (7)

beide both

beim = bei dem at/with/near the

das Bein, -e leg (B)

beisammen together

das Beispiel, -e example (3); zum Beispiel (z. B.) for example (3)

beißen (beißt), biss, gebissen to bite (9)

bei·treten (+ dat.) (tritt ... bei), trat ... bei, ist beigetreten to join

bekämpfen, bekämpft to fight against

bekannt well-known

der/die Bekannte, -n (ein Bekannter) acquaintance

bekennend admitted, avowed

bekommen (bekommt), bekam, bekommen to get; to receive (3)

belagern, belagert to besiege

belasten, belastet to load; to debit; belastendes Material incriminating evidence

beleben, belebt to liven up

belegen, belegt to cover; to take (a course) (4); das belegte Brot open-faced sandwich (8)

(das) Belgien Belgium (B)

belgisch Belgian (adj.)

beliebt popular (3)

bemerken, bemerkt to notice

benutzen, benutzt to use (7)

das Benzin gasoline (6)

der **Benzinverbrauch** gasoline consumption

berechnen (+ *dat.*), **berechnet** to charge (8)

der **Bereich, -e** sector, area (12)

bereichern, bereichert to enrich (12)

bereit ready; prepared

bereits already; just

der **Berg, -e** mountain (1); **in den Bergen wandern** to hike in the mountains (1); **in die Berge gehen** to go to the mountains (1)

die **Berghütte, -n** mountain cabin

der **Bergsteiger, -** / die **Bergsteigerin, -nen** mountaineer

der **Bericht, -e** report

Berliner (*adj.*) (of) Berlin; die **Berliner Mauer** the Berlin Wall; die **Berliner Weiße** *light, fizzy beer served with raspberry syrup*

der **Berliner, -** / die **Berlinerin, -nen** person from Berlin

(das) **Bern** Bern(e)

der **Beruf, -e** profession; career (1, 5); **Was sind Sie von Beruf?** What's your profession? (1)

der **Berufsberater, -** / die **Berufsberaterin, -nen** career counselor (5)

die **Berufsberatung, -en** job counseling

das **Berufsleben** career, professional life (12)

berufstätig working; employed

das **Berufsverbot, -e** *prohibition from practicing a particular profession*

beruhen (auf + *dat.*), **beruht** to be based (on)

berühmt famous (7)

berühren, berührt to touch

die **Besatzungszone, -n** occupation zone

beschädigen, beschädigt to damage

beschaffen, beschafft to get; to obtain

sich **beschäftigen** (mit + *dat.*), **beschäftigt** to occupy oneself (with); **beschäftigt** busy

der **Bescheid, -e** information; **Bescheid wissen** to know; to have an idea

beschließen (**beschließt**), **beschloss, beschlossen** to resolve; to decide

beschreiben (**beschreibt**), **beschrieb, beschrieben** to describe (11); **den Weg beschreiben** to give directions

die **Beschreibung, -en** description (B)

sich **beschweren** (bei + *dat.*), **beschwert** to complain (to) (8)

der **Besen, -** broom (6)

besetzt (*p.p. of* **besetzen**) occupied, taken

besichtigen, besichtigt to visit, sightsee (7)

besiedeln, besiedelt to settle

besiegen, besiegt to conquer (7)

der **Besitz** possessions (2)

besitzen (**besitzt**), **besaß, besessen** to possess

besonder- special, particular

besonders particularly (3)

(sich) (*dat.*) **besorgen, besorgt** to get (*o.s.*); to buy (*o.s.*)

bespitzeln, bespitzelt to spy on

besser better (2)

(sich) **bessern, gebessert** to improve

best- best

der **Bestandteil, -e** part, component

das **Besteck** silverware, cutlery (5)

bestehen (**besteht**), **bestand, bestanden** to exist; to last; to pass (*a test*); (aus + *dat.*) to consist (of)

besteigen (**besteigt**), **bestieg, bestiegen** to climb (7)

bestellen, bestellt to order (*food*) (8)

bestimmen, bestimmt to determine

bestimmt definite(ly); certain(ly) (3)

bestreuen, bestreut to sprinkle (8)

der **Besuch, -e** visit (3); **zu Besuch kommen** to visit (3)

besuchen, besucht to visit (1)

der **Besucher, -** / die **Besucherin, -nen** visitor

beten, gebetet to pray

der **Beton** concrete

betrachten, betrachtet to look at

der **Betrag, -̈e** amount (*of money*)

betragen (**beträgt**), **betrug, betragen** to amount to

betreffen (**betrifft**), **betraf, betroffen** to concern; to affect; **betroffen** upset; affected

betreten (**betritt**), **betrat, betreten** to enter

betreuen, betreut to take care of; to look after

betrunken drunk(en), drunkenly

das **Bett, -en** bed (1, 6); **ins Bett gehen** to go to bed (1)

sich **beugen, gebeugt** to bend down

die **Bevölkerung, -en** population

bevor (*subord. conj.*) before (11)

die **Bewachung** watch(ing); observation

sich **bewegen, bewegt** to move

sich **bewerben** (um + *acc.*) (**bewirbt**), **bewarb, beworben** to apply (for)

bewerten, bewertet to rate

bewirken, bewirkt to cause; to bring about

die **Bewirtung, -en** service

der **Bewohner, -** / die **Bewohnerin, -nen** occupant; inhabitant

bewundern, bewundert to admire

bewusstlos unconscious(ly)

bezahlen, bezahlt to pay (for) (4)

bezeichnen (als), **bezeichnet** to describe (as)

die **Beziehung, -en** relationship

beziehungsweise or; and . . . respectively

bezwingen (**bezwingt**), **bezwang, bezwungen** to defeat

die **Bibliothek, -en** library (4)

der **Bibliothekar, -e** / die **Bibliothekarin, -nen** librarian (5)

die **Biene, -n** bee (10)

das **Bier, -e** beer (2)

bieten (**bietet**), **bot, geboten** to offer

der **Bikini, -s** bikini (5)

bi-kulturell bicultural(ly)

das **Bild, -er** picture (2); **das Bild an die Wand hängen** to hang the picture on the wall (3); **Was zeigen Ihre Bilder?** What do your pictures show? (A)

bilden, gebildet to form

der **Bilderrahmen, -** picture frame

der **Bildhauer, -** / die **Bildhauerin, -nen** sculptor (12)

das **Bildnis, -se** portrait

billig cheap(ly), inexpensive(ly) (2)

binden (an + *acc.*) (**bindet**), **band, gebunden** to tie (to)

das **Bioei, -er** organic egg

die **Biografie, -n** biography

die **Biologie** biology (1)

der **Biomarkt, -̈e** organic produce market

das **Bioprodukt, -e** organic product

die **Birne, -n** pear (8)

bis (*prep. + acc.; subord. conj.*) until (2, 4, 11); **bis acht Uhr** until eight o'clock (2); **bis bald** so long; see you soon (A); **bis um vier Uhr** (**früh**) until four o'clock (in the morning) (4); **bis zu** as far as; up to (10)

bisher thus far; up to now

bisschen: ein bisschen a little (bit) (3); **kein bisschen** not at all (3)

der **Bissen, -** mouthful

bitte please (A); **Bitte schön?** Yes, please? May I help you? (7)

Bitte schön/sehr. There you go.

Unterschreib bitte hier. Sign here, please. (A)

bitten (um + *acc.*) (**bittet**), **bat, gebeten** to ask (for) (12)

blass pale(ly)

das **Blatt, -̈er** leaf; sheet (*of paper*)

blau blue (A, B); **blau machen** to take the day off (3); **der Blaue Reiter** *a group of artists in Munich* (1911–14)

die **Blaubeere, -n** blueberry

der **Blauwal, -e** blue whale (10)

bleiben (**bleibt**), **blieb, ist geblieben** to stay, remain; **sitzen bleiben** (**bleibt . . . sitzen**), **blieb . . . sitzen, ist sitzen geblieben** to remain seated; to be held back a grade; **stecken bleiben** (**bleibt . . . stecken**), **blieb . . . stecken, ist stecken geblieben** to get stuck (11)

bleichen, gebleicht to bleach

der **Bleistift, -e** pencil (A, B)

der **Blick, -e** look; glance; view

blind blind(ly)

der **Blinddarm, -̈e** appendix (11)

die **Blockflöte, -n** recorder (*type of flute*) (12)

blöd stupid(ly)

blond blond(e) (B)

bloß mere(ly); only

blühen, geblüht to bloom

die **Blume, -n** flower (3); **die Blumen gießen** to water the flowers (3)

der **Blumenkohl** cauliflower (8)

die **Bluse, -n** blouse (A)

das **Blut** blood (9, 11); **Blut abnehmen** to take blood (11)

der **Blutdruck** blood pressure (11); **niedrigen/hohen Blutdruck haben** to have low/high blood pressure (11)

die **Blüte, -n** bloom

bluten, geblutet to bleed (11)

das Blütenblatt, ¨er petal

der Boden, ¨ floor (B)

die Bohne, -n bean (8)

das Bonbon, -s drop, lozenge (11)

das Boot, -e boat (2)

die Börse, -n stock exchange (12)

der Börsenkrach, ¨e stock market crash (12)

böse evil, mean (9)

(das) Bosnien Bosnia

der Boss, -e boss

die Boutique, -n boutique (6)

bowlen, gebowlt to bowl

die Bowlingbahn, -en bowling alley

die Box, -en stereo speaker

boxen, geboxt to box (1)

die Branche, -n sector (12)

die Brandenburgischen Konzerte (pl.) the
  Brandenburg Concertos

braten (brät), briet, gebraten to fry (8)

der Braten, - roast (8)

die Bratwurst, ¨e (fried) sausage

brauchen, gebraucht to need; to use (1)

brauen, gebraut to brew

braun brown (A)

bräunen, gebräunt to brown, fry (8)

(das) Braunschweig Braunschweig, Brunswick

brausen, gebraust to roar; to rage

die Braut, ¨e bride (9)

die BRD = die Bundesrepublik Deutschland
  Federal Republic of Germany

brechen (bricht), brach, gebrochen to break (11);
  sich den Arm brechen to break one's arm (11)

breit broad, wide

die Bremse, -n brake (7)

bremsen, gebremst to brake (11)

brennen (brennt), brannte, gebrannt to
  burn (11)

der Brennofen, ¨ kiln (12)

das Brett, -er board; das schwarze Brett
  bulletin board

die Brezel, -n pretzel

der Brief, -e letter, epistle (1)

die Briefmarke, -n (postage) stamp (5)

die Brille, -n (eye)glasses (A)

bringen (bringt), brachte, gebracht to bring (2)

britisch British

der Brocken highest mountain in the Harz range

das Brot, -e (loaf of) bread (8); das belegte Brot
  open-face sandwich (8)

das Brötchen, - (bread) roll (8)

die Brücke, -n bridge (10)

der Bruder, ¨ brother (B)

die Bruderschaft, -en fraternity

der Brunnen, - well; fountain (9)

brutal brutal(ly)

das Bruttogehalt, ¨er gross salary

das Buch, ¨er book (A, B, 2)

der Bucheinband, ¨e book cover

buchen, gebucht to book (7)

die Bucht, -en bay (7)

sich bücken (nach + dat.), gebückt to bend
  down (toward)

das Bügeleisen, - iron (6)

bügeln, gebügelt to iron (6)

die Bulette, -n rissole, meatball, hamburger patty

(das) Bulgarien Bulgaria (B)

das Bundesausbildungsförderungsgesetz
  (BAföG) financial aid for students from the
  German government

das Bundesland, ¨er (German or Austrian) state

der Bundespräsident, -en (wk.) / die Bundesprä-
  sidentin, -nen (federal) president

die Bundesrepublik federal republic; die
  Bundesrepublik Deutschland Federal
  Republic of Germany

bunt colorful(ly)

das Burgenland Austrian state

der Bürger, - / die Bürgerin, -nen citizen (10)

bürgerlich bourgeois, middle-class

der Bürgerrechtskämpfer, - / die Bürgerrechts-
  kämpferin, -nen campaigner for civil rights

das Bürgertum bourgeoisie, middle class

das Büro, -s office (5); im Büro at the office (5)

die Bürste, -n brush (6)

der Bus, -se bus (2, 7)

der Busch, ¨e bush (9)

die Bushaltestelle, -n bus stop (10)

die Butter butter (8)

ca. = circa/zirka circa

das Café, -s café; im Café at the café (4)

die Cafeteria, -s cafeteria

das Camping camping (10)

der Campingplatz, ¨e campsite (10)

der Cartoon, -s cartoon

(der) Cäsar Caesar

das Casino, -s casino

die CD, -s CD, compact disc (A, 3)

der CD-Spieler, - CD player (2)

Celsius Celsius, centigrade (B); 18 Grad Celsius
  18 degrees Celsius (B)

der Cent, - cent (one hundredth of a euro)

der Champagner, - champagne

das Chaos chaos (5)

der Charakter, -e character; personality (12)

chatten, gechattet to chat (online) (1)

checken, gecheckt to check

der Chef, -s / die Chefin, -nen boss; director

die Chemie chemistry (1)

der Chemiker, - / die Chemikerin, -nen chemist

der Chili, -s chili (11)

(das) China China (B)

der Chinese, -n (wk.) / die Chinesin, -nen Chinese
  (person)

chinesisch Chinese (adj.)

(das) Chinesisch Chinese (language) (B)

die Chipkarte, -n chip card, smart card

cholerisch irascible, irascibly

der Chor, ¨e choir; chorus

der Christ, -en (wk.) / die Christin, -nen Christian
  (person)

der Christkindlmarkt, ¨e Christmas market

christlich Christian (adj.)

circa = zirka circa

der Clip, -s (video) clip

der Clown, -s clown (9)

die Cola, -s cola

die Collagetechnik, -en collage technique

das College, -s college

der Comic, -s comic strip; comic book

der Computer, - computer (2)

cool cool(ly); fabulous(ly)

die Creme, -s cream

ct = der Cent, - cent (one hundredth of a euro)

da (adv.) there (2); then; (subord. conj.) as, since

dabei in that connection; while doing so; (along)
  with it; dabei sein to be present; Ist ein/eine
  … dabei? Does it come with a . . . ? (6)

dabei·haben (hat … dabei), hatte … dabei,
  dabeigehabt to have (s.th.) with/on (s.o.)

da·bleiben (bleibt … da), blieb … da, ist
  dageblieben to stay, remain (there)

das Dach, ¨er roof (6)

der Dachboden, ¨ attic

der Dada(ismus) Dada(ism)

dadurch through it/them

dafür for it/them; for that reason; on behalf of it

dagegen against it/them; Haben Sie etwas
  dagegen? Do you have something for it
  (illness)? (11)

daheim at home (9)

daher therefore

dahin·kommen (kommt … dahin), kam … dahin,
  ist dahingekommen to get there

damalig (adj.) back then, at that time

damals (adv.) back then, at that time (9)

(das) Damaskus Damascus

damit (adv.) with it/them; (subord. conj.) so that (11)

danach after it/them; afterward (8, 10)

(das) Dänemark Denmark (B)

dänisch Danish (adj.)

der Dank thanks; vielen Dank many thanks (10)

die Dankbarkeit gratitude

danke thank you (A)

dann then (A)

daran at/on/to it/them

darauf after/for/on it/them; afterward, then; bald
  darauf soon thereafter (9)

darauffolgend following

daraufhin following that, thereupon

darin in it/them (6)

dar·stellen, dargestellt to represent, depict

darüber over/above/about it/them

das (def. art., neut. nom./acc.) the; (dem. pron., neut.
  nom./acc.) this/that; (rel. pron., neut. nom./acc.)
  which, who(m); Das ist … This/That is . . .
  (B); Das ist es ja! That's just it! (4); Das sind …
  These/Those are . . . (B)

dass (subord. conj.) that (11)

die Daten (pl.) data; persönliche Daten
  biographical information (1)

die **Datenverarbeitung** data processing
das **Datum, Daten** date (4); **Welches Datum ist heute?** What is today's date? (4)
die **Dauer, -** duration
der **Dauerauftrag, -̈e** standing order
dauern, gedauert to last (4)
die **Dauerwelle, -n** perm (11)
der **Daumen, -** thumb
davon of/from/about it/them
davon·laufen (läuft ... davon), lief ... davon, ist davongelaufen to run away
dazu to it/them; in addition (8)
dazu·kommen (kommt ... dazu), kam ... dazu, ist dazugekommen to turn up, arrive
dazu·schreiben (schreibt ... dazu), schrieb ... dazu, dazugeschrieben to add in writing
die **DDR = die Deutsche Demokratische Republik** German Democratic Republic (*former East Germany*)
der **Deckcode-Name, -n** (*wk.*) code name
die **Decke, -n** ceiling (B); blanket (11)
decken, gedeckt to cover; set (5); **den Tisch decken** to set the table (5)
die **Definition, -en** definition
deftig good and solid
dein(e) (*infor. sg.*) your (B, 2)
der **Delfin, -e** dolphin (10)
dem (*def. art., masc./neut. dat.*) the; (*dem. pron., masc./neut. dat.*) this/that; (*rel. pron., masc./neut. dat.*) which, whom
die **Demo, -s = die Demonstration, -en** (*coll.*) demonstration; rally
die **Demokratie, -n** democracy
demokratisch democratic(ally)
der **Demonstrant, -en** (*wk.*) / die **Demonstrantin, -nen** demonstrator
die **Demonstration, -en** demonstration; rally
demonstrieren, demonstriert to demonstrate
den (*def. art., masc. acc., pl. dat.*) the; (*dem. pron., masc. acc.*) this/that; (*rel. pron., masc. acc.*) which, whom
denen (*dem. pron., pl. dat.*) these/those; (*rel. pron., pl. dat.*) which, whom
denken (denkt), dachte, gedacht to think (4); (**an** + *acc.*) to think of (4); (**über** + *acc.*) to think about
denn (*coord. conj.*) for, because (9, 11); *particle used in questions:* **Wo willst du denn hin?** Where are you going? (A)
dennoch nevertheless
die **Deportation, -en** deportation
deportieren, deportiert to deport
deprimiert depressed (11)
der (*def. art., masc. nom., fem. dat./gen., pl. gen.*) the; (*dem. pron., masc. nom., fem. dat.*) this/that; (*rel. pron., masc. nom., fem. dat.*) which, who(m)
deren (*dem. pron., fem. gen., pl. gen.*) of this/that/these/those; (*rel. pron., fem. gen., pl. gen.*) of which, whose
derselbe, dasselbe, dieselbe(n) the same
der **Derwisch, -e** dervish

des (*def. art., masc./neut. gen.*) (of) the
deshalb therefore; that's why (4)
desinfizieren, desinfiziert to disinfect (11)
dessen (*dem. pron., masc./neut. gen.*) of this/that; (*rel. pron., masc./neut. gen.*) of which, whose
deutlich clear(ly); distinct(ly)
deutsch German (*adj.*)
(das) **Deutsch** German (*language*) (B); **auf Deutsch** in German
der/die **Deutsche, -n (ein Deutscher)** German (*person*) (B); **Ich bin Deutsche/r.** I am German. (B)
die **Deutsche Demokratische Republik (DDR)** German Democratic Republic (*former East Germany*)
die **Deutschkenntnisse** (*pl.*) knowledge of German (*language*)
der **Deutschkurs, -e** German (*language*) course; German class (A)
(das) **Deutschland** Germany (B); **die Bundesrepublik Deutschland** Federal Republic of Germany
deutschlandweit throughout Germany
deutschschweizerisch German-Swiss (*adj.*)
deutschsprachig German-speaking
deutschstämmig of German origin
der **Dezember** December (B)
der **Dialekt, -e** dialect
dich (*infor. sg. acc.*) you (2)
der **Dichter, -** / die **Dichterin, -nen** poet
dick large; fat (2)
dickköpfig headstrong
die (*def. art., fem. nom./acc., pl. nom./acc.*) the; (*dem. pron., fem. nom./acc., pl. nom./acc.*) this/that/these/those; (*rel. pron., fem. nom./acc., pl. nom./acc.*) which, who(m)
dienen (als), gedient to serve (as)
der **Diener, -** / die **Dienerin, -nen** servant (9)
der **Dienstag, -e** Tuesday (1)
dieser, dies(es), diese this, these; that, those (2, 4)
diesmal this time
die **Digitalkamera, -s** digital camera
diktatorisch dictatorial(ly)
die **Diktatur, -en** dictatorship
das **Ding, -e** thing (2)
die **Diphtherie** diphtheria (11)
das **Diplom, -e** degree; diploma
dir (*infor. sg. dat.*) you
direkt direct(ly)
der **Direktor, -en** / die **Direktorin, -nen** (school) principal; director (9)
der **Dirigent, -en** (*wk.*) / die **Dirigentin, -nen** (orchestra) conductor (5)
die **Disko, -s** disco (3)
die **Diskussion, -en** discussion
diskutieren, diskutiert to discuss (4)
die **Dissertation, -en** dissertation
die **DM = die D-Mark (Deutsche Mark)** German mark (*former monetary unit*)
doch however; nevertheless; yet; **doch!** yes (on the contrary)! (4)

der **Doktor, -en** / die **Doktorin, -nen** doctor
der **Dollar, -** dollar
der **Dom, -e** cathedral (10)
dominieren, dominiert to dominate
die **Donau** Danube (River)
der **Donnerstag, -e** Thursday (1)
doppelt double
das **Doppelzimmer, -** double room (5, 10)
das **Dorf, -̈er** village
der **Dorn, -en** thorn (9)
(das) **Dornröschen** Sleeping Beauty, Briar Rose
dort there (7)
dorthin there, thither, to a specific place
die **Dose, -n** can (8)
der **Dosenöffner, -** can opener (8)
der **Dozent, -en** (*wk.*) / die **Dozentin, -nen** lecturer
der **Drache, -n** (*wk.*) dragon (9)
das **Drama, Dramen** drama
dramatisch dramatic(ally)
der **Dramaturg, -en** (*wk.*) / die **Dramaturgin, -nen** dramaturge, theatrical adviser
dran = daran at/on/to it/them; **Du bist dran.** (*coll.*) It's your turn.
der **Drang** drive, urge; quest
drauf = darauf after/for/on it/them
draußen outside (11)
drei three (A)
dreigliedrig divided into three parts
dreimal three times (3)
dreißig thirty (A)
dreißigst- thirtieth
dreiundzwanzig twenty-three (A)
dreizehn thirteen (A)
dreizehnt- thirteenth (4)
dressieren, dressiert to train
drin = darin in it/them (6)
dringend urgent(ly) (2)
dritt- third (4); **das Dritte Reich** the Third Reich (Nazi Germany)
das **Drittel, -** third
die **Droge, -n** drug
die **Drogerie, -n** drugstore (6)
drucken, gedruckt to print
drücken, gedrückt to press
der **Drudenfuß, -̈e** pentagram
drum = darum therefore
der **Dschungel, -** jungle (7)
du (*infor. sg. nom.*) you
dumm dumb, stupid(ly) (6)
dümmlich simple-minded(ly)
dunkel dark (5)
dünn thin
durch (+ *acc.*) through (7); by means of
durchbluten, durchblutet to supply with blood
durcheinander in confusion
durch·greifen (greift ... durch), griff ... durch, durchgegriffen to take action
durchs = durch das through the
durch·schneiden (schneidet ... durch), schnitt ... durch, durchgeschnitten to cut through (8)

der **Durchschnitt** average; **im Durchschnitt** on average

durchschnittlich (on) average

sich **durch·setzen, durchgesetzt** to assert oneself

dürfen (darf), durfte, gedurft to be permitted (to), may (3); **nicht dürfen** must not

der **Durst** thirst (3); **Durst haben** to be thirsty (3)

die **Dusche, -n** shower (5)

(sich) **duschen, geduscht** to (take a) shower (1, 11)

die **DVD, -s** DVD

der **DVD-Spieler, -** DVD player (2, 3)

die **Dynamik** dynamic(s)

eben simply, just; just now

ebenfalls also, likewise

das **Ebenholz** ebony

ebenso likewise; just as

echt real(ly) (2)

die **EC-Karte, -n = die Eurocheque-Karte, -n** Eurocheque card (*debit card*)

die **Ecke, -n** corner (5); **(gleich) um die Ecke** (right) around the corner (5, 6)

eckig angular

die **EDV = die elektronische Datenverarbeitung** electronic data processing (12)

egal equal(ly), same (6); **Das ist mir egal.** It doesn't matter to me. (6)

der **Egoist, -en** (*wk.*) / die **Egoistin, -nen** egoist

die **Ehe, -n** marriage (12)

die **Eheleute** (*pl.*) married couple

ehemalig former

eher rather (12); more

der **Ehering, -e** wedding ring

der **Ehevertrag, ⸚e** prenuptial agreement (12)

die **Ehre, -n** honor

ehren, geehrt to honor

ei (*interj.*) oh

das **Ei, -er** egg (8); **gebratene Eier** (*pl.*) fried eggs (8); **gekochte Eier** (*pl.*) boiled eggs (8)

der **Eichbaum, ⸚e** oak tree

der/das **Eidotter** egg yolk

eifersüchtig jealous(ly) (3)

eigen own (6)

die **Eigenschaft, -en** trait, characteristic

eigensinnig stubborn(ly)

eigentlich actual(ly) (3)

sich **eignen, geeignet** to be suitable

die **Eile** hurry (3); **in Eile sein** to be in a hurry (3)

eilen, geeilt to hurry

eilig rushed (8); **es eilig haben** to be in a hurry (8)

ein, eine a(n); one (A); **ein bisschen** a little (bit) (3); some; **ein paar** a few (2)

einander one another, each other (3)

die **Einbahnstraße, -n** one-way street (7)

ein·biegen (biegt ... ein), bog ... ein, ist eingebogen to turn

ein·brechen (in + *acc.*) (bricht ... ein), brach ... ein, ist eingebrochen to break in(to); to break through

ins Eis einbrechen to go through the ice

der **Einbrecher, -** / die **Einbrecherin, -nen** burglar (9)

der **Einbruch, ⸚e** burglary; break-in

(sich) **ein·cremen, eingecremt** to put lotion on (*o.s.*) (11)

der **Eindruck, ⸚e** impression

einer, eine, ein(e)s one (*pron.*); **einfach** simple, simply (2); one-way (*trip*) (10)

die **Einfahrt, -en** driveway (11)

ein·fallen (+ *dat.*) (fällt ... ein), fiel ... ein, ist eingefallen to occur (*to s.o.*)

das **Einfamilienhaus, ⸚er** single-family home (6)

ein·führen, eingeführt to introduce

die **Einführung, -en** introduction (A)

der **Eingang, ⸚e** entrance

ein·geben (gibt ... ein), gab ... ein, eingegeben to give

ein·gehen (geht ... ein), ging ... ein, ist eingegangen to arrive; **darauf eingehen** to get into something

sich **ein·gewöhnen (in + *acc.*), eingewöhnt** to get accustomed (to)

ein·gravieren, eingraviert to engrave

die **Einheit** unity

einige some; several; a few

ein·jagen, eingejagt: jemandem Angst einjagen to scare someone

der **Einkauf, ⸚e** purchase

ein·kaufen, eingekauft to shop (for) (1); **einkaufen gehen** to go shopping (1, 5)

das **Einkommen, -** income (12)

ein·laden (lädt ... ein), lud ... ein, eingeladen to invite (2)

die **Einladung, -en** invitation (2)

ein·laufen (läuft ... ein), lief ... ein, ist eingelaufen to shrink

einmal once (4); for once; **Es war einmal ...** Once upon a time there was . . . ; **noch einmal** one more time; **Warst du schon einmal ...?** Were you ever . . . ? (4)

sich **ein·mischen, eingemischt** to interfere

ein·packen, eingepackt to pack up (1)

eins one (*cardinal number*) (A)

ein·sammeln, eingesammelt to gather, collect

der **Einsatz, ⸚e** deployment

ein·schalten, eingeschaltet to turn on (10)

ein·schlafen (schläft ... ein), schlief ... ein, ist eingeschlafen to fall asleep (7)

sich **ein·schreiben (schreibt ... ein), schrieb ... ein, eingeschrieben** to register, enroll

die **Einsicht, -en** view, look

ein·steigen (steigt ... ein), stieg ... ein, ist eingestiegen to board (10); to get in/on

ein·stellen, eingestellt to hire; to employ

die **Einstellung, -en** attitude (12)

(sich) **ein·teilen, eingeteilt** to divide up; to organize

eintönig monotonous(ly)

ein·tragen (trägt ... ein), trug ... ein, eingetragen to enter (*into a list or ledger*)

ein·treffen (trifft ... ein), traf ... ein, ist eingetroffen to arrive

die **Eintrittskarte, -n** admissions ticket (5)

einundzwanzig twenty-one (A)

der **Einwanderer, -** / die **Einwanderin, -nen** immigrant (12)

ein·wandern, ist eingewandert to immigrate (12)

die **Einwanderung** immigration

ein·werfen (wirft ... ein), warf ... ein, eingeworfen to break, smash (*a window*)

der **Einwohner, -** / die **Einwohnerin, -nen** inhabitant, resident

ein·zahlen, eingezahlt to pay in; to deposit

der **Einzelgänger, -** / die **Einzelgängerin, -nen** loner (12)

das **Einzelhandelsgeschäft, -e** retail shop, retail store

der **Einzelplatz, ⸚e** single seat

das **Einzelzimmer, -** single room (10)

ein·ziehen (zieht ... ein), zog ... ein, hat eingezogen to collect; to withdraw

ein·ziehen (in + *acc.*) (zieht ... ein), zog ... ein, ist eingezogen to move in(to)

einzig only; single; sole

das **Eis** ice; ice cream (2); **ins Eis einbrechen** to go through the ice

der **Eisbeutel, -** ice pack

das **Eiscafé, -s** ice cream parlor (8)

die **Eisenbahn, -en** railroad

das **Eisenwarengeschäft, -e** hardware store (6)

eiskalt ice-cold (8)

der **Eistee** iced tea

der **Elefant, -en** (*wk.*) elephant (9)

elegant elegant(ly) (8)

elektrisch electric(ally) (8)

der **Elektro** electro, electronic dance music

elektronisch electronic(ally); **die elektronische Datenverarbeitung (EDV)** electronic data processing (12)

der **Elektrotechniker, -** / die **Elektrotechnikerin, -nen** electrician; electronics technician

das **Element, -e** element

elf eleven (A)

das **Elfenbein** ivory (10)

elft- eleventh (4)

die **Eltern** (*pl.*) parents (B)

der **Elternteil, -e** parent

die **E-Mail, -s** e-mail (1, 2)

der **Emmentaler** Emmenthaler (cheese)

empfangen (empfängt), empfing, empfangen to receive

der **Empfänger, -** / die **Empfängerin, -nen** recipient; payee

empören, empört to outrage; **sich empören** to become outraged

das **Ende, -n** end

enden, geendet to end

endgültig final; conclusive(ly)

endlich finally (9)

das **Endspiel, -e** final (game)

die **Endung, -en** ending

eng tight, narrow, small (12); closely

sich **engagieren** (für + *acc.*), **engagiert** to commit oneself (to); **engagiert** (*adj.*) committed, involved

(das) **England** England (B)

der **Engländer**, - / die **Engländerin**, **-nen** English (*person*) (B)

englisch English (*adj.*)

(das) **Englisch** English (*language*) (B)

der **Enkel**, - / die **Enkelin**, **-nen** grandson/ granddaughter (5)

entartet (*adj.*) degenerate

entdecken, **entdeckt** to discover (4)

sich **entfernen** (von + *dat.*), **entfernt** to go away (from)

sich **entfremden** (von + *dat.*), **entfremdet** to become estranged (from)

entführen, **entführt** to kidnap

der **Entführer**, - / die **Entführerin**, **-nen** kidnapper

entgegnen, **entgegnet** to reply

entlang along (10)

entlang·fahren (fährt ... entlang), fuhr ... entlang, ist entlanggefahren to drive along

entlang·gehen (geht ... entlang), ging ... entlang, ist entlanggegangen to go along (10)

entlassen (entlässt), entließ, entlassen to release

(sich) **entscheiden** (entscheidet), entschied, entschieden to decide (4)

entscheidend decisive(ly)

entschlossen (*p.p. of* entschließen) resolute(ly)

entschuldigen, **entschuldigt** to excuse (10); **Entschuldigen Sie!** Excuse me! (10)

die **Entschuldigung**, **-en** excuse; **Entschuldigung!** Excuse me! (3)

entsetzlich terrible, terribly

entsetzt (*p.p. of* entsetzen) horrified

entspannen, **entspannt** to relax

entstammen (+ *dat.*), **ist entstammt** to come from

entstehen (aus + *dat.*) (entsteht), entstand, ist entstanden to originate (from)

entweder ... oder either . . . or

entwerfen (entwirft), entwarf, entworfen to design

entwickeln, **entwickelt** to develop

die **Entwicklungsland**, ⸚ er developing country

die **Entzündung**, **-en** infection (11); inflammation

entzündungshemmend anti-inflammatory

die **Epoche**, **-n** epoch, era, period

er (*pron., masc. nom.*) he, it

erarbeiten, **erarbeitet** to work on/out

die **Erbse**, **-n** pea (8)

die **Erdbeere**, **-n** strawberry (8)

die **Erde**, **-n** earth; ground; soil, dirt

die **Erdgeschichte** history of the earth

das **Erdgeschoss**, **-e** first floor, ground floor

die **Erdkunde** earth science; geography

das **Ereignis**, **-se** event

erfahren (erfährt), erfuhr, erfahren to find out, learn; to experience; to discover

die **Erfahrung**, **-en** experience

erfinden (erfindet), erfand, erfunden to invent (4)

der **Erfinder**, - / die **Erfinderin**, **-nen** inventor

die **Erfindung**, **-en** invention

der **Erfolg**, **-e** success; **Erfolg haben** to be successful

erfolgreich successful(ly)

erfüllen, **erfüllt** to fulfill

die **Erfüllung: in Erfüllung gehen** to become true

ergänzen, **ergänzt** to complete, fill in the blanks (4)

sich **ergeben** (aus + *dat.*) (ergibt), ergab, ergeben to arise (from)

das **Ergebnis**, **-se** result

ergehen (+ *dat.*) (ergeht), erging, ist ergangen to go (well or badly) (*for a person*)

erhalten (erhält), erhielt, erhalten to receive

erheben (erhebt), erhob, erhoben to raise

erhitzen, **erhitzt** to heat (8)

sich **erholen**, **erholt** to recuperate (11)

erinnern (an + *acc.*), **erinnert** to remind (*of s.o./ s.th.*); to commemorate (*s.o./s.th.*); sich **erinnern** (an + *acc.*), **erinnert** to remember (*s.o./s.th.*) (9)

die **Erinnerung**, **-en** memory, remembrance (4)

sich **erkälten**, **erkältet** to catch a cold (11)

die **Erkältung**, **-en** (head) cold (11)

erkennen (an + *dat.*) (erkennt), erkannte, erkannt to recognize (by)

erklären, **erklärt** to explain (5)

erklettern, **erklettert** to climb

sich **erkundigen** (nach + *dat.*), **erkundigt** to ask (about), get information (about) (10)

erlauben, **erlaubt** to permit (7)

die **Erlaubnis**, **-se** permission

erleben, **erlebt** to experience (3)

das **Erlebnis**, **-se** experience (7)

erledigen, **erledigt** to take care of; to handle; to settle

erleiden (erleidet), erlitt, erlitten to suffer

erlösen, **erlöst** to rescue, free (9)

ermitteln, **ermittelt** to investigate

ermöglichen, **ermöglicht** to make possible

ermorden, **ermordet** to murder

ernst serious(ly); **ernst nehmen** to take seriously

eröffnen, **eröffnet** to open (9); **ein Konto eröffnen** to open a bank account (5)

erreichbar reachable

erreichen, **erreicht** to reach (12); to achieve

erscheinen (erscheint), erschien, ist erschienen to appear

das **Erscheinungsjahr**, **-e** year of publication

erschießen (erschießt), erschoss, erschossen to shoot dead

erschrocken frightened

erst (*adv.*) first; not until (4); **erst mal** for now; **erst um vier Uhr** not until four o'clock (4)

erst- first (*ordinal number*) (4); **am ersten Oktober** on the first of October (4); **der erste Oktober** the first of October (4); **erster Klasse fahren** to travel first class (10); **im ersten Stock** on the second floor (6); **zum ersten Mal** for the first time (4)

erstarren, **ist erstarrt** to stand paralyzed

das **Erstaunen** astonishment

erstellen, **erstellt** to draw up

ersticken, **ist erstickt** to suffocate

erstmal *old spelling of* **erst mal** for now

das **Erststudium**, **Erststudien** undergraduate study

erteilen, **erteilt** to give

ertragen (erträgt), ertrug, ertragen to tolerate

erwachen, **ist erwacht** to wake up

erwachsen grown-up

erwarten, **erwartet** to expect (12)

die **Erwartung**, **-en** expectation

erwischen, **erwischt** to catch

erzählen, **erzählt** to tell (*a story, joke*) (3, 5); **Witze erzählen** to tell jokes (3)

das **Erzherzogtum**, ⸚er archduchy

erziehen (erzieht), erzog, erzogen to raise, bring up

der/die **Erziehungsberechtigte**, **-n** (**ein Erziehungsberechtigter**) parent or legal guardian

es (*pron., neut. nom./acc.*) it (B); **Gibt es ...?** Is there . . . ? / Are there . . . ? (A)

der **Esel**, - donkey

der/das **Essay**, **-s** essay

essen (isst), aß, gegessen to eat (2, 4); **zu Abend essen** to dine, have dinner (4); das **Essen** food

der **Essig** vinegar (8)

die **Essiggurke**, **-n** pickle

das **Esszimmer**, - dining room (6)

(das) **Estland** Estonia

etablieren, **etabliert** to establish

etwa approximately

etwas something (2, 4, 5); anything (5); somewhat; **etwas anderes** something else; **etwas Interessantes/Neues** something interesting/new (4); **Haben Sie etwas dagegen?** Do you have something for it (*illness*)? (11); **Sonst noch etwas?** Anything else? (5)

die **EU = die Europäische Union** European Union

euch (*infor. pl. pron., acc./dat.*) you; yourselves

euer, eu(e)re (*infor. pl.*) your

die **Eule**, **-n** owl

der **Euro**, - euro (*European monetary unit*) (7)

die **Eurocard** *European credit card*

(das) **Europa** Europe (B)

der **Europäer**, - / die **Europäerin**, **-nen** European (*person*)

die **Europäische Union (EU)** European Union

die **Euroscheckkarte**, **-n** Eurocheque Card (*debit card*) (12)

der **Euroschein**, **-e** banknote in euros; **der Zwanzigeuroschein**, **-e** twenty-euro note

die **Eurozone** *countries of the European Union in which the euro is the unit of currency*

evozieren, **evoziert** to evoke

ewig eternal(ly)

exakt exact(ly)

existieren, **existiert** to exist

exotisch exotic(ally) (7)

der **Exportartikel**, - export article

der **Expressionismus** expressionism

extra extra (10)

extrem extreme(ly)

der Extremismus extremism

der Extremist, -en (*wk.*) / **die Extremistin, -nen** extremist (12)

die Fabrik, -en factory (5); **in der Fabrik** in the factory (5)

das Fach, ⁻er academic subject (1)

die Fachhochschule, -n university of applied arts and sciences

der Fachleistungskurs, -e extension course

die Fähigkeit, -en ability, capability

fahren (fährt), fuhr, ist/hat gefahren to drive; to ride (2); **Auto fahren** to drive a car; **erster Klasse fahren** to travel first class (10); **ins Schwimmbad fahren** to drive/go to the swimming pool (1); **Kanu fahren** to go canoeing (10); **Rad fahren** to ride a bicycle (7); **Ski fahren** to ski (3)

Fahrenheit Fahrenheit (B)

der Fahrer, - / **die Fahrerin, -nen** driver (7)

der Fahrgast, ⁻e passenger

die Fahrkarte, -n ticket (4)

der Fahrkartenschalter, - ticket window (7)

der Fahrplan, ⁻e timetable, schedule

das Fahrrad, ⁻er bicycle (2, 7); **Fahrrad fahren** to ride a bicycle

der Fahrradhelm, -e bicycle helmet (5)

der Fahrstuhl, ⁻e elevator

die Fahrt, -en trip (10)

das Fahrzeug, -e vehicle (7, 11)

der Faktor, -en factor

der Fall, ⁻e fall, collapse; case; **auf jeden Fall** by all means (4)

fallen (fällt), fiel, ist gefallen to fall (9); **in Ohnmacht fallen** to faint (11); **schwer fallen** (+ *dat.*) to seem/feel difficult (*to s.o.*)

falls (*subord. conj.*) if; in case

falsch wrong(ly) (2); false(ly)

fälschen, gefälscht to fake

die Familie, -n family (B)

das Familienfest, -e family celebration (4)

der Familienname, -n (*wk.*) family name, surname (A, 1)

familienversichert covered by family health insurance

der Fan, -s fan, enthusiast

der Fanatiker, - / **die Fanatikerin, -nen** fanatic (12)

fangen (fängt), fing, gefangen to catch

das Fangen tag (*children's game*)

die Fantasie, -n imagination

fantastisch fantastic(ally)

die Farbe, -n color (A, 1); **Welche Farbe hat …?** What color is . . . ? (A)

die Farbensymbolik color symbolism

der Farbfilm color film

fassen, gefasst to grab, grasp

fast almost (5)

fasten, gefastet to fast

das Fast Food fast food

die Fauna fauna; animal life

der Februar February (B)

die Fee, -n fairy (9)

fegen, gefegt to sweep (5)

fehlen (+ *dat.*), **gefehlt** to lack; to be missing (6); to be wrong with, be the matter with (*a person*) (11)

die Feier, -n celebration, party (9)

feiern, gefeiert to celebrate (4, 5)

der Feiertag, -e holiday (4)

fein fine(ly) (8)

der Feind, -e / **die Feindin, -nen** enemy

das Feld, -er field (7)

das Fenster, - window (B); **unter dem Fenster** under the window (5)

die Fensterbank, ⁻e windowsill (5, 10)

die Fensterscheibe, -n windowpane (9)

die Ferien (*pl.*) vacation (1)

das Ferienhaus, ⁻er vacation house (4)

die Fernreise, -n long-distance trip

fern·sehen (sieht … fern), sah … fern, ferngesehen to watch TV (1)

das Fernsehen television

der Fernseher, - TV set (2)

die Fernsehsendung, -en TV show

das Fernsehzimmer, - TV room (10)

fertig ready; finished (3)

fest steady; fixed

das Fest, -e party; festival; holiday (4)

fest·nehmen (nimmt … fest), nahm … fest, festgenommen to arrest

fest·stehen (steht … fest), stand … fest, festgestanden to stand fast

fest·stellen, festgestellt to establish (8); to detect; to realize

die Fete, -n (*coll.*) party

fett fat; bold; **fett gedruckt** in bold print, boldface; **fette Jahre** good times, years of plenty

das Fett, -e fat

fettig fat(ty), greasy (8, 11)

feucht humid (B)

das Feuer, - fire (9)

die Feuerwehr fire department (11)

das Fieber fever (11)

die Figur, -en figure (12); character

der Film, -e film (2)

die Finanzen (*pl.*) finances

finanziell financial(ly)

finden (findet), fand, gefunden to find (2); **Wie findest du das?** How do you like that?

der Finger, - finger (11)

der Fingernagel, ⁻ fingernail (11)

(das) Finnland Finland (B)

die Firma, Firmen company, firm (3)

der Fisch, -e fish (8)

fischen, gefischt to fish

das Fischfilet, -s fish fillet

die Fläche, -n surface (7); area

die Flasche, -n bottle (5)

der Flaschenöffner, - bottle opener (8)

die Fledermaus, ⁻e bat (10)

das Fleisch meat (8)

das Fleischchüechli (*Swiss*) rissole, meatball, hamburger patty

fleißig industrious(ly) (12); diligent(ly)

die Fliege, -n fly (8)

fliegen (fliegt), flog, ist/hat geflogen to fly (1)

fliehen (flieht), floh, ist geflohen to flee

fließen (fließt), floss, ist geflossen to flow (7)

flippig (*coll.*) funky; stylish

der Flohmarkt, ⁻e flea market (2)

die Flora flora; plant life

der Fluch, ⁻e curse

fluchen, geflucht to curse, swear (11)

flüchten, ist geflüchtet to flee (11)

der Flug, ⁻e flight (9)

das Flugblatt, ⁻er pamphlet

der Flughafen, ⁻ airport (6)

das Flugzeug, -e airplane (7)

der Fluss, ⁻e river (7)

flüssig (*adj.*) liquid, fluid

die Focus-Frage, -n focus question

der Föhn, -e blow-dryer, hair-dryer

föhnen, geföhnt to blow-dry; **sich (die Haare) föhnen** to blow-dry (one's hair) (11)

die Folge, -n consequence, result; sequence

folgen (+ *dat.*), **ist gefolgt** to follow

folgend following

die Folklore folk music

foltern, gefoltert to torture

die Forderung, -en demand

die Forelle, -n trout (8)

die Form, -en form

die Formalität, -en formality (12)

das Formular, -e form (12)

fort·rennen (rennt … fort), rannte … fort, ist fortgerannt to run away

(sich) fort·setzen, fortgesetzt to continue

die Fortsetzung, -en continuation

das Foto, -s photo (1)

die Fotografie photography

fotografieren, fotografiert to take pictures (4)

die Fotomontage photomontage

die Frage, -n question (A); **eine Frage stellen** to ask a question (5)

fragen, gefragt to ask; **(nach + dat.)** to inquire (about); **nach dem Weg fragen** to ask for directions

der Franken, - (**der Schweizer Franken**) (*Swiss*) franc (8)

die Frankfurter, - frankfurter (sausage)

(das) Frankreich France (B)

der Franzose, -n (*wk.*) / **die Französin, -nen** French (*person*) (B)

französisch French (*adj.*)

(das) Französisch French (*language*) (B)

die Frau, -en woman; Mrs., Ms.; wife (A, B)

die Frauensache, -n woman's job, woman's concern

frei free(ly); empty, available (8); **in freier Natur** out in the open (country) (10); **Ist hier noch frei?** Is this seat available? (8)

der **Freigang** work-release day pass

frei·haben (hat ... frei), hatte ... frei, freigehabt to have free; to have time off

frei·lassen (lässt ... frei), ließ ... frei, freigelassen to set free

das **Freilichtmuseum, Freilichtmuseen** open-air museum

der **Freitag, -e** Friday (1)

freitags on Friday(s)

freiwillig voluntary; optional; voluntarily, willingly

die **Freizeit** leisure time (1)

fremd foreign

der/die **Fremde, -n (ein Fremder)** foreigner

der **Fremdenhass** xenophobia

die **Fremdsprache, -n** foreign language (5)

fressen (frisst), fraß, gefressen to eat (*said of an animal*) (9)

die **Freude, -n** joy; pleasure (9); **vor Freude** for/with joy

sich **freuen, gefreut (über** + *acc.***)** to be happy (about) (11); **(auf** + *acc.***)** to look forward (to)

der **Freund, -e** / die **Freundin, -nen** friend; boyfriend/girlfriend (A)

freundlich friendly (B)

die **Freundschaft, -en** friendship

der **Frieden, -** peace

der **Friedhof, ⁼e** cemetery

friedlich peaceful(ly)

frieren (friert), fror, gefroren to freeze

frisch fresh(ly) (8)

der **Friseur, -e** / die **Friseurin, -nen** hairdresser (5)

die **Frisur, -en** hairstyle

froh happy; cheerful

fröhlich happy; cheerful(ly)

der **Frosch, ⁼e** frog (9)

„**Der Froschkönig**" "The Frog Prince" (*fairy tale*)

die **Frucht, ⁼e** fruit

früh early (1); in the morning (4); **bis um vier Uhr früh** until four in the morning (4); **früher** former(ly); **morgen früh** tomorrow morning

der **Frühjahrsputz** spring cleaning (6)

der **Frühling, -e** spring (B); **im Frühling** in the spring (B)

das **Frühstück, -e** breakfast (2); **zum Frühstück** for breakfast

frühstücken, gefrühstückt to eat breakfast (1)

das **Frühstückszimmer, -** breakfast room/nook (10)

(sich) fühlen, gefühlt to feel (3, 11); to touch; **Ich fühle mich ...** I feel . . . (3); **sich wohl fühlen** to feel well (11); **Wie fühlst du dich?** How do you feel? (3)

führen, geführt to lead; **den Haushalt führen (**+ *dat.***)** to keep house (*for s.o.*); **Krieg führen** to wage war

der **Führerschein, -e** driver's license (4)

die **Führungsposition, -en** leadership position

füllen, gefüllt to fill

fünf five (A)

die **Fünf: eine Fünf** poor (*school grade*)

fünft- fifth (4)

fünfundzwanzig twenty-five (A)

fünfzehn fifteen (A)

fünfzehnt- fifteenth

fünfzig fifty (A)

die **Funktion, -en** function

funktionieren, funktioniert to work, function

für (+ *acc.***)** for (2); **was für** what kind of

furchtbar terrible, terribly (4)

sich **fürchten (vor** + *dat.***), gefürchtet** to be afraid (of) (10)

fürs = für das for the

der **Fuß, ⁼e** foot (B); **mit dem linken Fuß aufstehen** to get up on the wrong side of bed (4); **zu Fuß** on foot (3)

der **Fußball, ⁼e** soccer ball; soccer (A, 1)

der **Fußballplatz, ⁼e** soccer field

der **Fußgänger, -** pedestrian (7)

der **Fußgängerweg, -e** sidewalk (7)

die **Fußgängerzone, -n** pedestrian mall (10)

das **Futter** feed; fodder

füttern, gefüttert to feed (9)

die **Gabel, -n** fork (8)

der **Gang, ⁼e** gear (7)

die **Gang, -s** gang

ganz whole (2); complete(ly); quite (2); rather; **den ganzen Tag** all day long (1); **die ganze Nacht** all night long (3); **ganz gut** quite good; **ganz schön viel** quite a bit (3)

gar: gar kein(e) no . . . at all; **gar nicht** not at all, not a bit (3); **gar nichts** nothing at all

die **Garage, -n** garage (6)

der **Garten, ⁼** garden (6); yard; **im Garten** in the garden (4)

der **Gartenschlauch, ⁼e** garden hose (6)

die **Gasse, -n** narrow street; alley (10)

der **Gast, ⁼e** guest; patron, customer

der **Gastarbeiter, -** / die **Gastarbeiterin, -nen** foreign worker

das **Gästehaus, ⁼er** bed and breakfast (inn) (10)

die **Gastfamilie, -n** host family

das **Gastland, ⁼er** host country

die **Gaststätte, -n** restaurant (5); **in der Gaststätte** at the restaurant (5)

der **Gaul, ⁼e** horse

das **Gebäude, -** building (10)

geben (gibt), gab, gegeben to give (6); **(in** + *acc.***)** to put (into) (8); **eine Party geben** to throw a party; **Es gibt ...** There is/are . . . (6); **geben Sie mir** give me (A); **Gibt es ...?** Is there . . . ? / Are there . . . ? (A, 6); **sich einen Termin geben lassen** to get an appointment (11)

das **Gebet, -e** prayer

das **Gebirge, -** mountains, mountain range (7)

geboren born (1); **Wann sind Sie geboren?** When were you born? (1)

gebraten (p.p. of **braten)** roasted; broiled; fried (8); **gebratene Eier (**pl.**)** fried eggs (8)

der **Gebrauch, ⁼e** use (12)

gebrauchen, gebraucht to use

der **Gebrauchtwagen, -** used car (7)

die **Gebrüder (**pl.**)** brothers

gebückt (p.p. of **bücken)** bent over; **in gebückter Haltung** bending over, bending forward

die **Gebühr, -en** fee

die **Geburt, -en** birth

der **Geburtstag, -e** birthday (1, 2); **zum Geburtstag** for someone's birthday (2)

die **Geburtstagskarte, -n** birthday card (2)

der **Gedanke, -n (**wk.**)** thought; **sich Gedanken machen (über** + *acc.***)** to think (about)

gedenken (+ *dat.***) (gedenkt), gedachte, gedacht** to remember

das **Gedicht, -e** poem (3)

geduldig patient(ly) (12)

gefährlich dangerous(ly) (10)

gefahrlos safe(ly)

gefallen (+ *dat.***) (gefällt), gefiel, gefallen** to be to one's liking; to please (6); **es gefällt mir** I like it (6); **sich (etwas) gefallen lassen (**coll.**)** to put up with (*s.th.*)

der **Gefallen, -** favor

die **Gefangenschaft** captivity

das **Gefängnis, -se** prison; jail (6)

das **Gefrierfach, ⁼er** freezer compartment

die **Gefriertruhe, -n** freezer (8)

das **Gefühl, -e** feeling (3)

gegen (+ *acc.***)** against (9); around; **ein Medikament gegen** medicine for (11)

der **Gegenstand, ⁼e** object

gegenüber (+ *dat.***)** opposite; across (6); **(von** + *dat.***)** across from (10); **gleich gegenüber** right across the way (6)

der **Gegner, -** / die **Gegnerin, -nen** opponent

gegrillt (p.p. of **grillen)** grilled; broiled; barbecued (8)

geheim secret(ly); die **Geheime Staatspolizei (Gestapo)** Secret State Police (*in Nazi Germany*)

das **Geheimnis, -se** secret (5)

die **Geheimniskrämerei, -en** secret-mongering

die **Geheimzahl, -en** secret PIN (personal identification number) (12)

gehen (geht), ging, ist gegangen to go; to walk (A); **auf eine Party gehen** to go to a party (1); **einkaufen gehen** to go shopping (1, 5); **ich gehe lieber ...** I'd rather go . . . (2); **in die Berge gehen** to go to the mountains (1); **in Erfüllung gehen** to come true; **ins Bett gehen** to go to bed (1); **nach Hause gehen** to go home (1); **schief gehen** to go wrong; **Wie geht es dir? (**infor.**)** / **Wie geht es Ihnen? (**for.**)** How are you?

zur Uni gehen to go to the university (1); das **Gehirn, -e** brain (11)

gehören (+ *dat.***), gehört** to belong to (*s.o.*) (6); **(zu** + *dat.***)** to belong (*to s.th.*)

gehörlos deaf

gehorsam obedient(ly)

die **Geige, -n** violin (3)

der **Geist** spirit, mind

geistig mental(ly); intellectual(ly)

der **Geizhals, ⸚e** skinflint

gekocht (*p.p. of* **kochen**) cooked; boiled (8); **gekochte Eier** (*pl.*) boiled eggs (8)

das **Gel, -s** gel

gelb yellow (A)

das **Geld** money (2)

der **Geldautomat, -en** (*wk.*) automatic teller machine (ATM) (12)

die **Geldbörse, -n** purse; wallet

der **Geldbote, -n** (*wk.*) / die **Geldbotin, -nen** money runner

das **Geldgeschäft, -e** financial transaction

der **Geldschein, -e** note, bill (*of currency*) (12)

der/die **Geliebte, -n** (**ein Geliebter**) beloved friend, love (3)

gelingen (**gelingt**), **gelang, ist gelungen** to succeed

gelten (**als**) (**gilt**), **galt, gegolten** to be valid (as); to be regarded (as)

das **Gelüst, -e** craving

gemeinsam together; (in) common (11)

die **Gemeinschaft, -en** community

das **Gemisch, -e** mixture

gemischt (*p.p. of* **mischen**) mixed (8)

das **Gemüse, -** vegetable (8)

gemütlich cozy (10)

genau exact(ly) (B)

genauso just as

die **Generation, -en** generation

genießen (**genießt**), **genoss, genossen** to enjoy

der **Genosse, -n** (*wk.*) / die **Genossin, -nen** comrade

das **Genre, -s** genre

genug enough (3)

genügend sufficient(ly)

das **Genus, Genera** gender

die **Geografie** geography (B, 1)

geometrisch geometric(ally)

der **Gepard, -e** cheetah (10)

gerade right now; just (at the moment); straight; upright; **gerade stellen** to straighten (3)

geradeaus straight ahead (10)

geradewegs straight; directly

das **Gerät, -e** appliance (8)

das **Geräusch, -e** sound, noise (9)

das **Gericht, -e** court(house) (5); dish (8); **auf dem Gericht** at the courthouse (5)

der **Gerichtssaal, -säle** courtroom

gering low

gern(e) gladly (5); willingly; with pleasure; (*with verb*) to like to; **ich habe ... gern** I like (*s.o./s.th.*); **ich hätte gern** I would like (to have) (*s.th.*) (5); **Trägst du gern ...?** Do you like to wear . . . ? (A); **Wir singen gern.** We like to sing. (1)

der **Geruch, ⸚e** smell

gesalzen salted (8)

gesamt whole; combined

das **Geschäft, -e** store (2)

geschäftlich (*relating to*) business

die **Geschäftsfrau, -en** businesswoman

der **Geschäftsführer, -** / die **Geschäftsführerin, -nen** manager (8)

der **Geschäftsmann, Geschäftsleute** businessman

geschehen (**geschieht**), **geschah, ist geschehen** to happen; to occur

das **Geschenk, -e** present (2)

die **Geschichte, -n** history (1); story

die **Geschichtsklausur, -en** history test

das **Geschirr** (*sg.*) dishes (4, 5); **Geschirr spülen** to wash the dishes (4)

der **Geschirrspüler, -** dishwasher (5)

die **Geschirrspülmaschine, -n** dishwasher

die **Geschlechterrolle, -n** gender role

geschlechtertypisch gender-biased, typical for a particular sex

der **Geschmack, ⸚er** taste

die **Geschwister** (*pl.*) brother(s) and sister(s), siblings (B)

die **Geselligkeit** sociability; conviviality

die **Gesellschaft, -en** society

gesellschaftlich social(ly)

gesetzlich legal(ly); statutory

das **Gesicht, -er** face (B)

das **Gespräch, -e** conversation

gestalten, gestaltet to form; to create

die **Gestaltung, -en** design

das **Geständnis, -se** confession

die **Gestapo** = die **Geheime Staatspolizei** Secret State Police (*in Nazi Germany*)

gestehen (**gesteht**), **gestand, gestanden** to confess

gestern yesterday (4); **gestern Abend** last night (4)

gestresst (*p.p. of* **stressen**) (*coll.*) stressed out; under stress

das **Gesuch, -e** request; application

gesund healthy (8)

die **Gesundheit** health (11)

das **Getränk, -e** beverage (8)

getrennt separate(ly); separate checks (5)

die **Gewalt** violence (12); force

das **Gewehr, -e** rifle

gewinnen (**gewinnt**), **gewann, gewonnen** to win (4); **in der Lotterie gewinnen** to win the lottery (5)

das **Gewitter, -** storm; thunderstorm

gewöhnlich ordinary, ordinarily

das **Gewürz, -e** spice; seasoning (8)

gießen (**gießt**), **goss, gegossen** to pour (8); to water (3); **die Blumen gießen** to water the flowers (3)

die **Gießkanne, -n** watering can (6)

giftig poisonous (9)

der **Gipfel, -** mountaintop (7)

der **Gips** cast (*plaster*) (11)

die **Giraffe, -n** giraffe (10)

das **Girokonto, Girokonten** checking account (12)

die **Gitarre, -n** guitar (1)

der **Gitarrenverstärker, -** guitar amplifier

der **Gitarrist, -en** (*wk.*) / die **Gitarristin, -nen** guitarist

das **Glas, ⸚er** glass (5)

gläsern (*adj.*) (made of) glass (9)

die **Glatze, -n** bald head

glauben, geglaubt to believe (2)

gleich (*adj.*) equal, same (12); (*adv.*) right away, immediately; right, directly (6); **gleich gegenüber** right across the way (6); **gleich um die Ecke** right around the corner (6)

gleichgeschlechtlich same-sex

das **Gleis, -e** (set of) train tracks (10)

der **Gletscher, -** glacier (7)

glitzern, geglitzert to twinkle

das **Glück** luck; happiness (3); **Glück haben** to have luck, be lucky; **Viel Glück!** Lots of luck! Good luck! (3)

glücklich happy, happily (B)

gnadenlos merciless(ly)

gnädig gracious, kind, dear; **gnädige Frau** *very formal way of addressing a woman*

das **Gold** gold

golden gold(en)

der **Goldfisch, -e** goldfish (11)

das **Golf** golf (1)

der **Gott, ⸚er** god; God (12); **grüß Gott** good afternoon; hello (*for.; southern Germany, Austria*) (A)

der **Gourmet, -s** gourmet

der **Gouverneur, -e** governor

das **Grab, ⸚er** grave, tomb

der **Grad, -e** degree; **18 Grad Celsius** 18 degrees Celsius (B)

die **Grafik, -en** drawing; graphic(s)

der **Grafiker, -** / die **Grafikerin, -nen** graphic designer

die **Grammatik, -en** grammar (A)

das **Gras, ⸚er** grass

gratulieren (+ *dat.*), **gratuliert** to congratulate (6)

grau gray (A)

grauen, gegraut: es graut mir/mich I dread

grausam cruel(ly) (9)

greifen (**greift**), **griff, gegriffen** to grab, grasp (11)

grell gaudy, shrill; cool, neat (2)

die **Grenze, -n** border

(das) **Griechenland** Greece (B)

der **Grill, -s** grill, barbecue (8)

die **Grippe, -n** influenza, flu (11)

groß large, big; tall (B); great; in a big way; **ziemlich groß** pretty big (2)

großartig magnificent(ly)

(das) **Großbritannien** Great Britain (B)

die **Größe, -n** size; height (1)

die **Großeltern** (*pl.*) grandparents (B)

die **Großmutter, ⸚** grandmother (B)

größtenteils for the most part

der **Großvater, ⸚** grandfather (B)

grüezi hi (*Switzerland*) (A)

grün green (A)

der **Grund, ⸚e** reason; basis; **im Grunde** in principle; basically

gründen, gegründet to found

grundsätzlich in principle; fundamental(ly)

die **Grundschule, -n** elementary school (9)

das **Grundstück, -e** property, lot (*land*)

die **Gruppe, -n** group

der Gruselfilm, -e horror film (2)

der Gruß, -̈e greeting (9)

grüßen, gegrüßt to greet; to say hello to (10); grüß dich hello (infor.; southern Germany, Austria); grüß Gott good afternoon; hello (for.; southern Germany, Austria) (A)

die Grütze, -n groats; rote Grütze red fruit pudding

gucken, geguckt (coll.) to look (at); to watch

der Gummibaum, -̈e rubber tree

die Gurke, -n cucumber (8); saure Gurken (pl.) pickles (8)

der Gurt, -e strap

der Gürtel, - belt (2)

gut good; well; Das passt gut. That fits well. (11); Das steht / Die stehen dir gut! That looks / Those look good on you! (2)

Es sieht gut aus. It looks good. (2); ganz gut very good; quite well; guten Abend good evening (A); guten Morgen good morning (A); guten Tag good afternoon; hello (for.) (A); mach's gut take care (infor.) (A)

die Güte goodness; Du meine Güte! (coll.) My goodness!

das Guthaben, - bank balance (12)

das Gymnasium, Gymnasien high school, college preparatory school (6)

das Haar, -e hair (A, B, 11); Haare schneiden to cut hair (3); sich die Haare föhnen to blow-dry one's hair (11); sich die Haare kämmen to comb one's hair (11)

die Haarfarbe, -n color of hair (1)

die Haarmode, -n hairstyle

der Haarschnitt, -e haircut (2)

der Haarstreifen, - strip of hair

haben (hat), hatte, gehabt to have (A); Angst haben (vor + dat.) to be afraid (of) (3); es eilig haben to be in a hurry (8); Haben Sie etwas dagegen? Do you have something for it (illness)? (11); Hunger haben to be hungry (3); ich habe ... gern I like (s.o./s.th.); ich hätte gern I would like to (have) (s.th.) (5); Interesse haben an (+ dat.) to be interested in (5); Lust haben to feel like (doing s.th.) (3); recht haben to be right (2); Welche Farbe hat ...? What color is . . . ? (A)

der Habsburger, - Habsburg

das Hackfleisch ground beef (or pork) (8)

der Hafen, -̈ harbor, port (10)

das Hähnchen, - (grilled) chicken

der Hai, -e shark (10)

der Haken, - hook (8)

halb half; um halb drei at two thirty (1)

die Halbinsel, -n peninsula (7)

die Hälfte, -n half

hallo hi (infor.) (A)

der Hals, -̈e neck; throat (9)

die Halsentzündung, -en inflammation of the throat

die Halskette, -n necklace (2, 5)

die Halsschmerzen (pl.) sore throat (11)

das Halstuch, -̈er bandanna (1)

halten (hält), hielt, gehalten to hold (4); to keep; to stop (7); ein Referat halten to give a paper / oral report (4); halten für (+ acc.) to consider; to think of as; halten von (+ dat.) to think of (12)

die Haltestelle, -n stop (10)

die Haltung, -en posture

der Hamburger, - hamburger

hämisch malicious(ly)

der Hammer, -̈ hammer (8)

der Hamster, - hamster (10)

die Hand, -̈e hand (B); die Hand schütteln to shake hands (A)

handeln, gehandelt to act; (von + dat.) to be about

die Handlung, -en action; plot

der Handschuh, -e glove (2)

das Handtuch, -̈er hand towel (8)

handwerklich handy

das Handy, -s cellular phone (2)

hängen (hängt), hing, gehangen to hang, be in a hanging position (3)

hängen, gehängt to hang (up), put in a hanging position (3); das Bild an die Wand hängen to hang the picture on the wall (3)

(das) Hannover Hanover

harmlos harmless(ly)

hart hard

hartnäckig obstinate(ly), stubborn(ly)

der Hartz IV-Typ, -en (wk.) (coll.) person who collects unemployment benefits

der Hase, -n (wk.) hare

hassen, gehasst to hate (9)

hässlich ugly (2)

die Haube, -n bonnet; cap

häufig often, frequent(ly); common(ly)

Haupt- main (prefixed to nouns)

die Hauptabstammung, -en main line of descent

die Hauptstadt, -̈e capital city (B)

das Haus, -̈er house (1, 2, 6); home (2); nach Hause gehen to go home (1, 10); zu Hause sein to be at home (A, 1, 10)

die Hausarbeit, -en housework

der Hausarrest, -e house arrest

der Hausarzt, -̈e / die Hausärztin, -nen family doctor (11)

die Hausaufgabe, -n homework (assignment) (A)

der Hausbesitzer, - / die Hausbesitzerin, -nen homeowner

das Hausboot, -e houseboat (6)

das Häuschen, - small house, cottage

die Hausfrau, -en housewife, (female) homemaker (12)

der Haushalt, -e household; housekeeping (9)

häuslich domestic

der Hausmann, -̈er (male) homemaker (12)

der Hausmeister, - / die Hausmeisterin, -nen custodian (5)

das Hausmittel, - home remedy

die Hausnummer, -n house number (1)

der Hausschlüssel, - house key (9)

der Hausschuh, -e slipper

das Haustier, -e pet (10)

die Haut, -̈e skin (11)

das Heft, -e notebook (B)

heilen, geheilt to heal (5)

die Heilpflanze, -n medicinal plant

die Heimat, -en home, hometown, homeland (12)

das Heimatland, -̈er homeland (12)

die Heimatstadt, -̈e hometown (6)

heimlich secret(ly) (9)

das Heimweh homesickness (3); Heimweh haben to be homesick (3)

die Heirat, -en marriage

heiraten, geheiratet to marry (3, 5)

heiß hot (B)

heißen (heißt), hieß, geheißen to be called, to be named (A); Ich heiße ... My name is . . . (A); Wie heißen Sie? (for.) / Wie heißt du? (infor.) What's your name? (A)

heiter cheerful(ly)

die Heizung, -en heating

der Held, -en (wk.) / die Heldin, -nen hero/heroine

helfen (+ dat.) (hilft), half, geholfen to help (6)

hell light (6); bright(ly)

das Hemd, -en shirt (A)

her (to) here, hither; this way (10)

hin und her to and fro; back and forth; von (+ dat.) ... her as far as . . . is concerned

herauf·holen, heraufgeholt to bring up, retrieve

heraus out this way (10); (aus + dat.) out (of)

heraus·bringen (bringt ... heraus), brachte ... heraus, herausgebracht to bring out; to utter, say

heraus·finden (findet ... heraus), fand ... heraus, herausgefunden to find out

herausfordernd challenging(ly); provocative(ly)

die Herausforderung, -en challenge

heraus·kommen (kommt ... heraus), kam ... heraus, ist herausgekommen to come out this way (10)

heraus·springen (springt ... heraus), sprang ... heraus, ist herausgesprungen to jump out

sich heraus·stellen, herausgestellt to turn out

heraus·suchen, herausgesucht to pick out

herb sharp; harsh; bitter

die Herbergseltern (pl.) wardens of a youth hostel

der Herbst, -e fall, autumn (B)

der Herd, -e stove (5)

herein in this way (10)

herein·holen, hereingeholt to bring in

herein·kommen (kommt ... herein), kam ... herein, ist hereingekommen to get/go in this way (10)

her·gehen (geht ... her), ging ... her, ist hergegangen to go along

her·kommen (kommt ... her), kam ... her, ist hergekommen to come this way (10)

die Herkunft, -̈e origin (B); nationality

der Herr, -en (wk.) gentleman; Mr. (A); master

die Herrschaft, -en rule; dominion

her·stellen, hergestellt to produce
herum around, round about; um (+ acc.) ...
    herum around
herum·gehen (um + acc.) (geht ... herum),
    ging ... herum, ist herumgegangen to go
    around (s.th.)
herum·schwirren, ist herumgeschwirrt to buzz
    around
herum·tragen (trägt ... herum), trug ... herum,
    herumgetragen to carry around
herunter down (toward the speaker) (11)
herunter·klettern, ist heruntergeklettert
    to climb down (11)
herunter·kommen (kommt ... herunter), kam ...
    herunter, ist heruntergekommen to come
    down
herunter·werfen (wirft ... herunter), warf ...
    herunter, heruntergeworfen to throw down
das Herz, -en heart (11)
die Herzfrequenz, -en heart rate
der Herzinfarkt, -e heart attack
herzlich hearty, heartily
das Herzogtum, ⁼er duchy
die Herzschmerzen (pl.) heartache (11)
heute today (B); heute Abend this evening (2);
    heute früh this morning; heute Morgen this
    morning; Welcher Tag ist heute? What day is
    today? (1); Welches Datum ist heute? What is
    today's date? (4)
heutig (adj.) of today; present-day
die Hexe, -n witch (7, 9)
hier here (A); Ist hier noch frei? Is this seat
    available? (8)
hierher (to) here, hither
die Hilfe, -n help; Hilfe! Help! (11)
der Himmel, - sky; heaven(s)
himmlisch heavenly
hin (to) there, thither; that way (10)
die Hin- und Rückfahrt round-trip (7); hin und
    her to and fro; back and forth; hin und zurück
    there and back; round-trip (5, 10); Wo willst
    du denn hin? Where are you going? (A)
hinauf up that way (10)
hinauf·gehen (geht ... hinauf), ging ... hinauf, ist
    hinaufgegangen to go up that way (10)
hinaus·bringen (bringt ... hinaus), brachte ...
    hinaus, hinausgebracht to bring out
hinaus·werfen (wirft ... hinaus), warf ... hinaus,
    hinausgeworfen to throw out
hin·bringen (bringt ... hin), brachte ... hin,
    hingebracht to take (s.o/s.th. somewhere)
das Hindernis, -se obstacle
hinein in(ward) (9); (in + acc.) into
hinein·beißen (beißt ... hinein), biss ... hinein,
    hineingebissen to bite in
hinein·biegen (biegt ... hinein), bog ... hinein, ist
    hineingebogen to turn
hinein·geben (gibt ... hinein), gab ... hinein,
    hineingegeben to put in
hinein·geraten (in + acc.) (gerät ... hinein), geriet ...
    hinein, ist hineingeraten to get (into)

hinein·laufen (in + acc.) (läuft ... hinein), lief ...
    hinein, ist hineingelaufen to run (into)
hinein·mischen, hineingemischt to mix in
sich hinein·trauen, hineingetraut to dare to
    go inside
hin·fahren (fährt ... hin), fuhr ... hin, ist hinge-
    fahren to go/drive (that way)
die Hinfahrt, -en journey there; outbound journey;
    die Hin- und Rückfahrt round-trip (7)
hin·fallen (fällt ... hin), fiel ... hin, ist hingefallen
    to fall down (11)
hin·gehen (geht ... hin), ging ... hin, ist hingegan-
    gen to go that way (10)
sich hin·legen, hingelegt to lie down (11)
hin·richten, hingerichtet to execute
hin·schauen, hingeschaut to look
sich hin·setzen, hingesetzt to sit down
sich hin·stellen, hingestellt to stand; to position
    oneself
hinter (prep. + dat./acc.) behind; (adj.) back
hintereinander in a row (3)
der Hintergrund, ⁼e background
der Hinterhof, ⁼e courtyard
hinterlassen (hinterlässt), hinterließ, hinterlassen
    to leave behind
hinüber over that way (10)
hinüber·gehen (geht ... hinüber), ging ... hinüber,
    ist hinübergegangen to go over that way (10)
hinunter·gehen (geht ... hinunter), ging ... hinun-
    ter, ist hinuntergegangen to go/walk down
hinweg: über viele Jahrhunderte hinweg for many
    centuries
hin·weisen (auf + acc.) (weist ... hin), wies ...
    hin, hingewiesen to point (to)
hinzu·fügen, hinzugefügt to add
der Hirschbraten, - roast venison
historisch historical(ly)
der Hit, -s (coll.) hit
das Hobby, -s hobby (1)
hoch high(ly) (7); hohen Blutdruck haben to
    have high blood pressure (11)
das Hochhaus, ⁼er high-rise building (6)
hochqualifiziert highly qualified
der Hochschulabschluss, ⁼e college/university
    degree
die Hochschule, -n college, university
der Höchstsatz, ⁼e maximum rate
der Hochstuhl, ⁼e highchair
der Hochverrat high treason
die Hochzeit, -en wedding
hoffen, gehofft to hope (3)
höflich polite(ly)
die Höhe, -n height; amount (of money) (12)
der Höhepunkt, -e highlight (7)
die Höhle, -n cave
holen, geholt to fetch, (go) get (9)
(das) Holland Holland (B)
holländisch Dutch (adj.) (8)
das Holz, ⁼er wood (12)
die Holzschindel, -n wooden shingle
homogen homogeneous

der Honig honey (8)
hoppla oops
hören, gehört to hear; to listen (to) (1)
das Horoskop, -e horoscope
der Hörsaaldiener, - / die Hörsaaldienerin, -nen
    lecture hall custodian
die Hose, -n pants, trousers (A)
das Hotel, -s hotel (2, 5); im Hotel at the hotel (5)
hübsch pretty (A, 2)
der Hügel, - hill (7)
das Huhn, ⁼er chicken
die Hühnersuppe, -n chicken soup
der Hund, -e dog (2)
das Hundefutter dog food (5)
die Hunderasse, -n breed of dog
hundert hundred (A)
hundertst- hundredth (4)
der Hunger hunger (3); Hunger haben to be
    hungry (3)
hungrig hungry, hungrily (9)
die Hupe, -n horn (7)
hupen, gehupt to honk (7)
husten, gehustet to cough
der Husten, - cough (11)
das Hustenbier warm beer with honey
das Hustenbonbon, -s cough drop (11)
der Hustenreiz tickling in the throat; need
    to cough
der Hustensaft, ⁼e cough syrup (11)
der Hut, ⁼e hat (A)
der Hybrid, -e hybrid (car)
die Hymne, -n hymn; anthem

ich I
ideal ideal(ly) (12)
die Idee, -n idea (10)
identifizieren, identifiziert to identify
die Identität, -en identity
das Idol, -e idol
das Iglu, -s igloo (6)
ihm (dat.) him, it
ihn (acc.) him, it (2)
ihnen (dat.) them
Ihnen (for. dat.) you
ihr (dat. sg.) her; (infor. nom. pl.) you
ihr(e) her, its (1, 2); their (2)
Ihr(e) (for.) your (B, 2)
illegal illegal(ly) (12)
illusionslos without illusions
im = in dem in the
immer always (3); immer mehr more and more;
    immer noch still
die Immobilien (pl.) real estate
impfen (gegen + acc.), geimpft to vaccinate
    (against) (10)
das Importland, ⁼er importer, country that
    imports
das Impressum, Impressen imprint
in (+ dat./acc.) in; into; at (A, 4); im Ausland
    abroad (6); im Büro at the office (5); im ersten
    Stock on the second floor (6); im Frühling in

the spring (B); **im Internet surfen** to surf the Internet (1); **im Januar** in January (B); **im Moment** at the moment; right now (1); **in den Bergen wandern** to hike in the mountains (1); **in der Nähe** in the vicinity (6); **in der Schule** at school (5); **in der Woche** during the week (1); **in die Berge gehen** to go to the mountains (1); **in Eile sein** to be in a hurry (3); **ins Bett gehen** to go to bed (1); **ins Schwimmbad fahren** to drive/go to the swimming pool (1)

inbegriffen included (10)

indem (*subord. conj.*) while; as

indirekt indirect(ly)

die **Industrie, -n** industry

ineinander in one another; **sich ineinander verlieben** to fall in love with each other

der **Infinitiv, -e** infinitive

die **Informatik** computer science (1)

die **Information, -en** information (4)

(sich) **informieren** (**über** + *acc.*), **informiert** to inform (*o.s.*) (about) (12)

der **Inhalt, -e** contents

die **Initiative, -n** initiative

inklusive (inkl.) included (*utilities*) (6)

die **Innenstadt, ⁼e** downtown (6)

das **Innere (ein Inneres)** inside

ins = in das in(to) the

insbesondere especially

die **Inschrift, -en** inscription

die **Insel, -n** island (7)

insgesamt altogether

installieren, installiert to install

das **Institut, -e** institute

die **Instruktion, -en** instruction

das **Instrument, -e** instrument (12)

die **Integration, -en** integration (12)

der/die **Intellektuelle, -n (ein Intellektueller)** intellectual

intelligent intelligent(ly) (7)

die **Intelligenz, -en** intelligence

interessant interesting (7); **etwas Interessantes** something interesting (4)

das **Interesse, -n** interest (5); **Interesse haben an** (+ *dat.*) to be interested in (5)

interessieren, interessiert to interest (5); **sich interessieren für** (+ *acc.*) to be interested in (5)

international international(ly)

das **Internet** Internet; **im Internet surfen** to surf the Internet (1)

das **Interview, -s** interview (4)

interviewen, interviewt to interview

inzwischen in the meantime, meanwhile

der **I-Pod, -s** iPod (2)

der **Iran** Iran

irgendetwas something; anything

irgendwann sometime; anytime

(das) **Irland** Ireland (B)

(das) **Italien** Italy (B)

italienisch Italian (*adj.*)

(das) **Italienisch** Italian (*language*) (B)

ja yes; indeed (4); **Das ist es ja!** That's just it! (4); **wenn ja** if so

die **Jacke, -n** jacket (A)

die **Jackentasche, -n** jacket pocket

jagen, gejagt to hunt

der **Jäger, -** / die **Jägerin, -nen** hunter (9)

das **Jahr, -e** year (B); **seit zwei Jahren** for (the last) two years (4)

der **Jahrestag, -e** anniversary

die **Jahreszahl, -en** date (year)

die **Jahreszeit, -en** season (B)

das **Jahrhundert, -e** century

-jährig -year-old (*adj.*)

jährlich annual(ly)

das **Jahrzehnt, -e** decade (4)

der **Januar** January (B); **im Januar** in January (B)

japanisch Japanese (*adj.*) (8)

je ever; each; **je nach Betrag** depending on the amount

je (*interj.*): **Oh je!** Oh dear!

die **Jeans** (*pl.*) jeans (2)

die **Jeansjacke, -n** denim jacket

jedenfalls in any case (11)

jeder, jedes, jede each; every (3, 5); **auf jeden Fall** by all means (4); **jede Woche** every week (3)

jederzeit at any time

jedoch however

jeher: seit jeher always; since time immemorial

jemand someone, somebody (3)

jener, jenes, jene (*dem. pron.*) that, those

jetzig present, current

jetzt now (3)

jeweilig particular

jeweils each time; each; every

der **Job, -s** job

das **Joch, -e** yoke

joggen, ist gejoggt to jog

der **Joghurt** yogurt

journalistisch journalistic(ally)

der **Jude, -n** (*wk.*) / die **Jüdin, -nen** Jewish man/woman

jüdisch Jewish

die **Jugend** youth (9); young people

die **Jugendherberge, -n** youth hostel (10)

der/die **Jugendliche, -n (ein Jugendlicher)** young person

der **Jugendschutz** protection of young people

das **Jugendschutzgesetz, -e** law for the protection of minors

die **Jugendsünde, -n** youthful folly

(das) **Jugoslawien** Yugoslavia

der **Juli** July (B)

jung young (B)

der **Junge, -n** (*wk.*) boy

der **Juni** June (B)

der **Jux, -e** joke; prank

der **Kaffee** coffee (1)

der **Kaffeefilter, -** coffee filter (4)

die **Kaffeemaschine, -n** coffee machine (5)

die **Kaffeemühle, -n** coffee grinder (8)

der **Käfig, -e** cage (10)

kahl bald

(das) **Kairo** Cairo

der **Kaiser, -** / die **Kaiserin, -nen** emperor/empress

kaiserlich imperial

das **Kaiserreich, -e** empire

der **Kaiserschmarren** *pancake pieces sprinkled with powdered sugar and served with fruit sauce*

der **Kakao** cocoa; hot chocolate (8)

kalorienarm low in calories (8)

kalorienbewusst calorie-conscious (8)

kalt cold(ly) (B)

das **Kamel, -e** camel

die **Kamera, -s** camera (2)

der **Kamillentee** chamomile tea

der **Kamin, -e** hearth, fireplace

der **Kamm, ⁼e** comb

kämmen, gekämmt to comb (3); **sich (die Haare) kämmen** to comb one's hair (11)

der **Kampf, ⁼e** battle; struggle

kämpfen, gekämpft to fight (9)

(das) **Kanada** Canada (B)

der **Kanadier, -** / die **Kanadierin, -nen** Canadian (*person*) (B)

das **Känguru, -s** kangaroo (10)

das **Kaninchen, -** rabbit

das **Kanu, -s** canoe (10); **Kanu fahren** to go canoeing (10)

der **Kapitalismus** capitalism

kapitalistisch capitalistic

das **Kapitel, -** chapter (A)

das **Käppchen, -** little cap; little hood

kaputt broken (A)

kaputt·machen, kaputtgemacht to break; to ruin

Karl der Große Charlemagne

das **Karnickel, -** rabbit (*dialectal*)

(das) **Kärnten** Carinthia

die **Karotte, -n** carrot (8)

die **Karriere, -n** career

die **Karte, -n** card; ticket; map (1, 2)

die **Kartoffel, -n** potato (8)

der **Kartoffelbrei** mashed potatoes

der **Kartoffelchip, -s** potato chips

der **Käse, -** cheese (8)

die **Kasse, -n** ticket booth (5); cashier window (12); **an der Kasse** at the ticket booth (5)

das **Kassler, -s** *salted and smoked pork*

die **Kastanie, -n** chestnut

der **Kasus, -** (grammatical) case

die **Kategorie, -n** category

der **Kater, -** tomcat; hangover (11)

die **Katze, -n** cat (2)

der **Katzenliebhaber, -** / die **Katzenliebhaberin, -nen** cat lover

kauen, gekaut to chew (11)

kaufen, gekauft to buy (1)

der **Käufer, -** / die **Käuferin, -nen** buyer; customer

das **Kaufhaus, ⁼er** department store (5); **im Kaufhaus** at the department store (5)

(das) **Kaufland** *department store chain*

das **Kaufmannshaus, ⁼er** merchant's house

kaum hardly

die **Kaution, -en** security deposit

der **Kaviar, -e** caviar

kein(e) no; none (2); **gar kein(e)** no . . . at all; **kein bisschen** not at all (3); **kein Wunder** no wonder (4)

der **Keller, -** basement, cellar (4, 6)

der **Kellner, -** / die **Kellnerin, -nen** waiter/waitress (8)

kennen (kennt), kannte, gekannt to know, be acquainted with (B)

kennen·lernen, kennengelernt to meet, get acquainted with (1)

die **Kenntnisse** (*pl.*) skills; knowledge about a field (5)

kennzeichnen, gekennzeichnet to label; to characterize

der **Kern, -e** seed, pit

die **Kerze, -n** candle (3)

die **Kette, -n** chain

der **Kilometer, -** kilometer (2)

der **Kilometerstand** mileage (7)

das **Kind, -er** child (B)

der **Kindergarten, -̈** kindergarten (6)

der **Kinderreim, -e** nursery rhyme

der **Kinderwagen, -** baby carriage (7)

die **Kindheit** childhood (9)

das **Kino, -s** movie theater, cinema (1); **ins Kino gehen** to go to the movies (1)

die **Kinokarte, -n** movie ticket (2)

die **Kirche, -n** church (5); **in der Kirche** at church (5)

der **Kirchenbau, -ten** church building

das **Kissen, -** cushion, pillow

die **Kiwi, -s** kiwi (fruit)

Kl. = die **Klasse, -n** class

die **Klammer, -n** bracket; parenthesis

die **Klamotten** (*pl., coll.*) clothes

der **Klang, -̈e** sound; tone

die **Klapperschlange, -n** rattlesnake (10)

klar clear(ly); **Klar!** Of course! (2)

die **Klarinette, -n** clarinet

klasse (*coll.*) great

die **Klasse, -n** class (5, 10); grade, level (9); **erster Klasse fahren** to travel first class (10)

die **Klassenarbeit, -en** (written) class test

der **Klassenkamerad, -en** (*wk.*) / die **Klassenkameradin, -nen** classmate

der **Klassenlehrer, -** / die **Klassenlehrerin, -nen** homeroom teacher

das **Klassentreffen, -** class reunion (9)

die **Klassik** classical period

klassisch classical

klassizistisch classical

klauen, geklaut (*coll.*) to steal

das **Klavier, -e** piano (2)

die **Klavierstunde, -n** piano lesson

kleben, geklebt to stick, adhere; to be sticky

das **Kleid, -er** dress (A); (*pl.*) clothes

(sich) kleiden, gekleidet to clothe (*o.s.*)

der **Kleiderschrank, -̈e** clothes closet, wardrobe (6)

die **Kleidung** clothes (A, 2)

klein small, little; short (B)

klettern, ist geklettert to climb (9)

das **Klima, -s** climate

klingeln, geklingelt to ring (2)

klingen (wie) (klingt), klang, geklungen to sound (like) (11); (**nach** + *dat.*) to sound (like)

die **Klinke, -n** door handle

klopfen, geklopft to knock

der **Kloß, -̈e** dumpling

der **Klosterfriedhof, -̈e** cloister cemetery

der **Klub, -s** club; nightclub

km = der **Kilometer, -** kilometer

knapp meager; scarce(ly); just, barely (4)

die **Kneipe, -n** bar, tavern (4)

der **Knoblauch** garlic (8)

der **Knochen, -** bone

der **Knödel, -** dumpling (8)

der **Knopf, -̈e** button

knuspern (an + *dat.*)**, geknuspert** to nibble (at)

der **Koch, -̈e** / die **Köchin, -nen** cook, chef (5)

kochen, gekocht to cook (1); to boil

der **Koffer, -** suitcase

der **Kofferraum, -̈e** trunk (7)

der **Kognak, -s** cognac

der **Kohl** cabbage (8)

der **Kolibri, -s** hummingbird (10)

der **Kollege, -n** (*wk.*) / die **Kollegin, -nen** colleague, co-worker

(das) **Köln** Cologne

kolumbianisch Colombian (*adj.*)

das **Koma, -s** coma

kombinieren, kombiniert to combine (3)

der **Komfort** comfort

komisch funny, strange (10)

kommen (kommt), kam, ist gekommen to come (B); (**aus** + *dat.*) to come from (*a place*) (B); **auf andere Gedanken kommen** to keep one's mind off something; **sich etwas zuschulden kommen lassen** to do something wrong; **Woher kommst du?** Where do you come from? (*infor.*); **zu Besuch kommen** to visit (3)

kommentieren, kommentiert to comment on

der **Kommilitone, -n** (*wk.*) / die **Kommilitonin, -nen** fellow student

die **Kommode, -n** dresser (6); chest of drawers

die **Kommunikation, -en** communication

die **Komödie, -n** comedy

komponieren, komponiert to compose

der **Komponist, -en** (*wk.*) / die **Komponistin, -nen** composer

das **Kompositum, Komposita** compound noun

die **Konfession, -en** religious denomination, church (12)

der **Konflikt, -e** conflict

der **König, -e** / die **Königin, -nen** king/queen (9)

königlich royal

die **Konjunktion, -en** conjunction

können (kann), konnte, gekonnt to be able (to), can; may (3)

konservativ conservative(ly) (B)

das **Konservatorium, Konservatorien** conservatory

die **Konstellation, -en** constellation

der **Kontakt, -e** contact

der **Kontinent, -e** continent

das **Konto, Konten** bank account (5); **ein Konto eröffnen** to open a bank account (5)

der **Kontostand, -̈e** balance; account status

der **Kontrast, -e** contrast

der **Kontrolleur, -e** / die **Kontrolleurin, -nen** police inspector

kontrollieren, kontrolliert to check; to control; **das Öl kontrollieren** to check the oil (5)

kontrovers controversial(ly)

sich konzentrieren (auf + *acc.*)**, konzentriert** to concentrate (on)

der **Konzern, -e** group (of companies)

das **Konzert, -e** concert (1); concerto; **die Brandenburgischen Konzerte** (*pl.*) the Brandenburg Concertos; **ins Konzert gehen** to go to a concert (1)

die **Konzertkarte, -n** concert ticket (5)

der **Konzertsaal, -säle** concert hall

(das) **Kopenhagen** Copenhagen

der **Kopf, -̈e** head (B)

die **Kopfbedeckung, -en** headgear

das **Kopfkissen, -** pillow (6)

der **Kopfsalat, -e** lettuce (8)

die **Kopfschmerzen** (*pl.*) headache (11)

die **Kopfschmerztablette, -n** headache tablet (11)

der **Kopierladen, -̈** copy shop (10)

der **Korb, -̈e** basket

der **Korkenzieher, -** corkscrew (8)

das **Korn, -̈er** grain; corn

der **Körper, -** body (B)

körperlich physical(ly)

die **Körperpflege** personal hygiene

der **Korridor, -e** corridor, hall

korrigieren, korrigiert to correct (4)

das **Kosmetikprodukt, -e** cosmetic product

der **Kosmonaut, -en** (*wk.*) / die **Kosmonautin, -nen** cosmonaut

kosten, gekostet to cost (2, 6)

kostenlos free of charge

die **Köstlichkeit, -en** delicacy

das **Kostüm, -e** costume

die **Krabbe, -n** shrimp (8)

der **Krabbenkutter, -** shrimp boat

die **Kraft, -̈e** power

kräftig powerful(ly); strong(ly)

die **Krähe, -n** crow

krank sick (3)

das **Krankenhaus, -̈er** hospital (3, 5); **im Krankenhaus** in the hospital (5)

der **Krankenpfleger, -** / die **Krankenpflegerin, -nen** nurse (5)

krankenversichert covered by health insurance

die **Krankenversicherung, -en** health insurance

der **Krankenwagen**, - ambulance (11)
die **Krankheit**, -en illness, sickness (11)
das **Kraut**, ⸚er herb (8)
die **Kräuterbutter** herb butter (8)
die **Krawatte**, -n tie, necktie (A)
kreativ creative(ly)
der **Krebs**, -e crab; Cancer (*astrological sign*)
der **Kredit**, -e credit; loan; **einen Kredit aufnehmen** to take out a loan
der **Kreis**, -e circle; (administrative) district
das **Kreisarchiv**, -e district archives
der **Kreisverkehr**, -e traffic roundabout (10)
die **Kreuzung**, -en intersection (10)
der **Krieg**, -e war; **Krieg führen** to wage war
der **Kriegsdienst** military service
die **Kriegsgefangenschaft** captivity (as a prisoner of war)
die **Kriminalität** crime
kritisch critical(ly)
kritisieren, kritisiert to criticize
(das) **Kroatien** Croatia
die **Krokette**, -n croquette (8)
das **Krokodil**, -e crocodile (10)
der **Krokus**, -se crocus
krönen, gekrönt to crown
die **Küche**, -n kitchen (5); cooking (8); cuisine
der **Kuchen**, - cake (5)
die **Küchenarbeit**, -en kitchen work (5)
die **Küchenlampe**, -n kitchen lamp (5)
die **Küchenmaschine**, -n mixer (8)
der **Küchentisch**, -e kitchen table (5)
die **Küchenuhr**, -en kitchen clock (5)
die **Küchenwaage**, -n kitchen scale (5)
der **Kugelschreiber**, - ballpoint pen (4)
kühl cool(ly) (B)
der **Kühlschrank**, ⸚e refrigerator (5)
k. u. k. = **kaiserlich und königlich** imperial and royal (*pertaining to the dual monarchy of Austria-Hungary*)
kulinarisch culinary
die **Kultur**, -en culture (12)
der **Kulturminister**, - / die **Kulturministerin**, -nen minister for the arts
der **Kummer** sorrow; grief; trouble
sich **kümmern (um + acc.), gekümmert** to take care (of) (12); to pay attention (to)
der **Kunde**, -n (*wk.*) / die **Kundin**, -nen customer (12)
kündigen, gekündigt to quit, resign
die **Kunst**, ⸚e art (1)
der **Kunstalmanach**, -e art yearbook
die **Kunstgeschichte** art history (1)
die **Kunstgewerbeschule**, -n school of arts and crafts
der **Künstler**, - / die **Künstlerin**, -nen artist
künstlerisch artistic(ally)
die **Kunsttheorie**, -n art theory
der **Kurs**, -e (*academic*) course, class (A, 1); exchange rate
die **Kursfahrt**, -en cruise; boat trip
kurz short(ly) (A, B); brief(ly)

die **Kurzgeschichte**, -n short story
die **Kusine**, -n (female) cousin (B)
der **Kuss**, ⸚e kiss (4)
küssen, geküsst to kiss (9)
die **Küste**, -n coast (7)

labil unstable
das **Labor**, -s laboratory
lächeln, gelächelt to smile
lachen, gelacht to laugh (3); **vor Lachen** from laughing (so hard)
der **Lachs**, -e salmon
der **Laden**, ⸚store, shop
die **Lage**, -n place; position (10); location
die **Lampe**, -n lamp (B)
das **Land**, ⸚er land, country; state; country (*rural*) (6); **auf dem Land** in the country (6)
die **Landkarte**, -n map (7)
das **Landsäugetier**, -e land mammal (10)
die **Landschaft**, -en landscape; scenery; region
die **Landschaftskunde** study of the region
die **Landsleute** (*pl.*) compatriots
der **Landvogt**, ⸚e governor (*of an imperial province*)
lang long (A, B)
lange (*adv.*) a long time
die **Länge**, -n length
die **Langeweile** boredom (3); **Langeweile haben** to be bored (3)
lang·gehen (geht ... lang), ging ... lang, ist langgegangen (*coll.*) to go along
langsam slow(ly)
sich **langweilen, gelangweilt** to be bored
langweilig boring (2)
der **Laptop**, -s laptop (computer) (B)
lassen (lässt), ließ, gelassen to let (11); to leave alone; to have something done; **sich einen Termin geben lassen** to get an appointment (11); **sich etwas zuschulden kommen lassen** to do something wrong
der **Lastwagen**, - truck (7)
(das) **Latein** Latin (*language*) (1)
die **Laterne**, -n lamp; lantern
der **Lauf**, ⸚e course; **seinen Lauf nehmen** to take its course
laufen (läuft), lief, ist gelaufen to go; to run (A, 2); **im Wald laufen** to run in the woods (2); **Schlittschuh laufen** to go ice-skating (3)
laufend current; **sich auf dem Laufenden halten** to keep oneself up-to-date
die **Laune**, -n mood
die **Lausitz** Lusatia (*region on the German-Polish border*)
laut loud(ly)
lauten, gelautet to read, go, run (*of text, an utterance, words*)
die **Lautmalerei**, -en onomatopoeia
die **Lawine**, -n avalanche
das **Layout**, -s layout
der **Leadsänger**, - / die **Leadsängerin**, -nen lead singer
leben, gelebt to live (3)

das **Leben**, - life (9); **am Leben sein** to be alive (9)
lebendig alive
das **Lebensgefühl** awareness of life
das **Lebensmittel**, - food; groceries
das **Lebensmittelgeschäft**, -e grocery store
der **Lebensraum**, ⸚e living space; habitat
die **Leber**, -n liver (11)
der **Leberkäse** loaf made of minced liver, eggs, and spices
leblos lifeless
lecker delicious
das **Leder**, - leather
ledig unmarried (1)
leer empty (5)
legal legal(ly)
legen, gelegt to lay, put, place (*in a horizontal position*); **sich legen** to lie down
die **Legende**, -n legend
die **Lehre**, -n apprenticeship (5)
der **Lehrer**, - / die **Lehrerin**, -nen teacher, instructor (A, 1)
der **Lehrjunge**, -n (*wk.*) (*young male*) apprentice
die **Lehrkraft**, ⸚e teacher(s)
das **Lehrmädchen**, - (*young female*) apprentice
der **Leib**, -er body; belly
leicht easy, easily; light (6)
das **Leid** suffering
die **Leidenschaft**, -en passion
leider unfortunately (B)
leid·tun (tut ... leid), tat ... leid, leidgetan: to be sorry; **tut mir leid** I'm sorry (4, 5); to feel sorry for
leihen (leiht), lieh, geliehen to lend (5)
leise quiet(ly) (9); soft(ly)
die **Leistung**, -en achievement, accomplishment
leiten, geleitet to lead; to be head of
das **Leitungswasser** tap water
die **Lektüre**, -n reading material
das **Lenkrad**, ⸚er steering wheel (7)
lernen, gelernt to learn; to study (1)
lesen (liest), las, gelesen to read (A, 1); **Zeitung lesen** to read the newspaper (1)
(das) **Lettland** Latvia
letzt- last (4); **das letzte Mal** the last time (4); **letzten Montag** last Monday (4); **letzten Sommer** last summer (4); **letztes Wochenende** last weekend (4)
letzte Woche last week (4); **letztendlich** ultimately, in the end
leuchten, geleuchtet to shine
die **Leute** (*pl.*) people (7)
liberal liberal(ly) (9)
das **Licht**, -er light (3)
der **Lichtblick**, -e bright spot
der **Lichthof**, ⸚e light-well, atrium
lieb dear (7); beloved; sweet, lovable; **am liebsten** like (*to do s.th.*) best (7); **lieb haben** to love; to be fond of
die **Liebe**, -n love
lieben, geliebt to love (3)
lieber rather (2); **ich gehe lieber ...** I'd rather go . . . (2)

der **Liebeskummer** lovesickness (11)
der **Liebesroman, -e** romance novel (9)
liebevoll loving(ly)
lieblich charming(ly)
Lieblings- favorite (A)
die **Lieblingsbeschäftigung, -en** favorite activity (5)
das **Lieblingsfach, ⁼er** favorite subject (5)
die **Lieblingsfarbe, -n** favorite color (A)
der **Lieblingsname, -n** (*wk.*) favorite name (A)
(das) **Liechtenstein** Liechtenstein (B)
das **Lied, -er** song (7)
der **Liedermacher, - /** die **Liedermacherin, -nen** singer-songwriter
liegen (**liegt**), **lag, gelegen** to lie, be (in a horizontal position) (1); to recline; to be situated; **in der Sonne liegen** to lie in the sun (1); **liegen bleiben** (**bleibt ... liegen**), **blieb ... liegen, ist liegen geblieben** to remain lying down
der **Liegestuhl, ⁼e** deck chair (4)
lila purple (A)
die **Limo, -s** = die **Limonade, -n** soft drink; lemonade
lindern, gelindert to relieve, soothe
die **Linguistik** linguistics (1)
die **Linie, -n** line
link- (*adj.*), **links** (*adv.*) left; on/to the left (4, 10); **mit dem linken Fuß aufstehen** to get up on the wrong side of bed (4); **nach links** (to the) left
die **Linse, -n** lentil
die **Lippe, -n** lip (11)
der **Lippenstift, -e** lipstick
die **List, -en** deception, trick (9)
die **Liste, -n** list (5)
listen, gelistet to list
listig cunning(ly)
(das) **Litauen** Lithuania
der **Liter, -** liter (7)
die **Literatur, -en** literature (1)
das **Loch, ⁼er** hole (9)
der **Löffel, -** spoon (8)
logisch logical(ly)
der **Lohn, ⁼e** pay; wages, salary
die **Lokomotive, -n** locomotive (7)
los loose; away; **Was ist los?** What's happening? What's the matter?
lösen, gelöst to solve; **ein Rätsel lösen** to solve a puzzle/riddle (9); **sich lösen** to free oneself
los·fahren (**fährt ... los**), **fuhr ... los, ist losgefahren** to drive/ride off (4, 9)
los·gehen (**geht ... los**), **ging ... los, ist losgegangen** to set off; to get started
los·rennen (**rennt ... los**), **rannte ... los, ist losgerannt** to run off, start running
die **Lösung, -en** solution
der **Lösungsvorschlag, ⁼e** suggested solution
die **Lotterie, -n** lottery (5); **in der Lotterie gewinnen** to win the lottery (5)
der **Löwe, -n** (*wk.*) lion (10)
loyal loyal(ly)
die **Luft, ⁼e** air (7)

die **Luftmatratze, -n** air mattress (10)
lügen, log, gelogen to lie, tell a falsehood
die **Lunge, -n** lung (11)
die **Lungenentzündung** pneumonia (11)
die **Lust, ⁼e** desire (3); **Lust haben** to feel like (*doing s.th.*) (3)
lustig fun, funny (12); cheerful, jolly
lutschen, gelutscht to suck (11)
(das) **Luxemburg** Luxembourg
der **Luxus** luxury

machen, gemacht to make; to do; **blau machen** to take the day off (3); **mach's gut** take care (*infor.*) (A); **sauber machen** to clean (3); **selbst gemacht** homemade (8); **sich an die Arbeit machen** to get down to work; **Spaß machen** to be fun; **Urlaub machen** to take a vacation
die **Machtergreifung, -en** seizure of power
das **Mädchen, -** girl (9)
die **Mafia, -s** Mafia
der **Magen, ⁼** stomach (11)
die **Magen-Darm-Grippe** gastrointestinal flu
die **Magenschmerzen** (*pl.*) stomachache (11)
die **Magie** magic
magisch magical(ly) (12)
der **Magister, -** master's degree
mähen, gemäht to mow (5)
die **Mahlzeit, -en** meal (8)
(das) **Mähren** Moravia
der **Mai** May (B)
mailen, gemailt to send e-mail
der **Main** Main (*river*)
mal once; (*word used to soften commands*) (11); **Komm mal vorbei!** Come on over! (11)
das **Mal, -e** time (4); **das letzte Mal** the last time (4); **ein paar Mal** a few times; **zum ersten Mal** for the first time (4)
malen, gemalt to paint (12)
der **Maler, - /** die **Malerin, -nen** painter
die **Mama, -s** mama, mom
die **Mami, -s** mommy
man one (*pron.*); people, they; **Wie schreibt man das?** How do you spell that? (A)
manch- some
manchmal sometimes (B)
mangelhaft poor, deficient, unsatisfactory
der **Mann, ⁼er** man; husband (A, B)
männlich masculine; male
die **Mannschaft, -en** team (9)
der **Mantel, ⁼** coat; overcoat (A)
das **Märchen, -** fairy tale (9)
märchenhaft as in a fairy tale
der **Markt, ⁼e** market (10)
die **Marktkirche, -n** church on the market square
der **Marktplatz, ⁼e** marketplace; market square (6)
die **Marktwirtschaft, -en** market economy
die **Marmelade, -n** jam; marmalade (8)
der **März** March (B)
der **Maschinenbau** mechanical engineering (1)
das **Massaker, -** massacre

der **Massenmord, -e** mass murder
massieren, massiert to massage
das **Masterstudium, -studien** course of study for a master's degree
das **Material, -ien** material, substance (12)
die **Mathe** math
die **Mathematik** mathematics (1)
der **Mathematiker, - /** die **Mathematikerin, -nen** mathematician
das **Matterhorn** *mountain in Switzerland*
die **Mauer, -n** wall; **die Berliner Mauer** the Berlin Wall
das **Maul, ⁼er** mouth (of an animal) (9)
die **Maus, ⁼e** mouse (10)
das **Medikament, -e** medicine (11); **ein Medikament gegen** (+ *acc.*) medicine for (11)
die **Medizin** medicine
medizinisch medical(ly) (11)
das **Meer, -e** sea (1, 7); **ans Meer** to the sea (2); **im Meer schwimmen** to swim in the sea (1)
der **Meerrettich** horseradish
das **Meerschweinchen, -** guinea pig (10)
mehr more (7); **immer mehr** more and more; **nicht mehr** no longer; **nie mehr** never again
mehrere (*pl.*) several; **seit mehreren Tagen** for several days (11)
das **Mehrfamilienhaus, ⁼er** house with several apartments
mehrmals several times (5)
die **Mehrzimmerwohnung, -en** multi-bedroom apartment
meiden (**meidet**), **mied, gemieden** to avoid
die **Meile, -n** mile
der **Meilenstein, -e** milestone
mein(e) my (A, 2)
meinen, gemeint to mean; to think
die **Meinung, -en** opinion; **Ihrer Meinung nach** (*for.*) in your opinion
der **Meißel, -** chisel (12)
meist most(ly); **am meisten** mostly; the most; **die meisten** most (of)
meistens usually; mostly (8)
der **Meister, - /** die **Meisterin, -nen** master
die **Meisterschaft, -en** championship
melancholisch melancholy
(sich) **melden, gemeldet** to report
die **Mengenlehre** set theory
die **Mensa, Mensen** student cafeteria (2)
der **Mensch, -en** (*wk.*) person (2); human being; **Mensch!** (*coll.*) Man! Oh boy! (2)
menschengerecht suitable for humans
menschlich human
der **Mercedes** *make of car*
die **Messe, -n** trade fair
das **Messer, -** knife (8)
der **Meter, -** meter
die **Methode, -n** method
die **Metropolregion, -en** metropolitan area
die **Metzgerei, -en** butcher shop (6)
der **Mexikaner, - /** die **Mexikanerin, -nen** Mexican (*person*) (B)

mexikanisch Mexican (*adj.*) (8)

(das) Mexiko Mexico

mich (*acc.*) me

mies (*coll.*) crummy

die Miete, -n rent (6); **zur Miete** for rent

mieten, gemietet to rent (6)

der Mieter, - / die Mieterin, -nen renter (6)

das Mietrecht tenancy law, rental law

der Migrationshintergrund, -̈e immigrant
    background

die Mikrowelle, -n microwave (oven)

die Milch milk (8)

mildern, gemildert to relieve; to soothe

die Million, -en million (12)

Min. = **die Minute, -n** minute

mindestens at least

das Mineralwasser mineral water (8)

das Miniwörterbuch, -̈er minidictionary

die Minute, -n minute

mir (*dat.*) me; **mit mir** with me (3)

die Mischung, -en mixture

die Misshandlung, -en mistreatment

misstrauen (+ *dat.*), **misstraut** to mistrust

mit (+ *dat.*) with (A); **mit dem linken Fuß
    aufstehen** to get up on the wrong side of
    bed (4); **mit mir** with me (3)

der Mitarbeiter, - / die Mitarbeiterin, -nen
    co-worker; collaborator

der Mitbegründer, - / die Mitbegründerin, -nen
    cofounder

der Mitbewohner, - / die Mitbewohnerin, -nen
    roommate; housemate (2)

mit·bringen (**bringt ... mit**), **brachte ... mit,
    mitgebracht** to bring along (3)

der Mitbürger, - / die Mitbürgerin, -nen fellow
    citizen

miteinander with each other (3)

mit·fahren (**fährt ... mit**), **fuhr ... mit, ist
    mitgefahren** to ride/travel along

die Mitfahrzentrale, -n ride-share agency

das Mitglied, -er member

mithilfe (+ *gen.*) with the aid of

mit·kommen (**kommt ... mit**), **kam ... mit, ist
    mitgekommen** to come along

mit·machen, mitgemacht to participate; to join in

mit·nehmen (**nimmt ... mit**), **nahm ... mit,
    mitgenommen** to take along (3)

mit·schreiben (**schreibt ... mit**), **schrieb ... mit,
    mitgeschrieben** to write along (at the same
    time)

der Mitschüler, - / die Mitschülerin, -nen
    schoolmate, fellow pupil

mit·spielen, mitgespielt to play along, join in the
    game

der Mitstudent, -en (*wk.*) / **die Mitstudentin,
    -nen** fellow student (A)

der Mittag, -e midday, noon (3); **zu Mittag essen**
    to eat lunch

das Mittagessen, - midday meal, lunch (3); **zum
    Mittagessen** for lunch (3)

mittags at noon (2)

die Mitte middle, center; **in the middle of**

der Mittelfinger, - middle finger

das Mittelmeer Mediterranean Sea (B)

mitten in the middle (9); **mitten in der Nacht** in
    the middle of the night

die Mitternacht midnight; **um Mitternacht** at
    midnight

mittler- (*adj.*) middle

der Mittwoch, -e Wednesday (1)

mit·versorgen, mitversorgt to be equally
    responsible for taking care of

die Möbel (*pl.*) furniture (6)

das Möbelstück, -e piece of furniture (6)

möbliert furnished (6)

das Modalverb, -en modal verb

die Mode, -n fashion

das Modell, -e model, example

modern modern, in a modern fashion (6)

der Modeschnickschnack fashionable frills

der Modezeichner, - / die Modezeichnerin, -nen
    fashion designer

modisch fashionable, fashionably

mögen (mag), mochte, gemocht to like (to); to
    care for (1, 3); **möchte** would like (to) (2, 3)

möglich possible; **alles Mögliche** everything
    possible (2)

möglicherweise possibly

die Möglichkeit, -en possibility (5)

möglichst (+ *adv.*) as . . . as possible (6)

der Moment, -e moment (1); **im Moment** at the
    moment; right now (1)

die Monarchie, -n monarchy

der Monat, -e month (B)

monatlich monthly

das Monopol, -e monopoly

der Montag, -e Monday (1); **letzten Montag** last
    Monday (4)

montags on Monday(s)

das Moped, -s moped

der Mörder, - / die Mörderin, -nen murderer

morgen tomorrow (2); **morgen Abend** tomorrow
    evening; **morgen früh** tomorrow morning

der Morgen, - morning; **am Morgen** in the
    morning; **guten Morgen** good morning (A);
    heute Morgen this morning

das Morgengrauen dawn, daybreak

morgens in the morning(s)

die Morgentoilette morning grooming routine

(das) Moskau Moscow

das Motiv, -e motif, theme (12)

die Motorjacht, -en motor yacht

das Motorrad, -̈er motorcycle (1, 7); **Motorrad
    fahren** to ride a motorcycle (1)

das Motto, -s motto, slogan

die Möwe, -n seagull (10)

der MP3-Player, - MP3 player

der MP3-Spieler, - MP3 player (2, 5)

die Mücke, -n mosquito (10)

müde tired (3)

die Mühle, -n mill

der Müll trash; garbage (6)

der Mülleimer, - garbage can (8)

der Müllermeister, - / die Müllermeisterin, -nen
    master miller

die Müllerstochter, -̈ miller's daughter

multikulturell multicultural(ly)

(das) München Munich

Münchner (*adj.*) (of) Munich

der Mund, -̈er mouth (B)

die Mundharmonika, -s harmonica (12)

munter cheerful(ly); lively; wide awake

die Münze, -n coin

die Murmel, -n marble

die Muschel, -n mussel (8); seashell

das Museum, Museen museum (1); **ins Museum
    gehen** to go to a museum (1)

das Musical, -s musical (*stage play*)

die Musik, -en music (1)

der Musiker, - / die Musikerin, -nen musician

der Muskelkater, - sore muscles (11)

das Muskeltraining muscle exercise

das Müsli, -s granola

müssen (muss), musste, gemusst to have to,
    must (3); **nicht müssen** not to have to, not
    to need to

der Mut courage

mutig brave(ly)

die Mutter, -̈ mother (B)

die Muttersprache, -n mother tongue, native
    language

der Muttertag Mother's Day (4)

die Mutti, -s mom, mommy

die Mütze, -n cap (5)

mysteriös mysterious(ly)

na (*interj.*) well (3); so; **na, gut** well, okay; **na ja**
    all right; **na, klar** of course

nach (+ *dat.*) after; past; according to; toward; to
    (*a place*) (3, 10); **je nach Betrag** depending on
    the amount; **nach dem Weg fragen** to ask for
    directions; **nach Hause gehen** to go home
    (1, 10); **nach links** (to the) left; **nach oben**
    upwards; **um zwanzig nach fünf** at twenty
    after/past five (1)

der Nachbar, -n (*wk.*) / **die Nachbarin, -nen**
    neighbor (4)

das Nachbarhaus, -̈er house next door

nachdem (*subord. conj.*) after (9, 11)

nach·denken (über + *acc.*) **(denkt ... nach),
    dachte ... nach, nachgedacht** to think (about);
    to consider (7)

nacheinander one after the other

nach·forschen, nachgeforscht to investigate

nachher afterward

die Nachhilfe tutoring (3)

nachlässig lax; careless(ly)

der Nachmieter, - / die Nachmieterin, -nen
    subletter

der Nachmittag, -e afternoon (4); **am Nachmittag**
    in the afternoon; **heute Nachmittag** this
    afternoon

nachmittags afternoons, in the afternoon (4)

die **Nachricht, -en** report; message; (*pl.*) news (7)
nach·sehen (sieht ... nach), sah ... nach, **nachgesehen** to check; to go and see
die **Nachspeise, -n** dessert (8)
nächst- next; nearest
die **Nächstenliebe** charity, brotherly love
die **Nacht, -̈e** night (3); **die ganze Nacht** all night long (3); **mitten in der Nacht** in the middle of the night
der **Nachteil, -e** disadvantage (7)
das **Nachthemd, -en** nightshirt (2)
nachts nights, at night (4)
der **Nachttisch, -e** nightstand, bedside table (6)
der **Nacken, -** neck
der **Nagel, -̈** nail (8)
nah close, nearby (7)
nahe (+ *dat.*) near, close to
die **Nähe** closeness, proximity; vicinity (6); **in der Nähe** in the vicinity (6)
sich **nähern, genähert** to approach
der **Name, -n** (*wk.*) name (A, 1)
namens by the name of; called
nämlich namely; actually
die **Narbe, -n** scar (1)
die **Nase, -n** nose (11)
nass wet (3)
die **Nation, -en** nation
national national(ly)
der **Nationalfeiertag, -e** national holiday (4)
die **Nationalität, -en** nationality
nationalsozialistisch (*adj.*) National Socialist, Nazi
nativ native
die **Natur, -en** nature (9); disposition, temperament; **in freier Natur** out in the open (country) (10)
natürlich natural(ly) (2); of course
der **Naturschutz** nature conservation
der **Nazi, -s** Nazi
der **Nebel, -** fog, mist
neben (+ *dat./acc.*) next to (9); in addition to (3)
nebenan next door (5); **von nebenan** from next door (5)
die **Nebenkosten** (*pl.*) extra costs (*e.g., utilities*) (6)
das **Nebenzimmer, -** next room, adjacent room
der **Neffe, -n** (*wk.*) nephew (B)
negativ negative(ly)
nehmen (nimmt), nahm, genommen to take (A); **jemanden auf den Arm nehmen** to tease someone; to pull someone's leg
die **Neigung, -en** inclination; tendency
nein no (A)
nennen (nennt), nannte, genannt to name; to call; **sich nennen** to be called
nervös nervous(ly) (1)
das **Nest, -er** nest (10)
nett nice(ly) (3)
das **Netz, -e** net
das **Netzwerk, -e** network
neu new(ly) (A); **etwas Neues** something new (4)
der **Neubau, -ten** *building completed after 1 Dec. 1949*
neugierig curious(ly) (12)

neulich recently (9)
neun nine (A)
neunt- ninth (4)
neunundzwanzig twenty-nine (A)
neunzehn nineteen (A)
neunzehnt- nineteenth
neunzig ninety (A)
(das) **Neuseeland** New Zealand (B)
neuseeländisch of/from New Zealand
die **Neustadt, -̈e** new part of town
die **Neuzeit** modern era
nicht not (A); **gar nicht** not at all, not a bit (3); **nicht mehr** no longer; **nicht (wahr)?** isn't that right?
noch nicht not yet
die **Nichte, -n** niece (B)
nichts nothing (9); **gar nichts** nothing at all
nie never (2); **nie mehr** never again; **noch nie** never (before)
die **Niederlande** (*pl.*) the Netherlands (B)
niederländisch Dutch
sich **nieder·lassen (lässt ... nieder), ließ ... nieder,** **niedergelassen** to settle
(das) **Niederösterreich** Lower Austria
(das) **Niedersachsen** Lower Saxony
nieder·schlagen (schlägt ... nieder), schlug ... **nieder, niedergeschlagen** to knock down
nieder·schreiben (schreibt ... nieder), schrieb ... **nieder, niedergeschrieben** to write down
niedrig low; **niedrigen Blutdruck haben** to have low blood pressure (11)
niemals never
niemand no one, nobody (2)
die **Niere, -n** kidney (11)
die **Nierenentzündung** kidney infection (11)
das **Nikotin** nicotine
der **Nil** Nile (*river*)
das **Niveau, -s** level
noch even, still (B); yet; else; in addition; **immer noch** still; **Ist hier noch frei?** Is this seat available? (8); **noch ein(e)** another, an additional (one); **noch einmal** one more time; **noch nicht** not yet; **noch nie** never (before); **sonst noch** in addition; else; **Sonst noch etwas?** Anything else? (5)
die **Nominalphrase, -n** noun phrase
nord- north
(das) **Nordamerika** North America (B)
(das) **Nordbayern** Northern Bavaria
norddeutsch North German (*adj.*)
der **Norden** north
nordfriesisch North Frisian (*adj.*)
nördlich (von + *dat.*) north (of) (7)
nordöstlich (von + *dat.*) northeast (of) (7)
die **Nordsee** North Sea (B)
die **Nordwand, -̈e** north wall; north face (*of a mountain*)
nordwestlich (von + *dat.*) northwest (of) (7)
die **Norm, -en** norm
normal normal(ly) (5)
normalerweise normally (8)

(das) **Norwegen** Norway (B)
die **Not, -̈e** need; hardship; trouble
die **Note, -n** grade, mark (*in school*) (9)
das **Notebook, -s** notebook (computer)
der **Notfall, -̈e** emergency
nötig necessary; **nötig brauchen** to need urgently
die **Notiz, -en** note
die **Novelle, -n** novella
der **November** November (B)
die **Nudel, -n** noodle (8)
null zero (A)
der **Nullpunkt** freezing point, zero degrees Celsius (= 32 degrees Fahrenheit)
die **Nummer, -n** number (1)
das **Nummernschild, -er** license plate (7)
nun now; well
nur only (3)
(das) **Nürnberg** Nuremberg
die **Nuss, -̈e** nut (8)
die **Nusshecke, -n** nut thicket
nutzen, genutzt to use
nützen, genützt to do some good; to be of use
nützlich useful(ly) (10)

ob (*subord. conj.*) if, whether (6, 11)
der/die **Obdachlose, -n (ein Obdachloser)** homeless person
oben above (10); on top; upstairs; **nach oben** upwards
der **Oberarm, -e** upper arm
(das) **Oberösterreich** Upper Austria
die **Oberschule, -n** secondary school
das **Objekt, -e** object
das **Obst** fruit (8)
obwohl (*subord. conj.*) although (11)
oder (*coord. conj.*) or (A, 11)
die **Odyssee, -n** odyssey
offen open(ly)
öffentlich public(ly); **die öffentlichen Verkehrs-mittel** (*pl.*) public transportation (7)
offiziell official(ly)
öffnen, geöffnet to open (A)
oft often (A)
öfters now and then, once in a while
oftmals often
oh je (*interj.*) oh dear
ohne (+ *acc.*) without
die **Ohnmacht, -en** unconsciousness (11); **in Ohnmacht fallen** to faint (11)
das **Ohr, -en** ear (B)
die **Ohrenschmerzen** (*pl.*) earache (11)
der **Ohrring, -e** earring (A, 2)
okay (*coll.*) okay
ökologisch ecological(ly)
der **Oktober** October (B); **am ersten Oktober** on the first of October (4); **der erste Oktober** the first of October (4)
das **Oktoberfest, -e** Octoberfest (*annual beer festival in Munich*) (7)
das **Öl** oil (5, 8); **das Öl kontrollieren** to check the oil (5)

die Ölfarbe, -n oil color (*paint*) (12)
die Olive, -n olive (8)
die Oma, -s grandma (3)
das Omelett, -s omelet (8)
der Onkel, - uncle (B)
online online
der Onlinezugang, ⸚e online access
der Opa, -s grandpa
das Opfer, - sacrifice; victim
der Opi, -s grandpa
orange orange (*color*) (A)
die Orange, -n orange
der Orangensaft orange juice (8)
die Ordinalzahl, -en ordinal number
ordnen, geordnet to arrange, put in order
die Organisation, -en organization
organisch organic(ally)
die Orgel, -n organ (*musical instrument*) (12)
orientalisch oriental
der Orientexpress Orient Express (*train*)
das Original, -e original
der Ort, -e place (1, 5); town
der/die Ortsfremde, -n (ein Ortsfremder)
    stranger, nonresident
die Oskar-Nominierung, -en Oscar (Academy
    Award) nomination
ost- east
(das) Ostdeutschland (*former*) East Germany
der Osten east
das Ostern, - Easter
(das) Österreich Austria (B)
der Österreicher, - / die Österreicherin, -nen
    Austrian (*person*) (B)
österreichisch Austrian (*adj.*)
östlich (von + *dat.*) east (of) (7)
die Ostsee Baltic Sea (B)

paar: ein paar a few (2); a couple of; ein paar Mal
    a few times
das Paar, -e couple; pair (of)
packen, gepackt to pack (10)
der Pädagoge, -n (*wk.*) / die Pädagogin, -nen
    teacher; educational theorist
pädagogisch educational(ly)
das Paket, -e package (8)
die Palatschinke, -n *pancake with sweet filling*
der Papa, -s daddy, dad
der Papagei, -en parrot (10)
der Papi, -s daddy
das Papier, -e paper (B)
der Papierkorb, ⸚e wastebasket (3)
das Papiertuch, ⸚er paper towel (5)
der Paprika paprika
die Paprika, -s bell pepper
der Papst, ⸚e pope
parallel parallel
parat ready
das Parfüm, -e perfume (5)
der Park, -s park (1); im Park spazieren gehen to
    go for a walk in the park (1)
der Parkautomat, -en (*wk.*) parking meter

parken, geparkt to park (7)
die Parole, -n slogan
das Partizip, -ien participle
der Partner, - / die Partnerin, -nen partner (12);
    Arbeiten Sie mit einem Partner. Work with a
    partner. (A)
die Partnerschaft, -en partnership (12)
die Party, -s party (1, 2); auf eine Party gehen to
    go to a party (1)
der Pass, ⸚e passport (7)
passen, gepasst (+ *dat.*) to fit (6, 11); to suit;
    (zu + *dat.*) to go (with), fit in (with); Das
    passt gut. That fits well. (11)
passend fitting; proper
passieren, passiert to happen (4)
das Passwort, ⸚er password (7)
der Patient, -en (*wk.*) / die Patientin, -nen
    patient (5)
der Patrizier, - patrician
die Pause, -n recess, break (1); Pause machen to
    take a break
der Pazifik Pacific Ocean
das Pech pitch; bad luck; Pech haben to be
    unlucky
(das) Peking Beijing
der Pelz, -e fur
das Penizillin penicillin (4)
pennsylvanisch Pennsylvanian (*adj.*)
per per, by means of
perfekt perfect(ly)
die Person, -en person, individual (1)
der Personalausweis, -e (personal) ID card (1)
persönlich personal(ly); persönliche Daten
    biographical information (1)
die Persönlichkeit, -en personality
die Perspektive, -n perspective
pfälzisch of/from the Palatinate
die Pfanne, -n (frying) pan (5)
der Pfeffer, - (black) pepper (8)
das Pferd, -e horse (2, 9)
der Pfifferling, -e chanterelle (*type of mushroom*)
der Pfirsich, -e peach (8)
die Pflanze, -n plant (3, 6)
die Pflanzenheilkunde herbal medicine
das Pflaster, - adhesive bandage (11)
die Pflaume, -n plum (8)
pflegen, gepflegt to attend to; to nurse (5); to
    nurture
die Pflicht, -en duty; requirement; obligation (3)
pflichtbewusst conscientious(ly)
der Pflichtunterricht required instruction
pflücken, gepflückt to pick (9)
das Pharmaunternehmen, - pharmaceutical
    company
der Philosoph, -en (*wk.*) / die Philosophin, -nen
    philosopher
die Physik physics (1)
der Physiker, - / die Physikerin, -nen physicist
das Picknick, -s picnic (4)
das Piercing, -s piercing (2)
der Pilot, -en (*wk.*) / die Pilotin, -nen pilot (5)

der Pilz, -e mushroom (8)
die Pinnwand, ⸚e bulletin board
der Pinsel, - paintbrush (12)
der Pionier, -e Pioneer (*member of an East German
    youth organization*)
der Piranha, -s piranha (10)
die Pistole, -n pistol
die Pizza, Pizzen pizza (2)
das Plakat, -e poster; placard
der Plan, ⸚e plan (3)
planen, geplant to plan (9)
das Platin platinum
der Platz, ⸚e place; seat; room, space; plaza,
    square (3); Platz nehmen to take a seat
die Playliste, -n playlist
plötzlich sudden(ly) (9)
plus plus
(das) Polen Poland (B)
die Politik politics
politisch political(ly) (12)
die Polizei police; police station (5); auf der
    Polizei at the police station (5)
der Polizist, -en (*wk.*) / die Polizistin, -nen
    police officer (5)
die Pommes (frites) (*pl.*) French fries (8)
die Popmusik pop music
populär popular(ly)
das Portal, -e portal, gateway
das Portemonnaie, -s wallet
(das) Portugal Portugal (B)
(das) Portugiesisch Portuguese (*language*) (B)
(das) Posen Poznan (*city in Poland*)
positiv positive(ly)
das Possessivpronomen, - possessive adjective
die Post, - mail; post office (5); auf der Post at
    the post office (5)
das Poster, - poster (6)
die Postkarte, -n postcard (2)
potentiell potential(ly)
das Präfix, -e prefix
die Präposition, -en preposition
präsentieren, präsentiert to present
der Präsident, -en (*wk.*) / die Präsidentin, -nen
    president (5)
der Preis, -e price (7, 12); prize
preisgünstig at a favorable price; inexpensive(ly)
die Prellung, -en bruise
pressen, gepresst to press, squeeze
das Prestige prestige (5)
der Priester, - / die Priesterin, -nen priest/
    priestess (5)
prima great (6)
der Prinz, -en (*wk.*) / die Prinzessin, -nen
    prince/princess (9)
privat private(ly)
pro per (2)
die Probe, -n test; rehearsal
probieren, probiert to try; to taste (3)
das Problem, -e problem
problematisch problematic

die **Produktion**, -en production
der **Produzent**, -en (*wk.*) / die **Produzentin**, -nen producer
der **Professor**, -en / die **Professorin**, -nen professor (A, B)
der **Profikoch**, ‡e / die **Profiköchin**, -nen professional cook, chef
das **Programm**, -e program
das **Projekt**, -e project
die **Proportion**, -en proportion
protestantisch Protestant (*adj.*)
provisionsfrei without commission
das **Prozent**, -e percent, percentage (4)
prozentual by percentage
die **Prozentzahl**, -en percentage
der **Prozess**, -e trial
die **Prüfung**, -en test, exam (1)
die **Prüfungskommission**, -en examination committee
die **Prügel** (*pl.*) beating(s)
der **Psychiater**, - / die **Psychiaterin**, -nen psychiatrist (11)
psychisch psychological(ly), mental(ly)
der **Pudel**, - poodle
der **Pulli**, -s = der **Pullover**, - pullover; sweater (2)
der **Pullover**, - pullover; sweater
der **Punkt**, -e point (A); dot
punkten, gepunktet to score points
pünktlich punctual(ly); on time (4)
die **Pünktlichkeit** punctuality
pur pure
das **Putenschnitzel**, - turkey cutlet
putzen, geputzt to clean (6); **sich (die Zähne) putzen** to brush (one's teeth) (11)
der **Putzlappen**, - cloth, rag (for cleaning) (6)
die **Pyramide**, -n pyramid

qm = der **Quadratmeter**, - square meter (m²) (6)
das **Quadrat**, -e square
der **Quadratmeter**, - square meter (m²) (6)
quälen, gequält to torment
die **Qualität**, -en quality
die **Querflöte**, -n (transverse) flute (12)
die **Quickcard** *Austrian debit card*
die **Quittung**, -en receipt, check (8)
die **Quote**, -n proportion; rate; figures

das **Rad**, ‡er wheel (7); bicycle; **Rad fahren (fährt ... Rad), fuhr ... Rad, ist Rad gefahren** to ride a bicycle (7)
radeln, ist geradelt to ride a bicycle
der **Radfahrer**, - / die **Radfahrerin**, -nen bicyclist (7)
das **Radieschen**, - radish
das **Radio**, -s radio (2)
das **Radium** radium
die **Radtour**, -en bicycle tour (9)
die **Rakete**, -n rocket (7)
das **Ranking**, -s ranking
der **Ranzen**, - schoolbag; knapsack; satchel
der **Rapper**, - / die **Rapperin**, -nen rapper, rap singer

der **Rasen**, - lawn (5)
der **Rasenmäher**, - lawnmower (6)
der **Rasierapparat**, -e shaver, (electric) razor
sich rasieren, rasiert to shave (11)
die **Rasierklinge**, -n razor blade
das **Rasierwasser** aftershave lotion
der **Rat** (*pl.* Ratschläge) advice (5, 11)
die **Rate**, -n rate
raten (rät), riet, geraten to guess; (+ *dat.*) to advise (*s.o.*) (11)
das **Ratespiel**, -e guessing game; quiz
das **Rathaus**, ‡er town/city hall (1, 6); **auf dem Rathaus** at the town hall (1)
der **Ratschlag**, ‡e (piece of) advice (5, 11)
das **Rätsel**, - puzzle, riddle (9); **ein Rätsel lösen** to solve a puzzle/riddle (9)
die **Ratte**, -n rat (10)
rauchen, geraucht to smoke (3)
der **Raum**, ‡e room; space; area
die **Räumungsklage**, -n eviction notice
raus = **heraus** out
rauschen, gerauscht to rustle
reagieren, reagiert to react
die **Rechenart**, -en arithmetical operation
recherchieren, recherchiert to investigate
rechnen, gerechnet to do arithmetic
die **Rechnung**, -en bill; check (*in restaurant*) (4)
recht- (*adj.*); **rechts** (*adv.*) right; on/to the right (7, 10)
recht haben (hat ... recht), hatte ... recht, recht gehabt to be right (2)
rechtlich legal(ly)
der **Rechtsanwalt**, ‡e / die **Rechtsanwältin**, -nen lawyer
das **Rechtschreiben** spelling
das **Rededuell**, -e duel of words
reden, geredet to speak, talk
das **Referat**, -e report (3); (term) paper; **ein Referat halten** to give a paper / oral report (4)
der **Refrain**, -s refrain
das **Regal**, -e bookshelf, bookcase (2); rack
regelmäßig regular(ly) (11)
regeln, geregelt to regulate
der **Regen**, - rain (7); **bei Regen** in rainy weather (7)
der **Regenschirm**, -e umbrella (5)
die **Regierung**, -en government
das **Regime**, - regime
regimetreu loyal to the regime
die **Region**, -en region
regional regional(ly)
der **Regisseur**, -e / die **Regisseurin**, -nen stage/film director
registrieren, registriert to register; **sich registrieren lassen** to get registered
regnen, geregnet to rain; **es regnet** it is raining; it rains (B)
reiben (reibt), rieb, gerieben to rub
reich rich(ly)
das **Reich**, -e empire; kingdom; realm; **das Dritte Reich** the Third Reich (Nazi Germany)

der **Reifen**, - tire (7)
die **Reifenpanne**, -n flat tire (7)
die **Reihe**, -n row
die **Reihenfolge**, -n order, sequence (2, 4)
das **Reihenhaus**, ‡er row house, town house (6)
sich reimen, gereimt to rhyme
rein = **herein** in
die **Reinigung**, -en dry cleaner's (6)
der **Reis** rice (8)
die **Reise**, -n trip, journey (7); **auf Reisen sein** to be on a trip (7)
das **Reisebüro**, -s travel agency (6)
das **Reiseerlebnis**, -se travel experience (7)
der **Reiseführer**, - travel guidebook (5)
das **Reiseland**, ‡er tourist country
reisen, ist gereist to travel (1)
der/die **Reisende**, -n (ein Reisender) traveler (10)
der **Reisepass**, ‡e passport (1)
der **Reiseplan**, ‡e travel plan; itinerary
das **Reiseziel**, -e destination
reißen (reißt), riss, gerissen to tear, rip
reiten (reitet), ritt, ist geritten to ride (on horseback) (1); **Wellen reiten** to ride the waves, surf
der **Reiter**, - / die **Reiterin**, -nen (horseback) rider; **der Blaue Reiter** *a group of artists in Munich (1911–14)*
relativ relative(ly)
die **Religion**, -en religion (1)
religiös religious(ly) (B)
die **Renaissance** Renaissance
rennen (rennt), rannte, ist gerannt to run (7)
die **Reparatur**, -en repair
reparieren, repariert to repair (1)
der **Reporter**, - / die **Reporterin**, -nen reporter (4)
repräsentativ representative(ly)
die **Republik**, -en republic
republikanisch Republican (*adj.*)
reservieren, reserviert to reserve (7)
die **Residenz**, -en (royal) residence
die **Resonanz**, -en resonance
der **Rest**, -e rest, remainder
das **Restaurant**, -s restaurant (2)
das **Resultat**, -e result
retten, gerettet to save; to rescue
die **Rettichscheibe**, -n radish slice
die **Rettung** rescue; salvation
die **Revolution**, -en revolution
das **Rezept**, -e recipe; prescription (11)
die **Rezeption**, -en reception desk (10)
der **Rhein** Rhine (*river*)
der **Rhythmus**, Rhythmen rhythm
richten, gerichtet to direct; to turn; **sich richten (nach + *dat.*)** to depend (on); to comply (with)
der **Richter**, - / die **Richterin**, -nen judge (5)
richtig right(ly), correct(ly) (2)
die **Richtung**, -en direction (7)
riechen (riecht), roch, gerochen to smell (11)
der **Riese**, -n (*wk.*) / die **Riesin**, -nen giant (9)
riesig gigantic; tremendous(ly)
das **Rindfleisch** beef (8)

der **Ring**, -e ring (2)

der **Rock**, ⸚e skirt (A); (*sg. only*) rock music

das **Rockkonzert**, -e rock concert (11)

roh raw

die **Rolle**, -n role; part (4)

die **Rollenverteilung**, -en assignment of roles

der **Roman**, -e novel (5)

die **Romantik** Romantic period/movement

römisch Roman (*adj.*)

röntgen, geröntgt to X-ray (11)

rosa pink (A)

die **Rose**, -n rose; **die Weiße Rose** the White Rose (*name of an anti-Nazi resistance group*)

der **Rosenkohl** Brussels sprouts (8)

rostig rusty (8)

rot red (A); **rote Grütze** red fruit pudding

(das) **Rotkäppchen** Little Red Riding Hood

das **Roulette** roulette

der **Rücken**, - back (B)

die **Rückfahrt**, -en return journey; **die Hin- und Rückfahrt** round-trip (7)

rückgangig machen, gemacht to reverse

der **Rucksack**, ⸚e backpack (2)

die **Rückseite**, -n back (side); reverse (*of a coin*)

rufen (ruft), rief, gerufen to call, shout (7, 11)

ruhen, geruht to rest

ruhig quiet(ly), calm(ly) (B)

der **Ruhm** fame

(das) **Rumänien** Romania (B)

(das) **Rumpelstilzchen** Rumpelstiltskin

das **Rumpsteak**, -s rump steak (8)

rund round

der **Rundgang**, ⸚e walking tour

runter·bringen (bringt ... runter), brachte ... runter, runtergebracht = herunter·bringen to bring down

der **Rüssel**, - trunk (*of an elephant*) (10)

russisch Russian (*adj.*) (8)

(das) **Russisch** Russian (*language*) (B)

(das) **Russland** Russia (B)

rustikal country-style

rutschen, ist gerutscht to slide, slip (9)

rütteln, gerüttelt to shake

die **Sache**, -n thing (2); cause

die **Sachertorte**, -n *type of chocolate cake*

(das) **Sachsen** Saxony

sächsisch Saxon (*adj.*)

der **Saft**, ⸚e juice (8)

sagen, gesagt to say; to tell (A, 5)

die **Sahara** Sahara (Desert)

die **Sahne** cream

das **Sakko**, -s sports jacket (A)

die **Salami**, - salami

der **Salat**, -e salad (8)

die **Salatschüssel**, -n salad (mixing) bowl (5)

die **Salbe**, -n ointment

das **Salz** salt (8)

salzig salty (7)

die **Salzkartoffeln** (*pl.*) boiled potatoes (8)

sammeln, gesammelt to collect (10); to gather

der **Samstag**, -e Saturday (1); **am Samstag** on Saturday (2)

der **Samt** velvet

der **Sand**, -e sand (7)

die **Sandale**, -n sandal

die **Sandburg**, -en sandcastle (4)

sanft soft(ly); gentle, gently

der **Sänger**, - / die **Sängerin**, -nen singer

der **Sarg**, ⸚e coffin (9)

der **Satz**, ⸚e sentence (3)

die **Satzklammer**, -n sentence bracket

der **Satzteil**, -e part of sentence, clause

sauber clean (B); **sauber machen** to clean (3)

sauer sour (8); angry, angrily (5)

saure Gurken (*pl.*) pickles (8)

der **Sauerbraten**, - sauerbraten (*marinated beef roast*)

das **Sauerkraut** sauerkraut, pickled cabbage

saugen, gesaugt to vacuum; **Staub saugen** to vacuum (6)

die **Sauna**, -s sauna (11)

das **Schach** chess (1)

schade! too bad! (6)

schaden (+ *dat.*), **geschadet** to be harmful to (6)

schaffen (schafft), schuf, geschaffen to create

schaffen, geschafft to manage; to achieve; **jemanden aus dem Weg schaffen** to get someone out of the way

der **Schafskäse** feta cheese

der **Schal**, -s scarf (2)

die **Schallplatte**, -n (phonograph) record

der **Schalter**, - ticket booth (5); **am Schalter** at the ticket booth (5)

der **Schatten**, - shadow; shade (9)

der **Schatz**, ⸚e treasure (9)

schätzen, geschätzt to value

die **Schätzung**, -en estimate

schauen (an/auf + *acc.*), **geschaut** to look (at) (A)

schaufeln, geschaufelt to shovel (11)

der **Schauspieler**, - / die **Schauspielerin**, -nen actor/actress

der **Scheck**, -s check

die **Scheibe**, -n slice; windowpane (7)

der **Scheibenwischer**, - windshield wiper (7)

der **Scheiblettenkäse** processed cheese slices

die **Scheidung**, -en divorce (12)

der **Schein**, -e bill, note (*of currency*) (8)

scheinen (scheint), schien, geschienen to shine; to seem, appear

scheitern, gescheitert to fail

schenken, geschenkt to give (as a present) (5)

die **Schere**, -n scissors (8)

schick chic, stylish(ly), smart(ly) (2)

schicken, geschickt to send (2)

schief crooked; **schiefgehen** (*coll.*) to go wrong

die **Schiene**, -n train track (10)

schießen (schießt), schoss, geschossen to shoot

das **Schild**, -er sign (7)

schildern, geschildert to depict

die **Schildkröte**, -n turtle (10); tortoise

schimpfen, geschimpft to cuss; to scold (9)

der **Schinken**, - ham (8)

der **Schlaf** sleep (9)

der **Schlafanzug**, ⸚e pajamas

die **Schläfe**, -n temple

schlafen (schläft), schlief, geschlafen to sleep (2); **lange schlafen** to sleep late

der **Schlafsack**, ⸚e sleeping bag (2)

der **Schlafwagen**, - sleeping car (4)

das **Schlafzimmer**, - bedroom (6)

der **Schlag**, ⸚e (heart)beat

schlagen (schlägt), schlug, geschlagen to beat (8); to strike, hit (11)

der **Schlager**, - pop song

der **Schlagertext**, -e pop lyrics

das **Schlagzeug**, -e percussion, drums (12)

die **Schlange**, -n snake (10)

schlank slender, slim (B)

das **Schlauchboot**, -e inflatable dinghy (10)

schlecht bad(ly) (2)

die **Schleife**, -n bow, ribbon

schleudern, geschleudert to hurl

schließen (schließt), schloss, geschlossen to close, shut (A)

schließlich finally (7); after all

schlimm bad (11)

der **Schlittschuh**, -e ice skate (3); **Schlittschuh laufen** to go ice-skating (3)

das **Schloss**, ⸚er castle (9)

der **Schlossgang**, ⸚e castle passageway

der **Schluss**, ⸚e end (8); conclusion; **zum Schluss** in the end, finally (8); in conclusion

der **Schlüssel**, - key (9)

schmal narrow; thin

schmecken (+ *dat.*), **geschmeckt** to taste good (to) (6)

der **Schmerz**, -en pain (11)

sich schminken, geschminkt to put makeup on (11)

der **Schmuck** jewelry (2)

schmücken, geschmückt to decorate

schmutzig dirty (A)

der **Schnaps**, ⸚e spirit; schnapps

schnarchen, geschnarcht to snore

die **Schnecke**, -n snail (10)

der **Schnee** snow (9)

(das) **Schneewittchen** Snow White

schneiden (schneidet), schnitt, geschnitten to cut (3, 11); **Haare schneiden** to cut hair (3); **sich schneiden** to cut oneself (11)

schneien, geschneit to snow; **es schneit** it is snowing; it snows (B)

schnell quick(ly), fast (7)

der **Schnitt**, -e cut, incision; **im Schnitt** on average

das **Schnitzel**, - (veal/beef/pork) cutlet (8)

der **Schnupfen**, - cold (*with a runny nose*), sniffles (11)

die **Schnur**, ⸚e string (8)

der **Schnurrbart**, ⸚e mustache (A)

der **Schock**, -s shock (11)

schocken, geschockt (*coll.*) to shock

die **Schokolade**, -n chocolate

schon already (2, 4); indeed; **schon wieder** once again (3); **Warst du schon einmal ...?** Were you ever . . . ? (4)

schön pretty, beautiful; nice (B); **Bitte schön.** There you go.

Bitte schön? Yes please? May I help you? (7); **ganz schön viel** quite a bit (3)

das **Schönheitsideal, -e** ideal of beauty

der **Schrank, ⁓e** wardrobe (2); closet; cupboard (6)

die **Schranke, -n** barrier

der **Schrei, -e** cry; shout; scream

schreiben (schreibt), schrieb, geschrieben to write; to spell (A, 1); **(an +** *acc.***)** to write to; **(über +** *acc.***)** to write about; **eine SMS schreiben** to write a text message (1); **Wie schreibt man das?** How do you spell that? (A)

die **Schreibmaschine, -n** typewriter

der **Schreibtisch, -e** desk (2)

das **Schreibwarengeschäft, -e** stationery store (6)

schreien (schreit), schrie, geschrien to scream, yell (3)

die **Schrift, -en** script; writing

der **Schriftsteller, -** / die **Schriftstellerin, -nen** writer (5)

der **Schritt, -e** step

die **Schublade, -n** drawer (5)

schüchtern shy(ly) (B)

die **Schüchternheit** shyness

der **Schuh, -e** shoe (A)

das **Schuhgeschäft, -e** shoe store (6)

die **Schulbildung** education, schooling

schuld: schuld sein (an + *dat.***)** to be at fault (for)

die **Schuld, -en** debt; fault; guilt (12)

schulden, geschuldet to owe

die **Schule, -n** school (1, 5); **in der Schule** at school (5)

der **Schüler, -** / die **Schülerin, -nen** student; pupil (1)

der **Schulhof, ⁓e** schoolyard, playground

der **Schulleiter, -** / die **Schulleiterin, -nen** principal, headmaster

die **Schultasche, -n** book bag

die **Schulter, -n** shoulder (B)

die **Schuluniform, -en** school uniform

die **Schulzeit** school days

die **Schüssel, -n** bowl (8)

schütteln, geschüttelt to shake; **die Hand schütteln** to shake hands (A)

schützen, geschützt to protect

schwach weak(ly)

schwanger pregnant

schwarz black (A); **das schwarze Brett** bulletin board

das **Schwarzbier, -e** *very dark beer*

schwarzhaarig black-haired (9)

(das) **Schweden** Sweden (B)

(das) **Schwedisch** Swedish (*language*) (B)

schweigen (schweigt), schwieg, geschwiegen to become silent; to be silent, say nothing

das **Schweigen** silence

das **Schwein, -e** pig (9)

der **Schweinebraten, -** pork roast

das **Schweinefleisch** pork (8)

der **Schweinestall, ⁓e** pigpen (5)

die **Schweiz** Switzerland (B)

Schweizer Swiss (*adj.*); **der Schweizer Franken, -** Swiss franc (8)

der **Schweizer, -** / die **Schweizerin, -nen** Swiss (*person*) (B)

die **Schwellung, -en** swelling

schwer heavy, heavily; hard; difficult (3); **schwer verletzt** critically injured (11)

die **Schwester, -n** sister (B)

schwierig difficult (2)

die **Schwierigkeit, -en** difficulty

das **Schwimmbad, ⁓er** swimming pool (1, 5); **im Schwimmbad** at the swimming pool (5); **ins Schwimmbad fahren/gehen** to drive/go to the swimming pool (1)

schwimmen (schwimmt), schwamm, ist/hat geschwommen to swim (7); **im Meer schwimmen** to swim in the sea (1); **schwimmen gehen** to go swimming (1)

schwitzen, geschwitzt to sweat, perspire

sechs six (A)

sechst- sixth (4)

sechsundzwanzig twenty-six (A)

sechzehn sixteen (A)

sechzig sixty (A)

der **See, -n** lake (7)

die **Seele, -n** soul (12)

das **Segel, -** sail

segeln, ist/hat gesegelt to sail (1)

segnen, gesegnet to bless

sehen (sieht), sah, gesehen to see (2)

sehr very (B); **Bitte sehr.** There you go.

die **Seife, -n** soap (11)

der **Seiltänzer, -** / die **Seiltänzerin, -nen** tightrope walker

sein (ist), war, ist gewesen to be (A, 4)

sein(e) his, its (1, 2)

seit (*prep.*) since; for (4, 11); **seit mehreren Tagen** for several days (11); **seit zwei Jahren** for two years (4)

seitab off to the side

die **Seite, -n** side; page (6)

seitlich sideways

der **Sekretär, -e** / die **Sekretärin, -nen** secretary (5)

der **Sekt, -e** sparkling wine

die **Sekunde, -n** second (1)

selber, selbes, selbe same

selbst even; oneself, myself, yourself, himself, herself, itself; ourselves, yourselves, themselves; by (one)self; **selbst gemacht** homemade (8)

der **Selbstmord, -e** suicide

selbstverständlich of course (10)

selten rare(ly), seldom (8)

seltsam strange(ly)

das **Semester, -** semester (1)

die **Semesterferien** (*pl.*) semester break

das **Seminar, -e** seminar

der **Seminarraum, ⁓e** classroom (B)

die **Semmel, -n** (bread) roll

die **Sendung, -en** broadcast

der **Senf** mustard (8)

der **September** September (B)

die **Serviette, -n** napkin (8)

servus hello; good-bye (*infor.; southern Germany, Austria*) (A)

der **Sessel, -** armchair (2, 6)

setzen, gesetzt to put, place, set (*in a sitting position*) (7); **sich setzen** to sit down (A, 11)

das **Shampoo, -s** shampoo

sich oneself, himself, herself, itself, yourself; themselves, yourselves

sicher sure(ly) (1); of course; safe(ly)

die **Sicherheit, -en** safety

der **Sicherheitsgurt, -e** seat belt (7)

die **Sicherheitskraft, ⁓e** security officer

sicherlich certainly (3)

sichtbar visible, visibly

sie (*pron., fem. nom./acc.*) she, her, it; (*nom./acc. pl.*) they, them

Sie (*for. sg./pl.*) you

sieben seven (A)

siebenundzwanzig twenty-seven (A)

siebt- seventh (4)

siebzehn seventeen (A)

siebzig seventy (A)

die **Siedlung, -en** settlement

der **Sieg, -e** victory

signalisieren, signalisiert to signal; to indicate

silbern silver (*adj.*), silvery

die **Silvesternacht, ⁓e** night of New Year's Eve

simsen, gesimst (*coll.*) to text (1)

singen (singt), sang, gesungen to sing (1)

die **Single, -s** single (record)

sinken (sinkt), sank, ist gesunken to sink

der **Sinn, -e** sense; **im Sinn haben** to have in mind

sinnlich sensual(ly)

die **Situation, -en** situation

der **Sitz, -e** seat (7)

sitzen (sitzt), saß, gesessen to sit; to be in a seated position (4); **sitzen bleiben** to remain seated

das **Skateboard, -s** skateboard (3); **Skateboard fahren** to skateboard (3)

der **Ski, -er** ski (3); **Ski fahren** to ski (3)

die **Skihütte, -n** ski lodge (6)

der **Skorpion, -e** scorpion (10)

die **Slowakei** Slovakia (B)

(das) **Slowenien** Slovenia (B)

die **SMS** SMS, text message; **eine SMS schreiben** to write a text message (1)

das **Snowboard, -s** snowboard (1); **Snowboard fahren** to snowboard

das **Snowboarden** snowboarding

so so; such; that way (A); **das stimmt so** that's right; keep the change (8); **so viel** so much; **so was** something like that; some such thing

sobald (*subord. conj.*) as soon as

die **Socke, -n** sock (2)

das **Sofa, -s** sofa, couch (6)

sofort immediately (3)

sogar even

sogenannt so-called

der **Sohn**, ⸚e son (B)

das **Solarium**, **Solarien** tanning salon (11)

solcher, **solches**, **solche** such

sollen (**soll**), **sollte**, **gesollt** to be supposed to (3)

die **Solokarriere**, **-n** solo career

der **Solosänger**, **-** / die **Solosängerin**, **-nen** solo artist (singer)

der **Sommer**, **-** summer (B); **letzten Sommer** last summer (4)

sondern but, rather, on the contrary (A, 11)

die **Sonderschulpädagogik** special education

der **Song**, **-s** song

das **Songbuch**, ⸚er songbook (2)

der **Songwriter**, **-** / die **Songwriterin**, **-nen** songwriter

die **Sonne**, **-n** sun; **in der Sonne liegen** to lie in the sun (1)

das **Sonnenbaden** sunbathing

sonnenbaden gehen (**geht ... sonnenbaden**), **ging ... sonnenbaden**, **ist sonnenbaden gegangen** to go sunbathing (10)

der **Sonnenbrand**, ⸚e sunburn (10)

die **Sonnenbrille**, **-n** sunglasses (1, 2)

die **Sonnenmilch** suntan lotion (10)

der **Sonnenschirm**, **-e** sunshade; beach parasol (10)

der **Sonnenstrahl**, **-en** ray of sunlight

sonnig sunny (B)

der **Sonntag**, **-e** Sunday (1)

sonst otherwise (5); **sonst noch** in addition; else; **Sonst noch etwas?** Anything else? (5)

sonstig other

sortieren, **sortiert** to sort

die **Soße**, **-n** sauce (8); (salad) dressing

das **Souvenir**, **-s** souvenir (7)

sowie as well as

sowjetisch Soviet (*adj.*)

die **Sowjetunion** Soviet Union

sowohl als/wie as well as

sozial social(ly)

sozialdemokratisch Social Democratic

der **Sozialist**, **-en** (*wk.*) / die **Sozialistin**, **-nen** socialist (*person*)

sozialistisch socialist (*adj.*)

die **Sozialkunde** social studies (1)

die **Soziologie** sociology (1)

die **Spaghetti** (*pl.*) spaghetti (7)

die **Spalte**, **-n** column

(das) **Spanien** Spain (B)

spanisch Spanish (*adj.*)

(das) **Spanisch** Spanish (*language*) (B)

spannend suspenseful

die **Spannweite**, **-n** wingspan

sparen, **gespart** to save (*money*); (**auf** + *acc.*) to save up for

das **Sparkonto**, **Sparkonten** savings account (12)

der **Spaß**, ⸚e fun; **Spaß haben** to have fun; **Spaß machen** to be fun; **viel Spaß** have fun (A)

spät late (1); **später** later (1); **Wie spät ist es?** What time is it? (1)

die **Spätzle** (*pl.*) spaetzle (*kind of noodles*)

spazieren gehen (**geht ... spazieren**), **ging ... spazieren**, **ist spazieren gegangen** to go for a walk (1); **im Park spazieren gehen** to go for a walk in the park (1)

der **Speck** bacon (8)

speichern, **gespeichert** to store

die **Speisekarte**, **-n** menu (8)

der **Speisewagen**, **-** dining car

spekulieren, **spekuliert** to speculate

spenden, **gespendet** to donate

der **Sperrmüll** bulky waste

die **Spezialität**, **-en** specialty

speziell special; especially

der **Spiegel**, **-** mirror (6); *title of a German news magazine*

das **Spieglein**, **-** (*diminutive form of* der **Spiegel**) little mirror

das **Spiel**, **-e** game; match

spielen, **gespielt** to play (1)

der **Spieler**, **-** / die **Spielerin**, **-nen** player

der **Spielfilm**, **-e** theatrical feature film

der **Spielplatz**, ⸚e playground (9)

der **Spinat**, **-e** spinach

spitz pointed

der **Spitzbart**, ⸚e goatee

der **Spitzel**, **-** informer

der **Spitzname**, **-n** (*wk.*) nickname (1)

der **Sport** sport(s); physical education (1); **Sport treiben** to do sports (2)

die **Sporthose**, **-n** tights, sports pants (2)

sportlich athletic(ally) (B)

der **Sportplatz**, ⸚e sports field; playing field

der **Sportschuh**, **-e** athletic shoe (A)

die **Sporttasche**, **-n** athletic bag

die **Sportverletzung**, **-en** sports injury

die **Sprache**, **-n** language (B)

das **Sprachlabor**, **-s** language laboratory (4)

sprachlos speechless(ly)

der/das **Spray**, **-s** spray

sprechen (**spricht**), **sprach**, **gesprochen** to speak, talk (B); (**über** + *acc.*) to talk about

der **Sprechgesang** spoken song

die **Sprechsituation**, **-en** conversational situation (A)

die **Sprechstunde**, **-n** office hour (3)

die **Sprechstundenhilfe** (doctor's) receptionist

sprengen, **gesprengt** to water, sprinkle

das **Sprichwort**, ⸚er proverb, saying

springen (**springt**), **sprang**, **ist gesprungen** to jump (A)

die **Spritze**, **-n** shot, injection (11)

sprühen, **gesprüht** to spray

das **Spülbecken**, **-** sink (5)

spülen, **gespült** to wash; to rinse (4); **Geschirr spülen** to wash the dishes (4)

der **Spürsinn** intuition

der **Staat**, **-en** state (10); nation

staatlich state, government (*adj.*)

die **Staatsangehörigkeit**, **-en** nationality, citizenship (1)

der **Staatsbankrott**, **-e** government bankruptcy

die **Staatsbürgerschaft**, **-en** citizenship

das **Staatsbürgerschaftsrecht**, **-e** citizenship law

der **Staatchef**, **-s** / die **Staatschefin**, **-nen** head of state

das **Staatsexamen**, **-** *final university examination*

die **Staatspolizei** state police; **die Geheime Staatspolizei (Gestapo)** Secret State Police (*in Nazi Germany*)

die **Stadt**, ⸚e town, city (2, 6)

das **Stadtbild**, **-er** townscape, cityscape

das **Stadthaus Schlump** *an old building in Hamburg*

der **Stadtplan**, ⸚e city street map (10)

der **Stadtrand**, ⸚er city limits (6)

die **Stadtrundfahrt**, **-en** tour of the city (7)

der **Stadtteil**, **-e** district, neighborhood (6)

das **Stadtviertel**, **-** quarter, district, neighborhood (6)

die **Staffelei**, **-en** easel (12)

stammen (**aus** + *dat.*), **gestammt** to come (from), originate (in)

der **Stammgast**, ⸚e regular customer

ständig constant(ly)

der **Star**, **-s** star, celebrity

stark strong(ly); heavy, heavily; severe(ly) (11); (*coll.*) great

der **Start**, **-s** start

starten, **ist gestartet** to start; to take off

die **Stasi** (*coll.*) = die **Staatssicherheit** State Security (*former East German secret police*)

statt (+ *gen.*) instead of (12)

statt·finden (**findet ... statt**), **fand ... statt**, **stattgefunden** to take place (5)

die **Statue**, **-n** statue

der **Staub** dust; **Staub saugen** to vacuum (6); **Staub wischen** to (wipe) dust

der **Staubsauger**, **-** vacuum cleaner (6)

die **Stauchung**, **-en** compression

das **Staunen** amazement

das **Steak**, **-s** steak

stechen (**sticht**), **stach**, **gestochen** to prick; to sting; to bite (*of insects*) (10)

stecken, **gesteckt** to stick; to put; to be; **stecken bleiben** (**bliebt ... stecken**), **blieb ... stecken**, **ist stecken geblieben** to get stuck (11)

stehen (**steht**), **stand**, **gestanden** to stand (*be in a vertical position*) (2, 6); to be (situated); (+ *dat.*) to suit (6); (**für** + *acc.*) to stand (for); **Das steht / Die stehen dir gut!** That looks / Those look good on you! (2)

stehlen (**stiehlt**), **stahl**, **gestohlen** to steal (9)

die **Steiermark** Styria (*Austrian state*)

steigen (**steigt**), **stieg**, **ist gestiegen** to climb; to ascend; to increase

der **Stein**, **-e** stone (12)

steinern (*adj.*) (made of) stone

steinig stony, rocky

stellen, **gestellt** to stand up, put, place (upright) (3, 5); **eine Frage stellen** to ask a question (5); **gerade stellen** to straighten (3)

sterben (**stirbt**), **starb**, **ist gestorben** to die (9)

die **Stereoanlage**, **-n** stereo system (6)

der **Stern**, -e star

das **Sternzeichen**, - astrological sign, sign of the zodiac

die **Steuer**, -n tax

das **Stichwort**, ¨er keyword

sticken, gestickt to do embroidery

der **Stiefel**, - boot (A)

die **Stiefmutter**, ¨ stepmother (9)

der **Stiefsohn**, ¨e stepson

die **Stieftochter**, ¨ stepdaughter

der **Stiefvater**, ¨ stepfather (9)

der **Stift**, -e pen (A, B)

der **Stil**, -e style

die **Stille** quiet; silence

stillen, gestillt to still, stop

das **Stillleben**, - still life

die **Stimme**, -n voice (12)

stimmen, gestimmt to be right (8); **das stimmt so** that's right; keep the change (8); **Stimmt!** That's right!

die **Stimmung**, -en mood; atmosphere

das **Stipendium, Stipendien** scholarship (1)

die **Stirn**, -en forehead

das **Stirnband**, ¨er headband (A)

stöbern, gestöbert (coll.) to browse, rummage about

der **Stock**, ¨e stick; walking stick

der **Stock** (pl. **Stockwerke**) floor, story (6); **im ersten Stock** on the second floor (6)

das **Stockwerk**, -e floor, story (6)

stolpern, ist gestolpert to trip, stumble (9)

der **Stopp**, -s stop

stören, gestört to disturb (3)

der **Stoßzahn**, ¨e tusk (10)

stottern, gestottert to stutter

der **Strafzettel**, - (parking or speeding) ticket

der **Strand**, ¨e shore, beach (4, 7)

der **Strandkorb**, ¨e beach chair (10)

die **Strandpromenade**, -n (beach) promenade

die **Straße**, -n street, road (6)

die **Straßenbahn**, -en streetcar (7)

der **Straßenrand**, ¨er roadside

sich **sträuben, gesträubt** to stand on end, bristle (hair); to resist, be reluctant

der **Strauß**, ¨e bouquet

das **Streichholz**, ¨er match (8)

(sich) **streiten (streitet), stritt, gestritten** to argue, quarrel (9)

streng strict(ly) (9)

stricken, gestrickt to knit (3)

der **Strom**, ¨e current; electricity, power (8)

die **Strophe**, -n strophe; verse

der **Strudel**, - strudel (pastry)

die **Strumpfhose**, -n tights; pantyhose

das **Stück**, -e piece; slice (8)

der **Student**, -en (wk.) / die **Studentin**, -nen student (A, B)

das **Studentenheim**, -e dorm (2, 6)

das **Studentenleben** student life (4)

das **Studentenwerk**, -e student union

die **Studie**, -n study

das **Studienfach**, ¨er academic subject

der **Studiengang**, ¨e course of study

die **Studiengebühr**, -en registration fee, tuition

studieren, studiert to study; to attend a university/college (1)

der/die **Studierende**, -n (ein Studierender) student

das **Studium, Studien** university studies (1); course of studies (3)

der **Stuhl**, ¨e chair (B, 2)

die **Stunde**, -n hour (1, 2)

stundenlang for hours

der **Stundenplan**, ¨e schedule (1)

stürmen, gestürmt to storm

stürzen, ist gestürzt to fall

das **Substantiv**, -e noun

die **Suchanzeige**, -n housing-wanted ad (6)

die **Suche**, -n search

suchen, gesucht to look for (1)

die **Suchmaschine**, -n search engine

süd- south

(das) **Südafrika** South Africa

(das) **Südamerika** South America (B)

süddeutsch Southern German (adj.)

der **Süden** south

südlich (von + dat.) south (of) (7)

der **Südosten** southeast

südöstlich (von + dat.) southeast (of) (7)

südwestlich (von + dat.) southwest (of) (7)

der **Sünder**, - / die **Sünderin**, -nen sinner

super super

der **Superbowl** Super Bowl

der **Supermarkt**, ¨e supermarket (5, 6); **im Supermarkt** at the supermarket (5)

die **Suppe**, -n soup (8)

das **Surfbrett**, -er surfboard (2)

surfen, gesurft to surf, go surfing; **im Internet surfen** to surf the Internet (1)

das **Sushi** sushi

süß sweet(ly) (2); **voll süß** totally sweet (2)

die **Süßigkeit**, -en sweet, candy

der **Swimmingpool**, -s swimming pool

das **Symbol**, -e symbol

symbolisch symbolic(ally)

symbolisieren, symbolisiert to symbolize

der **Sympathisant**, -en (wk.) / die **Sympathisantin**, -nen sympathizer

sympathisch congenial(ly), appealing(ly)

das **Symphonieorchester**, - symphony orchestra

(das) **Syrien** Syria

das **System**, -e system

die **Szene**, -n scene

das **Szenepublikum** trendy following, in-crowd

die **Tabelle**, -n table; list

die **Tablette**, -n tablet, pill (11)

die **Tafel**, -n blackboard; whiteboard (A, B)

der **Tag**, -e day (1); **an welchem Tag?** on what day? (4); **den ganzen Tag** all day long (1); **eines Tages** one day; **guten Tag** good afternoon; hello (for.) (A); **seit mehreren Tagen** for several days (11); **Welcher Tag ist heute?** What day is today? (1)

das **Tagebuch**, ¨er diary (4)

der **Tagesablauf**, ¨e daily routine (1); course of (one's) day

die **Tageszeitung**, -en daily newspaper (5)

täglich daily (12)

das **Tal**, ¨er valley (7)

das **Talent**, -e talent (3)

der **Tank**, -s (fuel) tank (7)

tanken, getankt to fill up (with gas)

die **Tankstelle**, -n gas station (5); **an der Tankstelle** at the gas station (5)

die **Tante**, -n aunt (B)

tanzen, getanzt to dance (1)

die **Tanzfläche**, -n dance floor

die **Tanzschule**, -n dancing school

die **Tapete**, -n wallpaper

tapfer brave(ly) (9)

die **Tasche**, -n (hand)bag; purse; pocket (1)

die **Taschenlampe**, -n flashlight (9)

das **Taschentuch**, ¨er handkerchief (3)

die **Tasse**, -n cup (2, 5)

die **Tat**, -en act; deed

tätig active

die **Tätigkeit**, -en activity (6)

tätowieren, tätowiert to tattoo

der **Tätowierer**, - / die **Tätowiererin**, -nen tattoo artist

das **Tattoo**, -s tattoo

die **Taube**, -n pigeon; dove

der/die **Taubstumme**, -n (ein Taubstummer) deaf and dumb person

tauchen, hat/ist getaucht to dive (3)

tausend thousand

tausendmal a thousand times

das **Taxi**, -s taxi (3, 7)

der **Taxifahrer**, - / die **Taxifahrerin**, -nen taxi driver (5)

das/der **Techno** techno (music)

der **Teddy**, -s = der **Teddybär**, -en (wk.) teddy bear (A, 9)

der **Tee**, -s tea (4)

die **Teekanne**, -n teapot (8)

der **Teekessel**, - tea kettle (8)

der **Teenager**, - teenager

der **Teil**, -e part (7)

teilen, geteilt to divide

teil·nehmen (an + dat.) (nimmt ... teil), nahm ... teil, teilgenommen to participate (in s.th.)

das **Telefon**, -e telephone (1, 2); **am Telefon** on the phone (2)

das **Telefonat**, -e telephone call

telefonieren, telefoniert to telephone, talk on the phone (4)

die **Telefonkarte**, -n telephone card (2)

die **Telefonnummer**, -n telephone number (1)

die **Telefonzelle**, -n telephone booth (2)

der **Teller**, - plate (8)

die **Temperatur**, -en temperature

das **Tennis** tennis (1)

der **Teppich**, -e carpet (2); rug

der Termin, -e appointment (5, 11); **sich einen Termin geben lassen** to get an appointment (11)

der Terminkalender, - appointment calendar (11)

die Terrasse, -n terrace, deck (6)

der Test, -s test

der Tetanus tetanus (11)

teuer expensive(ly) (2)

der Teufel, - devil (12)

der Text, -e text (12)

das Theater, - theater (4)

das Thema, Themen theme, topic, subject (4)

der Thunfisch, -e tuna

(das) Thüringen Thuringia

das Ticket, -s ticket

tief deep(ly) (7)

das Tier, -e animal (3, 7, 10)

der Tierarzt, ⸚e / die Tierärztin, -nen veterinarian (11)

tippen, getippt to type (3, 6)

(das) Tirol Tyrol (*Austrian state*)

Tiroler (*adj.*) Tyrolean

der Tisch, -e table (B); **den Tisch abräumen** to clear the table (3); **den Tisch decken** to set the table (5)

das Tischtennis table tennis (3)

der Titel, - title

der Toaster, - toaster (8)

toben, getobt to rampage

die Tochter, ⸚ daughter (B)

der Tod, -e death (12)

die Todesart, -en way to die

die Todesgefahr, -en mortal danger

die Toilette, -n toilet (6)

das Toilettenpapier toilet paper (4)

die Toilettentasche, -n cosmetic bag

tolerant tolerant(ly) (7)

toll (*coll.*) neat, great (2); **das hört sich toll an** that sounds great (4)

die Tollwut rabies (10)

die Tomate, -n tomato (8)

der Ton, -e clay (12)

der Ton, ⸚e tone; musical note

der Topf, ⸚e pot, pan (5)

die Töpferscheibe, -n potter's wheel (12)

der Topflappen, - potholder (5)

das Topjahrzehnt, -e top decade

das Torhaus, ⸚er gatehouse

tot dead (9)

total total(ly) (4)

töten, getötet to kill (9)

der Totengang, ⸚e path of the dead

der Totenkopf, ⸚e skull; death's head

die Tour, -en tour; trip

der Tourismus tourism (10)

der Tourist, -en (*wk.*) / die Touristin, -nen tourist

die Tradition, -en tradition (4, 12)

traditionell traditional(ly)

tragen (trägt), trug, getragen to carry; to wear (A); **Trägst du gern ...?** Do you like to wear . . . ? (A)

die Tragödie, -n tragedy (12)

der Trailer, - trailer

trampen, ist getrampt to hitchhike (10)

der Tramper, - / die Tramperin, -nen hitchhiker

die Transaktion, -en transaction

transkontinental transcontinental(ly)

transportieren, transportiert to transport (7)

das Transportmittel, - means of transportation (7)

der Traum, ⸚e dream

träumen (von + *dat.*), geträumt to dream (of/about) (9)

traurig sad(ly) (B)

(sich) treffen (trifft), traf, getroffen to meet (2); **Treffen wir uns ...** Let's meet . . . (2)

treiben (treibt), trieb, getrieben to drive; to carry out, do; **Sport treiben** to do sports (2)

trennbar separable

(sich) trennen, getrennt to separate (7); to break up (*people*); to divide

die Treppe, -n stairway (6)

das Treppenhaus, ⸚er stairwell (10)

treten (tritt), trat, ist getreten to step

treu loyal(ly); true (9)

trinken (trinkt), trank, getrunken to drink (1)

das Trinkgeld, -er tip (8)

trivial trivial(ly); trite(ly)

trocken dry (11)

die Trompete, -n trumpet (12)

der Trost consolation

trotz (+ *gen.*) in spite of (12)

trotzdem in spite of that; nonetheless (12)

die Truppen (*pl.*) troops

(das) Tschechien Czech Republic (B)

(die) Tschechische Republik Czech Republic

tschüss bye (*infor.*) (A)

das T-Shirt, -s T-shirt (2)

tun (tut), tat, getan to do (1)

die Tür, -en door (A)

der Türke, -n (*wk.*) / die Türkin, -nen Turkish man/woman (12)

die Türkei Turkey (B)

türkisch Turkish (*adj.*)

(das) Türkisch Turkish (*language*) (B)

der Turnschuh, -e gym shoe

die Türschwelle, -n threshold

die Tüte, -n (paper or plastic) bag (11)

der TÜV = der Technische Überwachungsverein Technical Control Board (*German agency that checks vehicular safety*)

twittern, getwittert to use Twitter, "tweet"

der Typ, -en (*coll.*) character, person, guy

typisch typical(ly)

u. a. = unter anderem among others

die U-Bahn, -en = die Untergrundbahn, -en subway (7)

übel bad, nasty; **übel sein** (+ *dat.*) to feel sick, **mir ist übel** I feel sick

üben, geübt to practice; to exercise

über (+ *dat./acc.*) over (4); above; about; across; **übers Wochenende** over the weekend (4)

überall everywhere (10)

überfahren (überfährt), überfuhr, überfahren to run over (11)

überfallen (überfällt), überfiel, überfallen to hold up (*bank/store*)

überfliegen (überfliegt), überflog, überflogen to skim

überhaupt anyway; at all

überleben, überlebt to survive

überlegen, überlegt to consider, think about

übermorgen the day after tomorrow (9)

übermütig in high spirits, cocky

übernachten, übernachtet to stay overnight (6)

die Übernachtung, -en overnight stay

übernehmen (übernimmt), übernahm, übernommen to take on (7); to take over, adopt

überprüfen, überprüft to check, inspect

überqueren, überquert to cross, go across

überraschen, überrascht to surprise

überreden, überredet to convince, persuade

die Überredungskunst, ⸚e powers of persuasion

überrollen, überrollt to overrun

übers = über das over/about the

der Überschwang exuberance

übersetzen, übersetzt to translate (9)

überwachen, überwacht to monitor

die Überwachung, -en surveillance

überweisen (überweist), überwies, überwiesen to transfer (*money*)

die Überweisung, -en transfer (*of money*) (12)

überwiegen (überwiegt), überwog, überwogen to predominate

überzeugen, überzeugt to convince

überziehen (überzieht), überzog, überzogen to overdraw

der Überziehungskredit, -e overdraft protection (12)

üblich usual, customary

übrig remaining, left over

die Übung, -en exercise (A)

die UdSSR = die Union der Sozialistischen Sowjetrepubliken USSR, Soviet Union

die Uhr, -en clock (B); watch; (*sg. only*) o'clock; **bis acht Uhr** until eight o'clock (2); **bis um vier Uhr (früh)** until four o'clock (in the morning) (4); **erst um vier Uhr** not until four o'clock (4); **um sechs Uhr** at six o'clock (1); **um sieben Uhr zwanzig** at seven twenty (1); **Um wie viel Uhr ...?** At what time . . . ? (1); **Wie viel Uhr ist es?** What time is it? (1)

die Uhrzeit, -en time

die Ukraine Ukraine

um around; about; at; for; **(gleich) um die Ecke** (right) around the corner (5, 6); **um halb drei** at two thirty (1); **um sechs (Uhr)** at six o'clock (1); **um Viertel vor vier** at a quarter to four (1); **Um wie viel Uhr ...?** At what time . . . ? (1); **um zwanzig nach fünf** at twenty after/past five (1)

um ... zu (+ *inf.*) in order to (12)

um·bringen (bringt ... um), brachte ... um, umgebracht to kill

um·fallen (fällt ... um), fiel ... um, ist umgefallen to fall over (9)

umfassen, umfasst to embrace; to include

die Umfrage, -n survey (4)

der Umgang contact

umgeben (umgibt), umgab, umgeben to surround, enclose

die Umgebung, -en surrounding area, environs

um·gehen (mit + *dat.*) (geht ... um), ging ... um, umgegangen to treat, handle

sich um·gucken, umgeguckt (*coll.*) to look around

um·hängen, umgehängt to hang somewhere else

um·kippen, ist/hat umgekippt to turn over; to knock over (11)

die Umkleidekabine, -n dressing room (5)

ums = um das around/about/at/for the

der Umsatz, ⸚e sales, returns

der Umschlag, ⸚e cover; envelope; **warmer Umschlag** warm compress, poultice

um·schlagen (schlägt ... um), schlug ... um, ist/hat umgeschlagen to change

der Umstand, ⸚e circumstance

die Umstellung, -en adjustment

um·steigen (steigt ... um), stieg ... um, ist umgestiegen to change (*trains etc.*) (7)

die Umwelt environment

die Umweltkunde environmental studies

der Umweltschutz environmental protection

um·werfen (wirft ... um), warf ... um, umgeworfen to knock over/down

um·ziehen (zieht ... um), zog ... um, ist umgezogen to move (*to another residence*); (sich) **umziehen, hat umgezogen** to change clothes

der Umzug, ⸚e move, relocation

der Umzugsservice, -s moving service

unachtsam inattentive(ly)

unangenehm unpleasant(ly)

unbedingt without fail; absolute(ly)

und (*coord. conj.*) and (A, 11); **und so weiter (usw.)** and so forth

unerwartet unexpected(ly)

der Unfall, ⸚e accident (4)

(das) Ungarn Hungary (B)

ungeduldig impatient(ly) (10)

ungefähr approximate(ly) (7)

ungenügend inadequate(ly); unsatisfactory, unsatisfactorily

ungerecht unjust(ly), unfair(ly)

ungewöhnlich unusual(ly)

ungezogen naughty, naughtily; badly behaved

unglaublich incredible, incredibly (5)

unhöflich impolite(ly)

die Uni, -s (*coll.*) = **die Universität, -en** university (B, 1); **auf der Uni sein** to be at the university (1); **zur Uni gehen** to go to the university (1, 2)

die Union, -en union; **die Europäische Union (EU)** European Union

die Universität, -en university (B, 1, 5); **auf der Universität** at the university (5)

die Unizeitung, -en university newspaper (4)

unklug unwise(ly)

unmöglich impossible, impossibly

die Unmündigkeit dependence

uns (*acc./dat.*) us

unsaniert unrestored, unrenovated

unser(e) our (2)

unsympathisch uncongenial(ly); disagreeable, disagreeably; unpleasant(ly)

unten (*adv.*) below; down; downstairs

unter (+ *dat./acc.*) under, underneath (5); below, beneath; among (6); (*adj.*) lower; **unter anderem** among other things; **unter dem Fenster** under the window (5)

die Untergrundbahn, -en = die U-Bahn, -en subway (7)

sich unterhalten (unterhält), unterhielt, unterhalten to converse (9)

die Unterhaltung, -en conversation; entertainment

das Unterhemd, -en undershirt (2)

die Unterhose, -n underpants (2)

die Unterkunft, ⸚e lodging (10)

der Unterlass: ohne Unterlass incessantly

unternehmen (unternimmt), unternahm, unternommen to undertake

das Unternehmen undertaking; enterprise; company

der Unterricht class, instruction (11)

unterrichten, unterrichtet to teach, instruct (5)

der Unterschied, -e difference

unterschiedlich different; various(ly)

unterschreiben (unterschreibt), unterschrieb, unterschrieben to sign (1); **Unterschreib bitte hier.** Sign here please. (A)

die Unterschrift, -en signature (1)

unterstreichen (unterstreicht), unterstrich, unterstrichen to underline

unterstützen, unterstützt to support

die Unterstützung support

untersuchen, untersucht to investigate; to examine (5)

unterwegs underway; on the road (9)

unterzeichnen, unterzeichnet to sign

untreu disloyal; unfaithful

unvorhergesehen unforeseen; unexpected(ly)

unwichtig unimportant

unzufrieden dissatisfied

uralt very old, ancient

der Uranus Uranus (4)

urkundlich erwähnt mentioned in a document

der Urlaub, -e vacation (4, 5); **Urlaub machen** to take a vacation

der Urlauber, - / die Urlauberin, -nen vacationer

der Ursprung, ⸚e origin

ursprünglich original(ly)

das Urteil, -e verdict

die USA (*pl.*) USA (B)

der US-Amerikaner, - / die US-Amerikanerin, -nen American (from the USA) (*person*)

US-amerikanisch American (from the USA) (*adj.*)

usw. = und so weiter and so forth

die Utopie, -n utopia

der Valentinstag Valentine's Day (4)

der Vampir, -e vampire

die Vase, -n vase

der Vater, ⸚ father (B)

die Vaterstadt, ⸚e hometown

der Vati, -s dad, daddy

der Vegetarier, - / die Vegetarierin, -nen vegetarian (*person*)

sich verabreden (mit + *dat.*), verabredet to make a date (with), make an appointment (with)

die Verabredung, -en appointment; date (11)

sich verabschieden, verabschiedet to say goodbye, take leave

die Veränderung, -en change

das Verb, -en verb

der Verband, ⸚e bandage (11)

verbessern, verbessert to improve; to correct

verbieten (verbietet), verbot, verboten to forbid

verbinden (verbindet), verband, verbunden to connect (A); to combine

verboten (*p.p. of* **verbieten**) forbidden, prohibited (9)

verbrennen (verbrennt), verbrannte, verbrannt to burn (11); **sich (die Zunge) verbrennen** to burn (one's tongue) (11)

verbringen (verbringt), verbrachte, verbracht to spend (*time*) (3)

verdienen, verdient to earn (4)

der Verdienst, -e earnings

verdrängen, verdrängt to drive out, displace

verdutzt taken aback

der Verein, - e society, association

vereinen, vereint to unite

vereinigen, vereinigt to unite

verfallen (verfällt), verfiel, ist verfallen to decline; to deteriorate

die Verfassung, -en constitution; **körperliche und geistige Verfassung** physical and mental state

verfehlen, verfehlt to miss, not notice (10)

verfolgen, verfolgt to persecute

die Verfügung, -en order; **zur Verfügung** at one's disposal

die Vergebung, -en forgiveness

vergehen (vergeht), verging, ist vergangen to pass, go by (*time*)

vergessen (vergisst), vergaß, vergessen to forget (2)

vergiften, vergiftet to poison (9)

der Vergleich, -e comparison

vergleichbar comparable

vergleichen (vergleicht), verglich, verglichen to compare (7)

das Vergnügen pleasure (2); entertainment

vergnügt cheerful(ly); happy, happily

verhaften, verhaftet to arrest

sich verhalten (verhält), verhielt, verhalten to behave, act

das **Verhältnis**, -se relationship
verharren, verharrt to remain
sich **verheddern** (in + *dat.*), verheddert to get tangled up (in)
verheimlichen, verheimlicht to conceal, keep secret
sich **verheiraten** (mit + *dat.*), verheiratet to get married (to) (12)
verheiratet married (1, 12)
verhindern, verhindert to prevent
verhören, verhört to interrogate
verhungern, ist verhungert to starve (to death)
verkaufen, verkauft to sell (2, 5); **zu verkaufen** for sale
der **Verkäufer**, - / die **Verkäuferin**, -nen salesperson (5)
der **Verkehr** traffic (7, 11)
das **Verkehrsmittel**, - means of transportation; **die öffentlichen Verkehrsmittel** (*pl.*) public transportation (7)
das **Verkehrsschild**, -er traffic sign (7)
verkommen (verkommt), verkam, ist verkommen to degenerate, go bad
verlassen (verlässt), verließ, verlassen to leave; to abandon (11)
sich **verletzen**, verletzt to injure oneself (11)
verletzt injured (11); **schwer verletzt** critically injured (11)
der/die **Verletzte**, -n (ein Verletzter) injured person (11)
sich **verlieben** (in + *acc.*), verliebt to fall in love (with) (9, 12)
verliebt (sein) (to be) in love (4, 12)
verlieren (verliert), verlor, verloren to lose (7)
sich **verloben** (mit + *dat.*), verlobt to get engaged (to) (12); **verlobt sein** to be engaged (12)
vermieten, vermietet to rent out (6)
der **Vermieter**, - / die **Vermieterin**, -nen landlord/landlady (6)
vermischen, vermischt to mix
das **Vermögen**, - fortune
veröffentlichen, veröffentlicht to publish
die **Veröffentlichung**, -en publication
verpassen, verpasst to miss (9)
verraten (verrät), verriet, verraten to betray; to disclose, give away (*a secret*)
verreisen, ist verreist to go on a trip (3)
verrücken, verrückt to move, shift
verrückt crazy, crazily
verrühren, verrührt to stir together
verschieden different(ly); various(ly) (12)
verschlafen (verschläft), verschlief, verschlafen to sleep in, oversleep
verschlingen (verschlingt), verschlang, verschlungen to devour, swallow up
verschlossen reserved; taciturn
verschlucken, verschluckt to swallow; **sich verschlucken** (an + *dat.*), verschluckt to choke (on)
verschollen lost; missing
verschütten, verschüttet to spill

verschwinden (verschwindet), verschwand, ist verschwunden to disappear
versenden (versendet), versandte/versendete, versandt/versendet to send
die **Versetzung**, -en promotion (*to next grade in school*)
die **Versicherung**, -en insurance (5)
die **Version**, -en version
die **Verspätung**, -en lateness; delay (9)
versprechen (verspricht), versprach, versprochen to promise (7)
die **Verständigung** communication
das **Verständnis**, -se understanding
verstauen, verstaut to stow (7)
das **Versteck**, -e hiding place
(sich) **verstecken**, versteckt to hide (9)
verstehen (versteht), verstand, verstanden to understand (4)
sich **verstehen mit jemandem** to understand someone
verstummt speechless
versuchen, versucht to try, attempt (4)
verteilen, verteilt to distribute, hand out
die **Verteilung** distribution
der **Vertrag**, ⸚e contract (12)
vertrauen (+ *dat.*), vertraut to trust
vertreiben (vertreibt), vertrieb, vertrieben to drive (*s.o./s.th.*) out/away, expel
vertreten (vertritt), vertrat, vertreten to represent; to plead for
der **Vertreter**, - / die **Vertreterin**, -nen representative
verunglücken, verunglückt to have an accident
verurteilen, verurteilt to sentence; to condemn
verwalten, verwaltet to administer
die **Verwaltung**, -en administration
verwandeln, verwandelt to convert, transform; **sich verwandeln** (in + *acc.*) to change (into) (9)
der/die **Verwandte**, -n (ein Verwandter) relative (2)
verwanzen, verwanzt to bug, plant listening devices
verweisen (auf + *acc.*) (verweist), verwies, verwiesen to refer (to)
verwenden, verwendet to use
verwunschen cursed, enchanted (9)
verwünschen, verwünscht to curse, cast a spell on (9)
verzaubert (*p.p. of* verzaubern) bewitched
die **Verzeihung** forgiveness
verzichten (auf + *acc.*), verzichtet to do without, renounce (*s.th.*)
verzweifelt desperate(ly); despairing(ly)
der **Vetter**, -n (male) cousin (B)
das **Video**, -s video (9)
das **Videospiel**, -e video game (2)
viel (*sg.*) a lot (of), much (A); **viele** (*pl.*) many (A); **ganz schön viel** quite a bit (3); **Um wie viel Uhr ...?** At what time . . . ? (1); **vielen Dank** many thanks (10); **Viel Glück!** Lots of luck! Good luck! (3); **viel Spaß** have fun (A);

Wie viel ...? How much . . . ?; **Wie viele ...?** How many . . . ? (A); **Wie viel Uhr ist es?** What time is it? (1)
vielleicht perhaps (2); maybe
der **Vielvölkerstaat**, -en multinational state
vier four (A)
viert- fourth (4)
das **Viertel**, - quarter; **um Viertel vor vier** at a quarter to four (1)
vierundzwanzig twenty-four (A)
vierzehn fourteen (A)
vierzig forty (A)
vierzigst- fortieth
die **Villa**, **Villen** villa (6)
violett violet
die **Visakarte**, -n Visa card
die **Vision**, -en vision
der **Vogel**, ⸚ bird (10)
das **Vöglein**, - little bird
das **Volk**, ⸚er people
die **Volksmusik** folk music
die **Volkszählung**, -en census
voll full; full of; fully (10); **voll süß** totally sweet (2)
vollenden, vollendet to complete, finish
der **Volleyball**, ⸚e volleyball (1)
völlig fully, completely
vollkommen perfect(ly); flawless(ly) (12); complete(ly)
das **Vollkornbrot**, -e whole grain bread
vollständig complete(ly)
voll·tanken, vollgetankt to fill up (with gas) (5)
vom = **von dem** of/from/by the
von (+ *dat.*) of; from (A, 10); by; **von der Arbeit** from work (3); **von nebenan** from next door (5); **Was sind Sie von Beruf?** What's your profession? (1)
vor (+ *dat./acc.*) before; in front of; ago (4); because of; **um Viertel vor vier** at a quarter to four (1); **vor allem** above all; **vor Lachen** from laughing (so hard); **vor zwei Tagen** two days ago (4)
die **Voraussetzung**, -en prerequisite
voraussichtlich expected; probably
vorbei past, over (9); **an** (+ *dat.*) **... vorbei** by (10)
vorbei·fahren (fährt ... vorbei), fuhr ... vorbei, ist vorbeigefahren to go by
vorbei·fliegen (fliegt ... vorbei), flog ... vorbei, ist vorbeigeflogen to fly by
vorbei·gehen (an + *dat.*) (geht ... vorbei), ging ... vorbei, ist vorbeigegangen to go by (10)
vorbei·kommen (kommt ... vorbei), kam ... vorbei, ist vorbeigekommen to come by; to visit (3); **Komm mal vorbei!** Come on over! (11)
vorbei·schieben (schiebt ... vorbei), schob ... vorbei, vorbeigeschoben to push past
(sich) **vor·bereiten**, vorbereitet to prepare
die **Vorbereitung**, -en preparation
das **Vorbild**, -er role model, idol
vorder- (*adj.*) front
die **Vorderseite**, -n front (side); obverse (*of a coin*)

der **Vorfahre**, **-n** (*wk.*) ancestor (12)

die **Vorfahrt**, **-en** right-of-way (7)

vor·gehen (gegen + *acc.*) (geht ... vor), ging ... vor, ist vorgegangen to take action (against)

die **Vorgeschichte** prehistory

vorgestern the day before yesterday (4)

vor·haben (hat ... vor), hatte ... vor, vorgehabt to plan, intend

der **Vorhang**, **⸚e** drapery, curtain (6)

vor·heizen, vorgeheizt to preheat

vorhersagbar predictable

die **Vorhersage**, **-n** prediction

vor·kommen (kommt ... vor), kam ... vor, ist vorgekommen to occur; (+ *dat.*) to seem (to *s.o.*)

vor·lesen (liest ... vor), las ... vor, vorgelesen to read aloud (9)

die **Vorlesung**, **-en** lecture (4)

der **Vormittag**, **-e** late morning (4)

vormittags in the morning(s)

der **Vorname**, **-n** (*wk.*) first name, given name (A, 1)

vorne at the front; **von vorne** from the beginning

der **Vorreiter**, **-** / die **Vorreiterin**, **-nen** pioneer

vors = **vor das** in front of the

der **Vorschlag**, **⸚e** suggestion (5)

die **Vorspeise**, **-n** appetizer (8)

vor·spielen, vorgespielt to perform

(sich) **vor·stellen**, vorgestellt to introduce (*o.s.*); to present (*o.s.*) (6); **sich** (*dat.*) **etwas vorstellen** to imagine something (6)

der **Vorteil**, **-e** advantage (7)

der **Vortrag**, **⸚e** talk; lecture; presentation

der **Vulkan**, **-e** volcano

wach·rütteln, wachgerüttelt to rouse out of apathy

wachsen (wächst), wuchs, ist gewachsen to grow (9)

das **Wachstum** growth

der **Wachtmeister**, **-** / die **Wachtmeisterin**, **-nen** (police) constable

wagen, gewagt to dare; to risk

der **Wagen**, **-** car (7)

der **Waggon**, **-s** train car (7)

die **Wahl**, **-en** choice; election

wählen, gewählt to choose, select; to vote; to elect

wahlfrei optional

der **Wahlpflichtunterricht** compulsory class

der **Wahnsinn** insanity, madness

wahnsinnig crazy, crazily; insane(ly) (12)

wahr true (3); **nicht wahr?** isn't it so?

während (+ *gen.*) during (11); (*subord. conj.*) while

die **Wahrheit**, **-en** truth

wahrscheinlich probable, probably (1)

die **Währung**, **-en** currency (12)

der **Wald**, **⸚er** forest, woods (2, 7); **im Wald laufen** to run in the woods (2)

die **Walpurgisnacht** Walpurgis Night (*the witches' sabbath, April 30*)

der **Walzer**, **-** waltz (3)

die **Wand**, **⸚e** wall (B); **das Bild an die Wand hängen** to hang the picture on the wall (3)

die **Wandergans**, **⸚e** migratory goose

wandern, ist gewandert to hike (1); **in den Bergen wandern** to hike in the mountains (1)

der **Wanderschuh**, **-e** hiking shoe/boot (2)

die **Wanderung**, **-en** hike (7)

die **Wange**, **-n** cheek

wann when (B, 1); **Wann sind Sie geboren?** When were you born? (1)

warm warm(ly) (B); (*of room/apartment*) heated, heat included (6)

warnen, gewarnt to warn (7)

warten (auf + *acc.*), gewartet to wait (for) (7); **ein Auto warten** to do maintenance on a car

das **Wartezimmer**, **-** waiting room

warum why (3)

was what (B); **was für** (+ *acc.*) what kind of; **Was sind Sie von Beruf?** What's your profession? (1); **Was zeigen Ihre Bilder?** What do your pictures show? (A)

das **Waschbecken**, **-** (wash)basin (6)

die **Wäsche**, **-n** laundry (4)

(sich) **waschen** (wäscht), wusch, gewaschen to wash (*o.s.*) (2, 11)

der **Wäschetrockner**, **-** clothes dryer (8)

die **Waschmaschine**, **-n** washing machine (6)

der **Waschsalon**, **-s** laundromat (10)

das **Wasser** water

der **Wasserhahn**, **⸚e** faucet (5)

der **Wasservogel**, **⸚** waterfowl (10)

der **Wechselkurs**, **-e** exchange rate

wechseln, gewechselt to change; **Geld wechseln** to exchange money

wecken, geweckt to wake (*s.o.*) up (7)

der **Wecker**, **-** alarm clock (2)

weder ... noch neither . . . nor

weg away; **Wie weit weg?** How far away? (6)

der **Weg**, **-e** way; road; path; **den Weg beschreiben** to give directions; **nach dem Weg fragen** to ask for directions; **sich auf den Weg machen** to go on one's way, set off

weg·bringen (bringt ... weg), brachte ... weg, weggebracht to take out; to take away (5)

wegen (+ *gen.*) on account of; about (6)

weg·fahren (fährt ... weg), fuhr ... weg, ist weggefahren to drive off, leave

weg·führen, weggeführt to lead away

weg·gehen (geht ... weg), ging ... weg, ist weggegangen to go away, leave (4)

weg·laufen (läuft ... weg), lief ... weg, ist weggelaufen to run away

weg·nehmen (nimmt ... weg), nahm ... weg, weggenommen to take away

weg·stellen, weggestellt to put away (5)

weg·tragen (trägt ... weg), trug ... weg, weggetragen to carry away (9)

weg·trampen, ist weggetrampt to hitchhike away

weg·ziehen (zieht ... weg), zog ... weg, ist weggezogen to move away

wehen, geweht to blow

sich **wehren**, gewehrt to defend oneself

wehrhaft able to defend oneself

weh·tun (tut ... weh), tat ... weh, wehgetan to hurt (11)

weiblich female; feminine(ly)

(das) **Weihnachten** Christmas (4)

das **Weihnachtsgeschenk**, **-e** Christmas present (5)

weil (*subord. conj.*) because (3, 11)

das **Weilchen**, **-** little while

die **Weile**, **-n** while

Weimarer (*adj.*) (of) Weimar

der **Wein**, **-e** wine (7)

weinen, geweint to cry (3)

der **Weinkeller**, **-** wine cellar (6)

die **Weintraube**, **-n** grape (8)

weiß white (A); **die Weiße Rose** the White Rose (*name of an anti-Nazi resistance group*)

die **Weiße**: **die Berliner Weiße** light, *fizzy beer served with raspberry syrup*

weit far (6); **Wie weit weg?** How far away? (6)

weiter (*adj.*) additional; (*adv.*) farther; further; **und so weiter** (**usw.**) and so forth

die **Weiterbildung** continuing education

weiter·entwickeln, weiterentwickelt to develop further

weiter·gehen (geht ... weiter), ging ... weiter, ist weitergegangen to keep on walking (10)

weiter·helfen (hilft ... weiter), half ... weiter, weitergeholfen to help further

weiterhin still; in addition

weiter·leben, weitergelebt to go on living

welch- which, what (B); **an welchem Tag?** on what day? (4); **Welche Farbe hat ...?** What color is . . . ? (A); **Welcher Tag ist heute?** What day is today? (1); **Welches Datum ist heute?** What is today's date? (4)

die **Welle**, **-n** wave (10); well, shaft

die **Welt**, **-en** world (7); **alle Welt** (*coll.*) the whole world; everybody

weltweit worldwide; all over the world

wem whom (*dat.*) (5)

wen whom (*acc.*) (4)

die **Wende**, **-n** change

wenig (*sg.*) little; **wenige** (*pl.*) few; **am wenigsten** the least (8)

wenn (*subord. conj.*) if; when(ever) (2, 11); **wenn ja** if so

wer who (A, B)

werben (wirbt), warb, geworben to advertise

das **Werbeplakat**, **-e** advertising sign

die **Werbung**, **-en** advertisement

werden (wird), wurde, ist geworden to become (5)

werfen (wirft), warf, geworfen to throw (3)

das **Werk**, **-e** work, product (9)

die **Werkkunstschule**, **-n** college of applied arts

die **Werkstatt**, **⸚en** workshop; repair shop, garage (5)

das **Werkzeug**, **-e** tool (8)

wert worth

der Wert, -e value

wertvoll valuable, expensive (2)

weshalb why

wessen whose

west- west

(das) Westdeutschland (*former*) West Germany

der Westen west

westlich (von + *dat.*) west (of) (7)

das Wetter, - weather (B)

das Wettrennen, - race

die WG, -s = die Wohngemeinschaft, -en shared housing (6)

wichtig important (2)

die Wichtigkeit importance

wider·spiegeln, widergespiegelt to reflect

der Widerstand, ⸚e resistance

widmen, gewidmet to dedicate

wie how (B); Um wie viel Uhr ...? At what time . . . ? (1); Wie fühlst du dich? How do you feel? (3); Wie schreibt man das? How do you spell that? (A); Wie spät ist es? What time is it? (1); Wie viel ...? How much . . . ? Wie viele ...? How many . . . ? (A); Wie viel Uhr ist es? What time is it? (1); Wie weit weg? How far away? (6)

wieder again (3); schon wieder once again (3)

wiederholen, wiederholt to repeat (6)

das Wiederhören: auf Wiederhören good-bye (*on the phone*) (6)

wiederkehrend recurring

das Wiedersehen: auf Wiedersehen good-bye (A)

wiederum again

die Wiedervereinigung, -en reunification

(das) Wien Vienna

Wiener Viennese (*adj.*); das Wiener Schnitzel breaded veal cutlet

die Wiese, -n meadow, pasture (7)

wieso why

wild wild(ly)

die Wildnis, -se wilderness

das Wildschwein, -e wild boar (10)

willkommen welcome

der Wind, -e wind (9)

windig windy (B)

windsurfen gehen (geht ... windsurfen), ging ... windsurfen, ist windsurfen gegangen to go windsurfing (10)

der Winter, - winter (B)

wir we

wirken, gewirkt to work, take effect (11)

wirklich real(ly) (B)

die Wirklichkeit, -en reality

der Wirt, -e / die Wirtin, -nen host/hostess; innkeeper; barkeeper (10)

die Wirtschaft, -en economy; economics (1)

wirtschaftlich economic(ally)

wischen, gewischt to wipe (7); to mop (6); Staub wischen to (wipe) dust

wissen (weiß), wusste, gewusst to know (*as a fact*) (2); Bescheid wissen to know; to have an idea

die Wissenschaft, -en science

der Wissenschaftler, - / die Wissenschaftlerin, -nen scientist (12)

der Witz, -e joke (3); Witze erzählen to tell jokes (3)

wo where (B); Wo willst du denn hin? Where are you going? (A)

die Woche, -n week (1); in der Woche during the week (1); jede Woche every week (3); letzte Woche last week (4)

das Wochenende, -n weekend (1); am Wochenende over the weekend (1); letztes Wochenende last weekend (4)

das Wochenendhaus, ⸚er weekend cabin/ cottage

der Wochenplan, ⸚e weekly schedule

wodurch through what

wofür what for

wogegen against what

woher from where (B); whence

wohin where to (3); whither

wohl probably (12); well; sich wohl fühlen to feel well (11)

wohlbekannt well-known

der Wohlstand prosperity

der Wohnblock, -s *or* ⸚e residential block, apartment complex

wohnen (in + *dat.*), gewohnt to live (in) (B)

die Wohngemeinschaft, -en = die WG, -s shared housing (6)

das Wohnheim, -e dorm

der Wohnkomfort comfortable living

die Wohnmöglichkeit, -en living arrangements

der Wohnort, -e place of residence (1)

der/die Wohnraumbietende, -n (ein Wohnraum-bietender) person offering housing

der/die Wohnraumsuchende, -n (ein Wohn-raumsuchender) person looking for housing

die Wohnung, -en apartment (1, 2)

die Wohnungsbörse, -n apartment brokerage

die Wohnungssuche, -n search for an apartment; auf Wohnungssuche looking for a room or apartment

das Wohnviertel, - residential district

der Wohnwagen, - mobile home

das Wohnzimmer, - living room (6)

der Wolf, ⸚e wolf (9)

wollen (will), wollte, gewollt to want (to); to intend (to); to plan (to) (3); Wo willst du denn hin? Where are you going? (A)

womit with what, by what means

woran at/on/of what

worauf on/for what

das Wort, ⸚er/-e word; Worte words (*connected discourse*); Wörter words (*individual vocabulary items*) (A)

das Wörterbuch, ⸚er dictionary (2)

der Wortkasten, ⸚ word box

der Wortschatz, ⸚e vocabulary (A)

worüber about what

die Wunde, -n wound (11)

das Wunder, - miracle, wonder (4); kein Wunder no wonder (4)

wunderlich strange(ly)

sich wundern, gewundert to be surprised

wunderschön exceedingly beautiful(ly) (6)

der Wunsch, ⸚e wish

sich (*dat.*) wünschen, gewünscht to wish for

der Wunschzettel, - wish list (*of things one would like to have*)

die Wurst, ⸚e sausage (8); cold cuts

das Würstchen, - sausage; frank(furter); hot dog (8)

würzen, gewürzt to season (8)

die Wüste, -n desert (7)

wütend angry, angrily (3)

die Zahl, -en number (A); figure

zahlen, gezahlt to pay (for) (5); Miete zahlen to pay rent; Zahlen, bitte. The check, please.

zählen, gezählt to count (A); (zu + *dat.*) to be among

das Zahlenrätsel, - number puzzle

zahlreich numerous

die Zahlung, -en payment

das Zahlungsmittel, - means of payment (12)

offizielles Zahlungsmittel legal tender

zahm tame(ly) (10)

der Zahn, ⸚e tooth (11); sich die Zähne putzen to brush one's teeth (11)

der Zahnarzt, ⸚e / die Zahnärztin, -nen dentist (11)

die Zahnschmerzen (*pl.*) toothache (11)

die Zange, -n pliers; tongs (8)

zart tender(ly) (8)

der Zauber, - magic; charm

der Zauberer, - wizard

der Zaun, ⸚e fence (9)

z. B. = zum Beispiel for example (3)

das Zebra, -s zebra (10)

der Zebrastreifen, - crosswalk (10)

zehn ten (A)

zehnt- tenth (4)

das Zeichen, - sign

zeichnen, gezeichnet to draw (3, 5)

die Zeichnung, -en drawing

der Zeigefinger, - index finger

zeigen, gezeigt to show; Was zeigen Ihre Bilder? What do your pictures show? (A)

die Zeile, -n line

die Zeit, -en time (4); in letzter Zeit recently; lange Zeit (for) a long time; zu dieser Zeit at this time; zur Zeit at present

der Zeitgeschmack, ⸚er contemporary taste

die Zeitschrift, -en magazine

die Zeitung, -en newspaper (2); Zeitungen austragen to deliver newspapers (5); Zeitung lesen to read the newspaper (1)

das Zelt, -e tent (2)

zelten, gezeltet to camp (1)

der Zentimeter, - centimeter

zentral central(ly) (10)

die **Zentralheizung** central heating (6)

das **Zentrum, Zentren** center

der **Zeppelin, -e** zeppelin, dirigible (7)

zerbrechen (zerbricht), zerbrach, hat/ist zerbrochen to break into pieces

zerreißen (zerreißt), zerriss, zerrissen to tear (to pieces) (9)

zerschlagen (zerschlägt), zerschlug, zerschlagen to smash to bits

zerstören, zerstört to destroy

der **Zeuge, -n** (*wk.*) / die **Zeugin, -nen** witness (11)

das **Zeugnis, -se** report card

der **Ziegel, -** clay tile

ziehen (zieht), zog, ist gezogen to move (2); (*p.p. with* **haben**) to pull (8)

das **Ziel, -e** goal; destination (10)

ziellos aimless(ly)

ziemlich rather (2); **ziemlich groß** pretty big (2)

die **Zigarette, -n** cigarette (4)

die **Zigarre, -n** cigar (7)

das **Zimmer, -** room (1, 2)

die **Zimmersuche, -n** search for a room (*to rent*)

die **Zinsen** (*pl.*) interest (12)

zirka circa, about, approximately

der **Zirkus, -se** circus (9)

die **Zither, -n** zither

die **Zitrone, -n** lemon (8)

der **Zivilisationskritiker, -** / die **Zivilisationskritikerin, -nen** critic of civilization

der **Zoo, -s** zoo

zu (*adj.*) closed; (*adv.*) too (2); **zu viel** too much

zu (+ *dat.*) to (*a place*) (2, 10); for (*an occasion*) (2); for the purpose of; **bis zu** as far as; up to (10); **um ... zu** (+ *inf.*) in order to (12)

zu Abend essen to dine, have dinner (4); **zu Besuch kommen** to visit (3); **zu Fuß** on foot (3); **zu Hause sein** to be at home (A, 1, 10); **zum Arzt** to the doctor (3); **zum Beispiel (z. B.)** for example (3); **zum ersten Mal** for the first time (4); **zum Geburtstag** for someone's birthday (2); **zum Mittagessen** for lunch (3); **zum Schluss** in the end, finally (8); **zur Uni gehen** to go to the university (1, 2)

zu·bereiten, zubereitet to prepare (*food*) (8)

die **Zubereitung, -en** preparation (8)

zu·binden (bindet ... zu), band ... zu, zugebunden to tie shut

der **Zucker** sugar (8)

zu·decken, zugedeckt to cover (*with a blanket*) (11)

zu·drücken, zugedrückt to squeeze shut; **ein Auge zudrücken** to look the other way

zuerst first (4, 7)

zufällig accidental(ly) (9)

zufolge (+ *dat.*) according to

zufrieden satisfied

der **Zug, ⁻e** train (7, 10)

der **Zugang, ⁻e** access (12)

zugebunden (*p.p. of* **zubinden**) tied shut (8)

die **Zugfahrkarte, -n** train ticket (6)

die **Zugspitze** *mountain on the German-Austrian border*

zu·hören (+ *dat.*), **zugehört** to listen (to) (6); **hören Sie zu** listen (A)

die **Zukunft, ⁻e** future

zukünftig future (*adj.*)

zulässig permissible

zum = zu dem to/for the

zu·machen, zugemacht to close (3)

zumindest at least

zunächst at first

der **Zuname, -n** (*wk.*) surname, last name

die **Zunge, -n** tongue (11); **sich die Zunge verbrennen** to burn one's tongue (11)

zu·ordnen (+ *dat.*), **zugeordnet** to classify (as)

zur = zu der to/for the

zurecht·kommen (mit + *dat.*) **(kommt ... zurecht), kam ... zurecht, ist zurechtgekommen** to get along (with)

(das) **Zürich** Zurich

zurück back (9); **hin und zurück** there and back; round-trip (5, 10)

zurück·bekommen (bekommt ... zurück), bekam ... zurück, zurückbekommen to get back

zurück·bringen (bringt ... zurück), brachte ... zurück, zurückgebracht to bring back

zurück·führen (auf + *acc.*), **zurückgeführt** to lead back (to); to be attributable (to)

zurück·geben (gibt ... zurück), gab ... zurück, zurückgegeben to give back, return; to reply

zurück·gehen (geht ... zurück), ging ... zurück, ist zurückgegangen to go back

zurück·kehren, ist zurückgekehrt to come back, return

zurück·kommen (kommt ... zurück), kam ... zurück, ist zurückgekommen to come back, return (6)

zurück·rufen (ruft ... zurück), rief ... zurück, zurückgerufen to call back

zurück·treten (tritt ... zurück), trat ... zurück, ist zurückgetreten to step back; to step down

zurück·ziehen (zieht ... zurück), zog ... zurück, zurückgezogen to pull back, draw back; **sich zurückziehen** to withdraw

zusammen together (2)

die **Zusammenarbeit, -en** collaboration

der **Zusammenbruch, ⁻e** breakdown; collapse

zusammen·fassen, zusammengefasst to summarize

die **Zusammenfassung, -en** summary

zusammen·packen, zusammengepackt to pack up

sich zusammen·schließen (schließt ... zusammen), schloss ... zusammen, zusammengeschlossen to join together

sich zusammen·setzen (aus + *dat.*), **zusammengesetzt** to be composed (of)

zusammen·sitzen (mit + *dat.*) **(sitzt ... zusammen), saß ... zusammen, zusammengesessen** to sit together (with)

zusammen·stoßen (stößt ... zusammen), stieß ... zusammen, ist zusammengestoßen to crash (11)

zusammen·treffen (mit + *dat.*) **(trifft ... zusammen), traf ... zusammen, ist zusammengetroffen** to meet

zusätzlich additional, in addition

zu·schauen, zugeschaut to watch

zu·schnüren, zugeschnürt to tie up; to constrict

zuschulden: sich (*dat.*) **etwas zuschulden kommen lassen** to do something wrong

zu·sehen (+ *dat.*) **(sieht ... zu), sah ... zu, zugesehen** to watch

zu·sperren, zugesperrt to lock

der **Zustand, ⁻e** condition

die **Zutat, -en** ingredient (8)

(sich) zu·wenden (+ *dat.*) **(wendet ... zu), wandte ... zu, zugewandt** to turn toward

zu·winken (+ *dat.*), **zugewinkt** to wave to

zu·ziehen (zieht ... zu), zog ... zu, zugezogen to pull shut; to draw (*curtains*)

zwangsbeatmen, zwangsbeatmet to administer artificial respiration by force

zwanzig twenty (A)

der **Zwanzigeuroschein, -e** twenty-euro note (8)

zwanzigst- twentieth (4)

zwar to be sure

zwei two (A)

der **Zweifel, -** doubt

zweimal twice (5)

zweit: zu zweit arbeiten/leben to work/live together (*two people*)

zweit- second (4)

zweiundzwanzig twenty-two (A)

der **Zwerg, -e** dwarf (9)

die **Zwiebel, -n** onion (8)

zwingen (zwingt), zwang, gezwungen to force

zwischen (+ *dat./acc.*) between (7); among

die **Zwischenmiete, -n: zur Zwischenmiete** for sublet

die **Zwischenzeit** interim; **in der Zwischenzeit** in the meantime

zwölf twelve (A)

zwölft- twelfth (4)

(das) **Zypern** Cyprus

Vokabeln

Englisch-Deutsch

This list contains the words from the chapter vocabulary lists.

to abandon **verlassen (verlässt), verließ, verlassen** (11)

able: to be able (to) **können (kann), konnte, gekonnt** (3)

about **wegen** (+ *gen.*) (6)

above (*adv.*) **oben** (10); **über** (4)

abroad **im Ausland** (6); center for study abroad **das Auslandsamt, ⁻er** (1)

academic subject **das Fach, ⁻er** (1)

access **der Zugang** (12)

accident **der Unfall, ⁻e** (4)

accidental(ly) **zufällig** (9)

accordion **das Akkordeon, -s** (4)

account: bank account **das Konto, Konten** (5); checking account **das Girokonto, Girokonten** (12); on account of **wegen** (+ *gen.*) (6); to open a bank account **ein Konto eröffnen** (5); savings account **das Sparkonto, Sparkonten** (12)

acquainted: to get acquainted with **kennen·lernen, kennengelernt** (1)

across **gegenüber** (+ *dat.*) (6); across from **gegenüber von** (+ *dat.*) (10); right across the way **gleich gegenüber** (6)

activity **die Tätigkeit, -en** (6); favorite activity **die Lieblingsbeschäftigung, -en** (5)

actually **eigentlich** (3)

ad **die Anzeige, -n** (6); housing-wanted ad **die Suchanzeige, -n** (6)

addition: in addition **dazu** (8); in addition to **neben** (+ *dat./acc.*) (3)

address **die Adresse, -n** (1)

adhesive bandage **das Pflaster, -** (11)

admissions ticket **die Eintrittskarte, -n** (5)

advantage **der Vorteil, -e** (7)

advice **der Rat, Ratschläge** (5, 11)

to advise **raten** (+ *dat.*) **(rät), riet, geraten** (11)

afraid: to be afraid **Angst haben** (3); to be afraid of **sich fürchten vor** (+ *dat.*)**, gefürchtet** (10)

Africa **(das) Afrika** (B)

Afro-German (*adj.*) **afro-deutsch** (12)

after (*prep.*) **nach** (+ *dat.*) (3); (*subord. conj.*) **nachdem** (9, 11); at twenty after five **um zwanzig nach fünf** (1); the day after tomorrow **übermorgen** (9)

afternoon **der Nachmittag, -e** (4); afternoons, in the afternoon **nachmittags** (4); good afternoon (*for.*) **guten Tag** (A); good afternoon (*for.; southern Germany, Austria*) **grüß Gott** (A)

afterward **danach** (8, 10)

again **wieder** (3); once again **schon wieder** (3)

against **gegen** (+ *acc.*) (9)

age **das Alter** (1)

agency: travel agency **das Reisebüro, -s** (6)

agent: train agent **der/die Bahnangestellte, -n (ein Bahnangestellter)** (10)

ago **vor** (+ *dat.*) (4); two days ago **vor zwei Tagen** (4)

agreement: prenuptial agreement **der Ehevertrag, ⁻e** (12)

ahead: straight ahead **geradeaus** (10)

air **die Luft** (7); air mattress **die Luftmatratze, -n** (10)

airplane **das Flugzeug, -e** (7)

airport **der Flughafen, ⁻** (6)

alarm clock **der Wecker, -** (2)

albatross **der Albatros, -se** (10)

alive: to be alive **am Leben sein** (9)

all: all day long **den ganzen Tag** (1); all night long **die ganze Nacht** (3); by all means **auf jeden Fall** (4); not at all **kein bisschen** (3)

allergic **allergisch** (11)

alley **die Gasse, -n** (10)

almost **fast** (5)

along **entlang** (10); to bring along **mit·bringen (bringt ... mit), brachte ... mit, mitgebracht** (3); to go along **entlang·gehen (geht ... entlang), ging ... entlang, ist entlanggegangen** (10); to take along **mit·nehmen (nimmt ... mit), nahm ... mit, mitgenommen** (3)

aloud: to read aloud **vor·lesen (liest ... vor), las ... vor, vorgelesen** (9)

alphabet **das Alphabet, -e** (3)

the Alps **die Alpen** (*pl.*) (7)

already **schon** (2, 4)

also **auch** (A)

although (*subord. conj.*) **obwohl** (11)

always **immer** (3)

ambulance **der Krankenwagen, -** (11)

America **(das) Amerika** (B); North America **(das) Nordamerika** (B); South America **(das) Südamerika** (B)

American (*person*) **der Amerikaner, -** / **die Amerikanerin, -nen** (B)

among **unter** (+ *dat./acc.*) (6)

amount (*of money*) **die Höhe, -n** (12)

ancestor **der Vorfahre, -n** (*wk.*) (12)

and (*coord. conj.*) **und** (A, 11)

angry **wütend** (3); **sauer** (5)

to get angry **sich ärgern, geärgert** (11)

animal **das Tier, -e** (3, 7, 10)

to annoy **ärgern, geärgert** (3)

another: one another **einander** (3)

answer **die Antwort, -en** (A); to answer **antworten** (+ *dat.*)**, geantwortet** (4, 10); **beantworten, beantwortet** (7)

antibiotics **die Antibiotika** (*pl.*) (11)

any: in any case **jedenfalls** (11)

anything **etwas** (5); Anything else? **Sonst noch etwas?** (5)

apartment **die Wohnung, -en** (1, 2)

appendix **der Blinddarm, ⁻e** (11)

appetizer **die Vorspeise, -n** (8)

apple juice **der Apfelsaft** (8)

appliance **das Gerät, -e** (8)

to apply for **beantragen, beantragt** (12)

appointment **der Termin, -e** (5, 11); **die Verabredung, -en** (11); appointment calendar **der Terminkalender, -** (11); to get an appointment **sich einen Termin geben lassen** (11)

apprenticeship **die Lehre, -n** (5)

approximately **ungefähr** (7)

April **der April** (B)

Arabic (*language*) **(das) Arabisch** (B)

architect **der Architekt, -en** (*wk.*) / **die Architektin, -nen** (5)

area **der Bereich, -e** (12)

to argue **streiten (streitet), stritt, gestritten** (9)

arm **der Arm, -e** (B); to break one's arm **sich den Arm brechen** (11)

armchair **der Sessel, -** (2, 6)

army: German army **die Bundeswehr** (5); in the German army **bei der Bundeswehr** (5)

around the corner **um die Ecke** (5); right around the corner **gleich um die Ecke** (6)

arrival **die Ankunft, ⁻e** (7)

to arrive **an·kommen (kommt ... an), kam ... an, ist angekommen** (1)

art **die Kunst** (1); art history **die Kunstgeschichte** (1)

as **als** (5); as . . . as possible **möglichst** (+ *adv.*) (6); as far as **bis zu** (+ *dat.*) (10); as well **auch** (A); as what? **als was?** (5)

Asia **(das) Asien** (B)

to ask (for) **bitten (um + acc.) (bittet), bat, gebeten** (12); to ask about **sich erkundigen nach** (+ *dat.*), **erkundigt** (10); to ask a question **eine Frage stellen** (5)

asleep: to fall asleep **ein·schlafen (schläft ... ein), schlief ... ein, ist eingeschlafen** (7)

aspirin **das Aspirin** (11)

assignment **die Aufgabe, -n** (4)

at **an** (+ *dat.*) (2); **bei** (+ *dat.*) (2, 6, 10); **in** (+ *dat./acc.*) (4); at a bank **bei einer Bank** (6); at home **zu Hause** (A, 1, 10); **daheim** (9); at Monika's **bei Monika** (2); at night **nachts** (4); at noon **mittags** (2); at school **in der Schule** (5); at six o'clock **um sechs (Uhr)** (1); at the cafe **im Café** (4); at the courthouse **auf dem Gericht** (5); at the department store **im Kaufhaus** (5); at the gas station **an der Tankstelle** (5); at the moment **im Moment** (1); at the ticket booth **an der Kasse** (5); **am Schalter** (5); at the university **auf der Universität** (5); at two thirty **um halb drei** (1); At what time . . . ? **Um wie viel Uhr ...?** (1); at your parents' **bei deinen Eltern** (6)

athletic **sportlich** (B); athletic shoe **der Sportschuh, -e** (A)

ATM (automatic teller machine) **der Geldautomat, -en** (*wk.*) (12)

to attempt **versuchen, versucht** (4)

to attend to **pflegen, gepflegt** (5)

attendant: swimming-pool attendant **der Bademeister, - / die Bademeisterin, -nen** (5)

attention **die Achtung** (7); to pay attention **auf·passen, aufgepasst** (3); to pay attention to **achten auf** (+ *acc.*), **geachtet** (11)

attitude **die Einstellung, -en** (12)

attractive **attraktiv** (6)

August **der August** (B)

aunt **die Tante, -n** (B)

Australia **(das) Australien** (B)

Australian (*person*) **der Australier, - / die Australierin, -nen** (B)

Austria **(das) Österreich** (B)

Austrian (*person*) **der Österreicher, - / die Österreicherin, -nen** (B)

automatic teller machine (ATM) **der Geldautomat, -en** (*wk.*) (12)

autumn **der Herbst, -e** (B)

available **frei** (8); Is this seat available? **Ist hier noch frei?** (8)

away: How far away? **Wie weit weg?** (6); to carry away **weg·tragen (trägt ... weg), trug ... weg, weggetragen** (9); to put away **weg·stellen, weggestellt** (5); right away **gleich** (6); to take away **weg·bringen (bringt ... weg), brachte ... weg, weggebracht** (5)

baby **das Baby, -s** (7); baby carriage **der Kinderwagen, -** (7)

back (*adv.*) **zurück** (9); back then **damals** (9); to come back **zurück·kommen (kommt ... zurück), kam ... zurück, ist zurückgekommen** (6); there and back **hin und zurück** (10)

back (*n.*) **der Rücken, -** (B)

backpack **der Rucksack, ⁻e** (2)

bacon **der Speck** (8)

bad **schlecht** (2); **schlimm** (11); too bad! **schade!** (6)

bag **die Tasche, -n** (1); (*paper or plastic*) **die Tüte, -n** (11); sleeping bag **der Schlafsack, ⁻e** (2)

to bake **backen (bäckt), backte, gebacken** (5)

bakery **die Bäckerei, -en** (5); at the bakery **in der Bäckerei** (5)

balance: bank balance **das Guthaben** (12)

balcony **der Balkon, -e** (6)

ball **der Ball, ⁻e** (A, 1); soccer ball **der Fußball, ⁻e** (A, 1)

ballerina **die Ballerina, -s** (9)

ballet class **der Ballettunterricht** (9)

ballpoint pen **der Kugelschreiber, -** (4)

Baltic Sea **die Ostsee** (B)

banana **die Banane, -n** (8)

bandage **der Verband, ⁻e** (11); adhesive bandage **das Pflaster, -** (11)

bandanna **das Halstuch, ⁻er** (1)

bank **die Bank, -en** (5); at a bank **bei einer Bank** (6); at the bank **auf der Bank** (5); bank account **das Konto, Konten** (5); bank balance **das Guthaben** (12); bank employee **der/die Bankangestellte, -n (ein Bankangestellter)** (5); to open a bank account **ein Konto eröffnen** (5)

bar **die Kneipe, -n** (4)

barbecued **gegrillt** (8)

barely **knapp** (4)

barkeeper **der Wirt, -e / die Wirtin, -nen** (10)

baseball team **die Baseballmannschaft, -en** (9)

basement **der Keller, -** (4, 6)

basin **das Waschbecken, -** (6)

basketball **der Basketball, ⁻e** (2)

bat **die Fledermaus, ⁻e** (10)

bath, bathroom **das Bad, ⁻er** (6)

to bathe **baden, gebadet** (3); **(sich) baden, gebadet** (11)

bathrobe **der Bademantel, ⁻** (2)

bathtub **die Badewanne, -n** (6)

bay **die Bucht, -en** (7)

to be **sein (ist), war, ist gewesen** (A, 4)

beach **der Strand, ⁻e** (4, 7); beach chair **der Strandkorb, ⁻e** (10); beach parasol **der Sonnenschirm, -e** (10)

bean **die Bohne, -n** (8)

bear: teddy bear **der Teddybär, -en** (*wk.*) (A)

beard **der Bart, ⁻e** (B)

to beat **schlagen (schlägt), schlug, geschlagen** (8)

beautiful **schön** (B); exceedingly beautiful **wunderschön** (6)

because (*subord. conj.*) **weil** (3, 11); (*coord. conj.*) **denn** (9, 11)

to become **werden (wird), wurde, ist geworden** (5)

bed **das Bett, -en** (1, 6); bed-and-breakfast (inn) **das Gästehaus, ⁻er** (10); to get up on the wrong side of bed **mit dem linken Fuß auf·stehen** (4); to go to bed **ins Bett gehen** (1)

bedroom **das Schlafzimmer, -** (6)

bedside table **der Nachttisch, -e** (6)

bee **die Biene, -n** (10)

beef **das Rindfleisch** (8); ground beef **das Hackfleisch** (8)

beer **das Bier, -e** (2)

before (*subord. conj.*) **bevor** (11); the day before yesterday **vorgestern** (4)

to begin **beginnen (beginnt), begann, begonnen** (1); **an·fangen (fängt ... an), fing ... an, angefangen** (4)

Belgium **(das) Belgien** (B)

to believe **glauben, geglaubt** (2)

belly **der Bauch, ⁻e** (B)

to belong to **gehören** (+ *dat.*), **gehört** (6); to belong to (*an organization*) **an·gehören** (+ *dat.*), **angehört** (12)

beloved female friend **die Geliebte, -n** (3)

below **unter** (+ *dat./acc.*) (6)

belt **der Gürtel, -** (2); seat belt **der Sicherheitsgurt, -e** (7)

beneath **unter** (+ *dat./acc.*) (6)

beside **neben** (+ *dat./acc.*) (3)

besides **außerdem** (3, 10)

best: like (*to do*) best **am liebsten** (7)

better **besser** (2)

between **zwischen** (+ *dat./acc.*) (7)

beverage **das Getränk, -e** (8)

bicycle **das Fahrrad, ⁻er** (2, 7); bicycle helmet **der Fahrradhelm, -e** (5); bicycle tour **die Radtour, -en** (9); to ride a bicycle **Rad fahren (fährt ... Rad), fuhr ... Rad, ist Rad gefahren** (7)

bicyclist **der Radfahrer, - / die Radfahrerin, -nen** (7)

big **groß** (B); pretty big **ziemlich groß** (2)

bikini **der Bikini, -s** (5)

bill **die Rechnung, -en** (4); (*of currency*) **der Schein, -e** (8); **der Geldschein, -e** (12)

biographical information **persönliche Daten** (*pl.*) (1)

biology **die Biologie** (1)

bird **der Vogel, ⁻** (10)

birthday **der Geburtstag, -e** (1, 2); birthday card **die Geburtstagskarte, -n** (2); for someone's birthday **zum Geburtstag** (2)

bit: a little bit **ein bisschen** (3); not a bit **gar nicht** (3); quite a bit **ganz schön viel** (3)

to bite **beißen (beißt), biss, gebissen** (9); (*of insects*) **stechen (sticht), stach, gestochen** (10)

black **schwarz** (A); black-haired **schwarzhaarig** (9)

blackboard **die Tafel, -n** (A, B)

blanket **die Decke, -n** (11)

to bleed **bluten, geblutet** (11)

blond **blond** (B)

blood **das Blut** (9, 11); blood pressure **der Blutdruck** (11); to have low/high blood pressure **niedrigen/hohen Blutdruck haben** (11); to take blood **Blut ab·nehmen** (11)

blouse die Bluse, -n (A)

to blow-dry (one's hair) sich (die Haare) föhnen, geföhnt (11)

blue blau (A, B); blue whale der Blauwal, -e (10)

boar: wild boar das Wildschwein, -e (10)

to board ein·steigen (steigt ... ein), stieg ... ein, ist eingestiegen (10)

boat das Boot, -e (2)

body der Körper, - (B)

boiled gekocht (8); boiled eggs gekochte Eier (pl.) (8); boiled potatoes die Salzkartoffeln (pl.) (8)

to book buchen, gebucht (7)

book das Buch, ⸚er (A, B, 2)

bookcase, bookshelf das Regal, -e (2)

boot der Stiefel, - (A)

booth: telephone booth die Telefonzelle, -n (2); ticket booth die Kasse, -n (5), der Schalter, - (5); at the ticket booth an der Kasse (5), am Schalter (5)

bored: to be bored Langeweile haben (3)

boredom die Langeweile (3)

boring langweilig (2)

born geboren (1); When were you born? Wann sind Sie geboren? (1)

bottle die Flasche, -n (5); bottle opener der Flaschenöffner, - (8)

boutique die Boutique, -n (6)

bowl die Schüssel, -n (8); salad (mixing) bowl die Salatschüssel, -n (5)

to box boxen, geboxt (1)

boy: Oh boy! (coll.) Mensch! (2)

boyfriend der Freund, -e (A)

bracelet das Armband, ⸚er (2)

brain das Gehirn, -e (11)

to brake bremsen, gebremst (11)

brake die Bremse, -n (7)

brave tapfer (9)

bread das Brot, -e (8); farmer's bread das Bauernbrot, -e (5)

to break brechen (bricht), brach, gebrochen (11); to break (one's arm) sich den Arm brechen (11)

break die Pause, -n (1); breakfast das Frühstück, -e (2); breakfast room das Frühstückszimmer, - (10); to eat breakfast frühstücken, gefrühstückt (1)

to breathe atmen, geatmet (11)

bride die Braut, ⸚e (9)

bridge die Brücke, -n (10)

to bring bringen (bringt), brachte, gebracht (2); to bring along mit·bringen (bringt ... mit), brachte ... mit, mitgebracht (3)

broiled gebraten (8); gegrillt (8)

broken kaputt (A)

broom der Besen, - (6)

brother der Bruder, ⸚ (B)

brown braun (A); to brown bräunen, gebräunt (8)

to brush (one's teeth) sich (die Zähne) putzen (11)

brush die Bürste, -n (6)

Brussels sprouts der Rosenkohl (8)

building das Gebäude, - (10); high-rise building das Hochhaus, ⸚er (6)

Bulgaria (das) Bulgarien (B)

burglar der Einbrecher, - / die Einbrecherin, -nen (9)

to burn brennen (brennt), brannte, gebrannt (11); verbrennen (verbrennt), verbrannte, verbrannt (11); to burn (one's tongue) sich (die Zunge) verbrennen (11)

bus der Bus, -se (2, 7); bus stop die Bushaltestelle, -n (10)

bush der Busch, ⸚e (9)

but (coord. conj.) aber (A, 11); but (rather / on the contrary) sondern (A)

butcher shop die Metzgerei, -en (6)

butter die Butter (8); herb butter die Kräuterbutter (8)

to buy kaufen, gekauft (1)

by an ... vorbei (10); by all means auf jeden Fall (4)

bye (infor.) tschüss (A)

cabbage der Kohl (8)

café das Café, -s (4); at the café im Café (4)

cafeteria: student cafeteria die Mensa, Mensen (2)

cage der Käfig, -e (10)

cake der Kuchen, - (5)

calendar: appointment calendar der Terminkalender, - (11)

to call rufen (ruft), rief, gerufen (7, 11); to call up an·rufen (ruft ... an), rief ... an, angerufen (1)

called: to be called heißen (heißt), hieß, geheißen (A)

calm ruhig (B)

calorie: calorie-conscious kalorienbewusst (8); low in calories kalorienarm (8)

camera die Kamera, -s (2)

to camp zelten, gezeltet (1)

camping das Camping (10)

campsite der Campingplatz, ⸚e (10)

can (v.) können (kann), konnte, gekonnt (3)

can (n.) die Dose, -n (8); can opener der Dosenöffner, - (8); garbage can der Mülleimer, - (8); watering can die Gießkanne, -n (6)

Canada (das) Kanada (B)

Canadian (person) der Kanadier, - / die Kanadierin, -nen (B)

candle die Kerze, -n (3)

canoe das Kanu, -s (10)

canoeing: to go canoeing Kanu fahren (10)

cap die Mütze, -n (5)

capital city die Hauptstadt, ⸚e (B)

car das Auto, -s (A); der Wagen, - (7); car radio das Autoradio, -s (7); sleeping car der Schlafwagen, - (4); train car der Waggon, -s (7); used car der Gebrauchtwagen, - (7)

card die Karte, -n (1, 2); birthday card die Geburtstagskarte, -n (2); Eurocheque Card die Euroscheckkarte, -n (12); identification card der Ausweis, -e (10); personal ID card der Personalausweis, -e (1); telephone card die Telefonkarte, -n (2)

to care for mögen (mag), mochte, gemocht (3)

care: take care (infor.) mach's gut (A); to take care of sich kümmern um (+ acc.), gekümmert (12)

career der Beruf, -e (5); das Berufsleben (12); career counselor der Berufsberater, - / die Berufsberaterin, -nen (5); practical career training praktische Ausbildung (5)

carpet der Teppich, -e (2)

carriage: baby carriage der Kinderwagen, - (7)

carrot die Karotte, -n (8)

to carry away weg·tragen (trägt ... weg), trug ... weg, weggetragen (9); to carry out aus·führen, ausgeführt (12)

case: in any case jedenfalls (11)

cash das Bargeld (12); cash-free bargeldlos (12)

cashier window die Kasse, -n (12)

cast (plaster) der Gips (11)

to cast a spell on verwünschen, verwünscht (9)

castle das Schloss, ⸚er (9)

cat die Katze, -n (2)

to catch a cold sich erkälten, erkältet (11)

cathedral der Dom, -e (10)

cauliflower der Blumenkohl (8)

CD die CD, -s (A, 3); CD player der CD-Spieler, - (2)

ceiling die Decke, -n (B)

to celebrate feiern, gefeiert (4, 5)

celebration die Feier, -n (9); family celebration das Familienfest, -e (4)

cellar der Keller, - (4, 6); wine cellar der Weinkeller, - (6)

cellular phone das Handy, -s (2)

Celsius Celsius (B)

center for study abroad das Auslandsamt, ⸚er (1)

central zentral (10); central heating die Zentralheizung (6)

certainly bestimmt (3); sicherlich (3)

chair der Stuhl, ⸚e (B, 2); beach chair der Strandkorb, ⸚e (10); deck chair der Liegestuhl, ⸚e (4)

to change ändern, geändert (9); to change (trains) um·steigen (steigt ... um), stieg ... um, ist umgestiegen (7); to change into sich verwandeln in (+ acc.), verwandelt (9)

change: keep the change das stimmt so (8)

chaos das Chaos (5)

chapter das Kapitel, - (A)

to charge berechnen (+ dat.), berechnet (8)

to chat chatten, gechattet (1)

cheap billig (2)

to check the oil das Öl kontrollieren (5)

check (in restaurant) die Rechnung, -en (4); die Quittung, -en (8); separate checks getrennt (5)

checking account das Girokonto, Girokonten (12)

cheese der Käse (8)

cheetah der Gepard, -e (10)

chemistry die Chemie (1)

chess das Schach (1)

to chew kauen, gekaut (11)

chic schick (2)

child das Kind, -er (B)

childhood **die Kindheit** (9)

chili **der Chili** (11)

China **(das) China** (B)

Chinese (*language*) **(das) Chinesisch** (B)

chisel **der Meißel, -** (12)

chocolate: hot chocolate **der Kakao** (8)

Christmas **(das) Weihnachten** (4); Christmas present **das Weihnachtsgeschenk, -e** (5)

church **die Kirche, -n** (5); (*religious denomination*) **die Konfession, -en** (12); at church **in der Kirche** (5)

cigar **die Zigarre, -n** (7)

cigarette **die Zigarette, -n** (4)

cinema **das Kino, -s** (1)

circus **der Zirkus, -se** (9)

citizen **der Bürger, -** / **die Bürgerin, -nen** (10)

citizenship **die Staatsangehörigkeit, -en** (1)

city **die Stadt, ⸚e** (2, 6)

capital city **die Hauptstadt, ⸚e** (B); city limits **der Stadtrand, ⸚er** (6); city street map **der Stadtplan, ⸚e** (10); tour of the city **die Stadtrundfahrt, -en** (7)

class **der Kurs, -e** (A, 1); **die Klasse, -n** (5, 10); **der Unterricht** (11); ballet class **der Ballettunter-richt** (9); class reunion **das Klassentreffen, -** (9); German class **der Deutschkurs, -e** (A); to travel first class **erster Klasse fahren** (10)

classroom **der Seminarraum, ⸚e** (B)

clay **der Ton** (12)

to clean **sauber machen, sauber gemacht** (3); **putzen, geputzt** (6); to clean (up) **auf·räumen, aufgeräumt** (1); clean **sauber** (B); to wipe clean **ab·wischen, abgewischt** (6)

cleaner: dry cleaner's **die Reinigung, -en** (6); vacuum cleaner **der Staubsauger, -** (6)

cleaning: spring cleaning **der Frühjahrsputz** (6)

to clear **ab·räumen, abgeräumt** (3); to clear the table **den Tisch ab·räumen** (3)

clerk **der/die Angestellte, -n (ein Angestellter)** (7)

to climb **besteigen (besteigt), bestieg, bestiegen** (7); **klettern, ist geklettert** (9); to climb down **herunter·klettern, ist heruntergeklettert** (11)

clock **die Uhr, -en** (B); alarm clock **der Wecker, -** (2); kitchen clock **die Küchenuhr, -en** (5)

to close **schließen (schließt), schloss, geschlossen** (A); **zu·machen, zugemacht** (3)

close **nah** (7)

closet **der Schrank, ⸚e** (6); clothes closet **der Kleiderschrank, ⸚e** (6)

cloth (*for cleaning*) **der Putzlappen, -** (6)

clothes **die Kleidung** (A, 2); clothes closet **der Kleiderschrank, ⸚e** (6); clothes dryer **der Wäschetrockner, -** (8)

clown **der Clown, -s** (9)

coast **die Küste, -n** (7)

coat **der Mantel, ⸚** (A)

cocoa **der Kakao** (8)

coffee **der Kaffee** (1); coffee filter **der Kaffeefilter, -** (4); coffee grinder **die Kaffeemühle, -n** (8); coffee machine **die Kaffeemaschine, -n** (5)

coffin **der Sarg, ⸚e** (9)

cold (*adj.*) **kalt** (B); ice-cold **eiskalt** (8)

cold (*n.*) (*head cold*) **die Erkältung, -en** (11); to catch a cold **sich erkälten, erkältet** (11); cold (*with a runny nose*) **der Schnupfen, -** (11)

to collect **sammeln, gesammelt** (10)

college preparatory school **das Gymnasium, Gymnasien** (6)

color **die Farbe, -n** (A, 1); color of eyes **die Augenfarbe, -n** (1); color of hair **die Haarfarbe, -n** (1); favorite color **die Lieblingsfarbe, -n** (A); oil color (*paint*) **die Ölfarbe, -n** (12); What color is . . . ? **Welche Farbe hat ...?** (A)

to comb **kämmen, gekämmt** (3); to comb (one's hair) **sich (die Haare) kämmen, gekämmt** (11)

to combine **kombinieren, kombiniert** (3)

to come (from) **kommen (aus + dat.) (kommt), kam, ist gekommen** (B); to come back **zurück·kommen (kommt ... zurück), kam ... zurück, ist zurückgekommen** (6)

to come by **vorbei·kommen (kommt ... vorbei), kam ... vorbei, ist vorbeigekommen** (3)

Come on over! **Komm mal vorbei!** (11); to come out this way **heraus·kommen (kommt ... heraus), kam ... heraus, ist herausgekommen** (10)

to come this way **her·kommen (kommt ... her), kam ... her, ist hergekommen** (10); Does it come with a . . . ? **Ist ein/eine ... dabei?** (6)

common **gemeinsam** (11)

company **die Firma, Firmen** (3)

to compare **vergleichen (vergleicht), verglich, verglichen** (7)

to complain (to) **sich beschweren (bei + dat.), beschwert** (8)

to complete **ergänzen, ergänzt** (4)

computer **der Computer, -** (2); computer science **die Informatik** (1)

concert **das Konzert, -e** (1); concert ticket **die Konzertkarte, -n** (5); to go to a concert **ins Konzert gehen** (1); rock concert **das Rock-konzert, -e** (11)

conductor: orchestra conductor **der Dirigent, -en** (*wk.*) / **die Dirigentin, -nen** (5)

to congratulate **gratulieren (+ dat.), gratuliert** (6)

to connect **verbinden (verbindet), verband, verbunden** (A)

to conquer **besiegen, besiegt** (7)

conservative **konservativ** (B)

to consider **nach·denken (über + acc.) (denkt ... nach), dachte ... nach, nachgedacht** (7)

construction worker **der Bauarbeiter, -** / **die Bauarbeiterin, -nen** (5)

contract **der Vertrag, ⸚e** (12)

contrary: but (rather / on the contrary) **sondern** (A, 11); on the contrary! **doch!** (4)

conversational situation **die Sprechsituation, -en** (A)

to converse **sich unterhalten (unterhält), unterhielt, unterhalten** (9)

cook **der Koch, ⸚e** / **die Köchin, -nen** (5);

to cook **kochen, gekocht** (1)

cooked **gekocht** (8)

cooking **die Küche** (8)

cool **kühl** (B); (*coll.*) **grell** (2)

copy shop **der Kopierladen, ⸚** (10)

corkscrew **der Korkenzieher, -** (8)

corner **die Ecke, -n** (5); (right) around the corner **um die Ecke** (5, 6)

to correct **korrigieren, korrigiert** (4)

correct **richtig** (2)

to cost **kosten, gekostet** (2, 6)

cost: extra costs (*e.g., utilities*) **die Nebenkosten** (*pl.*) (6)

couch **das Sofa, -s** (6)

cough **der Husten** (11); cough drop **das Husten-bonbon, -s** (11); cough syrup **der Hustensaft, ⸚e** (11)

counselor: career counselor **der Berufsberater, -** / **die Berufsberaterin, -nen** (5)

to count **zählen, gezählt** (A)

country **das Land, ⸚er** (6); foreign countries **das Ausland** (6); in the country (*rural*) **auf dem Land** (6)

course **der Kurs, -e** (A, 1); course of studies **das Studium, Studien** (3); German course **der Deutschkurs, -e** (A); of course **selbstver-ständlich** (10); Of course! **Klar!** (2)

courthouse **das Gericht, -e** (5); at the courthouse **auf dem Gericht** (5)

cousin: female cousin **die Kusine, -n** (B); male cousin **der Vetter, -n** (B)

to cover **decken, gedeckt** (5); **zu·decken, zugedeckt** (11)

cozy **gemütlich** (10)

to crash (*airplane*) **ab·stürzen, ist abgestürzt** (11); (*cars*) **zusammen·stoßen (stößt ... zusammen), stieß ... zusammen, ist zusammengestoßen** (11)

crash: stock market crash **der Börsenkrach, ⸚e** (12)

crazy **verrückt** (B); **wahnsinnig** (12)

critically injured **schwer verletzt** (11)

crocodile **das Krokodil, -e** (10)

croquette **die Krokette, -n** (8)

crosswalk **der Zebrastreifen, -** (10)

cruel **grausam** (9)

to cry **weinen, geweint** (3)

cucumber **die Gurke, -n** (8)

culture **die Kultur, -en** (12)

cup **die Tasse, -n** (2, 5); **der Becher, -** (9)

cupboard **der Schrank, ⸚e** (6)

curious **neugierig** (12)

currency **die Währung, -en** (12)

to curse **verwünschen, verwünscht** (9); **fluchen, geflucht** (11)

cursed **verwunschen** (9)

curtain **der Vorhang, ⸚e** (6)

to cuss **schimpfen, geschimpft** (9)

custodian **der Hausmeister, -** / **die Hausmeisterin, -nen** (5)

customer **der Kunde, -n** (*wk.*) / **die Kundin, -nen** (12)

to cut **schneiden (schneidet), schnitt, geschnitten** (3); to cut (oneself) **(sich) schneiden** (11); to cut hair **Haare schneiden** (3); to cut off ab·schneiden (schneidet ... ab), schnitt ... ab, abgeschnitten (8); to cut through durch·schneiden (schneidet ... durch), schnitt ... durch, durchgeschnitten (8)

cutlery das Besteck (5)

cutlet das Schnitzel, - (8)

Czech Republic (das) Tschechien (B)

daily täglich (12); daily newspaper die Tageszeitung, -en (5); daily routine der Tagesablauf, ⁼e (1); der Alltag (4)

to dance tanzen, getanzt (1)

dangerous gefährlich (10)

dark dunkel (5)

data: data projector der Beamer, - (B); electronic data processing die EDV = elektronische Datenverarbeitung (12)

date das Datum, Daten (4); (appointment) die Verabredung, -en (11); What is today's date? Welches Datum ist heute? (4)

daughter die Tochter, ⁼ (B)

day der Tag, -e (1)

all day long den ganzen Tag (1); day after tomorrow übermorgen (9); day before yesterday vorgestern (4); for several days seit mehreren Tagen (11); on what day? an welchem Tag? (4); to take the day off blau machen (3); two days ago vor zwei Tagen (4); What day is today? Welcher Tag ist heute? (1)

dead tot (9)

dear lieb (7)

death der Tod, -e (12)

debt die Schuld, -en (12)

decade das Jahrzehnt, -e (4)

December der Dezember (B)

deception die List, -en (9)

to decide entscheiden (entscheidet), entschied, entschieden (4)

deck chair der Liegestuhl, ⁼e (4)

deep tief (7)

definitely bestimmt (3)

degree der Grad, -e (B)

delay die Verspätung, -en (9)

to deliver aus·tragen (trägt ... aus), trug ... aus, ausgetragen (5); to deliver newspapers Zeitungen aus·tragen (5)

Denmark (das) Dänemark (B)

denomination: religious denomination die Konfession, -en (12)

dentist der Zahnarzt, ⁼e / die Zahnärztin, -nen (11)

to depart ab·fahren (fährt ... ab), fuhr ... ab, ist abgefahren (4); ab·reisen, ist abgereist (10)

department: department store das Kaufhaus, ⁼er (5); at the department store im Kaufhaus (5); fire department die Feuerwehr (11)

departure die Abfahrt, -en (7)

depressed deprimiert (11)

to describe beschreiben (beschreibt), beschrieb, beschrieben (11)

description die Beschreibung, -en (B)

desert die Wüste, -n (7)

desire die Lust (3)

desk der Schreibtisch, -e (2)

dessert die Nachspeise, -n (8)

destination das Ziel, -e (10)

devil der Teufel, - (12)

diary das Tagebuch, ⁼er (4)

dictionary das Wörterbuch, ⁼er (2)

to die sterben (stirbt), starb, ist gestorben (9)

different verschieden (12)

difficult schwierig (2); schwer (3)

to dine zu Abend essen (4)

dinghy: inflatable dinghy das Schlauchboot, -e (10)

dining room das Esszimmer, - (6)

dinner: to have dinner zu Abend essen (4)

diphtheria die Diphtherie (11)

direction die Richtung, -en (7)

directly gleich (6)

director der Direktor, -en / die Direktorin, -nen (9)

dirty schmutzig (A)

disadvantage der Nachteil, -e (7)

disco die Disko, -s (3)

to discover entdecken, entdeckt (4)

to discuss diskutieren, diskutiert (4)

dish das Gericht, -e (8); dishes das Geschirr (4, 5); to wash the dishes Geschirr spülen, gespült (4)

dishwasher der Geschirrspüler, - (5)

to disinfect desinfizieren, desinfiziert (11)

district der Stadtteil, -e (6); das Stadtviertel, - (6)

to disturb stören, gestört (3)

to dive tauchen, hat/ist getaucht (3)

divorce die Scheidung, -en (12)

to do tun (tut), tat, getan (1); to do sports Sport treiben (treibt ... Sport), trieb ... Sport, Sport getrieben (2)

doctor der Arzt, ⁼e / die Ärztin, -nen (5, 11); doctor's office die Arztpraxis, Arztpraxen (11); eye doctor der Augenarzt, ⁼e / die Augenärztin, -nen (11); family doctor der Hausarzt, ⁼e / die Hausärztin, -nen (11)

to the doctor zum Arzt (3)

dog der Hund, -e (2); dog food das Hundefutter (5); hot dog das Würstchen, - (8)

dolphin der Delfin, -e (10)

door die Tür, -en (A); (from) next door (von) nebenan (5)

dorm das Studentenheim, -e (2, 6)

double room das Doppelzimmer, - (5, 10)

down (toward the speaker) herunter (11); to climb down herunter·klettern, ist heruntergeklettert (11); to fall down hin·fallen (fällt ... hin), fiel ... hin, ist hingefallen (11); to lie down sich hin·legen, hingelegt (11); to sit down sich setzen, gesetzt (11); to write down auf·schreiben (schreibt ... auf), schrieb ... auf, aufgeschrieben (11)

downtown die Heimatstadt, ⁼e (6)

dragon der Drache, -n (wk.) (9)

drapery der Vorhang, ⁼e (6)

to draw zeichnen, gezeichnet (3, 5)

drawer die Schublade, -n (5)

to dream träumen, geträumt (9)

dress das Kleid, -er (A)

dressed: to get dressed sich an·ziehen (zieht ... an), zog ... an, angezogen (11)

dresser die Kommode, -n (6)

dressing, salad dressing die Soße, -n (8)

dressing room die Umkleidekabine, -n (5)

to drink trinken (trinkt), trank, getrunken (1)

to drive fahren (fährt), fuhr, ist/hat gefahren (2); to drive off los·fahren (fährt ... los), fuhr ... los, ist losgefahren (4, 9)

driver der Fahrer, - / die Fahrerin, -nen (7); driver's license der Führerschein, -e (4); taxi driver der Taxifahrer, - / die Taxifahrerin, -nen (5)

driveway die Einfahrt, -en (11)

drop das Bonbon, -s (11); cough drop das Hustenbonbon, -s (11)

drugstore die Drogerie, -n (6)

drums das Schlagzeug, -e (12)

to dry (dishes) ab·trocknen, abgetrocknet (6); to dry oneself off sich ab·trocknen (11)

dry trocken (11); dry cleaner's die Reinigung, -en (6)

dryer: clothes dryer der Wäschetrockner, - (8)

dumb dumm (6)

dumpling der Knödel, - (8)

during während (+ gen.) (11); during the week in der Woche (1)

Dutch (adj.) holländisch (8)

duty die Pflicht, -en (3)

DVD player der DVD-Spieler, - (2, 3)

dwarf der Zwerg, -e (9)

each jeder, jedes, jede (3, 5); each other einander (3); with each other miteinander (3)

eagle der Adler, - (10)

ear das Ohr, -en (B)

earache die Ohrenschmerzen (pl.) (11)

early früh (1)

earring der Ohrring, -e (A, 2)

easel die Staffelei, -en (12)

east (of) östlich (von + dat.) (7)

easy leicht (6)

to eat essen (isst), aß, gegessen (2, 4); (said of an animal) fressen (frisst), fraß, gefressen (9); to eat breakfast frühstücken, gefrühstückt (1); to eat dinner zu Abend essen (4)

economics die Wirtschaft (1)

educated ausgebildet (12)

education die Schulbildung (5)

effect: to take effect wirken, gewirkt (11)

egg das Ei, -er (8); boiled eggs gekochte Eier (pl.) (8); fried eggs gebratene Eier (pl.) (8)

eight acht (A)

eighteen achtzehn (A)

eighth acht- (4)

eighty achtzig (A)

electric(al) elektrisch (8)

electricity **der Strom** (8)

electronic data processing **die EDV = elektronische Datenverarbeitung** (12)

elegant **elegant** (8)

elementary school **die Grundschule, -n** (9)

elephant **der Elefant, -en** (*wk.*) (9)

elevator **der Aufzug, ⸚e** (6)

eleven **elf** (A)

eleventh **elft-** (4)

else: Anything else? **Sonst noch etwas?** (5)

e-mail **die E-Mail, -s** (1, 2)

to emigrate **aus·wandern, ist ausgewandert** (12)

employee **die Arbeitskraft, ⸚e** (12); bank employee **der/die Bankangestellte, -n (ein Bankangestellter)** (5)

empty **leer** (5); **frei** (8); to empty **aus·leeren, ausgeleert** (3)

enchanted **verwunschen** (9)

end **der Schluss, ⸚e** (8); in the end **zum Schluss** (8)

engaged: to be engaged **verlobt sein** (12); to get engaged to **sich verloben mit** (+ *dat.*), **verlobt** (12)

engineering: mechanical engineering **der Maschinenbau** (1)

England **(das) England** (B)

English (*language*) **(das) Englisch** (B); (*person*) **der Engländer, - / die Engländerin, -nen** (B)

enough **genug** (3)

to enrich **bereichern, bereichert** (12)

equal **egal** (6); **gleich** (12)

to establish **fest·stellen, festgestellt** (8)

euro **der Euro, -** (7); twenty-euro note **der Zwanzigeuroschein, -e** (8)

Eurocheque Card **die Euroscheckkarte, -n** (12)

Europe **(das) Europa** (B)

even **noch** (B)

evening **der Abend, -e** (1, 4); evening meal **das Abendessen, -** (1); evenings **abends** (4); good evening **guten Abend** (A); in the evening **abends** (4), **am Abend** (4); this evening **heute Abend** (2)

ever: Were you ever . . . ? **Warst du schon einmal ...?** (4)

every **jeder, jede, jedes** (3); every week **jede Woche** (3)

everything **alles** (2); everything possible **alles Mögliche** (2)

everywhere **überall** (10)

evil **böse** (9)

exactly **genau** (B)

exam: high school graduation exam **das Abitur** (4)

to examine **untersuchen, untersucht** (5)

example **das Beispiel, -e** (3); for example **zum Beispiel (z. B.)** (3)

exceedingly beautiful **wunderschön** (6)

excellent **ausgezeichnet** (3)

exchange: stock exchange **die Börse, -n** (12)

excited: to get excited **sich auf·regen, aufgeregt** (11)

to excuse **entschuldigen, entschuldigt** (10); Excuse me! **Entschuldigung!** (3), **Entschuldigen Sie!** (10)

to execute **aus·führen, ausgeführt** (12)

exercise **die Übung, -en** (A)

exotic **exotisch** (7)

to expect **erwarten, erwartet** (12)

expensive **teuer** (2); **wertvoll** (2)

to experience **erleben, erlebt** (3); experience **das Erlebnis, -se** (7); travel experience **das Reiseerlebnis, -se** (7); to explain **erklären, erklärt** (5)

extra **extra** (10); extra costs (*e.g., utilities*) **die Nebenkosten** (*pl.*) (6)

extremist **der Extremist, -en** (*wk.*) (12)

eye **das Auge, -n** (B); color of eyes **die Augenfarbe, -n** (1); eye doctor **der Augenarzt, ⸚e / die Augenärztin, -nen** (11)

face **das Gesicht, -er** (B)

factory **die Fabrik, -en** (5); in the factory **in der Fabrik** (5)

Fahrenheit **Fahrenheit** (B)

to faint **in Ohnmacht fallen** (11)

fairy **die Fee, -n** (9); fairy tale **das Märchen, -** (9)

to fall **fallen (fällt), fiel, ist gefallen** (9); to fall asleep **ein·schlafen (schläft ... ein), schlief ... ein, ist eingeschlafen** (7); to fall down **hin·fallen (fällt ... hin), fiel ... hin, ist hingefallen** (11); to fall in love (with) **sich verlieben (in + acc.), verliebt** (9, 12); to fall over **um·fallen (fällt ... um), fiel ... um, ist umgefallen** (9)

fall (*autumn*) **der Herbst, -e** (B)

family **die Familie, -n** (B); family celebration **das Familienfest, -e** (4); family doctor **der Hausarzt, ⸚e / die Hausärztin, -nen** (11); family name **der Familienname, -n** (*wk.*) (A, 1)

famous **berühmt** (7)

fanatic **der Fanatiker, -** (12)

far **weit** (6); as far as **bis zu** (+ *dat.*) (10); How far away? **Wie weit weg?** (6)

farmer's bread **das Bauernbrot, -e** (5)

farmhouse **das Bauernhaus, ⸚er** (6)

fast **schnell** (7)

fat **dick** (2); **fettig** (8)

father **der Vater, ⸚** (B)

faucet **der Wasserhahn, ⸚e** (5)

favorite **Lieblings-** (A); favorite activity **die Lieblingsbeschäftigung, -en** (5); favorite color **die Lieblingsfarbe, -n** (A); favorite name **der Lieblingsname, -n** (*wk.*) (A); favorite subject **das Lieblingsfach, ⸚er** (5)

fear **die Angst, ⸚e** (3)

February **der Februar** (B)

to feed **füttern, gefüttert** (9)

to feel (sich) **fühlen, gefühlt** (3, 11); to feel like (*doing s.th.*) **Lust haben** (3); to feel well **sich wohl fühlen** (11); How do you feel? **Wie fühlst du dich?** (3); I feel . . . **Ich fühle mich ...** (3)

feeling **das Gefühl, -e** (3)

fellow student **der Mitstudent, -en** (*wk.*) / die Mitstudentin, -nen (A)

fence **der Zaun, ⸚e** (9)

to fetch **holen, geholt** (9)

fever **das Fieber** (11)

few: a few **ein paar** (2)

field **das Feld, -er** (7)

fifteen **fünfzehn** (A)

fifth **fünft-** (4)

fifty **fünfzig** (A)

to fight **kämpfen, gekämpft** (9)

figure **die Figur, -en** (12)

to fill in the blanks **ergänzen, ergänzt** (4); to fill out **aus·füllen, ausgefüllt** (1); to fill up (with gas) **voll·tanken, vollgetankt** (5)

film **der Film, -e** (2); horror film **der Gruselfilm, -e** (2)

filter: coffee filter **der Kaffeefilter, -** (4)

finally **schließlich** (7); **zum Schluss** (8); **endlich** (9)

to find **finden (findet), fand, gefunden** (2)

fine **fein** (8)

finger **der Finger, -** (11)

fingernail **der Fingernagel, ⸚** (11)

finished **fertig** (3)

Finland **(das) Finnland** (B)

fire **das Feuer, -** (9); fire department **die Feuerwehr** (11)

firm **die Firma, Firmen** (3)

first (*adj.*) **erst-** (4); (*adv.*) **zuerst** (4, 7); first floor **das Erdgeschoss, -e** (6); first name **der Vorname, -n** (*wk.*) (A, 1); the first of October **der erste Oktober** (4); for the first time **zum ersten Mal** (4); on the first of October **am ersten Oktober** (4); to travel first class **erster Klasse fahren** (10)

fish **der Fisch, -e** (8)

to fit **passen** (+ *dat.*), **gepasst** (6, 11); That fits well. **Das passt gut.** (11)

five **fünf** (A)

flashlight **die Taschenlampe, -n** (9)

flat tire **die Reifenpanne, -n** (7)

flawless **vollkommen** (12)

flea market **der Flohmarkt, ⸚e** (2)

to flee **flüchten, ist geflüchtet** (11)

flight **der Flug, ⸚e** (9)

to float **schwimmen (schwimmt), schwamm, ist geschwommen** (7)

floor **der Boden, ⸚** (B); (*story*) **der Stock, Stockwerke** (6); first floor **das Erdgeschoss, -e** (6); on the second floor **im ersten Stock** (6)

to flow **fließen (fließt), floss, ist geflossen** (7)

flower **die Blume, -n** (3); to water the flowers **die Blumen gießen (gießt), goss, gegossen** (3)

flu **die Grippe** (11)

flute: transverse flute **die Querflöte, -n** (12)

to fly **fliegen (fliegt), flog, ist/hat geflogen** (1)

fly **die Fliege, -n** (8)

food: dog food **das Hundefutter** (5)

foot **der Fuß, ⸚e** (B); on foot **zu Fuß** (3)

for (*prep.*) für (+ *acc.*) (2); seit (+ *dat.*) (4, 11); zu (+ *dat.*) (2); (*coord. conj.*) denn (9, 11); Do you have something for it (*illness*)? Haben Sie etwas dagegen? (11); for example zum Beispiel (z. B.) (3); for lunch zum Mittagessen (3); for several days seit mehreren Tagen (11); for someone's birthday zum Geburtstag (2); for the first time zum ersten Mal (4); for two years seit zwei Jahren (4); medicine for ein Medikament gegen (+ *acc.*) (11); forbidden verboten (9)

foreign ausländisch (12); foreign countries das Ausland (6); foreign language die Fremdsprache, -n (5)

foreigner der Ausländer, - / die Ausländerin, -nen (12)

forest der Wald, ⸚er (2, 7)

to forget vergessen (vergisst), vergaß, vergessen (2)

fork die Gabel, -n (8)

form das Formular, -e (12)

formality die Formalität, -en (12)

forty vierzig (A)

fountain der Brunnen, - (9)

four vier (A)

fourteen vierzehn (A)

fourth viert- (4)

franc (Swiss) der Schweizer Franken, - (8)

France (das) Frankreich (B)

frank(furter) das Würstchen, - (8)

free frei (8)

to free erlösen, erlöst (9)

freeway die Autobahn, -en (7)

freezer die Gefriertruhe, -n (8)

French (*language*) (das) Französisch (B); (*person*) der Franzose, -n (*wk.*) / die Französin, -nen (B); French fries die Pommes (frites) (*pl.*) (8)

fresh frisch (8)

Friday der Freitag (1)

fried gebraten (8); fried eggs gebratene Eier (*pl.*) (8)

friend der Freund, -e / die Freundin, -nen (A); beloved female friend die Geliebte, -n (3)

friendly freundlich (B)

fries: French fries die Pommes (frites) (*pl.*) (8)

frog der Frosch, ⸚e (9)

from von (+ *dat.*) (A, 10); aus (+ *dat.*) (10); from next door von nebenan (5); from where woher (B); from work von der Arbeit (3)

fruit das Obst (8)

to fry braten (brät), briet, gebraten (8); bräunen, gebräunt (8)

frying pan die Pfanne, -n (5)

fuel tank der Tank, -s (7)

full(y) voll (10)

fun lustig (12); have fun viel Spaß (A)

funny komisch (10); lustig (12)

furnished möbliert (6)

furniture die Möbel (*pl.*) (6); piece of furniture das Möbelstück, -e (6)

game: video game das Videospiel, -e (2)

garage die Werkstatt, ⸚en (5); die Garage, -n (6)

garbage der Müll (6); garbage can der Mülleimer, - (8)

garden der Garten, ⸚ (6); garden hose der Gartenschlauch, ⸚e (6); in the garden im Garten (4)

garlic der Knoblauch (8)

gas station die Tankstelle, -n (5); at the gas station an der Tankstelle (5)

gasoline das Benzin (6)

gaudy grell (2)

gear der Gang, ⸚e (7)

gentleman der Herr, -en (*wk.*) (A)

geography die Geografie (B, 1)

German (*language*) (das) Deutsch (B); (*person*) der/die Deutsche, -n (ein Deutscher) (B); German army die Bundeswehr (5); German class/course der Deutschkurs, -e (A); I am German. Ich bin Deutsche/r. (B); in the German army bei der Bundeswehr (5)

Germany (das) Deutschland (B)

to get bekommen (bekommt), bekam, bekommen (3); holen, geholt (9); to get acquainted with kennen·lernen, kennengelernt (1); to get an appointment sich einen Termin geben lassen (11); to get angry sich ärgern, geärgert (11); to get dressed sich an·ziehen (zieht ... an), zog ... an, angezogen (11); to get engaged to sich verloben mit (+ *dat.*), verlobt (12); to get excited sich auf·regen, aufgeregt (11); to get information about sich erkundigen nach (+ *dat.*), erkundigt (10); to get in this way herein·kommen (kommt ... herein), kam ... herein, ist hereingekommen (10); to get married to sich verheiraten mit (+ *dat.*), verheiratet (12); to get stuck stecken bleiben (bleibt ... stecken), blieb ... stecken, ist stecken geblieben (11); to get undressed sich aus·ziehen (zieht ... aus), zog ... aus, ausgezogen (11); to get up auf·stehen (steht ... auf), stand ... auf, ist aufgestanden (A, 1); to get up on the wrong side of bed mit dem linken Fuß auf·stehen (4); to get upset sich auf·regen, aufgeregt (11)

giant der Riese, -n (*wk.*) (9)

gifted begabt (9)

giraffe die Giraffe, -n (10)

girl das Mädchen, - (9)

girlfriend die Freundin, -nen (A)

to give geben (gibt), gab, gegeben (A, 6); (*as a present*) schenken, geschenkt (5)

to give a paper / oral report ein Referat halten (hält), hielt, gehalten (4); give me geben Sie mir (A)

given name der Vorname, -n (*wk.*) (A, 1)

glacier der Gletscher, - (7)

gladly gern (1, 5)

glass (*n.*) das Glas, ⸚er (5); (*adj.*) gläsern (9)

glasses (*pair of eyeglasses*) die Brille, -n (A)

glove der Handschuh, -e (2)

to go gehen (geht), ging, ist gegangen (A); laufen (läuft), lief, ist gelaufen (A); to go along entlang·gehen (geht ... entlang), ging ... entlang, ist entlanggegangen (10); to go away weg·gehen (geht ... weg), ging ... weg, ist weggegangen (4); to go by vorbei·fahren (fährt ... vorbei), fuhr ... vorbei, ist vorbeigefahren (10); to go canoeing Kanu fahren (10); to go for a walk spazieren gehen (geht ... spazieren), ging ... spazieren, ist spazieren gegangen (1); to go get holen, geholt (9); to go home nach Hause gehen (1); to go ice-skating Schlittschuh laufen (3); to go in this way herein·kommen (kommt ... herein), kam ... herein, ist hereingekommen (10); to go on a trip verreisen, ist verreist (3); to go out aus·gehen (geht ... aus), ging ... aus, ist ausgegangen (1); to go out (*power*) aus·fallen (fällt ... aus), fiel ... aus, ausgefallen (8); to go over that way hinüber·gehen (geht ... hinüber), ging ... hinüber, ist hinübergegangen (10); to go shopping ein·kaufen gehen (geht ... einkaufen), ging ... einkaufen, ist einkaufen gegangen (1, 5); to go that way hin·gehen (geht ... hin), ging ... hin, ist hingegangen (10); to go to a party auf eine Party gehen (1); to go to bed ins Bett gehen (1); to go to the mountains in die Berge gehen (1); to go to the movies ins Kino gehen (1); to go to the swimming pool ins Schwimmbad fahren (1); to go to the university zur Uni gehen (1); to go to work zur Arbeit gehen (1); to go up that way hinauf·gehen (geht ... hinauf), ging ... hinauf, ist hinaufgegangen (10); I'd rather go . . . Ich gehe lieber ... (2); Where are you going? Wo willst du denn hin? (A)

god, God der Gott, ⸚er (12)

goldfish der Goldfisch, -e (11)

golf das Golf (1)

good: good afternoon (*for.*) guten Tag (A); (*for.; southern Germany, Austria*) grüß Gott (A)

good evening guten Abend (A); Good luck! Viel Glück! (3); good morning guten Morgen (A); It looks good. Es sieht gut aus. (2); to taste good to schmecken (+ *dat.*), geschmeckt (6); That looks / Those look good on you! Das steht / Die stehen dir gut! (2)

good-bye auf Wiedersehen (A); (*infor.; southern Germany, Austria*) servus (A); (*on the phone*) auf Wiederhören (6)

to grab greifen (greift), griff, gegriffen (11)

grade (*level*) die Klasse, -n (9); (*mark*) die Note, -n (9)

graduation der Abschluss (9); high school graduation exam das Abitur (4)

grammar die Grammatik, -en (A)

granddaughter die Enkelin, -nen (5)

grandfather der Großvater, ⸚ (B)

grandma die Oma, -s (3)

grandmother die Großmutter, ⸚ (B)

grandparents die Großeltern (*pl.*) (B)

grandson der Enkel, - (5)

grape die Weintraube, -n (8)

to grasp greifen (greift), griff, gegriffen (11)

gray grau (A)

greasy fettig (8, 11)

great (coll.) toll (2); great! prima! (6); That sounds great. Das hört sich toll an. (4)

Great Britain (das) Großbritannien (B)

Greece (das) Griechenland (B)

green grün (A)

to greet grüßen, gegrüßt (10)

greeting der Gruß, ⸚e (9)

grill der Grill, -s (8)

grilled gegrillt (8)

grinder: coffee grinder die Kaffeemühle, -n (8)

ground beef (or pork) das Hackfleisch (8)

to grow wachsen (wächst), wuchs, ist gewachsen (9); to grow up auf·wachsen (wächst ... auf), wuchs ... auf, ist aufgewachsen (12)

guidebook: travel guidebook der Reiseführer, - (5)

guilt die Schuld, -en (12)

guinea pig das Meerschweinchen, - (10)

guitar die Gitarre, -n (1)

hair das Haar, -e (B, 11); black-haired schwarzhaarig (9); to blow-dry one's hair sich die Haare föhnen (11); color of hair die Haarfarbe (1); to comb one's hair sich die Haare kämmen (11); to cut hair Haare schneiden (schneidet), schnitt, geschnitten (3); with the short/long hair mit dem kurzen/langen Haar (A)

haircut der Haarschnitt, -e (2)

hairdresser der Friseur, -e / die Friseurin, -nen (5)

hall: town hall das Rathaus, ⸚er (1, 6); at the town hall auf dem Rathaus (1)

ham der Schinken (8)

hammer der Hammer, ⸚ (8)

hamster der Hamster, - (10)

hand die Hand, ⸚e (B); hand towel das Handtuch, ⸚er (8); to shake hands die Hand schütteln (A)

handkerchief das Taschentuch, ⸚er (3)

to hang (be in a hanging position) hängen (hängt), hing, gehangen (3); to hang (up) hängen, gehängt (3); auf·hängen, aufgehängt (8); to hang the picture on the wall das Bild an die Wand hängen (3); hangover der Kater, - (11)

to happen passieren, ist passiert (4)

happiness das Glück (3)

happy glücklich (B); to be happy about sich freuen über (+ acc.), gefreut (11)

harbor der Hafen, ⸚ (10)

hard schwer (3)

hardware store das Eisenwarengeschäft, -e (6)

harmful: to be harmful to schaden (+ dat.), geschadet (6)

harmonica die Mundharmonika, -s (12)

hat der Hut, ⸚e (A)

to hate hassen, gehasst (9)

to have haben (hat), hatte, gehabt (A); have fun viel Spaß (A); to have to müssen (muss), musste, gemusst (3)

head der Kopf, ⸚e (B); head cold die Erkältung, -en (11)

headache die Kopfschmerzen (pl.) (11); headache tablet die Kopfschmerztablette, -n (11)

headband das Stirnband, ⸚er (A)

to heal heilen, geheilt (5)

health die Gesundheit (11)

healthy gesund (8)

to hear hören, gehört (1)

heart das Herz, -en (11)

heartache die Herzschmerzen (pl.) (11)

to heat erhitzen, erhitzt (8)

heated, heat included warm (6)

heating: central heating die Zentralheizung (6)

heavy schwer (3); stark (11)

height die Größe, -n (1); die Höhe, -n (12)

hello (for.) guten Tag (A); (for.; southern Germany, Austria) grüß Gott (A); (infor.; southern Germany, Austria) servus (A); to say hello to grüßen, gegrüßt (10)

helmet: bicycle helmet der Fahrradhelm, -e (5)

to help helfen (+ dat.) (hilft), half, geholfen (6); Help! Hilfe! (11); May I help you? Bitte schön? (7)

her ihr(e) (1, 2)

herb butter die Kräuterbutter (8)

herbs die Kräuter (pl.) (8)

here hier (A)

hi (infor.) hallo (A); (Switzerland) grüezi (A)

to hide sich verstecken, versteckt (9)

high hoch (7); to have high blood pressure hohen Blutdruck haben (11); high-rise building das Hochhaus, ⸚er (6); high school das Gymnasium, Gymnasien (6); high school graduation exam das Abitur (4)

highlight der Höhepunkt, -e (7)

hike die Wanderung, -en (7); to hike wandern, ist gewandert (1); to hike in the mountains in den Bergen wandern (1)

hiking shoe der Wanderschuh, -e (2)

hill der Hügel, - (7)

him (acc.) ihn (2)

his sein(e) (1, 2)

history die Geschichte (1); history: art history die Kunstgeschichte (1)

to hit schlagen (schlägt), schlug, geschlagen (11)

to hitchhike trampen, ist getrampt (10)

hobby das Hobby, -s (1)

to hold halten (hält), hielt, gehalten (4)

hole das Loch, ⸚er (9)

holiday der Feiertag, -e (4); national holiday der Nationalfeiertag, -e (4)

Holland (das) Holland (B)

home das Haus, ⸚er (2); die Heimat, -en (12); at home zu Hause (A, 1, 10); daheim (9); to go home nach Hause gehen (1, 10); single-family home das Einfamilienhaus, ⸚er (6)

homeland die Heimat, -en (12); das Heimatland, ⸚er (12)

homemade selbst gemacht (8)

homemaker der Hausmann, ⸚er / die Hausfrau, -en (12)

homesick: to be homesick Heimweh haben (3)

homesickness das Heimweh (3)

hometown die Heimatstadt, ⸚e (6); die Heimat, -en (12)

homework die Hausaufgabe, -n (A)

honey der Honig (8)

to honk hupen, gehupt (7)

hook der Haken, - (8)

to hope hoffen, gehofft (3)

horn die Hupe, -n (7)

horror film der Gruselfilm, -e (2)

horse das Pferd, -e (2, 9)

hose: garden hose der Gartenschlauch, ⸚e (6)

hospital das Krankenhaus, ⸚er (3, 5); in the hospital im Krankenhaus (5)

host der Wirt, -e / die Wirtin, -nen (10)

hostel: youth hostel die Jugendherberge, -n (10)

hot heiß (B); hot chocolate der Kakao (8); hot dog das Würstchen, - (8)

hotel das Hotel, -s (2, 5); at the hotel im Hotel (5)

hour die Stunde, -n (1, 2); office hour die Sprechstunde, -n (3)

house das Haus, ⸚er (1, 2, 6); house key der Hausschlüssel, - (9); house number die Hausnummer, -n (1); row house, town house das Reihenhaus, ⸚er (6); vacation house das Ferienhaus, ⸚er (4)

houseboat das Hausboot, -e (6)

household der Haushalt, -e (9)

housekeeping der Haushalt, -e (9)

housemate der Mitbewohner, - / die Mitbewohnerin, -nen (2)

housewife die Hausfrau, -en (12)

housing: shared housing die WG, -s (die Wohngemeinschaft, -en) (6); housing-wanted ad die Suchanzeige, -n (6)

how wie (B); How do you feel? Wie fühlst du dich? (3); How do you spell that? Wie schreibt man das? (A); How far away? Wie weit weg? (6); how many . . . ? wie viele ...? (A)

humid feucht (B)

hummingbird der Kolibri, -s (10)

hundred hundert (A)

hundredth hundertst- (4)

Hungary (das) Ungarn (B)

hunger der Hunger (3)

hungry hungrig (9); to be hungry Hunger haben (3)

hunter der Jäger, - / die Jägerin, -nen (9)

to hurry sich beeilen, beeilt (8)

hurry die Eile (3); to be in a hurry in Eile sein (3); es eilig haben (8); to hurt weh·tun (tut ... weh), tat ... weh, wehgetan (11)

husband der Mann, ⸚er (B)

ice das Eis (2); ice-cold eiskalt (8); ice cream parlor das Eiscafé, -s (8); ice skate der Schlittschuh, -e (3); to go ice-skating Schlittschuh laufen (3) idea **die Idee, -n** (10)

ideal **ideal** (12)

identification card **der Personalausweis, -e** (1); **der Ausweis, -e** (10)

if (*subord. conj.*) **wenn** (2, 11); **ob** (6)

igloo **das Iglu, -s** (6)

illegal **illegal** (12)

illness **die Krankheit, -en** (11)

to imagine something **sich etwas vor·stellen, vorgestellt** (6)

immediately **sofort** (3)

immigrant **der Einwanderer, -** (12)

to immigrate **ein·wandern, ist eingewandert** (12)

impatient **ungeduldig** (10)

important **wichtig** (2)

in **in** (+ *dat./acc.*) (A, 4); **an** (+ *dat./acc.*) (4) in addition **dazu** (8); in addition to **neben** (+ *dat./acc.*) (3); in any case **jedenfalls** (11); in a row **hintereinander** (3); in it **drin/darin** (6); in January **im Januar** (B); in love **verliebt** (4); in order to **um ... zu** (12); in rainy weather **bei Regen** (7); in spite of **trotz** (+ *gen.*) (12); in the afternoon **nachmittags** (4); in the country (*rural*) **auf dem Land** (6); in the end **zum Schluss** (8); in the evening **am Abend** (4), **abends** (4); in the garden **im Garten** (4); in the German army **bei der Bundeswehr** (5); in the middle **mitten** (9); in the morning **früh** (4); in the spring **im Frühling** (B); in the vicinity **in der Nähe** (6); in this way **herein** (10); in(ward) **hinein** (9)

included **inbegriffen** (10); (*utilities*) **inklusive** (6); heat included **warm** (6)

income **das Einkommen** (12)

incredible **unglaublich** (5)

indeed **ja** (4)

industrious **fleißig** (12)

inexpensive **billig** (2)

infection **die Entzündung, -en** (11); kidney infection **die Nierenentzündung** (11)

inflatable dinghy **das Schlauchboot, -e** (10)

influenza **die Grippe** (11)

to inform oneself about **sich informieren über** (+ *acc.*), **informiert** (12)

information **die Information, -en** (4); biographical information **persönliche Daten** (*pl.*) (1); to get information about **sich erkundigen nach** (+ *dat.*), **erkundigt** (10)

ingredient **die Zutat, -en** (8)

injection **die Spritze, -n** (11)

to injure oneself **sich verletzen, verletzt** (11)

injured **verletzt** (11); critically injured **schwer verletzt** (11); injured person **der/die Verletzte, -n (ein Verletzter)** (11)

inn (bed-and-breakfast) **das Gästehaus, ¨er** (10)

innkeeper **der Wirt, -e / die Wirtin, -nen** (10)

insane **wahnsinnig** (12)

instead of **anstatt** (+ *gen.*) (12); **statt** (+ *gen.*) (12)

to instruct **unterrichten, unterrichtet** (5)

instruction **der Unterricht** (11)

instructor **der Lehrer, - / die Lehrerin, -nen** (A, 1)

instrument **das Instrument, -e** (12)

insurance **die Versicherung, -en** (5)

integration **die Integration** (12)

intelligent **intelligent** (7)

to intend (to) **wollen (will), wollte, gewollt** (3)

to interest **interessieren, interessiert** (5); to be interested in **Interesse haben an** (+ *dat.*) (5); **sich interessieren für** (+ *acc.*) (5)

interest **das Interesse, -n** (5); (*money*) **die Zinsen** (*pl.*) (12); interesting **interessant** (7); something interesting **etwas Interessantes** (4)

Internet: to surf the Internet **im Internet surfen** (1)

intersection **die Kreuzung, -en** (10)

interview **das Interview, -s** (4)

into **in** (+ *acc.*) (A)

to introduce **vor·stellen, vorgestellt** (6)

introduction **die Einführung, -en** (A)

to invent **erfinden (erfindet), erfand, erfunden** (4)

to investigate **untersuchen, untersucht** (5)

invitation **die Einladung, -en** (2)

to invite **ein·laden (lädt ... ein), lud ... ein, eingeladen** (2)

iPod **der I-Pod, -s** (2)

Ireland **(das) Irland** (B)

iron **das Bügeleisen, -** (6); to iron **bügeln, gebügelt** (6)

island **die Insel, -n** (7)

it **es** (B)

Italian (*language*) **(das) Italienisch** (B)

Italy **(das) Italien** (B)

its (*fem.*) **ihr(e)** (2); (*masc./neut.*) **sein(e)** (2)

ivory **das Elfenbein** (10)

jacket **die Jacke, -n** (A); sports jacket **das Sakko, -s** (A)

jail **das Gefängnis, -se** (6)

jam **die Marmelade, -n** (8)

January **der Januar** (B); in January **im Januar** (B)

Japanese (*adj.*) **japanisch** (8)

jealous **eifersüchtig** (3)

jeans **die Jeans** (*pl.*) (2)

jewelry **der Schmuck** (2)

joke **der Witz, -e** (3); to tell jokes **Witze erzählen** (3)

journey **die Reise, -n** (7)

joy **die Freude, -n** (9)

judge **der Richter, - / die Richterin, -nen** (5)

juice **der Saft, ¨e** (8); apple juice **der Apfelsaft** (8); orange juice **der Orangensaft** (8)

July **der Juli** (B)

to jump **springen (springt), sprang, ist gesprungen** (A)

June **der Juni** (B)

jungle **der Dschungel, -** (7)

just **knapp** (4); That's just it! **Das ist es ja!** (4)

kangaroo **das Känguru, -s** (10)

to keep: keep the change **das stimmt so** (8); to keep on walking **weiter·gehen (geht ... weiter), ging ... weiter, ist weitergegangen** (10)

kettle: tea kettle **der Teekessel, -** (8)

key **der Schlüssel, -** (9); house key **der Hausschlüssel, -** (9)

kidney **die Niere, -n** (11); kidney infection **die Nierenentzündung** (11)

to kill **töten, getötet** (9)

kiln **der Brennofen, ¨** (12)

kilometer **der Kilometer, -** (2)

kind **die Art, -en** (2)

kindergarten **der Kindergarten, ¨** (6)

king **der König, -e** (9)

to kiss **küssen, geküsst** (9)

kiss **der Kuss, ¨e** (4); kitchen **die Küche, -n** (5); kitchen clock **die Küchenuhr, -en** (5); kitchen lamp **die Küchenlampe, -n** (5); kitchen scale **die Küchenwaage, -n** (5); kitchen table **der Küchentisch, -e** (5); kitchen work **die Küchenarbeit, -en** (5)

knife **das Messer, -** (8)

to knit **stricken, gestrickt** (3)

to knock over **um·kippen, umgekippt** (11)

to know **kennen (kennt), kannte, gekannt** (B); **wissen (weiß), wusste, gewusst** (2)

knowledge about a field **die Kenntnisse** (*pl.*) (5)

labor **die Arbeitskraft, ¨e** (12)

laboratory: language laboratory **das Sprachlabor, -s** (4)

lake **der See, -n** (7)

lamp **die Lampe, -n** (B); kitchen lamp **die Küchenlampe, -n** (5)

landlord/landlady **der Vermieter, - / die Vermieterin, -nen** (6)

land mammal **das Landsäugetier, -e** (10)

language **die Sprache, -n** (B); foreign language **die Fremdsprache, -n** (5); language laboratory **das Sprachlabor, -s** (4)

laptop (computer) **der Laptop, -s** (B)

large **dick** (2)

last **letzt-** (4); last Monday **letzten Montag** (4); last night **gestern Abend** (4); last summer **letzten Sommer** (4); last week **letzte Woche** (4); last weekend **letztes Wochenende** (4); the last time **das letzte Mal** (4)

to last **dauern, gedauert** (4)

late(r) **spät(er)** (1); late morning **der Vormittag, -e** (4)

Latin (*language*) **das Latein** (1)

to laugh **lachen, gelacht** (3)

laundromat **der Waschsalon, -s** (10)

laundry **die Wäsche** (4)

lawn **der Rasen** (5); lawn mower **der Rasenmäher, -** (6)

to learn **lernen, gelernt** (1)

least: the least **am wenigsten** (8)

to leave **verlassen (verlässt), verließ, verlassen** (11)

lecture **die Vorlesung, -en** (4)

left **links** (4, 10)

leg **das Bein, -e** (B)

leisure time **die Freizeit** (1)

lemon die Zitrone, -n (8)

to lend leihen (leiht), lieh, geliehen (5)

to let lassen (lässt), ließ, gelassen (11); Let's meet . . . Treffen wir uns . . . (2)

letter der Brief, -e (1)

lettuce der Kopfsalat (8)

liberal liberal (9)

librarian der Bibliothekar, -e / die Bibliothekarin, -nen (5)

library die Bibliothek, -en (4)

license: driver's license der Führerschein, -e (4); license plate das Nummernschild, -er (7); license plate number die Autonummer, -n (11)

to lie liegen (liegt), lag, gelegen (1); to lie down sich hin·legen, hingelegt (11); to lie in the sun in der Sonne liegen (1)

Liechtenstein (das) Liechtenstein (B)

life das Leben, - (9); professional life das Berufsleben (12); student life das Studentenleben (4)

to light an·zünden, angezündet (3)

light (adj., color) hell (6); (adj., weight) leicht (6)

light (n.) das Licht, -er (3)

to like mögen (mag), mochte, gemocht (1, 3); to be to one's liking gefallen (+ dat.) (gefällt), gefiel, gefallen (6); Do you like to wear . . . ? Trägst du gern . . . ? (A); I like it. Es gefällt mir. (6); I would like ich hätte gern (5); like (to do) best am liebsten (7); We like to sing. Wir singen gern. (1); would like (to) möchte (2, 3)

limit: city limits der Stadtrand, ¨er (6)

linguistics die Linguistik (1)

lion der Löwe, -n (wk.) (10)

lip die Lippe, -n (11)

list die Liste, -n (5)

to listen zu·hören, zugehört (A)

to listen (to) hören, gehört (1); to listen to zu·hören (+ dat.), zugehört (6)

liter der Liter, - (7)

literature die Literatur (1)

little: a little bit ein bisschen (3)

to live leben, gelebt (3); to live (in) wohnen (in + dat.), gewohnt (B)

liver die Leber, -n (11)

living room das Wohnzimmer, - (6)

loaf of farmer's bread das Bauernbrot, -e (5)

locomotive die Lokomotive, -n (7)

lodge: ski lodge die Skihütte, -n (6)

lodging die Unterkunft, ¨e (10)

loner der Einzelgänger, - (12)

long lang (B); all day long den ganzen Tag (1); all night long die ganze Nacht (3); so long bis bald (A); with the long hair mit dem langen Haar (A)

to look schauen, geschaut (A); aus·sehen (sieht . . . aus), sah . . . aus, ausgesehen (2); It looks good. Es sieht gut aus. (2); to look at an·schauen, angeschaut (2); an·sehen (sieht . . . an), sah . . . an, angesehen (3); to look for suchen, gesucht (1); That looks / Those look good on you! Das steht / Die stehen dir gut! (2)

to lose verlieren (verliert), verlor, verloren (7); to lose weight ab·nehmen (nimmt . . . ab), nahm . . . ab, abgenommen (8, 11)

lot: a lot viel (A); Lots of luck! Viel Glück! (3)

lotion: suntan lotion die Sonnenmilch (10); to put lotion on sich ein·cremen, eingecremt (11)

lottery die Lotterie, -n (5); to win the lottery in der Lotterie gewinnen (5)

lounge der Aufenthaltsraum, ¨e (10)

to love lieben, geliebt (3); to be in love verliebt sein (4, 12); to fall in love (with) sich verlieben (in + acc.), verliebt (9, 12); love (beloved female friend) die Geliebte, -n (3)

lovesickness der Liebeskummer (11)

low: to have low blood pressure niedrigen Blutdruck haben (11); low in calories kalorienarm (8)

loyal treu (9)

lozenge das Bonbon, -s (11)

luck das Glück (3); Good luck! Lots of luck! Viel Glück! (3)

lunch das Mittagessen, - (3); for lunch zum Mittagessen (3)

lung die Lunge, -n (11)

machine: automatic teller machine (ATM) der Geldautomat, -en (wk.) (12); coffee machine die Kaffeemaschine, -n (5); washing machine die Waschmaschine, -n (6)

magical magisch (12)

makeup: to put makeup on sich schminken, geschminkt (11)

mall: pedestrian mall die Fußgängerzone, -n (10)

mammal: land mammal das Landsäugetier, -e (10)

man der Mann, ¨er (A, B); Man! (coll.) Mensch! (2)

manager der Geschäftsführer, - / die Geschäftsführerin, -nen (8)

mansion die Villa, Villen (6)

many viele (A); how many . . . ? wie viele . . . ? (A); many thanks vielen Dank (10)

map die Landkarte, -n (7); city street map der Stadtplan, ¨e (10)

March der März (B)

market der Markt, ¨e (10); flea market der Flohmarkt, ¨e (2); marketplace, market square der Marktplatz, ¨e (6); stock market crash der Börsenkrach, ¨e (12)

marmalade die Marmelade, -n (8)

marriage die Ehe, -n (12)

married verheiratet (1); to be married verheiratet sein (12); to get married to sich verheiraten mit (+ dat.), verheiratet (12)

to marry heiraten, geheiratet (3, 5)

match das Streichholz, ¨er (8)

material das Material, -ien (12)

mathematics die Mathematik (1)

matter: It doesn't matter to me. Das ist mir egal. (6); to be the matter with (a person) fehlen (+ dat.), gefehlt (11)

mattress: air mattress die Luftmatratze, -n (10)

May der Mai (B)

may (v.) dürfen (darf), durfte, gedurft (3); können (kann), konnte, gekonnt (3); May I help you? Bitte schön? (7)

meadow die Wiese, -n (7)

meal die Mahlzeit, -en (8); evening meal das Abendessen, - (1); midday meal das Mittagessen, - (3)

mean böse (9)

means: by all means auf jeden Fall (4); means of payment das Zahlungsmittel, - (12); means of transportation das Transportmittel, - (7)

meat das Fleisch (8)

mechanical engineering der Maschinenbau (1)

medical medizinisch (11)

medicine das Medikament, -e (11); medicine for ein Medikament gegen (+ acc.) (11)

Mediterranean Sea das Mittelmeer (B)

to meet treffen (trifft), traf, getroffen (2); begegnen (+ dat.), begegnet (6); Let's meet . . . Treffen wir uns . . . (2)

memory die Erinnerung, -en (4)

menu die Speisekarte, -n (8)

meter: square meter (m²) der Quadratmeter (qm), - (6)

Mexican (adj.) mexikanisch (8); Mexican (person) der Mexikaner, - / die Mexikanerin, -nen (B)

midday der Mittag, -e (3); midday meal das Mittagessen, - (3)

mileage der Kilometerstand (7)

milk die Milch (8)

million die Million, -en (12)

mineral water das Mineralwasser (8)

miracle das Wunder, - (4)

mirror der Spiegel, - (6)

to miss verpassen, verpasst (9); verfehlen, verfehlt (10); to be missing fehlen (+ dat.), gefehlt (6)

mixed gemischt (8)

mixer die Küchenmaschine, -n (8)

modern modern (6)

moment der Moment, -e (1); at the moment im Moment (1)

Monday der Montag (1); last Monday letzten Montag (4)

money das Geld (2)

month der Monat, -e (B)

to mop wischen, gewischt (6)

more mehr (7)

morning: good morning guten Morgen (A); in the morning früh (4); late morning der Vormittag, -e (4); until four in the morning bis um vier Uhr früh (4)

mosquito die Mücke, -n (10)

mostly meistens (8)

mother die Mutter, ¨ (B); Mother's Day der Muttertag (4)

motif das Motiv, -e (12)

motorcycle das Motorrad, ¨er (1, 7); to ride a motorcycle Motorrad fahren (1) mountain **der Berg, -e** (1); to go to the mountains **in die Berge gehen** (1); to hike in the mountains **in den Bergen wandern** (1); mountain range **das Gebirge, -** (7)

mountaintop **der Gipfel, -** (7)

mouse **die Maus, ̈e** (10)

mouth **der Mund, ̈er** (B)

mouth (of an animal) **das Maul, ̈er** (9)

to move **ziehen (zieht), zog, ist gezogen** (2)

movie: to go to the movies **ins Kino gehen** (1); movie theater **das Kino, -s** (1); movie ticket **die Kinokarte, -n** (2)

to mow **mähen, gemäht** (5)

mower: lawn mower **der Rasenmäher, -** (6)

MP3 player **der MP3-Spieler, -** (2, 5)

Mr. **der Herr, -en** (wk.) (A)

Mrs.; Ms. **die Frau, -en** (A)

much **viel** (A)

mug **der Becher, -** (9)

muscle: sore muscles **der Muskelkater, -** (11)

museum **das Museum, Museen** (1); to go to the museum **ins Museum gehen** (1)

mushroom **der Pilz, -e** (8)

music **die Musik** (1)

mussel **die Muschel, -n** (8)

must **müssen (muss), musste, gemusst** (3)

mustache **der Schnurrbart, ̈e** (A)

mustard **der Senf** (8)

my **mein(e)** (A, 2)

nail **der Nagel, ̈** (8)

name **der Name, -n** (wk.) (A, 1); family name **der Familienname, -n** (wk.) (A, 1); favorite name **der Lieblingsname, -n** (wk.) (A); first/given name **der Vorname, -n** (wk.) (A, 1); What's your name? **Wie heißen Sie?** (for.) / **Wie heißt du?** (infor.) (A)

named: to be named **heißen (heißt), hieß, geheißen** (A)

napkin **die Serviette, -n** (8)

narrow **eng** (12); narrow street **die Gasse, -n** (10)

national holiday **der Nationalfeiertag, -e** (4)

nationality **die Staatsangehörigkeit, -en** (1)

naturally **natürlich** (2)

nature **die Natur** (9)

near **bei** (+ dat.) (10)

nearby **nah** (7)

neat (coll.) **grell** (2); **toll** (2)

neck **der Hals, ̈e** (9)

necklace **die Halskette, -n** (2, 5)

to need **brauchen, gebraucht** (1)

neighbor **der Nachbar, -n** (wk.) / **die Nachbarin, -nen** (4)

neighborhood **der Stadtteil, -e** (6); **das Stadtviertel, -** (6)

nephew **der Neffe, -n** (wk.) (B)

nervous **nervös** (1)

nest **das Nest, -er** (10)

the Netherlands **die Niederlande** (pl.) (B)

never **nie** (2)

new **neu** (A); something new **etwas Neues** (4)

news **die Nachrichten** (pl.) (7)

newspaper **die Zeitung, -en** (2); daily newspaper **die Tageszeitung, -en** (5); to deliver newspapers **Zeitungen aus·tragen** (5); to read the newspaper **Zeitung lesen** (1); university newspaper **die Unizeitung, -en** (4)

New Zealand **(das) Neuseeland** (B)

next: (from) next door **(von) nebenan** (5); next to **neben** (+ dat./acc.) (9)

nice **nett** (3); (weather) **schön** (B)

nickname **der Spitzname, -n** (wk.) (1)

niece **die Nichte, -n** (B)

night **die Nacht, ̈e** (3); all night long **die ganze Nacht** (3); last night **gestern Abend** (4); nights, at night **nachts** (4)

nightshirt **das Nachthemd, -en** (2)

nightstand **der Nachttisch, -e** (6)

nine **neun** (A)

nineteen **neunzehn** (A)

ninety **neunzig** (A)

ninth **neunt-** (4)

no **nein** (A); **kein(e)** (2); no one **niemand** (2); no wonder **kein Wunder** (4)

nobody **niemand** (2)

noise **das Geräusch, -e** (9)

none **kein(e)** (2)

nonetheless **trotzdem** (12)

noodle **die Nudel, -n** (8)

noon **der Mittag, -e** (3); at noon **mittags** (2)

normal **normal** (5); normally **normalerweise** (8)

north (of) **nördlich (von** + dat.) (7)

North America **(das) Nordamerika** (B)

northeast (of) **nordöstlich (von** + dat.) (7)

North Sea **die Nordsee** (B)

northwest (of) **nordwestlich (von** + dat.) (7)

Norway **(das) Norwegen** (B)

nose **die Nase, -n** (11)

not **nicht** (A); not a bit **gar nicht** (3); not at all **kein bisschen** (3); not until (four o'clock) **erst (um vier Uhr)** (4)

note (of currency) **der Schein, -e** (8); **der Geldschein, -e** (12); twenty-euro note **der Zwanzigeuroschein, -e** (8)

notebook **das Heft, -e** (B)

nothing **nichts** (9)

to notice: not to notice **verfehlen, verfehlt** (10)

noticeable: to be noticeable **auf·fallen (fällt ... auf), fiel ... auf, ist aufgefallen** (12)

novel **der Roman, -e** (5); romance novel **der Liebesroman, -e** (9)

November **der November** (B)

now **jetzt** (3)

number **die Zahl, -en** (A); **die Nummer, -n** (1); house number **die Hausnummer, -n** (1); license plate number **die Autonummer, -n** (11); secret PIN (personal identification number) **die Geheimzahl, -en** (12); telephone number **die Telefonnummer, -n** (1)

nurse **der Krankenpfleger, -** / **die Krankenpflegerin, -nen** (5); to nurse **pflegen, gepflegt** (5)

nut **die Nuss, ̈e** (8)

obligation **die Pflicht, -en** (3)

o'clock: at six o'clock **um sechs (Uhr)** (1); until four o'clock **bis um vier Uhr** (4)

October **der Oktober** (B)

Octoberfest (annual beer festival in Munich) **das Oktoberfest, -e** (7)

of **von** (+ dat.) (A, 10); **aus** (+ dat.) (10); Of course! **Klar!** (2); **selbstverständlich** (10)

off: to take the day off **blau machen** (3)

office **das Büro, -s** (5); at the office **im Büro** (5); doctor's office **die Arztpraxis, Arztpraxen** (11); office hour **die Sprechstunde, -n** (3); post office **die Post** (5); at the post office **auf der Post** (5)

officer: police officer **der Polizist, -en** (wk.) / **die Polizistin, -nen** (5)

often **oft** (A)

Oh boy! (coll.) **Mensch!** (2)

oil **das Öl** (5, 8); to check the oil **das Öl kontrollieren, kontrolliert** (5); oil color (paint) **die Ölfarbe, -n** (12)

old **alt** (A)

olive **die Olive, -n** (8)

omelet **das Omelett, -s** (8)

on **an** (+ dat./acc.) (2, 4); Come on over! **Komm mal vorbei!** (11); on account of **wegen** (+ gen.) (6); on foot **zu Fuß** (3); on Saturday **am Samstag** (2); on the contrary **sondern** (11); on the contrary! **doch!** (4); on the first of October **am ersten Oktober** (4); on the phone **am Telefon** (2); on the road **unterwegs** (9); on the second floor **im ersten Stock** (6); on time **pünktlich** (4); on what day? **an welchem Tag?** (4)

once **einmal** (4); once again **schon wieder** (3)

one **eins** (A); one another **einander** (3); one-way (trip) **einfach** (10); one-way street **die Einbahnstraße, -n** (7)

onion **die Zwiebel, -n** (8)

only **nur** (3)

to open **öffnen, geöffnet** (A); **auf·machen, aufgemacht** (3); **eröffnen, eröffnet** (9)

to open a bank account **ein Konto eröffnen** (5); open: out in the open (country) **in freier Natur** (10); open-face sandwich **das belegte Brot, die belegten Brote** (8)

opener: bottle opener **der Flaschenöffner, -** (8); can opener **der Dosenöffner, -** (8)

opposite **gegenüber** (+ dat.) (6)

or (coord. conj.) **oder** (A, 11)

oral: to give an oral report **ein Referat halten** (4)

orange (adj.) **orange** (A)

orange (n.) **die Apfelsine, -n** (8); orange juice **der Orangensaft** (8)

orchestra conductor **der Dirigent, -en** (wk.) / **die Dirigentin, -nen** (5)

order **die Reihenfolge, -n** (2); in order to **um ... zu** (12); to order (food) **bestellen, bestellt** (8)

organ **die Orgel, -n** (12)

origin **die Herkunft, ̈e** (B)

other: each other **einander** (3); with each other **miteinander** (3)

otherwise **sonst** (5)

our **unser(e)** (2)

out (of) **aus** (+ *dat.*) (10); out in the open (country) **in freier Natur** (10); out this way **heraus** (10)

outside **draußen** (11)

oven **der Backofen, ⸚** (5)

over (*prep.*) **über** (+ *dat./acc.*) (4); (*adv.*) **vorbei** (9); Come on over! **Komm mal vorbei!** (11); to knock over **um·kippen, umgekippt** (11); over that way **hinüber** (10); over the weekend **am Wochenende** (1), **übers Wochenende** (4); to run over **überfahren (überfährt), überfuhr, überfahren** (11)

overcoat **der Mantel, ⸚** (A)

overdraft protection **der Überziehungskredit, -e** (12)

overnight: to stay overnight **übernachten, übernachtet** (6)

own **eigen** (6)

to pack **packen, gepackt** (10); to pack up **ein·packen, eingepackt** (1)

package **das Paket, -e** (8)

page **die Seite, -n** (6)

pain **der Schmerz, -en** (11)

to paint **malen, gemalt** (12)

paintbrush **der Pinsel, -** (12)

pan **der Topf, ⸚e** (5); **die Pfanne, -n** (5)

pants **die Hose, -n** (A); sports pants **die Sporthose, -n** (2)

paper **das Papier, -e** (B); to give a paper / oral report **ein Referat halten** (4); paper towel **das Papiertuch, ⸚er** (5); toilet paper **das Toilettenpapier** (4)

parasol: beach parasol **der Sonnenschirm, -e** (10)

parents **die Eltern** (*pl.*) (B); with your parents, at your parents' **bei deinen Eltern** (6)

to park **parken, geparkt** (7)

park **der Park, -s** (1); to go for a walk in the park **im Park spazieren gehen** (1)

parlor: ice cream parlor **das Eiscafé, -s** (8)

parrot **der Papagei, -en** (10)

part **der Teil, -e** (7)

particularly **besonders** (3)

partner **der Partner, -** / **die Partnerin, -nen** (12); work with a partner **arbeiten Sie mit einem Partner** (A)

partnership **die Partnerschaft, -en** (12)

party **die Party, -s** (1, 2); **die Feier, -n** (9); to go to a party **auf eine Party gehen** (1)

passport **der Reisepass, ⸚e** (1); **der Pass, ⸚e** (7)

password **das Passwort, ⸚er** (7)

past (*adv.*) **vorbei** (9); (*prep.*) at twenty past five **um zwanzig nach fünf** (1)

pasture **die Wiese, -n** (7)

patient (*adj.*) **geduldig** (12)

patient (*n.*) **der Patient, -en** (*wk.*) / **die Patientin, -nen** (5)

to pay **zahlen, gezahlt** (5); to pay (for) **bezahlen, bezahlt** (4); to pay attention **auf·passen, aufgepasst** (3); to pay attention to **achten auf** (+ *acc.*), **geachtet** (11); to pay off **ab·zahlen, abgezahlt** (12)

payment: means of payment **das Zahlungsmittel, -** (12)

pea **die Erbse, -n** (8)

peach **der Pfirsich, -e** (8)

pear **die Birne, -n** (8)

pedestrian **der Fußgänger, -** (7); pedestrian mall **die Fußgängerzone, -n** (10)

pen **der Stift, -e** (A, B); ballpoint pen **der Kugelschreiber, -** (4)

pencil **der Bleistift, -e** (A, B)

penicillin **das Penizillin** (4)

peninsula **die Halbinsel, -n** (7)

people **die Leute** (*pl.*) (7)

pepper (black) **der Pfeffer** (8)

per **pro** (2); per cent **das Prozent, -e** (4)

percussion **das Schlagzeug, -e** (12)

perfect **vollkommen** (12)

perfume **das Parfüm, -e** (5)

perhaps **vielleicht** (2)

perm **die Dauerwelle, -n** (11)

to permit **erlauben, erlaubt** (7)

permit: residence permit **die Aufenthaltserlaubnis, -se** (12); work permit **die Arbeitserlaubnis, -se** (12)

permitted: to be permitted (to) **dürfen (darf), durfte, gedurft** (3)

person **die Person, -en** (1); **der Mensch, -en** (*wk.*) (2)

personal ID card **der Personalausweis, -e** (1); secret PIN (personal identification number) **die Geheimzahl, -en** (12)

pet **das Haustier, -e** (10)

pharmacist **der Apotheker, -** / **die Apothekerin, -nen** (11)

pharmacy **die Apotheke, -n** (6)

phone **das Telefon, -e** (1, 2); cellular phone **das Handy, -s** (2); on the phone **am Telefon** (2); phone number **die Telefonnummer, -n** (1); to talk on the phone **telefonieren, telefoniert** (4)

photo **das Foto, -s** (1)

to photograph **fotografieren, fotografiert** (4)

physician **der Arzt, ⸚e** / **die Ärztin, -nen** (3, 5, 11)

physics **die Physik** (1)

piano **das Klavier, -e** (2)

to pick **pflücken, gepflückt** (9); to pick (*s.o.*) up (from a place) **ab·holen, abgeholt** (1)

pickles **saure Gurken** (8)

picnic **das Picknick, -s** (4)

picture **das Bild, -er** (2); to hang the picture on the wall **das Bild an die Wand hängen** (3); What do your pictures show? **Was zeigen Ihre Bilder?** (A)

piece **das Stück, -e** (8); piece of furniture **das Möbelstück, -e** (6)

piercing **das Piercing, -s** (2)

pig **das Schwein, -e** (9); guinea pig **das Meerschweinchen, -** (10)

pigpen **der Schweinestall, ⸚e** (5)

pillow **das Kopfkissen, -** (6)

pilot **der Pilot, -en** (*wk.*) / **die Pilotin, -nen** (5)

PIN: secret PIN (personal identification number) **die Geheimzahl, -en** (12)

pink **rosa** (A)

piranha **der Piranha, -s** (10)

pizza **die Pizza, Pizzen** (2)

to place (*in an upright position*) **stellen, gestellt** (3, 5)

to place (*in a sitting position*) **setzen, gesetzt** (7)

place **der Ort, -e** (1, 5); **der Platz, ⸚e** (3); **die Lage, -n** (10); marketplace **der Marktplatz, ⸚e** (6); to take place **statt·finden (findet ... statt), fand ... statt, stattgefunden** (5)

to plan **planen, geplant** (9)

to plan (to) **wollen (will), wollte, gewollt** (3)

plan **der Plan, ⸚e** (3)

plant **die Pflanze, -n** (3, 6)

plate **der Teller, -** (8); license plate **das Nummernschild, -er** (7); license plate number **die Autonummer, -n** (11)

to play **spielen, gespielt** (1)

player: CD player **der CD-Spieler, -** (2); DVD player **der DVD-Spieler, -** (2, 3); MP3 player **der MP3-Spieler, -** (2, 5)

playground **der Spielplatz, ⸚e** (9)

pleasant **angenehm** (6)

to please **gefallen** (+ *dat.*) **(gefällt), gefiel, gefallen** (6)

please **bitte** (A); Sign here, please. **Unterschreib bitte hier** (A); Yes please? **Bitte schön?** (7)

pleasure **das Vergnügen** (2); **die Freude, -n** (9); with pleasure **gern** (1)

pliers **die Zange, -n** (8)

plum **die Pflaume, -n** (8)

pneumonia **die Lungenentzündung** (11)

pocket **die Tasche, -n** (1)

poem **das Gedicht, -e** (3)

point **der Punkt, -e** (A)

to poison **vergiften, vergiftet** (9)

poisonous **giftig** (9)

Poland **(das) Polen** (B)

police: police officer **der Polizist, -en** (*wk.*) / **die Polizistin, -nen** (5); police station **die Polizei** (5); at the police station **auf der Polizei** (5)

political **politisch** (12)

pool: swimming pool **das Schwimmbad, ⸚er** (1, 5); at the swimming pool **im Schwimmbad** (5); to go to the swimming pool **ins Schwimmbad fahren** (1)

poor **arm** (9)

popular **beliebt** (3)

pork **das Schweinefleisch** (8); ground pork (or beef) **das Hackfleisch** (8)

port **der Hafen, ⸚** (10)

Portugal **(das) Portugal** (B)

Portuguese (*language*) **(das) Portugiesisch** (B)

position **die Lage, -n** (10)

possessions **der Besitz** (2)

possibility **die Möglichkeit, -en** (5)

possible: as . . . as possible **möglichst** (+ *adv.*) (6); everything possible **alles Mögliche** (2)

post office **die Post** (5); at the post office **auf der Post** (5)

postcard **die Postkarte, -n** (2)

poster **das Poster, -** (6)

pot **der Topf, ⸚e** (5)

potato **die Kartoffel, -n** (8)

boiled potatoes **die Salzkartoffeln** (*pl.*) (8)

potholder **der Topflappen, -** (5)

potter's wheel **die Töpferscheibe, -n** (12)

to pour **gießen (gießt), goss, gegossen** (8)

power **der Strom** (8)

practical (career) training **praktische Ausbildung** (5)

practical(ly) **praktisch** (5)

to practice **aus·üben, ausgeübt** (12)

prenuptial agreement **der Ehevertrag, ⸚e** (12)

preparation **die Zubereitung, -en** (8)

to prepare (*food*) **zu·bereiten, zubereitet** (8)

prescription **das Rezept, -e** (11)

to present **vor·stellen, vorgestellt** (6)

present **das Geschenk, -e** (2); Christmas present **das Weihnachtsgeschenk, -e** (5)

president **der Präsident, -en** (*wk.*) / **die Präsidentin, -nen** (5)

pressure: blood pressure **der Blutdruck** (11); to have low/high blood pressure **niedrigen/ hohen Blutdruck haben** (11)

prestige **das Prestige** (5)

pretty **hübsch** (A, 2); **schön** (B); pretty big **ziemlich groß** (2)

price **der Preis, -e** (7, 12)

priest **der Priester, -** / **die Priesterin, -nen** (5)

prince **der Prinz, -en** (*wk.*) (9)

princess **die Prinzessin, -nen** (9)

principal **der Direktor, -en** / **die Direktorin, -nen** (9)

prison **das Gefängnis, -se** (6)

probably **wahrscheinlich** (1); **wohl** (12)

processing: electronic data processing **die EDV = elektronische Datenverarbeitung** (12)

profession **der Beruf, -e** (1, 5); What's your profession? **Was sind Sie von Beruf?** (1)

professional life **das Berufsleben** (12)

professor **der Professor, -en** / **die Professorin, -nen** (A, B)

prohibited **verboten** (9)

projector: data projector **der Beamer, -** (B)

to promise **versprechen (verspricht), versprach, versprochen** (7)

protection: overdraft protection **der Überzie- hungskredit, -e** (12)

psychiatrist **der Psychiater, -** / **die Psychiaterin, -nen** (11)

public transportation **die öffentlichen Verkehrs- mittel** (*pl.*) (7)

to pull **ziehen (zieht), zog, gezogen** (8)

pullover **der Pullover, -** (**der Pulli, -s**) (2)

punctual **pünktlich** (4)

pupil **der Schüler, -** / **die Schülerin, -nen** (1)

purple **lila** (A)

purse **die Tasche, -n** (1)

to put (*in a sitting position*) **setzen, gesetzt** (7); (*in an upright position*) **stellen, gestellt** (3, 5); to put (into) **geben (in** + *acc.*) **(gibt), gab, gegeben** (8); to put away **weg·stellen, weggestellt** (5); to put lotion on **sich ein·cremen, eingecremt** (11); to put makeup on **sich schminken, geschminkt** (11); to put on (*clothes*) **an·ziehen (zieht ... an), zog ... an, angezogen** (3)

puzzle **das Rätsel, -** (9); to solve a puzzle **ein Rätsel lösen** (9)

to quarrel **streiten (streitet), stritt, gestritten** (9)

quarter: at a quarter to four **um Viertel vor vier** (1)

queen **die Königin, -nen** (9)

question **die Frage, -n** (A); to ask a question **eine Frage stellen** (5)

quick **schnell** (7)

quiet(ly) **ruhig** (B); **leise** (9)

quite **ganz** (2); quite a bit **ganz schön viel** (3)

rabies **die Tollwut** (10)

radio **das Radio, -s** (2); car radio **das Autoradio, -s** (7)

rag (*for cleaning*) **der Putzlappen, -** (6)

railroad **die Bahn, -en** (7)

rain **der Regen** (7); to rain **regnen, geregnet** (B)

rainy: in rainy weather **bei Regen** (7)

range: mountain range **das Gebirge, -** (7)

rare(ly) **selten** (8)

rat **die Ratte, -n** (10)

rather **ziemlich** (2); **lieber** (2); **eher** (12); but (rather / on the contrary) **sondern** (A); I'd rather go . . . **Ich gehe lieber ...** (2)

rattlesnake **die Klapperschlange, -n** (10)

to reach **erreichen, erreicht** (12)

to read **lesen (liest), las, gelesen** (A, 1); to read aloud **vor·lesen (liest ... vor), las ... vor, vorgelesen** (9); to read the newspaper **Zeitung lesen** (1)

ready **fertig** (3)

real(ly) **echt** (2); really **wirklich** (B)

receipt **die Quittung, -en** (8)

to receive **bekommen (bekommt), bekam, bekommen** (3)

recently **neulich** (9)

reception (desk) **die Rezeption, -en** (10)

recess **die Pause, -n** (1)

recorder (*type of flute*) **die Blockflöte, -n** (12)

recreation room **der Aufenthaltsraum, ⸚e** (10)

to recuperate **sich erholen, erholt** (11)

red **rot** (A)

refrigerator **der Kühlschrank, ⸚e** (5)

regularly **regelmäßig** (11)

relatives **die Verwandten** (*pl.*) (2)

religion **die Religion** (1)

religious **religiös** (B); religious denomination **die Konfession, -en** (12)

to remain **bleiben (bleibt), blieb, ist geblieben** (3) to remember **sich erinnern (an** + *acc.*)**, erinnert** (9)

remembrance **die Erinnerung, -en** (4)

to remove **ab·nehmen (nimmt ... ab), nahm ... ab, abgenommen** (11)

rent **die Miete, -n** (6); to rent **mieten, gemietet** (6); to rent out **vermieten, vermietet** (6)

renter **der Mieter, -** / **die Mieterin, -nen** (6)

to repair **reparieren, repariert** (1)

repair shop **die Werkstatt, ⸚en** (5)

to repeat **wiederholen, wiederholt** (6)

report **das Referat, -e** (3); to give a paper / oral report **ein Referat halten** (4)

reporter **der Reporter, -** / **die Reporterin, -nen** (4)

requirement **die Pflicht, -en** (3)

to rescue **erlösen, erlöst** (9)

to reserve **reservieren, reserviert** (7)

residence **der Wohnort, -e** (1); residence permit **die Aufenthaltserlaubnis, -se** (12)

to rest **sich aus·ruhen, ausgeruht** (11)

restaurant **das Restaurant, -s** (2); **die Gaststätte, -n** (5); at the restaurant **in der Gaststätte** (5)

reunion: class reunion **das Klassentreffen, -** (9)

rice **der Reis** (8)

riddle **das Rätsel, -** (9); to solve a riddle **ein Rätsel lösen** (9)

to ride **fahren (fährt), fuhr, ist/hat gefahren** (2); (*on horseback*) **reiten (reitet), ritt, ist geritten** (1); to ride a bicycle **Rad fahren (fährt ... Rad), fuhr ... Rad, ist Rad gefahren** (7); to ride a motorcycle **Motorrad fahren** (1); to ride off **los·fahren (fährt ... los), fuhr ... los, ist losgefahren** (9)

right (*adj.*) **richtig** (2); (*adv.*) **rechts** (10); to be right (*of a person*) **recht haben (hat ... recht), hatte ... recht, recht gehabt** (2); to be right, correct **stimmen, gestimmt** (8); right (away) **gleich** (6); right across the way **gleich gegenüber** (6); right around the corner **gleich um die Ecke** (6); right-of-way **die Vorfahrt, -en** (7); that's right **das stimmt so** (8); to the right **rechts** (7)

to ring **klingeln, geklingelt** (2)

ring **der Ring, -e** (2)

to rinse **spülen, gespült** (4)

river **der Fluss, ⸚e** (7)

road **die Straße, -n** (6); on the road **unterwegs** (9)

roast **der Braten, -** (8)

roasted **gebraten** (8)

rock concert **das Rockkonzert, -e** (11)

rocket **die Rakete, -n** (7)

role **die Rolle, -n** (4)

roll **das Brötchen, -** (8)

romance novel **der Liebesroman, -e** (9)

Romania **(das) Rumänien** (B)

roof **das Dach, ⸚er** (6)

room **das Zimmer, -** (1, 2); breakfast room **das Frühstückszimmer, -** (10); dining room **das Esszimmer, -** (6); double room **das Doppelzimmer, -** (5, 10); dressing room **die**

Umkleidekabine, -n (5); living room das Wohnzimmer, - (6); recreation room der Aufenthaltsraum, ⁼e (10); single room das Einzelzimmer, - (10); TV room das Fernsehzimmer, - (10); roommate der Mitbewohner, - / die Mitbewohnerin, -nen (2)

roundabout: traffic roundabout der Kreisverkehr (10)

round-trip hin und zurück (5, 10); die Hin- und Rückfahrt (7)

routine: daily routine der Tagesablauf, ⁼e (1); der Alltag (4)

row: in a row hintereinander (3); row house das Reihenhaus, ⁼er (6)

rump steak das Rumpsteak, -s (8)

to run laufen (läuft), lief, ist gelaufen (A, 2); rennen, ist gerannt (7); to run in the woods im Wald laufen (2); to run over überfahren (überfährt), überfuhr, überfahren (11)

rushed eilig (8)

Russia (das) Russland (B)

Russian (adj.) russisch (8); (language) (das) Russisch (B)

rusty rostig (8)

sad traurig (B)

to sail segeln, gesegelt (1)

salad der Salat, -e (8); salad (mixing) bowl die Salatschüssel, -n (5); salad dressing die Soße, -n (8)

salesperson der Verkäufer, - / die Verkäuferin, -nen (5)

salon: tanning salon das Solarium, Solarien (11)

salt das Salz (8)

salted gesalzen (8)

salty salzig (7)

same egal (6); gleich (12)

sand der Sand (7)

sandcastle die Sandburg, -en (4)

sandwich: open-face sandwich das belegte Brot, die belegten Brote (8)

Saturday der Samstag (1)

Saturday: on Saturday am Samstag (2)

sauce die Soße, -n (8)

sauna die Sauna, -s (11)

sausage die Wurst, ⁼e (8)

savings account das Sparkonto, Sparkonten (12)

to say sagen, gesagt (A, 5); to say hello to grüßen, gegrüßt (10)

scale: kitchen scale die Küchenwaage, -n (5)

scar die Narbe, -n (1)

scarf der Schal, -s (2)

schedule der Stundenplan, ⁼e (1)

scholarship das Stipendium, Stipendien (1)

school die Schule, -n (1, 3, 5); at school in der Schule (5); elementary school die Grundschule, -n (9); high school, college preparatory school das Gymnasium, Gymnasien (6); high school graduation exam das Abitur (4); school principal der Direktor, -en / die Direktorin, -nen (9)

schooling die Schulbildung (5)

science: computer science die Informatik (1)

scientist der Wissenschaftler, - / die Wissenschaftlerin, -nen (12)

scissors die Schere, -n (8)

to scold schimpfen, geschimpft (9)

scorpion der Skorpion, -e (10)

to scream schreien (schreit), schrie, geschrien (3)

sculptor der Bildhauer, - / die Bildhauerin, -nen (12)

sea das Meer, -e (1, 7); to swim in the sea im Meer schwimmen (1); to the sea ans Meer (2)

seagull die Möwe, -n (10)

to season würzen, gewürzt (8)

season die Jahreszeit, -en (B)

seasoning das Gewürz, -e (8)

seat der Sitz, -e (7); Is this seat available? Ist hier noch frei? (8); seat belt der Sicherheitsgurt, -e (7)

second (adj.) zweit- (4); on the second floor im ersten Stock (6)

second (n.) die Sekunde, -n (1)

secret (adj.) heimlich (9); secret PIN (personal identification number) die Geheimzahl, -en (12)

secret (n.) das Geheimnis, -se (5)

secretary der Sekretär, -e / die Sekretärin, -nen (5)

sector die Branche, -n (12); der Bereich, -e (12)

to see sehen (sieht), sah, gesehen (2); see you soon bis bald (A)

seldom selten (8)

to sell verkaufen, verkauft (2, 5)

semester das Semester, - (1)

to send schicken, geschickt (2)

sentence der Satz, ⁼e (3)

to separate trennen, getrennt (7)

separately, separate checks getrennt (5)

September der September (B)

sequence die Reihenfolge, -n (2, 4)

servant der Diener, - / die Dienerin, -nen (9)

service die Bedienung (8)

to set decken, gedeckt (5); setzen, gesetzt (7); to set the table den Tisch decken (5)

seven sieben (A)

seventeen siebzehn (A)

seventh siebt- (4)

seventy siebzig (A)

several: for several days seit mehreren Tagen (11); several times mehrmals (5)

severe stark (11)

shade, shadow der Schatten, - (9)

to shake hands die Hand schütteln, geschüttelt (A)

share die Aktie, -n (12)

shared housing die WG, -s (die Wohngemeinschaft, -en) (6)

shark der Hai, -e (10)

to shave sich rasieren, rasiert (11)

shirt das Hemd, -en (A); T-shirt das T-Shirt, -s (2)

shock der Schock, -s (11)

shoe der Schuh, -e (A); athletic shoe der Sportschuh, -e (A); hiking shoe der Wanderschuh, -e (2); shoe store das Schuhgeschäft, -e (6)

to shop (for) ein·kaufen, eingekauft (1)

shop: butcher shop die Metzgerei, -en (6); copy shop der Kopierladen, ⁼ (10); repair shop die Werkstatt, ⁼en (5)

shopping: to go shopping ein·kaufen gehen (geht ... einkaufen), ging ... einkaufen, ist einkaufen gegangen (1, 5)

shore der Strand, ⁼e (7)

short kurz (B); klein (B); with the short hair mit dem kurzen Haar (A)

shot die Spritze, -n (11)

shoulder die Schulter, -n (B)

to shout rufen (ruft), rief, gerufen (7)

to shovel schaufeln, geschaufelt (11)

to show: What do your pictures show? Was zeigen Ihre Bilder? (A)

shower die Dusche, -n (5); to shower (sich) duschen, geduscht (1, 11)

shrill grell (2)

shrimp die Krabbe, -n (8)

to shut schließen (schließt), schloss, geschlossen (A); tied shut zugebunden (8)

shy schüchtern (B)

siblings die Geschwister (pl.) (B)

sick krank (3)

sickness die Krankheit, -en (11)

side die Seite, -n (6)

sidewalk der Fußgängerweg, -e (7)

to sightsee besichtigen, besichtigt (7)

to sign unterschreiben (unterschreibt), unterschrieb, unterschrieben (1); Sign here, please. Unterschreib bitte hier. (A)

sign das Schild, -er (7); traffic sign das Verkehrsschild, -er (7)

signature die Unterschrift, -en (1)

silverware das Besteck (5)

simple, simply einfach (2)

since seit (+ dat.) (4, 11)

to sing singen (singt), sang, gesungen (1); We like to sing. Wir singen gern. (1)

single-family home das Einfamilienhaus, ⁼er (6); single room das Einzelzimmer, - (10)

sink das Spülbecken, - (5)

sister die Schwester, -n (B)

to sit sitzen (sitzt), saß, gesessen (4); to sit down sich setzen, gesetzt (A, 11)

situation: conversational situation die Sprechsituation, -en (A)

six sechs (A)

sixteen sechzehn (A)

sixth sechst- (4)

sixty sechzig (A)

skateboard das Skateboard, -s (3); to skateboard Skateboard fahren (fährt ... Skateboard), fuhr ... Skateboard, ist Skateboard gefahren (3)

ski der Ski, -er (3); to ski Ski fahren (fährt ... Ski), fuhr ... Ski, ist Ski gefahren (3); ski lodge die Skihütte, -n (6) skills die Kenntnisse (*pl.*) (5)

skin die Haut, -̈e (11)

skirt der Rock, -̈e (A)

sleep der Schlaf (9); to sleep schlafen (schläft), schlief, geschlafen (2)

sleeping bag der Schlafsack, -̈e (2); sleeping car der Schlafwagen, - (4)

slender schlank (B)

slice das Stück, -e (8)

to slide rutschen, ist gerutscht (9)

slim schlank (B)

to slip rutschen, ist gerutscht (9); aus·rutschen, ist ausgerutscht (11)

Slovakia die Slowakei (B)

Slovenia (das) Slowenien (B)

small klein (B); eng (12)

to smell riechen (riecht), roch, gerochen (11)

to smoke rauchen, geraucht (3)

snail die Schnecke, -n (10)

snake die Schlange, -n (10)

sniffles der Schnupfen, - (11)

snow der Schnee (9); to snow schneien, geschneit (B)

snowboard das Snowboard, -s (1)

so so (A); also (4)

so long bis bald (A)

so that (*subord. conj.*) damit (11)

soap die Seife, -n (11)

soccer (ball) der Fußball, -̈e (A, 1)

social studies die Sozialkunde (1)

sociology die Soziologie (1)

sock die Socke, -n (2)

sofa das Sofa, -s (6)

sold out ausverkauft (5)

to solve a puzzle/riddle ein Rätsel lösen, gelöst (9)

somebody, someone jemand (3)

something etwas (2, 4, 5); Do you have something for it (*illness*)? Haben Sie etwas dagegen? (11); something interesting/new etwas Interessantes/Neues (4)

sometimes manchmal (B)

son der Sohn, -̈e (B)

song das Lied, -er (7)

songbook das Songbuch, -̈er (2)

soon bald (9); see you soon bis bald (A); soon thereafter bald darauf (9)

sore muscles der Muskelkater, - (11); sore throat die Halsschmerzen (*pl.*) (11)

sorry: to be sorry leid·tun (+ *dat.*) (tut ... leid), tat ... leid, leidgetan (5); I'm sorry. Tut mir leid. (4, 5)

soul die Seele, -n (12)

to sound (like) klingen (wie) (klingt), klang, geklungen (11); That sounds great. Das hört sich toll an. (4)

sound das Geräusch, -e (9)

soup die Suppe, -n (8)

sour sauer (8)

south (of) südlich (von + *dat.*) (7)

South America (das) Südamerika (B)

southeast (of) südöstlich (von + *dat.*) (7)

southwest (of) südwestlich (von + *dat.*) (7)

souvenir das Souvenir, -s (7); das Andenken, - (10)

spaghetti die Spaghetti (*pl.*) (7)

Spain (das) Spanien (B)

Spanish (*language*) (das) Spanisch (B)

to speak sprechen (spricht), sprach, gesprochen (B)

specialized training die Ausbildung (5)

to spell schreiben (schreibt), schrieb, geschrieben (A); How do you spell that? Wie schreibt man das? (A)

spell: to cast a spell on verwünschen, verwünscht (9)

to spend (*money*) aus·geben (gibt ... aus), gab ... aus, ausgegeben (12); (*time*) verbringen (verbringt), verbrachte, verbracht (3)

spice das Gewürz, -e (8)

spite: in spite of trotz (+ *gen.*) (12)

spoon der Löffel, - (8)

sports der Sport (1); to do sports Sport treiben (treibt ... Sport), trieb ... Sport, Sport getrieben (2); sports jacket das Sakko, -s (A); sports pants die Sporthose, -n (2)

spring der Frühling, -e (B); in the spring im Frühling (B); spring cleaning der Frühjahrsputz (6)

to sprinkle bestreuen, bestreut (8)

sprout: Brussels sprouts der Rosenkohl (8)

square: market square der Marktplatz, -̈e (6); square meter (m²) der Quadratmeter (qm), - (6)

stairway die Treppe, -n (6)

stairwell das Treppenhaus, -̈er (10)

stamp die Briefmarke, -n (5)

to stand stehen (steht), stand, gestanden (2, 6); to stand up auf·stehen (steht ... auf), stand ... auf, ist aufgestanden (A)

state der Staat, -en (10)

station: gas station die Tankstelle, -n (5); at the gas station an der Tankstelle (5); police station die Polizei (5); at the police station auf der Polizei (5); train station der Bahnhof, -̈e (4, 5); at the train station auf dem Bahnhof (5)

stationery store das Schreibwarengeschäft, -e (6)

to stay bleiben (bleibt), blieb, ist geblieben (3); to stay overnight übernachten, übernachtet (6)

steak: rump steak das Rumpsteak, -s (8)

to steal stehlen (stiehlt), stahl, gestohlen (9)

steering wheel das Lenkrad, -̈er (7)

stepfather der Stiefvater, -̈ (9)

stepmother die Stiefmutter, -̈ (9)

stereo system die Stereoanlage, -n (6)

still noch (B)

to sting stechen (sticht), stach, gestochen (10)

stock die Aktie, -n (12); stock exchange die Börse, -n (12); stock market crash der Börsenkrach, -̈e (12)

stomach der Bauch, -̈e (B); der Magen, -̈ (11)

stomachache die Magenschmerzen (*pl.*) (11)

stone der Stein, -e (12)

to stop an·halten (hält ... an), hielt ... an, angehalten (7); halten (hält), hielt, gehalten (7)

to stop (*doing s.th.*) auf·hören (mit + *dat.*), aufgehört (1)

stop die Haltestelle, -n (10); bus stop die Bushaltestelle, -n (10)

store das Geschäft, -e (2); department store das Kaufhaus, -̈er (5); at the department store im Kaufhaus (5); hardware store das Eisenwarengeschäft, -e (6); shoe store das Schuhgeschäft, -e (6); stationery store das Schreibwarengeschäft, -e (6)

story der Stock, Stockwerke (6)

stove der Herd, -e (5)

to stow verstauen, verstaut (7)

straight ahead geradeaus (10)

to straighten gerade stellen, gerade gestellt (3)

strange komisch (10)

strawberry die Erdbeere, -n (8)

street die Straße, -n (6); city street map der Stadtplan, -̈e (10); narrow street die Gasse, -n (10); one-way street die Einbahnstraße, -n (7)

streetcar die Straßenbahn, -en (7)

strict streng (9)

string die Schnur, -̈e (8)

stuck: to get stuck stecken bleiben (bleibt ... stecken), blieb ... stecken, ist stecken geblieben (11)

student der Student, -en (*wk.*) / die Studentin, -nen (A, B); fellow student der Mitstudent, -en (*wk.*) / die Mitstudentin, -nen (A); student cafeteria die Mensa, Mensen (2); student life das Studentenleben (4)

to study (*at a university/college*) studieren, studiert (1)

to study (*for a test*) lernen, gelernt (1)

study: center for study abroad das Auslandsamt, -̈er (1); course of studies, university studies das Studium, Studien (3); social studies die Sozialkunde (1)

stupid dumm (6)

stylish schick (2)

subject das Thema, Themen (4); academic subject das Fach, -̈er (1); favorite subject das Lieblingsfach, -̈er (5)

subway die U-Bahn, -en (die Untergrundbahn, -en) (7)

to suck lutschen, gelutscht (11)

suddenly plötzlich (9)

sugar der Zucker (8)

suggestion der Vorschlag, -̈e (5)

to suit stehen (+ *dat.*) (steht), stand, gestanden (6)

suit der Anzug, -̈e (A)

summer der Sommer, - (B); last summer letzten Sommer (4)

sun: to lie in the sun in der Sonne liegen (1)

sunbathing: to go sunbathing sonnenbaden gehen (10)

sunburn der Sonnenbrand, -̈e (10)

Sunday **der Sonntag** (1)

sunglasses **die Sonnenbrille, -n** (1, 2)

sunny **sonnig** (B)

sunshade **der Sonnenschirm, -e** (10)

suntan lotion **die Sonnenmilch** (10)

supermarket **der Supermarkt, ⁻e** (5, 6); at the supermarket **im Supermarkt** (5)

supper **das Abendessen, -** (1)

supposed: to be supposed to **sollen (soll), sollte, gesollt** (3)

sure **sicher** (1)

to surf the Internet **im Internet surfen, gesurft** (1)

surface **die Fläche, -n** (7)

surfboard **das Surfbrett, -er** (2)

surname **der Familienname, -n** (*wk.*) (A, 1)

survey **die Umfrage, -n** (4)

to swear **fluchen, geflucht** (11)

Sweden **(das) Schweden** (B)

Swedish (*language*) **(das) Schwedisch** (B)

to sweep **fegen, gefegt** (5)

sweet **süß** (2); totally sweet **voll süß** (2)

to swim **schwimmen (schwimmt), schwamm, ist geschwommen** (7); to go swimming **schwimmen gehen (geht ... schwimmen), ging ... schwimmen, ist schwimmen gegangen** (1); to swim in the sea **im Meer schwimmen** (1)

swimming pool **das Schwimmbad, ⁻er** (1, 5); at the swimming pool **im Schwimmbad** (5); to go to the swimming pool **ins Schwimmbad fahren** (1); swimming pool attendant **der Bademeister, - / die Bademeisterin, -nen** (5)

swim(ming) trunks **die Badehose, -n** (5)

Swiss (*person*) **der Schweizer, - / die Schweizerin, -nen** (B); Swiss franc **der Schweizer Franken, -** (8)

to switch on **an·machen, angemacht** (3)

Switzerland **die Schweiz** (B)

syrup: cough syrup **der Hustensaft, ⁻e** (11)

system: stereo system **die Stereoanlage, -n** (6)

table **der Tisch, -e** (B); bedside table **der Nachttisch, -e** (6); to clear the table **den Tisch ab·räumen** (3); kitchen table **der Küchentisch, -e** (5); to set the table **den Tisch decken** (5); table tennis **das Tischtennis** (3)

tablet **die Tablette, -n** (11); headache tablet **die Kopfschmerztablette, -n** (11)

to take **nehmen (nimmt), nahm, genommen** (A); to take (*a course*) **belegen, belegt** (4); to take along **mit·nehmen (nimmt ... mit), nahm ... mit, mitgenommen** (3); to take a shower **(sich) duschen, geduscht** (11); to take away **weg·bringen (bringt ... weg), brachte ... weg, weggebracht** (5); to take blood **Blut ab·nehmen (nimmt ... ab), nahm ... ab, abgenommen** (11); take care (*infor.*) **mach's gut** (A); to take care of **sich kümmern um** (+ *acc.*), **gekümmert** (12); to take effect **wirken, gewirkt** (11); to take off (*clothes*) **aus·ziehen (zieht ... aus), zog ... aus,**

ausgezogen (3); to take on **übernehmen (übernimmt), übernahm, übernommen** (7); to take out (*a loan*) **auf·nehmen (nimmt ... auf), nahm ... auf, aufgenommen** (12); to take place **statt·finden (findet ... statt), fand ... statt, stattgefunden** (5); to take the day off **blau machen, gemacht** (3)

tale: fairy tale **das Märchen, -** (9)

talent **das Talent, -e** (3)

to talk on the phone **telefonieren, telefoniert** (4)

tall **groß** (B)

tame **zahm** (10)

tank: fuel tank **der Tank, -s** (7)

tanning salon **das Solarium, Solarien** (11)

to taste **probieren, probiert** (3); to taste good to **schmecken** (+ *dat.*), **geschmeckt** (6)

tavern **die Kneipe, -n** (4)

taxi **das Taxi, -s** (3, 7); taxi driver **der Taxifahrer, - / die Taxifahrerin, -nen** (5)

tea **der Tee** (4); tea kettle **der Teekessel, -** (8)

to teach **unterrichten, unterrichtet** (5)

teacher **der Lehrer, - / die Lehrerin, -nen** (A, 1)

team **die Mannschaft, -en** (9); baseball team **die Baseballmannschaft, -en** (9)

teapot **die Teekanne, -n** (8)

to tear **zerreißen (zerreißt), zerriss, zerrissen** (9)

to tease **ärgern, geärgert** (3)

teddy bear **der Teddybär, -en** (*wk.*) (A), **der Teddy, -s** (9)

to telephone **telefonieren, telefoniert** (4)

telephone **das Telefon, -e** (1, 2); telephone booth **die Telefonzelle, -n** (2); telephone card **die Telefonkarte, -n** (2); telephone number **die Telefonnummer, -n** (1)

to tell **erzählen, erzählt** (3, 5); **sagen, gesagt** (5); to tell jokes **Witze erzählen** (3)

teller: automatic teller machine (ATM) **der Geldautomat, -en** (*wk.*) (12)

ten **zehn** (A)

tender **zart** (8)

tennis **das Tennis** (1); table tennis **das Tischtennis** (3)

tent **das Zelt, -e** (2)

tenth **zehnt-** (4)

terrace **die Terrasse, -n** (6)

terrible **furchtbar** (4)

test **die Prüfung, -en** (1)

tetanus **der Tetanus** (11)

to text **simsen, gesimst** (1)

text **der Text, -e** (12); to write a text message **eine SMS schreiben** (1)

thank you **danke** (A)

thanks: many thanks **vielen Dank** (10)

that (*dem. pron.*) **dieser, dies(es), diese** (4);

over that way **hinüber** (10); That is . . . **Das ist ...** (B); That's just it! **Das ist es ja!** (4); that's why **deshalb** (4); that way **hin** (10); up that way **hinauf** (10)

that (*subord. conj.*) **dass** (11); so that (*subord. conj.*) **damit** (11)

theater **das Theater, -** (4); movie theater **das Kino, -s** (1)

their **ihr(e)** (2)

theme **das Thema, Themen** (4); **das Motiv, -e** (12)

then **dann** (A); back then **damals** (9)

there **da** (2); **dort** (7); Is/Are there . . . ? **Gibt es ...?** (A, 6); there and back **hin und zurück** (10); There is/are . . . **Es gibt ...** (6)

thereafter: soon thereafter **bald darauf** (9)

therefore **deshalb** (4)

these **diese** (2, 4); These are . . . **Das sind ...** (B)

thing **das Ding, -e** (2); **die Sache, -n** (2)

to think (about) **nach·denken (über** + *acc.*) **(denkt ... nach), dachte ... nach, nachgedacht** (7); to think (of/about) **denken (an** + *acc.*) **(denkt), dachte, gedacht** (4); to think of **halten von** (+ *dat.*) **(hält), hielt, gehalten** (12)

third **dritt-** (4)

thirst **der Durst** (3)

thirsty: to be thirsty **Durst haben** (3)

thirteen **dreizehn** (A)

thirteenth **dreizehnt-** (4)

thirty **dreißig** (A)

this **dieser, dies(es), diese** (2, 4); in this way **herein** (10); out this way **heraus** (10); this evening **heute Abend** (2); This is . . . **Das ist ...** (B); this way **her** (10)

thorn **der Dorn, -en** (9)

those **diese** (4); Those are . . . **Das sind ...** (B)

three **drei** (A); three times **dreimal** (3)

throat **der Hals, ⁻e** (9); sore throat **die Halsschmerzen** (*pl.*) (11)

through **durch** (+ *acc.*) (7)

to throw **werfen (wirft), warf, geworfen** (3)

Thursday **der Donnerstag** (1)

thus **also** (4)

ticket **die Karte, -n** (2); **die Fahrkarte, -n** (4); admissions ticket **die Eintrittskarte, -n** (5); concert ticket **die Konzertkarte, -n** (5); movie ticket **die Kinokarte, -n** (2); ticket booth **die Kasse, -n** (5), **der Schalter, -** (5); at the ticket booth **an der Kasse** (5), **am Schalter** (5); ticket window **der Fahrkartenschalter, -** (7); train ticket **die Zugfahrkarte, -n** (6)

tie **die Krawatte, -n** (A)

tied shut **zugebunden** (8)

tight **eng** (12)

tights **die Sporthose, -n** (2)

time **die Zeit, -en** (4); **das Mal, -e** (4); At what time . . . ? **Um wie viel Uhr ...?** (1); for the first time **zum ersten Mal** (4); leisure time **die Freizeit** (1); on time **pünktlich** (4); several times **mehrmals** (5); the last time **das letzte Mal** (4); three times **dreimal** (3); What time is it? **Wie spät ist es?** (1), **Wie viel Uhr ist es?** (1)

tip **das Trinkgeld, -er** (8)

tire **der Reifen, -** (7); flat tire **die Reifenpanne, -n** (7)

tired **müde** (3)

to **an** (+ *acc.*) (2); **zu** (+ *dat.*) (2, 10); **nach** (+ *dat.*) (3, 10); at a quarter to four **um Viertel vor** vier (1); to the doctor zum Arzt (3); to the right rechts (7); to the sea ans Meer (2); to the university zur Uni (2); up to bis zu (+ dat.) (10)

toaster der Toaster, - (8)

today heute (B); What day is today? Welcher Tag ist heute? (1); What is today's date? Welches Datum ist heute? (4)

together zusammen (2); gemeinsam (11)

toilet die Toilette, -n (6); toilet paper das Toilettenpapier (4)

tolerant tolerant (7)

tomato die Tomate, -n (8)

tomorrow morgen (2); the day after tomorrow übermorgen (9)

tongs die Zange, -n (8)

tongue die Zunge, -n (11) to burn one's tongue sich die Zunge verbrennen (11)

too auch (A); zu (2); too bad! schade! (6)

tool das Werkzeug, -e (8)

tooth der Zahn, ⸚e (11) to brush one's teeth sich die Zähne putzen (11)

toothache die Zahnschmerzen (pl.) (11)

topic das Thema, Themen (4)

total(ly) total (4); totally sweet voll süß (2)

tour: bicycle tour die Radtour, -en (9); tour of the city die Stadtrundfahrt, -en (7)

tourism der Tourismus (10)

towel: hand towel das Handtuch, ⸚er (8); paper towel das Papiertuch, ⸚er (5)

town die Stadt, ⸚e (6); town hall das Rathaus, ⸚er (1, 6); at the town hall auf dem Rathaus (1); town house das Reihenhaus, ⸚er (6)

track: train track die Schiene, -n (10); (set of) train tracks das Gleis, -e (10)

tradition die Tradition, -en (4, 12)

traffic der Verkehr (7, 11); traffic roundabout der Kreisverkehr (10); traffic sign das Verkehrsschild, -er (7)

tragedy die Tragödie, -n (12)

train der Zug, ⸚e (7, 10); train agent der/die Bahnangestellte, -n (ein Bahnangestellter) (10); train car der Waggon, -s (7); train station der Bahnhof, ⸚e (4, 5); at the train station auf dem Bahnhof (5); train ticket die Zugfahrkarte, -n (6); train track die Schiene, -n (10); (set of) train tracks das Gleis, -e (10); train trip die Bahnfahrt, -en (7)

training: practical (career) training praktische Ausbildung (5); specialized training die Ausbildung (5)

transfer (of money) die Überweisung, -en (12)

to translate übersetzen, übersetzt (9)

to transport transportieren, transportiert (7)

transportation: means of transportation das Transportmittel, - (7); public transportation die öffentlichen Verkehrsmittel (pl.) (7)

transverse flute die Querflöte, -n (12)

trash der Müll (6)

to travel reisen, ist gereist (1); to travel first class erster Klasse fahren (10)

travel: travel agency das Reisebüro, -s (6); travel experience das Reiseerlebnis, -se (7); travel guidebook der Reiseführer, - (5)

traveler der/die Reisende, -n (ein Reisender) (10)

treasure der Schatz, ⸚e (9)

tree der Baum, ⸚e (9)

trick die List, -en (9)

to trip stolpern, ist gestolpert (9)

trip die Reise, -n (7); die Fahrt, -en (10); to be on a trip auf Reisen sein (7); to go on a trip verreisen, ist verreist (3); round-trip die Hin- und Rückfahrt (7); train trip die Bahnfahrt, -en (7)

trouble der Ärger (9)

trout die Forelle, -n (8)

truck der Lastwagen, - (7)

true wahr (3); treu (9)

trumpet die Trompete, -n (12)

trunk der Kofferraum, ⸚e (7); (of an elephant) der Rüssel, - (10)

trunks: swim(ming) trunks die Badehose, -n (5)

to try probieren, probiert (3); versuchen, versucht (4)

T-shirt das T-Shirt, -s (2)

Tuesday der Dienstag (1)

Turkey die Türkei (B)

Turkish (language) (das) Türkisch (B); (person) der Türke, -n (wk.) / die Türkin, -nen (12)

to turn ab·biegen (biegt ... ab), bog ... ab, ist abgebogen (10); to turn off aus·machen, ausgemacht (3); to turn on an·machen, angemacht (3); ein·schalten, eingeschaltet (10)

turtle die Schildkröte, -n (10)

tusk der Stoßzahn, ⸚e (10)

tutoring die Nachhilfe (3)

TV room das Fernsehzimmer, - (10); TV set der Fernseher, - (2); to watch TV fern·sehen (sieht ... fern), sah ... fern, ferngesehen (1)

twelfth zwölft- (4)

twelve zwölf (A)

twentieth zwanzigst- (4)

twenty zwanzig (A); twenty-euro note der Zwanzigeuroschein, -e (8)

twenty-one einundzwanzig (A)

twice zweimal (5)

two zwei (A)

type die Art, -en (2); to type tippen, getippt (3, 6)

ugly hässlich (2)

umbrella der Regenschirm, -e (5)

uncle der Onkel, - (B)

unconsciousness die Ohnmacht (11)

under, underneath unter (+ dat./acc.) (5); under the window unter dem Fenster (5)

underpants die Unterhose, -n (2)

undershirt das Unterhemd, -en (2)

to understand verstehen (versteht), verstand, verstanden (4)

undressed: to get undressed sich aus·ziehen (zieht ... aus), zog ... aus, ausgezogen (11)

unemployed arbeitslos (12)

unfortunately leider (B)

university die Universität, -en (B, 1, 5); (coll.) die Uni, -s (B, 1); at the university auf der Universität (5); to be at the university auf der Uni sein (1); (to go) to the university zur Uni (gehen) (1, 2); university newspaper die Unizeitung, -en (4); university studies das Studium, Studien (1)

unmarried ledig (1)

until (prep.) bis (+ acc.) (2, 4, 11); (subord. conj.) bis (11); not until (four o'clock) erst (um vier Uhr) (4); until eight o'clock bis acht Uhr (2); until four in the morning bis um vier Uhr früh (4)

up to bis zu (+ dat.) (10); up that way hinauf (10)

upset: to get upset sich auf·regen, aufgeregt (11)

Uranus der Uranus (4)

urgent(ly) dringend (2)

USA die USA (pl.) (B)

to use brauchen, gebraucht (1); benutzen, benutzt (7)

use der Gebrauch, ⸚e (12)

used car der Gebrauchtwagen, - (7)

useful nützlich (10)

usually meistens (8)

vacation die Ferien (pl.) (1); der Urlaub, -e (4, 5); vacation house das Ferienhaus, ⸚er (4)

to vaccinate against impfen gegen (+ acc.), geimpft (10)

to vacuum Staub saugen, Staub gesaugt (6)

vacuum cleaner der Staubsauger, - (6)

Valentine's Day der Valentinstag (4)

valley das Tal, ⸚er (7)

valuable wertvoll (2)

various verschieden (12)

vegetable das Gemüse, - (8)

vehicle das Fahrzeug, -e (7, 11)

very sehr (B)

veterinarian der Tierarzt, ⸚e / die Tierärztin, -nen (11)

vicinity die Nähe (6); in the vicinity in der Nähe (6)

video das Video, -s (9); video game das Videospiel, -e (2)

view der Ausblick, -e (6)

vinegar der Essig (8)

violence die Gewalt (12)

violin die Geige, -n (3)

to visit besuchen, besucht (1); zu Besuch kommen (3); vorbei·kommen (kommt ... vorbei), kam ... vorbei, ist vorbeigekommen (3); besichtigen, besichtigt (7)

visit der Besuch, -e (3)

vocabulary der Wortschatz, ⸚e (A)

voice die Stimme, -n (12)

volleyball der Volleyball, ⸚e (1)

to wait warten, gewartet (7)

waiter/waitress der Kellner, - / die Kellnerin, -nen (8); die Bedienung (8) to wake up **auf·wachen, ist aufgewacht** (4); to wake (*s.o.*) (up) **wecken, geweckt** (7)

to walk **gehen (geht), ging, ist gegangen** (A); to go for a walk **spazieren gehen (geht ... spazieren), ging ... spazieren, ist spazieren gegangen** (1); to go for a walk in the park **im Park spazieren gehen** (1)

to keep on walking **weiter·gehen (geht ... weiter), ging ... weiter, ist weitergegangen** (10)

wall **die Wand, ⁻e** (B); to hang the picture on the wall **das Bild an die Wand hängen** (3)

waltz **der Walzer, -** (3)

to want (to) **wollen (will), wollte, gewollt** (3)

wardrobe **der Schrank, ⁻e** (2); **der Kleiderschrank, ⁻e** (6)

warm **warm** (B)

to warn **warnen, gewarnt** (7)

to wash **waschen (wäscht), wusch, gewaschen** (2); **spülen, gespült** (4); to wash (oneself) **(sich) waschen (wäscht), wusch, gewaschen** (11); to wash the dishes **Geschirr spülen, gespült** (4); washbasin **das Waschbecken, -** (6)

washing machine **die Waschmaschine, -n** (6)

wastebasket **der Papierkorb, ⁻e** (3)

to watch **an·sehen (sieht ... an), sah ... an, angesehen** (3); to watch out for **achten auf** (+ *acc.*), **geachtet** (11); to watch TV **fern·sehen (sieht ... fern), sah ... fern, ferngesehen** (1)

watch **die Armbanduhr, -en** (A)

to water **gießen (gießt), goss, gegossen** (3); to water the flowers **die Blumen gießen** (3)

water: mineral water **das Mineralwasser** (8)

waterfowl **der Wasservogel, ⁻** (10)

watering can **die Gießkanne, -n** (6)

wave **die Welle, -n** (10)

way: in this way **herein** (10); one-way street **die Einbahnstraße, -n** (7); out this way **heraus** (10); over that way **hinüber** (10); right across the way **gleich gegenüber** (6); right-of-way **die Vorfahrt, -en** (7); that way **hin** (10); this way **her** (10); up that way **hinauf** (10)

to wear **tragen (trägt), trug, getragen** (A); Do you like to wear . . . ? **Trägst du gern ...?** (A)

weather **das Wetter** (B); in rainy weather **bei Regen** (7)

Wednesday **der Mittwoch** (1)

week **die Woche, -n** (1); during the week **in der Woche** (1); every week **jede Woche** (3); last week **letzte Woche** (4)

weekend **das Wochenende, -n** (1); last weekend **letztes Wochenende** (4); over the weekend **am Wochenende** (1), **übers Wochenende** (4)

weight: to lose weight **ab·nehmen (nimmt ... ab), nahm ... ab, abgenommen** (8, 11)

well (*adv.*): as well **auch** (A); to feel well **sich wohl fühlen, gefühlt** (11); That fits well. **Das passt gut.** (11)

well (*interj.*) **na** (3); **also** (4)

well (*n.*) **der Brunnen, -** (9)

west (of) **westlich (von** + *dat.*) (7)

wet **nass** (3)

whale: blue whale **der Blauwal, -e** (10)

what **was** (B); At what time . . . ? **Um wie viel Uhr ...?** (1); on what day? **an welchem Tag?** (4); What color is . . . ? **Welche Farbe hat ...?** (A); What day is today? **Welcher Tag ist heute?** (1); What do your pictures show? **Was zeigen Ihre Bilder?** (A); What is today's date? **Welches Datum ist heute?** (4); What's your name? **Wie heißen Sie?** (*for.*) / **Wie heißt du?** (*infor.*) (A); What's your profession? **Was sind Sie von Beruf?** (1); What time is it? **Wie spät ist es?** (1), **Wie viel Uhr ist es?** (1)

wheel **das Rad, ⁻er** (7); potter's wheel **die Töpferscheibe, -n** (12); steering wheel **das Lenkrad, ⁻er** (7)

when **wann** (B, 1); (*subord. conj.*) **als** (5, 11); when(ever) (*subord. conj.*) **wenn** (2, 11); when I was eight years old **als ich acht Jahre alt war** (5); When were you born? **Wann sind Sie geboren?** (1)

whenever (*subord. conj.*) **wenn** (11)

where **wo** (B); from where **woher** (B); Where are you going? **Wo willst du denn hin?** (A); where to **wohin** (3)

whether (*subord. conj.*) **ob** (6, 11)

which **welch-** (B)

white **weiß** (A)

whiteboard **die Tafel, -n** (A, B)

who **wer** (A, B)

whole **ganz** (2)

whom (*acc.*) **wen** (4); (*dat.*) **wem** (5)

why **warum** (3); that's why **deshalb** (4)

wife **die Frau, -en** (B)

wild boar **das Wildschwein, -e** (10)

to win **gewinnen (gewinnt), gewann, gewonnen** (4); to win the lottery **in der Lotterie gewinnen** (5)

wind **der Wind, -e** (9)

window **das Fenster, -** (B); cashier window **die Kasse, -n** (12); ticket window **der Fahrkartenschalter, -** (7); under the window **unter dem Fenster** (5)

windowpane **die Scheibe, -n** (7); **die Fensterscheibe, -n** (9)

windowsill **die Fensterbank, ⁻e** (5, 10)

windshield wiper **der Scheibenwischer, -** (7)

windsurfing: to go windsurfing **windsurfen gehen** (10)

windy **windig** (B)

wine **der Wein, -e** (7); wine cellar **der Weinkeller, -** (6)

winter **der Winter, -** (B)

to wipe **wischen, gewischt** (7); to wipe clean **ab·wischen, abgewischt** (6)

wiper: windshield wiper **der Scheibenwischer, -** (7)

witch **die Hexe, -n** (7, 9)

with **mit** (+ *dat.*) (A); **bei** (+ *dat.*) (2, 6, 10); Does it come with a . . . ? **Ist ein/eine ... dabei?** (6); with each other **miteinander** (3);

with me **mit mir** (3); with pleasure **gern** (1); with the short/long hair **mit dem kurzen/langen Haar** (A); with your parents **bei deinen Eltern** (6)

witness **der Zeuge, -n** (*wk.*) / **die Zeugin, -nen** (11)

wolf **der Wolf, ⁻e** (9)

woman **die Frau, -en** (A, B)

wonder **das Wunder, -** (4); no wonder **kein Wunder** (4)

wood **das Holz, ⁻er** (12)

woods **der Wald, ⁻er** (2, 7); to run in the woods **im Wald laufen** (2)

word **das Wort, ⁻er** (A)

to work **arbeiten, gearbeitet** (1); work with a partner **arbeiten Sie mit einem Partner** (A)

to work (*take effect*) **wirken, gewirkt** (11); work **die Arbeit, -en** (1); **das Werk, -e** (9); from work **von der Arbeit** (3); to go to work **zur Arbeit gehen** (1); kitchen work **die Küchenarbeit, -en** (5); work permit **die Arbeitserlaubnis, -se** (12)

workbook **das Arbeitsbuch, ⁻er** (3)

worker **der Arbeiter, -** / **die Arbeiterin, -nen** (5); construction worker **der Bauarbeiter, -** / **die Bauarbeiterin, -nen** (5)

world **die Welt, -en** (7)

would like (to) **möchte** (2, 3)

wound **die Wunde, -n** (11)

to write **schreiben (schreibt), schrieb, geschrieben** (A, 1); to write a text message **eine SMS schreiben** (1); to write down **auf·schreiben (schreibt ... auf), schrieb ... auf, aufgeschrieben** (11)

writer **der Schriftsteller, -** / **die Schriftstellerin, -nen** (5)

wrong **falsch** (2); to be wrong with (*a person*) **fehlen** (+ *dat.*), **gefehlt** (11); to get up on the wrong side of bed **mit dem linken Fuß auf·stehen** (4)

to X-ray **röntgen, geröntgt** (11)

year **das Jahr, -e** (B); for two years **seit zwei Jahren** (4)

to yell **schreien (schreit), schrie, geschrien** (3)

yellow **gelb** (A)

yes (on the contrary)! **doch!** (4); Yes please? **Bitte schön?** (7)

yesterday **gestern** (4); the day before yesterday **vorgestern** (4)

you (*infor. sg. acc.*) **dich** (2)

young **jung** (B)

your (*for.*) **Ihr(e)** (B, 2); (*infor. sg.*) **dein(e)** (B, 2); (*infor. pl.*) **euer, eure** (2)

youth **die Jugend** (9); youth hostel **die Jugendherberge, -n** (10)

zebra **das Zebra, -s** (10)

zeppelin **der Zeppelin, -e** (7)

zero **null** (A)

Index

This index is divided into three subsections: Culture, Grammar, and Vocabulary. The notation "n" following a page number indicates that the subject is treated in a footnote on that page. Reading titles are included in the Culture section.

Culture

1989 in German history, 309
academic life and requirements, 55, 123, 143
academic year in Germany, 123
age-related laws, 118
alternative medicine, 374
apartment hunting, 215
apprenticeship and job training, 183
Austria, 274

Berlin Wall, the, 309
Blog Deutsch 101: Frau Schulz hat Geburtstag, 85–86
Bock, Kiymet Benita, 139

colors as symbols, 11
coolsten Studentenjobs, die, 179
counting, 14
credit cards, 414
currency, euro, 81

debit cards, 414
Deutsche Kastanien (Yüksel Pazarkaya), 408–411
doctors' visits, 382

East Germany, 309
EC-Karte, 414
euro, 81
European geography, 35

Filmlektüre: *Bella Martha*, 282–283
Filmlektüre: *Das Leben der Anderen*, 387
Filmlektüre: *Der Tunnel*, 187–188
Filmlektüre: *Die fetten Jahre sind vorbei*, 354–355
Filmlektüre: *Good bye Lenin!*, 220–221
Filmlektüre: *Hilfe!*, 59
Filmlektüre: *Im Juli*, 245
Filmlektüre: *Jenseits der Stille*, 155
Filmlektüre: *Lola rennt*, 90
Filmlektüre: *Nordwand*, 311
Filmlektüre: *Sophie Scholl — Die letzten Tage*, 418
Filmlektüre: *Soul Kitchen*, 122
Flegel, Georg, 269
Fünfter sein (Ernst Jandl), 382

gender equality, 404
German immigration in the United States, 349

German youth
    activities restricted by age, 118
    job training, 183
    online activities, 93
    schooling and school life, 123
    survey answers, 304
    values and attitudes, 28
Germany, position of in Europe, 35
Guten Tag, ich heiße ..., 64

health insurance, 382
Höch, Hannah, 371
Hofheinz-Döring, Margret, 79
Holbein, Ambrosius, 109
holidays and traditions, 148
home remedies, 374
housing, 206, 215
Hundertwasser, Friedensreich, 203
Husum, 344–345

job training, 183
Juttas neue Frisur, 379

Kandinsky, Wassily, 3
Kaube, Suzan Emine, 401

Leipzig, 175
leisure activities, 52, 93, 304
Lohse-Wächtler, Elfriede, 237
Lorelei, Die (Heinrich Heine), 240

Marc, Franz, 335
money, euro, 81
Motorradtour, Die (Christine Egger), 277–278
Musikszene: „36 Grad", 33
Musikszene: „A - N - N - A", 13
Musikszene: „Cüs Junge", 407
Musikszene: „Danke", 376
Musikszene: „Dieser Weg", 346
Musikszene: „Du hast den Farbfilm vergessen", 146
Musikszene: „Gewinner", 62
Musikszene: „Haus am See", 218
Musikszene: „Hawaii Toast Song", 273
Musikszene: „Junge", 88
Musikszene: „Mädchen, lach doch mal!", 243

Musikszene: „Millionär", 181
Musikszene: „Müssen nur wollen", 116
Musikszene: „Wir beide", 310

names, popular German, 6
natural medicine, 374

online activities, 93

payment options, 414
prohibitions by age, 118

Quickcard, 414

report cards in Germany, 123
restaurant behavior, 286
reunification in Germany, 309
Ringe fürs Leben zu zweit, 112–113
Rotkäppchen—Ein Märchen der Gebrüder Grimm, 318–319

Schmeck, Ingrid M., 301
schooling and school year in Germany, 55, 123
shopping and money, 81, 414
Spitzweg, Carl, 49
Stadt, Die (Theodor Storm), 343
Städteranking 2010, 211–212
Sternzeichen (Rafik Schami), 151
Switzerland, 252

travel, 338

university studies, 143

vacations, 338
values of German youth, 28
Volkswagen, 249
von Menzel, Adolph, 171

weather and climate, 32
work life, apprenticeship and training, 183
workplace gender equality, 404

youth. *See* German youth.

Ziegler, Doris, 25

Grammar

accusative case. *See also* case system.
  defined, 98
  objects in, with dative objects, 395
  of articles, 98 *table*
  of attributive adjectives, 292 *table*
  of negative article, 99 *table*
  of personal pronouns, 133 *table*
  of possessive adjectives, 102 *table*
  of question pronouns, 195
  of reflexive pronouns, 393, 393 *table*, 394 *table*
  of relative pronouns, 257–258, 258 *table*
  prepositions requiring, 429 *table*
  two-way prepositions and, 228–229, 229 *table*, 429 *table*
  with direction, 230–231
  with **möchte,** 100
  with prepositions for giving directions, 364
  with verbs of direction, 293–295
  word order of objects in, 395
accusative prepositions, 429 *table*
accusative reflexive pronouns, 393, 393 *table*, 394 *table*
adjectives
  accusative case of, 292 *table*
  attributive, 291, 292 *margin* (rules of thumb), 292 *table*, 297, 297 *table*, 424 *table*
  comparative and superlative of, 259–261
  dative case of, 297, 297 *table*
  endings of, explained, 20
  genitive case of, 423, 424 *table*
  nominative case of, 292 *table*
  overview, 291
  possessive, 47 *table*, 101–102, 102 *table*, 193 *table*
  predicate, 291
  rules of thumb for endings of, 292 *margin*
adverbs
  comparative and superlative of, 259–261
  of time, 298, 328–329
agent, expressing in the passive, 368, 368 *margin*
als
  meaning and usage of, 325, 328, 329 *table*
  with dependent-clause word order, 325
am, 21, 166
an, 197–198, 197 *table*. *See also* contractions of definite articles with prepositions; two-way prepositions.
an … vorbei, plus dative, 364, 364 *margin*
ans, 21
articles. *See also* definite articles.
  accusative, 98 *table*
  dative, 193 *table*
  endings of, explained, 20
  genitive, 423, 424 *table*
  indefinite, 20 *list*, 40 *table*
  listed, 20 *list*
  negative, 99 *table*
  nominative, 21 *table*, 40 *table*, 98 *table*
  with attributive adjectives, 291, 297
  with country names, 360

attributive adjectives, 291, 292 *margin* (rules of thumb), 292 *table*, 297, 297 *table*, 424 *table*
auf, 197–198, 197 *table*. *See also* contractions of definite articles with prepositions; two-way prepositions.
aus, to talk about place, 360, 360 *margin*, 360 *table*
auxiliary, 161. *See also* **haben; sein; werden.**

bei
  to talk about place, 360, 360 *margin*, 360 *table*
  with dative, 234–235
bis zu, 364, 364 *margin*
bitte, 362
bleiben, 161, 265, 429

capitalization
  of **Ihr** and **Sie,** 47 *margin*
  of nouns, 22 *margin*
case system, 20–21, 428–430 (summary review). *See also* accusative case; articles; attributive adjectives; dative case; genitive case; nominative case.
causality and purpose, 427
clauses
  dependent and independent, 397–398. *See also* dependent clause; independent clause; word order.
  relative, 257–258
comma, in relative clauses, 257
command forms, 4, 362–363 (summary)
  du-imperative, 106
  polite, 19
comparative, 259–261
  irregular forms of, 260 *list*
comparisons. *See* comparative; superlative.
complement, 71n, 74
compounds: da-compounds and wo-compounds, 263–264, 263 *list*, 264 *table*
conditional, 328
conjunctions. *See also* als; damit; dependent clause; nachdem; ob; weil; wenn.
  coordinating, 397–398, 397 *list*
  subordinating, 397–398, 398 *list*
contractions of definite articles with prepositions, 21 *list*, 197 *table*, 229 *margin*, 231 *margin*, 360 *margin list*
coordinating conjunctions, 397–398, 397 *list*

da-compounds, 263, 263 *list*, 264 *margin list*
damit, 427
dates, 165
dative case. *See also* case system.
  defined, 193
  endings for, 193, 193 *table*
  objects in, with accusative objects, 395
  of adjectives, 297, 297 *table*
  of articles and possessive adjectives, 193, 193 *table*
  of personal pronouns, 199–200, 199 *table*, 200 *table*

of plural nouns, 194
  of question pronoun, 195
  of reflexive pronouns, 394, 394 *table*
  of relative pronouns, 257–258, 258 *table*
  of weak masculine nouns, 194
  prepositions requiring, 234–235, 360–361, 429 *table*
  to indicate location, 197–198
  two-way prepositions and, 228–229, 229 *table*, 429
  verbs requiring, 194 *list*, 226, 226 *lists*, 430 *list*
  with **mit** and **bei,** 234–235
  with prepositions for giving directions, 364
  with prepositions of place, 360–361
  with **zu** and **nach** for direction, 230–231
  word order of objects in, 395
dative prepositions, 234–235, 360–361, 429 *table*
dative reflexive pronouns, 394, 394 *table*
dative verbs, 226, 226 *lists*, 430 *list*
definite articles, 40 table. *See also* articles.
  contractions of, with prepositions, 21 *list*, 197 *table*, 229 *margin*, 231 *margin*, 360 *margin list*
  with body parts and articles of clothing, 394
  with place names and **in,** 230
dependent clause, 397–398 (summary review)
  defined, 135
  indirect question as, 396–397
  modals in, 137
  relative clause, 257–258
  separable-prefix verbs in, 137, 232, 330
  with **nachdem,** 333
  with **weil** and **damit,** 427
  word order in, 135–136, 137, 232, 325, 333, 397–398
destination
  expressed with **nach** and **zu,** 360, 360 *table*, 361
  vs. location, 228–229, 229 *table*, 293–295. *See also* two-way prepositions.
determiners. *See* articles.
direction, in/auf vs. zu/nach, 230–231
directions, giving (with prepositions), 364
doch, 362
du
  du-imperative, 106, 362
  versus **Sie** or **ihr,** 23 *table*
dürfen, 131–132. *See also* modal verbs.
  present tense of, 132 *table*
  simple past tense of, 326 *table*
  subjunctive of, 365 *table*

ein-words. *See* articles.
endings. *See also* case system; *individual cases.*
  of articles and adjectives, 20
  of attributive adjectives, 291, 292 *margin* (rules of thumb), 292 *table*, 297, 297 *table*, 424 *table*
  of **welcher,** 77n
entlang, 364, 364 *margin*
expressing change with **werden,** 196
expressing possibility with **würde, hätte, wäre,** 426

feminine nouns
    and pronouns, 21–22
    plural forms of, 43–44, 43 table
formal *you*. See **Sie.**
fragen, passive voice, 367 table, 368 table
function to determine case, 428–429
future
    future tense and future time, 298
    future time expressed with **wenn** + present
        tense, 328, 329 table

ge-, in past participles, 163, 167, 265–266
gegenüber von, 364, 364 margin
gender, 21–22. See also articles; case system.
genitive case, 423–424, 423 table, 424 table, 429.
        See also case system.
genitive prepositions, 429 table
gern, 71

haben
    as auxiliary, 161, 161 list, 163 list, 167 list, 265
    as auxiliary for **-ieren** verbs, 168
    as auxiliary for inseparable-prefix verbs, 168
    as auxiliary for reflexive verbs, 393
    hätte gern, 366
    present tense of, 42 table
    simple past tense of, 267 table, 325
    subjunctive forms of, 426 table
hängen/hängen, 295
hätte, 426, 426 table
hätte gern, 366
heißen, 20 table, 429
hinter. See two-way prepositions.

-ieren verbs, past participles of, 168 list, 265 list
ihr
    in the imperative, 362
    versus **Sie** or **du,** 23 table
Ihr, capitalization of, 47 margin
im, 21, 166, 197, 198, 229 margin
imperative, 4, 362–363 (summary)
    du-imperative, 106, 362
    polite, 19
in. See also contractions of definite articles with
        prepositions; two-way prepositions.
    with the accusative case, 228–229, 239–231
    with the dative case, 197–198, 197 table, 228–229
indefinite articles. See articles.
independent clause, word order in, 232, 330,
        397–398
indirect questions, 328, 396–397, 396 margin
infinitive
    defined, 46
    of **-ieren** verbs, 168 list
    of inseparable-prefix verbs, 168 list
    of separable-prefix verbs, 75, 75 list, 167 list, 232
    plus **werden,** to talk about future events, 298
    with **möchte,** 100
    with modals, 130
    with **um ... zu,** 427
informal *you*. See **du; ihr.**

ins, 21, 231 margin
inseparable prefixes, 168 margin list, 266 margin list
inseparable-prefix verbs, past participles of,
        168 list, 266, 266 list
instructions. See imperative.
irregular comparative and superlative forms,
        260 list, 261 list
irregular past participles, 163 list

kein. See also articles.
    accusative forms of, 99 table
    dative forms of, 193 table
    nominative forms of, 99 table
kommen, present tense of, 46 table
können, 130. See also modal verbs.
    present tense of, 130 table
    simple past of, 326 table
    subjunctive forms of, 366 table

legen/liegen, 294, 295
likes and dislikes, expressing, 71
location
    expressed with **bei,** 360, 360 table
    vs. destination, 228–229, 229 table, 293–295.
        See also two-way prepositions.
    with the dative case, 197–198, 228–229, 229 table,
        293–295.

machen, simple past tense of, 330 table
main clause. See independent clause.
mal, 362
masculine nouns
    and pronouns, 21–22
    plural forms of, 43–44, 43 table
    weak, 194, 194 table
mit, 234–235
möchte
    as synonym of **wollen,** 366
    present tense of, 101 table
    to express desires, 100
modal verbs. See also **dürfen; können; mögen;**
        müssen; sollen; wollen.
    defined, 130
    in dependent clauses, 137, 232
    polite forms of, 365–366
    present tense of, 130 table, 132 table
    simple past tense of, 325–326, 326 table
    subjunctive form of, 365–366, 365 tables
    with separable-prefix verbs, 232
mögen, 130. See also **möchte;** modal verbs.
    present tense of, 130 table
    simple past tense of, 326 table
    subjunctive of, 365 table
müssen, 131–132. See also modal verbs.
    present tense of, 132 table
    simple past tense of, 326 table
    subjunctive of, 365 table

nach, 230–231, 360–361, 361 margin
nach Hause, 230
nachdem, 332–333

narration, in the past, 332–334
neben. See two-way prepositions.
negation, of **müssen** and **dürfen,** 132
negative article. See also articles.
    accusative, 99 table
    dative, 193 table
    nominative, 99 table
neuter nouns
    and pronouns, 21–22
    plural forms of, 43–44, 43 table
nicht gern, 71
nominative case. See also case system.
    of articles, 21 table, 40 table, 98 table
    of attributive adjectives, 292 table
    of negative article, 99 table
    of personal pronouns, 133 table, 199 table,
        200 table
    of possessive adjectives, 47 table, 102 table
    of question pronoun, 195
    of relative pronouns, 257
    of superlative adjectives, 261
    with verbs of identity, 429
nouns
    and word order of accusative and dative
        objects, 395
    capitalization of, 22 margin
    dative plural forms of, 194
    gender of, 21–22
    in the genitive, 423 table
    plural forms of, 43–44, 43 table, 194
    weak masculine, 194, 194 table
number. See articles; nouns; plural forms of nouns.
numbers, ordinal, 165

ob. See subordinating conjunctions.
objects. See also accusative case; dative case.
    accusative and dative together, 395
    dative, required by certain verbs, 430 list
ordinal numbers, 165
origin expressed with **aus** and **von,** 360, 360 table

participle, past. See past participles.
passieren, using **sein** as auxiliary, 168, 265
passive voice, 367–368
past. See past perfect tense; perfect tense; simple
        past tense.
past narration, 332–333
past participles
    formation of, 265–266
    irregular, 163 list
    of inseparable-prefix verbs, 168 list
    of separable-prefix verbs, 167 list, 232
    strong and weak, 163
    used in passive voice, 367–368, 367 margin
    used in perfect tense, 161
    with and without **ge-,** 167–168
    with **haben,** 163 list, 167 list
    with **sein,** 163 list, 167 list
past perfect tense, 332–333
past tenses. See past perfect tense; perfect tense;
        simple past tense.

perfect tense
    formation of, 161, 265–266
    of separable-prefix verbs, 232
    used in conversation, 161, 265
    versus simple past tense, 330
personal pronouns. *See also* **du; ihr; Sie.**
    accusative, 133 *table*
    dative, 199–200, 199 *table*, 200 *table*
    nominative, 45 *table*, 133 *table*, 199 *table*,
        200 *table*
    referring to people or animals, 263
place, prepositions of, 360–361
place, word order with, 230
placement vs. position. *See* destination vs.
    location.
plural forms of nouns, 43–44, 43 *table*
    dative, 194
politeness
    polite commands, 19
    polite requests with **dürfen,** 131
    Sie versus **du** or **ihr,** 23 *table*
    softening requests, 362
    subjunctive of modals used for, 365–366
possession
    expressed by genitive, 423–424, 429
    expressed in conversation with **von,** 423,
        423 *margin*
    expressed with possessive **s,** 47 *margin*
possessive adjectives
    accusative, 101–102, 102 *table*
    dative, 193 *table*
    genitive, 424 *table*
    nominative, 47 *table*, 101–102, 102 *table*
possibility expressed with **würde, hätte,**
    wäre, 426
predicate adjectives, 291
predicate nouns, 429
prefixes, inseparable, 168 *margin list*, 265 *margin list*
prefixes, separable, 167 *margin list*. *See also*
    separable-prefix verbs.
prepositions. *See also* **da-**compounds;
    wo-compounds; *individual prepositions.*
    contractions of, with definite articles, 21,
        197 *table*, 229 *margin*, 231 *margin*,
        360 *margin list*
    followed by relative pronoun, 258
    for giving directions, 364
    in questions about people, 263–264, 264 *table*
    mit and **bei** with dative, 234–235
    of location. *See* prepositions, two-way.
    of place, 360–361
    of time, 166
    requiring the accusative, 429 *table*. *See also*
        prepositions, two-way.
    requiring the dative, 234–235, 360–361,
        429 *table*. *See also* prepositions, two-way.
    requiring the genitive, 423, 423 *list*
    that cannot take **da(r)-,** 263 *margin*
    that determine case, 429 *table*
    two-way, 228–229, 229 *table*, 293–295, 429 *table*.
        See also **an; auf; in; über.**

present tense
    forms of, and exceptions, 69
    in the passive voice, 367 *table*
    meanings of, 69
    of **haben,** 42 *table*
    of **kommen,** 46 *table*
    of **möchte,** 101 *table*
    of modal verbs, 130 *table*
    of **reiten,** 69 *table*
    of **sein,** 41 *table*
    of separable-prefix verbs, 75, 232
    of **spielen,** 69 *table*
    of stem-vowel changing verbs, 104 *chart*
    of **werden,** 196 *table*
    to express the future, 298
probability expressed with **werden,** 298
pronouns. *See also* **du; ihr; Sie.**
    accusative reflexive, 393, 393 *table*, 394 *table*
    dative reflexive, 394, 394 *table*
    gender of, 21
    personal. *See* personal pronouns.
    question, 195
    reflexive, 19n, 393, 393 *table*, 394, 394 *table*
    relative, 257–258
    sich in command forms, 19
    word order of objects, 395

question pronouns, 195
questions
    about people, 263, 264 *table*
    about things and ideas, 263, 264 *table*
    indirect, 328, 396–397, 396 *margin*
    word order in, 76–77, 76 *table*
    yes/no, 77
question words, 76, 77, 396

reflexive pronouns
    accusative, 393, 393 *table*, 394 *table*
    dative, 394, 394 *table*
    in command forms, 19n
reflexive verbs, 393, 393 *list*
reiten, present tense of, 69 *table*
relative clauses, 257–258
relative pronouns, 257–258
requests. *See also* imperative.
    softening, 362

Satzklammer, 75, 101, 130 *margin,* 161
sein
    and the nominative case, 429
    as auxiliary, 161, 161 *list,* 163 *list,* 167 *list,* 265
    imperative forms of, 363
    present tense of, 41 *table*
    simple past tense of, 267 *table,* 325
    subjunctive forms of, 426 *table*
    using **sein** as its own auxiliary, 161, 264
    with predicate adjectives, 291
separable prefixes, 167 *margin list*
separable-prefix verbs, 75
    in dependent clauses, 137
    past participles of, 167 *list,* 232, 266, 266 *list*

perfect tense of, 232
    present tense of, 75, 232
    simple past tense of, 330
setzen/sitzen, 294, 295
sich, in command forms, 19. *See also* reflexive
    pronouns.
Sie. *See also* personal pronouns.
    capitalization of, 47 *margin*
    in the imperative, 19, 362, 363
    versus **du** or **ihr,** 23 *table*
simple past tense
    in the passive voice, 368 *table*
    of **haben,** 267 *table*
    of modals, 325–326, 326 *table*
    of **sein,** 267 *table*
    of strong verbs, 330, 331 *list*
    of weak verbs, 330, 330 *table*, 330 *list*
    of **werden,** 325–326, 326 *table*
    of **wissen,** 325, 327, 327 *table*
    with **als,** 328
    with **wenn,** 328
so ... wie, 259
sollen, 131–132. *See also* modal verbs.
    present tense of, 132 *table*
    simple past tense of, 326 *table*
    subjunctive of, 365 *table*
spielen, present tense of, 69 *table*
statements, word order in, 74
stellen/stehen, 293, 295
stem changes in the simple past tense of weak
    verbs, 330 *list*
stem-vowel changing verbs, 104 *chart*
    in the **du-**imperative, 106, 362
    past participle of, 163, 266 *list*
strong verbs, 163
    past participle of, 163, 266
    of location, 295, 295 *list*
    simple past tense of, 330–331, 331 *list*
subject, position of in sentence, 74. *See also* word
    order.
subjunctive
    of **haben, sein,** and **werden,** 426 *tables*
    of modal verbs, 365–366, 365 *tables*
    to be polite, 365–366
subordinating conjunctions, 396, 397–398, 398 *list*
superlative, 258–260
    before nouns, 261 *table*
    irregular forms of, 260 *list*, 261 *list*

telling time, 72–73
tense. *See individual tenses.*
time, expressing, 72–73, 166
time, prepositions of, 166
time expressions, 298, 328, 329 *table*
    word order with, 230
two-way prepositions, 228–229, 229 *table*, 293–295,
    429 *table*. *See also* **an; auf; in; über.**

über, 364, 364 *margin. See also* two-way
    prepositions.
um, 166

um ... zu, 427
unter. *See* two-way prepositions.

verb in second position, 74, 136, 398. *See also*
    word order.
verbs. *See also individual tenses; individual verbs;*
    infinitive; strong verbs; weak verbs.
  determining case, 429–430, 430 *list*
  -ieren, 168 *list*, 265 *list*
  inseparable-prefix, 168 *list*, 265 *list*
  of destination vs. location, 293–295
  reflexive, 393, 393 *list*
  requiring both accusative and dative objects,
    194 *list*
  requiring dative objects, 194 *list*, 226, 226 *lists*,
    430 *list*
  position of, 74, 136, 398. *See also* word order.
  separable-prefix. *See* separable-prefix verbs.
  stem-vowel changing, 104 *chart*
  strong. *See* strong verbs.
  using **sein** as auxiliary, 161, 161 *list*, 163 *list*, 167
    list, 265
  weak. *See* weak verbs.
voice. *See* passive voice.
von
  in the passive, 368, 368 *margin*
  to express possession in conversation, 423,
    423 *margin*
  to talk about place, 360, 360 *margin*
vor. *See* two-way prepositions.

wann, 328, 329 *table*
wäre, 426, 426 *table*
weak masculine nouns, 194, 194 *table*
weak past participles, 163, 265
weak verbs
  formation of past participle of, 163, 265
  of destination, 295, 295 *list*
  simple past tense of, 330, 330 *table*, 330 *list*
  with stem-vowel change in past participle,
    266 *list*
weil, 427
welcher, endings of, 77n
wenn, 328, 329 *table*
wer, wen, wem, 195, 263, 264 *table*
werden
  and the nominative case, 429
  present tense of, 196 *table*
  simple past tense of, 325–326, 326 *table*
  subjunctive forms of, 426 *table*
  to express change, 196
  used in the future tense, 298
  used to express probability, 298
  used to form passive, 367–368, 367 *table*,
    368 *table*
  uses of, 367 *margin* (summary)
will, 131 *margin. See also* **wollen.**
wir, in the imperative, 362, 363
wissen, simple past tense of, 325, 327, 327 *table*
wo, 228, 229 *table*
wo-compounds, 263–264, 264 *table*

woher, 46
wohin, 228, 229 *table*
wollen, 130. *See also* modal verbs.
  present tense of, 130 *table*
  simple past tense of, 326 *table*
  subjunctive forms of, 366 *table*
word order, 397–398 (summary review)
  in causal expressions, 427
  in dependent clauses, 135–136, 137, 232, 325,
    328, 330, 334–335, 396–397, 397–398
  in indirect questions, 328, 396–397, 396 *margin*
  in questions, 76–77, 76 *table*
  in relative clauses, 257
  in statements, 74
  in the imperative, 106
  in the perfect tense, 161
  of accusative and dative objects, 395
  Satzklammer, 75, 101, 130 *margin*, 161
  time before place, 230
  with **als,** 325
  with **gern** or **nicht gern,** 71
  with **möchte,** 101
  with modals, 232
  with **nachdem,** 332–333
  with prepositions for giving directions, 364
  with separable-prefix verbs, 75, 137, 232
  with **wann** in indirect questions, 328
würde, 426, 426 *table*

yes/no questions, 77

zu, 230–231, 360–361, 361 *margin. See also*
  contractions of definite articles with
  prepositions.
zu Hause, 231, 231 *margin*
zwischen. *See* two-way prepositions.

Vocabulary

abilities, 110, 128
academic subjects, 53, 67
accidents, 381, 384, 391
activities. *See* childhood and childhood
  activities; daily life and routine; leisure
  activities.
animals, 323, 350, 358–359
apartments and apartment hunting, 204, 213, 224
appliances, 184, 191, 275, 290
artists' tools and materials, 415, 421
asking for directions, 340, 358
auto parts, 246, 255

banking, 412, 421
beach activities, 347
belongings, 80, 83, 96, 172, 191
biographical information, 60, 67
birthdays and anniversaries, 147
body care, 375, 391–392
body parts, 28–29, 38, 375, 381, 391
breakfast. *See* meals.
buildings, 181, 191, 207, 209, 213, 224

calendar and dates, 147
car parts, 246, 255
childhood and childhood activities, 302, 305,
  307, 323
chores, 216–217, 302
city vocabulary, 181, 191, 207, 209, 213, 224, 358
classroom and schooling vocabulary, 18, 26, 38,
  67, 128, 159, 191
clothing and accessories, 8, 17, 87, 96
colors, 10, 17
commands, 4, 17
continents, 39
cooking, 279–280, 289
countries, 39

daily life and routine, 56, 68, 140, 153, 216–217,
  302, 375, 392
descriptions, 27, 38
dinner. *See* meals.
directions, 340, 358
doctors' visits. *See* health and health care.

fairy tales, 313, 323
family life, 402, 420. *See also* childhood; daily life
  and routine; household chores.
family relationships, 29, 38
favors and gifts, 172
feelings, 124, 128
finances, 412, 421
food and drink, 270–271, 279–280, 284, 289, 290
  cooking, 279–280, 289
  preparation, 289
  shopping, 279–280
furnishings, 80, 96, 184, 191, 224

garden terms, 224
gender roles, 402, 420
geography, 39, 238, 255
gifts, 83, 172, 191
giving directions, 340, 358
greeting and leave-taking, 12, 17

health and health care, 372, 381, 384,
  390–391
holidays, 159. *See also* vacations.
home furnishings, 80, 96, 184, 191, 224
household appliances, 184, 191, 275, 290
household chores, 216–217, 302
household items, 290. *See also* appliances;
  furnishings.
housing, 204, 213, 224

illness, 372, 381, 391–391

kinship terms, 29, 38
kitchen items, 184, 191, 275, 290

landscape features, 238, 255
languages, 39
leisure activities, 50, 67, 92, 110, 115, 142, 250.
  See also vacations.

living spaces, 204, 224
lunch. *See* meals.

married life. *See* family life.
meals, 270–271, 280, 290
   restaurant, 284, 290
money, 412, 421
multiculturalism, 405, 421
musical instruments, 415, 421

nationalities, 34, 39
nature, 31, 38, 323
neighborhoods, 181, 207, 209, 224
numbers
   cardinal, 14, 17
   ordinal, 159

objects, 80, 83, 96. *See also* gifts.
obligations, 114–115, 128
occupations, 176, 190–191
offices and stores, 181, 191
ordinal numbers, 159

personal descriptions, 27, 38, 60, 67
personal hygiene, 391–392
personal information, 60, 67
pets. *See* animals.
pharmacy and hospital, 391
physical and mental states, 124, 128
places, 67, 181, 191, 207, 209, 213, 224, 238, 255
plans, 110, 128
pleasures, 92
politeness formulas, 119
possessions, 80, 83, 96, 172, 191
professions, 176, 190–191

questions, 18

restaurant expressions, 284, 290
rooms, 204, 224
routine activities, 56, 68, 140, 153, 216–217, 302, 375, 392

school and classroom vocabulary, 18, 26, 38, 67, 128, 159, 191. *See also* school subjects.

school subjects, 53, 67
seasons and weather, 31, 38
shopping, 191, 279–280
states of being, 124, 128
stores, 191, 207, 209, 224
subjects, academic, 53, 67

talents, 110, 128
time expressions, 159
transportation, 242, 255
travel, 159, 250, 255, 336–337, 358

university studies, 53, 67, 159. *See also* classroom and schooling vocabulary.

vacations, 142, 159, 250, 255, 336–337, 347, 358
vehicles, 242, 246, 255

weather and seasons, 31, 38
workplaces, 181, 191

youth, 305, 323

Credits

Grateful acknowledgment is made for use of the following video stills, photographs, realia, and readings.

Video Stills

Photographs

Realia

Readings

ISLAND
Reykjavik

NORWEGEN
Oslo

SCHWEDEN
Stockholm

FINNLAND
Helsinki

ESTLAND
Tallinn

LETTLAND
Riga

LITAUEN
Wilna

(ZU RUSSLAND)

WEISSRUSS

Minsk

NORDSEE

OSTSEE

Schottland
Nordirland

IRLAND
Dublin

England
Wales

GROSSBRITANNIEN

London

Der Ärmelkanal

ATLANTISCHER
OZEAN

Kopenhagen
DÄNEMARK

DIE NIEDERLANDE
Amsterdam

Berlin

Brüssel
BELGIEN

Luxemburg

LUXEMBURG

Paris

FRANKREICH

Warschau

POLEN

DEUTSCHLAND

Prag
TSCHECHIEN

DIE SLOWAKEI

MOLDA

LIECHTENSTEIN
Bern
DIE SCHWEIZ

Wien
ÖSTERREICH

Budapest

UNGARN

RUMÄNIEN

Ljubljana
SLOWENIEN

Zagreb

Belgrad
SERBIEN

Bukarest

KROATIEN
BOSNIEN UND
HERZEGOWINA

MONACO

ANDORRA

Madrid

PORTUGAL

Lissabon

SPANIEN

Korsika

VATIKANSTADT
Rom

Sarajevo

MONTENEGRO
KOSOVO

Podgorica

Pristina
Tirana

Skopje

Sofia

BULGA

ITALIEN

ALBANIEN

MAZEDONIEN

Sardinien

Mallorca

GRIECHENLAND

Athen

Straße von
Gibraltar

Algier

Sizilien

Tunis
MALTA

MITTELMEER

Kre

Rabat

MAROKKO

TUNESIEN

Tripolis

ALGERIEN

LIBYEN